Tests

STAFF

Richard C. Sweetland, Ph.D.	Editor
Daniel J. Keyser, Ph.D.	Editor
William A. O'Connor, Ph.D.	Associate Editor
Terry Faulkner	Managing Editor
Susan P. Jesso	Assistant Managing Editor
Barry K. Hughes, M.A.	Editorial Associate
Randee Jae Shenkel, Ph.D.	Editorial Associate
Carl T. Edwards	Manuscript Editor
Richard Hardesty	Manuscript Editor

WRITING STAFF: Christine G. Becicka, Corliss Elena Cureton, Carl T. Edwards, Jane Pecinovsky Fowler, Richard Hardesty, Bernadette A. Hoyt, Charles A. McMurray, Jr.

RESEARCH STAFF: Ann B. Bonner, Todd Boysen, Corliss Elena Cureton, Russell Doll, Dayna L. Fuchs, Sandy Lerner, Dianne J. Lustig, Danny Mitchelson, Kelly Ray, Victoria J. Spain, Carrie A. Strathman, Deb Tooley, Janet R. Tyner.

COVER DESIGN: Hal Sandy

PRODUCTION ASSOCIATE: Connie Turner, Management Systems

Richard C. Sweetland, Ph.D.
Daniel J. Keyser, Ph.D.
Editors

William A. O'Connor, Ph.D.
Associate Editor

Sam Pirnazar, Ph.D.
Contributing Consultant

Library Edition
First Edition

a comprehensive
reference for assessments
in psychology,
education and business

Test Corporation of America
Kansas City

The first edition of **TESTS** was published in June, 1983
Second Printing—October, 1983

Library of Congress Cataloging in Publication Data

Main entry under title:

Tests : a comprehensive reference for assessments in psychology, education, and business.

Includes indexes.
1. Psychological tests. 2. Educational tests and measurements. 3. Business—Examinations. I. Sweetland, Richard C., 1931-   . II. Keyser, Daniel J., 1935-   .
BF176.T43   1983   150'28'7   83-5074
ISBN 0-9611286-0-7
ISBN 0-9611286-1-5 (lib. bdg.)

Printed in the United States of America

Table of Contents

Business & Industry Section

Foreword

Some years ago when I was a graduate student and working on a clinical team at the Peabody Child Study Center, I found myself inundated with the names of tests and procedures. The faculty, staff, and more advanced students tossed off references to these tests with ease, and I tried to look knowledgeable while mentally I was desperately racing through the filing cabinets in my mind trying to place the instrument in question. Later in my graduate program I took a course on psychoeducational appraisal of handicapped children. The instructor presented us with a list of what I thought were the most unusual tests I had ever seen and stated that we should become knowledgeable about these measuring devices. By "knowledgeable" he meant we should know the purpose, description, special utility, history, standardization, reliability, validity, strengths, weaknesses, and general evaluation of each instrument. He also informed us that we would have to search out and write up a review of every one of those esoteric tests as part of our work. After the groans had died down, he motivated us by telling us that we would then have a reference collection that would serve us well in our future professional work. How right he was!

I found the reference useful immediately in my clinical work and as the years went by I used it regularly. Futhermore, I found it very useful with students and colleagues who would want to familiarize themselves with a test that was new to them or to check a point of importance. Indeed, I still refer to that reference from time to time. Unfortunately, it became somewhat dated as time went by. I did try to keep up with the new tests as they came out and were adopted for use in the profession. The proliferation of tests eventually became such that I could not keep pace and I finally stopped adding to my collection. Of course, I used other standard references on tests but they were not always what I wanted. Sometimes I would simply want a brief description just so I would know what the test was about. Sometimes I would only be interested in a specific item such as cost or the target population. How I then wished for an expanded and updated version of my old collection.

Such a reference has now been developed to help the professional find a specific test and the basic information he needs. Dick Sweetland, Dan Keyser and their associates have compiled a reference volume, **TESTS**, that does just this job. It is an infinitely more comprehensive work, spanning as it does the fields of psychology, education, and business. I am sure that psychologists, educators, and human resource personnel will find this an eminently practical and useable reference work. I only wish I had enjoyed the ownership of such a reference for the last ten years.

S. Joseph Weaver, Ph.D.
Director of Psychology
Children's Rehabilitation Unit
Kansas University Medical Center
Kansas City, Kansas

Preface

As this first edition of **TESTS** is published, it seems appropriate to say a few words about the project's development and to recognize the contributions of the people who made the task possible.

TESTS was developed in response to our research needs. Colleagues for a number of years, we have pursued research interests involving the administration and interpretation of tests. One such project, begun in 1975, involved the exploration of computerized testing. The goal of this venture was to explore the feasibility of developing a computerized testing machine which could administer, score, and provide interpretive material for professionally qualified psychologists and educators.

As a part of this project, we began the task of studying as many tests as possible in terms of their adaptability to computer administration, scoring, and interpretation. What was encountered was a need for consistent codified information describing and cataloguing tests which are currently available for use by psychologists, educators, and human resource personnel.

As our research and data base on tests increased, so did our awareness of the need to make this research available to colleagues. The concept of a "quick search" reference book, designed by and for professionals, emerged. We were joined by dedicated psychologists, educators, human resource personnel as well as a staff of energetic and resourceful researchers and writers to accomplish the task over the next fourteen months.

We wish to express special appreciation to William A. O'Connor, Ph.D., Associate Editor, whose insightful and professional opinions always kept us aware of the project's high standards. Our thanks also go to Barry Hughes, Carl Edwards, Richard Hardesty, and Randee Shenkel, Ph.D., for their efforts in reviewing editorial content and guiding the writing staff.

Particular recognition must be given to Terry Faulkner and Susan Jesso who coordinated this project. Their persistence and dedication to quality proved to be a major factor in the fruition of this project.

Special thanks go to Ann Bonner who assisted us in new test research.

We are grateful to the many test publishers and authors who generously and graciously contributed their staff time, information, and support for this book.

Richard C. Sweetland, Ph.D.
Daniel Keyser, Ph.D.
Editors

Introduction

TESTS is a quick reference guide for psychologists, educators, and human resource personnel who search for tests both old and new which may prove valuable in meeting assessment needs.

Over 3,000 tests have been referenced and classified in a format which facilitates the location of tests available in the English language.

The main sections Psychology, Education, and Business, are divided in subgroups within each discipline. Considerable consultation was sought from professionals who use tests on a daily basis in order to establish groupings that would be practical and functional to the test administrator.

Each test has been given a primary classification and is described in detail in one of the sections and may be cross-referenced in a secondary category. For example, the Wechsler Adult Intelligence Scale, described within the Psychology section, is also cross-referenced under the Education section. This system of primary classification and cross-referencing is intended to organize and present the material to the administrator as clearly as possible without further expanding the number of categories and thus reducing the book's accessibility and ease of use.

The format and content of each test entry is designed to give the reader the information that is needed to decide whether or not a particular test is the "right" one for a given assessment need. The format chosen provides a statement of the test's purpose, a description of the test, relevant cost and availability information, a set of coded visual keys designed to assist in quick screening and the primary owner/publisher.

The PURPOSE statement for each test entry provides a plain-language statement of the test's intended applications. The purpose statement tells what a particular test measures, assesses, diagnoses, evaluates, or identifies, and in most cases indicates application.

The DESCRIPTION provides number of test items, type of test format (paper-pencil, true-false, projective, oral, observational, etc.), factors or variable measured, materials used, the manner in which the test is administered, foreign language availability, and special features according to the test owner's information.

The editors are aware of possibilities for error even though information is from a primary source. And although each test entry has been researched, screened, written, edited and read by professional test administrators, the editors ask that the reader understand that the job of checking and insuring accuracy of a book such as this is a process which will continue throughout the publication of subsequent editions.

The editors had originally designed **TESTS** to include a section presenting data concerning the validity and reliability of each test included in the book. It was soon discovered, however, that this was a project requiring a special publication. Many test publishers do not provide this data in catalogued information regarding their tests and many failed to include such data in the material which they sent to us in response to our requests. Furthermore, research on the validity and reliability of individual tests revealed that more than one set of data is available for many tests and that the conflicting information often proved confusing or misleading. While the purpose of **TESTS** from the outset had been to provide a quick reference of available tests, it soon became clear that an adequate presentation of validity and reliability data is more appropriate to an in-depth, critical review. After much consultation with cooperative publishers and concerned professionals, it was decided not to include a section on test validity and reliablity in this edition of **TESTS**. The editors strongly urge all test administrators to contact the test authors or publishers concerning statistical evidence of test validity and reliability.

In terms of style, the editors have chosen to use the commonly acceptable masculine pronoun and to use the word subject for the individual who is being assessed. In so doing, the editors do not intend to show any sexual bias or disregard for those being assessed. British spelling has been retained in proper titles.

How To Use **TESTS**

All tests are listed alphabetically according to test title under their designated subgroups and cross-referenced to other sections where appropriate.

The editors encourage readers to scan sections of the book relevant to their particular assessment needs. By following up on cross-references listed for related fields of testing, the reader will discover tests which will provide a new or more appropriate perspective to a particular assessment situation. For convenience there are six indices—table of contents, title, author, publisher, scoring service, and visually impaired.

The PURPOSE statement is set off by bars to direct the reader's attention to the most concise statement of what a test is designed to accomplish.

The KEYS are also designed for quick-scanning reference. They will appear in the following order:

child/teen/adult
grades

☞ ✍ : Symbolizes that an examiner is required.

✍ : Symbolizes that a test is self-administered.

Who May Order Tests

Test publishers adhere to the ethical standards for administering tests as established by appropriate professional organizations for psychology, education and business. The Test Corporation of America fully supports the ethical and professional standards as established by the various national and state professional organizations and encourages each test administrator to contact them. An individual ordering tests of a psychological nature, therefore, should have training and/or the appropriate supervision required by the standards of the American Psychological Association.

While some descriptions in **TESTS** state specific restrictions on test accessiblity, the inclusion of this information often reflects the wishes of the publisher or author; the fact that a test description does not list restrictions should not be taken to imply that such restrictions do not exist. Test administrators when ordering should ask each publisher for these standards or requirements for purchasing.

How To Order Tests

Order forms, catalogues, and further information regarding tests may be obtained from each publisher. Anyone interested in ordering a specific test should contact the publisher directly, using the Publishers Index which provides mailing addresses and phone numbers.

By necessity, the cost information included is selective and representative. Complete pricing for some tests (covering the various forms, kits, options, etc.) is so lengthy that it makes the inclusion of all cost variables prohibitive. Cost information is as accurate as the editors could establish at the time of publication.

Psychology

The tests presented and described in the Psychology Section have been selected on the basis of their appropriate usage in a clinical or counseling setting. In general, tests found in this section are those which might be used by a mental health professional rather than an educator or human resources specialist. Tests described under the six main subsections are those generally considered to be basically "clinically" oriented as opposed to "educationally" or "business" oriented.

The classification of tests on the basis of "typical usage or function" is, of course, an arbitrary one and the reader is encouraged to review the Education Section and Business Section for additional assessment techniques.

Psychology Section Index

Child and Child Development

THE BARBER SCALES OF SELF-REGARD FOR PRESCHOOL CHILDREN
Lucie W. Barber

child   Preschool

Purpose: Assesses level of development of young children. Used to help parents recognize and develop a child's self-regard.

Description: Multiple item paper-pencil assessment profile of seven developmental factors, each measured on a five-point scale. The factors are: purposeful learning skills, completing tasks, coping with fears, cooperating with parental requests, dealing with frustrations, social adjustment and developing imagination in play. Designed for parents with aid of professional educators. Work sheets direct parents to the next level of their child's development. Materials include packet containing the seven scales, a guide for parents and a profile guide with instructions. An examiner manual is also available. Self-administered. Suitable for group use.

Untimed: Varies

Range: Grades Preschool

Scoring: Examiner evaluated

Cost: Parents' packet $5.00; manual $6.50.

Publisher: Union College Character Research Project

BAYLEY SCALES OF INFANT DEVELOPMENT
Nancy Bayley

child

Purpose: Assesses early mental and psychomotor development. Used in the diagnosis of normal versus retarded development.

Description: Two scale test of infant mental and motor development. Mental Scale assesses sensory- perceptual behavior, learning ability, and early communication attempts. The Motor Scale measures general body control, coordination of large muscles, and skills in fine muscle control of hands. Materials include kit containing stimulus items, and the Infant Behavior Record for noting qualitative aspects of behavior. Examiner required. Not suitable for group use.

Untimed: 45 minutes

Range: Ages 2-30 months

Scoring: Examiner evaluated

Cost: Complete set (includes all necessary equipment, manual, 25 each of 3 record forms, carrying case) $187.00.

Publisher: The Psychological Corporation

BEHAVIOR RATING INSTRUMENT FOR AUTISTIC AND OTHER ATYPICAL CHILDREN (BRIAAC)
Bertram Ruttenberg, Beth Kalish, Charles Wenar, and Enid Wolf

child

Purpose: Evaluates the status of low functioning, atypical, and autistic children of all ages. Used to evaluate those who will not or cannot cooperate with formal testing procedures.

Description: Paper-pencil inventory of observations taken over a two-day period. Assesses a child's present level of functioning and measures behavioral change in eight areas: relationship to an adult, communication, drive for mastery, vocalization and expressive speech, sound and speech reception, social responsiveness, body movement (passive and active), and psychobiological development. Each of the eight scales begins with the most severe autistic behavior and progresses to behavior roughly comparable to that of a normally developing 3½ to 4½ year old. The complete BRIAAC includes: manual, report forms, individual scale score sheet, total score sheet, intrascale and, interscale profile forms, descriptive guides, and suggested individual plans. Examiner required. Not suitable for group use.

Untimed: Observed over two day period

Range: Autistic children of all ages

Scoring: Examiner evaluated

Cost: Complete kit (includes manual and all required forms) $165.00.

Publisher: Stoelting Co.

BEHAVIOUR STUDY TECHNIQUE
Isla Stamp

---

child   grades PRE-1

Purpose: Measures behavioral development and adjustment of preschool children. Identifies children in need of further testing and assistance.

Description: Multiple item observational instrument provides a checklist for systematic evaluation of behavior in preschool children, intended for use by kindergarten teachers. An extension of the test is presented in the manual for use by psychologists. This extension consists of a coding system which enables the psychologist to classify children as apparently mentally healthy, in need of some help in adjusting or urgently in need of referral for diagnosis and therapy. Australian norms provided of preschool and first grade children. The manual and score keys are restricted to use by psychologists. Materials include: questionnaire, teacher's guide revised 1979, psychologist's manual, and score keys. Examiner required.
AUSTRALIAN PUBLISHER

Untimed: Open ended

Range: Grades Preschool-1

Scoring: Hand key; examiner evaluated

Cost: Specimen set $4.35; 10 questionnaire $1.25; teacher's guide $4.25 (all remittances must be in Australian currency).

Publisher: The Australian Council for Educational Research Limited

---

THE BINGHAM BUTTON TEST
William Bingham

---

child

Purpose: Measures child's ability to discern color, shape, size and spatial relationships as an indication of preschool readiness.

Description: One jar and ten buttons of different colors and sizes are presented by the examiner to the child, who is asked to maneuver the buttons to reveal the child's ability to determine how colors, objects and space relate to each other. Also useful in the diagnosis of problems with visual perception or motor skills. Examiner required. Not suitable for groups.

Untimed: 25-30 minutes

Range: Ages 3-6 years

Scoring: Hand key

Cost: Complete set $4.00.

Publisher: Bingham Button Test

BIRTH TO THREE DEVELOP-MENTAL SCALE
Tina E. Bangs and Susan Dodson

child

Purpose: Assesses developmental delay in the behavioral categories of oral language, problem solving, social/personal, and motor activities. Used for educational planning and diagnosis.

Description: 85-item scale for early identification of developmental delay. Factors measured include: basic skills/perceptual motor, social/emotional/interest, auditory skills, reception, and expression. Materials include a manual, five different scoring forms, and one summary form. Data derived from the scale provide criterion-referenced feedback. Examiner required. Not for group use.

Untimed: Not available

Range: Ages Birth-3 years

Scoring: Examiner evaluated

Cost: Complete kit $38.00.

Publisher: Teaching Resources Corp.

BURKS' BEHAVIOR RATING SCALES, PRESCHOOL AND KINDERGARTEN
Refer to page 80.

THE BZOCH-LEAGUE RECEPTIVE-EXPRESSIVE EMERGENT LANGUAGE SCALE (REEL)
Kenneth R. Bzoch and Richard League

child

Purpose: Assesses emerging factors of expressive and receptive language

in children from birth to age 36 months. Identifies children in need of further evaluation.

Description: 132 item paper-pencil inventory measuring the development of language in infants. The child's overt speech and response behaviors are rated by parent or individual who has daily contact with the child and has opportunity for observation of the child's language behavior. Test items consist of statements of language behavior typical of children ages 0-36 months. The evaluator rates each item as being present or absent. Three expressive and three receptive factors are measured for each of 22 age levels. Three scores are derived: expressive language quotient, receptive language quotient, and overall language quotient. Results also yield receptive, expressive, and combined expressive and receptive language ages. Self-administered by evaluator. Not for group use.

Untimed: Not available

Range: Ages 0-36 months

Scoring: Examiner evaluated

Cost: 25 tests $12.95, manual (contact publisher).

Publisher: University Park Press, Inc.

CATTELL INFANT INTELLIGENCE SCALE
Psyche Cattell

child

Purpose: Assesses the mental development of infants.

Description: Test of early development. Items include rating infant verbalizations and motor control such as the manipulation of cubes, pencils, pegboards and other stimulus items. The test has been modified with items from the Gesell, Minnesota

Preschool, and Merrill-Palmer Scales and is applicable to a younger age range than the Stanford-Binet. Materials include a kit containing stimulus items. Examiner required. Not suitable for group use.

Untimed: 20-30 minutes

Range: Ages 3-30 months

Scoring: Examiner evaluated

Cost: Complete set (includes all necessary equipment, 25 record forms, carrying case) $175.00.

Publisher: The Psychological Corporation

COMMUNICATIVE EVALUATION CHART
Ruth M. Anderson, Madeline Miles and Patricia A. Matheny

child

Purpose: Assesses the development of overall abilities in language and visual-motor-perceptual skills in children from birth to age five. Identifies children in need of referral for clinical evaluation.

Description: Task assessment and oral response test measuring the development of skills required for speech development. Tasks are designed to cover the following areas: the coordination of the speech musculature, development of hearing acuity and auditory perception, acquisition of vowels and consonants, and growth of receptive and expressive language. Also evaluates a child's well-being, growth and development, motor coordination, and beginning visual-motor-perceptual skills. The examiner elicits responses from the child and evaluates the responses as: present, not present, or fluctuating. It is occasionally necessary to consult with parent, guardian, or pediatrician for pertinent information. Sub-divided into nine levels, with 14-36 items for each of the fol-

lowing age groups: 3, 6, or 9 months, 1, 1½, 2, 3, 4, or 5 years. Examiner required. Not for group use.

Untimed: 5-10 minutes

Range: Ages Birth-5

Scoring: Examiner evaluated

Cost: Test $1.00; 50 tests $37.50.

Publisher: Educators Publishing Service, Inc.

COMPREHENSIVE ASSESSMENT PROGRAM: BEGINNING EDUCATION ASSESSMENT (BEA)

child

Purpose: Assesses development of children ages four through six. Used for screening children for learning problems.

Description: Multiple item paper-pencil measure of student's cognitive growth with reading-, language-, and mathematics-related tasks. BEA consists of three separate but related test levels, four, five, and six. All tasks are examiner-paced to reduce anxiety and respond to individual needs. BEA may be used with CAP Achievement Series to provide continuous assessment from pre-kindergarten through high school. Examiner required. Suitable for group use.

Untimed: Open ended

Range: Ages 4-6

Scoring: Hand key; may be machine scored; computer scoring available

Cost: 35 hand scorable test booklets: level 4 $35.20; levels 5 and 6 $26.50; 35 machien scorable test booklets levels 5 and 6 $35.95; manual $6.30; hand key (specify level) $1.30; 35 record forms (specify level) $5.90; scoring service $.30 per pupil.

Publisher: Scott, Foresman and Company

COMPREHENSIVE DEVELOP-MENTAL EVALUATION CHART (CDEC)

Shirley Cliff, Diane Carr, Jennifer Gray, Carol Nyman and Sandra Redding

child

Purpose: Measures a child's developmental abilities from birth to three years of age. Used for evaluation by either transdisciplinary or conventional team approaches.

Description: Multiple item observational instrument to collect comprehensive data and follow a child's development. The CDE Chart includes evaluations of: gross motor, fine motor, muscle tone, reflexes, parental attitudes, height and weight, receptive language, head circumference, expressive language, cognitive/social development, feeding vision, hearing, and others. Examiner administered. Not for group use.

Untimed: 30 minutes

Range: Ages Birth-3

Scoring: Examiner evaluated

Cost: CDE packet (includes 2 charts and manual) $12.00.

Publisher: El Paso Rehabilitation Center

COMPREHENSIVE IDENTIFICATION PROCESS (CIP)
Refer to page 443.

DENVER DEVELOPMENTAL SCREENING TEST (DDST)
Wm. K. Frankenburg

child

Purpose: Evaluates a child's personal, social, fine and gross motor, language, and adaptive abilities as a means of identifying possible problems and screening for further evaluation.

Description: 105 item "pick and choose" test. The items are blocks, a bell, a ball, a bottle, raisins, rattle, yarn and a pencil. Items are presented to the child in chronological step-wise order to permit a more dynamic profile, like a growth curve, of a child's development. The examiner observes what the child does with the items and makes recommendations based on perceived abnormalities. Available in Spanish. Examiner required. Not for group use.

Untimed: 10-20 minutes

Range: Ages Birth-6 years

Scoring: Examiner evaluated

Cost: Kit $15.00; manual $8.00; 100 test forms $7.50.

Publisher: Ladoca Publishing Foundation

DEVELOPMENTAL ACTIVITIES SCREENING INVENTORY (DASI)
Refer to page 445.

THE DEVELOPMENTAL PROFILE II
Refer to page 446.

DIAL-DEVELOPMENT INDICATORS FOR THE ASSESSMENT OF LEARNING
Refer to page 447.

EXTENDED MERRILL-PALMER SCALE
Rachel Stutsman Ball, Philip Merrifield, and Leland H. Stott

child

Purpose: Measures intelligence in children ages 3-5.

Description: 16 item task assessment and oral response test of the mental processes of evaluation and production with both semantic and figural units. The 16 tasks include: tower building, ambiguous forms, food naming, dot joining, word meaning, pie completion, action agents, copying, round things, block sorting, following directions, 3-cube pyramid, 6-cube pyramid, action agents, stick manipulation, and design productions. Scores and percentile ranges are provided (at six intervals from ages 3-5 years) for four specific abilities (each one tested by four of the tasks). The abilities are: semantic production, figural production, semantic evaluation, and semantic production. The manual includes information on development of the test items, instructions for administering and scoring and case studies for 16 separate patterns of the four abilities at two age levels. Examiner required. Not for group use.

Timed: 45 minutes

Range: Ages 3-5

Scoring: Examiner evaluated

Cost: Complete kit (includes all test materials, record forms, scoring forms, manual, carrying case) $325.00.

Publisher: Stoelting Co.

THE FLINT INFANT SECURITY SCALE: FOR INFANTS AGED 3-24 MONTHS
Betty M. Flint

child

Purpose: Assesses an infant's mental health as well as the behavior of the mother (or other parent) as she interacts with the child.

Description: 74 item paper-pencil behavior scale assessing a child's sense of security and feeling of self-worth as well as parental behavior. When the "psychological parent" is other than the natural mother or father, the scale is of special value to physicians, social workers and child care agencies responsible for adoption placements and foster care. Examiner required. Not for group use.

CANADIAN PUBLISHER

Untimed: Not available

Range: Ages 3-24 months

Scoring: Examiner evaluated

Cost: Specimen set (manual, scoring booklet) $4.10.

Publisher: Guidance Centre

HOME SCREENING QUESTIONNAIRE (HSQ)
Refer to page 61.

HOUSTON TEST FOR LANGUAGE DEVELOPMENT
Margaret Crabtree

child

Purpose: Assesses verbal and non-verbal communication abilities in children from birth to six years of age. Diagnosis problems resulting from emotional deprivation, neurological disabilities, retardation, auditory or visual-motor deficits or environmental linguistic influence. Used to plan specific intervention procedures and to monitor the child's progress.

Description: Multiple item verbal and nonverbal checklist of communication abilities at two age levels. The Infant Scale consists of an observational checklist of linguistic and pre-linguistic skills characteristic of normal infants up to 18 months of age. The 2-6 Year test consists of 18 subtests which include both verbal and nonverbal tasks. The 18 subtests include: Self-Identity, Vocabulary, Body Orientation, Gesture, Auditory Judgments, Oral Monitoring with Toys, Sentence Length, Temporal Content, Syntax, Prepositions, Serial Counting, Counting Objects, Imitates Linguistic Structure, Imitated Prosodic Patterns, Imitates Designs, Drawing, Oral Monitoring while Drawing and Telling About Drawing. The manual provides normative data and information on reliability and validity. Individual child record forms serve as a work sheet, score sheet and permanent record of the test performance. Examiner required. Not for group use.

Untimed: 30 minutes

Range: Ages Birth-6 years

Scoring: Examiner evaluated

Cost: Complete kit (includes 25 record forms, vocabulary cards, and necessary manipulatives, manual) $78.00.

Publisher: Stoelting Co.

KAUFMAN INFANT AND PRE-SCHOOL SCALE (KIPS)
Harvey Kaufman

child

Purpose: Measures early high-level cognitive process and indicates possible need for intervention in normal children ages one month to four years, and in retarded children and adults with mental ages of four years or less. Used by special education and early childhood teachers, psychologists, and physicians for a variety of screening purposes.

Description: Multiple item task assessment and observation measure of high-level cognitive thinking. The child is observed and asked to perform a number of tasks indicative of his level. All test items are "maturational prototypes" which can be taught to enhance maturation. The KIPS covers three areas: general reasoning, storage, and verbal communication. Scores provided include an Overall Functioning Age (Mental Age) and an Overall Functioning Quotient. Based on a child's performance on the scale, the manual suggests types of activities and general experience the child needs for effective general adaptive behavior. Examiner required. Not for group use.

Untimed: 30 minutes

Range: Ages 1 month-4 years; mentally retarded of all ages

Scoring: Examiner evaluated

Cost: Complete kit (includes all manipulatives, stimulus cards, 10 evaluation booklets) $195.00.

Publisher: Stoelting Co.

KINDERGARTEN BEHAVIOURAL INDEX
Refer to page 453.

KNOX'S CUBE TEST (KCT)
Refer to page 453.

KOONTZ CHILD DEVELOP-
MENTAL PROGRAM:
TRAINING ACTIVITIES FOR
THE FIRST 48 MONTHS
Refer to page 453.

LINCOLN-OSERETSKY
MOTOR DEVELOPMENT
SCALE
Refer to page 534.

MARTIN DEVELOPMENT
ABILITY TEST FOR THE
BLIND
Refer to page 565.

McCARTHY SCALES OF CHIL-
DREN'S ABILITIES
Dorothea McCarthy

child

Purpose: Assesses intellectual and motor development of children 2½ to 8½ years of age.

Description: Measure of six aspects of children's thinking, motor, and mental abilities: Verbal, Ability, Short Term Memory, Numerical Ability, Perceptual Performance, Motor Coordination, and Lateral Dominance. Verbal, Numerical, and Perceptual performance scales are combined to yield the General Cognitive Index. Items involve puzzles, toy-like materials and game-like tasks. Six of the component scales which predict the child's ability to cope with school work in the early grades form the McCarthy Screening Test. Examiner required. Not suitable for group use.

Untimed: 45-60 minutes

Range: Ages 2½-8½ years

Scoring: Examiner evaluated

Cost: Complete set (includes all nec-

essary equipment, manual, 25 record forms, 25 drawing booklets, carrying case) $116.00.

Publisher: The Psychological Corporation

MEASUREMENT OF LAN-
GUAGE DEVELOPMENT
Refer to page 588.

MERRILL-PALMER SCALE
Rachel Stutsman

child

Purpose: Measures intelligence in children age 18 months through four years of age. Used as a substitute for, or a supplement to, the Binet Scale.

Description: 19 task assessment and oral response tests measure language skills, motor skills, dexterity, and matching. The 19 subtests are: Stutsman Color Matching Test, Wallin Pegboards A & B, Stutsman Buttoning Test, Stutsman Stick and String, Scissors, Stutsman Language Test, Stutsman Picture Formboards 1,2, & 3, Mare-Foal Formboard, Seguin-Goddard Formboard, Pintner-Manikin Test, Decroly Matching Game, Stutsman Nested Cubes, Woodworth-Wells Association Test, Stutsman Copying Test, Stutsman Pyramid Test, Stutsman Little Pink Tower Test, and Kohs Blocks. The test deals directly with the problem of resistance in the testing situation and provides a comprehensive listing of the many factors influencing a child's willingness to cooperate. Refused and omitted items are considered when arriving at a total score which may then be converted into mental age, sigma value, or percentile rank. The test is significant in its complete independence from The Stanford-Binet Scale. All subtests may be ordered separately. Examiner required. Not for group use.

Untimed: Not available

Range: Age 18 months-4 years

Scoring: Examiner evaluated

Cost: Complete kit (includes all tests, 50 record blanks, carrying case) $325.00.

Publisher: Stoelting Co.

MINNESOTA CHILD DEVELOP-MENT INVENTORY (MCDI)
Harold Ireton and Edward Thwing

child

Purpose: Measures child development based on mother's observations. Used for clinical evaluation and pre-school screening.

Description: 320 item paper-pencil, yes-no format inventory is completed by the mother to assess her child's current level of development. The inventory measures: the child's general development, gross motor, fine motor, expressive language, comprehension-conceptual, situation-comprehension, self-help and personal-social skills. For use primarily with mothers with a high school education. Self-administered, Suitable for group use.

Untimed: 20-30 minutes

Range: Ages 1-6½ years

Scoring: Hand key

Cost: Specimen set (includes manual, booklet, answer sheet, profile form) $11.00; 10 reusable booklets $8.00; 25 answer sheets $6.00; 25 profile forms (specify male or female) $6.00; scoring templates $15.00; manual $10.00.

Publisher: Behavior Science Systems, Inc.

MINNESOTA INFANT DEVEL-OPMENT INVENTORY (MIDI)
Harold Ireton and Edward Thwing

child

Purpose: Assesses infant development in the first fifteen months. Used for pediatric review, infant screening and maternal education regarding child development.

Description: 75 item paper-pencil inventory measures development in five areas: gross motor, fine motor, language, comprehension and personal-social. Allows the mother to report and describe her baby. The test does not yield scores, but rather provides a framework for making sound professional judgments and serves as an interview guide with the mother. For use primarily with mothers who have a high school education. Self-administered. Suitable for group use.

Untimed: 10 minutes

Range: Ages Birth-15 months

Scoring: Guidelines

Cost: Specimen set $1.00; 20 reusable booklets $12.00

Publisher: Behavior Science Systems, Inc.

PERCEPTUAL MOTOR EDUCA-TION SCALE
Refer to page 537.

PIP DEVELOPMENTAL CHARTS
Dorothy M. Jeffree and Roy McConkey

child

Purpose: Assesses the behavioral development of children from birth to five years of age. Identifies weaknesses in particular developmental areas. Provides a structured framework for recording a child's developmental progress. Useful for screening and survey purposes.

Description: Paper-pencil inventory provides a behavioral checklist and profile of the most important stages of development in the first five years of a child's life. Development is measured in five main areas: physical, social, eye-hand coordination, play, and language skills. Each of these five areas is sub-divided into developmental sections, each of which begins with a target behavior representing a "milestone" of development. Each section then lists the behavioral skills which lead up to that milestone, and the approximate ages at which these skills are "normally" acquired. The purpose of the charts is the evaluation and furthering of individual children's development, not normative comparisons. Use of the charts secures the active participation of the parents, and is particularly useful when developmental delay or handicap is suspected. Self-administered by evaluator under supervision of a psychologist. Suitable for group use. BRITISH PUBLISHER

Untimed: Not available

Range: Ages Birth-5

Scoring: Examiner evaluated

Cost: 10 charts £3.50 plus VAT

Publisher: Hodder and Stoughton

PRESCREENING DEVELOP-MENTAL QUESTIONNAIRE (PDQ)
Refer to page 459.

PRIMARY ACADEMIC SENTIMENT SCALE (PASS)
Refer to page 460.

PSYCHOLOGICAL STIMULUS RESPONSE
Eileen M. Mullen

child

Purpose: Assesses the underlying intelligence and functional age of severely cerebral palsied multihandicapped infants and young children and helps provide them with alternate ways of responding to questions and statements.

Description: An alternate response test measuring language, visual processing and general intelligence. Materials include a 100-page manual, 29 page vocabulary card booklet, a 20 page response card booklet and a 20 page protocol-score sheet book. In the vocabulary test the examiner shows the appropriate cards to the child. The child then chooses one of three cards presented and, if unable to speak, can respond with eye movements or by pointing. Examiner required. Not suitable for group use.

Untimed: 15 minutes

Range: Ages Birth-5

Scoring: Hand key

Cost: Complete set $35.00.

Publisher: Meeting Street School, Rhode Island Easter Seal Society

A QUICK SCREENING TEST OF MENTAL DEVELOPMENT
Refer to page 30.

THE REVISED DEVELOPMENTAL SCREENING INVENTORY
Hilda Knobloch and Frances Stevens

child

Purpose: Determines if a child is functioning at age level. Screens for abnormalities requiring more detailed examination.

Description: Multiple item, yes-no questionnaire covering 20 age levels. Tests five areas: adaptive, gross motor, fine motor, language, and person-social. The questions are answered by the child's parent or caregiver beginning with the earliest possible tasks able to be performed by an infant and proceeding to those requiring greater maturity. The maturity level is assigned by determining how well a child's behavior fits one age level constellation. Nine video tapes are available in addition to the questionnaire. Examiner required. Not for group use.

Untimed: 10-30 minutes

Range: Ages 4 weeks-36 months

Scoring: Examiner evaluated

Cost: 100 copies $35.00.

Publisher: Hilda Knobloch, M.D.

REYNELL DEVELOPMENTAL LANGUAGE SCALES- REVISED EDITION
Joan Reynell

child

Purpose: Assesses expressive language and verbal comprehension. Used for evaluation of early development.

Description: Multiple item two performance tests of expressive and receptive language development: Verbal Comprehension Scale and Expressive Language Scale.. Materials include necessary toys and pictures. Suitable for use with hearing impaired children. Revised from the Experimental Edition of the Scales. Examiner required. Not suitable for group use.
BRITISH PUBLISHER

Untimed: One hour

Range: Ages 1½-6 years

Scoring: Examiner evaluated

Cost: Complete kit (includes test

materials, manual and 35 record forms) £71.35 (payment in sterling for all overseas orders).

Publisher: NFER-Nelson Publishing Company

REYNELL-ZINKIN DEVELOPMENT SCALES FOR YOUNG VISUALLY HANDICAPPED CHILDREN
Joan Reynell and P. Zinkin

child

Purpose: Assesses development of blind and partially sighted babies and young children. Used for planning management and early education programs.

Description: Performance test of intellectual development, with separate subscales for the following areas: Social Adaptation, Sensori-Motor Understanding, Exploration of Environment, Response to Sound and Verbal Comprehension, Expressive Language and Communication. Assessment yields profile detailing strong and weak areas. Tables provided allow comparison to blind, partially sighted, and sighted children. For use by professionals responsible for the assessment and education of the handicapped, i.e., doctors, psychologists and teachers of blind and partially sighted children. Necessary materials include toys which examiner provides. The Motor Development component of the Reynell-Zinkin is currently being completed. Examiner required. Not suitable for group use.
BRITISH PUBLISHER

Untimed: Not available

Range: Blind, partially sighted and young mentally handicapped children

Scoring: Examiner evaluated

Cost: Specimen set £4.10; 25 record forms £2.20; manual £4.15 (payment in sterling for all overseas orders).

Publisher: NFER-Nelson Publishing Company

RING AND PEG TESTS OF BEHAVIOR DEVELOPMENT FOR INFANTS AND PRE-SCHOOL CHILDREN
Katherine M. Banham

child   grades

Purpose: Measures the development of infants and preschool children and helps to reveal the social and motivational factors influential in a child's development. Used for clinical assessment of infant-child development.

Description: Task assessment test measures five categories of behavioral performance and ability: umbulative, manipulative, communicative, social-adaptive, and emotive. The test covers a wider range of items than standard intelligence tests in order to provide the clinical psychologist with diagnostic information. The scale yields a point score and a behavior age for the whole test as well as for each of the five categories. A developmental quotient (D.Q.) may be derived from the full scale behavior age. Test kit includes minimally culture-bound manipulation objects (sanitary and relatively unbreakable), manual, test booklet and single scoring sheet. Examiner required. Not for group use.

Untimed: 45 minutes

Range: Ages Infants-Preschool

Scoring: Hand key

Cost: Professional examination kit (includes 25 tests and handbook) $20.00.

Publisher: Psychometric Affiliates

ROCKFORD INFANT DEVELOPMENTAL SCALES (RIDES)
Refer to page 462.

SEQUENCED INVENTORY OF COMMUNICATION DEVELOPMENT
D.L. Hedrick, E.M. Prather, and A.R. Tobin

child

Purpose: Evaluates the communication abilities of normal and retarded children between four months and four years of age.

Description: A paper-pencil test evaluating the language abilities of young infants and children. The test is planned for use in remedial programming of children with language disorders, mental retardation, and specific language problems. Examiner required. Not suitable for group use.

Untimed: Not available

Range: Ages 4 months-4 years; retarded children

Scoring: Examiner evaluated

Cost: Contact publisher

Publisher: University of Washington Press

THE SCHOOL READINESS CHECKLIST
Refer to page 463.

SCHOOL READINESS SCREENING TEST
Refer to page 464.

SCHOOL READINESS SURVEY
Refer to page 464.

SMITH-JOHNSON NONVER-BAL PERFORMANCE SCALE
Alathena J. Smith and Ruth E. Johnson

child

Purpose: Provides a nonverbal assessment of the developmental level of children ages 2-4 years. Used especially to evaluate hearing impaired, language delayed, culturally deprived, and handicapped children.

Description: 14 category examination using nonverbal tasks to measure the developmental level of a broad range of skills in young children. Each category consists of a series of subtasks presented in order of increasing difficulty. With the exception of two tasks, the examiner proceeds to the first task in the next category as soon as two consecutive tasks have been failed. All but one of the tasks are untimed. The test measures strengths and weaknesses across a broad range of skills without constricting the evaluation by labeling the child with a single quantitative score. Norms are provided for both hearing impaired and normals. Examiner required. Not for group use.

Untimed: 30-45 minutes

Range: Ages 2-4

Scoring: Hand key; examiner evaluated

Cost: Complete kit (includes test materials, record sheets, manual) $52.70.

Publisher: Western Psychological Services

STATE TRAIT ANXIETY INVENTORY FOR CHILDREN (STAIC)
Refer to page 90.

STEPS UP DEVELOPMENTAL SCREENING PROGRAM (SUDS)
Shirley Cliff and Diane Carr

child

Purpose: Screens children age three and under for a wide range of possible developmental problems. Can be used for evaluation by parents, social workers and day care center staff.

Description: Multiple item observation test in which 32 question cards are used by trained volunteers to check various functions. Different test cards are provided for each two-week category for children under one year; and for each three-month age category for children between one and three years. Each card contains questions screening areas of gross motor, fine motor. language, cognitive/social, vision, hearing, head circumference, congenitally dislocated hips, and convulsive disorders. The screening procedure takes less than five minutes per child, and is frequently given during the waiting period in public health clinics, hospital clinics, and physicians' offices. Examiner required.

Untimed: 5 minutes per screening

Range: Ages Birth-3

Scoring: Examiner evaluated

Cost: Steps Up kit (with manual) $60.00; 100 replacement cards $7.95; manual $10.00.

Publisher: El Paso Rehabilitation Center

STYCAR CHART OF DEVELOP-MENTAL SEQUENCES (REVISED EDITION, 1975)
Mary D. Sheridan

child

Purpose: Assesses normal development of children ages one month to five years. Used for clinical screening.

Description: Multiple item chart indicating steps in normal development. Includes testing procedures designed to supplement general pediatric examination. Available as wall chart or as a pocket size pamphlet. Not for public display in clinic waiting rooms. Available to medical doctors, speech therapists, and teachers of the deaf, blind and physically handicapped. Examiner required. Not suitable for group use.

BRITISH PUBLISHER

Untimed: Not available

Range: Ages 1 month-5

Scoring: Examiner evaluated

Cost: Pamphlet £.35; wall chart £1.05 (payment in sterling for all overseas orders).

Publisher: NFER-Nelson Publishing Company

STYCAR VISION TESTS
Refer to page 609.

SYMBOLIC PLAY TEST-EXPERIMENTAL EDITION (SPT)
Marianne Lowe and Anthony Costello

child

Purpose: Assesses necessary conditions for meaningful language development. Used for evaluating language potentialities of very young children.

Description: Multiple item test of early concept formation and symbolization. The examiner presents objects to the child and rates meaningful responses and connections that the child makes as expressed in spontaneous nonverbal play activities. Materials include a set of toys. A

videotape for the SPT is available. For use by all speech therapists completing training in 1973 or later, and medical doctors with a course in developmental pediatrics. Speech therapists completing training before 1973 must have undergone further training in this type of testing. Examiner required. Not suitable for group use.

BRITISH PUBLISHER

Untimed: 10-15 minutes

Range: Ages 12-36 months

Scoring: Examiner evaluated

Cost: Complete kit (25 record forms, set of toys, manual), £39.95; video tapes available (payment in sterling for all overseas orders).

Publisher: NFER-Nelson Publishing Company

VINELAND SOCIAL MATURITY SCALE
Edgar A. Doll

all ages

Purpose: Measures successive stages of social competence or adaptive behavior. Used to measure normal development or individual differences which may be significant in cases of handicaps such as mental deficiencies and emotional disturbances in order to plan therapy or individual education.

Description: 117 item interview covering eight categories: Self-help General, Self-help Eating, Self-help Dressing, Locomotion, Occupation, Communication, Self-direction, and Socialization. The examiner interviews a parent, close relative or other primary care-giver and enters the response against each item listed in the record form. Raw scores are converted to an age equivalent score (social age) which may be used to compute a social quotient. Materials include record form and manual.

Examiner required. Not for group use.

Untimed: 20-30 minutes

Range: Ages Birth-30 years

Scoring: Examiner evaluated

Cost: 25 record forms $4.75; manual $3.25.

Publisher: American Guidance Service

Intelligence and Related

AH4 GROUP TEST OF GENERAL INTELLIGENCE (REGULAR EDITION)
Refer to page 474.

AH5 GROUP TEST OF HIGH GRADE INTELLIGENCE
Refer to page 474.

ACER ADVANCED TEST B40 (REVISED)

teen, adult

Purpose: Measures intelligence of students ages 15 years and above.

Description: Multiple item paper-pencil test measures general mental abilities including both verbal and numerical reasoning items. The manual has been revised for this edition and the test has been standardized. Materials include: expendable booklet, score key, manual, and specimen set. Examiner required. Suitable for group use. AUSTRALIAN PUBLISHER

Untimed: One hour

Range: Ages 15 and older

Scoring: Hand key

Cost: Specimen set $2.75; 10 tests

$2.50 manual (with key) $2.50 (all remittances must be in Australian currency).

Publisher: The Australian Council for Educational Research Limited

ACER ADVANCED TEST N

teen, adult

Purpose: Measures intelligence of students ages 15 years and older.

Description: 76 item paper-pencil test contains both verbal and nonverbal items to measure verbal, numerical, and abstract reasoning abilities. Australian norms provided. Not available to government schools. Materials include: Eight-page booklet, manual (with key), and specimen set. Examiner required. Suitable for group use. AUSTRALIAN PUBLISHER

Timed: 60 minutes

Range: Ages 15 and older

Scoring: Hand key

Cost: Specimen Set $2.60; test $.60; manual (with key) $2.00 (all remittances must be in Australian currency).

Publisher: The Australian Council for Educational Research Limited

ACER INTERMEDIATE TEST F

child, teen

Purpose: Measures intelligence of students ages 10-14 years.

Description: 80 item pencil-paper test measures general mental abilities including; classification, jumbled sentences, number series, synonyms and antonyms, arithmetical and verbal problems, and proverbs. Materials include: four-page booklet, scoring key, manual, and specimen set. Australian norms provided. Examiner required. Suitable for group use. AUSTRALIAN PUBLISHER

Timed: 30 minutes

Range: Ages 10-14

Scoring: Hand key

Cost: Specimen set $4.50; 10 tests $2.50; key $.60; manual $5.00 (all remittances must be in Australian currency).

Publisher: The Australian Council for Educational Research Limited

---

ACER INTERMEDIATE TEST G

child, teen

Purpose: Measures intelligence of students ages 10-14 years.

Description: 75 item paper-pencil test measures general mental abilities including: analogies, classifications, synonyms, number and letter series, arithmetical and verbal reasoning questions, and proverbs. Materials include: four-page booklet, scoring key, manual, and specimen set. Australian norms provided. Not available to Australian government schools. Examiner required. Suitable for group use.
AUSTRALIAN PUBLISHER

Timed: 30 minutes

Range: Ages 10-14

Scoring: Hand key

Cost: Specimen set $5.85; 10 tests $2.50; key $.60; manual $5.00 (all remittances must be in Australian currency).

Publisher: The Australian Council for Educational Research Limited

---

ACER JUNIOR A TEST

child

Purpose: Measures intelligence of children ages 8.6- 11.11 years.

Description: 75 item paper-pencil test measures verbal, non-verbal, and quantitative reasoning abilities. Materials include: eight-page booklet, scoring key, manual, and specimen set. Examiner required. Suitable for group use.
AUSTRALIAN PUBLISHER

Timed: 30 minutes

Range: Ages 8.6-11.11

Scoring: Hand key

Cost: Specimen set $5.25; test $.50; key $1.25; manual $3.50 (all remittances must be in Australian currency).

Publisher: The Australian Council for Educational Research Limited

---

ACER JUNIOR NON-VERBAL TEST
Manual by D. Spearritt

child

Purpose: Measures intelligence of children ages 8.6-12 years.

Description: 60 item paper-pencil test measures general mental abilities using pictorial and diagrammatic analogies, and matrices. There are four sub- tests: time sequences, block series, diagrammatic analogies, and matrices. Australian norms are provided. Materials include: 16-page booklet, scoring key, manual, and specimen set. Examiner required. Suitable for group use.
AUSTRALIAN PUBLISHER

Timed: 34 minutes

Range: Ages 8.6-12

Scoring: Hand key

Cost: Specimen set $6.90; test $.90; key $2.40; manual $3.60 (all remittances must be in Australian currency).

Publisher: The Australian Council for Educational Research Limited

ACER HIGHER TESTS: WL-WQ, ML-MQ (SECOND EDITION) and PL-PQ

teen, adult

Purpose: Measures intelligence of students 13 years and older.

Description: 72 item paper-pencil test of general mental abilities is available in three forms: WL-WQ (for students age 13 years and older) and parallel forms ML-MQ and PL-PQ (for students age 15 years and older). The L section (36 items) of each form has a linguistic bias; the Q section (36 items) is quantitative. Australian norms are provided for both sections separately and for a combined score. Examiner required. Suitable for group use.
AUSTRALIAN PUBLISHER

Timed: Various times

Range: Ages 13 and older

Scoring: Hand key; examiner evaluated

Cost: Contact publisher.

Publisher: The Australian Council for Educational Research Limited

ACER LOWER GRADES GENERAL ABILITY SCALE

child

Purpose: Measures general mental abilities of children ages 6.6-9.0 years. Particularly useful with children who are just learning to read.

Description: 772 item paper-pencil test measures a child's mental development relative to his age group and independently of his ability to read. The test consists of four subtests (18 items each): Picture Vocabulary, Picture Arrangement, Picture Analogies, and Picture Series. The test as a whole measures the child's knowledge of concrete or abstract

concepts and his ability to discover logical sequence, particular relationships, and underlying principles. The four subtests are printed in two test booklets, Parts A and B. Australian norms are provided. Examiner required. Suitable for group use.
AUSTRALIAN PUBLISHER

Timed: Both sessions one hour each

Range: Ages 6.6-9

Scoring: Hand key

Cost: Specimen set $11.15; test (Parts A & B combined $.90; 4 score keys $3.00; manual $7.25 (all remittances must be in Australian currency).

Publisher: The Australian Council for Educational Research Limited

ADVANCED PROGRESSIVE MATIRCES (APM-1962)
J.C. Raven

teen, adult

Purpose: Assesses the mental ability of people with above-average intellectual ability by means of nonverbal abstract reasoning tasks. Used for school and vocational counseling and placement, as well as research.

Description: 48 item paper-pencil nonverbal test in two sets. Set I contains 12 problems and is used as a practice test for Set II, which consists of 36 problems. In each problem, the subject is presented with a pattern or figure design which has a part missing. The subject then selects one of six possible parts as the correct one. Answer sheets are provided. Examiner required. Suitable for group use. Standardized in Great Britain.
BRITISH PUBLISHER

Timed: 40 minutes

Untimed: 60 minutes

Range: Adolescent, adult

Scoring: Hand key

Cost: 25 Set I tests £22.00; 25 Set II

tests £51.00; 50 hand scorable record forms for Set I and Set II £2.95; plastic marking key £4.95 plus V.A.T.

Publisher: H.K. Lewis & Co. Ltd./ U.S. Distributor—The Psychological Corporation

ARTHUR POINT SCALE OF PERFORMANCE, FORM I
Grace Arthur

all ages

Purpose: Measures intelligence of children and adults. Used as a nonverbal supplement to the highly verbalized Binet tests, especially with people having language, speech, emotional, or cultural problems.

Description: Ten nonverbal task assessment subtests are used to measure intelligence. They are: Mare-Foal Formboard, Sequin-Goddard Formboard, Pintner- Paterson 2-Figure Formboard, Casuist Formboard, Pintner-Manikin Test, Knox-Kempf Feature Profile Test, Knox Cube Imitation Test, Healy Pictorial Completion Test 1, Kohs Block Design Test, and Porteus Mazes. Particularly useful in supplementing the Binet scale in cases where the environmental conditions have varied widely from those of the average child. The comparison is of value whether it confirms the Binet ratings or shows a disparity in verbal and nonverbal development. Examiner required. Not for group use.

Untimed: Not available

Range: Ages 4-adult

Scoring: Examiner evaluated

Cost: Complete kit (includes all tests, 50 record cards, manual) $395.00; 50 record cards $13.00.

Publisher: Stoelting Co.

ARTHUR POINT SCALE OF PERFORMANCE TESTS: REVISED FORM II
Grace Arthur

child, teen

Purpose: Measures mental abilities in difficult to assess children. Used to assess children with reading problems, delayed speech, hearing impairments, and non-English speaking subjects.

Description: A scale of five tests measuring mental abilities. The scale includes: Knox Cube Test (Arthur Revision); Seguin Formboard Test (Arthur Revision); Arthur Stencil Design Test I; Healy Picture Completion Test II; and Porteus Maze Test (Arthur Modification). Supercedes Form 1 of the Arthur Point Scales of Performance, and is more completely non-language. May be used independently or as a supplement to the Arthur Adaptation of the Leiter International Performance Scale. Examiner required. Not suitable for group use.

Untimed: 45-90 minutes

Range: Ages 5-15 years

Scoring: Examiner evaluated

Cost: Complete set (includes all necessary equipment for 5 tests, manual 100 record forms, carrying case) $200.00.

Publisher: The Psychological Corporation

THE BRITISH ABILITY SCALES
Refer to page 476.

COLOURED PROGRESSIVE MATRICES
J.C. Raven

child, adult

Purpose: Assesses the mental ability of young children and older adults who are mentally subnormal or impaired. Used for school and clinical counseling, and research.

Description: 36 item paper-pencil nonverbal test consisting of design and pattern problems printed in several colors, including the two easiest sets from SPM-1938, plus a dozen additional items of similar difficulty. In each problem, the subject is presented with a pattern or figure design which has a part missing. The subject then selects one of six possible parts as the correct one. Examiner required. Suitable for group use above age eight. Standard norms developed in Great Britain. BRITISH PUBLISHER

Untimed: 15-30 minutes

Range: Ages 5-11, adults

Scoring: Hand Key

Cost: Specimen set (includes 1 book of tests and 12 combined Coloured Matrices and Crichton Vocabulary Scale Forms) £9.10 plus V.A.T.; 25 tests £64.00.

Publisher: H.K. Lewis & Co. Ltd./ U.S. Distributor—The Psychological Corporation

COLUMBIA MENTAL MATURITY SCALE (CMMS)
Bessie B. Burgemeister, Lucille Hollander Blum and Irving Lorge

child

Purpose: Assesses mental ability. Used with children having physical or verbal impairments.

Description: 92 item test of general reasoning abilities. Items are arranged in a series of eight overlap-

ping levels. Level administered determined by child's chronological age. Items are printed on 95 (6" x 19") cards. Child responds by selecting from each series of drawings the one that does not belong. Materials include item cards and a Guide for Administration and Interpretation, which includes directions in Spanish. Examiner required. Not suitable for group use.

Untimed: 15-20 minutes

Range: Ages 3½-10 years

Scoring: Examiner evaluated

Cost: Examiner's kit (includes 95 item cards, guide) $110.00; 35 individual record forms $9.25.

Publisher: The Psychological Corporation

THE CULTURE FAIR SERIES: SCALES 1, 2, 3
Raymond B. Cattell and A.K.S. Cattell

all ages

Purpose: Measures individual intelligence for a wide range of ages (four years to adult) without, as much as possible, the influence of verbal fluency, cultural climate, and educational level. Identifies learning and emotional problems. Used in employee selection and placement, special education decisions, and college, career, and vocational counseling.

Description: Paper-pencil (except for part of Scale 1) tests are arranged in three scales to cover the age range of four years to adult. Test items are nonverbal and require only that subject be able to perceive relationships in shapes and figures. Scale 1 (for ages 4-8 and older retardates) differs from Scales 2 and 3 in not being wholly nonverbal or wholly group administered. Scale 1 consists of eight subtests, four of which must be individually administered. A set of cards and some common objects are required for two of the subtests. Scales 2 and 3 involve four paper-pencil subtests of perceptual tasks: completing series, classifying, solving incomplete designs, and evaluating conditions. Scale 2 can be used with children as young as eight years old as well as older children and adults. Scale 3 is more difficult than Scale 2 and obtains a greater refinement in the higher intelligence ranges for use with high school and college students and adults of superior intelligence. Choice of scales is based on the examiner's evaluation of the potential ability level to be tested. Scale 1 provides Mental age and IQ; Scales 2 and 3 provide percentiles (by age), IQ's, and special norms for untimed administration of Scale 2. Examiner required. Suitable for group use (except as noted for Scale 1). Available in Spanish.

Untimed: 22 minutes

Range: Ages 4-8 and older retardates

Scoring: Hand key

Cost: Scale 1 professional testing kit $21.25; Scale 1 specimen set $3.45; reusable classification test cards $8.60; 25 not reusable test booklets $9.50; scoring key $.70; handbook $2.25; Scales 2 and 3 professional examination kit $10.75; specimen set $4.65; 25 not reusable test booklets $8.00; 50 answer sheets (all Scales) $8.00; scoring keys (answer sheets) $1.05; scoring keys (test booklets $1.50; tape recording (Scale 2) $25.00; manual $2.80; and technical supplement $3.50.

Publisher: Institute for Personality and Ability Testing, Inc.

DEESIDE PICTURE TEST
W.G. Emmett

child

Purpose: Measures general intellec-

tual ability of children. Used for assessment at time of transfer from infant to junior school.

Description: 250 item paper-pencil test of general mental ability. Items are nonverbal, and are grouped into seven different sections. Each section preceeded by practice items. Conversion tables are given in the manual and an IQ score can be determined. A mental age norm is also available. Examiner required. Suitable for group use.
BRITISH PUBLISHER

Timed: 30 minutes

Range: Ages 5-11

Scoring: Hand key

Cost: 25 tests $15.00; manual and norms $2.50.

Publisher: Harrap, Ltd.-available from The Test Agency

EXTENDED MERRILL-PAL-MER SCALE
Refer to page 8.

FULL RANGE PICTURE VOCABULARY TEST (FRPV)
R.B. Ammons and H.S. Ammons

all ages

Purpose: Assesses individual intelligence. May be used for testing special populations such as physically handicapped, uncooperative, aphasic, or very young subjects.

Description: 50 item test of verbal comprehension. Items are matched on 16 cards. Subject points to one of four drawings which best represents a particular word. Subject may also respond by indicating yes or no as the examiner points to each drawing. No reading or writing is required of the subject. Materials include two parallel forms, A and B, which use the same set of stimulus plates. Examiner required. Not suitable for group use.

Untimed: 5-10 minutes

Range: Ages 2-adult

Scoring: Hand key; examiner evaluated

Cost: Set of plates, with instructions, norms and sample answer sheets $15.00; 25 answer sheets (specify Form A or B) $2.50; 100-$8.00.

Publisher: Psychological Test Specialists

GOODENOUGH-HARRIS DRAWING TEST
Florence L. Goodenough and Dale B. Harris

child, teen

Purpose: Assesses mental ability through nonverbal technique.

Description: Test measuring intelligence through three drawing tasks: Goodenough Draw-a-Man Test, Draw- a-Woman Test and the experimental Self-Drawing Scale. Man and woman drawings may be scored for the presence of up to 73 characteristics. Materials include Quality Scale Cards which are required for the short scoring method. Examiner required. Suitable for group use.

Untimed: 10-15 minutes

Range: Ages 3-15

Scoring: Hand key

Cost: Examiner's kit (includes test, manual, Quality Scale Cards) $13.25; 25 tests $10.50; manual $5.00; Quality Scale Cards $8.25.

Publisher: The Psychological Corporation

GRIFFITHS MENTAL DEVELOPMENT SCALES
Ruth Griffiths

child

Purpose: Measures cognitive/intellectual development in infants and children ages 2-8. Used for assessing need for remedial treatment and for assessing progress.

Description: 27 or 22 item test of intellectual development. Divided into two levels: Scale 1 (27 items) for children from birth to two, and Scale 2 (22 items) for children from ages two to eight. Some items appear on both scales. Factors measured include social development, fine and gross motor, hearing, eye-hand coordination, and speech. Materials include toys, form boards, pictures, and models packed in a carrying case. There are different materials for each age group. Two books by the author, *The Abilities of Babies* and *The Abilities of Young Children,* are available separately. They describe the methods employed in the development and standardization of the scales. Examiner required. Not suitable for group use. Available in Swedish and Italian. BRITISH PUBLISHER

Untimed: Not available

Range: Ages 0-8 years

Scoring: Examiner evaluated

Cost: Kit (0-2 Scale, 2-8 Extension Scale, "Abilities of Babies" manual, "Abilities of Young Children" manual) $440.00; 25 booklets $32.50; 25 forms $20.00

Publisher: The Test Agency-In U.S.A. available from Test Center, Inc., 7721 Holiday Drive, Sarasota, Florida 33581

GROUP TESTS-1974

child

Purpose: Assesses developmental intelligence. Used for psychological-educational evaluation.

Description: Six subtest measure of general intelligence. Three subtests are verbal, three are nonverbal. Test provides three scores: verbal, nonverbal, and total. Materials include three series: Junior Series for Standards 4 to 6, Intermediate Series for Standards 6 to 8 and Senior Series for Standards 8 to 10. Examiner required. Suitable for group use. SOUTH AFRICAN PUBLISHER

Timed: 2 ½ hours

Range: Ages Junior Standards 4 to 6; Intermediate Standards 6 to 8; Senior Standards 8 to 10

Scoring: Hand key; examiner evaluated

Cost: (In Rands) Junior test 2,00; manual 1,20; norms 0,30; scoring stencil 1,60; 10 answer sheets 0,70; Intermediate test 0,70; manual (for Intermediate and Senior) 3,70; norms 0,30; scoring stencils (Intermediate and Senior) 1,10; Senior test 0,50; norms 0,30 (orders from outside the RSA will be dealt with on merit).

Publisher: Human Sciences Research Council

HAPTIC INTELLIGENCE SCALE
Harriet C. Shurrager and Phil S. Shurrager

adult

Purpose: Measures the intelligence of blind and partially-sighted adults. Used as a substitute for or supplement to, the Wechsler Adult Intelligence Scale.

Description: Seven non-verbal (except for instructions) task assessment—subtests measure intelligence of blind and partially-sighted adults. The tests are: Digit Symbol, Object Assembly, Block Design, Plan- of-Search, Object Completion, Pattern Board, and Bead Arithmetic. Wechsler's procedures were followed in establishing age categories and statistical treatment of the data. Examiner required. Not for group use.

Timed: 90 minutes

Range: Adult blind

Scoring: Examiner evaluated

Cost: Complete kit (includes 25 record blanks, testing materials, manual) $450.00.

Publisher: Stoelting Co.

HEALY PICTORIAL COMPLETION TEST II
William Healy

all ages

Purpose: Measures mental ability and intelligence based on an individual's apperceptive ability. Used with all age groups as well as the mentally defective.

Description: Ten item task-assessment test of problems that are visual, non-language, and ideational measures of important apperceptive abilities. The test consists of two boards containing a total of eleven 5"x3½" pictures representing the sequence of events occurring during the day in the life of a school boy. A square piece of each picture is missing and the child must complete each test picture by selecting the proper square from the accompanying 60 choices. There is only one correct choice for each picture and the concepts embodied in the test items vary greatly according to difficulty. The 60 answer pieces are numbered on the back for scoring purposes. Examiner required. Not for group use.

Timed: 20 minutes

Range: Child, adolescent, adult

Scoring: Examiner evaluated

Cost: Complete set (includes test with manual, carrying case) $82.00.

Publisher: Stoelting Co.

THE IMMEDIATE TEST (IT)
Raymond J. Corsini

all ages

Purpose: Provides a rapid estimate of mental age and IQ. Designed primarily as an emergency test for use by clinical psychologists.

Description: 66 item verbal response test. The examiner reads words, obtains responses from the subject, and stops when the subject can no longer respond. The vocabulary items are carefully calibrated from the ten-year to the twenty-year level and were selected for their interest and their relative freedom from cultural and emotional effects. Scoring takes approximately five minutes and consists of a count of the words acceptable to the examiner. The test is especially adapted to adults who cannot be easily motivated to take the usual intelligence test. For use by clinical psychologists only. Examiner required. Not for group use.

Untimed: 5 minutes

Range: Ages 10-adult

Scoring: Examiner evaluated

Cost: 25 tests $3.00; manual $.75; specimen set $1.00.

Publisher: Sheridan Psychological Services, Inc.

JENKINS INTERMEDIATE NON-VERBAL TEST: ACER
adaptation
J. W. Jenkins

child, teen

Purpose: Measures intelligence of students ages 10-14 years.

Description: 80 item paper-pencil test measures nonverbal reasoning abilities. The diagrammatic test items are divided into five subtests, involving classification, serial ordering, and diagrammatic analogies. This test is an Australian adapatation (with Australian norms) of the "Scale of Non-Verbal Mental Ability" by Jenkins published by the National Foundation for Educational Research in England and Wales. Materials include: 16-page booklet, scoring key, manual, and specimen set. Examiner required. Suitable for group use.
AUSTRALIAN PUBLISHER

Timed: 24 minutes

Range: Ages 10-14

Scoring: Hand key

Cost: Specimen set $8.65; test $.90, key $2.50; manual $5.25 (all remittances must be in Australian currency).

Publisher: The Australian Council for Educational Research Limited

JENSEN ALTERNATION BOARD
Milton B. Jensen

teen, adult

Purpose: Measures an individual's ability to understand and repeat patterns. Used to establish learning age levels and to demonstrate consistency in measuring impaired performance in certain mental pathologies.

Description: A nonverbal, hand-eye-mental test using a switchboard device, 14"x10"x2½", containing a row of five individually switched lights, a sequence selector switch, and a privacy panel to prevent the subject from seeing which series the examiner selects. A single-position warm-up exercise is administered as an example, followed by three test series, each with a different pattern. The patterns are repeated until learned and totals for each series and a combined score are computed. Examiner required. Not suitable for group use.

Untimed: 15-20 minutes

Range: Adolescent, adult

Scoring: Hand key

Cost: Apparatus $88.00.

Publisher: Lafayette Instrument Company, Inc.

JUNIOR SOUTH AFRICAN INDIVIDUAL SCALES (JSAIS)-1979

child

Purpose: Assesses cognitive functioning of children. Used for psychological-educational diagnosis.

Description: 21 scale measure of various aspects of child's cognitive abilities. Twelve empirically selected scales yield the following IQ measures: general intellectual ability (GIQ), verbal ability (VIQ), and perceptual-performance ability (PIQ), as well as estimates of memory and quantitative ability. Any scale or group of scales may be used. Examiner required. Not suitable for group use.

SOUTH AFRICAN PUBLISHER

Untimed: Not available

Range: Ages 3-7

Scoring: Hand key; examiner evaluated

Cost: (In Rands) manual-part 1, 11,00; part II 12,10; part III 8,00; 10 answer booklets 7,80; 10 profile sheets (specify 3-5 years or 6-7 years) 1,40; vocabulary set 8,40; picture puzzles 10,30; number and quantity concepts 8,90; picture series 4,10; visual memory 4,70 per set; picture riddles 8,50 (orders from outside The RSA will be dealt with on merit).

Publisher: Human Sciences Research Council

KAHN INTELLIGENCE TEST (KIT:EXP): A CULTURE- MINI-MIZED EXPERIENCE
T.C. Kahn

all ages

Purpose: Assesses individual intelligence. May be used for the blind, deaf, or those from different educational and cultural backgrounds.

Description: Performance measure of several aspects of intelligence including concept formation, recall, and motor coordination. Special scale for assessment of intelligence with blind subjects is included. Requires no reading, writing, or verbal knowledge. Uses same materials as the Kahn Test of Symbol Arrangement (KTSA): 16 plastic objects, and a cloth strip containing 15 equal sized segments. Manual contains instructions on obtaining mental age, IQ, or developmental level. For use only by psychologists, psychiatrists, counselors and others with comparable training. Examiner required. Not suitable for group use.

Untimed: 15 minutes

Range: Ages Infant-adult

Scoring: Hand key; examiner evaluated

Cost: KIT:EXP complete set $52.00.

Publisher: Psychological Test Specialists

KASANIN-HANFMANN CONCEPT FORMATION TEST (VIGOTSKY TEST)

all ages

Purpose: Measures an individual's ability to think in abstract concepts. Used with uneducated adults, children, and special groups such as psychotic patients.

Description: Task-assessment test consisting of 22 blocks which the subject must analyze and sort. The blocks are of different colors, shapes, and sizes but are alike in some way. The subject must determine the common factor and sort the blocks according to this principle. Test kit includes manual and blocks. Examiner required. Not for group use.

Untimed: Not available

Range: Child, adolescent, adult

Scoring: Examiner evaluated

Cost: Complete test $49.00.

Publisher: Stoelting Co.

LEITER INTERNATIONAL PERFORMANCE SCALE (LIPS)
Russell G. Leiter

child, teen

Purpose: Measures intelligence and mental age for all individuals 2-18 years old including the deaf, cerebral palsied, non-English speaking, and culturally disadvantaged.

Description: Multiple item, nonverbal task assessment test of intelligence. The subject is required to match blocks with corresponding characteristic strips positioned in a sturdy wooden frame. The difficulty of the task increases at each level. The categories measured are: Concretistics (matching of specific relationships), Symbolic Transformation (judging relationships between two events), Quantitative Discriminations, Spatial Imagery, Genus Matching, Progression Discriminations, and Immediate Recall. Test materials include three trays of blocks and strips that make up 54 subtests. Tray 1 covers years 2-7, Tray 2 covers years 8-12 and Tray 3 covers years 13-17. Instructions for all age levels are delivered by easily-learned pantomime. The LIPS yields Mental Age and I.Q. The Binet-type year scale has four tests at each year level from Year II through Year XVI and six tests at year XVII. The test kit includes all materials, wooden frame, carrying case, 100 record cards and manual. Examiner required. Not for group use.

Untimed: 45 minutes

Range: Ages 2-18

Scoring: Examiner evaluated

Cost: Complete kit (includes all testing materials, 3 trays, manual and record forms) $495.00; 100 record forms $14.50.

Publisher: Stoelting Co.

LOGICAL REASONING
Alfred F. Hertzka and J.P. Guilford

teen, adult

Purpose: Measures critical thinking ability. Used for research and experiment.

Description: Multiple item paper-pencil, multiple-choice test measuring the "evaluation of semantic implications." This factor is defined as the ability to judge the logical soundness of meaningful conclusions. Norms provided for high school and college for both part and total scores. Restricted to A.P.A. members. Examiner required. Suitable for group use.

Untimed: 20 minutes

Range: High school, college, adult

Scoring: Hand key; may be computer scored

Cost: 25 tests $14.00; manual $.80; 25 answer sheets $3.50; scoring key $2.00.

Publisher: Sheridan Psychological Services, Inc.

MERRILL-PALMER SCALE
Refer to page 10.

MILL HILL VOCABULARY SCALE
J.C. Raven

teen, adult

Purpose: Measures an individual's ability to recall information and state it verbally. Used for diagnosis, counseling, and school placement.

Description: Multiple item paper-pencil vocabulary test consisting of two sets of words. For Set A the subject is given a stimulus word and required to select a synonym for it from a group of six words. For Set B, the subject provides a definition for each word. The scale can be used with an appropriate level of the Progressive Matrices Test. Materials include an expendable test booklet, a specimen set and a manual. Examiner required. Suitable for group use. BRITISH PUBLISHER

Untimed: 15 minutes

Range: Ages 14-adult

Scoring: Hand key; may be computer scored

Cost: 50 record forms £5.30; manual £1.95.

Publisher: H.K. Lewis & Co., Ltd./ U.S. Distributor—The Psychological Corporation

---

NAYLOR-HARWOOD ADULT INTELLIGENCE SCALE
G.F.K. Naylor and E. Harwood

adult

Purpose: Measures intelligence of adult individuals.

Description: Multiple item paper-pencil test provides an equivalent form of the Wechsler Adult Intelligence Scale (WAIS) which has been specifically adapted for use in Australia. Subtests of the scale are the same as for the WAIS. Some items relating specifically to Australia have been included and other inappropriate items excluded. Reliability of the test has been improved by excluding elementary items from the scoring or by reducing their number to a practical minimum, and, in some cases, by lengthening individual subtests. Materials include: complete set of test forms, manual, and record form. Examiner required. AUSTRALIAN PUBLISHER

Untimed: Not available

Range: Adult

Scoring: Hand key; examiner evaluated

Cost: Contact publisher.

Publisher: The Australian Council for Educational Research Limited

---

NON-LANGUAGE MULTI-MENTAL TEST
E.L. Terman, W.A. McCall and J. Lorge

all ages

Purpose: Measures basic intelligence of illiterate or language-handicapped persons including those who do not speak English or who are deaf. Used to determine linquistic handicaps.

Description: Multiple item picture test of abstract thinking and relationships of pictorial symbols. Adaptable for either simple verbal or pantomime directions. Administration and timing are flexible. May be administered to individuals or groups from second grade on. Materials include Forms A and B (verbal or pantomime), with instructions. Examiner required. Not for group use. CANADIAN PUBLISHER

Untimed: 30 minutes

Range: Grades 2 and above

Scoring: Hand key

Cost: Specimen test $1.00; 35 tests (Form A or Form B) $8.50.

Publisher: Institute of Psychological Research, Inc.

NON-LANGUAGE TEST OF VERBAL INTELLIGENCE
Refer to page 482.

OHIO CLASSIFICATION TEST
DeWitt E. Sell, Robert W. Scollay and Leroy N. Vernon

adult

Purpose: Assesses general mental ability. Used for evaluation of penal populations.

Description: Four subtest performance measure of general intellectual ability. Subtests include Block-Counting, Digit-Symbol, Number Series, and Memory Span for Objects. Directions given by examiner. Some reading required. May be used in any situation where a culture-fair measure of intelligence is needed. Examiner required. Not suitable for group use.

Timed: 20 minutes

Range: Adult

Scoring: Hand key

Cost: Specimen set $3.30; 25 tests $5.50; 100- $21.00; 25 answer sheets $2.20, 100-$7.70.

Publisher: Psychometric Affiliates

PICTORIAL TEST OF INTELLIGENCE
Refer to page 484.

PORTEUS MAZES
S.D. Porteus

all ages

Purpose: Assessment of mental ability of verbally handicapped subjects. Used in anthropological studies and in research on the effects of drugs and psychosurgery.

Description: Nonlanguage test of mental ability. Items are mazes. Materials include the Vineland Revision, Porteus Maze Extension, and Porteus Maze Supplement. Vineland Revision is the basic test, consisting of twelve mazes. The Porteus Maze Extension is a series of eight mazes designed for retesting and not intended for use as an initial test. Porteus Maze Supplement designed for third testing in clinical and research settings. Examiner required. Not suitable for group use.

Untimed: 25 minutes per scale

Range: Children-adults

Scoring: Examiner evaluated

Cost: Basic sets (include mazes and 100 score sheets) Vineland Revision $37.50; Porteus Maze Extension $27.75; Porteus Maze Supplement $26.50 (no score sheets).

Publisher: The Psychological Corporation

PROVERBS TEST
Donald R. Gorham

all ages

Purpose: Assesses abstract verbal

comprehension. Used for individual clinical evaluation, screening, and clinical research.

Description: 12 or 40 item power test measuring verbal comprehension. Subject is required to explain the meanings of proverbs. The 12 item free-answer format allows the subject to respond in his or her own words. A 40 item multiple-choice format is also available. Free response forms are scored for abstractness and pertinence on a three point scale; concrete score also available. Multiple-choice form is scored with a hand stencil. Materials include Forms I, II, and III for free-answer administration. Examiner required. Only multiple-choice form suitable for group use.

Untimed: Individual test 10-30 minutes; group multiple-choice test 20-40 minutes

Range: Child, adolescent, adult

Scoring: Hand Key; examiner evaluated

Cost: Complete kit (includes general manual, clinical manual, 10 each of Forms I, II, III, scoring cards, 10 Best Answer form booklets; scoring stencils) $13.00; 100 test blanks $8.00; 25 test booklets $8.00; 100 answer sheets $8.00.

Publisher: Psychological Test Specialists

A QUICK SCREENING TEST OF MENTAL DEVELOPMENT
Katherine M. Banham

child

Purpose: Assesses a child's mental development from six months to ten years of age. Identifies children in need of clinical evaluation. Used in clinics, hospitals, and special schools.

Description: Task assessment and observational instrument arranged in five behavioral categories. The test

booklet consists of brief descriptions of behavior in certain situations to be checked and scored directly on the booklet. Instructions for testing procedure are provided in the manual. Professional persons skilled in clinical interviewing procedures may administer the test but the interpretation of the test results should be done by persons trained in clinical psychology. The test provides a profile of scores in the five behavior categories for diagnostic purposes and educational guidance. Tentative norms provided for 50 children along with their scores on the Cattell Infant Scale and the Stanford Binet Scale. Examiner required. Not for group use.

Untimed: 30 minutes

Range: Ages 6 months-10 years

Scoring: Hand key

Cost: Specimen set $2.20; 25 tests $3.85; 100- $12.00.

Publisher: Psychometric Affiliates

QUICK TEST (QT)
R.B. Ammons and C.H. Ammons

all ages

Purpose: Assesses individual intelligence. May be used for evaluation of severely physically handicapped, those with short attention spans, or uncooperative subjects.

Description: 50 item test of general intelligence. Subject looks at plates with four line drawings and indicates which picture best illustrates the meaning of a given word. Answers are usually given by pointing. Requires no reading, writing or speaking. Usual administration involves presentation of 15 to 20 of the items. Items are administered until there have been six consecutive passes and six consecutive failures. Materials include plates with stimulus pictures, and three alternate forms. Examiner required. Group forms available.

Untimed: 3-10 minutes

Range: Ages 2-superior adult

Scoring: Hand key; examiner evaluated

Cost: Complete kit (manual, 3 plates, 100 record sheets, instruction cardboard, item cardboard) $16.00; 100 record sheets (specify form) $10.00; 3 plates $4.00; instruction cardboard $.80; item cardboard $.70; manual $5.60.

Publisher: Psychological Test Specialists

ROSS TEST OF HIGHER COG-NITIVE PROCESSES (ROSS TEST)
Refer to page 484.

SENIOR SOUTH AFRICAN INDIVIDUAL SCALE (SSAIS)-1964

child, teen

Purpose: Assesses general intelligence in children. Used for psychological-educational evaluation.

Description: Nine subtest measure of general intellectual ability. Five verbal subtests and four non-verbal subtests. Verbal, Non-Verbal and Total IQ may be obtained. Examiner required. Not suitable for group use. SOUTH AFRICAN PUBLISHER

Untimed: 50 minutes

Range: Ages 6-17

Scoring: Hand key; examiner evaluated

Cost: (In Rands) complete kit (includes manual, tests 1-9, globite holder, 2 examples of the answer sheets and practice samples) 102,00 (orders from outside The RSA will be dealt with on merit).

Publisher: Human Sciences Research Council

SHIPLEY INSTITUTE OF LIV-ING SCALE
W.C. Shipley

adult

Purpose: Measures the intellectual ability and impairment of adults and adolescents ages 15 years and older. Used for clinical assessment and counseling purposes in a wide variety of clinical, educational, personnel and counseling settings.

Description: 60 item, paper-pencil test measuring vocabulary and logical sequencing (abstract thinking) abilities. The test yields both an IQ estimate and a Conceptual Quotient (CQ) which expresses the extent to which the person's abstract thinking falls short of vocabulary. The CQ is particularly useful for assessing current impairment of intellectual functioning. Standardized on over 1,000 subjects. Examiner required. Suitable for group use.

Timed: 20 minutes

Range: Adults

Scoring: Hand key; computer scoring available

Cost: Kit (50 tests and manual) $9.20.

Publisher: Western Psychological Services

SLOSSON INTELLIGENCE TEST (SIT)/SLOSSON ORAL READING TEST (SORT)
Richard L. Slosson

all ages

Purpose: Measures the mental age, IQ, and reading level of children and adults. Used by psychologists, guidance counselors, special educators, learning disabilities teachers, and remedial reading teachers to provide a quick assessment of a person's mental abilities.

Description: 195 item oral screening instrument consisting of questions arranged on a scale of Chronological Age from one-half month to 27 years. A Basal Age is established at the point before which the subject gives an incorrect answer after giving at least ten correct answers in a row. Additional credit is then added for correct answers given above the Basal Age. The Basal Age plus added months credit are used to determine mental age and IQ. Norms provided include: percentiles, Normal Curve Equivalents, Stanine Categories, and T- Scores. The results can be used to predict reading achievement, to plan educational programs, to predict success and acceptance in college, to screen students for reading disabilities, and as an IQ test for the blind. Also includes the Slosson Oral Reading Test (SORT), which yields a reading grade level from primer into high school based on the ability to pronounce words at different levels of difficulty. Also used to identify reading handicaps. SIT item analysis available to identify strengths and weaknesses in eight learning areas. Examiner required. Not for group use.

Untimed: 10-20 minutes

Range: Child-adult (norms tables do not include infants with CA below 2).

Scoring: Examiner evaluated

Cost: Complete kit (includes Manual of Questions, directions, 1981 norms tables, 50 Slosson Oral Reading Tests, 50 score sheets for the Slosson Intelligence Test and vinyl binder) $35.00.

Publisher: Slosson Educational Publications, Inc.

SNIJDERS-OOMEN NON-VERBAL INTELLIGENCE SCALE (SON)
J. Th. Snijders and N. Snijders-Oomen

child, teen

Purpose: Assesses nonverbal intelligence of hearing defective children ages 5-17 years.

Description: Paper-pencil scale consisting of eight subtests which are combined under the headings Form, Combination, Abstraction and Immediate Memory. The full scale can also be divided into two shorter forms. Provides standard deviation IQ's and mental age for South Afrikaan speaking pupils. Available in Dutch and German. Examiner required. Suitable for individual use. DUTCH DISTRIBUTOR

Untimed: Not available

Range: Ages 3-16

Scoring: Examiner evaluated

Cost: Contact publisher.

Publisher: Swets Test Services

THE SOUTH AFRICAN INDIVIDUAL SCALE FOR THE BLIND (SAISB)-1979

child, teen

Purpose: Measures general intelligence of blind children ages 6-18. Used for psychological and educational evaluations.

Description: Nine subtest measure of general intellectual ability. Five subtests are verbal and four are non-verbal. Materials include Braillon sheets for Pattern Completion and Dominos subtests, form board and wooden blocks. Adapted from the New South African Individual Scale (NSAIS). Examiner required. Not

suitable for group use.
SOUTH AFRICAN PUBLISHER

Untimed: Not available

Range: Ages 6 years 10 months-18 years 3 months

Scoring: Hand key; examiner evaluated

Cost: Complete specimen (includes Pattern Completion, Rubberboard, Subtest 7, 8, 9 Form Board B, manual, vulvalite case, 2 sheets of cellophane paper and 2 general answer sheets (orders from outside The RSA will be dealt with on merit).

Publisher: Human Sciences Research Council

THE STANDARD PROGRES-SIVE MATRICES (SPM-1938)
J.C. Raven

---

all ages

Purpose: Measures an individual's mental ability through assessment of nonverbal abstract reasoning tasks. Used for school and vocational counseling and placement.

Description: 60 item paper-pencil nonverbal test in five sets of 12 problems each. In each problem, the subject is presented with a pattern or figure design which has a part missing. The subject then selects one of six possible parts as the correct one. The patterns are arrayed from simple to complex. The test is often used with the Mill Hill Vocabulary Scale. Examiner required. Suitable for group use. Standardized in Great Britain.
BRITISH PUBLISHER

Untimed: 45 minutes

Range: Ages 8-65

Scoring: Hand key; machine scored

Cost: Specimen set (includes book of tests, 5 matrices and Mill Hill Vocabulary record forms, sample machine scorable record form) £9.70 plus V.A.T.; 25 tests £48.00; 50 record forms £2.95; plastic marking key £4.95 plus VAT).

Publisher: H.K. Lewis & Co., Ltd./ U.S. Distributor—The Psychological Corporation

---

STANFORD-BINET INTEL-LIGENCE SCALE: FORM L-M
Lewis M. Terman and Maud A. Merrill

---

all ages

Purpose: Measures an individual's mental abilities. Used to substantiate questionable scores from group tests and when the subject has physical, language, or personality disorders which rule out group testing.

Description: 142 item verbal and nonverbal IQ test assessing the following factors: language, memory, conceptual thinking, reasoning, numerical reasoning, visual motor, and social reasoning. Measures IQ through individual assessment from ages two years through adulthood. In most cases, only 18-24 test items need be administered to a given subject. The basal age is established (year level at which all items are passed), and testing continues until the ceiling age is reached (year level at which all items are failed). Responses are then scored according to established procedures to yield mental age and IQ. Results identify children and adults who would benefit from specialized learning environments. Administered only by professionally trained, certified examiners. Examiner required. Not for group use.

Timed: 45-90 minutes

Range: Ages 2 and older

Scoring: Examiner evaluated

Cost: Examiner's kit, form L-M (includes manual, large and small printed card material, miniaturized objects) $123.75; 35 record booklets $14.01; 35 record forms $7.83.

Publisher: The Riverside Publishing Company

STANFORD-OHWAKI-KOHS BLOCK DESIGN INTELLIGENCE TEST FOR THE BLIND: AMERICAN REVISION
Richard M. Suinn and William L. Dauterman

teen, adult

Purpose: Measures intelligence of partially sighted and functionally blind individuals 16 years of age and older.

Description: Multiple item task assessment test uses tactile sense to identify and duplicate the Kohs design block test. This revision of the Ohwaki- Kohs Tactile Block Design Intelligence Test provides standardization on American subjects. Results yield percentile and IQ scores. Examiner required. Not for group use.

Timed: 1-2 hours

Range: Ages 16-adult

Scoring: Hand key; examiner evaluated

Cost: Complete kit (includes 1 set of test materials, 25 record forms, manual) $94.80.

Publisher: Western Psychological Services

THE TEST OF NONVERBAL INTELLIGENCE (TONI)
Linda Brown, Rita J. Sherbenu and Susan J. Dollar

all ages

Purpose: Provides a language-free measure of intelligence and reasoning. Used with subjects suspected of having difficulty in reading, writing, listening, or speaking, including the mentally retarded, stroke patients, bilingual and non-English speaking persons, speech or language handicapped, and the learning disabled.

Description: 50 item "point-to" response test assessing intellectual capacities in a format completely free of reading, writing, and verbalizing. The examiner pantomimes the instructions, and the subject responds by pointing to the selected answer. Test items use abstract symbols to present a variety of reasoning tasks, arranged in increasing order of complexity and difficulty. The test yields a TONI quotient and percentile ranks, accurately discriminating between retarded and normal subjects. Available in two equivalent forms. Examiner required. May be administered to small groups of up to five subjects.

Untimed: 20-30 minutes

Range: Ages 6-80

Scoring: Hand key

Cost: Complete kit (includes manual, picture book, 50 form A & 50 form B answer sheets in storage box) $63.00. Components available for separate purchase.

Publisher: PRO-ED

TIME APPRECIATION TEST
John N. Buck

all ages

Purpose: Measures intelligence for all ages over ten years. Used for initial screening and as an emergency intelligence test.

Description: 30 item paper-pencil test consisting of objective questions about various aspects of time. Provides mental age equivalent scores for children and adults, and adult intelligence quotients and classifications. Relatively high correlation with Stanford-Binet. Examiner required. Suitable for group use.

Untimed: 10 minutes

Range: Ages 10-adult

Scoring: Hand key

Cost: Complete kit (includes 50 tests, manual) $7.20.

Publisher: Western Psychological Services

WECHSLER SCALES: WECHSLER ADULT INTEL-LIGENCE SCALE (WAIS)
David Wechsler

teen, adult

Purpose: Measures intelligence in adolescents and adults

Description: 11 subtests divided into two major divisions yielding a verbal IQ, a performance IQ and a full scale IQ for persons age 16 and older. The Verbal section of the WAIS consists of the following subtests: Information, Comprehension, Arithmetic, Similarities, Digit Span and Vocabulary. The Performance or nonverbal section of the test consists of the following subtests: Digit Symbol, Picture Completion, Block Design, Picture Arrangement, and Object Assembly. Some units of the test require verbal responses from the subjects and others require the subject to manipulate test materials to demonstrate performance ability. Raw scores are converted into scale scores after the subject's performance has been recorded and scored on the provided answer form by the examiner. Examiner required. Not suitable for group use. Available in Spanish.

Untimed: 1 hour

Range: Ages 16-adult

Scoring: Examiner evaluated

Cost: Complete set (includes all necessary equipment, manual, 25 record forms) $87.50; complete set without carrying case $80.00.

Publisher: The Psychological Corporation

WECHSLER SCALES: WECHSLER ADULT INTEL-LIGENCE SCALE-REVISED (WAIS-R)
David Wechsler

teen, adult

Purpose: Assesses intelligence in adolescents and adults.

Description: 11 subtests divided into two major divisions yielding a verbal IQ, a performance IQ and a full scale IQ for persons age 16 and older. The Verbal section of the WAIS consists of the following subtests: Information, Comprehension, Arithmetic, Similarities, Digit Span and Vocabulary. The Performance or nonverbal section of the test consists of the following subtests: Digit Symbol, Picture Completion, Block Design, Picture Arrangement, and Object Assembly. Some units of the test require verbal responses from the subjects and others require the subject to manipulate test materials to demonstrate performance ability. Raw scores are converted into scale scores after the subject's performance has been recorded and scored on the provided answer form by the examiner. The WAIS-R is a revision of the 1955 WAIS edition. Examiner required. Not suitable for group use. Available in Spanish.

Untimed: 75 minutes

Range: Ages 16-adult

Scoring: Examiner evaluated

Cost: Complete set (includes all necessary equipment, manual, 25 record forms with carrying case) $87.50; complete without carrying case $80.00.

Publisher: The Psychological Corporation

WECHSLER SCALES: WECHSLER INTELLIGENCE SCALE FOR CHILDREN: 1949 EDITION (WISC)
David Wechsler

teen

Purpose: Measures intelligence for children ages 5-15.

Description: 12 subtests divided into two major divisions yielding a verbal IQ, a performance IQ and a full scale IQ for children tested individually. The Verbal section of the test consists of the following subtests: General Information, General Comprehension, Arithmetic, Similarities, Vocabulary, and Digit Span. The Performance section consists of the following subtests: Picture Completion, Picture Arrangement, Block Design, Object Assembly, Coding and Mazes. Some units of the test require verbal responses from the subjects and others require the subject to manipulate test materials to demonstrate performance ability. Raw scores are converted into scale scores after the subject's performance has been recorded and scored on the provided answer form by the examiner. The WISC-R is a more recently revised form of the 1949 WISC. Examiner required. Not suitable for group use. Available in Spanish.

Untimed: 1 hour

Range: Ages 5-15

Scoring: Examiner evaluated

Cost: Complete set (includes all equipment, manual, 25 record forms and test blanks, carrying case) $71.00; complete without carrying case $63.00.

Publisher: The Psychological Corporation

WECHSLER SCALES: WECHSLER INTELLIGENCE SCALE FOR CHILDREN- REVISED (WISC-R)
David Wechsler

child, teen

Purpose: Assesses mental ability in children.

Description: 12 subtests divided into two major divisions yielding a verbal IQ, a performance IQ and a full scale IQ for children tested individually. The Verbal section of the test consists of the following subtests: General Information, General Comprehension, Arithmetic, Similarities, Vocabulary, and Digit Span. The Performance section consists of the following subtests: Picture Completion, Picture Arrangement, Block Design, Object Assembly, Coding and Mazes. Some units of the test require verbal responses from the subjects and others require the subject to manipulate test materials to demonstrate performance ability. Raw scores are converted into scale scores after the subject's performance has been recorded and scored on the provided answer form by the examiner. The WISC-R is a more recently revised form of the 1949 WISC. Examiner required. Not suitable for group use. Available in Spanish.

Untimed: 1 hour

Range: Ages 6-16

Scoring: Examiner evaluated

Cost: Complete set (includes all necessary equipment, manual, 25 record forms, mazes, coding booklet, carrying case) $98.00; complete set without carrying case $90.00.

Publisher: The Psychological Corporation

WECHSLER SCALES: WECHSLER PRESCHOOL AND PRIMARY SCALE OF INTELLIGENCE (WPPSI)
David Wechsler

child

Purpose: Assesses intelligence in children ages 4- 6½.

Description: 10 subtests divided into two major divisions yielding a verbal IQ, a performance IQ and a full scale IQ for children tested individually. The Verbal section of the test consists of the following subtests: Information, Vocabulary, Arithmetic, Similarities, and Comprehension. (A supplementary Sentences Test is available within the Verbal section of test.) The Performance section consists of the following subtests: Animal House, Picture Completion, Mazes, Geometric Design, and Block Design. (An Animal House Retest unit is available within the Performance section.) Selected subtests require verbal responses while other require that the subject demonstrate abilities through manipulating test materials provided within the WPPSI test kit. Raw scores are converted to scale scores after examiner has recorded and scored subject responses on answer sheet. Examiner required. Not suitable for groups. Available in Spanish.

Untimed: 1 hour

Range: Ages 4-6½

Scoring: Examiner evaluated

Cost: Complete set (includes all necessary equipment, manual, 25 record forms, maze test, 50 geometric design sheets, with carrying case) $90.00; complete set without carrying case $77.50.

Publisher: The Psychological Corporation

WECHSLER MEMORY SCALE
Refer to page 54.

Learning Disabilities and Organic Dysfunction

ANALYTIC LEARNING DISABILITY ASSESSMENT (ALDA)
Refer to page 546.

BENDER VISUAL MOTOR GESTALT TEST
Lauretta Bender

all ages

Purpose: Assesses the visual-motor functions of individuals from age three years to adulthood. Also used in the evaluation of developmental problems in children, learning disabilities, retardation, psychosis, and organic brain disorders.

Description: Test consists of nine Gestalt cards: The subject is given the cards one at a time and asked to reproduce on blank paper the configuration or design shown on each card. Responses are scored according to the following criteria: development of the concepts of form, shape, and pattern; and orientation in space. Analysis of performance may indicate the presence of psychosis and maturational lags. Examiner required. Slides may be used for group administration.

Untimed: 15-20 minutes

Range: Ages 3 and older

Scoring: Examiner evaluated; Koppitz and Grune & Stratton provide scoring service.

Cost: Test cards $4.00; Monograph (instruction book) $10.00.

Publisher: American Orthopsychiatric Association

BENTON REVISED VISUAL RETENTION TEST
Arthur Benton

all ages

Purpose: Measures visual memory. Used as a supplement to usual mental examinations and in experimental research.

Description: Ten item test of visual perception, visual memory, and visuoconstructive abilities. Items are designs which are shown to subject one by one. Subject studies design and reproduces it as exactly as possible by drawing it on plain paper. Materials include Design Cards, and three alternate and equivalent forms, C, D, and E. Examiner required. Not suitable for group use.

Untimed: 5 minutes

Range: Ages 8-adult

Scoring: Examiner evaluated

Cost: Complete set (includes manual, Design cards-3 forms combined, 50 record forms) $15.50.

Publisher: The Psychological Corporation

BESSEMER SCREENING TEST
Refer to page 567.

THE BODER TEST OF READING-SPELLING PATTERNS
Refer to page 548.

THE BOOKLET CATEGORY TEST (BCT)
Nick A. DeFilippis and Elizabeth McCampbell

teen, adult

Purpose: Diagnoses brain dysfunction. Used for clinical assessment of brain damage.

Description: 208 item visually presented test of concept formation and abstract reasoning. Figures are presented one at a time to the subject who is asked to respond with a number between one and four. This is the booklet version of the Halstead Category Test. The first four subtests may be used to predict total error scores if time limitations do not allow for entire BCT. Examiner required. Not suitable for group use.

Untimed: 30-60 minutes

Range: Ages 16-adult

Scoring: Examiner evaluated

Cost: Complete set (includes BCT 2 volumes manual, and 25 scoring forms) $95.00.

Publisher: Psychological Assessment Resources, Inc.

CANTER BACKGROUND INTERFERENCE PROCEDURE (BIP) for the BENDER GESTALT TEST
Arthur Canter

teen, adult

Purpose: Assesses the probability of organic brain damage among individuals 15 years and older, and has some usefulness with children as young as 8 years old. Used for diagnosis and to plan rehabilitation programs.

Description: Ten item paper-pencil test. It uses the standard Bender Gestalt Test in which the subject is presented with stimulus cards and asked to copy the designs on a blank sheet of paper, and compares that with a Bender Gestalt Test in which the subject reproduces the designs on a special sheet with intersecting sinusoidal lines which provide a background "noise" or interference during the copying task. Scoring is a modification of the standard Pascal-Suttell system. The difference between the standard and the BIP results provides the basis for defining the level of impairment. Specific ranges of adequacy and inadequacy of performance are defined to permit a measure of impairment having a high probability of association with organic brain damage or disease. Examiner required. Not for group use.

Untimed: 20-30 minutes

Range: Ages 15-adult

Scoring: Examiner evaluated

Cost: Complete kit (includes 10 tests and manual) $11.50.

Publisher: Western Psychological Services

CHART OF INITIATIVE AND INDEPENDENCE

mental handicap

Purpose: Assesses capacity of mentally handicapped people. Used for placement decisions and ongoing assessments.

Description: Multiple item rating scale measure describing the behavior of mentally handicapped persons within a specific context such as an institution. Chart has four parts: Part One is directed at present capacity and level of opportunity; Part Two is directed at the future; Part Three is concerned with ward/hostel policy; Part Four is concerned with collecting other information such as IQ scores, medical condition, academic skills. Examiner required. Not suit-

able for group use.

BRITISH PUBLISHER

Untimed: Open ended

Range: Mentally handicapped

Scoring: Examiner evaluated

Cost: Manual (including Manual of Activities and PAF manual) £4.50; Manual of Activities £0.50; individual assessment forms and 1 copy residential policy forms £2.95; development programme forms and 1 copy residential policy forms £2.95; preliminary assessment forms plus 1 copy PAE manual £3.30 (payment in sterling for all overseas orders).

Publisher: NFER-Nelson Publishing Company

DIAGNOSTIC ANALYSIS OF READING ERRORS (DARE)
Refer to page 511.

DYSLEXIA SCHEDULE
Refer to page 549.

THE DYSLEXIA SCREENING SURVEY (DSS)
Robert E. Valett

child

Purpose: Evaluates basic neuropsychological skills for screening elementary pupils who may be dyslexic. Used to plan remedial strategies.

Description: 90 item paper-pencil test covering seven factors: I. Functional reading level, II. Reading potential, III. Significant reading discrepancy, IV. Specific processing skill deficiencies, V. Neuropsychological dysfunctions, VI. Associated factors, and VII. Development-remedial strategies. Administered individually in several steps including a compilation of available information and subsequent testing of paper-pencil and body- movement tasks which complete the survey. Recommended for use by special educators, remedial reading specialists, psychologists, and speech therapists, but is not restricted. Remedial methods are presented in the test author's book, *Dyslexia*. Examiner required. Not for group use.

Untimed: 30 minutes

Range: Grades 1-6

Scoring: Examiner evaluated

Cost: 10 forms $6.95.

Publisher: Pitman Learning, Inc.

ELIZUR TEST OF PSYCHO-ORGANICITY: CHILDREN & ADULTS
Abraham Elizur

all ages

Purpose: Differentiates between organic and non-organic brain disorders in individuals age 6 years to adult. Used by neurologists, psychologists, educators, counselors, and researchers.

Description: Multiple item task assessment test using drawings, digits, and blocks to eliminate "uni—dimensional" measurements. Test tasks are easily performed by subjects so as not to bias the results with intelligence factors. Separate instructions are provided for administering to adults and children. Results yield quantitative and qualitative measures with cutoff points provided for classifying examinees as organic. Examiner required. Not for group use.

Untimed: 10 minutes

Range: Ages 6-adult

Scoring: Hand key; examiner evaluated

Cost: Kit (10 protocol booklets, 1 set test materials, manual) $27.80.

Publisher: Western Psychological Services

FULD OBJECT-MEMORY EVALUATION
Paula Altman Fuld

adult

Purpose: Measures memory and learning in adults ages 70-90, regardless of vision, hearing, or language handicaps, cultural differences, or inattention problems.

Description: Ten common objects in a bag are presented to the patient to determine whether he can identify them by touch. The patient names the item, then pulls it out of the bag to see if he was right. After being distracted, the patient is asked to recall the items from the bag. The patient is then given four more chances to learn and recall the objects. The test provides separate scores for long-term storage, retrieval, consistency of retrieval and failure to recall items even after being reminded. It also provides a chance to observe naming ability, left-right orientation, stereognosis and verbal fluency. Separate norms are provided for total recall, storage, consistency of retrieval, ability to benefit from reminding and ability to say words in categories. Examiner required. Not for group use.

Timed: 60 seconds for each first trial, 30 seconds for each second trial

Range: Adult ages 70-90 years of age

Scoring: Examiner evaluated

Cost: Complete kit (includes all testing materials, manual, record forms) $21.00; 30 record forms $5.75.

Publisher: Stoelting Co.

FIVE TASK TEST
Refer to page 152.

FULLERTON LANGUAGE TEST FOR ADOLESCENTS (EXPERIMENTAL EDITION)
Refer to page 585.

GARDNER STEADINESS TESTER
Richard A. Gardner and Andrew K. Gardner

child, teen

Purpose: Measures one aspect of activity level in children suspected of minimal brain dysfunction; to be used in conjunction with a complete minimal brain dysfunction diagnostic battery.

Description: Nonverbal test measuring generalized hyperactivity, prolonged attention, motor impersistence, tremors, and choreiform movements. Materials consist of a special stylus and stylus plate, tone response, 1/100th-second stop clock, 60 minute timer, and control circuitry mounted on a 8" x 18" fiberesin board. The examiner demonstrates the device to the child and shows him how to hold it correctly. The child is then tested for three 60-second periods with 15 seconds of rest in-between. The total contact time for the three trials is allowed to accumulate on the clock. At the end, the total time is recorded and the clock reset. Examiner required. Not for group use.

Timed: Total time 3½ minutes

Range: Ages 5 years 0 months-14 years 11 months

Scoring: Hand key

Cost: Complete set $290.00.

Publisher: Lafayette Instrument Company, Inc.

GOLDSTEIN-SCHEERER TESTS OF ABSTRACT AND CONCRETE THINKING
Kurt Goldstein and Martin Scheerer

patients

Purpose: Measures impairment of the brain's abstract and concrete reasoning functions. Used for assessment of patients with brain injuries.

Description: Battery of performance tests assessing abstract and concrete reasoning. The Goldstein-Scheerer Cube Test requires subject to copy colored designs with blocks. The Gelb-Goldstein Color Sorting Test measures the ability to sort a variety of colors according to definite color concepts. The Goldstein-Scheerer Object Sorting Test requires the subject to sort a variety of simultaneously presented objects according to general concepts. The Weigl-Goldstein-Scheerer Color Form Sorting Test involves sorting different colored figures according to categories of color and form. The Goldstein-Scheerer Stick Test measures the subject's ability to copy figures composed of stick's and reproduce them from memory. Materials include all necessary equipment for the five tests. Examiner required. Not suitable for group use.

Untimed: 20-30 minutes

Range: Brain-injured patients

Scoring: Examiner evaluated

Cost: Complete set (includes all necessary equipment for all 5 tests, monograph, 50 each of 6 record forms) $163.50.

Publisher: The Psychological Corporation

GRASSI BASIC COGNITIVE EVALUATION
Joseph R. Grassi

child

Purpose: Identifies cognitive deficits in four to eight-year old children with brain dysfunction. Used by psychologists and educators for clinical assessment.

Description: Measures 27 different traits in visual, auditory and kinesthetic areas. Specially designed for children who are brain damaged, mentally retarded, cognitively disadvantaged or learning disabled. Materials include manual and record forms. Examiner-evaluated by trained psychologist or educator. Not for group use.

Untimed: 30 minutes

Range: Ages 4-8

Scoring: Examiner evaluated

Cost: Complete kit (includes 25 record forms and manual) $35.00.

Publisher: Joseph R. Grassi, Inc.

GRASSI BLOCK SUBSTITUTION TEST
Joseph R. Grassi

teen, adult

Purpose: Detects early symptoms of organic brain pathology in adolescents and adults. Used for clinical screening procedures.

Description: Task assessment test measuring abstract behavior as an indicator of organic brain pathology. Test materials consist of five specially designed semi-cubes and manual. Examiner must be a clinical psychologist with training and experience in the concepts of abstract versus concrete behavior. Examiner required. Not for group use.

Untimed: Not available

Range: Adolescent, adult

Scoring: Examiner evaluated

Cost: Test materials $30.00 (from Joseph R. Grassi, Inc.); manual $15.00 (from Charles C. Thomas Publisher, 2600 South 1st Street, Springfield, Illinois 62717, (217)789-8980).

Publisher: Joseph R. Grassi, Inc.

GROOVED PEGBOARD

all ages

Purpose: Measures hand-eye coordination and fine finger dexterity. Used as part of clinical neuropsychological evaluation battery in brain damage, alcoholism, aging, and epilepsy.

Description: Multiple-operation, manual test using a 4" x 4" mahogany box with a shallow well in the lid and a hole plate containing 25 keyed slots oriented in random directions and a set of 25 keyed pegs. The subject inserts all 25 pegs into the slots with one hand, then the other. Separate times are recorded for the dominant hand and the non-dominant hand. Used with the Trites Neuropsychological and the Halstead-Reitan Test Batteries. Also used to discriminate multiple sclerosis patients from those with other neurological diseases. Examiner required. Suitable for group use.

Untimed: 5 minutes

Range: Ages 5-adult

Scoring: Hand key

Cost: Complete kit $47.25; set of 30 replacement pegs $19.00.

Publisher: Lafayette Instrument Company, Inc.

HOOPER VISUAL ORGANIZA-
TION TEST (HVOT)
H. Elston Hooper

teen, adult

Purpose: Assesses organic brain pathology of the right hemisphere. Used for clinical diagnosis.

Description: 30 item pictorial test differentiating between functional and motivational disorders. The subject is presented drawings of simple objects cut into several parts and rearranged. He is asked to name the objects. A book of pictures is used for individual administration. Examiner required. Suitable for group use.

Untimed: 15 minutes

Range: Junior high school-adult

Scoring: Hand key

Cost: Complete $13.50 (booklet and manual).

Publisher: Brandywine Associates

HOUSTON TEST FOR
LANGUAGE DEVELOPMENT
Refer to page 8.

ILLINOIS TEST OF PSYCHO-
LINGUISTIC ABILITIES (ITPA)
Refer to page 586.

JORDAN LEFT-RIGHT
REVERSAL TEST (JLRRT)
Refer to page 550.

JOSEPH PRESCHOOL AND
PRIMARY SELF-CONCEPT
SCREENING TEST (JPPSST)
Jack Joseph

child

Purpose: Measures social-emotional development of children ages 3½-9 years. Used to identify children who may have learning difficulties due to negative self-appraisals, and to monitor progress in early childhood programs and special education classes. Useful in meeting requirements of P.L. 94-142.

Description: 16 item paper-pencil and oral response test in two parts. First, the child is asked to draw his own face on a blank figure of the corresponding sex. Then, the child is asked to answer two simple oral response questions and 13 questions asking the child to select from pairs of pictures the one with which he identifies more closely. The face drawing is evaluated qualitatively and the 15 questions are scored objectively. The test generates a Global Self-Concept Score based on five dimensions, and provides objective high-risk cut-off points. The effects of socially-desirable responses are corrected for at upper ranges (ages 5-9) and it develops both quantitative and qualitative indices regarding possible cognitive deficits, and experiential or receptive language lags. The manual provides normative data, measures of validity and reliability, item analysis, specific case illustrations, and research considerations. Examiner required. Not for group use.

Untimed: 5-7 minutes

Range: Ages 3½-9

Scoring: Examiner evaluated

Cost: Complete kit (includes manual, stimulus cards, identify reference drawings and 100 record forms) $56.00.

Publisher: Stoelting Co.

KAHN TEST OF SYMBOL ARRANGEMENT (KTSA)
Theodore C. Kahn

all ages

Purpose: Assesses personality dynamics and extent of cerebral competence. Used for individual diagnosis and therapy, as well as vocational counseling.

Description: Multiple task performance test of subject's cultural/symbolic thinking. Subject is required to sort plastic objects of varying size, color, thickness, and translucence in several ways. Examiner evaluates subject's symbol pattern, and compares it to patterns of normal and clinical groups. Materials include 16 plastic objects, a cloth strip containing 15 equal sized segments, and two manuals, administration and clinical. For use only by clinical psychologists, psychiatrists, counseling psychologists, school psychologists, and others with professional competence in clinical assessment. Examiner required. Not suitable for group use.

Untimed: 15 minutes

Range: Child, adolescent, adult

Scoring: Hand key; examiner evaluated

Cost: Complete kit (includes plastic objects, felt strip, 10 individual record sheets, manual, clinical manual) $50.00; 50 record sheets $15.00, replacement plastic objects $3.00 each; manual $4.00; clinical manual $6.00.

Publisher: Psychological Test Specialists

LEARNING DISABILITY RATING PROCEDURE (LDRP)
Refer to page 550.

LEARNING EFFICIENCY TEST (LET)
Refer to page 551.

LURIA-NEBRASKA NEURO-PSYCHOLOGICAL BATTERY
Charles J. Golden, Thomas A. Hammeke, and Arnold D. Purisch

teen, adult

Purpose: Assesses a broad range of neuropsychological functions for persons age 15 and older. Used to diagnose specific cerebral dysfunction and to select and assess rehabilitation programs.

Description: 269 item verbal, observational test. The discrete, scored items produce a profile for the following 14 scales: Motor, Rhythm, Tactile, Visual, Preceptive Speech, Expressive Speech, Writing, Reading, Arithmetic, Memory, Intellectual, Pathognomonic, Left Hemisphere, and Right Hemisphere. The battery has the ability to diagnose the presence of cerebral dysfunction, as well as to determine lateralization and localization. The test materials include: six stimulus cards, one tape cassette, and a few commonly available items such as a comb, a quarter, and a stopwatch. A manual provides instructions for administering the test, evidence of reliability and validity, interpretive guides, and copies of the *Administration and Scoring Booklet* and the *Patient Response Booklet*. The *Administration and Scoring Booklet* includes the Profile Form and Computation of Critical Level Tables. It is used to record all scores during the administration and provides the verbal instructions to be read to the patient. *The Patient Response Booklet* is provided for those items requiring written answers. An equivalent parallel form offering computer scoring and micro software (Form II) will be available in 1983. Examiner required. Not for group use.

Untimed: 1½-2½ hours

Range: Ages 15-adult

Scoring: Hand key; computer scoring available

Cost: Complete kit (includes manual, 6 stimulus cards, tape cassette, 5 scoring booklets, 5 patient response booklets, 1 set supplemental stimulus cards) $137.50.

Publisher: Western Psychological Services

LURIA'S NEUROPSYCHOLOGI-CAL INVESTIGATION
Anne-Lise Christensen

adult

Purpose: Diagnoses type and severity of brain injury as a basis for planning rehabilitational measures for brain-damaged adults.

Description: Oral response and task assessment test begins with a structure for preliminary conversation with the patient and goes on to measure the following neurological areas: motor functions, acoustico- motor organization, higher cutaneous and kinesthetic functions, higher visual functions, impressive speech, expressive speech, writing and reading, arithmetical skill, mnestic processes, and intellectual processes. Materials include: set of cards, manual, and text. Examiner required. Not for group use.

AUSTRALIAN DISTRIBUTOR

Untimed: Not available

Range: Adult

Scoring: Examiner evaluated

Cost: Contact publisher

Publisher: Munksgaard-distributed by The Australian Council for Education Research Limited

MANUAL ACCURACY AND SPEED TEST
Peter F. Briggs and Auke Tellegen

all ages

Purpose: Measures the level of motor development of normal and physically handicapped individuals. Used to evaluate treatment progress and as a basis for further testing and remediation.

Description: Five test nonverbal battery measuring manual motor skills. The examiner uses a master control console with an interval timer, 1/100th-second stop watch, counter and an adjustable stand, provided with the kit. The tests consist of Ballistic Tapping for rate of arm movement, Picking Up Nails for finger dexterity, Hole Steadiness for hand and arm control, Large Peg Placement for manual dexterity, and Small Peg Placement for eye-hand coordination. The materials are presented to the subject who is seated at the stand, adjusted to elbow height. All tasks are performed first with the right hand, then with the left, preceded by a practice session. The test is easily given to persons confined to wheelchairs. Examiner required. Not suitable for group use.

Untimed: 10 minutes

Range: Ages 4-39 years

Scoring: Hand key

Cost: Complete $1875.00.

Publisher: Lafayette Instrument Co., Inc.

MEMORY-FOR-DESIGNS TEST (MFD)
Frances K. Graham and Barbara S. Kendall

all ages

Purpose: Assesses perceptual-motor coordination. Used to differentiate between functional behavior disorders and those associated with brain injury.

Description: 15 item performance measure of perceptual- motor coordination. Items consist of designs on cardboard cards. Subject is shown a design for five seconds, then attempts to draw it from memory. This procedure is repeated for each of the 15 items. Materials include manual which summarizes research with the MFD. Diagnostic testing and evaluation should be closely supervised by a clinical or school psychologist, psychiatrist, neurologist, or pediatrician. Examiner required. Not suitable for group use.

Untimed: 10 minutes

Range: Ages 8½-60

Scoring: Hand key; examiner evaluated

Cost: Complete kit (revised general manual, set of 15 design cards, extra set of scoring examples and norms) $17.00; set of 15 design cards $15.00, utility scoring examples and norms $2.50; revised manual $5.00.

Publisher: Psychological Test Specialists

MINNESOTA PERCEPTO-DIAGNOSTIC TEST (MPD)
Gerald B. Fuller

all ages

Purpose: Assesses visual perception and visual motor abilities. Used to classify reading and learning disabilities and to identify individuals with emotionally disturbed or schizophrenic perception.

Description: Six item paper-pencil test consisting of Gestalt designs which the subject is asked to copy on a separate sheet of paper. The designs are individually presented to the subject on separate cards. Subject's

drawings are scored for degrees of rotation, separation, and distortion to decide whether the perception is normal, emotionally disturbed, or brain damaged. Also classifies the etiology of reading and learning disabilities as primary, secondary, or organic retardation, as well as measuring the maturational level of normal and retarded children. All Scores adjusted for both age and IQ. Available in separate scales for children and adults. Examiner required. Not for group use.

Untimed: 6-8 minutes

Range: Child scale ages 5-12; adult scale ages 13 and older

Scoring: Hand key; examiner evaluated

Cost: Manual $12.00; test cards $6.00; 50 record blanks $5.00.

Publisher: Clinical Psychology Publishing Co.

NEUROPSYCHOLOGICAL QUESTIONNAIRE: ADULT FORM
Fernando Melendez

teen, adult

Purpose: Evaluates possible conditions which may suggest underlying brain dysfunctions or other organic conditions in adults. Used as a symptom checklist for making appropriate referrals to other doctors, and for further neuropsychological testing.

Description: 59 item paper-pencil questionnaire to quickly review complaints, symptoms, and signs that may suggest brain dysfunction. Also serves as a reliable monitor in following course of recovery or decline of a person over a period of time. Examiner asks questions and requests elaboration when appropriate. Examiner required. Not for group use. Available in Spanish.

Untimed: 10-15 minutes

Range: Ages 16 and older

Scoring: Examiner evaluated

Cost: Complete kit (includes forms and manual) $12.00.

Publisher: Psychological Assessment Resources, Inc.

NEUROPSYCHOLOGICAL QUESTIONNAIRE: CHILDREN'S FORM
Fernando Melendez

child, teen

Purpose: Evaluates children suspected of having brain dysfunction. Used as part of a comprehensive evaluation that should include neuropsychological and pediatric neurological examination.

Description: 41 item pencil-paper questionnaire reviewing possible complaints, symptoms, and signs that suggest underlying brain dysfunction. The test stimulates the examiner into thinking about alternative problems and making appropriate referrals for further studies. Can be used as a basis for discussion with child's parents. Examiner required. Not for group use. Available in Spanish.

Untimed: 10-15 minutes

Range: Ages 6-16

Scoring: Examiner evaluated

Cost: Complete kit (includes forms and manual) $12.00.

Publisher: Psychological Assessment Resources, Inc.

NEUROPSYCHOLOGICAL SCREENING EXAM
John Preston

teen, adult

Purpose: Assesses probable learning disabilities and neurological impair-ment. Used in clinical settings by mental health professionals with some neuropsychological background.

Description: Multiple item paper-pencil test measuring the following neurological factors: level of consciousness, brain and behavioral abnormalities, handedness, verbal and language functioning, emotional problems, memory and cognitive functioning, and psychomotor development. Battery includes: screening exam (background information), examination record form, patient response record, stimulus cards, instructional audio tape for examiner, and three subtests from Halstead-Reitan battery which are purchased separately. Examiner required. Not suitable for group use.

Untimed: 50 minutes

Range: Ages 16-adult

Scoring: Examiner evaluated

Cost: Complete kit $38.00.

Publisher: The Wilmington Press

ORGANIC INTEGRITY TEST (OIT)
H.C. Tien

all ages

Purpose: Diagnose organic brain dysfunctions, psychoses and mental retardation. Used in neurology, psychometrics and assessment of perceptual lag.

Description: 20 card verbal test based on Tien's theory of chromaphilia in brain damage. The examiner shows the patient a card with one picture on it, followed by another card with two pictures on it, and asks the patient which of the pictures on the second card are like the first card. Persons with perceptual problems are more likely to make choices based on color similarities;

those with "perceptual lag" may be more likely to experience reading difficulties based on difficulty distinguishing form. Score based on percentage of correct answers with low score indicating dysfunction. Examiner required. Suitable for group use.

Untimed: 3-5 minutes

Range: Grades K-adult

Scoring: Hand key

Cost: Complete set (includes 20 cards and manual) $25.00.

Publisher: Psychodiagnostic Test Company

ORZECK APHASIA EVALUATION
Arthur Orzeck

all ages

Purpose: Measures the loss of ability to use and understand words in organic brain damaged patients. Used as a clinical screening tool or for research in the areas of organicity and aphasia.

Description: Multiple item oral response, clinical interview test measures signs of aphasia related to organic brain damage in three major areas: Apraxia, Agnosia, and Sensory Suppression. Examiner required. Not for group use.

Untimed: 30-40 minutes

Range: Child, adolescent, adult

Scoring: Hand key

Cost: Complete kit (includes 25 protocol booklets and manual) $9.90.

Publisher: Western Psychological Services

PEDIATRIC EXAMINATION OF EDUCATION READINESS (PEER)
Refer to page 457.

PERCEPTUAL MAZE TEST (PMT)
Janice Smith, David Jones and Alick Elithorn

all ages

Purpose: Assesses perceptual and intellectual skills. Used for diagnosis and localization of cerebral damage, particularly right hemisphere damage.

Description: Multiple item paper-pencil test of spatial abilities. Items are mazes consisting of a number of target dots superimposed upon the inter-section of a lattice background. Subject's task is to find a path along the lattice which passes through the greatest number of target dots. Several forms are available: Two parallel forms of the neuropsychiatric sets, NP1 and NP2, each with 12 test items. Mirrored versions, NP1M and NP2M, are also available. The VC Series, VC1 and VC2, each consist of 18 items. Mirror image sets VC1M and VC2M are also available. A special children's version of the PMT, with 16 items, is available for use with younger children. Examiner required. Suitable for group use. BRITISH PUBLISHER

Untimed: 20-30 minutes

Range: Ages 7-adult

Scoring: Hand key

Cost: 100 copies of Neuropsychiatric sets $35.00; 100 copies of the VC Series $50.00; 100 copies of children's version $50.00.

Publisher: Medical Research Council

THE PICTURE STORY LANGUAGE TEST (PSLT)
Refer to page 223.

PORCH INDEX OF COMMU-NICATIVE ABILITY (PICA)
Refer to page 591.

PRESCHOOL SCREENING INSTRUMENT
Refer to page 458.

PURDUE PERCEPTUAL-MOTOR SURVEY (PPMS)
Refer to page 538.

QUICK NEUROLOGICAL SCREENING TEST
Harold M. Sterling, Margaret Mutti and Norma V. Spalding

all ages

Purpose: Assesses neurological integration as it relates to the learning abilities of children, teen-agers, and adults.

Description: Multiple task, nonverbal test of 15 functions, each involving a motor task similar to those observed in neurological pediatric examinations. The areas measured include: maturity of motor development, skill in controlling large and small muscles, motor planning and sequencing, sense of rate and rhythm, spatial organization, visual and auditory perceptual skills, balance and cerebellar-vestibular function, and disorders of attention. Materials include geometric form reproduction sheets and flipcards printed with directions for administration and scoring. Scoring occurs simultaneously and neurodevelopmental difficulties result in an increasingly larger numerical score. Examiner required. Not suitable for group use.

Untimed: 20 minutes

Range: Grades K-12, adult

Scoring: Examiner evaluated

Cost: Manual $10.00; 25 scoring forms $6.00; 25 geometric form reproduction sheets $2.50; specimen set $10.00.

Publisher: Academic Therapy Publications

THE RAIL-WALKING TEST
S. Roy Heath

all ages

Purpose: Measures locomotor coordination. Screens for central nervous system disorder or injury.

Description: Task performance test assessing balance and motor coordination. The subject, shoes removed, is asked to walk "heel-to-toe" three items along each of three rails specifically constructed for the task. The first rail is four inches wide and nine feet long; the second rail is two inches wide and nine feet long: and the third rail is one inch wide and six feet long. Scores are based on the distance walked without falling off, with special weight given to each rail according to width. Directions are given for local construction of the test rails. Examiner required. Not for group use.

Untimed: 10 minutes

Range: Ages 6-adult

Scoring: Examiner evaluated

Cost: Instructions and norms $5.00.

Publisher: S. Roy Heath, Ph.D.

REITAN EVALUATION OF HEMISPHERIC ABILITIES AND BRAIN IMPROVEMENT TRAINING (REHABIT)
Ralph M. Reitan

all ages

Purpose: Diagnoses neuropsychological functions that may be impaired or deficient in both adults and children who may be suffering from brain damage or neurological dysfunction, specific neurocortical training sequences are included.

Description: Task assessment and oral response test, measure three fundamental areas of brain function: verbal and language functions (left hemisphere); visual-spatial, manipulatory, and sequential abilities (right hemisphere); and abstraction, reasoning, logical analysis, and ability to understand the essential nature of problem- situations (cerebral cortical functioning). Based on the results of the testing, five tracks of remedial training have been developed. Track A contains equipment and procedures that are specifically designed for developing expressive and receptive language and verbal skills. Track B also specializes in language and verbal materials, but includes elements of abstraction, reasoning, logical analysis, and organization. Track C includes various tasks that do not depend upon particular content as much as they do on reasoning, organization, and abstraction. Track D also emphasizes abstraction but uses material that requires the subject to deal with visual-spatial, sequential, and manipulatory skills. Track E specializes in tasks and materials that require the subject to exercise fundamental aspects of visual-spatial and manipulatory abilities. The training materials in each track are organized roughly from simple to complex; the subject is started at a level that is simple for him to perform satisfactorily. Examiner required. Not for group use.

Untimed: Not available

Range: Ages child-adult

Scoring: Examiner evaluated

Cost: Contact publisher.

Publisher: Ralph M. Reitan, Ph.D.

RILEY MOTOR PROBLEMS INVENTORY
Glyndon D. Riley

child

Purpose: Measures a child's oral, fine, and gross motor skills. Used to determine the need for further clinical evaluation.

Description: Multiple task, verbal test provides a quantified system of observing neurological signs which may indicate a need for referral and measures the motor component in any related syndrome. Differentiates between neurogenic and psychogenic disorders. Norms are provided for ages 4-9 years, with cutoff scores to indicate the need for further evaluation. Examiner required. Not for group use.

Untimed: 5-10 minutes

Range: Ages 4-9

Scoring: Hand key

Cost: Complete kit (includes 50 record forms, manual) $7.90.

Publisher: Western Psychological Services

SEQUIN-GODDARD FORM-BOARDS (TACTUAL PERFORMANCE TEST)

child, teen

Purpose: Measures spatial perception in children ages 5-14. Used in a variety of neuropsychological applications.

Description: Multiple-task examination of spatial perception, discrimination of forms, manual or construction ability, motor coordination, and the ability to meet new situations. The test materials consist of ten sturdy blocks cut in the geometric forms of semi-circle, triangle, cross, elongated hexagon, oblong, circle, square, flatted oval, star and lozenge, and a base with corresponding shapes cut into it. The child must place the blocks in the appropriate spaces on the formboard base. Two types of bases are available: one with raised geometric figures and one with flush geometric figures. Examiner required. Not for group use.

Untimed: Not available

Range: Ages 5-14

Scoring: Examiner evaluated

Cost: Formboard (used in Halstead-Reitan Battery) $75.00; formboard (used in Merrill-Palmer Scale) $64.50.

Publisher: Stoelting Co.

SHERMAN MENTAL IMPAIRMENT TEST
Murray H. Sherman

adult

Purpose: Measures mental impairment rapidly and objectively.

Description: Picture-card test administered, scored and interpreted in about ten minutes, providing a rapid measure for the objective determination of mental impairment. Standardized on young adults. Examiner required.
CANADIAN PUBLISHER

Untimed: 10 minutes

Range: Adult

Scoring: Examiner evaluated

Cost: Set of cards $5.00; manual $2.00.

Publisher: Institute of Psychological Research, Inc.

SINGLE AND DOUBLE SIMULTANEOUS STIMULATION TEST (SDSS)
Carmen C. Centofanti and Aaron Smith

all ages

Purpose: Assesses children and adults suspected of having central nervous system diseases or injuries. May be used with patients with confirmed lesions.

Description: Nonverbal, touch discriminations test which measures the accuracy with which subjects can identify single and double simultaneous tactile stimulation applied to the cheek and/or hand. Tests specific somatosensory functions and takes only a few minutes to administer and score. Correctly identifies two of every three patients with diverse types of acute cerebral lesions, and one of every two with chronic lesions, plus other persisting functional deficits. Especially useful when used in combination with the Symbol Digit Modalities Test. Examiner required. Not suitable for group use.

Untimed: 3-5 minutes

Range: Child, adolescent, adult

Scoring: Examiner evaluated

Cost: Complete kit (includes 50 score sheets and manual) $7.50.

Publisher: Western Psychological Services

SKLAR APHASIC SCALE: REVISED 1973
Refer to page 595.

SLOSSON DRAWING COORDINATION TEST (SDCT)
Richard L. Slosson

all ages

Purpose: Screens for serious forms of

brain dysfunction or damage and aids in the diagnosis of visual- perceptual or visual-motor coordination problems. Also indicates the possibility of severe emotional disturbances.

Description: 36 item paper-pencil screening test assessing eye-hand coordination. The subject is given 12 figures and asked to make three free-hand copies of each figure. The subject's copies are scored for degree of distortion indicative of brain damage or dysfunction, visual-motor coordination problems, emotional disturbances, or poor motivational attitude. Suggested cut-off scores provided. To fully evaluate these disorders the SDCT test should be used in conjunction with the Slosson Intelligence Test (or other intelligence test) to cover problems in which eye-hand coordination is not a factor. Test kit includes: Manual of Directions, Scoring Procedures, and two score sheets, and vinyl binder. Examiner required. Suitable for group use.

Untimed: 10-15 minutes

Range: Child-adult

Scoring: Hand key

Cost: Complete kit $25.00; 50 Slosson score sheets $7.00.

Publisher: Slosson Educational Publications, Inc.

SOUTHERN CALIFORNIA SENSORY INTEGRATION TESTS (SCSIT)
Refer to page 539.

SOUTHERN CALIFORNIA MOTOR ACCURACY TEST: REVISED
A. Jean Ayres

child

Purpose: Diagnoses perceptual-motor dysfunctions in atypical chil-

dren. Used in sensory integration.

Description: A manual, reflex test measuring the degree of sensory-motor integration of upper extremities of neurologically atypical children. Norms are provided for both left- and right-handed performance of children 4-8 years, at three performance speeds. Revised manual offers changes in both administration and scoring. The original test form may still be used, but only in conjunction with the new manual. Examiner required. Not for group use.

Untimed: 10-15 minutes

Range: Ages 4-8

Scoring: Hand key

Cost: Complete kit (includes 25 tests, manual, line measure) $22.50.

Publisher: Western Psychological Services

SPATIAL ORIENTATION MEMORY TEST
Refer to page 553.

STANDARDIZED ROAD-MAP TEST OF DIRECTION SENSE
Refer to page 540.

SYMBOL DIGIT MODALITIES TEST
Aaron Smith

all ages

Purpose: Measures individual brain damage. Used to screen and predict learning disorders and to identify children with potential reading problems.

Description: Multiple item test in which the subject is given 90 seconds to convert as many meaningless geometric designs as possible into their appropriate numbers according to the key provided. Useful as a screening device when group- administered; may be individually administered with an oral presentation for those who cannot take written tests. Since numbers are nearly universal, the test is virtually culture-free. Standardized on more than 3,600 boys and girls ages 8-17 years and 431 adults ages 18-75 years with norms given for each year by sex. Examiner required.

Timed: 90 seconds

Range: Ages 8-75

Scoring: Hand key

Cost: Complete kit (includes 50 tests, key, manual) $10.85.

Publisher: Western Psychological Services

TEST OF FACIAL RECOGNI-TION-FORM SL
A.L. Benton

adult

Purpose: Assesses the capacity of adults to discriminate and match faces of unfamiliar persons.

Description: Paper-pencil test of visual discrimination consisting of two parts. The first part is a 27 item short form which, in combination with the second part, constitutes the original 54 item or long form of the test. Normative data with age corrections are based on the performance of adult hospital controls.

Untimed: Not available

Range: Adult

Scoring: Examiner evaluated

Cost: Contact publisher.

Publisher: Oxford University Press

TEST OF PERCEPTUAL ORGANIZATION (TPO)
William T. Martin

adult

Purpose: Measures abstract reasoning abilities, psychomotor functioning, and the ability to follow specific, exacting instructions in an accurate manner. Identifies persons with emotional disturbance or perceptual-motor disabilities. Used for clinical research and screening purposes.

Description: Ten item paper-pencil test consisting of abstract reasoning and visual-motor tasks. Test items consist of written statements (instructions for plotting points on a map) which are presented in order of increasing difficulty. Subjects read the instructions and mark an "X" at each of the ten coordinate points on a street map containing 54 one-inch square blocks which are confined within a 6 x 9 inch area. Objective scoring discriminates between persons with emotional disturbance and/or perceptual-motor disabilities and those with one or few of these problems. Subjective analysis of the test protocol identifies those persons with emotional disturbances or intellect-abstraction problems. Clinical analysis must be done in terms of personality dynamics and visual-motor theory. Fourth grade reading level is required. Examiner required. Suitable for group use with an experienced examiner.

Timed: 10 minutes

Range: Adult

Scoring: Hand key; examiner evaluated.

Cost: Specimen set $7.25; examiner's set $25.00; 25 test forms $12.50; 100-$49.00; keys $2.25; 25 profile sheets $6.75; 100-$26.00; manual $5.50.

Publisher: Psychologists and Educators, Inc.

TRITES NEUROPSYCHOLOGI-CAL TEST BATTERY
Ronald L. Trites

all ages

Purpose: Measures psychomotor steadiness and eye-hand coordination. Used to detect brain damage in children and adults, to describe the extent of impairment, and document patient capabilities.

Description: Three battery manual test of various aspects of steadiness and perceptual ability. Groove Type Steadiness Testers are used to measure eye-hand coordination and other psycho-motor phenomena; the subject pushes a stylus through a gradually narrowing groove without touching the sides, in holes each of nine sizes. The units can be connected to a Tone Response device for immediate auditory feedback, and analyses can be made of the subject's total score to study the effects on steadiness of such variables as exercise, handedness, smoking, or alcohol consumption. The performance curve can also be analyzed for practice effects and fatigue. The third battery uses a Tapping Board, which has two 3½'' square stainless steel plates on either end of an 18'' fiberesin board. The subject is asked to tap the plates as rapidly as possible. A single impulse counter shows the effects of massed versus spaced trails, warm-up and fatigue effects, and end spurt. Social facilitation can be demonstrated by testing subjects alone or in groups. The manual presents age norms for subjects five through 15 with specific norms for males and females. Examiner required. Available in French.

Untimed: Not available

Range: Ages 5 years and older

Scoring: Examiner evaluated

Cost: Complete Set $2,000.00.

Publisher: Lafayette Instrument Company, Inc.

VISCO CHILD DEVELOPMENT SCREENING TEST (THE CHILDS TEST)
Refer to page 470.

WACHS ANALYSIS OF COGNITIVE STRUCTURES
Refer to page 471.

WECHSLER MEMORY SCALE
David Wechsler and C.P. Stone

adult

Purpose: Assesses memory functions. Used for adult subjects with special problems such as aphasics, elderly, and organically brain-injured.

Description: Brief, seven subtest scale yielding a memory quotient. Materials include two alternate forms, I and II. Examiner required. Not suitable for group use.

Untimed: Not available

Range: Adults

Scoring: Examiner evaluated

Cost: Specimen set (includes manual, Design Cards and both record forms) $2.65; 50 record forms $9.00 (specify form I or II); manual $1.75.

Publisher: The Psychological Corporation

WELLER-STRAWSER SCALES OF ADAPTIVE BEHAVIOR: FOR THE LEARNING DISABLED (WSSAB)
Refer to page 554.

THE WESTERN APHASIA BATTERY (WAB)
Andrew Kertesz

all ages

Purpose: Evaluates an individual's ability to read, write, and calculate; as well as the language functions of content, fluency, auditory comprehension, repetition and naming. Used to evaluate the severity of language impairment (aphasia) and the nonverbal skills of drawing, block design, and praxis.

Description: Three part test covering: (1) oral language; (2) reading, writing, calculation and praxis; and (3) nonverbal (apraxia, drawing, block design, calculation, Ravens) which is optional. The oral part requires a stopwatch, four Koh's blocks, and a Raven's Colored Progressive Matrices test to measure spontaneous speech, comprehension, naming, repetition, and thus aphasia. Subtests require conversational speech in response to questions and a picture interview. The reading and writing tests measure functional communication, spontaneous speech and fluency, and comprehension. Examiner required. Not for group use.

Timed: 60 minutes

Range: Child, adolescent, adult

Scoring: Examiner evaluated

Cost: Complete set $49.50.

Publisher: Grune & Stratton, Inc.

WISCONSIN CARD SORTING TEST (WCST)
David A. Grant and Esta A. Berg

teen, adult

Purpose: Assesses perseveration and abstract thinking. Used for neuropsychological assessment where brain lesions involving frontal lobes are suspected and to help discriminate frontal from non-frontal lesions when used in conjunction with more comprehensive ability testing.

Description: Multiple task, nonverbal test in which the subject is asked to match cards in two response decks to one of four stimulus cards for color, form, or number. Responses are recorded on a form for later scoring. The test provides measures of overall success and also of particular sources of difficulty. Examiner required. Not suitable for group use.

Untimed: Not available

Range: Ages 16-adult

Scoring: Examiner evaluated

Cost: Complete kit (includes card decks, response forms, manual) $60.00; 100 forms $10.00; manual $10.00.

Publisher: Psychological Assessment Resources, Inc.

WORD ORDER COMPREHENSION TEST
Refer to page 555.

Marriage and Family

Family

ACTUALIZING ASSESSEMENT BATTERY (AAB)
Refer to page 90.

ADAPTIVE BEHAVIOR INVENTORY OF CHILDREN (ABIC)
Jane R. Mercer and June F. Lewis

child

Purpose: Measurement of child's social role performance in family, peer group and community.

Description: 242 item inventory (interview format) measuring six aspects of adaptive behavior including: family, community, peer relations, non-academic school rules, earner/consumer, and self-maintenance. Items are divided into two sections. The first section is applicable to all children and the second consists of age-graded questions. Interviewer is usually a trained professional. This is one component of the System of Multicultural Pluralistic Assessment (SOMPA). Examiner required. Not suitable for group use. Available in Spanish.

Untimed: Not available

Range: Ages 5-11

Scoring: Hand key; examiner evaluated

Cost: Basic kit (includes manual, 6 keys, 25 record forms) $26.50.

Publisher: The Psychological Corporation

ADOLESCENT ALIENATION INDEX (AAI)
Refer to page 146.

THE AMERICAN HOME SCALE
W.A. Keer and H.H. Remmers

teen, adult

Purpose: Evaluates the cultural, aesthetic, and economic factors of a person's home environment. Used for counseling students or others who may be having problems due to their home environment.

Description: Multiple-item paper-pencil inventory assessing an individual's home environment. Construction is based on profile and factor analyses. Discriminates between sociological areas. Norms are based on over 16,000 eighth-grade students in over 42 American cities. Suitable for group use.

Timed: 40 minutes

Range: Grades 8-up

Scoring: Examiner evaluated

Cost: Specimen set $2.00; 25 surveys $2.75; 100- $10.00.

Publisher: Psychometric Affiliates

BORROMEAN FAMILY INDEX: FOR SINGLE PERSONS
Panos D. Bardis

teen, adult

Purpose: Measures attitudes and feelings of an individual toward his own family; useful for clinical assessment, family counseling, family attitude research and discussion in family education.

Description: 18 item paper-pencil test. Subject rates nine statements about "forces that attract yo to your family" from 0 (absent) to 4 (very strong) and nine statements about "forces that pull you away from your family" from 0 (does not pull you away at all) to 4 (very strong. May be self-administered. Suitable for group use.

Untimed: 10 minutes

Range: High school and up

Scoring: Examiner evaluated

Cost: Free.

Publisher: Panos D. Bardis

A FAMILISM SCALE
Panos D. Bardis

teen, adult

Purpose: Assesses individual attitudes toward both nuclear and extended families; useful for clinical evaluation, marriage and family counseling, research on the family, and discussion in family life education.

Description: 16 item paper-pencil test. Subject reads ten statements about nuclear family relationships and six statements about extended family relationships and rates them on the basis of their own personal beliefs on a scale from 0 (strongly disagree) to 4 (strongly agree). "Familism" score equals sum of 16 numerical responses. Theoretical range of scores: 0 (least familistic), to 64 (most familistic). Separate scores may be obtained for "nuclear family integration" and "extended family integration". May be self-administered. Suitable for group use.

Untimed: 10 minutes

Range: High school and up

Scoring: Examiner evaluated

Cost: Free.

Publisher: Panos D. Bardis

A FAMILISM SCALE: EXTENDED FAMILY INTEGRATION
Panos D. Bardis

teen, adult

Purpose: Measures attitudes toward the extended family (beyond the nuclear family, within the kinship group); useful for clinical assessment, marriage and family counseling, family attitude research and discussions in family education.

Description: Six item paper-pencil

test. Subject reads a list of statements concerning extended family relationships and rates them according to his or her personal beliefs on a scale from 0 (strongly disagree) to 4 (strongly agree). "Familism" score is the sum of the six numerical responses. Theoretical range of scores: 0 (least familistic), to 24 (most familistic). May be self-administered. Suitable for group use.

Untimed: 5 minutes

Range: High school annd up

Scoring: Examiner evaluated

Cost: Free.

Publisher: Panos D. Bardis

A FAMILISM SCALE: NUCLEAR FAMILY INTEGRATION
Panos D. Bardis

teen, adult

Purpose: Measures attitudes toward the solidarity of the nuclear family; useful for clinical assessmennt, marriage and family counseling, family attitude research, and discussion in family education.

Description: Ten item paper-pencil test. Subject rates ten statements about family relationships from 0 (strongly disagree) to 4 (strongly agree). "Familism" score equals sum total of ten numerical responses. Theoretical range of scores: 0 (least familistic) to 40 (most familistic). Self-administered. Suitable for use with groups or individuals.

Untimed: 5 minutes

Range: High school and up

Scoring: Hand key

Cost: Free.

Publisher: Panos D. Bardis

THE FAMILY ADJUSTMENT TEST (ELIAS FAMILY OPINION SURVEY)
Gabriel Elias and edited by H.H. Remmers

teen, adult

Purpose: Measures intrafamily Homeyness-Homelessness (acceptance-rejection) while appearing to be concerned only with attitudes toward general community life. Used for clinical evaluations and research.

Description: Paper-pencil or oral response projective test of adult and adolescent feeling sof family acceptance. The test booklet itself is entitled the Elias Family Opinion Survey to further this projective intent. The test yields ten subscores: attitudes toward mother, father, relatives preference, oedipal, independence struggle, parent-child friction, interparental friction, family status feeling, child rejection, and parental quality. Subtest scores and clinical indicators of a number of adjustment trends are provided as well as an overall index of feelings of intrafamily Homeyness-Homelessness. Percentile norms provided by sex for ages 12-13, 14-15, 16-18, and 19 and over. Interpretation is provided in terms of subtest profiles. Norms for specific parent-child relationships are also provided. No third party should be present if the test is administered orally. Examiner required. Paper-pencil format suitable for group use.

Timed: 45 minutes

Range: Adolescent and up

Scoring: Hand key; scoring service available

Cost: Specimen set (includes one test, manual, key) $2.50; 25 tests $6.00; 100-$22.00.

Publisher: Psychometric Affiliates

FAMILY ENVIRONMENT SCALE
Rudolf H. Moos and Bernice S. Moos

teen, adult

Purpose: Assesses characteristics of family environments; useful for family therapy.

Description: 90 item paper-pencil test measuring ten dimensions of family environments: cohesion, expresssiveness, conflict, independence, achievement orientation, intellectual-cultural orientation, active-recreational orientation, moral-religious emphasis, organization, and control. These dimensions are further grouped into three sets: Relationship, Personal Growth and System Maintenance. Materials include three forms: the Real Form (Form R), which measures perceptions of current family environments; the Ideal Form (Form I), measuring conceptions of ideal family environments; and the Expectancies Form (Form E), which measures expectations about family settings. Forms I and E are not published, however, instructions and items may be requested from the publisher. Examiner required. Suitable for group use.

Untimed: Not available

Range: Adolescent, adult

Scoring: Examiner evaluated

Cost: Specimen set $6.00; manual $5.00; key $.75; 25 reusable tests $4.00; 50 answer sheets $3.00; 50 profiles $3.00.

Publisher: Consulting Psychologists Press, Inc.

FAMILY PRE-COUNSELING INVENTORY PROGRAM
Richard B. Stuart and Freida Stuart

teen, adult

Purpose: Provides basic information about family members (adolescent or older) and establishes a basis for negotiating behavior changes. Used to counsel adolescents or families with adolescents and to evaluate counseling progress.

Description: Three separate paper-pencil test booklets to be filled out be family members: mother (103 items), father (84 items), and adolescent (86 items). Factors measured include: specific positive behaviors of family members, specific positive changes desired, family members' assets for bringing about change, family's goals and ways family can help attain them, shared activities, decision-making style within family, communication within family, parental and adolescent attitudes toward responsibilities, and privileges given to the adolescent. Emphasizes positive aspects of relationships and contracting for behavioral change. Average reading skill required. Self- administered. Suitable for group use.

Untimed: 45-60 minutes

Range: Adolescent-adult

Scoring: Examiner evaluated

Cost: 10 copies each of 3 different booklets and guide $26.95; 10 copies of any 1 booklet and guide $9.95.

Publisher: Research Press

FAMILY RELATIONSHIP INVENTORY (FRI)
Ruth B. Michaelson and Harry L. Bascom

all ages

Purpose: Evaluates family relation-

ships along positive' and negative' lines as an aid to child-adult counseling, family therapy, youth groups, high school instruction and marriage and family enrichment programs.

Description: 50 item card-sorting, game-like format measuring self-esteem, positive or negative perception of self and significant others, most and least esteemed family members, and closest and most distant relationships within the family. One numbered item is printed on each of 50 cards; items 1-25 have 'positive' valence, items 26-50 have 'negative' valence. The subject lists self and family members across the top of a tabulating form and assigns each item to self or a significant other, or to the 'wastebasket' column, and tallies the data on scoring forms with the help of a counselor. Materials include item cards, tabulating forms, scoring forms, a relationship wheel to graphically portray the responses, a Familygram to show family interrelationships, and a test manual. Examiner required. Suitable for groups.

Untimed: 30-45 minutes

Range: Ages 5-adult

Scoring: Examiner evaluated

Cost: Complete FRI kit (includes manual, 50 reusable item cards, 50 tabulating forms, 25 scoring forms, 50 individual relationship sheets, 25 Familygrams) $50.00.

Publisher: Psychological Publications, Inc.

FAMILY RELATIONS TEST-ADULT VERSION
Eva Bene and James Anthony

teen, adult

Purpose: Assesses memories of early family relationships. Used for evaluation for individual and family counseling and as a research tool.

Description: Multiple item test providing systematic recollection of early family experiences. Subject chooses figures from a large group to represent the family. The subject then assigns item cards indicating like or dislike, love or hate, or jealousy to each of the different figures. Memories regarding parental competence are also explored. Item content facilitates recollection of childhood family feelings. Examiner required. Not suitable for group use.
BRITISH PUBLISHER

Untimed: 20-25 minutes

Range: Ages 15 and up

Scoring: Examiner evaluated

Cost: Complete kit (set of figures, set of item cards, 25 scoring sheets, 25 older children record sheets, 25 younger children record sheets, manual) £28.95 (payment in sterling for all overseas orders).

Publisher: NFER-Nelson Publishing Company

FAMILY RELATIONS TEST-CHILDREN'S VERSION
Eva Bene and James Anthony

child, teen

Purpose: Assesses child's subjective perception of the interpersonal relationships in the family. Used for individual and family counseling and as a research tool.

Description: Multiple item test of child's perception of family relationships. Materials include a set of family figures and a pack of cards with a single emotion, attitude or sentiment printed on each card. Family figures are selected by the child to represent every member of the family. An additional figure is called "nobody". The child then assigns each card to a particular family member. Scoring consists of counting the number of items in each attitude area

for each figure. Results indicate relative psychological importance of each family member, whether feelings are positive, ambivalent or negative, and whether or not feelings are reciprocal. Materials include two item sets, one for ages 3-7 and one for ages 7-15. Examiner required. Not suitable for group use.
BRITISH PUBLISHER

Untimed: 20-25 minutes

Range: Ages 3-15

Scoring: Examiner required

Cost: Complete set (includes set of figures, set of items cards, 25 scoring sheets, 25 record sheets, 25 record/score sheets for younger children, and manual) £28.95 (payment in sterling for all overseas payments).

Publisher: NFER-Nelson Publishing Company

A FAMILY VIOLENCE SCALE
Panos D. Bardis

teen, adult

Purpose: Measures the degree of verbal and physical violence in an individual's family during childhood. Useful for clinical assessment, marriage and family counseling, research on attitudes toward family and violence, and classroom discussion.

Description: 25 item paper-pencil test. Subjects rate 25 statements about family violence on a scale from 0 (never) to 4 (very often). "Family violence" score equals the sum of the 25 numerical responses. Theoretical range of scores from: 0 (least violent), to 100 (most violent). Self-administered. Suitable for use with groups or individuals.

Untimed: 10 minutes

Range: High school and up

Scoring: Examiner evaluated

Cost: Free.

Publisher: Panos D. Bardis

THE FLINT INFANT SECURITY SCALE: FOR INFANTS AGE 3-24 MONTHS
Refer to page 8.

HOME INDEX
Refer to page 617.

HOME SCREENING QUESTIONNAIRE (HSQ)
C. Cooms, E. Gay, A. Vandal, C. Ker and W. Frankenberg

child

Purpose: Evaluates the quality of a child's home environment; useful as an indicator of need for further evaluation.

Description: 64 item paper-pencil test in two questionnaires; a 30 item blue form for children up to three years, and a 34 item white form for three-six year olds. Both forms have toy check lists. The parents fill out the questionnaires which are then scored by an examiner. Suspect results must be followed by an evaluation of the home by a trained professional to see if intervention is needed. Written at third and fourth-grade reading level. Self-administered.

Untimed: 15-20 minutes

Range: Ages Birth-6 years

Scoring: Hand key

Cost: 25 questionnaires $4.50; manual $4.50.

Publisher: Ladoca Publishing Foundation

INTERPERSONAL BEHAVIOR SURVEY (IBS)
Refer to page 158.

THE INTERPERSONAL CONFLICT SCALE (ICS)
Carol N. Hoskins and Philip R. Merrifield

adult

Purpose: Evaluates the level of conflict within a relationship through the partners' perceived feelings about each other's behavior. Used for research and counseling, especially in conflict resolution in a test-retest situation

Description: Paper-pencil test evaluating how successfully emotional interaction needs are being met by an existing relationship. Three forms are available, each with separate male and female inventories. The Primary Forms contain 80 items describing the dynamics of the relationship. Individuals rate their agreement or disagreement with the items according to their own perceptions. Alternate Forms A and B consist of 40 similar statements. Examiner required. Suitable for use with groups of couples.

Untimed: Not available

Range: Adults

Scoring: Hand key; examiner evaluated

Cost: Specimen set (includes manual, 3 sets of forms, keys) $4.00; 10 ICS (5m, 5f, key) $4.50, specify Primary or Alternate A or B; manual $1.00.

Publisher: Family Life Publications, Inc.

INTRA AND INTERPERSONAL RELATIONS
Refer to page 111.

INVENTORY OF ANGER COMMUNICATION (IAC)
Refer to page 111.

THE JONES-MOHR LISTENING TEST
Refer to page 833.

LIFE INTERPERSONAL HISTORY ENQUIRY (LIPHE)
Will Schutz

adult

Purpose: Evaluates an individual's retrospective account of relationship to parents before age six; useful for counseling and therapy.

Description: A paper-pencil report of early relationship with parents in areas of inclusion, control, and affection at both the behavioral and feeling levels. Separate scores are obtained for the father and the mother. May be self-administered but examiner recommended. Suitable for group use.

Untimed: Not available

Range: Adult

Scoring: Hand key

Cost: Sample set (including keys) $2.25; 25 tests $3.75.

Publisher: Consulting Psychologists Press, Inc.

MARYLAND PARENT ATTITUDE SURVEY (MPAS)
Donald Pumroy

adult

Purpose: Assesses parents' attitudes toward the way they rear their children; particularly useful as a research instrument.

Description: 95 item paper-pencil

test in which the subject chooses one of five pairs of A or B forced choice statements that best represent the parent's attitudes towards child rearing: indulgent, disciplinarian, protective, and rejecting. Indicates child rearing "type" or approach. Materials consist of a cover letter, a copy of the research article and scoring keys. Self- administered. Suitable for group use.

Untimed: 45 minutes

Range: Adult

Scoring: Hand key

Cost: Complete set $2.00.

Publisher: Donald K. Pumroy, Ph.D.

MATURITY STYLE MATCH—
Parent/Son/Daughter Forms
Paul Hersey, Kenneth H. Blanchard and Joseph W. Keilty

teen, adult

Purpose: Determines the relationship between parental style of influencing behavior and the child's maturity; helpful for family counseling.

Description: Six category paper-pencil test measuring how a parent tells, sells, participates and delegates; and the child's willingness and ability to handle certain activities and responsibilities. The subjects complete the inventory and compare their perceptions. The items are rated on a Likert scale from 'never' to 'almost always'. Suitable for children 12 and older. Test booklet includes scoring and interpretation material. Examiner/self-administered.

Untimed: Not available

Range: Ages 12 and older

Scoring: Hand key

Cost: 1-9 forms $1.95 each; 10-99 forms $1.65 each; 100-299 forms

$1.30 each; 300 or more forms $.95 each.

Publisher: Center for Leadership Studies

MOTHER-CHILD RELATIONSHIP EVALUATION
Robert M. Roth

adult

Purpose: Measures mothers' attitudes and how they relate to their children. Used for counseling and treatment programs.

Description: 48 item paper-pencil test. Each item consists of a statement to which the mother must respond on a five-point scale ranging from "Strongly Agree" to "Strongly Disagree." Measures four areas of mother-child relationships: acceptance, overprotection, overindulgence and rejection. Raw scores are converted to percentiles and T-scores for developing the profile. Examiner required. Suitable for group use.

Untimed: 30 minutes

Range: Adult

Scoring: Hand key

Cost: Kit (25 forms and manual) $9.90.

Publisher: Western Psychological Services

MOTIVATION AND POTENTIAL FOR ADOPTIVE PARENTHOOD SCALE (MPAPS)
B. W. Lindholm and J. Touliatos

adult

Purpose: Measures individual motivation and potential for adoptive parenthood. Used by caseworkers evaluating persons seeking to adopt children.

Description: 72 item paper-pencil test based upon the traits formalized by the Child Welfare League of America as standards for adoption services. The Motivation scale is composed of items covering both positive reasons for wanting to adopt, and lack of negative reasons for wanting to adopt. The Potential scale covers the following areas: attitude toward adoption and the natural parents of adopted children, acceptance and flexibility regarding the children that the applicants are willing to adopt, ability to use help relationships with one's family, relationships with one's spouse, relationships with one's friends, positive experiences with children, being able to enjoy and have a relationship with a child, being able to assume responsibility for others, and dealings with previous life situations. Self-administered. Suitable for group use.

Untimed: 20 minutes

Range: Adults

Scoring: Hand key

Cost: Specimen set $6.00; 35 scales $12.00; manual $3.00.

Publisher: Monitor

A RELIGION SCALE
Panos D. Bardis

teen, adult

Purpose: Measures attitudes toward religion; useful for clinical assessment, family, marriage, and other counseling, research on attitudes toward religion, and discussion in religion and social science classes.

Description: 25 item paper-pencil test. Subject reads 25 statements about religious issues and rates them on the basis of his own beliefs on a scale from 0 (strongly disagree) to 4 (strongly agree). Score is sum of 25 numerical responses. Theoretical range of scores: 0 (least religious), to

100 (most religious). May be self-administered. Suitable for group use.

Untimed: 10 minutes

Range: High school and up

Scoring: Examiner evaluated

Cost: Free

Publisher: Panos D. Bardis

SITUATIONAL PARENTING—
Parent Self or Parent Other
*Paul Hersey, Kenneth H.
Blanchard and John and
Anna Donaghue*

---

adult

Purpose: Evaluates parental style with child as an aid to family counseling and education.

Description: 12 situation, paper-pencil in test in two forms taken by the parent and a second person who observes the parent's behavior. It measures parent style (telling, selling, participating, delegating), flexibility and adaptability in relation to a specific child. The subjects fill out the forms, score them, matrix the results according to instructions and compare. There are separate forms for different age groups; early child (to age eight), intermediate (9-15) and young adult (16 and up). Examiner/self- administered.

Untimed: Not available

Range: Adult

Scoring: Hand key

Cost: 1-9 forms $1.95 each; 10-99 forms $1.65 each; 100-299 forms $1.30 each; 300 or more forms $.95 each.

Publisher: Center for Leadership Studies

TAYLOR-JOHNSON TEMPERA-MENT ANALYSIS
Refer to page 142.

Premarital and Marital Sex

ABORTION SCALE
Panos D. Bardis

---

teen, adult

Purpose: Measures attitudes toward many aspects of abortion; useful in clinical assessment, marriage and family counseling, research on attitudes toward abortion and discussion in family education.

Description: 25 item paper-pencil test. Subject reads statements about issues concerning abortion and rates them on the basis of his or her personal beliefs on a scale from 0 (strongly disagree) to 4 (strongly agree). Score equals sum of 25 numerical responses. Theoretical range of scores: 0 (lowest approval of abortion), to 100 (highest approval). Self-administered. Suitable for group use.

Untimed: 10 minutes

Range: High school and up

Scoring: Examiner evaluated

Cost: Free.

Publisher: Panos D. Bardis

BACKGROUND SCHEDULE
Marriage Council of Philadelphia

---

teen, adult

Purpose: Aids counselors of couples in a relationship by obtaining a wide range of relevant background material without using interview time to secure information, it is completed independently by the couple prior to their first interview.

Description: 39 item paper-pencil questionnaire; obtains from couples in a relationship independent answers to questions about vital statistics, religion, activities shared with partner, occupation, siblings, parental data, interaction between self and parent before teens, during teens, and at the present time. Not a psychological test. May be self-administered. Not suitable for use with groups.

Untimed: 30 minutes

Range: Couples in a relationship

Scoring: Examiner evaluated

Cost: Schedule $.20; 100-$15.00.

Publisher: Marriage Council of Philadelphia

BORROMEAN FAMILY INDEX: FOR MARRIED PERSONS
Panos D. Bardis

teen, adult

Purpose: Measures a married person's attitudes and feelings toward his or her own family (spouse and children, if any); useful for clinical assessment, family and marriage counseling, family attitude research, and discussions in family education.

Description: 18 item paper-pencil test. Subject rates nine statements about "forces that attract you to your family" on a scale from 0 (absent) to 4 (very strong) and nine statements about "forces that pull you away from your family" on a scale from 0 (does not pull you away at all) to 4 (very strong). Self-administered. Suitable for group use.

Untimed: 10 minutes

Range: High school and up

Scoring: Examiner evaluated

Cost: Free

Publisher: Panos D. Bardis

CALIFORNIA MARRIAGE READINESS EVALUATION
Morse P. Manson

adult

Purpose: Measures a couple's readiness for marriage and indicates potential difficulties and the areas where they are most likely to occur. Used for premarital counseling.

Description: 115 item paper-pencil inventory, consisting of 110 true-false questions and five projective completion items. Measures strengths and weaknesses in eight areas of marriage readiness within three general categories: personality (character structure, emotional maturity, marriage readiness), preparation for marriage (family experiences, dealing with money, planning ability), and interpersonal compatibility (marriage motivation and compatibility). Scores are provided for each of the eight areas measured, along with a total score which indicates overall readiness for marriage. Self-administered. Suitable for group use.

Untimed: 15-30 minutes

Range: Adult

Scoring: Hand key

Cost: Kit (25 forms and manual) $9.60.

Publisher: Western Psychological Services

CARING RELATIONSHIP INVENTORY (CRI)
Everett L. Shostrom

adult

Purpose: Measures the essential elements of caring (or love) in the two-person relationship existing between a man and a woman. Used as a basis for evaluation and discussion in marriage and family counseling.

Description: 83 item paper-pencil, true-false test consisting of a series of statements which the subject applies first to the other member of the couple (spouse, finance, etc.) and second to his or her "ideal" mate. Responses are scored on seven scales: Affection, Friendship, Eros, Empathy, Self Love,

Being Love and Deficiency Love. Separate forms are available for adult males and adult females. Test items were developed based on responses of criterion groups of successfully married couples, troubled couples in counseling, and divorced individuals. Percentile norms for successfully married couples are presented separately for men and women. Means and standard deviations are presented for troubled couples and divorced individuals. A component of the Actualizing Assessment Battery (AAB). Examiner required. Suitable for group use.

Untimed: 40 minutes

Range: Adults

Scoring: Hand scoring

Cost: Specimen set (includes manual and one copy of all forms) $3.00; 25 booklets (specify male or female) $7.50; 50 expendable profile sheets $4.00; 7 hand-scoring keys $3.00; manual $2.00.

Publisher: Educational and Industrial Testing Service

COITOMETER
Panos D. Bardis

teen, adult

Purpose: Measures an individual's knowledge of the anatomical and physiological aspects of coitus; useful for clinical assessment, marriage and family counseling, research on human sexuality, discussion in family and human sexuality classes.

Description: 50 item paper-pencil, true-false test. Test includes four-page instrument consisting of the questionnaire and a measure key. Self- administered. Suitable for group or individuals.

Untimed: 12 minutes

Range: High school and up

Scoring: Hand key

Cost: Free.

Publisher: Panos D. Bardis

COUPLE'S PRE-COUNSELING INVENTORY
Richard B. Stewart

adult

Purpose: Provides couples with information regarding expected roles in the treatment process and collects data from them concerning the feelings and behaviors which may be relevant to marriage, relationship and family counseling. Used prior to counseling and for periodic evaluation of progress in treatment.

Description: 133 item paper-pencil inventory covering the following areas of marital/family life: happiness with general areas of relationship, behaviors pleasing to each partner, level of communication, style of handling conflict, moods, effectiveness in everyday life, sexual satisfaction, level of agreement of child rearing issues, willingness to change, goals for treatment, and commitment to relationship. Emphasizes discovering strengths of relationship, as well as problem areas. Average reading skill required. Self-administered. Suitable for group use.

Untimed: 60 minutes

Range: Adults

Scoring: Examiner evaluated

Cost: Complete set (includes 10 booklets and guide) $14.95; guide $1.95.

Publisher: Research Press

A COURTSHIP ANALYSIS (CA) AND A DATING PROBLEMS CHECKLIST (DPCL)
Gelolo McHugh

all ages

Purpose: Assesses adolescent couples' social problems. Used in Family Living and Home Economics classes, Sunday schools, youth groups, and premarital counseling to stimulate conversation.

Description: Courtship Analysis is a 150 item paper-pencil questionnaire allowing partners in courtship to report on the dynamics of their relationship by indicating the presence or absence of positive and negative character traits and behaviors of their partner. The Dating Problems Checklist is a 125 item paper-pencil questionnaire which reports on the dating atmosphere in which respondents socialize. They respond by indicating whether or not a particular attitude or situation exists and if it is a problem for them. Examiner required. Suitable for group use.

Untimed: Not available

Range: Junior high-adult

Scoring: Examiner evaluated

Cost: Specimen set (includes manual and 2 copies of each form) $2.00; 10 copies (specify test) $4.50; manual $1.00.

Publisher: Family Life Publications, Inc.

A DATING SCALE
Panos D. Bardis

teen, adult

Purpose: Measures attitudes toward various aspects of dating; useful for clinical assessment, marriage and family counseling, research on attitudes toward dating and discussion in family education.

Description: 25 item paper-pencil test. Subject notes 25 statements about dating from 0 (strongly disagree) to 4 (strongly agree). Score equals sum total of 25 numerical responses. Theoretical range of scores: 0 (least liberal), to 100 (most liberal). Self-administered. Suitable for use with groups or individuals.

Untimed: 10 minutes

Range: High school and up

Scoring: Examiner evaluated

Cost: Free.

Publisher: Panos D. Bardis

ENGAGEMENT SCHEDULE
Marriage Council of Philadelphia

teen, adult

Purpose: Aids counselors working with couples engaged to be married by obtaining information about the couple's feelings and plans.

Description: 41 item paper-pencil questionnaire which secures independent responses from couples concerning facts about their engagement, feelings about future in-laws, feelings about their own parents, confiding, affection, need for more information about sex, number of children planned, and sharing interests and activities. Not to be considered as a measuring instrument for predicting future marriage possibilities or as a psychological test. The schedule is to be completed independently in the waiting room prior to the clients' first interview.

Untimed: 30 minutes

Range: Engaged couples

Scoring: Examiner evaluated

Cost: Schedule $.20; 100-$15.00.

Publisher: Marriage Council of Philadelphia

EROTOMETER: A TECHNIQUE FOR THE MEASUREMENT OF HETEROSEXUAL LOVE
Panos D. Bardis

teen, adult

Purpose: Measures the intensity of an individual's love for a member of the opposite sex; useful for clinical assessment, marriage and family counseling, research on love, and discussions in family and sex education.

Description: 50 item paper-pencil test. Subject reads statements concerning actual feelings, attitudes, desires, and wishes regarding one specific member of the opposite sex and rates them: 0 (absent), 1 (weak), 2 (strong). Score equals sum of 50 numerical responses. Theoretical range of scores: 0 (no love) to 100 (strongest love). Self- administered. Suitable for group use.

Untimed: 12 minutes

Range: High school and up

Scoring: Examiner evaluated

Cost: Free.

Publisher: Panos D. Bardis

FAMILY RELATIONS TEST-MARRIED COUPLES VERSION
Eva Bene

teen, adult

Purpose: Explores family interactions particularly between spouses and among parents and children. Used for marital and family counseling and as a research tool.

Description: Multiple item test measuring perception of family interactions. Subject chooses figures representing spouse and/or other family members. Items reflecting emotions, attitudes, or sentiments are assigned to each figure. May be used with children's and adult's versions to give a more complete picture of present and past family relationships. Examiner required. Not suitable for group use.
BRITISH PUBLISHER

Untimed: 20-25 minutes

Range: Married persons and parents

Scoring: Hand key; examiner evaluated

Cost: Complete kit (set of figures, set of item cards, 25 record sheets, 25 scoring sheets, manual) £29.15 (payment in sterling for all overseas orders).

Publisher: NFER-Nelson Publishing Company

GRAVIDOMETER
Panos D. Bardis

teen, adult

Purpose: Measures an individual's knowledge of the anatomical and physiological aspects of pregnancy. Used in clinical assessments, marriage and family counseling, research on human sexuality and family classes.

Description: 50 item paper-pencil true-false test measuring knowledge of human pregnancy. Self-administered. Suitable for group use.

Untimed: 12 minutes

Range: High school and up

Scoring: Hand key

Cost: Free.

Publisher: Panos D. Bardis

THE LOVE ATTITUDES INVENTORY (LAI)
David Knox

teen, adult

Purpose: Helps teachers and counselors teach the difference between romantic and realistic love. Used to promote discussion in adolescent and adult, family living and marriage classes, marital and premarital counseling.

Description: 30 statement paper-pencil questionnaire about love. The individual agrees or disagrees with each statement. Two additional long answer questions call for descriptions of loving behavior. Examiner required. Suitable for group use.

Untimed: Not available

Range: Adolescents-adults

Scoring: Examiner evaluated

Cost: Specimen set (includes manual and 2 forms) $2.00; 10 LAI $4.50; manual $1.00.

Publisher: Family Life Publications, Inc.

MARITAL CHECK-UP KIT
Millard J. Bienvenu

adult

Purpose: Identifies potential marital problems, facilitates communication, and encourages co- operative problem solving through positive intervention by a counselor.

Description: 6 paper-pencil exercises which facilitate a positive approach to marital self-evaluation. Each form can be completed prior to or as part of marital counseling or enrichment sessions. The exercises include: Positive Feedback Exercise (identifies positive personality traits), Marital Communication Exercise (identifies communication strengths and weaknesses), Marital Relationship Improvement Exercise (promotes understanding of individual feelings), Marital Relationship Assessment Exercise (promotes understanding of individual attitudes), Personality Pluses and Strengths (provides a self-evaluation of strengths brought to the marriage), and Feelings About Yourself (promotes discussion of feelings as they relate to spouse and marriage). Materials include forms for one couple and instructions. Part of Bienvenu Specimen Set. For administration by a trained counselor.

Untimed: Not available

Range: Adults

Scoring: Examiner evaluated

Cost: Per couple $3.60.

Publisher: Counseling and Self-Improvement Programs/Millard Bienvenu, Ph.D.

THE MARITAL COMMUNICATIONS INVENTORY
Millard J. Bienvenu, Sr.

adult

Purpose: Assesses communication in a troubled marriage and identifies communication problems. Stimulates group discussion in marriage enrichment programs and increases awareness of positive and negative communication patterns.

Description: 46 item paper-pencil questionnaire. Covers the following areas: feelings, emotions, economics, communication patterns and behaviors. Also includes an optional socioeconomic survey. Separate forms for male and female. Both husband and wife answer questions by indicating frequency of communication in each area. Materials include questionnaire forms and manual. Part of Complete Specimen Set and Bienvenu Specimen Set. Self- administered. Suitable for group use.

Untimed: Not available.

Range: Adults

Scoring: Hand key; examiner evaluated

Cost: Specimen set (manual, 1 male, 1 female, key) $2.00; manual $1.00; 10 MCI (5 female, 5 male) $4.50.

Publisher: Family Life Publications, Inc.

MARITAL SATISFACTION INVENTORY (MSI)
Douglas K. Snyder

adult

Purpose: Identifies separately for each spouse the nature and extent of marital distress. Used in marital and family counseling.

Description: 280 item (239 for couples with no children) paper-pencil true-false test. The inventory provides information from each spouse concerning nine basic measured dimensions of their marriage: affective communication, problem solving communication, time together, disagreement about finances, sexual dissatisfaction, role orientation, family history of distress, dissatisfaction with children, and conflict over childrearing. In addition, there is a validity scale and a global distress scale, which measures each individual's overall dissatisfaction with the marriage. The answer sheets are easily scored and the results for both spouses are then recorded on the same profile form, graphically identifying the areas of marital distress. Each spouse's scores can be individually evaluated as well as directly compared, thereby facilitating diagnostic and intervention procedures. Group mean profiles for each sex are provided for couples seeking general marital therapy, couples seeking divorce, couples with specific sexual dysfunctions, physically abused wives, and couples with specific distress around childrearing. A number of case illustrations are presented. Self-administered.

Untimed: 30-40 minutes

Range: Adult

Scoring: Hand key; computer scoring available

Cost: Complete kit (includes booklets, answer sheets, profile forms, key and manual) $17.50.

Publisher: Western Psychological Services

THE MARRIAGE ADJUST-MENT FORM (MAF)
Ernest Burgess

adult

Purpose: Measures a couple's level of adjustment to marriage. Used for marriage counseling.

Description: 93 item paper-pencil, multiple-choice questionnaire covering vital areas of marital adjustment. Couples complete the form in the presence of the counselor. Materials include questionnaire and instruction form. Available as part of a specimen set with the Marriage Prediction Schedule. Examiner required. Suitable for group use.

Untimed: Not available

Range: Adults

Scoring: Hand key; examiner evaluated

Cost: Specimen set (includes 1 copy, 1 Marriage Prediction Schedule, instruction sheet) $2.00; 10 MAF (includes instruction sheet) $4.50.

Publisher: Family Life Publications, Inc.

MARRIAGE ADJUSTMENT INVENTORY
Morse P. Manson and Arthur Lerner

adult

Purpose: Identifies the causes of marital tension and distress by revealing the couple's self-images and their images of each other. Used for marital and family counseling.

Description: 157 item paper-pencil, multiple-choice test measuring 12 common marital problem areas: Family Relations, Dominance, Immaturity, Neurotic Traits, Sociopathic Traits, Money Management, Children, Interests, Physical Abilities, Sexual and Incompatability. The couple indicates individually which of the problem statements apply to themselves, their spouse, or both of them. Provides four evaluative scores indicating severity of marital maladjustment. Self- administered. Suitable for group use.

Untimed: 10-15 minutes

Range: Adult

Scoring: Hand key

Cost: Kit (25 forms, manual) $9.80.

Publisher: Western Psychological Services

MARRIAGE ADJUSTMENT SCHEDULE 1A
Marriage Council of Philadelphia

teen, adult

Purpose: Aids counselors working with married couples by obtaining a wide range of relevant information; it is completed independently by couples prior to the first interview.

Description: 34 item paper-pencil test; secures independent responses about shared activities, feelings about those activities, problem areas in the marriage, and the sharing of responsibilities; also provides data on attitudes, feelings and problem areas for the counselor to review as he or she continues with the couple. Not to be considered a psychological test. Self-administered. Not for group use.

Untimed: 30 minutes

Range: Married couples

Scoring: Examiner evaluated

Cost: Schedule $.20; 100-$15.00.

Publisher: Marriage Council of Philadelphia

MARRIAGE ADJUSTMENT SCHEDULE 1B
Marriage Council of Philadelphia

teen, adult

Purpose: Provides the counselor with information concerning a couple's feelings, attitudes, and behavior regarding sex.

Description: 36 item paper-pencil schedule. The counselor completes the inventory during the counseling hour, using an interview format to survey the couple's feelings, attitudes, and behavior. Does not attempt to assess the couple's factual knowledge of human sexuality nor does it provide a psychological basis for counseling. Examiner required. Not for group use.

Untimed: Open ended

Range: Married couples

Scoring: Examiner evaluated

Cost: Schedule $.20; 100-$15.00.

Publisher: Marriage Council of Philadelphia

A MARRIAGE ANALYSIS (BGMA)
Daniel C. Blazier and Edgar T. Goosmans

adult

Purpose: Evaluates the progress of marriage counseling. Used to increase marriage counseling effectiveness.

Description: 113 item paper-pencil, multiple choice questionnaire exploring a couple's marital relationship. Investigates eight areas of marriage: role concepts, self-image, feelings toward spouse, emotional openness, knowledge of spouse, sexual adjustment and security, common traits, and meanings of marriage. Answers may be transferred to a profile sheet for visual assessment of marital adjustment. Materials include questionnaire, manual and profile sheet. Self-administered.

Untimed: Not available

Range: Adults

Scoring: Hand key; Examiner evaluated

Cost: Specimen set (includes manual, 2 forms profile sheet) $1.00; 10 BGMA (contains manual and profile sheets) $4.50.

Publisher: Family Life Publications, Inc.

A MARRIAGE EVALUATION (ME)
Henry Blount

adult

Purpose: Assesses a troubled couple's perceptions of marriage. Enables couples to evaluuate the status of their marriage and identifies areas in need of immediate discussion.

Description: 60 item paper-pencil, multiple-choice test assessing a couple's perception of their marriage. Topics include: readiness for marriage, decision making, values, communication, personal growth, commitment and expectation. Materials include test, manual and scoring instructions. Self- administered.

Untimed: 15 minutes

Range: Adults

Scoring: Hand key; examiner evaluated

Cost: Specimen set (includes manual and 2 tests) $2.00; 10 ME $4.50; manual $1.00.

Publisher: Family Life Publications, Inc.

THE MARRIAGE EXPECTATION INVENTORIES
P.J. McDonald

adult

Purpose: Evaluates an individual's marriage expectations in premarital and marriage enrichment counseling.

Description: 58 item, 8 page paper-pencil questionnaire. Investigates marital expectations in nine areas: love, communication, freedom, sex, money, selfishness, religion, relatives, and children. Respondents answer questions individually on separate forms and then share answers privately or in group discussion. Available in two forms: Form I for engaged couples and Form II for married couples. The two forms are identical except for wording. Materials include test forms and manual. Self-administered. Suitable for use with groups of couples. Test is part of Complete Specimen Set and Premarital Specimen Set.

Untimed: Not available

Range: Adults

Scoring: Examiner evaluated

Cost: Specimen set (includes manual, 2 copies of each form) $3.00; 10 MEI $4.50 (specify Form I or II) manual $2.50.

Publisher: Family Life Publications, Inc.

A MARRIAGE PREDICTION SCHEDULE (AMPS)
Ernest Burgess

teen, adult

Purpose: Measures a premarital couple's expectations of marriage. Used for compatibility evaluation in premarital counseling and in family living and marriage classes.

Description: 74 item paper-pencil,

multiple-choice questionnaire. The couple completes the form together and answers and scores are openly discussed. Materials include questionnaire and instruction sheet. Available as part of a specimen set with the Marriage Adjustment Form. Self-administered.

Untimed: Not available

Range: Adolescents-adults

Scoring: Hand key

Cost: Specimen set (includes 1 copy, 1 marriage adjustment form and instruction sheet) $2.00; 10 AMPS (includes instruction sheet) $4.50.

Publisher: Family Life Publications, Inc.

THE MARRIAGE ROLE EXPECTATION
Marie Dunn and J. Nicholas DeBonis (revision)

teen, adult   grades 10-UP

Purpose: Evaluates marital behavior expectations. Aids in evaluating potential marriage success. Used for premarital counseling and in high school family living classes.

Description: 71 item paper-pencil, multiple-choice test in in separate forms for males and females. Covers seven areas: authority, homemaking, child care, personal characteristics, social participation, education and employment/support. Materials include: test, profile, manual, and scoring key. Self-administered. Test is included in Complete Specimen Set and Premarital Specimen Set.

Untimed: 15-30 minutes

Range: High school-adult

Scoring: Hand key

Cost: Specimen set (includes manual, 2 forms, 2 profiles, key) $2.00; 10 REI (5 male, 5 female) $4.50; manual $1.00.

Publisher: Family Life Publication, Inc.

MENOMETER
Panos D. Bardis

teen, adult   grades 10-UP

Purpose: Measures an individual's knowledge of the anatomical and physiological aspects of menstruation; useful for clinical assessment, marriage and family counseling, research on human sexuality and discussion in family and human sexuality classes.

Description: 50 item paper-pencil, true-false test in which the subject marks the appropriate answers to be scored by the examiner with the key provided.

Untimed: 12 minutes

Range: High school and up

Scoring: Hand key

Cost: Free.

Publisher: Panos D. Bardis

MARRIAGE SCALE
J. Gustav White

adult

Purpose: Compares the opinions, attitudes, and beliefs of premarital or marital partners. Used for premarital, marital and family counseling.

Description: 21 item paper-pencil inventory measures factors related to marital life and compatibility. Each partner is asked to rate on a scale from one to ten statements pertaining to the following topics: mutual understanding, outlook on life, religion, love, intercommunication, objectional habits, pleasures, relatives, children, sex, occupation, interests, aesthetic tastes, finances, major plans, etc. After each subject completes his or her scale, the profile of each partner is copied onto the profile of the other partner for a direct comparison of their responses.

Four-page folder serves as a permanent file record. Not suitable for persons with below average reading ability. Self-administered. Suitable for use with groups of couples.

Untimed: 10-15 minutes

Range: Adult

Scoring: Hand key; examiner evaluated

Cost: Specimen set $4.00; 25 rating folders $12.50; 100-$49.00.

Publisher: Psychologists and Educators, Inc.

MIRROR-COUPLE RELATIONSHIP INVENTORY
Joan A. Hunt and Richard A. Hunt

teen, adult

Purpose: Measures an individual's attitudes towards self and partner; useful for personality assessment in marriage counseling.

Description: 336 item paper-pencil test containing 24 scales (11 content, 12 process, and one attitude) covering areas in family, careers, children, friends, parents, religion, money, sex, leisure time, future, personality, and freedom. Each set contains a male and female form. Self- administered. Suitable for group use.

Untimed: 30-45 minutes

Range: Adolescents, adults

Scoring: Computer scoring available

Cost: Specimen set (includes scoring) $10.00.

Publisher: Datascan

PAIR ATTRACTION INVENTORY (PAI)
Everett L. Shostrom

adult

Purpose: Measures aspects contrib-

uting to mate or friend selection in adult males and females. Used for premarital, marital and family counseling.

Description: 224 item paper-pencil test assessing the feelings and attitudes of one member of a male-female pair about the nature of the relationship. Percentile norms provided based on adult samples. A component of the Actualizing Assessment Battery (AAB). Examiner required. Suitable for group use.

Untimed: 30 minutes

Range: Adult

Scoring: Hand key

Cost: Kit (3 male, 3 female booklets, 50 answer sheets, 50 profiles, manual) $9.50; 25 booklets (specify male or female) $9.50; 50 answer sheets $4.75; 50 profile sheets $4.00; manual $2.00.

Publisher: Educational and Industrial Testing Service

A PILL SCALE
Panos D. Bardis

teen, adult   grades 10-UP

Purpose: Measuress attitudes toward the oral contraceptives; useful for clinical assessment, marriage and family counseling, family attitude research, and discussions in family and sex education.

Description: 25 item paper-pencil test. Subject reads statements concerning moral, sexual, psychological, and physical aspects of "the pill" and rates them on a scale from 0 (strongly disagree) to 4 (strongly agree). Score equals sum of 25 numerical responses. Theoretical range of scores: 0 (least liberal) to 100 (most liberal). May be self-administered. Suitable for group use.

Untimed: 10 minutes

Range: High school and up

Scoring: Examiner evaluated

Cost: Free.

Publisher: Panos D. Bardis

PREMARITAL COMMUNICATION INVENTORY
Millard Bienvenu

adult

Purpose: Evaluates the level of communication within a premarital relationship. Used to prepare couples in the communication skills required for a successful marriage and to identify trouble spots in communication.

Description: 40 item paper-pencil questionnaire. Covers the following areas: differences, feelings, anger, sex, opinions, in-laws, beliefs, criticism, manners, problem solving, depression, economics, future expectations, child rearing, personal problems, and future adjustments. Materials include: questionnaire, manual and scoring key. Part of Bienvenu Specimen Set. Administered by trained counselor or clergy.

Untimed: Not available

Range: Adults

Scoring: Hand key; examiner evaluated

Cost: PCI $.35; guide $1.25.

Publisher: Counseling and Self-Improvement Programs/Millard Bienvenu, Ph.D.

PRE-MARITAL COUNSELING INVENTORY
Richard B. Stuart and Freida Stuart

adult

Purpose: Assesses a couple's relationship before marriage. Identifies basic discrepancies in attitudes and expectations, measures each partner's understanding of the other and provides information that might assist accommodation of each other's positions and aid in premarital counseling.

Description: 94 item paper-pencil inventory administered separately to each member of a couple preparing for marriage. Factors covered include: religious background, family background, relationships with others, past marital history, history of relationship with prospective marital partner, marital role expectations, division of duties within marriage, and confidence in ability to handle various aspects of marriage. Average reading skill required. Self-administered. Suitable for group use.

Untimed: 60 minutes

Range: Adult

Scoring: Examiner evaluated

Cost: 10 booklets and guide $9.95; guide $1.95.

Publisher: Research Press

THE PREMARITAL COUNSELING KIT (PCK)
Millard J. Bienvenu, Sr.

adult

Purpose: Evaluates a premarital couple's relationship in preparation for marriage. Explores complexities of marriage with the couple through the guidance of a counselor or clergy man. Used for both premarital and marital counseling.

Description: Six separate forms comprising a series of counseling sessions. Form I compares the individuals' backgrounds and general indications of compatibility. Form II is a communication inventory to discover strengths and weaknesses in communication skills. Form III provides incomplete sentences for elaborating on areas of the relationship about which either person feels unsure. Form IV covers strengths and problem areas to be worked on in the relationship. Form V is an evaluation summary for the counselor. Form VI is the marriage preparation programming forum for specific recommendations of activities and discussion for the couple in preparation for marriage. Recommended for use over a period of at least three counseling sessions. Part of the Bienvenu Specimen Set, Complete Specimen Set and Premarital Specimen Set.

Untimed: Not available

Range: Adults

Scoring: Examiner evaluated

Cost: Introductory kit (includes manual and forms for one couple) $5.00; manual $2.50; PCK-5 (5 couples) $10.00.

Publisher: Family Life Publications, Inc.

RELATIONSHIP SATISFACTION SURVEY
Rose Lucas

teen, adult

Purpose: Assesses marital conflicts and issues. Used in couple, family and marital counseling.

Description: 120 item paper-pencil survey assessing the following factors of a relationship: communication patterns, emotional factors, child rearing practices, habits, affection, career, finances, social-recreational activities, and values. Most helpful when both partners cooperate in filling out the survey. Self-administered. Suitable for group use.

Untimed: 25 minutes

Range: 16 and older

Scoring: Examiner evaluated

Cost: 50 survey forms $15.00.

Publisher: The Wilmington Press

A RELIGIOUS ATTITUDES INVENTORY (CCEA)
Crane and Coffer

teen, adult

Purpose: Assesses religious belief for consideration in marital and premarital counseling. Determines religious compatibility and promotes ddiscussion of religious attitudes. Used in marriage enrichment and religion classes.

Description: 107 item paper-pencil inventory covering areas such as: responsibility, belief, and child rearing. Individuals respond to statements by degree of agreement or disagreement. Scores are then transferred to a profile sheet for comparison. Materials include inventory, profiles and manual.

Untimed: Not available

Range: Adolescents-adults

Scoring: Examiner evaluated

Cost: Specimen set (includes manual, 2 profiles, 2 inventories) $2.00; 10 CCRA (includes profiles) $4.50; manual $1.00.

Publisher: Family Life Publications, Inc.

THE SEX ATTITUDES SURVEY (SAS)
Gelolo McHugh

adult

Purpose: Examines sexual attitudes. Used in marital and premarital counseling, adult sex education, counselor-teacher training, and sexual and marital enrichment programs.

Description: 107 item paper-pencil survey which helps to promote understanding, growth and sharing about sexual attitudes. Statements cover areas such as: intercourse, sex roles, sex dreams and homo- and heterosexuality. Subjects respond to each statement on an agree-disagree basis. Responses can be connected to form an individual profile for comparison of specific disagreements. Materials include manual and test. Test is included in The Sex Educators and Counselor's Package.

Untimed: Not available

Range: Adults

Scoring: Examiner evaluated

Cost: Specimen set (includes manual and two forms) $2.00; 10 kits $4.50; manual $1.00.

Publisher: Family Life Publications, Inc.

SEX KNOWLEDGE AND ATTITUDE TEST (SKAT)
Harold I. Lief and David Reed

teen, adult   grades 13-UP

Purpose: Assesses an individual's sexual knowledge and attitudes. Useful as a research annd educational tool.

Description: 106 item paper-pencil test. The sexual knowledge section contains 71 items (only 50 are scored, the others are teaching items). The sexual attitudes section contain 35 items (32 are scored) in four subsections: heterosexual relationships, sexual myths, abortion, and autoeroticism. Using medical students for the norm, attitudes are measured for "conservatism" vs "liberalism". Inappropriate for those with less than a college education. Available in Spanish. Self-administered. Suitable for group use.

Untimed: 30-45 minutes

Range: Ages 18 and older

Scoring: Hand key: may be computer scored

Cost: Test booklet $1.00; answer sheet $.25; manual $2.50; norms

booklet $.50; set of scoring keys $3.00; Sexual Performance Evaluation $2.00; set of 7 SKAT related articles $3.00.

Publisher: Marriage Council of Philadelphia

THE SEX KNOWLEDGE INVENTORY-FORM X (SKI-X)
Gelolo McHugh

teen, adult   grades 10-UP

Purpose: Facilitates discussion of basic sex facts and the emotional aspects of sexuality. Used for marital and premarital counseling, for college and high school sex education, and counselor- educator training.

Description: 80 item paper-pencil multiple-choice test assesses knowledge of and attitudes toward sexual behavior. Aids teachers and counselors in dispelling sexual myths and teaching facts. Materials include: reusable test booklet, manual, answer sheets and see-through scoring key. The test is included in the Complete Specimen Set, Premarital Set, and Sex Educators and Counselor's Package.

Untimed: Not available

Range: High school-adult

Scoring: Hand key; examiner evaluated

Cost: Specimen set (includes manual, 1 test booklet, 2 answer sheets) $2.00; 1-9 Test Booklets $1.35 each; 10 answer sheets $3.00; key $5.00; manual $3.50.

Publisher: Family Life Publications, Inc.

THE SEX KNOWLEDGE INVENTORY-FORM Y (SKI-Y)
Gelolo McHugh

teen, adult

Purpose: Measures knowledge and function of sexual anatomy, and correct medical vocabulary. Used for marital and premarital counseling, pre- or post- testing for sex-education classes (high school and college level) and churches and clinics.

Description: 98 item paper-pencil inventory consisting of three parts. Part I (20 items) uses side view drawings of external and internal male and female sex organs, which the subject must match with their correct names. Part II (30 items) consists of matching organ names or drawings with a description of their function. Part III (48 items) consists of matching vocabulary words (covering all aspects of sexuality) with their correct definition. Materials include test manual and scoring key. This test is included in the Complete Specimen Set, Premarital Set, and Sex Educators and Counselor's Package.

Untimed: Not available

Range: Adolescent-adult

Scoring: Hand key

Cost: Specimen set (includes manual, 2 tests, scoring key) $2.00; 10 tests $4.50; manual $1.00.

Publisher: Family Life Publications, Inc.

SEXOMETER
Panos D. Bardis

teen, adult   grades 10-UP

Purpose: Assesses an individual's knowledge of human reproductive anatomy and physiology. Useful for clinical assessment, marriage and family counselinng, research on sex knowledge, and discussion in family

and sex information.

Description: 50 item paper-pencil test consisting of short answer and identification questions concerning human reproduction, anatomy, function, and physiology, disease, birth control, and sexual behavior. Materials include three page test form and two page answer key. May be self-administered. Suitable for group use.

Untimed: 15 minutes

Range: High school and up

Scoring: Hand key

Cost: Free.

Publisher: Panos D. Bardis

THE SEXUAL CONCERNS CHECKLIST (SCC)
Lester A. Kirkendall

teen, adult

Purpose: Determines an individual's most important sexual concerns so that counselors or teachers can address clients' or students' specific needs. Use for sex education, sexual counseling, premarital and marital counseling, marriage enrichment programs and research.

Description: Paper-pencil checklist containing human sexuality questions. Four forms are available containing statements of concerns appropriate to each of the following groups: male/female adolescents and male/female adults. The adolescent forms concern knowledge, attitudes and specific problems related to adolescents. The adult forms cover the same areas as well as sexual function problems. The test is included in The Complete Specimen Set and the Sex Educators and Counselors' Package.

Untimed: Not available

Range: Adolescents and adults

Scoring: Examiner evaluated

Cost: Specimen set (4 forms and

manual $3.00; 10 forms (5 male, 5 female, specify adult or adolescent) $4.50.

Publisher: Family Life Publications, Inc.

SEXUAL COMMUNICATION INVENTORY (SCI)
Millard Bienvenu

adult

Purpose: Evaluates the level and type of communication about sexual matters within an established relationship. Used for marital counseling and enrichment programs.

Description: Paper-pencil test designed to help a couple overcome inhibitions in talking about their sexual relationship through an examination of their communication patterns. Part I consists of 30 statements concerning frequency and pattern of sexual communication and desire for change. Part II consists of incomplete sentences for a self report of sexual feelings, ability to communicate, and desire for change. Part III surveys general background information to aid the counselor. Materials include: the inventory, manual, and scoring key. Part of Bienvenu Specimen Set. For use by trained psychologists only.

Untimed: Not available

Range: Adults

Scoring: Hand key; examiner evaluated

Cost: Marital form $.35; guide $.75.

Publisher: Counseling and Self-Improvement Programs/Millard Bienvenu, Ph.D.

THE SEXUAL COMPATABILITY TEST
Arthur L. Foster

adult

Purpose: Assesses a couple's sexual relationship. Used to plan sex therapy programs and to predict success of sexual treatment.

Description: 101 item paper-pencil test assessing the following factors: sexual satisfaction, sexual dysfunction, variety, communication, interests or desires, and a broad range of sexual activities. Materials include: test form, answer sheet, and manual. Couples must have an ongoing sexual relationship of at least one year. Self-administered. Suitable for use with groups of couples.

Untimed: One hour

Range: Adult

Scoring: Hand key; examiner evaluated, computer scoring available.

Cost: Complete test $30.00.

Publisher: The Phoenix Institute of California

SOCIO-SEXUAL KNOWLEDGE AND ATTITUDES TEST (SSKAT)
Joel Wish, Katherine F. McCombs and Barbara Edmonson

adult

Purpose: Measures sexual knowledge and attitudes of the developmentally disabled of all ages. Used for educational and clinical counseling, planning, and placement.

Description: 227-page Stimulus Picture Book presents realistic pictures illustrating "Yes or No" and point-to response questions relevant to 14 socio- sexual topic areas. Anatomy Terminology, Menstruation, Dating,

Marriage, Intimacy, Intercourse, Pregnancy and Childbirth, Birth Control, Masturbation and Homosexuality, Veneral Disease, Alcohol and Drugs, Community Risks and Hazards, and a Terminology Check. Subjects to be tested must have visual and verbal comprehension; expressive language requirements are minimal. This is a criterion test to determine what the subject knows, believes, and does not know about human sexuality. It does not establish standards. Normative data is based on developmentally disabled ages 14-42, although SSKAT is also valuable in determining sexual knowledge and attitudes of non-retarded persons of all ages. The manual presents data on reliability and item- total correlations for each subtest. Examiner required. Not for group use.

Untimed: Open ended

Range: Developmentally disabled 18-42

Scoring: Examiner evaluated

Cost: Complete kit (includes record forms, stimulus picture book, manual) $95.00.

Publisher: Stoelting Co.

VASECTOMY SCALE: ATTITUDES
Panos D. Bardis

teen, adult   grades 10-UP

Purpose: Measures attitudes toward the social and psychological aspects of vasectomy; useful for clinical assessment, marriage and family counseling, research on human sexuality, and discussions in family and sex education.

Description: 25 item paper-pencil test. Subject rates 25 statements concerning vasectomy on a scale from 0 (strongly disagree) to 4 (strongly agree). Score equals sum total of 25 numerical responses. Theoretical range of scores: 0 (lowest approval at vasectomy) to 100 (highest approval). May be self-administered. Suitable for group use.

Untimed: 10 minutes

Range: High school and up

Scoring: Examiner evaluated

Cost: Free.

Publisher: Panos D. Bardis

Personality: Normal and Abnormal, Assessment and Treatment

Child

BURK'S BEHAVIOR RATING SCALES
Harold F. Burks

child, teen   grades 1-9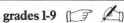

Purpose: Indentifies patterns of behavior problems in children in grades 1-9. Used as an aid to differential diagnosis.

Description: 110 item paper-pencil inventory with which a parent or teacher rates the child on the basis of descriptive statements of observed behavior. Nineteen subscales measure: excessive self-blame, anxiety, withdrawal, dependency, suffering, sense of persecution, aggressiveness, resistance, poor ego strength, physical strength, coordination, intellectuality, academics, attention, impulse control, reality contact, sense of identity, anger control, and social conformity. The Parent's Guide and the Teacher's Guide define each of the scales, present possible causes for the problem behavior, and offer suggestions on how to deal with the undesirable behavior from the point of view of parent or teacher. The manual discusses: causes and manifestations and possible intervention approaches for each of the subscales; usability with special groups such as educable mentally retarded; educationally and orthopedically handicapped; and speech and hearing handicapped.

Untimed: 15-20 minutes

Range: Grades 1-9

Scoring: Hand key

Cost: Complete kit (includes 20 booklets and profile sheets, manual, 2 parents' guides, 2 teachers' guides) $14.00.

Publisher: Western Psychological Services

BURK'S BEHAVIOR RATING SCALES, PRESCHOOL AND KINDERGARTEN EDITION
Harold F. Burks

child   grades PRE-K

Purpose: Identifies patterns of behavior problems in children ages 3-6. Used to aid differential diagnosis.

Description: 105 item paper-pencil inventory with which a parent or teacher rates the child on the basis of descriptive statements of observed behavior. 19 subscales are measured: excessive self-blame, anxiety, withdrawal, dependency, suffering, sense of persecution, aggressiveness, and resistance as well as poor ego strength, physical strength, coordination, intellectuality, attention, impulse control, reality contact,

sense of identity, anger control, and social conformity. This inventory is a downward extension of Burk's Behavior Rating Scale.

Untimed: 15-20 minutes

Range: Grades Preschool and Kindergarten

Scoring: Hand key

Cost: Complete kit (includes 20 profile sheets and booklets, manual) $12.30.

Publisher: Western Psychological Services

CALIFORNIA CHILD Q-SET
Jeanne H. Block and Jack Block

child

Purpose: Describes individual behavior and personality in contemporary psychodynamic terms. Used for research in child development.

Description: 100 item formulation of personality descriptions. Items are descriptive personality statements which are sorted from most to least applicable to the subject. Materials include individual 2¼" x 3½" cards. Examiner required. Not suitable for group use.

Untimed: Not available

Range: Child

Scoring: Examiner evaluated

Cost: Q-Sort Deck $6.00.

Publisher: Consulting Psychologists Press, Inc.

CHILD ANXIETY SCALE (CAS)
John S. Gillis

child

Purpose: Diagnoses adjustment problems in children ages 6-8 years. Helps to prevent emotional and behavioral disorders in later life by identifying children who would benefit from therapeutic intervention at an early age. Used for clinical evaluations and educational and personal counseling.

Description: Paper-pencil test measures anxiety-based disturbances in young children. Test items are based on extensive research of the form anxiety takes in the self-report of 6-8 year olds. An audio-cassette tape is used to present the questionnaire items, and brightly colored, easy- to-read answer sheets are specially designed for use with children of this age group. The CAS manual contains: reliability and validity information, scoring instructions, and percentiles and standard scores for both sexes separately and combined. Examiner required. Suitable for group use.

Untimed: Not available

Range: Ages 6-8

Scoring: Hand key

Cost: CAS professional examination kit $19.45; CAS manual $2.70; 50 handscoring answer sheets, scoring key $3.75; cassette tape $7.25.

Publisher: Institute for Personality and Ability Testing, Inc.

CHILD OBSERVATION GUIDE
Refer to page 615.

THE CHILDREN'S APPERCEPTION TEST (CAT-A)
Leopold Bellak and Sonya Sorel Bellak

child

Purpose: Assesses personality in children ages 3-10 years. Used in clinical

evaluation and diagnosis.

Description: Ten item oral response projective personality test measures the traits, attitudes and psychodynamics involved in the personalities of children ages 3-10 years. Each test item consists of a picture of animals in a human social context through which the child becomes involved in conflicts, identities, roles, family structures, etc. Examinees are asked to tell a story about each picture. Also includes: informational material on the history, nature and purpose of CAT, Ego Function Graph, test interpretation, use of the Short Form, research possibilities, and bibliography. Examiner required. Not suitable for group use. The following foreign language versions are available: Spanish, Indian, French, German, Japanese, Flemish, Portugese, and Italian.

Untimed: 20-30 minutes

Range: Ages 3-10

Scoring: Examiner evaluated

Cost: Complete kit (includes pictures and manual) $14.00.

Publisher: C.P.S., Inc.

THE CHILDREN'S APPERCEPTION TEST-HUMAN FIGURES (CAT-H)
Leopold Bellak and Sonya Sorel Bellak

child

Purpose: Assesses personality in children ages 3-10 years. Used for clinical evaluation and diagnosis.

Description: Ten item oral response projective personality test measures the traits, attitudes and psychodynamics involved in the personalities of children ages 3-10 years. The test consists of ten pictures of human figures in situations of concern to children: conflicts, identities, roles, family structure, etc. Also included: a review of the literature concerning the use of animal vs. human figures in projective techniques, a discussion of the process of transposing animal figures to human forms, a copy of Haworth's Schedule of Adaptive Mechanisms in CAT Responses and bibliography. Examiner required. Not suitable for group use. Spanish, Portugese, Flemish, and Japanese versions also available.

Untimed: 20-30 minutes

Range: Ages 3-10

Scoring: Examiner evaluated

Cost: Complete kit (10 pictures and manual) $14.00.

Publisher: C.P.S., Inc.

THE CHILDREN'S APPERCEPTION TEST-SUPPLEMENT (CAT-S)
Leopold Bellak, Sonya Sorel Bellak

child

Purpose: Assesses personality in children ages 3-10 years. Used for clinical evaluation and diagnosis.

Description: Ten item oral response projective personality test measures the traits, attitudes and psychodynamics at work in the personalities of children ages 3-10 years. The test items consist of ten pictures using animal figures to present the children with family situations which are common, but not as universal as those of the Children's Apperception Test. Situations depicted are: prolonged illness, physical disability, mother's pregnancy, separation of parents, etc. The picture plates are constructed like pieces of a large jigsaw puzzle, with irregularly-shaped outlines. Children who do not relate stories readily can manipulate these forms in play techniques. Also included: infor-

mational material on test techniques and bibliography. Examiner required. Not suitable for group use. Versions available in the following foreign languages: Spanish, French, Flemish, and Italian.

Untimed: 20-30 minutes

Range: Ages 3-10

Scoring: Examiner evaluated

Cost: Complete kit (10 pictures and manual) $14.00.

Publisher: C.P.S., Inc.

CHILDREN'S PERSONALITY QUESTIONNAIRE (CPQ)
Rutherford B. Porter and Raymond B. Cattell

child, teen

Purpose: Assesses personality development in children ages 8-12 years. Used for clinical evaluations and educational and personal counseling.

Description: 140 item paper-pencil test measures 14 primary personality traits useful in predicting and evaluating the course of personal, social, and academic development. Traits measured include emotional stability, self-concept level, excitability, and self-assurance. Scores for extraversion, anxiety and other broad trait patterns are obtained as combinations of the primary scales. Percentiles and standard scores are presented for both sexes together and separately. The test is available in four equivalent forms: A,B,C, and D. Each form is divided into two parts for scheduling convenience in school settings. Third grade reading level required. Examiner required. Suitable for group use. Available in Spanish and German.

Untimed: 30-60 minutes per form

Range: Ages 8-12

Scoring: Hand key; scoring and interpretation services available

Cost: Professional examination kit $14.80; CPQ specimen set $2.95; handbook $6.25; manual $1.95; 25 reusable tests $9.00; 50 answer sheets $6.00; 50 profile sheets $6.00; 50 answer-profile sheets $7.00; scoring key for answer sheets $6.00; scoring key for test booklet $3.00; scoring service $2.28-$3.80 each depending on quantity.

Publisher: Institute for Personality and Ability Testing, Inc.

CHILDREN'S SCALE OF SOCIAL ATTITUDES
Glen D. Wilson, David K.B. Nias, and Paul M. Insel

child, teen

Purpose: Assesses social attitudes in school children. Used for research in personality, developmental and social psychology, education and sociology.

Description: 50 item paper-pencil test of social attitudes. Items are single words representing social issues familiar to children. Children respond by agreeing or disagreeing with each item. Factors measured yield scores on Conservatism, Religiosity, Punitiveness, Ethnocentrism and Hedonism. Modeled on the Wilson-Patterson Attitude Inventory for adults. Examiner required. Suitable for group use. BRITISH PUBLISHER

Untimed: 15 minutes

Range: Ages 8-14

Scoring: Examiner evaluated

Cost: Contact publishers.

Publisher: NFER-Nelson Publishing Company

CONOLEY-HARRISON PROJECTED SELF-CONCEPT INVENTORY (ENGLISH/SPANISH) (PSCI)
Refer to page 634.

DRISCOLL PLAY KIT
G.P. Driscoll

child

Purpose: Assesses dynamics of personality development and adjustment in children. Used for diagnosis and as a therapy tool.

Description: Procedure for systematic observation of children's doll play. Materials include case which opens to form a house, a family of five plastic dolls, and 37 pieces of furniture. For use by psychologists, pediatricians, or researchers. Examiner required. Not suitable for group use.

Untimed: Not available

Range: Children

Scoring: Examiner evaluated

Cost: Contact publisher.

Publisher: The Psychological Corporation

EARLY SCHOOL PERSONALITY QUESTIONNAIRE (ESPQ)
Raymond B. Cattell, Richard W. Coan, and IPAT Staff

child

Purpose: Measures personality in children in the early school years (ages 6-8). Used for clinical evaluation and educational and personal counseling.

Description: 160 item paper-pencil test uses a pictorial answer sheet to facilitate personality testing at an early age. Questions are read aloud by the teacher (an optional tape recording may be used instead) and the students mark their answers on the specially designed answer sheet. To use the answer sheet, children need only be able to discriminate the letter A from the letter B and to recognize pictures of a bird, cat, tree, flower, and other common objects. Percentiles and standard scores are provided for both sexes separately and together. The test is divided into two equal parts (80 items each) for scheduling convenience. Examiner required. Suitable for group use. Available in Spanish.

Untimed: Not available

Range: Ages 6-8

Scoring: Hand key

Cost: ESPQ professional examination kit $8.50; manual $4.50; 25 child's answer booklets $4.00; 50 profile sheets $4.00; 2 scoring keys $3.50; tape recording $25.00.

Publisher: Institute for Personality and Ability Testing, Inc.

FROST SELF-DESCRIPTION QUESTIONNAIRE
B.P. Frost

child, teen

Purpose: Diagnoses various aspects of a child's feelings of anxiety, aggression, affiliation, and submission for use by school psychologists to identify such children.

Description: 107 item paper-pencil, true-false test covering 14 scales of anxiety: test, social, worry and tension, concentration, separation from family, spatial separation, body damage, and free-floating anxiety, externailized aggression, internalized aggression, projective aggression, denial affiliation, and submission. Materials consist of a booklet, answer sheet, and answer keys. Use

restricted to psychologists. Available in Spanish and Japanese. Examiner required. Suitable for group use.

Untimed: 15 minutes

Range: Ages 8-14

Scoring: Hand key

Cost: Manual $2.50; 25 questionnaire booklets $15.00; 25 answer sheets $7.50; 4 keys $4.00; specimen set $7.50.

Publisher: B.P. Frost

INTERMEDIATE PERSONALITY QUESTIONNAIRE FOR INDIAN PUPILS (IPQI)-1974
Refer to page 635.

JOSEPH PRESCHOOL AND PRIMARY SELF-CONCEPT SCREENING TEST (JPPSST)
Refer to page 43.

MICHIGAN PICTURE TEST, REVISED
Max L. Hutt

child, teen   grades 3-12

Purpose: Differentiates between emotionally maladjusted children (Grades 3-12) and emotionally well-adjusted children. Diagnoses type and severity of conflicts and identifies children in need of rehabilitative/psycho-therapeutic procedures.

Description: Oral response projective test measures school age children for degree of emotional adjustment or maladjustment, areas of emotional conflict, and types of emotional conflict. Four "Core" pictures (presented to both sexes) yield scores on several emotional areas. Eight additional pictures for boys and eight pictures for girls yield information about areas and types of conflict. The students are presented with the picture cards one at a time and asked to make up stories about them. Scoring employs simple objective methods along with characteristics of partially-structured projective tests. Examiner required. Suitable for group use.

Untimed: Short form, 15 minutes; long form , 1 hour

Range: Grades 3-12

Scoring: Hand key; examiner evaluated

Cost: Complete set $49.00; 50 record forms $11.00; set of pictures $21.50; manual $18.00.

Publisher: Grune & Stratton, Inc.

MISSOURI CHILDREN'S PICTURE SERIES (MCPS)
J.O. Sines, J.D. Pauker, L.K. Sines

---

child, teen

Purpose: Measures child personality characteristics as a means to screen school-age children for personality difficulties and to evaluate in terms of clinical diagnosis.

Description: 238 item test consisting of picture diagrams of everyday situations printed on 3 x 5 cards which the examiner presents to the children, asking them to select those which look like fun and those which do not. The examiner separates the cards by color dividers to score the answers on the following scales: Conformity, Masculinity/Femininity, Maturity, Aggression, Introversion, Hyperactivity, Sleep Disturbance, and Systematic Complaint. The results yield information regarding the possibility of personality difficulties. Available only to psychologists, trained teachers and counselors. Examiner required. Suitable for group use.

Untimed: 25 minutes

Range: Ages 5-16

Scoring: Hand key

Cost: Specimen set $40.00.

Publisher: Psychological Assessment and Services, Inc.

PERSONALITY INVENTORY FOR CHILDREN (PIC)
Robert D. Wirt, David Lachar, James E. Klinedist, Philip D. Seat, and William E. Broen

---

child, teen

Purpose: Evaluates the personality attributes of children ages 3-16. Used by professionals for counseling and identification of learning and social disabilities.

Description: 600 item paper-pencil, true-false inventory, filled out by a parent. It provides comprehensive profiles based on the model of the Minnesota Multiphasic Personality Inventory (MMPI). A total of 33 scales are measured. The 16 primary scales are graphically presented on the Profile Form, they consist of three validity scales and the following clinical and screening scales: Adjustment, Development, Family Relations, Anxiety, Social Skills, Achievement, Somatic Concern, Delinquency, Psychosis, Intellectual Screening, Depression, Withdrawal, and Hyperactivity. An additional 17 experimental scales (not included on the Profile Form) are also provided: Adolescent Maladjustment, Ego Strength, Infrequency, K (defensiveness), Sex Role, Somatization, Aggression, Cerebral Dysfunction, Excitement, Internalization, Learning Disability Prediction, Asocial Behavior, Delinquency Prediction, Externalization, Introversion- Extroversion, Reality Distortion, and Social Desirability. Norms and profiles are available for two age groups: 3-5 years and 6-16 years. Revised format allows administration of two short forms of inventory, providing information on shortened Clinical Scales and Factor

Scales. Examiner-administered. Not for group use.

Untimed: Not available

Range: Ages 3-16

Scoring: Hand key; computer scoring available

Cost: Complete kit $42.20; 10 booklets $9.70; 100 profile forms $9.50 (specify ages 3-5 or 6-16 years); 100 answer sheets $9.50; scoring templates $24.50.

Publisher: Western Psychological Services

PERSONALITY RATING SCALE
S. Mary Amantora

child, teen   grades K-12

Purpose: Assesses personality strengths and weaknesses of children from Kindergarten to Grade 12. Identifies children in need of further psychological evaluation.

Description: 22 item paper-pencil test of personality functioning. Items are characteristics of good and poor habits of interaction acquired in childhood and strengthened in early adolescence which affect personality development and the process of maturation. Rating scale may be completed by the child, teacher, or peers. For use in Grades 4-12; in Kindergarten through Grade 3 with special instructions as given in manual. May be self-administered. Suitable for group use.

Untimed: 30-40 minutes for 10-15 classmates

Range: Grades K-12

Scoring: Hand key; examiner and student evaluated

Cost: Specimen set $1.25; complete kit (includes 35 scales and 35 pupil rating sheets, 3 class record sheets, key, manual) $4.25; additional manuals $.35 each.

Publisher: Educators'/Employers' Tests and Services Associates

---

PLAY AND TELL CARDS: A THERAPEUTIC GAME
Robert Gordon

child

Purpose: Allows children to verbalize thoughts and fears in a nonthreatening environment. Aids in building a therapeutic relationship by stimulating dialogue and establishing rapport between child and therapist.

Description: 80 item interview guide consisting of cards which present topics to be discussed during a game of checkers. After each move in the game, the child selects a card and discusses it with the therapist. The cards ask questions about home, family, emotions, relationships, school, values, safety, health, discipline, thought processes, conflicts, and fears. Checkers and board not provided. Examiner required. Suitable for group use.

Untimed: Not available

Range: Ages 6-12

Scoring: Examiner evaluated

Cost: Complete set (includes cards and instructions) $13.00.

Publisher: The Wilmington Press

THE PRESCHOOL BEHAVIOR QUESTIONNAIRE
Lenore B. Behar and Samuel Stringfield

child

Purpose: Screens preschool age children for symptoms that indicate behavior problems. Used by child psychologists to determine individual need and placement.

Description: 30 item paper-pencil observational scale consisting of behavioral statements which a teacher or parent rates "Doesn't Apply," "Applies Sometimes," or "Certainly

Applies" for the child in question. Measures hostile-aggressive, anxious, and distractible behaviors. Materials include score sheet, answer sheet, and manual. Self-administered by parent or teacher; scored by child psychologist. Not for group use.

Untimed: 10 minutes

Range: Ages 3-6

Scoring: Hand key; examiner evaluated

Cost: Complete kit (50 score sheets and answer sheets, manual) $10.00.

Publisher: Lenore Behar

PRESCHOOL SELF-CONCEPT PICTURE TEST (PS-CPT)
Refer to page 638.

PSYCHOLOGICAL EVALUATION OF CHILDRENS HUMAN FIGURES DRAWING (HFD)
Elizabeth M. Koppitz

child

Purpose: Assesses a child's mental maturity, personality characteristics, and family relationships. Used to screen school beginners, as part of a psychological test battery, and to measure progress.

Description: Multiple-item, paper-pencil test in which the child draws "one whole person" and answers three questions. The drawing is scored and analyzed for developmental items, emotional indicators, and content. Factors measured include mental maturity, self-concept, attitudes (concerns, anxiety, conflict), and interpersonal relationships. Examiner required. Suitable for group use. Available in German, Spanish, and Japanese.

Untimed: 5-12 minutes

Range: Ages 5-12

Scoring: Examiner evaluated

Cost: Manual $26.00; 100 scoring sheets $14.50.

Publisher: Grune & Stratton, Inc.

ROBERTS APPERCEPTION TEST FOR CHILDREN
Glen E. Roberts and Dorthea S. McArthur

child, teen

Purpose: Identifies emotionally disturbed children (ages 6-15). Used for clinical diagnosis, particularly with those children just entering counseling or therapy.

Description: 16 item oral response test in which the child is shown a series of line-drawings and is asked to make up stories about each of them. The stimuli cards are realistic illustrations of adults and children in up-to-date clothing. They emphasize every-day interpersonal events of contemporary life and include (in addition to the standard situations of the TAT and CAT) situations such as: parental disagreement, parental affection, observation of nudity, and school and peer interpersonal events. Stimuli are chosen to elicit psychologically meaningful responses and the following clinical areas are measured and reported on the "Interpersonal Chart": Conflict, Anxiety, Aggression, Depression, Rejection, Punishment, Dependency, Support, Closure, resolution, Unresolved Indicator, Maladaptive Outcome, and Deviation Response. Other measures include: Ego Functioning Index, an Aggression Index, and a Levels of Projection Scale. Objective scoring methods have high interrater reliability. Normative data collected on Caucasian children, although preliminary studies indicate that the test is probably valid with children of several different ethnic backgrounds. The stimuli consist of

27 8½" x 11" cards, only 16 of which are used, depending on the sex of the child. The manual includes a number of case studies and examples. Examiner required. Not for group use.

Untimed: 20-30 minutes

Range: Ages 6-15

Scoring: Examiner evaluated

Cost: Complete kit (1 set of test pictures, 10 record booklets, manual) $35.00

Publisher: Western Psychological Services

SCHOOL APPERCEPTION METHOD (SAM)
Irving L. Solomon and Bernard D. Starr

child, teen   grades K-9

Purpose: Assesses the emotional and cognitive frame of mind of children and adolescents. Used for clinical evaluations.

Description: 12 item oral response projective test consisting of 12 drawings - plus 12 alternates - focused on school situations. The scenes are designed to elicit school-oriented fantasies, feelings, attitudes, and perceptions. Manual included. Examiner required. Suitable for group use.

Untimed: Not available

Range: Grades K-9

Scoring: Examiner evaluated

Cost: Complete kit (24 pictures plus manual) $25.50.

Publisher: Springer Publishing Company

SCHOOL CHILD STRESS SCALE (SCSS)
Justin Pikunas

child, teen   grades 1-8

Purpose: Measures the intensity of stress present in severely retarded and/or mentally deficient children from 1st-8th grade. Used to identify children who need special adjustment counseling.

Description: Multiple item oral response questionnaire examining a child's levels of efficiency and adjustment in dealing with the stress often encountered by severely retarded and mentally deficient children. The examiner reads through the three-page instrument, questions the child and records the answers. Examiner required. Not for group use.

Untimed: 20 minutes

Range: Grades 1-8

Scoring: Examiner evaluated

Cost: Per testing form (includes guidelines for interpretation), $2.00; 10 or more $1.00.

Publisher: Justin Pikunas, Ph.D.

SELF-CONCEPT ADJECTIVE CHECKLIST
Alan J. Politte

child   grades K-8

Purpose: Measures personality and self-concept. Used for diagnosis, screening and measuring changes due to therapy.

Description: 114 item paper-pencil test of self-concept. Items are traits which are categorized as Physical Traits, Social Values, Intellectual Abilities and Miscellaneous. Children in gardes K-3 check "I Am" or "I Am Not" for each item. Children in grades 4-8 have the additional choice of an "I Would Like To Be" column.

Item may be rated by the student or an observer. Examiner required. Suitable for group use.

Untimed: 10 minutes

Range: Elementary school level

Scoring: Hand key; examiner evaluated

Cost: Specimen set $4.00; 25 rating checklist $12.50; 100-$49.00.

Publisher: Psychologists and Educators, Inc.

STATE-TRAIT ANXIETY INVENTORY FOR CHILDREN (STAIC)
Charles D. Spielberger

child, teen   grades 4-8

Purpose: Assesses anxiety in children. Used for research screening and treatment evaluation.

Description: Two 20-item scales measuring two types of anxiety: state anxiety (A-State), and trait anxiety (A-Trait). The A-State scales ask how the child feels at a particular moment in time, while the A-Trait scales ask how he generally feels. Based on the same concept as the State-Trait Anxiety Inventory and is used in conjunction with the adult form manual. Self-administered. Suitable for group use.

Untimed: 10-20 minutes

Range: Grades 4-8

Scoring: Hand key; examiner evaluated

Cost: Specimen set $4.00; manual $2.00; key $.75; 25 expendable tests $2.25.

Publisher: Consulting Psychologists Press, Inc.

Adolescent and Adult

ACUTALIZING ASSESSMENT BATTERY (AAB)
Everett L. Shostrom

adult

Purpose: Measures an individual's sense of actualization with himself and within his relationships with others. Used for a wide variety of counseling situations by therapists, marriage and family counselors, personnel administrators and school psychologists.

Description: Four paper-pencil tests measuring 13 dimensions of a person's sense of actualization: being, weakness, synergistic integration, time orientation, core centeredness, love, trust in humanity, creative living, mission, strength, manipulation awareness, anger, and potentiation. The Personal Orientations Dimensions (POD) and the Personal Orientation Inventory (POI) primarily measure intrapersonal actualizing, while the Caring Relationship Inventory (CRI) and the Pair Attraction Inventory (PAI) primarily measure interpersonal actualizing. The AAB may be scored locally by using the POI, CRI, and PAI or may be sent to EITS for scoring. Results are reported through the AAB Interpretation Brochure, a six- page booklet containing descriptions and profiles for each of the four tests. Examiner required. Suitable for group use.

Untimed: Not available

Range: Adult

Scoring: Hand key; computer scoring available

Cost: Sample AAB Packet (includes sample booklet answer sheet, manual for each AAB instrument plus one scoring certificate) $9.75; AAB scoring (POD, CRI, PAI, POI) $4.00; AAB

Interpretaion Brochure (local scoring of POI, CRI, PAI) package of 25, $5.50; package of 100-$19.50.

Publisher: Educational and Industrial Testing Service

ADJECTIVE CHECK LIST (ACL)
Harrison Gough and Alfred Heilbrun, Jr.

teen, adult   grades 9-UP

Purpose: Describes self and relations with others; useful for personality assessment and research.

Description: 300 item paper-pencil test of up to 37 dimensions of personality including four Method of Response Scales, 15 Need Scales, nine Topical Scales, five Transactional Scales, and four Origence-Intellectence Scales. Items are adjectives which are checked if they apply to self and also may be answered with reference to others. Scores need not be obtained on all 37 scales. Self-administered. Suitable for group use. Available in Spanish.

Untimed: 15-20 minutes

Range: Grades 9-16; adult

Scoring: Computer scoring necessary

Cost: Specimen set $11.95; manual $11.00; 25 check lists $4.00; 25 profiles $1.75.

Publisher: Consulting Psychologists Press, Inc.

ADULT STRESS INVENTORY (ASI)
Justin Pikunas

teen, adult

Purpose: Measures the intensity of stress present in adults and adolescents 16 years and older. Used to identify individuals in need of counseling in order to deal more efficiently with stress.

Description: Two page paper-pencil inventory examining the effects of stress on the subject's personal efficiency, adjustment, and physical health. Sixth-grade reading level required. Test results are compared to college student sample. Self- administered. Suitable for group use.

Untimed: 15 minutes

Range: Ages 16-adult

Scoring: Hand key

Cost: Testing form $1.00; 10 or more $1.50.

Publisher: Justin Pikunas

AFFECT SCALE
Ricardo Girona

teen, adult

Purpose: Assesses adult adjustment and self concept. Used for educational and clinical screening and to evaluate psychotherapy progress.

Description: Multiple item paper-pencil test of individual perception of self and others, using 18 pair- choices of adjectives or dimensions, each with a seven-scale intensity rating. Materials include scorable booklets and scoring keys. Self- administered. Suitable for group use.

Untimed: 15 minutes

Range: Ages 16-adult

Scoring: Hand key; examiner evaluated

Cost: Scale $.30.

Publisher: Dr. Ricardo Girona

Ai3Q MEASURE OF OBSESSIONAL OR ANAL CHARACTER
Paul Kline

all ages

Purpose: Measures degree of obsessional or anal personality characteristics. Used for research studies of personality, vocational guidance, and clinical studies of neuroses.

Description: 30 item paper-pencil measure of obsessiveness, a construct derived from Freudian theory. Items are marked either yes or no. Differentiates groups identified by raters as being high or low on obsessive characteristics. Examiner required. Suitable for group use.
BRITISH PUBLISHER

Untimed: 10 minutes

Range: Grades sixth-formers, intelligent adults

Scoring: Examiner evaluated

Cost: Specimen set £4.25; 25 questionnaires £1.65; manual £3.95 (payment in sterling for all overseas orders).

Publisher: NFER-Nelson Publishing Company

ALCADD TEST
Morse P. Manson

adult

Purpose: Measures extent of alcohol addiction. Used for diagnosis, therapy and research.

Description: Paper-pencil inventory measures extent of alcohol addiction by measuring areas of maladjustment. Not an instrument for detecting alcoholics. Examiner required. Suitable for group use.

Untimed: 5-10 minutes

Range: Adult

Scoring: Hand key

Cost: Complete kit (includes 20 tests, manual, key) $9.80.

Publisher: Western Psychological Services

ANXIETY SCALE FOR THE BLIND
Richard E. Hardy

teen, adult

Purpose: Measures manifest anxiety among blind and partially sighted people. Used for clinical evaluations by psychologists, psychiatrists, and trained counselors.

Description: 78 item true-false test measuring the level of anxiety present in blind and partially sighted children and recently modified adults. The subject is given a roll of tickets to be placed to the right or left of the table to indicate true or false as the items are read. Originally developed for use in residential schools with students of high school age, it is useful in other contexts as well. Still experimental in nature and must be used only by psychologists, psychiatrists and other qualified counselors. Examiner required. Not for group use.

Untimed: Not available

Range: Ages 13-adult

Scoring: Examiner evaluated

Cost: Scale $4.00.

Publisher: American Foundation for the Blind

ASSOCIATION ADJUSTMENT INVENTORY (AAI)
Martin M. Bruce

adult

Purpose: Evaluates the extent to which the subject is maladjusted, immature, and deviant in ideation'; useful as an aid to predicting potential deviant behavior.

Description: 100 item test in which the subject selects one of four words to associate with a stimulus word, thus allowing the examiner to screen for ideational deviation, general psychosis, depression, hysteria, withdrawal, paranoia, rigidity, schizophrenia, impulsiveness, sociopathy, psych- somapathia, and anxiety. The answers are compared to "norms" to measure significant deviation. Available in Spanish and German. Examiner/self-administered. Suitable for groups.

Range: Adult

Scoring: Hand key

Cost: Specimen set with IBM scoring stencil $10.90; specimen set with hand key $8.53; package of tests used with IBM answer sheets $15.30. Package of tests with hand key $15.30; manual $4.35; package of profile sheets $6.05.

Publisher: Martin M.Bruce, Ph.D. Publishers

BEHAVIOR STATUS INVENTORY (BSI)
William T. Martin

---

teen, adult

Purpose: Measures behavioral traits of adults and adolescents in mental health settings. Used to evaluate emotionally disturbed, brain-damaged, and mentally retarded patients. Used to monitor patient progress in response to therapy.

Description: 91 item observational inventory assessing seven behavioral areas: personal appearance, manifest (obvious) behavior, attitude, verbal behavior, social behavior, work behavior, and cognitive behavior. An aide or staff member familiar with the individual can complete the questionnaire, rating each of the behavioral statements from 1 to 4 as it applies to the patient based upon observed behavior during the past week. Scores for each of the seven subscales as well as a Total Patient Asset Score are derived. Item analysis and subscale scores can be machine scored for one time or ongoing patient and/or program analysis. Administered by the evaluator. Suitable for group use.

Untimed: No time limit

Range: Adolescent, adult

Scoring: Examiner evaluated

Cost: Specimen set $4.00; 25 forms $12.50; 100- $49.00; 25 profile sheets $5.50; 100-$21.00.

Publisher: Psychologists and Educators, Inc.

BEM SEX-ROLE INVENTORY (BSRI)
Sandra L. Bem

---

adult

Purpose: Measures masculinity and femininity. Used for research on psychological androgyny.

Description: 60 item paper-pencil measure of integration of masculinity and femininity. Items are three sets of twenty personality characteristics: masculine, feminine, and neutral. Subject indicates on a seven-point scale how well each characteristic describes him. Materials include a 30 item short form. Self-administered. Suitable for group use.

Untimed: 10 minutes

Range: Adult

Scoring: Hand key

Cost: Specimen set $8.00; manual $7.50; key $.75; 25 expendable inventories $2.75; computer scoring instructions $5.00.

Publisher: Consulting Psychologists Press, Inc.

THE BLACK INTELLIGENCE TEST OF CULTURAL HOMOGENEITY (BITCH)
Robert L. Williams

teen, adult

Purpose: Measures white Americans' sensitivity to the black experience and black Americans' identification with the black experience. Used in racial relations seminars or interracial workshops.

Description: 41 item paper-pencil multiple-choice test providing a culture-specific measure of racial attitudes. Two forms available. Self-administered. Suitable for group use.

Untimed: 20 minutes

Range: Ages 16-adult

Scoring: Hand key

Cost: Complete set (includes 20 tests, directions, key) $22.00; manual $3.75.

Publisher: Robert L. Williams & Associates, Inc.

BLOOM SENTENCE COMPLETION ATTITUDE SURVEY
Wallace Bloom

teen, adult

Purpose: Assesses adult and student attitudes toward self and other important factors in everyday living. Used to identify change in an individual over time and to compare individuals and groups.

Description: 40 item paper-pencil free response test consisting of sentence stems which the subject is asked to complete in his own words. The responses measure attitudes toward: age mates or people, physical self, family, psychological self, self directedness, education or work (depending on which version is used), accomplishment, and irritants. Two

versions are available: one for adults and one for unmarried students. Scoring system facilitates use of the test as both an objective and projective instrument. Examiner required. Suitable for group use.

Untimed: 25 minutes

Range: Unmarried students-adult

Scoring: Examiner evaluated

Cost: Both versions - complete kit (includes 30 test forms, 30 analysis record forms, manual) $24.00 each.

Publisher: Stoelting Co.

THE BROOK REACTION TEST OF INTERESTS AND TEMPERAMENT
Refer to page 614.

CALIFORNIA PSYCHOLOGICAL INVENTORY (CPI)
Harrison G. Gough

teen, adult

Purpose: Assesses normal adult personality as an aid to educational, clinical, counseling and vocational guidance.

Description: 480 item paper-pencil test of 18 socially desirable behavioral tendencies: dominance, capacity for status, sociability, social presence, self-acceptance, sense of well-being, responsibility, socialization, self-control, tolerance, good impression, communality, achievement via conformance, achievement via independence, intellectual efficiency, psychological-mindedness, flexibility, and femininity. Assists counselors of non- psychiatrically disturbed clients by measuring personality characteristics important for social living and social interaction. Self-administered. Available in Spanish, French, Italian, and German.

Untimed: 45-60 minutes

Range: Adolescent, adult

Scoring: Hand key

Cost: Counselor's kit (includes 5 reusable tests, 25 answer sheets, 25 profiles, set of stencils, manual) $17.50.

Publisher: Consulting Psychologists Press, Inc.

CALIFORNIA Q-SORT DECK
Jack Block adapted by Daryl Bem

adult

Purpose: Describes individual personality in contemporary psychodynamic terms. Used for research.

Description: 100 item test used to formulate personality descriptions. Items are descriptive personality statements on cards which are sorted from most to least applicable to the subject's experience. Materials include individual 2¼" x 3½" cards and a Sorting Guide. May be sorted by professionals or laymen. Examiner required. Not for group use.

Untimed: Not available

Range: Adult

Scoring: Examiner evaluated

Cost: Q-Sort Deck $4.00; guide and 50 recording pads $5.50.

Publisher: Consulting Psychologists Press, Inc.

CARLSON PSYCHOLOGICAL SURVEY (CPS)
Kenneth A. Carlson

teen, adult

Purpose: Assesses and classifies criminal offenders. Used to evaluate persons presenting behavioral or substance abuse problems and to analyze the effects of intervention programs.

Description: 50 item paper-pencil questionnaire in a five- category response format with space for respondent's comments. The scales are: Chemical Abuse, Thought Disturbance, Antisocial Tendencies, Self- Depreciation, and Validity. The test is designed for offenders, those charged with crimes, and others who have come to the attention of the criminal justice or social welfare systems. The results are classified into 18 offender types as described in the manual. The subjects must have at least a fourth-grade reading level. Use restricted to APA registered psychologists. Examiner required. Suitable for group use.

Untimed: 15 minutes

Range: Adolescent, adult

Scoring: Hand key

Cost: Complete set $15.00.

Publisher: Research Psychologists Press, Inc.

CENTER FOR EPIDEMIOLOGIC STUDIES-DEPRESSION SCALE (CES-D)

adult

Purpose: Measures symptoms associated with depression in adults. Used to identify high risk groups for research and screening.

Description: A 20 item paper-pencil test which may be read to a subject by an examiner or completed in privacy by the client. The subject is asked to rank his experiences and feelings for the past week on a 0 to 3 scale: Less than once a day (0) to Most or All of the time (3). Questions deal with symptoms of depressed mood, lack of energy, insomnia and appetite loss. Scales are weighted for scoring and interpretation. Self-administered. Suitable for group use. Available in Spanish.

Untimed: 5 minutes

Range: Adult

Scoring: Hand key

Cost: Contact publisher.

Publisher: Center for Epidemiologic Studies

CHARACTER ASSESSMENT SCALE
Paul F. Schmidt

adult

Purpose: Assesses a person's moral strength and weaknesses. Allows individuals to explore their moral character. Useful in pastoral counseling and clinical psychology.

Description: 225 item paper-pencil test that measures a series of eight moral character strengths and weaknesses. The moral character strengths examined are humility, compassion, peacemaking, resourcefulness, enthusiasm, sexual integrity, physical fitness and honesty. Weaknesses include pride, envy, resentment, greed, laziness, lust, gluttony and denial. Subject reads each item and marks the answer true or false. Self-administered. Suitable for group use.

Untimed: 45 minutes

Range: Adult

Scoring: Hand key: examiner evaluated; scoring service available

Cost: Test package $12.00; answer sheets $5.00; scoring service $5.00, manual $8.00.

Publisher: Paul F. Schmidt, Ph.D.

CLINICAL ANALYSIS QUESTIONNAIRE (CAQ)
Raymond B. Cattell and IPAT Staff

teen, adult

Purpose: Evaluates personality and psychiatric/psychological difficulties as a measure of primary behavioral dimensions in adults and adolescents over 16 years of age. Used for clinical diagnosis, evaluation of therapeutic progress, and vocational and rehabilitation guidance.

Description: 272 item paper-pencil multiple-choice test measures 16 personality factors (the 16PF factors) as well as hypochondriasis, agitated depression, suicidal depression, anxious depression, guilt, energy level, boredom, and five other dimensions in the pathology domain. Norms are provided for adults, college men and women, and special adolescent norms for Part II. The manual contains profiles for a number of special groups, including alcoholics, narcotic addicts, various types of neurotic and psychotic disorders, criminals and others. The test has been organized in two parts so that the entire test need not be given in a single sitting. Sixth-grade reading level required. Self-administered. Suitable for group use.

Untimed: 2 hours

Range: Ages 16 and older

Scoring: Hand key; computer scoring services available.

Cost: Computer Profile and Interpretation $4.50- $12.00; 25 reusable test booklets $17.50; also ARION II Teleprocessing $22.00-$24.00.

Publisher: Institute for Personality and Ability Testing, Inc.

COMPREHENSIVE PERSONAL ASSESSMENT SYSTEM: ADJECTIVE SELF-DESCRIPTION (ASD)
Donald J. Veldman and George V.C. Parker

teen, adult

Purpose: Evaluates an individual's assessment of his own personality traits.

Description: 56 item paper-pencil, multiple-choice test of self-evaluated personality characteristics. Measures seven factor-analytic derived traits. Self-administered. Suitable for group use.

Untimed: 15 minutes

Range: Adolescent, adult

Scoring: Hand key; computer scoring available

Cost: 100 forms $1.30; manual $2.25.

Publisher: Research and Development Center for Teacher Education

COMPREHENSIVE PERSONAL ASSESSMENT SYSTEM: DIRECTED IMAGINATION (DI)
Donald J. Veldman and S. L. Menaker

teen, adult College

Purpose: Assesses the concerns and attitudes of college-age students.

Description: Four item paper-pencil projective test measuring a broad array of psychological characteristics. Each test item consists of a timed (4-minute) story-writing exercise which provides a projective sample of the subject's thinking. Examiner required. Suitable for group use.

Timed: 16 minutes

Range: College-age students

Scoring: Examiner evaluated

Cost: 100 forms $3.90; manual $2.50.

Publisher: Research and Development Center for Teacher Education

COMPREHENSIVE PERSONAL ASSESSMENT SYSTEM: ONE-WORD SENTENCE COMPLETION (OWSC)
Donald J. Veldman, S.L. Menaker, and R.F. Peck

teen, adult College

Purpose: Provides information for clinical assessment of personality.

Description: 62 item paper-pencil projective personality test. Test items consist of sentences with single word blanks to be filled in by the subject. Primarily for the assessment of normal adults and adolescents; normed for college age individuals. Keypunch response forms for computer processing are optionally available. Self-administered. Suitable for group use.

Untimed: Not available

Range: College-age only

Scoring: Examiner evaluated; may be computer scored

Cost: 100 forms $3.90; manual $1.75.

Publisher: Research and Development Center for Teacher Education

COMPREHENSIVE PERSONAL ASSESSMENT SYSTEM: SELF REPORT INVENTORY (SRI)
Oliver H. Bown

teen, adult

Purpose: Assesses the perception of adults and adolescents concerning their attitudes toward self and others.

Description: 48 item paper-pencil, multiple-choice test evaluating a person's self-image of his phenomenological world. Measures eight subareas. Self-administered.

Suitable for group use.

Untimed: 20 minutes

Range: Adolescents, adults

Scoring: Hand key; computer scoring available

Cost: 100 forms $3.90.

Publisher: Research and Development Center for Teacher Education

---

COMREY PERSONALITY SCALES (CPS)
Andrew L. Comrey

teen, adult   grades 10-UP

Purpose: Measures major personality characteristics of adults and high school and college students. Used in educational, clinical and business settings where personality structure and stability are important.

Description: 180 item paper-pencil test consisting of scales for each of eight Personality Dimensions (20 items each), a Validity Scale (8 items), and a Response Bias Scale (12 items). Subjects respond to items according to seven-point scales ranging from "Never" or "Definitely Not", to "Always" or "Definitely". The eight personality scales are: Trust vs. Defensiveness, Orderliness vs. Lack of Orderliness, Social Conformity vs. Rebelliousness, Activity vs. Lack of Energy, Emotional Stability vs. Neuroticism, Extraversion vs. Introversion, Masculinity vs. Femininity, and Empathy vs. Egocentrism. The Profile presents a description of the personality structure of "normal" socially functioning individuals. Extreme scores on any of thee scales may provide a clue as to the scales may provide a clue as to the source of current difficulties, predict future problems, aid in selection of therapy programs and screen job applicants. Norms presented as T-scores for male and female college students. Examiner required. Suitable for group use.

Untimed: 30-50 minutes

Range: High school, college and adult

Scoring: Hand key; computer scoring available

Cost: Specimen set (includes manual and all forms) $3.00; 25 reusable test booklets $9.50; 50 answer sheets $5.75; 500-$45.00; 50 computer answer sheets $6.50; 500-$60.00; 50 profile sheets $4.00; 500-$37.50; handbook $7.95; manual $2.50.

Publisher: Educational and Industrial Testing Service

COPING OPERATIONS PREFERENCE ENQUIRY (COPE)
Will Schutz

adult

Purpose: Measures individual preference for certain types of coping or defense mechanisms; useful for counseling and therapy.

Description: Six item paper-pencil test measuring the characteristic use of five defense mechanisms: denial, isolation, projection, regression, and turning-against-the-self. Each item describes a person and his behavior in a particular situation. The respondent rank orders five alternative ways he might feel, which represent the inventory's five coping mechanisms. Materials include separate forms for men and women. May be self- administered but examiner recommended. Suitable for group use.

Untimed: Not available

Range: Adult

Scoring: Examiner evaluated

Cost: Specimen set $.50, 25 tests (specify male or female) $6.00.

Publisher: Consulting Psychologists Press, Inc.

CORNELL WORD FORM
Arthur Weider

adult

Purpose: Assesses an individual's adaptive mechanisms. Used in a variety of clinical and research settings.

Description: Multiple item paper-pencil test employing a modification of the word association technique. For each test item, the subject selects one word of a pair of printed responses that he associates with a given stimulus word. Analysis of the responses contributes to a descriptive sketch of the subject's adaptive mechanisms in a manner not easily apparent. Self-administered. Suitable for group use.

Untimed: 5 minutes

Range: Adult

Scoring: Examiner evaluated

Cost: Specimen set $2.00; 25 copies $7.00; 100- $25.50.

Publisher: Dr. Arthur Weider

CORRECTIONAL INSTITUTIONS ENVIRONMENT SCALE (CIES)
Rudolf H. Moos

adult

Purpose: Assesses the social environment of juvenile and adult correctional facilities.

Description: 90 item paper-pencil true-false test of nine aspects of social environment: involvement, support, expressiveness, autonomy, practical orientation, personal problem orientation, order and organization, clarity, and staff control. Materials include four forms: the Real Form (Form R), measuring perceptions of current correctional program; the 36 item Short Form (Form S); the Ideal Form (Form I), which measures con-

ceptions of an ideal program; and the Expectations Form (Form E), measuring expectations of a new program. Forms I and E are not published, but items and instructions appear in the Appendix of the CIES manual. Items and subscales are similar to those used in the Ward Atmosphere Scale. One of a series of nine Social Climate Scales. Examiner administered. Suitable for group use.

Untimed: 20-30 minutes

Range: Adult

Scoring: Hand key; examiner evaluated

Cost: Specimen set $6.00; 50 reusable tests $4.00; 50 answer sheets $3.00; 50 profiles $3.00; key $.75; manual $5.00.

Publisher: Consulting Psychologists Press, Inc.

CROWN-CRISP EXPERIMENTAL INDEX (CCEI)
Sidney Crown and A.H. Crisp

teen, adult

Purpose: Diagnoses psychoneurotic illness and personality disorder. Used for clinical screening and research, measuring change before and after defined intervention, and comparison of defined groups. Suitable for all ages from late adolescence and with a wide range of intelligence levels.

Description: 48 item paper-pencil questionnaire consists of six sub-tests designed to facilitate the rapid quantification of common symptoms and traits relevant to six conventional categories of psychoneurotic illness and personality disorder: free-floating anxiety, phobic anxiety, obsessionality, somatic anxiety, depression, and hysterical traits. The index provides a profile which can be related to the scores of defined groups. The manual includes reliability and validity data and statistics relating CCEI scores to age, sex, and social class. Restricted to senior staff members of any recognized medical or educational institution, medical doctors, and BPS and APA members. Examiner required.

BRITISH PUBLISHER

Untimed: 5-10 minutes

Range: Adolescent, adult

Scoring: Examiner evaluated

Cost: Specimen set £3.00; 20 questionnaires £1.75 plus VAT; scoring template £.85 plus VAT; manual £2.25.

Publisher: Hodder & Stoughton

CURTIS COMPLETION FORM
James W. Curtis

teen, adult

Purpose: Evaluates the emotional adjustment of older adolescents and adults. Used for employment situations to screen individuals whose emotional adjustment makes them poor employment risks. Also useful in educational and industrial counseling to identify those who would benefit from clinical treatment.

Description: Multiple item, paper-pencil, free response, sentence completion test which measures emotional adjustment. It is similar to a projective test, but is scored using relatively objective, standardized criteria. Examiner required. Suitable for group use. Available in Spanish and French.

Untimed: 30 minutes

Range: Adolescents, adults

Scoring: Examiner evaluated

Cost: Kit (25 forms and manual) $10.50.

Publisher: Western Psychological Services

DEPRESSION ADJECTIVE CHECK LIST (DACL)
Bernard Lubin

teen, adult   grades 10-UP

Purpose: Differentiates between "depressed" and "non- depressed" high school and college students and adults. Used for counseling, group screening and large-scale studies on depression.

Description: 34 item paper-pencil checklist measures transient depressive moods, feelings, or emotions. Seven parallel forms provide for repeated measurement of these factors. The checklists consist of adjectives to which the subject responds by checking those which describe how he feels at the time of testing. Forms A,B,C, and D contain 32 items each; Forms E,F, and G contain 34 items each. None of the adjectives appear on more than one of the four Check Lists A,B,C, or D, or on more than one of the three Lists E,F, or G. Norms are presented for male and female normals and for depressed patients. Self-administered; examiner scored. Suitable for group use.

Untimed: 5 minutes per form

Range: High school, college and adult

Scoring: Hand key

Cost: Specimen set (includes manual and one copy of all forms) $3.25; 25 checklists (specify form) $3.75; key $2.50; manual $2.50.

Publisher: Educational and Industrial Testing Service

DESCRIBING PERSONALITY
Refer to page 634.

DYNAMIC PERSONALITY INVENTORY (DPI) and LIKES AND INTERESTS TEST (LIT)
T.G. Grygier

teen, adult

Purpose: Assesses general personality organization. Used for individual counseling and personnel selection.

Description: 325 item paper-pencil test of personality. Items include objects, concepts, and activities associated with various personality traits and defense mechanisms. Includes measures of interpersonal relationships, aggression, creativity, drive, and ego strength. Subject indicates like or dislike for each item. Materials include separate score sheets standardized for males versus females, neurotics versus normals, college students and general population. A shorter edition of the DPI, the Likes and Interests Tests (LIT), uses a special score sheet and was constructed for personnel selection and other industrial applications. Self-administered. Suitable for group use.
BRITISH PUBLISHER

Untimed: 40 minutes

Range: Minimum age 17, minimum IQ 80

Scoring: Hand key; examiner evaluated

Cost: Specimen set £4.95; LIT specimen set £4.95 (payment in sterling for all overseas orders).

Publisher: NFER-Nelson Publishing Company

EDWARDS PERSONAL PREFERENCE SCHEDULE (EPPS)
A.L. Edwards

teen, adult

Purpose: Assesses an individual's

personality. Used for both personal counseling and personality research.

Description: Paper-pencil, forced-choice test designed to show relative importance of 15 needs and motives: achievement, deference, order, exhibition, autonomy, affiliation, intraception, succorance, dominance, abasement, nurturance, change, endurance, heterosexuality, and aggression. Social Desirability score may also be obtained. Self-administered. Suitable for group use.

Untimed: 45 minutes

Range: Ages 18-adult

Scoring: Hand key; may be machine scored; NCS scoring service available

Cost: Specimen set (includes schedule booklet, hand-scorable answer document and template; IBM 805 and NCS answer documents, manual) $3.50.

Publisher: The Psychological Corporation

EGO-IDEAL AND CONSCIENCE DEVELOPMENT TEST (EICDT)
R.N. Cassel

child, teen

Purpose: Helps evaluate an individual's ego-ideal or conscience, defined as the pattern of characteristics and emotional states held as desirable for oneself. Used as an index of parole or probation readiness for delinquents and to assess a person's knowledge of social expectations when confronted with problems.

Description: 80 item paper-pencil, multiple-choice test of the extent to which the examinee agrees with the mainstream of U.S. society regarding solutions to social problems. The test consists of eight sections of ten items each. It yields a total score reflecting general agreement with society, as well as the eight section scores representing ego-ideal and conscience development within each of the eight parts: Home and Family, Inner Development, Community Relations, Rules and Law, School and Education, Romance and Psychosexual, Economic Sufficiency, and Self-Actualization. Two parallel forms have been validated. Interpretation forms are available which describe the scale scores in detail and provide a normed profile for each examinee. The manual describes the test rationale, gives directions for administering, scoring and interpreting the test, and provides a complete description of the psychometric analyses of this instrument. Examiner/self-administered. Suitable for group use.

Untimed: 60 minutes

Range: Ages 12-18

Scoring: Hand key

Cost: 35 tests $24.00; 35 answer sheets $3.00; 35 interpretation forms $4.00; scoring stencil $2.50; manual $3.00; specimen set $6.00; specify form A or B for each item.

Publisher: Monitor

EGO STATE INVENTORY
David G. McCarley

teen, adult

Purpose: Evaluates individual personality dynamics and interpersonal relations. Used in schools, industry, correctional institutions, and hospitals to acquire information about the internal dynamics of an individual from a transactional analytic view.

Description: 52 item paper-pencil, multiple-choice test covering five ego states: Punitive Parent, Nurturing Parent, Adult, Rebellious Child, Adaptive Child. Each item consists of a cartoon drawing of two or more people in a recognizable social situation. One person in each of the cartoons is making a statement or asking a question, and the subject chooses from five possible responses the one he imagines the second person would make. The test is hand scored with five stencils corresponding to the five ego states. Examiner required. Suitable for group use.

Timed: 20-30 minutes

Range: Adolescent, adult

Scoring: Hand key; examiner evaluated

Cost: Complete kit (includes workbook containing cartoons, manual with 5 scoring stencils and 100 answer sheets) $47.50.

Publisher: Stoelting Co.

EIGHT STATE QUESTIONNAIRE: FORMS A & B (8SQ)
James P. Curran and Raymond B. Cattell

teen, adult

Purpose: Assesses the state of mind of adults and adolescents age 17 and older. Measures experimental manipulations of a person's moods as well as progress of related therapeutic intervention. Used for clinical evaluation and personal counseling.

Description: Multiple item paper-pencil questionnaire measures eight important mood states: anxiety, stress, depression, regression, fatigue, guilt, extraversion, and arousal. Available in two equivalent forms to allow for accurate retesting. Standard scores and percentiles are presented for men and women together, men alone, women alone, and male prisoners. Sixth-grade reading level required. Self-administered. Suitable for group use.

Untimed: 30 minutes

Range: Ages 17-adult

Scoring: Hand key

Cost: Specimen set $4.00; manual

$2.80; 25 reusable test booklets (for both Forms A & B) $12.50; 50 answer sheets $8.00; 50 profile sheets $5.50 and scoring key $3.50.

Publisher: Institute for Personality and Ability Testing, Inc.

THE EMPATHY TEST
Refer to page 816.

EMOTIONS PROFILE INDEX
Robert Plutchik and Henry Kellerman

teen, adult

Purpose: Measures personality traits and conflicts in adults and adolescents. Used for counseling and guidance, therapy, and diagnostic evaluations.

Description: 62 item paper-pencil test with a forced-choice format. It presents bipolar pairs of words and requires the subject to choose which of the two words best describes self. Four bipolar scales measure the following eight dimensions of emotions: Timid vs. Aggressive, Trustful vs. Distrustful, Controlled vs. Dyscontrolled, and Gregarious vs. Depressed. A unique circular profile displays percentile scores and compares the basic personality dimensions. Norms are provided on 1,000 adult men and women. Data is also given for certain special groups. Examiner required. Suitable for group use.

Untimed: 10-15 minutes

Range: Adolescent, adult

Scoring: Hand key

Cost: Complete kit (includes 25 tests and profile sheets, manual) $12.90.

Publisher: Western Psychological Services

EYSENCK PERSONALITY INVENTORY (EPI)
H.J. Eysenck and S.B.G. Eysenck

teen, adult   grades 10-UP

Purpose: Measures extraversion and neuroticism, the two dimensions of personality which account for most personality variance. Used for counseling, clinical evaluation and research.

Description: 57 item paper-pencil yes-no inventory measures two independent dimensions of personality, Extraversion-Introversion and Neuroticism- Stability. A falsification scale provides for detection of response distortion. Scores are provided for three scales: E- Extraversion, N- Neuroticism, and L-Lie. Available in equivalent Forms A and B for pre- and post-testing and Industrial Form A-I. College norms presented in percentile form for both Forms A and B separately and combined. Adult norms presented for Form A-I. Self-administered. Suitable for group use. Available in Spanish.

Untimed: 10-15 minutes

Range: High school, college and adult

Scoring: Hand key; computer scoring available

Cost: Specimen set (manual and one copy of all forms) $3.00; 25 EPI inventories $3.75; 100-$14.00 (specify Form A, B, or Industrial) keys $2.00; manual $2.00.

Publisher: Educational and Industrial Testing Service

EYSENCK PERSONALITY QUESTIONNAIRE (EPQ)
H.J. Eysenck and S.B.G. Eysenck

teen, adult

Purpose: Measures the personality dimensions of extraversion, emotionality and toughmindedness (psychoticism in extreme cases) in individuals age 7 through adult. Used for clinical diagnosis, educational guidance, occupational counseling, personnel selection and placement, and market research.

Description: 90 item paper-pencil yes-no inventory measuring three important dimensions of personality: Extraversion-Introversion (21 items), Neuroticism-Stability (23 items), and Psychoticism (25 items). 21 items provide data for the falsification scale. The questionnaire deals with normal behaviors which become pathological only in extreme cases, hence use of the term "toughmindedness" is suggested for non- pathological cases. An 81 item Junior Form is also available for testing at lower ages. Scores are provided for E-Extraversion, N-Neuroticism or emotionality, P-Psychoticism or toughmindedness, and L-Lie. College norms presented in percentile form for both Form A and B separately and combined. Adult norms provided for an industrially employed sample. Self-administered. Suitable for group use.

Untimed: 10-15 minutes

Range: Ages 7-adult

Scoring: Hand key

Cost: Specimen set (includes manual and one copy of each form) $3.25; 25 forms $4.50; 100-$16.00; (specify both forms and keys), keys $2.75; manual $2.00.

Publisher: Educational and Industrial Testing Service

FEAR SURVEY SCHEDULE (FSS)
Joseph Wolpe and Peter J. Lang

adult

Purpose: Evaluates the manner in which an individual deals with fear-related situations. Particularly useful in the practice of behavior therapy.

Description: Multiple item paper-pencil survey of a patient's reactions to a variety of possible sources of maladaptive emotional reactions. The reactions tapped by the survey are nearly always fearful, fear-tinged, or fear-related--and always unpleasant. Since it is necessary in the application of behavior therapy to obtain a coherent picture of the stimulus antecedents of neurotic reactions, the Schedule frequently saves a great deal of effort in revealing reactions to many stimulus classes in a short time. Examiner required. Suitable for group use.

Untimed: Not available

Range: Adult

Scoring: Examiner evaluated

Cost: 25 response forms and manual $5.00; 100- $14.50.

Publisher: Educational and Industrial Testing Service

THE FORTY-EIGHT ITEM COUNSELING EVALUATION TEST: REVISED
Frank B. McMahon, Jr.

teen, adult

Purpose: Assesses the personal and emotional problems of adolescents and adults. Used by high school and college counselors.

Description: 48 item paper-pencil true-false personality questionnaire. The test employs a "double- question" technique in which each item actually consists of two questions: (1) an introductory question probing a specific aspect of behavior or personality, and (2) a contingency question which qualifies and amplifies the introductory question. Responses are evaluated in six problem areas: anxiety, compulsion, depression, socialization, goals, and inadequacy. Total Score indicates severity of maladjustment and Subscores provide insights into each of the six problem areas. Examiner required. Suitable for group use.

Untimed: 10-20 minutes

Range: Adolescent, adult

Scoring: Hand key

Cost: Complete kit (includes 25 tests and manual) $10.40.

Publisher: Western Psychological Services

FUNDAMENTAL INTERPERSONAL RELATIONS ORIENTATION-FEELINGS (FIRO-F)
Will Schutz

adult

Purpose: Evaluates an individual's characteristic feelings toward others; used to assess both individual and interactional traits as an aid to counseling and therapy.

Description: 54 item paper-pencil test measuring six dimensions of feelings toward others: expressed significance, expressed competence, expressed loveability, wanted significance, wanted competence, and wanted loveability. Dimensions parallel the three dimensions of the FIRO-B. May be self-administered, although an examiner is recommended to assist in the assessment/interpretation process. Suitable for group use.

Untimed: 15-20 minutes

Range: Adult

Scoring: Hand key

Cost: Sample set (includes tests and key) $4.00; 25 tests $3.25.

Publisher: Consulting Psychologists Press, Inc.

GENERAL HEALTH QUESTIONNAIRE (GHQ)
D. Goldberg

teen, adult

Purpose: Screens for psychiatric disorders among respondents in community settings, such as primary care or among general medical outpatients.

Description: Multiple item self-report, paper-pencil measure of psychiatric problems. Test requires a minimum of subjective responses by the examinee. Items aimed at detecting disorders which may be relevant to subject's presence in a medical clinic. Three forms are available: GHQ-60, GHQ- 30, a short form, and GHQ-28, for research studies requiring more than one severity score. Available to psychiatrists, qualified medical doctors, and clinically experienced psychologists. Self- administered. Suitable for group use.
BRITISH PUBLISHER

Untimed: Not available

Range: Adolescent, adult

Scoring: Examiner evaluated

Cost: Specimen set £3.75; 25 GHQ-28 £1.95; 25 GHQ-30 £1.95; 25 GHQ-60 £3.25 (payment in sterling for all overseas orders).

Publisher: NFER-Nelson Publishing Company

GORDON PERSONAL PROFILE AND INVENTORY (GPP- I)
Leonard V. Gordon

teen, adult

Purpose: Assesses an individual's personality. Used for individual counseling.

Description: Paper-pencil measure of eight aspects of personality. Personal Profile measures ascendancy, responsibility, emotional stability, and sociability. Four traits combine to yield Self-Esteem score. Personal Inventory measures cautiousness, original thinking, personal relations, and vigor. Respondents mark one item in each group of three as being most like them and one as being least like them. Self-administered. Suitable for group use.

Untimed: 15 minutes for each instrument

Range: Adolescent, adult

Scoring: Hand key; may be machine scored

Cost: Specimen set (includes booklet, key, manual for both profile and inventory) $13.75.

Publisher: The Psychological Corporation

GROUP ENVIRONMENT SCALE (GES)
Rudolf H. Moos

teen, adult

Purpose: Assesses social climate of therapeutic, social, or task-oriented groups.

Description: 90 item paper-pencil true-false test of ten aspects of group social environments: cohesion, leader support, expressiveness, independence, task orientation, self-discovery, anger and aggression, order and organization, leader con-

trol, and innovation. These scales are grouped into three dimensions: Relationship, Personal Growth, and System Maintenance and System Change. Materials include the Real Form (Form R), measuring perceptions of a current group; the Ideal Form (Form I), which measures conceptions of an ideal group; and the Expectations Form (Form E), measuring expectations of a new group. Forms I and E are not published, but items and instructions may be requested from the publisher. One of a series of nine Social Climate Scales. Examiner administered. Suitable for group use.

Untimed: 20-30 minutes

Range: Adult

Scoring: Examiner evaluated; hand key

Cost: Specimen set $6.00; manual $5.00; key $.75; 25 reusable tests $4.00; 40 answer sheets $3.00; 50 profiles $3.00.

Publisher: Consulting Psychologists Press, Inc.

GROUP PSYCHOTHERAPY EVALUATION SCALE
Clifton E. Kew

adult

Purpose: Evaluates behavior and ego strength as a measure of a person's suitability for group therapy techniques. Discriminates between patients who can function in a group setting and those who would be overwhelmed with anxiety in the group experience.

Description: Paper-pencil inventory measuring cognitive, emotional, and behavioral aspects of a patient in terms of his group functioning ability. The therapist rates the patient from 0-4 in four areas: amount of communication and relatedness, and capacity for change and involvement. The therapist then rates himself on amount of verbal activity and direction of therapist verbal activity. Suggested cutoff scores provided for patients most and least suited for group therapy. Administered by therapist. Not for group use.

Untimed: 5 minutes

Range: Adult

Scoring: Examiner evaluated

Cost: Free (distributed by Educational Testing Service).

Publisher: Clifton E. Kew

GROUP SHORR IMAGERY TEST (GSIT)
Joseph E. Shorr

adult

Purpose: Evaluates a person's use of imagery and assesses self-image, areas of conflict, and strategies for coping with the world. Used for in-depth personality analysis.

Description: 15 item paper-pencil projective personality test. Subjects (listening to a tape cassette) are asked to imagine a particular situation and then to expand (in writing) in a directed way upon the image evoked. These imaginary situations are used to reveal a wide range of personality variables including: the individual's personal world, relationships between self and others, self-image, sexual attitudes, and internal and external forces acting upon the individual. Responses are quantitatively scored according to degree of conflict within the subject's personality. Not limited by intelligence; minimally culture bound. The manual includes: instructions for scoring, a sample of the theoretical basis for in-depth personality analysis and normative data. Examiner required. Suitable for group use.

Untimed: One hour

Range: Adult

Scoring: Examiner evaluated

Cost: Complete set $44.50.

Publisher: Institute for Psycho-Imagination Therapy

GROWTH PROCESS INVENTORY (GPI)
Everett L. Shostrom

adult

Purpose: Measures self-actualization. Used for research in the area of humanistic psychology.

Description: Multiple item paper-pencil test measures healthy actualizing dimensions as well as character disorders. Measurement is related to the DSM III and provides for the diagnosis of character types. Examiner required. Suitable for group use in research applications.

Untimed: Not available

Range: Adult

Scoring: Hand key; computer scoring available

Cost: 25 test booklets $9.50; 50 answer sheets $5.50; 50 profile sheets $4.00; manual $2.75.

Publisher: Educational and Industrial Testing Service

GUILFORD-ZIMMERMAN TEMPERAMENT SURVEY (GZTS)
J.P. Guilford and Wayne S. Zimmerman

teen, adult   grades 10-UP

Purpose: Measures personality traits. Used for personnel selection, vocational guidance and clinical practice.

Description: 300 item paper-pencil measure of ten factor- analytically derived traits that have proved to be most uniquely measurable. They are: general activity, restraint, ascendance, sociability, emotional stability, objectivity, friendliness, thoughtfulness, personal relations, and masculinity/femininity. C-scale, centile, and T- scale norms provided for high school and college students and adults. Restricted to A.P.A. members. Examiner required. Suitable for group use.

Untimed: 45 minutes

Range: Grades 10-adult

Scoring: Hand key; may be computer scored

Cost: 25 tests $14.00; 25 answer sheets $4.50; 25 profile charts $3.50; manual $4.00; scoring set $5.00.

Publisher: Sheridan Psychological Services, Inc.

HARROWER PSYCHODIAGNOSTIC INKBLOT TEST
Molly Harrower

teen, adult

Purpose: Measures an individual's perceptual-cognitive abilities related to aspects of personality. With a standard inkblot test in a form that can be group, individually and self-administered. Used as an alternative to the Rorschach test, with significantly related results.

Description: Ten item paper-pencil test consisting of a set of ten inkblot cards (8" x 10") printed in color on forms on which the subject marks responses. These forms can be kept as part of the subject's permanent record. The protocol booklet provides for recording data, responses, scoring, profiles, interpretations, and includes all ten inkblots in miniature and in color as a location form. The manual includes many colored plates, case studies, frequency counts of responses, and extensive research data. Examiner required. Suitable for group use. May be self-administered.

Untimed: 20 minutes

Range: Ages 16-adult

Scoring: Examiner evaluated

Cost: Kit (1 set test cards, manual, 5 protocol booklets, 5 expendable inkblots) $43.00.

Publisher: Western Psychological Services

HIGH SCHOOL PERSONALITY QUESTIONNAIRE (HSPQ)
Raymond B. Cattell and Mary D. Cattell

teen

Purpose: Identifies adolescents (ages 12-18 years) with high potentials for dropping out of school, drug abuse, and low achievement. Used in correctional situations to facilitate parent-teacher, parent- officer and parent-clinic cooperation.

Description: 142 item paper-pencil questionnaire measures 14 primary personality dimensions such as stability, tension, warmth, and enthusiasm. Scores for anxiety, extraversion, creativity, leadership, and other broad trait patterns are also obtained. The test is available in four equivalent forms: A,B,C, and D. Percentiles and standard scores are provided for boys, girls, and combined. Sixth-grade reading level required. Examiner required. Suitable for group use. Available in Spanish.

Untimed: 45-60 minutes per form

Range: Ages 12-18

Scoring: Hand key; scoring and interpretation services available

Cost: HSPQ Professional examination kit $16.35; specimen set $3.20; handbook $5.75; manual $2.25; 25 reusable test booklets $9.00; 50 machine- scorable answer sheets $6.00; 50 handscoring answer sheets $5.50; 50 handscoring answer-profile sheets $6.50; and 2 scoring keys $3.80.

Publisher: Insititute for Personality and Ability Testing, Inc.

HOFFER-OSMOND DIAGNOSTIC TEST (HOD)
Abram Hoffer, Humphrey Osmond, and Harold Kelm

teen, adult

Purpose: Diagnoses the degree and nature of psychiatric illness. Monitors treatment and establishes prognosis. Used by mental health practitioners to screen for mental illness.

Description: 145 item true-false test measuring the amount of paranoia, depression, and perceptual distortion in patients age 13 and older. Each test item consists of a statement printed on a card. The subject reads each card and either answers on a separate answer sheet or places the card in a true or false box. If the patient is illiterate, the items may be read aloud. Helps determine when a patient requires hospitalization or is ready to be discharged from the hospital. Materials include: 145 test cards, manual, score sheet and test booklet. Self-administered under clinical supervision. Suitable for group use.

Untimed: 30 minutes

Range: Ages 13-adult

Scoring: Hand key

Cost: Complete test $36.50; HOD text $22.50.

Publisher: Behavior Science Press

HOW WELL DO YOU KNOW YOURSELF
Thomas N. Jenkins

teen, adult   grades 10-UP

Purpose: Assesses normal personality. Used for educational guidance.

Description: Multiple item paper-pencil test of 17 personality traits: Irritability, Practicality, Punctuality, Novelty-loving, Vocational Assurance, Cooperativeness, Ambitiousness, Hypercriticalness, Dejection, General Morale, Persistence, Nervousness, Seriousness, Submissiveness, Impulsiveness, Dynamism, and Emotional Control. Two additional measures of response style are included, Consistency and Test Objectivity. Examiner required. Suitable for group use.

Untimed: 20 minutes

Range: High school, college, adults

Scoring: Hand key

Cost: Complete kit (includes 3 test booklets of each edition and manual) $8.25; 25 tests (specify Secondary, College or Personnel) $16.50; 100-$65.00; keys $5.50; manual $5.50.

Publisher: Psychologists and Educators, Inc.

HUMAN RELATIONS INVENTORY
Raymond S. Bernberg

teen, adult   grades 10-UP

Purpose: Measures a person's tendency toward social (or lawful) conformity. Differentiates between conformist and non-conformist individuals.

Description: Multiple-item paper-pencil test measuring an individual's sense of social conformity. Social conformity is defined and tested in terms of moral values, positive goals, reality testing, ability to give affection, tension level and impulsivity. The test is constructed using the "direction of perception" technique and the purpose of the test is effectively disguised from subjects to insure more valid results. Discriminates between samples of law violators and ordinary conformists. Norms provided for senior high school boys, college students, regular church-goers, Los Angeles Police officers, male inmates of a California youth prison, adult male inmates of the Los Angeles County Jail and adult female inmates of the Los Angeles County Jail. Examiner required. Suitable for group use.

Untimed: Not available

Range: Senior high school-adult

Scoring: Examiner evaluated

Cost: Specimen set $2.00; 25 inventories $2.75; 100-$10.00.

Publisher: Psychometric Affiliates

INCOMPLETE SENTENCES TASK
Barbara Lanyon and Richard Lanyon

teen, adult   grades 7-UP

Purpose: Identifies potential emotional problems in students from junior high school through college so that intervention can begin before problems become too severe.

Description: 39 item paper-pencil test consisting of incomplete sentence stems which the subject completes in his own words. The test is both projective and psychometric and measures the following factors: hostility, anxiety, and dependency. Scoring is based on examples for each item found in the manual. Two forms are available: a School Form, for grades 7-12, and a College Form for college-age adolescents. Norms are provided for three groups: School Form (Grades 7-9), School Form (Grades 10-12), and College Form. Self-administered. Suitable for group use.

Untimed: 15-20 minutes

Range: Grades 7-12, college

Scoring: Examiner evaluated

Cost: Complete kit (includes 30 test

forms and manual; specify school or college form) $16.00.

Publisher: Stoelting Co.

INTERPERSONAL CHECK LIST (ICL)
R. LaForge and R. Suczek

adult

Purpose: Describes individual perception of another personality. Useful for clinical and social research.

Description: 134 item paper-pencil checklist for describing self or another person. Each item belongs to one of 16 inter-personal categories and one of four intensity levels. Summary variables: Dominance, Love, Number of Items Endorsed, and Average Intensity of Endorsed Items. The subject is required to describe one or more persons, possibly self or a hypothetical person, by checking items. Materials include one-page test and manual. Examiner required. Suitable for group use.

Untimed: 15 minutes

Range: Adult

Scoring: Computer scored

Cost: Tests free and may be duplicated; technical report, Using The ICL, $12.00.

Publisher: Rolfe LaForge

INTERPERSONAL RELATIONS QUESTIONNAIRE (IRQ)- 1981

teen

Purpose: Assesses personal adjustment in adolescence. Used for counseling and guidance.

Description: 260 or 100 item paper-pencil test of 12 components of adjustment: self-confidence, self-esteem, self-control, nervousness, health, family influences, personal freedom, general sociability,

sociability with the opposite sex, sociability with the same sex, moral sense and formal relations. Items are answered on a four point scale. 100 item abridged questionnaire provides more general indication of adjustment involving five commponents. Examiner required. Suitable for group use. Publisher notes that this test is "normed on Whites and Indians only."
SOUTH AFRICAN PUBLISHER

Untimed: 2 hours; abridged questionnaire, 1 hour

Range: Ages 12-15

Scoring: Hand key; examiner evaluated

Cost: (In Rands) Questionnaire 0,90; 10 answer sheets 0,80; scoring stencil (positive items) 4,20; scoring stencil (negative items) 4,30; Test Profiles 2,20; manual 7,70 (orders from outside of the RSA will be dealt with on merit).

Publisher: Human Sciences Research Council

INTRA AND INTERPERSONAL RELATIONS

child, teen

Purpose: Measures the relationship with self and parental figures. Used for counseling and assessment.

Description: Paper-pencil test of relationships with self and others. Scale also measures relationship between the real and ideal selves. Indicates self-acceptance. Examiner required. Suitable for group use. Publisher notes that this test is "normed on Blacks only."
SOUTH AFRICAN PUBLISHER

Untimed: 30 minutes

Range: Grades Standards 9 and 10

Scoring: Hand key; examiner evaluated

Cost: (In Rands) Test booklet 2,20; manual 7,80; 10 answer sheets 0,30; scoring stencil 1,30 (orders from outside The RSA will be dealt with on merit).

Publisher: Human Sciences Research Council

INVENTORY OF ANGER COMMUNICATION (IAC)
Millard Bienvenu

teen, adult

Purpose: Helps individuals learn about their style of handling anger. Used in counseling and as a teaching tool.

Description: 30 item paper-pencil, multiple choice questionnaire. Covers areas such as: handling anger, confrontation, expression of feelings, and measurement of anger. Materials include: questionnaire, manual, scoring key. Examiner preferred but may be self-administered. Suitable for group use.

Untimed: 15 minutes

Range: Ages 15 and older

Scoring: Hand key; examiner evaluated

Cost: IAC $.35; guide $1.50.

Publisher: Counseling and Self-Improvement Programs/ Millard Bienvenu, Ph.D.

INVENTORY OF INDIVIDUALLY PERCEIVED GROUP COHESIVENESS
Refer to page 817.

IPAT ANXIETY SCALE (or SELF-ANALYSIS FORM)
Raymond B. Cattell, Ivan H. Scheier, and IPAT Staff

teen, adult   grades 10-UP

Purpose: Measures anxiety in senior high school students and adults of most educational levels. Used for both clinical diagnosis and psychological research on anxiety.

Description: 40 item paper-pencil questionnaire measures the five principal 16 PF factors of anxiety, which are: emotional instability (C-), suspiciousness (L+), guilt-proneness (O+), low integration (Q3-), and tension (Q4+). Norms provided for adult, college, and high school populations, with both separate and combined sex tables. Sixth-grade reading level required. Examiner required. Suitable for group use. Available in Spanish.

Untimed: 10 minutes

Range: Senior high school-adult

Scoring: Hand key

Cost: Anxiety Scale testing kit (includes handbook, test booklet (not reusable), scoring key) $6.65; Anxiety Scale Handbook $5.75; scoring key $.70; 25 test booklets (not reusable) $3.60.

Publisher: Institute for Personality and Ability Testing, Inc.

IPAT DEPRESSION SCALE
Samuel E. Krug and James E. Laughlin

adult

Purpose: Diagnoses depression in adults of most educational levels. Used for both clinical diagnosis and psychological research on depression.

Description: 40 item paper-pencil questionnaire diagnoses and measures depression in adults. Test validation blended two distinct strategies-- factor analysis and contrasted-groups--to insure both construct and empirical validity. Norms provided for adult, college, prison, and certain clinical populations. Fifth-grade reading level required. Self-administered. Available in Spanish.

Untimed: 10 minutes

Range: Adult

Scoring: Hand key

Cost: Complete kit $5.00; manual $4.20; 25 not reusable test booklets $3.75; scoring key $.70.

Publisher: Institute for Personality and Ability Testing, Inc.

JACKSON PERSONALITY INVENTORY (JPI)
Douglas N. Jackson

teen, adult

Purpose: Assesses personality characteristics of normal people who have average and above-average intelligence. Used to evaluate behavior in a wide range of settings including those involving work, education, organizations, interpersonal, and high- level performance.

Description: 320 item paper-pencil, true-false test covering 15 substantive scales and one validity scale. The scales are: Anxiety, Breadth of Interest, Complexity, Conformity, Energy Level, Innovation, Interpersonal Affect, Organization, Responsibility, Risk Taking, Self Esteem, Social Adroitness, Social Participation, Tolerance, Value Orthodoxy, and Infrequency. Materials include a manual, reusable test booklets, answer sheet, and template and profiles. Norms are based on random college sampling. This test differs from the Personality Research Form in terms of the nature of the variables measured and is a further refinement of substantive psychometric and computer-based strategies for scale development. Suitable for group use.

Untimed: 1 hour

Range: Adolescent, adult

Scoring: Hand key

Cost: Complete set $25.00.

Publisher: Research Psychologists Press, Inc.

JESNESS BEHAVIOR CHECKLIST
Carl F. Jesness

teen

Purpose: Assesses the social behavior of adolescents. Used to evaluate behavioral change in school or institutional settings.

Description: 80 item paper-pencil rating scale measuring 14 bi-polar behavioral tendencies: unobtrusiveness vs. obtrusiveness, friendliness vs. hostility, responsibility vs. irresponsibility, considerateness vs. inconsiderateness, independence vs. dependence, rapport vs. alienation, enthusiasm vs. depression, sociability vs. poor peer relations, conformity vs. non-conformity, calmness vs. anxiousness, effective communication vs. inarticulateness, insight vs. unawareness and indecisiveness, social control vs. attention-seeking, and anger control vs. hypersensitivity. Materials include an Observer Form for ratings by teachers and therapists and a Self-Appraisal Form for self-evaluation. Self-administered. Suitable for group use.

Untimed: 10-20 minutes

Range: Adolescents

Scoring: Hand key; scoring service available

Cost: Specimen set (no key) $2.75; manual $2.50; key $10.00.

Publisher: Consulting Psychologists Press, Inc.

JUNG PERSONALITY QUESTIONNAIRE (JPQ)-1982

all ages

Purpose: Assesses personality. The aim of the questionnaire is to assist vocational guidance in particular.

Description: Multiple item, paper-pencil test of personality based on the theory of Carl Gustav Jung. Personality factors measured are extraversion, introversion, thought, feeling, sensation, intuition, judgement, and perception. Examiner required. Suitable for group use. SOUTH AFRICAN PUBLISHER

Untimed: Not available

Range: Grades Standard 7-Standard 10, and post school level

Scoring: Hand key; examiner evaluated; machine scoring available

Cost: (In Rands) Test booklet 1,00; 10 answer sheets (machine-3881) 0,90; scoring stencil 4,10 (orders from outside The RSA will be dealt with on merit).

Publisher: Human Sciences Research Council

KATZ ADJUSTMENT SCALES (KAS)
Martin M. Katz

adult

Purpose: Describes and measures an individual's social behavior, symptoms, and performance. Evaluates personal and social adjustment. Used for both normal and mentally disordered persons.

Description: 225 item paper-pencil test consisting of five scales, plus a self-report form. Measures 12 factors: emotional stability, general psychopathology, belligerance, expansiveness, negativism, anxiety, helplessness, suspiciousness, with drawal and retardation, nervousness, confusion hyperactivity bizarreness, level of performance and satisfaction with level of socially-expected activities. Test is administered to a relative or "significant other" in a position to observe subject for at least seven weeks. Useful as an experimental study of various mental disorders as perceived by the United States and other cultures and the evaluation of treatments. May be administered by interview if observer is illiterate. Available in 12 European and Asian languages. Materials include scale, list of references and brief manual. Self-administered. Not for group use.

Untimed: 20-30 minutes

Range: Adults

Scoring: Hand key; computer scoring available

Cost: Complete kit (includes scale, references list, manual) $15.00.

Publisher: Martin M. Katz, Ph. D.

KUNDU INTROVERSION-EXTRAVERSION INVENTORY (K.I.E.I.)
Ramanath Kundu

teen, adult

Purpose: Assesses the introversion-extroversion dimension of adolescent and adult personalities. Used for clinical diagnosis, research, guidance and placement.

Description: Multiple-item, paper-pencil test measuring introversion and extroversion. Minimum English reading level is required. Self-administered. Suitable for group use.
PUBLISHED IN INDIA

Untimed: 15 minutes

Range: Adolescent, adult

Scoring: Hand key

Cost: (In Rupees) Specimen set 50-00Rs.; 25 reusable booklets 160-00Rs.; 10 manuals with scoring 100-

00Rs.; 100 answer sheets 180-00Rs.

Publisher: Ramanath Kundu

KUNDU'S NEUROTIC PERSONALITY INVENTORY (K.N.P.I.)
Ramanath Kundu

teen, adult

Purpose: Assesses degrees of neeuroticism. Used for clinical diagnosis, research guidance, and employee selection.

Description: 66 item paper-pencil test measuring neuroticism. Minimum English reading level required. Self-administered. Suitable for group use.
PUBLISHED IN INDIA

Untimed: 15 minutes

Range: Adolescent, adult

Scoring: Hand key

Cost: (In Rupees) Specimen set 50-00Rs.; 25 reusable booklets 160-00Rs.; 10 manuals with scoring 75-00Rs.; 100 answer sheets 180-00Rs.

Publisher: Ramanath Kundu

LEWIS COUNSELING INVENTORY
D.G. Lewis and P.D. Pumfrey

teen

Purpose: Measures self-perceived problems of adolescents. Used for individual counseling and screening for pupils most in need of guidance.

Description: 46 item paper-pencil test measuring need for professional help. Items include six Lie scale items, and a series of direct statements scored in six areas: relationship with teeachers, relationship with family, irritability, social confidence, relationship with peers, and health. Pupil indicates agree or disagree for all items. Inventory may

be followed by Part 2, a short questionnaire allowing the pupil to expand on specifics about his or her perceived problems. Response patterns may indicate type of help needed. Examiner required. Suitable for group use.
BRITISH PUBLISHER

Untimed: Part I, 10-15 minutes and Part II, 15 minutes

Range: Adolescents

Scoring: Hand key

Cost: Specimen set £3.90; 25 Part I £2.65; 25 Supplementary Questionnaires £0.90; 6 keys £5.60; manual £3.70 (Payment in sterling for all overseas orders).

Publisher: NFER-Nelson Publishing Company

LIFE EVENT SCALE-ADOLESCENTS
R. Dean Coddington

teen

Purpose: Assesses significant events occurring in an adolescent's life. Used for clinical evaluation and counseling of adolescents.

Description: 50 item paper-pencil questionnaire measuring the frequency of selected important events in an adolescent's family and social life. Scores are provided for three areas: family events over which the adolescent had no control (17 items), desirable extrafamilial events (18 items), and undesirable extrafamilial events (15 items). Total extrafamilial event scores and total scores are easily computed. Items are weighted for scoring purposes according to criteria provided by pediatricians, teachers and mental health workers dealing with children and adolescents. Materials include the one-page test form and instruction manual. Examiner required. Suitable for group use.

Untimed: 5 minutes

Range: Adolescents

Scoring: Examiner evaluated

Cost: Contact publisher.

Publisher: Psychological Assessment Resources, Inc.

THE LEEDS SCALES FOR THE SELF-ASSESSMENT OF ANXIETY AND DEPRESSION
R.P. Snaith, C.W.K. Bridge and Max Hamilton

adult

Purpose: Measures severity of depression and anxiety. Used for individual counseling and therapy.

Description: 15 item paper-pencil test of patient's self-report of depression and anxiety. Four scale scores are obtained: Depression Specific Scale, Anxiety Specific Scale, Depression General Scale, and Anxiety General Scale. Specific scales provide a measure of the severity of diagnosed affective illness. Self-administered. Suitable for group use.
BRITISH PUBLISHER

Untimed: Not available

Range: Adult

Scoring: Hand key

Cost: Specimen set (includes answer sheet, specific and general scale stencils manual) $8.80; keys $4.40; 50 answer sheets $8.40; manual $2.80.

Publisher: Psychological Test Publications--available from The Test Agency

LIFE POSITION IN TRANSACTIONAL ANALYSIS
Hunter H. Wood

adult

Purpose: Measures a person's Life Position in the theoretical framework of Transactional Analysis. Used in situations where personality characteristics and predictions are relevant.

Description: 32 item paper-pencil, true-false test consisting of a series of attitudinal statements with which the subject must either agree or disagree. Responses are evaluated to measure a person's life position on four scales: I'm OK, You're OK; I'm not OK, You're OK; I'm OK, You're not OK; and I'm not OK, You're not OK. Examiner required. Suitable for group use.

Untimed: 15-20 minutes

Range: Adult

Scoring: Examiner evaluated

Cost: 30 forms, $7.00.

Publisher: Stoelting Co.

THE MACC BEHAVIORAL ADJUSTMENT SCALE: REVISED 1971
Robert B. Ellsworth

adult

Purpose: Measures adjustment to hospital and community of psychiatric patients independent of their pathology. Used to measure treatment progress, to evaluate patients for release and to determine their adjustment after release.

Description: 16 item paper-pencil inventory of objective questions which can be answered quickly by anyone familiar with the patient. The test provides scores for Mood, Cooperation, Communication, and Social Contact, as well as a Total Adjustment Score. Standardized on over 1,400 patients. Self-administered by the evaluator. Suitable for group use.

Untimed: 10 minutes

Range: Adult psychiatric patients

Scoring: Hand key

Cost: Complete kit (includes 25 scales and manual) $5.80.

Publisher: Western Psychological Services.

MANSON EVALUATION
Refer to page 820.

MARTIN S-D INVENTORY
William T. Martin

teen, adult

Purpose: Identifies persons with depressive and suicidal tendencies. Serves as a screening instrument for suicide prevention centers and mental health facilities. Also used for research on suicide and depression.

Description: 50 item paper-pencil inventory measuring behavioral and cognitive aspects related to depression and suicide. Subjects rate statements (both negative and positive) on a scale from 1 to 4 as they apply to their own beliefs and behavior. A total Adjusted Score is derived, with norms provided for normals, depressed persons, and psychiatric patients. Suggested cutoff scores are provided for persons considered "depressed," moderately depressed," and "significantly depressed." May be used in conjunction with the S-D Proneness Checklist. 12 page pamphlet on suicide/depression also available. Administered by examiner. Suitable for group use.

Untimed: 15 minutes

Range: Adolescent, adult

Scoring: Hand key; examiner evaluated

Cost: Specimen set $7.25; 25 tests $6.75; 100- $26.00; scoring templates $2.25; manual $5.50.

Publisher: Psychologists and Educators, Inc.

MATHEMATICS ANXIETY RATING SCALE
Richard M. Suinn

teen, adult   grades COLLEGE-UP

Purpose: Measures college students' anxieties regarding situations involving the use of mathematics. Used for screening and diagnostic purposes, research on mathematics anxiety, and as a means for developing anxiety hierarchies for desensitization therapy.

Description: 98 item paper-pencil test assessing the level of a student's mathematics anxiety. Test items refer to situations involving the use of mathematics. The student is asked to rate how anxious he is made by each situation on a five- point scale from "Not at all" to "Very much." Norms available for college students. Use restricted to APA membership guidelines. Self- administered. Suitable for group use.

Untimed: 45 minutes

Range: College-adult

Scoring: Hand key

Cost: 100 scales $50.00.

Publisher: Rocky Mountain Behavioral Science Institute, Inc.

MATHEMATICS ANXIETY RATING SCALE-A (MARS-A)
Richard M. Suinn

child, teen   grades 7-12

Purpose: Measures students' anxieties regarding situations involving the use of mathematics. Used for screening and diagnostic purposes, research on mathematics anxiety, and as a means for developing anxiety hierarchies for desensitization therapy.

Description: 98 item paper-pencil test assessing the level of a student's mathematics anxiety. Test items refer to situations involving the use of mathematics. The student is asked to rate how anxious he is made by each situation on a five- point scale from "Not at all" to "Very much." Norms available for junior and senior high school students by grade and by sex. Use restricted to APA membership guidelines. Self-administered. Suitable for group use.

Untimed: 20-30 minutes

Range: Junior high-high school

Scoring: Hand key

Cost: 100 scales $50.00.

Publisher: Rocky Mountain Behavioral Science Institute, Inc.

MAUDSLEY PERSONALITY INVENTORY (MPI)
H. J. Eysenck

teen, adult   grades 10-UP

Purpose: Measures the personality dimensions of Extraversion-Introversion and Neuroticism- Stability in high school and college students and adults. Used for industrial and educational prediction and screening, clinical evaluation, and research.

Description: 48 item paper-pencil checklist measuring two pervasive and independent dimensions of personality: Extraversion-Introversion (24 items) and Neuroticism-Stability (24 items). Test items are selected on the basis of item and factor analyses. Scores provided for E-Extraversion and N-Neuroticism. College norms presented in percentile and stanines, with other norms for many clinical and occupational subgroups. Examiner required. Suitable for group use.

Untimed: 10-15 minutes

Range: High school, college and adults

Scoring: Hand key

Cost: Specimen set (manual and one

copy of all forms) $3.00; 25 inventories $3.75; 100-$14.00; keys $2.00; manual $2.00.

Publisher: Educational and Industrial Testing Service

MILLON ADOLESCENT PERSONALITY INVENTORY (MAPI)
Theodore Millon, Catherine J. Green and Robert B. Meagher, Jr.

---

teen

Purpose: Evaluates adolescent personality as an aid to clinical assessment, academic and vocational guidance; identifies student behavioral and emotional problems.

Description: 150 item paper-pencil, true-false test covering eight personality style scales, eight expressed concern scales (such as peer security), and four behavioral correlates scales (such as impulse control). Clinical version available to those with experience in the use of self-administered clinical tests. Suitable for group use.

Untimed: 20-30 minutes

Range: Ages 13-19

Scoring: Computer scored

Cost: Clinical version from $7.50; Guidance version from $3.70; each includes profile and interpretation.

Publisher: NCS Interpretive Scoring Systems

MILLON BEHAVIORAL HEALTH INVENTORY (MBHI)
Theodore Millon, Catherine Green and Robert B. Meagher, Jr.

---

teen, adult

Purpose: Assesses attitudes of physically ill adults toward daily stress factors and health care personnel. Used for clinical evaluation of possible psychosomatic complications.

Description: 150 item paper-pencil, true-false inventory. The scales cover: eight basic coping styles (e.g. cooperation), six psychogenic attitudes (e.g. chronic tension), three psychosomatic correlatives (e.g. allergic inclinations), and three prognostic indexes (e.g. pain treatment responsivity). The test is designed for use with medical patients by examiners experienced in the use of clinical instruments. Self-administered. Suitable for group use.

Untimed: 20 minutes

Range: Ages 18 and older

Scoring: Computer scoring by NCS

Cost: Profile and interpretation from $7.50; Arion II teleprocessing from $20.00.

Publisher: NCS Interpretive Scoring Systems

MILLON CLINICAL MULTIAXIAL INVENTORY (MCMI)
Theodore Millon

---

teen, adult

Purpose: Diagnoses emotionally disturbed adults. Used to screen individuals who may require more intensive clinical evaluation and treatment.

Description: 175 item paper-pencil, true-false test evaluating adults who have psychological or psychiatric difficulties. The test covers three categories which include: eight basic personality patterns (DSM-III,Axis II) reflecting a patient's lifelong traits existing prior to the behavioral dysfunctions; three pathological personality disorders (DSM-III,Axis II) reflecting chronic or severe abnormalities, and nine clinical symptom syndromes (DSM-III,Axis I) describing episodes or states in which active pathological processes are clearly evidenced. This instrument is intended for use only with psychiatric-emotionally disturbed populations. The examiner must be experienced in the use of clinical tests. Interpretation is available exclusively from NCS, and test results are available immediately via Arion II teleprocessing. Self-administered. Suitable for group use.

Untimed: 25 minutes

Range: Ages 18 and older

Scoring: Computer scored

Cost: Profile and interpretation from $7.50; Arion II teleprocessing from $20.00.

Publisher: NCS Interpretive Scoring Systems

THE MINNESOTA MULTIPHASIC PERSONALITY INVENTORY: NEW GROUP FORM (FORM R)
Strake R. Hathaway and Charnley McKinley

teen, adult

Purpose: Assesses individual personality. Used for clinical diagnosis and research on psychopathology.

Description: 566 item true-false test of ten clinical variables or factors of personality: hypochondriasis, depression, hysteria, psychopathic-deviate, masculinity-femininity, paranoia, psychasthenia, schizophrenia, hypomania and social introversion. Scores are also obtained on four validity scales: Question, Lie (L), Validity (F), and Defensiveness (K). Items required for these fourteen basic scores are grouped as items 1-399. Items used only in research are presented as items 400-566. Materials include hardcover question booklet with step-down pages. Individual and Old Group Forms are also available. Personality scores are plotted on profile sheet reflecting standard deviations from the Mean. Self-administered. Suitable for group and individual use. Available in 45 languages.

Untimed: 45-90 minutes

Range: Ages 16 and older

Scoring: Hand key; examiner evaluated; computer scoring available

Cost: Test booklet $7.75; 25 answer sheets $5.00; answer keys (includes manual) $12.50.

Publisher: University of Minnesota Press--distributed exclusively by: NCS Interpretive Scoring Systems

THE MINNESOTA MULTIPHASIC PERSONALITY INVENTORY: THE INDIVIDUAL FORM (MMPI)
Strake R. Hathaway and Charnley McKinley

teen, adult

Purpose: Assesses individual personality. Used for clinical diagnosis and research on psychopathology.

Description: 550 item true-false test of ten clinical variables or factors of personality: hypochondriasis, depression, hysteria, psychopathic-deviate, masculinity-femininity, paranoia, psychasthenia, schizophrenia, hypomania and social introversion. Scores are also obtained on four validity scales: Question, Lie (L), Validity (F), and Defensiveness (K). Materials include 550 cards to which the individual responds. Personality scores are plotted on profile sheet reflecting standard deviations from the Mean. Old and New Group Forms are also available. Examiner required. Available in 45 languages.

Untimed: 90 minutes

Range: Ages 16 and older

Scoring: Hand key; examiner evaluated; computer scoring available

Cost: 25 recording sheets $5.00; item cards $54.00; answer keys (includes manual) $18.00.

Publisher: University of Minnesota Press--distributed exclusively by: NCS Interpretive Scoring Systems

THE MINNESOTA MULTI-PHASIC PERSONALITY INVENTORY: OLD GROUP FORM
Strake R. Hathaway and Charnley McKinley

teen, adult

Purpose: Assesses individual personality. Used for clinical diagnosis and research on psychopathology and mental health.

Description: 566 item true-false test of ten clinical variables or factors of personality: hypochondriasis, depression, hysteria, psychopathic-deviate, masculinity-femininity, paranoia, psychasthenia, schizophrenia, hypomania and social introversion. Scores are also obtained on four validity scales: Question, Lie (L), Validity (F), and Defensiveness (K). Subjects respond to items on separate answer sheet. Individual and New Group Forms are also available. Personality scores are plotted on profile sheet reflecting standard deviations from the Mean. Self-administered. Suitable for group and individual use. Available in 45 languages.

Untimed: 45-90 minutes

Range: Ages 16 and older

Scoring: Hand key; examiner evaluated; computer scoring available

Cost: 10 test booklets $6.00; 25 machine-scored answer sheets $5.00; 25 hand-scored answer sheets $3.40; hand-scored answer keys $3.40; 25 case summary and profile forms $3.20; tape recorded version of MMPI $38.00.

Publisher: University of Minnesota Press--distributed exclusively by: NCS Interpretive Scoring Systems

MIRROR-COUPLE RELATIONSHIP INVENTORY
Refer to page 74.

MISKIMINS SELF-GOAL-OTHER DISCREPANCY SCALE (MSGO-I & MSGO-II)
R. W. Miskimins

teen, adult

Purpose: Measures a person's self-concept in terms of the way that person sees himself, the way he would like to be, and the way he believes others see him. Used for clinical diagnosis and research.

Description: Paper-pencil test assessing social, emotional, and general aspects of a person's self-concept. Available in two forms: MSGO-I contains 15 items plus five blank items in which the subject or examiner can insert his own dimensions; and MSGO- II, which contains 12 items plus four blank items presented with a simplified format and wording for use with younger people, seriously debilitated individuals, or the educationally handicapped.
The two forms differ slightly in item content and administration, but use the same rating procedure and yield nearly identical results. For each test item the subject rates himself three times on a scale consisting of bipolar adjectives separated by a nine-point Likert scale. For example, if the dimension being rated is "good person--bad person," the subject first answers for the way he sees himself, then for his goal in this dimension, and finally for the way he believes others perceive him.
When scores for all items have been combined, it is possible to determine discrepancies between "Self" and "Goal" and between "Self" and "Others." A greater discrepancy indicates a lower self-concept. A profile of each subject's responses can be drawn, and interpretative data are available for the most common types of profiles. In addition, the MSGO-I yields 28 subscores (19 of which significantly distinguish between normal and psychiatric populations)

and the MSGO-II yields seven sub-scores. Use restricted to APA membership guidelines. Examiner required. Suitable for group use.

Untimed: Not available

Range: Adolescent, adult

Scoring: Hand key; may be computer scored

Cost: 100 scales and profiles $50 (specify I or II); manual $14.00.

Publisher: Rocky Mountain Behavioral Science Institute, Inc.

MOONEY PROBLEM CHECKLIST
R.L. Mooney and L. V. Gordon

teen, adult   grades 7-UP

Purpose: Identifies individuals who want or need help with personal problems. Used for individual counseling.

Description: Multiple-item, paper-pencil, self-assessment of personal problems. Subjects read examples of problems, underline those of "some concern", circle those of "most concern", and write a summary in their own words. Areas covered vary from form to form, but include health and physical development, home and family, boy and girl relations, morals and religion, courtship and marriage, economic security, school or occupation, and social and recreational. Materials include separate checklists for junior high students, high school students, college students, and adults. Self-administered. Suitable for group use.

Untimed: 30 minutes

Range: Grades 7-12, college, adult

Scoring: Hand key; may be machine scored

Cost: Examiner's kit (materials without separate answer documents, junior high, high school, college, adult) $3.25; examiner kit (with separate answer documents, junior high,

high school, college) $3.50. Both include checklist and manual.

Publisher: The Psychological Corporation

MULTIPLE AFFECT ADJEC-TIVE CHECK LIST (MAACL)
Marvin Zuckerman and Bernard Lubin

teen, adult   grades 10-UP

Purpose: Measures anxiety, depression, and hostility in high school and college students and adults. Used for clinical evaluation and research applications.

Description: 132 item paper-pencil inventory of adjectives, available in three forms. The Today Form measures current affect states with instructions to check those adjectives which describe how the subject feels at the time of testing. The In-General Form instructs the subject to check those adjectives which describe a more general state of their feelings. The third form uses computer scoring and allows for verbally presented instructional sets. Scores are provided for A-Anxiety, D- Depression and H-Hostility. The Today Form is sensitive to changes in affect resulting from examination anxiety among college students, perceptual isolation, therapy sessions, combat training, and intake of alcohol. College student and adult job applicant norms are presented in the form of T-score equivalents. Means and standard deviations are presented for a variety of clinical groups and experimental situations. Self- administered; examiner scored. Suitable for group use.

Untimed: 5 minutes for each form

Range: High school, college and adult

Scoring: Hand key; computer scoring available

Cost: Specimen set (manual and one copy of all forms) $3.25; 25 Check

Lists $3.75; 100-$14.00; 100 computer check lists $14.50; 500-$59.00; 25 recording forms $2.00; keys $2.00; manual $2.00.

Publisher: Educational and Industrial Testing Service

MYERS-BRIGGS TYPE INDICATOR (MBTI)
Isabel Briggs Myers and Katharine C. Briggs

teen, adult   grades 9-UP

Purpose: Measures personality dispositions and interests based on Jung's theory of types; used in personal, vocational, marital counseling, executive development programs, and personality research.

Description: 166 to 126 item paper-pencil test of four bi-polar aspects of personality: Introversion-Extroversion, Sensing-Intuition, Thinking-Feeling, and Judging-Perceptive. The subjects are classified as one of two "types" on each scale. The test is heavily influenced by Jungian theories of personality types and the ways in which these types express their personality traits through perceptions, judgments, interests, values and motivations. A theoretical background in dynamic psychology is helpful in maximizing the benefits of research compiled for this test. Materials include Form F (166 items) and Form G (126 items) which eliminates 40 items not scored on the four standard scales. Self-administered. Suitable for group use.

Untimed: 20-30 minutes

Range: Grades 9-12 and adults

Scoring: Hand key

Cost: Counselor's kit (specify Form F or G, includes manual, key 5 tests, 25 answer sheets) $27.50.
Publisher: Consulting Psychologists Press, Inc.

NEUROTICISM SCALE QUESTIONNAIRE (NSQ)
Raymond B. Cattell and Ivan H. Scheier

teen, adult   grades 10-UP

Purpose: Measures neuroticism in senior high school students and adults of most educational levels. Used for clinical evaluation, personal counseling, and research on neuroticism.

Description: 40 item paper-pencil questionnaire measures degree of "neurotic trend" in adults and adolescents. Standard scores are provided for men, women, and men and women together. Sixth-grade reading level required. Self-administered. Suitable for group use.

Untimed: 10 minutes

Range: Senior high school students-adults

Scoring: Hand key

Cost: Testing kit $5.50; handbook $4.70; 25 test booklets (not reusable) $4.25; scoring key $.70.

Publisher: Institute for Personality and Ability Testing, Inc.

OBJECTIVE ANALYTIC BATTERIES (O-A)
Raymond B. Cattell and James M. Schueiger

teen, adult

Purpose: Evaluates personality in adults and adolescents age 14 and above. Used for clinical evaluations, research on personality source traits, and personal counseling.

Description: Ten paper-pencil tests provide an objective measure of ten personality source traits: ego strength, anxiety, independence, extraversion, regression, control, cortertia, depression, and others. The batteries are arranged in a kit, from which tests for half an hour, an hour, two hours, etc., may be scheduled, according to purpose and testing time. The handbook for the O-A Kit combines practical tests with broad developments in psychometry (defining validity, reliability, function fluctuation, state-trait differences) and in personality theory concerning the source-trait structures and their mode of interaction. The handbook is explicitly designed as supportive reading and realistic illustration for courses on personality theory. Norms are calculated directly for each of the ten factors; norm base covers ages 14-30 years; age trends included for other situations. Examiner required. Suitable for group use.

Untimed: 30 minute test

Range: Ages 14 and older

Cost: Professional testing kit $89.50; handbook $37.50; test kit $32.00; 10 expendable booklets (OA359) $8.50; (OA360) $4.75; (OA361) $4.50; 25 answer sheets (OA362); $8.00; audio tapes (OA363) $7.00; (OA347) set of 5 $32.50; score summary sheets for handscoring available from IPAT.

Publisher: Institute for Personality and Ability Testing, Inc.

OBJECT RELATIONS TECHNIQUE
H. Phillipson

teen, adult

Purpose: Assesses interpersonal relations. Used for individual therapy and counseling.

Description: 12 item projective test of interpersonal relations. Items are cards presenting important interpersonal situations in varying environmental and emotional contexts. Subject makes up a story about each picture. Evaluation of responses is based on object relations theory in psychoanalysis. Materials include set of 12 stimulus plates. Examiner required. Not suitable for group use. BRITISH PUBLISHER

Untimed: 1 hour

Range: Adolescent, adult

Scoring: Examiner evaluated

Cost: Set of 12 plates £14.30; handbook £2.90 (payment in sterling for all overseas orders).

Publisher: NFER-Nelson Publishing Company

THE OFFER SELF-IMAGE QUESTIONNAIRE FOR ADOLESCENTS
Daniel Offer

teen

Purpose: Assesses teen-agers self-image and personality adjustment as an aid to clinical counseling.

Description: 130 item pencil and paper test evaluating five categories of personal imagery: psychological selves, sexual selves familial selves and coping selves measured on a scale of six responses ranging from 'Describes me very well' to 'Does not describe me at all.' The test is standard scored. A low standard score indicates that the takers do not deal adequately with their feelings and environment. A high score indicates a good ability to cope. Materials consist of a test booklet, manual, and score sheet. Subjects are asked to read the front page of the booklet and provide the requested personal information, asking questions of the examiner if necessary. Examiner preferred but not required. May be administered to groups.

Untimed: 40 minutes

Range: Ages 13-19

Scoring: Examiner evaluated

Cost: Manual $12.00; M/F questionnaire $1.00 each; answer sheet $.15; scoring service per questionnaire $1.00.

Publisher: Institute for Psychosomatic & Psychiatric Research & Training

OMNIBUS PERSONALITY INVENTORY (OPI)
P.A. Histe, T.R. McConnell, H.D. Webster, and G.D. Yonge

teen, adult   grades 11-UP

Purpose: Assesses selected personality factors, values and interests of students relevant to an academic activity. Used to understand and differentiate among students in an educational context.

Description: 385 item paper-pencil inventory of 14 aspects of personality including Thinking Introversion, Theoretical Orientation, Aestheticism, Complexity, Autonomy, Religious Orientation, Social Extraversion, Impulse Expression, Personal Integration, Anxiety Level, Altruism, Practical Outlook, Masculinity-Femininity, and Response Bias. An "Intellectual Disposition Catagory" is determined for each individual by combining his standings on six of the regular scales. Examiner required. Suitable for group use.

Untimed: 45-60 minutes

Range: Grades 11-12, college, adult

Scoring: Hand key; computer scoring available

Cost: 25 inventory booklets $11.25; 50 machine scorable answer sheets $7.75; 50 hand scorable answer sheets $8.00; manual $4.75; specimen set $6.50.

Publisher: The Psychological Corporation

PAIN APPERCEPTION TEST
Refer to page 184.

A PARTIAL INDEX OF MODERNIZATION: MEASUREMENT OF ATTITUDES TOWARD MORALITY
Panos D. Bardis

teen, adult   grades 10-UP

Purpose: Measures attitudes toward traditional concepts of sin; useful for clinical assessment, counseling, research on religion and morals, and discussions in religion and social science classes.

Description: Ten item paper-pencil test. Subjects rate ten statements about sin and morality from 0 (least amount of agreement) to 10 (highest amount of agreement). Score equals sum of the ten numerical responses. Theoretical range of scores: 0 (least modern) to 100 (most modern). May be self- administered. Suitable for group use.

Untimed: 5 minutes

Range: Grades High school and up

Scoring: Examiner evaluated

Cost: Free.

Publisher: Panos D. Bardis

THE PERSONAL AUDIT
Refer to page 823.

PERSONAL DISTRESS INVENTORY AND SCALES
Alan Bedford and Graham Foulds

adult

Purpose: Measures personal illness and personality deviance. Used for personality assessment, individual counseling, evaluation of treatment and research.

Description: Four multiple item, paper-pencil tests of personality deviance. The Delusion-Symptoms-State Inventory (DSSI) is an 84 item self-report instrument measuring a wide range of current symptomology. There are 12 sets of seven items each, corresponding to acute psychiatric symptoms. The Personal Disturbance Scale (DSSI/SaD) consists of the seven state anxiety and seven depression items from the full DSSI. Both total and separate scores for the two scales may be obtained. The DSSI/NS (Neurotic Symptoms) is also derived from the DSSI and consists of the five sets of items measuring neurotic symptoms. The Personality Deviance Scales (PDS) covers the three dimensions of Extrapunitiveness, Intropunitiveness and Dominance. Each dimension consists of 12 items scored on a four point scale. Examiner required. Suitable for group use.
BRITISH PUBLISHER

Untimed: Not available

Range: Adult

Scoring: Hand key; examiner evaluated

Cost: Specimen set (includes single copies of each manual and questionnaire; no keys) £3.95 (payment in sterling for all overseas orders).

Publisher: NFER-Nelson Publishing Company

PERSONALITY AND PERSONAL ILLNESS QUESTIONNAIRES
T.M. Caine, G.A. Foulds and K. Hope

adult

Purpose: Evaluates personality structure and psychological functioning of adults. Identifies individuals with neurotic, psychotic, or aggressive

tendencies. Used for screening and diagnostic purposes.

Description: Multiple item, paper-pencil true-false inventory consists of two tests which measure two levels of psychological functioning. The Hysteroid-Obsessoid Questionnaire (HOQ) measures components of personality present in neurotics, while the Hostility and Direction of Hostility Questionnaire (HDHQ) samples a wide range of possible manifestations of aggression, hostility, or punitiveness. Materials include: HOQ-- questionnaire, manual, scoring key; HDHQ-- questionnaire, manual, scoring key, clinical diagrams for neurotics and psychotics. Examiner required.

Untimed: Not available

Range: Adult

Scoring: Hand key; examiner evaluated

Cost: Contact publisher.

Publisher: Hodder & Stoughton-- distributed by The Australian Council for Educational Research Limited

---

PERSONAL ORIENTATION DIMENSIONS (POD)
Everett L. Shostrom

adult

Purpose: Measures attitudes and values in terms of concepts of the actualizing person, one who is more fully functioning and lives a more enriched life. Used to introduce humanistic value concepts, to indicate a person's level of positive mental health and to measure the effects of various treatment and training techniques.

Description: 260 item paper-pencil, two-choice test consists of bi-polar pairs of statements of comparative values and behavior judgements. Subject must choose the statement from each pair which is closest to his beliefs. Items are stated both negatively and positively with the opposites dictated not by word choice but by context. Test-items are non-threatening in order to facilitate communication of the results and provide a positive approach for measuring the following personality dimensions: Orientation (time orientation and core centeredness), Polarities (strength/weakness and love/anger), Integration (synergistic integration and potentiation), and Awareness (being, trust in humanity, creative living, mission, and manipulation awareness). Test results indicate whether (and to what degree) an individual is actualizing or non-actualizing. A component of the Actualizing Assessment Battery (AAB). Examiner required. Suitable for group use.

Untimed: 30-40 minutes

Range: Adult

Scoring: Hand key; computer scoring available

Cost: Specimen set (manual, one copy of all forms) $2.25; 25 reusable test booklets $9.50; 50 answer sheets (Digital or NCS) $5.50; Edits scoring- without profile $.60, with profile $.95.

Publisher: Educational and Industrial Testing Service

PERSONAL ORIENTATION INVENTORY (POI)
Everett L. Shostrom

teen, adult   grades 10-UP

Purpose: Measures values and behaviors important in the development of actualizing persons. Used in counseling and group training sessions, and as a pre- and post-therapy measure to indicate a person's level of positive mental health.

Description: 150 item paper-pencil,

two-choice test consisting bi-polar pairs of statements of comparative values and behavioral judgements. The subject must choose the statement from each pair closest to his beliefs. The inventory is scored for two major scales and ten subscales: Time Ratio, Support Ratio, Self-Actualizing Value, Existentiality, Feeling Reactivity, Spontaneity, Self-Regard, Self-Acceptance, Nature of Man, Synergy, Acceptance of Aggression, Capacity for Intimate Contact. College norms presented in percentile scores. Adult mean scores and profiles provided. Means, standard deviations, and plotted profiles for clinically nominated "self-actualized" and "non-self-actualized" groups as well as for many other clinical and industrial samples. A component of the Actualizing Assessment Battery (AAB). Examiner required. Suitable for group use.

Untimed: 30 minutes

Range: High school, colleges, adults

Scoring: Hand key; computer scoring available

Cost: Specimen set (includes manual and all forms) $3.75; 25 reusable test booklets $10.50; 50 profile sheets $4.00; set of 14 hand-scoring stencils $10.00; handbook $12.95; manual $2.75.

Publisher: Educational and Industrial Testing Service

PERSONAL PREFERENCE SCALE
Maurice H. Krout and Johanna Krout

adult

Purpose: Assesses aspects of personality that are usually available only through projective tests. Used for clinical evaluations, vocational guidance, and industrial placement.

Description: 100 item paper-pencil,

multiple-choice test consisting of ten subtests of ten items each. Test items are drawn from everyday activities which relate to a variety of early experiences. The subject rates each item on a three-point scale according to personal likes and dislikes, and the responses indicate important attitudes and personality traits derived from those early experiences. Factors measured include: adventuresomeness vs. security-seeking, communicativeness vs. taciturnity, optimism vs. pessimism, altruism vs. punitivism, emotional lability vs. emotional rigidity, aspiration level, assertiveness level, sentimentality, and impersonal affiliativeness. Hand-scoring takes less than two minutes. A guide for interpretation is available, but more sophisticated approaches in terms of personality development and structure will yield more valuable insights from the scores. In industrial applications, specific subtests have proven most valuable in discriminating between workers who were well-motivated and successful with certain operations and those who were poorly suited for such work. In clinical settings, the information this test provides is confirmed by the results of other paper-pencil personality tests. Self-administered. Suitable for group use.

Untimed: 20 minutes

Range: Adult

Scoring: Hand key

Cost: Test $.65 (free guide with each set of fifty purchased).

Publisher: Johanna Krout Tabin, Ph.D.

PERSONAL QUESTIONNAIRE RAPID SCALING TECHNIQUE (PQRST)
David Mulhall

teen, adult

Purpose: Measures changes in feelings, beliefs and symptoms. Used for clinical and educational counseling.

Description: Multiple item, paper-pencil test of issues important to an individual. In cooperation with a consultant, respondent defines set of constructs to be measured. Constructs may include feelings, attitudes on behavior. Technique provides framework through which intensity of each construct can be measured. Materials include two forms, PQ10 and PQ14. PQ10 contains slightly fewer constructs. Availability limited to experienced psychologists or persons of equivalent qualifications. Examiner required. Not suitable for group use.
BRITISH PUBLISHER

Untimed: Not available

Range: Adolescent, adult

Scoring: Hand key

Cost: Specimen set £9.90 (payment in sterling for all overseas orders).

Publisher: NFER-Nelson Publishing Company

PHSF RELATIONS QUESTIONNAIRE-1970
Refer to page 620.

THE PICTORIAL STUDY OF VALUES
Charles Shooster

adult

Purpose: Examines personal values. Used for self- awareness programs, discussion groups and research on values and mores. Suitable for illiterates and non-English speaking persons.

Description: Multiple item, paper-pencil test measuring reactions to six basic value areas: social, political, economic, religious, aesthetic, and theoretical. Test items are composed of interesting photographs. The test correlates as well with self-judgements of personal values as does the verbal Allport-Vernon-Lindzey Study of Values and the six areas are similarly independent. College norms provided. Examiner required. Suitable for group use.

Untimed: 20 minutes

Range: Adult

Scoring: Examiner evaluated

Cost: Specimen set $2.20; 25 tests $3.85; 100- $12.00.

Publisher: Psychometric Affiliates

THE PICTURE IDENTIFICATION TEST
Jay L. Chambers

teen, adult

Purpose: Assesses a person's effectiveness in dealing with combative, personal and competitive motivational dimensios. Used for personality analysis and research in psychotherapy.

Description: Multiple item two part paper-pencil test. The subject is presented a card with 12 photographs representing a variety of facial expressions (6 male, 6 female photographs, ages 21-23 years). Part I, subject rates the person's expression in each picture from 1 (very positive) to 5 (very negative). Part II, subject is given a list of 22 needs (based on Murray's Need System) and 3 time dimension items (past, present, and future). The subject rates each of the 12 pictures for the 25 items on a scale

of 1 (very definite expression of the motive) to 5 (definintely does not express the motive). The ratings are computer analyzed by the author and yield two types of scores. A multidimensional scale analysis which yields 3 dimension scales: Combative, Personal, and Competitive. Specific attitudes scores are also computed for each need. These attitude scores are correlated with target dimension need locations to provide an attitude score for each dimension. Self-administered. Suitable for group use.

Untimed: 45-60 minutes

Range: Adolescent, adult

Scoring: Computer scored

Cost: Manual $13.00, scoring and interpretation $3.00.

Publisher: Jay L. Chambers, Ph.D.

POLYFACTORIAL STUDY OF PERSONALITY
Ronald H. Stark

adult

Purpose: Diagnoses the subject's personality as an aid to the clinical evaluation of the individual's relationship with others.

Description: 300 item pencil and paper true-false test measuring eleven aspects of psychopathology: hypochrondriasis, sexual identification, anxiety, social distance, sociopathy, depression, compulsivity, repression paranoia, schizophrenia and hyperaffectivity. Self-administered. Suitable for group use.

Untimed: 45 minutes

Range: Adult

Scoring: Hand key

Cost: Specimen set $9.35; manual $3.99; IBM scoring stencil $5.40; Package of profile sheets $6.05; package of IBM answer sheets $6.05.

Publisher: Martin M. Bruce, Ph.D. Publishers

PROFILE OF MOOD STATES (POMS)

Douglas M. McNair, Maurice Lorr, and Leo Droppleman

teen, adult

Purpose: Assesses affect or mood in individuals 18 years and older. Used to measure response of outpatients to various therapeutic approaches, including drug evaluation studies.

Description: 65 item paper-pencil test measuring six dimensions of affect or mood: Tension-Anxiety, Depression-Dejection, Anger-Hostility, Vigor- Activity, Fatigue-Inertia, and Confusion- Bewilderment. An alternative POMS-Bipolar Form measures mood dimensions in terms of six bipolar affective states identified in recent research. These dimensions are: Composed-Anxious, Elated-Depressed, Agreeable-Hostile, Engergetic-Tired, Clearheaded-Confused, and Confident-Unsure. The POMS-Bipolar Form is available at present for research use. Norms are provided for POMS for college and outpatient populations. Examiner required. Suitable for group use.

Untimed: 3-5 minutes

Range: Ages 18-adult

Scoring: Hand key, computer scoring available

Cost: Specimen set (includes manual and all forms) $3.00; 25 inventories $3.75; 100-$14.00; 25 profile sheets $4.00; 50-$4.00 (specify college or outpatient); keys $3.00; manual $2.50.

Publisher: Educational and Industrial Testing Service

THE PROJECTIVE ASSESSMENT OF AGING METHOD (PAAM)

Bernard D. Starr, Marcella Bakur Weiner and Marilyn Rabetz

adult

Purpose: Assesses the adaptations, potential crisis situations, and areas of conflict unique to the phenomenology of aging. Used for clinical evaluation.

Description: 28 item oral response projective test consisting of 31 drawings for use in clinical administration: 14 standard pictures with male/female alternatives, and 14 alternates. The scenes are related to aging and elicit feelings, attitudes, and perceptions of the subjects that give clues to their emotional and cognitive frame of mind. Examiner required. Not for group use.

Untimed: Not available

Range: Adult

Scoring: Examiner evaluated

Cost: Complete kit (includes 28 cards and manual) $35.00.

Publisher: Springer Publishing Company

PROJECTIVE PERSONALITY TEST (Analagous to the TAT)

adult

Purpose: Evaluates basic personality characteristics. Intended for use exclusively with Black African subjects.

Description: 16-18 picture cards provide the stimuli for a projective personality test analagous to the TAT. Each picture presents some degree of ambiguity to facilitate a variety of interpretations. Where humans are depicted, Black characters are used except where the situation "requires a Caucasian." There is one set of cards for each of the following groups: urban men, urban women, rural men, and rural women. Use is restricted to competent persons properly registered with either the South African Medical and Dental Council or Test Commission of the Republic of South Africa. Examiner required. Not for group use.

SOUTH AFRICAN PUBLISHER

Untimed: Open ended

Range: Black adults

Scoring: Examiner evaluated

Cost: (In Rands) complete kit 78,000; manual (separately) 30,00.

Publisher: National Institute for Personnel Research

PSYCHIATRIC DIAGNOSTIC INTERVIEW (PDI)
Ekkehard Othmer, Elizabeth C. Penick, and Barbara J. Powell

---

adult　　

Purpose: Identifies 15 of the most frequently encountered psychiatric disorders. Used in all phases of diagnostic screening, intake and followup.

Description: Multiple item, verbally administered, oral response test consisting of easily understood questions, most of which require only a "yes" or "no" answer. Clinicians and trained support personnel can quickly obtain diagnostic summaries evaluating the following basic syndromes: Organic Brain Syndrome, Alcoholism, Drug Dependency, Mania, Depression, Schizophrenia, Antisocial Personality, Hysteria (Briquet Syndrome), Anorexia Nervosa, Obsessive-Compulsive Neurosis, Phobic Neurosis, Anxiety Neurosis, Mental Retardation, Homosexuality and Transsexualism. In addition, there are three derived syndromes:

Polydrug Abuse, Schizoaffective Disorder and Manic- Depressive Disorder. The questions for each of the basic syndromes are divided into four sections. If the simple response criteria, as indicated on the Recording Booklet, are not met, the interviewer omits and remainder of the questions for that syndrome and proceeds to the next syndrome. All positive syndromes are recorded on the Time Profile, graphically displaying which syndromes were positive, the patient's age when they were positive, and how long they were positive. Examiner required. Not suitable for group use.

Untimed: 15-60 minutes

Range: Adult

Scoring: Examiner evaluated; computer scoring available

Cost: Kit (1 reusable test booklet, 10 recording booklets, manual) $25.00.

Publisher: Western Psychological Services

PSYCHOLOGICAL SCREENING INVENTORY (PSI)
Richard I. Lanyon

---

teen, adult　grades 10-UP　

Purpose: Identifies adults and adolescents who may need more extensive mental health examination or professional attention. A quick, non-threatening screen for use in clinics, hospitals, schools, courts and reformatories.

Description: 130 item, true-false test covering five scales: Alienation, Social Nonconformity, Discomfort, Expression, and Defensiveness. Materials include a manual, question and answer sheet, scoring template, and profile. Use restricted to certified psychologists. Examiner required. Suitable for group use. Available in Spanish.

Untimed: 15 minutes

Range: High school-adult

Scoring: Hand key

Cost: Complete kit $33.00

Publisher: Research Psychologists Press, Inc.

PSYCHOTIC INPATIENT PROFILE
Maurice Lorr and Norris D. Vestre

adult

Purpose: Measures behavior patterns of adult psychiatric patients. Used with difficult patients and to evaluate treatment progress.

Description: 96 item paper-pencil inventory consists of questions about the subject's behavior which a nurse or psychiatric aide answers by indicating frequency of observation from "Not at all" to "Nearly always." Analysis of the responses provides objective and quantitative measures of 12 syndromes of observable psychotic behavior: Excitement, Hostile Belligerence, Paranoid Projection, Anxious Depression, Retardation, Seclusiveness, Care Needed, Psychotic Disorganization, Grandiosity, Perceptual Distortion, Depressive Mood, and Disorientation. The six-page test booklet is a revised and expanded version of the Psychotic Reaction Profile. Norms are provided for men and women, both drug-free and drug treated. Examiner required. Suitable for group use.

Untimed: 20-30 minutes

Range: Adult psychiatric patients

Scoring: Hand key

Cost: Complete kit (includes 20 forms, manual) $9.50.

Publisher: Western Psychological Services

PURPOSE IN LIFE (PIL)
James C. Crumbaugh and Leonard T. Maholick

---

adult

Purpose: Measures degree to which an individual has found meaning in life. Used with addicted, retired, handicapped, and philosophically confused individuals for purposes of clinical assessment, student counseling, vocational guidance, and rehabilitation.

Description: 34 item paper-pencil test assessing man's major motivations in life. Subjects must rate 20 statements according to their own beliefs, complete 13 sentence stems, and write an original paragraph describing their aims, ambitions, and goals in life. Based on Viktor Frankl's "will to meaning," The test embraces his logotherapeutic orientation in recognition of threat of the existential vacuum. Norms provided for mental patients and normals. Fourth-grade reading level required. Self-administered. Suitable for group use. Available in Spanish.

Untimed: 10-15 minutes

Range: Adults

Scoring: Scoring service available

Cost: Specimen set (includes test, manual, bibliography) $3.00; 25 tests $4.00; 100-$14.00.

Publisher: Psychometric Affiliates

QUIT SMOKING NOW PROGRAM
Robert Gordon

---

teen, adult

Purpose: Evaluates a person's addiction to smoking cigarettes. Used by therapists to assist patients who wish to quit smoking.

Description: 40 item paper-pencil

survey assessing the causes and nature of individual's addiction to smoking, and their commitment to change as they attempt to quit. After the initial survey is completed, the therapist graphs on the Progress Chart the number of cigarettes smoked versus days of treatment. Monitoring cards are placed in front of patients' cigarette packages and are used for recording frequency and time of smoking. May be used in conjunction with hypnosis, behavioral techniques, and/or counseling. Self-administered. Suitable for group use.

Untimed: Not available

Range: Adolescent, adult

Scoring: Examiner evaluated

Cost: Kit (includes 25 smoking surveys, 25 progress charts, 25 monitors and instructions) $18.00.

Publisher: The Wilmington Press

RORSCHACH CONCEPT EVALUATION TECHNIQUE
Paul McReynolds

adult

Purpose: Measures an individual's conceptual deviance that may be related to various aspects of personality. Used for clinical analysis.

Description: Multiple-item, paper-pencil test (for groups) or oral response (for individuals). The procedure requires five "yes" or "no" answers for each Rorschach card which yields three scores: J Score, a measure of "conceptual precision", V Score, a measure of "conceptual conformity"; and C Score, a measure of "overall conceptual deviance." Examiner required. Suitable for group use.

Untimed: 10 minutes

Range: Adult

Scoring: Examiner evaluated

Cost: Kit (25 booklets and manual) $9.00.

Publisher: Western Psychological Services

ROTTER INCOMPLETE SENTENCES BLANK
Julian B. Rotter

teen, adult

Purpose: Assesses personality of adolescents and adults.

Description: 40 item paper-pencil test of personality. Items are stems of sentences to be completed by the subject. Responses may be classified into three categories: unhealthy responses, neutral responses, and positive or healthy responses. Materials include a High School, College, and Adult Form. Self-administered. Suitable for individuals and groups.

Untimed: 20-40 minutes

Range: Adolescent, adult

Scoring: Hand key; examiner evaluated

Cost: 25 blanks (specify High School, College or Adult) $3.75; manual $6.00.

Publisher: The Psychological Corporation

SCHOOL MOTIVATION ANALYSIS TEST (SMAT)
Samuel E. Krug, Raymond B. Cattell, and Arthur B. Sweney

teen

Purpose: Assesses the psychological motivations of adolescents ages 12-18 years. Used for clinical evaluation, educational and personal counseling, and psychological research on adolescent motivations.

Description: 190 item paper-pencil, multiple-choice test measures ten important achievement, social, and comfort needs of 12 to 18 year olds. Six of the needs are basic drives: ptotectiveness, caution, self-assertion, sexual identity, aggressiveness, and self-indulgence. Four are interests that develop and mature through learning experiences: interest in school, dependency, responsibility, and self-fulfillment. Test items consist of objective devices which are less susceptible to deliberate faking or distortion than standard questionnaires or checklists. For each of the ten interest areas, scores measure drive or need level, satisfaction level, degree of conflict, and total motivational strength. Norms provided for males and females separately. Fourth-grade reading level required. Examiner required. Suitable for group use.

Untimed: 46-60 minutes

Range: Ages 12-18

Scoring: Hand key; computer scoring service available

Cost: Specimen set $8.85; handbook $4.60; 25 reusable test booklets $22.00; 50 answer sheets $8.00; 3 scoring keys $6.75; individual scoring report $2.28-$3.80 each depending upon quantity.

Publisher: Institute for Personality and Ability Testing, Inc.

THE SHUTZ MEASURES: ELEMENT B-BEHAVIOR
Will Schutz

adult

Purpose: Measures a respondent's perception of his own behavior. Used for personal growth, assessment, training and development by counselors, psychologists, and team trainers.

Description: 54 item paper-pencil test consisting of behavioral descriptions which subjects are asked to rate in terms of "The Way It Is" and "The Way I Want It to Be." Factors measured include: expressed-received and perceived-wanted aspects of the behavioral dimensions: inclusion, control and openness. This measure is an expansion of Fundamental Interpersonal Relations Orientation (FIRO) Theory. May be self-administered. Facilitator helpful. Suitable for group use.

Untimed: 15 minutes

Range: Adult

Scoring: Hand key

Cost: Complete set (materials for 10 participants) $30.00; trainer's pkg. (manual, each of 5 tests) $50.00.

Publisher: University Associates, Inc.

THE SCHUTZ MEASURES: ELEMENT F-FEELINGS
Will Schutz

adult

Purpose: Measures a respondent's perception of his feelings. Useful for personality assessment, personal growth, and training and development.

Description: 54 item paper-pencil test consisting of behavioral descriptions which subjects are asked to rate according to how "I Feel" and how "I Want to Feel." Factors measured include: expressed- received and perceived-wanted aspects of the feeling dimensions: significance, competence and likeability. This measure is an expansion of Fundamental Interpersonal Relations Orientation (FIRO) Theory. May be self-administered. Facilitator helpful. Suitable for group use.

Untimed: 15 minutes

Range: Adult

Scoring: Hand Key

Cost: Complete set (materials for 10 participants) $30.00; trainer's pkg. (manual, each of 5 tests) $50.00.

Publisher: University Associates, Inc.

THE SCHUTZ MEASURES: ELEMENT R- RELATIONSHIPS
Will Schutz

adult

Purpose: Measures two respondents' perception of their relationship. Used for team building, family therapy, conflict resolution, training and development.

Description: 54 item paper-pencil test consisting of two forms: "Me to You" and "You to Me." Respondents rate descriptions of "The Way It Is" and "The Way I Want It to Be" in terms of their relationship. Factors measured include: expressed-received and perceived-wanted aspects of the behavioral dimensions of inclusion, control, and openness and the feelings dimensions of significance, competence and likeability. This measure is an expansion of Fundamental Interpersonal Relations Orientation (FIRO) Theory. May be self-administered. Facilitator helpful. Suitable for group use.

Untimed: 20-25 minutes

Range: Adult

Scoring: Hand key

Cost: Complete set (material for 10 participants) $30.00; trainer's pkg. (manual, each of 5 tests) $50.00

Publisher: University Associates, Inc.

THE SCHUTZ MEASURES: ELEMENT S-SELF-CONCEPT
Will Schutz

adult

Purpose: Evaluates an adult's self-concept. Used in personal growth; analysis, counseling and training and development of counselors.

Description: 54 item paper-pencil test consisting of statements to be rated in terms of "I" and "I Want To." Factors measured include: perceived-wanted aspects of the dimensions self-inclusion (presence); self-control (vs. spontaneity); self-openness (awareness); self-significance; self-competence; and self-like. This measure is an expansion of Fundamental Interpersonal Relations Orientation (FIRO) Theory. May be self-administered. Facilitator helpful. Suitable for group use.

Untimed: 15 minutes

Range: Adult

Scoring: Hand key

Cost: Complete set (material for 10 participants) $30.00; trainer's pkg. (manual, each of 5 tests) $50.00

Publisher: University Associates, Inc.

S-D PRONENESS CHECKLIST
William T. Martin

teen, adult

Purpose: Identifies persons with depressive and suicidal tendencies. Used by persons and agencies involved in suicide prevention and may be administered via telephone.

Description: 30 item paper-pencil inventory assesses a person's level of depression and suicide tendencies. Any trained counselor can complete the questionnaire, based on information gained through interviews and observation. The evaluator rates each of the statements on a five-point scale from "Does Not Apply" to "Most Significant." Three scores are derived: Suicidal Score, Depression Score, and Total Suicide-Depression Proneness Score. Interpretative guidelines provided with each form, including suicide correction factors. Twelve page pamphlet on suicide/

depression also available. Self-administered by examiner. Not for group use.

Untimed: Open ended

Range: Adolescents and up

Scoring: Examiner evaluated

Cost: Specimen set $4.00; 25 rating forms $6.75; 100-$26.00.

Publisher: Psychologists and Educators, Inc.

THE SEEKING OF NOETIC GOALS TEST (SONG)
James C. Crumbaugh

teen, adult

Purpose: Measures the strength of a person's motivation to find meaning in life. Used for pre- and post- testing of logotherapy programs with addicted, retired, handicapped, and philosophically confused individuals.

Description: 20 item paper-pencil test consisting of statements which the subject rates from 1 to 7 according to his or her own beliefs. Used in conjunction with the Purpose In Life Test to predict therapeutic success. The manual includes a discussion of the test's rationale, validity, reliability, administration, scoring, norms, and other technical data. Fourth-grade reading level required. Self-administered. Suitable for group use.

Untimed: 10 minutes

Range: Adolescent, adult

Scoring: Scoring service available

Cost: Specimen set (includes one test and manual) $3.00; 25 tests $4.00; 100-$14.00.

Publisher: Psychometric Affiliates

SELF-INTERVIEW INVENTORY
H. Birnet Hovey

adult

Purpose: Measures a person's level of emotional adjustment and identifies persons with neurotic tendencies. Useful for self-awareness and counseling programs with both psychiatric and normal patients.

Description: 185 item paper-pencil inventory containing a high loading level of unique content. A Composite Neurotic score is derived from sub-scores on current complaints, emotional insecurity, and guilt feelings. A Composite Maladjustment score is derived from subscores on pre-psychotic and psychotic behavior and childhood illness. Two validating scores are also provided: one on carefulness, and one on truthfulness of response. Validated and cross-validated on neuropsychiatric and control groups. Norms provided for control groups.

Untimed: Not available

Range: Adults

Scoring: Hand key

Cost: Specimen set $3.30; 25 inventories $3.85; 100-$12.00; 25 answer sheets $2.20; 100-$7.70; 25 profiles $2.20; 100-$7.70.

Publisher: Psychometric Affiliates

THE SELF-PERCEPTION INVENTORY (SPI)
Refer to page 622.

SELF-RATING ANXIETY SCALE (SAS)
William W.K. Zung

all ages

Purpose: Assesses intensity of anxiety symptoms. Used for clinical diagnosis and research on anxiety.

Description: 20 item paper-pencil measure of anxiety. Each item is a specific characteristic of anxiety. Subject checks "None" or "A little of the time," "Some of the time," "Good part of the time," or "Most" or "All of the time" for each item. Materials include the booklet, *The Measurement of Anxiety*, with directions, keys, norms and multiple copies of the scale. Examiner required. Suitable for group use.
BRITISH PUBLISHER

Untimed: 5 minutes

Range: Clinical patients

Scoring: Hand key

Cost: Contact publisher.

Publisher: Warner/Chilcott

SELF-RATING DEPRESSION SCALE (SDS)
William W.K. Zung

all ages

Purpose: Assesses intensity of depressive symptoms. Used for clinical diagnosis and research on depression.

Description: 20 item paper-pencil measure of anxiety. Each item is a specific characteristic of depression. Subject checks "None" or "A little of the time," "Some of the time," "Good part of the time," or "Most" or "All of the time" for each item. Materials include the booklet, *The Measurement of Anxiety*, with directions, keys, norms and 12 copies of the scale. Examiner required. Suitable for group use. Available in Chinese, Czech, Dutch, French, German, Italian, Japanese, Slovak, Spanish, Swedish and Thai.

Untimed: 5 minutes

Range: Clinical patients

Scoring: Hand key; examiner

evaluated

Cost: Contact publisher.

Publisher: Merrell-National Laboratories

SELF-RATING PSYCHIATRIC INVENTORY LIST (SPIL)
William W.K. Zung

all ages

Purpose: Assesses psychiatric symptomatology. Used for diagnosis, evaluation of treatment outcome and research.

Description: 88 item self-report, paper-pencil measure of psychiatric symptoms, for which subject checks one of the following: "None- or A little of the time," "Some of the time," "Good part of the time," or "Most or All of the time." Scores are obtained in seven areas: Psychoticism, Elation, Depression, Anxiety, Neuroticism, Emotional Status and Drug Abuse. Self-administered. Suitable for group use.

Timed: 5 minutes

Range: Clinical patients

Scoring: Hand key; examiner evaluated; may be computer scored.

Cost: Contact publisher.

Publisher: William W.K. Zung, M.D.

THE SENIOR APPERCEPTION TECHNIQUE (SAT)
Leopold Bellak and Sonya Sorel Bellak

adult

Purpose: Assesses personality in individuals 60 years of age and older. Used by psychiatrists, psychologists, physicians, nurses and social workers for clinical evaluation and diagnosis.

Description: 16 item oral response

projective personality test measures the traits, attitudes, and psychodynamics involved in the personalities of individuals age 60 years and older. Each test item consists of a picture of human figures in situations of concern to the aged. The examinee is asked to tell a story about each picture. Also includes informational material on technique, administration, research possibilities and bibliography. Examiner required. Not suitable for group use. Spanish and Japanese versions available.

Untimed: 20-30 minutes

Range: 60 and older

Scoring: Examiner Evaluated

Cost: Complete kit (pictures and manual) $13.00.

Publisher: C.P.S., Inc.

SENTENCE COMPLETION TEST
Floyd S. Irvin

teen, adult   grades 10-UP

Purpose: Assesses personality functioning. Used for clinical counseling and academic guidance.

Description: 90 item paper-pencil test of six aspects of personality: Self Concept, Parental Attitude, Peer Attitude, Need for Achievement, Learning Attitude, and Body Image. Items are sentence stems which the subject completes. Items are scored on a five point scale ranging from outright positive to outright negative. Examiner required. Not suitable for group use.

Untimed: 15 minutes

Range: Grades Secondary and college level

Scoring: Hand key; examiner evaluated.

Cost: Specimen set $5.50; 25 forms $6.75; 100- $26.00.

Publisher: Psychologists and Educators, Inc.

SHORR IMAGERY TEST (SIT)
Joseph E. Shorr

teen, adult

Purpose: Evaluates a person's use of imagery and assesses self-image, areas of conflict, and strategies for coping with the world. Used for in-depth personality analysis.

Description: 15 item orally administered/oral response projective personality test. The respondent is asked to imagine a particular situation and then to expand in a directed way upon the image evoked. These imaginary situations are used to reveal a wide range of personality variables: the individual's personal world, relationships between self and others, self-image, sexual attitudes, and internal and external forces acting upon the person. Answers are recorded by the examiner and quantitatively scored according to the degree of conflict within the subject's personality. Not limited by intelligence; suitable for use with the blind, illiterate, and physically handicapped. Minimally culture bound. Examiner required. Not for group use.

Untimed: One hour

Range: Late adolescent-adult

Scoring: Examiner evaluated

Cost: Complete set $37.50.

Publisher: Institute for Psycho-Imagination Therapy

SHORT IMAGINAL PROCESSES INVENTORY (SIPI)
G.J. Huba, J.L. Singer, C.S. Aneshensel and J.S. Antrobus

teen, adult

Purpose: Evaluates the content and style of an individual's daydreams and general inner experience. Used for personal assessment, to study the relation of inner experience to other psychological functions and to investigate group differences in imaginal processes.

Description: 45 item paper-pencil test consisting of five alternative responses covering three scales: Positive-Constructive Daydreaming, Guilt and Fear of Failure Daydreaming and Poor Attentional Control. Responses are recorded in the question and answer booklet and hand scored. Materials include profiles and scoring templates. Suitable for group use.

Untimed: 10 minutes

Range: Adolescent, adult

Scoring: Hand key

Cost: Complete kit $14.50.

Publisher: Research Psychologists Press, Inc.

SIXTEEN PERSONALITY FACTOR QUESTIONNAIRE
Raymond B. Cattell and IPAT Staff

teen, adult

Purpose: Evaluates the normal, adult personality. Used for clinical evaluations, personnel selection and placement, vocational and educational guidance, marriage counseling, and psychological research on personality.

Description: 105-187 item paper-pencil test (depending on which of the five forms is used) measuring 16 primary personality traits including levels of assertiveness, emotional maturity, shrewdness, self-sufficiency, tension, warmth, impulsivity, sensitivity. Test results have specific applications for business, psychotherapy and education.

For business and industry, the 16PF predicts important job related criteria such as length of time an employee is likely to remain with the company, sales effectiveness, work efficiency, tolerance for routine and other specific measures. In diagnostic and therapeutic settings, measures are provided for anxiety, neuroticism, rigidity and other behavior trends. Educators and school psychologists can use the 16PF to counsel college-bound and university students and to identify potential drop-outs, drug users, low achievers, etc. Occupational profile data (based on more than 11,000 cases) are summarized in the handbook for use in vocational and rehabilitation counseling.

Four forms of the 16PF are available. Forms A and B (seventh-grade reading level) consist of 187 items each. Forms B and C (sixth-grade reading level) consist of 105 items each. Form E (third-grade reading level) consists of 128 items in a forced-choice format with large type and shorter, more concrete items.

Four types of computer-analyzed reports are available: the 16PF Narrative Scoring Report provides a complete report for each individual, including descriptions of all significant personality characteristics as well as relevant vocational and occupational comparisons; the Personal Career Development Profile provides information about individual strengths, behavioral attributes, and gratifications to accomplish personal career development objectives; the Karson Clinical Report provides an in-depth analysis of underlying personality dynamics in clinical terms for use in psychiatric and psychological applications; and the Marriage Counseling Report examines individual and joint strengths and weaknesses in the personality organization of two individuals.

The 16PF Manual is a nontechnical guide for administration, scoring, and basic interpretation of Forms A, B, C, and D and is provided with the Examination Sets/Specimen Kits. The 16PF Handbook, which must be ordered separately, is the primary source of technical information on the 16PF. A videotape recording of Form A test booklet in American Sign Language is available. Form E test booklet is also available on cassette tape. Examiner required. Suitable for group-, individual-, and self-administration. Available in Spanish and German.

Untimed: 45-60 minutes

Range: Ages 16 and older

Scoring: Hand key; computer scoring available

Cost: 25 reusable test booklets (specify For A, B, C, or D) $14.25; 50 OpScan answer sheets $6.50; 50 handscoring answer sheets (specify Form A or B, Form C or D, or Form E) $5.50; 50 profile sheets $5.40; 50 handscoring answer-profile sheets (specify Form A or Form B, Form C or Form D or Form E) $6.40.

Publisher: Institute for Personality and Ability Testing, Inc.

SOMATIC INKBLOT SERIES (SIS)
Wilfred A. Cassell

teen, adult

Purpose: Assesses an individual's body perception and general personality dynamics. Used to evaluate the psychopathological significance of somatic symptoms, conversion reactions, and sexual dysfunction.

Description: 20 item verbal examination consisting of 20 cards, each containing a carefully designed inkblot. The cards are presented individually to the subject who describes his perceptions and associations to the examiner. The inkblots are oriented towards body perceptions. The subject's awareness of somatic similaritiess in the inkblots is used to provide clinical data of a projective nature regarding conscious-unconscious somatic attitudes as well as general psychodynamics. The SIS is accompanied by Dr. Wilfred Cassell's book, *Body Symbolism,* which describes scoring techniques. An examiner qualified in projective techniques is required. Not suitable for group use.

Untimed: 45 minutes

Range: Adolescent, adult

Scoring: Examiner evaluated; scoring service available

Cost: Set of cards and scoring sheets $45.00.

Publisher: Aurora Publishing

SOUTH AFRICAN PERSONALITY QUESTIONNAIRE

teen, adult   grades 10-UP

Purpose: Measures general personality traits in the context of South African society. Used for employee screening and selection. Suitable for matriculants and higher.

Description: 150 item paper-pencil test. Consists of bipolar forced-choice items which measure the following personality traits: social responsiveness, dominance, hostility, flexibility, and anxiety. Use is restricted to competent persons properly registered with either the South African Medical and Dental Council or Test Commission of the Republic of South Africa. Examiner required. Suitable for group use.
SOUTH AFRICAN PUBLISHER

Untimed: Open ended

Range: College, adult

Scoring: Hand key; examiner evaluated

Cost: (In Rands) Reusable book 3,60; 25 answer sheets 1,80; scoring key (per set) 12,00; manual 7,20.

Publisher: National Institute For Personnel Research

STATE-TRAIT ANXIETY INVENTORY (STAI)
Charles D. Spielberger, Richard L. Gorusch and Robert E. Lushene

teen, adult   grades 7-UP

Purpose: Evaluates individual anxiety levels as an aid to clinical screening for anxiety-prone students, as an indicator of current anxiety level of therapy and counseling clients, and as a research tool.

Description: Two 20 item paper-pencil tests of two aspects of anxiety, state (A-State) and trait (A-Trait). The A-Trait Scale asks the subject to indicate how they "generally" feel, the A-State how they feel "at a particular moment in time". Self- administered. Suitable for group use. Available in Spanish.

Untimed: 15 minutes

Range: Grades Junior high school-adult

Scoring: Hand key

Cost: Specimen set (includes tests, manual, key) $6.75; 25 tests $2.25; key $.75; manual $6.00; 25 tests in Spanish $4.50; Spanish manual $7.50.

Publisher: Consulting Psychologists Press, Inc.

STRUCTURED AND SCALED INTERVIEW TO ASSESS MALADJUSTMENT (SSIAM)
Barry J. Gurland

adult

Purpose: Identifies problems in social adjustment and rates them quantitatively. Used for clinical evaluations of mental patients.

Description: 32-page interview booklet including scales, profile chart, and instructions for administering and rating the interview. Eleven ratings are provided (five for deviant behavior, one for friction with others, three for distress, and two inferential) for five areas (work, social-leisure, family, marriage, and sex), plus 11 overall ratings. Examiner required. Not for group use.

Range: Adult

Scoring: Examiner evaluated

Cost: 10 copies (includes scales, profile chart, instructions) $24.00.

Publisher: Springer Publishing Company

STUDY OF VALUES (REVISED 1964 BRITISH EDITION)
S. Richardson

teen, adult

Purpose: Measures an individual's basic personality values. Used for counseling and research.

Description: Paper-pencil test of six basic interests and motives: theoretical, economic, aesthetic, social, political and religious. First published in 1931 and revised in 1951 and 1960, the current edition has a new scale form, standardized in Great Britain. New items are added, but the form and intention of the original are maintained. Materials include booklets and manual. Examiner required. Suitable for group use.

CANADIAN PUBLISHER

Untimed: 20 minutes

Range: Ages 16 and older

Scoring: Examiner evaluated

Cost: Specimen set $13.70; 25 booklets $27.36; manual $11.01.

Publisher: Institute of Psychological Research, Inc.

STYLE OF MIND INVENTORY (SMI)
Daniel Fetler

---

teen, adult   grades 13-UP

Purpose: Describes the patterns of an individual's traits, values and beliefs as related to Greek', Roman' and Hebrew' styles of thought. Used to help evaluate character, who we think we are and how we got that way.

Description: 99 item paper-pencil inventory examining the relationship between Greek, Roman, and Hebrew Minds, or ways of thinking, and the subject's traits, values and beliefs. The test is based on the author's observation that what we think of as *the Mind is, among other things, an historical creation* conditioned by various styles of thought, many of which contain at least one "nutty" idea leading to misunderstanding and cultural tension. The inventory deals with three types of questions. The first ten cover 30 attitudes, inclinations or traits which may or may not correspond with certain values. The second section concerns 30 values involving character and ethics, and examines the distinction between "ought" and "is". The third section covers the issues of faith and belief, the norm being the limitations of reason and the senses. The most important scores are the first choices under Values and Beliefs. It is recommended that the examiner discuss with students each question and ask them the reason for their choices. In private interviews it is best to administer the test orally and to scramble the order of the items in each question. Self- administered and examiner evaluated.

Untimed: 60 minutes

Range: College students, adults

Scoring: Examiner evaluated; may be computer scored

Cost: The Fetler Therapy $3.00

Publisher: Daniel Fetler & Associates

SUICIDE PROBABILITY SCALE (SPS)
John G. Cull and Wayne S. Gill

---

all ages

Purpose: Predicts the probability of suicidal behavior. Used by clinicians to assess the probability that a person may be of harm to himself or herself.

Description: 36 item paper-pencil test. The subject responds to statements on a four-point scale, ranging from "None or little of the time," to "Most or all of the time," indicating how the statements would be descriptive of his or her behavior or feelings. The test format itself makes no mention of suicide. Scoring takes only a minute or two and yields an SPS Index, which translates into a probability of engaging in suicidal behavior. Cutoff scores indicating level of probable suicide behavior, interpretive guidelines, and clinical strategies for each level are presented in the manual. The test is standardized on nearly 1,000 people from the ages of ten to sixty-five, including whites, blacks, and hispanics and has been validated on normals and clinical groups with documented, serious suicide attempts. Examiner required. Suitable for group use.

Untimed: 5-10 minutes

Range: Ages 10-65

Scoring: Hand key

Cost: Complete kit (includes 10 tests and manual) $9.95.

Publisher: Western Psychological Services

SUINN TEST OF ANXIETY BEHAVIOR SCALE (STABS)
Refer to page 640.

SURVEY OF INTERPERSONAL VALUES
Leonard V. Gordon

teen, adult   grades 10-UP

Purpose: Measures an individual's values through assesssing what is important in relationships with others. Used to measure values associated with adjustment and performance for selection, placement employment counseling and research purposes.

Description: 30 item paper-pencil inventory assessing personal values. Each test item consists of a triad of value statements. For each triad, examinees must indicate most and least important valuues. Assesses six values: support, conformity, recognition, independence, benevolence, and leadership. Self-administered. Suitable for group use.

Untimed: 15 minutes

Range: High school-adult

Scoring: Hand key

Cost: 25 test booklets $19.00; scoring stencil $3.40; examiner's manual $6.40.

Publisher: Science Research Associates

SURVEY OF PERSONAL VALUES
Refer to page 830.

TASKS OF EMOTIONAL DEVELOPMENT TEST
Refer to page 622.

TAYLOR-JOHNSON TEMPERAMENT ANALYSIS
Robert M. Taylor and Lucille P. Morrison

teen, adult

Purpose: Clinical assessment of personality; also usable for premarital, marital and family counseling, and educational and vocational guidance.

Description: 180 item paper-pencil test measuring common personality traits to assist in assessing individual adjustment and formulation of overall counseling plan. Regular edition has special feature allowing "criss-cross" testing where questions are answered as applied to self and again as applied to significant other (e.g., husband's perception of both self and spouse, and vice versa), thereby adding the dimension of interpersonal perception to counseling perspective. Eighth-grade reading level required. Secondary edition is presented in direct question format with simplified vocabulary for lower-level readers. Fifth-grade reading level required; not designed for "criss-cross." Evaluation is presented as bipolar graphs of trait-pairs: nervous/composed, depressive/light-hearted, active-social/quiet, expressive-responsive/inhibited, sympathetic/indifferent, subjective/objective, dominant/submissive, hostile/tolerant, and self-disciplined/impulsive. The following additional scales are available when Psychological Publications computer Scoring Service is utilized: emotional pressure (stress), adequacy of self-image (self-esteem), preference for privacy, outwardly poised, alienating, passive-aggressive, potential for marital adjustment, parenting effectiveness, leadership, and sales. Self-administered. Suitable for administering to groups and individuals. Available in Spanish, French, German and Portuguese.

Untimed: 20 minutes

Range: Regular edition Ages 15-adult;

Secondary edition ages 11-19 and adult poor readers.

Scoring: Hand key; computer scoring available

Cost: Basic package includes (manual, handscoring stencils, pens, ruler, 5 test booklets--regular or secondary, 50 handscoring answer sheets and 50 profiles) $62.50; counselor's kit (includes manual, handscoring stencils, pens and ruler) $50.00; practice scoring training packet $5.00; manual $40.00; 10 test booklets $5.00; 50 handscoring answer sheets $5.00; 50 computer scoring answer sheets $4.50; 50 profiles percentile shaded, sten or student sten $5.00.

Publisher: Psychological Publications, Inc.

TEST ANXIETY PROFILE (TAP)
Refer to page 641.

TEST OF BEHAVIORAL RIGIDITY (TBR)
K. Warner Schaie and Iris A. Parham

adult

Purpose: Measures ability to adjust to the stress imposed by constant environmental change.

Description: Multiple item, paper-pencil test of three aspects of rigidity: personality-perceptual, motor-cognitive, and psychomotor speed. The subject is asked to copy a writing passage, write a list of opposites and fill out a 70 item questionnaire. Examiner required. Suitable for group use.

Untimed: 30 minutes

Range: Ages 20-70

Scoring: Hand key

Cost: Specimen set (includes testts and manual) $4.00.

Publisher: Consulting Psychologists Press, Inc.

THEMATIC APPERCEPTION TEST (TAT)
Henry Alexander Murray

teen, adult

Purpose: Assesses personality through projective technique focusing on dominate drives, emotions, sentiments, complexes, attitudes, and conflicts.

Description: 20 item projective type test in which a subject is shown pictures one at a time and asked to makke up a story about each picture. The examiner records the subject's stories for later analysis. The projective test seeks to measure, among other things, the subject's temperament, level of emotional maturity, observational ability, intellectuality, imagination, psychological insight, creativity, sense of reality and factors of family and psychic dynamics. Generally the subject is asked to make up stories based on ten cards in each of two sessions. A trained examiner is required. Not suitable for groups.

Untimed: 1 hour per series

Range: Ages 14-40

Scoring: Examiner evaluated

Cost: Specimen set $11.50; manual $1.50.

Publisher: Harvard University Press

TIME QUESTIONNAIRE (TQ)
Robert Yufit and Bonnie Benzies

teen, adult

Purpose: Evaluates an individual's feelings about the past, present, and future. Used for the exploration and quantitative assessment of suicide potential.

Description: Multiple item, four page, paper-pencil or oral, semi-projective measure of feelings about the present, future and past. The TQ is composed of three types of items: multiple-choice, open- ended, and rating scales. Provides an index of time perspective found to be related to suicide potential. Examiner required. Not suitable for group use.

Untimed: 15 minutes

Range: Ages 16-81

Scoring: Examiner evaluated

Cost: Specimen set $4.00; manual $3.75; 25 expendable questionnaires $6.00.

Publisher: Consulting Psychologists Press, Inc.

TRANSACTIONAL ANALYSIS LIFE POSITION SURVEY (TALPS)
F.D. Kramer and B. Strade

---

adult

Purpose: Measures of an individual's life position as defined in Transactional Analysis, "I'm OK" and "You're OK" dimensions. Used for personnel screening, personal assessment, and counseling aid, and as a before-and-after measure for teachers presenting TA to large groups.

Description: 40 item paper-pencil test of attitudes toward self and others. Both "I'm OK" and "You're OK" scores are normed in percentiles for various age groups. The normed scores can be charted on a life position graph of the Report Form. Useful as both a discussion-starter and as a tool for in- depth analysis. Self-administered. Suitable for group use.

Untimed: 10-15 minutes

Range: Adult

Scoring: Hand key

Cost: Specimen set $6.00; 35 surveys $10.00; 2 scoring stencils $3.00; 35 report forms $5.00; manual $3.00.

Publisher: Monitor

TRIADAL EQUATED PERSONALITY INVENTORY
United Consultants Research Staff

---

adult

Purpose: Assesses personality. Used as a predictor of job success, and as a measure of personal adjustment.

Description: 633 item paper-pencil test of personality. Items are simple adjectives equated for response popularity. 21 self-image scores are obtained: dominance, self-confidence, decisiveness, independence, toughness, suspicion, introversion, activity, depression, foresight, industriousness, warmth, enthusiasm, conformity, inventiveness, persistence, sex drive, recognition, drive, cooperativeneess, humility-tolerance, and self- control. Examiner required. Suitable for group use.

Untimed: 50-120 minutes

Range: Adult

Scoring: Examiner evaluated

Cost: Professional examination kit for 24, $24.00.

Publisher: Psychometric Affiliates

A VIOLENCE SCALE
Panos D. Bardis

---

teen, adult   grades 10-UP

Purpose: Measures attitudes toward violence (words and actions aimed at property damage and personal injury); useful for clinical assessment, marriage and family counseling, research on violence, and discussions in social science classes..

Description: 25 item paper-pencil test. Subjects rate 25 statements concerning various aspects of violence on a scale from 0 (strongly disagree) to 44 (strongly agree); the "violence" score equals the sum of 25 numerical responses. Theoretical range of scores: 0 (lowest approval of violence), to 100 (highest approval). May be self-administered. Suitable for group use.

Untimed: 10 minutes

Range: High school and up

Scoring: Examiner evaluated

Cost: Free.

Publisher: Panos D. Bardis

WAHLER PHYSICAL SYMPTOMS INVENTORY
H. J. Wahler

adult

Purpose: Discriminates between patients with medical ailments and those with psychogenic complaints. Used to screen new patients.

Description: 42 item paper-pencil test. Each item consists of a physical problem on which the subjects must rate themselves on a six-point frequency scale from "Almost Never" to "Nearly Every Day." The test is quickly administered and scored and helps identify conversion hysteria, hypocondriasis, and psychophysiological reactions as well as physically determined disorders. Self- administered. Suitable for group use.

Untimed: 15-20 minutes

Range: Psychiatric patients, adult

Scoring: Hand key

Cost: Complete kit (Includes 50 inventory pads, manual) $8.50.

Publisher: Western Psychological Services

WESTERN PERSONALITY INVENTORY
Morse P. Manson

adult

Purpose: Diagnoses presence and degree of alcoholism. Useful in alcohol rehabilitation programs.

Description: Paper-pencil test consisting of a six-page form which combines into one test booklet the "Manson Evaluation," which identifies the potential alcoholic personality, and the "Alcadd Test," which measures extent of alcohol addiction. Examiner required. Suitable for group use.

Untimed: 15-20 minutes

Range: Adult

Scoring: Hand key

Cost: Kit (25 tests, manual) $9.75.

Publisher: Western Psychological Services

WHITAKER INDEX OF SCHIZOPHRENIC THINKING (WIST)
Leighton C. Whitaker

teen, adult grades 8-UP

Purpose: Provides an index of schizophrenic thinking. Used for intake screening.

Description: 25 item paper-pencil, multiple-choice tests which diiscriminates between schizophrenic and non- schizophrenic thinking. The test can be completed by anyone with an eighth-grade education. Easily scored with standardized cutoff scores to quickly identify schizophrenicc thought patterns. Available in two equivalent forms. A newly published (1980) manual provides the following information: discussion of relevant diagnostic issues and the development of WIST, directions for administration and scoring, standardization and validity data, discussion of diagnostic and clinical uses, case illustrations, references, and specimen copies of the test forms. Self-administered. Suitable for group use.

Untimed: 15 minutes

Range: Grades 8/adult mental patients

Scoring: Hand key

Cost: Kit (10 each of Forms A & B, key, manual) $15.25.

Publisher: Western Psychological Services

WILLIAMS AWARENESS SENTENCE COMPLETION (WASC)
Robert L. Williams

teen, adult

Purpose: Measures ethnic awareness and consciousness of Black Americans.

Description: 40 item paper-pencil sentence completion test pertaining to Black awareness as manifested in four factors: pro-White, anti-Black, pro-Black, and anti-White sentiments. Self-administered. Suitable for group use.

Untimed: 20 minutes

Range: Ages 16-adult

Scoring: Examiner evaluated

Cost: Complete (includes tests and manual) $12.00.

Publisher: Robert L. Williams & Associates, Inc.

WITTENBORN PSYCHIATRIC RATING SCALES (REVISED)
J.R. Wittenborn

teen, adult

Purpose: Measures observed behavior of mental patients. Used to facilitate diagnosis and appraise pro-

gress in therapy.

Description: Multiple item, paper-pencil clinician rating of mental patients' behavior. Rating on 52 symptom scales are combined to yield nine cluster scores. Cluster scores are defined in standard psychiatric nomenclature. Manual contains information on administration and scoring. Examiner required. Not suitable for group use.
BRITISH PUBLISHER

Untimed: 15-25 minutes

Range: Adolescent and adult mental patients

Scoring: Examiner evaluated

Cost: Specimen set £2.10; 25 rating scales £7.60 manual £1.65 (payment in sterling for all overseas orders).

Publisher: NFER-Nelson Publishing Company

Multi-Levels

ADOLESCENT ALIENATION INDEX (AAI)
F.K. Heussenstamm

teen

Purpose: Identifies emergent or developing alienation in adolescents. Provides a measure of incipient estrangement that may give clues to personality disjunctures long before behavioral symptoms are evident.

Description: 41 item paper-pencil test. Students choose between two self-descriptive statements for each test item. Covers facets of youthful alienation such as: normlessness, meaninglessness, powerlessness, self-estrangement, and social isolation. Form A offers separate answer sheets for ease of test-taking and scoring. Form C offers consumable test forms designed for students with less sophisticated test-taking skills. Norms are based upon suburban white, urban black, and rural Mexican-American high school students and upon black Job Corps enrollees. Self- administered. Suitable for group use.

Timed: 20 minutes

Range: Ages 12-19

Scoring: Hand key

Cost: 35 AAI (Form A or C) $8.00; 100-$20.00; 35 AAI answer sheets (Form A) $3.00; 100-$6.00; AAI scoring stencil (Form A) $2.50; AAI scoring guide (Form C) $2.50; AAI manual $3.00; AAI specimen set (specify form) $6.00.

Publisher: Monitor

ADOLESCENT SEPARATION ANXIETY TEST
Henry G. Hansburg

all ages

Purpose: Evaluates the emotional and personality patterns with which children and adolescents react to separation experiences; used by clinical psychologists as a therapeutic tool when separation disorders are suspected.

Description: 12 item verbal response test consisting of illustrations of severe and mild separation experiences ranging from a picture of a child being transferred to a new class to a picture of a child and father standing at the mother's coffin. Each picture has a set of 17 statements describing a range of possible feelings associated with the situation depicted. The subjects look at each picture, then tell the examiner which statements best describe their reactions. Measures interaction of attachment, individuation, hostility, fear-anxiety-pain syndrome, defensiveness, and self-evaluation (self-

esteem, self-love identity). The diagnostic categories most frequently used with the instrument consist of mild, strong, severe anxious attachment, hostile anxious attachment, hostile detachment, and excessive self-sufficiency or dependence. The test has been used experimentally with whole families. Volume I and Volume II handbooks are recommended for use with the examination. Examiner required. Not suitable for group use.

Untimed: 20 minutes

Range: Ages 9-adult

Scoring: Examiner evaluated

Cost: Complete kit (Volumes I and II, boy test, girl test, evaluation pads) $22.50; Volume I ST of Adolescent Separation Problems $6.95; Volume II Separation Disorders $8.96; tests $3.00 (specify for boy or girl); 30 evaluation sheets $6.00.

Publisher: Robert E. Krieger Publishing Company, Inc.

AUDITORY PROJECTIVE TEST
S. Braverman and H. Chevigny

all ages

Purpose: Assesses personality of blind people through a projective auditory technique. Test parallels the Thematic Apperception Test (TAT).

Description: A three-part tape-recorded form of scenes from the Thematic Apperception Test. In the first part, the client listens to a scene spoken unemotionally in an artificial language between various role-playing characters, such as an older man and a young man, an older woman and a boy, and a man and a woman. As in other projective tests, the client is asked to develop a story based upon the stimulus presented. In the second section, English is used instead of the artificial language. In the third section, sound effects are presented, such as a stormy background with footsteps entering a house, a train with a whistle and screeching auto brakes, and running footsteps and gunshots. Interpretation consists of noting the themes, conflicts, style, and other aspects of the stories as they relate to the stimuli used. Examiner required. Not suitable for group use.

Untimed: Not available

Range: Ages 4 and older

Scoring: Contact publisher

Cost: Not available.

Publisher: American Foundation for the Blind

BARRON-WELSH ART SCALE
Frank Barron and George S. Welsh

all ages

Purpose: Evaluates individual personality traits through response to figures. Used for counseling and research.

Description: 86 item paper-pencil test of preference for black and white figures. Subject expresses "like" or "dislike" for each figure. Includes items from the Revised Art Scale. The items on this test are also included in the 400 item Welsh Figure Preference Test. Measures creativity. Examiner required. Suitable for group use.

Untimed: 15 minutes

Range: Ages 6-adult

Scoring: Hand key

Cost: Specimen set (does not include manual) $1.00; 25 test booklets $16.25; 50 hand scorable answer sheets $4.50; manual $7.50.

Publisher: Consulting Psychologists Press, Inc.

THE TEST OF SOCIAL INSIGHT: YOUTH EDITION and ADULT EDITION
Russell N. Cassel

all ages

Purpose: Appraises characteristic mode of reaction of the individual in reacting to interpersonal (social) problems, providing one aspect to subject's understanding of, and capacity to adapt to, acceptable patterns of culture in U.S.

Description: 60 item paper-pencil multiple choice test measuring five ways of responding to interpersonal problems: withdrawal, passivity, cooperation, competition, and aggression. The potential conflict areas dealt with include home and family, authority figures, avocational contacts, and work interests. Available in youth and adult editions, with a fifth grade reading level required for both. Examiner required. Suitable for group use.

Untimed: 30-40 minutes

Range: Ages Youth edition 10-18; Adult edition 18 and older

Scoring: Hand key

Cost: Specimen set $6.33; manual $4.00; package of tests $16.45; package of profile sheets $6.05; IBM scoring stencils $5.78; IBM answer sheets $6.05.

Publisher: Martin M. Bruce, Ph.D. Publishers

BEHAVIORAL DEVIANCY PROFILE
Betty Ball and Rita Weinberg

all ages

Purpose: Diagnoses deviancy and disturbance in children and adolescents who have moderate to severe social and emotional problems. Used to compare deviance of physical, psychological, and social factors in a child before and after intervention, and to improve the observations of staff in mental health and educational programs.

Description: Multiple item, paper-pencil questionnaire in which the examiner records the child's observed behavior in four major developmental areas: physical and motor development, cognitive development, speech and language development, and social and emotional development. The profile looks at the total functioning of the child via a developmental and dynamic method. Severity of behavior, duration, and age appropriateness of the behavior are considered. Examiner required. Not for group use.

Untimed: Observation time

Range: Ages 3-21

Scoring: Examiner evaluated

Cost: Complete kit (includes manual and 15 record booklets) $14.00.

Publisher: Stoelting Co.

THE BLACKY PICTURES
Gerald S. Blum

all ages

Purpose: Clinical assessment of personality dynamics. Used for psychodynamically oriented research.

Description: 68 item paper-pencil, picture test of personality, using a set of 12 pictures. Subject views pictures, makes up a story and answers 6-7 multiple choice or short answer questions for each picture then sorts pictures according to preference. Helps determine conflicts and defenses in area of psychosexual development. Also suitable as a semi-structured projective test of psychosexual stages of development. Materials include the pictures, inquiry booklets, record blanks and a manual. Administered individually to ages 5 to adult. May be administered

to groups using slides of pictures. Examiner required. Slides not yet available commercially. Available in Italian.

Untimed: 45 minutes

Range: Ages 5-adult

Scoring: Examiner evaluated

Cost: Complete set (includes 12 pictures, inquiry booklets, manual and 25 record blanks) $32.00.

Publisher: Psychodynamic Instruments

BRISTOL SOCIAL ADJUSTMENT GUIDES
Refer to page 614.

BUTTONS: A PROJECTIVE TEST FOR PRE- ADOLESCENTS AND ADOLESCENTS
Refer to page 615.

CHILD DEVELOPMENT CENTER Q-SORT (CDCQ)
Frances Fuchs Schachter

all ages   grades PRE-UP

Purpose: Measures personality development at all ages and identifies personality types. Used by clinicians, counselors, and teachers to assess degree of normality and changes in the individual's personality picture.

Description: Multiple item observational test consisting of 113 Sort Deck Cards, each representing a personality characteristic. The examiner sorts the cards according to the prominence of each characteristic for the person being evaluated. A personality profile is then developed based on the following seven factors: Independence/Dependence, Affectivity, Relations with People, Relations with Self, Relations with Inanimate Objects, Heterosexual Relationships,

Ego, and Superego. The personality profile of the person being evaluated is compared with that of an "ideal" individual of the same age and sex. The ideal profiles are based on a consensus of mental health experts for each developmental level. The CDCQ also yields an overall index of personality adjustment or psychological well-being to be used in evaluation and follow-up work. A complete CDCQ set includes a CDCQ Sort Deck, distribution cards, manual and 30 record forms, and ideal male and female profiles for the age level ordered. Examiner administered. Suitable for group use.

Untimed: Open ended

Range: Grades Preschool-adult

Scoring: Examiner evaluated

Cost: Complete kit for each level $35.00 each.

Publisher: Stoelting Co.

CHILDREN'S DEPRESSION SCALE
Moshe Lange and Miriam Tisher

child, teen

Purpose: Measures depression in children ages 9-16 years. Identifies depressed children in need of further evaluation.

Description: 66 test items, 48 "depressive" and 18 "positive", measure six aspects of childhood depression: effective response, social problems, self-esteem, preoccupation with own sickness of death, guilt, and pleasure. Items are presented on cards which the child sorts into five boxes ranging from "very right" to "very wrong" according to how he feels the item applies to himself. A separate set of cards, identical in content but appropriately reworded is provided for use with parents, teachers, or other adults familiar with the child. Complete set of materials include: two sets of 66 cards, five boxes, record form, and manual. Examiner required. Not for group use.

AUSTRALIAN PUBLISHER

Untimed: Not available

Range: Ages 9-16

Scoring: Examiner evaluated

Cost: Contact publisher.

Publisher: The Australian Council for Educational Research Limited

CHILDREN'S INTERACTION MATRIX (CIM)
Wm. Fawcett Hill

child   grades 1-6

Purpose: Assesses suitability of grade school children for assignment to counseling group or other small groups. Useful in determining group composition.

Description: 64 item paper-pencil test that determines the child's overall acceptance of small groups, what they talk about, and their manner and degree of participation. Child reads statements describing a group situation and marks his reaction on the answer sheet scale. Examiner/self-administered. Suitable for use with groups.

Untimed: 20 minutes

Range: Gradeschool

Scoring: Hand key; computer scoring available

Cost: Monograph $4.00; manual $3.00; computer programs $2.00 each.

Publisher: William Fawcett Hill

COLUMBUS: PICTURE ANALYSIS OF GROWTH TOWARD MATURITY, THIRD EDITION
M.J. Langeveld

child, teen

Purpose: Measures a child's level of maturity and self reliance. Used as an aid to explore and analyze developmental processes of children ages 5-18.

Description: 24 item oral response projective test assessing social and emotional adjustment and maturity. Each test item consists of a picture card designed to elicit the child's perception of himself and his relationships with parents, peers, and educators. Manual includes: guides for interpreting the child's responses, detailed analyses of the test illustrations, and practical applications for testing and diagnostic purposes. Examiner required. Not for group use. Available in German

Untimed: Not available

Range: Ages 5-18

Scoring: Examiner evaluated

Cost: Complete kit (includes 24 picture cards and manual) $55.75.

Publisher: Karger

COOPERSMITH SELF-ESTEEM INVENTORIES (CSEI)
Stanley Coopersmith

all ages

Purpose: Measures attitudes toward the self in social, academic, and personal contexts. Used for individual diagnosis, classroom screening, prepost evaluations, and clinical and research studies.

Description: 58 or 25 item paper-pencil test of self- attitudes in four areas: Social Self-Peers, Home- Parents, School-Academic, and General-Self. Related to academic achievement and to personal satisfaction in school and adult life. Materials include three forms: the 58 item School Form, 25 item School Short Form, and 25 item Adult Form. Self-administered. Suitable for group use.

Untimed: 15 minutes

Range: Ages: School Form (8-15); Adult Form (15- adult)

Scoring: Hand key

Cost: 25 School Form test booklets $5.00; 25 Adult Form test $3.00; keys-adult $1.00, school $1.75; manual, no available price.

Publisher: Consulting Psychologists Press, Inc.

EDUCATION APPERCEPTION TEST
Refer to page 617.

ENVIRONMENTAL DEPRIVATION SCALE
Gerald R. Pascal and William O. Jenkins

all ages

Purpose: Clinical measurement of an individual's environmental deprivation. Predicts recidivism of offenders, mental hospital patients, and others who exhibit maladaption.

Description: 16 item paper-pencil test measuring environmental support/deprivation. Items include: employment, income, debts, parental relationship, education, and fear. Behavior interviewing techniques are used in face-to-face contact with subjects ages 10 through adult. Scoring is a forced-choice technique: "0" for no deprivation, "1" for deprivation. Useful to pinpoint areas requiring intervention. Materials include manual and test answer sheet. Juvenile version available. Examiner required.

Not for group use.

Untimed: 40 minutes

Range: Ages 10-adult

Scoring: Hand key

Cost: Complete kit (includes 25 test forms and manual) $35.00.

Publisher: Behavior Science Press

EYSENCK-WITHERS PERSON-ALITY INVENTORY
Sybil B.G. Eysenck

Purpose: Evaluates personality structure and adjustment of subnormal patients (those with IQ's between 50 and 80). Identifies individuals with tendencies toward mental illness or toward criminal or hostile behavior. Used for clinical diagnosis and screening.

Description: Multiple item, paper-pencil questionnaire measures important dimensions of a person's personality structure. Responses are scored on three scales: neuroticism, extraversion/introversion, and psychoticism. Norms are based on 400 subnormal patients having IQ's of between 50 and 80. Restricted to senior staff members of any recognized medical or educational institution, medical doctors, and BPS and APA members. Examiner required. Not suitable for group use. BRITISH PUBLISHER

Untimed: Not available

Range: IQ range 50-80

Scoring: Hand key; examiner evaluated

Cost: Specimen set £1.45; 20 questionnaires £1.50 plus VAT; scoring key 70p. plus VAT; manual 60p.

Publisher: Hodder & Stoughton

FIVE TASK TEST
Charlotte Buhler and Kathryn Mandeville

all ages

Purpose: Evaluates general aspects of personality and emotionality, manual skills, and possible brain damage in children age 8 or older, adolescents, and adults. Used in clinical studies, diagnosis, and psychological evaluations.

Description: Five simple, non-threatening performance tasks are used to examine and reveal general aspects of personality and manual skills which may indicate brain damage. The first part of the test requires the subject to cut out three designs (circle, heart, star) plus one design of the subjects choice. In the second part, the subject solves the problem presented by Terman's Ball and Field Task. Qualitative and quantitative scoring provided for cut-out designs. Ball and Field Task qualitatively classified into one of three solution groups: Normal, Borderline, or Problematic. Examiner required. Suitable for group use.

Untimed: 15 minutes

Range: Ages 8-adult

Scoring: Examiner evaluated

Cost: Complete kit (includes 1 set colored paper, 25 ball and field task sheets, 10 record booklets, manual) $15.40.

Publisher: Western Psychological Services

FORER STRUCTURED SEN-TENCE COMPLETION TEST
Bertram F. Forer

all ages

Purpose: Evaluates personality dynamics and interrelationships of individuals 13 years and older. Used for clinical evaluation.

Description: 100 item paper-pencil, sentence-completion test available in separate forms for men, women, adolescent boys, and adolescent girls. Test items are highly structured for wide coverage of attitude-value systems and to point out evasiveness, individual differences, and defense mechanisms. Objective interpretation assisted by checklist. Examiner required. Suitable for group use.

Untimed: 40-60 minutes

Range: Adolescent, adult

Scoring: Examiner evaluated

Cost: 25 tests $7.10; 25 checklists $7.10; manual $4.50 (specify adolescent or adult; male or female).

Publisher: Western Psychological Services

FOUR PICTURE TEST
D. J. VanLennep and R. Houwink

all ages

Purpose: Assesses personality. Used for diagnosis and individual counseling.

Description: Four item projective test of personality. Subject looks at four pictures for one minute. The pictures are then removed and the subject is asked to write a single story based on memory in which all four pictures are used. Materials include four picture cards and manual. Examiner required. Suitable for group use.
DUTCH PUBLISHER

Untimed: 30-45 minutes

Range: Ages 10 and older

Scoring: Examiner evaluated

Cost: Contact publisher.

Publisher: Martinus Nijhoff

FRANCK DRAWING COMPLETION TEST
K. Franck

all ages

Purpose: Evaluates the relationship of sex role to mental illness in both children and adults. Used as a supplementary clinical tool for research purposes.

Description: 36 item paper-pencil projective personality test consists of stimulus figures from which the examinee is required to make complete drawings. These are analyzed according to a number of criteria to give a quantitative score which may be placed on a masculinity-femininity continuum. The author's notes on some interpretations of the drawings are included in the manual to provide hypotheses for further research. Materials include: eight-page expendable test booklet, scoring sheet, manual, scoring key, and specimen set. Examiner required. Not for group use.
AUSTRALIAN PUBLISHER

Untimed: 15 minutes

Range: Child, adult

Scoring: Hand key, examiner evaluated

Cost: Contact publisher.

Publisher: The Australian Council for Educational Research Limited

---

FUNDAMENTAL INTERPERSONAL RELATIONS ORIENTATION-BEHAVIOR (FIRO-B)
Will Schutz

all ages

Purpose: Measures characteristic behavior toward other people; used in individual and group psychotherapy, executive development programs, and as a measure of compatibility in relationships.

Description: 54 item paper-pencil test measuring six dimensions of behavior toward others; expressed inclusion, expressed control, expressed affection, wanted inclusion, wanted control, and wanted affection. Optional materials include the FIRO-BC, a form developed for use with children. May be self-administered, although an examiner is recommended to assist in assessment/interpretation process. Suitable for group use.

Untimed: 20 minutes

Range: Child, adult

Scoring: Hand key

Cost: Sample set (includes tests and key) $1.00; 25 tests (specify FIRO-B or FIRO-BC) $3.25.

Publisher: Consulting Psychologists Press, Inc.

GRID TEST OF SCHIZO-PHRENIC THOUGHT DISORDER
D. Bannister and Fay Fransella

all ages

Purpose: Identifies schizophrenic thought disorder. Used for diagnosis of schizophrenia.

Description: Multiple item test of thought disorder based on ranking photographs of people on various dimensions. Eight photographs are presented to the subject. Subject is required to rank the pictures from most to least likely to be Kind. Subject then is asked to rank pictures for Stupid, Selfish, Sincere, Mean, Honest. Responses are scored on the basis of consistency and intensity. The relationship between the sorting categories, rather than the "correctness" of the sorts, is the most important evaluative factor. Materials include eight photographs. Examiner

required. Not suitable for group use. BRITISH PUBLISHER

Untimed: 20 minutes

Range: Child, adolescent, adult

Scoring: Examiner evaluated

Cost: Specimen set (pictures, manual, record sheet, analysis sheet) $9.60; set of pictures $4.80; 50 analysis sheets $8.40; manual $4.80.

Publisher: Psychological Test Publishers-Available from The Test Agency

GROUP PERSONALITY PROJECTIVE TEST (GPPT)
R.N. Cassel and T.C. Kahn

all ages

Purpose: Measures major personality characteristics. Used to screen potentially pathological personalities.

Description: 90 item paper-pencil test measuring seven aspects of personality including: tension, nurturance, withdrawal, neuroticism, affiliation, succorance, and total. Items are stick drawings accompanied by five descriptive or interpretative statements, one of which must be chosen by the subject as being most accurate. Self- administered. Suitable for group use.

Untimed: 40 minutes

Range: Ages 11 and older

Scoring: Hand key; examiner evaluated

Cost: Examiner's set (includes manual, 7 scoring keys, 12 test booklets, 100 answer and profile sheets) $27.00; 25 test booklets $25.00; 100 answer and profile sheets $13.00; scoring keys $4.00; manual $4.00.

Publisher: Psychological Test Specialists

THE HAND TEST, Revised 1983
Edwin E. Wagner

all ages

Purpose: Measures attitudes and action tendencies in individuals ages 6 to adult that are likely to be expressed in overt behavior, particularly aggression. Used for diagnosis and screening.

Description: Ten item oral response, projective test. The subject is asked to describe the activities portrayed by picture cards which present hands in different positions. Responses to the non- threatening task are scored on a variety of qualitative and quantitative indices to measure potential behavior toward persons and objects in the environment, pathological inefficiency and social withdrawal. Reading skill is not required. Scoring takes a few minutes. The manual presents normative data on over 120 normals and a variety of clinical groups. Validity and reliability data on over 2,600 evaluations. Examiner required. Not for group use.

Untimed: 10 minutes

Range: Ages 6-adult

Scoring: Examiner evaluated

Cost: Kit (10 scoring booklets, 1 set picture cards, manual) $35.00.

Publisher: Western Psychological Services

HARTMAN VALUE PROFILE (HVP)
Robert S. Hartman

all ages

Purpose: Assesses a person's capacity to value and indicates presence of emotional or existential problems. Used for mental health screening, personnel evaluation, research, educational program evaluation, assessment of special education class needs, and development of individual goals.

Description: Multiple item, paper-pencil or oral response inventory measuring a person's capacity to value in terms of both intellectual and emotional capacities. Scores are provided on the following scales: world concept-self concept potentials, cognitive-affective domain relationships, social- emotional handicaps, and interpersonal compatibility. Computer processing makes large scale screening possible, while in-depth analysis provides significant psychiatric and psychological insight. Available in three forms (regular, card, and pictorial) making testing possible with subjects from age five to adult. Self- administered; supervision required. Suitable for group use. Available in Spanish.

Untimed: 20-30 minutes

Range: Ages 5-adult

Scoring: Hand key; examiner evaluated; computer scoring available

Cost: 35 Profile forms $4.80; Profile card form $8.00; Profile pictorial form $10.00; 35 keys $2.50; manual $12.00.

Publisher: Research Concepts

HILL INTERACTION MATRIX-A (HIM-A)
William Fawcett Hill

teen, adult

Purpose: Assesses adolescents' and adults' suitability for assignment to counseling groups or other small groups. Useful in determining group composition and diagnosing problem members.

Description: 64 item paper-pencil test measures the person's overall acceptance of small groups, their discussion topic preferences and their participation tendencies. Subject reads statements describing a group situation and marks his reaction on the six-position answer sheet scale for each item. Hill Interaction B available with more sophisticated language. Examiner/self- administered. Suitable for use with groups. Available in German.

Untimed: 20 minutes

Range: Adolescent, adult

Scoring: Hand key; computer scoring available

Cost: Monograph $4.00; manual $3.00; computer programs $2.00 each.

Publisher: William Fawcett Hill

HILL INTERACTION MATRIX-B (HIM-B)
William Fawcett Hill

teen, adult

Purpose: Assesses suitability of adolescents and adults for assignment to counseling groups or other small groups. Useful in determining group composition.

Description: 64 item paper-pencil test measures the person's overall acceptance of small groups, their discussion topic preferences, and their style of participation. Subject reads statements describing a group situation and marks his reaction on the six-position answer sheet scale for each item. Hill Interaction A available with simpler language. Examiner/self-administered. Suitable for group use. Available in German.

Untimed: 20 minutes

Range: Adolescent, adult

Scoring: Hand key; computer scoring available

Cost: Monograph $4.00; manual $3.00; computer programs $2.00 each.

Publisher: William Fawcett Hill

HILL INTERACTION MATRIX-G (HIM-G)
William Fawcett Hill

teen, adult

Purpose: Assesses verbal interaction in counseling/encounter groups. Can be used to estimate current functioning of a group and to determine group development through repeated evaluation.

Description: 74 item paper-pencil test that measures the work mode, topic preference, risk-taking ration and therapist/member interaction ratio of a group. Subject observes, listens or views a tape recording, or reads a transcript of a group session and marks the amount of interaction for each item on a seven point scale. Examiner/self- administered. Suitable for group use.

Untimed: 20 minutes

Range: Adolescent, adult

Scoring: Hand key; computer scoring available

Cost: Monograph $4.00; manual $3.00; computer programs $2.00 each.

Publisher: William Fawcett Hill

HOLTZMAN INKBLOT TECHNIQUE (HIT)
W.H. Holtzman

all ages

Purpose: Assesses individual personality. Used for diagnosis and therapy planning.

Description: 45 item projective measure of personality. Items are inkblots, to which examinee gives one response each. Some inkblots are asymmetric and some are in one color other than black. An objective scoring system has been developed. Materials include two alternate and equivalent forms A and B for a total of 90 stimulus cards. Examiner required. Not suitable for group use.

Untimed: Not available

Range: Ages 5-adult

Scoring: Examiner evaluated

Cost: Complete set (includes 45 inkblots, 25 record forms with summary sheets, scoring guide), Form A $112.00; Form B $112.00; combined A,B $210.00; monograph $29.50.

Publisher: The Psychological Corporation

HOSTILITY AND DIRECTION OF HOSTILITY QUESTIONNAIRE (HDHQ)
A. T.M. Caine, G.A. Foulds and K. Hope

all ages

Purpose: Measures an individual's tendency toward aggressive or hostile reactions. Used for clinical and research purposes.

Description: Paper-pencil questionnaire measures a wide range of possible manifestations of aggression, hostility, or punitiveness. Two forms available, one for use with neurotic patients and one for use with psychotic patients. Restricted to senior staff members of any recognized medical or educational institution, medical doctors, and BPS and APA members. Examiner required. BRITISH PUBLISHER

Untimed: Not available

Range: Child, adolescent, adult

Scoring: Examiner evaluated

Cost: Specimen set, £2.35 plus VAT.

Publisher: Hodder & Stoughton

HOUSE-TREE-PERSON TECHNIQUE: REVISED MANUAL (H-T-P)
John N. Buck

all ages

Purpose: Assesses personality disturbances in individuals in psychotherapy, school and research settings. May be used with the culturally disadvantaged, educationally deprived, mentally retarded, and the aged.

Description: Multiple item, paper-pencil and oral response test which provides a projective study of personality. The test consists of two steps. The first is nonverbal, creative, and almost completely unstructured, requiring the subject to make a freehand drawing of a house, a tree, and a person. The second step is verbal, apperceptive, and more formally structured, giving the subject an opportunity to describe, define, and interpret other drawings and their respective environments. Quantitative scoring norms for adults are provided. Examiner required. Not for group use.

Untimed: 15-20 minutes

Range: Adolescent, adult

Scoring: Hand key; examiner evaluated

Cost: Manual $27.50

Publisher: Western Psychological Services

THE IES TEST
Lawrence A. Dombrose and Morton S. Slobin

all ages

Purpose: Assesses relative strengths of various personality forces. Used for individual diagnosis, clinical evaluation and research.

Description: 57 item, four subtest

projective measure of personality. Picture Title is a 12 item test in which the subject creates titles for pictures. Picture Story Completion requires the subject to select a cartoon to end each of thirteen incomplete cartoon stories. Photo-Analysis consists of nine men's photographs with two objectively scored questions about each. Arrow- Dot subtest is a set of 23 graphic problems requiring the subject to draw a line from an arrow to a dot goal without creating or crossing carriers. All responses are scored impulse (I), Ego (E), or superego (S). Use limited to psychologists, psychiatrists, and other professionals in the areas of clinical and research psychology. Examiner required. Not suitable for group use.

Untimed: 30 minutes

Range: Ages 10 and older

Scoring: Examiner evaluated

Cost: Complete kit (Picture Title cards, Picture Story Completion cards, Photo-Analysis cards, 25 Arrow-Dot test forms, 25 record forms, separate instruction cards, general manual, heavy storage boxes) $43.50; 100 record forms $10.00; 25 Arrow- Dot forms $9.00; manual $6.00.

Publisher: Psychological Test Specialists

INFORMATION TEST ON DRUGS AND DRUG ABUSE
Refer to page 271.

INTERPERSONAL BEHAVIOR SURVEY (IBS)
Paul A. Mauger, David R. Adkinson, Suzanne K. Loss, Gregory Firestone and J. David Hook

adult

Purpose: Distinguishes assertive and aggressive behaviors among adolescents and adults. Used for assertiveness training, marriage counseling, and a variety of clinical uses.

Description: 272 item paper-pencil test. The subject responds to present-tense statements written at the sixth-grade reading level to provide sensitivity to ongoing changes. The test is scored as follows: eight aggressiveness scales (including a scale which measures general aggressiveness over a broad range of behaviors, feelings, and attitudes), nine assertiveness scales (including one which is a general assertiveness scale over a broad range of behaviors), three validity scales, and three relationship scales (Conflict Avoidance, Dependency, and Shyness). Two shorter forms are available: a 38-item form provides a general sampling of behaviors and takes approximately ten minutes to complete; a 133-item form provides information on all sscales and takes approximately 30 minutes to complete. The Profile Form provides a display of raw scores, T-scores, and percentiles. Norms are provided for adult males, adult femaales, high school students, college students, and blacks. The manual presents validity and reliability data, interpretive guidelines, and number of illustrated cases. Self-administered. Suitable for group use.

Untimed: 10-45 minutes

Range: High School-adult

Scoring: Hand key

Cost: Complete kit (includes 5 booklets, 20 profile forms, 20 answer sheeets, key, manual) $24.75.

Publisher: Western Psychological Services

INTER-PERSON PERCEPTION TEST (IPPT)
F.K. Heussenstamm and R. Hoepfner

all ages

Purpose: Assesses individual and group status on interpersonal perception or social cognition. Used to evaluate changes accompanying sensitivity training, counseling, or psychotherapy. Also used to select personnel who must interact with people and for research purposes.

Description: 40 item paper-pencil, multiple-choice test in which the subject is asked to select one of four alternative facial photographs which expresses the same thoughts, feelings, and intentions as the given exemplar. The faces used for the 40 items are divided equally by sex and by ethnicity (10 each for Caucasions, Negroes, Mexican-Americans, and Oriental-Americans). Each item has been constructed with the aid of representatives of its respective age, sex, and ethnic group and has undergone intensive validation within samples of its representative group. With photographs of faces the only item content, the test is concerned primarily with abilities of social sensitivities, and is relatively free of verbal intelligence aspects. Form AC uses faces of children and youths. Form AA uses faces of adults. Reusable forms are provided with separate answer sheets. Examiner required. Self-administered. Suitable for group use.

Timed: 20 minutes

Range: Ages 7-76

Scoring: Hand key

Cost: Specimen set (specify form) $6.00; 35 tests (Form AA or AC) $30.00; 35 answer sheets (Form AA or AC) $3.00; scoring stencil (Form AA or AC) $2.50; manual $3.00.

Publisher: Monitor

THE JESNESS INVENTORY
Carl F. Jesness

child, teen

Purpose: Evaluates personality disorders predictive of a social tendencies. Used to classify disturbed children and adolescents for treatment.

Description: 155 item paper-pencil test of 11 personality characteristics: social maladjustment, value orientation, immaturity, autism, alienation, manifest aggression, withdrawal, social anxiety, repression, denial, and asocial. Distinguishes delinquents from non-delinquents. Administration requires either test booklets or tape recorder and tape. Examiner/self-administered.

Untimed: 20-30 minutes

Range: Ages 8-18

Scoring: Hand key

Cost: Specimen set (no key) $3.25; manual $3.00; key $5.50; cassette tapes $10.00.

Publisher: Consulting Psychologists Press, Inc.

LAW ENCOUNTER SEVERITY SCALE (LESS)
A.D. Witherspoon, E.K. deValera and W.O. Jenkins

all ages

Purpose: Assesses the severity of an individual's law encounter. Used for counseling purposes and follow-up studies with parolees and probationers.

Description: 38 item oral response test measures any criminal offense in terms of frequency, variety, severity, and consequences. Items are classified in five groups, ranging from no encounter to those felony offenses for which the offender is sentenced to prison for more than one year. Data is obtained through face-to-face interviews, with the examiner using behavioral interviewing techniques. Can be used as a criterion for criminal acts. Examiner required. Not for group use.

Untimed: 30 minutes

Range: Ages 10-adult

Scoring: Hand key

Cost: Complete kit (includes 25 test forms and manual) $25.00.

Publisher: Behavior Science Press

LOUISVILLE BEHAVIOR CHECKLIST
Lovick C. Miller

child, teen

Purpose: Measures the entire range of social and emotional behaviors indicative of psychopathological disorders in children and adolescents. Used as an intake screening device.

Description: 164 item paper-pencil, true-false inventory. It helps parents record their children's behavior by asking questions which provide relevant information on a number of interpretive scales. The three available forms for three different age groups and the scales measured by each form are listed below. Scale measures for Form E1 (Ages 4- 6 years) are Infantile Aggression, Hyperactivity, Antisocial Behavior, Aggression, Social Withdrawal, Sensitivity, Fear, Inhibition, Intellectual Deficit, Immaturity, Cognitive Disability, Normal Irritability, Prosocial Deficit, Rare Deviance, Neurotic Behavior, Psychotic Behavior, Somatic Behavior, Sexual Behavior, School Disturbance Predictor and Severity Level. Scale measures for Form E2 (Ages 7-12) are Infantile Aggression, Hyperactivity, Antisocial Behavior, Aggression, Social Withdrawal, Sensitivity, Fear, Inhibition, Academic Disability, Immaturity, Learning Dis-

ability, Normal Irritability, Prosocial Deficit, Rare Deviance, Neurotic Behavior, Psychotic Behavior, Somatic Behavior, Sexual Behavior, and Severity Level. Scales measures for Form E3 (Ages 13-17 years) are Egocentric- Explosive, Destructive-Assaultive, Social Delinquency, Adolescent Turmoil, Apathetic Isolation, Neuroticism, Dependent-Inhibited, Academic Disability, Neurological or Psychotic Abnormality, General Pathology, Longitudinal, Severity Level, and Total Pathology. Standardized on multi-ethnic groups representative of urban Mid-American students. Forms E1 and E2 have general and clinical norms, Form E3 has only clinical norms. Norms are provided by sex and age for Form E1, and by sex only for Forms E2 and E3. the manual provides a number of case studies. Examiner required.

Untimed: 20-30 minutes

Range: Ages 4-17

Scoring: Hand key; computer scoring available

Cost: Complete for all ages $79.20; kit, form E1 ages 4-6, form E2 ages 7-12, form E3 ages 13-17, specify form $27.50, (each kit includes reusable questionnaires, answer-profile sheets, key, manual) $27.50.

Publisher: Western Psychological Services

MALADAPTED BEHAVIOR RECORD (MBR)
W.O. Jenkins, A.D. Witherspoon, E.D. de Valera, and John M. McKees

all ages

Purpose: Assesses behavioral maladaption of individuals age 10 years and older and predicts the likelihood of habitual relapse of maladaptive individuals and groups. Used for counseling purposes with offender groups and drug and alcoohol abuse cases, as well as for predicting parole success.

Description: 16 item oral response test measures response categories such as: working conditions, amount of income, employer interactions, work attendance, alcohol use, gambliing, money management, fighting, psychological adjustment, etc. Data is obtained through face-to-face interviews, with examiner using behavioral interviewing techniques. Each item is scored as "maladaption" or "no maladaption." Juvenile version available. Examiner required. Not for group use.

Untimed: 40 minutes

Range: Ages 10-adult

Scoring: Hand key

Cost: Complete kit (includes 25 test forms and manual) $35.00.

Publisher: Behavior Science Press

MODES OF EXISTENCE TEST
S. Roy Heath

teen, adult

Purpose: Assesses personality in terms of temperament and emotional and intellectual maturity. Used for student and employee counseling when temperament and maturity are important factors.

Description: 11 item paper-pencil test measuring a person's self-concept of his personality. The test items consist of personality descriptions from which the subject is asked to select the three which most closely approximate the way he sees himself. The subject then ranks each of the three selected descriptions on a ladder chart according to how closely each represents his sense of self. The subject then selects and records which of the 11 personality descriptions are least like his sense of self. The examiner scores the responses according to three dimensions of temperament

related to Heath's model of ego-functioning (group cooperative, group competitive, or group independent) and three levels of intellectual and emotional maturity (high, medium, and low). Not applicable for those below 12 years of age; sixth-grade reading level required. Self-administered. Suitable for group.

Untimed: 20 minutes.

Range: Ages 12-adult

Scoring: Examiner evaluated

Cost: $2.00 per copy.

Publisher: S. Roy Heath, Ph.D.

MUTUALLY RESPONSIBLE FACILITATION INVENTORY (MRFI)
Thomas D. Gnagey

teen, adult

Purpose: Guides analysis of how the individual helps others and provides assistance in planning personal goals and activities to handle such things as teacher-pupil problems, family friction and business relationships.

Description: 25 item paper-pencil test measuring the following categories of behavior: being needed, ability to "play by the rules", seeking positive relationships, involvement with others, giving and accepting love. The individual uses the outline provided to analyze how he assists others to grow in each of the categories and to plan an approach to further personal growth. Self-administered. Suitable for group use.

Untimed: 30 minutes

Range: Ages 12-adult

Scoring: Examiner evaluated

Cost: Instructions and 20 inventory forms $3.75; 100 additional forms $10.00.

Publisher: Facilitation House

MY SELF CHECK LIST (MSCL)
Robert E. Valett

child, teen grades 1-12

Purpose: Determines self-esteem levels of primary and secondary school students. Used by counselors and educators to assess possible personal problems.

Description: 40 item, paper-pencil self-concept inventory in a "yes-no-not sure" format. There are ten incomplete sentences and five written "strengths and weakness" sections covering self-concept in personal, social, school, and family settings. Can be used as an informal and non-threatening vehicle for individual or group clinical and school discussions. Examiner required. Suitable for group use. Available in Spanish.

Untimed: 20 minutes

Range: Grades Primary-secondary levels

Scoring: Examiner evaluated

Cost: 10 booklets and manual $4.95.

Publisher: Pitman Learning, Inc.

PERSONAL AJUSTMENT INVENTORY
Carl Rogers

child

Purpose: Measures personality adjustment of children ages 9-13 years. Diagnoses type and degree of emotional disturbance and the child's methods of dealing with his problems.

Description: Multiple item, paper-pencil, multiple-choice test requires the child to respond to questions which might be asked by any skilled interviewer, indicating feelings about self, peers, and family. Four diagnostic scores are obtained: personal inferiority, social maladjustment, family maladjustment, and daydreaming. Materials include: separate expendable test booklets for boys and girls, manual, and specimen set. Examiner required. Suitable for group use.

Untimed: 40-50 minutes

Range: Ages 9-13

Scoring: Examiner evaluated

Cost: Contact publisher.

Publisher: Associated Press-distributed by The Australian Council for Educational Research Limited

PERSONALITY DESCRIPTIONS
Union College Character Research Project

child, teen grades PRE-12

Purpose: Determines an individual's general personality characteristics as well as those pertaining to religious orientation. Used for observing spiritual and character growth.

Description: Multiple item, paper-pencil projective self- description test of nine personality factors: outstanding characteristics, activities and interests, growing up, coaching and school, social relationships, emotional security and self- confidence, imagination and curiosity, community and vocational interests, philosophy of life (for junior and senior high), and home and family. Designed for eight age levels, male or female. Distinctive personality traits are obtained by modification process from age-level norms. Materials include age-level forms and instructions. May be administered individually or to groups. Examiner evaluated. Suitable for group use.

Untimed: 20-30 minutes

Range: Grades Nursery-senior high

Scoring: Examiner evaluated

Cost: Each form $.25 (specify age and sex); sample set of 16 $3.00.

Publisher: Union College Character Research Project

PERSONALITY RESEARCH FORM (PRF)
Douglas N. Jackson

all ages

Purpose: Assesses personality traits relevant to the functioning of an individual in a variety of situations. Used in self-improvement courses, guidance centers, and for personnel selection.

Description: Multiple item, paper-pencil, true-false test in five forms. Forms AA and BB contain 440 items covering 22 areas of normal functioning. Form E has 352 items in 22 scales. Forms A and B have 300 items in 15 scales. The 22 scales are: Abasement, Achievement, Affiliation, Aggression, Autonomy, Change, Cognitive Structure, Defendance, Dominance, Endurance, Exhibition, Harm-Avoidance, Impulsivity, Nurturance, Order, Play, Sentience, Social Recognition, Succorance, Understanding, Infrequency, and Desirability. A 90-minute cassette tape with simplified wording is available for use with those who have limited verbal skills or sight or reading problems. Materials include a manual, reusable test booklet, answer sheets, profiles, scoring template, cassette tape and tape mmanual. Must be administered by certified psychologist. Suitable for group use. Form E available in French.

Timed: Form E, 1 hour; Forms A & B, 45 minutes; Forms AA & BB, 1¼ hours; plus cassette tape, 90 minutes

Range: Grades 6-adult

Scoring: Hand key

Cost: Specimen set $25.00.

Publisher: Research Psychologists Press, Inc.

PICTURE WORLD TEST
Charlotte Buhler and Morse P. Manson

all ages

Purpose: Evaluates the manner in which an individual views his or her relationship to the rest of the world. Used by educators and counselors to gain insights into defenses, escapes, social reactions, and adjustments.

Description: Nonverbal, projective test in which the subject is given 12 pictures of common scenes such as farms, slums, churches, universities, and factories, which are to be stuck on a large sheet of drawing paper in any arrangement. The subject then completes his or her "world" by drawing in all connecting and related items such as roads, people, etc. This projective task explores reactions to life and world, people, groups, situations, institutions, and authority. Examiner required. Not for group use.

Untimed: 15-20 minutes

Range: Ages 6-adult

Scoring: Examiner evaluated

Cost: Complete kit (includes 1 set of scenes, 10 protocol booklets, manual) $25.80.

Publisher: Western Psychological Services

PIKUNAS GRAPHOSCOPIC SCALE (PGS)
Justin Pikunas

all ages

Purpose: Assesses an individual's cognitive development, emotionality and adjustment. Used by clinical and school psychologists to build rapport, test deficits and evaluate various forms of psychopathology.

Description: Nonverbal test using a single sheet containing ten framed, partial drawings containing perceptual cues in various colors. The subject is asked to add to the drawings with the results providing an indication of self-expressive balance, intelligence, creativity, emotional disturbance, and some forms of psychopathology. Materials include the test, graphic scale, and manual. Examiner required. Suitable for group use.

Untimed: PGSI (K to 8th grade), 20 minutes; PGSII (9th grade to adult), 30 minutes

Range: Child, adolescent, adult

Scoring: Examiner evaluated

Cost: Specimen set (specify PGSI or II) $6.75.

Publisher: University Press of America

POLITTE SENTENCE COMPLETION TEST (PSCT)
Refer to page 638.

THE Q-TAGS TEST OF PERSONALITY
Arthur G. Storey and Louis I. Masson

all ages

Purpose: Measures individual personality traits. Used for counseling, self-examination and research.

Description: 54 card test of five factors of personality: assertive, effective, hostile, reverie, and social. Subjects are required to sort cards and in so doing are able to describe themselves as they are and as they wish to be. Developed with norms for age, grade, occupation, and sex based on a wide range of subjects. Materials include cards, a paradigm, sorting instructions, and manual. Self-administered. Suitable for group use.
CANADIAN PUBLISHER

Untimed: 30 minutes

Range: Ages 6 and older

Scoring: Examiner evaluated

Cost: Specimen set (includes 4 series of 54 tags, 4 paper boards, manual, list of directions, 25 answer sheets) $4.00; 25 answer sheets $10.00.

Publisher: Institute of Psychological Research, Inc.

ROHDE SENTENCE COMPLETIONS
Amanda R. Rohde

all ages

Purpose: Evaluates basic drives and feelings of individuals with a mental age of 10 years and older. Used for clinical studies, diagnosis, and psychological evaluation.

Description: 65 item paper-pencil test consisting of sentence stems eliciting information from a broad range of potential behavioral reaction. Examiner required. Suitable for group use.

Untimed: 40 minutes

Range: Ages 10-adult

Scoring: Examiner evaluated

Cost: 25 tests $7.10.

Publisher: Western Psychological Services

ROKEACH VALUE SURVEY
Milton Rokeach

all ages

Purpose: Measures personal values and provides objective feedback about them in comparison with reference group. Used for value therapy, values clarification and to change socially undesirable values.

Description: 36 item ranking test requiring minimum literacy. Values are printed on gummed labels which respondent arranges in rank order. Test assesses values which are divided into terminal ("comfortable life" and "world peace") and behavioral ("loving" and "ambition"). Self-administered. Suitable for group use. Translated in Spanish, French, German, Czech, Japanese, Vietnamese, Russian, Hungarian, Swedish, Chinese, Lithuanian, Hebrew.

Untimed: 15 minutes

Range: Ages 11-adult

Scoring: Examiner evaluated; can be computer scored.

Cost: Test $.50-$1.00 (depending on quantity).

Publisher: Halgren Tests

RORSCHACH PSYCHODIAGNOSTIC TEST
Hermann Rorschach

all ages

Purpose: Evaluates personality through projective technique. Used in clinical evaluation.

Description: Ten card oral response projective personality test. The subject is asked to interpret what he sees in ten inkblots, based on the assumption that the individual's perceptions and associations are selected and organized in terms of his motivations, impulses, and other underlying aspects of personality. Extensive scoring systems have been developed. Although many variations are in use, this entry refers only to the Psychodiagnostic Plates first published in 1921. Materials include: inquiry charts, tabulation sheets, and set of 10 inkblots. Set of 10 Kodaslides of the inkblots may be imported on request. Trained examiner required.

Untimed: Not available

Range: Ages 3 and older

Scoring: Examiner evaluated

Cost: Contact publisher.

Publisher: Hans Huber-distributed by Grune & Stratton (U.S.A.)

ROSENZWEIG PICTURE-FRUSTRATION STUDY (P-F)
Saul Rosenzweig

all ages

Purpose: Measures aggression in personality. Used in clinical counseling.

Description: Eight page leaflet series, paper-pencil test of an individual's response patterns to everyday frustration or stress. Consists of 24 cartoon pictures, each depicting two persons in a frustrating situation, one being the frustrator. Requires the subject to write or tell the first response that comes to mind for the anonymous frustrated person in the second picture. Measures three types of aggression (obstacle-dominance, ego-defense, and need-persistence), and three directions of aggression (extraggression, imaggression and intraggression). Nine factors, derived by combining the types and directions of aggression, constitute the score. For optimal scoring, individual administration is followed by inquiry. Standardization includes scoring and retest reliabilities with correlations of 65-85 percent agreement or better. Materials consist of examination blanks (25 or 100), scoring blanks (25 or 100), basic manual and supplement for the age level desired (4-12, 12-18, and 18 or over).

Timed: 15 minutes

Range: Ages 4-adult

Scoring: Hand key

Cost: 25 examination blanks $12.50; 100-$36.00; 25 scoring blanks $3.00; 100-$8.00; basic manual $6.00; supplement $14.50.

Publisher: Dr. Saul Rosenzweig

SELF-PERCEPTION INVENTORY
William T. Martin

teen, adult

Purpose: Evaluates an individual's personality and measures general level of adjustment. Used for screening procedures clinical research on personality, and evaluation of therapeutic progress.

Description: 200 item paper-pencil true-false test of personality. Test items consist of symptomatic and descriptive statements which are grouped according to the following syndromes: consistency, self actualization, supervision, rigidity-dogmatism, authoritarianism, anxiety, depression, and paranoia. Subscale scores are provided for each syndrome. General Adjustment and General Maladjustment Scores are then derived from these subscales to provide an index of personality patterning. Suitable for individual's 12 years and older with fifth-grade reading ability. Examiner required. Suitable for group use.

Untimed: 20-35 minutes

Range: Ages 12 and over

Scoring: Hand key

Cost: Specimen set (includes manual) $7.25; examiner's manual (includes 10 tests, 25 answer sheets, 25 profile sheets, keys, and manual) $31.00; 25 tests $22.00; 100-$86.00; 25 answer and 25 profile sheets $5.50 each; keys $7.25; manual $5.50.

Publisher: Psychologists and Educators, Inc.

STROOP COLOR AND WORD TEST
Charles Golden

all ages   grades 2-UP

Purpose: Evaluates personality, cognition, stress response, psychiatric disorders, and other psychological phenomena. Used to differentiate normal subject and non-brain damaged psychiatric subjects from brain damaged subjects.

Description: Multiple item response test of an individual's ability to separate word and color stimuli and react to them independently. The test consists of three pages: a Word Page containing color words printed in black ink; a Color Page with a series of X's printed in colored inks; and a Word-Color page on which the words on the first page are printed in the colors of the second page except that the word and color do not match. The subject is given all three pages and asked to read the Word Page. He is then asked to name the colors of the X's on the Color Page. Then he must name the color of the ink in which the words on the Word- Color Page are printed, ignoring the semantic meaning of the words. The test requires only a second grade reading level. Examiner required. Not for group use.

Timed: 5 minutes

Range: Grades 2 and up

Scoring: Examiner evaluated

Cost: Complete kit (includes manual, 25 sets of 3 sheets) $42.50.

Publisher: Stoelting Co.

SYMBOL ELABORATION TEST (S.E.T.)
Johanna Krout Tabin

all ages

Purpose: Assesses personality. Used for individual evaluation and cross-cultural research.

Description: 11 item projective measure of personality. Items are simple line figures. Subjects use each line figure as a beginning stimulus for their own drawings, then answer seven brief questions aimed at eliciting feelings and associations. Factors measured include: concepts of maleness and femaleness; views of interactions between same- sex, opposite sex, and mixed-groups; handling of aggression; diffuse and sexual anxiety; and self- concept. Examiner required. Suitable for group use.

Untimed: 30 minutes

Range: All ages

Scoring: Examiner evaluated

Cost: Test booklet $1.15; complete manual (includes standardization) $15.00, guide $6.50.

Publisher: Johanna Krout Tabin, Ph.D.

TENNESSEE SELF CONCEPT SCALE
William H. Fitts

teen, adult

Purpose: Measures an individual's self-concept in terms of identity, feelings, and behavior. Used for a wide range of clinical and educational applications.

Description: 100 item paper-pencil test consisting of self- descriptive statements which subjects use to rate themselves on a scale from 1 (completely false) to 5 (completely true). Can be used with persons 12 years or older who have at least a sixth-grade reading level, whether they are psychologically disturbed or healthy. Two forms are available. Both forms use the same test booklet and procedures, with different answer-profile sheets. The Counseling Form (Form C) is appropriate if the results are to be used directly with the subject and provides a number of measures, including response defensiveness, a total score, and self- concept scales that reflect "What I Am," "How I Feel," and "What I Do," the scales include: Identify, Self Satisfaction,

Behavior, Physical Self, Moral-Ethical Self, Personal Self, Family Self, and Social Self. It does not require scoring keys. The Clinical and Research Form (Form C & R) yields additional measures which might be intimidating to the subject, including the following six empirical scales (special scoring keys are required): Defensive Position, General Maladjustment, Psychosis, Personality Disorder, Neurosis, and Personality Integration. Self-administered. Suitable for group use.

Untimed: 10-20 minutes

Range: Ages 12-adult

Scoring: Hand key

Cost: Complete kit (includes 10 reusable test booklets, 20 Form C answer-profile sheets, manual) $12.90.

Publisher: Western Psychological Services

THEMATIC APPERCEPTION TEST (TAT-Z)-1976

adult

Purpose: Measures personality characteristics. Used for assessment and diagnosis of abnormal personality.

Description: Ten card projective measure of personality. It uses the method of choosing cards which reveal, ter alia, the level of westernization and adjustment to western demands. Subject chooses pictures which relate to the following ten areas: degree and direction of acculturation, family relationships, father-son relationship, mother-son relationship, attitude toward black authority, attitude toward white authority, self-concept, heterosexual relationships, social relationships, and handling of aggression. Examiner required. Not suitable for group use. Publisher notes that this test is "normed on Blacks only."
SOUTH AFRICAN PUBLISHER

Untimed: 2 hours

Range: For adults only

Scoring: Hand key; examiner evaluated

Cost: (In Rands) test album 18,80; answer book 0,30; manual 8,90; interpretation form 0,20; 10 shortened answer books 3,00 (orders from outside The RSA will be dealt with on merit).

Publisher: Human Sciences Research Council

THEMES CONCERNING BLACKS (TCB)
Robert L. Williams

all ages   grades PRE-UP

Purpose: Assesses culturally specific attitudes of black people. Used as a personality or diagnostic test.

Description: 20 item oral response projective test assessing the feelings and attitudes of black Americans to their ethnic experience in American society. Each test item consists of a picture card depicting some facet of the black experience. The subject is asked to elaborate on each card. Must be administered by a trained psychologist for diagnostic purposes. May be administered to groups with slides and projector.

Untimed: 30 minutes

Range: Grades Preschool-adult

Scoring: Examiner evaluated

Cost: Complete (includes 20 cards and manual) $30.00.

Publisher: Robert L. Williams & Associates, Inc.

TWITCHELL-ALLEN THREE DIMENSIONAL PERSONALITY TEST (T-A 3-DPT)
Doris Twitchell Allen

all ages

Purpose: Evaluates general and specific personality structure for adults and children ages 3 to 100 years. Useful for clinical diagnosis and research on personality and as guides for psychotherapy.

Description: Four action and oral response tests provide a projective evaluation of an individual's personality. Test materials consist of 28 small objects, all of an ambiguous or abstract nature (some of which are suggestive of human forms). The four subtests are: Pre-Naming Story, in which the subject is asked to choose one or more of the objects and make up a story and dramatize with the pieces as he tells it; Naming Test, in which the subject is asked to name 14 designated objects; Post-Naming Story, which allows the subject to tell a second story, since now there is more familiarity with the pieces; the Fein Testing of Limits (for intra familial relations), in which the examiner arranges 3 designated objects in a designated pattern (according to test directions) and asks the subject to tell a story about the examiner's chose pieces. The following types of responses are recorded by the examiner: gestures, general behavior, constructions with the test forms, vocalizations (everything the subject says, not just the stories and names), sequence, and tiem. May be administered to the blind with only minor procedural adaptations. Examiner required. Not for group use. Shorter form available.

Untimed: 1 hour

Range: Ages 3 and over

Scoring: Examiner evaluated

Cost: Complete set (includes instructions and recording forms) $60.00.

Publisher: Doris Twitchell Allen, Ph.D.

VISUAL-VERBAL TEST, 1981 EDITION
Marvin J. Feldman and James Drasgrow

Purpose: Measures conceptual thinking and abstraction in schizophrenics. Used for diagnosis and assessment related to therapy.

Description: 42 item oral response test measuring conceptual deviancy in schizophrenic patients. Each item consists of a stimulus card depicting four items. The examinee is required to formulate two different concepts for each card using three of the four items. The test items are based upon simple concepts such as color, form, size, structural similarities, naming, and position. Normative data provided for normals, schizophrenics and special groups. Examiner required. Not for group use.

Untimed: 30-40 minutes

Range: Schizophrenic patients

Scoring: Hand key

Cost: Kit (set of test cards, 10 protocol booklets, manual) $21.50.

Publisher: Western Psychological Services

WAHLER SELF-DESCRIPTION INVENTORY
H.J. Wahler

adult

Purpose: Measures the extent to which individuals emphasize their favorable and unfavorable characteristics in self-evaluations. Used to identify those who may be "overcompensating" for real or imagined inadequacies, or who have poor self-images.

Description: 66 item paper-pencil test. Each test item is a descriptive statement which the subjects use to rate themselves on a nine-point scale from "Not at all like me," to "Beyond question very much like me." Scoring provides information about defensiveness, maladjustment, potential for change, and actual change during treatment. Standardized cutoff scores are provided to identify possible deviations from normal populations. Sixth-grade reading level required. Self-administered. Suitable for group use.

Untimed: 10-15 minutes

Range: Adult

Scoring: Hand key

Cost: Complete kit (includes 50 inventory sheets, manual, key) $11.20.

Publisher: Western Psychological Services

WELSH FIGURE PREFERENCE TEST (WFPT)
George S. Welsh

all ages

Purpose: Evaluates individual personality traits through reactions to figures. Used for counseling and research.

Description: 400 item paper-pencil test of preference for types of black-and-white figures. Subject responds by indicating "likes" or "dislikes" for each figure. Scales include Conformity, Male- Female, Neuropsychiatric, Consensus, Origence, Intellectence, Barron-Welsh Original Art Scale, Revised Art Scale, Repression, Anxiety, Children, Movement, Figure-Ground Reversal, Sex Symbol, and several measuring preferences for specific kindss of geometric figures. All scales need not be scored. Barron-Welsh Art Scale (86 items) is available separately. Examiner required. Suitable for group use.

Untimed: 50 minutes

Range: Ages 6-adult

Scoring: Must make own stencils

Cost: Experimental kit (includes 5 test booklets, 25 answer sheets, manual) $19.50; 10 reusable test booklets $22.75; 50 handscorable answer sheets $4.50.

Publisher: Consulting Psychologists Press, Inc.

WIDE RANGE INTELLIGENCE-PERSONALITY TEST (WRIPT)
Joseph F. Jastak

all ages

Purpose: Measures general mental ability and personality structure. Used for clinical diagnosis and research relating personality to intelligence, academic achievement, and vocational aptitudes and performances.

Description: Ten paper-pencil subtests measuring verbal, numerical, pictorial, spatial, social competency, and other abilities. Provides a ''g'' (global) or intelligence score, and identifies the extent to which this general factor influences behavior. Also provides cluster (lobal) scores for language, reality set, motivation, and psychomotor skills. Offers several areas of special effectiveness: measuring mental abilities through a wide range of abilities; studying personality make-up; measuring changes in specific personality traits due to age, health, education, or other factors; demonstrating the role of group (lobal) factors in schooling, job selection, and social adjustment; studying variances contributing to the diagnosis of mental retardation, mental illness, learning disabilities, and anti-social and asocial behavior; showing how cultural neglect or environmental limits influence a person's over-all functioning; and many research

applications. Examiner Required. Suitable for group use. Limited to Educational/Psychological professionals.

Timed: 50 minutes

Range: Ages 9 years 6 months-adult

Scoring: Hand key

Cost: Manual $19.55; 25 test forms $15.90; scoring stencil $11.90.

Publisher: Jastak Assessment System

WILSON-PATTERSON ATTITUDE INVENTORY
Glenn D. Wilson

teen, adult

Purpose: Assesses attitudes, including general conservatism. Used for attitude research.

Description: Paper-pencil test of attitudes. Provides a measure of general conservatism. Additional factors include two orthogonal principal component factors: conservatism-liberalism and realism- idealism; and four oblique primary factors: militarism-punitiveness, anti-hedonism, ethnocentrism-intolerance, religion-puritanism. Examiner required. Suitable for group use.
BRITISH PUBLISHER

Untimed: 15 minutes

Range: Ages 12 and up

Scoring: Hand key

Cost: Specimen set £6.70; 25 questionnaires £2.15; scoring keys £1.70; manual £5.05 (payment in sterling for all overseas orders).

Publisher: NFER-Nelson Publishing Company

Research

Ai3Q MEASURE OF OBSESSIONAL OR ANAL CHARACTER
Refer to page 92.

ALTERNATE USES (AU)
Paul R. Christensen, J.P. Guilford, Philip R. Merrifield and Robert C. Wilson

teen, adult   grades 7-UP

Purpose: Measures ability to produce spontaneously ideas in response to objects or other ideas. Useful for research and experiment.

Description: Multiple item, paperpencil test measuring spontaneous flexibility, defined as the ability to produce a variety of class ideas in connection with an object or other unit of thought. This ability is also known as the "divergent production of semantic classes." Forms B and C are equivalent. Norms are provided for sixth-grade, ninthgrade, and college students. Restricted to A.P.A. members. Examiner required. Suitable for group use.

Timed: 12 minutes

Range: Junior high school-adult

Scoring: Examiner evaluated

Cost: Manual $3.50; 25 tests $7.00; scoring guide $.75.

Publisher: Sheridan Psychological Services, Inc.

ASSOCIATIONAL FLUENCY (AF)
Paul R. Christensen and J.P. Guilford

teen, adult   grades 7-UP

Purpose: Measures the ability to produce spontaneously meaningful words. Useful in research and experimental applications.

Description: Multiple item, paperpencil test measures the factor of "divergent production of semantic relations," which is defined as the ability to produce efficiently ideas bearing prescribed relations to other ideas or to produce alternate relations. Form A employs adjectives while Form B employs verbs (the forms are equivalent). In each case, the task is to list as many words as possible that bear a specified meaningful relation to the stimulus words. Instructions are included in the manual. Norms are provided for ninth-grade and college students. Restricted to A.P.A. members. Examiner required. Suitable for group use.

Timed: 4 minutes

Range: Junior high school-adult

Scoring: Examiner evaluated

Cost: 25 testts $7.00; scoring guide $.75.

Publisher: Sheridan Psychological Services, Inc.

BAY AREA FUNCTIONAL PERFORMANCE EVALUATION-RESEARCH EDITION (BaFPE)
Judith S. Bloomer and Susan K. Williams

Purpose: Assesses abilities needed by patient to perform certain concrete intellectual functions satisfactorily in daily life. Used for counseling, and research on treatment and training programs in occupational therapy and special education.

Description: Two category paper-pencil observation test of the subject's general ability to act on the environment in goal-directed ways and to relate to other people. The examination consists of two major subtests: Task Oriented Assessment (TOA) and Social

Interaction Scale (SIS). The TOA is a five-task measuring general ability to be goal- directed. The five tasks, (sorting sheets, bank deposit slip, house floor plan, block design, and draw-a-person), measure ten functional components of behavior: paraphrase, productive decision- making, motivation, organization of time and materials, mastery and self-esteem, frustration tolerance, attention span, ability to abstract, verbal or behavioral evidence of thought or mood disorder, and ability to follow instructions leading to correct task completion. Examiner rates subject's performance on each task. Materials include a demographic data sheet.

The SIS is a behavioral rating scale of general ability to relate appropriately to other people within the environment. Seven basic categories of social interaction are measured: response to authority figures, verbal communication, psychomotor behavior, independence/dependence, socially appropriate behavior, ability to work with peers, and participation in group or program activities. Each category rated on a one to five scale. SIS is rated by a clinician who observes the client in a daily social situation. The TOA is administered individually by an examiner.

Timed: 40-60 minutes per client

Range: Psychiatric or neurological patients, mentally retarded adults

Scoring: Hand key

Cost: Complete kit (includes reusable items, expendable forms for testing 25 subjects, manual) $75.00.

Publisher: Consulting Psychologists Press, Inc.

BEM SEX-ROLE INVENTORY (BSRI)
Refer to page 93.

CARTOON PREDICTIONS (SICP)
Maureen O'Sullivan and J.P. Guilford

teen, adult   grades 10-UP

Purpose: Measures ability to understand a sequence of behaviors and predict the next step in the sequence. Used in research.

Description: Multiple item, paper-pencil, multiple-choice test of an individual's cognition of behavioral implications--the ability to predict what is most likely to happen next in a sequence of behaviors. Each test item shows a single cartoon-like scene with characters in a readily grasped situation. The subject selects from among the alternative pictures the one that shows what is most likely to happen next in terms of the psychological states of the persons concerned. Norms are provided for tenth-grade and college students. Restricted to A.P.A. members. Examiner required. Suitable for group use.

Timed: 8 minutes

Range: High school-adult

Scoring: Hand key

Cost: 25 tests $14.00; manual $3.50; 25 answer sheets $3.50; scoring key $2.00.

Publisher: Sheridan Psychological Services, Inc.

CALIFORNIA CHILD Q-SET
Refer to page 81.

CALIFORNIA Q-SORT DECK
Refer to page 95.

CHILDREN'S EMBEDDED FIGURES TEST (CEFT)
Stephen A. Karp and Norma Konstadt

child

Purpose: Assesses cognitive style in perceptual tasks; useful for measuring field dependence in studies of psychological differentiation.

Description: 25 item verbal-manual test of perceptual processes including field dependence-independence. Performance related to analytic ability, social behavior, and body concept. Materials include cut-out models of two forms, 38 plates for the 25 items and 13 practice items, clear plastic envelopes to protect plates, and a star rubber stamp. Washable-ink stamp pad required. Subject finds simple forms in complex figures and stamps correct choice. Examiner required. Not suitable for group use.

Untimed: Open ended

Range: Ages 5-12

Scoring: Examiner evaluated

Cost: Test kit (includes 50 record sheets and all test materials) $17.50.

Publisher: Consulting Psychologists Press, Inc.

CHILDREN'S SCALE OF SOCIAL ATTITUDES
Refer to page 84.

COMMUNITY-ORIENTED PROGRAMS ENVIRONMENT SCALE (COPES)
Rudolf H. Moos

adult

Purpose: Assesses social environments of community- based psychiatric treatment programs.

Description: 100 item paper-pencil, true-false test of ten aspects of social environment: involvement, support, spontaneity, autonomy, practical orientation, personal problem orientation, anger and aggression, order and organization, program clarity, and staff control. Materials include the Real Form (Form R), which measures perceptions of a current program; the 40 item Short Form (Form S); the Ideal Form (Form I), measuring conceptions of an ideal program; and the Expectations Form (Form E), which measures expectations of a new program. Forms I and E are not published, but items and instructions are printed in the Appendix of the COPES manual. Items are modified from the Ward Atmosphere Scale. One of a series of nine Social Climate Scales. Examiner administered.

Untimed: 20 minutes

Range: Adult

Scoring: Hand key

Cost: Specimen set $4.50; manual $3.50; key $.75; 25 reusable tests $4.00; 50 answer sheets $3.00; 50 profiles $3.00.

Publisher: Consulting Psychologists Press, Inc.

CONSEQUENCES (CQ)
Paul R. Christensen, P.R. Merrifield and J.P. Guilford

teen, adult   grades 7-UP

Purpose: Measures ability to produce spontaneously original ideas in response to associated ideas. Used for research and experiment.

Description: Multiple item, paper-pencil test measuring two factors: ideational fluency (divergent production of semantic units), and originality (divergent production of semantic transformations). Originality in this test is shown by giving remotely associated ideas which are likely to require revisions of other ideas. Ideational fluency is scored by count of obvious responses. Originality is scored by count of remote responses. Available in two equivalent forms (AI and AII). One manual covers both forms. The Review set includes this manual and a portion of CQAI. Norms are provided for ninth-grade and engineering students. Restricted to A.P.A. members. Examiner required. Suitable for group use.

Timed: 10 minutes

Range: Junior high school-adult

Scoring: Examiner evaluated

Cost: 25 test booklet $10.00; manual $5.00; scoring guide $1.50.

Publisher: Sheridan Psychological Services, Inc.

CORNELL CLASS REASONING TEST
Refer to page 362.

CORNELL CONDITIONAL REASONING TEST, FORM X
Refer to page 362.

CORNELL CRITICAL THINKING TEST, LEVEL X
Refer to page 362.

CORNELL CRITICAL THINKING TEST. LEVEL Z
Refer to page 363.

THE C.P.H. (COLORADO PSYCHOPATHIC HOSPITAL) PATIENT ATTITUDE SCALE
Marvin W. Kahn and Nelson F. Jones

adult

Purpose: Assesses a mental patient's attitudes about hospital treatment. Useful for examining ward programs and comparing what happens in the hospital with the patient's social station in life, and as a research tool.

Description: 45 item paper-pencil test scored on a five- point Likert scale ranging from strongly agree to strongly disagree. The five attitude dimensions are: authoritarian control and non-psychological orientation; negative hospital orientation, external control, cause and treatment; mental illness and treatment as the hospital supplies regressive dependence; letdown of control or therapeutic gainarbitrary restriction. Materials include scales and manual. Selfadministered. Suitable for group use.

Untimed: 10-30 minutes

Range: Adult

Scoring: Hand key

Cost: Specimen set $3.50.

Publisher: Marvin W. Kahn, Ph.D.

CROWN-CRISP EXPERIENTAL INDEX (CCEI)
Refer to page 99.

CURRENT AND PAST PSYCHOPATHOLOGY SCALES (CAPPS)
Jean Endicott and The Research Assessment and Training Unit

all ages

Purpose: Assesses past and present psychiatric functioning. Used for diagnosis of psychopathology.

Description: 171 scales and checklist items measuring psychiatric signs and symptoms. Covers broad range of material similar to the Psychiatric Evaluation Form with the addition of items covering history relevant to severity, prognosis, and diagnosis. The CAPPS is filled out by the examiner after a clinical workup or through client interview. Examiner required. Not suitable for group use.

Untimed: 1-2 hours with interview

Range: Student-adult

Scoring: Examiner evaluated; computer diagnosis available

Cost: Booklet with scoresheets $1.00; scoresheet $.20; suggested procedure/training $.20; 6 pt. rating $.20; Fortran Program (scoring) $60.00 with tape-$75.00; Family Evaluation Form (FEF) booklets $1.00; scoring system $1.50; Fortran Scoring scales $60.00; Program and tapefile $75.00.

Publisher: Biometrics Research/ Research Assessment and Training Unit-N.Y. State Psychiatric Institute

DECORATION (DEC)
Sheldon Gardner, Arthur Gershon, Philip R. Merrifield and J.P. Guilford

teen, adult   grades 10-UP

Purpose: Measures ability to add meaningful decorations to simple drawings. Used for research and experimentation.

Description: Paper-pencil test measuring the "divergent production of figural implications" which is the ability to add meaningful details to what is given. Subjects are presented with outlines of well-known articles of furnishings and asked to add decorative lines. Artistic quality is not important, figural ideas are. Scored by a simple count of acceptable responses. Restricted to A.P.A. members. Examiner required. Suitable for group use.

Timed: 12 minutes

Range: High school-adult

Scoring: Examiner evaluated

Cost: 25 tests $11.00; manual $.80; scoring guide $.80.

Publisher: Sheridan Psychological Services, Inc.

DEFENSE MECHANISMS INVENTORY
Goldine C. Gleser

teen, adult

Purpose: Assesses an individual's use of such defense mechanisms as projection and reversal. Used only for research.

Description: Ten vignettes (male and female forms) determining defense responses to a variety of situations are presented to the subject. There are five possible responses to each vignette corresponding with the following five defense mechanisms: Turning against an Object, Projection, Principalization, Turning against Self, and Reversal. Each vignette is followed by four questions: "What would you do?", "What would you like to doo?", "What do you think?", and "How do you feel?". The materials include male and female forms, answer sheets and male and female profiles. Self-administered. Suitable for group use. Available in German, and French.

Untimed: 40 minutes

Range: Ages 16 and older

Scoring: Hand key

Cost: 50 test booklets (specify male or female) $3.50; 10 answer sheets $3.50; 50 profiles $3.50; specimen set $2.50.

Publisher: Goldine C. Gleser, Ph.D.

EDWARDS PERSONAL PREFERENCE SCHEDULE (EPPS)
Refer to page 101.

EFFECTIVENESS-
MOTIVATION SCALE
Refer to page 447.

EMBEDDED FIGURES TEST
(EFT)
Herman Witkin

all ages

Purpose: Assesses cognitive style in perceptual tasks; useful in counseling.

Description: 12 item verbal-manual test of perceptual processes including field dependence-independence. Performance related to analytic ability, social behavior, body concept, and preferred defense mechanisms. Materials include cards with complex figures, cards with simple figures and a stylus for tracing. Two alternate forms are available. Stopwatch with second hand is also needed. Task requires subject to locate and trace a previously seen simple figure within a larger complex figure.

Untimed: 10-45 minutes

Range: Ages 10-adult

Scoring: Examiner evaluated

Cost: Test kit (includes card set, stylus, 50 recording sheets) $11.00.

Publisher: Consulting Psychologists Press, Inc.

ENVIRONMENTAL RESPONSE
INVENTORY (ERI)
George E. McKechnie

adult

Purpose: Measures individual dispositions toward different physical/psychological environments. Used for research in retirement counseling, environmental planning, architecture and urban design.

Description: 184 item paper-pencil measure of eight aspects of how people think about the physical environment: Pastoralism, Urbanism, Environmental Adaptation, Stimulus Seeking, Environmental Trust, Antiquarianism, Need Privacy, and Mechanical Orientation. Subject indicates degree of agreement/disagreement on a five-point scale. Currently intended for research use only. Self- administered. Suitable for group use.

Untimed: 30 minutes

Range: Adult

Scoring: Hand key

Cost: Specimen set (no key) $7.50; manual $7.00; key $6.00.

Publisher: Consulting Psychologists Press, Inc.

EXPRESSIONAL FLUENCY (EF)
Paul R. Christensen and J.P. Guilford

teen, adult   grades 7-UP

Purpose: Measures the ability to produce spontaneously statements of organized thought. Useful in research and experimental applications.

Description: Multiple item, paper-pencil test measures the factor of "divergent production of semantic systems," which is defined as the ability to produce efficiently appropriate verbal expressions of organized thought. Instructions are included in the manual. Norms are provided for ninth-grade students. Restricted to A.P.A. members. Examiner required. Suitable for group use.

Timed: 8 minutes

Range: Junior high school-adult

Scoring: Examiner evaluated

Cost: 25 tests $10.00.

Publisher: Sheridan Psychological Services, Inc.

EXPRESSION GROUPING (SIEG)
Maureen O'Sullivan and J.P. Guilford

teen, adult   grades 10-UP

Purpose: Measures ability to understand facial expressions and body language. Used for counseling and research.

Description: Multiple item, paper-pencil, multiple-choice test. Measures the "cognition of behavioral classes," defined as the abiliity to look at a number of pictured expressions involving different parts of the body, deciding what psychological state or momentary disposition they indicate in common. Norms provided for tenth-grade and college students. Restricted to A.P.A. members. Examiner required. Suitable for group use.

Timed: 10 minutes

Range: High school-adult

Scoring: Hand key

Cost: 25 tests $14.00; manual $3.50; 25 answer sheets $3.50; scoring key $2.00.

Publisher: Sheridan Psychological Services, Inc.

FAMILY HISTORY-RESEARCH DIAGNOSTIC CRITERIA (FH-RDC)
Jean Endicott and The Research Assessment and Training Unit

teen, adult

Purpose: Provides criteria for diagnosis of mental disorders in family background. Used for psychiatric evaluation.

Description: 26 item checklist measure of existence of mental disorders in family history. Clinician rates items based on interview of a family member about other family members. Examiner required. Not suitable for group use.

Untimed: 30-120 minutes, depending upon size of family

Range: Student-adult

Scoring: Examiner evaluated

Cost: Booklet with scoresheet $1.50; parent work and data sheet $.15; sibling work and data sheet $.15; child work and data sheet $.15; mate work and data sheet $.15; summary data sheet 1 or 2 $.20 each; sample set of all scoresheets $1.00; case vignettes and keys $1.50.

Publisher: Biometrics Research/ Research Assessment and Training Unit-N.Y. State Psychiatric Insititute

FAMILY RELATIONS TEST-ADULT VERSION
Refer to page 59.

FAMILY RELATIONS TEST-CHILDREN'S VERSION
Refer to page 60.

FAMILY RELATIONS TEST-MARRIED COUPLES VERSION
Refer to page 68.

FAMOUS SAYINGS (FS)
Refer to page 816.

FLUENCY (FLU)
Paul R. Christensen and J.P. Guilford

teen, adult   grades 7-UP

Purpose: Measures divergent-thinking abilities in terms of words, expressions, and ideas. Used for research and experiment.

Description: Four paper-pencil, multiple-choice tests measuring aptitudes for verbalized creative thinking. Each test covers a distinct area in the divergent-thinking process. The tests are: Word Fluency (WF), Expressional Fluency (EF), Ideational Fluency (IF), and Associational Fluency (AF). Often referred to as the Christensen- Guilford Fluency Tests, the tests share a common manual and review set. All tests are administered in expendable booklets. Scoring guides are essential to decision as to acceptability of responses to test items. Restricted to A.P.A. members. Examiner required. Suitablle for group use.

Timed: 24 minutes

Range: Junior high school-adult

Scoring: Examiner evaluated

Cost: Specimen set $6.00; manual (includes screening for EF & WF) $5.00.

Publisher: Sheridan Psychological Services, Inc.

GLOBAL ASSESSMENT SCALE (GAS)
Jean Endicott and The Research Assessment and Training Unit

teen, adult　　　

Purpose: Assesses general level of psychopathology. Used for diagnosis.

Description: Multiple item measure of overall individual functioning. Information from family, case records, and clinical workup are used to rate client's overall health or sickness on a 100 point scale. Examiner required. Not suitable for group use.

Untimed: After evaluation, 2 minutes

Range: Student-adult

Scoring: Examiner evaluated

Cost: Scale $.25; case vignettes and keys $1.50; instructions/examples $.50.

Publisher: Biometrics Research/ Research Assessment and Training Unit-N.Y. State Psychiatric Institute

---

GROUP EMBEDDED FIGURES TEST (GEFT)
Philip K. Oltman, Evelyn Raskin and Herman A. Witkin

all ages　　　

Purpose: Assesses cognitive style in perceptual tasks; useful in counseling.

Description: 25 item paper-pencil test of perceptual processes including field dependence-independence. Performance related to analytic ability, social behavior, body concept, and preferred defense mechanisms. Subjects find one of eight simple figures in the complex designs, marking them in pencil. Examiner required. Designed for group use.

Untimed: 20 minutes

Range: Ages 10-adult

Scoring: Hand key

Cost: Sample set (manual not included) $1.25; manual $3.50; 25 tests $23.00; scoring key $.75.

Publisher: Consulting Psychologists Press, Inc.

GROWTH PROCESS INVENTORY (GPI)
Refer to page 107.

GUILFORD-ZIMMERMAN APTITUDE SURVEY (GZAS)
Refer to page 716.

IDEATIONAL FLUENCY (IF)
Paul R. Christensen and J.P. Guilford

teen, adult   grades 7-UP

Purpose: Measures ability to express meaningful ideas. Useful in research and experimental applications.

Description: Multiple item, paper-pencil test measures the factor of "divergent production of semantic units" by requiring the subject to produce efficiently many ideas fulfilling meaningful specifications. Instructions are included in the manual. Norms are provided for ninth-grade and college students. Restricted to A.P.A. members. Examiner required. Suitable for group use.

Timed: 12 minutes

Range: Junior high school-adult

Scoring: Examiner evaluated

Cost: 25 tests $10.00; scoring guide $.60.

Publisher: Sheridan Psychological Services, Inc.

THE IES TEST
Refer to page 157.

IMAGERY OF CANCER
Jeanne Achterberg and G. Frank Lawlis

Purpose: Evaluates the process of disease. Helps patients to understand cancer and mobilize their psychological resources to combat its progress. Bridges the gap between subjective holistic opinions and predictive science. Used for clinical evaluations, behavioral medicine, and rehabilitation counseling.

Description: Paper-pencil and oral response test combines guided imagery/relaxation procedures, patient drawings of disease-related images and a structured interview. After scoring the imagery and interview content along 14 dimensions, a total score is derived. This score reflects the overall quality of the patient's imagery and is highly predictive of long-term disease status. Examiner required. Suitable for group use. CANADIAN PUBLISHER

Untimed: Open ended

Range: Not available

Scoring: Hand key

Cost: Professional examination kit $25.70; handbook $9.75; Image-CA interview record and 25 scoring sheets $8.45; and Relaxation and Guided Imagery Tape $7.50.

Publisher: Institute for Personality and Ability Testing, Inc.

INTERPERSONAL CHECK LIST (ICL)
Refer to page 110.

AN INVENTORY OF ATTITUDES TOWARD BLACK/WHITE RELATIONS IN UNITED STATES
James H. Morrison

teen, adult

Purpose: Initiates discussions of black-white relations in training sessions. Used as a self-exam to sensitize a person to his attitudes towards race relations and for research.

Description: 28 item paper-pencil inventory measuring attitudes toward black-white relations in the United States on an integrationist-separationist continuum. Instructions are read to the subjects, who are allowed as much time as necessary to complete the test. Requires a 10th grade reading level. Self-administered. Suitable for group use.

Timed: 25 minutes

Range: Adolescents, adults

Scoring: Hand key

Cost: Specimen set (includes inventory and manual) $2.00; 20 tests (with manual) $4.00.

Publisher: James H. Morrison

JENKINS ACTIVITY SURVEY (JAS)
C. David Jenkins

adult

Purpose: Identifies persons with the "coronary-prone behavior pattern" or "Type A" behavior. Used for research and clinical screening.

Description: 52 item paper-pencil test of several aspects of Type A behavior including speed and impatience, job involvement and hard driving and competitive. Items include questions about behavior found useful in medical diagnosis. Scores associated with future risk of heart disease. Self- administered. Suitable for group use.

Untimed: Not available

Range: Adults

Scoring: Scoring service available

Cost: 25 questionnaires $13.75; 10 questionnaires with prepared scoring certificates $87.50; manual $4.00.

Publisher: The Psychological Corporation

JUNIOR EYSENCK PERSONALITY INVENTORY (JEPI)
Sybil B. G. Eysenck

child, teen

Purpose: Measures the major personality dimensions of children ages 7-16.

Used as a research instrument.

Description: 60 item paper-pencil yes-no inventory measures Extraversion-Introversion (24 items) Neuroticism- Stability (24 items). Twelve of the items constitute a falsification scale for the detection of response distortion. Scores are provided for E- Extraversion, N- Neuroticism and L-Lie. Norms available for selected samples of majority and minority children. Examiner required. Suitable for group use. Available in Spanish.

Untimed: 10 minutes

Range: Ages 7-16

Scoring: Hand Key

Cost: Specimen set (manual and one copy of all forms) $3.00; 25 inventories $4.50; key $2.00; manual $2.00.

Publisher: Educational and Industrial Testing Service

KATZ-ZALK OPINION QUESTIONNAIRE
Refer to page 627.

KIRTON ADAPTION-INNOVATION INVENTORY
M. J. Kirton

teen, adult

Purpose: Evaluates an individual's adaptive and innnovative characteristics. Used for research in occupational psychology.

Description: Paper-pencil test of response to organizational change based on a scale ranging from an ability to "do things better," to the ability to "do things differently." Responses are related to concepts of creativity, problem solving and decision-making. The test is a research tool and should not be used for evaluating individuals. Materials include

---

response sheet, manual and key. Examiner required. Suitable for group use.
CANADIAN PUBLISHER

Untimed: 10-15 minutes

Range: Adolescents, adults

Scoring: Hand key

Cost: Specimen set $27.52; 25 response sheets $18.87; key $7.33; manual $18.20.

Publisher: Institute of Psychological Research, Inc.

KUNDU INTROVERSION-EXTRAVERSION INVENTORY (K.I.E.I.)
Refer to page 114.

KUNDU'S NEUROTIC PERSONALITY INVENTORY (K.N.P.I.)
Refer to page 114.

LEISURE ACTIVITIES BLANK (LAB)
George McKechnie

adult

Purpose: Assesses an individual's past and future leisure and recreation activities. Used for research and counseling.

Description: 120 item paper-pencil test of recreational time use. Items are a list of recreational activities. Respondents indicate extent of past participation and expected future participation. Responses scored on six Past Scales: Mechanics, Crafts, Intellectual, Slow Living, Sports, and Glamour Sports; eight Future Scales: Adventure, Mechanics, Crafts, Easy Living, Intellectual, Ego- Recognition, Slow-Living, and Clean Living. There are two validity scales. Self-administered. Suitable for group use.

Untimed: 15-20 minutes

Range: Adult

Scoring: Hand Key

Cost: Specimen set (no key) $5.25; manual $5.00; 25 tests $3.25; 25 profiles $3.00; scoring stencils $10.00.

Publisher: Consulting Psychologists Press, Inc.

MAKING OBJECTS (MO)
Sheldon Gardner, Arthur Gershon, Philip R. Merrifield and J. P. Guilford

teen, adult   grades 10-UP

Purpose: Measures the ability to combine figural elements to produce specific objects. Used for research and experiment.

Description: Multiple item, paper-pencil test measuring the "divergent production of figural systems." This test is parallel to those measuring expressional fluency in the verbal or semantic category. The factor might be called "figural expressional fluency," or, more precisely, "visual-figural expressional fluency." Given a collection of very simple figural elements, the subject is told to construct specified objects by combining those elements. Scored by a simple count of acceptable responses. Norms provided for ninth-grade students and adults. Restricted to A.P.A. members. Examiner required. Suitable for group use.

Timed: 6 minutes

Range: Junior high school-adult

Scoring: Examiner evaluated

Cost: 25 tests $7.00; manual $1.50; scoring guide $.50.

Publisher: Sheridan Psychological Services, Inc.

MARYLAND PARENT ATTITUDE SURVEY (MPAS)
Refer to page 62.

MASLACH BURNOUT INVENTORY (MBI)
Christina Maslach and Susan E. Jackson

adult

Purpose: Evaluates emotional exhaustion and cynicism among members of helping professions as an aid to research on cause, effect, and duration of "burnout" syndrome.

Description: 22 item paper-pencil test of three burnout aspects: exhaustion, personal accomplishment, and depersonalization. Each item is answered on two dimensions, frequency and intensity. Demographic Data Sheet may be used to obtain general information. Examiner/self-administered.

Untimed: 20-30 minutes

Range: Adult

Scoring: Examiner evaluated

Cost: Not available.

Publisher: Consulting Psychologists Press, Inc.

MASTER ATTITUDE SCALES
Refer to page 627.

MATCH PROBLEMS (MP)
Raymond M. Berger and J.P. Guilford

teen, adult   grades 7-UP

Purpose: Measures an individual's originality in transforming figure conceptions. Used for research and experiment.

Description: Multiple item, paper-pencil test measuring the "divergent production of figural transformations," first known as "adaptive flexibility." The parallel ability in the verbal category is originality (divergent production of semantic transformations). Scored by simple count of acceptable responses. Norms provided for ninth- grade students and young adult males. Restricted to A.P.A. members. Examiner required. Suitable for group use.

Timed: 14 minutes

Range: Junior high school-adult

Scoring: Examiner evaluated

Cost: 25 tests $10.00; manual $2.50; scoring key $1.00.

Publisher: Sheridan Psychological Services, Inc.

MATCH PROBLEMS V (MPV)
Philip R. Merrifield and J.P. Guilford

teen, adult   grades 7-UP

Purpose: Measures the ability to revise conceptions of figures, but at a lower level of difficulty than the match problems test. Used for research and experiment.

Description: Multiple item, paper-pencil test measuring the "divergent production of figural transformations," first known as "adaptive flexibility." The parallel ability in the verbal category is originality (divergent production of semantic transformations). An alternate, shorter form of Match Problems, measuring the same factor at a lower level of task complexity. Scored by simple count of acceptable responses. Norms provided for ninth-grade students. Restricted to A.P.A. members. Examiner required. Suitable for group use.

Timed: 10 minutes

Range: Junior high school-adult

Scoring: Examiner evaluated

Cost: 25 tests $7.00; manual $2.50; scoring key $1.00.

Publisher: Sheridan Psychological Services, Inc.

MEMORY FOR EVENTS (ME)
J.P. Guilford

teen, adult grades 7-UP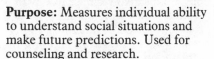

Purpose: Measures the ability to remember events in sequence. Used for psychological research on semantic systems.

Description: Multiple item, paper-pencil test measuring "memory for semantic systems." This is the ability to learn and remember the temporal order of a sequence of facts. Test booklets are reusable. The answer sheets, manual, and review set come in forms that cover both the ME test and the Memory for Meanings test. Norms provided for entering college students. Restricted to A.P.A. members. Examiner required. Suitable for group use.

Timed: 12 minutes

Range: Junior high school-adult

Scoring: Hand key

Cost: 25 tests $14.00; 25 answer sheets $3.50; manual $.75; key $2.00.

Publisher: Sheridan Psychological Services, Inc.

MEMORY FOR MEANINGS (MM)
Ralph Hoepfner and J.P. Guilford

teen, adult grades 7-UP

Purpose: Measures the ability to remember the meaning of new words. Used for research and experiment.

Description: Multiple item, paper-pencil test measuring "memory for semantic units." The subject is required to remember the meanings of a number of words, showing this by recognizing very close synonyms. Test booklets are reusable; the answer sheets, manual, and review set come in forms that cover both the MM test and the Memory for Events test. Norms provided for entering college students. Restricted to A.P.A. members. Examiner required. Suitable for group use.

Timed: 12 minutes

Range: Junior high school-adult

Scoring: Hand key

Cost: 25 tests $14.00; 25 answer sheets $3.50; manual $.75; key $2.00.

Publisher: Sheridan Psychological Services, Inc.

MINNESOTA SATISFACTORI-NESS SCALE (MSS)
Refer to page 821.

MISSING CARTOONS (SIMC)
Richard deMille, Maureen O'Sullivan and J.P. Guilford

teen, adult grades 10-UP

Purpose: Measures individual ability to understand social situations and make future predictions. Used for counseling and research.

Description: Paper-pencil, multiple-choice test. Measures three factors of social cognition, listed in order of importance: cognition of behavioral systems (situations), cognition of behavioral units (momentary dispositions), and cognition of behavioral implications (predictions). Each test item shows a four-part cartoon strip, with no verbal content, with one picture missing. The subject selects the most appropriate alternative cartoon to complete the meaning of the strip. Norms provided for tenth-grade and college students. Restricted to A.P.A. members. Examiner required. Suitable for group use.

Timed: 16 minutes

Range: Grades High school-adult

Scoring: Hand key

Cost: 25 tests $20.00; manual $3.50; 25 answer sheets $3.50; scoring key $2.00.

Publisher: Sheridan Psychological Services, Inc.

MULTIPLE AFFECT ADJECTIVE CHECK LIST (MAACL)
Refer to page 121.

NEW USES (NU)
Ralph Hoepfner and J.P. Guilford

teen, adult   grades 10-UP

Purpose: Measures the ability to redefine and find new ways of looking at things. Used for research and experiment.

Description: Multiple item, paper-pencil test measuring the structure-of-intellect ability of "convergent production of semantic transformations." This involves the capacity to redefine. A low score on this test probably indicates "functional fixedness," which serves as an inhibitor in problem solving by preventing insights. Norms provided for entering college students. Restricted to A.P.A. members. Examiner required. Suitable for group use.

Timed: 9 minutes

Range: High school-adult

Scoring: Examiner evaluated

Cost: 25 test $7.00; manual $.50; scoring guide $1.00.

Publisher: Sheridan Psychological Services, Inc.

PAIN APPERCEPTION TEST
Leonard Small

adult

Purpose: Examines the emotional aspects of pain. Used in settings where pain might be experienced or anticipated.

Description: 25 item oral response projective test assesses pain's emotional aspects (within a psychological context). It measures the individual's perception of intensity and duration of pain focusing on total reactions and not just thresholds. The test items consist of picture cards dealing with three major groups of pain situations: felt pain sensations; anticipation versus felt-sensation of pain; and self-inflicted versus other-inflicted pain. Responses are recorded by the examiner on the Protocol Sheet. Adult normative data are provided. Examiner required. Suitable for group use.

Untimed: 15-20 minutes

Range: Adult

Scoring: Examiner evaluated

Cost: Complete kit (includes 25 protocol sheets, 1 set of plates, manual) $25.60.

Publisher: Western Psychological Services

PERTINENT QUESTIONS
Raymond M. Berger and J.P. Guilford

teen, adult   grades 10-UP

Purpose: Measures conceptual foresight. Used for experiment and research.

Description: Multiple item, paper-pencil test measuring the cognition of semantic implications. This is the ability to see implications of a meaningful kind, as in having anticipations, in being aware of consequences, and in making predictions. Norms provided for college groups. Restricted to A.P.A. members. Examiner required. Suitable for group use.

Timed: 12 minutes

Range: High school-adult

Scoring: Examiner evaluated

Cost: 25 tests; manual $1.00; scoring guide $2.00.

Publisher: Sheridan Psychological Services, Inc.

THE PICTORIAL STUDY OF VALUES
Refer to page 127.

PICTURE SITUATION TEST
Refer to page 825.

PLOT TITLES (PT)
Raymond M. Berger and J.P. Guilford

teen, adult   grades 10-UP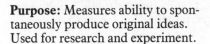

Purpose: Measures ability to spontaneously produce original ideas. Used for research and experiment.

Description: Multiple item, paper-pencil test measuring two factors: ideational fluency (divergent production of semantic units), and originality (divergent production of semantic transformations). Originality in this test is seen in the production of ideas of high quality with respect to the criterion of "cleverness." Ideational fluency is scored by a count of non-clever responses; originality is scored by a count of clever responses. Available in two equivalent forms (AI and B). Norms provided for ninth-grade and architecture students. Restricted to

A.P.A. members. Examiner required. Suitable for group use.

Timed: 6 minutes

Range: Grades High school-adult

Scoring: Examiner evaluated

Cost: 25 tests $7.00; manual $2.50; scoring guide $1.00.

Publisher: Sheridan Psychological Services, Inc.

PORTEUS MAZES
Refer to page 29.

POSSIBLE JOBS (PJ)
Arthur Gershon and J.P. Guilford

teen, adult   grades 7-UP

Purpose: Measures the ability to elaborate upon given information. Used for research and experiment.

Description: Multiple item, paper-pencil test measuring "divergent production of semantic implications", which is defined as the ability to elaborate upon given information or to suggest alternative deductions or extensions. Scored by a simple count of acceptable responses. Norms provided for ninth- and tenth-grade students. Restricted to A.P.A. members. Examiner required. Suitable for group use.

Timed: 10 minutes

Range: Grades Junior high school-adult

Scoring: Examiner evaluated

Cost: 25 test booklets $7.00; manual $1.50; scoring guide $.60.

Publisher: Sheridan Psychological Services, Inc.

PROBLEM APPRAISAL SCALES (PAS)

Jean Endicott and The Research Assessment and Training Unit

teen, adult

Purpose: Assesses psychiatric functioning. Use for diagnosis of psychopathology.

Description: Multiple item measure of broad range of psychiatric signs and symptoms consisting of 40 scales and 1 check list item. The PAS covers the same areas as the Psychiatric Evaluation Form (PEF) with the addition of items covering physical functioning and intellectual development. The PAS is filled out by the examiner after a clinical workup. Examiner required. Not suitable for group use.

Untimed: After clinical workup, 3-5 minutes

Range: Student-adult

Scoring: Examiner evaluated; computer primary scale scores

Cost: Scale $.25; interview guide $.50; suggested procedures and instruction $.40; summary scale scores/tables $.50.

Publisher: Biometrics Research/ Research Assessment and Training Unit-State Psychiatric Institute

PROFILE OF MOOD STATES (POMS)

Refer to page 129.

PROVERBS TEST

Refer to page 29.

PSYCHIATRIC EVALUATION FORM (PEF)

Jean Endicott and The Research Assessment and Training Unit

teen, adult

Purpose: Assesses current psychiatric functioning. Used for diagnosis of psychopathology.

Description: Multiple item measure of broad range of psychiatric symptoms consisting of 27 scales and 2 checklist items. The PEF measures the same areas as the Psychiatric Status Schedule, with the addition of characteristics of present illness and major reason for admission. The PEF is filled out by the examiner based on a clinical workup or client interview. Examiner required. Not suitable for group use.

Untimed: 25-50 minutes total interview

Range: Student-adult

Scoring: Examiner evaluated; computer scored for summary scales

Cost: Booklet with scoresheet $2.50; scoresheet $.20; manual of instructions $1.00; teaching tape and key $4.00; summary scale scores $.55; editing/coding instructions $.20; Fortran program $60.00; program and tapefile $75.00.

Publisher: Biometrics Research/ Research Assessment and Training Unit-N.Y. State Psychiatric Institute

PSYCHIATRIC STATUS SCHEDULE (PSS)

Jean Endicott and The Research Assessment and Training Unit

teen, adult

Purpose: Assesses current psychiatric functioning. Used for diagnosis of psychopathology.

Description: 321 item measure of psychopathology, organicity, alcoholism, or drug abuse. Subject's role as wage earner, housekeeper, student, mate, and parent are also covered. Items are true-false and checklist. Interviewer answers items based on meeting with subject. Materials include 21 page stepdown booklet. Covers many of the same areas as the Psychiatric Evaluation Form (PEF). Examiner required. Not suitable for group use.

Untimed: 30-50 minutes

Range: Student-adult

Scoring: Hand key; examiner evaluated; compuuter scoring available

Cost: Booklet with scoresheet $3.50; scoresheet $.30; suggested procedure and training $.20; manual $1.50; teaching tape and key $4.00; scale score summary $1.50; editing/coding instructions $.20; hand stencils $5.00; Fortran program $60.00; program and tapefile $75.00.

Publisher: Biometrics Research/ Research Assessment and Training Unit-N.Y. State Psychiatric Institute

---

REACTION TIME TESTING
Refer to page 538.

REACTION TO EVERYDAY SITUATIONS-TEST
Refer to page 827.

RESEARCH DIAGNOSTIC CRITERIA (RDC)
Jean Endicott and The Research Assessment and Training Unit

teen, adult

Purpose: Provides criteria for diagnosis of mental disorders and subtypes of disorders. Used for diagnosis of affective and schizophrenic disorders.

Description: 25 item measure of pre-

sent or previous illnesses. Items are a list of 25 diagnoses: preesent, past, life-time. Clinician checks applicable diagnosis based on clinical workup or Schedule for Affective Disorders and Schizophrenia (SADS) interview. Examiner required. Suitable for group use.

Untimed: After clinical workup, 10-15 minutes

Range: Student-adult

Scoring: Examiner evaluated

Cost: Booklet $1.50; scoresheet $.25; checklist $.50; suggested training procedures $.40; case record training exercise $7.00; CR training exercise testing $6.00; editing/coding instructions $.20.

Publisher: Biometrics Research/ Research Assessment and Training Unit-N.Y. State Psychiatric Institute

---

ROKEACH VALUE SURVEY
Refer to page 164.

SCHEDULE FOR AFFECTIVE DISORDERS AND SCHIZO-PHRENIA (SADS)
Jean Endicott and The Research Assessment and Training Unit

teen, adult

Purpose: Describes psychopathology of the past week and current episode of illness. Used as an aid to diagnose and to estimate prognosis and severity.

Description: Measure of recent psychopathology consisting of over 200 scales and many checklist items. Examiner rates items based on subject interview, case records, and clinical workup. Similar in concept to the Schedule for Affective Disorders and Schizophrenia--Life-time Version (SADS-L) and Schedule for Affective Disorders and Schizophrenia--Change Version (SADS-C). Must be used in conjunction with the Research Diagnostic Criteria (RDC). Examiner required. Not suitable for group use.

Untimed: 90-120 minutes

Range: Ages 12-adult

Scoring: Examiner evaluated; computer summary scale scores

Cost: SADS booklet $2.00; SADS scoresheet $.30; SADS, SAD-L, RDC suggested procedures $.50; SADS, SADS-L instructions $.50; SADS, SADS-L, RDC Clars, $7.00; summary scale booklet $1.50; editing/coding instructions $.40; Fortran program $60.00; program and tape-file $75.00.

Publisher: Biometrics Research/ Research Assessment and Training Unit-N.Y. State Psychiatric Institute

SCHEDULE FOR AFFECTIVE DISORDERS AND SCHIZO-PHRENIA--CHANGE VERSION (SADS-C)
Jean Endicott and The Research Assessment and Training Unit

teen, adult

Purpose: Assesses change in psychopathological symptoms for the previous week. Used in diagnosis and treatment planning.

Description: Measure of symptom changes over the last week consisting of 29 scaled items and several checklist items. Examiner rates items based on subject interview and clinical records. Part of a series including Schedule for Affective Disorders and Schizophrenia (SADS) and Schedule for Affective Disorders and Schizophrenia--Life-time Version (SADS-L). Examiner required. Not suitable for group use.

Untimed: 20-30 minutes

Range: Student-adult

Scoring: Examiner evaluated; computerized summary scale scores

Cost: Booklet $1.00; scoresheet $.20; summary scale booklet $1.00; editing/coding instructions $.20; Fortran program $60.00; with tape $75.00.

Publisher: Biometrics Research/ Research Assessment and Training Unit-N.Y. State Psychiatric Institute

SCHEDULE FOR AFFECTIVE DISORDERRS AND SCHIZO-PHRENIA--LIFE-TIME VERSION (SADS-L)
Jean Endicott and The Research Assessment and Training Unit

teen, adult

Purpose: Assesses clinical history of psychopathology. Used for differential diagnosis of mental disorders.

Description: Measure of history relevant to diagnosis, prognosis and severity of illness consisting of several scales and numerous checklist items. Examiner rates items based on subject interview, case records, and clinical workup. Items similar to the Schedule for Affective Disorders and Schizophrenia (SADS) and Schedule for Affective Disorders and Schizophrenia--Change Version (SADS- C). Must be used in conjunction with the Research Diagnostic Criteria (RDC). Examiner required. Not suitable for group use.

Untimed: If not ill, 45 minutes; In an episode, 45-90 minutes

Range: Student-adult

Scoring: Examiner evaluated; computer scoring available

Cost: SADS-L booklet $1.00; scoresheet $.25; editing/codiing instruction $.20; summary data program $60.00; editing program $60.00; program with tapefile $75.00.

Publisher: Biometrics Research/

Research Assessment and Training
Unit-N.Y. State Psychiatric Institute

SEEING PROBLEMS (SP)
*Phillip R. Merrifield and J.P.
Guilford*

teen, adult   grades 7-UP 👉 ✏️

Purpose: Measures the ability to see
and anticipate problems. Used for
research on semantics.

Description: Multiple item, paper-
pencil test measuring the cognition of
semantic implications. This is the
ability to see implications of a meaningful kind, as in having
anticipations, in being aware of consequences, and in making
predictions. Norms provided for high
school graduates. Restricted to
A.P.A. members. Examiner
required. Suitable for group use.

Timed: 4 minutes

Range: Junior high school-adult

Scoring: Examiner evaluated

Cost: 25 tests $7.00; manual $2.00;
scoring guide $1.25.

Publisher: Sheridan Psychological
Services, Inc.

SKETCHES (SKET)
*Arthur Gershon, Sheldon
Gardner, Philip R. Merrifield
and J.P. Guilford*

teen, adult   grades 7-UP 👉 ✏️

Purpose: Measures the ability to
make abstract figures into recognizable objects. Used for research and
experiment.

Description: 48 item paper-pencil
test measuring figural fluency (divergent production of figural units); the
ability to produce efficiently a variety
of units of visual-figural information
in response to specifications. Four

basic, simple figures are given, each
repeated 12 times. The taker is asked
to transform each one into a recognizable object. Scored by a simple count
of acceptable objects produced.
Norms provided for ninth-grade students and young adult males.
Restricted to A.P.A. members.
Examiner required. Suitable for
group use.

Timed: 8 minutes

Range: Junior high school-adult

Scoring: Examiner evaluated

Cost: 25 tests $12.00; manual $.75;
scoring guide $.60.

Publisher: Sheridan Psychological
Services, Inc.

SLOAN ACHROMATOPSIA TEST
Munsel Color

all ages 👉 ✏️

Purpose: A research test to screen
the congenital achromat in populations that are completely colorblind
and to measure how such persons see
color.

Description: A visual-verbal test
consisting of seven neutral gray scales
each displaying 17 steps between
black and white. The scales are
mounted on red, orange, yellow,
green, blue, and magenta color references. The subject is asked to select
the gray on the scale which appears to
match the color reference mounted
behind it. Examiner required. Not
for group use.

Untimed: 3-4 minutes

Range: Ages 6-adult

Scoring: Examiner evaluated

Cost: Complete $75.00.

Publisher: Munsell Color

SMOKING AND HEALTH
Refer to page 273.

SOCIAL TRANSLATIONS (SIST)
Maureen O'Sullivan and J.P. Guilford

teen, adult   grades 10-UP

Purpose: Measures individual ability to understand behavioral change and psychological relationships. Useful for counseling and research.

Description: Paper-pencil multiple-choice test. A completely verbal measure of the "cognition of behavioral transformations" and to a lesser degree the additional factor of "cognition of behavioral relations," the ability to appreciate what kind of psychological relation occurs between two people who are communicating with each other. Norms provided for tenth-grade and college students. Restricted to A.P.A. members. Examiner required. Suitable for group use.

Timed: 8 minutes

Range: High school-adult

Scoring: Hand key

Cost: 25 tests $10.00; manual $3.50; 25 answer sheets $3.50; scoring key $2.00.

Publisher: Sheridan Psychological Services, Inc.

SPORTS EMOTION TEST (SET)
E.R. Oetting and C.W. Cole

athletes

Purpose: Evaluates emotional responses of athletes prior to and during competition. Used as a research instrument.

Description: 132 item paper-pencil rating scale measuring four response areas: feelings of anxiety, concentration, intensity, and physical readiness. Subjects rate each response area on a 7-point scale according to how they feel at different times: 24 hours before, at breakfast, just before, and just after the start of the event, and just after "something goes wrong." Materials include: expendable test booklets, profile sheets, and manual. Suitable for group use. Supervision of a trained psychologist required.

Timed: 20 minutes

Range: Not available

Scoring: Examiner evaluated

Cost: 100 scales and profiles $50.00; manual $12.00.

Publisher: Rocky Mountain Behavioral Science Institute, Inc.

STANFORD HYPNOTIC SUSCEPTIBILITY SCALE
André M. Weitzenhoffer and Ernest R. Hilgard

teen, adult   grades 13-UP

Purpose: Measures hypnotic susceptibility. Used for teaching, research, and experimentation in hypnosis.

Description: Multiple item test of subject's responsiveness to hypnotic suggestions. Includes verbatim instructions for inducing and testing hypnotic states. Subject's scores are based on a 12 point scale. Materials include three forms: A, B, and C. Forms A and B are equivalent; Form C contains more difficult items and a wider variety of hypnotic experiences. Restricted to APA guidelines. Examiner required. Not suitable for group use.

Untimed: 40 minutes

Range: College-adult

Scoring: Hand key

Cost: Forms A, B and C $6.50; A and

B kit (includes both scales, scoring sheets, interrogatory blanks for 50 subjects) $12.50; pad of 25 score sheets $2.00; pad of 50 Form A and B interrogatory blanks $3.25; Form C kit $9.00.

Publisher: Consulting Psychologists Press, Inc.

STANFORD PROFILE SCALES OF HYPNOTIC SUSCEPTIBILITY
André M. Weitzenhoffer and Ernest R. Hilgard

teen, adult   grades 13-UP

Purpose: Assesses differential susceptibility to a variety of hypnotic state suggestions. Used for teaching, research, and experimentation in hypnosis.

Description: Multiple item test of hypnotic susceptibility yielding 25 scores in six areas: agnosia and cognitive distortion, positive hallucinations, negative hallucinations, dreams and regressions, amnesia and post-hypnotic compulsions, and total susceptibility. Materials include two roughly equivalent forms, I and II. Both must be administered to yield the profile. Profile scales may be used with subjects chosen by the Stanford Hypnotic Susceptibility Scale. Examiner required. Not suitable for group use.

Range: College-adult

Scoring: Examiner evaluated

Cost: Specimen set $6.00; 25 of each form scoring booklets $12.50; 100 profile sheets $6.00; manual $4.75.

Publisher: Consulting Psychologists Press, Inc.

STUDY OF VALUES
Refer to page 630.

STUDY OF VALUES (REVISED 1964 BRITISH EDITION)
Refer to page 140.

SWANSEA EVALUATION PROFILE FOR SCHOOL ENTRANTS
R. Evans, P. Davies, N. Ferguson and P. Williams

child

Purpose: Evaluates mental ability and background of children ages 4 to 5. Used to identify those in need of special education.

Description: Three section paper-pencil profile which includes: home background, initial adjustment to school, and a cognitive test battery measuring child development. Test is experimental and is not yet available for classroom use, but is produced in limited quantities for research. Materials include set of three tests. Examiner required. Not for group use.
CANADIAN PUBLISHER

Timed: Section 1, 5 minutes; Section 2, 5 minutes; Section 3, 30 minutes

Range: Ages 4.11-5

Scoring: Examiner evaluated

Cost: Contact publisher.

Publisher: Institute of Psychological Research, Inc.

SYMBOL IDENTITIES
Ralph Hoepfner

teen, adult   grades 10-UP

Purpose: Measures ability to deal with and differentiate symbols. May be used as a research tool.

Description: Multiple item, paper-pencil test measuring the "evaluation of symbolic units." Subjects are presented with pairs of sets of symbols (words, names, numbers) and required to determine whether the pair members are exactly alike or different. Norms provided for 10th grade students. Restricted to A.P.A. members. Examiner required. Suitable for group use.

Timed: 4 minutes

Range: High school, college, adult

Scoring: Examiner evaluated

Cost: 25 tests $7.00; manual $.80; scoring key $1.50.

Publisher: Sheridan Psycholgical Services, Inc.

TEST ANXIETY INVENTORY (TAI)
Charles D. Spielberger

teen, adult grades 10-UP

Purpose: Measures individual differences in anxiety over taking tests. Used for research.

Description: 20 item paper-pencil test of two major components of test anxiety, worry and emotionality. Respondents report how frequently they experience specific anxiety symptoms around examinations. Similar in structure and concept to the A-Trait Scale of the State-Trait Anxiety Inventory. May be self-administered. Suitable for group use.

Untimed: 5-10 minutes

Range: High school and college

Scoring: Hand key

Cost: Specimen set $4.00; manual $3.25; key $.50; 25 expendable tests $3.00.

Publisher: Consulting Psychologists Press, Inc.

TEST OF BASIC ASSUMPTIONS
James H. Morrison and Martin Levit

teen, adult

Purpose: Diagnoses philosphical preferences. Used to examine assumptions about reality or philosophy and for research and group discussion.

Description: 20 item paper-pencil measure of realism, idealism, and pragmaticism. Instructions are read to the subjects, who are allowed as much time as they need. Minimum 12th grade reading level necessary. Not to be used for prediction purposes. Self-administered. Suitable for group use.

Untimed: 40 minutes

Range: Adolescent, adult

Scoring: Hand key

Cost: Specimen set (includes manual, 1 score sheet, 1 test) $2.00; 25 tests (includes score sheets and manual) $4.30.

Publisher: James H. Morrison

WIDE RANGE INTELLIGENCE-PERSONALITY TEST (WRIPT)
Refer to page 170.

WILSON-PATTERSON ATTITUDE INVENTORY
Refer to page 170.

WORD FLUENCY (WF)
Paul R. Christensen and J.P. Guilford

teen, adult grades 7-UP

Purpose: Measures the ability to produce spontaneously words useful in research and experimental applications.

Description: Multiple item, paper-pencil test measures the "divergent production of symbolic units" by requiring the subject to produce rapidly words fulfilling specified symbolic (letter) properties. Instructions are included in the manual. Norms are provided for ninth-grade students. Restricted to A.P.A. members. Examiner required. Suitable for group use.

Timed: 4 minutes

Range: Junior high school-adult

Scoring: Examiner evaluated

Cost: 25 tests $7.00.

Publisher: Sheridan Psychological Services, Inc.

Education

The tests described in the Education Section are grouped by subtopic on the basis of usage in an educational or school setting. These are tests which would typically be used by educators or professionals concerned with the cognitive and emotional growth and development of persons of all ages. Typically, professionals who utilize tests listed in the Education Section are school psychologists, school counselors, and classroom teachers.

Since the classification of tests by "function or usage" (i.e. use by schools rather than mental health centers) is somewhat arbitrarily determined, the reader is encouraged to check for additional tests which may by helpful in meeting their testing needs in the Psychology Section and Business Section.

Education Section Index

Academic Subjects

Business Education

**ACT PROFICIENCY EXAMINA-
TION PROGRAM-BUSINESS:
ACCOUNTING: LEVEL I**
Refer to page 297.

**ACT PROFICIENCY EXAMINA-
TION PROGRAM-BUSINESS:
ACCOUNTING: LEVEL II**
Refer to page 297.

**ACT PROFICIENCY EXAMINA-
TION PROGRAM-BUSINESS:
ACCOUNTING: LEVEL III Area 1,
2, 3**
Refer to page 298.

**ACT PROFICIENCY EXAMINA-
TION PROGRAM-BUSINESS:
BUSINESS ENVIRONMENT AND
STRATEGY**
Refer to page 298.

**ACT PROFICIENCY EXAMINA-
TION PROGRAM-BUSINESS:
FINANCE: LEVEL I**
Refer to page 299.

**ACT PROFICIENCY EXAMINA-
TION PROGRAM-BUSINESS:
FINANCE: LEVEL II**
Refer to page 299.

**ACT PROFICIENCY EXAMINA-
TION PROGRAM-BUSINESS:
FINANCE: LEVEL III**
Refer to page 299.

**ACT PROFICIENCY EXAMINA-
TION PROGRAM-BUSINESS:
MANAGEMENT OF HUMAN
RESOURCES: LEVEL I**
Refer to page 300.

**ACT PROFICIENCY EXAMINA-
TION PROGRAM-BUSINESS:
MANAGEMENT OF HUMAN
RESOURCES: LEVEL II**
Refer to page 300.

**ACT PROFICIENCY EXAMINA-
TION PROGRAM-BUSINESS:
MANAGEMENT OF HUMAN
RESOURCES: LEVEL III**
Refer to page 301.

**ACT PROFICIENCY EXAMINA-
TION PROGRAM-BUSINESS:
MARKETING: LEVEL I**
Refer to page 301.

ACT PROFICIENCY EXAMINA-TION PROGRAM-BUSINESS: MARKETING: LEVEL II
Refer to page 301.

ACT PROFICIENCY EXAMINA-TION PROGRAM-BUSINESS: MARKETING: LEVEL III
Refer to page 302.

ACT PROFICIENCY EXAMINA-TION PROGRAM-BUSINESS: OPERATIONS MANAGEMENT: LEVEL I
Refer to page 302.

ACT PROFICIENCY EXAMINA-TION PROGRAM-BUSINESS: OPERATIONS MANAGEMENT: LEVEL II
Refer to page 303.

CLERICAL SKILLS SERIES
Refer to page 762.

COLLEGE LEVEL EXAMINA-TION PROGRAM (CLEP) BUSINESS: MONEY and BANKING
Refer to page 343.

COLLEGE LEVEL EXAMINA-TION PROGRAM (CLEP) BUSINESS: INTRODUCTION to MANAGEMENT
Refer to page 341.

COLLEGE LEVEL EXAMINA-TION PROGRAM (CLEP) BUSINESS: INTRODUCTORY BUSINESS LAW
Refer to page 342.

COLLEGE LEVEL EXAMINA-TION PROGRAM (CLEP) BUSINESS: INTRODUCTORY MARKETING
Refer to page 342.

COMMERCIAL TESTS-1962

teen

Purpose: Assesses abilities important in commercial fields. Used for vocational guidance.

Description: Multiple item, paper-pencil test battery measuring six areas of commercial abilities: Arithmetic Part I and II, Comparison, Synonyms, Alphabetizing, and Spelling and Punctuation. Materials include two alternate and equivalent forms, A and B. Examiner required. Suitable for group use.
SOUTH AFRICAN PUBLISHER

Untimed: 1 hour

Range: Standards 6-8

Scoring: Hand key; examiner evaluated

Cost: (In Rands) Test booklet (specify form A or B) 0,30; 10 answer sheets (specify form) 0,40; scoring key (specify A or B) 1,10 each; manual 0,80 (orders from outside The RSA will be dealt with on merit).

Publisher: Human Sciences Research Council

HIETT DIAMOND JUBILEE SERIES SHORTHAND TEST
V.C. Hiett

teen   grades 10-12

Purpose: Assesses shorthand achievement of high school and college students. Used as mid-year or end-of-year exam.

Description: 125 item paper-pencil test of characters, dictation, and notes interpretation. Examiner required. Suitable for group use.

Timed: 40 minutes

Range: Grades High school

Scoring: Hand key

Cost: Specimen set $1.50; test $.15 each; manual $.15; key $.15.

Publisher: Bureau of Educational Measurements

HIETT SIMPLIFIED SHORT-HAND TEST
V.C. Hiett and H.E. Schrammel

teen   grades 10-12

Purpose: Assesses shorthand achievement of high school and college students. Used as first and second semester exam.

Description: 125 item paper-pencil test of reading and writing of Gregg shorthand system. Examiner required. Suitable for group use.

Timed: 40 minutes

Range: Grades High school

Scoring: Hand key

Cost: Specimen set $1.50; test $.15 each; manual $15.00; key $.15.

Publisher: Bureau of Educational Measurements

NATIONAL BUSINESS COMPETENCY TESTS
N.B.E.A. Competency Test Committee

teen, adult   grades 10-UP

Purpose: A series of tests which evaluate office skills of high school and college students to see if skills learned meet entry level demands of employers.

Description: Six tests in two areas: typewriting and office procedures. Materials include test booklet for all tests, and manual including answer key. Examiner required. Suitable for group use.

Range: Grades High school and college

Scoring: Hand key

Cost: Review set (6 tests and 4 manuals) $5.00.

Publisher: National Business Education Association

NATIONAL BUSINESS COMPETENCY TESTS: OFFICE PROCEDURES
N.B.E.A. Competency Test Committee

teen, adult   grades 10-UP

Purpose: Assesses proficiency in entry-level office skills, excluding use of the typewriter. Used for student and program evaluations.

Description: Multiple item, paper-pencil test consisting of two parts. Part 1, Office Services, consists of 12 subtests. Each subtest consists of performing a task commonly found in office work and taught in the classroom, such as checking, proofreading, telephoning, mail services, and filling out a job application form. Part 2 consists of nine jobs involving computation and accounting services, including: payroll, accounting forms, and computation. Responses are scored for accuracy, completeness, and neatness. Parts 1 and 2 may be given on separate days. Examiner required. Suitable for group use.

Timed: Two 50 minute periods

Range: Grades High school and college

Scoring: Hand key

Cost: Test $.75.

Publisher: National Business Education Association

NATIONAL BUSINESS COMPETENCY TESTS: TYPEWRITING
N.B.E.A. Competency Test Committee

teen, adult   grades 10-UP

Purpose: Assesses typing skills of advanced high school and college typing students.

Description: Multiple item test of typing speed and accuracy consisting of two parts designed to be administered on separate days. Part 1 consists of two five-minute timed writing exercises requiring line-for-line copying. Part 2 requires a full class-period and consists of five typing jobs to be completed as accurately as possible in the allotted time. Tasks include: information to be filled in on a form with horizontal lines, a business letter, a 3-column table with headings, a 2-page report manuscript with footnotes, and an invoice. Materials required: typewriter, paper, carbon paper, and correction materials. Examiner required. Suitable for group use.

Timed: Two 50 minute periods

Range: Grades High school and college

Scoring: Hand key

Cost: Test $.75.

Publisher: National Business Education Association

NATIONAL BUSINESS ENTRANCE TESTS
N.B.E.A. Test Committee

teen, adult   grades 10-UP

Purpose: Assesses proficiency in clerical and general office skills. Used in business for employment and placement purposes. Used in schools for grading purposes and to prepare students for the Official Testing Series.

Description: Six tests measuring an applicant's rate of production at tasks requiring certain well defined office skills. The tests include: Business Fundamentals and General Information Test, Bookkeeping Test, General Office Clerical Test, Machine Calculation Test, Stenographic Test, and Typewriting Test. An attempt is made in all tests to simulate actual working conditions. Norms and suggested cutoff scores provided. Examiner required. Suitable for group use.

Untimed: Varies

Range: Grades High school and college/adults in business

Scoring: Hand key

Cost: Review set (includes 6 tests and 4 manuals) $5.00.

Publisher: National Business Education Association

NATIONAL BUSINESS ENTRANCE TESTS-BOOK-KEEPING TEST
N.B.E.A. Test Committee

teen, adult   grades 10-UP

Purpose: Assesses proficiency in entry-level bookkeeping skills. Used for selection and placement of office workers.

Description: Multiple-item, paper-pencil test assessing the ability to accurately perform bookkeeping tasks under timed conditions. Measures the following factors: understanding of bookkeeping principles and practices, ability to follow instructions, practical ability in carrying out bookkeeping problems, and accuracy in computation. Candidates are provided with columnar cash records, journals, and ledger accounts and asked to make basic bookkeeping entries based on this information. Examiner required. Suitable for group use.

Timed: 2 hours

Range: Grades High school and college/adults in business

Scoring: Hand key

Cost: Test $.75.

Publisher: National Business Education Association

NATIONAL BUSINESS ENTRANCE TESTS-BUSINESS FUNDAMENTALS AND GENERAL INFORMATION TEST
N.B.E.A. Test Committee

teen, adult   grades 10-UP

Purpose: Measures general verbal, numerical, and mental abilities. Used in business for employment and placement purposes.

Description: 100 item paper-pencil, multiple-choice test measuring general mental abilities. Measures command of certain fundamentals including: spelling, plurals, grammar, proper use of words, the solving of arithmetic problems, ability to remember, judgment, and general information about everyday affairs. Examiner required. Suitable for group use.

Timed: 45 minutes

Range: Grades High school and college/adults in business

Scoring: Hand key

Cost: Test $.75.

Publisher: National Business Education Association

NATIONAL BUSINESS ENTRANCE TESTS-MACHINE CALCULATION TEST
N.B.E.A. Test Committee

teen, adult   grades 10-UP

Purpose: Measures ability to perform machine calculations. Used for selection and placement of entry-level office workers.

Description: Multiple item, paper-pencil test assessing the ability to work under timed conditions with a machine calculator to provide figures for a variety of accounting and statistical tables. Computational tasks are similar to actual office duties and include the following topics: invoices, computing averages, yearly summaries, comparative reports, and statistical reports. Test items emphasize quick and accurate computation rather than the ability to organize the material being quantified. Examiner required. Suitable for group use.

Timed: 2 hours

Range: Ages High school and college/adults in business

Scoring: Hand key

Cost: Test $.75.

Publisher: National Business Education Association

NATIONAL BUSINESS ENTRANCE TESTS-STENOGRAPHIC TEST
N.B.E.A. Test Committee

teen, adult   grades 10-UP

Purpose: Assesses the ability to take

dictation and transcribe it into business letters and inter- office communications. Used for selection and placement of stenographers.

Description: 13 item test requiring applicants to take shorthand notes and transcribe dictated material into usable letters under conditions similar to those found in the typical office. Twelve business letters and one inter-office communication are dictated at the rate of 80 words-per-minute. Applicants provide their own notebook and pencil for taking notes, and the entire dictation section (including pauses between items) comprises 30 minutes 15 seconds. Applicants are then given 90 minutes to transcribe the material into typed copy. At the beginning of the transcription period, applicants are given a transcription folder containing 12 sheets of letterhead paper, 8 manifold carbon sets, and one sheet of white paper, along with appropriate information as to format and special requirements of the letters. Examiner required. Suitable for group use.

Timed: 120 minutes

Range: Grades High school and college/adults in business

Scoring: Hand key

Cost: Test $.75.

Publisher: National Business Education Association

NM CONSUMER RIGHTS AND RESPONSIBILITIES TEST (NMCRRT)
S. P. Klein

teen   grades 9-12

Purpose: Measures understanding of consumer rights and responsibilities. Used for program evaluation and needs assessment.

Description: 20 item paper-pencil, multiple-choice test of a student's understanding of consumer protection laws, economic conditions and terms, insurance, purchase payment plans, personal finance, and product information. The test booklets are reusable and the scoring employs a lay-over stencil. The reliability and norms have been determined from samples of ninth- and twelfth- grade secondary students. Examiner required. Suitable for group use.

Timed: 20 minutes

Range: Grades 9-12

Scoring: Hand key

Cost: Specimen set $5.00; 35 tests $10.00; 35 answer sheets $3.00; scoring stencil $2.00; manual $2.00.

Publisher: Monitor

THE OHIO VOCATIONAL ACHIEVEMENT TESTS IN BUSINESS AND OFFICE EDUCATION-- ACCOUNTING/ COMPUTING CLERK
Refer to page 416.

THE OHIO VOCATIONAL ACHIEVEMENT TESTS IN BUSINESS AND OFFICE EDUCATION--CLERK-STENOGRAPHER
Refer to page 417.

THE OHIO VOCATIONAL ACHIEVEMENT TESTS IN BUSINESS AND OFFICE EDUCATION--DATA PROCESSING
Refer to page 418.

THE OHIO VOCATIONAL ACHIEVEMENT TESTS IN BUSINESS AND OFFICE EDUCATION--GENERAL OFFICE CLERK
Refer to page 418.

THE OHIO VOCATIONAL ACHIEVEMENT TESTS IN DISTRIBUTIVE EDUCATION--GENERAL MERCHANDISING
Refer to page 422.

REICHERTER-SANDERS TYPEWRITING
Richard F. Reicherter and M. W. Sanders

teen   grades 10-12

Purpose: Assesses typing achievement of high school students. Used as first or second year exam

Description: 150 item test in the form of work samples by which speed and accuracy may be measured. Test requires typewriter and examiner. Suitable for group use.

Timed: 36 minutes

Range: Grades High school

Scoring: Hand key

Cost: Specimen set $1.50; test $.15; manual $.20; key $.20.

Publisher: Bureau of Educational Measurements

RUSSELL-SANDERS BOOKKEEPING TEST
Raymond B. Russell and M. W. Sanders

teen   grades 10-12

Purpose: Assesses bookkeeping knowledge of high school students. Used as first and second semester exam.

Description: 90 item paper-pencil test of journalizing transactions, classification of accounts, adjusting and closing entries, and solving practical problems. Examiner required. Suitable for group use.

Timed: 40 minutes

Range: Grades High school

Scoring: Hand key

Cost: Specimen set $1.50; test $.15; manual $.20; key $.20.

Publisher: Bureau of Educational Measurements

SRA TYPING 5
Refer to page 784.

SRA TYPING SKILLS TEST
Refer to page 784.

STUDENT OCCUPATIONAL COMPETENCY ACHIEVEMENT TESTING: ACCOUNTING/ BOOKKEEPING
Refer to page 432.

STUDENT OCCUPATIONAL COMPETENCY ACHIEVEMENT TESTING: GENERAL MERCHANDISING
Refer to page 433.

STUDENT OCCUPATIONAL COMPETENCY ACHIEVEMENT TESTING: GENERAL OFFICE
Refer to page 433.

STUDENTS TYPEWRITING TESTS
N.B.E.A. Test Committee

teen, adult   grades 10-UP

Purpose: Assesses typing skills of high school and college students through their first four semesters of typing instruction.

Description: Multiple item test of typing skill assessing speed and accuracy arranged in four levels. Test I (administered after the first semester of instruction) consists of two 5-minute timed writing exercises: one from printed copy and one from handwritten copy. Test II (after the second semester) consists of one 5-minute timed writing exercise, and three exercises emphasizing accuracy rather than speed: typing a business letter with corrections, a tabulation, and a manuscript. Test III (after the third semester) and Test IV (after the fourth semester) are similar to Test II, presenting appropriately more difficult typing tasks. Materials required: Typewriter, paper, carbon paper, and correction materials. Examiner required. Suitable for group use.

Timed: 35 minutes

Range: Grades High school and up

Scoring: Examiner evaluated

Cost: Set of 4 tests and manual $3.00; (specify semester level) $.75.

Publisher: National Business Education Association

TEST OF CONSUMER COMPETENCIES (TCC)
Thomas Stanley, E. Thomas Garman and Richard Brown

teen   grades 8-12

Purpose: Measures student knowledge of the marketplace, including money management and health ser-vices. Used to evaluate consumer education courses and as a pre-and-post test.

Description: Multiple item, paper-pencil test available in two alternate forms. Each item is keyed to one of fourteen basic concepts to help the teacher identify those which have been mastered and those which require further study. The test includes the following concepts: the individual consumer in the market place, money management, con-sumer credit, housing, food, transportation, clothing, health ser-vices, drugs and cosmetics, recreation, furnishings and appliances, insurance, savings and investments, taxes, the consumer in society. Examiner required. Suitable for group use.

Timed: 45 minutes

Range: Grades 8-12

Scoring: Hand key; examiner evaluated, computer scoring available.

Cost: Complete kit (includes 20 test booklets and manual of directions) $14.00.

Publisher: Scholastic Testing Service, Inc.

English and Related

Preschool, Elementary and Junior High School

BASIC SKILLS TEST--WRITING-ELEMENTARY-FORMS A AND B
IOX Assessment Associates

child   grades 5-6

Purpose: Measures student's end-of-elementary school achievement in the basic writing skills. Also useful in determination of grade promotion and program evaluation.

Description: 35 item paper-pencil test with optional writing sample. Measures student's ability to select complete sentences; spell, capitalize and punctuate correctly; use verbs, adjectives, adverbs and pronouns correctly; and express ideas in writing. This test preceeds the IOX Basic Skills Test--Writing-Secondary Level. Examiner required. Suitable for group use.

Untimed: 30-45 minutes

Range: Grades 5 and 6

Scoring: Hand key, may be computer scored

Cost: 25 BW-A2 $37.50; teacher's guide BW-G2 $3.95; 25 BW-B2 $27.50; test manual BTM-2 $3.95; 50 answer sheets BA-2 $6.95.

Publisher: IOX Assessment Associates

CARROW ELICITED LANGUAGE INVENTORY (CELI)
Refer to page 582.

DIAGNOSTIC SPELLING TEST
Denis Vincent and Jenny Claydon

child

Purpose: Assesses spelling skills. Used for diagnosing individual student weaknesses.

Description: Multiple item, paper-pencil test of spelling skills. Items include editing and correcting a passage of text and recognizing common letter groups in nonsense words. Diagnostic Spelling Test also contains a questionnaire measuring attitudes toward spelling, a short dictation passage, and a short section measuring understanding of alphabetical order. Materials include two parallel and equivalent forms, A and B. Examiner required. Suitable for group use. BRITISH PUBLISHER

Untimed: Not available

Range: Ages 8-12

Scoring: Hand key; examiner evaluated

Cost: Specimen set (includes pupils' forms A and B and manual) £2.55; 25 forms (specify A or B) £4.25 (payment in sterling for all overseas orders).

Publisher: NFER-Nelson Publishing Company

DOS AMIGOS VERBAL LANGUAGE SCALES
Refer to page 230.

GATES-McKILLOP-HOROWITZ READING DIAGNOSTIC TESTS
Refer to page 495.

HOLLINGSWORTH-SANDERS JUNIOR HIGH LITERATURE TEST
Leon Hillingsworth and M.W. Sanders

teen   grades 7-8

Purpose: Assesses literature achievement of junior high students. Used as first or second semester exam.

Description: 115 item paper-pencil test of selection content, authorship, comprehension of quotations, and literary appreciation. Examiner required. Suitable for group use.

Timed: 40 minutes

Range: Grades 7 and 8

Scoring: Hand key

Cost: Specimen set $1.50; test $.15; manual $.20; key $.20.

Publisher: Bureau of Educational Measurements

HOYUM-SANDERS ENGLISH TESTS
Vera Davis Hoyum and M.W. Sanders

child   grades 2-8

Purpose: Assesses English achievement of students. Used as first or second semester exam.

Description: 95-120 item paper-pencil tests for elementary (grades 2-4), intermediate (grades 5-6), and junior high (grades 7-9) students. Factors measured include sentence recognition, capitalization, punctuation, contractions, spelling, usage, and alphabetization. Examiner required. Suitable for group use.

Timed: 40 minutes

Range: Grades 2-8

Scoring: Hand key

Cost: Test $.18; manual $.20; key $.20.

Publisher: Bureau of Educational Measurements

THE HUNTER-GRUNDIN LITERACY PROFILES LEVELS 1, 2, 3, 4 AND 5
Elizabeth Hunter-Grundin and Hans U. Grundin

child, teen

Purpose: Assesses child's progress in reading and language development. Used for directing teaching towards a wider range of language and literacy skills.

Description: Battery of brief, paper-pencil and oral tests of five components of literacy skills including reading for meaning, attitude toward reading, spelling, free writing, and spoken language. Divided in five levels: Level 1, 6 ½-8 years; Level 2, 8-9 years; Level 3, 9-10 years; Level 4, 10-11 + years; and Level 5, 11-12 + years. Reading for Meaning passage is different at each

level. Score correlates with Schonell Reading Test, Holborn Reading Scale and the Neale Analysis of Reading Ability. Examiner required. Suitable for group use with the exception of the Spoken Language subtest, which must be administered individually. BRITISH PUBLISHER

Timed: Levels 1 and 2, 40 minutes; Levels 3, 4, 5, 35 minutes

Range: Ages 6½-13½

Scoring: Hand key; examiner evaluated

Cost: Complete kit for each level (includes manual, keys, 35 tests for each area plus picture) $35.00. Cumulative record is included for Level 1.

Publisher: The Test Agency

KANSAS ELEMENTARY SPELLING TEST
Connie Moritz and M.W. Sanders

child   grades 3

Purpose: Assesses spelling achievement of students in grade 3. Useful as a comparison measure.

Description: 85 item pencil and paper test of correct spelling recognition. Two sets of forms for each semester available. Examiner required. Suitable for group use.

Timed: 15 minutes

Range: Grade 3

Scoring: Hand key

Cost: Specimen set $1.50; test $.15; manual $.20; key $.20.

Publisher: Bureau of Educational Measurements

KANSAS INTERMEDIATE SPELLING TEST
Alice Robinson and M. W. Sanders

child   grades 4-6

Purpose: Assesses spelling achievement of upper elementary students. Useful as a comparison measure.

Description: 85 item pencil-paper test of correct spelling recognition. Two sets of forms for each semester available. Examiner required. Suitable for group use.

Timed: 15 minutes

Range: Grades 4-6

Scoring: Hand Key

Cost: Specimen set $1.50.

Publisher: Bureau of Educational Measurements

KANSAS JUNIOR HIGH SPELLING TEST
Mary T. Williams and M. W. Sanders

teen   grades 7-8

Purpose: Assesses spelling achievement of junior high students. Used as a comparison measure.

Description: 85 item paper-pencil test of correct spelling recognition. Two sets of forms for each semester available. Examiner required. Suitable for group use.

Timed: 15 minutes

Range: Grades 7-8

Scoring: Hand key

Cost: Specimen set $1.50.

Publisher: Bureau of Educational Measurements

LISTENING COMPREHENSION TESTS IN ENGLISH FOR STANDARDS 5 and 8
Refer to page 374.

METROPOLITAN LANGUAGE INSTRUCTIONAL TESTS
Refer to page 376.

PHONOVISUAL DIAGNOSTIC TESTS
Edna B. Smith and Mazie Lloyd

child

Purpose: Assesses students' knowledge of the sounds of the letters of the alphabet. Used to determine strengths and weaknesses in the use of phonics.

Description: 24 item paper-pencil test consisting of 24 words dictated to the student to write. The test measures initial and final consonant sounds, short and long vowels, vowel spelling, 22 initial blends and 14 final blends. Examiner required. Suitable for group use.

Untimed: 5-10 minutes

Scoring: Examiner evaluated

Cost: Complete set $4.50.

Publisher: Phonovisual Products, Inc.

THE SIMILES TEST
Refer to page 543.

SOUTH AFRICAN WRITTEN LANGUAGE TEST (SAWLT)- 1981

grades ii-Standard 5

Purpose: Measures written language

ability of English speaking primary school students. Used for educational guidance.

Description: Test of written language which requires the subject to write a passage in response to a stimulus photo. Materials include the stimulus photo, which should be provided to each subject in group administrations. Examiner required. Suitable for group use.

SOUTH AFRICAN PUBLISHER

Untimed: 30 minutes

Range: Grade ii-Standard 5

Scoring: Hand key; examiner evaluated

Cost: (In Rands) manual 7,20; stimulus photo 1,20; writing pad 0,50; scoring pad 1,20 (orders from outside The RSA will be dealt with on merit).

Publisher: Human Sciences Research Council

PRETOS-YEARS 3-7-- PROOFREADING TESTS OF SPELLING
Cedric Croft, Alison Gilmore, Neil Reid and Peter Jackson

child   grades 3-7

Purpose: Measures ability to discriminate between misspelled and correctly spelled words. Used for giving diagnostic information about individual spelling accomplishments.

Description: Multiple item, paper-pencil tests of spelling achievement. Items are reading passages containing misspelled words. Child is required to detect spelling mistakes, correct words identified as misspelled, and indicate lines of text without mistakes. Divided into five overlapping tests for use with different grade levels. Each test is made up of three or four paragraphs consisting of 12-14 lines of text, with two having no misspelled words. Examiner

required. Suitable for group use.

PUBLISHED IN NEW ZEALAND

Timed: 30 minutes

Range: Ages 3-7

Scoring: Hand key; examiner evaluated

Cost: Complete kit (includes 40 test booklets, 1 manual, 1 score key) $12.50 per year level (all remittances must be in New Zealand currency).

Publisher: New Zealand Council for Educational Research

TEST OF WRITTEN ENGLISH (TWE)
Velma R. Anderson and Sheryl K. Thompson

child   grades 1-6

Purpose: Measures written language skills of elementary school children and older remedial students. Used to screen for mastery in areas of capitalization, punctuation, written expression, and paragraph writing.

Description: Multiple item, paper-pencil form on which the student corrects various errors of capitalization, punctuation, and usage, and is asked to write a brief paragraph. Items in each skill area are grouped according to difficulty from grade one through six, with remedial activities provided for each of the areas tested. Items may be read by the students themselves or by the examiner so that even poor readers can be accurately evaluated. A conversion table is provided for translating score into approximate grade-level placement. Examiner-required. Not for group use.

Untimed: 30 minutes

Range: Grades 1-6 and older remedial students

Scoring: Hand key

Cost: Manual $10.00; 25 test forms $6.00; specimen set $10.00.

Publisher: Academic Therapy Publications

TEST OF WRITTEN SPELLING (TWS)
Stephen C. Larsen and Donald D. Hammill

child, teen   grades 1-8

Purpose: Measures student's spelling abilities by using both words which are easily predictable by their sound and words which are more irregular. Identifies spelling strengths and weaknesses of students Grades 1-8.

Description: 60 item paper-pencil test assessing student spelling performance with three groups of words: words readily predictable in sound-spelling pattern, words less predictable, and both types of words presented together. Spelling Age, Spelling Quotient, and Spelling Grade Equivalent are provided for each of the three groups. Test items developed after review of 2,000 spelling rules, with words drawn from ten basal spelling programs. Examiner required. Suitable for group use.

Untimed: 20 minutes

Range: Grades 1-8

Scoring: Examiner evaluated

Cost: Complete (includes manual, 50 answer sheets, class profile sheet, storage box) $26.00. Separate purchase of components available.

Publisher: PRO-ED

TESTS ON NEWBERY MEDAL AWARD BOOKS

child

Purpose: Measures students' content recall of specific Newbery Award books. Used to encourage reading and to quickly check whether a student has read a particular book.

Description: Ten item paper-pencil tests in three versions for each of 53 Newbery Award titles up to 1974. The titles include: *Strawberry Girl, 21 Ballons, Rabbit Hill*, and *The Slave Dancer.* Materials include test and answer key. Examiner required. Suitable for group use.

Untimed: 50 minutes

Range: Ages 10-12

Scoring: Hand key

Cost: Test book $2.45.

Publisher: The Perfection Form Company

VISUAL MEMORY SCALE (VMS)
Refer to page 509.

VOCABULARY COMPREHENSION SCALE (VCS)
Tina E. Bangs

child

Purpose: Evaluates a young child's comprehension of pronouns and words of position, quality, quantity, and size. Used for instructional programming and remediation work.

Description: 61 item test in which the subject responds to the examiner's spoken directions by manipulating the appropriate item, such as card, dolls, cubes, cylinders, buttons in a box, a garage, fence, ladder, a tea set, etc., which are included among the materials. The data collected can be used to plan activities for developing vocabulary needed to enter kindergarten or first grade. Suggestions for teaching unfamiliar words and concepts are included in the test manual. Examiner required. Not for group use.

Untimed: Not available

Range: Ages 2-6

Scoring: Examiner evaluated

Cost: Complete $52.00.

Publisher: Teaching Resources Corporation

WRITE: JUNIOR HIGH
CTB/McGraw-Hill

---

teen   grades 7-9

Purpose: Measures the competencies of junior high school students in writing and communication skills. Used to identify student needs and implement correctional/remedial instruction.

Description: Two-section paper-pencil test consisting of a multiple-choice section and a writing sample section. The multiple-choice section measures student's ability related to mechanics, punctuation, usage, vocabulary, spelling, organization, and format. The writing section requires two samples of written communications in response to hypothetical situations. Examiner required. Suitable for group use.

Timed: 50 minutes per section

Range: Grades Junior high school

Scoring: Hand key; computer scoring available

Cost: Specimen set (includes a sample of the objective test, writing topics, manual, computer and hand scored answer sheets, writing guide, class summary sheet and a test reviewer's guide) $7.25.

Publisher: CTB/McGraw-Hill

WRITING PROFICIENCY PROGRAM/INTERMEDIATE SYSTEM (WPP/IS)
Richard M. Bossone

---

child, teen   grades 6-9

Purpose: Assesses the writing skills of students in grades 6-9. Used by composition teachers.

Description: Four test assessment includes a 70 item, multiple choice, paper-pencil test measuring 14 objectives: adjectives and adverbs, sentence fragments, pronouns, verb tense, subject/verb agreement, misplaced modifiers, conjunctions, run-together sentences, capitalization, quotation and end marks, commas, topic/supporting sentences, sentence sequence, and use of transitions; and three writing exercises including the descriptive, narrative and persuasive forms. Tests are an integral part of a program that includes instructional materials for the teacher. Examiner required. Suitable for group use.

Timed: 50 minutes

Range: Grades 6-9

Scoring: Hand key; computer scoring available

Cost: Specimen set (includes objective test book, Writing Exercise 1, manual, computer and hand scoring answer sheets and a sampling of their other accessories) $13.45.

Publisher: CBT/McGraw-Hill

High School and College

ACT PROFICIENCY EXAMINATION PROGRAM-ARTS AND SCIENCES: SHAKESPEARE
Refer to page 296.

ACT PROFICIENCY EXAMINATION PROGRAM-ARTS AND SCIENCES: FRESHMAN ENGLISH
Refer to page 296.

ADMISSIONS TESTING PROGRAM: TEST OF STANDARD WRITTEN ENGLISH (TSWE)
Refer to page 318.

AMERICAN LITERATURE-ESSAY TESTS

teen   grades 10-12

Purpose: Measures student content recall of a specific American novel, and evaluates writing skills through paragraph organization and content. Used as a literature course post-test.

Description: Five paper-pencil essay questions. For each of 111 American Literature titles including: *An American Tragedy, Black Like Me, Johnny Tremain, On the Beach, The Perfect Tribute,* and *The Red Pony.* Materials include test questions and guidelines. Examiner required. Suitable for group use.

Untimed: 50 minutes

Range: Grades 10-12

Scoring: Examiner evaluated

Cost: Test including guidelines $.40.

Publisher: The Perfection Form Company

AMERICAN LITERATURE 50 Q TESTS

teen   grades 7-12

Purpose: Measures high school student content recall of a specific American novel. Used as a literature post-test.

Description: 50 paper-pencil, multiple-choice questions for each of 167 titles compiled alphabetically and divided in two volumes. Tests are available for all titles including: *Across 5 Aprils, Christy, Ethan Frome, Intruder in the Dust, Rumble Fish, Swiftwater,* *Watership Down* and *The Yearling.* Examiner required. Suitable for group use.

Untimed: 50 minutes

Range: Grades 7-12

Scoring: Hand key

Cost: Two volumes of 75 tests each $30.00 each volume.

Publisher: The Perfection Form Company

AP EXAMINATION: ENGLISH-ENGLISH LANGUAGE
Refer to page 322.

AP EXAMINATION: ENGLISH-ENGLISH LITERATURE
Refer to page 323.

BARRETT-RYAN ENGLISH TEST
E.R. Barrett and Theresa M. Ryan

teen   grades 9-12

Purpose: Measures English language achievement of high school students. Suitable as first or second semester exam for both survey and diagnostic purposes.

Description: 150 item paper-pencil, multiple-choice test of punctuation, correct usage, capitalization, sentence structure, verb usage, grammar, and diction. Examiner required. Suitable for group use.

Timed: 50 minutes

Range: Grades 9-12

Scoring: Hand key

Cost: Specimen set $1.50; test $.18; manual $.20; key $.20.

Publisher: Bureau of Educational Measurements

BASIC SKILLS TEST-WRITING-SECONDARY-FORMS A AND B
IOX Assessment Associates

teen   grades 8-11

Purpose: Measures minimum competency of high school students in the basic writing skills. Useful for program evaluation.

Description: 20 item paper-pencil test with optional writing sample. Measures student's competency in using words correctly, checking mechanics, selecting correct sentences, and expressing ideas in writing. This test succeeds the IOX Basic Skills Test-Writing-Elementary Level. Examiner required. Suitable for group use.

Untimed: 30-45 minutes

Range: Grades 8-11

Scoring: Hand key; may be computer scored

Cost: 25 BW-A1 $37.50; 25 BW-B1 $37.50; teacher's guide BW-G1 $3.95; 50 answer sheets $6.95.

Publisher: IOX Assessment Associates

CLARKE READING SELF-ASSESSMENT SURVEY (SAS)
Refer to page 338.

COLLEGE LEVEL EXAMINATION PROGRAM (CLEP) GENERAL EXAMINATION: ENGLISH COMPOSITION
Refer to page 345.

COLLEGE LEVEL EXAMINATION PROGRAM (CLEP) HUMANITIES: AMERICAN LITERATURE
Refer to page 347.

COLLEGE LEVEL EXAMINATION PROGRAM (CLEP) HUMANITIES: ANALYSIS AND INTERPRETATION OF LITERATURE
Refer to page 348.

COLLEGE LEVEL EXAMINATION PROGRAM (CLEP) HUMANITIES: COLLEGE COMPOSITION
Refer to page 348.

COLLEGE LEVEL EXAMINATION PROGRAM (CLEP) HUMANITIES: FRESHMAN ENGLISH
Refer to page 349.

COLLEGE LEVEL EXAMINATION PROGRAM (CLEP) HUMANITIES: ENGLISH LITERATURE
Refer to page 348.

COOPERATIVE ENGLISH TESTS
Refer to page 360.

DIAGNOSTIC READING TESTS: (DRT) SECTION I-VOCABULARY
Refer to page 518.

END-OF-YEAR EXAMINATIONS FOR COLLEGE-BOUND STUDENTS, GRADES 9-12
Commission on English

teen   grades 9-12

Purpose: Measures proficiency in English skills considered necessary for college-bound students. Used to determine progress in writing competence from grade to grade.

Description: Three section paper-pencil test consisting of three comprehensive questions in language, literature, and composition. These questions are followed by actual student answers, ranging from excellent to poor; each answer is analyzed and evaluated, allowing teachers to compare their students' achievement with that of students throughout the country. The examinations are designed for use at the end of grades 9, 10, 11, and 12. This is a companion volume to *12,000 Students and Their English Teachers*, also compiled by the Commission on English, which has been charged with examining the state of English teaching in th U.S. and making recommendations for improving its quality. Examiner required. Suitable for group use.

Untimed: Not available

Range: Grades 9-12

Scoring: Examiner evaluated

Cost: Manual $4.00.

Publisher: College Board Publications

ENGLISH AND WORLD LITERATURE-50 Q
Wayne DeMouth

teen   grades 11-12

Purpose: Measures high school student knowledge of English and world writers. Used as a regular course post-tests.

Description: 50 paper-pencil, multiple-choice questions for each of 135 titles including: *The Aeneid, Darkness at Noon, Fireweed, Hamlet, Lord Jim, Of Human Bondage*. Examiner required. Suitable for group use.

Untimed: 50 minutes

Range: Grades 11-12

Scoring: Hand key

Cost: Test and key $.40.

Publisher: The Perfection Form Company

ENGLISH KNOWLEDGE AND COMPREHENSION
S. Chatterji and Manjula Maukerjee

teen

Purpose: Measures knowledge and comprehension of English of students ages 14-16 years.

Description: 67 item paper-pencil test arranged in two separately timed parts assessing knowledge and comprehension of the English language. Part I consists of 29 items with a 20 minute time limit; Part II consists of 38 items with a one hour time limit. Useful with students whose native language is not English, but who have been taught in English language schools. Examiner required. Suitable for group use.
PUBLISHED IN INDIA

Timed: 80 minutes

Range: Ages 14-16

Scoring: Hand key; examiner evaluated

Cost: (In Rupees) Complete kit (includes 25 booklets, 100 answer sheets, key, manual) 90Rs.

Publisher: Manasayan

ENGLISH WORLD LITERATURE-ESSAY TESTS

teen   grades 10-12

Purpose: Measures high school student content recall of a specific title in English World Literature and evaluates writing skills through paragraph organization and content. Used as a unit post- test.

Description: Five paper-pencil essay questions for each of 93 titles including: *Anna Karenina, Dracula, Everyman, The Hobbit, Les Miserable, A Piece of String.* Materials include test questions and guide book. Examiner required. Suitable for group use.

Untimed: 50 minutes

Range: Grades 10-12

Scoring: Examiner evaluated

Cost: Test and evaluation guidelines $.40.

Publisher: The Perfection Form Company

ENNIS-WEIR ARGUMENTATION TEST, LEVEL X

teen grades 10-12

Purpose: Assesses ability for critical thinking. Used for instruction regarding informal logic.

Description: Essay test of critical thinking ability. Test stimulus is a letter to the editor of a fictional newspaper. Students read the letter and then write an essay evaluating each of its eight paragraphs as well as the letter as a whole. Areas of competence covered include: getting the point, seeing the reasons and assumptions, stating one's point, and offering good reason. Self-administered. Suitable for group use.

Untimed:

Range: Grades High school and college

Scoring: Examiner evaluated; scoring service

Cost: Test and criterion sheet for grading $.50; manual $1.00; scoring service $1.00 per test.

Publisher: Illinois Thinking Project

GRAMMAR TEST PACKET
Kenneth Stratton and George Christian

teen grades 10-12

Purpose: Assesses skills in grammar. Used for indentifying student strengths and weaknesses as part of an educational evaluation.

Description: Ten paper-pencil test of grammar skills. Both diagnostic and achievement tests are available in four areas: parts of speech, parts of the sentence, joining parts of the sentence, and punctuation and capitalization. Six other areas are covered by shorter tests designed to be used as measures of student knowledge: nouns, pronouns, verbs, adjectives and adverbs, prepositions, conjunctions and interjections, correct usage, variety in sentence arrangement. Examiner required. Suitable for group use.

Untimed: Not available

Range: Grades High school

Scoring: Hand key

Cost: Set of tests for 25 $5.95.

Publisher: Stratton-Christian Press, Inc.

HOSKINS-SANDERS LITERATURE TEST
Thomas Hoskins and M.W. Sanders

teen grades 9-12

Purpose: Assesses literature achievement of high school students. Useful as first or second semester exam.

Description: 150 item paper-pencil, multiple-choice test of general literary content of 35 classical selections. Factors measured are content of selection, authorship, recognition and understanding of selections by English and American authors. Examiner required. Suitable for group use.

Timed: 40 minutes

Range: Grades 9-12

Scoring: Hand key

Cost: Specimen set $1.50; test $.15; manual $.10; key $.20.

Publisher: Bureau of Educational Measurements

INTERPERSONAL COMMU-NICATION INVENTORY (ICI)
Refer to page 817.

JOURNALISM TEST
Francis Miller and Kenneth Stratton

teen   grades 10-12

Purpose: Assesses journalism skills. Used for diagnosing strengths and weaknesses and measuring student achievement.

Description: Multiple item, paper-pencil test of major journalism areas: judgment of news values, paragraphing, sentence variety, news sources, sports, judgment of feature values, speech- interview stories, editorials, make-up, headlines, terminology, copyreading, style, columns, and advertising. Item types include true-false and identifying errors. Examiner required. Suitable for group use.

Untimed: Not available

Range: Grades High school

Scoring: Hand key

Cost: Test $.29 each (minimum order of 10).

Publisher: Stratton-Christian Press, Inc.

MYTHOLOGY TESTS

teen   grades 9-12

Purpose: Measures recall of information read in specific mythology texts. Used as a mythology unit post-test.

Description: 100 item and 50 item paper-pencil, multiple- choice tests. There are separate tests for each of three books: *The Greek Way* and *The Roman Way* both by Edith Hamilton, and *Gods and Myths of Northern Europe* by Ellis Davidson. Materials include test questions, teachers guide and student guide. Examiner required. Suitable for group use.

Untimed: 55 minutes

Range: Grades 9-12

Scoring: Hand key

Cost: Book$2.50-$2.95 each; 50 Q test $.25; 100 Q test $.40; teacher guide $.95; student guide $.30.

Publisher: The Perfection Form Company

NATIONAL ACHIEVEMENT TESTS: ENGLISH, READING and VOCABULARY TESTS-COLLEGE ENGLISH-FOR HIGH SCHOOL and COLLEGE
Refer to page 380.

NATIONAL ACHIEVEMENT TESTS: ENGLISH, READING and VOCABULARY TESTS-ENGLISH
Refer to page 381.

NATIONAL ACHIEVEMENT TESTS: ENGLISH, READING and VOCABULARY TESTS-VOCABULARY (Grades 7-Up)
Refer to page 382.

READING, COMPREHENSION, GRAMMAR USAGE AND STRUCTURE, AND VOCABULARY TESTS
William A. McCartney

teen   grades 10-13

Purpose: Assesses English knowledge or potential of students seeking to enter four-year colleges. Used to predict degree of success in freshman composition or other English classes, and for admission and placement.

Description: 198 item paper-pencil battery of three tests designed to be used together but which may be taken separately to measure performance in the following areas: Reading Comprehension (48 multiple-choice items based on 16 short selections), Grammar, Usage, and Structure (100 two-choice items based on logic of expression, idiom, and good taste), Vocabulary (50 five-choice items which call for recognition of synonyms). Examiner required. Suitable for group use.

Timed: 2 hours complete battery

Range: Grades High school and college freshmen

Scoring: Hand key; may be computer scored

Cost: Contact publisher.

Publisher: William A. McCartney

SANDERS-FLETCHER SPELLING TEST
Gwen Fletcher and M. W. Sanders

teen   grades 9-12

Purpose: Measures spelling achievement of high school students. Used as first or second semester exam.

Description: 150 item paper-pencil test of common words. Examiner required. Suitable for class use.

Timed: 30 minutes

Range: Grades 9-12

Scoring: Hand key

Cost: Specimen set $1.50; test $.15; manual $.20; key $.20.

Publisher: Bureau of Educational Measurements

SANDERS-FLETCHER VOCABULARY TEST
Gwen Fletcher and M. W. Sanders

teen   grades 10-UP

Purpose: Measures vocabulary proficiency of high school and college students. Used as a measure of scholastic aptitude.

Description: 100 item paper-pencil test of general vocabulary words. Examiner required. Suitable for group use.

Timed: 40 minutes

Range: Grades High school and college

Scoring: Hand key

Cost: Specimen set $1.50; test $.15; manual $.20; key $.20.

Publisher: Bureau of Educational Measurements

SENIOR ENGLISH TEST
Refer to page 430.

SPIRIT MASTER TESTS

teen   grades 9-12

Purpose: Evaluates high school students' content recall of specific books used in reading programs. Used as a post-test.

Description: 50 item paper-pencil, two page tests in multiple-choice, true-false and matching format for each of 33 titles. Sample test titles:

The Bell Jar, Go Ask Alice, The Illustrated Man and *Old Yeller.* Materials consist of spirit masters, answer sheet, and scoring key. Examiner required. Suitable for group use and in some cases as student self-test.

Untimed: Not available

Range: Grades 9-12

Scoring: Hand key

Cost: Each master $1.25.

Publisher: The Perfection Form Company

STRUCTURE TESTS, ENGLISH LANGUAGE (STEL)
Jeanette Best and Donna Ilyin

teen, adult grades 10-UP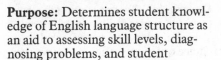

Purpose: Determines student knowledge of English language structure as an aid to assessing skill levels, diagnosing problems, and student placement.

Description: 50 item paper-pencil, multiple-choice test in beginning, intermediate and advanced levels, with two levels of difficulty for each category (one test, six separate forms). The student selects which of three statements is written in correct English, following standard examination procedures. Test can be used with an oral interview, such as the Ilyin Oral Interview Test. Examiner required. Suitable for group use.

Untimed: 30 minutes per test

Range: Secondary-adult

Scoring: Hand key

Cost: Package containing 20 tests and answer sheets (specify level) $8.95.

Publisher: Newbury House Publishers, Inc.

TEST OF EVERYDAY WRITING SKILLS (TEWS)
CTB/McGraw-Hill

teen grades 10-12

Purpose: Assesses a student's competency in writing or composition skills. Used by educators as an evaluation tool for both students and curriculum.

Description: Two component paper-pencil test: multiple- choice and writing sample. The multiple-choice component consists of three subtests: composition skills, spelling, and paragraph organization. It measures performance in spelling, paragraph organization, grammar, usage, and language mechanics. Examiner required. Suitable for use with groups.

Timed: 50 minutes for each component

Range: Grades High school

Scoring: Hand key; computer scoring available

Cost: Specimen key (includes a sample of a test book, manual, machine-score answer sheet, writing guide, users manual and a test reviewer's guide) $7.25.

Publisher: CTB/McGraw-Hill

WALTON-SANDERS ENGLISH TEST
Charles E. Walton and M. W. Sanders

teen grades 9-13

Purpose: Assesses ability of high school and college students to use English grammar and structure correctly. Used as first or second semester exam.

Description: 150 item paper-pencil test of spelling, pronunciation, punctuation, sentence structure, word forms, verbs, pronouns, and prepositions. Examiner required. Suitable for group use.

Timed: 50 minutes

Range: Grades 9-12 and college freshman

Scoring: Hand key

Cost: Specimen set $1.50; test $.15; manual $.20; key $.20.

Publisher: Bureau of Educational Measurements

WESTERN MICHIGAN UNIVERSITY ENGLISH QUALIFYING EXAM
Refer to page 407.

WORD UNDERSTANDING (WU)
Refer to page 409.

WRITE: SENIOR HIGH
CTB/McGraw-Hill

teen   grades 10-12

Purpose: Assesses writing skills of high school students. Used to identify student needs and implement remedial instruction.

Description: Two section paper-pencil test consisting of a multiple-choice section and a writing sample section. The multiple-choice section measures student's ability related to mechanics, punctuation, usage, vocabulary, spelling organization, and format. The writing section requires two samples of written communications in response to hypothetical situations. Examiner required. Suitable for group use.

Timed: 50 minutes for each section.

Range: Grades Senior high school

Scoring: Hand key; computer scor-

ing available

Cost: Specimen set (includes a sample of the objective test book, writing topic sheet, manual, machine and hand-scorable answer sheet, writing sample gguide, class summary sheet, test reviewer's guide) $7.25.

Publisher: CTB/McGraw-Hill

WRITING PROFICIENCY PROGRAM (WPP)
Richard M. Bossone

teen   grades 9-13

Purpose: Assesses the expository writing skills of students in grades 9-13. Used by teachers of composition.

Description: Two paper-pencil tests: test 1 for grades 9- 10; test 2 for grades 11-13. Each test consists of a multiple-choice question section plus a writing sample. Objectives measured in the multiple-choice section include sentence structure, word usage, punctuation and mechanics, capitalization, spelling, the paragraph, the essay, and a business letter. Tests are an integral part of a program that includes instructional components for the teacher. Examiner required. Suitable for use with groups.

Timed: 50 minutes

Range: Grades 9-13

Scoring: Hand key; computer scored

Cost: Specimen set (includes test 1, test 2, manual, computer answer sheet, hand score answer sheet, a writing booklet, sample teacher resource file, activity card, and mastery test, handbook, class summary sheet and test reviewer's guide) $13.45.

Publisher: CTB/McGraw-Hill

Multi-Level

BILINGUAL SYNTAX MEASURE (BSM)
Refer to page 230.

COOPER-McGUIRE DIAGNOS-TIC WORD ANALYSIS TEST
Refer to page 361.

DIAGNOSTIC SCREENING TEST: LANGUAGE 2ND ED. (DST: LANGUAGE)
Thomas D. Gnagey and Patricia A. Gnagey

child, teen   grades K-13

Purpose: Determines ability to write English and diagnoses common problems in the use of the language.

Description: 120 item multiple-choice, paper-pencil test measuring and diagnosing the ability to understand sentence structure, grammar, punctuation, capitalization, spelling, formal and applied knowledge of the rules of writing, and total written language skill. Examiner explains procedure to individuals or groups, and reads the test if students have poor reading skills. Material includes a tear-sheet of individualized classroom recommendations, an index of how solid or spotty each skill is, a pretest, percentile ranks, T scores and grade equivalents. Examiner required. Suitable for groups.

Untimed: 5-15 minutes

Range: Grades Kindergarten-13

Scoring: Hand key

Cost: Manual and 20 test forms $14.00; 100 additional test forms $25.00.

Publisher: Facilitation House

DIAGNOSTIC SCREENING TEST: SPELLING 3RD ED. (DST: SPELLING)
Thomas D. Gnagey

child, teen   grades 1-15

Purpose: Measures student ability to spell words and diagnoses common spelling problems.

Description: 78 item pencil-paper test measuring sight vs. phonics orientation, verbal vs. written processing efficiency, sequential vs. gross visual memory, sequential vs. gross auditory memory, and good vs. poor spelling potential. The examiner, using the test form, pronounces words and the student spells them orally; the examiner then repronounces difficult words and student writes them. The test also provides an index of how spotty or solid each skill is. Includes pretest, percentile ranks, T scores, grade equivalents, and separate A and B forms. Examiner required. Suitable for group use.

Untimed: 5-10 minutes

Range: Grades 1-15

Scoring: Hand key

Cost: Manual and 20 tests (form A) $12.00; 100 additional tests (Form A) $21.00; 100 additional tests (form B) $21.00; 20 additional tests (form B) $6.50.

Publisher: Facilitation House

DIAGNOSTIC SPELLING POTENTIAL TEST (DSPT)
John Arena

all ages

Purpose: Compares an individual's spelling efficiency with such skills as decoding, utilization of phonetic generalizations, visual recall, and matching auditory with visual representations. Used to identify learning and language deficiencies for possible remediation.

Description: Multiple item paper-pencil battery consisting of four subtests: Spelling, Word Recognition, Visual Recognition, and Auditory-Visual Recognition, and two parallel forms which can be used for pre-and-post-testing. Tables are provided for converting raw scores to standard scores, percentile ranks, and grade ratings. Scores and percentiles may be plotted on a profile chart to interpret subtest scores. Words representing unique American-English spellings are excluded, so the test can be used in other English-speaking countries. The test is most effective when given individually, but three of the subtests can be administered to groups. Examiner required.

Untimed: 25-40 minutes

Range: Ages 7-adult

Scoring: Hand key

Cost: Manual $15.00; 25 forms A-1 and B-1 (Spelling/Word Recognition) $6.00; 25 forms A-2 and B-2 (Visual/Auditory-Visual Recognition) $6.00; specimen set $15.00.

Publisher: Academic Therapy Publications

ENGLISH LANGUAGE SKILLS ASSESSMENT IN A READING CONTEXT (ELSA)
Donna Ilyin, Cecelia Doherty, Laurie Freid Lee and Lynn Levy

all ages

Purpose: Measures student understanding of the meaning and grammatical correctness of English language statements as an aid to placement and learning progress.

Description: 25 item paper-pencil, multiple-choice test in five versions: beginning conversation, beginning narration, intermediate conversation, intermediate narration, and advanced narration. The student selects one of four words which best completes the sentence in the conversation or story.

The test has been used in federal accountability reports for funding. Self-administered. Suitable for group use.

Untimed: 30 minutes

Range: Grades Upper elementary-college

Scoring: Hand key

Cost: Complete set;(includes 25 tests, 50 answer sheets and 80 answer keys) $8.95; manual $3.95; free sample kit.

Publisher: Newbury House Publishers, Inc.

ENGLISH PROGRESS TESTS SERIES

child, teen

Purpose: Assesses English skills for children ages 7 to 14. Used for measuring individual pupil progress.

Description: Series of 13 paper-pencil tests providing continuous assessment of reading skills. English Progress Test A, for ages 8 to 9, measures general progress in English. Test A2, ages 7 to 9, covers rhymes, plurals, spelling, vocabulary, pronouns, tenses and reading comprehension. Test B2, ages 8 to 10, requires the child to provide rhymes and opposites, to spell and punctuate, and to write sentences. Test B3, ages 8 to 9, uses multiple- choice questions to assess ability to use words correctly. Test C2, requires written answers covering spelling, punctuation, vocabulary, and comprehension, and is for ages 9 to 11. Test C3, ages 9 to 10, tests basic punctuation, vocabulary and comprehension. Children are also required to join pairs of sentences into longer sentences, and to construct acceptable sentences. Test D3, ages 10 to 11, consists of 50 questions assessing the ability to use words correctly, elementary punctuation, and comprehension of a poetry and a prose passage. Tests E and E2 both include 12 different types of questions testing grammatical usage, written expression, vocabulary comprehension and punctuation. E2 is for ages 11 to 12; Test E has only a provisional standardization and is for ages 12 to 13. Test F2, ages 12 to 13, consists of questions of the "creative response" type, and cover grammatical usage, written expression, vocabulary, comprehension and punctuation. Test F3, ages 12 to 13, provides an assessment of the ability to use words in a way that is contextually correct, and to underrstand their meanings. Test G, ages 13 to 14, consists of ten different exercises assessing English progress by various means, including comprehension passages, questions requiring correction for spelling and punctuation, and transforming direct speech to reported speech. Examiner required. Suitable for group use.

BRITISH PUBLISHER

Untimed: 40 minutes for each test

Range: Ages 7-14

Scoring: Hand key

Cost: Specimen set primary (includes A2, A, B2, B3, C2, C3, D2, D3, pupils forms and a sample manual) £2.00; specimen set secondary (includes D2, D3, E2, E, F2, F3, G) pupil forms and sample manual) £1.80 (payment in sterling for all overseas orders).

Publisher: NFER-Nelson Publishing Company

GRADED WORD SPELLING TEST
P.E. Vernon

child, teen, adult

Purpose: Measures spelling ability. Suitable for use with students from the age of six years, extending to the level of spelling reached by well-educated adults.

Description: 80 item paper-pencil test measures students ability to correctly spell words which are presented to them orally. Each word is placed in the

context of a short sentence, and the test items are graded in order of difficulty. The particular items to be used on any one occasion are selected from the 80-word list according to the age and ability of the pupils to be tested; no pupil takes the whole test. The test is contained in a single reusable booklet and is designed to be administered orally. Full instructions for administration, scoring, and interpretation and provided. Norms are given as quotients (for chronological ages 5:6 to 17:6 +) and as Spelling Ages (5:7 to 15:10). Examiner required. Suitable for group use.

BRITISH PUBLISHER

Untimed: 30 minutes

Range: Ages 6 and older

Scoring: Hand key

Cost: Test booklet £1.25.

Publisher: Hodder & Stoughton

INTERNATIONAL SOCIETY FOR PHILOSOPHICAL ENQUIRY VOCABULARY FORM A

adult

Purpose: Measures knowledge of vocabulary at a high level of achievement (expected ceiling circa 170 A.Q.). Used as preparation for the supervised vocabulary test, Form B.

Description: 70 item paper-pencil, multiple-choice test provides a high level measure of linguistic aptitude. Subjects are asked to select from four choices the one word most closely "related" to the given test-item word. Norms available from top 6% to top 00.002%. Answers and norms printed on the back of the test form. Self-administered. Suitable for group use.

Untimed: Not available

Range: Adult

Scoring: Self-scored

Cost: Test $3.00.

Publisher: Harding Tests

INTERNATIONAL SOCIETY FOR PHILOSOPHICAL ENQUIRY VOCABULARY FORM B

adult

Purpose: Measures knowledge of vocabulary at a high level of achievement. Provides best accuracy with the top 6% to top 00.13% of the population.

Description: 136 item paper-pencil, multiple-choice test provides a high level measure of linguistic ability. Subjects are asked to select from three choices the one word most closely "related" to the given test-item word. Answers and norms printed on the back of the test form. Supervision required. Suitable for group use.

Untimed: Not available

Range: Adult

Scoring: Self-scored

Cost: Test $3.00.

Publisher: Harding Tests

LANGUAGE INVENTORY FOR TEACHERS (LIT)
Arlene Cooper and Beverly A. School

child, teen   grades PRE-9

Purpose: Assesses ability of children and older students who have language difficulties in reading and writing. Used to determine areas of deficiency which require remedial intervention.

Description: Multiple item, paper-pencil sequence of more than 500 language tasks corresponding to 13 long-range goals, five for spoken language and eight for written language. They are ordered by type and difficulty to correspond to the hierarchical development of language concepts. Testing is started at a point where the student is expected to have success and discontinued when several errors have been made. Following the guidelines in the manual, the items the student misses may be translated directly into instructional objectives. The test is designed to help teachers write comprehensive and detailed Individualized Education Programs (IEPs). Examiner required. Not for group use.

Untimed: 30 minutes

Range: Grades Preschool-junior high and older students with language difficulty

Scoring: Hand key

Cost: Manual $10.00; 25 record forms $6.00; specimen set $10.00.

Publisher: Academic Therapy Publications

LANGUAGE PROFICIENCY TEST (LPT)
Joan E. Gerald and Gloria Weinstock

teen, adult

Purpose: Evaluates an individual's ability to use the English language, especially those whose lack of skill prevents them from succeeding at work or school. Used to identify competency levels and to detect specific deficiencies of English as a second language (ESL) student.

Description: Multiple-item, paper-pencil, criterion- referenced, test in three major sections: aural/oral, reading, and writing. It covers nine areas of language functioning, including an optional translation section for ESL students. Each section was designed with subtests of increasing difficulty to provide scores indicating the most appropriate levels of instruction for the student. Scores for each subtest are converted to a percentage and plotted on a profile chart that indicates the level of proficiency. Materials are appropriate in content for the mature student who has low-level skills. Most of the nine subtests can be group-administered; the two which measure low-level functioning require individual administration and are optional for native English students. Examiner required.

Untimed: 90 minutes

Range: Grades 7-adult

Scoring: Hand key

Cost: Manual $7.50; 10 test booklets $15.00; specimen set $7.50.

Publisher: Academic Therapy Publications

MILL HILL VOCABULARY SCALE
Refer to page 28.

THE PICTURE STORY LANGUAGE TEST (PSLT)
Helmer R. Myklebust

child, teen

Purpose: Determines a child's ability to express ideas through writing. Used to evaluate differences between learning disabled, mentally retarded, emotionally disturbed, reading disabled, and speech handicapped, and to diagnose childhood dyslexia.

Description: Multiple-item, paper-pencil test in which examiner places picture on an easel and asks the children to write the best story they can about it. Factors measured include: number of words written, number of sentences, number of words per sentence, syntax accuracy, and success in expression of meaning. Administration for groups of less than ten children. Trained examiner is required.

Untimed: 15-20 minutes

Range: Ages 7-17

Scoring: Hand key; examiner

evaluated.

Cost: Test $16.00; 50 record forms $19.50; Development and Disorders of Written Language, Vol. I-The Picture Story Language Test $28.00; Vol. II-Norms for Exceptional Children $28.00.

Publisher: Grune & Stratton, Inc.

PRI READING SYSTEMS (PRI/RS)
CTB/McGraw-Hill

child, teen   grades K-9

Purpose: Assesses reading and language arts skills in Grades K-9. Used for diagnosis and placement of students.

Description: Multiple item, paper-pencil test of four aspects of language arts skills: oral language, word attack and usage, comprehension, and applications. Divided into five levels spanning grades K-9. For each skill, measurement can take place at three levels of specificity: the skill level; Category Objectives Assessment level; and Instructional Objectives Assessment level. These three approaches are included in System 1 of the PRI/RS, which assesses skills by level, and System 2, which assesses skill clusters across levels. Materials include instructional materials for teaching, reinforcing and monitoring progress. Examiner required. Suitable for group use.

Untimed: Not available

Range: Grades Level A, grades K-1; level B, grades 1- 2; level C, grades 2-3; level D, grades 4-6; level E, grades 7-9 + .

Scoring: Hand key; computer scoring available

Cost: Contact publisher.

Publisher: CTB/McGraw-Hill

PRI/RS: SYSTEM 1, GRADED APPROACH, INSTRUCTIONAL OBJECTIVES INVENTORY
CTB/McGraw-Hill

child, teen grades K-9

Purpose: Assesses instructional objectives in reading and language arts. Used for providing specific instructional information.

Description: Multiple item, paper-pencil test of four language arts areas: oral language, word attack and usage, comprehension, and applications. Divided into five levels spanning grades K-9. Measures of broader skills may be obtained using the Category Objectives Test. Materials include Locator Tests, short reading vocabulary and comprehension tests for determining appropriate test level. Examiner required. Suitable for group use.

Untimed: Not available

Range: Grades K-9

Scoring: Hand key; computer scoring available

Cost: Examination kit (includes an assortment of test books, answer sheets, manuals and keys, overview chart, and class record sheet for various levels) $13.45.

Publisher: CTB/McGraw-Hill

PRI/RS: SYSTEM 1, GRADED APPROACH, CATEGORY OBJECTIVES TEST
CTB/McGraw-Hill

child, teen grades K-9

Purpose: Assesses category objectives in reading and language arts. Used for providing instructional information on mastery of category objectives.

Description: Multiple item, paper-pencil test of four language arts areas: oral language, word attack and usage, comprehension, and applications. Divided into five levels spanning grades K-9. Measures of more specific skills may be obtained by using the Instructional Objectives Test. Materials include Locator Tests, short reading vocabulary and comprehension tests for determining appropriate test level. Examiner required. Suitable for group use.

Untimed: Not available

Range: Grades K-9

Scoring: Hand key; computer scoring available

Cost: Examination kit $13.45.

Publisher: CTB/McGraw-Hill

PRI/RS: SYSTEM 2, MULTI-GRADED APPROACH TO ASSESSMENT AND INSTRUCTION
CTB/McGraw-Hill

child, teen grades K-9

Purpose: Assesses skill levels in reading and language arts. Used for diagnosis of instructional needs.

Description: Multiple item, paper-pencil test of four skill areas: oral language, word attack and usage, comprehension, and applications. Divided into five levels spanning grades K-9. Used in a two-stage assessment approach. First stage consists of a Placement Test which indicates which level of a skill area within the cluster is the appropriate instructional level for the student. Skill Area Diagnostic Test is then administered to determine specific instructional objectives which have or have not been mastered. Examiner required. Suitable for group use.

Untimed: Not available

Range: Grades K-9

Scoring: Hand key; computer scoring available

Cost: Examination kit $19.50.

Publisher: CTB/McGraw-Hill

SPAR (SPELLING AND READING) TESTS
Dennis Young

child, teen

Purpose: Measures the ability to read and write of children ages 7-15 years. Identifies students in need of remedial attention (designed to discriminate particularly among lower ability levels).

Description: Multiple-item, paper-pencil test consists of two sections (Spelling and Reading) which provide a complementary approach to testing literacy at a simple level. The spelling items are presented in the manual as "banks," allowing the user to select ten matched tests without overlap and many more with partial overlap. The Reading test follows the same format as D. Young's "Group Reading Test" and can be scored using the same templates. Parallel forms A and B are available. Examiner required. Suitable for group use. BRITISH PUBLISHER

Untimed: Not available

Range: Ages 7-15.11

Scoring: Hand key

Cost: Specimen set £1.25; 20 test copies (specify form) 95p per set, manual 95p.

Publisher: Hodder & Stoughton

SPELLING TESTS (ENGLISH)-1964

child, teen

Purpose: Measures ability to spell English words correctly. Used for educational evaluation and placement.

Description: Four paper-pencil tests of spelling ability. Series 2 is designed for Standards 1-3, Series 3 for Standards 3-5, Series 4 for Standards 6-8, and Series 5 for Standards 9-10. Afrikaans-speaking students may need to be administered a series below their actual standard level. Materials include two alternate forms, A and B, for each series. Examiner required. Suitable for group use. Test to be discontinued in near future. SOUTH AFRICAN PUBLISHER

Timed: 45 minutes

Range: Grades Standards 1-10

Scoring: Hand key, examiner evaluated

Cost: (In Rands) 10 tests (specify form and series number) 0,30; manual 0,60; scoring key (specify form) 0,40 (all orders outside The RSA will be dealt with on merit).

Publisher: Human Sciences Research Council

TEST OF WRITTEN LANGUAGE (TOWL)
Donald D. Hammill and Stephen C. Larsen

child, teen   grades 2-12

Purpose: Identifies students grades 2-12 who have problems in written expression, pinpointing specific areas of deficit.

Description: Paper-pencil, free-response test in which students are given a theme and asked to write a story about it. Yields information in six areas of writing competence: thematic maturity, spelling, vocabulary, word usage, style, and handwriting. Information derived is from an analysis of a sample of continuous writing, as well as from an analysis of subtest performance. Materials include answer and profile sheets and a manual which includes a section dealing with informal methods for evaluating the quality of written products. Standardized on 3,418 students with the same characteristics as those reported in the 1980 census. Examiner required. Available in Spanish.

Untimed: Varies

Range: Grades 2-12

Scoring: Examiner evaluated

Cost: Complete kit (includes examiner manual, 50 student response sheets, 50 profile sheets) $46.00.

Publisher: PRO-ED

TESTS OF PROFICIENCY IN ENGLISH
Refer to page 403.

TESTS OF PROFICIENCY IN ENGLISH--LISTENING TESTS
Refer to page 404.

TESTS OF PROFICIENCY IN ENGLISH--READING TESTS
Refer to page 404.

TESTS OF PROFICIENCY IN ENGLISH--SPEAKING TESTS
Refer to page 405.

TESTS OF PROFICIENCY IN ENGLISH--WRITING TESTS
Refer to page 405.

WOODCOCK LANGUAGE PROFICIENCY BATTERY (WLPB)
Refer to page 408.

Fine Arts

BELWIN-MILLS SINGING ACHIEVEMENT TEST
Richard W. Bowles

child, teen   grades 1-UP

Purpose: Measures achievement in sight singing of written music. Used for progress records in sight singing, chair placement or class assignment in choral organizations, and assessment of sight singing skills.

Description: 14 item test of a person's ability to sight read and sing written music. Test items consist of 8-bar passages arranged in order of increasing difficulty. All passages are in the key of C; a variety of time signatures are presented. Students are scored for the number of measures correctly sung for each item. Examiner required. Not for group use.

Untimed: Not available

Range: Grades Elementary-college

Scoring: Hand key

Cost: 48 score sheets $2.50.

Publisher: Belwin Mills Publishing Corporation

FARNUM MUSIC TEST
Stephen Farnum

teen

Purpose: Measures student musical achievement and ability as a way of helping teachers distinguish individuals with talent from those without.

Description: Multiple item paper-pencil test covering music symbols, notation, tonal patterns, and cadence. The symbol section measures eye focus speed and reaction speed to stimuli. Notation test measures ability to differentiate between written notes and different ones played on the piano. With tonal patterns, the student identifies which of four tones has been changed. In cadence testing, the student indicates whether a tone should rise or fall to complete a musical phrase. Materials include: 16 page manual for testing, scoring, and selecting beginning band members; a 12-inch LP phonograph record; answer sheets; and correction keys. Examiner required. Suitable for group use.

Untimed: 40-45 minutes

Range: ages 10-16 years

Scoring: Hand key

Cost: Test kit $12.75, answer sheets $12.00 per hundred.

Publisher: Bond Publishing Company

FARNUM STRING SCALE
Stephan Farnum

child, teen   grades 4-12

Purpose: Measures student performance and progress playing stringed instrumentts. Useful in placing individuals in orchestras.

Description: A performance test in which the student is presented a series of musical exercises of increasing difficulty to sight-read. The performance level is recorded by noting the number of errors in the execution. Materials consist of an exercise book and scoring sheets. Examiner required. Not suitable for group use.

Untimed: 10-15 minutes

Range: Grades 4-12

Scoring: Examiner evaluated

Cost: Testing book $6.00; 100 score sheets $12.95.

Publisher: Hal Leonard Publishing Corporation

INDIANA-OREGON MUSIC DISCRIMINATION TEST
Newell H. Long

child, teen   grades 5-UP

Purpose: Assesses the development of a students musical taste. Used in music appreciation classes.

Description: Multiple item, paper-pencil test in which the examiner plays a 12-inch LP record. The students listen and record their responses on an answer sheet. Materials include the record, test manual, and scoring key. Examiner required. Suitable for group use.

Untimed: 25-45 minutes

Range: Grades 5 and up

Scoring: Hand key

Cost: Complete (includes 12" LP, manual, 3 answer sheets, 2 scoring keys) $12.50.

Publisher: Midwest Music Tests

KWALWASSER MUSIC TALENT TEST
Jacob Kwalwasser

all ages   grades 4-UP

Purpose: Measures musical aptitude. A very short test used from fourth grade up and for any level experience.

Description: 50 item aurally administered paper-pencil test assessing musical talent. Form A consists of 50 three-tone patterns which are repeated with variation in pitch, tone, rhythm, or loudness. Alternate Form B consists of 40 items which present the same features in a more simplified form. Record player and examiner required. Suitable for group use.

Timed: 10 minutes

Range: Grades 4-college

Scoring: Hand key; examiner evaluated

Cost: Contact publisher.

Publisher: Belwin Mills Publishing Corporation

MODERN PHOTOGRAPHY COMPREHENSION
Martin M. Bruce

teen, adult

Purpose: Assesses individual's knowledge of photography as an aid to vocational guidance and a measure of classroom progress.

Description: 40 item paper-pencil multiple-choice test designated to measure photographic understanding. Rated on a scale of superior, high average, average, low average, and very low. Materials include a manual and grading keys. Self-administered. Suitable for group use.

Untimed: 20-25 minutes

Range: Adolescent-adult

Scoring: Hand key

Cost: Specimen test $3.20; 25 tests $15.30; manual $.66; keys $.66.

Publisher: Martin M. Bruce, Ph.D. Publishers

MUSICAL APTITUDE TESTS-MUSAT J and MUSAT S
Refer to page 379.

THE OHIO VOCATIONAL ACHIEVEMENT TESTS IN GRAPHICS COMMUNICATION-COMMERCIAL ART
Refer to page 423.

SEASHORE MEASURES OF MUSICAL TALENTS
C.E. Seashore

all ages   grades 4-UP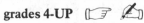

Purpose: Assesses abilities funda-mental to the development of musical proficiency.

Description: Six auditorily presented tests measuring aspects of auditory discrimination: Pitch, Loudness, Time, Timbre, Rhythm and Total Memory. Scores relatively unrelated to amount of formal musical training. Materials include audio test stimulus on record or reel-to-reel tape. Examiner required. Suitable for group use.

Untimed: 1 hour total

Range: Grades 4-12; college; adult

Scoring: Hand key; may be machine scored

Cost: Complete set (includes audio stimulus, 50 IBM 805 answer documents, key, manual); Record Version $30.00; tape version reel-to-reel $37.50.

Publisher: The Psychological Corporation

SIMONS MEASUREMENTS OF MUSIC LISTENING SKILLS

child   grades 1-3

Purpose: Measures attainment of music listening objectives common to most primary school music curricula.

Description: Multiple item non-verbal criterion referenced test of nine separate music listening objectives. All instructions and test items are tape recorded. Set includes: manual, five cassette recordings, 30 answer booklets, overhead transparencies of test pages, and scoring mask. Examiner required. Suitable for group use.

Timed: Three 25 minute periods

Range: Grades 1-3

Scoring: Hand key

Cost: Contact publisher.

Publisher: Stoelting Co.

WATKINS-FARNUM PERFORMANCE SCALE
Stephan Farnum and John Watkins

child, teen   grades 4-12

Purpose: Measures student performance and progress in playing musical instruments. Used to place individuals in musical groups.

Description: Multiple item performance test in which the student is presented a series of musical exercises of increasing difficulty to sight-read. The performance level is recorded by noting the number of errors in the execution. Materials consist of an exercise book and scoring sheets. A second version (Form B) provides a different set of exercises. Examiner required. Not suitable for groups.

Untimed: 10-15 minutes

Range: Grades 4-12

Scoring: Examiner evaluated

Cost: Testing book $9.00; 100 score sheets $7.00.

Publisher: Hal Leonard Publishing Corporation

WING STANDARDISED TESTS OF MUSICAL INTELLIGENCE
H.D. Wing

all ages

Purpose: Measures a child's mental capacity for the study of music. Used with individuals from age 8 to adult to determine levels and groupings for the study of music.

Description: Standardized ear tests measuring analysis of chords, pitch discrimination, memory for pitch, harmony appreciation, intensity appreciation, rhythm appreciation and phasing appreciation. Tests are played on piano, then recorded. Easy to administer to ages eight and above. Administered in one time period for older student and in two shorter periods for younger children. Used to screen musically bright children to study musical instruments and to select children capable of studying to G.C.E. levels. Materials include manual, answer sheets, key, monograph and tape. Examiner required. Suitable for group use.
BRITISH PUBLISHER

Timed: Playing time 45-50 minutes

Range: Ages 8-adult

Scoring: Hand key

Cost: Contact publisher.

Publisher: NFER-Nelson Publishing Company

Foreign Language and English as a Second Language

AP EXAMINATION: FRENCH LANGUAGE
Refer to page 323.

AP EXAMINATION: FRENCH LITERATURE
Refer to page 324.

AP EXAMINATION: GERMAN LANGUAGE
Refer to page 324.

AP EXAMINATION: SPANISH-- SPANISH LANGUAGE
Refer to page 329.

AP EXAMINATION: SPANISH-- SPANISH LITERATURE

Refer to page 330.

AP EXAMINATION: LATIN--- VERGIL AND CATULLUS- HORACE

Refer to page 326.

BILINGUAL SYNTAX MEASURE (BSM)

Marina K. Burt, Heidi C. Dulay and Eduardo Hernandez

child, teen   grades K-12

Purpose: Measures children's mastery of basic oral syntactic structures in both English and Spanish. Used for diagnosis and placement in bilingual and other special language programs.

Description: Multiple item measure to test strengths and weaknesses in basic language construction by using cartoon-type pictures and simple questions to elicit natural speech patterns. The BSM also places pupils in a proficiency level category (in both English and Spanish). Scores on the BSM may be used for determining "English readiness" or "program exit" in bilingual and other special programs. Available at two levels. BSMI foor grades K-2; BSMII for grades 3-12. Manual provides proficiency ratings and equivalent Law categories established by federal guidelines. English (BSM-E) and Spanish (BSM-S) versions available. Examiner required. Not suitable for group use.

Untimed: 10-15 minutes

Range: Grades K-12

Scoring: Hand key

Cost: Complete set (includes picture booklet, 35 english child/student response booklets, English manual, 35 Spanish child/student response booklets, Spanish manual, class records, technical handbook, expanding envelope) BSMI $82.50; BSMII $87.00.

Publisher: The Psychological Corporation

COLLEGE LEVEL EXAMINA- TION PROGRAM (CLEP) MODERN LANGUAGES: COL- LEGE FRENCH LEVELS 1 AND 2

Refer to page 352.

COLLEGE LEVEL EXAMINA- TION PROGRAM (CLEP) MODERN LANGUAGES: COL- LEGE GERMAN LEVELS 1 AND 2

Refer to page 352.

COLLEGE LEVEL EXAMINA- TION PROGRAM (CLEP) MODERN LANGUAGES: COL- LEGE SPANISH LEVELS 1 AND 2

Refer to page 353.

CRANE ORAL DOMINANCE TEST (CODT)

Refer to page 583.

DOS AMIGOS VERBAL LAN- GUAGE SCALES

Donald E. Critchlow

child, teen

Purpose: Measures a child's ability to understand English and Spanish words. Used to determine dominant language proficiency, so that primary-language instruction, English as a Second Language programs, or remediation may be planned.

Description: 85 item verbal test in English and Spanish consisting of 85 word scales and their opposites. The examiner dictates each stimulus word, and the child responds with a word which has the opposite meaning. Words that have unique American-English spellings are excluded, so the test can be used in other English-speaking countries. Examiner must be fluent in English and Spanish. Not suitable for group use.

Untimed: 20 minutes

Range: Ages 5-13

Scoring: Hand key

Cost: Manual $5.50; 25 recording forms $6.00; specimen set $5.50.

Publisher: Academic Therapy Publications

EMPORIA FIRST YEAR LATIN TEST

Bernadine Sitts, Lillian Wall, Minnie Miller and M. W. Sanders

teen   grades 10-12

Purpose: Assesses achievement of high school students in first year Latin courses. Used as first or second semester exam.

Description: 85 item paper-pencil test of Latin forms, syntax, derivatives, and simple paragraphs for comprehension. Examiner required. Suitable for class use.

Timed: 40 minutes

Range: Grades High school

Scoring: Hand key

Cost: Specimen set $1.50; test $.15; manual $.20; key $.20.

Publisher: Bureau of Educational Measurements

EMPORIA SECOND YEAR LATIN TEST

Bernadine Sitts, Lillian Wall, Minnie Miller and M. W. Sanders

teen   grades 10-12

Purpose: Assesses achievement of high school students in second year Latin courses. Used as first or second semester exam.

Description: 90 item paper-pencil test of vocabulary, forms, syntax, derivatives, background material, and reading comprehension. Examiner required. Suitable for class use.

Timed: 40 minutes

Range: Grades High school

Scoring: Hand key

Cost: Specimen set $1.50; test $.15; manual $.20; key $.20.

Publisher: Bureau of Educational Measurements

ENGLISH FIRST AND SECOND LANGUAGE TESTS

Purpose: Measures understanding of English as a first or second language. Used for educational placement and guidance.

Description: 19 separate paper-pencil tests of English comprehension for each standard or level of pupil. Particular subtests vary, but generally include Language Usage, Vocabulary, Reading Comprehension, and Spelling. Exclusing English first language, standards; and English second language, Standard 6. Materials include two alternate forms, A and B, for each standard. Examiner required. Suitable for group use.
SOUTH AFRICAN PUBLISHER

Untimed: Not available

Range: Grade 2/Sub ii-Standard 10

Scoring: Hand key; examiner evaluated

Cost: Contact publisher (orders from outside The RSA will be dealt with on merit).

Publisher: Human Sciences Research Council

FIRST YEAR FRENCH TEST
Minnie M. Miller and Jean M. Leblon

teen   grades 10-12

Purpose: Assesses high school student achievement in first year French courses. Useful as end-of- course exam.

Description: 100 item paper-pencil test of vocabulary, pronunciation, structure, and reading. Examiner required. Suitable for group use.

Timed: 50 minutes

Range: Grades High school

Scoring: Hand key

Cost: Specimen set $1.50; test $.15; manual $.20; key $.20.

Publisher: Bureau of Educational Measurements

FIRST YEAR SPANISH TEST
Oscar F. Hernandaz and Minnie M. Miller

teen   grades 10-12

Purpose: Assesses high school student achievement in first year Spanish courses. Useful as end-of-course exam.

Description: 100 item paper-pencil test of vocabulary, pronunciation, structure, and reading. Examiner required. Suitable for group use.

Timed: 50 minutes

Range: Grades High school

Scoring: Hand key

Cost: Specimen set $1.50; test $.15;

manual $.20; key $.20.

Publisher: Bureau of Educational Measurements

FRENCH COMPREHENSION TESTS
H.C. Barik

child   grades 1-8

Purpose: Measures French listening comprehension. Used with students involved in French immersion programs or intensive French programs at early grade levels.

Description: 45 item paper-pencil multiple-choice test assessing listening comprehension in French. Answer choices are presented in picture form. Consists of three sections: words and sentences, questions, and stories. Separate test manuals for Primer (K) level and Level 1. Optional reel-to-reel tape available for test administration. Examiner required. Suitable for group use. CANADIAN PUBLISHER

Untimed: 40 minutes

Range: Grades Primary school

Scoring: Hand key

Cost: 35 Primer level tests $18.50; tape $15.00 (specify test) 35 Level 1 tests $20.50; test manual (specify test) $4.50 (Canadian exchange).

Publisher: Ministry of Education-Ontario

JAPANESE PROFICIENCY TEST (JPT)

teen, adult   College

Purpose: Evaluates level of proficiency in Japanese of American or other English speaking students. Used for measuring achievement in language programs.

Description: 130 item paper-pencil

---

test of three aspects of proficiency in Japanese: listening comprehension, reading comprehension and Japanese character recognition. Items are multiple choice; the stimulus material for the listening comprehension section is recorded in standard modern Japanese. Audio equipment is required for listening comprehension stimulus material. Examiner required. Suitable for group use.

Timed: 120 minutes

Range: Grades College and university students

Scoring: Computer scored

Cost: $15.00 per examinee.

Publisher: Educational Testing Service

LANGUAGE PROFICIENCY TESTS (LPT)-1972

teen

Purpose: Measures language proficiency. Used for educational placement and diagnosis.

Description: Multiple item paper-pencil test of proficiency in English and Afrikaans. Separate materials available for Standards 9 and 10. Examiner required. Suitable for group use. Publisher notes that this test is "normed on Blacks only."

Timed: 2½ hours

Range: Grades Standards 9 and 10

Scoring: Hand key; examiner evaluated

Cost: (In Rands) Test (specify Standard 9 or 10) 0,40; manual 2,30; scoring stencil (specify Standard 9 or 10) 0,90; 10 answer sheets 0,60 (orders from outside The RSA will be dealt with on merit).

Publisher: Human Sciences Research Council

LISTENING COMPREHENSION GROUP TEST (LCGT)
Donna Ilyin

teen, adult

Purpose: Measures the ability of non-native speakers of English to comprehend and wriite English as an aid to student placement, screening, and diagnosis.

Description: Two part verbal-picture, paper-pencil test for use in English as a Second Language (ESL) and bilingual programs. The picture test (LCPT) measures listening comprehension by having the subject look at a picture or series of pictures and listen to the examiner make a statement about them, followed by questions. The subject then answers each question by selecting one of three pictures and the words 'yes' and 'no', which are written on a separate piece of paper. The written test (LCWT) is intended for intermediate and advanced ESL students, who look at a picture series, listen to a story, look at other related pictures, listen to the examiner's questions, and write one-sentence answers. Examiner required. Suitable for group use.

Untimed: 30 minutes for picture test; 45 minutes for written test

Range: Ages 14-85

Scoring: Hand key

Cost: Picture booklet $2.95; technical guide $5.95; manual $4.50; includes 50 answer sheets and 2 keys $5.95; complete written test (includes 50 answer sheets) $5.96.

Publisher: Newbury House Publishers, Inc.

MODERN LANGUAGE APTI-TUDE TEST (MLAT)
Refer to page 377.

MODERN LANGUAGE ASSO-CIATION-COOPERATIVE FOREIGN LANGUAGE TESTS
Educational Testing Service/ MLA

teen, adult   grades 10-UP

Purpose: Measures competency in French, German, Italian, Russian or Spanish. Used for student evaluation and curriculum planning in foreign language programs.

Description: Multiple subtests measure Listening, Speaking, Reading and Writing skills for each language. Available on two levels: Level L, 1st and 2nd year high school instruction or 1st and 2nd semester college; Level M, 3rd and 4th year high school instruction or 3rd or 4th semester college instruction. The tests are conducted entirely in the foreign language tested. Materials include test booklets, an optional individual writing test booklet, listening tape, speaking tape, answer sheet, key and manual. Examiner required. Suitable for group use.

Timed: Listening 25 minutes; speaking 10 minutes; reading 35 minutes; writing 35 minutes

Range: Grades High school/college

Scoring: Hand key; examiner evaluated; computer scoring available

Cost: Complete test books $14.00 per pkg. (pkg. includes 10 reusable tests for all three areas and directions, specify language and level); all components may be ordered separately.

Publisher: CTB/McGraw-Hill

PIMSLEUR LANGUAGE APTI-TUDE BATTERY
Paul Pimsleur

child, teen   grades 6-12

Purpose: Assesses aptitude for learning languages. Used for screening potential foreign language students and grouping for instruction.

Description: Test battery assessing aptitude for learning modern languages. Six parts include information on student's grade point average, interest in studying a foreign language, verbal ability and auditory ability. Materials include test tape providing auditory stimuli for parts 5 and 6. Examiner required. Suitable for group use.

Untimed: 50-60 minutes

Range: Grades 6-12

Scoring: Hand key; computer scoring service available

Cost: Specimen set (includes manual, test, class record, IBM 805 and 1230 answer documents) $15.00; basic scoring services $.60 per student.

Publisher: The Psychological Corporation

SECONDARY LEVEL ENGLISH PROFICIENCY TEST (SLEP)
Educational Testing Service

teen

Purpose: Assesses English language proficiency of non- native speakers. Used as admissions test by private secondary schools and as a placement test by both public and private secondary schools.

Description: 150 item paper-pencil test of two components of English proficiency, listening comprehension and reading comprehension--structure and vocabulary. Does not measure productive language skills.

Tape recorder is required to administer listening comprehension sections, and materials include the necessary cassette tape. Examiner required. Suitable for group use.

Timed: 80 minutes

Range: Ages 12-17

Scoring: Hand key; computer scoring available

Cost: Complete kit $75.00 (reusable materials, 25 test booklets, 500 answer sheets, 1 cassette, 2 keys, manual); specimen set $7.00 (1 each, test booklet, answer sheet, tape, manual).

Publisher: Educational Testing Service

SECOND YEAR FRENCH TEST
Minnie M. Miller and Jean M. Leblon

teen   grades 10-12

Purpose: Assesses achievement of high school students in second year French courses. Used as end-of-course exam.

Description: 100 item paper-pencil test of vocabulary, pronunciation, structure, reading, and simple facts about France. Examiner required. Suitable for group use.

Timed: 50 minutes

Range: Grades High school

Scoring: Hand key

Cost: Specimen set $1.50; test $.15; manual $.20; key $.20.

Publisher: Bureau of Educational Measurements

SPANISH AND LATIN AMERICAN LIFE AND CULTURES
Minnie Miller and Beulah Aiken

teen   grades 10-UP

Purpose: Assesses achievement of high school and college students in Spanish and Latin American life and culture. Used as end-of-course exam for Spanish classes.

Description: 100 item paper-pencil test of geography, history, art, literature, and customs. Examiner required. Suitable for group use.

Timed: 40 minutes

Range: Grades High school and college

Scoring: Hand key

Cost: Specimen set (includes test, key, manuals) $1.50.

Publisher: Bureau of Educational Measurements

SPANISH/ENGLISH READING AND VOCABULARY SCREENING TEST (SERVS)

child   grades 1-4

Purpose: Assesses student's dominant language. Used for determining appropriate language for testing.

Description: Multiple item, paper-pencil pretest of dominant language. Reduces frustration and inappropriate testing by indentifying whether Spanish or English is most appropriate language for achievement testing. Three forms of SERVS are available. Form BC is designed for screening students before testing at Grades 1 and 2. Form HS, Hand-Scorable, is designed primarily for use with Grade 3 students, who mark their answers in the test book. Form MS, Machine Scorable, is designed for students in Grade 4 or above. Developed for use with CTBS--Espanol. Examiner required. Suitable for group use.

Untimed: Not available

Range: Grades 1-4

Scoring: Hand key; computer scoring available

Cost: Multi-level examination kit $10.35.

Publisher: CTB/McGraw-Hill

TESTS OF BASIC LITERACY IN THE SOTHO LANGUAGE-1982

teen, adult

Purpose: Measures literacy skills of adults and Higher Primary Level students. Used for educational and vocational guidance.

Description: Multiple item tests of literacy skills in three South African languages: South Sotho, North Sotho, and Tswana. Each test consists of three subtests: reading comprehension of items related to practical knowledge, reading comprehension of continuous prose and a cursive letter, and writing skill from dictation. Materials include two forms for each test. Examiner required. Suitable for group use. SOUTH AFRICAN PUBLISHER

Untimed: 1½ hours

Range: Grades Higher Primary Level-adult

Scoring: Examiner evaluated

Cost: Contact publisher (orders from outside The RSA will be dealt with on merit).

Publisher: Human Sciences Research Council

TEST OF ENGLISH AS A FOREIGN LANGUAGE (TOEFL)
Educational Testing Service

adult

Purpose: Assesses proficiency in English for non-native speakers. Used as college admission test and placement test.

Description: 150 item test of three aspects of English ability: listening, structure and written expression, and reading comprehension and vocabulary. Items are four-option multiple choice and involve comprehension of spoken and written language. Institutional TOEFL is available by special arrangement with ETS. Examiner required. Suitable for group use.

Timed: 120 minutes

Range: Adult

Scoring: Computer scored

Cost: Saturday $21.00 per student; Friday $29.00 per student; Overseas $23.00 and $31.00.

Publisher: Educational Testing Service

TEST OF SPOKEN ENGLISH (TSE)
Educational Testing Service

adult

Purpose: Assesses proficiency in spoken English for non-native speakers. Used for evaluating applicants for graduate level teaching assistantships and certification in health related professions.

Description: 20 item test of spoken English. Stimulus material is provided by test tape and test book. Answers are taped; tapes are evaluated by two raters at ETS. Four scores are provided: Overall Comprehensibility Score and Three area scores-grammar, fluency, and pronounciation. Materials include a Speaking Proficiency in English Assessment Kit (SPEAK) for instructional use. Examiner required. Suitable for group use.

Untimed: Not available

Range: Adult

Scoring: Computer scored; examiner evaluated

Cost: $30.00 per test; SPEAK test form and rater training materials $300.00.

Publisher: Educational Testing Service

TESTS OF PROFICIENCY IN ENGLISH

Refer to page 403.

TESTS OF PROFICIENCY IN ENGLISH-LISTENING TESTS

Refer to page 404.

TESTS OF PROFICIENCY IN ENGLISH-READING TESTS

Refer to page 404.

TESTS OF PROFICIENCY IN ENGLISH-SPEAKING TESTS

Refer to page 405.

TESTS OF PROFICIENCY IN ENGLISH-WRITING TESTS

Refer to page 405.

Mathematics

Basic Math Skills

ASSESSMENT OF SKILLS IN COMPUTATION (ASC)
CTB/McGraw-Hill

child, teen   grades 7-9

Purpose: Diagnoses a student's computation skill strengths and needs and indicates the instruction required to improve. Used by junior high school teachers.

Description: Two-section paper-pencil test of 36 items each measuring com-

putational skills required in activities such as reading a graph, buying records on sale, measuring shelves, or redecorating a room. Examiner required. Suitable for group use.

Timed: 50 minutes, 2 sessions

Range: Grades Junior high school

Scoring: Hand key; computer scoring available

Cost: Specimen set (includes a test book, manual, a machine and hand-score answer sheet, class summary sheet, an objectives matrix, a text reviewer's guide) $7.25.

Publisher: CTB/McGraw-Hill

BASIC MATHEMATICS TESTS SERIES

child, teen

Purpose: Measures understanding of basic mathematical principles. Used for diagnosis of individual children's abilities.

Description: Five paper-pencil tests of understanding of fundamental relationships and processes in mathematics. Test A, for ages 6 to 8, consists of 40 items measuring a range of math skills. Test B, ages 8 to 9, has 40 items assessing more complex relationships. Test C, ages 9 to 10, is a 50 item test covering area, graphical representation, symmetry, inequality, elementary knowledge of sets, and decimals and fractions. Test DE, ages 10 to 12, covers symmetry, tabulation, fractions. Test DE, ages 10 to 12 covers symmetry, tabulation, fractions, elementary algebra, basic spatial ability and graphical representation. Test FG, ages 12 to 14, consists of 55 questions covering a wide range of mathematical thinking. Examiner required. Suitable for group use.
BRITISH PUBLISHER

Untimed: 1 hour

Range: Ages 7-15

Scoring: Hand key

Cost: Specimen set primary (includes pupils Forms A, B, C, DE and manual) £1.80; specimen set secondary (includes pupils Forms DE, FG plus manuals for DE and FG) £2.40 (payment in sterling for all overseas orders).

Publisher: NFER-Nelson Publishing Company

BASIC NUMBER DIAGNOSTIC TEST
W.E.C. Gillham

child

Purpose: Measures number skill of children ages 5-7 years and older children who are deficient in the use of numbers. Diagnoses what a child can and cannot do so that specific teaching objectives can be determined. Suitable for all children scoring below a 7½-year reading age on the Basic Number Screening Test.

Description: Multiple item paper-pencil and oral response test covers the basic number skills that a normally developing 7-year-old child should have mastered. Test items are arranged in approximate order of difficulty within twelve categories of skills progressing from reciting, copying, and writing numbers to dealing with simple addition and subtraction. The format allows close observation of the child's strategies and errors, thus providing a basis for remedial assistance. The test is intended to be given at regular intervals so that a child's progress can be charted and teaching requirements revised. Where appropriate, both test and retest items are provided. Approximate age-norms are provided. Examiner required. Not for group use.
BRITISH PUBLISHER

Untimed: 15-20 minutes

Range: Ages 5-9

Scoring: Examiner evaluated

Cost: Specimen set £1.00; 20 tests

£3.00 per set, manual 85p.

Publisher: Hodder & Stoughton

BASIC NUMBER SCREENING TEST
W.E.C. Gillham and K.A. Heese

child

Purpose: Evaluates basic number skills of children ages 7-12 years. Used for survey and screening purposes. Identifies children in need of further testing and possibly remedial attention.

Description: Multiple item paper-pencil test measures proficiency with numbers and understanding of number concepts. Two parallel forms, A and B, may be used simultaneously to minimize the risk of copying and for test-retest programs. Norms are presented as Number Ages (7:0 to 12:0). The manual contains instructions for administering and scoring the test. Examiner required. Suitable for group use.
BRITISH PUBLISHER

Untimed: 30 minutes

Range: Ages 7-12

Scoring: Hand key

Cost: Specimen set 95p.; 20 tests (specify form) £1.65; manual 70p.

Publisher: Hodder & Stoughton

BASIC SKILLS TEST--MATHEMATICS ELEMENTARY-FORMS A AND B
IOX Assessment Systems

child   grades 5-6

Purpose: Measures student's end-of-elementary school achievement in basic mathematics skills. Useful for minimum competency testing, determination of grade promotion, or program evaluation.

Description: 30 item paper-pencil test

measures student's performance in basic calculations with whole numbers, fractions and decimals; word problems requiring single arithmetic operations and measurement units; and interpreting tables and graphs. This test preceeds the IOX Basic Skill Test--Mathematics-Secondary Level.

Untimed: 30-45 minutes

Range: Grades 5 and 6

Scoring: Hand key, may be computer scored

Cost: 25 BM-A2 $37.50; 25 BM-B2 $37.50; teacher's guide BM-G2 $3.95; test manual BTM-2 $3.95; 50 BA- 2 answer sheets $6.95.

Publisher: IOX Assessment Systems

BASICS OF OPERATIONS (GRADES 1-3)
B. J. Beeson and Sam Adams

child   grades 1-3

Purpose: Measures the ability of third- and fourth- grade students to add and subtract. Used to assess student progress and determine remedial needs.

Description: 335 item paper-pencil test. Measures basic knowledge of addition and subtraction as well as readiness for multiplication and division. The teacher reads the directions/questions in the beginning sections. Other sections can be completed independently. Examiner required. Suitable for group use.

Untimed: 30 minutes

Range: Grades 1-3

Scoring: Examiner evaluated

Cost: Contact publisher.

Publisher: Dr. Charles Sauls

COMMON FRACTIONS
Sam Adams

child, teen   grades 6-8

Purpose: Measures the ability of fifth- through eighth- grade students to work with common fractions. Diagnoses individual needs in this area.

Description: 172 item paper-pencil test measuring 49 concepts and computational skills necessary for understanding and working with common fractions. The student may complete the entire test or that portion related to a particular operation. Examiner required. Suitable for group use.

Untimed: 45 minutes

Range: Grades 6-8

Scoring: Examiner evaluated

Cost: Contact publisher.

Publisher: Dr. Charles Sauls

CSMS DIAGNOSTIC MATHS TESTS

child, teen

Purpose: Assesses levels of conceptual understanding in mathematics. Used for matching teaching methods and materials to individual child needs.

Description: Ten paper-pencil tests of mathematics concepts. CSMS Number Operations, for ages 11 to 12, asks pupils to identify which of the four basic operations are required to solve every day problems, and to invent problems which fit particular arithmetic expressions. CSMS Graphs Test, ages 13 to 16, examines child's understanding of important ideas regarding graphical representation. CSMS Ratio and Proportion Test, ages 13 to 16, assesses knowledge of ideas related to ratios and proportion. CSMS Fractions Tests 1 and 2, for ages 11 to 13 and 14 to 15, consist of problems in diagrammatic and word problem form, as well as

computations. Test 2 looks at all four operations on fractions. CSMS Measurement Test, ages 11 to 14, assesses knowledge of fundamental principles of length, area, and volume. CSMS Place Value and Decimals Test, ages 11 to 16, examines understanding of principles, structure and meaning of decimals. CSMS Reflection and Rotation Test classifies performance into several levels based on difficulty of the items. CSMS Algebra Test ages 13 to 15, and CSMS Vectors Test, ages 14 to 16, both measure knowledge in their specific areas.
BRITISH PUBLISHER

Untimed: 40-60 minutes for each test

Range: Ages 10-13.09

Scoring: Examiner evaluated

Cost: Contact publisher

Publisher: NFER-Nelson Publishing Company

DECIMAL FRACTIONS
B. J. Beeson and Lionel O. Pellegrin

child, teen   grades 6-8

Purpose: Measures the ability of fifth-through eighth- grade students to work with decimal fractions. Diagnoses individual needs in this area.

Description: 129 item paper-pencil test measuring 43 concepts and computational skills required to understand and work with decimal fractions. Examiner required. Suitable for group use.

Untimed: 45 minutes

Range: Grades 6-8

Scoring: Examiner evaluated

Cost: Contact publisher.

Publisher: Dr. Charles Sauls

DIAGNOSTIC ABILITIES IN MATH (D.A.M. TEST)
Francis T. Sganga

Slow Learner

Purpose: Measures knowledge of basic mathematics. Used for student placement and remediation.

Description: 220 item paper-pencil test in two sections. Part I is a timed test with 160 problems testing instant recall of fundamentals of addition, subtraction, multiplication, and division. Part II is a diagnostic test which consists of 60 problems covering whole numbers, fractions, and decimals. Examiner required. Suitable for group use.

Timed: Part I, 30 minutes; Part II, 3 hours

Range: Slow Learner, Remedial Basic Math Student

Scoring: Hand key

Cost: 10 test booklets, teacher instructions, answer key $22.95.

Publisher: Mafex Associates, Inc.

DIAGNOSTIC MATHEMATICS INVENTORY (DMI)
CTB/McGraw-Hill

child, teen   grades 1.5-UP

Purpose: Assesses student mastery of mathematics objectives. Used for providing diagnostic information for teachers, and for prescribing group and individual learning activities.

Description: Multiple item paper-pencil tests of 325 objectives taught in traditional and contemporary mathematics curriculums. Items are multiple- choice, one per objective. Divided into seven overlapping levels spanning grades 1.5-7.5. Recommended grade ranges are: Level A, Grades 1.5-2.5; Level B, Grades 2.5-3.5; Level C, Grades 3.5-4.5;

Level D, Grades 4.5-5.5; Level E, Grades 5.5-6.5; Level F, Grades 6.5-7.5; and Level G, Grades 7.5 and beyond. Materials include Practice Exercises, Learning Activities Guide, and Guide to Ancillary Materials. Examiner required. Suitable for group use.

Untimed: Not available

Range: Level A grades 1.5-2.5; Level B grades 2.5- 3.5; Level C grades 3.5-4.5; Level D grades 4.5- 5.5; Level E grades 5.5-6.5; Level F grades 6.5- 7.5; Level G grades 7.5 and over

Scoring: Hand key; computer scoring available

Cost: Multi-level examination kit (includes assorted tests, answer sheets, manuals and guides from different levels) $19.50. Specimen set for a specific level $7.25.

Publisher: CTB/McGraw-Hill

DIAGNOSTIC MATH TESTS

child, teen

Purpose: Assesses skills in arithmetic. Used for determining nature of specific pupil problems.

Description: Three paper-pencil tests of math ability: Diagnostic Arithmetic Tests, Standards 2 to 8; Diagnostic Tests in Basic Algebra, Standards 7 and 8; and Mathematics Tests, Diagnostic, Primary Level, Standards 1 to 5. Each test is divided into subtests. Aspects tested by the Diagnostic Tests in Basic Algebra are basic operations; simple algebraic expressions and linear equations; sets; exponents; number systems; ratio, rate, and proportion; substitution; and factors. Examiner required. Suitable for group use.
SOUTH AFRICAN PUBLISHER

Untimed: Not available

Range: Grades Standards 1-8

Scoring: Hand key; examiner evaluated

Cost: Contact publisher (orders outside The RSA will be dealt with on merit).

Publisher: Human Sciences Research Council

DIAGNOSTIC SCREENING TEST: MATH (DST:MATH)
Thomas D. Gnagey

---

child, teen   grades 1-10

Purpose: Determines ability to use numbers in computation, including percentages and metric measurements, and assesses achievement levels in 72 individual math processes.

Description: 72 item paper-pencil test in two sections of 36 items each: basic computation and specialized procedures; covering multiplication, division, use of zero, manipulation, decimals, simple fractions, fraction manipulation, time, sequencing, money, U.S. and metric measurement and percentages. The examiner explains the procedure and student completes the problems, using test forms A or B. Material also includes a tearsheet of individualized classroom recommendations, a consolidation index of how solid or spotty each skill is. A pretest, percentile ranks, T scores and grade equivalents. Examiner required. Suitable for group use.

Untimed: 3-20 minutes

Range: Grades 1-10

Scoring: Hand key

Cost: Manual and 20 tests (Form A) $12.00; 100 additional tests (Form A) $21.00; 100 additional tests (Form B) $21.00; 20 additional tests (Form B) $6.50.

Publisher: Facilitation House

EMPORIA ELEMENTARY ARITHMETIC TEST
Patricia M. Pease and M. W. Sanders

child   grade 1

Purpose: Assesses arithmetic achievement of primary school students. Used as first or second semester exam.

Description: 130 item paper-pencil test of fundamental operations and reasoning problems. Examiner required. Suitable for group use.

Timed: 40 minutes

Range: Grade 1

Scoring: Hand key

Cost: Specimen set $1.50.

Publisher: Bureau of Educational Measurements

EMPORIA INTERMEDIATE ARITHMETIC TEST
Ruth Otterstrom and M. W. Sanders

child   grades 4-6

Purpose: Assesses arithmetic achievement of elementary school students. Used as first or second semester exam.

Description: 130 item paper-pencil test of computation, comprehension, and problem solving. Examiner required. Suitable for group use.

Timed: 50 minutes

Range: Grades 4-6

Scoring: Hand key

Cost: Specimen set $1.50.

Publisher: Bureau of Educational Measurements

EMPORIA JUNIOR HIGH SCHOOL ARITHMETIC TEST
Ieleen Engleson and M. W. Sanders

teen   grades 7-9

Purpose: Assesses arithmetic achievement of junior high students. Used as first or second semester exam.

Description: 130 item paper-pencil test of computation, problem solving, and concepts. Examiner required. Suitable for class administration and group use.

Timed: 50 minutes

Range: Grades 7-9

Scoring: Hand key

Cost: Specimen set $1.50.

Publisher: Bureau of Educational Measurements

EMPORIA PRIMARY ARITHMETIC TEST
Patricia M. Pease and M. W. Sanders

child, teen   grade 1

Purpose: Assesses arithmetic achievement of primary school students. Useful as first or second semester exam.

Description: 130 item paper-pencil test of basic arithmetic skills. Examiner required. Suitable for group use.

Timed: 20 minutes

Range: Grade 1

Scoring: Hand key

Cost: Test $.20; manual $.20; key $.20.

Publisher: Bureau of Educational Measurements

ESSENTIAL MATHEMATICS
L.M. Bental

child, teen

Purpose: Assesses mathematic skills. Used in diagnosis of specific mathematics deficiencies and planning of remedial activities.

Description: Multiple item paper-pencil tests of knowledge important in learning mathematics. Topics covered include conservations, sets, the four rules, place value, fractions, decimals, time and length. Not age-normed, emphasis is on evaluation of specific tasks. Test booklet may be retained for future reference. Examiner required. Not suitable for group use.
BRITISH PUBLISHER

Untimed: 30 minutes

Range: Ages 7-14

Scoring: Hand key; examiner evaluated

Cost: 10 tests £3.35; manual £0.95 (payment in sterling for all overseas orders).

Publisher: NFER-Nelson Publishing Company

EVERYDAY SKILLS TEST: MATHEMATICS
Refer to page 360.

GRADED ARITHMETIC-MATHEMATICS TEST--METRIC EDITION
P.E. Vernon and K.M. Miller

child, teen

Purpose: Measures arithmetic and mathematics skills of children 6-16 years old. May be used with the visually impaired.

Description: Multiple item paper-pencil test of achievement in arithmetic and mathematics is arranged in separate forms for Junior and Senior students, with a slight overlap to achieve continuity within the test as a whole. The Junior form is intended for students ages 6-12 years; the Senior form for students ages 11-16 years. The manual provides relevant technical data and full instructions for administering the test, including an "oral" version for use with the visually impaired. The answers are clearly presented to facilitate scoring, and advice given on the acceptability of various alternative forms of response. Norms are provided as Mathematics Ages (5:0 to 17:1) and as deviation quotients (for chronological ages 5:3 to 18:0 +). Examiner required. Suitable for group use.
BRITISH PUBLISHER

Untimed: 30 minutes

Range: Junior Edition, Ages 6-12; Senior Edition, Ages 11 and older

Scoring: Hand key

Cost: Specimen set £1.25, 20 tests (specify form) £1.60 per set, manual 85p.

Publisher: Hodder & Stoughton

GROUP MATHEMATICS TEST: SECOND EDITION
Dennis Young

child

Purpose: Measures mathematical understanding of children ages 6-12 years.

Description: Multiple item paper-pencil test measures simple mathematical skills and understanding. The item content of this second edition is the same as the first edition. The revised manual provides new norms and slightly revised instructions for administration. Separate tables of quotients are given to cover a wide range of ability, from Infants (ages 6:5 to 7:10) and first-year Juniors (ages 6:5 to 7:10) to less able pupils up to age 12:10. Examiner required. Suitable for group use. BRITISH PUBLISHER

Untimed: Not available

Range: Ages 6.5 to 8.10

Scoring: Examiner evaluated

Cost: Specimen set £1.50; 20 tests (specify form) £1.50; manual £1.25.

Publisher: Hodder & Stoughton

KEYMATH DIAGNOSTIC ARITHMETIC TEST
Austin Connolly, William Nachtman and E.M. Pritchett

child   grades K-6

Purpose: Diagnoses children's arithmetic skills to identify areas of weakness for remedial instruction.

Description: Three category test covering: Content, (numeration, fractions, geometry and symbols), Operations, (addition, subtraction, multiplication, division, mental computation, and numerical reasoning), and Applications, (word problems, missing elements, money, measurement and time). The examiner displays a test plate to the student and asks a test question, recording the response on an individual record form. Only those items within the student's functional range are administered. Materials include test plates bound into an easel, manual and a package of 25 diagnostic records. Grade equivalents, grade percentile ranks, and normal curve equivalents for grades 2-6 are available. Diagnostic information provided includes total test performance, area performance in content, operations, and applications, subtest performance, and subtest item performance. A KeyMath Metric Supplement to assess metric measurement skills is available. Examiner required. Not

for group use.

Untimed: 30-40 minutes

Range: Grades K-6

Scoring: Examiner evaluated

Cost: Complete kit $43.50; 25 diagnostic records $7.35; Metric Supplement Test plates and manual $6.50; 25 Metric Supplement record forms $3.75.

Publisher: American Guidance Service

KRAMER PRESCHOOL MATH INVENTORY (KPMI)
Robert E. Kramer

child

Purpose: Analyzes mathematical skills and concepts in preschool children. Used to determine need for remedial instruction.

Description: Multiple item inventory covering seven categories and 77 concepts which measures academic/cognitive, receptive, and expressive factors. Materials include the manual, scoring and record forms, and a 21-item Math Screen, which can be administered to groups and indicates the amount of individualized instruction needed in addition to regular classroom work. The inventory itself can only be administered to individuals. Examiner required.

Untimed: Not available

Range: Ages 3-6½

Scoring: Examiner evaluated

Cost: Complete $53.00.

Publisher: Teaching Resources Corporation

LEICESTER NUMBER TEST
W.E.C. Gillham and K.A. Hesse

child

Purpose: Measures basic number skills of individual students and class groups ages 7-9 years old. Identifies students in need of special help. Indicates areas in need of special attention with the class as a whole.

Description: Multiple item paper-pencil test assesses a child's understanding of basic concepts of the number system as well as his grasp of the "four rules" of conventional calculation. Intended for use as a general screening test to be given at the beginning of the school year. Norms provided for ages 7:1 to 9:0. Examiner required. Suitable for group use.
BRITISH PUBLISHER

Untimed: Not available

Range: Ages 7.1 to 9.0

Scoring: Examiner evaluated

Cost: Specimen set 95p; 20 tests £4.25 per set; manual 80p.

Publisher: Hodder & Stoughton

MATHEMATICS ATTAINMENT TESTS SERIES

child, teen

Purpose: Measures understanding of mathematics. Used to identify individual student strengths and weaknesses.

Description: Seven paper-pencil tests of mathematics attainment: Test A, ages 7 to 8; Test B, ages 8 to 10; Test C1, ages 9 to 12; Test C3, ages 9 to 10; Test DE1, ages 10 to 12; Test DE2, ages 10 to 11; and Test EF, ages 11 to 13. Tests A and B are orally administered, and are varied in content and style. Tests C1, C3, DE1, and DE2 are written tests in which

computation is kept to a minimum. Questions cover graphs, simple geometry, base, series and number patterns, fractions, arithmetical processes and equations. Test EF consists of 60 multiple-choice items measuring number concepts, space operations, geometry and tabular/graphical representation. Examiner required. Suitable for group use.
BRITISH PUBLISHER

Untimed: 50 minutes for each test

Range: Ages 7-13.06

Scoring: Hand key; examiner evaluated

Cost: Specimen set primary (includes pupil forms A, B, C1, C3, DE1, DE2 and sample manual) £1.50; specimen set secondary (includes pupil forms C1, DE1, DE2, and sample manual) £1.50 (payment in sterling for all overseas orders).

Publisher: NFER-Nelson Publishing Company

MATH TESTS GRADE i/SUB A-STANDARD 10

Purpose: Measures understanding of mathematics. Used for educational evaluation and placement.

Description: 19 separate paper-pencil tests of mathematics achievement and understanding. Particular subtests vary, but generally include Mechanical, Insight, and Problem Solving. Materials include two alternate forms, A and B, for all standards except Grade i/Sub A. Examiner required. Suitable for group use.
SOUTH AFRICAN PUBLISHER

Untimed: Not available

Range: Grade i/Sub A-Standard 10

Scoring: Hand key; examiner evaluated

Cost: Contact publisher (orders from outside The RSA will be dealt with on merit).

Publisher: Human Sciences Research Council

METROPOLITAN MATHEMATICS INSTRUCTIONAL TESTS
Refer to page 376.

MINIMUM ESSENTIALS FOR MODERN MATHEMATICS
Ernest Hayes

---

child, teen   grades 6-8

Purpose: Measures mathematical aptitude among children Grades 6-8. Used to group students for math instruction.

Description: 55 item paper-pencil test measures the understanding of important basic concepts in present day mathematics. Special symbolization has been avoided to extend the use to classes in modern mathematics as well as regular mathematics. Examiner required. Suitable for group use.

Timed: 40 minutes

Range: Grades 6-8

Scoring: Hand key

Cost: Complete set (includes 30 booklets, manuals for administration and interpretation, scoring key, 30 record sheets) $5.50. Manual of statistical information sent on request.

Publisher: Hayes Educational Tests

NATIONAL ACHIEVEMENT TESTS for ELEMENTARY SCHOOLS: ARITHMETIC AND MATHEMATICS--ALGEBRA TEST FOR ENGINEERING AND SCIENCE
Refer to page 382.

NATIONAL ACHIEVEMENT TESTS for ELEMENTARY SCHOOLS: ARITHMETIC AND MATHEMATICS--AMERICAN NUMERICAL TEST
Refer to page 382.

NATIONAL ACHIEVEMENT TESTS for ELEMENTARY SCHOOLS: ARITHMETIC AND MATHEMATICS--ARITHMETIC FUNDAMENTALS
Refer to page 383.

NATIONAL ACHIEVEMENT TESTS for ELEMENTARY SCHOOLS: ARITHMETIC AND MATHEMATICS--ARITHMETIC (FUNDAMENTALS AND REASONING)
Refer to page 383.

NATIONAL ACHIEVEMENT TESTS for ELEMENTARY SCHOOLS: ARITHMETIC AND MATHEMATICS--ARITHMETIC REASONING
Refer to page 384.

NATIONAL ACHIEVEMENT TESTS for ELEMENTARY SCHOOLS: ARITHMETIC AND MATHEMATICS--ARITHME-TIC- 3-6 (FUNDAMENTALS and REASONING)
Refer to page 383.

NATIONAL ACHIEVEMENT TESTS for ELEMENTARY SCHOOLS: ARITHMETIC AND MATHEMATICS--FIRST YEAR-ALGEBRA TEST
Refer to page 384.

NATIONAL ACHIEVEMENT TESTS for ELEMENTARY SCHOOLS: ARITHMETIC AND MATHEMATICS--GENERAL MATHEMATICS
Refer to page 385.

NATIONAL ACHIEVEMENT TESTS for ELEMENTARY SCHOOLS: ARITHMETIC AND MATHEMATICS--PLANE GEOMETRY, SOLID GEOME-TRY AND PLANE TRIGONOMETRY TESTS
Refer to page 385.

NOTTINGHAM NUMBER TEST
W.E.C. Gillham and K.A. Hesse

child

Purpose: Measures basic knowledge or arithmeticc among children ages 9-11 years. Identifies students in need of further testing. Groups students according to ability for teaching purposes.

Description: Two multiple item paper-pencil subtests measure knowledge and understanding of basic arithmetic. The first part assesses basic number concepts (series and place-value). The second part assesses basic calculation skills (the "four rules" of formal arithmetic). Items of each type are presented in varied order, but are graded for difficulty, and are identified by symbols in the scoring column. Separate norms are provided for the two subtests as well as for the test as a whole. Examiner required. Suitable for group use.
BRITISH PUBLISHER

Untimed: Not available

Range: Ages 9.1-11

Scoring: Examiner evaluated

Cost: Specimen set 95p.; 20 tests

£3.00 per set; manual 80p.

Publisher: Hodder & Stoughton

NUMBER TEST DE
B. Barnard

child

Purpose: Measures understanding of basic number processes. Used for educational evaluation.

Description: Multiple item paper-pencil test of four basic processes: addition, subtraction, multiplication and division. Test DE uses the principle that knowledge of these processes will allow the child to apply them and use them logically. Examiner required. Suitable for group use.
BRITISH PUBLISHER

Untimed: 50 minutes

Range: Ages 10.06-12.06

Scoring: Hand scoring

Cost: 10 tests £1.95; manual £0.55 (payment in sterling for all overseas orders).

Publisher: NFER-Nelson Publishing Company

PEABODY MATHEMATICS READINESS TEST (PMRT)
Refer to page 457.

PORTLAND PROGNOSTIC TEST FOR MATHEMATICS
Ernest Hayes

child, teen   grades 6.5-9

Purpose: Measures mathematical aptitude among children Grades 7-9. Used to group students for math instruction, measure achievement, and predict success in algebra classes, especially for the more competent math student.

Description: 59 item paper-pencil

tests provides an inventory of basic arithmetic concepts useful for prognosis and measuring achievement. Grade 9, Forms A and B (for testing at the end of grade 8) is designed to predict success in grade 9, grade 8, Forms A and B (for testing at the end of grade 7 or beginning of grade 8) is designed to predict success in grade 8 accellerated mathematics; grade 7, Forms A and B (for testing at the end of grade 6 or beginning of grade 7) is the same test as grade 8 but with special norms for identifying students who can profit from an accellerated mathematics program in grade 7. The norms developed include: percentile ranks, T-scores, deviation scores, predicted achievement and stanines. Examiner required. Suitable for group use.

Timed: 40 minutes

Range: Grades 6.5-9

Scoring: Hand key

Cost: Complete set (includes 30 booklets, manuals for administration and interpretation, scoring key, 30 record sheets) $5.50. Manual of statistical information sent on request.

Publisher: Hayes Educational Tests

PROFILE OF MATHEMATICAL SKILLS
Norman France

---

child, teen

Purpose: Measures mathematics achievement. Used for diagnosis of specific student strengths and weaknesses.

Description: Multiple item, paper-pencil, criterion- referenced tests of mathematics skills. Divided into two levels. Level 1, ages 8 to 13, measures addition, subtraction, multiplication, division, operations, measurement and money, and extensions. Level 2, ages 10 to 15, measures these same areas plus fractions, decimal fractions and percentages, and diagrams. Tests are administered over the normal course of mathematics lessons.. Examiner required. Suitable for group use.

BRITISH PUBLISHER

Untimed: 30 minutes

Range: Ages 8-15

Scoring: Hand key; examiner evaluated

Cost: Specimen set (includes Level 1 and Level 2 pupil's booklet profile chart, teacher's book) £2.55 (payment in sterling for all overseas orders).

Publisher: NFER-Nelson Publishing Company

READINESS FOR OPERATIONS (K-3)
Sam Adams and Charles Sauls

---

child   grades K-3

Purpose: Measures student understanding of math concepts which are prerequisite to addition and subtraction. Used to determine readiness for kindergarten mathematics and to assess remedial needs of first and second grade students.

Description: 48 item paper-pencil test measuring 16 concepts. These include: one-to-one correspondence (pictures of objects), one-to-one correspondence (symbols), matching equal sets, matching numerals, matching numerals and names, recognizing numerals, writing numbers, separating subsets, recognizing cardinal numbers, sequencing through ten, writing numerals for set, and basic meaning of addition. Examiner reads aloud the directions for each test item; no reading required of the examinees. Examiner required. Suitable for group use.

Untimed: 30 minutes

Range: Grades K-3

Scoring: Examiner evaluated

Cost: Contact publisher.

Publisher: Dr. Charles Sauls

SEQUENTIAL ASSESSMENT OF MATHEMATICS INVENTORY-CLASSROOM TEST (SAMI-CLASSROOM)
Fredricka K. Reisman

child, teen   grades K-8

Purpose: Assesses math performance at the classroom level points out curriculum strengths and weaknesses, and yields a profile of the group's standing.

Description: Multiple item paper-pencil test of eight areas of mathematics: math language, ordinality, number/notation, measurement, geometry, computation, word problems, and math applications. Class scores may suggest a need for further testing of some students. Test kit includes 30 tests for specific K-8 grade levels, and a manual. Examiner required. Intended for group use.

Untimed: 40 minutes

Range: Grades K-8

Scoring: Hand key

Cost: Contact publisher.

Publisher: Charles E. Merrill Publishing Company

SEQUENTIAL ASSESSMENT OF MATHEMATICS INVENTORY-INDIVIDUAL ASSESSMENT BATTERY (SAMI)
Fredricka K. Reisman

child, teen   grades K-8

Purpose: Assesses math performance of elementary school students to provide detailed diagnosis of an individual's strengths and weaknesses. Useful for referral to gifted or remedial classes.

Description: 300 item paper-pencil test measuring math performance in eight content areas: math language, ordinality, number/notation, measurement, geometry, computation, word problems, and math applications. Test kit includes stimulus manual, response form and teacher record form. Examiner required. Not suitable for group use.

Untimed: 30-60 minutes

Range: Grades K-8

Scoring: Hand key

Cost: Contact publisher.

Publisher: Charles E. Merrill Publishing Company

SKILLCORP COMPUTER MANAGEMENT SYSTEM--MATH

child   grades K-6

Purpose: Assesses math skill deficiencies. Used to diagnose individual deficiencies in math and prescribe resources for reteaching.

Description: 60 criterion referenced tests determine math skill deficiences for grades K-6. Microcomputer prints prescription for individual students or groups to reteach skills not mastered. All skills tested are cross-referenced to major publisher materials. Materials include test administration manual or test cassette, and test cards for each grade level. Examiner required. Suitable for group use.

Timed: Varies on each test

Range: Grades K-6

Scoring: Hand key; may be computer scored

Cost: Contact publisher.

Publisher: Skillcorp Software, Inc.

STANFORD MEASUREMENT SERIES-STANFORD DIAGNOSTIC MATHEMATICS TEST (SDMT)
Refer to page 398.

THE STAFFORDSHIRE TEST OF COMPUTATION
M.E. Hebron and W. Pattinson

child, teen

Purpose: Measures computational skills of children age seven to fifteen. Used for identifying specific weaknesses of individual pupils.

Description: 31 item paper-pencil test of addition, subtraction, multiplication, and division. Items require knowledge of decimal currency, metric measures, and common commercial transactions. Subject must have some ability to deal with numbers. Examiner required. Suitable for group use.
BRITISH PUBLISHER

Untimed: Not available

Range: Ages 7-15

Scoring: Hand key

Cost: 50 test sheets $7.50; manual and norms $3.00.

Publisher: Harrap Ltd.-available from The Test Agency and Pendragon House, Inc. (U.S.A.)

STEENBURGEN DIAGNOSTIC-PRESCRIPTIVE MATH PROGRAM AND QUICK MATH SCREENING TEST
Fran Steenburgen Gelb

child   grades 1-6

Purpose: Determines an elementary school student's exact level of functioning in mathematics. Used to plan programs for children and older remedial students whose math skills

are still at the elementary level.

Description: Multiple item paper-pencil screening test. It measures ability in simple addition subtraction, one-digit carrying, aaddition of mixed numbers, and long division. The items are arranged in a sequential hierarchy according to the grade level when each skill is introduced (Level I includes problems appropriate for grades one through three; Level II, grades four through six). Scores can be plotted on a profile sheet that shows a graphic representation of progress made from pre-to-post- test. After strengths and weaknesses are identified, the student can be introduced to the diagnostic-prescriptive program consisting of 55 reproducible worksheets, to be used until skills are mastered. The format of the screening test does not overstimulate hyperactive or distractible children. Examiner required. Suitable for group use.

Untimed: 10 minutes

Range: Grades 1-6 and older remedial students with elementary level math skills.

Scoring: Hand key

Cost: Complete program $25.00; Level I (grades 1-3) 25 test forms and 25 profile sheets $7.00; Level II (grades 4-6) 25 test forms and 25 profile sheets $7.00.

Publisher: Academic Therapy Publications

TESTS OF COMPETENCE IN MATHEMATICS
Frances C. Morrison

child, teen   grades 4-9

Purpose: Assesses mathematics achievement of students in grades 4-9. Provides information on specific areas of strengths and weaknesses. Used as a pre- or post-course test.

Description: Three paper-pencil, multiple-choice subtests of 50 items each measuring mastery of computational skills, mathematical concepts, and word problems. Material covered includes: fractional and decimal knowledge, computational skills, geometry, and metric measurement. Subtest Level 4-5 is intended mainly for use at end of grade 4 or beginning of grade 5; Level 6-7 for end of grade 6 or beginning of grade 7; and Level 8-9 for end of grade 8 or beginning of grade 9. Examiner required. Suitable for group use.
CANADIAN PUBLISHER

Timed: 30 minutes per session

Range: Grades 4-9

Scoring: Hand key

Cost: Specimen set (includes test booklets part I and II, answer sheet, key, manual) for Level 4-5 $3.70; for Level 6-7 $4.05; for Level 8-9 $4.25.

Publisher: Guidance Centre

WORKING WITH WHOLE NUMBERS
Sam Adams and Leslie Ellis

child, teen   grades 4-8

Purpose: Assesses ability to add, subtract, multiply, and divide. Used to plan remedial approaches for students in grades 4-8.

Description: 575 item paper-pencil test in two sections measuring mastery of the four basic arithmetic operations using whole numbers. Survey portion measures concepts and is administered by the teacher. Second portion measures ability with facts and is completed independently. Examiner required. Suitable for group use.

Untimed: 45 minutes

Range: Grades 4-8

Scoring: Examiner evaluated

Cost: Contact publisher.

Publisher: Dr. Charles Sauls

Y' MATHEMATICS SERIES
Dennis Young

child

Purpose: Measures achievement in mathematics of children ages 7-11 years. Assesses individual and class progress in the study of mathematics and identifies strengths or weaknesses of curriculum and teaching methods.

Description: Four paper-pencil tests measure mathematics achievement in four overlapping stages, (Y1, Y2, Y3 and Y4) covering the overall age range from 7:5 to 11:10 years. Y1 (ages 7:5 to 8:10) and Y2 (ages 8:5 to 9:10) each consists of three sections: orally-presented items, computation, and written problems. This format helps to identify those students whose mathematical ability is being under-estimated because of reading difficulties. An additional table of quotients for Y2 is provided for use with older backward and slow reading children up to age 14:10. Y3 (ages 9:5 to 10:10) and Y4 (ages 10:5 to 11:10) each contain two sections: computation and written problems. All four stages require an examiner. Suitable for group use.
BRITISH PUBLISHER

Timed: Single class period

Range: Y1, ages 7.5-8.10; Y2, ages 8.5-9.10; Y3, ages 9.5-10.10; Y4, ages 10.5-11.10.

Scoring: Examiner evaluated

Cost: Specimen set £2.50; 20 tests (specify form) £1.75 per set; manual (specify level) 80p.

Publisher: Hodder & Stoughton

YARDSTICKS

child

Purpose: Assesses achievement in mathematics. Used for regular measurement of student progress.

Description: Multiple item paper-pencil test of mathematics skills applicable to the teaching curriculum. Divided into six different tests. Level 1, 6 year olds; Level 2, 7 year olds; Level 3, 8 year olds; Level 4, 9 year olds; Level 5, 10 year olds; and Level 6, 11 year olds. Each test is broken down into teaching objectives for that age group. There are five questions per objective in Levels 1-3, ten in Levels 4-6. Examiner required. Suitable for group use.
BRITISH PUBLISHER

Untimed: Not available

Range: Ages 6-12

Scoring: Hand key; examiner evaluated

Cost: Complete kit (includes 30 pupil's books, 1 answer book, and 1 management guide for the appropriate level) Level 1, 2 or 3--£28.00 each; Level 4, 5, 6--£34.00 each (payment in sterling for all overseas orders).

Publisher: NFER-Nelson Publishing Company

Upper Math Skills

ACER ARITHMETIC TESTS

child, teen   grades K-11

Purpose: Measures achievement in arithmetic. Used for diagnosing individual student strengths and weaknesses.

Description: 13 multiple-choice,

paper-pencil tests of basic mathematics skills: addition, subtraction, multiplication, and division. Tests are ACER Arithmetic Test Form C, for years 4-7; ACER Class Achievement Test in Mathematics (CATIM), a criterion-reference test for years 4-5; ACER Class Achievement Test in Mathematics (CATIM), years 6- 7; ACER Lower Grades Number Concepts Test; ACER Mathematics Profile Series, measuring Operations at years 4-10, and Space, Measurement, and Number at years 7-10; ACER Mathematics Tests (AM Series); ACER Test of Reasoning in Mathematics, years 8-11; Diagnostic Fractions Test-Seville, years 6-8; Diagnostic Number Tests-Seville, years 4-8; Henshaw Secondary Mathematics Test, years 8-10; Mathematics Evaluation Procedures K-2, years K-4; New Zealand Item Bank: Mathematics, years 3-8. Examiner required. Suitable for group use.
AUSTRALIAN PUBLISHER

Timed: Varies

Range: Grades K-Year 11

Scoring: Hand key

Cost: Test booklet prices range from $.50 to complete sets, $90.00. For further information write to ACER.

Publisher: The Australian Council for Educational Research Limited

ACER NUMBER TEST
Refer to page 760.

AMERICAN HIGH SCHOOL MATHEMATICS EXAMINATION (AHSME)

teen   grades 7-12

Purpose: Assesses skills and conceptual knowledge of pre-calculus mathematical students. Test was designed to provide challenging problems to create and sustain an interest in mathematics.

Description: 30 item paper-pencil, multiple-choice test assessing proficiency in the concepts and skills associated with pre-calculus mathematics with emphasis on intermediate algebra and plane geometry. Participating high schools must register each fall with the Regional Examination Coordinators. Each school makes its own decision as to the number of participants (for official status the minimum number of participants per school is three), though the test is open to all students with the necessary background. The test is administered in the U.S.A., Canada, England, Finland, Belgium, Hungary, Ireland, Israel, Italy, Jamaica, Luxembourg, Australia, Colombia, and in other American and foreign schools abroad. Examiner required. Suitable for group use. Available in Spanish, Braille, and large-print editions.

Timed: 90 minutes

Range: Junior high school-12

Scoring: Hand key

Cost: Specimen sets of prior examinations are $.35 each.

Publisher: MAA Committee on High School Contests

AP EXAMINATION: COMPUTER SCIENCE
Refer to page 322..

AP EXAMINATION: MATHEMATICS--CALCULUS AB
Refer to page 326.

AP EXAMINATION: MATHEMATICS--CALCULUS BC
Refer to page 327.

BASIC SKILLS TEST MATHEMATICS--SECONDARY-FORMS A AND B
IOX Assessment Systems

teen   grades 8-11

Purpose: Measures minimum competency of high school students in basic mathematic skills. Also useful for program evaluation.

Description: 25 item paper-pencil tests examines student's ability to perform basic calculations and solve everyday problems requiring single arithmetic operations, multiple arithmetic operations, and formulas. (This test succeeds the IOX Basic Skills Test--Mathematics-Elementary Level.) Examiner required. Suitable for group use.

Untimed: 30-45 minutes

Range: Grades 8-11

Scoring: Hand key; may be computer scored

Cost: 24 BM-Al $37.50; 25 BM-Bl $37.50; teacher's guide BM-Gl $3.95; BTM-1 test manual $3.95; 50 answer sheets $6.95.

Publisher: IOX Assessment Systems

COLLEGE LEVEL EXAMINATION PROGRAM (CLEP) BUSINESS: ELEMENTARY COMPUTER PROGRAMMING, FORTRAN IV
Refer to page 341.

COLLEGE LEVEL EXAMINATION PROGRAM (CLEP) BUSINESS: COMPUTERS AND DATA PROCESSING
Refer to page 340.

COLLEGE LEVEL EXAMINA-
TION PROGRAM (CLEP)
GENERAL EXAMINATION:
MATHEMATICS
Refer to page 346.

COLLEGE LEVEL EXAMINA-
TION PROGRAM (CLEP)
MATHEMATICS: CALCULUS
WITH ELEMENTARY
FUNCTIONS
Refer to page 349.

COLLEGE LEVEL EXAMINA-
TION PROGRAM (CLEP)
MATHEMATICS: COLLEGE
ALGEBRA
Refer to page 349.

COLLEGE LEVEL EXAMINA-
TION PROGRAM (CLEP)
MATHEMATICS: COLLEGE
ALGEBRA-TRIGONOMETRY
Refer to page 350.

COLLEGE LEVEL EXAMINA-
TION PROGRAM (CLEP)
MATHEMATICS: STATISTICS
Refer to page 350.

COLLEGE LEVEL EXAMINA-
TION PROGRAM (CLEP)
MATHEMATICS:
TRIGONOMETRY
Refer to page 350.

COOPERATIVE MATHEMATICS
TESTS
Refer to page 361.

DOPPELT MATHEMATICAL
REASONING TEST
J.E. Doppelt

adult   Graduate Students

Purpose: Measures mathematical reasoning ability. Used for admitting graduate students.

Description: Multiple item paper-pencil test of mathematical reasoning ability. Developed to provide a high-level measure of mathematical skills comparable to the Miller Analogies Test and Advanced Personnel Test. Examiner required. Suitable for group use.

Untimed: Not available

Range: Graduate students

Scoring: Scoring service available

Cost: Contact publisher.

Publisher: The Psychological Corporation

EMPORIA STATE ALGEBRA II
TEST
Stanley J. Laughlin and Howard P. Schwartz

teen   grades 10-12

Purpose: Assesses algebra aptitude of high school students. Used as Algebra II preassessment test and for program evaluation.

Description: 50 item paper-pencil test of general knowledge for Algebra II courses. Test is criterion- referenced with seven goals and 17 objectives being evaluated. Examiner required. Suitable for group use.

Timed: 50 minutes

Range: High school

Scoring: Hand key

Cost: Test $.25; manual $.20; key $.20.

Publisher: Bureau of Educational Measurements

NM CONSUMER MATHEMATICS TEST (NMCMT)
S.P. Klein

teen   grades 9-12

Purpose: Measures ability to solve consumer problems using basic arithmetic operations. Used for program evaluation and needs assessment.

Description: 20 item paper-pencil, multiple-choice test of ability to solve problems involving measures and prices, addition, subtraction, multiplication, and division in a consumer context. The test booklets are reusable and the scoring is by lay-over stencil. The reliability and norms have been determined from samples of ninth- and twelfth- grade secondary students. Examiner required. Suitable for group use.

Timed: 20 minutes

Range: Grades 9-12

Scoring: Hand key

Cost: Specimen set $5.00; 35 tests $10.00; 100 $17.00; 35 answer sheets $3.00; scoring stencil $2.00; manual $2.00.

ORLEANS-HANNA ALGEBRA PROGNOSIS TEST
Refer to page 387.

ORLEANS-HANNA ALGEBRA PROGNOSIS TEST (REVISED)
Refer to page 387.

SENIOR MATHEMATICS TEST

teen

Purpose: Assesses basic mathematics skills. Used for allocation of students to engineering courses.

Description: 50 item paper-pencil test of basic elementary mathematics needed in any engineering course. Topics covered include common units of measurement, decimal and other fractions, averages, percentages, indices and simple algebra and geometry. May be used in conjunction with the Senior English Test. Examiner required. Suitable for group use.
BRITISH PUBLISHER

Timed: 45 minutes

Range: Ages 16-18

Scoring: Not available

Cost: 10 tests £1.95; manual £0.75 (payment in sterling for all overseas orders).

Publisher: NFER-Nelson Publishing Company

TEST OF PERFORMANCE IN COMPUTATIONAL SKILLS (TOPICS)
CTB/McGraw-Hill

teen   grades 10-12

Purpose: Measures a high school student's proficiency in basic mathematical skills. Used to identify student needs and institute remedial instruction.

Description: 72 item, 2-section, paper-pencil test that measures student's ability to use basic mathematics skills in adult-like situations involving such things as price lists, timecards, deposit slips, maps, checkbook records, etc. Examiner required. Suitable for group use.

Timed: 50 minutes each section

Range: Senior high school

Scoring: Hand key; computer scoring available

Cost: Specimen set (includes a sample test book, manual, machine and hand-score answer sheet, class summary sheet, and objective matrix and a test reviewer's guide) $7.25.

Publisher: CTB/McGraw-Hill

Religious Education

BECOMING THE GIFT (BTG)
Merton P. Strommen

teen, adult   grades 8-12

Purpose: Helps young people express their values, beliefs and concerns and assists them in deciding on directions for personal growth. Designed for persons with a Christian orientation. Useful for one-on-one counseling sessions with a caring adult, group sharing and individual study and growth.

Description: 176 item paper-pencil survey assessing the attitudes and beliefs of church-oriented high school students. Subscales include: family unity, parental understanding, lack of self- confidence, personal faults, classroom relationships, national issues, God relationship, orientation for change, moral responsibility, meaningful life, religious participation, self regard, human relations, God awareness, and Biblical concepts. The young person receives a computer analyzed profile in a sealed envelope, together with a 64-page self-study guide, Becoming the Gift, which explains the profile, guides the youth in interpreting the results, helps identify areas where faith or values need to grow, and provides suggestions for dealing with these areas. Group profiles are available which provide a composite description of a youth group while protecting the confidentiality of the individuals. Profiles also available for sub-groups, such as boys, girls, seniors, etc. Self-administered. Suitable for group use.

Untimed: 45 minutes

Range: Grades 8-12

Scoring: Computer scored

Cost: Per individual (includes test booklet, answer sheet, profile, self-study guide, manual) $5.75; group profiles $22.00 each.

Publisher: Search Institute

NEW YOUTH RESEARCH SURVEY (NYRS)
Merton P. Strommen

teen, adult   grades 8-12

Purpose: Provides information on the attitudes and beliefs of church-related youth groups.

Description: 248 item paper-pencil survey assessing the concerns, beliefs, values, and perceptions of the members of church-related youth groups. Subscales include: family unity, parental understanding, lack of self-confidence, personal faults, classroom relationships, national issues, God relationships, orientation for change, religious participation, moral responsibility, meaningful life, self regard, human relations, God awareness, Biblical concepts, interest in help, youth group vitality, and adult caring. Yields computer analyzed scale scores and response frequencies for the youth group as a whole. Individual profiles also available. Norms available for the following denominations: Ecuminical, Lutheran, Southern Baptist, Roman Catholic, and parochial high schools. Self-administered. Suitable for group use.

Untimed: 1-1½ hours

Range: Grades 8-12

Scoring: Computer scored

Cost: Complete $3.75 per person.

Publisher: Search Institute

STANDARDIZED BIBLE CONTENT TESTS
AABC Commission on Testing and Measurement

adult

Purpose: Evaluates individual knowledge of the Bible. Useful for college entrance examinations, class assignment and to compare national and institutional norms.

Description: 150 item paper-pencil, multiple-choice test is six equivalent forms. Measures Biblical knowledge: people, history, doctrine, geography, and quotations. Recommended for institutions of higher education. Self-administered. Suitable for group use. Available in Spanish.

Timed: 45 minutes

Range: Adult

Scoring: Hand key

Cost: Tests $.60 each or 100 for $40.00; answer sheets $.07 each or 100 $5.00; scoring key $.75; test manual $5.00.

Publisher: American Association of Bible Colleges

STRAIT BIBLICAL KNOWLEDGE TEST
Jim Strait

teen, adult   grades 10-UP

Purpose: Assesses Biblical knowledge of students and adults. Used as a pretest or end-of-course exam.

Description: 100 item paper-pencil test of general content of Old (Form 1) and New (Form 2) Testaments. Examiner required. Suitable for group use.

Timed: 40 minutes

Range: High school-adult

Scoring: Hand key

Cost: 35 tests $8.50; 35 answer sheets $4.55; key $.10.

Publisher: Bureau of Educational Measurements

Science

General Science

ACER SCIENCE TESTS

child

Purpose: Measures achievement in science courses. Used for diagnosis of individual student strengths and weaknesses.

Description: 13 multiple-choice, paper-pencil tests of basic science subjects. Tests are ACER Biology Tests-Form 5, 15 item tests for year 11; ACER Biology Tests-Form 6, 19 item tests for year 12; ACER Chemistry Item Bank; ACER Chemistry Diagnostic Tests-Form 5, a diagnostic and achievement test for year 11; ACER Chemistry Test Item Collection (CHEMTIC), year 12; ACER Physics Unit Tests, years 11 and 12; Tests of Perceptions of Scientists and Self, a test of science attitudes for years 9-12; Test of Science-Related Attitudes (TOSRA); and Understanding in Science Test, a test of science concepts for years 7 and 8. Examiner required. Suitable for group use.
AUSTRALIAN PUBLISHER

Timed: 40-55 minutes

Range: Years 9-12

Scoring: Hand key

Cost: Test booklets range from $.60 to $13.00 for complete sets. Fur further information write to ACER.

Publisher: The Australian Council for Educational Research Limited

ACT PROFICIENCY EXAMINA-TION PROGRAM-ARTS AND SCIENCES: ANATOMY AND PHYSIOLOGY
Refer to page 294.

ACT PROFICIENCY EXAMINA-TION PROGRAM-ARTS AND SCIENCES: EARTH SCIENCE
Refer to page 295.

ACT PROFICIENCY EXAMINA-TION PROGRAM-ARTS AND SCIENCES: PHYSICAL GEOLOGY
Refer to page 296.

ADVANCED HIGH SCHOOL CHEMISTRY TESTS

teen, adult   grades 10-UP

Purpose: Measures achievement in advanced or honors courses in high school chemistry. Evaluates student strengths and weaknesses and aids in assigning grades.

Description: 50 or 60 item paper-pencil test covering ten areas of high school chemistry: atomic structure; chemical bonding; thermodynamics; kinetics; solids, liquids, gases and solutions; acid-base chemistry; electrochemistry; chemical periodicity; descriptive chemistry and stoichiometry; and laboratory procedures and techniques. Items are multiple-choice questions. Materials include Forms 1977 (50 items), 1980 (60 items), and 1982 (60 items). For use only by authorized chemistry teachers and administrators. Examiner required. Suitable for group use.

Timed: Form 1982 ADV-110 minutes; Form 1980-100 minutes; Form 1977-80 minutes

Range: High school, college

Scoring: Hand key

Cost: Specimen set $5.00; 25 tests $15.00; 25 answer sheets $3.00; scoring stencil $1.00.

Publisher: Examinations Committee-American Chemical Society

ANALYTICAL CHEMISTRY TESTS

adult   Graduate Students

Purpose: Measures achievement in college analytical chemistry courses. Used for placement of graduate students.

Description: 35 or 40 item paper-pencil, multiple-choice test measuring knowledge of analytical chemistry. Materials include Form 1977-A (35 items) and Form 1981-A (40 items). For use only by authorized chemistry teachers and administrators. Examiner required. Suitable for group use.

Timed: Form 1981-A, 90 minutes; Form 1977-A, 110 minutes

Range: Graduate students

Scoring: Hand key

Cost: Specimen set $5.00; 25 tests $18.00; 25 answer sheets $3.00; scoring stencils $1.00.

Publisher: Examinations Committee-American Chemical Society

ANALYTICAL CHEMISTRY TESTS (QUANTITATIVE ANALYSIS)

teen, adult   College

Purpose: Measures achievement in undergraduate analytical chemistry courses. Evaluates student strengths and weaknesses and aids in assigning grades.

Description: 50 item paper-pencil

test covering the following topics in analytical chemistry: gravimetric, volumetric, spectrophotometric, electrometric analysis, compleximetry, pH and buffers, solubility, analytical separations, data evaluation, oxidation-reduction, and indicators. Materials include Form 1974 and Form 1982. For use only by authorized chemistry teachers and administrators. Examiner required. Suitable for group use.

Timed: Form 1982, 90 minutes; Form 1974, 110 minutes

Range: College

Scoring: Hand key

Cost: Specimen set $5.00; 25 tests $18.00; 25 answer sheets $3.00; scoring stencil $1.00.

Publisher: Examinations Committee-American Chemical Society

AP EXAMINATION: BIOLOGY-- GENERAL BIOLOGY
Refer to page 321.

AP EXAMINATION: CHEM- ISTRY--GENERAL CHEMISTRY
Refer to page 321.

AP EXAMINATION: PHYSICS B
Refer to page 328.

AP EXAMINATION: PHYSICS C
Refer to page 329.

BIOCHEMISTRY TESTS

teen, adult   College

Purpose: Measures achievement in undergraduate general biochemistry courses. Evaluates prospective graduate students and serves as a comprehensive final examination for undergraduate courses.

Description: 60 item paper-pencil test covering topics in general biochemistry. Forty percent of the items deal with properties and structure-function relationships of biological molecules, and sixty percent cover intermediary metabolism and its control, the biochemistry of information macromolecules, and biochemical methods. Materials include Forms 1977 and 1982. For use only by authorized chemistry teachers and administrators. Examiner required. Suitable for group use.

Timed: Forms 1982, 1977-120 minutes

Range: College

Scoring: Hand key

Cost: Specimen set $5.00; 25 tests $18.00; 25 answer sheets $3.00; scoring stencil $1.00.

Publisher: Examinations Committee-American Chemical Society

BORMAN-SANDERS ELEMEN- TARY SCIENCE
Ina M. Borman and M. W. Sanders

---

child   grades 5-6

Purpose: Assesses general science achievement of elementary students. Used as end of first or second semester exam.

Description: 100 item paper-pencil test of general physical science concepts and facts. Examiner required. Suitable for group use.

Timed: 40 minutes

Range: Grades 5 and 6

Scoring: Hand key

Cost: Specimen set $1.50; test $.15; manual $.20; key $.20.

Publisher: Bureau of Educational Measurements

BRIEF ORGANIC CHEMISTRY TEST

teen, adult   College

Purpose: Measures achievement in undergraduate organic chemistry courses. Evaluates student strengths and weaknesses, and aids in assigning grades.

Description: 70 item paper-pencil test measuring topics in organic chemistry including: bonding, isomerism, functional group recognition, IUPAC nomenclature, physical properties, acidity and basicity, characteristic reactions of major functional groups, reaction mechanisms, qualitative organic analysis, applications, lipids, carbohydrates, and proteins. For use only by authorized chemistry teachers and administrators. Examiner required. Suitable for group use.

Timed: 90 minutes

Range: College

Scoring: Hand key

Cost: Specimen set $5.00; 25 tests $18.00; 25 answer sheets $3.00; scoring stencils $1.00.

Publisher: Examinations Committee-American Chemical Society

BRIEF QUALITATIVE ANALYSIS TEST

teen, adult   College

Purpose: Measures achievement in undergraduate qualitative analysis courses. Evaluates student strengths and weaknesses and aids in assigning grades.

Description: 35 or 50 item paper-pencil test assessing knowledge of qualitative analysis. Materials include Form 1973-B (50 items) and Form 1977-B (35 items). May be given in combination with any of the General

Chemistry tests. For use only by authorized chemistry teachers and administrators. Examiner required. Suitable for group use.

Untimed: 50 minutes

Range: College

Scoring: Hand key

Cost: Specimen set $5.00; 25 tests $18.00; 25 answer sheets $3.00; scoring stencils $1.00.

Publisher: Examinations Committee-American Chemical Society

EMPORIA CHEMISTRY TEST
A. J. Ericson and M. W. Sanders

teen   grades 10-12

Purpose: Assesses chemistry achievement of high school students. Used as end of first or second semester exam.

Description: 100 item paper-pencil test of chemistry definitions, formulas, equations, principles, theories, and problems. Examiner required. Suitable for group use.

Timed: 40 minutes

Range: High school

Scoring: Hand key

Cost: Specimen set $1.50; Test $.15; manual $.20; key $.20.

Publisher: Bureau of Educational Measurements

EMPORIA GENERAL SCIENCE TEST
Donald Cross and M. W. Sanders

teen   grades 10-12

Purpose: Assesses general science achievement of high school students. Used as end of first or second semester exam.

Description: 90 item paper-pencil test of wide variety of topics in general science. Examiner required. Suitable for group use.

Timed: 40 minutes

Range: High school

Scoring: Hand key

Cost: Specimen set $1.50; test $.15; manual $.20; key $.20.

Publisher: Bureau of Educational Measurements

EMPORIA PHYSICS TEST
Gerald L. Witten and M. W. Sanders

---

teen   grades 10-12

Purpose: Assesses high school student knowledge of physics. Used as end of first or second semester exam.

Description: 90 item paper-pencil test of general physics concepts such as mechanics, heat, magnetism, electricity, and sound. Examiner required. Suitable for group use.

Timed: 40 minutes

Range: High school

Scoring: Hand key

Cost: Specimen set $1.50; test $.15; manual $.20; key $.20.

Publisher: Bureau of Educational Measurements

GENERAL CHEMISTRY FORM 1981-B (BRIEF TEST)

teen, adult   College

Purpose: Measures achievement in first year college chemistry courses. Evaluates student strengths and weaknesses and aids in assigning grades.

Description: 50 item paper-pencil test measuring proficiency in material traditionally included in a first year college chemistry course. Questions are comparable in difficulty to those on the 1981 General Chemistry Tests. For use only by authorized chemistry teachers and administrators. Examiner required. Suitable for group use.

Untimed: 50 minutes

Range: College

Scoring: Hand key

Cost: Specimen set $5.00; 25 answer sheets $3.00; scoring stencils $1.00.

Publisher: Examinations Committee-American Chemical Society

GENERAL CHEMISTRY TESTS

teen, adult   College

Purpose: Measures achievement in first year college chemistry courses. Evaluates student strengths and weaknesses and aids in assigning grades.

Description: 80 item paper-pencil test measuring the following chemistry subject areas: states of matter, stoichiometry, carbon chemistry, solutions, acid-based chemistry, equilibria, electrochemistry and redox, thermodynamics and kinetics, descriptive chemistry, special topics, and laboratory skills. Materials include 1975, 1977, 1979 and 1981 forms. "Scrambled" forms, with items in different order, are also available. For use only by authorized chemistry teachers and administrators. Examiner required. Suitable for group use.

Timed: Form 1981-110 minutes; Forms 1979, 1977, 1975-115 minutes

Range: College

Scoring: Hand key; examiner evaluated; beginning with 1970 forms, the answer sheets are designed for machine scoring

Cost: Specimen set $5.00; 25 tests $18.00; 25 answer sheets $3.00; scoring stencils $1.00.

Publisher: Examinations Committee-

American Chemical Society

GENERAL-ORGANIC-BIO-LOGICAL CHEMISTRY (FOR ALLIED HEALTH SCIENCES PROGRAM) TEST

teen, adult   College

Purpose: Measures achievement in courses covering basic materials in general, organic, and biological chemistry. Used for unit or end-of-semester examination.

Description: 180 item paper-pencil test measuring proficiency in three areas of chemistry: general chemistry, organic chemistry, and biological chemistry. Each subtest has two parts, Part A (40 items) and Part B (20 items). For use only by authorized chemistry teachers and administrators. Examiner required. Suitable for group use.

Timed: 165 minutes

Range: College

Scoring: Hand key

Cost: Specimen set $5.00; 25 tests $18.00; 25 answer sheets $3.00; scoring stencil $1.00.

Publisher: Examinations Committee-American Chemical Society

INORGANIC CHEMISTRY TESTS

teen, adult   College

Purpose: Measures achievement in undergraduate inorganic chemistry courses. Assesses student strengths and weaknesses and assists graduate level placement of entering students.

Description: 60 item paper-pencil test covering theoretical and descriptive inorganic chemistry. Topics include: nomenclature, bonding, structure, reaction mechanisms, coordination chemistry, and thermodynamics of inorganic elements and compounds. Materials include Forms 1976 and 1981. For use only by authorized chemistry teachers and administrators. For use only by authorized chemistry teachers and administrators. Examiner required. Suitable for group use.

Timed: Forms 1981, 1976-110 minutes

Range: College

Scoring: Hand key

Cost: Specimen set $5.00; 25 tests $18.00; 25 answer sheets $3.00; scoring stencils $1.00.

Publisher: Examinations Committee-American Chemical Society

INORGANIC CHEMISTRY TESTS (I)

adult   Graduate Students

Purpose: Measures achievement in college inorganic chemistry courses. Used for placement of graduate students.

Description: 60 item paper-pencil, multiple-choice test measuring knowledge of inorganic chemistry. Materials include Forms 1976-I and 1981-I. For use only by authorized chemistry teachers and administrators. Examiner required. Suitable for group use.

Timed: 110 minutes

Range: Graduate students

Scoring: Hand key

Cost: Specimen set $5.00;; 25 tests $18.00; 25 answer sheets $3.00; scoring stencils $1.00.

Publisher: Examinations Committee-American Chemical Society

INSTRUMENTAL DETER-MINATIONS (ANALYSIS) TESTS

teen, adult College

Purpose: Measures achievement in undergraduate instrumental determinations courses. Evaluates student strengths and weaknesses and aids in assigning grades.

Description: 60 or 75 item paper-pencil test assessing knowledge of instrumental methods. Materials include Form 1971 (60 items) and Form 1981 (75 items). Form 1981 is 25% spectroscopy; 15% electroanalytical; 10% separations; 15% instrumentation; 5% each thermal, NMR, mass spectroscopy, radioactivity, and choice of method; and 10% other items such as x-ray, internal standard methods, titration curves, kinetics, etc. Form 1971 is 25% electroanalytical chemistry; 20% spectrophotometry; 15% instrumentation; 10% chromatography; 10% choice of method for an analytical situation; and 20% other including NMR, EPR, emission spectroscopy and kinetics. For use only by authorized chemistry teachers and administrators. Examiner required. Suitable for group use.

Timed: Form 1981-120 minutes; Form 1971-110 minutes

Range: College

Scoring: Hand key

Cost: Specimen set $5.00; 25 tests $18.00; 25 answer sheets $3.00; scoring stencils $1.00.

Publisher: Examinations Committee-American Chemical Society

MULTIPLE-CHOICE BIOLOGY and ADVANCED MULTIPLE-CHOICE BIOLOGY
R. Soper, D. Robinson, S.T. Smith

teen

Purpose: Assesses knowledge of biology. Used to prepare students for objective biology exams.

Description: Multiple item paper-pencil, multiple-choice tests measuring understanding of biological concepts. Multiple-Choice Biology(80 pages) is suitable for CSE and "O" level students. *Advanced Multiple-Choice Biology* (112 pages) deals with more complex concepts; suitable for "A" level students. Answers provided in the back of the book for all tests. Examiner required. Suitable for group use.
BRITISH PUBLISHER

Untimed: Not available

Range: Grades Sixth Form- 'O' level

Scoring: Hand key; examiner evaluated

Cost: Each book, $4.00.

Publisher: Harrap, Ltd.-available from Pendragon House, Inc. (U.S.A.)

MULTIPLE-CHOICE CHEMISTRY and ADVANCED MULTIPLE-CHOICE CHEMISTRY
J.A.S. Rees

teen

Purpose: Assesses knowledge of chemistry. Used to prepare students for objective chemistry exams.

Description: Multiple item paper-pencil, multiple-choice tests measuring achievement of chemistry knowledge and concepts. Multiple-Choice Chemistry(96 pages) is suitable for "O" level students. *Advanced Multiple-Choice Chemistry* (100 pages) covers more complex topics; suitable for "A" level students. Answers provided in the back of the book for all tests. Suitable for group use. BRITISH PUBLISHER

Untimed: Not available

Range: Grades O-A Level

Scoring: Hand key; examiner evaluated

Cost: Each book, $5.00.

Publisher: Harrap, Ltd.-available from Pendragon House, Inc. (U.S.A.)

MULTIPLE-CHOICE PHYSICS
R. W. Adams

teen

Purpose: Assesses knowledge of physics. Used for preparing students for objective physics exams and to stimulate class discussion.

Description: Multiple item paper-pencil, multiple-choice tests measuring knowledge and understanding of physics concepts expected of students who have completed a modern five-year physics syllabus. Suitable for CSE or "O" level students. Materials contained in one 83-page book. Suitable for group use. BRITISH PUBLISHER

Untimed: Not available

Range: Grades CSE and O level

Scoring: Hand key; examiner evaluated

Cost: Book, $4.50.

Publisher: Harrap Ltd.-available from Pendragon House, Inc. (U.S.A.)

NATIONAL ACADEMIC APTITUDE TESTS--NON-VERBAL INTELLIGENCE
Refer to page 412.

NM CONCEPTS OF ECOLOGY TEST-LEVEL 1 (NMCET-1)
S. P. Klein

child, teen   grades 6-8

Purpose: Measures an individual's understanding of the concepts of ecology from micro to macro systems. Used for program evaluation and needs assessment.

Description: 20 item paper-pencil, multiple-choicee test of a student's understanding of natural resources, pollution, plant/animal dependencies, life processes, natural balance, geographic evolution and conservation, and natural adaptation. The test booklets are reusable and scoring employs a lay-over stencil. The reliability and norms have been determined from a sample of sixth-grade students. Examiner/self-administered. Suitable for group use.

Timed: 20 minutes

Range: Grades 6-8

Scoring: Hand key

Cost: Specimen sheet $5.00; 35 tests (specify Level 1 or 2) $10.00; 100-$27.00; 35 answer sheets (specify Level 1 or 2) $3.00; 100-$6.00; scoring stencil $2.00; manual $2.00.

Publisher: Monitor

NM CONCEPTS OF ECOLOGY TEST-LEVEL 2 (NMCET-2)
S. P. Klein

teen   grades 9-12

Purpose: Measures an individual's understanding of the basic concepts of ecology and conservation. Used for program evaluation and needs assessment.

Description: 20 item paper-pencil, multiple-choice test measures student's understanding of life processes, plant/animal dependencies, geographic evolution and conservation, soil connservation, and natural adaptation. The test booklets are reusable, and scoring employs a lay-over stencil. The reliability and norms have been determined from samples of ninth and twelfth-grade secondary stuudents. Examiner/self-administered. Suitable for group use.

Timed: 20 minutes

Range: Grades 9-12

Scoring: Hand key

Cost: Specimen set $5.00; 35 tests (specify Level 1 or 2) $10.00; 100-$27.00; 35 answer sheets (specify Level 1 or 2) $3.00; 100-$6.00; scoring stencil $2.00; manual $2.00.

Publisher: Monitor

ORGANIC CHEMISTRY TESTS

teen, adult   College

Purpose: Measures achievement in undergraduate organic chemistry courses. Evaluates student strengths and weaknesses and aids in assigning grades.

Description: 70 item paper-pencil test measuring diverse aspects of organic chemistry including theoretical concepts, acid and basic character of organic compounds, stereochemistry, various reaction types associated with organic molecules, reaction mechanisms, spectroscopic identification of organic structures, and synthetic sequences. Materials include Forms 1982, 1978, and 1974. For use only by authorized chemistry teachers and administrators. Examiner required. Suitable for group use.

Timed: Forms 1982, 1978-115 min-

utes; Form 1974-110 minutes

Range: College

Scoring: Hand key

Cost: Specimen set $5.00; 25 tests $18.00; 25 answer sheets $3.00; scoring stencils $1.00.

Publisher: Examinations Committee-American Chemical Society

ORGANIC CHEMISTRY TESTS (O)

adult   Graduate Students

Purpose: Measures achievement in college organic chemistry courses. Used for placement of graduate students.

Description: 70 or 75 item paper-pencil, multiple-choice test measuring knowledge of organic chemistry. Materials include Forms 1977-O (75 items) and 1981-O (70 items). For use only by authorized chemistry teachers and administrators. Examiner required. Suitable for group use.

Timed: Form 1981-O, 90-120 minutes; Form 1977-O, 110 minutes

Range: Graduate students

Scoring: Hand key

Cost: Specimen set $5.00; 25 tests $18.00; 25 answer sheets $3.00; scoring stencils $1.00.

Publisher: Examinations Committee-American Chemical Society

PHYSICAL CHEMISTRY TESTS

adult   College

Purpose: Measures achievement in undergraduate physical chemistry courses. Evaluates student strengths and weaknesses and aids in assigning grades.

Description: Three 45 item paper-pencil subtests measuring three aspects of physical chemistry; thermodynamics, chemical dynamics, and quantum chemistry. Subtests may be administered separately. Thermodynamics covers: fundamental laws, state functions, criteria for equilibrium, solutions, and electrochemistry. Chemical Dynamics covers: rate theories, kinetic theory of gases, and transport phenomena. Quantum chemistry covers fundamental laws of quantum mechanics and their applications. Each subtest is divided into two parts: Part A (30 items) and Part B (15 items). Three forms are available. Form 1973 has all three subtests, Form 1976 only Thermodynamics, and Form 1981 only Chemical Dynamics. The Entire physical Chemistry Sequence, Form 1975, is also available. This 40 item test may be given at the end of the Physical Chemistry Tests, and covers chemical thermodynamics, chemical kinetics and transport phenomena, and quantum chemistry and spectroscopy. For use only by authorized chemistry teachers and administrators. Examiner required. Suitable for group use.

Timed: Part A, 50 minutes; Part B, 40 minutes

Range: College

Scoring: Hand key

Cost: Specimen set $5.00; 25 tests $18.00; 25 answer sheets $3.00; scoring stencils $1.00.

Publisher: Examinations Committee-American Chemical Society

PHYSICAL CHEMISTRY FOR THE LIFE SCIENCES TEST

teen, adult   College

Purpose: Measures achievement in undergraduate course in physical chemical taught for life science students. Evaluates student strengths and weaknesses and aids in assigning grades.

Description: 50 item paper-pencil test measuring comprehension of principles of physical chemistry. Topic areas include: thermodynamics, solutions and equilibria, dynamics, quantum chemistry, and macromolecules. For use only by authorized chemistry teachers and administrators. Examiner required. Suitable for group use.

Timed: 90 minutes

Range: College

Scoring: Hand key

Cost: Specimen set $5.00; 25 tests $18.00; 25 answer sheets $3.00; scoring stencils $1.00.

Publisher: Examinations Committee-American Chemical Society

PHYSICAL CHEMISTRY TESTS (P)

adult   Graduate Students

Purpose: Measures achievement in college Physical Chemistry courses. Used for placement of graduate students.

Description: 60 item paper-pencil, multiple-choice test measuring knowledge of physical chemistry. Materials include Forms 1977-P and 1981-P. For use only by authorized chemistry teachers and administrators. Examiner required. Suitable for group use.

Timed: Form 1981-P, 150-180 minutes; Form 1977-P, 120 minutes

Range: Graduate students

Scoring: Hand key

Cost: Specimen set $5.00; 25 tests $18.00; 25 answer sheets $3.00; scoring stencils $1.00.

Publisher: Examinations Committee-American Chemical Society

POLYMER CHEMISTRY TEST

teen, adult College

Purpose: Measures achievement in upper level undergraduate and lower level graduate courses in polymer chemistry. Evaluates student strengths and weaknesses and aids in placement and admission of graduate students.

Description: 60 item paper-pencil test covering five areas of polymer chemistry subject matter: organic, thermo-kinetics, characterization, physical behavior, and general. Materials include Forms 1977 and 1982. For use only by authorized chemistry teachers and administrators. Examiner required. Suitable for group use.

Timed: 120 minutes

Range: College

Scoring: Hand key

Cost: Specimen set $5.00; 25 tests $18.00; 25 answer sheets $3.00; scoring stencils $1.00.

Publisher: Examinations Committee-American Chemical Society

REGULAR HIGH SCHOOL CHEMISTRY TESTS

teen grades 10-12

Purpose: Measures achievement in first-year high school chemistry courses. Identifies student strengths and weaknesses and aids in assigning grades.

Description: 80 item paper-pencil test measuring understanding of fundamental concepts and application of basic principles in chemistry. Areas tested include: introductory concepts, physical concepts, atomic and molecular concepts, and solutions concepts. Materials include 1975, 1977, 1979, and 1981 forms. "Scrambled" forms, with items in

different order, are also available. For use only by authorized chemistry teachers and administrators. Examiner required. Suitable for group use.

Timed: Form 1981, 110 minutes; Forms 1979, 1977, 1975, 80 minutes

Range: High school

Scoring: Hand key

Cost: Specimen set $5.00; 25 tests $15.00; 25 answer sheets $3.00; scoring stencils $1.00.

Publisher: Examinations Committee-American Chemical Society

SCIENTIFIC KNOWLEDGE AND APTITUDE TEST
Refer to page 393.

STUDENT OCCUPATIONAL COMPETENCY ACHIEVEMENT TESTING: HORTICULTURE
Refer to page 444.

TOLEDO CHEMISTRY PLACEMENT EXAMINATION
Refer to page 406.

Health Science

ACT PROFICIENCY EXAMINATION PROGRAM-ADULT NURSING
Refer to page 306.

ACT PROFICIENCY EXAMINATION PROGRAM-ART AND SCIENCES: FOUNDATION OF GERONTOLOGY
Refer to page 295.

**ACT PROFICIENCY EXAMINA-
TION PROGRAM-NURSING:
COMMONALITIES IN NURSING
CARE, AREA I**
Refer to page 306.

**ACT PROFICIENCY EXAMINA-
TION PROGRAM-NURSING:
COMMONALITIES IN NURSING
CARE, AREA II**
Refer to page 307.

**ACT PROFICIENCY EXAMINA-
TION PROGRAM-NURSING:
DIFFERENCES IN NURSING
CARE, AREA I**
Refer to page 307.

**ACT PROFICIENCY EXAMINA-
TION PROGRAM-NURSING:
DIFFERENCES IN NURSING
CARE, AREA II**
Refer to page 308.

**ACT PROFICIENCY EXAMINA-
TION PROGRAM-NURSING:
DIFFERENCES IN NURSING
CARE, AREA III**
Refer to page 308.

**ACT PROFICIENCY EXAMINA-
TION PROGRAM-NURSING:
FUNDAMENTALS OF NURSING**
Refer to page 309.

**ACT PROFICIENCY EXAMINA-
TION PROGRAM-NURSING:
HEALTH RESTORATION, AREA I**
Refer to page 309.

**ACT PROFICIENCY EXAMINA-
TION PROGRAM-NURSING:
HEALTH RESTORATION, AREA
II**
Refer to page 309.

**ACT PROFICIENCY EXAMINA-
TION PROGRAM-NURSING:
HEALTH SUPPORT, AREA I**
Refer to page 310.

**ACT PROFICIENCY EXAMINA-
TION PROGRAM-NURSING:
HEALTH SUPPORT, AREA II**
Refer to page 310.

**ACT PROFICIENCY EXAMINA-
TION PROGRAM-NURSING:
MATERNAL AND CHILD NURS-
ING, ASSOCIATE DEGREE**
Refer to page 311.

**ACT PROFICIENCY EXAMINA-
TION PROGRAM-NURSING:
MATERNAL AND CHILD NURS-
ING, BACCALAUREATE
DEGREE**
Refer to page 311.

**ACT PROFICIENCY EXAMINA-
TION PROGRAM-NURSING:
NURSING HEALTH CARE**
Refer to page 311.

**ACT PROFICIENCY EXAMINA-
TION PROGRAM-NURSING:
OCCUPATIONAL STRATEGY,
NURSING**
Refer to page 312.

COLLEGE LEVEL EXAMINA-TION PROGRAM (CLEP) NURSING: FUNDAMENTALS of NURSING
Refer to page 354.

COLLEGE LEVEL EXAMINA-TION PROGRAM (CLEP) NURSING: MEDICAL-SURGICAL NURSING
Refer to page 354.

EMPORIA ELEMENTARY HEALTH TEST
Gary Adamson and Merritt W. Sanders

child, teen   grades 6-9

Purpose: Assesses health achieve-ment of students in grades 6, 7, and 8. Useful as end-of-course exam.

Description: 60 item paper-pencil, multiple-choice exam measuring knowledge of rules and principles of healthful living as well as health atti-tudes. Two sets of forms available for each semester. Examiner required. Suitable for group use.

Timed: 30 minutes

Range: Grades 6-8

Scoring: Hand key

Cost: Specimen set $1.50; test $.15; manual $.20; key $.20.

Publisher: Bureau of Educational Measurements

EMPORIA HIGH SCHOOL HEALTH TEST
Ron Blaylock and Merritt W. Sanders

teen   grades 10-12

Purpose: Assesses health knowledge of high school students. Useful as

end-of-course exam.

Description: 60 item paper-pencil multiple-choice test measuring knowledge of basic facts and rules fundamental to healthful living, and attitudes toward basic health rules. Student is given test booklet and answer sheet. Examiner required. Suitable for group use.

Timed: 30 minutes

Range: High school

Scoring: Hand key

Cost: Specimen set $1.50.

Publisher: Bureau of Educational Measurements

FAST-TYSON HEALTH KNOWLEDGE TEST
Charles G. Fast

teen   grades 12-13

Purpose: Measures discrimination and judgment in matters of personal health. Used to counsel high school and college students, upgrade their health knowledge, and for pre- and post-testing in curriculum studies.

Description: 100 item paper-pencil multiple-choice test assessing a stu-dent's knowledge of factors contributing to personal health. Thir-teen areas are covered: personal health, exercise, relaxation and sleep, nutrition and diet, consumer health, contemporary health problems, tobacco, alcohol, drugs and narcot-ics, safety and first aid, communicable and non-communica-ble diseases, mental health, and sex and family life. Norms provided for college freshmen and high school seniors. Available in two forms, A and B, both of which contain the same questions in different orders. Examiner required. Suitable for group use.

Untimed: 40-50 minutes

Range: High school seniors and college freshmen

Scoring: Hand key

Cost: One form: 50 copies $60.00, 100 copies for $110.00; Forms A and B combined: 50 copies $75.00, 100 copies $130.00.

Publisher: Charles G. Fast

HUMAN REPRODUCTION
H. Frederick Kilander and Glenn C. Leach

teen   grades 10-13

Purpose: Measures high school and college students' knowledge of the human reproductive system. Used for health and human sexuality courses.

Description: 33 item paper-pencil muultiple-choice test assessing knowledge of human reproduction. Self- administered. Suitable for group use.

Timed: 30 minutes

Range: Senior high-college freshmen

Scoring: Hand key

Cost: Free

Publisher: Glenn C. Leach, Ed.D.

INFORMATION TEST ON DRUGS AND DRUG ABUSE
Glenn C. Leach and H. Frederick Kilander

teen   grades 10-13

Purpose: Measures high school and college students' knowledge of drugs and drug abuse. Used for drug abuse counseling.

Description: 30 item paper-pencil multiple-choice test concerning legal and illegal drug use. Self- administered. Suitable for group use.

Timed: 30 minutes

Range: Senior high-college freshmen

Scoring: Hand key

Cost: Free

Publisher: Glenn C. Leach, Ed.D.

KILANDER-LEACH HEALTH KNOWLEDGE
H. Frederick Kilander and Glen C. Leach

teen   grades 10-13

Purpose: Measures general knowledge of high school and college students about health. Used as a pre- or end-of-course exam for high school health education classes.

Description: 100 item paper-pencil, multiple-choice test measuring health knowledge. Factors included are: personal health, nutrition, community health, sanitation, communicable diseases, safety, first aid, family living, and mental health. Self- administered; proctor desirable. Suitable for group use.

Untimed: 45-50 minutes

Range: Senior high-college freshmen

Scoring: Hand key

Cost: 100 booklets $25.00; 35 answer sheets $12.50; guide $1.00.

Publisher: Glenn C. Leach, Ed.D.

NATIONAL ACHIEVEMENT TESTS: HEALTH and SCIENCE TESTS-HEALTH EDUCATION
John S. Shaw, Maurice E. Troyer, and Clifford L. Brownell

teen   grades 7-UP

Purpose: Assesses knowledge of health. Used for educational evaluation.

Description: Paper-pencil test of newer phases of health information. Includes problems with which students in high school and college should be familiar. Materials include two equivalent forms, A and B. Part of the National Achievement Series. Examiner required. Suitable for group use.

Timed: 40 minutes

Range: Grades 7-12 and college

Scoring: Hand key

Cost: Specimen set (includes one test, manual and key) $2.20; 25 tests $5.50; 100 tests $21.00; 25 answer sheets $2.20; 100-$7.70.

Publisher: Psychometric Affiliates

NATIONAL ACHIEVEMENT TESTS: HEALTH AND SCIENCE TESTS--GENERAL BIOLOGY
Lester D. Crow and James G. Murray

teen   grades 9-12

Purpose: Assesses achievement in general biology for students in grades 9 through 12. Used for identification of student strengths and weaknesses as part of an educational evaluation.

Description: Multiple item paper-pencil test of student's knowledge of uses, processes, and results; important biological scientists; and miscellaneous facts of biology. Part of the National Achievement Series. Examiner required. Suitable for group use.

Timed: 35 minutes

Range: Grades 9-12

Scoring: Hand key

Cost: Specimen set (includes one test, manual and key) $2.00; 25 tests $5.50, 100-$21.00

Publisher: Psychometric Affiliates

NETHERNE STUDY DIFFICUL-TIES BATTERY FOR STUDENT NURSES (SDB)
James Patrick S. Robertson

teen, adult

Purpose: Assesses intellectual difficulties interfering with the academic performance of student nurses. Also used for selecting student nurses, and for diagnosis after student failure.

Description: Battery of 14 paper-pencil tests measuring skills important in studying nursing. Areas covered include understanding and use of words, scientific information, learning from a text, checking accuracy (spelling, numbers, names) learning from a diagram, summarizing ability (paragraphs, drawings, diagrams), following directions, speed ability (associations, handwriting, freehand drawing). Materials include re-usable study sheets. Examiner required. Suitable for group use.
BRITISH PUBLISHER

Timed: 2½ hours for completion of all tests

Range: Student nurse

Scoring: Hand key

Cost: Contact distributor.

Publisher: Psychological Research Department, Netherne Hospital distributed by NFER-Nelson Publishing Company

NUTRITION INFORMATION TEST
H. Frederick Kilander and Glenn C. Leach

teen, adult   grades 10-UP

Purpose: Determines knowledge and attitudes of high school and college students

Description: 33 item paper-pencil

multiple-choice test dealing with various aspects of nutrition including: calories, diseases, physical health, weight control, etc. Self-administered. Suitable for group use.

Untimed: 15 minutes

Range: Secondary-college

Scoring: Hand key

Cost: Free.

Publisher: Glenn C. Leach, Ed.D.

THE OHIO VOCATIONAL ACHIEVEMENT TESTS IN HEALTH OCCUPATIONS EDUCATION--DENTAL ASSISTING
Refer to page 424.

THE OHIO VOCATIONAL ACHIEVEMENT TESTS IN HEALTH OCCUPATIONS EDUCATION--DIVERSIFIED HEALTH OCCUPATION
Refer to page 425.

THE OHIO VOCATIONAL ACHIEVEMENT TESTS IN HEALTH OCCUPATIONS EDUCATION--MEDICAL ASSISTING
Refer to page 425.

SCIENCE TESTS-STANDARD 5 THROUGH STANDARD 8 HIGHER GRADE

child, teen

Purpose: Assesses achievement in science courses. Used for educational evaluation and placement.

Description: Six paper-pencil tests of science knowledge in Standards 5 through 8 Higher Grade. General Science-Standard 5 consists of Measurement of Matter, Heat, Mag-

netism and Biology. Physical Science-Standard 6 has three subtests: Matter Classification of Matter, Oxygen, Hydrogen, Carbon Dioxide, Water, and Force, Work, Energy, and Electricity. Physical Science-Standard 7 is very similar to Standard 6. Standard 8 and above measures 8 aspects of physical science: Light; Sound; Heat, Work, and Energy; Electricity; Atomic Structure; chemical Reactions; Acids, bases, and salts; and Chemical reactions and electricity. Biology tests for Standards 6 and 7, measure some of the following areas: reproduction, growth and development, nutrition, and gaseous exchange during respiration. Examiner required. Suitable for group use.
SOUTH AFRICAN PUBLISHER

Untimed: Not available

Range: Standard 5-Standard 8 Higher Grade

Scoring: Hand key; examiner evaluated

Cost: Contact publisher (orders from outside The RSA will be dealt with on merit).

Publisher: Human Sciences Research Council

SMOKING AND HEALTH
H. Frederick Kilander

---

teen, adult   grades

Purpose: Assesses an individual's commitment to and knowledge of smoking. Used for analysis of smoking behavior and research.

Description: 33 item paper-pencil test of objective and multiple-choice questions on smoking. Self- administered. Suitable for group use.

Timed: 25 minutes

Range: Senior high-college freshmen

Scoring: Hand key

Cost: Free.

Publisher: Glenn C. Leach, Ed.D.

STUDENT OCCUPATIONAL COMPETENCY ACHIEVEMENT TESTING: PRACTICAL NURSING
Refer to page 435.

Social Studies

ACT PROFICIENCY EXAMINATION PROGRAM-ARTS AND SCIENCES: AFRO-AMERICAN HISTORY
Refer to page 294.

ACT PROFICIENCY EXAMINATION PROGRAM-ARTS AND SCIENCES: AMERICAN HISTORY
Refer to page 294.

ACT PROFICIENCY EXAMINATION PROGRAM-CRIMINAL JUSTICE: CRIMINAL INVESTIGATION
Refer to page 304.

ACT PROFICIENCY EXAMINAA-TION PROGRAM-CRIMINAL JUSTICE: INTRODUCTION TO CRIMINAL JUSTICE
Refer to page 304.

ACT PROFICIENCY EXAMINATION PROGRAM- EDUCATION: EDUCATIONAL PSYCHOLOGY
Refer to page 304.

ACT PROFICIENCY EXAMINATION PROGRAM- EDUCATION: HISTORY OF AMERICAN EDUCATION
Refer to page 305.

AMERICAN GOVERNMENT TEST

teen   grades 8-12

Purpose: Evaluates high school student understanding of government, with strong emphasis on political action and dynamics of American Politics. Used for course testing.

Description: 100 paper-pencil, multiple-choice questions in each of six tests. The tests are: Fundamentals of Government, Executive Branch, Legislative Branch, Civil Liberties and American Law, State and Local Government, and a Final Test. Materials include test booklets, answer sheet, manual and key. Examiner required. Suitable for group use.

Untimed: 50 minutes

Range: Grades 8-12

Scoring: Hand key

Cost: Single test with answer sheet $.45; complete set of 6 tests $2.60; 30 additional answer sheets $1.20.

Publisher: The Perfection Form Company

AMERICAN HISTORY MAP TEST FOLIO

teen   grades 10-12

Purpose: Measures high school student understanding of American History through map reading skills. Used for teaching or testing.

Description: 100 item paper-pencil, multiple-choice test. Items cover knowledge of history, politics, religion and other areas for each of 21 map titles including: New World Explorations, French and Indian War, World War I, America and Europe. Questions are posed on basic outline maps which students check to complete the questions. Examiner required. Suitable for group use.

Untimed: Not available

Range: High school

Scoring: Hand key

Cost: Test $1.25; tests-30 classroom sets (one set includes 21 map tests-one for each title) $27.95.

Publisher: The Perfection Form Company

AMERICAN HISTORY TEST

child, teen   grades 7-9

Purpose: Evaluates junior high school student knowledge of specific periods of American History. Used as unit tests.

Description: 75 paper-pencil objective questions in separate tests for each of 12 periods from Colonial America to Post World War II. Materials include test, answer sheet, and answer key. Examiner required. Suitable for group use.

Untimed: 50 minutes

Range: Junior high

Scoring: Hand key

Cost: Test (includes answer key and sheet) $.45; complete set $4.75; 30 additional answer sheets $1.20.

Publisher: The Perfection Form Company

AMERICAN HISTORY TESTS

teen   grades 10-12

Purpose: Evaluates senior high school student knowledge of specific periods in American History. Used for unit post-tests.

Description: 100 paper-pencil, multiple-choice questions in each of 13 tests covering American History from the Colonial Period to Post World Ward II and the present, plus two semester tests and final exam. Materials include test book, answer sheets, and answer key. Examiner required. Suitable for group use.

Untimed: 50 minutes

Range: Senior high

Scoring: Hand key

Cost: Test (includes answer sheet and key) $.45; 13 tests $3.95; 30 additional answer sheets $1.20.

Publisher: The Perfection Form Company

AP EXAMINATION: HISTORY-- AMERICAN HISTORY
Refer to page 325.

AP EXAMINATION: HISTORY-- EUROPEAN HISTORY
Refer to page 325.

BASIC ECONOMICS TEST (BET)
John F. Chizmar and Ronald S. Halinski

child   grades 4-6

Purpose: Measures elementary school students' understanding of economic principles. Used to assess curricular development and to determine the effectiveness of materials and teaching strategies.

Description: 38 item paper-pencil, multiple-choice test in A and B forms covering: basic economic concepts, economic systems, micro-economics, resource allocation, macro-economics, and economic institutions. Examiner required. Suitable for

group use.

Timed: 50 minutes

Range: Grades 4-6

Scoring: Hand key; may be computer scored

Cost: Manual and answer key $3.00; 25 test booklets (A or B) $6.00.

Publisher: Joint Council on Economic Education

BLACK HISTORY: A TEST TO CREATE AWARENESS AND AROUSE INTEREST
Gregory C. Coffin, Elsie F. Harley and Bessie M.L. Rhodes

---

child   grade 5

Purpose: Creates awareness and interest in Black history; not intended as a measure of factual knowledge. Used to supplement class studies.

Description: 100 item paper-pencil test intended to create awareness of distortions or omissions of Black history in the basic curriculum and history books. May be self-administered. Suitable for use with groups.

Untimed: 1 hour

Range: Grade 5

Scoring: Hand key

Cost: 30 copies $50.00.

Publisher: Coffin Associates

CASS-SANDERS PSYCHOLOGY TEST
Dal H. Cass and Merritt W. Sanders

---

teen, adult   grades 10-UP

Purpose: Assesses psychology course achievement of high school and college students. Used as end-of- course exam.

Description: 125 item paper-pencil

---

test of basic facts, rules, and principles covered in a beginning psychology course. Examiner required. Suitable for group use.

Timed: 50 minutes

Range: High school and college

Scoring: Hand key

Cost: Specimen set $1.50; test $.20; manual $.20; key $.20.

Publisher: Bureau of Educational Measurements

COLLEGE LEVEL EXAMINATION PROGRAM (CLEP) AMERICAN HISTORY I: EARLY COLONIZATIONS to 1877
Refer to page 340.

COLLEGE LEVEL EXAMINATION PROGRAM (CLEP) AMERICAN HISTORY II: 1865 to the PRESENT
Refer to page 340.

COLLEGE LEVEL EXAMINATION PROGRAM (CLEP) EDUCATION: EDUCATIONAL PSYCHOLOGY
Refer to page 344.

COLLEGE LEVEL EXAMINATION PROGRAM (CLEP) EDUCATION: HUMAN GROWTH and DEVELOPMENT
Refer to page 345.

COLLEGE LEVEL EXAMINATION PROGRAM (CLEP) GENERAL EXAMINATION: HUMANITIES
Refer to page 346.

**COLLEGE LEVEL EXAMINA-
TION PROGRAM (CLEP)
GENERAL EXAMINATION:
SOCIAL SCIENCE and HISTORY**
Refer to page 347.

**COLLEGE LEVEL EXAMINA-
TION PROGRAM (CLEP)
INTRODUCTORY
MACROECONOMICS**
Refer to page 356.

**COLLEGE LEVEL EXAMINA-
TION PROGRAM (CLEP)
INTRODUCTORY
MICROECONOMICS**
Refer to page 356.

**COLLEGE LEVEL EXAMINA-
TION PROGRAM (CLEP)
NURSING: BEHAVIORAL SCI-
ENCES FOR NURSES**
Refer to page 353.

**COLLEGE LEVEL EXAMINA-
TION PROGRAM (CLEP)
SOCIAL SCIENCES: AFRO-
AMERICAN HISTORY**
Refer to page 355.

**COLLEGE LEVEL EXAMINA-
TION PROGRAM (CLEP)
SOCIAL SCIENCES: AMERICAN
GOVERNMENT**
Refer to page 355.

**COLLEGE LEVEL EXAMINA-
TION PROGRAM (CLEP)
SOCIAL SCIENCES: GENERAL
PSYCHOLOGY**
Refer to page 356.

**COLLEGE LEVEL EXAMINA-
TION PROGRAM (CLEP)
WESTERN CIVILIZATION I:
ANCIENT NEAR EAST to 1648**
Refer to page 357.

**COLLEGE LEVEL EXAMINA-
TION PROGRAM (CLEP)
WESTERN CIVILIZATION II:
1648 to The PRESENT**
Refer to page 357.

**CPRI QUESTIONNAIRES (Q-71,
Q-74, Q-75, Q-76)**
Refer to page 625.

ECONOMICS TESTS

teen   grades 10-12

Purpose: Measures high school student economic knowledge over a semester course. Used as unit post-tests.

Description: 100 item paper-pencil test of the following four areas: concepts in economics (price, income and personal growth), money (banking and insurance), international trade, and a final exam. Materials include test, answer sheet and key. Examiner required. Suitable for group use.

Untimed: Not available

Range: Grades 10-12

Scoring: Hand key

Cost: Test (includes answer sheet and key) $.45; complete set $2.20; 30 additional answer sheets $1.20.

Publisher: The Perfection Form Company

EMPORIA AMERICAN GOVERNMENT TEST

Earl Rohrbaugh, Robert Zevier and David J. Hurt

teen   grades 10-12

Purpose: Measures high school student understanding of American government. Used as pretest and/or end- of-course exam.

Description: 75 item paper-pencil, multiple-choice test of the theory and facts of American government. Test also assesses student ability to apply knowledge to hypothetical problems and situations. Examiner required. Suitable for group use.

Untimed: 50-60 minutes

Range: High school

Scoring: Hand key

Cost: Specimen set $1.50; test $.20; manual $.20; key $.20.

Publisher: Bureau of Educational Measurements

EMPORIA AMERICAN HISTORY TEST

Shirley Meares, Merritt W. Sanders

teen   grades 10-12

Purpose: Assesses high school student understanding of American history. Used as end-of-course exam.

Description: 120 item paper-pencil general survey test of concepts, historical events, vocabulary, and people covered in a one-year American history course. Examiner required. Suitable for group use.

Timed: 40 minutes

Range: High school

Scoring: Hand key

Cost: Specimen set $1.50; test $.15; manual $.20; key $.20.

Publisher: Bureau of Educational Measurements

HOLLINGSWORTH-SANDERS GEOGRAPHY TEST

Leon Hollingsworth and M.W. Sanders

child, teen   grades 5-7

Purpose: Assesses student achievement in geography course work. Used as end-of-course exam.

Description: 65 item paper-pencil objective test of geographical facts, principles, cause and effect, and map study. Examiner required. Suitable for group use.

Timed: 30 minutes

Range: Grades 5-7

Scoring: Hand key

Cost: Specimen set $1.50; test $.15; manual $.20; key $.20.

Publisher: Bureau of Educational Measurements

HOLLINGSWORTH-SANDERS INTER HISTORY TEST

Leon Hollingsworth and M.W. Sanders

child   grades 5-6

Purpose: Assesses history achievement of upper elementary students. Used as first or second semester exam.

Description: 55 item paper-pencil test of historical facts as well as application of information and reasoning. Examiner required. Suitable for group use.

Timed: 30 minutes

Range: Grades 5-6

Scoring: Hand key

Cost: Specimen set $1.50; test $.15; manual $.20; key $.20.

Publisher: Bureau of Educational Measurements

HUMAN LOYALTY EXPRESSIONAIRE
Theodore F. Lentz

---

teen, adult   College

Purpose: Measures human loyalty and global awareness for use in peace and global studies courses.

Description: 172 item paper-pencil test in three sections of 104, 50, and 18 items. The subject agrees or disagrees with each statement. Recommended for adults and college and university students. Self- administered. Suitable for group use.

Timed: 45 minutes

Range: College and university students

Scoring: Hand key

Cost: 3 forms of questionnaire, scoring keys, and norms. $7.00 (book). Questionnaires can be reproduced at no further charge.

Publisher: Peach Research Laboratory

INFORMETER: AN INTERNATIONAL TECHNIQUE FOR THE MEASUREMENT OF POLITICAL INFORMATION
Panos D. Bardis

---

teen   grades 10-UP

Purpose: Measures political knowledge and awareness of local, national, and international affairs. Used for research on political information in the general population and discussion in social sciences classes

---

Description: 100 item paper-pencil test. Subject is asked to list important names, dates, events, and issues in response to specific questions about politics, government, and current events. May be self- administered and evaluated. Suitable for group use.

Untimed: 15 minutes

Range: High school and up

Scoring: Examiner evaluated

Cost: Free.

Publisher: Panos D. Bardis

JUNIOR HIGH SCHOOL TEST OF ECONOMICS
Committee for the Development of a Junior High School Test of Economics

---

teen   grades 7-9

Purpose: Tests junior high school students' understanding of economics; used to evaluate classroom progress and effectiveness of teaching materials.

Description: 40 item paper-pencil examination of students' knowledge of economic facts and concepts. Concepts tested are: scarcity, opportunity costs, supply and demands, GNP, money, prices and inflation, government taxation and spending, Economic growth, and government policies to achieve full employment and price stability. Materials include test booklet and answer sheet. Examiner required. Suitable for group use.

Timed: 40 minutes

Range: Grades 7-9

Scoring: Hand key; may be computer scored

Cost: Manual with answer key $3.00; 25 tests $6.00.

Publisher: Joint Council on Economic Education

MEARES-SANDERS JUNIOR HIGH SCHOOL HISTORY TEST
Shirley Meares and M. W. Sanders

teen   grades 7-8

Purpose: Assesses history achievement of junior high students. Used as first or second semester exam.

Description: 100 item paper-pencil test of historical factual knowledge as well as application of information and reasoning. Examiner required. Suitable for class use.

Timed: 40 minutes

Range: Grades 7-8

Scoring: Hand key

Cost: Specimen set $1.50; test $.15; manual $.20; key $.20.

Publisher: Bureau of Educational Measurements

THE MULTI-ETHNIC AWARENESS SURVEY
Gregory C. Coffin, Nancy S. Coffin, Bessie L. Rhodes and Robert E. Rhodes

child, teen   grades 5-UP

Purpose: Creates awareness of and arouses interest in the historical role of seven American ethnic groups: Blacks, Asians, Jews, Irish, Italians, Latinos, and Native Americans. The test is used as a supplement to the curriculum, not a measure of factual knowledge.

Description: 100 item paper-pencil inventory designed to create awareness of the contributions of seven major ethnic groups to America's history. Self- administered. Suitable for group use.

Untimed: 1 hour

Range: Grades 5 and up

Scoring: Hand key

Cost: Complete set $50.00.

Publisher: Coffin Associates

PRIMARY TEST OF ECONOMIC UNDERSTANDING
Donald G. Davison and John H. Kilgore

child   grades 2-3

Purpose: Reveals a child's understanding of economic concepts typically taught in grades 2 and 3. Useful for diagnosis and to evaluate effectiveness of teaching materials.

Description: 32 item paper-pencil yes-no, test. Child must answer both questions correctly to be scored correct. The examiner reads the questions aloud and the child writes 'yes' or 'no' for each one. Materials include test and answer key. Examiner required. Suitable for group use.

Untimed: 40 minutes

Range: Grades 2-3

Scoring: Hand key

Cost: Manual and answer key $3.00; 25 test booklets $6.00.

Publisher: Bureau of Business and Economic Research/University of Iowa

REVISED TEST OF UNDERSTANDING IN COLLEGE ECONOMICS
Phillip Saunders

teen, adult   College

Purpose: Serves as a measuring instrument for controlled experiments in the teaching of introductory college economics. Used for research and to compare one college course with another.

Description: 90 item paper-pencil examination consisting of three subtests, each in comparable A and B forms. Each form contains 30 questions dealing with recognition and understanding, and simple and complex application of macro, micro and hybrid economic principles. The Macro test covers the measurement of aggregate economic performance, aggregate supply, productive capacity and growth, income and expenditure approach to aggregate demand and fiscal policy, monetary approach to aggregate demand, policy combination, and practical problems of stabilization. The Micro test covers basic economic problems, markets and market failure, externalities, government intervention and regulation, income distribution and government redistribution. The Hybrid test covers material from both the Macro and Micro tests. Examiner required. Suitable for group use.

Timed: 45 minutes

Range: College students

Scoring: Hand key; may be computer scored

Cost: Manual $3.00; 25 test booklets $6.00 (specify form).

Publisher: Joint Council on Economic Education

SARE-SANDERS CONSTITUTION TEST
Harold V. Sare and Merritt .W. Sanders

teen   grades 10-12

Purpose: Assesses high school student knowledge of U.S. Constitution. Used as end of first or second semester exam.

Description: 125 item paper-pencil test of the vocabulary, history, and application of the U.S. Constitution. Examiner required. Suitable for group use.

Timed: 40 minutes

Range: High school

Scoring: Hand key

Cost: Specimen set $1.50; test $.15; manual $.20; key $.20.

Publisher: Bureau of Educational Measurements

SARE-SANDERS SOCIOLOGY TEST
Harold Sare and Merritt W. Sanders

teen   grades 10-12

Purpose: Assesses sociology achievement of high school students. Used as end-of-course exam.

Description: 142 item paper-pencil test of customs, folkways, mores, traditions, and social problems. Examiner required. Suitable for group use.

Timed: 40 minutes

Range: High school

Scoring: Hand key

Cost: Specimen set $1.50; test $.20; manual $.20; key $.20.

Publisher: Bureau of Educational Measurements

SANDERS-BULLER WORLD HISTORY TEST
Merritt W. Sanders and Robert Buller

teen   grades 10-12

Purpose: Assesses world history achievement of high school students. Used as first or second semester exam.

Description: 100 item paper-pencil test of ancient, medieval, and modern history. Examiner required. Suitable for class use.

Timed: 40 minutes

Range: High schoool

Scoring: Hand key

Cost: Specimen set $1.50; test $.15;

manual $.20; key $.20.

Publisher: Bureau of Educational Measurements

TEST OF ECONOMIC ACHIEVEMENT
J.D. Thexton

teen

Purpose: Measures achievement of students in Canadian secondary school economics courses at the Grade 12 and Grade 13 level.

Description: 50 item paper-pencil test measuring knowledge, understanding, and application of knowledge in economics. Examiner required. Suitable for group use. CANADIAN PUBLISHER

Timed: 1 hour

Range: Grades 12 and 13 (Canadian)

Scoring: Hand key

Cost: Specimen set (includes 1 manual, 1 key, 1 test A and B, 1 answer sheet) $15.10; class set for 10 $33.00.

Publisher: Guidance Centre

TEST OF ECONOMIC LITERACY (TEL)
John C. Soper

teen   grades 11-12

Purpose: Measures senior high school students' knowledge of economic systems and theory. Used to evaluate the quality of instruction and effectiveness of materials used.

Description: 46 item paper-pencil test in A and B forms covering seven content areas: basic economic problems, economic systems, microeconomics, resource allocation and economic distribution, macro-economics, economic stability and growth, world economy, economic institutions, and concepts for evaluat-

ing economic actions and policies. Examiner required. Suitable for group use. Available in Spanish.

Untimed: 40 minutes

Range: Grades 11 and 12

Scoring: Hand key

Cost: Manual with answer key $3.00; 25 form A $6.00; 25 form B $6.00; single copy of Spanish language test $1.00.

Publisher: Joint Council on Economic Education

TEST OF UNDERSTANDING IN PERSONAL ECONOMICS
Joint Council on Economic Education

teen   grades 9-12

Purpose: Measures high school students' understanding of personal economics, including principles and operations; used as course review and to determine effectiveness of instruction.

Description: 50 item paper-pencil, multiple-choice test of the student's knowledge of economics. Materials include test book and answer sheets. Examiner required. Suitable for group use.

Timed: 45 minutes

Range: Grades 9-12

Scoring: Hand key

Cost: Manual with answer key $3.00; 25 test booklets $6.00.

Publisher: Joint Council on Economic Education

WORLD HISTORY MAP TEST FOLIO
Earl Brightwater

teen   grades 9-12

Purpose: Measures high school student understanding of world history through map reading skills. Used as transparencies and unit teaching aids.

Description: 100 item paper-pencil, multiple-choice test. Test covers knowledge of history, politics, religion and other areas for each of 20 map titles including: Roman Empire, Europe 1812, and the Far East. Questions are posed in basic outline maps which students check to complete the questions. Examiner required. Suitable for group use.

Untimed: 50 minutes

Range: Grades 9-12

Scoring: Hand key

Cost: Test (includes answer sheet and key) $1.25; test set (includes 30 sets of 20 maps) $29.95.

Publisher: The Perfection Form Company

WORLD HISTORY TEST

teen   grades 8-12

Purpose: Measures high school student recall of factual information from specific periods in World History. Used as unit tests.

Description: 100 item paper-pencil test covering each of 16 periods from The Earliest Civilizations to New Imperialism and Russian History, plus two semester tests and a final exam. Materials include test, answer key and answer sheets. Examiner required. Suitable for group use.

Untimed: 50 minutes

Range: Grades 8-12

Scoring: Hand key

Cost: Test (includes answer sheet and key) $.45; complete set $6.25; 30 additional answer sheets $1.20.

Publisher: The Perfection Form Company

ZIMMERMAN-SANDERS SOCIAL STUDIES TEST
John J. Zimmerman and Merritt W. Sanders

teen   grades 7-8

Purpose: Assesses social studies achievement of junior high students. Used as end-of-course exam.

Description: 85 item paper-pencil test of basic areas of history, geography, and civics. Examiner required. Suitable for group use.

Timed: 30 minutes

Range: Grades 7-8

Scoring: Hand key

Cost: Specimen set $1.50; test $.15; manual $.20; key $.20.

Publisher: Bureau of Educational Measurements

Achievement and Aptitude

Academic

ACADEMIC APTITUDE TEST (AAT)-1974

teen

Purpose: Assesses academic abilities. Used for vocational guidance.

Description: Battery including ten tests of specific academic aptitudes: Nonverbal Reasoning, Verbal Reasoning, English Vocabulary, English Reading Comprehension, Numerical Comprehension, Afrikaans Vocabulary, Afrikaans Reading Comprehension,

Squares, Spatial Perception (3D) and Mathematical Proficiency. Materials include demonstration model. Examiner required. Suitable for group use. Publisher notes that this test is "standardized for Blacks only."
SOUTH AFRICAN PUBLISHER

Timed: 7 hours

Range: Standard 10

Scoring: Hand key; examiner evaluated

Cost: (In Rands) test booklet 2,40; manual 5,00; demonstration model 3,80; 10 answer sheets 1,00; scoring stencil 3,90 (orders from outside The RSA will be dealt with on merit).

Publisher: Human Sciences Research Council

ACADEMIC APTITUDE TEST (AAT)-1976

teen, adult

Purpose: Assesses academic abilities at the university level. Used for vocational guidance.

Description: Multiple item battery of tests measuring ten specific academic aptitudes: Nonverbal Reasoning, Verbal Reasoning, English Vocabulary, English Reading Comprehension, Numerical Comprehension, Afrikaans Vocabulary, Afrikaans Reading Comprehension, Squares, Spatial Perception (3D) and Mathematical Proficiency. Materials include demonstration model. Examiner required. Suitable for group use. Publisher notes that this test is "standardized for Blacks only."
SOUTH AFRICAN PUBLISHER

Timed: 7 hours

Range: First year university students

Scoring: Hand key; examiner evaluated

Cost: (In Rands) test booklet 2,10; manual 5,50; demonstration model 3,80; 10 answer sheets 1,00; scoring stencil 3,90 (orders from outside The RSA will be dealt with on merit).

Publisher: Human Sciences Research Council

ACER TESTS OF LEARNING ABILITY (TOLA)

child, teen

Purpose: Measures the language and reasoning aspects of general intellectual ability which are important for academic success for students ages 8.6-13.2 years.

Description: Multiple-item paper-pencil test of general academic aptitude is available at two levels: TOLA 4 (Year 4 of schooling or ages 8.6-11.5 years) and TOLA 6 (Year 6 of schooling or ages 10.3-13.2 years). Each level contains three separately timed subtests: Verbal Comprehension (vocabulary); General Reasoning (problem solving in a mathematical framework); and Syllogistic Reasoning (verbal analogies). Australian norms are provided in the form of stanines and percentile ranks. Examiner required. Suitable for group use.
AUSTRALIAN PUBLISHER

Timed: 33 minutes

Range: TOLA 4, ages 8.6-11.5; TOLA 6, ages 10.3-13.2

Scoring: Hand key

Cost: Specimen set (includes both levels) $15.25; test (specify level) $.90; 10 answer sheets (specify level) $1.25; score key (specify level) $.60; manual $12.00 (all remittances must be in Australian currency.

Publisher: The Australian Council for Educational Research Limited

ACHIEVEMENT AND SPECIAL ABILITIES TESTING PROGRAMS: PROFESSIONAL EXAMINATIONS DIVISION
The Psychological Corporation

teen, adult

Purpose: Assesses special abilities and achievements of students and adults. Used for selection and admission of applicants and students to various programs and schools.

Description: Nine multiple item, multiple-choice, paper- pencil tests of special ability and achievement. They include the following:
COOPERATIVE ENTRANCE EXAMINATION PROGRAM: A test developed for the Archdiocese of New York and the Diocese of Brooklyn to assist in review of qualifications of students who wish to enter participating Catholic high schools.
TESTS FOR ACCOUNTING: For high school, college, and professional levels to assess the promise and achievement of prospective accounting students, enrolled accounting students, and graduate accountants.
NAACOG HOME STUDY MODULE: A self-administered examination based on the continuing education program of the Nurses Association of the American College of Obstretricians and Gynecologists.
COMPREHENSIVE TEST IN NURSING: A three-hour examination covering communicable disease nursing, medical nursing, nutrition, pharmacology, and surgical nursing.
PROFICIENCY TEST IN PRACTICAL NURSING: A test on medical-surgical nursing, pharmacology, nutrition, maternal and child care, and general nursing information.
MODULAR ACHIEVEMENT TESTING UNITS: A test on subject matter of nursing and other health sciences for use in educational and service settings to evaluate students and practitioners.
QUALIFYING EXAMINATION SERVICES FOR SECURITIES AND EXCHANGE ORGANIZATIONS: Used by the National Association of Securities Dealers, New York Stock Exchange, American Stock Exchange, Pacific Coast Stock Exchange, and Chicago Board of Trade.
TESTS FOR CONTINUING EDUCATION: Tests of evaluation of performance on audiovisual modules.

ASSESS TEST PROGRAM: A self-administered examination for nurse licensure. Examiner administered tests are given in designated test centers. Applicants must complete and file an application and the appropriate fee by specific deadlines. For specific content and cost information, contact the publisher.

Timed: Approximately 4 hours per test

Range: Students and adults

Scoring: Computer scoring service provided

Cost: Contact publisher.

Publisher: The Professional Examinations Division/The Psychological Corporation

---

ACHIEVEMENT TEST
College Board Achievement Test Development Committees

teen   grades 10-12

Purpose: Measures high school student knowledge of a particular subject and the ability to apply that knowledge in a specified subject area. Used to predict how well the student will do in a college- level course, and for admissions selection and course placement.

Description: 14 paper-pencil, multiple-choice tests, each an hour long and ranging from 60 to 100 questions each, are given in the following areas: English composition (with and without essay), literature, American history and social studies, European history and world cultures, mathematics level I, mathematics level II, French, German, Hebrew, Latin, Spanish, biology, chemistry, and physics. The examinations are multiple-choice, except for English composition, which includes a 20-minute essay. One point is given for each correct answer, and a fraction of a point is deducted for each wrong answer. Scores are reported on a scale of 200 to 800. Most tests are given five times a year, and the fee entitles a student to take as many as three tests on one date. The achievement tests, together with the Scholastic Aptitude Test (SAT), are offered through the Admissions Testing Program (ATP) of the College Board. For students with disabilities, the ATP offers special testing arrangements, including extended-time administrations of the achievement tests. Examiner required. Administered in group settings.

Timed: 60 minutes per test

Range: Senior high school

Scoring: Computer scored

Cost: Contact publisher.

Publisher: The College Board

ACHIEVEMENT TEST: ENGLISH--ENGLISH COMPOSITION
College Board Achievement Test Development Committees

teen　grades 10-12　

Purpose: Measures high school student ability to write clear and effective prose in standard English. Used to predict college performance and by some schools for admissions selection and course placement.

Description: Multiple item, paper-pencil, multiple-choice and essay test in two forms. One is administered only in December and requires the student to answer approximately 70 multiple-choice questions and write a brief essay. The second form, offered at four other times during the year, consists of about 90 multiple-choice questions, with no writing involved. The various types of questions test the student's understanding of the relationship between ideas in a sentence, awareness of tone and meaning of words, sensitivity to wordiness and

ambiguity, and knowledge of the structure and idiom of the written English that is acceptable to college teachers. The essay test (given only in December) is a 20-minute assignment, preceded by a quotation or statement intended to stimulate the writer's thoughts on the subject. It gives an opportunity for the writer to demonstrate quality of self-expression. Graded by high school and college English teachers, the essay comprises one-third of the total English Composition score, which is reported on a 200 to 800 scale This achievement test together with the Scholastic Aptitude Test (SAT), is offered through the Admissions Testing Program (ATP) of the College Board. For students with disabilities, the ATP has available special testing arrangements including extended time administrations of the achievement test. Examiner required.

Timed: 60 minutes

Range: Senior high school

Scoring: Computer scored

Cost: Contact publisher.

Publisher: The College Board

ACHIEVEMENT TEST: ENGLISH--LITERATURE
College Board Achievement Test Development Committees

teen　grades 10-12　

Purpose: Assesses high school student understanding and interpretation of works of literature. Used to predict college performance and by some schools for admissions selection and course placement.

Description: 60 item paper-pencil, multiple-choice test based on passages drawn from poetry, fiction, drama, and prose written in English from the Renaissance to the present. Some questions ask for analysis or summation of parts of or whole passages; others ask that elements of style (such as rhythm, rhyme, and metaphor) be related to the meaning, mood, or structure of the passage. The student is not expected to have read or studied any of the passages, but to be able to examine them using developed skills. One point is given for each correct answer and a fraction of a point is deducted for each wrong answer. Scores are reported on a scale of 200 to 800. This achievement test (given five times a year), together with the Scholastic Aptitude Test (SAT), is offered through the Admissions Testing Program (ATP) of the College Board. For students with disabilities, the ATP has available special testing arrangements including extended time administrations of the achievement test. Examiner required.

Timed: 60 minutes

Range: Senior high school

Scoring: Computer scored

Cost: Contact publisher.

Publisher: The College Board

ACHIEVEMENT TEST: HISTORY AND SOCIAL STUDIES--AMERICAN HISTORY AND SOCIAL STUDIES
College Board Achievement Test Development Committees

teen   grades 10-12

Purpose: Evaluates high school student knowledge of American history and social studies. Used to predict college performance and by some schools for admissions selection and course placement.

Description: 100 item, paper-pencil, multiple-choice test of knowledge of 19th and 20th century American history in the political, social, economic, diplomatic, intellectual, and cultural fields. The test also covers social studies concepts, methods, and gen-

eralizations as they are encountered in the study of history. One point is given for each correct answer and a fraction of a point is deducted for each wrong answer. Scores are reported on a scale of 200 to 800. This achievement test (given five times a year), together with the Scholastic Aptitude Test (SAT), is offered through the Admissions Testing Program (ATP) of the College Board. For students with disabilities, the ATP has available special testing arrangements including extended time administrations of the achievement test. Examiner required.

Timed: 60 minutes

Range: Senior high school

Scoring: Computer scored

Cost: Contact publisher.

Publisher: The College Board

ACHIEVEMENT TEST: HISTORY AND SOCIAL STUDIES--EUROPEAN HISTORY and WORLD CULTURES
College Board Achievement Test Development Committees

teen   grades 10-12

Purpose: Measures high school student understanding of the development of Western and non-Western cultures, comprehension of fundamental social science concepts, and the ability to use basic historical techniques. Used to predict college performance and by some schools for admissions selection and course placement.

Description: 100 item paper-pencil, multiple-choice test, half of which deals with Western Europe, while the remainder covers other areas. Most of the questions cover the period from the middle of the 15th century to the present. Subjects covered include political and diplomatic history, intellectual and cultural history, and social and economic history. One point is given for each correct answer and a fraction of a point is deducted for each wrong answer. Scores are reported on a scale of 200 to 800. This achievement test (given five times a year), together with the Scholastic Aptitude Test (SAT), is offered through the Admissions Testing Program (ATP) of the College Board. For students with disabilities, the ATP has available special testing arrangements including extended time administrations of the achievement test. Examiner required.

Timed: 60 minutes

Range: Senior high school

Scoring: Computer scored

Cost: Contact publisher.

Publisher: The College Board

ACHIEVEMENT TEST: MATHE-MATICS--MATHEMATICS LEVEL I
College Board Achievement Test Development Committees

teen   grades 10-12

Purpose: Determines high school student level of skill in mathematics typical of three years of college preparatory work. Used to predict college performance and by some schools for admissions selection and course placement.

Description: A broad range, cumulative, paper-pencil, multiple-choice examination. About half the questions are concerned with algebra and plane Euclidean geometry. The remainder cover aspects of coordinate geometry, trigonometry of the right triangle, functions and functional notation for composition and inverse, space perception of simple solids, mathematical reasoning, and the nature of proof. One point is given for each correct answer and a fraction of a point is deducted for each wrong

answer. Scores are reported on a scale of 200 to 800. This achievement test (given five times a year), together with the Scholastic Aptitude Test (SAT), is offered through the Admissions Testing Program (ATP) of the College Board. For students with disabilities, the ATP has available special testing arrangements including extended time administrations of the achievement test. Examiner required.

Timed: 60 minutes

Range: Senior high school

Scoring: Computer scored

Cost: Contact publisher.

Publisher: The College Board

ACHIEVEMENT TEST: MATHE-MATICS--MATHEMATICS LEVEL II
College Board Achievement Test Development Committees

teen   grades 10-12

Purpose: Determines the level of skill of high school students who have taken college preparatory-level mathematics for 3½ years or more. Used to predict college performance and by some schools for admissions selection and course placement.

Description: A paper-pencil, multiple-choice test which overlaps that of Mathematics Level I. However, the questions in this test concentrate on more advanced work, calling for a greater depth of understanding and sophistication and stressing aspects that are prerequisites for calculus. The Level II test is composed of nearly equal parts of algebra, geometry, trigonometry, functions, and a miscellaneous category consisting of such topics as sequences and limits, logic and proof, probability and statistics, and number theory. One point is given for each correct answer and a fraction of a point is deducted for each wrong answer. Scores are reported on a scale of 200 to 800. This achievement test (given five times a year), together with the Scholastic Aptitude Test (SAT), is offered through the Admissions Testing Program (ATP) of the College Board. For students with disabilities, the ATP has available special testing arrangements including extended time administrations of the achievement test. Examiner required.

Timed: 60 minutes

Range: Senior high school

Scoring: Computer scored

Cost: Contact publisher.

Publisher: The College Board

ACHIEVEMENT TEST: FOREIGN LANGUAGES--FRENCH
College Board Achievement Test Development Committees

teen   grades 10-12

Purpose: Measures high school student vocabulary mastery, grammatical control, and reading comprehension of French. Used to predict college performance and by some schools for admissions selection and course placement.

Description: Multiple item, paper-pencil, multiple-choice test of ability and knowledge in three areas: Vocabulary Mastery, the knowledge of the meaning of words and idiomatic expressions as they appear in the written and spoken forms of the language; Grammatical Control, the identification of usage that is structurally correct and appropriate in context; and Reading Comprehension, the overall meaning of passages in various styles and levels of writing, as well as specific details. One point is given for each correct answer and a fraction of a point is deducted for each wrong answer. Scores are reported on a scale of 200 to 800.

This achievement test (given five times a year), together with the Scholastic Aptitude Test (SAT), is offered through the Admissions Testing Program (ATP) of the College Board. For students with disabilities, the ATP has available special testing arrangements including extended time administrations of the achievement test. Examiner required.

Timed: 60 minutes

Range: Senior high school

Scoring: Computer scored

Cost: Contact publisher.

Publisher: The College Board

ACHIEVEMENT TEST: FOREIGN LANGUAGES--GERMAN
College Board Achievement Test Development Committees

teen   grades 10-12

Purpose: Measures high school student vocabulary mastery, grammatical control, and reading comprehension of German. Used to predict college performance and by some schools for admissions selection and course placement.

Description: Multiple item, paper-pencil, multiple-choice test of ability and knowledge in three areas: Vocabulary Mastery, the knowledge of the meaning of words and idiomatic expressions as they appear in the written and spoken forms of the language; Grammatical Control, the identification of usage that is structurally correct and appropriate in context; and Reading Comprehension, the overall meaning of passages in various styles and levels of writing, as well as specific details. One point is given for each correct answer and a fraction of a point is deducted for each wrong answer. Scores are reported on a scale of 200 to 800. This achievement test (given five times a year), together with the Scholastic Aptitude Test (SAT), is offered through the Admissions Testing Program (ATP) of the College Board. For students with disabilities, the ATP has available special testing arrangements including extended time administrations of the achievement test. Examiner required.

Timed: 60 minutes

Range: Senior high school

Scoring: Computer scored

Cost: Contact publisher.

Publisher: The College Board

gram (ATP) of the College Board. For students with disabilities, the ATP has available special testing arrangements including extended time administrations of the achievement test. Examiner required.

Timed: 60 minutes

Range: Senior high school

Scoring: Computer scored

Cost: Contact publisher.

Publisher: The College Board

ACHIEVEMENT TEST: FOREIGN LANGUAGES--HEBREW
College Board Achievement Test Development Committees

teen   grades 10-12

Purpose: Measures high school student vocabulary mastery, grammatical control, and reading comprehension of Hebrew. Used to predict college performance and by some schools for admissions selection and course placement.

Description: Multiple item, paperpencil, multiple-choice test of ability and knowledge in three areas: Vocabulary Mastery, the knowledge of the meaning of words and idiomatic expressions as they appear in the written and spoken forms of the language; Grammatical Control, the identification of usage that is structurally correct and appropriate in context; and Reading Comprehension, the overall meaning of passages in various styles and levels of writing, as well as specific details. One point is given for each correct answer and a fraction of a point is deducted for each wrong answer. Scores are reported on a scale of 200 to 800. This achievement test (given five times a year), together with the Scholastic Aptitude Test (SAT), is offered through the Admissions Testing Pro-

ACHIEVEMENT TEST: FOREIGN LANGUAGES--LATIN
College Board Achievement Test Development Committees

teen   grades 10-12

Purpose: Measures high school student vocabulary mastery, grammatical control, and reading comprehension of Latin. Used to predict college performance and by some schools for admissions selection and course placement.

Description: Multiple item, paperpencil, multiple-choice test of ability and knowledge in three areas: Vocabulary Mastery, the knowledge of the meaning of words and idiomatic expressions as they appear in the written and spoken forms of the language; Grammatical Control, the identification of usage that is structurally correct and appropriate in context; and Reading Comprehension, the overall meaning of passages in various styles and levels of writing, as well as specific details. One point is given for each correct answer and a fraction of a point is deducted for each wrong answer. Scores are reported on a scale of 200 to 800. This achievement test (given five times a year), together with the Scholastic Aptitude Test (SAT), is offered through the Admissions Testing Program (ATP) of the College Board. For students with disabilities, the ATP has available special testing arrangements including extended time administrations of the achievement test. Examiner required.

Timed: 60 minutes

Range: Senior high school

Scoring: Computer scored

Cost: Contact publisher.

Publisher: The College Board

ACHIEVEMENT TEST: FOREIGN LANGUAGES--SPANISH
College Board Achievement Test Development Committees

---

teen   grades 10-12

Purpose: Measures high school student vocabulary mastery, grammatical control, and reading comprehension of Spanish. Used to predict college performance and by some schools for admissions selection and course placement.

Description: Multiple item, paper-pencil, multiple-choice test of ability and knowledge in three areas: Vocabulary Mastery, the knowledge of the meaning of words and idiomatic expressions as they appear in the written and spoken forms of the language; in Grammatical Control, the identification of usage that is structurally correct and appropriate in context; and Reading Comprehension, the overall meaning of passages in various styles and levels of writing, as well as specific details. One point is given for each correct answer and a fraction of a point is deducted for each wrong answer. Scores are reported on a scale of 200 to 800. This achievement test (given five times a year), together with the Scholastic Aptitude Test (SAT), is offered through the Admissions Testing Program (ATP) of the College Board. For students with disabilities, the ATP has available special testing arrangements including extended time

administrations of the achievement test. Examiner required.

Timed: 60 minutes

Range: Senior high school

Scoring: Computer scored

Cost: Contact publisher.

Publisher: The College Board

ACHIEVEMENT TEST: SCIENCES--BIOLOGY
College Board Achievement Test Development Committees

---

teen   grades 10-12

Purpose: Measures high school student knowledge of biology and the skills of comprehension, application, analysis, synthesis, and evaluation that have been acquired for using that knowledge. Used to predict college performance and by some schools for admissions selection and course placement.

Description: Multiple item, paper-pencil, multiple-choice test of the following topics: cellular structure and function; organismal reproduction, development, growth, nutrition, structure, and function; genetics, evolution, systematics, ecology, and behavior. There also are test questions that require interpretation of experimental data, understanding of scientific methods and laboratory techniques, and knowledge of biology history. One point is given for each correct answer and a fraction of a point is deducted for each wrong answer. Scores are reported on a scale of 200 to 800. This achievement test (given five times a year), together with the Scholastic Aptitude Test (SAT), is offered through the Admissions Testing Program (ATP) of the College Board. For students with disabilities, the ATP has available special testing arrangements including extended time administrations of the achievement test. Examiner required.

Timed: 60 minutes

Range: Senior high school

Scoring: Computer scored

Cost: Contact publisher.

Publisher: The College Board

ACHIEVEMENT TEST: SCIENCES--CHEMISTRY
College Board Achievement Test Development Committees

teen   grades 10-12

Purpose: Measures high school student knowledge of chemistry and the skills in comprehension, application, analysis, synthesis, and evaluation that have been acquired for using that knowledge. Used to predict college performance and by some schools for admissions selection and course placement.

Description: Multiple item, paper-pencil, multiple-choice test. It covers areas such as kinetic-molecular theory and the three states of matter; atomic structure, quantitative relations, chemical bonding and molecular structure, the nature of chemical reactions, interpretation of chemical equilibria and reaction rates, electrochemistry, nuclear chemistry and radiochemistry, physical and chemical properties of the more familiar metals, transition elements, and nonmetals and of the more familiar compounds. One point is given for each correct answer and a fraction of a point is deducted for each wrong answer. Scores are reported on a scale of 200 to 800. This achievement test (given five times a year), together with the Scholastic Aptitude Test (SAT), is offered through the Admissions Testing Program (ATP) of the College Board. For students with disabilities, the ATP has available special testing arrangements including extended time

administrations of the achievement test. Examiner required.

Timed: 60 minutes

Range: Senior high school

Scoring: Computer scored

Cost: Contact publisher.

Publisher: The College Board

ACHIEVEMENT TEST: SCIENCES--PHYSICS
College Board Achievement Test Development Committees

teen   grades 10-12

Purpose: Measures high school student knowledge of physics and the skills in comprehension, application, analysis, synthesis, and evaluation that have been acquired for using that knowledge. Used to predict college performance and by some schools for admissions selection and course placement.

Description: Multiple item, paper-pencil, multiple-choice test comprised of questions distributed as follows among the major areas of physics: mechanics, 40 percent; electricity and magnetism, 20 percent; geometric optics and waves, 20 percent; heat and kinetic theory, 10 percent, and modern physics, 10 percent. One point is given for each correct answer and a fraction of a point is deducted for each wrong answer. Scores are reported on a scale of 200 to 800. This achievement test (given five times a year), together with the Scholastic Aptitude Test (SAT), is offered through the Admissions Testing Program (ATP) of the College Board. For students with disabilities, the ATP has available special testing arrangements including extended time administrations of the achievement test. Examiner required.

Timed: 60 minutes

Range: Senior high school

Scoring: Computer scored

Cost: Contact publisher.

Publisher: The College Board

THE ACT ASSESSMENT
The American College Testing Program

---

teen, adult   grades 7-UP

Purpose: Assesses academic achievement of high school students. The program is a comprehensive system of data collection, processing and reporting designed to help students and counselors develop post-secondary plans and to help colleges develop instructional programs suited to the needs and characteristics of their applicants.

Description: 219 item paper-pencil test consisting of four separately timed sections: the English usage section is 40 minutes long and consists of 75 items; the mathematics usage section is 50 minutes long and consists of 40 items; the social studies reading section is 35 minutes long and consists of 52 items; the natural sciences reading section is 35 minutes long and consists of 52 items. The student must take all four sections of the test. Also included are a student profile section and interest inventory. The test is administered five times each year at designated ACT test centers to college-bound students and is also available at certain college campuses under residual testing. Examiner required. Suitable for group use.

Timed: 4 subtests-195 minutes; untimed for handicapped

Range: Junior, senior, post-high school

Scoring: Scored by publisher

Cost: Basic test fee $9.50 (New York $11.50), includes 3 score reports. Additional score reports $2.00 each.

Publisher: The American College Testing Program

ACT PROFICIENCY EXAMINATION PROGRAM (ACT PEP)
The American College Testing Program

---

adult

Purpose: Assesses college level academic achievement. Used to grant college credit and/or advanced placement in academic courses to students entering the New York Regents External Degree Program or other participating institutions.

Description: 49 paper-pencil tests measure achievement in a wide range of fields: Arts and Sciences (8 tests), Business (18 tests), Criminal Justice (2 tests), Education (4 tests), Nursing (17 tests). Most of the tests are objective (125-150 items), some are multiple-choice and essay, and some are all essay. College level achievement is measured from introductory to advanced levels of study. There are no restrictions on who may take the tests. Certain tests are administered nationwide in May and November only. Designed for New York External Degree Program. Others should contact the institution from which they are seeking credit for information. ACT test results are accepted at 600 participating colleges.

Timed: 3-7 hours per test

Range: Adult

Scoring: Examiner evaluated and/or scored by ACT

Cost: Varies in fee structure from $40.00-$235.00.

Publisher: The American College Testing Program

ACT PROFICIENCY EXAMINATION PROGRAM--ARTS AND SCIENCES: AFRO-AMERICAN HISTORY
The American College Testing Program

adult

Purpose: Measures knowledge and understanding of the history of Black Americans. Used to grant college credit and/or advanced placement in academic courses.

Description: Multiple item paper-pencil, multiple-choice test. Measures knowledge of facts, events and themes during the periods 1500-1865 (from the beginning of slavery through the Civil War); 1865-1909 (Reconstruction and its aftermath), and 1909-1968 (beginning of the 20th Century through the civil rights era). Designed for the New York Regents External Degree Program; others should contact the institution from which they are seeking credit for information. Examiner required. Suitable for group use.

Timed: 3 hours

Range: Adult

Scoring: Scored by ACT

Cost: Fee $40.00.

Publisher: The American College Testing Program

ACT PROFICIENCY EXAMINATION PROGRAM--ARTS AND SCIENCES: AMERICAN HISTORY
The American College Testing Program

adult

Purpose: Measures knowledge and understanding of American historical facts and events. Used to grant college credit and/or advanced

placement in academic courses.

Description: Multiple item paper-pencil, multiple-choice and essay test. Measures knowledge of historical events from the colonial period to the present, and the ability to discuss and interpret their historical significance. Designed for the New York Regents External Degree Program; others should contact the institution from which they are seeking credit for information. Administered in May and November only. Examiner required. Suitable for group use.

Timed: 3 hours

Range: Adult

Scoring: Examiner evaluated and scored by ACT

Cost: Fee $60.00.

Publisher: The American College Testing Program

ACT PROFICIENCY EXAMINATION PROGRAM--ARTS AND SCIENCES: ANATOMY AND PHYSIOLOGY
The American College Testing Program

adult

Purpose: Measures knowledge and understanding of anatomy and physiology. Used to grant college credit and/or advanced placement in academic courses.

Description: Multiple item paper-pencil, multiple-choice test. Items are based on anatomical terminology and facts, physiological concepts and principles, and the structure and function of body cells, tissues, organs, and systems. Emphasis is placed on systems that maintain, integrate, and control bodily functions. Designed for the New York Regents External Degree Program; others should contact the institution from which they are seeking credit for information. Examiner required. Suitable for group use.

Timed: 3 hours

Range: Adult

Scoring: Scored by ACT

Cost: Fee $40.00.

Publisher: The American College Testing Program

ACT PROFICIENCY EXAMINA-TION PROGRAM-ARTS AND SCIENCES: EARTH SCIENCE
The American College Testing Program

adult

Purpose: Measures proficiency in the earth sciences: astronomy, geology, meteorology, and oceanography. Used to grant college credit and/or advanced placement in academic courses.

Description: Multiple item paper-pencil test consisting of both essay and multiple-choice questions. Items include the areas of astronomy, geology, meteorology, and oceanography and are based upon their interrelationships and mans' interaction with the earth, atmosphere, and the oceans. Students must be able to read charts, manipulate data, and understand the operation of scientific instruments. Designed for the New York Regents External Degree Program; others should contact the institution from which they are seeking credit for information. Examiner required. Suitable for group use.

Timed: 3 hours

Range: Adult

Scoring: Examiner evaluated and scored by ACT

Cost: Fee $60.00.

Publisher: The American College Testing Program

ACT PROFICIENCY EXAMINA-TION PROGRAM-ARTS AND SCIENCES: FOUNDATION OF GERONTOLOGY
The American College Testing Program

adult

Purpose: Measures knowledge and understanding of the biological, psychological, and social aspects of aging. Used to grant college credit and/or advanced placement in academic courses.

Description: Multiple item paper-pencil, multiple-choice test. Items are based on material normally taught in a one-semester introductory course in gerontology at the undergraduate level. Measures the ability to describe, understand, and analyze issues pertaining to the functioning and well-being of the elderly. Emphasis is placed on an awareness of the needs and realities involved in both the normal aspects of aging and problems associated with aging. Designed for the New York Regents External Degree Program; others should contact the institution from which they are seeking credit for information. Examiner required. Suitable for group use.

Timed: 3 hours

Range: Adult

Scoring: Scored by ACT

Cost: Fee $40.00.

Publisher: The American College Testing Program

ACT PROFICIENCY EXAMINATION PROGRAM-ARTS AND SCIENCES: FRESHMAN ENGLISH
The American College Testing Program

adult

Purpose: Measures proficiency in English composition and literary criticism. Used to grant college credit and/or advanced placement in academic courses.

Description: Multiple item paper-pencil test consisting of both multiple-choice (Part I) and essay questions (Part II). Items are based on specific works of fiction (short story and novel), nonfiction (essay and autobiography), drama, and poetry; on literary terminology; on the nature and characteristics of the various genres and their relationship to content; and on the concepts of prosody. The exam requires the ability to write a good composition. Designed for the New York Regents External Degree Program; others should contact the institution from which they are seeking credit for information. Examiner required. Suitable for group use.

Timed: 3 hours

Range: Adult

Scoring: Examiner evaluated and scored by ACT

Cost: Fee $60.00.

Publisher: The American College Testing Program

ACT PROFICIENCY EXAMINATION PROGRAM-ARTS AND SCIENCES: PHYSICAL GEOLOGY
The American College Testing Program

adult

Purpose: Measures proficiency in the study of physical geology. Used to grant college credit and/or advanced placement in academic courses.

Description: Multiple item paper-pencil, multiple-choice test covering material normally taught in introductory undergraduate courses in physical geology. Measures knowledge and understanding of the following areas: the processes which form the earth through geologic time; the structure, composition, and evolution of the earth; and the landforms created by the processes which form the earth. Designed for the New York Regents External Degree Program; others should contact the institution from which they are seeking credit for information. Examiner required. Suitable for group use.

Timed: 3 hours

Range: Adult

Scoring: Scored by ACT

Cost: Fee $40.00.

Publisher: The American College Testing Program

ACT PROFICIENCY EXAMINATION PROGRAM-ARTS AND SCIENCES: SHAKESPEARE
The American College Testing Program

adult

Purpose: Measures knowledge of Shakespeare, his plays, and the historical and literary context in which the plays were written. Used to grant college credit and/or advanced placement in academic courses.

Description: Multiple item paper-pencil test consisting of both multiple-choice questions (Part I) and essay questions (Part II). Items are based on specific plays of Shakespeare, their dates, sources, and textual history; the life of Shakespeare; and the conventions and customs of the Elizabethan theater. Designed for the New York Regents External Degree Program; others should contact the institution from which they are seeking credit for information. Examiner required. Suitable for group use.

Timed: 3 hours

Range: Adult

Scoring: Examiner evaluated and scored by ACT

Cost: Fee $60.00.

Publisher: The American College Testing Program

ACT PROFICIENCY EXAMINATION PROGRAM- BUSINESS: ACCOUNTING: LEVEL I
The American College Testing Program

adult

Purpose: Measures knowledge and understanding of basic accounting concepts, principles, and procedures. Used to grant college credit and/or advanced placement in academic courses.

Description: Multiple item paper-pencil, multiple-choice test. Measures knowledge of terms, the ability to apply appropriate techniques in recording, analyzing, and summarizing financial data, and interpreting and reporting financial results. Students other than those enrolled in the New York Regents External Degree

Program should contact the institution from which they are seeking credit for information. Examiner required. Suitable for group use.

Timed: 3 hours

Range: Adult

Scoring: Scored by ACT

Cost: Fee $50.00.

Publisher: The American College Testing Program

ACT PROFICIENCY EXAMINATION PROGRAM- BUSINESS: ACCOUNTING: LEVEL II
The American College Testing Program

adult

Purpose: Measures proficiency in financial accounting, cost accounting, and the handling of financial data. Used to grant college credit and/or advanced placement in academic courses.

Description: Multiple item paper-pencil test consisting of both essay and multiple-choice questions. Items are based upon financial accounting concepts, terminology, and theory as recommended by the American Institute of Certified Public Accountants and the Financial Accounting Standards Board; the solution to financial and cost accounting problems; and the preparation of financial budgets and statements. Designed for the New York Regents External Degree Program; others should contact the institution from which they are seeking credit for information. Administered in May and November only. Examiner required. Suitable for group use.

Timed: 3 hours

Range: Adult

Scoring: Examiner evaluated and scored by ACT

Cost: Fee $125.00.

Publisher: The American College Testing Program

ACT PROFICIENCY EXAMINATION PROGRAM-BUSINESS: ACCOUNTING: LEVEL III, AREA I, II, III

The American College Testing Program

adult

Purpose: Measures knowledge of accounting based upon business law, federal income taxation, auditing and cost analysis, income concepts, valuation basis, measurements, and other professional issues. Used to grant college credit and/or advanced placement in academic courses.

Description: Multiple item paper-pencil essay test in three levels: Accounting, Auditing, and Advanced Accounting. Accounting Area I measures detailed knowledge of business law and federal income taxation and the ability to integrate and interpret data. Accounting Area II measures knowledge of auditing and cost analysis. Auditing items are based upon CPA examinations of financial statements and auditor's reports as well as professional ethics and responsibility. Area III includes advanced accounting theory and special problems. Students are awarded credit only if all three examinations are completed successfully. Designed for the New York Regents External Degree Program; others should contact the institution from which they are seeking credit for information. Examiner required. Suitable for group use.

Timed: 9 hours total, 3 hours per area

Range: Adult

Scoring: Examiner evaluated by ACT

Cost: Fee per area $125.00.

Publisher: The American College Testing Program

ACT PROFICIENCY EXAMINATION PROGRAM-BUSINESS: BUSINESS ENVIRONMENT AND STRATEGY

The American College Testing Program

adult

Purpose: Measures knowledge of the concepts and principles of general management decision making and corporate strategy formulation, as well as the ability to apply that knowledge to specific situations. Used to grant college credit and/or advanced placement in academic courses.

Description: Multiple item paper-pencil test consisting of both multiple-choice and essay questions. Items are based on the relationship between a manager and his environment, the formulation of corporate policy and strategy, and the integration of facts from these two areas. The essay questions include case incidents which students must analyze and choose a particular course of action, demonstrating ability to integrate (1) a working knowledge of the functional areas of business (accounting, finance, marketing, personnel, and production) and (2) an understanding of the impact of the social, political, and economic environments in which the business operates. Designed for the New York Regens External Degree Program; others should contact the institution from which they are seeking credit for information. Examiner required. Suitable for group use.

Timed: 4 hours

Range: Adult

Scoring: Examiner evaluated and computer scored by ACT

Cost: Fee $125.00

Publisher: The American College Testing Program

ACT PROFICIENCY EXAMINA-TION PROGRAM-BUSINESS: FINANCE: LEVEL I
The American College Testing Program

adult

Purpose: Measures proficiency in the areas of money and banking and corporation finance. Used to grant college credit and/or advanced placement in academic courses.

Description: Multiple item paper-pencil, multiple-choice test. Items are based upon concepts, definitions, and terminology in the areas of money and banking and corporation finance. Questions on money and banking require an analytical as well as a descriptive knowledge of the area, and questions in both areas assume an understanding of the principles of macro-economics and micro-economics. Students must solve problems requiring simple computations and apply analytic procedures to practical situations. Designed for the New York Regents External Degree Program; others should contact the institution from which they are seeking credit for information. Examiner required. Suitable for group use.

Timed: 3 hours

Range: Adult

Scoring: Scored by ACT

Cost: Fee $50.00.

Publisher: The American College Testing Program

ACT PROFICIENCY EXAMINA-TION PROGRAM-BUSINESS: FINANCE: LEVEL II
The American College Testing Program

adult

Purpose: Assesses proficiency in the areas of advanced corporation finance, security analysis and portfolio management, and financial institutions and markets. Used to grant college credit and/or advanced placement in academic courses.

Description: Multiple item paper-pencil test consisting of both objective and essay questions. Items are based upon financial facts and concepts and their relationships, the analysis of given situations, and the solutions of presented problems. Designed for the New York Regents External Degree Program; others should contact the institution from which they are seeking credit for information. Examiner required. Suitable for group use.

Timed: 4 hours

Range: Adult

Scoring: Examiner evaluated and scored by ACT

Cost: Fee $125.00.

Publisher: The American College Testing Program

ACT PROFICIENCY EXAMINA-TION PROGRAM-BUSINESS: FINANCE: LEVEL III
The American College Testing Program

adult

Purpose: Measures proficiency in financial analysis. Used to grant college credit and/or advanced placement in academic courses.

Description: Multiple item paper-pencil essay test arranged in two parts. Items for both sections are based upon the principles of finance, the interrelationships among the areas of finance, the analytic tools and measures of financial performance, and alternative solutions to financial problems. Part I covers advanced coporation finance, security analysis, and portfolio management. Part II covers financial institutions and markets. Designed for the New York Regents External Degree Program; others should contact the institution from which they are seeking credit for information. Examiner required. Suitable for group use.

Timed: 7 hours

Range: Adult

Scoring: Examiner evaluated

Cost: Fee $235.00.

Publisher: The American College Testing Program

ACT PROFICIENCY EXAMINATION PROGRAM-BUSINESS: MANAGEMENT OF HUMAN RESOURCES: LEVEL I
The American College Testing Program

---

adult

Purpose: Measures proficiency in management of human resources. Used to grant college credit and/or advanced placement in academic courses.

Description: Multiple item paper-pencil, multiple-choice test. Items are based upon facts, terminology, concepts, and theories in the area of human relations as applied to individual and group behavior, organization dynamics, organizational development, functions of management and the development of management thought. Designed for the New York Regents External Degree Program; others should contact the institution from which they are seeking credit for information. Examiner required. Suitable for group use.

Timed: 3 hours

Range: Adult

Scoring: Scored by ACT

Cost: Fee $50.00.

Publisher: The American College Testing Program

ACT PROFICIENCY EXAMINATION PROGRAM-BUSINESS: MANAGEMENT OF HUMAN RESOURCES: LEVEL II
The American College Testing Program

---

adult

Purpose: Measures proficiency in the management of human resources. Used to grant college credit and/or advanced placement in academic courses.

Description: Multiple item paper-pencil test consisting of both essay and objective questions. Items are based upon factual material applied to given situations in the areas of: management theories related to management practice, functions of management, organization dynamics, individual and group behavior, and personnel administration and labor relations. Designed for the New York Regents External Degree Program; others should contact the institution from which they are seeking credit for information. Examiner required. Suitable for group use.

Timed: 4 hours

Range: Adult

Scoring: Examiner evaluated and scored by ACT

Cost: Fee $125.00.

Publisher: The American College Testing Program

ACT PROFICIENCY EXAMINATION PROGRAM-BUSINESS: MANAGEMENT OF HUMAN RESOURCES: LEVEL III
The American College Testing Program

adult

Purpose: Measures proficiency in the management of human resources. Used to grant college credit and/or advanced placement in academic courses.

Description: Multiple item paper-pencil essay test. Items are based on knowledge in given situations in the areas of evolution of management thought, functions of management, individual and group behavior, organization dynamics, organizational development, and business policy. A knowledge of content from supporting courses in related areas of business is assumed. Designed for the New York Regents External Degree Program; others should contact the institution from which they are seeking credit for information. Examiner required. Suitable for group use.

Timed: 7 hours

Range: Adult

Scoring: Examiner evaluated

Cost: Fee $235.00.

Publisher: The American College Testing Program

ACT PROFICIENCY EXAMINATION PROGRAM-BUSINESS: MARKETING: LEVEL I
The American College Testing Program

adult

Purpose: Assesses proficiency in areas of marketing management and analysis; products, pricing, promotion, distribution, and legal and social issues. Used to grant college credit and/or advanced placement in academic courses.

Description: Multiple item paper-pencil, multiple-choice test. Measures the following aspects of marketing management and analysis: knowledge of marketing terminology, concepts, and trends; comprehension of marketing conditions, strategies, principles, and theories; ability to explain marketing procedures and theories and anticipate their effects; and ability to explain advantages and disadvantages of using various principles and techniques in defined situations. Designed for the New York Regents External Degree Program; others should contact the institution from which they are seeking credit for information. Examiner required. Suitable for group use.

Timed: 3 hours

Range: Adult

Scoring: Scored by ACT

Cost: Fee $50.00.

Publisher: The American College Testing Program

ACT PROFICIENCY EXAMINATION PROGRAM-BUSINESS: MARKETING: LEVEL II
The American College Testing Program

adult

Purpose: Asseses proficiency in the

application of factual material to given situations in the areas of marketing research, consumer behavior, marketing communications, and distribution. Used to grant college credit and/or advanced placement in academic courses.

Description: Multiple item test consisting of both objective and essay questions. Covers the following aspects of marketing: knowledge of terminology, facts, and resources; comprehension of concepts and strategies, including the purposes, conditions, advantages, and limitations of each; ability to explain advantages and disadvantages of using various principles and techniques in defined situations; and ability to apply principles and procedures to specific situations. Designed for the New York Regents External Degree Program; others should contact the institution from which they are seeking credit for information. Examiner required. Suitable for group use.

Timed: 4 hours

Range: Adult

Scoring: Examiner evaluated and scored by ACT

Cost: Fee $125.00.

Publisher: The American College Testing Program

ACT PROFICIENCY EXAMINA-TION PROGRAM-BUSINESS: MARKETING: LEVEL III
The American College Testing Program

adult

Purpose: Measures knowledge of industrial and consumer marketing approaches. Used to grant college credit and/or advanced placement in academic courses.

Description: Multiple item paper-

pencil essay test consisting of case incidents and case studies which the examinee must analyze and discuss. Items are based upon the economic, cultural, psychological, and social characteristics of industrial and consumer markets. The following areas are included: evolution of marketing and marketing policy, management, strategies, and procedures. Designed for the New York Regents External Degree Program; others should contact the institution from which they are seeking credit for information. Examiner required. Suitable for group use.

Timed: 7 hours

Range: Adult

Scoring: Examiner evaluated

Cost: Fee $235.00.

Publisher: The American College Testing Program

ACT PROFICIENCY EXAMINA-TION PROGRAM-BUSINESS: OPERATIONS MANAGEMENT: LEVEL I
The American College Testing Program

adult

Purpose: Assesses proficiency in the skills required for quantitative operations analysis. Used to grant college credit and/or advanced placement in academic courses.

Description: Multiple item paper-pencil, multiple-choice test. The test covers the following areas: knowledge of the terminology and basic principles of statistics, mathematics, and operations management; comprehension of analytic procedures and situations in which they apply; uses and interpretations of statistics and graphical data; uses, advantages, and disadvantages of analytic techniques; ability to apply knowledge of descriptive and inferential statistics and probability to the solution of problems requiring simple computation. Designed for the New York Regents External Degree Program; others should contact the institution from which they are seeking credit for information. Examiner required. Suitable for group use.

Timed: 3 hours

Range: Adult

Scoring: Scored by ACT

Cost: Fee $50.00.

Publisher: The American College Testing Program

ACT PROFICIENCY EXAMINATION PROGRAM-BUSINESS: OPERATIONS MANAGEMENT: LEVEL II
The American College Testing Program

adult

Purpose: Measures proficiency in material covered in intermediate undergraduate courses in operations management and quantitative decision making. Used to grant college credit and/or advanced placement in academic courses.

Description: Multiple item paper-pencil test consisting of objective, essay, and computational questions. Items are based upon the concepts and techniques of operations management and involve determining the solution to problems typically encountered in the field. Assesses the level of learning expected of a student with a minor concentration in operations management. Designed for the New York Regents External Degree Program; others should contact the institution from which they are seeking credit for information. Examiner required. Suitable for group use.

Timed: 4 hours

Range: Adult

Scoring: Examiner evaluated and scored by ACT

Cost: Fee $125.00.

Publisher: The American College Testing Program

ACT PROFICIENCY EXAMINATION PROGRAM-BUSINESS: OPERATIONS MANAGEMENT: LEVEL III
The American College Testing Program

adult

Purpose: Measures proficiency in operations management. Used to grant college credit and/or advanced placement in academic courses.

Description: Multiple item paper-pencil test consisting of essay and computational questions. Items are based upon the application of knowledge and concepts to given situations involving such areas as production system design, forecasting methodology, programming and planning, quality control, inventory, management, queing, statistical decision making, and simulation. Designed for the New York Regents External Degree Program; others should contact the institution from which they are seeking credit for information. Examiner required. Suitable for group use.

Timed: 7 hours

Range: Adult

Scoring: Examiner evaluated

Cost: Fee $235.00.

Publisher: The American College Testing Program

ACT PROFICIENCY EXAMINA-TION PROGRAM-CRIMINAL JUSTICE: CRIMINAL INVESTIGATION

The American College Testing Program

adult

Purpose: Assesses proficiency in the study of criminal investigation. Used to grant college credit and/or advanced placement in academic courses.

Description: Multiple item paper-pencil, multiple-choice test. Items are based upon the history of criminal investigation, the role of the investigator, and the elements and techniques of investigation, including uses, implications, and legal and practical limitations. Designed for the New York Regents External Degree Program; others should contact the institution from which they are seeking credit for information. Examiner required. Suitable for group use.

Timed: 3 hours

Range: Adult

Scoring: Scored by ACT

Cost: Fee $40.00.

Publisher: The American College Testing Program

ACT PROFICIENCY EXAMINA-TION PROGRAM-CRIMINAL JUSTICE: INTRODUCTION TO CRIMINAL JUSTICE

The American College Testing Program

adult

Purpose: Measures proficiency in the basic functions and aspects of the criminal justice system. Used to grant college credit and/or advanced placement in academic courses.

Description: Multiple item paper-pencil, multiple-choice test. Items are based upon the terminology, classifications, trends, and theories of criminal justice; the roles of the police, the courts, and corrections; their interrelationships; and the historical development of the criminal justice system. Designed for the New York Regents External Degree Program; others should contact the institution from which they are seeking credit for information. Examiner required. Suitable for group use.

Timed: 3 hours

Range: Adult

Scoring: Scored by ACT

Cost: Fee $40.00.

Publisher: The American College Testing Program

ACT PROFICIENCY EXAMINA-TION PROGRAM- EDUCATION: EDUCATIONAL PSYCHOLOGY

The American College Testing Program

adult

Purpose: Assesses proficiency in the material covered by introductory college courses in educational psychology or in the psychological foundations of education. Used to grant college credit and/or advanced placement in academic courses.

Description: Multiple item paper-pencil, multiple-choice test. Covers terminology, concepts, theories, and principles in the following areas: individual growth and development; learning and instruction; the influence of social, cultural, and environment factors; and measurement. No classroom or tutorial experience is assumed. Designed for the New York Regents External Degree Program; others should contact the institution from which they are seeking credit for information. Examiner required. Suitable for group use.

Timed: 3 hours

Range: Adult

Scoring: Scored by ACT

Cost: Fee $40.00.

Publisher: The American College Testing Program

ACT PROFICIENCY EXAMINATION PROGRAM- EDUCATION: CORRECTIVE AND REMEDIAL INSTRUCTION IN READING
The American College Testing Program

adult

Purpose: Assesses proficiency in corrective and remedial reading instruction. Used to grant college credit and/or advanced placement in academic courses.

Description: Multiple item paper-pencil, multiple-choice test. Items are based upon the following aspects of teaching reading from the primary grades through secondary school: planning programs for pupils, parents' role, relationship between the reading teacher and the school support staff, and personal responsibilities of the reading teacher. Designed for the New York Regents External Degree Program; others should contact the institution from which they are seeking credit for information. Examiner required. Suitable for group use.

Timed: 3 hours

Range: Adult

Scoring: Scored by ACT

Cost: Fee $40.00.

Publisher: The American College Testing Program

ACT PROFICIENCY EXAMINATION PROGRAM- EDUCATION: HISTORY OF AMERICAN EDUCATION
The American College Testing Program

adult

Purpose: Assesses proficiency in the study of history of American education. Used to grant college credit and/or advanced placement in academic courses.

Description: Multiple item paper-pencil test consisting of objective and essay questions. Items are based upon the influence of English-European heritage on American education, important events in the development of American education, the influence of those events on contemporary education policy and practice, and the relationships between education and various societal factors. Designed for the New York Regents External Degree Program; others should contact the institution from which they are seeking credit for information. Examiner required. Suitable for group use.

Timed: 3 hours

Range: Adult

Scoring: Examiner evaluated and scored by ACT

Cost: Fee $60.00.

Publisher: The American College Testing Program

ACT PROFICIENCY EXAMINATION PROGRAM- EDUCATION: READING INSTRUCTION IN THE ELEMENTARY SCHOOL
The American College Testing Program

adult

Purpose: Assesses proficiency in elementary school reading instruction.

Used to grant college credit and/or advanced placement in academic courses.

Description: Multiple item paper-pencil, multiple-choice test. Items are based on terms, concepts, and methods related to the following areas of reading instruction: assessment, goal setting, materials, methodologies, instructional management, instruction, evaluation, parental role, school support staff, and personal responsibilities of the teacher. Designed for the New York Regents External Degree Program; others should contact the institution from which they are seeking credit for information. Examiner required. Suitable for group use.

Timed: 3 hours

Range: Adult

Scoring: Scored by ACT

Cost: Fee $40.00.

Publisher: The American College Testing Program

ACT PROFICIENCY EXAMINATION PROGRAM-NURSING: ADULT NURSING
The American College Testing Program

adult

Purpose: Assesses proficiency in adult nursing care. Used to grant college credit and/or advanced placement in academic courses.

Description: Multiple item paper-pencil, multiple-choice test. Items are based on material normally taught in an upper-division sequence of courses in medical- surgical nursing or adult nursing at the baccalaureate level. Designed for and standardized at the B.A. degree level in conjunction with the New York Regents External Degree Program; others should contact the institution from

which they are seeking credit for information. Examiner required. Suitable for group use.

Timed: 3 hours

Range: Adult

Scoring: Scored by ACT

Cost: Fee $40.00.

Publisher: The American College Testing Program

ACT PROFICIENCY EXAMINATION PROGRAM-NURSING: COMMONALITIES IN NURSING CARE, AREA I
The American College Testing Program

adult

Purpose: Assesses proficiency in dealing with basic nursing problems. Used to grant college credit and/or advanced placement in academic courses.

Description: Multiple item paper-pencil, multiple-choice test. Items are based upon common nursing problems and nursing care as they are related to the comfort, rest, and activity of man; nutrition; elimination; and the integument. Knowledge and understanding of technical vocabulary, anatomy, physiology, and pharmacology is assumed. Designed for and standardized at the A.A. degree level in conjunction with New York Regents External Degree Program; others should contact the institution from which they are seeking credit for information. Examiner required. Suitable for group use.

Timed: 3 hours

Range: Adult

Scoring: Scored by ACT

Cost: Fee $50.00.

Publisher: The American College Testing Program

ACT PROFICIENCY EXAMINATION PROGRAM-NURSING: COMMONALITIES IN NURSING CARE, AREA II
The American College Testing Program

adult

Purpose: Assesses proficiency in dealing with common nursing problems. Used to grant college credit and/or advanced placement in academic courses.

Description: Multiple item paper-pencil, multiple-choice test. Items are based upon common nursing problems and nursing care as they are related to fluid and electrolyte balance, asepsis, communication, interpersonal relations, safe environment, and oxygenation. Knowledge and understanding of technical vocabulary, anatomy, physiology, and pharmacology are assumed. Designed for and standardized at the A.A. degree level in conjunction with the New York Regents External Degree Program; others should contact the institution from which they are seeking credit for information. Examiner required. Suitable for group use.

Timed: 3 hours

Range: Adult

Scoring: Scored by ACT

Cost: Fee $50.00.

Publisher: The American College Testing Program

ACT PROFICIENCY EXAMINATION PROGRAM-NURSING: DIFFERENCES IN NURSING CARE, AREA I
The American College Testing Program

adult

Purpose: Assesses proficiency in nursing care related to diseases and common health care problems of children and adults encountered in clinical situations, including the specific fields of oxygenation and cell growth. Used to grant college credit and/or advanced placement in academic courses.

Description: Multiple item paper-pencil, multiple-choice test. Measures four areas of basic nursing care: (1) knowledge of anatomy, physiology, pathophysiology, physical and emotional development, and psychosocial aspects of acute and long-terms health problems; (2) comprehension of the causes, symptoms, and relationships between common and specific manifestations involving oxygenation and cell growth; (3) comprehension of the effects and relative advantages and disadvantages of various treatments; and (4) ability to apply knowledge of differences in nursing care related to oxygenation and cell growth and resulting from specific health problems and the individual's response to clinical situations. Knowledge of anatomy, physiology, pharmacology, and nutrition is assumed. Designed for and standardized at the A.A. degree level in conjunction with the New York Regents External Degree Program; others should contact the institution from which they are seeking credit for information. Examiner required. Suitable for group use.

Timed: 3 hours

Range: Adult

Scoring: Scored by ACT

Cost: Fee $50.00.

Publisher: The American College Testing Program

ACT PROFICIENCY EXAMINA-TION PROGRAM-NURSING: DIFFERENCES IN NURSING CARE: AREA II

The American College Testing Program

adult

Purpose: Assesses proficiency in nursing care related to diseases and common health problems of children and adults encountered in clinical situations, including the specific fields of behavioral responses and body secretions. Used to grant college credit and/or advanced placement in academic courses.

Description: Multiple item paper-pencil, multiple-choice test. Measures four areas of basic nursing care: (1) knowledge of anatomy, physiology, pathophysiology, physical and emotional development, and psychosocial aspects of acute and long-term health problems; (2) comprehension of the causes, symptoms, and relationships between common and specific manifestations involving behavioral responses and body secretions; (3) comprehension of the effects and relative advantages and disadvantages of various treatments; and (4) ability to apply knowledge of differences in nursing care related to behavioral responses and body secretions resulting from specific health problems and the individual's response to clinical settings. Knowledge of anatomy, physiology, pharmacology, and nutrition is assumed. Designed for and standardized at the A.A. degree level in conjunction with the New York Regents External Degree Program; others should contact the institution from which they are seeking credit for information. Examiner required. Suitable for group use.

Timed: 3 hours
Range: Adult
Scoring: Scored by ACT

Cost: Fee $50.00.
Publisher: The American College Testing Program

ACT PROFICIENCY EXAMINA-TION PROGRAM-NURSING: DIFFERENCES IN NURSING CARE: AREA III

The American College Testing Program

adult

Purpose: Assesses proficiency in nursing care related to diseases and common health problems of children and adults encountered in clinical situations, including the specific fields of infectious process, tissue trauma, and the neuromuscular network. Used to grant college credit and/or advanced placement in academic courses.

Description: Multiple item paper-pencil, multiple-choice test. Measures four areas of basic nursing care: (1) knowledge of anatomy, physiology, pathophysiology, physical and emotional development, and psychosocial aspects of acute and long-term health problems; (2) comprehension of the causes, symptoms, and relationships between common and specific manifestations involving the infectious process, tissue trauma, and the neuromuscular network; (3) comprehension of the effects and relative advantages and disadvantages of various treatments; and (4) ability to apply knowledge of differences in nursing care related to the infectious process, tissue trauma, and neuromuscular network resulting from specific health problems and the individual's response to clinical situations. Knowledge of anatomy, physiology, pharmacology, and nutrition is assumed. Designed for and standardized at the A.A. degree level in conjunction with the New York Regents External Degree Program;

others should contact the institution from which they are seeking credit for information. Examiner required. Suitable for group use.

Timed: 3 hours

Range: Adult

Scoring: Scored by ACT

Cost: Fee $50.00.

Publisher: The American College Testing Program

ACT PROFICIENCY EXAMINATION PROGRAM-NURSING: FUNDAMENTALS OF NURSING
The American College Testing Program

adult

Purpose: Assesses proficiency in nursing skills and procedures. Used to grant college credit and/or advanced placement in academic courses.

Description: Multiple item paper-pencil, multiple-choice test measuring terms, facts, and trends and the ability to apply principles and theories to nursing situations. Examination is based on conventional nursing content. Designed for and standardized for the A.A. degree level in conjunction with the New York Regents External Degree Program; others should contact the institution from which they are seeking credit for information. Examiner required. Suitable for group use.

Timed: 3 hours

Range: Adult

Scoring: Scored by ACT

Cost: Fee $40.00.

Publisher: The American College Testing Program

ACT PROFICIENCY EXAMINATION PROGRAM-NURSING: HEALTH RESTORATION, AREA I
The American College Testing Program

adult

Purpose: Assesses proficiency in nursing care and intervention aimed at health restoration for individuals, families, and communities. Used to grant college credit and/or advanced placement in academic courses.

Description: Multiple item paper-pencil, multiple-choice test. Items are based on the interrelationship between the nursing process and changes in the client system (individual, family, community). The nursing process is emphasized as the framework for assisting client adaptation to change in a way that promotes restoration, palliation, habilitation, and rehabilitation. Designed for and standardized at the B.A. degree level in conjunction with the New York Regents External Degree Program; others should contact the institution from which they are seeking credit for information. Examiner required. Suitable for group use.

Timed: 3 hours

Range: Adult

Scoring: Scored by ACT

Cost: Fee $50.00.

Publisher: The American College Testing Program

ACT PROFICIENCY EXAMINATION PROGRAM-NURSING: HEALTH RESTORATION, AREA II
The American College Testing Program

adult

Purpose: Assesses proficiency in

nursing care and intervention aimed at health restoration of individuals, families, and communities. Used to grant college credit and/or advanced placement in academic courses.

Description: Multiple item paper-pencil, multiple-choice test. Items are based on the interrelationship between the nursing process and changes in the client system (individual, family, community). The nursing process is emphasized as the framework for assisting client adaptation to change in a way that promotes restoration, palliation, habilitation, and rehabilitation. Designed for and standardized at the B.A. degree level in conjunction with the New York Regents External Degree Program; others should contact the institution from which they are seeking credit for information. Examiner required. Suitable for group use.

Timed: 3 hours

Range: Adult

Scoring: Scored by ACT

Cost: Fee $50.00.

Publisher: The American College Testing Program

ACT PROFICIENCY EXAMINATION PROGRAM-NURSING: HEALTH SUPPORT, AREA I
The American College Testing Program

adult

Purpose: Assesses proficiency in health support approaches. Used to grant college credit and/or advanced placement in academic courses.

Description: Multiple item paper-pencil, multiple-choice test. Items cover the patterns that influence wellness and their interrelationships and potential barriers to wellness: rhythmicity, culture and ethnicity, values, socioeconomic status, and client per-

ception of patterns. The examination emphasizes use of the nursing process to support health of the client throughout the life cycle. Client spectrum includes individuals, families, and communities. Designed for the New York Regents External Degree Program; others should contact the institution from which they are seeking credit for information. Examiner required. Suitable for group use.

Timed: 3 hours

Range: Adult

Scoring: Scored by ACT

Cost: Fee $50.00.

Publisher: The American College Testing Program

ACT PROFICIENCY EXAMINATION PROGRAM-NURSING: HEALTH SUPPORT, AREA II
The American College Testing Program

adult

Purpose: Assesses the use of the nursing process in supporting the health of the client throughout the life cycle. Used to grant college credit and/or advanced placement in academic courses.

Description: Multiple item paper-pencil, multiple-choice test. Items focus on alterations of developmental, sustenal, activity, or life-space patterns that place the client (individual, family, community) at high risk for major health problems. Emphasis is placed on nursing actions related to prevention, teaching and counseling, screening, and early detection with regard to the need of the clients. Designed for and standardized at the B.A. degree level in conjunction with the New York Regents External Degree Program; others should contact the institution from which they are seeking credit for information. Examiner required.

Suitable for group use.

Timed: 3 hours

Range: Adult

Scoring: Scored by ACT

Cost: Fee $50.00.

Publisher: The American College Testing Program

ACT PROFICIENCY EXAMINA-TION PROGRAM-NURSING: MATERNAL AND CHILD NURSING, ASSOCIATE DEGREE
The American College Testing Program

adult

Purpose: Assesses proficiency in maternal and child nursing. Used to grant college credit and/or advanced placement in academic courses.

Description: Multiple item paper-pencil, multiple-choice test. Items are based on knowledge of facts, trends, and terminology, and on the ability to recognize and apply theories of nursing care and principles of interpersonal relationships, nutrition, and pharmacology to a variety of health care situations. Also assesses the ability to utilize the nursing process (assessment, planning, implementation, and evaluation) as it relates to the nursing care of the family during the childbearing cycle. Designed for and standardized at the A.A. degree level in conjunction with the New York Regents External Degree Program; others should contact the institution from which they are seeking credit for information. Examiner required. Suitable for group use.

Timed: 3 hours

Range: Adult

Scoring: Scored by ACT

Cost: Fee $40.00.

Publisher: The American College Testing Program

ACT PROFICIENCY EXAMINA-TION PROGRAM-NURSING: MATERNAL AND CHILD NURSING, BACCALAURATE DEGREE
The American College Testing Program

adult

Purpose: Measures proficiency in maternal and child nursing. Used to grant college credit and/or advanced placement in academic courses.

Description: Multiple item paper-pencil, multiple-choice test. Items are based upon the physiology and pathophysiology of maternal and child nursing, the theoretical framework of family functioning, and the application of the nursing process to practical situations. Designed for and standardized at the B.A. degree level in conjunction with the New York Regents External Degree Program; others should contact the institution from which they are seeking credit for information. Examiner required. Suitable for group use.

Timed: 3 hours

Range: Adult

Scoring: Scored by ACT

Cost: Fee $40.00.

Publisher: The American College Testing Program

ACT PROFICIENCY EXAMINA-TION PROGRAM-NURSING: NURSING HEALTH CARE
The American College Testing Program

adult

Purpose: Measures proficiency in basic nursing care. Used to grant college credit and/or advanced placement in academic courses.

Description: Multiple item paper-pencil, multiple-choice test. Items are based upon basic concepts in health and the interrelationships of the psychosocial and cultural factors that affect health. Emphasis is placed on the health continuum, the health care delivery system, and factors influencing common health deviations as these apply to and influence the practice of nursing. Designed for and standardized at the A.A. degree level in conjunction with the New York Regents External Degree Program; others should contact the institution from which they are seeking credit for information. Examiner required. Suitable for group use.

Timed: 3 hours

Range: Adult

Scoring: Scored by ACT

Cost: Fee $50.00.

Publisher: The American College Testing Program

ACT PROFICIENCY EXAMINA-TION PROGRAM-NURSING: OCCUPATIONAL STRATEGY, NURSING

The American College Testing Program

---

adult

Purpose: Assesses an individual's knowledge and understanding of the roles and functions of the technical nurse as that individual contributes to the current practice of nursing within the legal limitations placed on the profession. Used to grant college credit and/or advanced placement in academic courses.

Description: Multiple item paper-pencil, multiple-choice test. Covers the health team, the nursing team, and the legal guidelines to nursing

practice within both the context of the history and the current framework of the health care delivery system. Also covers knowledge and understanding of how licensure, nursing organizations, and education influence the technical nurse's function, as well as ethical guidelines for nursing practice. Designed for and the standardized at the A.A. degree level in conjunction with the New York Regents External Degree Program; others should contact the institution from which they are seeking credit for information. Examiner required. Suitable for group use.

Timed: 3 hours

Range: Adult

Scoring: Scored by ACT

Cost: Fee $50.00.

Publisher: The American College Testing Program

ACT PROFICIENCY EXAMINA-TION PROGRAM-NURSING: PROFESSIONAL STRATEGIES, NURSING

The American College Testing Program

---

adult

Purpose: Measures knowledge and understanding of the professional role within the occupation of nursing. Used to grant college credit and/or advanced placement in academic courses.

Description: Multiple item paper-pencil, multiple-choice test. Primary focus is on professional practice and the health care delivery system. Other areas tested include the understanding of the development of the profession of nursing, professional organizations, and the evolution of nursing practice and education. Designed for and standardized at the A.A. degree level in conjunction with the New York Regents External

Degree Program; others should contact the institution from which they are seeking credit for information. Examiner required. Suitable for group use.

Timed: 3 hours

Range: Adult

Scoring: Scored by ACT

Cost: Fee $50.00.

Publisher: The American College Testing Program

ACT PROFICIENCY EXAMINATION PROGRAM-NURSING: PSYCHIATRIC/MENTAL HEALTH NURSING
The American College Testing Program

adult

Purpose: Assesses proficiency in Psychiatric/Mental Health Nursing. Used to grant college credit and/or advanced placement in academic courses.

Description: Multiple item paper-pencil, multiple-choice test. Items are based on terminology, principles, and dynamics in the areas of personality development, family development, and psychological dysfunctions, as they relate to nursing assessment, planning, intervention, and evaluation. This test is designed for and standardized at the B.A. degree level in conjunction with the New York Regents External Degree Program; others should contact the institution from which they are seeking credit for information. Examiner required. Suitable for group use.

Timed: 3 hours

Range: Adult

Scoring: Scored by ACT

Cost: Fee $40.00.

Publisher: The American College Testing Program

ADMISSIONS EXAMINATIONS: PROFESSIONAL EXAMINATIONS DIVISION
The Psychological Corporation

teen, adult　grades 10-UP

Purpose: Assesses students' readiness to enter various health and medical schools and colleges. Used for admission and guidance of students seeking to enter post-high school studies.

Description: Nine paper-pencil admissions examinations include: Allied Health Professions Test (AHPAT), Entrance Examination for Schools of Health Related Technologies (EESRT), Pharmacy College Admissions Test (PACT), Optometry College Admission Test (OCAT), Veterinary Aptitude Test (VAT), Entrance Examination for Schools of Nursing, Entrance Examination for Schools of Practical/Vocational Nursing, Aptitude Test for Allied Health Programs, and Allied Health Entrance Examination. The Professional Examinations Division (PED) provides testing services to certification boards, professional registries, and national associations in connection with professional licensing, certification, counseling, admissions, scholarships, and personnel selection. PED also offers related consulting services. Applicants must complete and file an application and the appropriate fee by specific deadlines. Results are sent to the applicant and schools or colleges designated by the applicant approximately three to six weeks following the date of testing. Tests are given at designated test centers. For specific content and cost information, contact the publisher. Examiner required. Suitable for group use.

Timed: 4 hours approximately per test

Range: High school-adult

Scoring: Computer scoring service

provided

Cost: Contact publisher.

Publisher: The Professional Examinations Division/The Psychological Corporation

---

ADMISSIONS EXAMINATIONS: PROFESSIONAL EXAMINATIONS DIVISION: ALLIED HEALTH ENTRANCE EXAMINATION
The Psychological Corporation

teen, adult   grades 10-UP

Purpose: Assesses aptitude and achievement of students seeking admission to short-term assistant and technician educational programs. Used for admissions and selection.

Description: Multiple item, multiple-choice, paper-pencil test for applicants to short-term assistant and technician educational programs. See Admissions Examinations: Professional Examinations Division of The Psychological Corporation. Examiner required. Suitable for group use.

Untimed: Not available

Range: High school-adult

Scoring: Scoring service provided by publisher

Cost: Contact publisher.

Publisher: The Professional Examinations Division/The Psychological Corporation

---

ADMISSIONS EXAMINATIONS: PROFESSIONAL EXAMINATIONS DIVISION: ALLIED HEALTH PROFESSIONS ADMISSIONS TEST (AHPAT)
The Psychological Corporation

teen, adult   grades 10-UP

Purpose: Assesses students' readi-

ness for entering into upper division majors in programs leading to baccalaureate and post-baccalaureate degrees in allied health professions. Used for admissions and selection.

Description: Multiple item, multiple-choice, paper-pencil test measures verbal ability, quantitative ability, biology principles and concepts, chemistry principles including inorganic and organic chemistry, and reading comprehension. See Admissions Examinations: Professional Examinations Division of The Psychological Corporation. Examiner required. Suitable for group use.

Untimed: Not available

Range: High school-adult

Scoring: Scoring service provided by publisher

Cost: Fee $15.00.

Publisher: The Professional Examinations Division/The Psychological Corporation

---

ADMISSIONS EXAMINATIONS: PROFESSIONAL EXAMINATIONS DIVISION: APTITUDE TEST FOR ALLIED HEALTH PROGRAMS
The Psychological Corporation

teen, adult   grades 10-UP

Purpose: Assesses aptitude and achievement of students seeking admission to allied health educational programs. Used for admissions and selection.

Description: Multiple item, multiple-choice, paper-pencil test designed for students applying to allied health educational programs. See Admissions Examinations: Professional Examinations Division of The Psychological Corporation. Examiner required. Suitable for group use.

Untimed: Not available

Range: High school-adult

Scoring: Scoring service provided by publisher

Cost: Contact publisher.

Publisher: The Professional Examinations Division/The Psychological Corporation

---

ADMISSIONS EXAMINATIONS: PROFESSIONAL EXAMINATIONS DIVISION: ENTRANCE EXAMINATION FOR SCHOOLS OF HEALTH RELATED TECHNOLOGIES (EESRT)
The Psychological Corporation

teen, adult   grades 10-UP

Purpose: Measures general academic and scientific knowledge with emphasis on the physical sciences for applicants seeking admission to one or two- year post high school programs in health-related technologies. Used for admissions and selection.

Description: Multiple item, multiple-choice, paper-pencil test measures verbal ability, quantitative ability, science, reading comprehension, and space relations. See Admissions Examinations: Professional Examinations Division of The Psychological Corporation. Examiner required. Suitable for group use.

Untimed: Not available

Range: High school-adult

Scoring: Scoring service provided by publisher

Cost: Contact publisher.

Publisher: The Professional Examinations Division/The Psychological Corporation

---

ADMISSIONS EXAMINATIONS: PROFESSIONAL EXAMINATIONS DIVISION: ENTRANCE EXAMINATION FOR SCHOOLS OF NURSING
The Psychological Corporation

teen, adult   grades 10-UP

Purpose: Assesses students' readiness for entering a post-high school nursing school. Used for admissions and selection.

Description: Multiple item, paper-pencil test designed to assist in the admission and guidance of students entering nursing school. See Admissions Examinations: Professional Examinations Division of The Psychological Corporation. Examiner required. Suitable for group use.

Untimed: Not available

Range: High school-adult

Scoring: Scoring service provided by publisher

Cost: Contact publisher.

Publisher: The Professional Examinations Division/The Psychological Corporation

---

ADMISSIONS EXAMINATIONS: PROFESSIONAL EXAMINATIONS DIVISION: ENTRANCE EXAMINATION FOR SCHOOLS OF PRACTICAL/VOCATIONAL NURSING
The Psychological Corporation

teen, adult   grades 10-UP

Purpose: Assesses aptitude and achievement of students seeking admission to schools of practical or vocational nursing. Used for admissions and selection.

Description: Multiple item, multiple-choice, paper-pencil test designed for programs admitting students being prepared to become practical or vocational nurses. See Admissions Examinations: Professional Examinations Division of The Psychological Corporation. Examiner required. Suitable for group use.

Untimed: Not available

Range: High school-adult

Scoring: Scoring service provided by publisher

Cost: Contact publisher.

Publisher: The Professional Examinations Division/The Psychological Corporation

---

ADMISSIONS EXAMINATIONS: PROFESSIONAL EXAMINATIONS DIVISION: OPTOMETRY COLLEGE ADMISSION TEST
The Psychological Corporation

teen, adult   grades 10-UP

Purpose: Assesses aptitude and achievement of students seeking admission to colleges of optometry. Used for admissions and selection.

Description: Multiple item, multiple-choice, paper-pencil test measures verbal ability, quantitative ability, biology principles and concepts, organic and inorganic chemistry knowledge, physics knowledge with emphasis on light, and study- reading ability. See Admissions Examinations: Professional Examinations Division of The Psychological Corporation. Examiner required. Suitable for group use.

Untimed: Not available

Range: High school-adult

Scoring: Scoring service provided by publisher

Cost: Fee $25.00.

Publisher: The Professional Examinations Division/The Psychological Corporation

---

ADMISSIONS EXAMINATIONS: PROFESSIONAL EXAMINATIONS DIVISION: PHARMACY COLLEGE ADMISSION TEST (PCAT)
The Psychological Corporation

teen, adult   grades 10-UP

Purpose: Assesses aptitude and achievement of students seeking admission to colleges of pharmacy. Used for admissions and selection.

Description: Multiple item, multiple-choice, paper-pencil test designed to assist in the admission and guidance of students seeking admission to pharmacy colleges. See Admissions Examinations: Professional Examinations Division of The Psychological Corporation. Examiner required. Suitable for group use.

Untimed: Not available

Range: High school-adult

Scoring: Scoring service provided by publisher

Cost: Contact publisher.

Publisher: The Professional Examinations Division/The Psychological Corporation

---

ADMISSIONS EXAMINATIONS: PROFESSIONAL EXAMINATIONS DIVISION: VETERINARY APTITUDE TEST (VAT)
The Psychological Corporation

teen, adult   grades 10-UP

Purpose: Assesses aptitude and achievement of students seeking admission to colleges of veterinary medicine. Used for admissions and selection.

Description: Five multiple item paper-pencil tests measure abilities related to scholastic performance: reading comprehension, quantitative ability, biology, chemistry, and study reading. In addition, applicant performance on these measures is combined in a total score to provide a single index of scholastic aptitude. See Admissions Examinations: Professional Examinations Division of The Psychological Corporation. Examiner required. Suitable for group use.

Untimed: Not available

Range: High school-adult

Scoring: Scoring service provided by publisher

Cost: Fee $20.00.

Publisher: The Professional Examinations Division/The Psychological Corporation

---

ADMISSIONS TESTING PROGRAM (ATP)

teen   grades 11-12

Purpose: Assists students, high schools, colleges, universities, and scholarship agencies with post- secondary educational planning and decision-making through a battery of aptitude and achievement tests.

Description: The ATP consists of the Scholastic Aptitude Test (SAT), the Test of Standard Written English (TSWE), and Achievement Tests, and the Student Descriptive Questionnaire (SDQ). Closely related to the ATP are the Student Search Service, the Summary Reporting Service, and the Validity Study Service. The SAT, TSWE, and Achievement Tests are described in separate entries. The Student Descriptive Questionnaire, answered by about 91% of all students who take the ATP, provides additional information and specific characteristics (background, academic record, extra-curricular activities, etc.) about the student. The Student Search Service assists colleges and scholarship pro-

grams in identifying students with certain characteristics based on the SDQ. Students are included by their response on the SDQ and a search is conducted quarterly for colleges and programs requesting it. Handicapped students may be tested under special arrangements such as extended time administrations, with special editions of the SAT and TSWE (large type, braille, cassette) or with the use of a reader, manual translator, or an amanuensis. Tests for registered students are given at specified times by membership schools. Pre-enrollment required. Examiner required. Suitable for group use.

Timed: See specific test

Range: Junior or senior year of high school

Scoring: Computer scored

Cost: Contact publisher.

Publisher: The College Board Publications

ADMISSIONS TESTING PROGRAM: PRELIMINARY SCHOLASTIC APTITUDE TEST/NATIONAL MERIT (PSAT/NM)

teen   grade 11

Purpose: Assesses high school student verbal and mathematical reasoning abilities and evaluates readiness for college level study. Used as a preview of the Scholastic Aptitude Test and serves as the qualifying test for student competitions conducted by the National Merit Scholarship Corporation: the National Merit Scholarship Program and the National Achievement Scholarship Program for Outstanding Negro Students.

Description: 115 item paper-pencil, multiple-choice test that measures verbal and mathematical achievement and aptitude. The verbal section consists of 65 questions of four types: antonyms, sentence completions, analogies, and reading comprehension. The mathematical section consists of 50 questions applying graphic, spatial, numerical, symbolic, and logical techniques at a knowledge level no higher than elementary algebra and geometry. Special testing arrangements can be made for away- from school testing, for students abroad, for students with visual and other handicaps. Examiner required. Suitable for group use.

Timed: 1 hour 40 minutes

Range: Junior year of high school

Scoring: Computer scored

Cost: $4.25 per student.

Publisher: The College Board Publications

ADMISSIONS TESTING PROGRAM: SCHOLASTIC APTITUDE TEST (SAT)

teen   grades 11-12

Purpose: Measures verbal and mathematic reasoning abilities that are related to successful performance in college. Used to supplement secondary school records and other information in assessing readiness for college level work.

Description: 135 item paper-pencil, multiple-choice test measuring reading comprehension, vocabulary, and mathematical problem solving ability involving arithmetic reasoning, algebra, and geometry. The test consists of two verbal sections of 85 questions including 25 antonyms, 20 analogies, 15 sentence completions, and 25 reading questions; and two mathematical sections of 50 questions including approximately two-thirds multiple-choice and one-third quantitative comparison questions. Examiner required. Suitable for group use.

Timed: 2½ hours

Range: Junior or senior year of high school

Scoring: Computer scored

Cost: Contact publisher.

Publisher: The College Board Publications

ADMISSIONS TESTING PROGRAM: TEST OF STANDARD WRITTEN ENGLISH (TSWE)

teen   grades 11-12

Purpose: Evaluates a student's ability to recognize standard written English. Used by colleges to help place students in appropriate freshman English courses.

Description: 50 item paper-pencil, multiple-choice test of basic principles of grammar and usage as well as more complicated writing problems. This test is administered with the Scholastic Aptitude Test. Examiner required. Suitable for group use.

Timed: 30 minutes

Range: Junior or senior years of high school

Scoring: Computer scored

Cost: Contact publisher.

Publisher: The College Board Publications

AP EXAMINATION: ADVANCED PLACEMENT PROGRAM

teen   grades 10-12

Purpose: Measures academic achievement in a wide range of fields. Used by participating colleges to grant credit and placement in these fields to more gifted or advanced students and to measure the effectiveness of a school's Advanced Placement (AP) Program.

Description: The AP examinations are a part of the AP Program, which provides course descriptions, examinations, and curricular materials to high schools in order to allow those students who wish to pursue college level studies while still in secondary school to receive advanced placement and/or credit upon entering college. The AP Program provides descriptions and examinations on 24 introductory college courses in the following 13 fields: art, biology, chemistry, computer science, English, French, German, history, Latin, mathematics, music, physics, and Spanish.

No test is longer than three hours, some are shorter. All examinations are paper-pencil tests (except for the art portfolios) with an essay or problem- solving section and another section consisting of multiple-choice questions.

Using the operational services provided by the Educational Testing Service, the AP Examinations are administered in May by schools throughout the world. Any school may participate; it need only appoint an AP coordinator and order its examinations in time. The current fee for each examination is $42. Fee reductions are available for students with acute financial need. In June the examinations are graded on a five-point scale: 5, extremely well qualified; 4, well qualified; 3, qualified; 2, possibly qualified; 1, no recommendation. In early July, the grades are sent to the students, their desginated colleges, and their schools. Booklets on Beginning and Advanced Placement Course and Grading the Advanced Placement Examination are available in most fields. Films and booklets describing the AP Program as a whole are also available. Examiner required for all tests. Intended for group use.

Timed: 3 hours maximum

Range: Secondary school

Scoring: Computer scored

Cost: Per student $42.00.

Publisher: The College Board

AP EXAMINATION: ART--HISTORY OF ART

teen   grades 10-12

Purpose: Measures academic achievement in the study of art history. Used by participating colleges to grant credit and placement to more gifted or advanced students. Also measures the effectiveness of a school's AP Program in art history.

Description: Multiple item paper-pencil test arranged in two sections. Section I is a multiple-choice test of student's acquisition of factual or objective aspects of history of art. Questions in this section test the student's knowledge about the history of Western Art from antiquity to present. Test items include names of artists, schools, movements, chronological periods and specific dates, and the subjects styles, plus techniques of particular works of art. Section II has two parts. Part A is a series of short-answer questions testing the student's familiarity with a wide range of visual types and their historical significance. Test items here involve a comparison of related works of art. Section II, Part B is an essay test of the student's ability to deal with style development, treatment of a theme in art, the influence of historical context on works of art, and the influence of style from one given period to another. Administered in May through Educational Testing Services in schools throughout the world; graded in June on a five- point scale from 5 (extremely well qualified) to 1 (no recommendation). Grades are sent in July to the students, their designated colleges, and their schools. Fee reductions available for students with acute financial need.

Available to all schools. Examiner required.

Untimed: 3 hours
Range: Secondary school
Scoring: Computer scored
Cost: Per student $42.00.
Publisher: The College Board

AP EXAMINATION: ART-- STUDIO ART (DRAWING)

teen   grades 10-12

Purpose: Evaluates academic achievement in the study of basic drawing skills. Used by participating colleges to grant credit and placement to more gifted or advanced students. Also measures the effectiveness of a school's AP Program in studio art.

Description: Student portfolios are evaluated according to criteria which parallel specialized drawing curricula at college and university levels. Students are asked to show evidence of experience and skill in perceptual and conceptual aspects of drawing. Portfolios are evaluated for quality, concentration (depth), and breadth. For evaluation of quality, students submit four original drawings to be judged in terms of their artistic "success." For evaluation of concentration, students submit up to 20 drawings (slides required) which demonstrate in-depth work with a single concept or medium. For evaluation of breadth, students submit 14-20 additional slides of their drawings to demonstrate their exposure to and experience in a wide range of drawing alternatives. Detailed instructions for shipping, sizes of works to be submitted, and acceptable mediums are contained in the course description. Administered in May through Educational Testing Service in schools throughout the world; graded in June on a five-point scale from 5 (extremely well

qualified) to 1 (no recommendation). Grades are sent in July to the students, their designated colleges, and their schools. Fee reductions available for students with acute financial need. Available to all schools. Examiner required.

Untimed: Not available
Range: Secondary school
Scoring: Computer scored
Cost: Per student $42.00.
Publisher: The College Board

AP EXAMINATION: ART-- STUDIO ART (GENERAL PORTFOLIO)

teen   grades 10-12

Purpose: Evaluates general academic achievement in the study of studio art. Used by participating colleges to grant credit and placement to more gifted or advanced students. Also measures the effectiveness of a school's AP Program in Studio Art.

Description: Student portfolios are evaluated for three factors; quality, concentration (depth), and breadth. For evaluation of quality, students submit four original works in their original form to be judged in terms of artistic "success." For evaluation of concentration, students are asked to show evidence of work which reveals an in-depth artistic investigation (accompanied by a written commentary). For evaluation of breadth, students must submit slides of six drawings, as well as slides of six additional works which address the following six artistic factors: technique, color, design, spatial, content, and three-dimensional. Detailed instructions for shipping, size of works to be submitted, and acceptable mediums are included in the course description. Administered in May through Educational Testing Service in schools throughout the world; graded in June on a five-point scale from 5 (extremely well qualified) to 1 (no recommendation). Grades are sent in July to the students, their designated colleges, and their schools. Fee reductions available for students with acute financial need. Available to all schools. Examiner required.

Untimed: Not available

Range: Secondary school

Scoring: Computer scored

Cost: Per student $42.00.

Publisher: The College Board

AP EXAMINATION: BIOLOGY--GENERAL BIOLOGY

teen   grades 10-12

Purpose: Measures academic achievement in the study of biology. Used by participating colleges to grant credit and placement to more gifted or advanced students. Also measures the effectiveness of a school's AP Program in biology.

Description: Multiple item paper-pencil test consists of a 90-minute multiple-choice section and a 75-minute free-response section. Both sections test the student's knowledge and understanding of the three major subdivisions of biology: molecular and cellular, organismal, and populational. Part of the multiple-choice section includes questions on experimental situations. For the free-response section, three pairs of questions are presented (one pair for each subdivision), and students are required to answer one question from each pair. Administered in May through Educational Testing Service in schools throughout the world; graded in June on a five-point scale from 5 (extremely well qualified) to 1 (no recommendation). Grades are sent in July to the students, their designated colleges, and their

schools. Fee reductions available for students with acute financial need. Available to all schools. Examiner required.

Untimed: 3 hours maximum

Range: Secondary school

Scoring: Computer scored

Cost: Per student $42.00.

Publisher: The College Board

AP EXAMINATION: CHEMISTRY--GENERAL CHEMISTRY

teen   grades 10-12

Purpose: Measures academic achievement in the study of chemistry. Used by participating colleges to grant credit and placement to more gifted or advanced students. Also measures the effectiveness of a school's AP Program in chemistry.

Description: Multiple item paper-pencil test in two parts. Part I is an 85 item multiple-choice test for which 105 minutes are allotted (45% of the final grade). Part II (55% of the final grade; allotted 75 minutes) consists of several comprehensive problems and essay topics which allow the student to demonstrate reasoning abilities by the application of chemical principles to problem solving. Both cover the following areas of fundamental chemistry: structure of matter, states of matter, reactions, descriptive chemistry, and laboratory work. Non-programmable hand calculators are allowed. Administered in May through Educational Testing Service in schools throughout the world; graded in June on a five- point scale from 5 (extremely well qualified) to 1 (no recommendation). Grades are sent in July to the students, their designated colleges, and their schools. Fee reductions available for students with acute financial need. Available to all schools. Examiner required.

Untimed: 3 hours maximum

Range: Secondary school

Scoring: Computer scored

Cost: Per student $42.00.

Publisher: The College Board

AP EXAMINATION: COMPUTER SCIENCE

teen   grades 10-12

Purpose: Measures academic achievement in the study of computer science. Used by participating colleges to grant credit and placement to more gifted or advanced students. Also measures the effectiveness of a school's AP Program in computer science.

Description: Multiple item paper-pencil test in two equally weighted parts: (1) a multiple-choice section, and (2) a free-response section requiring the students to design, write, and document programs and procedures. Both sections include the following topics: programming methodology, features of programming languages, data types and structures, linear data structures, algorithms, and applications of computing. Knowledge of computer systems and social implications of computing are tested in questions on other topics. Details on equipment needed are included in the course guide. Administered in May through Educational Testing Service in schools throughout the world; graded in June on a five-point scale from 5 (extremely well qualified) to 1 (no recommendation). Grades are sent in July to the students, their designated colleges, and their schools. Fee reductions available for students with acute financial need. Available to all schools. Examiner required.

Untimed: 3 hours maximum

Range: Secondary school

Scoring: Computer scored

Cost: Per student $42.00.

Publisher: The College Board

AP EXAMINATION: ENGLISH-- ENGLISH LANGUAGE

teen   grades 10-12

Purpose: Measures academic achievement in the study of English language and composition. Used by participating colleges to grant credit and placement to more gifted or advanced students. Also measures the effectiveness of a school's AP Program in English language and composition.

Description: Multiple item paper-pencil test arranged in two parts: Part I (60 minutes; 40% of the final grade) employs multiple-choice questions to test a student's skill at recasting sentences and analyzing the rhetoric of prose passages. Part II (90 minutes; 60% of the final grade) requires students to demonstrate their skill at composition directly by writing several essays of varying lengths invarious rehetorical modes. Both parts test abilities to recognize and work with the following factors: kinds and levels of diction, varieties of sentence structures, logical and functional semantic relationships, modes of discourse, aims of discourse, various rehetorical strategies, and appropriate relationships among author, audience and subject. Administered in May through Educational Testing Service in schools throughout the world; graded in June on a five-point scale from 5 (extremely well qualified) to 1 (no recommendation). Grades are sent in July to the students, their designated colleges, and their schools. Fee reductions available for students with acute financial need. Available to all schools. Examiner required.

Untimed: 3 hours maximum

Range: Secondary school

Scoring: Computer scored

Cost: Per student $42.00.

Publisher: The College Board

AP EXAMINATION: ENGLISH-- ENGLISH LITERATURE

teen   grades 10-12

Purpose: Measures academic achievement in the study of English literature and composition. Used by participating colleges to grant credit and placement to more gifted or advanced students. Also measures the effectiveness of a school's AP Program in English literature and composition.

Description: Multiple item paper-pencil test in two parts: Part I (60 minutes; 40% of the final grade) employs multiple-choice questions that test the student's reading of selected passages. Part II (90 minutes; 60% of the final grade) requires writing as a direct measure of the student's ability to read and interpret literature. Both parts measure the following critical and compositional skills: the use of modes of discourse, the recognition of assumptions underlying various rhetorical strategies, and the awareness of the resources of language (connotation, metaphor, irony, syntax, and tone). Administered in May through Educational Testing Service in schools throughout the world; graded in June on a five-point scale from 5 (extremely well qualified) to 1 (no recommendation). Grades are sent in July to the students, their designated colleges, and their schools. Fee reductions available for students with acute financial need. Available to all schools. Examiner required.

Untimed: 3 hours maximum

Range: Secondary school

Scoring: Computer scored

Cost: Per student $42.00.

Publisher: The College Board

AP EXAMINATION: FRENCH LANGUAGE

teen   grades 10-12

Purpose: Measures academic achievement in the study of the French language. Used by participating colleges to grant credit and placement to more gifted or advanced students. Also measures the effectiveness of a school's AP Program in French language.

Description: Multiple item paper-pencil test evaluates level of performance in the use of the French language, both in understanding written and spoken French, and in responding with ease in correct and idiomatic French. Listening and reading skills are tested in the multiple-choice section. Writing and speaking skills are tested in the free response section. The portion of the examination devoted to each skill counts for one-fourth of the final grade. The examination as a whole tests the following objectives: ability to understand spoken French in both formal and conversational situations; the development of an ample vocabulary; and the ability to express ideas accurately and resourcefully both orally and in writing. Students' oral responses are taped, requiring that all students be familiar with whatever equipment is to be used in the examination. Administered in May through Educational Testing Service in schools throughout the world; graded in June on a five-point scale from 5 (extremely well qualified) to 1 (no recommendation). Grades are sent in July to the students, their designated colleges, and their schools. Fee reductions available for students with acute financial need. Available to all schools.

Examiner required.

Timed: 3 hours maximum

Range: Secondary school

Scoring: Computer scored

Cost: Per student $42.00.

Publisher: The College Board

AP EXAMINATION: FRENCH LITERATURE

teen   grades 10-12

Purpose: Measures academic achievement in the study of French literature and language. Used by participating colleges to grant credit and placement to more gifted or advanced students. Also measures the effectiveness of a school's AP Program in French literature.

Description: Multiple item paper-pencil test in two sections. Section I (60 minutes; one-third of the final grade) employs multiple-choice questions to test the student's ability to understand and analyze literary prose and poetry in French. Section II (120 minutes; two-thirds of final grade) consists of an essay part and a literary analysis part. As a whole, the examination measures understanding of the works of French literature on the reading list provided the AP Program as well as the ability to interpret and analyze literary texts, and competence in the use of written French. Administered in May through Educational Testing Service in schools throughout the world; graded in June on a five-point scale from 5 (extremely well qualified) to 1 (no recommendation). Grades are sent in July to the students, their designated colleges, and their schools. Fee reductions available for students with acute financial need. Available to all schools. Examiner required.

Timed: 3 hours maximum

Range: Secondary school

Scoring: Computer scored

Cost: Per student $42.00.

Publisher: The College Board

AP EXAMINATION: GERMAN LANGUAGE

teen   grades 10-12

Purpose: Measures academic achievement in the study of the German language. Used by participating colleges to grant credit and placement to more gifted or advanced students. Also measures the effectiveness of a school's AP Program in German.

Description: Multiple item paper-pencil test consists of two sections. Section I (120 minutes; two-thirds of the final grade) is a multiple-choice test for listening comprehension and reading skills. Section II (60 minutes; one-third of the final grade) is a free-response essay test of writing skills. Speaking ability is not tested. The test evaluates level of performance in the use of the German language. Administered in May through Educational Testing Service in schools throughout the world; graded in June on a five-point scale from 5 (extremely well qualified) to 1 (no recommendation). Grades are sent in July to the students, their designated colleges, and their schools. Fee reductions available for students with acute financial need. Available to all schools. Examiner required.

Timed: 3 hours maximum

Range: Secondary school

Scoring: Computer scored

Cost: Per student $42.00.

Publisher: The College Board

AP EXAMINATION: HISTORY-- AMERICAN HISTORY

teen   grades 10-12

Purpose: Measures academic achievement in the study of American history. Used by participating colleges to grant credit and placement to more gifted or advanced students. Also measures the effectiveness of a school's AP Program in American history.

Description: Multiple item paper-pencil test in two equally weighted sections. Section I (75 minutes) employs multiple-choice questions to test the student's factual knowledge, breadth of preparation, and knowledge-based analytical skills. Section II consists of two parts: Part A (40 minutes), in which students answer a document- based essay question; and Part B (50 minutes), in which students answer one of five standard essay questions. The essay questions test the student's mastery of historical interpretation and the ability to express views and knowledge in writing. Both sections cover the period from the earliest colonial settlements to the present (with emphasis on the nineteenth and twentieth centuries) and cover the following topics: political institutions, behavior, public policy, social and economic change, diplomacy, and international relations, and cultural and intellectual developments. Administered in May through Educational Testing Service in schools throughout the world; graded in June on a five-point scale from 5 (extremely well qualified) to 1 (no recommendation). Grades are sent in July to the students, their designated colleges, and their schools. Fee reductions available for students with acute financial need. Available to all schools. Examiner required.

Timed: 3 hours maximum

Range: Secondary school

Scoring: Computer scored

Cost: Per student $42.00.

Publisher: The College Board

AP EXAMINATION: HISTORY-- EUROPEAN HISTORY

teen   grades 10-12

Purpose: Measures academic achievement in the study of European history. Used by participating colleges to grant credit and placement to more gifted or advanced students. Also measures the effectiveness of a school's AP Program in European history.

Description: Multiple item paper-pencil test in two equally weighted sections. Section I (75 minutes) is a multiple-choice test dealing with concepts, major historical facts, and historical analysis. Section II consists of two parts: Part A (45 minutes) is a document-based essay question, and Part B (45 minutes) requires the student to answer one of six standard essay questions. Students are expected to demonstrate a knowledge of basic chronology of major events and trends from approximately 1450 to the 1980's (high Renaissance to present). Test items cover the following historical themes: intellectual-cultural, social- economic, and political-diplomatic. Administered in May through Educational Testing Service in schools throughout the world; graded in June on a five-point scale from 5 (extremely well qualified) to 1 (no recommendation). Grades are sent in July to the students, their designated colleges, and their schools. Fee reductions available for students with acute financial need. Available to all schools. Examiner required.

Timed: 3 hours maximum

Range: Secondary school

Scoring: Computer scored

Cost: Per student $42.00.

Publisher: The College Board

AP EXAMINATION: VERGIL AND CATULLUS-HORACE

teen   grades 10-12

Purpose: Measures academic achievement in the study of Latin. Used by participating colleges to grant credit and placement to more gifted or advanced students. Also measures the effectiveness of a school's AP Program in Latin.

Description: Multiple item paper-pencil test consists of three parts: a multiple-choice section which tests students' ability to read and understand Latin poetry at sight, and two free response sections which measure the students' ability to comprehend and interpret the material read in the two specific courses on Vergil and Catullus- Horace. Students may elect to take either or both of the free response sections (each one represents roughly one semester of college work). Students are expected to be able to translate accurately the poetry they are reading from Latin into English and demonstrate a grasp of grammatical structures and vocabulary used. Other important factors include: stylistic analysis, awareness of political, social and cultural backgrounds of the works being read, and awareness of the classical influences of later literature. Administered in May through Educational Testing Service in schools throughout the world; graded in June on a five-point scale from 5 (extremely well qualified) to 1 (no recommendation). Grades are sent in July to the students, their designated colleges, and their schools. Fee reductions available for students with acute financial need. Available to all schools. Examiner required.

Timed: 3 hours maximum

Range: Secondary school

Scoring: Computer scored

Cost: Per student $42.00.

Publisher: The College Board

AP EXAMINATION: MATHE-MATICS--CALCULUS AB

teen   grades 10-12

Purpose: Measures academic achievement in the study of calculus. Used by participating colleges to grant credit and placement to more gifted or advanced students. Also measures the effectiveness of a school's AP Program in calculus.

Description: Multiple item paper-pencil test in two equally weighted parts: (1) a multiple-choice test of proficiency in a wide variety of topics; (2) a problem section requiring students to demonstrate their ability to carry out proofs and solve problems involving a more extended chain of reasoning. Topics covered include: elementary functions, differential calculus, and integral calculus. The use of specific functions is emphasized, rather than their theoretical development and basis. Calculus AB level is not generally as difficult as Calculus BC level. Administered in May through Educational Testing Service in schools throughout the world; graded in June on a five-point scale from 5 (extremely well qualified) to 1 (no recommendation). Grades are sent in July to the students, their designated colleges, and their schools. Fee reductions available for students with acute financial need. Available to all schools. Examiner required.

Timed: 3 hours maximum

Range: Secondary school

Scoring: Computer scored

Cost: Per student $42.00.

Publisher: The College Board

AP EXAMINATION: MATHE-MATICS--CALCULUS BC

teen   grades 10-12

Purpose: Measures academic achievement in the study of calculus. Used by participating colleges to grant credit and placement to more gifted or advanced students. Also measures the effectiveness of a school's AP Program in calculus.

Description: Multiple item paper-pencil test in two equally weighted parts: (1) a multiple-choice test of proficiency in a wide variety of topics (2) a problem section requiring students to demonstrate their ability to carry out proofs and solve problems involving a more extended chain of reasoning. Topics covered include: elementary functions, differential calculus, integral calculus, sequences and series, and elementary differential equations. Calculus BC level is generally more difficult and involves more theoretical reasoning than Calculus AB level. Administered in May through Educational Testing Service in schools throughout the world; graded in June on a five-point scale from 5 (extremely well qualified) to 1 (no recommendation). Grades are sent in July to the students, their designated colleges, and their schools. Fee reductions available for students with acute financial need. Available to all schools. Examiner required.

Timed: 3 hours maximum

Range: Secondary school

Scoring: Computer scored

Cost: Per student $42.00.

Publisher: The College Board

AP EXAMINATION: MUSIC--LISTENING AND LITERATURE

teen   grades 10-12

Purpose: Measures academic achievement in the study of music listening and literature. Used by participating colleges to grant credit and placement to more gifted or advanced students. Also measures the effectiveness of a school's AP Program in music.

Description: Multiple item paper-pencil test measuring knowledge of musical styles and forms. The test contains 70 minutes of questions specific to music listening and literature, and a 40-minute test of the Aural Perception Component (APC). The APC is also a part of the AP Music Theory exam and is taken only once if both tests are taken in the same year. In the specific questions section, multiple-choice and free response questions (using both aural and visual stimuli) address the structural aspects (70 percent) and historical and cultural aspects (30 percent) of music. The APC requires the student to distinguish among various scales, meters, and rhythms, to identify cadence and texture types, and to recognize formal structure and function. Administered in May through Educational Testing Service in schools throughout the world; graded in June on a five-point scale from 5 (extremely well qualified) to 1 (no recommendation). Grades are sent in July to the students, their designated colleges, and their schools. Fee reductions available for students with acute financial need. Available to all schools. Examiner required.

Timed: 110 minutes

Range: Secondary school

Scoring: Computer scored

Cost: Per student $42.00.

Publisher: The College Board

AP EXAMINATION: MUSIC--MUSIC THEORY

teen   grades 10-12

Purpose: Measures academic achievement in the study of music theory. Used by participating colleges to grant credit and placement to more gifted or advanced students. Also measures the effectiveness of a school's AP Program in music theory.

Description: Multiple item paper-pencil test measure of the student's understanding of musical structure and compositional procedures. Three kinds of questions are included: multiple-choice based on recorded music; multiple-choice based not on aural materials, but on general musical knowledge; and free response questions of various lengths, some of which are based on recorded music. Also included is a 40-minute test of the Aural Perception Component (this component is also a part of the AP Music Listening and Literature exam and is taken only once if both tests are taken in the same year). The following fundamentals are covered: terminology and notational skills, elementary composition, visual analysis, and aural skills. The Aural Perception Component (APC) requires the student to discriminate among various scales, meters, and rhythms; to identify cadence and texture types; and to recognize formal structure and function. Administered in May through Educational Testing Service in schools throughout the world; graded in June on a five- point scale from 5 (extremely well qualified) to 1 (no recommendation). Grades are sent in July to the students, their designated colleges, and their schools. Fee reductions available for students with acute financial need. Available to all schools. Examiner required.

Timed: 3 hours maximum

Range: Secondary school

Scoring: Computer scored

Cost: Per student $42.00.

Publisher: The College Board

AP EXAMINATION: PHYSICS B

teen   grades 10-12

Purpose: Measures academic achievement in the study of physics as a basis for more advanced work in the life sciences, medicine, geology, and related fields. Used by participating colleges to grant credit and placement to more gifted or advanced students. Also measures the effectiveness of a school's AP Program in physics.

Description: Multiple item paper-pencil test consists of two equally weighted sections (90 minutes each): one multiple-choice section and one free response section. Five general topics are covered: mechanics, kinetic theory and thermodynamics, electricity and magnetism, waves and optics, and modern physics. Calculus is not required. Administered in May through Educational Testing Service in schools throughout the world; graded in June on a five-point scale from 5 (extremely well qualified) to 1 (no recommendation). Grades are sent in July to the students, their designated colleges, and their schools. Fee reductions available for students with acute financial need. Available to all schools. Examiner required.

Timed: 3 hours maximum

Range: Secondary school

Scoring: Computer scored

Cost: Per student $42.00.

Publisher: The College Board

AP EXAMINATION: PHYSICS C

teen   grades 10-12

Purpose: Measures academic achievement in the study of physics as a basis for more advanced study in the physical sciences and engineering. Used by participating colleges to grant credit and placement to more gifted or advanced students. Also measures the effectiveness of a school's AP Program in physics.

Description: Paper-pencil test in two parts (90 minutes each): one part for mechanics, and one part for electricity and magnetism. Students may take either or both parts, each with a separate grade representing roughly one semester of college level work. The parts are divided equally (in time and scoring weight) between a multiple-choice section and a free response section. The Mechanics part covers the following topics: kinematics; Newton's Laws of Motion; work, energy, and power; systems of particles (statics); rotational motion; and oscillations and gravitation. The Electricity and Magnetism part covers the following topics: electrostatics, electric current and circuits, capacitance and capacitors, magnetostatics, and electromagnetism. Use of calculus is required (when appropriate) for both parts. Administered in May through Educational Testing Service in schools throughout the world; graded in June on a five-point scale from 5 (extremely well qualified) to 1 (no recommendation). Grades are sent in July to the students, their designated colleges, and their schools. Fee reductions available for students with acute financial need. Available to all schools. Examiner required.

Timed: 3 hours maximum

Range: Secondary school

Scoring: Computer scored

Cost: Per student $42.00.

Publisher: The College Board

AP EXAMINATION: SPANISH-- SPANISH LANGUAGE

teen   grades 10-12

Purpose: Measures academic achievement in the study of the Spanish language. Used by participating colleges to grant credit and placement to more gifted or advanced students. Also measures the effectiveness of a school's AP Program in Spanish.

Description: Paper-pencil and oral response test consists of two sections. Section I (90 minutes) employs multiple-choice questions and tests listening and reading comprehension skills (including mastery of grammatical structure and vocabulary). Section II (75 minutes), a free response section, tests the active skills of speaking and writing. The portion of the examination devoted to each skill counts for one-fourth of the composite score. The test evaluates general ability to understand written and spoken Spanish and to write and speak easily and idiomatically. Students must be trained in the use of examination equipment in order to insure that their oral responses are properly recorded. Administered in May through Educational Testing Service in schools throughout the world; graded in June on a five-point scale from 5 (extremely well qualified) to 1 (no recommendation). Grades are sent in July to the students, their designated colleges, and their schools. Fee reductions available for students with acute financial need. Available to all schools. Examiner required.

Timed: 3 hours maximum

Range: Secondary school

Scoring: Computer scored

Cost: Per student $42.00.

Publisher: The College Board

AP EXAMINATION: SPANISH-- SPANISH LITERATURE

teen   grades 10-12

Purpose: Measures academic achievement in the study of Spanish literature. Used by participating colleges to grant credit and placement to more gifted or advanced students. Also measures the effectiveness of a school's AP Program in Spanish.

Description: Paper-pencil test consisting of two equally weighted parts: (1) a multiple-choice section on aural comprehension, literary analysis, the reading comprehension of passages, and the analysis of two poems; and (2) a free-response section on literary interpretation and analysis and skill in writing critical, expository prose in Spanish. Section 2 contains two essays. Each essay deals with two or more of the authors required by the AP Program in Spanish Literature. Students are asked to analyze and discuss in Spanish, works that they have read (no choice of authors is given). Administered in May through Educational Testing Service in schools throughout the world; graded in June on a five-point scale from 5 (extremely well qualified) to 1 (no recommendation). Grades are sent in July to the students, their designated colleges, and their schools. Fee reductions available for students with acute financial need. Available to all schools. Examiner required.

Timed: 3 hours maximum

Range: Secondary school

Scoring: Computer scored

Cost: Per student $42.00.

Publisher: The College Board

APTITUDE TEST FOR ADULTS (AA)-1979

child, teen

Purpose: Assesses specific aptitudes. Used for psycho-educational evaluation.

Description: 225 item paper-pencil test of nine specific aptitudes including Comparison, Figural Series, Calculations, Reasoning, Mechanical Insight, Spatial Visualization (2-D), Classification, Spatial Visualization (3-D) and Spare Parts. Examiner required. Suitable for group use. Publisher notes that this test is "normed on Blacks only."
SOUTH AFRICAN PUBLISHER

Timed: 3½

Range: Standard 5 to 10

Scoring: Hand key; examiner evaluated

Cost: (In Rands) test booklet 3,90; manual 9,10; 10 answer sheets 1,20; scoring stencil 3,80 (orders from outside The RSA will be dealt with on merit).

Publisher: Human Sciences Research Council

APTITUDE TESTS FOR INDIAN SOUTH AFRICANS- JATISA and SATISA

child, teen

Purpose: Assesses aptitudes of Indian children. Used for vocational guidance.

Description: Multiple item paper-pencil test batteries. JATISA designed for Standards 6 to 8; SATISA for Standards 9 and 10. JATISA consists of 10 subtests: Verbal Reasoning, Series Completion, Social Insight, Language Usage, Numerical Reasoning, Spatial Perception (2-D), Spatial Perception

(3-D), Visual Arts, Clerical Speed and Accuracy and Mechanical Insight. SATISA tests the following 11 areas: Verbal Reasoning, Numerical Reasoning, Spatial Perception (3-D), Series Completion, Mechanical Insight, Classification, Spatial Perception (2-D), Comparison, Language Usage, Memory and Filing. Examiner required. Suitable for group use.

SOUTH AFRICAN PUBLISHER

Timed: Junior, 3½ hours; Senior 4½ hours

Range: Grades Junior, Standards 6-8; Senior, Standard 9 and 10

Scoring: Hand key; examiner evaluated

Cost: (In Rands) Junior-test plus photos 1,10; manual 9,10; scoring stencil 5,00; 10 answer sheets 0.90; Senior-tests A or B 2,10 each; 10 answer sheets I, 0,60; 10 answer sheets II 0,60; manual 6,30; scoring stencils I, II, III, IV 3,40 each (orders from outside The RSA will be dealt with on merit).

Publisher: Human Sciences Research Council

APTITUDE TESTS FOR SCHOOL BEGINNERS (ASB)-1974

child

Purpose: Assesses aptitudes of children beginning school. Used for placement, program planning, and prediction of future achievement.

Description: Multiple item paper-pencil test of eight areas important in the early school years: Perception, Spatial, Reasoning, Numerical, Gestalt, Coordination, Memory, and Verbal Comprehension. Yields differential aptitude profile rather than IQ-type score. Administration during the first two months of the school year is recommended. Examiner required.

Suitable for group use.

SOUTH AFRICAN PUBLISHER

Timed: 7 hours

Range: Ages 5-8 years

Scoring: Hand key; examiner evaluated

Cost: (In Rands) 10 tests 3,00; 10 tests of Verbal Comprehension 0,70; scoring key 0,60; manual 5,70 (orders from outside The RSA will be dealt with on merit).

Publisher: Human Sciences Research Council

APU ARITHMETIC TEST and APU VOCABULARY TEST
S.J. Closs and Michael Hutchings

child, teen

Purpose: Measures vocabulary and arithmetic skills of children 11 to 18 years old. Used in schools and colleges as well as in vocational guidance, industrial selection, and similar situations where an overall indication of verbal and arithmetical skills is required.

Description: Two paper-pencil tests measure vocabulary and arithmetic skills. The APU Vocabulary Test contains 75 items which have been culled from newspapers and magazines to ensure that the range of difficulty is realistic and that the scores give a valid indication of understanding of vocabulary in current use. Materials include reusable test booklets and separate answer sheets which can be scored using a template. Norms provided for ages 11-17 years. The APU Arithmetic Test contains 50 items which cover the whole range from basic skills to percentages, sets, ratios, and elementary statistics. The test is fully metricated. Scoring employs a specially-designed key provided in the manual. Norms provided for ages 11-18 years. Examiner required. Suitable for group use.

BRITISH PUBLISHER

Timed: Arithmetic, 25 minutes; Vocabulary, 15 minutes

Range: Ages 11-18

Scoring: Hand key

Cost: Arithmetic specimen set 60p; 20 tests £2.00 per set; manual 50p; Vocabulary specimen set 75p; 20 tests £1.80 per set; 20 answer sheets 90p plus VAT; template 60p plus VAT; manual 60p.

Publisher: Hodder & Stoughton

ASSESSMENT OF BASIC COM-PETENCIES (ABC)
Jwalla P. Somvaru

child, teen   grades PRE-9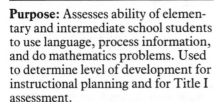

Purpose: Assesses ability of elementary and intermediate school students to use language, process information, and do mathematics problems. Used to determine level of development for instructional planning and for Title I assessment.

Description: Multiple item, verbal, and paper-pencil test. It covers 11 defined test areas in three broad domains. Language skills covers reading, decoding, comprehending expressions, producing expressions, and understanding words. Information Processing covers relating, organizing, and observing and Mathematics Skills covers solving problems, understanding concepts, and knowing numbers and operations. The test is individually administered with the student and examiner on opposite sides of a table. Scoring provides a raw score, level of competence, developmental age, grade equivalent, standard score, and percentile. Since the battery is both criterion and norm-referenced, two kinds of response forms are included: the diagnostic version, which enables the user to observe performance primarily in terms of clusters of skills;

and the developmental version, which enables the user to observe performance primarily in terms of developmental level. All items relate to specific objectives which can be placed onto Individualized Education Program (I.E.P.). Materials included. Examiner required. Not suitable for group use.

Timed: 2 hours

Range: Preschool-Grade 9

Scoring: Hand key; examiner evaluated

Cost: Starter set $414.00.

Publisher: Scholastic Testing Service, Inc.

AUSTRALIAN ITEM BANK

child, teen

Purpose: Assesses achievement in academic subjects. Used for providing items for classroom and final examinations.

Description: Multiple item paper-pencil test consisting of items in science, social science, and mathematics. Subject banks available separately or as a complete set. Examiner required. Suitable for group use.

AUSTRALIAN PUBLISHER

Untimed: Not available

Range: Years 8-12

Scoring: Not available

Cost: Complete set $90.00; Mathematics and Science Item Bank $36.00 each; Social Science Item Bank $18.00 (all remittances must be in Australian currency).

Publisher: The Australian Council for Educational Research Limited

BASIC EDUCATIONAL SKILLS INVENTORY (BESI)

child, teen

Purpose: Assesses proficiency in basic classroom skills and diagnoses specific numerical and verbal skill deficits. Used to establish Individualized Education Programs and to monitor student response to remedial intervention.

Description: Multiple item paper-pencil tests available in two levels of two tests each. Level A measures reading (362 items) and mathematics (221 items) readiness. Level B measures reading (427 items) and mathematics (407 items) skill development. Both levels assess 33 reading skill areas such as pre-reading skills, alphabet, phonic analysis and synthesis, sight recognition, word patterns, etc.; and 30 mathematics skill areas such as quantitative concepts, counting skills, basic number proficiency, number words, sequencing and ordering, basic computation, fractions, decimals, etc. All skill areas are cross-referenced to the Prescriptive Materials Retrieval System (PMRS) to aid in selection of proper remediation materials. Examiner required. Suitable for group use.

Untimed: Not available

Range: Ages 4-12

Scoring: Examiner evaluated

Cost: Complete $124.95; BESI Read-Levels A and B $45.00; BESI Math-Levels A and B $87.50 (each kit contains all materials needed for 35 students).

Publisher: B.L. Winch & Associates

BASIC EDUCATIONAL SKILLS TEST (BEST)
Ruth Segel and Sandra Golding

child   grades 1-5

Purpose: Determines ability of elementary school children and older remedial students to read, write, and do arithmetic. Used to screen for group placement and program planning.

Description: 75 item paper-pencil examination consisting of three subtests: Reading, Writing-Spelling, and Mathematics. Materials include a manual, test plates, and recording forms, which correlate performance on each item with relevant perceptual modalities (auditory, visual, vocal, and haptic). Examiner required. Not suitable for group use.

Untimed: 20 minutes

Range: Grades 1-5 and older remedial students

Scoring: Hand key

Cost: Manual $7.50; test plates $18.00; 25 recording forms $6.00; specimen set $7.50.

Publisher: Academic Therapy Publications

BASIC MATHEMATICS TESTS SERIES
Refer to page 237.

BASIC SCHOOL SKILLS INVENTORY-DIAGNOSTIC (BSSI-D)
Donald D. Hammill and James E. Leigh

child

Purpose: Determines the special learning needs of children, pinpointing both the general areas and the specific readiness skills that need remedial attention. Results of this testing-for-teaching- approach-to-assessment provide practical knowledge for teaching children the items they do not know.

Description: 110 item paper-pencil test enabling the examiner to view a child's performance individually or compared with his peers. Measures six areas of school performance: daily living skills, spoken language, reading readiness, writing readiness, math readiness, and classroom behavior. Materials include picture cards and answer sheets. Standardization sample of 376 children are in general the same as those in the 1980 U.S. Census. A companion test is the Basic School Skills Inventory--Screen. Examiner required. Not for group use.

Untimed: Not available

Range: Ages 4-0 to 6-11

Scoring: Examiner evaluated

Cost: Complete (includes examiner manual, 50 answer sheets, picture cards, storage box) $42.08.

Publisher: PRO-ED

BASIC SCHOOL SKILLS INVENTORY-SCREEN (BSSI-S)
Donald P. Hammill and James E. Leigh

child

Purpose: Diagnoses children who are "high risk" for school failure, who need more in depth assessment, and who should be referred for further evaluation. Assesses a child's overall readiness for school.

Description: 20 item paper-pencil observational screening device. Examines: daily living skills, spoken language, reading readiness, writing readiness, math readiness, and classroom behavior. The examiner checks off answers known about the child;

further investigation may be needed for some items. Standardization sample of 376 children are in general the same as those in the 1980 U.S. Census. A companion test is the Basic School Skills Inventory--Diagnostic. Examiner required. Not for group use.

Untimed: 5-8 minutes

Range: Ages 4-0 to 6-11

Scoring: Examiner evaluated

Cost: Complete (includes examiner manual and 50 answer sheets) $14.00.

Publisher: PRO-ED

BASIC SKILLS ASSESSMENT PROGRAM (BSAP)
Educational Testing Service

all ages

Purpose: Evaluates how well the individual applies academic skills to everyday situations. Used to screen students needing special help in basic skills.

Description: 210 item paper-pencil, multiple-choice test of reading, writing skills, and mathematics. Assesses comprehension of everyday skills such as understanding consumer information, reading newspapers, making a simple calculation and writing letters and completing job applications. The test can be used as a high school graduation requirement to judge attainment of minimal proficiency in basic skills. Examiner required. Suitable for group use.

Timed: 45 minutes

Range: 7-adult

Scoring: Hand key; computer scoring available

Cost: Reusable combined test books for 35 $61.25; 100 answer sheets $16.00; set of 5 scoring stencils $4.50 (specify form).

Publisher: CTB/McGraw-Hill

BASIC SKILLS INVENTORY K-12
Los Angeles County Test Development Center

child, teen   grades K-12

Purpose: Assesses competencies in reading, language arts, and mathematics. Used for end of year evaluation.

Description: 24 to 36 item paper-pencil tests of basic academic skills. Divided into six levels: Level A, grades K-1; Level B, grades 1-2; Level C, grades 2-3; Level I, grades 4-6; Level II, grades 7-9; Level III, grades 10-12. Reading, language arts and mathematics tests are available at each level, as is a combined test with items in all three areas. Factors measured include difficulty, fit, and error factor. Test is criterion-referenced rather than norm-reference. Examiner required. Suitable for group use.

Untimed: 45 minutes

Range: Grades K-12

Scoring: Computer scored

Cost: Individual test booklets $.75 each; combined test $1.50 each.

Publisher: Intran Corporation

BENCH MARK MEASURES
Aylett Cox

child, teen

Purpose: Assesses a student's general phonic knowledge, including reading, writing, and spelling, as a means of diagnosing particular deficiencies and to gauge progress during remediation.

Description: Three paper-pencil, verbal tests arranged in sequence to cover four areas of remedial language: alphabet and dictionary skills, reading, handwriting, and spelling. The alphabet and reading sections must be administered individually, while the handwriting and spelling schedules can be given to groups. The Bench Mark Measures kit contains step-by-step directions for administration, along with reading passages and spelling lists. The Guide to Bench Mark Measures contains a description of testing, scoring and evaluation. The Graphs of Concepts and Multisensory Introduction shows the graphemes and concepts in the order taught in the Alphabetic Phonics curriculum. Summary sheets are used to record responses and mark errors. This examination was designed primarily for use with the Alphabetic Phonics curriculum, the three levels of which correspond to the Bench Mark's alphabet, reading, and writing schedules. It can, however, be used with any student as a diagnostic tool and should be administered by a trained examiner in a quiet setting. The last two sections can be given to small groups.

Untimed: 30 minutes-1 hour for each of the four levels; 2-4 hours in total

Range: Ungraded-measures a student's mastery during remediation

Scoring: Examiner evaluated

Cost: Complete kit $55.00; summary sheets $10.00; graph $1.25.

Publisher: Educators Publishing Service, Inc.

BRISTOL ACHIEVEMENT TESTS
Alan Brimer, general editor

child, teen

Purpose: Measures achievement in basic academic skills. Used for evaluation of student progress and identification of an individual's strengths and weaknesses.

Description: Multiple item paper-pencil tests of achievement in English language, mathematics, and study skills. English Language Tests measure word meaning, paragraph meaning, sentence organization, organization of ideas, and spelling and punctuation. Mathematics Tests cover the following areas: number, reasoning, space, measurement and arithmetical laws and processes. Study Skills Tests measure properties, structures, processes, explanations and interpretation. Tests are available at five levels for ages 8 through 13. Materials include two parallel forms, A and B. Examiner required. Suitable for group use. BRITISH PUBLISHER

Timed: Various timings

Range: Ages 8-14

Scoring: Hand key; examiner evaluated

Cost: Teacher's set for each area of achievement (includes one each of the parallel forms A and B, 2 marking keys, profile and manual) £2.25 (payment in sterling for all overseas orders).

Publisher: NFER-Nelson Publishing Co.

CALIFORNIA ACHIEVEMENT TESTS: FORMS C AND D (CAT/C&D)
CTB McGraw-Hill

child, teen   grades K-12.9

Purpose: Assesses achievement in basic academic skills. Used for making educational decisions leading to improvement in instruction.

Description: Multiple item paper-pencil measures of basic curricular areas of reading, language and mathematics. Divided into ten overlapping levels spanning kindergarten through grade 12. Level 10 is a "readiness" instrument for children in kindergarten derived from Form S of the Comprehensive Tests of Basic Skills. Levels 11-19 are composed of separate

tests that combine to yield scores in Total Reading, Spelling, Total Language, Total Mathematics, and Reference Skills. Spelling not available at Level 11; Reference Skills tested only at Levels 14-19. Alternate form, Form D, available for Levels 13-19. Examiner required. Suitable for group use.

Timed: Depending on level, complete battery up to 2 hours 48 minutes

Range: Grades K-12.9

Scoring: Hand key; computer scoring available

Cost: Multi-level examination kit $19.50; specimen set (specify primary, intermediate, or secondary) $10.35.

Publisher: CTB/McGraw-Hill

CANADIAN COGNITIVE ABILITIES TEST (CCAT)
E. Wright, R. Thorndike and E. Hagan

child, teen   grades K-12

Purpose: Measures cognitive development of students in grades K-3 (primary battery) and 3-12 (multilevel edition). Used for placement, counseling, and class planning.

Description: Primary battery (K-3) is a 76-90 item paper-pencil test of the following concepts: relational, multimental, quantitative, and oral. Multilevel battery (3-12) is a 240 item paper-pencil test of the following abilities: verbal (vocabulary, sentence completion, verbal classification, verbal analogies), quantitative (relations, number series, equations), and non-verbal (figure classification, analysis and synthesis). Examiner required. Not for group use. CANADIAN PUBLISHER

Timed: 1 hour 38 minutes

Range: Grades K-12

Scoring: Hand key; computer scoring available

Cost: Booklet $4.75; 500 answer sheets $80.00; scoring mask $6.15; manual $8.25.

Publisher: Nelson Canada

CANADIAN TESTS OF BASIC SKILLS: HIGH SCHOOL EDITION (CTBS)
E. King, D. Scannel, et al

teen

Purpose: Assesses high school student progress in developing basic educational skills. Used for class planning and counseling.

Description: 233 to 242 item paper-pencil test of achievement in the following areas: reading comprehension, mathematics, using sources of information, and written expression. The test has a multilevel format with Canadian norms. Examiner required. Suitable for group use. CANADIAN PUBLISHER

Timed: 2 hours 40 minutes

Range: Ages 14-18

Scoring: Hand key; computer scoring available

Cost: Booklet $4.95; 500 answer sheets $80.00; scoring masks $6.15; teacher's guide $7.95.

Publisher: Nelson Canada

CANADIAN TESTS OF BASIC SKILLS (MULTILEVEL EDITION) (CTBS)
E. King, A. Hieronymus, et al

child, teen

Purpose: Assesses student progress in developing basic educational skills. Used for group placement and curriculum planning.

Description: 350 to 465 item paper-pencil measure of achievement in: vocabulary, reading comprehension, spelling, capitalization, punctuation, usage, visual materials, reference materials, math concepts, math problems, and math computation. The test is timed, scaled to grade, and Canadian normed. One multilevel, reusable booklet is appropriate for all grades 3-8. Examiner required. Suitable for group use. CANADIAN PUBLISHER

Timed: 4 hours, 40 minutes

Range: Ages 8-14

Scoring: Hand key; computer scoring available

Cost: Booklet $4.95; 500 answer sheets $90.00; scoring mask $6.15; teacher's guide $7.95.

Publisher: Nelson Canada

CANADIAN TESTS OF BASIC SKILLS (PRIMARY BATTERY) (CTBS)
E. King, A. Hieronymus, et al

child

Purpose: Assesses progress of K-3 students in developing basic educational skills. Used for class grouping and evaluation.

Description: 157 to 539 item paper-pencil test of the following: vocabulary, reading comprehension, spelling, capitalization, punctuation, usage, visual materials, reference materials, mathematic concepts, problems, and computations. The test is scaled to grade. Examiner required. Suitable for group use. CANADIAN PUBLISHER

Timed: 2 hours 30 minutes-3 hours 55 minutes

Range: Ages 5-8

Scoring: Hand key

Cost: 25 booklets $21.45; scoring masks $9.25; teacher's guide $6.35.

Publisher: Nelson Canada

CLARKE READING SELF-ASSESSMENT SURVEY (SAS)
John H. Clarke and Simon Wittes

teen, adult   grades 9-UP

Purpose: Measures student language skills prior to beginning the first semester in college. Used for self-assessment and counseling.

Description: Multiple item paper-pencil instrument which diagnoses strengths and weaknesses in reading, conceptualization, and written expression, with suggestions for skill improvement. Test booklet contains instructions for the student, multiple- choice questions, answers, scoring guide and graphic profile. Self-administered. Suitable for group use.

Untimed: 1 hour

Range: Grades 9-adult

Scoring: Hand key

Cost: Survey $4.00; 10-$25.00.

Publisher: Academic Therapy Publications

CLASSROOM LEARNING SCREENING (CLS)
Carl H. Koenig and Harold P. Kunzelman

child   grades 1-6

Purpose: Screens small groups of elementary school students of varying abilities for performance in reading, math and spelling in order to identify those who need special help.

Description: 30 item paper-pencil test using stimulus cards and an audio tape to assess current performance and learning rates of individuals in such groups as resource rooms or special education classes. Materials include an audiotape, cards, spirit duplicating masters, and a handbook. Examiner required. Suitable for group use.

Untimed: 5 minutes

Range: Grades 1-6

Scoring: Hand key

Cost: Complete kit (includes handbook, spirit duplicating masters, stimulus cards, audiotape) $59.95; student booklets (specify level) $36.00; examiner's manual $5.95.

Publisher: Charles E. Merrill Publishing Company

COGNITIVE ABILITIES TEST, FORM 3 (CogAT)
Robert L. Thorndike and Elizabeth P. Hagen

child, teen   grades K-12

Purpose: Assesses the verbal, quantitative, and other abstract cognitive skills that are important in learning activities. Used with students from Kindergarten through Grade 12 to identify those who need help in developing general cognitive skills, to aid in the diagnosis of learning disabilities, and to plan individualized instructional programs.

Description: Multiple item paper-pencil test measuring the development of students' cognitive skills as an indicator of potential academic success. Level 1 (84 items) for Grades K-1 and Level 2 (98 items) for Grades 2-3 comprise the Primary Battery which measures the following factors: oral vocabulary, relational concepts, object classification, and quantitative concepts. Levels A-H (240 items each) comprise the Multilevel Edition for use with Grades 3-12. Each level (A-H) contains a verbal battery assessing vocabulary, sentence completion, classification, and analogies; and a quantitative battery assessing relations, number series, and equation building. Also available is a nonverbal battery measuring figure classification, analogies, and synthesis. All levels are normed concurrently with the Iowa Tests of Basic Skills and the Tests of Achievement and Proficiency to provide comparisons of achievement and abilities test scores. Examiner required. Suitable for group use.

Timed: 32-34 minutes, Multilevel Edition

Untimed: 54-56 minutes, Primary Battery

Range: Grades K-1 (Level 1), Grades 2-3 (Level 2, Grades 3-12 (Level A-H)

Scoring: Hand key; computer scoring available

Cost: 35 Levels 1 or 2 Primary Battery-MRC machine- scorable test booklets (includes examiner's manual) $24.75; Multilevel Edition-complete test booklet for Levels A-H $2.97 each; 35 MRC answer sheets (includes examiner's manual) $12.60 per level. Examiner's manual $4.17.

Publisher: The Riverside Publishing Company

COLLEGE LEVEL EXAMINATION PROGRAM (CLEP)

teen, adult   grades 12-UP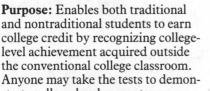

Purpose: Enables both traditional and nontraditional students to earn college credit by recognizing college-level achievement acquired outside the conventional college classroom. Anyone may take the tests to demonstrate college-level competency, no matter where or how this knowledge was acquired: through formal study, private reading, employment experience, noncredit courses, adult classes, TV/radio/cassette courses, military/industrial/business training, or advanced work in regular high school courses.

Description: Five General Examinations and 46 Subject Examinations assess college-level proficiency in a wide range of fields. The General Examinations measure achievement in five basic areas of the liberal arts: English Composition, Humanities, Mathematics, Natural Sciences, and Social Sciences and History. Each of these examinations tests material usually covered in the first two years of college and often referred to as the general or liberal education requirement. The Subject Examinations measure achievement in specific college courses and are used to grant exemption from and credit for these courses.

The examinations are not based on a particular syllabus, but rather, stress concepts, principles, relationships, and applications of course material. Constructed to differentiate among several levels of mastery, they contain questions of varying difficulty. All CLEP tests are constructed by committees composed of teachers and scholars from colleges and universities in all parts of the United States.

Test content is based on a curriculum survey prepared by the Educational Testing Service and completed by colleges and universities throughout the country. The survey enables the committees to determine test specifications according to current curriculum standards, testbooks, and methods of teaching. Examinations are administered during the third week of each month at more than 900 test centers located on college and university campuses throughout the country (the General Examination in English Composition with essay is available in June and October only).

Approximately one month after the test date, test scores and a booklet explaining them are sent to the candidates, as well as to colleges, universities, or other recipients as specified by the candidates. If the optional essay section of a Subject Examination is taken, it is sent for grading to the institution receiving the score. Institutions honoring CLEP test scores for credit are listed in "Moving Ahead with CLEP," available free from the publisher. Examiner required. Suitable for group use.

Timed: 90 minutes per test

Range: High school seniors-college; adult

Scoring: Computer scoring provided

Cost: Contact publisher.

Publisher: The College Board

COLLEGE LEVEL EXAMINA-TION PROGRAM (CLEP) AMERICAN HISTORY I: EARLY COLONIZATIONS TO 1877

teen, adult   grades 12-UP

Purpose: Measures proficiency in the material commonly covered in one-semester introductory college courses on the early period of American history.

Description: 120 item paper-pencil, multiple-choice test assessing knowledge and understanding of American history from the Spanish and French colonizations to the end of Reconstruction (1877). Coverage of the colonial period emphasizes the development of the English colonies, while the emphasis of the test as a whole is on the period of nationhood. Candidates are expected to be able to describe, characterize, analyze, and explain major historical phenomena in the following categories: political institutions and behavior and public policy, social and economic change, cultural and intellectual developments, and diplomacy and international relations. An optional essay section assesses the ability to present organized, logical historical arguments dealing with the topics covered in the objective section. Examiner required. Suitable for group use.

Timed: 90 minutes

Range: High school seniors-college;

adult

Scoring: Computer scoring provided

Cost: Contact publisher.

Publisher: The College Board

COLLEGE LEVEL EXAMINA-TION PROGRAM (CLEP) AMERICAN HISTORY II: 1865 TO THE PRESENT

teen, adult   grades 12-UP

Purpose: Measures college level competency in the study of American history from 1865 to the present.

Description: 120 item paper-pencil test covering the period of American History from the end of the Civil War to the present: 1865 to 1914, and 1915 to the present. Content coverage is political institutions and behavior and public policy, social and economic change, cultural and intellectual developments, and diplomacy and international relations. An optional 90 minute essay section is also offered. Examiner required. Suitable for group use.

Timed: 90 minutes; optional essay 90 minutes

Range: High school seniors-college; adult

Scoring: Computer scoring provided

Cost: Contact publisher.

Publisher: The College Board

COLLEGE LEVEL EXAMINA-TION PROGRAM (CLEP) BUSINESS: COMPUTERS and DATA PROCESSING

teen, adult   grades 12-UP

Purpose: Measures proficiency in the material commonly taught in introductory one-semester college courses in computers and data processing.

Description: 100 item paper-pencil,

multiple-choice test assessing knowledge and understanding of concepts of computer programming and data processing which are applicable to a variety of programming languages. The test assumes a general knowledge of hardware and software, but does not emphasize hardware design or language-specific programming techniques. Arranged in two sections of 50 items each, the test covers the following topics: hardware, data, software, systems concepts, and miscellaneous historical and state-of-the-art topics. An optional essay section contains five questions dealing in depth with important topics in computer programming and data processing. Examiner required. Suitable for group use.

Timed: 90 minutes

Range: High school seniors-college; adult

Scoring: Computer scoring provided

Cost: Contact publisher.

Publisher: The College Board

COLLEGE LEVEL EXAMINATION PROGRAM (CLEP) BUSINESS: ELEMENTARY COMPUTER PROGRAMMING, FORTRAN IV

teen, adult   grades 12-UP

Purpose: Measures knowledge, understanding and skill equivalent to that gained from a college-level one-semester course in FORTRAN IV computer programming.

Description: 100 item paper-pencil objective test measuring those elements of FORTRAN IV which are common to most users. Topics covered include: constants, variables, arrays, logic expressions, statement functions and function subprograms; subscripts, GOTO, Data, Dimension, explicit type, Common, Equivalence; subroutine subpro-

grams; logical and arithmetic IF; Arithmetic expressions, DO; Read and Write. Fifteen percent of the test questions are embedded within program segments. Examiner required. Suitable for group use.

Timed: 90 minutes

Range: High school seniors-college; adult

Scoring: Computer scoring provided

Cost: Contact publisher.

Publisher: The College Board

COLLEGE LEVEL EXAMINATION PROGRAM (CLEP) BUSINESS: INTRODUCTION to MANAGEMENT

teen, adult   grades 12-UP

Purpose: Measures understanding of the material taught in introductory courses in the essentials of management and organization.

Description: 199 item paper-pencil test assessing the following areas: knowledge of manpower and human resources, operational aspects of management, functional aspects of management, and miscellaneous aspects of management. The optional essay section contains five questions measuring the ability to relate the concepts of management to current issues and to bring together material drawn from different parts of the subject. Examiner required. Suitable for group use.

Timed: 90 minutes

Range: High school seniors-college; adult

Scoring: Computer scoring provided

Cost: Contact publisher.

Publisher: The College Board

COLLEGE LEVEL EXAMINATION PROGRAM (CLEP) BUSINESS: INTRODUCTORY ACCOUNTING

teen, adult   grades 12-UP

Purpose: Assesses the level of accounting skills expected of a person with one year of college accounting or equivalent on-the-job training.

Description: 80 item paper-pencil objective test measuring proficiency in financial accounting and managerial accounting. Assesses the following accounting skills: familiarity with accounting concepts and terminology, the ability to prepare and use financial reports issued for internal and external purposes, and the ability to apply accounting techniques to simple problem situation involving computations. An optional essay section tests the candidates abilities to apply general concepts and procedures to stated problems and to combine material from various areas of accounting. Silent hand calculators are allowed. Examiner required. Suitable for group use.

Timed: 90 minutes

Range: High school seniors-college; adult

Scoring: Computer scoring provided

Cost: Contact publisher.

Publisher: The College Board

COLLEGE LEVEL EXAMINATION PROGRAM (CLEP) BUSINESS: INTRODUCTORY BUSINESS LAW

teen, adult   grades 12-UP

Purpose: Measures knowledge and understanding of the function of contracts in American business law at the introductory undergraduate level.

Description: 100 item paper-pencil objective test assessing six major content categories: history and sources of American law, American legal systems and procedures, contracts, agency and employment, sales, and miscellaneous. Optional essay portion measures ability to select pertinent material and present it in an organized manner dealing with case materials or business law concepts. Examiner required. Suitable for group use.

Timed: 90 minutes

Range: High school seniors-college; adult

Scoring: Computer scoring provided

Cost: Contact publisher.

Publisher: The College Board

COLLEGE LEVEL EXAMINATION PROGRAM (CLEP) BUSINESS: INTRODUCTORY MARKETING

teen, adult   grades 12-UP

Purpose: Measures proficiency in the material usually covered in introductory one-semester college courses in the fundamentals of marketing.

Description: 100 item paper-pencil, multiple-choice test assessing knowledge and understanding of the principles of marketing. Test items concern marketing interactions, marketing functions and institutions, and selected issues and topics related to marketing problems, strategies, and decisions. The test assumes a basic knowledge of demographic and economic trends, wholesaling and retailing institutional structures, and the classification of consumer and industrial goods. Four optional essay questions test the ability to apply marketing principles to basic marketing problems. Candidates who have business experience equivalent to a course in introductory marketing will be well-prepared for the exam.

Examiner required. Suitable for group use.

Timed: 90 minutes

Range: High school seniors-college; adult

Scoring: Computer scoring provided

Cost: Contact publisher.

Publisher: The College Board

COLLEGE LEVEL EXAMINATION PROGRAM (CLEP) BUSINESS: MONEY and BANKING

teen, adult   grades 12-UP

Purpose: Measures competency in the basic material covered in a one semester college-level money and banking course.

Description: 100 item paper-pencil objective assessing knowledge and understanding of the banking system in the United States. The test is concerned with the use of actual knowledge in new situations and in problem-solving contexts, as well as the analysis and understanding of economic relationships and the basic interpretation of appropriate materials. Material covered includes: money and supply, commercial banking, monetary theory, monetary policy implementation, international monetary relations, and problems in monetary policy. The three optional essay questions measure the ability to relate principles to current issues and assimilate various materials learned in the course. Examiner required. Suitable for group use.

Timed: 90 minutes

Range: High school seniors-college; adult

Scoring: Computer scoring provided

Cost: Contact publisher.

Publisher: The College Board

COLLEGE LEVEL EXAMINATION PROGRAM (CLEP) DENTAL AUXILIARY EDUCATION: DENTAL MATERIALS

teen, adult   grades 12-UP

Purpose: Measures proficiency in the subject commonly covered in an introductory one-semester course in dental materials for students of dental hygiene or dental assisting (but not for students of dental laboratory technology).

Description: Multiple item paper-pencil test assessing knowledge and understanding of dental materials and their use in the practice of dentistry. Covers the following topics: structure and properties of materials, gypsum products, impression materials, synthetic resins, dental cements, science of metals (including tarnish and corrosion), dental amalgams, direct filling gold, castings, porcelain, and miscellaneous abrasives, tools, dentifrices. Examiner required. Suitable for group use.

Timed: 90 minutes

Range: High school seniors-college; adult

Scoring: Computer scoring provided

Cost: Contact publisher.

Publisher: The College Board

COLLEGE LEVEL EXAMINATION PROGRAM (CLEP) DENTAL AUXILIARY EDUCATION: HEAD, NECK and ORAL ANATOMY

teen, adult   grades 12-UP

Purpose: Measures proficiency in the material commonly taught in an introductory one-semester course in head, neck, and oral anatomy for students of dental hygiene, dental assisting, or dental laboratory technology.

Description: Multiple item paper-pencil test assessing knowledge and understanding of head, neck and oral anatomy. Covers the following topics: osteology, myology, angiology, neurology, orally related structures, oral landmarks, and anthrology. Examiner required. Suitable for group use.

Timed: 90 minutes

Range: High school seniors-college; adult

Scoring: Computer scoring provided

Cost: Contact publisher.

Publisher: The College Board

COLLEGE LEVEL EXAMINATION PROGRAM (CLEP) DENTAL AUXILIARY EDUCATION: ORAL RADIOGRAPHY

teen, adult   grades 12-UP

Purpose: Measures competency in oral radiography.

Description: Multiple item, paper-pencil objective exam assessing knowledge of material usually covered in an introductory course in oral radiography for students of dental hygiene and dental assisting. Topics covered include: X-radiation physics, biological effects, radiation hygiene and safety, technique, film, film processing, mounting and viewing, and radiographic analysis. The development committee recommends colleges supplement the exam with a practical test of their own. Examiner required. Suitable for group use.

Timed: 45 minutes

Range: High school seniors-college; adult

Scoring: Computer scoring provided

Cost: Contact publisher.

Publisher: The College Board

COLLEGE LEVEL EXAMINATION PROGRAM (CLEP) DENTAL AUXILIARY EDUCATION: TOOTH MORPHOLOGY AND FUNCTION

teen, adult   grades 12-UP

Purpose: Measures competency in tooth morphology and function.

Description: Paper-pencil objective test assessing knowledge of material usually covered in an introductory course in tooth morphology and function for students of dental hygiene, dental assisting, and dental laboratory technique. Topics covered are: tooth development and eruption, morphology of dentition (primary and secondary), function (interaction), abnormalities. Examiner required. Suitable for group use.

Timed: 45 minutes

Range: High school seniors-college; adult

Scoring: Computer scoring provided

Cost: Contact publisher.

Publisher: The College Board

COLLEGE LEVEL EXAMINATION PROGRAM (CLEP) EDUCATION: EDUCATIONAL PSYCHOLOGY

teen, adult   grades 12-UP

Purpose: Measures competency in educational psychology at the introductory college course level.

Description: 100 item paper-pencil objective test assessing knowledge and comprehension of basic information, concepts, and principles that pertain to the psychology of education. The exam measures one's ability to integrate various aspects of this content as it applies to teaching situations and problems. The categories are: theories and theorist, teaching, education, development, motivation, learning. The optional essay section assesses factors such as: accuracy of information, comprehensiveness and relevance of treatment, organization of materials, approach to problems from a psychological frame of reference and logic and imaginativeness. Examiner required. Suitable for group use.

Timed: 90 minutes

Range: High school seniors-college; adult

Scoring: Computer scoring provided

Cost: Contact publisher.

Publisher: The College Board

COLLEGE LEVEL EXAMINATION PROGRAM (CLEP) EDUCATION: HUMAN GROWTH and DEVELOPMENT

teen, adult   grades 12-UP

Purpose: Measures knowledge and understanding of the subject matter usually covered in introductory one-semester college courses called Human Growth and Development, Child Psychology, or Child Development.

Description: 90 item paper-pencil, multiple-choice test assessing proficiency in the field of child development, with concentration placed on the periods of early and middle childhood. Test items measure three levels of mastery: knowledge of facts, terminology and theory; understanding of concepts and principles; and ability to apply what has been learned to particular problems or situations. The examination covers the following topics: theoretical foundations (major views of development), research strategies and methadology, biological aspects of development, perceptual and sensorimotor development, cognitive development, language development,

emotional development, personality, intelligence testing, influences of schooling, social development, family relations and childrearing practices, learning, and atypical behavior and development. An optional essay section consisting of four questions covers the same material as the objective section and measures the ability to select pertinent material and present it in an organized and logical manner. Examiner required. Suitable for group use.

Timed: 90 minutes

Range: High school seniors-college; adult

Scoring: Computer scoring provided

Cost: Contact publisher.

Publisher: The College Board

COLLEGE LEVEL EXAMINATION PROGRAM (CLEP) GENERAL EXAMINATION: ENGLISH COMPOSITION

teen, adult   grades 12-UP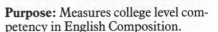

Purpose: Measures college level competency in English Composition.

Description: Multiple item, paper-pencil test available in two editions: Edition One has two 45 minute objective sections, 130 questions; Edition Two has one 45 minute, 65 question objective section and 45 minute essay section. Both editions measure competency in writing expository essays that follow the conventions of standard written English. The exam is concerned with Freshman English students' acquired knowledge, not technical vocabulary or imaginative writing.

Section One of both editions deals primarily with logical and structural relationships within the sentence. Section Two of Edition One (multiple-choice items) deals with logical arrangement of ideas, use of evidence and adaptation of language to purpose and audience. Section Two of Edition Two (essay questions) requires an expository essay to demonstrate skill at presenting a point of view, developing a logical argument and providing supporting evidence. Examiner required. Suitable for group use.

Timed: 90 minutes

Range: High school seniors-college; adult

Scoring: Computer scoring provided

Cost: Contact publisher.

Publisher: The College Board

COLLEGE LEVEL EXAMINATION PROGRAM (CLEP) GENERAL EXAMINATION: HUMANITIES

teen, adult   grades 12-UP

Purpose: Measures college level knowledge of literature, art and music.

Description: 150 item paper-pencil objective exam. Covers the following topics: drama, poetry, fiction, nonfiction, visual arts, music, performing arts, and architecture. Measures cultural interests and humanities subject matter understanding in three ways: recollection or recognition of specific information; comprehension and application of concepts; and, analysis and interpretation of various works of art. Examiner required. Suitable for group use.

Timed: 90 minutes

Range: High school seniors-college; adult

Scoring: Computer scoring provided

Cost: Contact publisher.

Publisher: The College Board

COLLEGE LEVEL EXAMINATION PROGRAM (CLEP) GENERAL EXAMINATION: MATHEMATICS

teen, adult   grades 12-UP

Purpose: Measures college level competency in general mathematics.

Description: 90 item paper-pencil test consisting of two parts. Part A consists of 40 questions that measures facility in arithmetic, elementary algebra, geometry and data interpretation. The first 25 questions required special directions and involve comparing quantities in two columns. The remaining 15 questions are objective. Part B consists of 50 objective questions on sets, logic, real number systems, probability and statistics and miscellaneous topics. Calculators are not permitted. Examiner required. Suitable for group use.

Timed: 90 minutes

Range: High school seniors-college; adult

Scoring: Computer scoring provided

Cost: Contact publisher.

Publisher: The College Board

COLLEGE LEVEL EXAMINATION PROGRAM (CLEP) GENERAL EXAMINATION: NATURAL SCIENCE

teen, adult   grades 12-UP

Purpose: Measures college level competency in introductory biological and physical science areas.

Description: 120 item paper-pencil objective test consisting of two 45 minute timed sections--one concerning biological science, the other physical science. The exam should not be considered appropriate as a prerequisite for more advanced study than the subject exams in General

Biology and General Chemistry. Emphasis is given to role of science in our contemporary society, to the knowledge and application of the basic principles and concepts of science, and to the understanding of scientific information and data that may be presented. Content of exam is as follows: origin and evolution of life, cell study, development in organisms, population biology with an emphasis in econogy, atomic and nuclear structure, chemical compounds/molecular structure, thermodynamics, classical mechanics and relativity, electrical and magnetism, the universe, and the Earth. Examiner required. Suitable for group use.

Timed: 90 minutes

Range: High school seniors-college; adult

Scoring: Computer scoring provided

Cost: Contact publisher.

Publisher: The College Board

COLLEGE LEVEL EXAMINATION PROGRAM (CLEP) GENERAL EXAMINATION: SOCIAL SCIENCE and HISTORY

teen, adult   grades 12-UP

Purpose: Measures the level of knowledge and understanding expected of college students meeting a distributional or general education requirement in social sciences-history.

Description: 125 item paper-pencil, multiple-choice test addressing a wide range of topics from the social sciences and history. Covers subject matter from introductory college courses in political science, economics, sociology, social physhology, United States History, Western Civilization, and African- Asian civilizations. Test items assess knowledge of terminology, facts, conventions, methodology, concepts, principles, generalizations, and theories in the fields listed above, as well as the ability to apply these abstractions to particulars. Examiner required. Suitable for group use.

Timed: 90 minutes

Range: High school seniors-college; adult

Scoring: Computer scoring provided

Cost: Contact publisher.

Publisher: The College Board

COLLEGE LEVEL EXAMINATION PROGRAM (CLEP) HUMANITIES: AMERICAN LITERATURE

teen, adult   grades 12-UP

Purpose: Measures familiarity with American prose and poetry from colonial time to mid-twentieth century.

Description: 110 item paper-pencil test measuring competency level comparable to a one year college survey course in American literature. Knowledge of critical and historical literacy terms is assumed. Areas covered include: the Colonial and Early National period, the period since World War II, and the periods of religion and Early Naturalism. Also covers writers of the Romantic and Modern period. The remaining questions assess knowledge of content of particular literary works: their characters, plots, settings, and themes. Some knowledge is needed of historical and social settings, authors and their influence and relations of literary works and traditions. The optional 90 minute essay section contains three questions two of which must be answered. The section tests the candidate's ability to make organized statements on American literature that are pertinent and informed. Examiner required. Suit able for group use.

Timed: 90 minutes; optional essay section 90 minutes

Range: High school seniors-college; adult

Scoring: Computer scoring provided

Cost: Contact publisher.

Publisher: The College Board

COLLEGE LEVEL EXAMINATION PROGRAM (CLEP) HUMANITIES: ANALYSIS AND INTERPRETATION OF LITERATURE

teen, adult   grades 12-UP

Purpose: Measures college level competency equivalent to a one-year undergraduate course in literature.

Description: 100 item paper-pencil objective test assessing the ability to read prose and poetry with understanding and respond to nuances of meaning, tone, mood, imagery and style.
The optional essay section assesses the ability to write well- organized critical essays on given passage of poetry and on general literary questions. Examiner required. Suitable for group use.

Timed: 90 minutes

Range: High school seniors-college; adult

Scoring: Computer scoring provided

Cost: Contact publisher.

Publisher: The College Board

COLLEGE LEVEL EXAMINATION PROGRAM (CLEP) HUMANITIES: COLLEGE COMPOSITION

teen, adult   grades 12-UP

Purpose: Assesses knowledge of the

theoretical aspects of writing and the ability to put into practice the principles of standard written English.

Description: 100 item paper-pencil objective test measuring proficiency in English Composition. Topics include: the sentence, the paragraph and essay, style, logic in writing, library information, and manuscript format and documentation. An optional 90 minute essay section provides three questions, two of which are to be answered. Examiner required. Suitable for group use.

Timed: 90 minutes; optional essay section 90 minutes

Range: High school seniors-college; adult

Scoring: Computer scoring provided

Cost: Contact publisher.

Publisher: The College Board

COLLEGE LEVEL EXAMINATION PROGRAM (CLEP) HUMANITIES: ENGLISH LITERATURE

teen, adult   grades 12-UP

Purpose: Measures college-level competency in English literature.

Description: 100 item paper-pencil objective test assessing proficiency in the study of English literature. Knowledge of common literary terms and forms as well as major authors and texts is assumed. Many items are based on passages and poems. Other areas include: literary background, content of major works, chronology, author identification, material patterns and literary references. The candidate is also asked to analyze elements of form, perceive meanings, and identify tone, mood and style. The optional 90 minute essay section contains three topics, one of which is required. A second essay must be written on one of the other two topics. Examiner required. Suitable for group use.

Timed: 90 minutes; optional essay 90 minutes

Range: High school seniors-college; adult

Scoring: Computer scoring provided

Cost: Contact publisher.

Publisher: The College Board

COLLEGE LEVEL EXAMINATION PROGRAM (CLEP) HUMANITIES: FRESHMAN ENGLISH

teen, adult   grades 12-UP

Purpose: Measures a candidate's ability to recognize and apply principles of good writing.

Description: 100 item paper-pencil objective test measuring sensitivity in reading and skill in judging and controlling language on the assumption that these abilities are closely related to the ability to write well. One third of the exam requires the analysis of short passages of prose and poetry; both for comprehension of content and for judgment of structure and style. One third of the test is devoted to considerations of style and logical development. The final third focuses on clear syntax, correct usage, and correct punctuation. The optional essay section allows a candidate to demonstrate writing skills in three sustained writing tasks. The topics present concrete problems that involve personal knowledge and require control and flexibility in the use of language. Examiner required. Suitable for group use.

Timed: 90 minutes; optional essay section 90 minutes

Range: High school seniors-college; adult

Scoring: Computer scoring provided

Cost: Contact publisher.

Publisher: The College Board

COLLEGE LEVEL EXAMINATION PROGRAM (CLEP) MATHEMATICS: CALCULUS with ELEMENTARY FUNCTIONS

teen, adult   grades 12-UP

Purpose: Measures skills and concepts usually covered in a one-year college course in calculus with elementary functions.

Description: 45 item paper-pencil objective test assesses a person's intuitive understanding of calculus and experience with its methods and application. Knowledge of preparatory mathematics (algebra, plane and solid geometry, trigonometry and analytical geometry) is assumed. Topics covered include: elementary functions, differential calculus, and integral calculus. Examiner required. Suitable for group use.

Timed: 90 minutes

Range: High school seniors-college; adult

Scoring: Computer scoring provided

Cost: Contact publisher.

Publisher: The College Board

COLLEGE LEVEL EXAMINATION PROGRAM (CLEP) MATHEMATICS: COLLEGE ALGEBRA

teen, adult   grades 12-UP

Purpose: Measures college level competency equivalent to one-semester college algebra course.

Description: 80 item paper-pencil objective exam consisting of questions that require the solution of routine or straightforward problems and understanding and application of concepts and skills to situations that may not be familiar. The exam assesses understanding and knowledge of basic algebraic operations: linear equations and inequities and their graphs, quadratic equation and their graphs, functions, exponential and logarithmic functions, and theory of equations. Also includes sets, the real number system, complex numbers, systems of equations, sequence and series, matrix addition and multiplication, evaluation of determinants and mathematical induction. Examiner required. Suitable for group use.

Timed: 90 minutes

Range: High school seniors-college; adult

Scoring: Computer scoring provided

Cost: Contact publisher.

Publisher: The College Board

COLLEGE LEVEL EXAMINATION PROGRAM (CLEP) MATHEMATICS: COLLEGE ALGEBRA-TRIGONOMETRY

teen, adult   grades 12-UP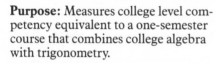

Purpose: Measures college level competency equivalent to a one-semester course that combines college algebra with trigonometry.

Description: 80 item paper-pencil, multiple-choice test consisting of two 40-item sections. One section is devoted entirely to algebra, the other to trigonometry. The test as a whole provides a single score based on the entire 90-minute test. For descriptions of test content, refer to College Algebra and College Trigonometry descriptions. Examiner required. Suitable for group use.

Timed: 90 minutes

Range: High school seniors-college; adult

Scoring: Computer scoring provided

Cost: Contact publisher.

Publisher: The College Board

COLLEGE LEVEL EXAMINATION PROGRAM (CLEP) MATHEMATICS: STATISTICS

teen, adult   grades 12-UP

Purpose: Measures college-level competency equivalent to a one-semester course in probabilities and statistics.

Description: 60 item paper-pencil objective test assessing levels of understanding in elementary statistical inference, probabilities, descriptive statistics, random variables and expected values. Other content categories include: sampling and problems related to distributions, combinations, and permutations. The test book contains two tables: the normal curve and the student's distribution. The 90 minute optional essay section covers the same general content areas as the multiple-choice test and consists of four questions that may require either computation or discussion or both. Examiner required. Suitable for group use.

Timed: 90 minutes

Range: High school seniors-college; adult

Scoring: Computer scoring provided

Cost: Contact publisher.

Publisher: The College Board

COLLEGE LEVEL EXAMINATION PROGRAM (CLEP) MATHEMATICS: TRIGONOMETRY

teen, adult   grades 12-UP

Purpose: Measures knowledge and ability equivalent to a one semester course with primary emphasis on analytical trigonometry.

Description: 80 item paper-pencil objective test assessing academic achievement in analytical trigonometry. The following areas are considered: trigonometric functions and their relationships, cofunction relationships, reciprocal relationships, Pythagorean relationships, functions of two angles, functions of double angles, functions of half angles, and identities. Other topics include: trigonometric equations and inequalities graphs of trigonometric function and trigonometry of the triangle including the law of sines and cosines as well as inverse functions and the trigonometric form of complex numbers. Examiner required. Suitable for group use.

Timed: 90 minutes

Range: High school seniors-college; adult

Scoring: Computer scoring provided

Cost: Contact publisher.

Publisher: The College Board

COLLEGE LEVEL EXAMINATION PROGRAM (CLEP) MEDICAL TECHNOLOGY: CLINICAL CHEMISTRY

teen, adult   grades 12-UP 👉 ✍

Purpose: Measures knowledge normally gained in courses offered during the clinical portion of four year medical technology programs.

Description: 100 item paper-pencil objective test assessing the following areas: general chemical principles, general clinical chemistry principles, instrumentation for important techniques, specific analysis of biologic fluids, quality control, clinical pathology, toxicology, and biochemistry, physiology and genetics. Examiner required. Suitable for group use.

Timed: 90 minutes

Range: High school seniors-college; adult

Scoring: Computer scoring provided

Cost: Contact publisher.

Publisher: The College Board

COLLEGE LEVEL EXAMINATION PROGRAM (CLEP) MEDICAL TECHNOLOGY: HEMATOLOGY

teen, adult   grades 12-UP 👉 ✍

Purpose: Measures knowledge normally gained in courses offered during the clinical portion of four-year medical technology programs.

Description: 100 item paper-pencil objective test covering the following areas: development and components of blood, collection of specimens, hemoglobin disorders, and coagulation and hemostasis. Examiner required. Suitable for group use.

Timed: 90 minutes

Range: High school seniors-college; adult

Scoring: Computer scoring provided

Cost: Contact publisher.

Publisher: The College Board

COLLEGE LEVEL EXAMINATION PROGRAM (CLEP) MEDICAL TECHNOLOGY: IMMUNOHEMATOLOGY AND BLOOD BANKING

teen, adult   grades 12-UP 👉 ✍

Purpose: Measures knowledge normally gained in courses offered during the clinical portion of four-year medical technology programs.

Description: 100 item paper-pencil objective test. Covers the following areas: history and general principles of blood transfusion; the antigen-antibody reaction; ABO blood type system; M, K, and P blood types; the Rh system; the Kell and Duffy blood types; the Lewis types; other blood systems; detection of new blood type system; pretransfusion procedures; leukocyte and platelet groups; blood types in anthropology and forensic pathology; auto-immune acquired hemolytic anemia; principles of blood banking procedures and serologic tests on donor blood. Examiner required. Suitable for group use.

Timed: 90 minutes

Range: High school seniors-college; adult

Scoring: Computer scoring provided

Cost: Contact publisher.

Publisher: The College Board

COLLEGE LEVEL EXAMINATION PROGRAM (CLEP) MEDICAL TECHNOLOGY: MICROBIOLOGY

teen, adult   grades 12-UP

Purpose: Measures college-level competency normally gained in a one-semester course in microbiology.

Description: 100 item paper-pencil objective test assessing both the knowledge of microbiology and the analytical abilities that are important in the first course. The test covers: nature of microorganisms, virology, nutrition and metabolism of bacteria, microbial genetics, control of micro-organisms, microbiology of water, microbiology of foods, basis of infectious disease, resistance and immunity, the pathogenic cocci and diseases they cause, gram-negative enteric bacteria, other gram-negative bacteria, gram-positive bacilli, the spirochetes and spirochetal diseases (3%), and soil and non- pathogens. Examiner required. Suitable for group use.

Timed: 90 minutes

Range: High school seniors-college; adult

Scoring: Computer scoring provided

Cost: Contact publisher.

Publisher: The College Board

COLLEGE LEVEL EXAMINATION PROGRAM (CLEP) MODERN LANGUAGES: COLLEGE FRENCH LEVELS 1 AND 2

teen, adult   grades 12-UP

Purpose: Measures knowledge and ability equivalent to that of students who have completed from two to four semesters of college level French.

Description: Multiple item paper-pencil test assessing proficiency in the skills typically achieved from the end of the first year through the second year of college level French. Both levels are incorporated into a single examination measuring knowledge and ability in the following areas: vocabulary mastery, grammatical control, reading comprehension, and listening comprehension. Examiner required. Suitable for group use.

Timed: 90 minutes

Range: High school seniors-college; adult

Scoring: Computer scoring provided

Cost: Contact publisher.

Publisher: The College Board

COLLEGE LEVEL EXAMINATION PROGRAM (CLEP) MODERN LANGUAGES: COLLEGE GERMAN LEVELS 1 AND 2

teen, adult   grades 12-UP

Purpose: Measures knowledge and ability equivalent to that of students who have completed from two to four semesters of college level German.

Description: Multiple item paper-pencil test assessing proficiency in the skills typically achieved from the end of the first year through the second year of college level German. Both levels are incorporated into a single examination measuring knowledge and ability in the following areas: vocabulary mastery, grammatical control, reading comprehension, and listening comprehension. Examiner required. Suitable for group use.

Timed: 90 minutes

Range: High school seniors-college; adult

Scoring: Computer scoring provided

Cost: Contact publisher.

Publisher: The College Board

COLLEGE LEVEL EXAMINATION PROGRAM (CLEP) MODERN LANGUAGES: COLLEGE SPANISH LEVELS 1 AND 2

teen, adult   grades 12-UP

Purpose: Measures knowledge and ability equivalent to that of students who have completed from two to four semesters of college level Spanish.

Description: Multiple item paper-pencil test assessing proficiency in the skills typically achieved from the end of the first year through the second year of college level Spanish. Both levels are incorporated into a single examination measuring knowledge and ability in the following areas: vocabulary mastery, grammatical control, reading comprehension, and listening comprehension. Examiner required. Suitable for group use.

Timed: 90 minutes

Range: High school seniors-college; adult

Scoring: Computer scoring provided

Cost: Contact publisher.

Publisher: The College Board

COLLEGE LEVEL EXAMINATION PROGRAM (CLEP) NURSING: ANATOMY, MICROBIOLOGY, PHYSIOLOGY

teen, adult   grades 12-UP

Purpose: Measures subject matter knowledge covered during first year ADN programs. Provides Licensed Practical Nurses and others with an opportunity to gain credit toward the first year of study in an ADN program.

Description: 75 item paper-pencil objective test assessing general proficiency in anatomy, physiology, and microbiology. Topics covered include basic physiological: food, elimination, sex, and security (integrity of organism); internal and external environment. Examiner required. Suitable for group use.

Timed: 90 minutes

Range: High school seniors-college; adult

Scoring: Computer scoring provided

Cost: Contact publisher.

Publisher: The College Board

COLLEGE LEVEL EXAMINATION PROGRAM (CLEP) NURSING: BEHAVIORAL SCIENCES for NURSES

teen, adult   grades 12-UP

Purpose: Measures knowledge of subject matter covered during first year ADN programs.

Description: Multiple-item paper-pencil test assessing knowledge of sociology and psychology. Approximately 60 percent of the questions are from the field of sociology. Topics covered include: social change, the family, social institutions and their functions, process of socialization norms, mores, social roles, culture, demography and crime and crime rate. Questions from the field of psychology make up 35 percent of the test. Topics covered include: child development, personality, social psychology, clinical and abnormal psychology and mental health. Examiner required. Suitable for group use.

Timed: 90 minutes

Range: High school seniors-college; adult

Scoring: Computer scoring provided

Cost: Contact publisher.

Publisher: The College Board

COLLEGE LEVEL EXAMINATION PROGRAM (CLEP) NURSING: FUNDAMENTALS of NURSING

teen, adult   grades 12-UP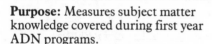

Purpose: Measures subject matter knowledge covered during first year ADN programs.

Description: Multiple item paper-pencil test assessing proficiency in the fundamental skills of nursing. Test includes: introduction to nursing fundamentals, communication, stress and adaptation, nutrition (fluid and electrolyte balance), rest and comfort, elimination, providing safe environment, observation and assessment, special therapeutics. Examiner required. Suitable for group use.

Timed: 90 minutes

Range: High school seniors-college; adult

Scoring: Computer scoring provided

Cost: Contact publisher.

Publisher: The College Board

COLLEGE LEVEL EXAMINATION PROGRAM (CLEP) NURSING: MEDICAL-SURGICAL NURSING

teen, adult   grades 12-UP

Purpose: Measures knowledge of subject matter covered during first year ADN program.

Description: Multiple item paper-pencil test covering the areas of study and content presented in the first year of two-year ADN programs. Major topics covered are: transport to and from the cells (cardiovascular); exchange of gases (respiratory); immobility (digestive and renal); and aging. Examiner required. Suitable for group use.

Timed: 90 minutes

Range: High school seniors-college; adult

Scoring: Computer scoring provided

Cost: Contact publisher.

Publisher: The College Board

COLLEGE LEVEL EXAMINATION PROGRAM (CLEP) SCIENCES: GENERAL BIOLOGY

teen, adult   grades 12-UP

Purpose: Measures proficiency in the material usually covered in a one-year biology course at the college level.

Description: 120 item paper-pencil, multiple-choice test assessing knowledge and understanding in three broad areas of the biological sciences: molecular and cellular, organismal, and populational. Test items measure three levels of proficiency: knowledge of facts, principles, and processes of biology; understanding of the means by which information is collected, how it is interpreted, how one hypothesizes and synthesizes from available information, and how one draws conclusions and makes further predictions; and understanding that science is a human endeavor with social consequences. An optional essay section covers the same material and measures the ability to select pertinent material and present it in an organized and logical manner. Examiner required. Suitable for group use.

Timed: 90 minutes

Range: High school seniors-college; adult

Scoring: Computer scoring provided

Cost: Contact publisher.

Publisher: The College Board

COLLEGE LEVEL EXAMINATION PROGRAM (CLEP) SCIENCES: GENERAL CHEMISTRY

teen, adult   grades 12-UP

Purpose: Determines college-level competency in general chemistry.

Description: 80 item paper-pencil objective test requires the candidate to demonstrate knowledge of the material that institutes the core topics of introductory college chemistry courses and to interpret and apply this material in ways not necessarily familiar to the candidate. The following areas are covered: structure of matter, status of matter, reaction types, equations and stoichiometry, kinetics, equilibrium, thermodynamics, descriptive chemistry, and experimental chemistry. The use of slide rules and calculators is permitted. The content of the optional essays section includes essays, equations, and quantitative problems. Examiner required. Suitable for group use.

Timed: 90 minutes

Range: High school seniors-college; adult

Scoring: Computer scoring provided

Cost: Contact publisher.

Publisher: The College Board

COLLEGE LEVEL EXAMINATION PROGRAM (CLEP) SOCIAL SCIENCES: AFRO-AMERICAN HISTORY

teen, adult   grades 12-UP

Purpose: Measures college-level competency in the material covered in a one semester course in Afro-American History.

Description: 100 item paper-pencil objective test covers: the African experience and the relationship fo Africa to the discovery of America, the Afro- American experience from Colonial America through Reconstruction to about 1900, and the Afro-American experience in the United States from about 1900 to the present. The optional essay section offers a choice of two questions in three broad areas: African background through Colonial America, the black experience from the American Revolution through the First World War, and the black experience from 1919 to the Present. Examiner required. Suitable for group use.

Timed: 90 minutes

Range: High school seniors-college; adult

Scoring: Computer scoring provided

Cost: Contact publisher.

Publisher: The College Board

COLLEGE LEVEL EXAMINATION PROGRAM (CLEP) SOCIAL SCIENCES: AMERICAN GOVERNMENT

teen, adult   grades 12-UP

Purpose: Measures college level competency in the study of American government and politics.

Description: 100 item paper-pencil objective test consisting of two sections of 50 items each. Areas tested include: institutions and policy processes; presidency, executive branch and congress; federal courts and civil liberties; political parties and pressure groups; political beliefs and behavior; and constitutional underpinnings of American democracy. The optional essay section offers a choice of writing on any three of four topics offered. Examiner required. Suitable for group use.

Timed: 90 minutes

Range: High school seniors-college; adult

Scoring: Computer scoring provided

Cost: Contact publisher.

Publisher: The College Board

COLLEGE LEVEL EXAMINATION PROGRAM (CLEP) SOCIAL SCIENCES: GENERAL PSYCHOLOGY

teen, adult   grades 12-UP

Purpose: Measures college-level competency in general psychology.

Description: 100 item paper-pencil objective test assessing basic facts, concepts, and principles of general psychology. The examination covers: physiology and behavior, perceptual and sensory experience, motivation and emotion, learning, cognition, life- span development, personality and adjustment, behavior disorders, social psychology, measurement and statistics, history and philosophy. An optional essay section is included. Examiner required. Suitable for group use.

Timed: 90 minutes

Range: High school seniors-college;

adult

Scoring: Computer scoring provided

Cost: Contact publisher.

Publisher: The College Board

COLLEGE LEVEL EXAMINATION PROGRAM (CLEP) SOCIAL SCIENCES: INTRODUCTORY MACROECONOMICS

teen, adult   grades 12-UP

Purpose: Measures college-level competency in introductory macroeconomics.

Description: The 90 item paper-pencil objective test assessing knowledge and understanding of determinants of aggregate demand on the monetary and/or fiscal policies that are appropriate to achieve particular policy objectives. Materials covered on the examination include basic or generic concepts and macroeconomic concepts. A 90 minute optional essay section is offered. Examiner required. Suitable for group use.

Timed: 90 minutes

Range: High school seniors-college; adult

Scoring: Computer scoring provided

Cost: Contact publisher.

Publisher: The College Board

COLLEGE LEVEL EXAMINATION PROGRAM (CLEP) SOCIAL SCIENCES: INTRODUCTORY MICROECONOMICS

teen, adult   grades 12-UP

Purpose: Measures college-level competency in introductory microeconomics.

Description: 90 item paper-pencil objective test requiring students to apply analytical techniques to hypothetical situations and to analyze and evaluate interpretations or criticism of government policies on the basis of simple theoretical models. The test emphasizes analytical capabilities rather than factual understanding of United States institutions and policies. The test covers basic or generic concepts and microeconomic concepts. A 90 minute optional essay section is included. Examiner required. Suitable for group use.

Timed: 90 minutes; optional essay 90 minutes

Range: High school seniors-college; adult

Scoring: Computer scoring provided

Cost: Contact publisher.

Publisher: The College Board

COLLEGE LEVEL EXAMINATION PROGRAM (CLEP) WESTERN CIVILIZATION I: ANCIENT NEAR EAST TO 1648

teen, adult   grades 12-UP

Purpose: Measures college level competency in the study of western civilization: Ancient Near East to 1648.

Description: 120 item paper-pencil, 90 minute objective test covering six broad historical periods as follows: Ancient Near East, Ancient Greece and Hellenistic Civilization, Ancient Rome, Medieval History, Renaissance and Reformation, and Early Modern Europe 1560-1648. The optional essay section requires the candidate to write three essays, one from each of three chronological areas. Examiner required. Suitable for group use.

Timed: 90 minutes; optional essay 90 minutes

Range: High school seniors-college; adult

Scoring: Computer scoring provided

Cost: Contact publisher.

Publisher: The College Board

COLLEGE LEVEL EXAMINATION PROGRAM (CLEP) WESTERN CIVILIZATION II: 1648 to the PRESENT

teen, adult   grades 12-UP

Purpose: Measures college-level competency in the study of Western Civilization from 1648 to the Present.

Description: 120 item paper-pencil objective exam covering twelve broad historical periods: Absolutism and Constitutionalism, 1648-1715; Competition for Empire and Economic Expansion; The Scientific View of the World; Enlightenment and Enlightened Despotism; The French Revolution and Napoleonic Europe; The Industrial Revolution; Political Developments, 1815-1848; Politics and Diplomacy in the Age of Nationalism, 1850-1914; Economy, Culture and Imperialism, 1850-1914; The First World War, the Russian Revolution, and Postwar Europe, 1914-1924; Europe between the Wars; The Second World War and Contemporary Europe. The exam measures a person's ability to identify the causes and effects of major events in history, to analyze, interpret, and evaluate historical materials, and to reach conclusions. A 90-minute optional essay section is included. Examiner required. Suitable for group use.

Timed: 90 minutes; optional essay 90 minutes

Range: High school seniors-college; adult

Scoring: Computer scoring provided

Cost: Contact publisher.

Publisher: The College Board

COMPREHENSION TEST FOR COLLEGE OF EDUCATION STUDENTS
E.L. Black

adult

Purpose: Assesses abilities of students who have not been in school for several years and screens for academic placement.

Description: 60 item paper-pencil, multiple-choice test measuring reading comprehension. Test questions are based on eight passages of prose, each with a different kind of subject matter and style of language. Provides diagnostic information regarding student reading comprehension. Materials include booklets and manual. Examiner required. Suitable for group use. CANADIAN PUBLISHER

Untimed: Not available

Range: Adult

Scoring: Examiner evaluated

Cost: Specimen set $8.55; 25 booklets $46.39; manual $7.54.

Publisher: Institute of Psychological Research, Inc.

COMPREHENSIVE ASSESSMENT PROGRAM: ACHIEVEMENT SERIES
John W. Wick and Jefferey K. Smith

child, teen

Purpose: Assesses student achievement in basic academic areas. Used for evaluating individual or group status; planning instructional improvement; monitoring student progress; and evaluating program effectiveness.

Description: 11 test levels. Levels 4-6 (pre-kindergarten through grade 1) emphasize children's capabilities to perform given tasks to ascertain their level of development. Levels 7-12 (grades 2-8) measure achievement in reading, language and mathematics. Levels 13 and 14 (grades 9-12) test achievement in reading, language, writing, mathematics, science, and social studies. When combined with Developing Cognitive Abilities Test, the level of student performance in relation to abilities can be determined. Examiner required; suitable for group use.

Untimed: Varies with level and test

Range: Ages 4-18

Scoring: Hand key; computer scoring available

Cost: 35 test booklets $26.50-$35.95 (specify level and machine- or hand-scorable); key $1.30 (specify level); manual $5.90.

Publisher: Scott, Foresman and Company

COMPREHENSIVE ASSESSMENT PROGRAM: HIGH SCHOOL SUBJECT TESTS
Louis A. Gatta

teen   grades 9-12

Purpose: Measures student's proficiency in common high school courses. Also used in analyzing instruction and planning.

Description: Multiple item, individual tests for the 15 most commonly taught courses at the secondary level; general mathematics, algebra, geometry, health, consumer education, biology, chemistry, physical science, American history, American government, world geography, world history, language, literature and vocabulary, and writing and mechanics. Self-scoring answer sheets. Examiner required. Suitable for group use.

Timed: 40 minutes

Range: Grades 9-12

Scoring: Hand key: computer scoring available

Cost: 35 test booklets $21.95; 35 answer wheets $12.50; manual $6.50; directions for administration $2.85; 35 machine-scorable answer sheets $9.00 (specify subject).

Publisher: Scott, Foresman and Company

COMPREHENSIVE TESTING PROGRAM (CTP) LEVELS 1 AND 2
Committees of teachers and curriculum specialists

---

child   grades 2,3

Purpose: Evaluates first, second and third grader's basic knowledge and progress in learning. Used for guidance and to improve instruction.

Description: 225 item paper-pencil test of skills in reading, writing, word analysis, and mathematics at levels one and two (grades one through beginning of third). Offered only to members of the Educational Records Bureau. Designed for groups. Examiner required.

Untimed: 150 minutes

Range: Grades 2 and 3

Scoring: Hand key; computer scoring available

Cost: 20 package booklets $19.00; manual $4.00.

Publisher: Educational Records

COMPREHENSIVE TESTING PROGRAM (CTP) LEVELS 3, 4 and 5
Committees of teachers and curriculum specialists

---

child, teen   grades 1-12

Purpose: Measures the verbal and mathematical skills of students

Grades 1-12. Used for guidance counseling, evaluation of student progress, and monitoring the effectiveness of instructional programs.

Description: Paper-pencil, multiple-choice tests arranged in five levels: Levels 1 and 2 for testing Grade 1 through early Grade 3; and levels 3, 4, and 5 for testing from the end of Grade 3 through Grade 12. Levels 1 and 2 contain 225 items and consist of four subtests: Mathematics, Reading, Word Analysis, and Writing Skills. Levels 3, 4, and 5 contain 300 items and consist of seven subtests: Verbal Aptitude, Quantitative Aptitude, Reading Comprehension, Mathematics, Mechanics of Writing, Vocabulary, and English Expression. For Levels 1 and 2, students mark their answers in machine-scorable test booklets; Levels 3, 4, and 5 use separate answer sheets. Use restricted to schools with ERB membership. Examiner required. Suitable for group use.

Timed: 260 minutes

Range: Grades 1-12

Scoring: Hand key; computer scoring available

Cost: 20 booklets $31.00; manual $4.00.

Publisher: Educational Records Bureau

COMPREHENSIVE TESTS OF BASIC SKILLS (FORMS S AND T)

---

child, teen   grades K-12.9

Purpose: Measures achievement in language, number, and problem-solving skills.

Description: Three to six test measure of academic skills. Form S is divided into seven levels: Level A, Grades K-1.3; Level B, Grades K.6-1.9; Level C, Grades 1.6-2.9;

Level 1, Grades 2.5-4.9; Level 2, Grades 4.5-6.9; Level 3, Grades 6.5-8.9; and Level 4, Grades 8.5-12.9. Levels A and B test reading, language and mathematics skills. Level C also measures science and social studies, while Levels 1-4 have an additional Reference Skills Test. Alternate form tests (Form T) are available only for Levels 1-4. Superseded by CTBS Forms U and V. Examiner required. Suitable for group use. Also available in Spanish as CTBS-Espanol.

Timed: Complete battery up to 4 hours 15 minutes, varies by level.

Range: Grades K-12.9

Scoring: Hand key; computer scoring

Cost: Multilevel examination kits $20.00; specimen sets (specify level) $7.50. May order complete batteries or divisions of batteries independently.

Publisher: CTB/McGraw-Hill

COMPREHENSIVE TESTS OF BASIC SKILLS: FORMS U AND V (CTBS/U AND V)

child, teen   grades K-12.9

Purpose: Measures achievement in language, number, and problem-solving skills. Used for evaluating attainment of fundamental academic goals.

Description: Three to seven test measure of academic skills. Form U is divided into ten levels: Level A, Grades K.0-K.9; Level B, Grades K.6-1.6; Level C, Grades 1.0-1.9; Level D, Grades 1.6-2.9; Level E, Grades 2.6-3.9; Level F, Grades 3.6-4.9; and Level G, Grades 4.6-6.9; Level H, Grades 6.6-8.9; Level J, Grades 8.6-12.9; and Level K, Grades 11.0-12.9. Level A tests reading and mathematics skills. Level B and C test reading, language and mathematics. Levels D and E test these areas as

well as science, social studies, and spelling, while Levels F through K also add a Reference Skills Test. Alternate form tests (Form V) are available at Levels D-J. Replaces CTBS Forms S and T. Examiner required. Suitable for group use.

Timed: Complete battery from 1 hours, 8 minutes - 4 hours, 50 minutes

Range: Grades K-12.9

Scoring: Hand key; computer scoring

Cost: Multilevel examination kits $19.50; specimen sets (specify primary, intermediate or secondary) $10.35.

Publisher: CTB/McGraw-Hill

COOPERATIVE ENGLISH TESTS
Educational Testing Service

teen   grades 9-14

Purpose: Measures achievement of high school and college students in reading comprehension and written expression. Used to screen students who are advanced or lacking in basic English abilities and for placement in the appropriate level of instruction.

Description: 210 test paper-pencil test is designed to assess a student's mastery of basic English skills. Four subtests are independently available: Reading Comprehension Part I, measures vocabulary; Reading Comprehension Part II, measures level and speed of comprehension in varied style and content; English Expression Part I, measures effectiveness in conveying exact meaning; English Expression Part II, measures mechanics in usage, spelling, punctuation, capitalization. Two levels are available for each subtest: Level 1 for grades 12-14; Level 2 for grades 9-12. Examiner required. Suitable for group use.

Timed: 40 minutes each section

Range: Grades 9-14

Scoring: Hand key; computer scoring available

Cost: 20 reusable test books $18.40 (specify level) 100 answer sheets $16.00.

Publisher: CTB/McGraw-Hill

COOPERATIVE MATHEMATICS TESTS
Educational Testing Service

---

teen   grades 7-14

Purpose: Measures achievement in major content areas from junior high school arithmetic through calculus.

Description: Multiple item test assesses comprehension of basic concepts, techniques and unifying principles of mathematics. All tests are 40 minutes except the 80 minute calculus and geometry tests. The following subtests are used: Arithmetic, basic concepts without emphasis on commercial applications (grades 7-9); Structure of the Number System, concepts underlying the structure of real number system (grades 7-8); Algebra, concepts and skills up to quadratic equations, inequalities, number line, and field properties in limited amounts (grades 8-9); Algebra II, concepts and skills, inequalities and absolute value included (grades 9-12); Geometry Part I, standard course in Euclidean geometry and Part II, advanced understanding, proof, spatial reasoning (grades 9- 12); Trigonometry, functional and numerical trigonometry (grades 9-14); Algebra III, traditional topics and contemporary material such as inequalities and functional notation (grades 9- 14; Analytic Geometry, suitable for one-semester course or combined analytic geometry-calculus course (grades 9-14); Calculus, Part I, algebraic

functions, emphasis on differential calculus and Part II, transcendental functions, emphasis on integral calculus (grades 9-14). Separate norms for college engineering, education, and liberal arts students are available. Subtests may be ordered independently. Examiner required. Suitable for group use.

Timed: 40 or 80 minutes

Range: Grades 7-14

Scoring: Hand key; computer scoring available

Cost: 20 tests $11.00 (specify title); 100 answer sheets $16.00; manual $7.50.

Publisher: CTB/McGraw-Hill

COOPER-McGUIRE DIAGNOS-TIC WORD ANALYSIS TEST
*J. Louis Cooper and
Marion L. McGuire*

---

all ages

Purpose: Measures achievement of word mastery skills. Used for class skill grouping, diagnostic testing, and preparing Individualized Education Programs.

Description: 32 paper-pencil subtests assess three areas: readiness for word analysis (tests R1-R5), phonics (tests P1-P7) and structural analysis (tests S1- S10). Administration too soon after instruction can invalidate the scores. Examiner required. Suitable for group use.

Untimed: 5 minutes

Range: Test administered based on reader instructional level

Scoring: Hand key

Cost: Complete kit (includes pre and post masters, manual, directions for administration, class record charts, and tape allowing testing for several hundred children) less than $100.00.

Publisher: Croft, Inc.

CORNELL CLASS REASONING TEST
Robert H. Ennis, William L. Gardiner, Richard Morrow, Dieter Paulus, and Lucille Ringel

child, teen   grades 1-12

Purpose: Assesses level of logical competence in deductive reasoning. Used for research in school systems.

Description: 72 item paper-pencil measure of class reasoning ability. Items give a supposition, then ask the subject to indicate whether a related statement is true, may be true, or false. Self- administered. Suitable for group use.

Timed: 50 minutes

Range: Grades 1-12

Scoring: Hand key; computer scoring available

Cost: Test booklet with answer key $.50.

Publisher: Illinois Thinking Project

CORNELL CONDITIONAL REASONING TEST, FORM X
Robert H. Ennis, William L. Gardiner, John Guzzetta, Richard Morrow, Dieter Paulus, and Lucille Ringel

child, teen   grades 1-12

Purpose: Assesses a subject's ability or level of conditional reasoning. Used for research in the areas of competence.

Description: 72 item paper-pencil measure of conditional reasoning. Items give two conditions or assumptions; the subject is then asked to indicate whether a conclusion based on those assumptions is true, may be true, or false. Self-administered. Suitable for group use.

Timed: 50 minutes

Range: Grades 1-12

Scoring: Hand key; computer scoring available

Cost: Test booklet with answer key $.50.

Publisher: Illinois Thinking Project

CORNELL CRITICAL THINKING TEST, LEVEL X
Robert H. Ennis and Jason Millman

child, teen   grades 4-12

Purpose: Assesses abilities for critical thinking. Used for research, the teaching of critical thinking, or the admission to positions or areas requiring ability for critical thinking.

Description: 71 item paper-pencil measure of critical thinking. Divided into four sections. The first section asks for the bearing of information on a hypothesis. Second section measures ability to judge the reliability of information. Third section tests ability to judge whether a statement follows from premises. The fourth section deals with the identification of assumptions. Somewhat easier than Level Z. Examiner required for grades 4-6. Suitable for group use.

Timed: 50-62 minutes, depends on grade.

Range: Grades 4-12

Scoring: Hand key; computer scoring available

Cost: Test $.50 each; answer sheet $.03; manual $1.50.

Publisher: Illinois Thinking Project

CORNELL CRITICAL THINKING TEST, LEVEL Z
Robert H. Ennis and Jason Millman

teen, adult   grades 13-UP

Purpose: Assesses abilities for critical thinking. Used for research, the teaching of critical thinking, or the admission to positions or areas requiring ability for critical thinking.

Description: 52 item paper-pencil measure of critical thinking. Divided into seven sections directed at assessing ability to: tell whether a statement follows from premises; detect equivocal arguments; judge reliability of observations and authenticity of sources; judge direction of support for a hypothesis; find assumptions of various types. Somewhat more difficult than Level X. Self-administered. Suitable for group use.

Timed: 50 minutes

Range: Undergraduate and graduate

Scoring: Hand key; computer scoring available

Cost: Test $.50 each; answer sheet $.03; manual $1.50.

Publisher: Illinois Thinking Project

CRITERION TEST OF BASIC SKILLS
Kerth Lundell, William Brown and James Evans

child   grades 1-6

Purpose: Assesses elementary school student reading and arithmetic skills. Used by teachers for classroom placement.

Description: Multiple item paper-pencil subtests covering reading and arithmetic. The reading test measures: letter recognition, letter sounding, blending, sequencing, special sounds, and sight words. The arithmetic test measures: number and numerical recognition, addition, subtraction, multiplication, and division. After scoring, both portions of the test can be transferred to a graphic profile of each student's strengths and weaknesses. Materials include recording forms, problem sheets, a stimulus cards booklet, and manual, which contains activities correlated to the skill areas assessed. Examiner required. Suitable for group use.

Untimed: 10-15 minutes

Range: Grades 1-6

Scoring: Hand key

Cost: Manual $10.00; 25 math recording forms $6.00; 25 reading recording forms $6.00; 25 math problems sheets $2.50; stimulus cards booklet $6.00; specimen set $10.00.

Publisher: Academic Therapy Publications

CURRICULUM REFERENCED TESTS OF MASTERY (CRTM)
Darrell Sabers et al

child, teen   grades 1-12

Purpose: Evaluates the academic performance of individual students, classes, schools, and districts. Helps administrators and teachers determine the effects of instruction and make curricular decisions.

Description: Multiple item paper-pencil achievement test of reading, language arts, and mathematics skills. The Standard Edition offers 150 reading items and 299 mathematics items. The Custom Edition allows school districts to select from an Objectives Bank containing 478 reading items and 792 mathematics items. Scoring for the tests are norm- and curriculum-referenced. Examiner required. Suitable for group use.

Untimed: Varies

Range: Grades 1-12

Scoring: Hand key; examiner evaluated; computer scoring available

Cost: Contact publisher

Publisher: Charles E. Merrill Publishing Company

DENTAL ADMISSION TEST (DAT)
American Dental Association

adult   grades 14-UP

Purpose: Measures general academic ability, scientific understanding and perceptual ability of potential dental school students. Required of all candidates for admission to U.S. dental schools.

Description: 290 item paper-pencil, competitive examination in four sections: Quantitative Reasoning (50 items); Reading Comprehension (50 items): Natural Sciences, including biology and general and organic chemistry (100 items); and Perceptual Ability (90 items). Given only to those who have completed at least one year of college, including courses in natural sciences, although two or more years of college experience are recommended. No books, slide rules, paper, calculators, or other resource material is permitted in the exam room. Administered bi-annually in specific cities only. Examiner provided through the American Dental Association.

Timed: ½ day

Range: College sophomore and older

Scoring: Computer scored

Cost: Fee $25.00 per person

Publisher: American Dental Association

DETROIT TESTS OF LEARNING APTITUDE
Harry J. Baker

all ages

Purpose: Measures concentration and comprehension skills for professional diagnosis of individual learning disabilities.

Description: 19 category, examiner-led test, covering pictorial and verbal absurdities, pictorial and verbal opposites, oral ommissions, social adjustment, free association, memory for design, number ability, and likenesses and differences. Eight classifications are measured within each category: reasoning and comprehension, practical judgment, verbal ability, time and space relationships, number ability, auditory attentive ability, visual attentive ability, and motor ability. Materials consist of record booklets and forms, examiner's handbook and supplement, book of pictorial materials and a sample packet. The examiner, depending upon the subtest, shows response cards or reads to the pupils and records their responses. Must be administered individually by trained professionals.

Untimed: 35-40 minutes

Range: Ages 3-adult

Scoring: Hand key; examiner evaluated

Cost: 35 record booklets $12.75; examiner's handbook and 8 record forms $9.80; handbook supplement $3.75; pictorial materials $7.50; specimen set $17.95; set of 8 record forms $2.75.

Publisher: Bobbs-Merrill

DIAGNOSTIC ABILITIES IN MATH (D.A.M. TEST)
Refer to page 240.

DIAGNOSTIC SCREENING TEST: ACHIEVEMENT--SOCIAL STUDIES, SCIENCE, LITERATURE and THE ARTS (DST: ACHIEVEMENT)

Refer to page 567.

DIAGNOSTIC SKILLS BATTERY (DSB)

O.F. Anderhalter, STS staff and consultants

child, teen   grades 1-8

Purpose: Evaluates student abilities in reading, mathematics, and elementary school language arts. Used for pre- and post-testing.

Description: Multiple item paper-pencil test battery covers 30-40 objectives for each of the following skills areas: reading, mathematics, and language arts (not included in Form 12). The battery is based on selected "terminal" objectives from the more detailed Analysis of Skills series. Level 12 covers grades 1-3 and does not include language arts; Level 34 covers grades 3-5; Level 56 covers grades 5-7; and Level 78 covers grades 7-9. The Standard Scoring Service offers two plans. Plan I reports class lists of norm-referenced scores and Plan II gives Performance Profiles showing both norm- and objective-based information. Both plans provide summary information. Scoring options include Normal Curve Equivalent scores for Title I use and an Individual Skills Analysis. DSB is available as a program or a School Purchase Program (STS scoring only). Examiner required. Intended for group use.

Timed: 2 hours, 40 minutes

Range: Grades 1-8

Scoring: Hand key; computer scoring available

Cost: Specimen set (specify level and form) $2.00.

Publisher: Scholastic Testing Service, Inc.

DIFFERENTIAL APTITUDE TEST BATTERY

Manjula Makerjee

child, teen

Purpose: Identifies specific areas of academic aptitude for students ages 11-13 years.

Description: 547 item paper-pencil test consisting of seven subtests measuring aptitude in several academic fields. The tests include: English Knowledge and Comprehension, Clerical Aptitude I (speed), Clerical Aptitude II, Abstract Reasoning, Verbal Reasoning, Mathematics Knowledge and Comprehension, Scientific Aptitude, and Mechanical Comprehension. The scores from the subtests can be used to predict success in various education fields, such as the humanities, science, commerce, etc. Eighth-grade reading level required. Examiner required. Suitable for group use.
PUBLISHED IN INDIA

Untimed: Not available

Range: Ages 11-13

Scoring: Hand key; examiner evaluated

Cost: Contact publisher

Publisher: Manasayan

DIFFERENTIAL APTITUDE TESTS (DAT) FORMS S AND T

teen   grades 8-12

Purpose: Assesses aptitude. Used for educational and vocational guidance in junior and senior high schools.

Description: Multiple item paper-pencil test of eight abilities including verbal reasoning, numerical ability, abstract reasoning, clerical speed and accuracy, mechanical reasoning, space relations, spelling, and language usage. A ninth score is obtained by summing verbal reasoning and numerical ability scores. Materials include two alternate forms, S and T. Career Planning Questionnaire is optional. Superseded by DAT Forms V and W. Examiner required. Suitable for group use.

Timed: Complete battery, 3 hours

Range: Grades 8-12

Scoring: Hand key; may be machine scored; computer scoring service available

Cost: Specimen set (includes test, various answer documents, directions and norms) Form S or Form T $8.00; DAT Career Planning Service Information Packet (includes counselor's manual, questionnaire, glossary, interpretive report) $4.00.

Publisher: The Psychological Corporation

DIFFERENTIAL APTITUDE TESTS (DAT) FORMS V AND W
G.K. Bennett, H.G. Seashore and A.G. Wesman

teen   grades 8-12

Purpose: Assesses scholastic aptitude. Used for educational and vocational guidance in junior and senior high schools.

Description: Multiple item paper-pencil test of eight scholastic abilities including verbal reasoning, numerical ability, abstract reasoning, clerical speed and accuracy, mechanical reasoning, space relations, spelling, and language usage. A ninth score is obtained by adding verbal reasoning and numerical ability scores. Materials include two alternate and equivalent forms, V and W. Career

Planning Questionnaire is optional. Supersedes DAT Forms S and T. Examiner required. Suitable for group use.

Timed: Complete battery, 3 hours

Range: Grades 8-12

Scoring: Hand key; may be machine scored; computer scoring service available

Cost: Specimen set (includes test, direction; administrator's handbook; MRC and NCS answer documents and sheets NC; list of correct answers, order for scoring service, sample profile forms) $7.50; DAT Career Planning Service Information Packet (includes counselor's manual, directions, glossary, sample career planning report; explanation of school summary report; MRC answer document; orientation booklet) $5.00.

Publisher: The Psychological Corporation

DOPPELT MATHEMATICAL REASONING TEST
Refer to page 254.

EDUCATIONAL ABILITIES SCALES

teen

Purpose: Assesses abilities important to educational achievement. Used for identifying individual pupil strengths and weaknesses.

Description: Multiple item battery of five pencil-paper tests covering the following abilities: mechanical, spatial, symbolic, scientific process and inference, and clerical speed and accuracy. Student uses a special pen to mark answers, getting immediate feedback about accuracy. Student "answers until correct." Equivalent scores are given for each ability,

allowing comparison between different abilities. Materials include special pens. Examiner required. Suitable for group use.
BRITISH PUBLISHER

Untimed: Not available

Range: Ages 13-15

Scoring: Examiner evaluated

Cost: Student's book £1.65; 10 answer sheets £1.60; 12 special pens £4.00 (payment in sterling for all overseas orders).

Publisher: NFER-Nelson Publishing Company

EDUCATIONAL DEVELOPMENT SERIES (ED SERIES)
O.F Anderhalter, R.H. Bauernfeind, V.M. Cashen, Mary E. Greig, Walter Lifton, George and Jackie Mallinson, Joseph Papenfuss, and Neil Vail

---

child, teen   grades 2-12

Purpose: Assesses elementary and high school student academic aptitude and achievement and gathers information concerning school and career plans and interests. Used to screen those who need counseling because of conflicts between achievement, ability and ambition.

Description: Multiple item paper-pencil test. The Complete Battery covers the following areas: interests, future plans, verbal and nonverbal reasoning ability, reading, english, mathematic skills, science achievement, social science achievement, and career planning. Three other formats can be drawn from the Complete Battery booklet: Core Achievement Battery, Basic Skills Battery, and Ability/Skills Battery. The Upper Primary/Lower Primary Basic Skills Battery is the only one with a separate booklet. Six series are available. The R, S, T, and U series are based on up-to-date objectives

and modern views of social studies and career planning. The B and C series are longer (5 ½ hours per battery) and stress more traditional objectives. All Primary Forms are shorter.

Standard Scoring and Reporting Service offers two plans. Plan I returns alphabetical lists of names, school and career plans, raw scores, local stanines, and national norm scores, as well as a Group Summary Report. Plan II provides a performance profile and diagnostic information for each student. Optional services and materials include item analysis, IBM Work cards, Rank Order Lists, Listings for Other Groupings, Summaries for Other Groupings, Student Score Folders, Growth Profiles, Technical Report, and a Manual for Hand-Scoring and Interpreting. Examiner required. Suitable for group use.

Timed: 4 hours

Range: Lower primary 2-3; upper primary 3-4; elementary 4-6, advanced 6-0; senior 9-12

Scoring: Hand key; examiner evaluated; computer scoring available

Cost: Specimen set (specify level and form) $2.00.

Publisher: Scholastic Testing Service, Inc.

ENGLISH FIRST AND SECOND LANGUAGE TESTS
Refer to page 231.

EVERYDAY SKILLS TEST (EDST)
CTB/McGraw-Hill

---

teen   grades 10-12

Purpose: Measures the high school student's skills in reading and mathematics. Used by educators to monitor instruction, evaluation, and establishment of minimum proficiency levels.

Description: Consists of two tests, reading and mathematics, that evaluate skills required in everyday life. See Everyday Skills Test: Reading and Everyday Skills Test: Mathematics. Examiner required. Suitable for group use.

Timed: 2 hours

Range: High school

Scoring: Hand key; computer scoring available

Cost: Specimen set (includes one: reading book, math book, machine-score answer sheet, class record sheet, manual, test reviewer's guide) $7.25.

Publisher: CTB/McGraw-Hill

EVERYDAY SKILLS TEST: READING

teen   grades 10-12

Purpose: Measures the high school student's skill in reading. Used by educators to monitor and evaluate instruction, and to establish minimum proficiency levels.

Description: A two-part, 95 item paper-pencil test. Part A consists of 45 items over objectives such as reading and comprehending labels, telephone directories, medical instructions, preparation directions, store directories, want ads, outdoor signs, tax forms, transportation schedules, job applications, driver's handbooks, newspaper reports, and the meaning of abbreviations. Part B contains: 20 items on the use of reference materials that measure the ability to use library materials; and 30 items over graphic materials that emphasize the understanding of legends and symbols, the perception of relationships, drawing conclusions, and interpreting data on maps, diagrams, graphs and tables. Examiner

required. Suitable for use with groups.

Timed: 1 hour

Range: High school

Scoring: Hand key; computer scoring available

Cost: 35 tests $16.45; 50 machine-score answer sheets $5.50.

Publisher: CTB/McGraw-Hill

EVERYDAY SKILLS TEST: MATHEMATICS

teen   grades 10-12

Purpose: Measures the high school student's skill in mathematics. Used by educators to monitor and evaluate instruction, and to establish minimum proficiency levels.

Description: 63 item, two-part paper-pencil test. Part A consists of 27 items measuring student's understanding of interest rate, discount rate, cost comparison, travel time, time calculation, spending behavior, sales tax, currency, and income tax calculation. Part B consists of 36 items applying basic arithmetic operations to whole numbers, decimals, fractions, mixed numerals, exponents, and literal expressions. Examiner required. Suitable for group use.

Timed: 1 hour

Range: High school

Scoring: Hand key; computer scoring available

Cost: 35 tests $13.65; 50 machine-score answer sheets $5.50.

Publisher: CTB/McGraw-Hill

GENERAL ABILITY TESTS: NUMERICAL (GAT-NUMERICAL)
Refer to page 798.

GENERAL ABILITY TESTS: PERCEPTUAL (GAT-PERCEPTUAL)

Refer to page 799.

GENERAL ABILITY TESTS: VERBAL (GAT-VERBAL)

Refer to page 799.

GENERAL EDUCATIONAL PERFORMANCE INDEX

Don F. Seaman and Anna Seaman

adult

Purpose: Assesses adult students' preparedness to take the General Educational Development (GED) test. Also indicates academic areas where the student is weak.

Description: 168 item paper-pencil test that measures students' competency in writing, social studies, science, reading and mathematics. Examiner required. Suitable for group use.

Timed: 2½-3 hours

Range: Adult

Scoring: Hand key

Cost: 25 level AA tests $34.10; 25 level BB tests $34.10; teacher's set manual and AA & BB scoring template $6.90; 50 answer sheets $9.00.

Publisher: Steck-Vaughn Co.

GENERAL TESTS OF LANGUAGE AND ARITHMETIC FOR STUDENTS (GTLAS)-1972

child   grades 1-2

Purpose: Assesses academic achievement. Used for Primary Teacher's Certificate of the Department of Training and Education.

Description: Multiple item paper-pencil measure of proficiency in arithmetic, English, and Afrikaans. Materials include two alternate forms, A and B. Examiner required. Suitable for group use. Test to be discontinued in near future. SOUTH AFRICAN PUBLISHER

Timed: 8 hours

Range: 1st and 2nd year students

Scoring: Hand key; examiner evaluated

Cost: (In Rands) Test-form A 1,70; form B 4,40; manual 8,40; 10 answer sheets 0,50; scoring stencil form A 2,60; scoring stencil form B 2,90 (order from outside The RSA will be dealt with on merit).

Publisher: Human Sciences Research Council

GOYER ORGANIZATION OF IDEAS TEST

Robert S. Goyer

teen   grades 9-UP

Purpose: Measures ability to organize ideas verbally and to assess an individual's general mental ability. Used to place undergraduates in upper level courses and to screen students from areas in which they might not succeed.

Description: 30 item paper-pencil, multiple-choice test of ability to perceive oral-visual-written stimuli and to analyze and synthesize the ideas selected. The total process applied involves the following identifiable skill categories: *Component* (part-whole) relationships (including dependence- independence, significance-insignificance, coordination of ideas); *Sequential* relationships (including chronological, cause-to-effect, climax, topical); *Material-to-purpose* (relevance) relationships (including recognition of central or unifying idea, exclusion of ideas lacking consistency with total group); and *Transitional* (connective) relationships (including use of relational words and phrases based on total pattern of communication. Self-administered. Suitable for group use. Available in Korean.

Untimed: 50-60 minutes

Range: 9th grade-adult; nursing school applicants

Scoring: Hand key; may be computer scored

Cost: Test booklet $2.00; answer key with normative summary $20.00.

Publisher: Robert S. Goyer, Ph.D.

GRADUATE MANAGEMENT ADMISSION TEST (GMAT)

adult   College Graduates

Purpose: Measures developed abilities related to success in graduate schools of management. Used in admissions to graduate schools of management.

Description: Multiple-choice paper-pencil test measuring general verbal and quantitative abilities. Does not measure proficiency in undergraduate business or economics courses. Test is administered four times annually at centers established by the publisher and registration materials available at no charge. Examiner required. Suitable for group use.

Untimed: 4 hours

Range: College graduates

Scoring: Computer scored

Cost: Contact publisher.

Publisher: Educational Testing Service

GRADUATE RECORD EXAMINATIONS (GRE)

adult   College Graduates

Purpose: Measures academic abilities

and knowledge of graduate school applicants. Used by graduate schools for screening qualifications of applicants and by organizations for selecting fellowship recipients.

Description: Multiple item paper-pencil battery of advanced achievement and aptitude tests. GRE offers a General Test measuring verbal, quantitative and analytical abilities. Also offered are 20 Subject Tests in: Biology, Chemistry, Computer Science, Economics, Education, Engineering, French, Geography, Geology, German, History, Literature in English, Mathematics, Music, Philosophy, Physics, Political Science, Psychology, Sociology, and Spanish. Tests are administered on specified dates at centers established by the publisher. Examiner required. Suitable for group use.

Untimed: Not available

Range: College graduates

Scoring: Computer scored

Cost: Contact publisher.

Publisher: Educational Testing Service

GROUP LITERACY ASSESSMENT
Frank A. Spooncer

child

Purpose: Measures overall ability of children at the stage of transfer from primary to secondary education to deal effectively with written material. Identifies students in need of help. Indicates standards within a school district. Suggests appropriate follow-up procedures for both class groups and individual students.

Description: Multiple item paper-pencil test of written verbal abilities consists of two sections. In the first section, the student has to identify and correct mistakes in a simple

story. In the second section, the story is continued as a modified cloze text. Children are required to use and combine pictorial, contextual and grammatical cues offered by continuous prose. The test measures their ability to note significant details, to carry information in short-term memory, and to make inferential judgments, while at the same time giving useful information about the student's spelling skills. Norms are presented as deviation quotients for ages 10.6 to 12.6 and reading age equivalents for ages 7 to 14. Scoring requires an average of two minutes per paper. Examiner required. Suitable for group use.
BRITISH PUBLISHER

Untimed: 30 minutes

Range: Ages 10.6-12.6

Scoring: Hand key

Cost: Specimen set £1.50; 20 test forms £1.25 per set; manual £1.25.

Publisher: Hodder & Stoughton

GUIDANCE TEST BATTERY FOR SECONDARY PUPILS (GBS)-1981

teen

Purpose: Measures scholastic achievement. Used for educational guidance.

Description: Paper-pencil test of pupils' proficiency in English, Afrikaans, Mathematics, Nonverbal Reasoning, and Verbal Reasoning. Materials include two forms, A and B. Examiner required. Suitable for group use. Publisher notes that this test is "normed on Blacks only."
SOUTH AFRICAN PUBLISHER

Timed: 3½ hours

Range: Standard 8

Scoring: Hand key; examiner evalu-

ated; machine scoring available

Cost: (In Rands) Test (a or B) 1,20 each; instructions and norms 1,40; scoring stencil 1,90; 10 answer sheets (machine and hand scoring) 0,70 (orders from outside The RSA will be dealt with on merit).

Publisher: Human Sciences Research Council

INITIAL EVALUATION TESTS IN ENGLISH AND MATHEMATICS

child, teen

Purpose: Measures achievement in English and math. Used for educational evaluation at the beginning of a new standard.

Description: Nine tests measuring achievement in English and mathematics. Initial Evaluation Tests in English are available at Standards 5 and 8. Seven Initial Evaluation Tests in Mathematics are available, for Standards 1 to 7. Materials include two alternate forms, A and B, for each of the nine tests. Tests should be administered as soon as possible after the beginning of the school year. Examiner required. Suitable for group use.
SOUTH AFRICAN PUBLISHER

Untimed: Not available

Range: English-Standard 5-8; mathematics-Standards 1-7

Scoring: Hand key; examiner evaluated

Cost: Contact publisher (orders from outside The RSA will be dealt with on merit).

Publisher: Human Sciences Research Council

INTELLIGENCE TESTS
Refer to page 481.

IOWA TESTS OF BASIC SKILLS, FORMS 7 AND 8 (ITBS)
A.N. Hieronymous, E.F. Lindquist and H.D. Hoover

child, teen   grades K-9

Purpose: Assesses the development of basic academic skills in students Grades K-9. Identifies individual student's strengths and weaknesses and evaluates the effectiveness of instructional programs.

Description: Multiple item paper-pencil tests assessing proficiency in the basic skills required for academic success. All levels assess combinations of the following skills: vocabulary, reading, language, spelling, capitalization, punctuation, usage, work-study, visual materials, reference materials, mathematics concepts, problem solving, and computation. Listening and word analysis are also measured at the primary level. Levels 5-8 (157-539 items each), for use with Grades K-3.5, comprise the Primary Battery, which uses machine-scorable test booklets. Levels 9-14 (350-465 items each), for use with Grades 3-8/9, comprise the Multilevel Edition, which uses test booklets and separate answer sheets. Normed concurrently with the Cognitive Abilities Test for reliable comparisons between attained and expected achievement scores. Examiner required. Suitable for group use.

Timed: 244 minutes, Complete Battery, 139 minutes, Basic Battery, Multilevel Edition

Untimed: 150-235 minutes, depending on form, Primary Battery

Range: Primary Battery grades K-3.5 (Levels 5-8); Multilevel-Grades 3-8/9 (Levels 9-14)

Scoring: Hand key; computer scoring available

Cost: 25 level 5 or 6 Primary Battery machine-scorable test booklets $22.41 per level; 25 level 7 or 8 Complete Battery tests $30.90 per level; Basic Battery (includes Teacher's Guide) $22.41; Multilevel Edition Test Battery (levels 9-14) $2.97 each. Basic Battery $1.98; 35 MRC answer sheets (includes Teacher's Guide) $12.60 per level; Teacher's Guide $4.17.

Publisher: The Riverside Publishing Company

IOWA TESTS OF EDUCATIONAL DEVELOPMENT (ITED): FORMS X7 AND Y7
E.F. Lindquist and Leonard S. Feldt

teen   grades 9-12

Purpose: Measures adolescent and adult learning skills and abilities and general educational development. Identifies strengths and weaknesses in content skill areas (although not a test of specific curriculum areas or minimal competencies) and monitors educational development.

Description: 357 item paper-pencil achievement test assessing knowledge and application of skills of analysis. Factors measured include: recognizing good writing, solving quantitative problems, critically analyzing social issues, understanding nontechnical scientific reports, recognizing sound scientific inquiry methods, using common information sources and tools, and perceiving subtle meanings and moods in literature. Available in two levels (Level I for grades 9-10; Level II for grades 11-12) with overlapping items. Norm referenced. Examiner required. Suitable for group use.

Timed: 240 minutes

Range: Grades 9-12, semesters 1 and 2

Scoring: Hand key; computer scoring available

Cost: Rental and scoring for student $2.30; test booklets scoring $1.55; 25 tests $41.25; review set $4.10.

Publisher: Science Research Associates, Inc.

JUNIOR APTITUDE TESTS (JAT)-1974

child, teen

Purpose: Measures aptitude. Used for educational counseling.

Description: Multiple item paper-pencil test of ten specific aptitudes: classification, reasoning, number ability, synonyms, comparison, spatial 2 D, spatial 3 D, memory (paragraph), memory (words and symbols), and mechanical insight. Examiner required. Suitable for group use.
SOUTH AFRICAN PUBLISHER

Untimed: 2¾ hours

Range: Standards 5-8

Scoring: Hand key; examiner evaluated; machine scoring available

Cost: (In Rands) Test booklet 0,90; 10 answer sheets (T1-T6), 0,60; 10 answer sheets (T7-T10) 0,60; scoring stencil for 1224 2,20; scoring stencil for 1225 2,90; manual 5,20; 10 machine answer sheets 1,50 (order from outside The RSA will be dealt with on merit).

Publisher: Human Sciences Research Council

KERBY LEARNING MODALITY TEST, REVISED 1980
Refer to page 550.

KUHLMANN ANDERSON TESTS (KA): 8TH EDITION
F. Kuhlmann and Rose Anderson

child, teen   grades K-12

Purpose: Evaluates academic ability

and potential among students from kindergarten to Grade 12. Used for group placement and to diagnose individual learning abilities.

Description: 80 to 130 item (depending on level) paper-pencil test in eight different booklets covering the following grades: K-kindergarten; A-Grade 1; B-Grade 2; CD-Grades 3-4; D-Grades 4-5; EF-Grades 5-7; G-Grades 7-9; and H-Grades 9-12. The yielded scores are mental age, deviation IQ, grade percentile rank, IQ percentile rank, stanine, and for grades 7-12 only, separate verbal and quantitative grade percentiles. Norms have been based on a large national sampling of socio-economic, ethnic, and social diversity. Only STS answer sheets may be machine-scored. Examiner required. Suitable for group use.

Timed: 50-75 minutes

Range: Grades K-12

Scoring: Hand key; computer scoring available

Cost: 20 booklets $10.00-$16.00; 50 answer sheets $10.00; sample set $3.00.

Publisher: Scholastic Testing Service, Inc.

LANGUAGE FACILITY TEST
Refer to page 587.

LEARNING SCREEN (LS)
Carl H. Koenig and Harold P. Kunzelman

child   grades 1-6

Purpose: Provides a large-scale assessment of elementary school performance in reading, writing and arithmetic for placement and program planning by school districts, individual schools, and classes.

Description: Multiple item paper-

pencil test measuring performance and learning in reading, math and spelling. Administered over a ten-day period to either groups or individuals, although it is designed for large-group use where students show widely varying performance. Materials include a manual, student booklets, reading cards, audio tapes, and class ranking forms. Examiner required.

Untimed: 3 minutes per child for 10 days

Range: Grades 1-6

Scoring: Hand key

Cost: Specimen set (includes examiners manual, class ranking form, "How to Practice" manual, one score form for each level, one reading card for each level, and one audiotape for level 1S/2f) $16.95; 25 student booklets $36.50 (specify level); examiner's manual $5.95.

Publisher: Charles E. Merrill Publishing Company

LISTENING COMPREHENSION TESTS IN ENGLISH FOR STANDARDS 5 and 8

child, teen

Purpose: Measures ability to understand spoken English. Used for educational evaluation.

Description: Multiple item, paper-pencil tests of listening comprehension for students in Standards 5 and 8. Pupils listen to recorded questions and mark answers on answer sheet. Materials include a cassette tape with questions for two alternate forms, A and B. Examiner required. Suitable for group use.
SOUTH AFRICAN PUBLISHER

Untimed: 50 minutes

Range: Standards 5 and 8

Scoring: Hand key; examiner evaluated

Cost: (In Rands) Standard 5 manual 3,70; cassette 7,40; 10 answer sheets A 0,30; 10 answer sheets B 0,40; scoring stencils (specify A or B) 1,80; Standard 8 manual 4,00; cassette 7,40; 10 answer sheets A 0,30; 10 answer sheets B 0,40; scoring stencil A or B 1,80 each (orders outside The RSA will be dealt with on merit).

Publisher: Human Sciences Research Council

MATHEMATICS ATTAINMENT TESTS SERIES
Refer to page 245.

MATH TESTS--GRADE i/SUB A-STANDARD 10
Refer to page 245.

MEASURE OF ACADEMIC PROGRESS (MAP)
Wayne Adams, David Sheslow and Lynn Erb

---

child, teen   grades K-8

Purpose: Determines the approximate grade level at which a student is performing. Used with students Grades K-8 to identify those who are operating above or below their expected grade level.

Description: 160 item paper-pencil test containing approximately five items per grade level (K-8) in each of the following categories: mathematics, spelling, word recognition, and passage comprehension. Also provides an informal handwriting checklist. Student must produce rather than identify the correct response. "Drop-back and discontinue" rules establish basal and ceiling levels. Score is the highest grade level where all items are passed. Test items are tied to actual content taught at each grade level. Examiner required. Not for group use.

Untimed: 20-30 minutes

Range: Grades K-8

Scoring: Hand key

Cost: Contact publisher.

Publisher: Charles E. Merrill Publishing Company

MEDICAL COLLEGE ADMISSION TEST
Association of American Medical College

---

teen, adult   grades 13-UP 🖝 ✐

Purpose: Primarily assists medical school admission committees in the evaluation of candidates primarily applying to medical school.

Description: One full day of examinations assessing academic achievement and aptitude of medical school applicants. The examinations are administered in four sections: Science Knowledge (presents biology, chemistry, and physics in separate assessment areas as a partial assessment of science achievement), Science Problems (intermingles biology, chemistry, and physics to assess the application of knowledge in solving problems), Skills Analysis: Reading (presents information in reading passages to assess analytical and reasoning skills, Quantitative (assesses analytical and reasoning skills using questions involving quantitative material). The new MCAT Student Manual includes: test day schedule, descriptions of the tests, and comprehensive guidelines for preparing for the test. Prerequisite subjects for the science subtests are usually covered in one-year introductory courses in biology, general chemistry, organic chemistry, and physics. The examinations are administered in the spring and fall of each year at centers established and supervised by the American College

Testing Program. Examiner required. Suitable for group use.

Timed: 12 hours

Range: College students and adults

Scoring: Computer scored

Cost: Regular exam (on Saturday) $45.00; Sunday exam $50.00; student manual $5.75.

Publisher: Association of American Medical Colleges

METROPOLITAN ACHIEVEMENT TEST: 5TH EDITION-SURVEY BATTERY
Irving H. Balow, Roger Farr, Thomas P. Hogan, and George A. Prescott

---

child, teen   grades K-12.9 🖝 ✐

Purpose: Assesses school achievement. Used for measuring performance of large groups of students.

Description: Multiple item paper-pencil tests of school achievement. Divided into 8 levels: Preprimer, Grade K.0-K.5; Primer, Grade K.5-1.4; Primary 1, Grade 1.5-2.4; Primary 2, Grade 2.5-3.4; Elementary, Grade 3.5-4.9; Intermediate, Grade 5.0-6.9; Advanced 1, Grade 7.0-9.9; and Advanced 2, Grade 10.0-12.9. The Basic Battery for all eight levels consists of tests in reading comprehension, mathematics and language. The Complete Battery for Primary 1 through Advanced 1 adds Social Science and Science tests to the basic three. Materials include two alternate and equivalent forms, JS and KS, at Primer through Advanced 2 levels. Metropolitan Reading, Mathematics and Language Instructional Tests provide more in-depth analyses than does the Survey Battery. Examiner required. Suitable for group use.

Timed: Varies

Range: Grades K.0-12.9

Scoring: Hand key; may be machine scored; scoring service available

Cost: Specimen sets (includes test, Teacher's Manual for Administering and Interpreting; Preprimer includes practice test and directions; Intermediate and Advanced 1 and 2 include handscorable answer document) specify level $6.00 each.

Publisher: The Psychological Corporation

METROPOLITAN LANGUAGE INSTRUCTIONAL TESTS
Irving H. Balow, Roger Farr, Thomas P. Hogan, and George A. Prescott

child, teen   grades K.5-9.9 ☞ ✎

Purpose: Assesses basic skill areas in language arts. Used for providing prescriptive information on educational performance of individual pupils.

Description: Multiple item series of paper-pencil tests measuring major components of language arts skills including listening comprehension, punctuation and capitalization, usage, grammar and syntax, spelling and study skills. Divided into six levels: Primer, Grade K.5-1.4; Primary 1, Grade 1.5-2.4; Primary 2, Grade 2.5-3.4; Elementary, Grade 3.5-4.9; Intermediate, Grade 5.0-6.9; and Advanced 1, Grade 7.0-9.9. Each level assesses three to six of the above component areas. One in a series of instructional tests related to the Metropolitan Achievement Test Survey Battery. Examiner required. Suitable for group use.

Timed: Varies

Range: Grades K.5-9.9

Scoring: Scoring service available

Cost: Specimen sets (includes test, Teacher's Manual for Administering and Interpreting; Intermediate and Advanced 1 (includes handscorable answer document)-specify level-$6.00 each.

Publisher: The Psychological Corporation

METROPOLITAN MATHEMATICS INSTRUCTIONAL TESTS
Thomas P. Hogan, Roger Farr, George A. Prescott, and Irving H. Balow

child, teen   grades K.5-9.9 ☞ ✎

Purpose: Assesses mathematics skills and competence. Used for providing prescriptive information on educational performance of individual pupils.

Description: Multiple item series of paper-pencil tests measuring major components of mathematics skills including numeration, geometry and measurement, problem solving and operations: whole numbers, laws and properties, fractions and decimals, and graphs and statistics. Divided into six levels: Primer, Grade K.5-1.4; Primary 1, Grade 1.5-2.4; Primary 2, Grade 2.5-3.4; Elementary, Grade 3.5-4.9; Intermediate, Grade 5.0-6.9; and Advanced 1, Grade 7.0-9.9. Each level assesses four to seven of the above components. One in a series of instructional tests related to the Metropolitan Achievement Test Survey Battery. Examiner required. Suitable for group use.

Timed: Varies

Range: Grades K.5-9.9

Scoring: Hand key; may be machine scored; scoring service available

Cost: Specimen sets (includes test, Teacher's Manual for Administering and Interpreting; Intermediate and Advanced 1 (includes handscorable answer document)-specify level-$6.00 each

Publisher: The Psychological Corporation

METROPOLITAN READINESS TESTS (MRT)
Refer to page 455.

METROPOLITAN READINESS TEST: 1965 EDITION
Refer to page 455.

MILLER ANALOGIES TEST
W.S. Miller

adult College

Purpose: Assesses information and verbal reasoning ability. Used for admission of students to graduate school.

Description: 100 item paper-pencil test of verbal reasoning ability. Items are multiple-choice analogies. Braille and large-type editions available. Distribution restricted and test administered at specified licensed university centers. Examiner required. Suitable for group use.

Untimed: Not available

Range: College students

Scoring: Scoring service available

Cost: Contact publisher.

Publisher: The Psychological Corporation

MINIMUM ESSENTIALS TEST (MET)
William K. Rice, Jr., Thomas R. Guskey, Carole Lachman Perlman, and Marion F. Rice

teen, adult grades 8-UP

Purpose: Academic achievement measure of minimum basic skills. Used as minimum competency test or as final examination for basic essentials course.

Description: 124 item paper-pencil test of basic skills in reading, language and mathematics. The test provides information on student's ability to apply basic skills to life situations. An optional writing test is included which requires student to write one paragraph based on a given cartoon depiction. The academic and life skills sections may be used independently. Standards of acceptable performance are determined by local district. Examiner required. Suitable for group use.

Timed: Basic academic skills--45 minutes; basic life skills--45 minutes; writing sample--20 minutes

Range: Grades 8-12; adult

Scoring: Hand key; computer scoring available

Cost: Specimen set $6.50; 35 test booklets $24.85; 35 answer sheets $7.95; manual $4.30; key $1.30; directions for administration $1.90; norms booklet $4.35.

Publisher: Scott, Foresman and Company

MODERN LANGUAGE APTITUDE TEST (MLAT)
J.B. Carroll and S.M. Sapon

teen, adult grades 9-UP

Purpose: Assesses the ease with which students will learn a foreign language.

Description: Five part series of exercises in learning various aspects of language: number learning (aural), phonetic script (audio-visual), spelling clues, words in sentences, and paired associates. Number learning and phonetic script require use of a reel-to-reel or cassette tape recorder. Other three parts may be used as Short Form. Materials include test tapes with instructions and auditory stimuli. Examiner required. Suitable for group use.

Untimed: Short form, 30 minutes;

complete test, 1 hour

Range: Grades 9-12, college, adult

Scoring: Hand key; may be machine scored

Cost: Specimen set (includes test, IBM 805 answer document and key, practice exercise sheet, manual) $3.25; reel-to-reel tape $14.00; cassette tape $14.00; 25 tets $7.25; 50 IBM 805 answer documents $7.25.

Publisher: The Psychological Corporation

MORAY HOUSE TESTS

child, teen

Purpose: Assesses academic aptitude by measuring mathematic, English language, and verbal reasoning skills. Used with all ages from 8.6 to 14.0 years.

Description: 15 paper-pencil tests measures mathematics, English, and verbal reasoning abilities at a number of different levels providing both standardized and unstandardized tests. Three tests cover mathematical reasoning and arithmetic computation. Achievement is effectively measured whether the children are taught by "old" or "new" methods. The MHM (Junior)2 for ages 8.6 to 10.6 and the MHM 4, 4a, 7, 9, and 10 for ages 10.0 to 12.0 are both standardized tests, while the MHM (Advanced)1 for ages 12.0 to 14.0 is not standardized.

Four tests measure the following English language skills: vocabulary, punctuation, and ability to select the most appropriate completion (semantically or syntactically) together with a substantial element of general comprehension of prose and poetry. MHE (Junior)5 and 6 for ages 8.6 to 10.6, MHE 41 and 42 for ages 10.0 to 12.0, and MHE (Advanced)1 and 2 for ages 12.0 to 14.0 are standardized, while the MHE (Advanced)3 and 4

for is not standardized.

The eight Verbal Reasoning Tests relate less directly to current attainment and schooling than the English and Mathematics tests and as such have a semi-predictive function. The MHT (Junior)2, 4, 6, and 7 for ages 8.6 to 10.6, the MHT 82, 86, 87, 88, and 89 for ages 10.0 to 12.0 the MHT 12/1 for ages 11.0 to 13.0, the MHT (Advanced)10 for ages 12.0 to 14.0, and the MHT (Adult)1 for ages 13.6 to 17.6 are all standardized while MHT 8/1 for ages 7.3 to 8.6, MH Vernier 8 for ages 10.0 to 12.0, and MHT (Advanced)14 for ages 12.0 to 14.0 are not standardized.

Normative data are available for all the tests but are derived from smaller samples (usually a single LEA) in the case of the unstandardized tests. Available to schools with the permission of the local Chief Education Officer. Examiner required. Suitable for group use.

BRITISH PUBLISHER

Untimed: 45 minutes each

Range: Age varies with level

Scoring: Examiner evaluated

Cost: Tests range in price from £4.50 to £6.50 for 20 copies. For further information contact publisher.

Publisher: Hodder & Stoughton

MULTILEVEL ACADEMIC SKILLS INVENTORY: READING PROGRAM (MASI)
Kenneth W. Howell, Stanley H. Zucker and Mada Kay Morehead

child, teen   grades 1-8

Purpose: Assesses student reading and language arts performance in general and in detail to help teachers and school psychologists plan instructional strategies and refer students to remedial programs.

Description: Multiple item reusable paper-pencil test in three levels measuring decoding, reading comprehension, vocabulary, handwriting, and spelling. A Survey Test samples performance over a wide range of objectives. The Placement Test assesses abilities in more detail with a content area, and a Specific Level Test examines subskills in detail. Materials include a manual, diagnostic batteries, survey and placement test booklets, response booklets, and record forms. Examiner required. Suitable for group use.

Untimed: Varies

Range: Grades 1-8

Scoring: Examiner evaluated

Cost: Complete set $69.00.

Publisher: Charles E. Merrill Publishing Company

MULTILEVEL ACADEMIC SKILLS INVENTORY: MATH PROGRAM (MASI)
Kenneth W. Howell, Stanley H. Zucker and Mada Kay Morehead

child, teen   grades 1-8

Purpose: Assesses student math performance in general and in detail to help teachers and school psychologists plan instructional strategies and refer students to remedial programs.

Description: Multiple item reusable paper-pencil test in three levels measuring computation, application of skills with money, time and temperature, problem- solving, metric measurement, addition, subtraction, multiplication, division, fractions decimals, ratios, percent and geometry. A Survey Test samples performance over a wide range of objectives. The Placement Test assesses abilities in more detail with a content area, and a Specific Level Test examines subskills in detail. Materials include a manual, diagnostic batteries, survey and placement

test booklets, response booklets, and record forms. Examiner required. Suitable for group use.

Untimed: Varies

Range: Grades 1-8

Scoring: Examiner evaluated

Cost: Complete set $69.00.

Publisher: Charles E. Merrill Publishing Company

MUSICAL APTITUDE TESTS-- MUSAT J and MUSAT S

child, teen

Purpose: Assesses musical aptitude. Used for educational evaluation.

Description: Two tests of musical ability; MUSAT J is for pupils in Standards 1 to 5, and MUSAT S is for pupils in Standards 6 to 10. MUSAT J measures ability to perceive seven aspects of music: interval, harmony, timbre, rhythm, duration, speed, and counting units. MUSAT S measures ten aptitudes: for interval, harmony, timbre, rhythm, duration, speed, counting, loudness of tone, intonation and selective listening. Materials include records containing music specially composed for this test. Record player required for test administration. Group should not contain more than 20 students. Examiner required. Suitable for group use.
SOUTH AFRICAN PUBLISHER

Untimed: Junior-1½ hours; Senior-2½ hours

Range: Junior, Standards 1-5; Senior, Standards 6-10.

Scoring: Hand key, examiner evaluated

Cost: (In Rands) Junior--Complete kit (includes container and 2 records) 8.90; 10 answer sheets 1,0,90; 10 answer sheets 2 0,80; scoring stencils 1,80; manual 3,90; Senior--complete kit (includes container and 3 records) 11,20; 10 answer sheets I or II 0,70 each; scoring stencils 2,20; manual 3,90 (orders from outside The RSA will be dealt with on merit)

Publisher: Human Sciences Research Council

NATIONAL ACADEMIC APTI-TUDE TESTS--VERBAL INTELLIGENCE
Andrew Kobal, J. Wayne Wrightstone, Karl R. Kunze, edited by A.J. MacElroy

teen, adult   grades 12-UP

Purpose: Assesses mental aptitudes important in academic and professional work. Used for evaluation of applicants for employment and school programs.

Description: Three verbal, paper-pencil tests of mental aptitudes. Three tests cover the following: general information, academic and general science, mental alterness, comprehension, judgment, arithmetic reasoning, comprehension of relations, logical selection, analogies, classification. Norms are provided for all grades from 7 through 12, college students, administrative and executive employees, physicians, lawyers and other professionals. Examiner required. Suitable for group use.

Timed: 40 minutes

Range: Ages High school and adult

Scoring: Hand key

Cost: Specimen set $2.20; 25 tests $8.00; 100- $29.00.

Publisher: Psychometric Affiliates

NATIONAL ACHIEVEMENT TESTS: ENGLISH, READING and VOCABULARY TESTS-- AMERICAN LITERACY TEST
John J. McCarty

adult

Purpose: Assesses literacy in adults. Used for detecting the functionally illiterate.

Description: 50 item paper-pencil test of vocabulary or depth of literacy. Items require knowledge of approximate synonyms. Discriminates degrees of literacy from illiterate through highly sophisticated. Examiner required. Suitable for group use.

Timed: 4 minutes

Range: Adult

Scoring: Hand key

Cost: Specimen set (includes one test, manual and key) $2.00; 25 scales $3.85; 100-$12.00.

Publisher: Psychometric Affiliates

NATIONAL ACHIEVEMENT TESTS: ENGLISH, READING and VOCABULARY TESTS-- COLLEGE ENGLISH--FOR HIGH SCHOOL and COLLEGE
A. C. Jordon

teen, adult   grades 10-UP

Purpose: Assesses achievement in English of high school and college students. Used for evaluating prospective college students.

Description: Multiple item paper-pencil test of a range of English skills. Areas covered include: ability to use correct capitalization; ability to punctuate correctly; skill in the use of syntax; ability to determine the correct agreement of subject and verb; skill related to sentence structure; ability to use modifiers correctly; and knowledge of language principles.

Materials include two equivalent forms, A and B. Examiner required. Suitable for group use.

Timed: 45 minutes

Range: High school and post secondary

Scoring: Hand key

Cost: Specimen set (includes one test, manual and key) $2.20; 25 tests $5.50; 100-$21.00.

Publisher: Psychometric Affiliates

NATIONAL ACHIEVEMENT TESTS: ENGLISH, READING and VOCABULARY TESTS-- ENGLISH
R.K. Speer and Samuel Smith

teen   grades 7-12

Purpose: Assesses achievement in English for students in grades 7 through 12. Used for identification of student strengths and weaknesses as part of an educational evaluation.

Description: Multiple item paper-pencil test of knowledge and skill in English. Areas assessed include word usage; skill in the use of punctuation; vocabulary; ability to select correct, sensible sentences; ability to identify or express ideas; and ability to identify or express feelings. Emphasis is placed on power of self-expression and judgment. Materials include two equivalent forms, A and B. Examiner required. Suitable for group use.

Timed: 40 minutes

Range: Grades 7-12, inclusive

Scoring: Hand key

Cost: Specimen set (includes one test, manual and key) $2.20; 25 tests $8.00; 100-$21.00.

Publisher: Psychometric Affiliates

NATIONAL ACHIEVEMENT TESTS: ENGLISH, READING and VOCABULARY TESTS-- READING
R.K. Speer and Samuel Smith

teen, adult   grades 7-UP

Purpose: Assesses reading achievement of students in grades 7 through 12 and college. Used for identification of student strengths and weaknesses as part of an educational evaluation.

Description: Multiple item paper-pencil test of skills important in reading achievement including vocabulary; word discrimination; sentence meaning; noting details; and interpreting paragraphs. Materials include equivalent forms, A and B. Examiner required. Suitable for group use.

Timed: 40 minutes

Range: Grades 7-12 and college

Scoring: Hand key

Cost: Specimen set (includes 1 test, manual and key) $2.20; 25 tests $8.00; 100-$29.00; plus shipping.

Publisher: Psychometric Affiliates

NATIONAL ACHIEVEMENT TESTS: ENGLISH, READING and VOCABULARY TESTS-- VOCABULARY
R.K. Speer and Samuel Smith

child, teen   grades 3-8

Purpose: Assesses vocabulary knowledge of children in grades 3 through 8. Used as part of an educational evaluation.

Description: Multiple item paper-pencil test of vocabulary knowledge. For each item, the important word is printed in capital letters in a meaningful sentence. Pupil selects a synonym from a group of words, each of which fits perfectly into the same

sentence. Base words are more difficult than synonym. Materials include
two equivalent forms, A and B.
Examiner required. Suitable for
group use.

Timed: 15 minutes

Range: Grades 3-8, inclusive

Scoring: Hand key

Cost: Specimen set (includes one
test, manual and key) $2.00; 25 tests
$8.00; 100-$29.00.

Publisher: Psychometric Affiliates

NATIONAL ACHIEVEMENT TESTS: ENGLISH, READING and VOCABULARY TESTS-- VOCABULARY
R.K. Speer and Samuel Smith

teen   grades 7-UP

Purpose: Assesses vocabulary knowledge of children in grades 7 to 12 and
college. Used as part of an educational evaluation.

Description: Multiple item paper-
pencil test of knowledge and judgment related to word meaning and
word discrimination. Materials
include two equivalent forms, A and
B. Examiner required. Suitable for
group use.

Timed: 15 minutes

Range: Grades 7-12 and college

Scoring: Hand key

Cost: Specimen set (includes one
test, manual and key) $2.20; 25 tests
$2.75; 100-$10.00.

Publisher: Psychometric Affiliates

NATIONAL ACHIEVEMENT TESTS for ELEMENTARY SCHOOLS: ARITHMETIC and MATHEMATICS--ALGEBRA TEST FOR ENGINEERING AND SCIENCE
*A.B. Lonski and edited by John
Kinsella*

teen

Purpose: Assesses achievement in
intermediate algebra. Used for
screening students planning registration in an engineering college or
technical school.

Description: Paper-pencil test of
algebra knowledge. Items represent
mistakes made in algebra by college
freshmen who failed the subject in
engineering and science courses. Test
represents minimum essentials for
entry into regular freshmen mathematics. Examiner required. Suitable
for group use.

Untimed: Not available

Range: Post secondary school

Scoring: Hand key

Cost: Specimen set (includes one
test, key and manual) $3.30; 25 tests
$10.00; 100-$38.00; 25 answer sheets
$2.20; 100-$7.70; plus shipping.

Publisher: Psychometric Affiliates

NATIONAL ACHIEVEMENT TESTS for ELEMENTARY SCHOOLS: ARITHMETIC and MATHEMATICS--AMERICAN NUMERICAL TEST
John J. McCarty

child

Purpose: Assesses arithmetic and
numerical ability. Used for educational evaluation and vocational
guidance.

Description: Sixty item paper-pencil
test arranged in sequences of the four

basic arithmetical operations. Items require numerical alertness and adaptation. Materials include two equivalent forms, A and B. Examiner required. Suitable for group use.

Timed: 4 minutes

Range: Elementary

Scoring: Hand key

Cost: Specimen set (includes one test, key and manual) $2.00; 25 tests $2.75; 100 tests $10.00, plus shipping.

Publisher: Psychometric Affiliates

NATIONAL ACHIEVEMENT TESTS for ELEMENTARY SCHOOLS: ARITHMETIC and MATHEMATICS--ARITHMETIC FUNDAMENTALS

Robert K. Speer and Samuel Smith

child, teen   grades 3-8

Purpose: Assesses achievement in basic arithmetic skills for children in grades 3 through 8. Used for identification of strengths and weaknesses as part of an educational evaluation.

Description: Multiple item paper-pencil test of three basic areas of arithmetic skills: speed and accuracy in computation; judgment, speed, and accuracy in comparing computations; and skill and understanding, without special reference to speed. Materials include two equivalent forms, A and B. Examiner required. Suitable for group use.

Timed: 45 minutes

Range: Grades 3-8, inclusive

Scoring: Hand key

Cost: Specimen set (includes one test, key and manual) $2.20; 25 tests $5.00; 100 tests $18.00; plus shipping.

Publisher: Psychometric Affiliates

NATIONAL ACHIEVEMENT TESTS for ELEMENTARY SCHOOLS: ARITHMETIC and MATHEMATICS--ARITHMETIC (FUNDAMENTALS AND REASONING)

Robert K. Speer and Samuel Smith

teen   grades 6-8

Purpose: Assesses achievement in arithmetic for children in grades 6 to 8. Used for identification of strengths and weaknesses as part of an educational evaluation.

Description: Five part paper-pencil test of arithmetic reasoning and fundamentals. Areas measured include fundamentals, number comparisons, mathematical judgments, problem reading, and problem solving. Special norms for students with high and low IQs are provided. Materials include two equivalent forms, A and B. Examiner required. Suitable for group use.

Timed: 30 minutes each part

Range: Grades 6-8

Scoring: Hand key

Cost: Specimen set (includes one test, key and manual) $2.20; 25 tests $5.50; 100 tests $21.00.

Publisher: Psychometric Affiliates

NATIONAL ACHIEVEMENT TESTS for ELEMENTARY SCHOOLS: ARITHMETIC and MATHEMATICS--ARITHME-TIC- 3-6 (FUNDAMENTALS AND REASONING)

Robert K. Speer and Samuel Smith

child   grades 3-6

Purpose: Assesses achievement in arithmetic for children in grades 3 to 6. Used for identification of strengths and weaknesses as part of an educational evaluation.

Description: Five part paper-pencil test of arithmetic reasoning and fundamentals. Areas measured include computation, arithmetical judgments, problem reading, and problem solving. Special norms for students with high and low IQs are provided. Materials include two equivalent forms, A and B. Examiner required. Suitable for group use.

Timed: 30 minutes for each part

Range: Grades 3-6

Scoring: Hand key

Cost: Specimen set (includes one test, key and manual) $2.20; 25 tests $5.50; 100 tests $21.00.

Publisher: Psychometric Affiliates

NATIONAL ACHIEVEMENT TESTS for ELEMENTARY SCHOOLS: ARITHMETIC and MATHEMATICS--ARITHMETIC REASONING
Robert K. Speer and Samuel Smith

child, teen   grades 3-8

Purpose: Assesses achievement in arithmetic reasoning skills for children in grades 3 to 8. Used for identification of strengths and weaknesses as part of an educational evaluation.

Description: Four part paper-pencil test of factors of judgment and reasoning beyond those covered by the usual tests on the subject. Includes not only standard material but also important judgment and practical aspects of arithmetic. Materials include two equivalent forms, A and B. Examiner required. Suitable for group use.

Timed: 40 minutes

Range: Grades 3-8 inclusive

Scoring: Hand key

Cost: Specimen set (includes one test, key and manual) $2.20; 25 tests $5.50; 100 tests $21.00.

Publisher: Psychometric Affiliates

NATIONAL ACHIEVEMENT TESTS for ELEMENTARY SCHOOLS: ARITHMETIC and MATHEMATICS--FIRST YEAR-ALGEBRA TEST
Ray Webb and Julius H. Hlavaty

teen

Purpose: Assesses achievement in first year algebra. Used for identification of strengths and weaknesses as part of an educational evaluation.

Description: Paper-pencil test of pupil's knowledge of first year algebra. Part of the National Achievement Series. Materials include two equivalent forms, A and B. Examiner required. Suitable for group use.

Timed: 40 minutes

Range: Secondary school

Scoring: Hand key

Cost: Specimen set (includes one test, key and manual) $4.40; 25 tests $6.00; 100-$20.00; 25 answer sheets $2.20; 100-$7.70.

Publisher: Psychometric Affiliates

NATIONAL ACHIEVEMENT TESTS for ELEMENTARY SCHOOLS: ARITHMETIC and MATHEMATICS--GENERAL MATH
Stanley J. Lejeune

child   grades 4-6

Purpose: Assesses achievement in general mathematics skills for children in grade 4 through 6. Used for identification of strengths and weaknesses as part of an educational evaluation.

Description: Multiple item paper-pencil test of student comprehension of 11 major topics in general mathematics: numeration system; addition, subtraction, multiplication and division; common fractions; decimal fractions and per cent; measurements; geometry; solving written problems; graphs and scale drawings; set terminology; mathematical structure; and money. General Math is an untimed power test. Materials include two equivalent forms, A and B. Examiner required. Suitable for group use.

Untimed: Approximately 2-3 class periods

Range: Grades 4-6

Scoring: Hand key

Cost: Specimen set (includes one test, key and manual) $3.30; 25 tests $5.50; 100 tests $21.00; 25 answer sheets $2.20; 100-$7.70.

Publisher: Psychometric Affiliates

NATIONAL ACHIEVEMENT TESTS for ELEMENTARY SCHOOLS: ARITHMETIC and MATHEMATICS--GENERAL MATHEMATICS
Harry Eisner

teen   grades 7-9

Purpose: Assesses achievement in general mathematics for children in grades 7 to 9. Used for identification of strengths and weaknesses as part of an educational evaluation.

Description: Multiple item paper-pencil test of student's knowledge of essential concepts, skills, and insights which should be developed in junior high school mathematics. Abilities measured include arithmetic, algebraic and geometric concepts, applications, problem analysis, and reasoning. Materials include two equivalent forms, A and B. Examiner required. Suitable for group use.

Timed: 10 minutes, Section 1; 15 minutes, Section 2; 27 minutes, Section 3

Range: Grades 7-9

Scoring: Hand key

Cost: Specimen set (includes one test, key and manual) $2.20; 25 tests $5.50; 100 tests $21.00.

Publisher: Psychometric Affiliates

NATIONAL ACHIEVEMENT TESTS for ELEMENTARY SCHOOLS: ARITHMETIC and MATHEMATICS--PLANE GEOMETRY, SOLID GEOMETRY, AND PLANE TRIGONOMETRY TESTS
Ray Webb and Julius H. Hlavaty

teen

Purpose: Assesses achievement in geometry and trigonometry. Used for identification of strengths and weaknesses as part of an educational evaluation.

Description: Three paper-pencil tests measuring essential concepts, skills and insight in three content areas: plane and solid geometry, and plane trigonometry. Materials include two equivalent forms, A and B. Examiner required. Suitable for group use.

Timed: 40 minutes

Range: Secondary school

Scoring: Hand key

Cost: Specimen set (includes one test, key and manual) $4.40; 25 tests $6.00; 100-$20.00; 25 answer sheets $2.20; 100-$7.70.

Publisher: Psychometric Affiliates

NATIONAL EDUCATIONAL DEVELOPMENT TEST (NEDT)
Science Research Associates and T.G. Thurstone

teen   grades 9-10

Purpose: Assesses students' strengths and weaknesses in English, math, and social studies and natural sciences reading. Predicts success in college and serves as a practice instrument for college admissions exams.

Description: 209 item paper-pencil test measuring ability to apply rules and principles of grammar and general English usage, understand mathematical concepts and apply principles in solving quantitative problems, comprehend reading selections, and apply critical reading skills. Examiner required; used only in schools that are designated test centers. Suitable for group use.

Timed: 150 minutes

Range: Grades 9-10 (October and February administrations)

Scoring: Computer scored

Cost: Test materials and scoring service/student $3.00.

Publisher: Science Research Associates, Inc.

ONTARIO ASSESSMENT INSTRUMENT POOL (OAIP)

teen   grades 4-13

Purpose: Evaluates student achievement and program effectiveness in Ontario Province Schools. Measures pupils' mastery of predetermined educational objectives. Used as a unit pre- or post-test. May be used with any other educational assessment device.

Description: Paper-pencil assessment instruments covering a variety of school subjects in both French and English. The following unit test titles are available: Chemistry I, II, III, and IV, Senior Division (grades 11-13); English I and II, Intermediate Division (grades 7-10); Anglais I, Junior Division Writing and Speaking (grades 4- 6); Anglais, Intermediate Division I writing and speaking (grades 7-10); French as a Second Language, Junior and Intermediate Divisions, (Grades 6-10); Francais au cycle moyen I, Savior écrire, savoir parler (grades 4-6); Francais au cycle intermédiaire I, Savoir écrire, savoir parler (grades 7-10); Geography, Intermediate Division (grades 7-10); Géographie (L'amérique du nord) au cycle intermédiaire (grades 7-10); Geography (Canada) Intermediate Division (grades 7-10); Géographie (le Canada) au cycle intlérmediare (grades 7-10); History, Intermediate Division (grades 7-10); History Part II, Intermediate Division (grades 7-10); Mathematics, Intermediate Division (grades 7-10); Mathematique au cycle intermediaire (grades 7-10); Physics, Senior Division (grades 11-13); Physique au cycle superieur, (grades 11-13).
The Pool will be made available to all teachers in systems within the Ontario province. Materials may be used separately or in groups. They include test booklets, information sheets and manuals. Examiner required. Suitable for individual or group use.
CANADIAN PUBLISHER

Untimed: Varies

Range: Grades 4-13

Scoring: Not available

Cost: $15.00 per pool.

Publisher: Ministry of Education-Ontario

ORLEANS-HANNA ALGEBRA PROGNOSIS TEST
Joseph B. Orleans and Gerald S. Hanna

teen   grades 7-11

Purpose: Evaluates a student's probability of success in learning first-year algebra. Used in counseling, selecting or grouping algebra students.

Description: Multiple item test of three variables related to prognosis of success in algebra: proficiency, aptitude, and interest. Superseded by the 1982 Orleans-Hanna Algebra Prognosis Test (Revised). Examiner required. Suitable for group use.

Timed: 40 minutes

Range: Grades 7-11

Scoring: Hand key; may be machine scored; computer scoring service available

Cost: 35 tests with manual $19.50; 35 MRC machine- scorable answer documents $5.75; key $2.00; 35 IBM 805 answer documents $4.25; key $2.00; 35 IBM 1230 answer documents $5.50; key $2.00; 35 Op Scan answer documents $5.50; key $2.00.

Publisher: The Psychological Corporation

ORLEANS-HANNA ALGEBRA PROGNOSIS TEST (REVISED)
Gerald S. Hanna and Joseph B. Orleans

teen   grades 7-UP

Purpose: Identifies students likely to have difficulties in an algebra course. Used in counseling, selecting, and grouping algebra students.

Description: Multiple item test of three variables related to prognosis of success in an algebra course: aptitude, achievement, and interest and motivation. Items include question-

naire and work samples. Students indicate recent grades and estimate of algebra grade on questionnaire, then complete the 60 item work sample. Revision of the 1968 Orleans-Hanna Algebra Prognosis Test. Examiner required. Suitable for group use.

Timed: 40 minutes

Range: Grades 7 and up

Scoring: Hand key; may be machine scored; computer scoring service available

Cost: 35 tests with manual $19.25; 35 hand-scorable answer documents $4.25; keys $2.50; 35 NCS machine-scorable answer documents $5.50; 25 student report forms $4.25.

Publisher: The Psychological Corporation

OTIS-LENNON MENTAL ABILITY TEST
Arthur S. Otis and Roger T. Lennon

child, teen   grades K.5-12

Purpose: Assesses general mental ability or scholastic aptitude.

Description: Multiple item test of a broad range of cognitive abilities. Divided into six levels: Primary I and II, Kindergarten-Grade 1; Elementary I and II, Grades 1-6; Intermediate, Grades 7-9; and Advanced, Grades 10-12. No reading required at first three levels. Materials include two alternate and equivalent forms, J and K. Replaces Otis Quick-Scoring Mental Ability Tests. Examiner required. Suitable for group use.

Timed: Varies

Range: Grades K.5-12

Scoring: Hand key; may be machine scored; computer scoring service available

Cost: Specimen set (includes test, key for hand scoring booklet, manual, norms conversion booklet) specify level $4.50 each.

Publisher: The Psychological Corporation

OTIS-LENNON SCHOOL ABILITY TEST (OLSAT)
Arthur S. Otis and Roger T. Lennon

child, teen grades 1-12

Purpose: Measures abstract thinking and reasoning ability. Used for prediction of success in cognitive, school-related activities.

Description: Multiple item test of abilities emphasized in school. Items use verbal, figural, and numerical stimuli. Divided into five levels: Primary I, Grade 1; Primary II, Grades 2-3; Elementary, Grades 4-5; Intermediate, Grades 6-8; Advanced, Grades 9-12. No reading required of pupils in grades 1, 2, and 3. Materials include two alternate and equivalent forms, R and S. Form R may be used in conjunction with the Metropolitan Achievement Tests: 5th Edition. Examiner required. Suitable for group use.

Timed: Varies

Range: Grades 1-12

Scoring: Hand key; may be machine scored; computer scoring service available

Cost: Specimen set (includes test, manual, parent/teacher report) specify level $4.75 each.

Publisher: The Psychological Corporation

PEABODY INDIVIDUAL ACHIEVEMENT TEST (PIAT)
Lloyd M. Dunn and Fredrick C. Markwardt, Jr.

all ages

Purpose: Provides an overview of individual scholastic attainment. Used to screen for areas of weakness requiring more detailed diagnostic testing.

Description: 402 item test of mathematics (84 items), reading recognition (84 items), reading comprehension (66 items), spelling (84 items), and general information (84 items), including science, social studies, fine arts and sports. Materials include two easel kits containing test plates, 25 record booklets, and a manual. Derived scores are grade equivalents, grade percentile ranks, age equivalents, age percentile ranks, and standard scores by age or grade. Examiner required. Not suitable for group use.

Untimed: 30-50 minutes

Range: Ages 5-adult

Scoring: Examiner evaluated

Cost: Complete kit, regular edition $64.50; special plastic edition $76.50; training tape $7.50; 25 record booklets $6.35.

Publisher: American Guidance Service

PIMSLEUR LANGUAGE APTITUDE BATTERY
Refer to page 234.

PROFICIENCY BATTERIES-JSPB, SPB, APP and SPT- HP

all ages

Purpose: Assesses achievement in scholastic fields. Used for selection and placement of students and applicants.

Description: Four paper-pencil measures of proficiency in a range of scholastic fields. The JSPB is designed for pupils in Standards 5 to 7, and measures proficiency in First Language (English or Afrikaans), Mathematics, Natural Sciences, Geography, History and Second Language. The SPB is for pupils in Standards 8 to 10, and measures Social Sciences, Commercial Sciences, Natural Sciences, Arithmetic and home language, English or Afrikaans. APP tests proficiency in Social Sciences, Commercial Sciences, Natural Sciences, Mathematical Sciences and their home language, and is designed for use with first-year university students. The SPT-HP is for adults whose proficiency is at the higher primary level, and measures performance in Mathematics, English, and Afrikaans. Examiner required. Suitable for group use.
SOUTH AFRICAN PUBLISHER

Timed: JSPB 2½ hours; SPB 1¾ hours; APB 1¾ hours.

Range: JSPB, Standards 5-7; SPB, Standards 8-10; APB, college level

Scoring: Hand key; examiner evaluated

Cost: (In Rands) JSPB--test 2,00; 10 answer sheets 0,70; scoring stencil 2,40; manual 2,20; SPB--test 0,80; 10 answer sheets 0,60; scoring stencil and manual 1,00 each; APB--test 0.90; 10 answer sheets 0,60; scoring stencil 1,00; manual 2,40; SPT-HP-- test 0,50; manual 2,30; scoring stencil 1,50; 10 answer sheets 0,50 (orders from outside The RSA will be dealt with on merit).

Publisher: Human Sciences Research Council

PROGRESSIVE ACHIEVEMENT TESTS

Warwick Elley, Neil Reid, David Hughes, Cedric Croft, and Peter Jackson

child, teen

Purpose: Measures school achievement. Used for educational assessment.

Description: Five paper-pencil tests of school achievement. PAT: Reading Vocabulary consists of multiple-choice items requiring child to select best synonym from five alternatives. PAT: Listening Comprehension measures child's ability to understand orally presented material. Child chooses best answer from four alternatives presented in multiple-choice format. PAT: Reading Comprehension consists of graded reading passages followed by five to seven multiple-choice questions. PAT: Mathematics is a 50 item multiple-choice test of achievement in knowledge, computation, understanding, and application. PAT: Study Skills measures skills in three broad areas: knowledge and use of common reference materials; reading and interpreting graphic and tabular materials; and general reading study skills. Examiner required. Suitable for group use.
PUBLISHED IN NEW ZEALAND

Timed: 30-40 minutes

Range: Ages 7-15

Scoring: Hand key; examiner evaluated

Cost: Contact publisher.

Publisher: New Zealand Council for Educational Research

A PSYCHOEDUCATIONAL INVENTORY OF BASIC LEARNING ABILITIES
Robert E. Valett

child, teen   grades 1-8

Purpose: Evaluates basic learning ability of elementary and junior high students who may have learning disabilities. Used by educators and psychologists to determine pupil strengths and weaknesses and to select educational objectives.

Description: 53 item paper-pencil test of six skill areas: gross motor (14 items); sensory-motor (7 items); perceptual-motor (15 items); language (7 items); conceptual (6 items) and social (4 items). Usually administered a section at a time on one- to-one basis. The student marks responses in a workbook record and the examiner rates the responses on a special profile form. Correlated lessons for use with inventory are in an auxiliary paperback book *The Remediation of Learning Disabilities.* Examiner required. Not suitable for group use.

Untimed: 50 minutes

Range: Grades 1-8

Scoring: Examiner evaluated

Cost: 10 inventories and workbook $14.95. Auxiliary book (contains correlated lessons for use with the inventory) $18.50.

Publisher: Pitman Learning

PSYCHO-EDUCATIONAL BATTERY (PEB)
Lillie Pope

all ages   grades K-UP

Purpose: Identifies learning problems of children and adults. Used to develop individualized teaching plans.

Description: Multiple item paper-pencil observational instrument measuring the following aspects of a student's functioning: motor performance, sensory and perceptual performance, language cognition and memory, and reading, spelling, and arithmetic skills. The examiner completes the inventory based on observations of the student. Some additional probing by the evaluator may be necessary. Interpretation of the inventory yields a psycho-educational assessment of skills and deficits in young children and all age groups for special needs populations. The subjects should be within a normal range of behavior and gross motor skills. Two forms are available: Level Y (Kindergarten to Grade 6) and Level O (junior high to adult). The PEB consists of five components: Student Recording Form; Evaluator Recording Form; Family, Social, and Medical History; Visual Pack; and Teacher's Referral Form. Examiner required. Not for group use.

Untimed: 1-2 hours

Range: Grades K-adult

Scoring: Examiner evaluated

Cost: Complete kit (specify Level Y, K-6 or Level O, Jr. High-adult) $24.95; part A, recording forms $7.50; part B, evaluator's form $9.95; part C, family, social and medical history $7.50; part D, visual pack $7.50; part E, teacher's referral form $4.95.

Publisher: Book Lab

PUPIL RECORD OF EDUCATIONAL BEHAVIOR (PREB)
Ruth Cheves

child   grades PRE-6

Purpose: Evaluates a child's level and pattern of functioning in visual-motor, auditory, language, and mathematical skills. Used for instructional programming.

Description: Multiple item, visual-motor test. It profiles performance over a range of developmental skills, including: gross-motor coordination and fine- motor skills, visual-motor integration, auditory and visual perception, association and generalization, language development, and mathematical concepts. In addition to the guide and record booklets, the materials include guide and record booklets and a variety of cards (shape, color, picture/word, etc.), jigsaw puzzles, stencils, cubes, pegboard with pegs, whistle, and scissors. Examiner required. Not suitable for group use.

Untimed: Not available

Range: Preschool-primary (no norms available)

Scoring: Examiner evaluated

Cost: Complete $76.00.

Publisher: Teaching Resources Corporation

QUICKSCREEN
Janet B. Fudala

child   grades K-2

Purpose: Measures the ability of young children to read, write and use numbers. Identifies those who may have speech, language or learning problems. Used to implement P.L. 94-142.

Description: Multiple item, paper-pencil, verbal test available at three levels: Kindergarten (with four equivalent forms A, B, C, and D) and First and Second Grades (with A and B equivalent forms) to facilitate administration to a whole class at one time. The kindergarten level consists of four subtests: Name Writing, Figure Copying, Story, and Sentence Repetition. The first-grade level consists of five subtests: Name Writing, Figures, Words, Story, and Sentences. The second-grade level consists of five subtests: Name Writing, Fig-

ures, Story, Cognitive, and Sentences. Cutoff scores are provided to identify students with "High" or "Possible" risk of potential learning disability so they can be referred for more detailed evaluation. The manual provides evidence of reliability and validity, detailed instructions for administration and scoring, case studies, and recommended materials and tests for subsequent evaluation and remediation. The Score Sheet provides for a summary of the entire classroom and the Scoring Summary Card summarizes scoring procedures (Grades 1 and 2) on an easy-to-refer-to card to facilitate scoring. Examiner required. Suitable for group use.

Untimed: 15-25 minutes

Range: Grades K-2

Scoring: Hand key

Cost: Complete: Kindergarten kit $14.75; First Grade kit $19.90; Second Grade kit $19.90; complete set for 3 grades $52.50 (each kit contains test booklets, score sheets, templates, a summary card, manual).

Publisher: Western Psychological Services

RICHMOND TESTS OF BASIC SKILLS
A.N. Hieronymus, E.F. Lindquist and Norman France

child, teen

Purpose: Assesses child's progress in academic work. Used for diagnosing areas of general strengths and weaknesses.

Description: Multiple item, paper-pencil measure of progress in five areas: vocabulary, reading comprehension, language skills, study skills and mathematics. Separated into 11 individual tests: Vocabulary, Reading Comprehension, Spelling, Use of Capital Letters, Punctuation, Usage, Map Reading, Reading

Graphs and Tables, Knowledge and Use of Reference Materials, Mathematics Concepts, and Mathematics Problem Solving. Divided into six levels for ages 8 to 14. Materials include a 96 page book incorporating all 11 tests for all six levels of difficulty. Examiner required. Suitable for group use.
BRITISH PUBLISHER

Timed: Various timings

Range: Ages 8-14

Scoring: Hand key; computer scoring service available

Cost: 30 pupils' books £58.50; 25 answer sheets £7.80; keys (specify level) £2.65; teacher's guide £2.65; table of norms £2.30 (payment in sterling for all overseas orders).

Publisher: NFER-Nelson Publishing Company

SCHOLASTIC APTITUDE TEST BATTERIES FOR STANDARDS 2, 3 AND 5-SATB AND JSATB

child

Purpose: Assesses academic and scholastic aptitudes. Used for psycho-educational counseling.

Description: Multiple item test batteries measuring a broad range of scholastic aptitudes. SATB applies to Standards 2 and 3, and JSATB to Standard 5. SATB measures mathematics, non-verbal reasoning ability, and proficiency in English, Afrikaans, and one of seven mother tongues: Northern Sotho, Southern Sotho, Tswanga, Tsonga, Venda, Xhosa, and Zulu. JSATB assesses abilities in language, mathematics, and verbal and nonverbal reasoning ability. Examiner required. Suitable for group use. Publisher notes that this test is "normed on Blacks only."
SOUTH AFRICAN PUBLISHER

Timed: SATB, 3 hours; JSATB, 2½ hours

Range: Standards 2, 3 and 5

Scoring: Hand key; examiner evaluated

Cost: (In Rands) SATB test booklet (specify language) 0,60; manual 1,40; 10 answer sheets 1,00; scoring stencil 1,20; JSATB test booklet 2,40; answer sheet, not available; scoring stencil, not available; manual 6,70 net (orders from outside The RSA will be dealt with on merit).

Publisher: Human Sciences Research Council

SCHOOL AND COLLEGE ABILITY TESTS II (SCAT II)
Educational Testing Service

child, teen   grades 3.5-14

Purpose: Measures verbal and quantitative ability at four different levels. Used to estimate current level, growth and success in basic skill areas.

Description: 100 item paper-pencil test measures verbal skills (50 verbal analogies) and mathematical abilities (50 quantitative comparisons). Available in four levels: Level I (grades 13 fall-14 spring; Level II (grades 9 spring-12 spring); Level III (grades 6 spring-9 fall); Level IV (grades 3 spring-6 fall). Examiner required. Suitable for group use.

Timed: 40 minutes

Range: Grades 3.5-14

Scoring: Hand key; computer scoring available

Cost: 20 reusable test books $11.20 (specify level); 100 answer sheets $16.00; manual $4.50 (specify level).

Publisher: CTB/McGraw-Hill

SCHOOL AND COLLEGE ABILITY TESTS (SCAT III)
Educational Testing Service

child, teen   grades 3.5-12.9

Purpose: Measures a student's understanding of words through the use of analogies and the understanding of fundamental number operations through items of quantitative comparison.

Description: 100 item paper-pencil test measures verbal and mathematical skills and is used to measure both students' achievements and class performance. The SCAT III is based on SCAT II with the metric system incorporated and any unintended racial or ethnic bias deleted. The tests are available for three levels: Elementary (grades 3.5-6.5); Intermediate (grades 6.5-9.5); Advanced (grades 9.5-12.9). Examiner required. Suitable for group use.

Timed: 40 minutes

Range: Grades 3.5-12.9

Scoring: Hand key; computer scoring available

Cost: 25 reusable test books $15.40 (specify level); 100 answer sheets $20.00; scoring stencil $2.25 each (specify level).

Publisher: CTB/McGraw-Hill

SCIENTIFIC KNOWLEDGE AND APTITUDE TEST
S. Chatterji

teen

Purpose: Measures the scientific knowledge and aptitude of high school students.

Description: 72 item paper-pencil test assessing scientific knowledge and aptitude. Useful with students whose native language is not English, but who have been taught in English

language schools. Examiner required. Suitable for group use. PUBLISHED IN INDIA

Timed: 60 minutes

Range: Ages 15-16

Scoring: Hand key; examiner evaluated

Cost: (In Rupees) complete kit (includes 25 booklets, 100 answer sheets, manual, key) Rs90.

Publisher: Manasayan

SCRE PROFILE ASSESSMENT SYSTEM

child, teen

Purpose: Assesses school achievement. Used for educational evaluation.

Description: Multiple item, paper-pencil tests for academic achievement for students in Years 7 and above. Examiner required. Suitable for group use. DISTRIBUTED BY AUSTRALIAN PUBLISHER

Untimed: Not available

Range: Grades Year 7 and above

Scoring: Not available

Cost: Contact distributor.

Publisher: Scottish Council for Research in Education- distributed by The Australian Council for Educational Research Limited

SENIOR APTITUDE TESTS (SAT)-1969
F.A. Fouché and N.F. Alberts

teen

Purpose: Measures scholastic aptitude. Used for educational counseling.

Description: Multiple item, paper-pencil test of 12 specific aptitudes: verbal comprehension, calculations, disguised words, comparison, pattern completion, figural series, spatial 2 D, spatial 3 D, memory (paragraph), memory (symbols), coordination, and writing speed. Examiner required. Suitable for group use.

SOUTH AFRICAN PUBLISHER

Timed: 2 hours to complete

Range: Grades Standards 8-10

Scoring: Hand key; examiner evaluated; machine scoring available

Cost: (In Rands) test booklet 1,90; 10 answer sheets T11-T12 0,40; 10 answer sheets T1-T6, T7- T10 (specify form) 0,70; 10 profile sheets 0,70; scoring stencil (T1-T6) 2,10; scoring stencil (T7- T10) 1,60; manual 5,60; 10 machine answer sheets 1,10 (orders from outside The RSA will be dealt with on merit).

Publisher: Human Sciences Research Council

SEQUENTIAL TESTS OF EDUCATIONAL PROGRESS: CIRCUS LEVELS A-D

child   grades PRE-3.5

Purpose: Assesses achievement of preprimary-grade 3 students. Used to diagnose instructional needs of the child and evaluate curriculum.

Description: Multiple item testing program which includes subtests and teacher completed instruments. The test assesses children's interests, problem solving, prereading and reading skills, mathematics concepts and perceptual-motor coordination. Level A is for nursery school and beginning K; Level B, K.5-1.5; Level C, 1.5-2.5; Level D, 2.5-3.5. A slide presentation with accompanying script is available. "El Circo" is a Spanish version of Level A. Examiner required. Suitable for group use.

Untimed: 30 minutes per test

Range: Grades Prekindergarten-3.5

Scoring: Hand key; computer scoring available

Cost: Test prices range from $8.00-$31.00 for a package of 25 depending on test title (specify level).

Publisher: CTB/McGraw-Hill

SEQUENTIAL TESTS OF EDUCATIONAL PROGRESS (STEP II)

Educational Testing Service

teen, adult   grades 13-UP

Purpose: Measures achievement levels in language, mathematics, science, and social studies. Used to assess academic mastery, diagnose deficiencies and plan curriculum.

Description: Multiple item paper-pencil battery of tests designed for grades 13 fall to 14 spring. The battery includes five subtests which may be ordered independently. The 65 item English Expression Test assesses the ability to evaluate correctness and effectiveness of sentences and proficiency in standard written English. The 60 item Reading Test measures the ability to read and comprehend a variety of materials. The 50 item Mathematics Basic Concepts Test measures: ability to recall facts and perform mathematical manipulation; comprehension of mathematical concepts; problem solving techniques; numerical operations such as algebraic relations and statistics. The 50 item Science Test measures: knowledge and understanding of fundamental science concepts; comprehension and application of this knowledge; and mastery of science skills. The 85 item Social Studies Test measures: student development skills and understanding of social change, the interdependence of individuals, communities, and societies; the way society directs and regulates behavior of its members;

and the nature of a democratic society. All subtests are available in equivalent forms A and B. Examiner required. Suitable for group use.

Timed: 40 minutes per test

Range: Grades 13-14/college students

Scoring: Hand key; computer scoring available

Cost: 20 reusable booklets and instructions $13.00 or $15.00 (specify subject).

Publisher: CTB/McGraw-Hill

SEQUENTIAL TESTS OF EDUCATIONAL PROGRESS (STEP III: LEVELS E-J)
Educational Testing Service

child, teen   grades 3.5-12.9

Purpose: Measures achievement in language, mathematics, science, and social studies. Used to assess individual and group academic mastery and to evaluate curriculum program.

Description: Multiple item, comprehensive testing program consisting of eight tests: Reading, Vocabulary, Writing Skills, Mathematic Computation, Mathematic and Basic Concepts, Study Skills/Listening, Social Studies, and Science. Designed for grades 3.5 to 12.9 with six levels available. To test across grade levels, multi-level tests are available and are selected on the basis of a short language and math "locator test" to determine the appropriate test level for each student. Examiner required. Suitable for group use.

Timed: 40 minutes per test

Range: Grades 3.5-12.9

Scoring: Hand key; computer scoring available

Cost: Complete battery for 35 students $34.65 (specify level); one multi-level test book $3.80 each.

Publisher: CTB/McGraw-Hill

SOCIAL AND PREVOCATIONAL INFORMATION BATTERY-T (SPIB-T)
Refer to page 560.

SRA ACHIEVEMENT SERIES FORMS 1-2 (ACH 1-2)
Robert A. Naslund, Louis P. Thorpe and D. Welty Lefever

child, teen   grades K-12

Purpose: Assesses general scholastic achievement of students from kindergarten to grade 12.

Description: Multiple item paper-pencil academic achievement test. Assesses the following areas: reading, math, language, science, and social studies. Includes optional section on reference materials. Tests are norm referenced, establishing eight levels of proficiency. Two equivalent forms available for each test. Examiner required. Suitable for group use.

Timed: 3-5 hours

Range: Grades K-12

Scoring: Hand key; computer scoring available

Cost: Components priced separately per level. Forms 1 and 2, Level A: 25 booklets $31.25; 25 practice sheets $1.90; manual $.85; key $1.45; 100 profile sheets $11.40; sample set $3.00.

Publisher: Science Research Associates, Inc.

SRA PAC PROGRAM
Robert A. Naslund, Louis P. Thorpe and D. Welty Lefever

child, teen   grades 4-10

Purpose: Assesses general academic achievement of students grades 4-10. Used in student screening, grade placement and scheduling.

Description: Multiple item paper-pencil test measuring academic achievement in reading, math, language, science, social studies, and knowledge of reference materials. Educational Ability Series (EAS) and Kuder General Interest Survey are optionally available. The test is a norm- referenced, shortened version of the SRA Achievement Series. Examiner required. Suitable for group use.

Timed: 3 hours

Range: Grades 4-10

Scoring: Hand key; computer scoring available

Cost: Contact publisher.

Publisher: Science Research Associates, Inc.

STANFORD MEASUREMENT SERIES-STANFORD ACHIEVEMENT TEST: 6TH EDITION
Richard Madden, Eric F. Gardner, Herbert C. Rudman, Bjorn Karlsen, and Jack C. Merwin

child, teen   grades 1.5-9.9 〖☞ ✑〗

Purpose: Assesses school achievement status of children in grades 1 through 9.

Description: Six level battery of paper-pencil tests measuring achievement in school. Six levels are Primary Level I, Primary Level II, Primary Level III, Intermediate Level I, Intermediate Level II, Advanced Level. Primary Level I measures the following areas: vocabulary, reading comprehension, word study skills, mathematics concepts, mathematics computation, spelling, and listening comprehension. Primary Level II tests these areas plus Mathematics applications, social science and science. Language is added at Primary Level III and Intermediate Levels I

and II. The advanced Level drops the word study skills and listening comprehension subtests. Superseded by Stanford Achievement Test: 7th Edition. Examiner required. Suitable for group use.

Timed: Varies

Range: Grades 1.5-9.9

Scoring: Hand key; computer scoring service available

Cost: Specimen set (includes complete battery, teacher's directions, norms booklet; primary and intermediate levels include practice test and directions) $5.00 (specify, Primary I, II or III, Intermediate I or II, or Advanced).

Publisher: The Psychological Corporation

STANFORD MEASUREMENT SERIES-STANFORD ACHIEVEMENT TEST: 7TH EDITION
Eric F. Gardner, Herbert C. Rudman, Bjorn Karlsen, and Jack C. Merwin

child, teen   grades 1.5-9.9 〖☞ ✑〗

Purpose: Assesses school achievement status of children from first through tenth grade.

Description: Multiple item paper-pencil test of 9, 10 or 11 aspects of school achievement. The Stanford Achievement Test is divided into six levels: Primary 1, Primary 2, Primary 3, Intermediate 1, Intermediate 2, and Advanced. Primary 1 and 2 test nine achievement areas: word study skills, word reading, reading comprehension, vocabulary, listening comprehension, spelling concepts of number, mathematics computation, and environment. The next three higher levels measure same areas with the exception of word reading and environment. Instead, language/English, mathematics applications, science, and social science are assessed. The Advanced Level assesses the same skills, omitting only word study skills. Together with the Stanford Early School Achievement Test and the Stanford Test of Academic Skills, the Stanford Achievement Test provides for continuous assessment throughout the school years. Examiner required. Suitable for group use.

Timed: Varies

Range: Grades 1.5-9.9

Scoring: Hand key; computer scoring service available

Cost: Specimen set (includes complete battery booklet, teacher's directions, norms booklet) $7.00. Specify Primary 1, 2 or 3, Intermediate 1 or 2, Advanced, or Task 1 and 2; SESAT 1 and 2, $6.00.

Publisher: The Psychological Corporation

STANFORD MEASUREMENT SERIES-STANFORD EARLY SCHOOL ACHIEVEMENT TEST: 1ST EDITION (SESAT)
Richard Madden and Eric F. Gardner

child   grades K.1-1.8

Purpose: Assesses school achievement status of children at the Kindergarten and first grade level.

Description: Multiple item paper-pencil test of what the child has learned prior to entry into formal school instruction. SESAT is divided into two levels: Level I for Kindergarten, and Level II for first graders. SESAT includes the following subtests at both levels: environment, mathematics, letters and sounds, and aural comprehension. Level II also measures word reading and sentence reading. Superseded by second edition of SESAT. Examiner required. Suitable for group use. Available in Spanish.

Timed: Level I, 1 hour, 30 minutes; Level II, 2 hours, 20 minutes

Range: Grades K.1-1.8

Scoring: Hand key; computer scoring service available

Cost: Specimen set (includes test and directions) $4.00 (specify level I or level II).

Publisher: The Psychological Corporation

STANFORD MEASUREMENT SERIES-STANFORD EARLY SCHOOL ACHIEVEMENT TEST: 2ND EDITION (SESAT)
Richard Madden, Eric F. Gardner and Cathy S. Collins

child   grades K.0-1.9

Purpose: Assesses school achievement status of children at the Kindergarten and first grade level.

Description: Multiple item paper-pencil test of five or six aspects of school achievement. SESAT is divided into two levels: SESAT 1, for Kindergarten children, and SESAT 2 for children from mid-kindergarten through first grade. SESAT 1 tests five achievement areas: sounds and letters, word reading, listening to words and stories, mathematics, and environment. SESAT 2 tests these same areas as well as reading comprehension. Together with the Stanford Achievement Test: 7th Edition, and the Stanford Test of Academic Skills, the SESAT provides for continuous assessment throughout the school years. Examiner required. Suitable for group use.

Timed: Total battery, 2 hours, 25 minutes

Range: Grades K.0-1.9

Scoring: Hand key; computer scoring service available

Cost: Specimen set (includes complete battery book, teacher's

directions, norms booklet) $6.00 (specify SESAT 1 or 2).
Publisher: The Psychological Corporation

STANFORD MEASUREMENT SERIES-STANFORD ACHIEVEMENT TEST: 1ST EDITION (TASK)
Eric F. Gardner, Robert Callis, Jack C. Merwin, and Richard Madden

teen   grades 8-13

Purpose: Assesses school achievement status of children in grades 8 through 13.

Description: Multiple item paper-pencil test of three achievement areas: reading, English, and mathematics. Divided into three levels: Level I, Grades 8-10; Level II, Grades 10-12; College Edition, Grade 13. Materials include two alternate and equivalent forms, A and B. TASK scores related to those of other Stanford Batteries (SESAT), Stanford Achievement Test). Superseded by second edition of TASK. Examiner required. Suitable for group use.

Timed: Total battery, 2 hours

Range: Grades 8-13

Scoring: Hand key; computer scoring service available

Cost: Specimen set (includes test, manual) $5.00 (specify Level I and II or Level II College).

Publisher: The Psychological Corporation

STANFORD MEASUREMENT SERIES-STANFORD ACHIEVEMENT TEST: 2ND EDITION (TASK)
Eric F. Gardner, Robert Collis, Jack C. Merwin, and Herbert C. Rudman

teen   grades 8-13

Purpose: Assesses school achievement status of children in grades 8 through 13.

Description: Multiple item paper-pencil test of seven aspects of school achievement. TASK is divided into two levels, TASK 1 and TASK 2. Both measure reading comprehension, vocabulary, spelling, language/English, mathematics, science, and social science. Together with the SESAT and the Stanford Achievement Test, the TASK provides for continuous assessment throughout the school years. Examiner required. Suitable for group use.

Timed: Total battery 3 hours, 5 minutes

Range: Grades 8-13

Scoring: Hand key; computer scoring service available

Cost: Specimen set (includes complete battery book, teacher's directions, norms booklet) $7.00 (specify TASK 1 or 2).

Publisher: The Psychological Corporation

STANFORD MEASUREMENT SERIES-STANFORD DIAGNOSTIC MATHEMATICS TEST (SDMT)
Leslie S. Beatty, Richard Madden, Eric F. Gardner, and Bjorn Karlsen

child, teen   grades 1.5-13

Purpose: Identifies individual pupil needs in area of mathematics.

Description: Multiple item paper-pencil test of three mathematics skill areas: number system and numeration, computation, and applications. SDMT is divided into four levels: red, Grades 1.5-4.5; green, Grades 3.5-6.5; brown, Grades 5.5-8.5; and blue, Grades 7.5-13. Materials include manual with prescriptive teaching strategies and two alternate and equivalent forms, A and B. Linked statistically with the Stanford Achievement Test Series. Examiner required. Suitable for group use.

Timed: Varies

Range: Grades 1.5-13

Scoring: Hand key; computer scoring service available

Cost: Specimen set (includes test, manual, instructional placement report. Green, brown and blue levels also include hand-scorable answer document) $4.50 (specify red, green brown or blue level).

Publisher: The Psychological Corporation

STANFORD MEASUREMENT SERIES-STANFORD DIAGNOSTIC READING TEST (SDRT)
Bjorn Karlsen, Richard Madden and Eric F. Gardner

child, teen grades 1.5-13

Purpose: Measures major components of the reading process. For use in diagnosing specific pupil needs.

Description: Multiple item paper-pencil test of four aspects of reading including comprehension, decoding, vocabulary, and rate. Cutoff scores indicate need for remedial programming. SDRT is divided into four levels: red, Grades 1.5-3.5; green, Grades 2.5-5.5; brown, Grades 4.5-9.5; and blue, Grades 9-13. Materials include handbooks with instructional suggestions and instructional materials. Two alternate and

equivalent forms, A and B. Linked statistically with the Stanford Achievement Test Series. Examiner required. Suitable for group use.

Timed: Varies

Range: Grades 1.5-13

Scoring: Hand key; computer scoring service available

Cost: Specimen set (includes test, manual, instructional placement report, brown and blue levels also includes answer document) $4.50 (specify red, green, brown or blue level).

Publisher: The Psychological Corporation

STECK-VAUGHN PLACEMENT SURVEY FOR ADULT BASIC EDUCATION
Beth Phillips

adult

Purpose: Determines entry point for students in Adult Basic Education.

Description: 105 and 141 items (on Level 1 and Level 2 tests, respectively.) Paper-pencil test that assesses student's ability in reading, language and mathematics. Student reads a 60-word screening list to determine the proper test level. Examiner required. Suitable for group use except Level 1 reading portion.

Untimed: 45 minutes

Range: Adult

Scoring: Hand key

Cost: 25 form 1-K of L $66.00; 25 answer sheets $6,00; 25 form 2-M of Q $66.00; 50 answer sheets $6.00.

Publisher: Steck-Vaughn Company

STEENBURGEN DIAGNOSTIC-PRESCRIPTIVE MATH PROGRAM AND QUICK MATH SCREENING TEST

Refer to page 250.

STS-HIGH SCHOOL PLACEMENT TEST (HSPT)

teen   grades 8.9-9.3

Purpose: Measures eighth-grader's ability to read, write and do arithmetic. Used for appropriate high school placement.

Description: 298 item paper-pencil test of verbal ability (60 items), quantitative ability (52 items), reading skills (62 items), mathematics skills (64 items), and language skills (60 items). Optional tests include Mechanical Aptitude, Science, and Catholic Religion (40 items). For these Closed Edition tests schools may purchase the test materials and hand-score them, or they may lease the test materials and use the standard scoring service. The Closed Edition offers new materials each year, with security insured (no specimen sets available). One of the optional tests may be selected free-of-charge with the Closed Edition. The Open Edition is a reprint of a recent Closed Edition, for which specimen sets are available. The Standard Service includes scoring and reporting the following information: alphabetical lists of names, raw scores, percentiles, and IQ's for the Ability subtests, raw scores, percentiles, and GE for the Skills subtests and T composite raw scores and percentiles for all the subtests combined; Rank Order List Reports; Group Summary Statistical Report; an interpretive manual, To The Test User. Additional scoring options are: Alternate Rank Order Listings, Summary for Other Groupings, Individual Item Analysis, Group Item Analysis, IBM Work Cards, and Student address information. Optional materials for both editions are: Student Record Cards, Student Score Folders, To The Test User, and Technical Reports. Examiner required. Intended for group use.

Timed: 2½ hours

Range: Grades 8.9-9.3

Scoring: Hand key; may be computer scored

Cost: Specimen set $2.00.

Publisher: Scholastic Testing Service, Inc.

SURVEY OF BASIC COMPETENCIES (SBC)

Jwalla P. Somwaru

child, teen

Purpose: Measures ability of children ages 3-15 to read, write and do arithmetic. Used to identify those who have learning problems and to screen for further testing with the Assessment of Basic Competencies diagnostic battery, and for Title I assessment.

Description: 138 item verbal response, paper-pencil test consisting of four subtests: Information Processing (36 items), Language (36 items), Reading (30 items), and Mathematics (36 items). The test is individually administered, with the child and examiner on opposite sides of a desk. Scoring provides a raw score, a Developmental Age, a Grade Equivalent, and operating range (in terms of grade). Starter set includes the manual, one reusable test, 20 response forms, and a carrying case. Examiner required. Not suitable for group use.

Untimed: 30 minutes

Range: Ages 3-15

Scoring: Hand key

Cost: Starter set $54.50.

Publisher: Scholastic Testing Service, Inc.

TESTS OF ACHIEVEMENT AND PROFICIENCY FORM T (TAP)

Dale Scannell in cooperation with Oscar M. Haugh, Alvin H. Schild and Gilbert Ulmer

teen   grades 9-12

Purpose: Measures high school student progress in learning such basic skills as reading, writing, mathematics and science. Used for evaluation and career planning.

Description: Multiple item, paperpencil battery. The complete battery has 353-365 items in six subtests covering: reading comprehension, mathematics, written expression, using sources of information, social studies, and science. The basic battery has 233-242 items, depending on the level administered, and measures reading, mathematics, writing, and sources of information. Objective, primarily norm-referenced score information allows students to compare their performance to that of others in their grade, and makes them aware of those areas where they have been the most and least successful. The test is normed concurrently with the Cognitive Abilities Test for Reliable comparisons between attained and anticipated achievement test scores. In order for the norms to be useful, those taking the test should be representative of students included in the norming sample. Examiner required. Suitable for group use.

Timed: Complete Battery, 240 minutes; Basic Battery, 160 minutes

Range: Grades 9-12

Scoring: Hand key; computer scoring available

Cost: Complete Battery test booklet for Levels 15-18 (single copy) $2.97; Basic Battery test booklets for levels 15-18 (single copy) $2.25; 35 MRC answer sheets, Teacher's Guide, 35 student report folders, and materials necessary for machine scoring (specify level) $12.60. Two MRC scoring masks price per level $8.01.

Publisher: The Riverside Publishing Company

TESTS OF ACHIEVEMENT IN BASIC SKILLS (TABS)

EdITS Staff

child, teen   grades 2-13

Purpose: Evaluates individual student progress in reading, mathematics and geometry skills from second-grade to the first year of college. Used to measure overall class and school achievement growth related to specific academic objectives.

Description: Multiple item, paperpencil criterion referenced tests of student achievement. They are available in the areas of mathematics and reading comprehension at four ability levels: Level A for grades 2-4, Level B for grades 4-6, Level C for grades 7-9, and Level D for grades 10-13. The TABS-MATH Level B, for example, is designed for use with students whose achievement level approximates those in grades 4, 5 and 6. Two parallel forms are available, Form 1 and Form 2, each of which consists of 66 items arranged in three parts. Part I, Arithmetic Skills, consists of 30 items measuring basic arithmetic skills. Part II, Geometry-Measurement-Application, consists of 25 items measuring basic geometric concepts, arithmetic measurements and application to practical problems. Part III, Modern Concepts, consists of 11 items measuring modern mathematics concepts. Examiner required. Intended for group use.

Untimed: Not available

Range: Grades 2-first year of college

Scoring: Scoring service available

Cost: Contact publisher.

Publisher: Educational and Industrial Testing Service

TESTS OF ADULT BASIC EDUCATION (TABE)
CTB/McGraw-Hill

adult

Purpose: Measures the proficiency of adults in reading, mathematics and language. Used by educators to identify individual weaknesses, establish level of instruction, and measure growth after instruction.

Description: Multiple item paper-pencil test provided for three levels: Level D, grades 6 thru 9; Level M, grades 4 thru 6; and Level E, grades 2 thru 4. Levels D and M are subdivided into reading (testing vocabulary and comprehension), mathematics (testing computation, concepts and problems), and language (testing mechanics and expression, and spelling). Level E contains reading and math tests only. A Practice Exercise is included to reduce anxiety and provide some experience in test-taking procedures, and a Locator Test is used to determine the appropriate test level. Examiner required. Suitable for group use.

Timed: Level D, 2 hours, 17 minutes; Level M, 2 hours, 29 minutes, Level E, 1 hours, 28 minutes

Range: Adult

Scoring: Hand key; computer scoring available

Cost: Multi-Level Examination Kit (including descriptive brochure, practice exercise and locator test, practice exercise and locator answer sheet, test book and manual for all levels, battery answer sheet, group record sheet, and test Reviewer's Guide) $7.25.

Publisher: CTB/McGraw-Hill

TEST OF BASIC EXPERIENCES (TOBE2)
Refer to page 467.

TEST OF CHILDREN'S LEARNING ABILITY-- INDIVIDUAL VERSION
J. Haynes, S. Hegarty, X. Perryer, and C. Gipps

child

Purpose: Assesses learning ability. Used for individual evaluation of children with language deficiencies or for whom English is not the home language.

Description: Multiple item performance test of learning ability. Test consists of five subtests: classification of objects according to various perceptual characteristics, number seriation, intuition of relationships in nonverbal analogies, and paired-associate and auditory rote learning. Administration involves teaching a skill, allowing the child practice, then testing. Useful as supplement to existing instruments to compensate for cultural biases in other tests. Examiner required. Not suitable for group use.
BRITISH PUBLISHER

Untimed: Not available

Range: Ages 7-8

Scoring: Hand key

Cost: Complete kit £34.00 (payment in sterling for all overseas orders).

Publisher: NFER-Nelson Publishing Company

TEST OF COGNITIVE SKILLS (TCS)
CTB/McGraw-Hill

child, teen   grades 2-12

Purpose: Assesses skills important to success in school settings. Used for predicting school achievement and screening students for further evaluation.

Description: Multiple item paper-pencil test of four areas of cognitive skills: sequences, analogies, memory, and verbal reasoning. The Sequences Test measures the student's ability to comprehend a rule or principle implicit in a pattern or sequence of figures, letters or numbers. The Analogies Test measures the student's ability to see concrete or abstract relationships and to classify objects or concepts according to common attributes. The Memory Test measures the student's ability to recall previously presented materials. The Verbal Reasoning Test measures the student's ability to discern relationships and reason logically. Divided into five levels spanning grades 2 through 12. Following scores are available: Number of Correct Responses (NCR), Age or Grade Percentile Rank, Stanine, Scale Score, and Cognitive Skills Index. Examiner required. Suitable for group use.

Untimed: 1 hour

Range: Grades 2-12

Scoring: Hand key; computer scoring available

Cost: Multilevel Examination kit (with assorted test booklets and answer sheets for different levels, handbook, record sheet) $19.50. Specimen set (specify level) $7.25.

Publisher: CTB/McGraw-Hill

TEST OF ENQUIRY SKILLS

child

Purpose: Measures achievement. Used as part of an educational evaluation.

Description: Multiple item paper-pencil test of learning skills for students in years 7-10. Materials include a set of masters and handbook. Examiner required. Suitable for group use.
AUSTRALIAN PUBLISHER

Untimed: 30 to 40 minutes each

Range: Ages 7-10

Scoring: Examiner evaluated

Cost: Complete set (includes masters and handbook) $15.50; handbook $4.00 (all remittances must be in Australian currency).

Publisher: The Australian Council for Educational Research Limited

TESTS OF PROFICIENCY IN ENGLISH
C. Gipps and E. Ewen

child

Purpose: Measures English comprehension and intelligibility of children whose native language/dialect differs from the English required in junior-level schools. Used as a diagnostic guide and to monitor progress.

Description: Four separate tests, paper-pencil or oral, of skills in listening, speaking, reading and writing. Each test is measured in four ascending levels related to words, sentences, and extended units of communication. Scores are based on relationship of content and skills measured rather than by general norms. At least one term should elapse if test is repeated with the same child. Test is not a teaching tool

and no strict structure is required if children can express themselves appropriately in speech and writing. Also useful for child placement. Materials include four separate manuals, ten tests for each skill level in each category, a general guide and cassettes as indicated in the following separate descriptions. Examiner required.
BRITISH PUBLISHER

Untimed: Not available

Range: Ages 7-11

Scoring: Examiner evaluated

Cost: Costs follow. Payment in sterling for all overseas orders.

Publisher: NFER-Nelson Publishing Company

TESTS OF PROFICIENCY IN ENGLISH--LISTENING TESTS
C. Gipps and E. Ewen

child

Purpose: Measures English listening comprehension of children whose native language or dialect differs from the English required in junior-level schools. Used for student placement and monitoring.

Description: Multiple item oral test in four progressive levels of listening and comprehension; each level composed of 10 subtests. Picture materials may be used as a stimulus. Tape recorder required. Pronunciation is not a criterion unless it interferes with intelligibility. Materials include 10 tests each for Listening One, Listening Two, Listening Three (part 1), and Listening Three (part 2); as well as cassettes for Listening Two and Three, part 1 and for Listening Three, part 2. Examiner required.
BRITISH PUBLISHER

Untimed: Not available

Range: Ages 7-11

Scoring: Examiner evaluated

Cost: 10 Listening One tests £3.15; 10 Listening Two tests £2.10; 10 Listening Three Part 1 tests £0.85; 10 Listening Three Part 2 tests £2.10; cassette for Listening Two and Three Part 1 £4.60; cassette for Listening Three Part 2 £4.60; manual £0.65.

Publisher: NFER-Nelson Publishing Company

TESTS OF PROFICIENCY IN ENGLISH--READING TESTS
C. Gipps and E. Ewen

child

Purpose: Measures reading comprehension of children whose native language or dialect differs from the English required in junior-level schools. Identifies specific strengths and weakness for each child tested.

Description: Four progressive levels of reading comprehension, each level with 10 subtests. Picture materials may be used as stimulus. Tests are independent of reading ability and pronunciation is not a criterion unless it interferes with intelligibility. Used for placement and monitoring. Materials include 10 tests each for Reading One, Reading Two, Reading Three, part one, and Reading Three, part two. Also includes manual. Examiner required. Suitable for group use.
BRITISH PUBLISHER

Untimed: Not available

Range: Ages 7-11

Scoring: Examiner evaluated

Cost: 10 Reading One tests £3.15; 10 Reading Two tests £2.10; 10 Reading Three Part 1 tests £1.70; 10 Reading Three Part 2 tests £1.70; manual £0.55.

Publisher: NFER-Nelson Publishing Company

TESTS OF PROFICIENCY IN ENGLISH--SPEAKING TESTS
C. Gipps and E. Ewen

child

Purpose: Measures comprehension of children whose native language or dialect differs from the English required in junior-level schools. Used for student placement and monitoring.

Description: Multiple item oral response tests in four progressive levels of speaking abilities, each with 10 subtests. Picture materials may be used as a stimulus. Tape recorder required. Tests are as open ended as possible and pronunciation is not a criterion unless it interferes with intelligibility. Materials include manual and 10 tests each for Speaking One, Speaking Two, part 1; Speaking Two, part 2; Speaking Three, part 2. Examiner required. Not for group use.
BRITISH PUBLISHER

Untimed: Not available

Range: Ages 7-11

Scoring: Examiner evaluated

Cost: 10 Speaking One tests £1.95; 10 Speaking Two, Part 1 tests £1.70; 10 Speaking Two, Part 2 tests £1.70; 10 Speaking Three, Part 2 tests £0.95; manual £0.55.

Publisher: NFER-Nelson Publishing Company

TESTS OF PROFICIENCY IN ENGLISH--WRITING TESTS
C. Gipps and E. Ewen

child

Purpose: Measures comprehension of children whose native language or dialect differs from the English required in junior-level schools. Used for student placement and monitoring.

Description: Multiple item paper-pencil test of writing performance consisting of four progressive levels of 10 subtests each. Picture materials may be used as a stimulus. Tests are as open-ended as possible and spelling is not a criterion. Materials include manual and ten tests each for Writing One, Writing Two, part 1, Writing Two, part 2; Writing Three, part 1, and Writing Three, part 2. Examiner required. Suitable for group use.
BRITISH PUBLISHER

Untimed: Not available

Range: Ages 7-11

Scoring: Examiner evaluated

Cost: 10 Writing One tests £1.70; 10 riting Two, Part 1 tests £1.10; 10 Writing Two, Part 2 tests £0.85; 10 Writing Three, Part 1 tests £0.85; 10 Writing Three, Part 2 tests £0.85; manual £0.55.

Publisher: NFER-Nelson Publishing Company

TEST OF SCHOLASTIC ABILITIES
Neil Reid, Peter Jackson, Alison Gilmore, and Cedric Croft

child, teen

Purpose: Measures student's current status in broad language and numerical reasoning abilities. Used as beginning step in educational assessment.

Description: 70 item paper-pencil test of basic scholastic abilities. Items are multiple-choice and completion type. Abilities measured are school-related but do not involve skills taught directly in the classroom. Divided into three levels: Primary, Intermediate and Secondary. Examiner required. Suitable for group use.
PUBLISHED IN NEW ZEALAND

Timed: 30 minutes for

administration

Range: Ages 9-14

Scoring: Examiner evaluated

Cost: Contact publisher.

Publisher: New Zealand Council for Educational Research

THE 3-R'S TEST: ACHIEVEMENT EDITION
Nancy S. Cole, E. Roger Trent and Dena C. Wadell

child, teen   grades K-12

Purpose: Measures proficiency in reading, language arts, and mathematics skills of students from Kindergarten through Grade 12.

Description: Multiple item paper-pencil test assessing verbal and mathematical performance of students from kindergarten through high school. The reading sections measure: vocabulary, comprehension, word skills, and study skills. The mathematics sections measure computation and problem solving abilities. Levels 6-8 contain 59- 65 items and use machine-scorable test booklets. Levels 9-18 contain 125 items and use separate answer sheets. Two alternate editions are available: the Achievement and Abilities Edition for levels 9-18 which combines verbal and quantitative abilities tests along with the achievement battery, enabling a comparison of actual achievement to expected performance; and a Class-Period Edition (40 minutes), which contains a less detailed version of Form A. Examiner required. Suitable for group use. Available in Spanish (levels 6-14 only).

Timed: 100 minutes, Levels 9-17/18; 90-95 minutes, Levels 6-8

Range: Grades K-12

Scoring: Hand key; computer scoring available

Cost: 25 Form A or B MRC machine-scorable test booklets for Level 6, 7 or 8 $23.50 per level; 25 machine-scorable booklets for Level 9 $29.50; 35 Achievement Test booklets for Levels 9-17/18 $22.75 per level; Teacher's Manual for Levels 9-12 or Levels 13-17/18 $3.30.

Publisher: The Riverside Publishing Company

TOLEDO CHEMISTRY PLACEMENT EXAMINATION

teen, adult   College

Purpose: Predicts performance in college chemistry. Used for placement in appropriate chemistry course.

Description: 60 or 67 item paper-pencil multiple-choice test assessing readiness for college chemistry. Materials include two forms, 1974 and 1981. Form 1981 (60 items) measures three areas: general mathematics, general chemical knowledge, and specific chemical knowledge. Form 1975 (67 items) is arranged into five parts. For use only by authorized chemistry teachers and administrators. Examiner required. Suitable for group use.

Timed: Form 1981-55 minutes; Form 1974-55 minutes

Range: College students

Scoring: Hand key

Cost: Specimen set $5.00; 25 tests $18.00; 25 answer sheet $3.00; scoring stencils $1.00.

Publisher: Examinations Committee-American Chemical Society

TRANSITIONAL ASSESSMENT MODULES

child

Purpose: Assesses school achievement in English and mathematics. Used for identification of students having learning difficulties.

Description: Eighteen paper-pencil test modules measuring English and mathematics achievement. Eight English modules include auto-biographical essay, descriptive essay, explanatory essay, story- writing essay, sentence writing, punctuation, Cloze-Technique--reading comprehension, and reading comprehension passages and questions. There are 10 Mathematics Modules, each with 12 questions: numbers; addition; subtraction; multiplication; division; properties of the four operations; shapes; ratio, proportion and percentage; money; and problems devised after the first nine modules. Examiner required. Suitable for group use.
BRITISH PUBLISHER

Untimed: Not available

Range: Children in last term at junior school

Scoring: Examiner evaluated

Cost: Specimen set English modules (includes one each of modules 1-8, English manual, and record form) £2.30; specimen set, Maths modules (includes one each of modules 1-10, Maths manual and a record form) £2.90 (payment in sterling for all overseas orders).

Publisher: NFER-Nelson Publishing Company

VERBAL REASONING TESTS SERIES

child, teen

Purpose: Measures general scholastic ability. Used for educational evaluation.

Description: Six paper-pencil tests of verbal reasoning. Question types include analogies, similarities,

opposites, codes, odd-man-out, jumbled sentences, classifications and syllogisms. The six tests and the ages they are designed for are: Verbal Test BC, ages 8 to 10; Verbal Test CD, ages 9 to 11; Verbal Test C, ages 9 to 11; Verbal Test D, Ages 10 to 12; Verbal Test EF, ages 11 to 13; Verbal Test GH, ages 13 to 15. All tests make extensive use of written English, and may not be suitable for poor readers. Examiner required. Suitable for group use.
BRITISH PUBLISHER

Timed: Varies with each test

Range: Ages 8-15

Scoring: Hand key

Cost: Primary specimen set (includes 1 pupil's booklet BC, CD, C, D and sample manual) £1.20; Secondary specimen set (includes 1 pupil's booklets D, EF, GH and sample manual) £1.00 (payment in sterling for all overseas orders.)

Publisher: NFER-Nelson Publishing Company

WESTERN MICHIGAN UNIVERSITY ENGLISH QUALIFYING EXAM (EQE)
Bernadine P. Carlson

teen, adult   grades 15-UP

Purpose: Assesses level of English usage skills for graduate students and college juniors and seniors. Used for academic placement, as a criterion for graduation, and as evaluation of skills for graduate work.

Description: 195 item paper-pencil, multiple-choice test consisting of six parts: grammatical errors (30 items), punctuation for meaning (45 items), sentence structure (30 items), spelling (30 items), word usage (30 items), and reading comprehension and rhetorical style (30 items). Test items consist of sentences taken from papers written by students of this level. Specimen booklet available. Examiner required. Suitable for group use.

Timed: 100 minutes

Range: College juniors or seniors; graduate students

Scoring: Hand key; computer scoring available

Cost: Contact publisher.

Publisher: Bernadine P. Carlson

WIDE RANGE ACHIEVEMENT TEST (WRAT)
Joseph F. Jastak and Sarah Jastak

---

child, teen   grades 5-UP

Purpose: Measures the basic educational skills of word recognition, spelling and arithmetic, and identifies individual's with learning difficulties. Used for educational placement, measuring school achievement, vocational assessment, job placement and training.

Description: Three paper-pencil subtests (50-100 items per subtest) assessing the coding skills of: Reading (recognizing and naming letters and pronouncing printed words), Spelling (copying marks resembling letters, writing name and printing words), and Arithmetic (counting, reading number symbols, oral, and written computation). Test consists of two levels printed on the same form: Level I for ages 5-11 and Level II for ages 12-adult. Optional word lists for both levels of the reading and spelling tests are offered on plastic cards, and a recorded pronunciation of the lists is provided on cassette tape. The tape itself can be used to administer the spelling section. A One Level edition is available for clinicians and teachers who are willing to spend more time in testing in order to be able to analyze error patterns. A Large Print edition is available for those who require

magnification of reading material. Normed for age rather than grade for better accuracy. In conjunction with other tests, such as the Wechsler Scales, WRAT is useful for determining personality structure. Restricted to Educational and Psychological professionals. Examiner required. Spelling and Arithmetic subtests are suitable for group use. Reading subtest must be individually administered

Timed: 10 minutes each subtest

Range: Ages 5 and older

Scoring: Examiner evaluated

Cost: Manual $13.00; 50 test forms $9.25.

Publisher: Jastak Assessment Systems

WOODCOCK LANGUAGE PROFICIENCY BATTERY (WLPB)
Richard W. Woodcock

---

all ages   grades PRE-UP

Purpose: Measures oral language, reading and written language in either English or Spanish. Used to diagnose learning disabilities in children and adults and for instructional planning.

Description: Multiple item battery of eight subtests taken from the Woodcock-Johnson Psycho-Educational Battery. It measures the following factors: picture vocabulary, antonyms-synonyms, analogies, letter-word identification, word attack, passage comprehension, dictation, and proofing. Within the school-age range, the WLPB-English can be administered to students having English as their second language. If the Spanish form also is given, the overview can include a description of proficiency in each language in each area of skill. Materials, in both forms, include the battery, response booklets, and manual. Examiner required. Not for group use. Available in Spanish.

Untimed: Not available

Range: Preschool-adult

Scoring: Examiner evaluated

Cost: English form $46.00; Spanish form $50.00.

Publisher: Teaching Resources Corporation

WOODCOCK-JOHNSON PSYCHO-EDUCATIONAL BATTERY (WJPEB)
Richard W. Woodcock and Mary Bonner Johnson

all ages   grades PRE-UP

Purpose: Evaluates individual cognitive ability, scholastic achievement, and interest level. Used to diagnose learning disabilities, and for instructional planning, vocational rehabilitation counseling, and research.

Description: 27 test battery in three parts, some paper and pencil. It can be administered in its entirety or as single tests or clusters to meet specific appraisal needs. Part one tests cognitive ability in areas such as picture vocabulary, sentence memory, visual-auditory learning, antonyms-synonyms, and concept formation. Part two covers letter-word identification, calculation, dictation, proofing, and science. Part three tests interest levels in reading, mathematics, language, and physical and social fields. Materials include the test books, response booklets, cassette tape, and a technical manual, which also may be ordered separately. Not for group use. Examiner required. Available in Spanish.

Untimed: Varies

Range: Preschool-adult

Scoring: Examiner evaluated; computer scored

Cost: Complete set $125.00.

Publisher: Teaching Resources Corporation

WORD AND NUMBER ASSESSMENT INVENTORY (WNAI)
Charles B. Johansson

teen, adult   grades 9-UP

Purpose: Measures individual aptitude for words and numbers. Useful for career and school counseling and employment screening.

Description: 80 item paper-pencil, multiple-choice test consisting of 50 vocabulary and 30 mathematics items on combined question-answer forms. The scores are compared to those of individuals at several educational levels and in a number of occupations. Self-administered. Suitable for group use.

Untimed: 60 minutes

Range: Grades 9-adult

Scoring: Computer scored

Cost: Profile and interpretation from $3.50.

Publisher: NCS Interpretive Scoring Systems

WORD UNDERSTANDING (WU)
R. Hoepfner, M. Hendricks and R.H. Silverman

teen   grades 7-12

Purpose: Measures verbal comprehension and vocabulary. Used for personal and program evaluation.

Description: 32 item paper-pencil, multiple-choice test consisting of two separately timed parts, each with 16 items arranged in order of difficulty. Each part is timed at four minutes. Scores reflect the breadth and depth of vocabulary. Two forms are available Form A is a reusable form for which answers are recorded on answer sheets (lay-over stencil available for scoring). Form C is a consumable form for subjects who may be expected not to perform well on answer-sheet tests (response guide available for scoring). This test has been normed on over 1,300 junior-high school students. Examiner required. Suitable for group use.

Timed: 8 minutes

Range: Grades 7-12

Scoring: Hand key

Cost: Specimen set (specify form) $3.00; 35 tests (Form A or C) $7.00; 35 answer sheets (Form A) $3.00; scoring stencil (Form A) $2.00; scoring guide (Form C) $1.00; manual $1.00.

Publisher: Monitor

Vocational

ACADEMIC-TECHNICAL APTITUDE TESTS-ATA AND SATA
Refer to page 653.

EMPORIA CLOTHING TEST
Margaret C. Parkman, Patricia Duncan and Merritt W. Sanders

teen   grades 10-12

Purpose: Assesses clothing course achievement and knowledge. Useful as end-of-course exam.

Description: 100 item paper-pencil, multiple-choice test measuring knowledge of construction, choice of materials, finishes, design, care and repair of clothing, care and management of household furnishings. Examiner required. Suitable for group use.

Timed: 40 minutes

Range: Grades High school

Scoring: Hand key

Cost: Specimen set $1.50; test $.15; manual $.20; key $.20.

Publisher: Bureau of Educational Measurements

EMPORIA FOOD TEST
Margaret C. Parkman, Patricia Duncan and M. W. Sanders

teen   grades 10-12

Purpose: Assesses foods course knowledge of high school students. Used as end-of-course exam.

Description: 105 item paper-pencil test of food preparation, nutrient values, meal planning, marketing, care and preservation. Examiner required. Suitable for group use.

Timed: 40 minutes

Range: Grades High school

Scoring: Hand key

Cost: Specimen set $1.50; test $.15; manual $.20; key $.20.

Publisher: Bureau of Educational Measurements

EMPORIA INDUSTRIAL ARTS TEST
Elton Amburn, David E. Hill and M. W. Sanders

teen   grades 10-12

Purpose: Assesses industrial arts achievement of high school students. Used as end-of-course exam.

Description: 80 item paper-pencil test of woodworking, wood finishing, sheet metal working, and welding. Examiner required. Suitable for group use.

Timed: 40 minutes

Range: High school

Scoring: Hand key

Cost: Specimen set $1.50; test $.15; manual $.20; key $.20.

Publisher: Bureau of Educational Measurements

GARNETT COLLEGE TEST IN ENGINEERING SCIENCE (REVISED EDITION)
I. MacFarlane Smith

---

teen, adult   College

Purpose: Assesses knowledge of engineering. Used for selection of students for Technical Colleges.

Description: 110 item paper-pencil test of knowledge in engineering science. Divided into two parts. The first part deals with mechanics, the second with heat, electricity and magnetism. The 1971 revision incorporated the SI system of units. Examiner required. Suitable for group use.
BRITISH PUBLISHER

Timed: 60 minutes

Range: College students

Scoring: Hand key

Cost: Specimen set £2.80, 25 booklets £6.45; manual £1.50 (payment in sterling for all overseas orders).

Publisher: NFER-Nelson Publishing Company

INDUSTRIAL ARTS APTITUDE TEST
Dale Hogan, Elton Amburn and Kevin Hogan

---

teen, adult   grades 7-UP

Purpose: Assesses woodworking aptitude of junior high, high school, and college students.

Description: 50 item paper-pencil test covering knowledge of terms, concepts, problem-solving techniques, and outcomes of woodworking class. Examiner required. Suitable for group use.

Timed: 45 minutes

Range: Grades Junior high school and up

Scoring: Hand key

Cost: Specimen set $1.50; test $.18; manual $.20; key $.20.

Publisher: Bureau of Educational Measurements

INTUITIVE MECHANICS (WEIGHTS AND PULLEYS)
Refer to page 855.

MECHANICAL APTITUDE TEST
Refer to page 855.

MINNESOTA ENGINEERING ANALOGIES TEST
M.D. Dunnette

---

adult

Purpose: Measures engineering achievement and mathematical reasoning ability. Used for selection and placement of engineers, and admission of graduate students.

Description: Multiple item paper-pencil test of engineering skills and potential. Items are multiple-choice analogies. Examiner required. Suitable for group use.

Untimed: Not available

Range: Engineers and graduate school applicants

Scoring: Scoring service available

Cost: Contact publisher.

Publisher: The Psychological Corporation

NATIONAL ACADEMIC APTI-TUDE TESTS--NON-VERBAL INTELLIGENCE
Andrew Kobal, J. Wayne Wrightstone, and Karl R. Kunze; edited by A.J. MacElroy

teen, adult   grades 10-UP

Purpose: Assesses mental abilities. Used for indicating aptitudes for academic training in areas such as engineering, chemistry and other sciences.

Description: Three nonverbal, paper-pencil tests of mental aptitudes: Nonverbal Test of Spatial Relations, Comprehension of Physical Relations, and Graphic Relations. Items include pictorial and graphic work. Detects ability for handling nonverbal materials at a higher mental level. Examiner required. Suitable for group use.

Timed: 26 minutes

Range: High school and adult

Scoring: Hand key

Cost: Specimen set $2.20; 25 tests $8.00; 100- $29.00.

Publisher: Psychometric Affiliates

NIIP TESTS-ENGINEERING SELECTION TEST BATTERY

adult

Purpose: Assesses general intellectual ability and specific skills. Used for selecting student, professional and industrial engineering applicants.

Description: 22 paper-pencil tests measuring general and specific intellectual abilities. Manual for the Engineering Selection Test Battery (1980 Revision) gives administration details and scoring procedure for tests GT82, GT90A/B, GT70/70B, EA2A, EA4, VDM (old edition),

VMD (1979 revision), and MI (Mechanical Information). Group Test 90A (GT90A) is a four part test of general intelligence and verbal aptitude for adults of above average educational attainment. Group Test 90B (GT90B) is an alternative test to GT90A, with similar but different items.

Group Test 70 (GT70) is a three part general intelligence test for use with groups of above average educational attainment. The first part and the answer sheets for Parts 2 and 3 are printed in an 8 page disposable booklet. Parts 2 and 3 are presented in a 16 page reusable booklet. Group Test 70B (GT70B) is an alternative test to GT70. The first part is identical, second and third parts are similar but different.

Engineering Arithmetic Test 2A (EA2A) is a decimalized test of attainment in arithmetic. Engineering Arithmetic Test 4 (EA4) is a metricated test based on EA2A. Group Test 82 (GT82) is a four part test of comprehension of shapes and spatial relationships.

Form Relations Group Test is an eight part test of comprehension of shapes and spatial relationships. Vincent Mechanical Diagrams Group Test (VMD) is an eight part test consisting of simple mechanical problems. The VMD has been replaced by the Vincents Mechanical Diagrams Test-1979 Revision. There are now four subtests rather than eight, and the Test takes half as long to administer. In addition to the tests and manual for the Engineering Selection Test Battery, Engineering Apprentice Battery Profile Charts are available.

Group Test 91 (GT91) is a verbal test of general intelligence for use with groups of below-average educational attainment, and is used for industrial applicants. Group Test 72 (GT72) is a nonverbal test of general intelligence for groups of below average educational attainment. Group Test 73

(GT73) is an alternative test to GT72, with different questions but similar item type. Group Tests 80a and 81 (GT80a and GT81) are tests of comprehension of shapes and spatial relationships. GT80a consists of four parts, GT81 of two parts. Mechanical Information Test (MI) is a test of knowledge of common workshop terms for use with applicants for engineering apprenticeships.

There are also four clerical tests in the NIIP Test Series: Group Tests 20, 61A, 64, and 66A. Group Test 20 (GT20) tests speed and accuracy in checking numbers and names. Group Test 61A (GT61A) tests speed and accuracy in filing, classifying and checking. Group Test 64 (GT64) is a test of spelling. Group Test 66A (GT66A) is a two part test of attainment in arithmetic. Examiner required. Suitable for group use. BRITISH PUBLISHER

Timed: Various timings per test

Range: Adults of above-average educational attainment

Scoring: Hand key

Cost: Contact publisher.

Publisher: NFER-Nelson Publishing Company

NUTRITION KNOWLEDGE AND INTEREST QUESTIONNAIRE
G. Darrell Passwater

child, teen   grades 9-12

Purpose: Assesses high school students' knowledge of nutrition and determines what else they want to know in that area. Used for high school curriculum planning.

Description: 56 item paper-pencil test consists of 50 multiple-choice questions and six written answer items covering six general areas, as follows: (1) Physical, mental, emotional, social, and economic factors

affecting an individual's diet; (2) interprets relationships between nutritional status and disease; (3) assesses the interrelationships of diet, activity and other factors that regulate weight control; (4) distinguishes between food fads and fallacies and those diets based on scientific principles of nutrition; (5) examines emergency trends in society that influence dietary patterns; and (6) develops a plan of nutritional behaviors that promote health. Materials include test booklets, manual and answer sheet. Examiner required. Suitable for group use.

Untimed: Not available

Range: Grades 9-12 (and general use with adult population)

Scoring: Examiner evaluated

Cost: Complete kit (includes 35 student test booklets, 35 test answer sheets, 1 teacher's manual/answer key) $13.95; 35 student answer sheets $2.95; teacher's manual/answer key $1.95

Publisher: Teacher College Press

THE OHIO VOCATIONAL ACHIEVEMENT TEST PROGRAM

teen   grades 11-12

Purpose: Measures senior high school students' abilities and understanding of specific vocational areas. Used to evaluate teaching objectives and materials and for counseling and program supervision.

Description: Tests junior and senior vocational high school students in 11 vocational areas. Part of a test battery package which includes the California Short Form Test of Academic Aptitude (SFTAA). The complete battery, to be administered on any three consecutive days during the first three weeks of March in Ohio (non-Ohio at all times), reveals the correlation of student academic and vocational aptitude. Measures student ability to solve problems, analyze data, use abstractions in specific situations and assemble parts to form a complete structure. Also assesses student knowledge of principles and specifics. Test booklets are controlled and must be returned after use. Examiner required. Suitable for group use.

Timed: SFTAA, 1 hour; Parts I and II 2½ hours each

Range: Grades 11 and 12 in secondary vocational programs

Scoring: Computer scoring provided

Cost: Testing loan service (includes test booklets, answer sheets, scoring service). Ohio students $1.25 each; out of state students $2.50 each for March administration, $3.50 at other times.

Publisher: Instructional Materials Laboratory: The Ohio State University

metric patterns. Each test is timed separately. They precede the Ohio Vocational Achievement Tests which together complete the battery package. The battery is administered any three consecutive days during the first three weeks of March in Ohio. Non-Ohio at all times. The test booklet, answer document and instruction booklet are controlled items to be returned after use. Examiner required. Suitable for group use.

Timed: 1 hour

Range: Grades 11 and 12 in secondary vocational programs

Scoring: Computer scoring provided

Cost: Testing loan service (includes test booklets, answer sheets, scoring service). Ohio students $1.25 each; out of state students $2.50 each for March administration, $3.50 at other times.

Publisher: Instructional Materials Laboratory: The Ohio State University

---

THE OHIO VOCATIONAL ACHIEVEMENT TEST PROGRAM CALIFORNIA SHORT FORM TEST OF ACADEMIC APTITUDE, LEVEL 5 (SFTAA)

teen   grades 11-12

Purpose: Helps evaluate student comprehension word and idea relationships. Used in senior high school vocational programs to evaluate achievement and provide motivation.

Description: 85 item paper-pencil, multiple-choice test in two parts. The Language section contains a 25- item test of word meaning, verbal comprehension and word relationships; and a 20-item memory test based on a story read to students. The Non-Language section consists of a 20-item analogies test of literal or symbolic relationships and a 20-item sequence test of numerical and geo-

---

THE OHIO VOCATIONAL ACHIEVEMENT TESTS in AGRICULTURAL EDUCATION--AGRICULTURAL BUSINESS

teen   grades 11-12

Purpose: Evaluates and diagnoses achievement for instructional improvement in agricultural business. May be used for vocational guidance in an overall program.

Description: 300 item two-part paper-pencil test: Part I in 5 sections, 146 items, covers: 1) Agricultural Careers, 2) Human Relations, 3) Office Procedures, 4) Agricultural Service-Animals and 5) Advertising and Promotions. Part II in 4 sections, 162 items, contains 6) Agricultural Services-Plants, 7) Sales, 8) Marketing and Storage and 9) Money Management. Administered to groups.

Timed: Parts I and II, 2½ hours each

Range: Grades 11 and 12 in secondary vocational programs

Scoring: Computer scoring provided

Cost: Testing loan service (includes test booklets, answer sheets, scoring service). Ohio students $1.25 each; out of state students $2.50 each for March administration, $3.50 at other times.

Publisher: Instructional Materials Laboratory: The Ohio State University

THE OHIO VOCATIONAL ACHIEVEMENT TESTS in AGRICULTURAL EDUCA-TION--AGRICULTURAL MECHANIC

teen   grades 11-12

Purpose: Evaluates and diagnoses achievement for instructional improvement in agricultural mechanics. May be used for vocational guidance in an overall program.

Description: 343 item paper-pencil, multiple-choice test in two parts. Part I (7 sections, 167 items) covers: engine service and repair, carburetions systems, diesel engines, cooling systems, hydraulic systems, brakes and steering, and equipment assembly. Part II (7 sections, 176 items) covers: charging systems and accessories, cranking systems, ignition systems, power trains and transmissions, metal fabrication and refinishing, heating, ventilation and air conditioning, and personal development. Test is part of Ohio Vocational Test package which includes the California Short Form Test of Academic Aptitude, Level 5. Examiner required. Suitable for group use.

Timed: Parts I and II, 2½ hours each

Range: Grades 11 and 12 in secondary vocational programs

Scoring: Computer scoring provided

Cost: Testing loan service (includes test booklets, answer sheets, scoring service). Ohio students $1.25 each; out of state students $2.50 each for March administration, $3.50 at other times.

Publisher: Instructional Materials Laboratory: The Ohio State University

THE OHIO VOCATIONAL ACHIEVEMENT TESTS in AGRICULTURAL EDUCA-TION--FARM MANAGEMENT

teen   grades 11-12

Purpose: Evaluates and diagnoses achievement for instructional improvement in farm management. May be used for vocational guidance in an overall program.

Description: 304 item paper-pencil, multiple-choice test. Part I (5 sections, 137 items) covers: plan and work supervision, farm record analysis, buildings and structures, finance operations, and inventory. Part II (6 sections, 167 items) covers: planning crop enterprises, marketing products, planning livestock enterprises, equipment and machinery, general management duties, and employment procedures. Test accompanies the California Short Form Test of Academic Aptitude, Level 5. Examiner required. Suitable for group use.

Timed: Parts I and II, 2½ hours each

Range: Grades 11 and 12 in secondary vocational programs

Scoring: Computer scoring provided

Cost: Testing loan service (includes test booklets, answer sheets, scoring service). Ohio students $1.25 each; out of state students $2.50 each for March administration, $3.50 at other times.

Publisher: Instructional Materials Laboratory: The Ohio State University

THE OHIO VOCATIONAL ACHIEVEMENT TESTS in AGRICULTURAL EDUCATION--HORTICULTURE

teen   grades 11-12

Purpose: Evaluates and diagnoses achievement for instructional improvement in horticulture. May be used for vocational guidance in an overall program.

Description: 349 item paper-pencil, multiple-choice test in two parts. Part I (6 sections, 181 items) covers: soil and plant science, production floriculture, retail floriculture, garden center, personal development, and fruit and vegetable production. Part II (4 sections, 168 items) covers: turf services, nursery, landscaping, and equipment and mechanics. Examiner required. Suitable for group use.

Timed: Parts I and II, 2½ hours each

Range: Grades 11 and 12 in secondary vocational programs

Scoring: Computer scoring provided

Cost: Testing loan service (includes test booklets, answer sheets, scoring service). Ohio students $1.25 each; out of state students $2.50 each for March administration, $3.50 at other times.

Publisher: Instructional Materials Laboratory: The Ohio State University

THE OHIO VOCATIONAL ACHIEVEMENT TESTS in AGRICULTURAL EDUCATION--PRODUCTION AGRICULTURE

teen   grades 11-12

Purpose: Evaluates and diagnoses achievement for instructional improvement in production agriculture. May be used for vocational guidance in an overall program.

Description: 353 item paper-pencil, multiple-choice test in two parts. Part I (6 sections, 177 items) covers: beef production, sheep production, soybean production, crop chemical application, and agriculture instruction. Part II (6 sections, 176 items) covers: operator equipment maintenance, diary production, corn production, swine production, forage production, and employment procedures. Examiner required. Suitable for groups use.

Timed: Parts I and II, 2½ hours each

Range: Grades 11 and 12 in secondary vocational programs

Scoring: Computer scoring provided

Cost: Testing loan service (includes test booklets, answer sheets, scoring service). Ohio students $1.25 each; out of state students $2.50 each for March administration, $3.50 at other times.

Publisher: Instructional Materials Laboratory: The Ohio State University

THE OHIO VOCATIONAL ACHIEVEMENT TESTS in BUSINESS AND OFFICE EDUCATION-- ACCOUNTING/ COMPUTING CLERK

teen   grades 11-12

Purpose: Evaluates and diagnoses achievement for instructional improvement in accounting/computing clerk area. May be used for vocational guidance in an overall program.

Description: 321 item paper-pencil, multiple-choice test in two parts. Part I (5 sections, 159 items) covers: sales and receivables, payroll records, maintaining inventory records and files, completing the accounting cycle, and worksheet information. Part II (5 sections, 162 items) covers: processing purchases and payables, specialized accounting and office functions, cash receipts and payments, mechanical and electronic data accounting and employment procedures. Examiner required. Suitable for group use.

Timed: Parts I and II, 2½ hours each

Range: Grades 11 and 12 in secondary vocational programs

Scoring: Computer scoring provided

Cost: Testing loan service (includes test booklets, answer sheets, scoring service). Ohio students $1.25 each; out of state students $2.50 each for March administration, $3.50 at other times.

Publisher: Instructional Materials Laboratory: The Ohio State University

---

THE OHIO VOCATIONAL ACHIEVEMENT TESTS in BUSINESS AND OFFICE EDUCATION--CLERK-STENOGRAPHER

teen   grades 11-12

Purpose: Evaluates and diagnoses achievement for instructional improvement in clerk-stenographer area. May be used for vocational guidance in an overall program.

Description: 278 item two-part, paper-pencil, multiple- choice test. Part I (3 sections, 159 items) covers:

dictation, correspondence and financial records. Part II (4 sections, 119 items) covers: communications, copy reproduction, record management, and personal development-employment. Examiner required. Suitable for group use.

Timed: Parts I and II, 2½ hours each

Range: Grades 11 and 12 in secondary vocational programs

Scoring: Computer scoring provided

Cost: Testing loan service (includes test booklets, answer sheets, scoring service). Ohio students $1.25 each; out of state students $2.50 each for March administration, $3.50 at other times.

Publisher: Instructional Materials Laboratory: The Ohio State University

---

THE OHIO VOCATIONAL ACHIEVEMENT TESTS in BUSINESS AND OFFICE EDUCATION--CLERK TYPIST

teen   grades 11-12

Purpose: Evaluate and diagnoses achievement for instructional improvement in clerk typing programs. May be used for vocational guidance in an overall program.

Description: 332 item two-part, paper-pencil, multiple-choice test. Part I (5 sections, 164 items) covers: letters, envelopes and memos, filing, proofreading and editing, mail procedures, employment procedures and human relations. Part II (5 sections, 168 itesm) covers: reports, manuscripts and forms, accounting/calculating, telephone and receptionist, machine transcription/word processing, reprographics. Examiner required. Suitable for group use.

Timed: Parts I and II, 2½ hours each

Range: Grades 11 and 12 in secondary vocational programs

Scoring: Computer scoring provided

Cost: Testing loan service (includes test booklets, answer sheets, scoring service). Ohio students $1.25 each; out of state students $2.50 each for March administration, $3.50 at other times.

Publisher: Instructional Materials Laboratory: The Ohio State University

THE OHIO VOCATIONAL ACHIEVEMENT TESTS in BUSINESS AND OFFICE EDUCATION--DATA PROCESSING

teen   grades 11-12

Purpose: Evaluates and diagnoses achievement for instructional improvement in data processing. May be used for vocational guidance in an overall program.

Description: 346 item two-part, paper-pencil, multiple- choice test. Part I (5 sections, 166 items) covers: computer systems, clerical procedures, programming languages, human relations, and automated electronic D.P. equipment. Part II (5 sections, 180 items) covers: flow charting, data entry, operations, business math-accounting, and employment procedures. Examiner required. Suitable for group use.

Timed: Parts I and II, 2½ hours each

Range: Grades 11 and 12 in secondary vocational programs

Scoring: Computer scoring provided

Cost: Testing loan service (includes test booklets, answer sheets, scoring service). Ohio students $1.25 each; out of state students $2.50 each for March administration, $3.50 at other times.

Publisher: Instructional Materials Laboratory: The Ohio State University

THE OHIO VOCATIONAL ACHIEVEMENT TESTS in BUSINESS AND OFFICE EDUCATION--GENERAL OFFICE CLERK

teen   grades 11-12

Purpose: Evaluates and diagnoses achievement for instructional improvement in general office area. May be used for vocational guidance in an overall program.

Description: 285 item paper-pencil, multiple-choice test in two parts. Part I (5 sections, 148 items) covers: typing forms and reports, reprographics, employment seeking, composition and editing, and records management. Part II (6 sections, 137 items) covers: receptionist duties, letters and correspondence, financial records, telephone communications, word processing, and accounting functions. Examiner required. Suitable for group use.

Timed: Parts I and II, 2½ hours each

Range: Grades 11 and 12 in secondary vocational programs

Scoring: Computer scoring provided

Cost: Testing loan service (includes test booklets, answer sheets, scoring service). Ohio students $1.25 each; out of state students $2.50 each for March administration, $3.50 at other times.

Publisher: Instructional Materials Laboratory: The Ohio State University

THE OHIO VOCATIONAL ACHIEVEMENT TESTS in BUSINESS AND OFFICE EDUCATION--WORD PROCESSING

teen   grades 11-12

Purpose: Evaluates and diagnoses achievement for instructional improvement in word processing. May by used for vocational guidance in an overall program.

Description: 345 item paper-pencil, multiple-choice test in two parts. Part I (5 sections, 170 items) covers: typing and transcription, reprographics, word processing concepts and procedures, business transactions, and proofreading and editing. Part II (5 sections, 175 items) covers: automated wordprocessing equipment, receptionist duties, composition and dictation, records management, and employment procedures. Examiner required. Suitable for groups use.

Timed: Parts I and II, 2½ hours each

Range: Grades 11 and 12 in secondary vocational programs

Scoring: Computer scoring provided

Cost: Testing loan service (includes test booklets, answer sheets, scoring service). Ohio students $1.25 each; out of state students $2.50 each for March administration, $3.50 at other times.

Publisher: Instructional Materials Laboratory: The Ohio State University

THE OHIO VOCATIONAL ACHIEVEMENT TESTS in CONSTRUCTION TRADES-- CARPENTRY

teen   grades 11-12

Purpose: Evaluates and diagnoses achievement for instructional improvement in carpentry. May be used for vocational guidance in an overall program.

Description: 325 item paper-pencil, multiple-choice, two part test. Part I (7 sections, 159 items) covers: blueprint reading, surveying, foundations, floor framing, wall and ceiling framing, insulation, and mathematics and estimating. Part II

(4 sections, 166 items) covers: roof framing, roofing, exterior finish, and interior finish. Examiner required. Suitable for group use.

Timed: Parts I and II, 2½ hours each

Range: Grades 11 and 12 in secondary vocational programs

Scoring: Computer scoring provided

Cost: Testing loan service (includes test booklets, answer sheets, scoring service). Ohio students $1.25 each; out of state students $2.50 each for March administration, $3.50 at other times.

Publisher: Instructional Materials Laboratory: The Ohio State University

THE OHIO VOCATIONAL ACHIEVEMENT TESTS in CONSTRUCTION TRADES-- CONSTRUCTION ELECTRICITY

teen   grades 11-12

Purpose: Evaluates and diagnoses achievement for instructional improvement in construction electricity. May be used for vocational guidance in an overall program.

Description: 317 item paper-pencil, multiple-choice, two- part test. Part I (5 sections, 158 items) covers: basic electricity, National Electric Code, planning and layout, rough-in wiring, and finish wiring. Part II (6 section, 159 items) covers: safety, service entrance, motors and controls, low voltage systems, electricians' mathematics, and tools and personal development. Examiner required. Suitable for group use.

Timed: Parts I and II, 2½ hours each

Range: Grades 11 and 12 in secondary vocational programs

Scoring: Computer scoring provided

Cost: Testing loan service (includes test booklets, answer sheets, scoring service). Ohio students $1.25 each; out of state students $2.50 each for March administration, $3.50 at other times.

Publisher: Instructional Materials Laboratory: The Ohio State University

THE OHIO VOCATIONAL ACHIEVEMENT TESTS in CONSTRUCTION TRADES--HEATING, AIR CONDITIONING AND REFRIGERATION

teen   grades 11-12

Purpose: Evaluates and diagnoses achievement for instructional improvement in heating, air conditioning and refrigeration. May be used for vocational guidance in an overall program.

Description: 302 item two-part, paper-pencil, multiple- choice test. Part I (4 sections, 151 items) covers: installing refrigeration and air conditioning equipment, troubleshooting refrigeration and air conditioning equipment- electrical, troubleshooting refrigeration and air conditioning equipment-mechanical, and service and repair of refrigeration and air conditioning equipment-electrical. Part II (6 sections, 151 items) covers: service and repair of refrigeration and air conditioning equipment- mechanical, installing warm air heating systems, troubleshooting warm air heating-electrical, troubleshooting warm air heating systems- mechanical, service and repair warm air heating systems-mechanical, service and repair warm air heating systems-electrical. Examiner required. Suitable for group use.

Timed: Parts I and II, 2½ hours each

Range: Grades 11 and 12 in secondary vocational programs

Scoring: Computer scoring provided

Cost: Testing loan service (includes test booklets, answer sheets, scoring service). Ohio students $1.25 each; out of state students $2.50 each for March administration, $3.50 at other times.

Publisher: Instructional Materials Laboratory: The Ohio State University

THE OHIO VOCATIONAL ACHIEVEMENT TESTS in CONSTRUCTION TRADES--MASONRY

teen   grades 11-12

Purpose: Evaluates and diagnoses achievement for instructional improvement in masonry. May be used for vocational guidance in an overall program.

Description: 299 item paper-pencil, multiple-choice test in two parts. Part I (5 sections, 154 items) covers: job site and material preparation, lay brick and block to a line, lay brick and block with a plumb rule, fireplaces and chimneys, arches. Part II (5 sections, 145 items) covers: miscellaneous masonry construction, concrete masonry, surveying, mathematics and blueprint reading, and personal development. Examiner required. Suitable for group use.

Timed: Parts I and II, 2½ hours each

Range: Grades 11 and 12 in secondary vocational programs

Scoring: Computer scoring provided

Cost: Testing loan service (includes test booklets, answer sheets, scoring service). Ohio students $1.25 each; out of state students $2.50 each for March administration, $3.50 at other times.

Publisher: Instructional Materials Laboratory: The Ohio State University

THE OHIO VOCATIONAL ACHIEVEMENT TESTS in DISTRIBUTIVE EDUCATION-- APPAREL AND ACCESSORIES

teen   grades 11-12

Purpose: Evaluates and diagnoses achievement for instructional improvement in apparel and accessories. May be used for vocational guidance in an overall program.

Description: 346 item paper-pencil, multiple-choice test in two parts. Part I (5 sections, 174 items) covers: cashiering, merchandise display, sales, stock-keeping and inventory control, and first line management. Part II (5 sections, 172 items) covers: product knowledge, receiving and marking merchandise, support functions, customer services and obtain employment. Examiner required. Suitable for group use.

Timed: Parts I and II, 2½ hours each

Range: Grades 11 and 12 in secondary vocational programs

Scoring: Computer scoring provided

Cost: Testing loan service (includes test booklets, answer sheets, scoring service). Ohio students $1.25 each; out of state students $2.50 each for March administration, $3.50 at other times.

Publisher: Instructional Materials Laboratory: The Ohio State University

THE OHIO VOCATIONAL ACHIEVEMENT TESTS in DISTRIBUTIVE EDUCATION-- FOOD MARKETING

teen   grades 11-12

Purpose: Evaluates and diagnoses achievement for instructional improvement in food marketing. May be used for vocational guidance in an overall program.

Description: 383 item paper-pencil, multiple-choice test in two parts. Part I (5 sections, 188 items) covers: employment procedures, human relations, business principles, communications, and financial operations. Part II (6 sections, 195 items) covers: public relations, service technology, product information, pricing, operations, and advertising and display. Examiner required. Suitable for group use.

Timed: Parts I and II, 2½ hours each

Range: Grades 11 and 12 in secondary vocational programs

Scoring: Computer scoring provided

Cost: Testing loan service (includes test booklets, answer sheets, scoring service). Ohio students $1.25 each; out of state students $2.50 each for March administration, $3.50 at other times.

Publisher: Instructional Materials Laboratory: The Ohio State University

THE OHIO VOCATIONAL ACHIEVEMENT TESTS in DISTRIBUTIVE EDUCATION-- FOOD SERVICE PERSONNEL

teen   grades 11-12

Purpose: Evaluates and diagnoses achievement for instructional improvement in food service. May be used for vocational guidance in an overall program.

Description: 316 item paper-pencil, multiple-choice test in two parts. Part I (5 sections, 154 items) covers: restaurant management, inventory and purchasing procedures, business principles, waiter- waitressing, and cashiering. Part II (7 sections, 162 items) covers: employment procedures, human relations, communications, selling principles, advertising, product-service information, and safety and housekeeping.

Examiner required. Suitable for group use.

Timed: Parts I and II, 2½ hours each

Range: Grades 11 and 12 in secondary vocational programs

Scoring: Computer scoring provided

Cost: Testing loan service (includes test booklets, answer sheets, scoring service). Ohio students $1.25 each; out of state students $2.50 each for March administration, $3.50 at other times.

Publisher: Instructional Materials Laboratory: The Ohio State University

THE OHIO VOCATIONAL ACHIEVEMENT TESTS in DISTRIBUTIVE EDUCATION-- GENERAL MERCHANDISING

teen   grades 11-12

Purpose: Evaluates and diagnoses achievement for instructional improvement in general merchandising. May be used for vocational guidance in an overall program.

Description: 352 item paper-pencil, multiple-choice test in two parts. Part I (6 sections, 188 items) covers: employment procedures, human relations, business principles, communications, and financial transactions. Part II (7 sections, 164 items) covers: selling, marketing, cashiering, inventory procedures, housekeeping and security, advertising and display, and product and service technology. Examiner required. Suitable for group use.

Timed: Parts I and II, 2½ hours each

Range: Grades 11 and 12 in secondary vocational programs

Scoring: Computer scoring provided

Cost: Testing loan service (includes test booklets, answer sheets, scoring service). Ohio students $1.25 each; out of state students $2.50 each for March administration, $3.50 at other times.

Publisher: Instructional Materials Laboratory: The Ohio State University

THE OHIO VOCATIONAL ACHIEVEMENT TESTS in ELECTRONICS--COMMUNICA- TION PRODUCTS ELECTRONICS

teen   grades 11-12

Purpose: Evaluates and diagnoses achievement for instructional improvement in industrial electronics. May be used for vocational guidance in an overall program.

Description: 338 item paper-pencil, multiple-choice test in two parts. Part I (6 sections, 176 items) covers: personal development, DC electronics, AC electronics, active electronic devices, electronic circuitry and electronic test equipment. Part II (7 section, 162 items) covers: audio systems, radio receiver, TV receiver systems, transmitter systems, antenna and transmission systems and digital logic systems. Examiner required. Suitable for groups use.

Timed: Parts I and II, 2½ hours each

Range: Grades 11 and 12 in secondary vocational programs

Scoring: Computer scoring provided

Cost: Testing loan service (includes test booklets, answer sheets, scoring service). Ohio students $1.25 each; out of state students $2.50 each for March administration, $3.50 at other times.

Publisher: Instructional Materials Laboratory: The Ohio State University

THE OHIO VOCATIONAL ACHIEVEMENT TESTS in ELECTRONICS--INDUSTRIAL ELECTRONICS

teen   grades 11-12

Purpose: Evaluates and diagnoses achievement for instructional improvement in industrial electronics. May be used for vocational guidance in an overall program.

Description: 326 item, two-part, paper-pencil, multiple- choice test. Part I (7 sections, 168 items) covers: personal development; selling, installating and testing equipment; fabricate circuits and enclosures; DC electronics; AC electronics; semiconductors; and test equipment. Part II (6 sections, 158 items) covers: analog electronic equipment, digital logic, digital electronic circuits, troubleshooting and analysis, special electronic devices, and electromechanical devices. Examiner required. Suitable for groups use.

Timed: Parts I and II, 2½ hours each

Range: Grades 11 and 12 in secondary vocational programs

Scoring: Computer scoring provided

Cost: Testing loan service (includes test booklets, answer sheets, scoring service). Ohio students $1.25 each; out of state students $2.50 each for March administration, $3.50 at other times.

Publisher: Instructional Materials Laboratory: The Ohio State University

THE OHIO VOCATIONAL ACHIEVEMENT TESTS in GRAPHICS COMMUNICATION--COMMERICAL ART

teen   grades 11-12

Purpose: Evaluates and diagnoses achievement for instructional improvement in commercial art. May be used for vocational guidance in an overall program.

Description: 311 item, two-part, paper-pencil, multiple- choice test. Part I (5 sections, 153 items) covers: drawing, design, illustration, technique, and color. Part II (5 sections, 158 items) covers: drafting, mechanical, photography, layout, and typography. Examiner required. Suitable for group use.

Timed: Parts I and II, 2½ hours each

Range: Grades 11 and 12 in secondary vocational programs

Scoring: Computer scoring provided

Cost: Testing loan service (includes test booklets, answer sheets, scoring service). Ohio students $1.25 each; out of state students $2.50 each for March administration, $3.50 at other times.

Publisher: Instructional Materials Laboratory: The Ohio State University

THE OHIO VOCATIONAL ACHIEVEMENT TESTS in GRAPHICS COMMUNICATION--DRAFTING

teen   grades 11-12

Purpose: Evaluates and diagnoses achievement for instructional improvement in drafting. May be used for vocational guidance in an overall program.

Description: 320 item paper-pencil, multiple-choice test in two parts. Part I (10 sections, 170 items) covers: geometric drawing, orthographic projection, pictorial drawing, sectional views, auxiliary views, drafting materials, equipment and reproduction methods, dimensioning, production- working drawings, fastening methods, and industrial materials and processes. Part II (7 sections, 150 items) covers: intersections and developments, mechanisms, architectural drawings, structural drawings, electrical drawings, civil engineering drawings, and mathematics. Examiner required. Suitable for group use.

Timed: Parts I and II, 2½ hours each

Range: Grades 11 and 12 in secondary vocational programs

Scoring: Computer scoring provided

Cost: Testing loan service (includes test booklets, answer sheets, scoring service). Ohio students $1.25 each; out of state students $2.50 each for March administration, $3.50 at other times.

Publisher: Instructional Materials Laboratory: The Ohio State University

THE OHIO VOCATIONAL ACHIEVEMENT TESTS in GRAPHICS COMMUNICATION--LITHOGRAPHIC PRINTING

teen   grades 11-12

Purpose: Evaluates and diagnoses achievement for instructional improvement in lithographic printing. May be used for vocational guidance in an overall program.

Description: 318 item paper-pencil, multiple-choice test in two parts. Part I (6 sections, 169 items) covers: layout and design, composing, paste up, proofing, camera and film processing, and stripping. Part II (3 sections, 149 items) covers: platemaking and proofs, off-set presses, and finishing operations. Examiner required. Suitable for group use.

Timed: Parts I and II, 2½ hours each

Range: Grades 11 and 12 in secondary vocational programs

Scoring: Computer scoring provided

Cost: Testing loan service (includes

test booklets, answer sheets, scoring service). Ohio students $1.25 each; out of state students $2.50 each for March administration, $3.50 at other times.

Publisher: Instructional Materials Laboratory: The Ohio State University

THE OHIO VOCATIONAL ACHIEVEMENT TESTS in HEALTH OCCUPATIONS EDUCATION--DENTAL ASSISTING

teen   grades 11-12

Purpose: Evaluates and diagnoses achievement for instructional improvement in dental assistant. May be used for vocational guidance in an overall program.

Description: 344 item, two-part, paper-pencil, multiple- choice test. Part I (7 sections, 167 items) covers: anatomy, microbiology and sterilization, dental emergencies and pharmacology, dental laboratory, restorative and impression materials, preventive dentistry, and ethics and personal development. Part II (7 sections, 177 items) covers: radiology, dental office management, chairside assisting-basic, chairside assisting-prosthetics, chairside assisting-oral surgery and pathology, chairside assisting-other specialties, and expanded duties. Examiner required. Suitable for group use.

Timed: Parts I and II, 2½ hours each

Range: Grades 11 and 12 in secondary vocational programs

Scoring: Computer scoring provided

Cost: Testing loan service (includes test booklets, answer sheets, scoring service). Ohio students $1.25 each; out of state students $2.50 each for March administration, $3.50 at other times.

Publisher: Instructional Materials Laboratory: The Ohio State

University

THE OHIO VOCATIONAL ACHIEVEMENT TESTS in HEALTH OCCUPATIONS EDUCATION--DIVERSIFIED HEALTH OCCUPATION

teen   grades 11-12

Purpose: Evaluates and diagnoses achievement for instructional improvement in health occupation areas. May be used for vocational guidance in an overall program.

Description: 288 item paper-pencil, multiple-choice test in two parts. Part I (7 sections, 125 items) covers: orientation, emergency first aid, dental assisting skills, medical assisting skills, communications and office skills, laboratory skills, and preparing for the world of work. Part II (9 sections, 155 items) covers: asepsis, vital signs, positioning and draping, physical examinations, transfer and ambulation, patient units, patient personal care, pre-op care, and emergencies. Examiner required. Suitable for group use.

Timed: Parts I and II, 2½ hours each

Range: Grades 11 and 12 in secondary vocational programs

Scoring: Computer scoring provided

Cost: Testing loan service (includes test booklets, answer sheets, scoring service). Ohio students $1.25 each; out of state students $2.50 each for March administration, $3.50 at other times.

Publisher: Instructional Materials Laboratory: The Ohio State University

THE OHIO VOCATIONAL ACHIEVEMENT TESTS in HEALTH OCCUPATIONS EDUCATION--MEDICAL ASSISTING

teen   grades 11-12

Purpose: Evaluates and diagnoses achievement for instructional improvement in medical assistant areas. May be used for vocational guidance in an overall program.

Description: 339 item, two-part, paper-pencil, multiple-choice test. Part I (5 section, 170 items) covers: personal development, body systems, clinical skills, medications, and medical office skills. Part II (8 sections, 169 items) covers: sterilization, laboratory skills, E.K.G., X-ray, diet and nutrition, first aid, medical terminology, and medical office computation. Examiner required. Suitable for group use.

Timed: Parts I and II, 2½ hours each

Range: Grades 11 and 12 in secondary vocational programs

Scoring: Computer scoring provided

Cost: Testing loan service (includes test booklets, answer sheets, scoring service). Ohio students $1.25 each; out of state students $2.50 each for March administration, $3.50 at other times.

Publisher: Instructional Materials Laboratory: The Ohio State University

THE OHIO VOCATIONAL ACHIEVEMENT TESTS in HOME ECONOMICS EDUCATION--COMMUNITY AND HOME SERVICES

teen   grades 11-12

Purpose: Evaluates and diagnoses achievement for instructional improvement in community and home services. May be used for vocational guidance in an overall program.

Description: 354 item two-part, paper-pencil, multiple-choice test. Part I (6 sections, 179 items) covers: personal care for patient, vital signs, lift, move and transport patients, special care, infant and child care, and food service. Part II (9 sections, 175 items) covers: care of cleaning equipment, care of furnishings, care of resilient and masonry floors, care of draperies, upholstery and carpeting, room care, care of restrooms, care of public areas, laundry service, and careers and employment. Examiner required. Suitable for group use.

Timed: Parts I and II, 2½ hours each

Range: Grades 11 and 12 in secondary vocational programs

Scoring: Computer scoring provided

Cost: Testing loan service (includes test booklets, answer sheets, scoring service). Ohio students $1.25 each; out of state students $2.50 each for March administration, $3.50 at other times.

Publisher: Instructional Materials Laboratory: The Ohio State University

THE OHIO VOCATIONAL ACHIEVEMENT TESTS in HOME ECONOMICS EDUCATION--FABRIC SERVICE

teen   grades 11-12

Purpose: Evaluates and diagnoses achievement for instructional improvement in fabric services. May be used for vocational guidance in an overall program.

Description: 391 item, two-part, paper-pencil, multiple-choice test. Part I (7 sections, 184 items) covers: alteration specialist, custom dressmaker, custom tailor, fabric

coordinator, fashion coordinator, power machine operator, and dry cleaner. Part II (8 sections, 187 items) covers: interior design specialist, drapery consultant, drapery maker, drapery installer, slipcover maker, upholsterer, refinisher, and careers and employment. Examiner required. Suitable for group use.

Timed: Parts I and II, 2½ hours each

Range: Grades 11 and 12 in secondary vocational programs

Scoring: Computer scoring provided

Cost: Testing loan service (includes test booklets, answer sheets, scoring service). Ohio students $1.25 each; out of state students $2.50 each for March administration, $3.50 at other times.

Publisher: Instructional Materials Laboratory: The Ohio State University

THE OHIO VOCATIONAL ACHIEVEMENT TESTS in HOME ECONOMICS EDUCATION--FOOD SERVICES

teen   grades 11-12

Purpose: Evaluates and diagnoses achievement for instructional improvement in food services. May be used for vocational guidance in an overall program.

Description: 376 item paper-pencil, multiple-choice, two-part test. Part I (5 sections, 185 items) covers: baker, cook-chef, pantry worker, caterer, and dietary aide. Part II (5 sections, 191 items) covers: dining room service, cafeteria line, sanitation and safety, storeroom operations, and careers and employment. Examiner required. Suitable for group use.

Timed: Parts I and II, 2½ hours each

Range: Grades 11 and 12 in secondary vocational programs

Scoring: Computer scoring provided

Cost: Testing loan service (includes test booklets, answer sheets, scoring service). Ohio students $1.25 each; out of state students $2.50 each for March administration, $3.50 at other times.

Publisher: Instructional Materials Laboratory: The Ohio State University

THE OHIO VOCATIONAL ACHIEVEMENT TESTS in HOME ECONOMICS EDUCATION--NURSERY SCHOOL TEACHER AIDE

teen grades 11-12

Purpose: Evaluates and diagnoses achievement for instructional improvement in nursery school teacher aide programs. May be used for vocational guidance in an overall program.

Description: 269 item paper-pencil, multiple-choice test in two parts. Part I (7 sections, 146 items) covers: child care careers, center administration, maintenance, program planning, evaluation, special need children, and health and safety. Part II (5 sections, 123 items) covers: activity selection, structured activity preparation, unstructured activity supervision, routine activity supervision, and nutrition and snacks. Examiner required. Suitable for group use.

Timed: Parts I and II, 2½ hours each

Range: Grades 11 and 12 in secondary vocational programs

Scoring: Computer scoring provided

Cost: Testing loan service (includes test booklets, answer sheets, scoring service). Ohio students $1.25 each; out of state students $2.50 each for March administration, $3.50 at other times.

Publisher: Instructional Materials Laboratory: The Ohio State University

THE OHIO VOCATIONAL ACHIEVEMENT TESTS in METAL TRADES--MACHINE TRADES

teen grades 11-12

Purpose: Evaluates and diagnoses achievement for instructional improvement in machine trades. May be used for vocational guidance in an overall program.

Description: 306 item, two-part, paper-pencil, multiple- choice test. Part I (6 sections, 146 items) covers: orientation, bench work, power sawing, drilling machines, lathes, and blueprint reading. Part II (6 sections, 160 items) covers: milling machine, shaper-planer, abrasive machining, heat treating and applied metallurgy, applied match, and applied science. Examiner required. Suitable for group use.

Timed: Parts I and II, 2½ hours each

Range: Grades 11 and 12 in secondary vocational programs

Scoring: Computer scoring provided

Cost: Testing loan service (includes test booklets, answer sheets, scoring service). Ohio students $1.25 each; out of state students $2.50 each for March administration, $3.50 at other times.

Publisher: Instructional Materials Laboratory: The Ohio State University

THE OHIO VOCATIONAL ACHIEVEMENT TESTS in METAL TRADES--WELDING

teen grades 11-12

Purpose: Evaluates and diagnoses achievement for instructional improvement in welding. May be used for vocational guidance in an overall program.

Description: 333 item, two-part, paper-pencil, multiple- choice test. Part I (3 sections, 168 items) covers: labor and management, oxyacetylene welding, and shielded metal arc welding. Part II (4 sections, 165 items) covers: tungsten arc welding, gas metal arc welding, resistance welding, and blueprint and math. Examiner required. Suitable for group use.

Timed: Parts I and II, 2½ hours each

Range: Grades 11 and 12 in secondary vocational programs

Scoring: Computer scoring provided

Cost: Testing loan service (includes test booklets, answer sheets, scoring service). Ohio students $1.25 each; out of state students $2.50 each for March administration, $3.50 at other times.

Publisher: Instructional Materials Laboratory: The Ohio State University

THE OHIO VOCATIONAL ACHIEVEMENT TESTS in PERSONAL SERVICES-- COSMETOLOGY

teen   grades 11-12

Purpose: Evaluates and diagnoses achievement for instructional improvement in Cosmetology. May be used for vocational guidance in an overall program.

Description: 338 item paper-pencil, multiple-choice test in two parts. Part I (6 sections, 173 items) covers: sanitation, scalp care, manicure, hair shaping, hair styling, and facials. Part II (4 sections, 165 items) covers: permanent waving, hair coloring, applied science, and shop management and mathematics. Examiner required. Suitable for group use.

Timed: Parts I and II, 2½ hours each

Range: Grades 11 and 12 in secondary vocational programs

Scoring: Computer scoring provided

Cost: Testing loan service (includes test booklets, answer sheets, scoring service). Ohio students $1.25 each; out of state students $2.50 each for March administration, $3.50 at other times.

Publisher: Instructional Materials Laboratory: The Ohio State University

THE OHIO VOCATIONAL ACHIEVEMENT TESTS in TRADE AND INDUSTRIAL EDUCATION: AUTOMOTIVE-- AUTO BODY MECHANIC

teen   grades 11-12

Purpose: Evaluates and diagnoses achievement for instructional improvement in auto body mechanics. May be used for vocational guidance in an overall program.

Description: 335 item paper-pencil, multiple-choice, two- part test. Part I (6 sections, 169 items) covers: welding, repair and straightening, patch and fill, fiberglass repair, panel replacement, and refinishing. Part II (8 sections, 166 items) covers: trim and hardware, glass replacement, frame and unit body repair, suspension systems, engine cooling systems, air conditioning, electrical systems, and shop management and operations. Examiner required. Suitable for group use.

Timed: Parts I and II, 2½ hours each

Range: Grades 11 and 12 in secondary vocational programs

Scoring: Computer scoring provided

Cost: Testing loan service (includes test booklets, answer sheets, scoring service). Ohio students $1.25 each; out of state students $2.50 each for

March administration, $3.50 at other times.

Publisher: Instructional Materials Laboratory: The Ohio State University

THE OHIO VOCATIONAL ACHIEVEMENT TESTS in TRADE AND INDUSTRIAL EDUCATION: AUTOMOTIVE-- AUTOMOTIVE MECHANICS

teen   grades 11-12

Purpose: Evaluates and diagnoses achievement for instructional improvement in automotive mechanics. May be used for vocational guidance in an overall program.

Description: 325 item paper-pencil, multiple-choice, two- part test. Part I (7 sections, 169 items) covers: service management, lubrication and preventive maintenance, engine service and repair, cooling systems, fuel and exhaust systems, ignition systems, and cranking systems. Part II (9 sections, 156 items) covers: charging systems, accessory systems, transmissions, drive line, emission systems, brake systems, steering systems, suspension systems, heating, ventilation and air conditioning systems. Examiner required. Suitable for group use.

Timed: Parts I and II, 2½ hours each

Range: Grades 11 and 12 in secondary vocational programs

Scoring: Computer scoring provided

Cost: Testing loan service (includes test booklets, answer sheets, scoring service). Ohio students $1.25 each; out of state students $2.50 each for March administration, $3.50 at other times.

Publisher: Instructional Materials Laboratory: The Ohio State University

THE OHIO VOCATIONAL ACHIEVEMENT TESTS in TRADE AND INDUSTRIAL EDUCATION: AUTOMOTIVE-- DIESEL MECHANIC

teen   grades 11-12

Purpose: Evaluates and diagnoses achievement for instructional improvement in industrial electronics. May be used for vocational guidance in an overall program.

Description: 332 item paper-pencil, multiple-choice test in two parts. Part I (6 sections, 168 items) covers: engine service and repair, fuel systems, intake systems, charging and cranking systems, electrical and ignition systems, hydraulic systems. Part II (8 sections, 164 items) covers: cooling systems, drive line, steering systems, suspension systems, brake systems, heating and air conditioning systems, lubrication and preventive maintenance, and service management. Examiner required. Suitable for group use.

Timed: Parts I and II, 2½ hours each

Range: Grades 11 and 12 in secondary vocational programs

Scoring: Computer scoring provided

Cost: Testing loan service (includes test booklets, answer sheets, scoring service). Ohio students $1.25 each; out of state students $2.50 each for March administration, $3.50 at other times.

Publisher: Instructional Materials Laboratory: The Ohio State University

THE OHIO VOCATIONAL ACHIEVEMENT TESTS in TRADE AND INDUSTRIAL EDUCATION: AUTOMOTIVE-- SMALL ENGINE REPAIR

teen   grades 11-12

Purpose: Evaluates and diagnoses achievement for instructional improvement in small engine repair. May be used for vocational guidance in an overall program.

Description: 332 item paper-pencil, multiple-choice test in two parts. Part I (7 sections, 170 items) covers: tools and fasteners, fuel and exhaust systems, cooling and lubrication systems, short block and governor systems, charging and electrical systems, starting systems, mechanics' mathematics. Part II (8 sections, 162 items) covers: ignition systems, valve train systems, troubleshooting, lawn and garden equipment, motorcycle equipment, marine equipment, snowmobile equipment, and business and shop operations. Examiner required. Suitable for group use.

Timed: Parts I and II, 2½ hours each

Range: Grades 11 and 12 in secondary vocational programs

Scoring: Computer scoring provided

Cost: Testing loan service (includes test booklets, answer sheets, scoring service). Ohio students $1.25 each; out of state students $2.50 each for March administration, $3.50 at other times.

Publisher: Instructional Materials Laboratory: The Ohio State University

SENIOR ENGLISH TEST

teen

Purpose: Assesses English skills. Specially designed for allocation of entrants to engineering courses.

Description: 56 item paper-pencil test of the following English skills: comprehension, vocabulary and written expression. Examiner required. Suitable for group use.
BRITISH PUBLISHER

Timed: 60 minutes

Range: Ages 16-18

Scoring: Hand key

Cost: 10 tests £1.95; manual £0.75 (payment in sterling for all overseas orders).

Publisher: NFER-Nelson Publishing Company

STUDENT OCCUPATIONAL COMPETENCY ACHIEVEMENT TESTING (SOCAT)

teen

Purpose: Measures achievement of students in vocational education programs. Used for grade assignment, identifying curriculum strengths and weaknesses, and evaluation of job applicants.

Description: Multiple item tests of skills and knowledge in 19 vocations fields: Accounting/Bookkeeping, Agricultural Mechanics, Auto Body, Auto Mechanics, Construction Electricity, Drafting, General Merchandising, General Office, Heating and Air Conditioning, Horticulture, Industrial Electronics, Machine Trades, Practical Nursing, Printing, Radio and TV Repair, Refrigeration, Sewn Products, Small Engine Repair, and Welding. Each SOCAT consists of two parts, written and performance. Written tests are multiple choice, and cover factual knowledge, technical information, understanding of principles, and problem solving abilities related to the occupation. The performance tests are administered in a laboratory, school shop, or clinical setting, and enables students to demonstrate knowledge and skills of competent craft persons. Mental aptitude tests are available for administration at same time as the competency test. Examiner required. Suitable for group use.

Untimed: Not available

Range: Secondary and postsecondary vocational students

Scoring: Scoring service provided

Cost: Contact publisher.

Publisher: National Occupational Competency Testing Institute

STUDENT OCCUPATIONAL COMPETENCY ACHIEVEMENT TESTING: AUTO MECHANICS

teen

Purpose: Measures achievement of students in vocational auto mechanics programs. Used for assigning grades, identifying curriculum strengths and weaknesses, and evaluating job applicants.

Description: Two-part test of skills and knowledge in auto mechanics. The written test is multiple-choice and covers the following areas: brakes, front end, engine repair, engine tune-up, automatic transmission, manual transmission/rear axle, electrical systems, and heating/air conditioning. The performance test measures abilities in three areas: maintain and repair brake system, perform minor tune-up, and maintain and repair electrical systems. Examiner required. Suitable for group use.

Untimed: Not available

Range: Secondary and postsecondary vocational students

Scoring: Scoring service provided

Cost: Contact publisher.

Publisher: National Occupational Competency Testing Institute

STUDENT OCCUPATIONAL COMPETENCY ACHIEVEMENT TESTING: AUTO BODY

teen

Purpose: Measures achievement of students in vocational auto body programs. Used for grade assignment, identifying curriculum strengths and weaknesses, and evaluating job applicants.

Description: Two-part test of skills and knowledge in auto body. The written test is multiple-choice, and covers the following areas: soldering and brazing, safety, welding, hand tools and power tools, math and science, body preparation and painting, basic knowledge, terminology, and customer relations. The performance test measures abilities in four areas: welding, sheet metal repair, panel construction, and painting. Examiner required. Suitable for group use.

Untimed: Not available

Range: Secondary and postsecondary vocational students

Scoring: Scoring service provided

Cost: Contact publisher.

Publisher: National Occupational Competency Testing Institute

STUDENT OCCUPATIONAL COMPETENCY ACHIEVEMENT TESTING: AGRICULTURE MECHANICS

teen

Purpose: Measures achievement of students in vocational agriculture mechanics programs. Used for grade assignment, identifying curriculum strengths and weaknesses, and evaluating job applicants.

Description: Two-part test of skills and knowledge in agriculture mechanics. The written test is multiple-choice, and covers the following areas: orientation and safety, agricultural mechanic skills, agricultural power and machinery, agricultural electrical power and processing, agricultural structures, and soil and water management. The performance test measures abilities in six areas: shielded metal arc welding, oxycetylene cutting, wheel bearings, electrical installation, agricultural structures, and farm level. Examiner required. Suitable for group use.

Untimed: Not available

Range: Secondary and postsecondary vocational students

Scoring: Scoring service provided

Cost: Contact publisher.

Publisher: National Occupational Competency Testing Institute

STUDENT OCCUPATIONAL COMPETENCY ACHIEVEMENT TESTING: ACCOUNTING/ BOOKKEEPING

teen

Purpose: Measures achievement of students in vocational accounting/ bookkeeping programs. Used for grade assignment, identifying curriculum strengths and weaknesses, and evaluating job applicants.

Description: Two-part test of skills and knowledge in accounting and bookkeeping. The written test is multiple-choice, and covers the following areas: processing purchases and payables, sales and receivables, cash receipts and cash payments, processing payroll and related records, inventory. filing and records management, operating mechanical and electronic accounting devices, completing the accounting cycle, performing general office functions, obtaining employment as an accounting/computing clerk. The performance test measures abilities in

six area: journalizing business transactions, posting from specialized journals, payroll procedures, banking and banking procedures, worksheet and statement preparation, and locating source data. Examiner required. Suitable for group use.

Untimed: Not available

Range: Secondary and postsecondary vocational students

Scoring: Scoring service provided

Cost: Contact publisher.

Publisher: National Occupational Competency Testing Institute

STUDENT OCCUPATIONAL COMPETENCY ACHIEVEMENT TESTING: CONSTRUCTION ELECTRICITY

teen

Purpose: Measures achievement of students in vocational construction electricity programs. Used for grade assignment, identifying curriculum strengths and weaknesses, and evaluating job applicants.

Description: Two-part test of skills and knowledge in construction electricity. The written test is multiple-choice, and covers the following areas: orientation, tools and equipment, blueprints, planning and layout, electronics, AC electricity, transformers, SC motors and starters, branch circuits, wiring methods, and lighting, heating and air conditioning, and low voltage. The performance test measures abilities in three areas: planning and layout, wiring methods, and service installation. Examiner required. Suitable for group use.

Untimed: Not available

Range: Secondary and postsecondary vocational students

Scoring: Scoring service provided

Cost: Contact publisher.

Publisher: National Occupational Competency Testing Institute

STUDENT OCCUPATIONAL COMPETENCY ACHIEVEMENT TESTING: DRAFTING

teen

Purpose: Measures achievement of students in vocational drafting programs. Used for grade assignment, identifying curriculum strengths and weaknesses, and evaluating job applicants.

Description: Two-part test of skills and knowledge in drafting. The written test is multiple-choice, and covers the following areas: interpretation of drawings, machine drawing, architectural drawing, mathematical calculations, electrical/electronic drawing, sheet metal drawing, mapping and cartography, and computer-assisted drawing. The performance test measures abilities in six areas: orthographic projection, sectioning, auxiliary, threads, production/detail, and specialty areas. Examiner required. Suitable for group use.

Untimed: Not available

Range: Secondary and postsecondary vocational students

Scoring: Scoring service provided

Cost: Contact publisher.

Publisher: National Occupational Competency Testing Institute

STUDENT OCCUPATIONAL COMPETENCY ACHIEVEMENT TESTING: GENERAL MERCHANDISING

teen

Purpose: Measures achievement of students in vocational general merchandising programs. Used for grade assignment, identifying curriculum strengths and weaknesses, and evaluating job applicants.

Description: Two-part test of skills and knowledge in general merchandising. The written test is multiple-choice, and covers the following areas: communication, human relations, merchandising, operations, management, and sales. The performance test measures abilities in three areas: mechanics of completing a sale and handling money, human relations/communications and product knowledge-selling. Examiner required. Suitable for group use.

Untimed: Not available

Range: Secondary and postsecondary vocational students

Scoring: Scoring service provided

Cost: Contact publisher.

Publisher: National Occupational Competency Testing Institute

STUDENT OCCUPATIONAL COMPETENCY ACHIEVEMENT TESTING: GENERAL OFFICE

teen

Purpose: Measures achievement of students in vocational general office programs. Used for grade assignment, identifying curriculum strengths and weaknesses, and evaluating job applicants.

Description: Two-part test of skills and knowledge in general office work. The written test is multiple-choice, and covers the following areas: office recordkeeping, filing and records management, personal business management for the executive, job seeking and behavior on the job, machine transcription, production typing, modern office technology, business dynamics, and business communications. The performance test measures abilities in six areas: letter writing, envelope preparation, tabulation, office filing, machine calculation, and forms preparation. Examiner required. Suitable for group use.

Untimed: Not available

Range: Secondary and postsecondary vocational students

Scoring: Scoring service provided

Cost: Contact publisher.

Publisher: National Occupational Competency Testing Institute

STUDENT OCCUPATIONAL COMPETENCY ACHIEVEMENT TESTING: HEATING AND AIR CONDITIONING

teen

Purpose: Measures achievement of students in vocational heating and air conditioning programs. Used for grade assignment, identifying curriculum strengths and weaknesses, and evaluating job applicants.

Description: Two-part test of skills and knowledge in heating and air conditioning. The written test is multiple-choice, and covers the following areas: related math and science, installation and service, electricity, controls, solar heating, and gas and oil furnaces. The performance test measures abilities in two areas: troubleshoot and repair a cooling and/or a heating system and fabricate a heat exchanger. Examiner required. Suitable for group use.

Untimed: Not available

Range: Secondary and postsecondary vocational students

Scoring: Scoring service provided

Cost: Contact publisher.

Publisher: National Occupational Competency Testing Institute

STUDENT OCCUPATIONAL COMPETENCY ACHIEVEMENT TESTING: HORTICULTURE

teen

Purpose: Measures achievement of students in vocational horticulture programs. Used for grade assignment, identifying curriculum strengths and weaknesses, and evaluating job applicants.

Description: Two-part test of skills and knowledge in horticulture. The written test is multiple-choice, and covers the following areas: arboriculture/landscaping/nursery/turf, floriculture/floristry/greenhouse management, and vegetables/small fruits/tree fruits. The performance test measures abilities in these same three areas. Examiner required. Suitable for group use.

Untimed: Not available

Range: Secondary and postsecondary vocational students

Scoring: Scoring service provided

Cost: Contact publisher.

Publisher: National Occupational Competency Testing Institute

STUDENT OCCUPATIONAL COMPETENCY ACHIEVEMENT TESTING: INDUSTRIAL ELECTRONICS

teen

Purpose: Measures achievement of students in vocational industrial electronics programs. Used for grade assignment, identifying curriculum strengths and weaknesses, and evaluating job applicants.

Description: Two-part test of skills and knowledge in industrial electronics. The written test is multiple-choice, and covers the following areas: basic theory, DC concepts, test equipment, AC concepts, vacuum tubes, solid state devices, power supplies and rectification, amplifier circuits and operation, digital electronics, and miscellaneous circuits and components. The performance test measures abilities in seven areas: desolder PC board, component testing, oscilloscope, circuit timing, photosensitive transducer, logic circuit, and power supply. Examiner required. Suitable for group use.

Untimed: Not available

Range: Secondary and postsecondary vocational students

Scoring: Scoring service provided

Cost: Contact publisher.

Publisher: National Occupational Competency Testing Institute

STUDENT OCCUPATIONAL COMPETENCY ACHIEVEMENT TESTING: MACHINE TRADES

teen

Purpose: Measures achievement of students in vocational machine trades programs. Used for grade assignment, identifying curriculum strengths and weaknesses, and evaluating job applicants.

Description: Two-part test of skills and knowledge in machine trades. The written test is multiple- choice, and covers the following areas: bench work, sawing, drilling, lathes, milling, grinding, and related theory. The performance test measures abilities in seven areas: layout, measurement, drilling and hole forming, lathe operations, milling machine operations, bench work, and safety. Examiner required. Suitable for group use.

Untimed: Not available

Range: Secondary and postsecondary vocational students

Scoring: Scoring service provided

Cost: Contact publisher.

Publisher: National Occupational Competency Testing Institute

STUDENT OCCUPATIONAL COMPETENCY ACHIEVEMENT TESTING: PRACTICAL NURSING

teen

Purpose: Measures achievement of students in vocational practical nursing programs. Used for grade assignment, identifying curriculum strengths and weaknesses, and evaluating job applicants.

Description: Two-part test of skills and knowledge in practical nursing. The written test is multiple- choice, and covers the following areas: anatomy and physiology, medical/surgical nursing, basic nursing, maternal and child health, and personal/vocational relationships. The performance test measures abilities in ten areas: make an occupied bed, take vital signs, demonstrate sterile technique/ indwelling catheter, administration of oral medication, administration of an intramuscular injection, administration of subcutaneous medication, tube feeding, perineal care, collection of clean catch/midstream urine specimen, and transfer patient from bed to wheelchair. Examiner required. Suitable for group use.

Untimed: Not available

Range: Secondary and postsecondary vocational students

Scoring: Scoring service provided

Cost: Contact publisher.

Publisher: National Occupational Competency Testing Institute

STUDENT OCCUPATIONAL COMPETENCY ACHIEVEMENT TESTING: PRINTING

teen

Purpose: Measures achievement of students in vocational printing programs. Used for grade assignment, identifying curriculum strengths and weaknesses, and evaluating job applicants.

Description: Two-part test of skills and knowledge in printing. The written test is multiple-choice, and covers the following areas: layout and design, composition, copy preparation, darkroom, stripping and platemaking, presswork, and finishing/paper. The performance test measures abilities in six areas: layout and design, composition, copy preparation, darkroom, stripping, and presswork. Examiner required. Suitable for group use.

Untimed: Not available

Range: Secondary and postsecondary vocational students

Scoring: Scoring service provided

Cost: Contact publisher.

Publisher: National Occupational Competency Testing Institute

---

STUDENT OCCUPATIONAL COMPETENCY ACHIEVEMENT TESTING: RADIO AND TV REPAIR

teen

Purpose: Measures achievement of students in vocational radio and TV repair programs. Used for grade assignment, identifying curriculum strengths and weaknesses, and evaluating job applicants.

Description: Two-part test of skills and knowledge in radio and TV repair. The written test is multiple-

choice, and covers the following areas: basic skills, television receiver circuits, audio systems, radio receivers, tape players/recorders, television antennas, digital and logic circuits, safety, and customer services. The performance test measures abilities in three areas: perform color television setup procedures, diagnose and repair AM/FM receiver and repair black and white television. Examiner required. Suitable for group use.

Untimed: Not available

Range: Secondary and postsecondary vocational students

Scoring: Scoring service provided

Cost: Contact publisher.

Publisher: National Occupational Competency Testing Institute

---

STUDENT OCCUPATIONAL COMPETENCY ACHIEVEMENT TESTING: REFRIGERATION

teen

Purpose: Measures achievement of students in vocational refrigeration programs. Used for grade assignment, identifying curriculum strengths and weaknesses, and evaluating job applicants.

Description: Two part test of skills and knowledge in refrigeration. The written test is multiple- choice, and covers the following areas: nomenclature; valves, gauges, controls; electricity; related math and science; installation and service; and safety. The performance test is divided into three parts measuring different aspects of troubleshooting and repairing refrigeration systems. Examiner required. Suitable for group use.

Untimed: Not available

Range: Secondary and postsecondary vocational students

Scoring: Scoring service provided

Cost: Contact publisher.

Publisher: National Occupational Competency Testing Institute

STUDENT OCCUPATIONAL COMPETENCY ACHIEVEMENT TESTING: SEWN PRODUCTS

teen

Purpose: Measures achievement of students in vocational sewn product programs. Used for grade assignment, identifying curriculum strengths and weaknesses, and evaluating job applicants.

Description: Two-part test of skills and knowledge in sewn products occupations. The written test is multiple-choice, and covers the following areas: textiles, pressing, industrial sewing methods, operation of equipment, fitting garments, altering finished garments, and construction. The performance test measures abilities in seven areas: machine usage, industrial sewing machine maintenance, industrial sewing methods, garment construction methods, taking body measurements, pattern alterations, and alteration of finished garments. Examiner required. Suitable for group use.

Untimed: Not available

Range: Secondary and postsecondary vocational students

Scoring: Scoring service provided

Cost: Contact publisher.

Publisher: National Occupational Competency Testing Institute

STUDENT OCCUPATIONAL COMPETENCY ACHIEVEMENT TESTING: SMALL ENGINE REPAIR

teen

Purpose: Measures achievement of students in vocational small engine repair programs. Used for grade assignment, identifying curriculum strengths and weaknesses, and evaluating job applicants.

Description: Two-part test of skills and knowledge in small engine repair. The written test is multiple-choice, and covers the following areas: ignition, fuel, governors, starters, valves-ports, engine block components-cooling, compression-lubrication, powered equipment mechanisms, shop procedures-safety, and theory-shop arithmetic. The performance test measures abilities in five areas: check engine and start disassembly, complete disassembly and check and measure parts, reassemble engine and operate, invoicing parts, and use of time. Examiner required. Suitable for group use.

Untimed: Not available

Range: Secondary and postsecondary vocational students

Scoring: Scoring service provided

Cost: Contact publisher.

Publisher: National Occupational Competency Testing Institute

STUDENT OCCUPATIONAL COMPETENCY ACHIEVEMENT TESTING: WELDING

teen

Purpose: Measures achievement of students in vocational welding programs. Used for grade assignment, identifying curriculum strengths and weaknesses, and evaluating job applicants.

Description: Two-part test of skills and knowledge in welding occupations. The written test is multiple-choice, and covers the following areas: nomenclature, welding symbols, basic welding information, electricity, basic metallurgy, shielded-metal arc welding, related math and science, and safety. The performance test measures abilities in four areas: oxyacetylene welding, shielded metal arc welding, gas metal arc welding, and gas tungsten arc welding. Examiner required. Suitable for group use.

Untimed: Not available

Range: Secondary and postsecondary vocational students

Scoring: Scoring service provided

Cost: Contact publisher.

Publisher: National Occupational Competency Testing Institute

---

TECHNICAL TESTS-1962

teen

Purpose: Measures technical abilities. Used for vocational guidance.

Description: Multiple item paper-pencil test battery measuring six areas of technical abilities: Arithmetic Part I and II, Mechanical Insight, Form Perception Part I and II, and a Tool Test. Materials include a bilingual test booklet (English, Afrikaans). Examiner required. Suitable for group use.
SOUTH AFRICAN PUBLISHER

Untimed: 1½ hours

Range: Ages 13-15 years old

Scoring: Hand key; examiner evaluated

Cost: (In Rands) test 0,40; 10 answer sheets 0,50; key 0,60; manual 0,70 (orders from outside The RSA will be dealt with on merit).

Publisher: Human Sciences Research Council

TRADE APTITUDE TEST (TRAT)-1982
Refer to page 682.

Educational Development and Preschool Readiness

ACER CHECKLISTS FOR SCHOOL BEGINNERS

child   grades PRE-1

Purpose: Measures school readiness of preschool and kindergarten children. Identifies children in need of further evaluation and developmental assistance.

Description: Multiple item paper-pencil checklist consists mostly of single task activities which are scored plus or minus, depending on whether or not the child has displayed the developmental behavior presented in the test item. Areas covered include: social development, motor skills, memory and attention, and language skills. Two forms are available: one for use by teachers in the classroom setting, and one for use by parents. The items may be checked in any order; most may be completed on the basis of informal observation. The child's behavioral development, based on the results of the checklist, is assessed to provide a measure of the child's readiness for participation in formal school situations. Materials include: checklist for teacher use, checklist for parent use, class record sheet, and manual. Self-administered by evaluator. Suitable for group use. The following foreign language versions are available by special arrangement: Arabic, Greek, Italian, Maltese, Serbo-Croatian (Yugoslav), Spanish, and Turkish.
AUSTRALIAN PUBLISHER

Untimed: Not available

Range: Preschool-1

Scoring: Examiner evaluated

Cost: Specimen set $6.00; 30 teachers' checklists, 30 parents' checklist and class record form $11.50; individual class record forms $.60 (all remittances must be in Australian currency).

Publisher: The Australian Council for Educational Research Limited

THE ABC INVENTORY
Normand Adair and George Blesch

child

Purpose: Assesses the school readiness of preschoolers and provides an index of a child's maturity upon entering school. Identifies children in need of further evaluation and assistance. Provides a basis for better parent-teacher understanding.

Description: Oral response and task performance test assessing a child's general level of maturity and development. The four sections of the test require the child to perform the following tasks: (1) draw a man, (2) answer language questions such as "what has wings" or "tell me the color of grass," (3) answer cognitive questions such as "what is ice when it melts" or "how do we hear," and (4) motor activity tasks, such as counting four squares, folding a paper triangle, repeating four digits, and copying a square. Examiner required. Not for group use.

Untimed: 8-9 minutes

Range: Ages 3½-6½

Scoring: Examiner evaluated

Cost: 50 inventories $6.50.

Publisher: Educational Studies and Development

ACER EARLY SCHOOL SERIES

child   Preschool

Purpose: Measures perceptual, verbal and numerical skills needed by children entering kindergarten. Used for readiness screening; identifies children in need of further evaluation and assistance.

Description: Multiple item, paper-pencil tests of ten readiness skills: auditory discrimination, recognition of initial consonant sounds, number, figure formation, prepositions, pronouns, verb tense, negation, and comprehension. Overall Word Knowledge score is also obtained. Materials include separate administration booklet for each test, and a handbook entitled Early Identification and Intervention. Examiner required. Suitable for group use. AUSTRALIAN PUBLISHER

Untimed: Not available

Range: Preschool

Scoring: Hand key

Cost: Complete kit (includes 5 of each test, individual test score keys, manuals) $43.00 (all remittances must be in Australian currency).

Publisher: Australian Council for Educational Research Limited

ADAPTIVE BEHAVIOR SCALE FOR INFANTS AND EARLY CHILDHOOD (ABSI)
Henry Leland, Mandana Shoaee, Douglas McElwain, and Rachael Christie

child

Purpose: Describes the adaptive behavior of infants and young children as an aid to effective program planning and preschool placement. The scales are especially useful with the mentally retarded, developmentally disabled and physically handicapped.

Description: 63 item interview examination covering seven domains, with an additional 80 item review test of potential maladaptive social behavior. The domains measured are: adaptive behavior, independent functioning and physical development, communication skills, conceptual skills, play skills, self-direction and personal responsibility, and socialization. Helpful in discovering major psychological problems which may be developing, indications of possible brain damage or other sensory-motor problems, and indications of possible delays in cognitive and communication development. The test is administered by an examiner acting as a third party to a parent or teacher or other individual who has thorough knowledge of the child. Examiner required. Not suitable for group use.

Untimed: 45 minutes

Range: Infant-6 years

Scoring: Examiner evaluated

Cost: Specimen set $8.00.

Publisher: The Nisonger Center, Ohio State University

ADELPHI PARENT ADMINISTERED READINESS TEST (A.P.A.R.T.)
Pnina S. Klein

child

Purpose: Identifies learning disabilities and language problems of preschool children. Used for counseling and to help parents understand the relationship between ability and academic achievement.

Description: 42 item paper-pencil examination in 10 subtests covering: Concept Formation, Letter Form Recognition, Writing Ability, Knowledge of Numbers, Visual Perception, Visual Memory, Comprehension and Memory, Auditory Sequential Memory, Recognition of Facial Expressions of Emotion, and Creative Ability. Parent reads directions to the child, records responses and scores the test. To be administered 4-6 months before entering first grade. May be administered in languages other than English.

Untimed: 20 minutes

Range: Ages 5 years, 2 months-6 years, 3 months

Scoring: Hand key; examiner evaluated

Cost: 10 tests $24.95.

Publisher: Mafex Associates, Inc.

ANTON BRENNER DEVELOPMENTAL GESTALT TEST OF SCHOOL READINESS
Anton Brenner

child

Purpose: Assesses school readiness for kindergarten and first grade. Used to identify those who need special attention.

Description: Multiple item, oral response and task assessment test uses Gestalt and developmental principles to measure children's conceptual and perceptual abilities. The test provides a quantitative and qualitative evaluation of a child's perceptual-conceptual development and identifies three special groups: early maturing and/or gifted; slowly maturing and/or retarded; and emotionally disturbed. Almost "culture free." It can be used with non-English speaking and culturally deprived children. Examiner required. Not for group use.

Untimed: 5 minutes

Range: Ages 5-6

Scoring: Hand key; examiner evaluated

Cost: Complete kit (includes 20 booklets, manual, 1 set of test materials) $18.40.

Publisher: Western Psychological Services

ASSESSMENT IN NURSERY EDUCATION
Margaret Bate and Marjorie Smith

child

Purpose: Assesses development of children ages 3 to 5. Used for identifying strengths and weaknesses and for monitoring progress.

Description: Multiple item, observational assessment of five major developmental areas: social skills and social thinking, talking and listening, thinking and doing, manual and tool skills, and physical skills. Assessment is by observed and demonstrated ability to perform special tasks. Materials include Outlines of Model People, Pictures and Picture Story Cards, Set of Shapes for Copying, Set of Shapes for Cutting Out, and Guideline Patterns for Drawing. Video tapes demonstrating assessment are also available. Examiner required. Not suitable for group use. BRITISH PUBLISHER

Untimed: Observation time

Range: Ages 3-5

Scoring: Examiner evaluated

Cost: Complete kit (1 manual, 1 Colour Selection Booklet, 1 Individual Record Form, 1 set of Outlines of Model People, 2 Pictures and 2 Sets of Picture Story Cards, 1 set of Shapes for Cutting Out and Guideline Patterns for Drawing) £15.50; video recordings set in three parts £105.00 (payment in sterling for all overseas orders).

Publisher: NFER-Nelson Publishing Company

ATTITUDE TO SCHOOL QUESTIONNAIRE (ASQ)
Refer to page 624.

THE BARBER SCALES OF SELF-REGARD FOR PRESCHOOL CHILDREN
Refer to page 3.

BASIC SCHOOL SKILLS INVENTORY-DIAGNOSTIC (BSSI-D)
Refer to page 333.

BASIC SCHOOL SKILLS INVENTORY-SCREEN (BSSI-S)
Refer to page 334.

BEHAVIOUR STUDY TECHNIQUE
Refer to page 4.

THE BINGHAM BUTTON TEST
Refer to page 4.

BIRTH TO THREE DEVELOPMENTAL SCALE
Refer to page 5.

BOEHM TEST OF BASIC CONCEPTS
Ann E. Boehm

child   grades K-2

Purpose: Evaluates young child's mastery of concepts used in school instruction. Used for screening for referral to special services.

Description: 50 item paper-pencil, multiple-choice picture test of concepts related to quantity, space, and time. Child responds to oral instructions by marking one of several pictures. Materials include two alternate forms, A and B, measuring knowledge of the same concepts. Examiner required. Suitable for individual or small group use. Available in Spanish.

Untimed: 15-20 minutes

Range: Grades K-2

Scoring: Hand key

Cost: 30 test booklets 1 and 2 (includes directions class record and key) $12.25 (specify form A or B); manual $1.75; Spanish directions (form A or B) $1.25.

Publisher: The Psychological Corporation

BRACKEN BASIC CONCEPT SCALE-DIAGNOSTIC SCALE (BBCS-DIAG)
Bruce A. Bracken

child

Purpose: Measures a child's ability to acquire concepts such as color, quantity and time sequence. Used by speech pathologists and school psychologists to screen students for special attention.

Description: 258 item verbal "point-to" test using picture stimuli to evaluate 11 categories of basic concept acquisition. They are: Color, Shape, Size, Quantity, Counting, Letter Identification, Direction/Position, Time/Sequence, Texture, Comparisons, and Social/Emotional Responses. The examiner shows a picture to the child and records the "point-to" response on a diagnostic scale form provided with the test package. The test is influenced by expressive language deficits or physical disabilities. Examiner required. Not suitable for group use.

Untimed: 20-40 minutes

Range: Ages 2½-8

Scoring: Examiner evaluated

Cost: Contact publisher.

Publisher: Charles E. Merrill

Publishing Company

BRACKEN BASIC CONCEPT SCALE-SCREENING TEST (BBCS-SCREENING)
Bruce A. Bracken

child

Purpose: Helps identify children whose ability to distinguish concepts is below age-level expections. Useful as a guide to further testing.

Description: Two 30 item paper-pencil, multiple-choice tests. Two books of picture stimuli test different concepts of approximately equal difficulty in eight categories of basic concept acquisition. It yields a single norm referenced standard score. Suitable for use with groups.

Timed: 20-30 minutes

Range: Ages 2½-8

Scoring: Hand key

Cost: Contact publisher.

Publisher: Charles E. Merrill Publishing Company

COGNITIVE SKILLS ASSESSMENT BATTERY
Ann E. Boehm and Barbara Slater

child   grades PRE-K

Purpose: Assesses preschool and kindergarten children's progress relative to teaching goals in cognitive and physical-motor areas. Used by teachers for curriculum planning and to match classroom goals with cognitive skills.

Description: 64 item verbal test using easel cards to measure: orientation towards environment, discrimination of similarities and differences, comprehension and concept formation, coordination, and immediate and delayed memory. The easel is placed between examiner and child and the child is introduced to the task. The examiner goes through the cards asking questions and recording the responses. Materials include easel and 64 cards, response sheets, manual, eight blocks, watch, and paper and pencils. Test does not provide criteria levels and no total score is obtained. Examiner should be a teacher, learning disability specialist, or school psychologist. Examiner required. Not suitable for group use. Available in Japanese.

Untimed: 20-25 minutes

Range: Preschool and kindergarten

Scoring: Examiner evaluated

Cost: Complete kit (includes card easel, assessor's manual, class record sheet, 30 pupil response sheets) $48.95; manual $3.50; specimen set (includes assessor's manual, class record sheet, pupil response sheet, 1 sample easel page) $3.95.

Publisher: Teachers College Press

COMMUNICATIVE EVALUATION CHART
Refer to page 6.

COMPREHENSIVE ASSESSMENT PROGRAM: BEGINNING EDUCATION ASSESSMENT (BEA)
Refer to page 6.

COMPREHENSIVE IDENTIFICATION PROCESS (CIP)
R. Reid Zehrbach

child

Purpose: Evaluates the mental and physical development of young children. Used to identify those in need of special medical, psychological or

educational help before entering kindergarten or the first grade.

Description: Multiple item, verbal response and task- assessment test of eight areas of child development: cognitive-verbal, fine motor, gross motor, speech and expressive language, hearing, vision, social/affective, and medical history. The screening kit contains administrator's and interviewer's manuals, screening booklet, 35 parent interview forms, 35 observation of behavior forms, 35 speech and expressive language forms, 35 record folders, and the materials required for the tasks (blocks, balls, beads, buttons, crayons, etc.). The screening can be administered by trained paraprofessionals supervised by professionals in the preschool area. Suggestions for dealing with various cultural and language backgrounds are included. CIP helps meet the Child Find requirements of PL94-142. Examiner required. Not for group use.

Untimed: 30 minutes

Range: Ages 2½-5 ½

Scoring: Examiner evaluated

Cost: CIP screening kit $80.00.

Publisher: Scholastic Testing Service, Inc.

CONCEPT ASSESSMENT KIT-- CONSERVATION (CAK)
Marcel L. Goldschmid and Peter M. Bentler

child

Purpose: Assesses cognitive development among preschool and early-school age children. Used to assess the effect of training based on Piaget's theories.

Description: Multiple item, task-assessment and oral response test of the development of the concept of conservation. Three forms are available. Two parallel forms A and B measure conservation in terms of two-dimensional space, number, substance, continuous quantity, discontinuous quantity, and weight. Form C measures conservation in terms of area and length. Test items are constructed to assess the child's conservation behavior as well as assessing his comprehension of the principle involved. The items require the child to indicate the presence or absence of conservation as well as to specify the reason for this judgment. CAK is relatively independent of IQ while correlating significantly with school performance. The parallel forms provide for assessment of the effect of training, and Form C allows for testing of transfer effects of the training. Norms are provided separately for boys and girls for ages 4-7. Examiner required. Not for group use.

Untimed: 15 minutes per form

Range: Ages 4-7

Scoring: Hand key

Cost: Complete kit (Forms A, B, C manual) $26.50; 25 Recording A or B Forms (separate four-page instruction sheet) $4.50; 25 C Forms, $4.00; manual $1.75.

Publisher: Educational and Industrial Testing Service

COOPERATIVE PRESCHOOL INVENTORY
Bettye M. Caldwell

child   Preschool

Purpose: Assesses achievement in areas necessary for school success. Used to screen children entering school and to estimate the degree of disadvantage the child may have.

Description: 64 item paper-pencil test used to reveal the child's knowledge of self, ability to follow directions, verbal expressions, basic numerical concepts and sensory attributes. Necessary items for testing are: recording leaflet, blank sheet of paper, three small cars, eight large crayons, one box of checkers, and three cardboard boxes. Examiner required. Not suitable for group use. Available in Spanish.

Untimed: 15 minutes

Range: Preschool

Scoring: Hand key

Cost: Directions for administering and scoring $1.00; 20 recording forms $6.25; handbook $3.75.

Publisher: CTB/McGraw-Hill

CREATIVITY TESTS FOR CHILDREN (CT)
J.P. Guilford, et al.

child   grades 4-UP

Purpose: Measures creative thinking among children grade 4 and above by assessing verbal and nonverbal modes of expression. Used for counseling, group placement and research.

Description: Ten paper-pencil tests measure different aspects of divergent production. Both semantic (verbal) and visual-figural abilities are tested in the CT battery tests. The tests are: Names for Stories, What To Do With It, Similar Meanings, Writing Sentences, Kinds Of People, Make Something Out Of It, Different Letter Groups, Making Objects, Hidden Letters, and Adding Decorations. It is recommended that the battery as a whole be used. Seven of the ten tests are adaptations of adult forms for the same factors. The Manual of Interpretations, Profile Chart, and Review Set cover the entire battery; tests, scoring guides, and Administrative Manuals may be ordered for individual tests. Alternate forms are available. Norms provided for fourth- and sixth-grade students. Restricted to A.P.A.

members. Examiner required. Suitable for group use.

Timed: 100 minutes

Range: Grades 4 and up

Scoring: Examiner evaluated

Cost: 25 tests of any given test $7.00; interpretation manual $7.00; administration manual for entire battery $10.00; or $1.75/individual test; 25 profile charts $3.50; scoring guide per test $.75.

Publisher: Sheridan Psychological Services, Inc.

THE DARVILLE TEST-THE BRITISH PICTURE VOCABULARY SCALE

child, teen

Purpose: Assesses vocabulary in children. Used for screening children with language and cognitive delays.

Description: Multiple item picture test of receptive vocabulary. Child indicates which of four pictures on a page best illustrates the meaning of a stimulus word. No oral or written response is required. Materials include test plates and both a short and long form. Adapted from the Peabody Picture Vocabulary Test for use in Britain. Examiner required. Not suitable for group use.
BRITISH PUBLISHER

Untimed: Not available

Range: Ages 2½-18

Scoring: Hand key; examiner evaluated

Cost: Complete kit (includes manual, long form test plates with stand, short form test plates, 25 long form test records, 25 short form test records) may be ordered through NFER-Nelson.

Publisher: NFER-Nelson Publishing Company

DEL RIO LANGUAGE SCREENING TEST (ENGLISH/SPANISH) (DRLST)
Refer to page 584.

DEVELOPMENTAL ACTIVITIES SCREENING INVENTORY (DASI)
Rebecca R. Fewell and Mary Beth Langley

child

Purpose: Assesses developmental skills and abilities in infants and young children. Used for early detection of disabilities for determination of remedial teaching.

Description: 55 item paper-pencil and manual dexterity test. It measures academic/cognitive and basic skills/perceptual motor factors, and can be presented in different sequences in one or two sittings. Instructions are given either visually or verbally. The developmental skills studied include fine-motor manipulation, cause-effect relationships, associations, number concepts, size discriminations, and sequencing. Materials include a kit of manipulative materials such as cubes, a peg board and pegs, a form board, beads, rings, an assortment of cards, cups, bowls, and plastic shapes; student response forms. The manual suggests instructional programs which can be used before a comprehensive remedial program is developed. The inventory can be modified for use with the visually or hearing impaired. Examiner required. Not suitable for group use.

Untimed: Not available

Range: 6 months-5 years (no norms are provided)

Scoring: Examiner evaluated

Cost: Complete $99.00.

Publisher: Teaching Resources

Corporation

THE DEVELOPMENTAL PROFILE II
Gerald D. Alpern, Thomas Boll and Marsha Shearer

child

Purpose: Evaluates the age-equivalent physical, social and mental development of normal or handicapped young children. Used for counseling, school planning, and research.

Description: 186 item interview test of five areas: Physical, Self-Help, Social, Academic, and Communication. Developmental-age scores are derived by interviewing a parent or by teacher observation. The scales are graded from birth to age 4 by half-year increments, then by years through age nine. Also provides an IQ equivalency score. Materials include test books, profile and scoring forms, and a manual and step-by-step procedures for administering and interpreting. Also available on computer diskette. Examiner required. Suitable for group use. Available in Spanish.

Untimed: 20-40 minutes

Range: Ages Birth-9

Scoring: Examiner evaluated

Cost: Complete set $23.50; manual $18.25; 30 profile and scoring forms $8.25; computer diskette $165.00

Publisher: Psychological Development Publications

DEVELOPMENTAL TASK ANALYSIS
Robert E. Valett

child   grades PRE-6

Purpose: Measures the basic developmental tasks necessary for success in learning. Useful for preschool and early childhood counseling, special education and selecting learning objectives.

Description: 100 item paper-pencil test of four basic skills: Social and personal (23 items); perceptual (42 items); language (15 items) and thinking (15 items). Each test is rated 0-3, from "has not begun to learn" to "well learned with no difficulties." Items of special concern are described in each section. Materials include a five-page form and rating scale plus 10 six-page forms. Administered by parents or teachers. Not suitable for group use.

Untimed: 20 minutes

Range: Preschool and primary

Scoring: Examiner evaluated

Cost: 10 forms $3.95.

Publisher: Pitman Learning, Inc.

DEVELOPMENTAL TASKS FOR KINDERGARTEN READINESS (DTKR)
Walter J. Lesiak

child

Purpose: Assesses prior to kindergarten, a child's skills and abilities as they relate to performance in kindergarten. Provides school personnel with an average profile of children entering their classes as an aid to curriculum planning.

Description: 12 subtests, using auditory and visual stimuli, assessing the following areas: social development, receptive and expressive oral language, visual-motor skills, and cognitive development. Each subtest provides items arranged in order of difficulty. The examiner asks questions and/or shows stimulus cards to the child, the child responds, and the examiner records judgments and observations of the response for diagnostic and prescriptive use. Examiner required. Not for group use.

Untimed: 20 minutes

Range: Ages 4½-6½

Scoring: Hand key; examiner evaluated

Cost: Complete kit $30.00; manual $7.00; cards $6.00; 25 record booklets $18.50.

Publisher: Clinical Psychology Publishing Company, Inc.

DIAL-DEVELOPMENT INDICATORS FOR THE ASSESSMENT OF LEARNING
Carol Mardell and Dorothea S. Goldenberg

child

Purpose: Assesses a child's general developmental level. Used for screening of potentially delayed children who need professional evaluation.

Description: 28 item multidimensional developmental assessment of abilities in four skill areas: gross motor, fine motor, concepts and communication. Behavior is reviewed and the child's picture is taken. Administered by team of para-professionals and professionals at four stations. DIAL kit contains plastic dials and stands, blocks, scissors, beanbags, cutting cards, scoresheets, primary pencil, colored marking pens, tape and clipboard. Supplemental materials: small mirror or camera, playdough, and balance beam are also needed, and may be ordered from the publisher. DIAL-R will also be available after August, 1983. Examiner required. Not suitable for group use.

Untimed: 20-30 minutes

Range: Ages 2½-5½/preschool

Scoring: Examiner evaluated

Cost: Complete kit (includes consumable materials for 50 children),

$139.95; 50 scoresheets $3.50; 100 cutting cards $3.50.

Publisher: Childcraft Education Corporation

EARLY CHILDHOOD ENVIRONMENT RATING SCALE
Refer to page 648.

EARLY SCHOOL INVENTORY
Joanne R. Nurss and Mary E. McGauvran

child   grades K-1

Purpose: Assesses children in Kindergarten and first grade for potential school problems.

Description: Eighty-two item checklist for recording observed physical, language, socio-emotional, and cognitive development. Teacher indicates whether or not the child demonstrates each behavior. May be used with Metropolitan Readiness Test to provide additional information. Examiner required. Not suitable for group use.

Untimed: Open ended

Range: Kindergarten and first grade

Scoring: Examiner evaluated

Cost: 35 inventories $10.75

Publisher: The Psychological Corporation

EFFECTIVENESS-MOTIVATION SCALE
J. Sharp and D.H. Stott

child

Purpose: Measures different levels of effective motivation of preschool children. Used for screening prior to school, for research, and for assessing changes in functioning.

Description: Paper-pencil scale consisting of descriptions of behavior in eleven common areas of social and individual play. Scale is completed by teacher based on day-to-day observation of child's play behavior. Teacher selects most common observed behaviors in each area, which are added to give the following scores: effectiveness (E), withdrawal (W) and inconsequential behaviors (Q). Available to research and educational psychologists working through nursery and playgroup teachers. Examiner required. Not suitable for group use. BRITISH PUBLISHER

Untimed: 5-10 minutes

Range: 3-5 years

Scoring: Hand key

Cost: Specimen set £5.15; 25 tests £6.25; 25 scoring forms £1.95; manual £5.10 (payment in sterling for all overseas orders).

Publisher: NFER-Nelson Publishing Company

EL CIRCO, 1980
Educational Testing Service

child   grades PRE-1

Purpose: Identifies instructional needs in the areas of language and math for Spanish-speaking children. Used to evaluate early childhood bilingual curricula.

Description: Four paper-pencil tests assessing the skills of Spanish-speaking children. The Language Check assesses if a child's Spanish skills are sufficient to complete the other measures in Spanish: Para que sirven las palabra, 38 item measure of receptive language skills in Spanish; What Words Are For, 30 item measure of receptive language skills in English; Cuánto y cuantos; 39 item measure of mathematical skills (counting, relationships, and numerical concepts).

Examiner required. Suitable for group use.

Untimed: 15-30 minutes

Range: Preschool-grade 1

Scoring: Hand key

Cost: 30 tests $24.60; Language Check $7.20; manual $6.50.

Publisher: CTB/McGraw-Hill

THE FIRST GRADE READINESS CHECKLIST
John J. Austin

child   Kindergarten

Purpose: Evaluates a child's readiness for first grade work. Used to determine the learning experiences at which the child can be expected to succeed, and for school placement.

Description: 54 item paper-pencil "yes-no" test, of the subject's comprehension, age and growth, practical skills, attitudes and interests, memory for numbers, and general knowledge. A parent's kit is available in addition to the checklist and manual. Self-administered by parents or teachers. Not suitable for group use.

Untimed: 15 minutes

Range: End of kindergarten year

Scoring: Examiner evaluated

Cost: Parent's kit (includes set: condensed version of handbook plus 4 sample checklists 2 of each) $4.00; 50 checklists $8.00; manual $6.95.

Publisher: Research Concepts

FIRST GRADE SCREENING TEST (FGST)
John E. Pate and Warren W. Webb

child   grades K-1

Purpose: Evaluates school readiness. Used for identification of children who need individual assessment and remedial attention.

Description: Multiple item paper-pencil measure of school readiness. Areas measured include vocabulary, general knowledge, body image, emotional maturity, child's perceptions of parents and appropriate play, visual-motor coordination, ability to follow directions and memory. Materials include separate test booklets for boys and girls. Examiner required. Suitable for group use.

Timed: Kindergarten, 45 minutes; Grade 1, 30 minutes

Range: Kindergarten and first grade

Scoring: Examiner evaluated

Cost: Specimen set (a Girl's and a Boy's Test Booklet and manual), $4.50; 25 test booklets (specify boy or girl) $9.50; manual $4.25.

Publisher: American Guidance Service

FROSTIG DEVELOPMENTAL TEST OF VISUAL PERCEPTION
Marianne Frostig and Associates

child   grades PRE-3

Purpose: Assesses perceptual skills to help evaluate children referred for learning difficulties or neurological handicaps.

Description: 41 item test of five operationally-defined perceptual skills: Eye-Motor Coordination, Figure-Ground, Constancy of Shape, Position in Space, and Spatial Relationships. Correlated with reading achievement in normal first grade classroom. Materials include 11 demonstration cards showing various shapes and figures. Examiner provides regular and colored pencils, and crayons. Blackboard necessary for group administration. Individual and group administration. Examiner required. Available from foreign publishers in Spanish, French, German, Italian, Dutch, Japanese, and Swedish.

Untimed: 30-45 minutes

Range: Nursery school-grade 3

Scoring: Hand key

Cost: Specimen set (includes test booklet, manual, monograph), demonstration cards, set of score keys) $6.00; 25 tests $11.50.

Publisher: Consulting Psychologists Press, Inc.

THE GESELL PRESCHOOL TEST
Gesell Institute

child

Purpose: Assesses the behavioral, emotional and physical development of children ages 2½-6 years. Used for screening purposes, early intervention or diagnosis depending on the qualifications of the examiner. Meets Child Find Requirements of P.L. 94-142.

Description: 13 tests assessing a wide range of developmental factors in preschoolers. Cube Test measures eye-hand coordination, motor skill, attention span, level of functioning in a structured fine motor task, and ability to understand and follow directions. Interview Questions section assesses clarity of speech and accuracy of information. Pencil and Paper Tests section (Name, Numbers and Copy Form) assess visual perception and neuro-muscular and eye-hand coordination. Incomplete Man section assesses perceptual functioning by requiring the child to draw additional parts to a partially drawn human figure. Discriminates Prepositions section measures understanding of words and concepts related to spatial position. Digit Repetition section assesses ability to focus attention, hold information, repeat information in order given, and short term memory. Picture Vocabulary section assesses verbal intelligence. Color Forms section measures recognition of similar shapes. Action Agent section assesses language comprehension. Three-Hole Formboard section measures form discrimination ability and general adaptability. Indentifying Letters and Numbers section measures academic abilities against standard norms. Motor section assesses patterns of comprehension, manipulation, and gross motor activity. Developmental schedules section provide behavioral age level in all areas tested.

Also yields an effective personality profile. Materials include: test manual, 50 pre-collated test recording sheets, recording sheets, developmental schedules, set of ten cubes, bean-bag, picture vocabulary booklet, two-sided chart of letters and numbers, three-hold formboard, color forms, copy forms, pellets (non-toxic) and bottle, and complimentary case. Additional interpretive and instructional guides available. Examiner required. Not for group use.

Untimed: 40 minutes

Range: Ages 2½-6

Scoring: Examiner evaluated

Cost: Complete $129.95 (item PS-22)

Publisher: Programs for Education, Inc.

THE GESELL SCHOOL READINESS TEST-COMPLETE BATTERY
Gesell Institute

child

Purpose: Determines if a child is ready to begin Kindergarten, assesses a child's readiness for grade promotion (Grades 1-3), and evaluates whether or not a child has been placed at the proper grade level for his abilities. Used by school psychologists, educators, early childhood specialists, and child development professionals.

Description: Seven subtests measuring the adaptive behavior and visual-perceptual skills necessary for successful performance in school from Kindergarten to Grade 3. The Cube Test measures eye-hand coordination, motor skills, attention span, and level of functioning in a structured fine motor task. The Interview Questions Test assesses clarity of speech and accuracy of information. The Pencil and Paper Tests (Name, Numbers and Copy Forms) assess visual perception, neuro-muscular and eye-hand coordination, and general level of maturity.

The Incomplete Man Test measures perceptual functioning by asking the child to draw additional parts to an incomplete human figure. The Right and Left Test measures the ability to name parts of the body, distinguish right from left, and follow single and double commands. The Visual Tests assess understanding of directions, ability to carry out orders and the ability to hold and recall information. The Animals and Interests Test measures verbal abilities while providing clues about the child's tempo and organization of thinking and capacity to attend.

Materials include: pre-collated recording sheets sufficient for 50 students, a textbook of administration procedures and background information, the visual stimuli cards, cubes, and cylinders required for the various tests, a Sample School Readiness Test (for practice and preparation), and carrying case. Examiner required. Not for group use.

Untimed: 40 minutes

Range: Ages 4½-9

Scoring: Examiner evaluated

Cost: Complete $66.00 (item 142)

Publisher: Programs for Education, Inc.

GOODMAN LOCK BOX
Joan Goodman

child   Preschool

Purpose: Screens preschool children for mental retardation, fine motor problems, and distractibility/hyperactivity. Used as a non- threatening warm-up instrument for more extensive preschool screening.

Description: Multiple-task assessment test of a preschool child's ability to organize a free-choice situation. The child is presented with a box with ten locked doors to open and investigate, with a toy behind each door. The manner in which the child removes the toys is observed to determine whether a child is systematic and organized, or poorly focused and distractible. The test relies entirely on spontaneous behavior (no questions are asked). It supplements, without duplicating, other intelligence tests. Norms are provided at six-month intervals for normally developing children. and at yearly intervals for mentally retarded children. Examiner required. Not for group use.

Timed: 6½ minutes

Range: Preschool

Scoring: Examiner evaluated

Cost: Complete kit (includes testing materials, manual, record forms) $295.00.

Publisher: Stoelting Co.

HESS SCHOOL READINESS SCALE (HSRS)
Richard J. Hess

child

Purpose: Measures the general mental ability of young children. Used to determine readiness to enter school and to predict classroom success.

Description: 45 item paper-pencil, verbal test consisting of 12 subtests. They are: Pictoral Identification, Discrimination of Animal Pictures, Picture Memory, Form Perception and Discrimination, Comprehension and Discrimination, Copying Geometric Forms, Paper Folding, Number Concepts, Digital Memory Span, Opposite Analogies, Comprehension, and Sentence Memory Span. All subtests are presented with verbal instructions. Materials include the manual, guide for administering, a counting frame, 4"x4" paper package, triangle paper package, 5½"x8½" paper package, scoring forms, pencil, and case. Examiner required. Not suitable for group use.
BRITISH PUBLISHER

Timed: 120 minutes

Range: Ages 3 years, 6 months-7 (mental ag to 3.0 to 7.6)

Scoring: Hand key; examiner evaluated

Cost: Complete kit $34.95.

Publisher: Mafex Associates, Inc.

INFANT RATING SCALE (IRS)
G.A. Lindsay

child

Purpose: Evaluates a child's developing skills and behavior, and provides an overall picture of the child's developmental progress compared with his peer group. Identifies children "at risk" in one or more areas and helps the teacher respond appropriately. Used with children ages 5-7½ years.

Description: 25 item paper-pencil observational instrument rates on a five-point scale the child's strengths and weaknesses in the following developmental areas: language, early learning and motor skills, behavior, social integration, and general development. The IRS has two levels: Level 1 is suitable for children ages

5-5½, Level 2 is intended for children ages 7-7½. The teacher completes a form for each pupil, and enters the ratings on a separate profile/record sheet. This gives a broad overview of the child's areas of strength and weakness, as well as a comparison of the child with others of the same age, in terms of subtests and total scores. When Level 2 is used later with the same pupil, the Scale forms part of a consecutive monitoring procedure to facilitate the planning of an individualized educational strategy, as the child progresses from the Infants to the Junior School. Full statistical details, together with practical illustrations of the uses and interpretations of the IRS, are given in the manual. Self- administered. Suitable for group use.
BRITISH PUBLISHER

Untimed: Not available

Range: Ages Level 1, 5-5½; Level 2, 7-7½

Scoring: Examiner evaluated

Cost: Specimen set (Levels 1 and 2) £2; manual £1.50.

Publisher: Hodder & Stoughton

KAUFMAN DEVELOPMENTAL SCALE (KDS)
Harvey Kaufman

child

Purpose: Evaluates school readiness, developmental deficits, and all levels of retardation for normal children through age nine, and the mentally retarded of all ages. Used in programming accountability.

Description: 270 item task-assessment test consisting of behavioral evaluation items which are actually expandable teaching objectives. The KDS yields a Developmental Age and Developmental Quotient, as well as individual age-scores and quotients for the following areas of behavioral

development: Gross Motor, Fine Motor, Receptive, Expressive, Personal Behavior, and Inter-personal Behavior. Examiner required. Not for group use.

Untimed: Not available

Range: Normal children through 9 years; all ages mentally retarded

Scoring: Examiner evaluated

Cost: Complete kit (includes testing materials, manual, 25 record forms, carrying case) $180.00.

Publisher: Stoelting Co.

KAUFMAN INFANT AND PRE-SCHOOL SCALE (KIPS)
Refer to page 9.

KEELE PRE-SCHOOL ASSESSMENT GUIDE
Stephen Tyler

child   Preschool

Purpose: Assesses child development. Used for identification of strengths and weaknesses and for individual program planning.

Description: Two part outline of a child's developmental abilities. Section I assesses social behavior, while Section II covers the areas of cognition, language, socialization, and physical skills. Performance may be plotted on a circular chart. Examiner required. Not suitable for group use.
BRITISH PUBLISHER

Untimed: Completed in stages over a number of days

Range: Preschool age children

Scoring: Examiner evaluated

Cost: 25 record forms £2.10; manual £1.35 (payment in sterling for all overseas orders).

Publisher: NFER-Nelson Publishing Company

KINDERGARTEN BEHAVIOURAL INDEX
Enid M. Banks

child

Purpose: Measures behavioral development of children ages 5½-6 years. Identifies children in need of further evaluation and assistance.

Description: Paper-pencil checklist records the behavioral responses of children in the normal kindergarten classroom situation. Test items represent the various areas of development considered relevant to future academic learning. The index may be used as a screening technique to identify children whose present functioning indicates a lack of readiness for formal tasks such as learning to read. It may also be used as a guide to specific remediation requirements. Materials include manual and teaching guide, individual record forms, and class record sheet. Self-administered by evaluator. Suitable for group use.
AUSTRALIAN PUBLISHER

Untimed: Not available

Range: Ages 5½-6

Scoring: Examiner evaluated

Cost: Specimen set (package plus manual) $9.50; 40 individual record forms and one class record sheet $6,00; individual class record sheets $.60; manual $3.50 (all remittances must be in Australian currency).

Publisher: The Australian Council for Educational Research Limited

KNOX'S CUBE TEST (KCT)
Mark Stone and Benjamin Wright

child, teen

Purpose: Measures short-term memory and attention span, which together constitute the most elementary stage of mental activity, of children and adults. Used to evaluate deaf, language-impaired, and foreign-speaking persons.

Description: Multiple-task assessment test of attention span and short-term memory. It measures how accurately an individual can repeat simple rhythmic figures which are tapped out for him by the examiner. Test materials include four cubes attached to a wooden base and a separate tapping block. Directions can be delivered in pantomime. The manual provides procedures and rationale for administering, scoring, and interpreting a comprehensive version of KCT which incorporates all previous versions. This revision utilizes Rasch measurement procedures to develop an objective psychometric variable, along which both items and persons can be positioned. Examiner required. Not for group use.

Timed: Not available

Range: Junior version ages 2-8; Senior version ages 8 and older

Scoring: Examiner evaluated

Cost: Both versions complete (includes all testing materials, manual and record forms) $23.00 each.

Publisher: Stoelting Co.

KOONTZ CHILD DEVELOPMENTAL PROGRAM: TRAINING ACTIVITIES FOR THE FIRST 48 MONTHS
Charles W. Koontz

child

Purpose: Evaluates the development of normal and retarded children who are functioning at developmental levels of 1 to 48 months. Used for evaluating and developing skills and can be modified for use with the hearing and visually impaired.

Description: 550 item paper-pencil inventory of observable performance items arranged to parallel development in a normal child. Parent, teacher, or therapist checks off those specific behaviors which have been observed in the child's routine activities. This establishes the level of functioning in each of four areas of evaluation. Progress is recorded in relation to performance items and training activities have been designed to reinforce and develop each skill. The test pages are made of cardboard and are divided in such a way as to make it possible to have different developmental age levels of each of the four areas appear at the same item. Consequently, the person working with a child who is functioning at different levels in any of the four areas can have all the appropriate activities visable at the same time. Administered by the person doing the evaluation. Not for group use.

Untimed: Not available

Range: Ages 1-48 months

Scoring: Hand key

Cost: Complete kit (includes 25 record cards and manual) $21.60.

Publisher: Western Psychological Services

KRAMER PRESCHOOL MATH INVENTORY (KPMI)
Refer to page 244.

MANCHESTER SCALES OF SOCIAL ADAPTATION
E.A. Lunzer

---

child, teen

Purpose: Measures social competence in children. Used for individual evaluation.

Description: Two part measure of social adaptation: Social Perspective and Self-Direction. Each part yields scores on 4 or 5 subscales such as

General Knowledge in Science, General Knowledge in Current Affairs, Self-Help and Handling Money. Examiner required. Not suitable for group use.
BRITISH PUBLISHER

Untimed: 25 minutes

Range: Ages 5-15

Scoring: Hand key

Cost: Specimen set £4.50; 25 score sheets £1.70; manual £3.55 (payment in sterling for all overseas orders).

Publisher: NFER-Nelson Publishing Company

MEETING STREET SCHOOL SCREENING TEST
Peter Hainsworth and Marion Siqueland

---

child

Purpose: Identifies kindergarten and first-grade children with learning disorders. Used to minimize subsequent learning failure and behavioral upset.

Description: 15 item paper-pencil test in three five-item subtests. The motor patterning subtest includes the ability to hop, skip, move on command, fine finger dexterity, and ability to imitate examiner's hand gestures. The visual-perceptual subtest includes copying geometric and letter forms, drawing when commanded, and tapping block patterns in sequence. The language subtest includes repetition of short phrases and sentences and nonsense words, counting forward and backward, sequencing time concepts and describing an abstract picture. The examiner uses a spiral-bound manual and a four page record booklet containing worksheet, scoresheet, behavior rating scale, and performance grid. Normative tables for tests and scores are provided at one-half year levels based on 1966 census figures. Examiner required. Not for

group use.

Untimed: 20 minutes

Range: Ages 5-7½

Scoring: Hand key; examiner evaluated

Cost: Manual $12.00; 50 record forms $5.00; 100 record forms $9.00.

Publisher: Meeting Street School, Easter Seal Society of Rhode Island, Inc.

METROPOLITAN READINESS TESTS (MRT)
Joanne R. Nurss and Mary E. McGauvran

child   grades K-1

Purpose: Assesses underlying skills important for early school learning. For use in identification of each individual child's needs.

Description: Multiple item paper-pencil test of skills important for learning reading, mathematics, and for developing language. The test is divided into two levels. Level I yields scores in three areas: Visual Area, Language Area and Pre-Reading Skills Composite. Level II gives scores in six areas: Auditory Area, Visual Area, Language Area, Quantitative Area, Pre-Reading Skills Composite, and Battery Composite. Materials include two alternate and equivalent forms, P and Q. Examiner required. Suitable for group use.

Timed: Level 1, 80-90 minutes, Level II, 80 minutes

Range: Grades K-1

Scoring: Computer scoring service available

Cost: Specimen set (includes test, manual parts I and II, parent-teacher report, Early School Inventory for each level) $6.00.

Publisher: The Psychological Corporation

METROPOLITAN READINESS TEST: 1965 EDITION
Gertrude H. Hildreth, Nellie L. Griffiths and Mary E. McGauvran

child   grades K-1

Purpose: Assesses underlying skills important for early school learning.

Description: Multiple item paper-pencil test of skills important for learning reading, writing and developing language in Kindergarten and first grade. Materials include two alternate and equivalent forms, A and B. May be used with the Early School Inventory and the Handbook for Skill Development Activities for Young Children. Superseded by the 1976 Metropolitan Readiness Test. Examiner required. Suitable for group use.

Timed: 1 hour (3 sittings)

Range: Grades K-1

Scoring: Hand key

Cost: Specimen set (includes test, manual key, class record) $4.00; 35 tests (includes manual, key, class record-form A or B) $20.00; manual $2.25; keys (specify form A or B) $1.75; class record $1.00.

Publisher: The Psychological Corporation

McCARTHY SCALES OF CHILDREN'S ABILITIES
Refer to page 10.

McCARTHY SCREENING TEST
Dorothea McCarthy

child

Purpose: Predicts a child's ability to cope with schoolwork in the early grades. For use in early identification of children "at risk" for school problems.

Description: Six scale test of mental abilities: right- left orientation, verbal memory, draw-a-person, numerical memory, conceptual grouping, and leg coordination. Children having learning disabilities or other handicaps perform less well than do children without problems. Materials include card for right-left orientation, tape and blocks. Scales are drawn from the McCarthy Scales of Children's Abilities. Examiner required. Not suitable for group use.

Untimed: 20 minutes

Range: Ages 4-6.5

Scoring: Examiner evaluated

Cost: Complete set (includes all necessary equipment, manual, 25 record forms, 25 drawing booklets, carrying case) $47.50.

Publisher: The Psychological Corporation

MINNESOTA CHILD DEVELOPMENT INVENTORY (MCDI)
Refer to page 11.

MINNESOTA PRESCHOOL INVENTORY (MPI)
Harold Ireton and Edward Thwing

child

Purpose: Measures a child's readiness for kindergarten. Used by educators, psychologists, physicians, and other professionals to assess the child's current development, readiness skills, social and emotional adjustment, and symptoms.

Description: 150 item paper-pencil inventory completed by the mother. The inventory measures: self-help, fine motor, expressive language, comprehension, memory, letter recognition, number comprehension, immaturity, hyperactivity, behavior problems, emotional problems, motor, language, somatic and sensory symptoms. For use primarily with mothers with a high school education. Self-administered. Suitable for group use.

Untimed: 15 minutes

Range: Ages 41/2-5½

Scoring: Hand key

Cost: Specimen set (includes manual, booklet, answer sheet, profile form) $11.00; 25 reusable booklets $14.00; 25 answer sheets $6.00; 25 profile forms $6.00; scoring templates $12.00; manual $10.00.

Publisher: Behavior Science Systems, Inc.

THE MINNESOTA PRESCHOOL INVENTORY (MPI) FORM 34
Harold Ireton and Edward Thwing

child

Purpose: Determines readiness of three and four-year old children to enter preschool.

Description: Multiple item paper-pencil inventory used by the mother to review a child's development, adjustment and symptoms. Materials include Form 34 booklets, answer sheets, Form 34 profile forms and manual. Examiner evaluated
CANADIAN PUBLISHER

Untimed: Not available

Range: Ages 3-4

Scoring: Examiner evaluated

Cost: Specimen set (includes instructions, Form 34 booklet, MPI answer sheet, Form 34 profile form) $5.21; 25 Form 34 booklets $17.85; 25 answer sheets $8.95; 25 Form 34 profile forms $8.95; manual $14.88.

Publisher: Institute of Psychological Research, Inc.

PARENT READINESS EVALUATION OF PRESCHOOLERS (PREP)
A. Edward Ahr

child

Purpose: Evaluates verbal and mental abilities of preschool children. Used to assess educational readiness.

Description: 190 item verbal, manual test to ascertain educational readiness in preschoolers by parent. Also aids parents to help the child learn at home by pointing out strengths and weaknesses. Used in conjunction with the handbook entitled Developing Your Child's Skills and Abilities at Home. Examiner required. Not for group use.

Untimed: 30 minutes

Range: Ages 3 years, 9 months-5 years, 6 months

Scoring: Hand key

Cost: Test $2.50.

Publisher: Priority Innovations, Inc.

PEABODY MATHEMATICS READINESS TEST (PMRT)
Otto C. Bassler, Morris I. Beers, Lloyd I. Richardson, and Richard L. Thurman

child   grades K-1

Purpose: Measures the ability of average (4 to 6 years) and special education (4 to 6 mental age) children to complete first grade mathematics. Used for diagnosis and placement.

Description: Multiple item examination assesses the readiness factors of number, containment, size, shape, configuration, and drawing which have been proven to identify students who later display poor mathematics achievement. An Activity Manual provides activities to assist in prescriptive remediation. Examiner required. Suitable for group use.

Timed: 20 minutes

Range: 4-6 mental age (grades K-1)

Scoring: Hand key; examiner evaluated

Cost: Starter set (includes manual, 20 test booklets and performance records, plus activity manual) $22.46.

Publisher: Scholastic Testing Service, Inc.

PEDIATRIC EXAMINATION OF EDUCATIONAL READINESS (PEER)
Melvin D. Levine

child

Purpose: Detects high-prevalence, 'low-severity' disabilities in young children which are critical to success in school. Used for diagnosis, screening, research, and professional training.

Description: A verbal, paper-pencil, show-tell measure of six developmental areas: orientation, gross motor, visual-fine motor, sequential, linguistic, and preacademic skills. the child is asked to identify pictures and copy some of them with a pencil; tasks are presented to the child using numerous miscellaneous items (keys, tennis balls, blocks) contained in the PEER kit; sentences are provided for language assessment. The examination produces an empirical description of what occurred when a child was asked to perform age-appropriate tasks. The information can then be used to help plan health, education and developmentally oriented services. Examiner administered. Not suitable for group use.

Untimed: 1 hours

Range: Ages 4-6

Scoring: Examiner evaluated

Cost: Record forms and stimulus

booklet $16.00; examiner's manual $6.50; stimulus booklet $4.00; kit $6.50; specimen set $1.50; complete set $29.00.

Publisher: Educators Publishing Service, Inc.

PERCEPTUAL MOTOR EDUCATION SCALE
Refer to page 537.

PRE-ACADEMIC LEARNING INVENTORY (PAL)
Mildred H. Wood and Fay M. Layne

child

Purpose: Assesses readiness of young children to handle academic tasks. Used to diagnose strengths and weaknesses in order to plan educational and remedial programs.

Description: Multiple item, checklist examination covering these nine areas: language development, speech development, concept development, body concept, auditory channel development, visual channel development, visual-motor integration, eye-hand coordination, and gross-motor coordination. Materials include stimulus pictures and cards, record booklets and sheets, eye-hand coordination activity sheets, and parent-child activity leaflets. Scoring is by the checklist method. Examiner required. Not for group use.

Untimed: 30-35 minutes

Range: Ages 4½-6

Scoring: Hand key; examiner evaluated

Cost: Manual $5.00; stimulus pictures $6.00; 10 child's record booklets $5.00; 25 eye-hand coordination activity sheets $1.00; 25 parent-child activity leaflets $2.50; 25 accountability record sheets $1.50; visual memory stimulus card $1.00; specimen set $5.00.

Publisher: Academic Therapy Publications

PRESCHOOL EMBEDDED FIGURES TEST (PEFT)
Susan W. Coates

child

Purpose: Assesses individual perceptual processes, including field dependence. Used for counseling and research.

Description: 24 item nonverbal test of cognitive functioning and styles. Items are complex black and white line drawings in which the subject is to find an embedded triangle. Materials include plates with complex figures, clear plastic envelopes, and one simple figure. Examiner required. Not suitable for group use.

Timed: 15 minutes

Range: Ages 3-6

Scoring: Examiner evaluated

Cost: Complete kit (includes manual, plates, 25 record sheets). $10.00.

Publisher: Consulting Psychologists Press, Inc.

PRESCHOOL LANGUAGE SCALE (PLS)
Refer to page 592.

PRESCHOOL SCREENING INSTRUMENT
Stephen Paul Cohen

child

Purpose: Identifies pre-kindergarten children who have learning disabilities. Used to meet P.L. 94-142 screening requirements.

Description: Multiple item, task-assessment test. The child is told in a fun manner that he will be "playing some games" with the examiner, who administers the following subtests: figure drawing, circle drawing, tower building, cross drawing, block design, square drawing, broad jumping, balancing, ball throwing, hopping, whole name, picture responses, comprehension, and oral vocabulary. The child's responses are evaluated in seven developmental areas: visual-motor perception, fine motor development, gross motor skills, language development, verbal fluency, conceptual skills, and speech and behavioral problems. Examiner required. Not for group use.

Untimed: 5-8 minutes

Range: Ages 4 years-5 years, 3 months (tables extend down to 3-0 years)

Scoring: Examiner evaluated

Cost: Complete kit (includes 25 student record books, manual, 16 wooden blocks, picture story card, and 6 kindergarten-size pencils) $48.00.

Publisher: Stoelting Co.

PRESCHOOL SELF-CONCEPT PICTURE TEST (PS-CPT)
Refer to page 638.

PRESCREENING DEVELOPMENTAL QUESTIONNAIRE (PDQ)
W.K. Frankenburg, W. VanDoorninck, T. Liddell, and N. Dick

child

Purpose: Determines if children can perform certain skills that most children their age can do; useful as indicator for further testing.

Description: 97 item, paper-pencil test administered by the parents, who are given response forms color-coded by age, with 10 questions appropriate for each age group. Examiners must have at least a high school education. Examiner required. Suitable for groups. Available in Spanish and French.

Untimed: 2-5 minutes

Range: Ages 3 months to 6 years

Scoring: Hand key

Cost: 100 forms $6.00 (order by age group): 3-5 months, green form; 6-8 months, both green and pink forms; 9-12 months, pink form; 13-15 months, both pink and yellow forms; 16-24 months, yellow forms; 2 yrs. 1 month-2 yrs. 9 months, both yellow and blue forms; 3-4, blue forms; 4 yrs. 3 months-4 yrs. 9 months, both blue and while forms; 5-6 white form; directions and interpretive instructions included.

Publisher: Ladoca Publishing Foundation

PRESCRIPTIVE TEACHING SERIES
Sue Martin

child, teen   grades 1-8

Purpose: Measures individual child development. Used for assessment of child's strengths and weaknesses and for planning educational experiences.

Description: Six scale test of development in the following areas: visual, visual-motor, motor, auditory, reading and language, and math. Visual Skills Test is composed of 22 skills with 104 sub-items. Visual-Motor Skills Booklet is composed of 28 items in four areas: body imagery, spatial orientation, visual-motor discrimination, and writing skills. Motor Skills booklet consists of 166 items. Auditory Skills Booklet is made up of 31 items in several areas: auditory stimuli, speech response to auditory stimuli, oral reading and phonetic analysis. Reading and Language Skills booklet is composed of 152 skills; Math Skills is composed of 315 skills. Examiner required. Not suitable for group use.

Untimed: Each rating period 15 minutes

Range: Grades 1-8

Scoring: Hand key; examiner evaluated

Cost: Specimen set (includes 1 copy all booklets and manual) $7.25; examiner's set (includes 10 copies all booklets and manual) $37.50; 25 Visual Skills, 25 Visual-Motor Skills $12.50 each; 25 Motor Skills, 25 Auditory Skills, 25 Reading and Language Skills $16.50 each, 25 Math Skills $27.50.

Publisher: Psychologists and Educators, Inc.

PRIMARY ACADEMIC SENTIMENT SCALE (PASS)
Glen Robbins Thompson

child

Purpose: Assesses a child's motivation for learning, level of maturity and parental independence. Used to screen for school readiness and develop academic moivation plans.

Description: 38 item verbal scale yielding two scores: sentiment quotient (interest in academics) and dependency stanine (child's interdependence on parents). The child is shown pictures of various activities and asked to point to how he feels: a happy, neutral or sad face. Examiner required. Suitable for group use.

Untimed: 30 minutes

Range: 4 years 4 months-7 years 3 months

Scoring: Hand key

Cost: 10-99 forms $1.30.

Publisher: Priority Innovations, Inc.

PRIMARY EDUCATION PROGRAM: DIAGNOSTIC TEST FOR CLASSIFICATION/COMMUNICATION SKILLS (PEP)
Margaret C. Wang and Lauren B. Resnick

child

Purpose: Measures the ability of young children to match, sort and name things. Used by teahers for individual curriculum planning.

Description: Multiple item, picture-book, verbal test of a child's ability to match like objects, discriminate shapes and sizes, name colors and shapes, and handle descriptions of size, length, width and height. One test is provided for each objective. Materials include a progress chart and a 108-page spiral-bound manual containing color illustrations on glossy paper. Examiner required. Not suitable for group use.

Untimed: Not available

Range: Ages 3-6

Scoring: Hand key; examiner evaluated

Cost: Complete kit $27.95.

Publisher: Mafex Associates, Inc.

PRIMARY EDUCATION PROGRAM: DIAGNOSTIC TESTS FOR QUANTIFICATION SKILLS
Margaret C. Wang and Lauren B. Resnick

child

Purpose: Assesses entry-level quantification skills of preschool and primary grade children. Used for group placement and to check instructional progress.

Description: Eight unit verbal test covering 56 objectives: Nine in counting and comprehending one-to-one correspondences to the number 5; nine in counting and comprehending one-to-one correspondences to the number 10; seven in numerals to the number 5; seven in numerals 6-10; seven in comparison of sets; four in seriation and ordinal position; seven in addition and subtraction; and six in adding and subtracting equations. Materials include a spiral-bound manual, progress chart, and handbook with all necessary instructions. Examiner required. Not for group use.

Untimed: Not available

Range: Ages 3-6

Scoring: Hand key; examiner evaluated

Cost: Complete kit $22.95.

Publisher: Mafex Associates, Inc.

PRIMARY MENTAL ABILITIES (PMA) READINESS LEVEL I
L.L. Thurstone and Thelma Gwinn Thurstone

child   grades K-1

Purpose: Assesses learning readiness of kindergarten and first grade students. Provides information about level of development compared with other children. Used in planning materials and instruction rates, identifying special needs, facilitating grouping and communicating with parents.

Description: 90 item paper-pencil test measures auditory discrimination, verbal meaning, perceptual speed, number facility, spatial relations. Grade-based normative information available. Examiner required. Suitable for group use.

Untimed: 60 minutes

Range: Grades K-1

Scoring: Hand key

Cost: Complete set (includes 30 copies each of 4 test booklets and student

profile folders, 1 examiner's manual, and 1 user's manual) $24.75; specimen set $3.00.

Publisher: Science Research Associates, Inc.

THE PRIMARY VISUAL MOTOR TEST
Refer to page 537.

PSYCHOLOGICAL EVALUATION OF CHILDRENS HUMAN FIGURES DRAWING (HFD)
Refer to page 88.

PUPIL RECORD OF EDUCATIONAL BEHAVIOR (PREB)
Refer to page 390.

RAPID EXAM FOR EARLY REFERRAL (REFER)
Carl H. Koenig and Harold P. Kunzelman

child   grades PRE-K

Purpose: Identifies potential learning problems of preschool and kindergarten children by gathering data about a child's language and non-language skills, in both receptive and expressive channels, as a guide to placement in special programs.

Description: Multiple item, examiner-guided, verbal, paper- pencil test in which the child responds to questions, draws loops, and touches parts named by the examiner. The results identify children who need special help or are candidates for accelerated programs. Related Challenge' materials are available for follow-up. Examiner required. Not suitable for group use.

Untimed: 5 minutes

Range: Preschool and kindergarten

Scoring: Examiner evaluated

Cost: Manual and scoreforms $21.90; specimen set $12.95.

Publisher: Charles E. Merrill Publishing Company

(REVISED) PRE-READING SCREENING PROCEDURES
Refer to page 566.

REYNELL-ZINKIN DEVELOPMENTAL SCALES FOR YOUNG VISUALLY HANDICAPPED CHILDREN
Refer to page 13.

RILEY PRESCHOOL DEVELOPMENTAL SCREENING INVENTORY
Clara M.D. Riley

child   grades PRE-1

Purpose: Measures readiness of young children to attend school and identifies those most likely to need assistance. Used for counseling and to meet the requirements of P.L. 94-142.

Description: Multiple item, observational test of children's developmental age and self-concept to determine serious development and maturity problems. Can be administered at the beginning of pre-school, kindergarten or first-grade. Developed and widely used in Head Start Programs. Provides suggested cut-off scores. Examiner required. Suitable for group use. Test instructions are in both Spanish and English.

Untimed: 15-20 minutes

Range: Preschool-grade 1

Scoring: Examiner evaluated

Cost: Complete kit (includes 25 tests and manual) $9.80.

Publisher: Western Psychological Services

ROCKFORD INFANT DEVELOPMENTAL SCALES (RIDES)
Project RHISE

child

Purpose: Evaluates the level of a child's skill and behavioral development. Used for initial assessment by special education teachers to guide and objectify their observations of a child.

Description: Multiple item paper-pencil evaluation of 308 developmental behaviors arranged by age into five skill areas: personal-social/self-help, fine motor/adaptive, receptive language, expressive language, and gross motor. Each behavioral item is determined to be present, emerging or absent. Test results relate these single items to major developmental patterns and competencies. The format calls for one eight-page booklet per child. An Individual Child Progress Graph on the back page shows progress and allows comparison of level across developmental areas. The manual contains a section detailing development, and use and interpretation of RIDES. The entries for all 308 behaviors provide scoring criteria, developmental significance, equipment specifications, and references to further information, along with an appendix containing master equipment list, skill group listings, notes, and bibliography. The Starter Set includes manual and 20 checklists. Examiner required. Not for group use.

Untimed: Varies

Range: Birth-4 years

Scoring: Hand key

Cost: Starter set $33.56.

Publisher: Scholastic Testing Service, Inc.

SANTA CLARA PLUS COMPUTER MANAGEMENT SYSTEM

child

Purpose: Assesses cognitive and affective skills of children ages 3½-7. Used for diagnostic and prescriptive mastery of objectives for kindergarten and special education students.

Description: Multiple test kit assessing 60 cognitive and 12 affective skills (one item per objective). Child is directed to perform an activity; the examiner monitors the tasks and rates the child's performance; results are transferred to a profile chart or micro-computer diskette for analysis and prescription. Prescriptive materials provided. Examiner required. Suitable for group use.

Untimed: Not available

Range: Ages 3½-7

Scoring: Hand key; may be computer scored

Cost: Complete $160.00 plus $50.00 per diskette for each additional classroom; package of test cards $4.00.

Publisher: Skillcorp Software, Inc.

SCHOOL ENTRANCE CHECKLIST
John McLeod

child   grades K-1

Purpose: Gathers relevant social data about a child just entering school.

Description: 18 item paper-pencil questionnaire to be filled out by parents or guardians at the time a child enters school. Recommended for routine survey and screening. The School Entrance Checklist contains the most pertinent questions from the Dyslexia Schedule, but contains only 18 of the Dyslexia Schedule's 89 questions to avoid overwhelming the parent. The School Entrance Checklist may be sent home for the parents to complete and return. Self-administered.

Untimed: 20-30 minutes

Range: Kindergarten and grade 1

Scoring: Examiner evaluated

Cost: Under 100-$.50 each; over 100-$.45 each.

Publisher: Educators Publishing Service, Inc.

THE SCHOOL READINESS CHECKLIST
John J. Austin and J. Clayton Lafferty

child

Purpose: Determines a child's readiness for kindergarten work. Used to educate parents about learning patterns and to help with preschool clinics and meetings.

Description: 43 item paper-pencil test in yes-no format of the subject's comprehension, age and growth, practical skills, attitudes and interests, memory for numbers, and general knowledge. Materials include booklets with white child or black child illustrations. Self-administered by parents and teachers. Not suitable for group use. Manual available in Spanish.

Untimed: 15 minutes

Range: Kindergarten readiness

Scoring: Examiner evaluated

Cost: Specimen set (includes condensed version of Ready-or-Not Handbook, 2 kindergarten, 2 1st grade) $4.00; manual $6.95; 50 checklists $8.00.

Publisher: Research Concepts

SCHOOL READINESS SCREENING TEST
Gesell Institute

child

Purpose: Measures coordination, motor skills and verbal ability of young children. Used to determine developmental readiness for kindergarten.

Description: Multiple task, verbal, manual and paper-pencil examination in five subtests measuring predominant adaptive behavior. Subtests are: (1) Cube Test measures eye-hand coordination, motor skills, attention span, level of functioning in a structured fine motor task (2) Interview questions to reveal speech clarity and accuracy of information; (3) Paper-pencil tests of visual perception, neuro-muscular, eye-hand coordination, general maturity level; (4) Incomplete Man, to provide clues to perceptual functioning by having child complete a human figure; (5) Animals and Interests to test verbal abilities, provide clues about a child's tempo, organization of thinking, capacity to attend. Materials: manual, 50 recording sheets, developmental schedules, 10 cubes, bean-bag, picture vocabulary booklet 2-sided letters and numbers chart. 3-hole formboard, color forms, copy forms, non-toxic pellets bottle. Examiner required. Not suitable for group use.

Untimed: 20 minutes

Range: Ages 4½-5

Scoring: Examiner evaluated

Cost: Complete kit $62.00.

Publisher: Programs for Education, Inc.

SCHOOL READINESS SURVEY
F.L. Jordan and James Massey

child

Purpose: Assesses a child's understanding of numbers, colors, words and forms. Used to determine readiness for kindergarten.

Description: 95 item paper-pencil, verbal test consisting of eight school readiness subtests: Number Concept, Discrimination of Form, Color Naming, Symbol Matching, Speaking Vocabulary, Listening Vocabulary, General Information, and General Readiness. Parent-administered scores correlated with teacher-administered scores. Materials include suggestions to parents for developing child's skill areas. Parents must supply two pencils and a marker. Can be administered by parents. Examiner required.

Untimed: Not available

Range: Ages 4-6

Scoring: Examiner evaluated

Cost: Specimen set $1.00; manual $.75; 25 surveys $13.00.

Publisher: Consulting Psychologists Press, Inc.

SCHOOL READINESS TEST (SRT)
Oliver F. Anderhalter

child   grades K-1

Purpose: Determines individual and group readiness for first grade. Used to identify and diagnose students with skill deficiencies.

Description: Multiple item, paper-pencil, verbal test designed for children entering the first grade. It reveals readiness for formal instruction by assessing seven skill areas: Word Recognition, Identifying Letters, Visual Discrimination, Auditory Discrimination, Comprehension and Interpretation, Handwriting Readiness, and Number Readiness. The test results show each child at one of six readiness levels which can be the basis for placement. Examiner required. Suitable for group use.

Manual available in Spanish.

Timed: 60 minutes

Range: End of kindergarten-first 3 weeks of grade 1

Scoring: Hand key; examiner evaluated

Cost: Complete set (includes 35 booklets, manual, scoring key, class record sheet) $19.50.

Publisher: Scholastic Testing Service, Inc.

SCHOOLREADINESS TESTS FOR BLIND CHILDREN (STBC)

child

Purpose: Assesses cognitive abilities of blind children. Used for determining school readiness.

Description: Seven subtest measure of cognitive skills important to school readiness including Information Test, Kinesthesis Test, Vocabulary Test, Number Concept Test, Motor Development Test, Memory Test, and Reasoning Test. Examiner may make subjective evaluations of child's perseverance, readiness to follow instructions and social adjustment. Examiner required. Not suitable for group use.
SOUTH AFRICAN PUBLISHER

Untimed: 1½ hours

Range: Blind children

Scoring: Examiner evaluated

Cost: (In Rands) Complete kit (includes 10 biographical questionnaires, 10 answer sheets, container, apparatus and manual) 99,70 (orders from outside The RSA will be dealt with on merit).

Publisher: Human Sciences Research Council

SCREENING TEST OF ACADEMIC READINESS (STAR)
A. Edward Ahr

child

Purpose: Measures mental ability and emotional development of young children. Used to determine readiness to enter school.

Description: 50 item paper-pencil, 'point-to' test consisting of eight subtests. They are: Picture Vocabulary, Letters, Picture Completion, Copying, Picture Description, Human Figure, Relationships, and Numbers. The examiner asks the child to point to, or mark in the answer book as instructed. For instance, marking the orange where it is shown with four other objects, or matching the tame animal where shown with three wild animals. The child's understanding of the world is evaluated by asking him or her to identify objects, copy simple figures, or identify an object after hearing a description of it, such as a knife among other items in a picture. Examiner required. Suitable for group use.

Untimed: 1 hour

Range: Ages 4-6

Scoring: Hand key

Cost: Specimen set $4.00; test $1.30.; manual included with 35 orders.

Publisher: Priority Innovations, Inc.

SCREENING TEST FOR THE ASSIGNMENT OF REMEDIAL TREATMENT
A. Edward Ahr

child

Purpose: Assesses the skill development of children ages 4 years 6 months to 6 years 5 months. Identifies children in need of further evaluation for potential learning difficulties. Also used to evaluate kindergarten and grade 1 instructional programs.

Description: 50 item orally administered test assessing the basic skills required for successful performance in kindergarten and grade 1. Measures the following factors: visual memory, auditory memory, visual-motor coordination, and visual discrimination. Each test item consists of four pictures presented on one page in the test booklet. The examiner instructs the child to look at each page, then provides a task for the pictures presented for each test item: select the correct answer, copy the pictures or remember what is pictured for delayed response. Examiner required. Suitable for group use.

Timed: 45 minutes

Range: Ages 4 years 6 months to 6 years 5 months

Scoring: Hand key

Cost: Specimen set $4.00.

Publisher: Priority Innovations, Inc.

SEQUENCED INVENTORY OF COMMUNICATION DEVELOPMENT
Refer to page 14.

SENTENCE IMITATION SCREENING TEST (SIST)
Merlin J. Mecham and J. Dean Jones

child

Purpose: Identifies children who have problems in handling syntactic transformational rules. Used to screen Head Start and early education classes for students who are in need of more extended diagnostic testing.

Description: 90 item oral response

test consisting of three sets of 30 items each. Measures the following factors: production (imitation) of syntactic transformational rules, language processing, short-term memory span, and verbal imitative performance. The examiner says the stimulus sentences and the child is asked to repeat them. The child's responses are tape-recorded and analyzed later for specified types of errors. Test kit includes manual (with stimulus sentences) and 50 score sheets. Examiner required. Not for group use.

Untimed: 5-10 minutes

Range: Ages 3-6 years

Scoring: Examiner evaluated

Cost: Manual and 50 score sheets $10.50.

Publisher: Communication Research Associates, Inc.

S.O.I. LEARNING ABILITIES TEST
Mary Meeker and Robert Meeker

child   grades 1-6

Purpose: Measures learning abilities of elementary and intermediate school children. Used for cognitive clinical assessment, diagnosis, screening for giftedness, and to identify specific learning deficiencies.

Description: 430 item paper-pencil, multiple-choice and free response test. The test measures 24 of the factors identified by Guilford's Structure-of-Intellect model. The operations of Cognition, Memory, Evaluation, Convergent Production, and Divergent Production are applied to Figural, Symbolic, and Semantic content. Available in five forms: two equivalent forms, A and B; and a career-vocational form; and two shorter forms (200 items each), one for gifted-screening and one for special education use. The shorter forms use 12 subtest factors. All use printed test forms and a manual with visual aids for group presentations. The test is administered to groups or individuals by an examiner who leads the child/children through the test booklet. Training in administration and usage is required. Examiner required. Suitable for group use in some situations.

Untimed: Not available

Range: Grades 1-6 and intermediate school level

Scoring: Hand key; examiner evaluated; computer scoring available

Cost: Cost information available from Western Psychological Services or: S.O.I. Institute, 343 Richmond Street, El Segundo, CA 90245.

Publisher: Western Psychological Services

SWANSEA EVALUATION PROFILE FOR SCHOOL ENTRANTS
Refer to page 191.

THE TACTILE TEST OF BASIC CONCEPTS

child

Purpose: Assesses the visually impaired child's mastery of concepts that are commonly found in preschool and primary grade instructional materials and that are essential to understanding oral communications from teachers and fellow pupils. Used with children from kindergarten to grade 2 who require braille and other tactile media.

Description: 50 item tactile test of verbal comprehension and conceptual development of visually impaired children. Five practice cards are provided to familiarize the child with the test task and to determine if he is familiar with the raised outline forms

used in the test (circle, square, triangle, rectangle). The 50 test items are identical to those of the Boehm Test of Basic Concepts, presented with raised outline forms. A few items consist of simple raised outline drawings. BTBC test manual included for use in interpreting the test results. Examiner required. Not for group use.

Untimed: Not available

Range: Visually impaired children K-2

Scoring: Not available

Cost: Complete set (5 practice cards, 50 test cards, 1 class record form, TTBC test manual, BTBC test manual) $30.00.

Publisher: American Printing House for the Blind

TEST OF BASIC EXPERIENCES (TOBE2)
Margaret H. Moss

child   grades K-1

Purpose: Measures degree to which young children have acquired concepts and experiences related to effective school participation. Used for evaluation of school readiness.

Description: Multiple item battery of paper-pencil tests measuring quantity and quality of children's early experiences. Divided into two overlapping levels, K and L, covering preschool programs through grade one. Each level has four tests: Language, Mathematics, Science, and Social Studies. Each TOBE item consists of a verbal stimulus, read by the examiner, and four pictured responses. Level K can be used in the spring of prekindergarten, the fall and spring of kindergarten, and the fall of first grade. Level L is for use in the spring of kindergarten and the fall and spring of first grade. Available materials include an

Instructional Activities Kit with materials for teaching concepts and skills. Examiner required. Suitable for group use. Administration directions available in Spanish.

Untimed: 45 minutes for each test

Range: Grades K-1

Scoring: Hand key; computer scoring available

Cost: Specimen set for either level K or L (includes machine and hand-scorable test books, manual with key, norms and data book, a practice test, class evaluation record, and a test reviewer's guide) $7.25.

Publisher: CTB/McGraw-Hill

TEST OF EARLY LEARNING SKILLS (TELS)
Jwalla P. Somwaru

child

Purpose: Assesses the cognitive skills of preschool and kindergarten children at the beginning of their formal education. Used to evaluate individual strengths and weaknesses and to plan instruction.

Description: 54 item verbal response test consisting of three subtests: Thinking Skills (18 items), Language Skills (18 items), and Number Skills (18 items). The TELS is individually administered, with the child and examiner on opposite sides of a table. Scoring provides diagnostic information, raw scores and a Developmental Age. The Starter Set contains: a manual, one reusable test, 20 response forms, manipulatives, and carrying case. Examiner required. Not suitable for group use.

Untimed: 30 minutes

Range: Ages 3½-5½

Scoring: Hand key; examiner evaluated

Cost: Starter set $54.50.

Publisher: Scholastic Testing Service, Inc.

TEST OF LINGUISTIC AWARENESS IN READING READINESS (LARR Test)
Refer to page 507.

UNIFORM PERFORMANCE ASSESSMENT SYSTEM (UPAS)
Owen R. White, et al

all ages

Purpose: Evaluates the social and behavioral development of handicapped individuals. Used by psychologists and special educators to set Individualized Education Program objectives and measure progress.

Description: 250 item verbal response test using stimulus cards to introduce tasks for measuring five categories of performance: pre-academic/fine motor skills, communication skills, social/self-help skills, gross motor development, and behavior management. Test kit includes: stimulus cards, record forms and manual. Examiner required. Not for group use.

Untimed: Varies; some subtests timed

Range: Ages 0-adult

Scoring: Examiner evaluated

Cost: Complete (includes stimulus cards, record forms, manual) $70.00.

Publisher: Charles E. Merrill Publishing Company

UTAH TEST OF LANGUAGE DEVELOPMENT
Refer to page 600.

VALETT DEVELOPMENTAL SURVEY OF BASIC LEARNING ABILITIES

Refer to page 562.

VALETT INVENTORY OF CRITICAL THINKING (VICTA)
Robert E. Valett

child, teen

Purpose: Assesses problem-solving skills and abilities of children and older exceptional pupils who have developmental difficulties. Used at the beginning of a diagnostic session to establish rapport with a child.

Description: 100 item verbal response examination of sensory-perceptual exploration, intuitive organization, concrete relationships, representational concepts, and propositional logic. The test consists of problems dealing with these 10 critical thinking abilities: knowledge, analysis, calculation, verbal conceptualization, synthesis, comprehension, application, humor, evaluation, and imagination. A quantitative evaluation of the student's critical thinking ability is provided by determing the percentage of tasks passed at each of the five developmental stages and comparing that figure with the child's age. Only items of appropriate difficulty for a child are tested. Examiner required. Not suitable for group use.

Untimed: 40 minutes

Range: Ages 4-15 and older exceptional pupils with developmental difficulties

Scoring: Examiner evaluated

Cost: Manual $7.50; 25 record forms $6.00; specimen set $7.50.

Publisher: Academic Therapy Publications

THE VANE KINDERGARTEN TEST (VKT)
Julia R. Vane

child   Kindergarten

Purpose: Evaluates the academic potential of young children and identifies those for whom remedial help may be necessary.

Description: Multiple item, task assessment, oral response test consisting of three parts. In the first part, the child is shown pictures of three shapes (circle, square, hexagon) and asked to copy them on a sheet of paper. In the second part, the child turns the paper over and draws a picture of a man. In the third part, the child identifies as many words as possible from a list of 12 words arranged in order of difficulty. All 12 words are rarely used, except with exceptionally bright children. The child's responses are assessed in a number of areas: eye-hand coordination, vocabulary development, emotional adjustment, hearing deficiency. Examiner required. Suitable for group use.

Untimed: 10 minutes

Range: Kindergarten

Scoring: Examiner evaluated

Cost: Manual $4.00; 50 record sheets $3.50.

Publisher: Clinical Psychology Publishing Company, Inc.

VINELAND SOCIAL MATURITY SCALE

Refer to page 16.

VISCO CHILD DEVELOPMENT SCREENING TEST (THE CHILDS TEST)
Susan J. Visco and Carmela R. Visco

child

Purpose: Assesses the development of learning abilities and skills in children ages 3-7 years. Identifies children with possible learning disabilities who should be referred for diagnostic evaluation.

Description: 118 item task performance test measuring the basic skills and abilities required in the learning process. The following factors are evaluated: Processing Functions (visual perceptuomotor, auditory-visual-motor integration, visual vocal, and auditory vocal), Abilities (sequencing, language, numerical, syntax, and articulation), and Cognition (cognitive efficiency). In addition to the materials included in the kit, the following items are required: a stopwatch, a small table, 2 chairs, a tape for a line, a small cup, and a flight of stairs. Examiner required. Not for group use.

Untimed: 25-30 minutes

Range: Ages 3-7

Scoring: Hand key; examiner evaluated

Cost: Program contains: Overview Manual, Test Administration and Scoring Manual, 20 individualized record booklets, 9 one-inch cubes, 7 numerical Gestalt cards, 25 labels and functions picture cards, felt strip with 4 buttons, felt strip with 4 button holes $43.00; 10 extra record booklets $8.90; orientation and training sound filmstrip $19.00.

Publisher: Educational Activities, Inc.

VISUAL PATTERN RECOGNITION TEST DIAGNOSTIC SCHEDULE AND TRAINING MATERIALS
Diane Montgomery

child

Purpose: Assesses pre-reading behaviors and skills of children ages 4 years 7 months to 5 years 6 months. Identifies children who are lacking specific skills and suggests relevant learning programs for both groups and individuals.

Description: Four task performance tests assessing a child's competencies and difficulties regarding readiness for reading instruction. The tests provide a behavioral assessment of the child in terms of motivation, attention span, and distractibility, while an analysis is also being made of visual pattern recognition skills and sub- skills of the reading process. The child's responses to the visual problems are direct and not mediated by verbal behavior, and the administration can take place without oral instructions.
Children who have difficulty completing the test are easily identified, and teaching materials can be constructed to help them learn the critical rules for recognition required for reading. Useful for classroom teachers, pediatricians, educational psychologists, clinical psychologists, and teachers of the mentally handicapped. Specimen Set includes: manual, 25 score sheets, subtests 1A, 1B, 1C, and 1D (1 copy each), but no counters or sticks. The Complete Set includes: manual, 25 score sheets, subtests 1A and 1B (1 copy each), subtests 1C and 1D (25 copies each), and a set of sticks and counters. Examiner required. Not for group use.
BRITISH PUBLISHER

Untimed: 15-25 minutes

Range: Ages 4 years 7 months to 5

years 6 months

Scoring: Hand key

Cost: Complete set £9.00; 25 score sheets £1.25; subtests A1 £0.95; subtests 1B £0.75; 25 subtests 1C £0.95; 25 subtests 1D £0.95; set coloured counters £2.45; set sticks and counters £0.65; manual £3.20.

Publisher: NFER-Nelson Publishing Company

VOCABULARY COMPREHENSION SCALE (VCS)
Refer to page 209.

WACHS ANALYSIS OF COGNITIVE STRUCTURES
Harry Wachs and Lawrence J. Vaughan

---

child

Purpose: Measures the development of learning ability among young children and suggests activities to stimulate learning growth as described in *Thinking Goes to School: Piaget's Theory in Practice.* Used especially with the learning disabled and the culturally disadvantaged.

Description: An observational examination. The examiner watches the child perform tasks based on Piaget's theories of measuring cognitive development in terms of "body" and "sense" thinking. The inventory consists of 15 clusters of tasks divided into subtests made up of a variety of manipulative, visual-sensory, and body movement actions which are grouped into four areas of assessment: identification of objects, object design, graphic design, and general movement. The test is primarily nonverbal and culture fair and has been used successfully with children having language and mental deficiencies and hearing deficits. Standardized on white and minority children with percentile and standard scores presented for each of the four areas of assessment as well as the total test at six month age intervals. A profile sheet enhances communication with parents. Manual includes a curriculum guide and supplemental diagnostic tasks for more indepth analysis. Examiner required. Not for group use.

Untimed: 30-45 minutes

Range: Ages 3-5 years 11 months

Scoring: Hand key; examiner evaluated

Cost: Complete kit (includes test materials, 10 record books and profile sheets, manual, carrying case) $219.00.

Publisher: Western Psychological Services.

YELLOW BRICK ROAD (YBR)
Christine Kallstrom

---

child   Preschool

Purpose: Identifies functional strengths and weaknesses in preschool children. Used for kindergarten screening and instructional programming.

Description: 24 item paper-pencil, motor, vision test specifically designed to follow the Wizard of Oz theme. It is divided into these four batteries: Motor, Visual, Auditory, and Language, with each battery subdivided into six test units. Materials include the manual, battery booklets for administration and scoring, and the testing materials (manipulatives). Can be administered individually by an examiner or in a group setting, with volunteers, aides, and parents assisting the examiners.

Untimed: 45 minutes

Range: Preschool

Scoring: Examiner evaluated

Cost: Complete $52.00.

Publisher: Teaching Resources
Corporation

Intelligence and Related

ACER ADVANCED TEST AL-AQ (SECOND EDITION) and BL-BQ

teen, adult

Purpose: Measures intelligence of students ages 15 years and older at secondary and tertiary levels.

Description: Multiple item paper-pencil intelligence test is available in two parallel forms, AL-AQ (second edition) and BL-BQ. The L section of both forms deal with linguistic items; the Q section with quantitative items. Norms are presented for upper secondary level and first year samples from TAFE colleges and Colleges of Advanced Education. Materials include: expendable booklets for each section (AL, BL, AQ OR BQ), scoring keys for each section, manual, and specimen set. Examiner required. Suitable for group use.
AUSTRALIAN PUBLISHER

Timed: AL, BL-15 minutes; AQ, BQ-20 minutes

Range: Ages 15 years and older

Scoring: Hand key; examiner evaluated

Cost: Contact publisher.

Publisher: The Australian Council for Educational Research, Ltd.

ACER ADVANCED TEST B40 (REVISED)
Refer to page 17.

ACER ADVANCED TEST N
Refer to page 17.

ACER HIGHER TESTS: WL-WQ, ML-MQ (SECOND EDITION) and PL-PQ
Refer to page 19.

ACER INTERMEDIATE TEST F
Refer to page 17.

ACER INTERMEDIATE TEST G
Refer to page 18.

ACER JUNIOR A TEST
Refer to page 18.

ACER JUNIOR NON-VERBAL TEST
Refer to page 18.

ACER LOWER GRADES GENERAL ABILITY SCALE
Refer to page 19.

ACTIVITIES FOR ASSESSING CLASSIFICATION SKILLS (EXPERIMENTAL EDITION)
Rachel Gal-Choppin

child

Purpose: Diagnosis problems in classification skills. Used for identification of children needing remedial assistance in this cognitive area.

Description: Series of four activities assessing classification skills. Four activities become progressively more difficult. In each activity children must cut and re-group pictures of shapes and objects according to different properties, then explain what they have done. Performance judged against set criteria. Administered in informal classroom situation. Materials include two forms, A for ages 7 to 8, and B for ages 9 to 11 and older. Examiner required. Suitable for group use. BRITISH PUBLISHER

Untimed: 50 minutes

Range: Ages 7-12

Scoring: Examiner evaluated against set criteria

Cost: Specimen set £5.40; 5 class record forms £1.35; 1 activities 1-4 form (specify A or B) £0.95 (payment in sterling for all overseas orders).

Publisher: NFER-Nelson Publishing Company

ADVANCED PROGRESSIVE MATRICES (APM-1962)
Refer to page 19.

AH1, x and y
A. W. Heim, K. P. Watts and V. Simmonds

child

Purpose: Assesses perceptual or non-verbal reasoning skills. Used for classroom evaluation of poor readers.

Description: Four subtest, paper-pencil measure of nonverbal reasoning. Subtests are: Series, Likes, Analogues, and Differents. Items are multiple-choice, and are presented in pictorial or diagrammatic format. Materials include two parallel forms, X and Y. Examiner required. Suitable for group use. BRITISH PUBLISHER

Timed: up to 45 minutes

Range: Ages 7-11

Scoring: Hand key

Cost: AH1 specimen set £12.60; 25 booklets (specify form) £8.95; key £4.35 plus VAT; manual £7.45 (payment in sterling for all overseas orders).

Publisher: NFER-Nelson Publishing Company

AH2/AH3-GROUP TEST OF GENERAL ABILITY
A. W. Heim, K. P. Watts and V. Simmonds

all ages

Purpose: Assesses general reasoning ability. Used for evaluating intelligence.

Description: 120 item paper-pencil test of three areas of reasoning ability: Verbal (V), Numerical (N) and Perceptual (P). There are 40 items in each area, and all items are multiple-choice with six response alternatives. Perceptual subtest presents items in diagrammatic and pictorial formats. Profile of the subject, showing areas of strength and weakness, may be constructed. Materials include two parallel forms, AH2 and AH3. Developed as an alternative to the AH4 Group Tests of Intelligence. Examiner required. Suitable for group use. BRITISH PUBLISHER

Timed: Short time-28 minutes; Longer time-42 minutes

Range: Ages 10-adult

Scoring: Hand key

Cost: Specimen set £9.40; 25 question books (specify form) £20.80; 25 answer sheets (specify form) £4.40; marking keys £1.55 each; manual £3.75 (payment in sterling for all overseas orders).

Publisher: NFER-Nelson Publishing Company

AH4 GROUP TEST OF GENERAL INTELLIGENCE (REGULAR EDITION)
A. W. Heim

all ages

Purpose: Measures general intellectual ability. Used for evaluation of children, adults, or selected groups with below average levels of intelligence.

Description: Multiple item paper-pencil test of general intelligence. There are two major sections. The first tests verbal and numerical skills, and the second uses items presented in diagrammatic form. Items require deductive reasoning, understanding of everyday words, observing details accurately, and following simple instructions exactly. Most items are multiple-choice, although a few require more extensive answers. Examiner required. Suitable for group use. BRITISH PUBLISHER

Timed: 10 minutes for each part

Range: Over 10 years of age and cross section of the adult population

Scoring: Hand key; computer scoring service available

Cost: Specimen set £2.95; 25 booklets £8.75; 25 answer sheets £1.65 plus VAT; key £0.45 plus VAT; manual £2.05 (payment in sterling for all overseas orders).

Publisher: NFER-Nelson Publishing Company

AH5 GROUP TEST OF HIGH GRADE INTELLIGENCE
A. W. Heim

teen, adult

Purpose: Assesses general intellectual ability. Used for evaluating subjects of above average intelligence.

Description: Two-part, paper-pencil test of intelligence. The first part is comprised of verbal and numerical problems, the second of problems in diagrammatic form. Majority of items are multiple-choice. Emphasis is on deductive reasoning, but test also requires accurate observation, attention to detail, and ability to appreciate shades of meaning. Examiner required. Suitable for group use. BRITISH PUBLISHER

Timed: 20 minutes for each part

Range: Ages 13-college and university level

Scoring: Hand key

Cost: Specimen set £3.50; 25 booklets £7.25; 25 answer sheets £2.10 plus VAT; key £2.05 and manual £0.80 plus VAT (payment in sterling for all overseas orders).

Publisher: NFER-Nelson Publishing Company

AH6-GROUP TESTS OF HIGH LEVEL INTELLIGENCE
A. W. Heim, K. P. Watts and V. Simmonds

teen, adult

Purpose: Assesses general learning ability. Used for evaluating above average subjects from age 16 through university age.

Description: Two separate paper-pencil tests of general reasoning: SEM, for use with Scientists, Engineers and Mathematicians (whether potential or qualified), and AG, for use with professions such as historians, linguists, teachers, or economists. Both tests include verbal, numerical and diagrammatic items, but differ in proportion of each item type. Form AG is one-half verbal, while Form SEM has equal proportions of the three item types. Similar in concept to AH5, but suitable for a somewhat higher age range.

Examiner required. Suitable for group use.
BRITISH PUBLISHER

Timed: Form AG, 35 minutes and Form SEM, 40 minutes

Range: 16 years old up to college and university level

Scoring: Hand key

Cost: Specimen set £4.95; 25 AG booklets £9.90; 25 AG answer sheets £2.40; 25 SEM booklets £8.40; 25 SEM answer sheets plus VAT; manual £2.65 (payment in sterling for all overseas orders).

Publisher: NFER-Nelson Publishing Company

AH VOCABULARY SCALE
A. Heim, K. P. Watts and V. Simmonds

all ages

Purpose: Measures vocabulary level. Used for assessment of intellectual ability.

Description: Multiple item paper-pencil test of vocabulary arranged in six sets: P, Q, R, S, T, and U. Each set contains 40 items and difficulty level increases throughout the scale. Designed for the following age groups: P and Q for ages 9-11, Q and R for 12-14 year olds, R and S for ages 15-16, S and T for students at colleges and universities, T and U for university graduates. Usually used in conjunction with tests of verbal and nonverbal reasoning. Examiner required. Suitable for group use.
BRITISH PUBLISHER

Untimed: 20 minutes per set

Range: Ages 9-university graduates

Scoring: Hand key

Cost: Specimen set (includes all test booklets and manual) £7.00; 25 booklets (specify set) £5.80; 25 answer sheets (specify set) £4.40 plus VAT; keys (specify set) £1.50 plus

VAT; manual £4.65 (Payment in sterling for all overseas orders).

Publisher: NFER-Nelson Publishing Company

ARTHUR POINT SCALE OF PERFORMANCE TEST: REVISED FORM II
Refer to page 20.

BARSCH LEARNING STYLE INVENTORY
Refer to page 556.

BICULTURAL TEST OF NON-VERBAL REASONING-- BTNR-(ENGLISH/SPANISH)
Allen S. Toronto

child   grades 1-6

Purpose: Measures a child's reasoning abilities using nonverbal stimuli and responses.

Description: Multiple item, nonverbal test consists of three subtests: Differences, Similarities and Analogies. The child is presented with picture stimuli, then identifies a difference, a similarity, or an analogy by pointing to one of several line drawings. The test is designed for a mixed population of Anglo- and Mexican-American children. Examiner required. Not suitable for group use.

Untimed: 25 minutes

Range: Elementary school children

Scoring: Hand key; examiner evaluated

Cost: Complete kit (includes reusable picture stimuli, instructions, norms, statistical information, 30 scoring forms) $37.45; 30 scoring forms $3.50.

Publisher: National Educational Laboratory Publishers, Inc.

BLOOMER LEARNING TEST (BLT)

Richard H. Bloomer

child, teen   grades 1.5-11 +

Purpose: Determines strengths and weaknesses in learning patterns of individual pupils for purposes of planning remedial or compensatory educational programs. Useful with special groups such as learning disabled, emotionally disturbed, and gifted, as well as normal students.

Description: Ten paper-pencil subtests, each sufficiently reliable to be used alone and in any order. The subtests measure activity, visual and auditory short-term memory, visual apprehension, serial learning, recall, relearning, association, paired associate learning, concept recognition and production, and problem solving. Also evaluates simple learning IQ, problem solving IQ, and full learning IQ. The ten subtests are contained in a loose-leaf binder. The number of items ranges from 4-64 multiple-choice type. Each student has an answer form; and the scores are calculated on a student record form. No reading except for individual words is required. Examiner required. Suitable for group use.

Timed: Rate of Responding-8 minutes; Association-5 minutes

Range: Grades 1.5-11 +

Scoring: Hand key; examiner evaluated

Cost: Manual, test stimuli, answer forms, record forms, scoring key $78.00.

Publisher: Brador Publications, Inc.

THE BRITISH ABILITY SCALES

Colin D. Elliott, David J. Murray and Lea S. Pearson

child, teen

Purpose: Assesses cognitive ability. Used for individual, educational and clinical evaluations.

Description: 23 scales measure cognitive ability. Scales are classified along three major dimensions: stimulus presentation mode, response mode and behavioral characteristics. Behavioral characteristics dimension is divided into speed and five major areas of processes. Each scale may be administered on its own or in combination with any other scales. Most scales have short-form versions. Examiner required. Suitable for group use.
BRITISH PUBLISHER

Timed: Open ended

Range: Ages Supplementary Preschool and Early School Scales, 2½-8; School Age Scales, 5-17

Scoring: Examiner evaluated

Cost: Complete set £60.26; complete set School Age Scales £115.00 (payment in sterling for all overseas orders).

Publisher: NFER-Nelson Publishing Company

CHILDREN'S ABILITIES SCALES

child

Purpose: Assesses children's intellectual abilities. Used for describing individual strengths and weaknesses, and for identifying learning difficulties.

Description: Battery of paper-pencil tests covering verbal, nonverbal and spatial abilities. Student uses special pen to mark answers and get

immediate feedback about correctness. Student continues to "answer until correct." The test manual explains the relationship between tests and thereby allows teacher to build a profile of the child's abilities. Materials include special pens. Examiner required. Suitable for group use.
BRITISH PUBLISHER

Untimed: Not available

Range: Ages 10-12

Scoring: Hand key; examiner evaluated

Cost: Pupil's book £1.25; 10 answer sheets £1.60; 12 special pens £4.00 (payment in sterling for all overseas orders).

Publisher: NFER-Nelson Publishing Company

COLOURED PROGRESSIVE MATRICES
Refer to page 21.

COLUMBIA MENTAL MATURITY SCALE (CMMS)
Refer to page 21.

COMPOUND SERIES TEST (CST)
Refer to page 796.

COMPREHENSIVE ASSESSMENT PROGRAM DEVELOPING COGNITIVE ABILITIES TEST
Donald L. Beggs and John T. Mouw

child, teen   grades 2-12

Purpose: Identifies intellectual strengths and weaknesses in groups and individuals. Used to compare learning ability to academic achieve-

ment; identify students for gifted programs; evaluate curricular alternatives.

Description: 80 item paper-pencil test that measures verbal, quantitative, and spatial abilities. Tests for grades 3-12 provide information about the individual's skills in application, analysis and synthesis as well as his knowledge and comprehension. When administered with the Comprehensive Assessment Program: Achievement Series, it will show the level of student performance in relation to abilities. Examiner required. Suitable for group use.

Timed: 50 minutes

Range: Ages 7-18; Grades 2-12 (emperical out-of- level norms available)

Scoring: Hand key; computer scoring available

Cost: 35 test booklets $17.80-$23.40 (specify level and machine- or hand-scorable); 35 answer sheets $7.95; directions for administration $1.95; manual $6.25; key $3.80.

Publisher: Scott, Foresman and Company

THE CULTURE FAIR SERIES: SCALES 1, 2, 3
Refer to page 21.

DEESIDE PICTURE TEST
Refer to page 22.

ESSENTIAL INTELLIGENCE TESTS
F.J. Schonell and R.H. Adams

child

Purpose: Measures general intelligence of children ages 7 to 12. Also used with older children who have a reading age of at least 7½.

Description: Two multiple-item paper-pencil tests measuring intelligence. Materials include Essential Intelligence Test Form A and Essential Intelligence Test Form B. Separate manuals of directions are available for Form A and Form B. Examiner required.
BRITISH PUBLISHER

Untimed: Not available

Range: Ages 7-12½

Scoring: Examiner evaluated

Cost: 20 form A tests £2.65; form A manual 45p.; 20 form B tests £2.65; form B manual 45p.

Publisher: Oliver and Boyd/Longman, Inc. (U.S.A.)

EXPRESSIVE ONE-WORD PICTURE VOCABULARY TEST (EOWPVT)
Morrison F. Gardner

child

Purpose: Assesses a child's verbal intelligence. Used to screen for possible speech defects, to evaluate bilingual student fluency in English, and to determine preschool placement.

Description: 110 item verbal test of definitional and interpretational skills. It consists of 100 pictures which are presented one at a time to the subject who is asked to name each picture while the examiner records the response. The requirement for the student to name what is seen can be a more precise measure of verbal maturity than when he chooses an already-named picture from an array. Scoring tables yield deviation IQs, percentiles, and mental age equivalents. Materials include test plates which show only one stimulus picture at a time and a set of Spanish recording forms. Examiner required. Not

suitable for group use. Available in Spanish.

Untimed: 20 minutes

Range: Ages 2-12

Scoring: Hand key

Cost: Manual $10.00; test plates $25.00; 25 recording forms (Spanish or English) $6.00; specimen set $10.00.

Publisher: Academic Therapy Publications

FULL RANGE PICTURE VOCABULARY TEST (FRPV)
Refer to page 22.

GRIFFITHS MENTAL DEVELOPMENT SCALES
Refer to page 23.

GROUP TESTS FOR 5/6 AND 7/8 YEAR OLDS-1960

child

Purpose: Assesses intellectual ability. Used for measurement of school readiness.

Description: Six subtest measure of general intellectual ability. Materials include bilingual (English, Afrikaans) test booklets. Child should be able to handle a pencil and follow instructions without emotional distress. Examiner required. Suitable for group use.
SOUTH AFRICAN PUBLISHER

Untimed: Not time limit

Range: Ages 5/6 and 7/8

Scoring: Hand key; examiner evaluated

Cost: (In Rands) 10 tests for 5/6 1,60; 10 tests for 7/8 1,70; manual 3,10 (orders from outside The RSA will be dealt with on merit).

Publisher: Human Sciences Research Council

GROUP TEST FOR INDIAN PUPILS-1968

child, teen

Purpose: Measures general mental ability. Used for psycho-educational evaluation.

Description: Six subtest paper-pencil measure of general mental ability. Three subtests are verbal and three are nonverbal. Test provide three scores, verbal, nonverbal and total. Divided into three series, Junior, Intermediate and Senior. Two alternative forms are available for the Junior and Intermediate Series. Examiner required. Suitable for group use. SOUTH AFRICAN PUBLISHER

Timed: 2 hours

Range: Ages Junior 10-13; Intermediate 13-16; Senior 16-19

Scoring: Hand key; examiner evaluated

Cost: (In Rands) Junior Form A test booklet 1,70; Junior Form B test booklet 1,40; Intermediate Form A test booklet 1,40; Intermediate Form B 1,70; Senior test booklets 1,40; manual 5,00; scoring stencils-Junior A 2,10; Junior B 2,40; Intermediate A & B 1,80 each; Senior 1,90 (orders from outside The RSA will be dealt with on merit).

Publisher: Human Sciences Research Council

GROUP TESTS-1974
Refer to page 24.

HARDING SKYSCRAPER FORM B-C
Chris Harding

adult

Purpose: Measures mental abilities at a high level of achievement. Originally developed to serve the selection needs of the International Society for Philosophical Enquiry. Used with candidates in the 140-173 Ability Quotient range, with a ceiling of 181 + .

Description: 40 item paper-pencil test measures the integration of thinking, creative, and informational abilities to yield a single unified score called the Ability Quotient (A.Q.). Using multiple-choice and short answer questions for Section B, and incomplete analogies (each with four choices) for Section C, the test measures Convergent, Divergent, and Condivergent thinking processes. Supervision required. Suitable for group use. AUSTRALIAN PUBLISHER

Untimed: 1½-2 hours

Range: Adult

Scoring: Scored by publisher

Cost: Test $2.00; scoring $5.00.

Publisher: Harding Tests

HARDING W87 TEST
Chris Harding

adult

Purpose: Measures mental abilities at a high level of achievement. Developed to replace the Harding Skyscraper as the entrance test of the International Society for Philosophical Enquiry (ISPE). Suitable for individuals with Ability Quotient 140-173.

Description: 64 item paper-pencil test measures the integration of

thinking, creative, and informational abilities. The test consists of two parts. Set I (34 items) uses multiple-choice and free response questions to test verbal, numerical and logical reasoning abilities. Set-II (30 items) provides incomplete word-analogies, requiring the subject to choose from ten possible words to complete the analogy. The test as a whole measures Convergent, Divergent and Condivergent thinking processes. This test may be obtained only from IPSE, who wishes to control its use. Supervision required. Suitable for group use.
AUSTRALIAN PUBLISHER

Untimed: 3 hours

Range: Adult

Scoring: Publisher scored

Cost: Contact publisher.

Publisher: Harding Tests

HEALY PICTORIAL COMPLETION TEST I
William Healy

child

Purpose: Measures mental ability and intelligence based on an individual's apperceptive ability. Used with all ages, though primarily for those with a child-type mind.

Description: Ten item task-assessment test using a picture board with ten pieces missing so that the scene is incomplete. The missing pieces are of uniform size and shape, and the subject must select the ten correct insets from the 50 choices presented and insert them in their proper places to complete the scene. Errors are rated in two categories: logical errors and total errors. Observation of the child's approach to the task provides information about the child's mental control and processes of association. The instrument is particularly useful with defectives and aberrational indi-

viduals. This test is also included in the Arthur Point Scale of Performance, Form I. Examiner required. Not for group use.

Timed: 20 minutes

Range: Children/aberrational individuals

Scoring: Examiner evaluated

Cost: Test with manual and carrying case $71.00.

Publisher: Stoelting Co.

INDIVIDUAL SCALE FOR INDIAN SOUTH AFRICANS (ISISA)-1971
R. J. Prinsloo and F.W.O. Heinichen in collaboration with D.J. Swart

child, teen

Purpose: Assesses intelligence in Indian pupils. Used for psychological-educational evaluation.

Description: Ten subtest measure of general intellectual ability. Five subtests are verbal, five nonverbal. Scores obtained include vocabulary, comprehension, similarities, problems, memory, pattern completion, blocks, absurdities, formboard, and mazes. Test may be administered in an abbreviated form. Adapted for Indians from the New South African Individual Scale. Examiner required. Not suitable for group use.
SOUTH AFRICAN PUBLISHER

Untimed: 80 minutes

Range: Ages 8-17

Scoring: Hand key; examiner evaluated

Cost: (In Rands) Complete specimen set (includes 2 pattern completions, 2 mazes, 2 answer sheets) 63,00 (orders from outside The RSA will be dealt with on merit).

Publisher: Human Sciences Research Council

INTELLIGENCE TESTS

child, teen

Purpose: Measures general intelligence of secondary school pupils.

Description: Several tests assessing the reasoning abilities of secondary school pupils. The Cotswold Tests provide measures of Mental Ability and English Ability for two age levels: 10- 12½ years and 8½-9½ years. The Kelvin Tests include: Infant, Reading and Mental Tests. The Ryburn tests are available for two levels: junior and senior. The Cotswold Personality Assessment provides three preference scores (things, people, ideas) and three attitude scores (using one's hands, being with other people, talking about school) for students ages 11-16. The last test of the battery is the Orton Intelligence Test for students ages 9-14 years. Instructions and norms are available for all tests, as well as a booklet entitled *Spotlight on Reasoning*, which contains 40 sets of exercises, both verbal and nonverbal. BRITISH PUBLISHER

Timed: Varies

Range: Secondary school students

Scoring: Not available

Cost: 20 Cotswold tests (specify title) £1.60; 20 Kelvin tests (specify title £1.60; 20 Ryburn tests (specify junior or senior) £1.60; 100 Cotswold Personality Assessment £7.95; 20 Orton Intelligence tests £1.40; instructions and norms for all tests 20p.

Publisher: Robert Gibson-Publisher

JENKINS INTERMEDIATE NON-VERBAL TEST: ACER adaptation
Refer to page 25.

JUNIOR SOUTH AFRICAN INDIVIDUAL SCALES (JSAIS)-1979
Refer to page 26.

KAUFMAN DEVELOPMENTAL SCALE (KDS)
Refer to page 452.

KOHS BLOCK DESIGN TEST
S.C. Kohs

Mental Ages 3-19

Purpose: Measures intelligence for persons with a mental age of 3-19 years. Useful in testing individuals who have language and hearing handicaps as well as the disadvantaged and those who do not speak English.

Description: Multiple item, task-assessment test consisting of 17 cards containing colored designs and 16 colored blocks which the subject uses to duplicate the designs on the cards. Performance is evaluated for Attention, Adaptation and Auto- Criticism. The results are said to be less affected by school training than the Binet tests. This test is also included in the Merrill-Palmer and Arthur Performance Scales. Complete set includes cubes, cards, manual, and 50 record blanks. Examiner required. Suitable for group use.

Timed: Up to 40 minutes

Range: Mental Ages 3-19

Scoring: Examiner evaluated

Cost: Complete kit (includes blocks, cards, manual, and 50 record blanks) $55.00.

Publisher: Stoelting Co.

LEITER INTERNATIONAL PER-FORMANCE SCALE (LIPS)
Refer to page 27.

NEW SOUTH AFRICAN GROUP TEST (NSAGT)-1965

child, teen

Purpose: Assesses intellectual ability. Used for psychological and educational evaluation.

Description: Six subtest measure of general intellectual ability. Three subtests are verbal and three are non-verbal. Test is available at three levels, Junior, Intermediate and Senior. Materials include two equivalent forms for the Junior and Senior Series, but only one for the Intermediate Series. Available only to departments of education and private schools, or to schools training teachers for the purpose of training and research. Examiner required. Not suitable for group use.
SOUTH AFRICAN PUBLISHER

Timed: 2 hours

Range: Form J/K, ages 8-11; Form G, ages 10-14; Form S/T, ages 13-17

Scoring: Hand key; examiner evaluated; machine scoring available

Cost: (In Rands) Form J test 0,30; Form G test 0,60; Form S/T test 0,30; Intermediate manual 1,10; Junior and Senior manual 1,60; scoring stencils (specify form) 0,40 each; 10 answer sheets 0,40; 10 machine answer sheets 1,10 (orders from outside The RSA will be dealt with on merit).

Publisher: Human Sciences Research Council

NON-LANGUAGE TEST OF VERBAL INTELLIGENCE
S. Chatterji and Manjula Mukerjee

child

Purpose: Measures verbal intelligence of children ages 8-12 years, but uses a non-language medium to achieve this measure. Used to test groups of children with differing linguistic or cultural backgrounds. Also identifies children whose academic backwardness is due to linguistic difficulty, not lack of verbal ability.

Description: 62 item, paper-pencil, multiple-choice test consisting entirely of pictured test items. The test consists of four parts: analogy, classification, opposites, and picture arrangement. The candidates are required to record their answers on a separate answer sheet; test booklets are reusable. The examiner's manual includes detailed instructions for administration, evaluation and interpretation of the test. Examiner required. Suitable for group use.
PUBLISHED IN INDIA

Timed: 45 minutes

Range: Ages 8-12

Scoring: Hand key; examiner evaluated

Cost: Contact publisher.

Publisher: Statistical Publishing Society

NON-READERS INTELLIGENCE TEST-THIRD EDITION and ORAL VERBAL INTELLIGENCE TEST
Refer to page 551.

NON-VERBAL REASONING TESTS SERIES

child, teen

Purpose: Assesses non-verbal reasoning ability. Used for evaluation of poor readers.

Description: Four paper-pencil tests of basic reasoning using geometric shapes and pictures. All questions appear in pictorial or diagrammatic form. Pictures Test A, ages 7 to 8, uses three types of questions in picture form. In the first section, the child chooses the picture different from a set; in the second section children choose one of five alternative patterns to complete a story or pattern; the third section presents analogues in pictorial form. Non-Verbal Test BD, ages 8 to 11, consists of questions relating to geometric shapes, cyphers, similarities, analogues, and series. Non-Verbal Test DH, ages 10 to 15, contains two main types of questions. The first requires the child to select one of five small squares that will complete the overall series or pattern contained in a larger square. Other questions are series type. Administration can be either in the full 96 question form or as a shorter 64 question test. Spatial Test EG, ages 11 to 14, is designed to measure spatial aptitude in association with general aptitude. All tests are preceeded by oral instructions and practice items. Examiner required. Suitable for group use. BRITISH PUBLISHER

Timed: Varies with each test

Range: Ages 7-15

Scoring: Hand key

Cost: 10 picture tests £3.10; manual £0.55; 10 tests BD £3.25; manual £0.65; 10 tests DH £4.15; 10 answer sheets £0.85 plus VAT; manual £0.55; 10 tests EG £3.40; manual £0.65 (Payment in sterling for all overseas orders).

Publisher: NFER-Nelson Publishing Company

NONVERBAL TEST OF COGNITIVE SKILLS (NTCS)
G. Orville Johnson and Herbert F. Boyd

child   grades K-7

Purpose: Assesses school related abilities in children for grades K-7.

Description: Multiple item, nonverbal test in which the examiner uses pantomime to guide the child in the manipulation of blocks, color cubes, dominos, picture stimuli, and Knox cubes to measure the following skills and abilities: reasoning, rote memory, recognition and memory of patterns, visual memory, discrimination, space and spatial relationships, conceptual thinking, recognition of and ability to deal with quantities, quantitative memory, and visual motor perception. Examiner required. Not for group use.

Timed: 25-30 minutes

Range: Grades K-7

Scoring: Examiner evaluated

Cost: Test kit $150.00.

Publisher: Charles E. Merrill Publishing Company

OREGON ACADEMIC RANKING TEST
Charles H. Derthick

child   grades 3-7

Purpose: Identifies exceptionally bright young children in Grades 3-7. Used for placement in enriched or gifted programs.

Description: Multiple item paper-pencil test measuring creativity and abstract thinking to determine academic or learning ability. The test uses eight types of test items which are designed to be interesting and challenging. responses are scored for both quantity and quality. Norms include cut-off scores to identify children in the top three percent of the school population. Examiner required. Not suitable for group use.

Untimed: 30 minutes

Range: Grades 3-7

Scoring: Hand key; examiner evaluated

Cost: Kit $7.90 (20 tests, manual)

Publisher: Western Psychological Services.

PICTORIAL TEST OF INTELLIGENCE
Joseph L. French

child

Purpose: Measures general ability of three to eight year old children. Used for curriculum planning and evaluation.

Description: Multiple item, oral, picture test in six sections. The subtests are: Picture Vocabulary, Information and Comprehension, Form Discrimination, Similarities, Size and Number, and Immediate Recall. The examiner presents picture cards on which are represented four possible answers and asks questions of the child. The cards are designed so that the examiner, by observing eye movement, can also determine the response of children who are physically handicapped. Materials include cards, manual and record forms. Examiner required. Not for group use.
CANADIAN PUBLISHER

Untimed: 45 minutes

Range: Ages 3-8

Scoring: Hand key

Cost: Complete test kit (includes record forms and manual) $190.00; 35

record forms $22.00; manual $22.00.

Publisher: Institute of Psychological Research, Inc.

QUICK TEST (QT)
Refer to page 30.

ROSS TEST OF HIGHER COGNITIVE PROCESSES (ROSS TEST)
John D. Ross and Catherine M. Ross

child

Purpose: Assesses abstract and critical thinking skills among gifted and non-gifted intermediate grade students. Used to screen students for special programs, and to evaluate program effectiveness.

Description: 105 item paper-pencil, multiple-choice test in eight sections, each dealing with a specific level of higher cognitive processes within the areas of analysis, synthesis and evaluation. Test is taken in two sittings. Responses may be recorded directly in the student test booklet or on optional answer sheet. Materials include overlays for scoring of answer sheets and a cassette tape of test. Examiner required. Suitable for group use.

Timed: First sitting, 50 minutes; second sitting 55 minutes

Range: Grades 4-6

Scoring: Hand key

Cost: Manual $10.00; 10 test booklets $15.00; 50 answer sheets $5.00; hand-key $2.00; cassette tape test $10.00; specimen set $10.00.

Publisher: Academic Therapy Publications

SENIOR SOUTH AFRICAN INDIVIDUAL SCALE (SSAIS)-1964
Refer to page 31.

SLOSSON INTELLIGENCE TEST (SIT)/SLOSSON ORAL READING TEST (SORT)
Refer to page 31.

SNIJDERS-OOMEN NON-VERBAL INTELLIGENCE SCALE (SON)
Refer to page 32.

THE SOUTH AFRICAN INDIVIDUAL SCALE FOR THE BLIND (SAISB)-1979
Refer to page 32.

THE STANDARD PROGRESSIVE MATRICES (SPM-1938)
Refer to page 33.

STANFORD-BINET INTELLIGENCE SCALE: FORM L-M
Refer to page 33.

SYSTEM OF MULTICULTURAL PLURALISTIC ASSESSMENT (SOMPA)
Jane R. Mercer and June F. Lewis

child

Purpose: Assesses cognitive abilities, sensorimotor abilities and adaptive behavior of children ages 5 to 11. Used for assessment of children from varied cultural backgrounds.

Description: Multiple instrument measure of various aspects of functioning of children from diverse cultural backgrounds. SOMPA has two major components: The Parent Interview and Student Assessment Materials. The Parent Interview takes place in the home, and includes administration of the Adaptive Behavior Inventory for Children (ABIC), Sociocultural Scales, Health History Inventories. Student Assessment Materials data are collected in the school environment, and include Physcial Dexterity Tasks, Weight by Height, Visual Acuity, Auditory Acuity, Bender Visual Motor Gestalt Test (sold separately), and the WISC-R, or WPPSI (sold separately). Interpretation of SOMPA should be done by psychologist or a qualified team. Examiner required. Not suitable for group use. Parent Interview available in Spanish.

Untimed: Parent interview, 60 minutes; individual, 20 minutes in addition to time required for Wechsler and Bender-Gestalt

Range: Ages 5-11

Scoring: Examiner evaluated

Cost: Basic kit (includes parent interview manual, 25 parent interview record forms, ABIC scoring keys, student assessment manual, 25 student assessment record forms, 25 profile folders, technical manual) $75.00.

Publisher: The Psychological Corporation

TEST OF CONCEPT UTILIZATION (TCU)
Richard L. Crager

child, teen

Purpose: Measures the abilities of children and adolescents to think conceptually. Used by teachers to identify a child's conceptual strengths, especially underachievers and those with learning disabilities.

Description: 50 item oral response test consisting of 50 pairs of colored pictures of common objects. The child must indicate how they are alike. Analysis of the responses provides qualitative and quantitative assessments of five areas of conceptual thinking: color, shape, relational function, homogeneous function, and abstract function. Norms provided for ages 5-18 years. *The Development of Concepts: A Manual for the Test of Concept Utilization* (104 pages) includes all scoring instructions, standardization, normative data, and chapters on clinical and educational uses of the test. The new (1980) manual, *Concepts in the Classroom: A Manual for the Educational Use of the Test of Conceptual Utilization*, provides instructions for a short scoring procedure. New TCU studies are presented but do not include administration instructions or normative data, and the original manual is still needed to administer and interpret the test. Examiner required. Not for group use.

Untimed: 10 minutes

Range: Ages 5-18

Scoring: Hand key

Cost: Complete kit (includes 1 set test plates, 5 pads protocol sheets, 5 scoring booklets, 2 manuals, 5 short scoring forms) $49.50.

THE TEST OF NONVERBAL INTELLIGENCE (TONI)
Refer to page 34.

TIME APPRECIATION TEST
Refer to page 34.

THE VANE-L SCALE
Refer to page 600.

VERBAL POWER TEST OF CONCEPT EQUIVALENTS
E. Francesco

teen, adult

Purpose: Assesses general intelligence and verbal ability of adults and adolescents 14 years and older.

Description: 75 item paper-pencil test consisting of pairs of words which the subject must decide are either the "same" or "different". A minimum fourth-grade reading ability is required. Available in two equivalent forms for retesting. Standardized on over 1,000 subjects. Examiner required. Suitable for group use.

Untimed: 10 minutes

Range: Ages 14-adult

Scoring: Hand key

Cost: Complete kit (includes 50 tests, manual, key) $9.30.

Publisher: Western Psychological Services

WECHSLER SCALES: WECHSLER ADULT INTELLIGENCE SCALE (WAIS)
Refer to page 35.

WECHSLER SCALES: WECHSLER ADULT INTELLIGENCE SCALE-REVISED (WAIS-R)
Refer to page 35.

WECHSLER SCALES: WECHSLER INTELLIGENCE SCALES FOR CHILDREN: 1949 EDITION (WISC)
Refer to page 36.

WECHSLER SCALES: WECHSLER INTELLIGENCE SCALES FOR CHILDREN-REVISED (WISC-R)
Refer to page 36.

WECHSLER SCALES: WECHSLER PRESCHOOL AND PRIMARY SCALE OF INTELLIGENCE (WPPSI)
Refer to page 37.

WILLIAMS INTELLIGENCE TEST FOR CHILDREN WITH DEFECTIVE VISION
M. Williams

child, teen

Purpose: Assesses intelligence in blind children and those with visual impairments. Used for individual evaluation.

Description: Series of performance tests measuring intelligence. Materials include Braille cards. Test has

been standardized on British children whose visual acuity did not amount to more than approximately 6/36 according to the Snellen Chart. Examiner required. Not suitable for group use.
BRITISH PUBLISHER

Untimed: Not available

Range: Ages 5-15

Scoring: Examiner evaluated

Cost: Complete kit (includes 12 record forms, handbook, set of 3 Braille cards, set of materials) £45.55 (payment in sterling for all overseas orders).

Publisher: Distributed by NFER-Nelson Publishing Company

Reading

Elementary

ACER SILENT READING TEST-FORM C

child

Purpose: Measures achievement in reading. Used for diagnosis of individual student strengths and weaknesses as part of an educational evaluation.

Description: Multiple item, paper-pencil tests of three components of reading achievement: Word Knowledge, Speed of Reading, and Reading for Meaning. Word Knowledge Test is a vocabulary test of 100 commonly used words graded in order of difficulty. Child chooses synonym from among five alternatives. Speed of Reading Test estimates amount read silently in about three minutes. Reading for Meaning

Test is a comprehension test of 30 short paragraphs with two multiple-choice questions asked about each paragraph. Examiner required. Suitable for group use.

AUSTRALIAN PUBLISHER

Timed: Varies

Range: Ages 9-12 inclusive

Scoring: Hand key

Cost: Specimen set $8.25; 10 tests Part 1 $2.50; Part 2 and 3 $.50 each; key $2.50; manual $4.50 (all remittances must be in Australian currency).

Publisher: The Australian Council for Educational Research Limited

---

ANALYTICAL READING INVENTORY, 2ND EDITION
Mary Lynn Woods and Alden J. Moe

---

child, teen   grades 1-9

Purpose: Analyzes reading skills to help classroom teachers and reading specialists make remediation decisions.

Description: 170 items of graded word lists and reading passages which measure strengths and weaknesses in word attack and comprehension skills, level of reading achievement and potential for reading growth. Examiner evaluated, individually administered. Not suitable for group use.

Untimed: Variable

Range: Grades 2-9

Scoring: Examiner evaluated

Cost: Complete package (includes student record summary sheets, qualitative analysis summary sheets, graded word lists, graded reading passages) $9.95.

Publisher: Charles E. Merrill Publishing Company

BASIC SKILLS TEST-READING-ELEMENTARY-FORMS A and B
IOX Assessment Associates

---

child   grades 5-6

Purpose: Measures student's end-of-elementary school achievement in basic reading skills. Used in determining minimum competency or grade promotion; program evaluation.

Description: 35 item paper-pencil test measures student's ability to comprehend word meaning and syntax; identify sequences, main ideas and details; and use a dictionary and common reference sources. This test preceeds The IOX Basic Skills Test-Reading-Secondary Level. Examiner required. Suitable for group use.

Untimed: 30-45 minutes

Range: Grades 5 and 6

Scoring: Hand key

Cost: 25 BR-A2 tests $37.50; 25 BR-B2 tests $37.50; teacher's guide BR-G2 $3.95; test manual BTM-2 $3.95.

Publisher: IOX Assessment Associates

BURT WORD READING TEST
Scottish Council For Research In Education

---

all ages

Purpose: Measures word reading skills of children with reading ages 6.4-12.0 years. Also assesses the reading performance of class groups. Identifies children in need of special reading assistance. Used in planning individual and class instructional approaches.

Description: Multiple item, oral response test of word reading skills requires the student to read from a Test Card, which consists of 100 words printed in decreasing size of type and graded in approximate order of difficulty. The student's achievement on the test provides a basis for making decision about appropriate teaching and reading materials, instructional groupings, etc. This 1974 revised edition offers up-to-date normative data and establishes present-day levels of difficulty of the words. A separate version revised and standardized for use in New Zealand is also available. Norms are provided for both versions for students 6-13 years old. Examiner required. Suitable for group use. BRITISH PUBLISHER

Untimed: 5-10 minutes

Range: Ages 5 and older

Scoring: Examiner evaluated

Cost: 20 tests £1.25 per set, manual 90p. net c.

Publisher: Hodder & Stoughton

COMPREHENSION TEST: EARLY PRIMARY, PRIMARY AND INTERMEDIATE
Marion L. McGuire and Marguerite J. Bumpus

child, teen

Purpose: Measures mastery levels in reasoning and problem solving.

Description: Multiple item paper-pencil test which measures comprehension objectives. The Comprehension Test is written for three reading levels: Early Primary, reading level 1.2-2.2; Primary, reading level 2.2-3.2; Intermediate, reading level 4.0-6.0. The test measures mastery of twelve objectives assigned to four categories: Literal A-1 recognition detail, A-2 translations of detail, A-3 pattern signal words, A-4 pattern signal words; Interpretive B-1 implied detail, B-2 pattern of organization, B-3 inferred main idea; Analytic C-1 determine problem, C-2 select hypothesis, C-3 distinguish relevant details; Critical D-2 select criterion for judgment, D-2 make judgment based on criterion. The student must be able to read the test

reasonably well. Examiner required. Suitable for group use.

Untimed: 20 to 25 minutes

Range: Students at 1.2-6 Reader level

Scoring: Hand key; computer scoring with TRS 80

Cost: Complete kit (includes pre and post test masters allowing testing for 200 to 300) $39.95 (specify level).

Publisher: Croft, Inc.

THE DELAWARE COUNTY SILENT READING TESTS-LEVEL 1 AND LEVEL 1[2]
Delaware County Reading Council

child   grade 1

Purpose: Measures first-graders' ability to read and write. Used to provide reading instruction and as a post-test of teaching effectiveness.

Description: 20 item paper-pencil, multiple-choice test covering four major areas: interpretation of ideas, organization of ideas, vocabulary, and structural analysis of words. Examiner distributes story and test booklets and writes the following words on a chalkboard: 'paragraph', 'sentences', 'word', 'underline', 'write', 'letter', and 'number'. These words are not usually found in typical second-grade reading materials. The examiner guides the pupils in pronouncing the words and tells them the may ask for help in figuring out which words correspond to the appropriate constructions in the story. Examiner required. Suitable for group use.

Untimed: 45-50 minutes

Range: Grade 1

Scoring: Hand key

Cost: Pupil test $.10; story booklet $.15; teacher's guide included with each order of 25; additional teacher guides and answer keys $.10 each;

specimen set $3.50.

Publisher: Delaware County Intermediate Unit

DELAWARE COUNTY SILENT READING TESTS-LEVEL 2 AND LEVEL 2[2]
Delaware County Reading Council

child   grade 2

Purpose: Measures second-graders' ability to read and write. Used to provide reading instruction and as a post-test of teaching effectiveness.

Description: 20 item paper-pencil, multiple-choice test covering four major areas: interpretation of ideas, organization of ideas, vocabulary, and structural analysis of words. Examiner distributes story and test booklets and writes the following words on a chalkboard: 'paragraph', 'sentence', 'question', 'underline', 'title', and 'root'. These words are not usually found in typical second-grade reading materials. The examiner guides the pupils in pronouncing the words and tells them they may ask for help in figuring out which words correspond to the appropriate constructions in the story. Examiner required. Suitable for group use.

Untimed: 45-50 minutes

Range: Grade 2

Scoring: Hand key

Cost: Pupil test $.10; story booklet $.15; teacher's guide included with each order of 25; additional teacher's guides and answer keys $.10 each; specimen set $3.50.

Publisher: Delaware County Intermediate Unit

THE DELAWARE COUNTY SILENT READING TESTS-LEVEL 3 AND LEVEL 3[2]
Delaware County Reading Council

child   grade 3

Purpose: Measures third-graders' ability to read and write. Used to provide reading instruction and as a post-test of teaching effectiveness.

Description: 20 item paper-pencil, multiple-choice test covering four major areas: interpretation of ideas, organization of ideas, vocabulary, and structural analysis of words. Examiner distributes story and test booklets and writes the following words on a chalkboard: 'sentences', 'opposite', 'paragraph', 'syllable', 'root', and 'blank spaces'. These words are not usually found in typical third-grade reading materials. The examiner guides the pupils in pronouncing the words and tells them the may ask for help in figuring out which words correspond to the appropriate constructions in the story. Examiner required. Suitable for group use.

Untimed: 45-50 minutes

Range: Grade 3

Scoring: Hand key

Cost: Pupil test $.10; story booklet $.15; teacher's guide included with each order of 25; additional teacher guides and answer keys $.10 each; specimen set $3.50.

Publisher: Delaware County Intermediate Unit

THE DELAWARE COUNTY SILENT READING TESTS: LEVELS 4-8
Delaware County Reading Council

child, teen   grades 4-8

Purpose: Measures intermediate grade students' reading achievement and ability to express ideas in writing. Used to evaluate progress, for classroom placement and counseling.

Description: 20 item paper-pencil, multiple-choice and short answer test with separate forms for grades 4-8. The student answers questions from a story booklet covering four areas: interpretation of ideas (8 items), organization of ideas (2 items), vocabulary (7 items), and structural analysis of words (3 items). Scores are ranked as excellent, good, average, poor, or very poor. Examiner required. Suitable for group use.

Untimed: 45-50 minutes

Range: Grades 4-8

Scoring: Hand key

Cost: Pupil test $.10; story booklet $.15; teacher's guide included with each order of 25; additional teacher guides and answer keys $.10 each; specimen set $3.50.

Publisher: Delaware County Intermediate Unit

DIAGNOSTIC READING SCALES, REVISED (DRS)
George D. Spache

child

Purpose: Identifies a student's strengths and weaknesses in reading. Used by educators to determine placement and prescribe instruction.

Description: A multiple item, verbal test consisting of a series of graduated scales containing three word- recog-

nition lists, twenty-two reading selections, and twelve phonics and word analysis tests. The word-recognition list yields a tentative level of performance and is used to determine the student's entry level to the reading selections, which in turn are used to establish three reading levels for the student--instructional level (oral reading), independent level (silent reading and comprehension), and potential level (auditory comprehension). The word analysis and phonics tests measure the following skills: recognition of initial and final consonants, consonant digraphs and blends, short and long vowel sounds, vowels with r, vowel dophthongs and digraphs, common syllables and phonograms, initial consonants presented auditorily; auditory discrimination of minimal word pairs; initial consonant substitution; and blending of word parts. Examiner required. Not suitable for group use.

Timed: Not available

Range: Beginning readers and above

Scoring: Examiner evaluated

Cost: Specimen set (includes test book, record book, representative pages of the manual, and a test reviewer's guide) 1981 edition $7.25; 1972 edition $10.35.

Publisher: CTB/McGraw-Hill

DOMAIN PHONIC TEST KIT
J. McLeod and J. Atkinson

child

Purpose: Diagnoses reading disabilities due to uncertainty about phonic structures and provides appropriate remedial approaches.

Description: Multiple item, oral response tests assessing strengths and weaknesses of a student's knowledge of phonic structures. Analysis sheets indicate which of the Domain Phonic Workshop sheets should be used to

remedy weaknesses once they are identified. Student progress is monitored in the record book. The manual includes complete instructions for use of the kit and gives examples of typical cases. Examiner required.
BRITISH PUBLISHER

Untimed: Not available

Range: Primary school students

Scoring: Not available

Cost: Complete kit (includes manual, 2 sets of phonic tests, 5 record books, 5 phonic workshops) £7.65; 5 record books £1.25; 5 phonic workshops £4.65; manual £1.05.

Publisher: Oliver and Boyd/Longman, Inc. (U.S.A.)

DOREN DIAGNOSTIC READING TEST OF WORD RECOGNITION SKILLS
Margaret Doren

child   grades 1-4

Purpose: Assesses why a child has difficulty reading. Used with groups to identify a level from which reading instruction should proceed.

Description: 12 category paper-pencil measure of word recognition skills in the following areas: Letter Recognition, Beginning Sounds, Whole Word Recognition, Words within Words, Speech Consonants, Ending Sounds, Blending, Rhyming, Vowels, Discriminate Guessing, Spelling, and Sight Words. The examiner reads the directions printed in the manual and encourages the students to follow the same directions in their test booklets. Samples are provided at the beginning of each subtest. Scores are graphed on an Individual Skill Profile for each student and overall class performance is recorded on the Class Composite Record. The test is designed to provide in a group situation the detailed diagnosis which

otherwise could be obtained only by individual testing. Examiner required. Suitable for group use.

Untimed: 1-3 hours

Range: Grades 1-4

Scoring: Hand key; examiner evaluated

Cost: Manual $3.00; 25 test booklets $9.50; key $8.25.

Publisher: American Guidance Service

DURRELL ANALYSIS OF READING DIFFICULTY: THIRD EDITION
Donald D. Durrell and Jane H. Catterson

child   grades 1-6

Purpose: Assesses reading behavior. Used in diagnosis, measurement of prereading skills, and planning remedial programs.

Description: Multiple item series of tests and situations measuring ten reading abilities: oral reading, silent reading, listening comprehension, listening vocabulary, word recognition/word analysis, spelling, auditory analysis of words and word elements, pronunciation of word elements, visual memory of words, and pre-reading phonics abilities. Supplementary paragraphs are provided for oral and silent reading to be used in supplementary testing or retesting. Materials include a spiral-bound booklet containing items to be read and a tachistoscope with accompanying test card. Examiner required. Not suitable for group use.

Untimed: 30-45 minutes

Range: Grades 1-6

Scoring: Examiner evaluated

Cost: Examiner's kit (includes 5 record booklets, tachistoscope, reading booklet, manual) $16.00.

Publisher: The Psychological

Corporation

EARLY DETECTION OF READING DIFFICULTIES

child

Purpose: Assesses reading skills. Used for diagnosing individual reading deficiencies.

Description: Multiple item test for reading screening of children in Years 1 and 2. Available materials include set of two test booklets and guide, and a textbook, *The Patterning of Complex Behavior.* Examiner required. Suitable for group use. DISTRIBUTED BY AUSTRALIAN PUBLISHER

Untimed: Not available

Range: Years 1 and 2

Scoring: Not available

Cost: Set of 2 test booklets and guide $18.50 (all remittances must be in Australian currency).

Publisher: Heineman-distributed by The Australian Council for Educational Research Limited

EMPORIA PRIMARY READING TEST
Marjorie Barnett and M.W. Sanders

child   grade 1

Purpose: Assesses general reading achievement of primary school students. Used to determine a student's actual reading level.

Description: 65 item paper-pencil test of reading achievement and readiness of beginners. Examiner required. Suitable for group use.

Timed: 15 minutes

Range: Grade 1

Scoring: Hand key

Cost: Specimen set $1.50.

Publisher: Bureau of Educational Measurements

EMPORIA READING TEST: ELEMENTARY
Marjorie Barnett and M.W. Sanders

child   grades 2-3

Purpose: Assesses general reading achievement of primary school students. Useful for determining student's actual reading level.

Description: 65 item paper-pencil test of word recognition, sentence and paragraph comprehension. Examiner required. Suitable for group use.

Timed: 25 minutes

Range: Grades 2-3

Scoring: Hand key

Cost: Specimen set $1.50.

Publisher: Bureau of Educational Measurements

EMPORIA READING TEST: INTERMEDIATE
Donald E. Carline, Ed L. Eaton and M.W. Sanders

child   grades 4-6

Purpose: Assesses general reading achievement of elementary school students. Useful for determining student's actual reading level.

Description: 65 item paper-pencil test of general comprehension. Examiner required. Suitable for group use.

Timed: 25 minutes

Range: Grades 4-6

Scoring: Hand key

Cost: Specimen set $1.50.

Publisher: Bureau of Educational Measurements

EMPORIA READING TEST: JUNIOR HIGH SCHOOL
Donald E. Carline, Stanford Studer, Ed L. Eaton, and M.W. Sanders

teen grades 7-8

Purpose: Assesses general reading achievement of junior high school students. Useful for determining student's actual reading level.

Description: 65 item paper-pencil test of general comprehension. Examiner required. Suitable for group use.

Timed: 25 minutes

Range: Grades 7-8

Scoring: Hand key

Cost: Specimen set $1.50.

Publisher: Bureau of Educational Measurements

EVERYDAY SKILLS TEST: READING
Refer to page 368.

THE FLORIDA KINDERGARTEN SCREENING BATTERY
Paul Satz and Jack Fletcher

child Kindergarten

Purpose: Identifies Kindergarten children at high risk for subsequent reading disabilities. Permits early identification of learning problems prior to the beginning of reading instruction.

Description: Multiple item battery of five tests screens children for potential reading problems. The battery of tests includes: Peabody Picture Vocabulary Test-Revised, Beery Developmental Test of Visual-Motor Integration, Recognition- Discrimination Test, Finger Localization Test, and Alphabet Recitation. May be administered by supervised paraprofessionals. Examiner required. Not suitable for group use.

Untimed: 20 minutes

Range: Kindergarten

Scoring: Not available

Cost: Complete kit (includes all tests, 50 record forms, manual) $99.00.

Publisher: Psychological Assessment Resources, Inc.

GAPADOL READING COMPREHENSION TESTS
McLeod and Anderson

child

Purpose: Measures reading comprehension. Used for identifying student achievement as part of an educational evaluation.

Description: Multiple item tests of reading achievement using the Cloze technique. Student fills in words omitted from reading passages. GAP Reading Comprehension Test is for years 4-6, and has two alternate forms, R and B. GAPADOL Reading Comprehension is for years 5-10. Examiner required. Suitable for group use.
DISTRIBUTED BY AUSTRALIAN PUBLISHER

Timed: 15 minutes

Range: Ages 1-10

Scoring: Examiner evaluated

Cost: Contact ACER.

Publisher: Heineman-distributed by The Australian Council for Educational Research Limited

GATES-McKILLOP-HOROWITZ READING DIAGNOSTIC TESTS
Arthur I. Gates, Anne S. McKillop and Elizabeth C. Horowitz

child   grades 1-6

Purpose: Evaluates oral reading, spelling, and writing skills of children in grades 1 to 6, and diagnoses reading difficulties of older students. Used for class grouping and curriculum planning.

Description: 11 part verbal, paper-pencil test of the following abilities: oral reading, isolated word recognition, knowledge of word parts, recognizing and blending common word parts, reading words, giving letter sounds, naming letters, identifying vowel sounds, auditory blending and discrimination, and an informal writing sample. Not all parts need be given to every student. Materials include a test materials booklet containing a tachistoscope (for word flash tests), pupil record book, and manual. Examiner required. Not for group use.

Untimed: 60 minutes

Range: Grades 1-6

Scoring: Examiner evaluated

Cost: Test materials (contains tachistoscope) $3.50; 30 pupil record booklets $13.50; manual of directions $1.50; specimen set (includes test materials, 1 pupil record booklet, manual of directions) $5.25.

Publisher: Teachers College Press

GILLINGHAM-CHILDS PHONICS PROFICIENCY SCALES: SERIES I, BASIC READING AND SPELLING; SERIES II, ADVANCED READING
Sally B. Childs and Ralph de S. Childs

child, teen   grades 1-8

Purpose: Evaluates student progress in the mastery of phonic and beginning reading skills to provide teachers with an index of remedial progress.

Description: Multiple item, primarily verbal examination in two series: (I) Basic Reading and Spelling, and (II) Advanced Reading. Series I has 12 scales dealing with basic reading and spelling skills: letter-sound relationships, three-letter words, consonant digraphs and blends, one-syllable words ending with f, l, or s; vowel-consonant-ewords; syllabication rules; sight words; and suffix rules. The teacher uses the Reading Booklet for dictation of the spelling words, since the reading and spelling words are the same. Series II has 16 scales for advanced reading skills: alternating phonograms; hard and soft sounds of cand g; long vowel sounds; 'Wild Old Words' (nonsense words); vowel dipthongs and digraphs, words irregular for reading; and more advanced syllabication rules. There is no spelling test in Series II. The teacher should be familiar with the pronunciation of nonsense words. The original version of the scales was developed by Anna Gillingham; these have been strengthened in their revised version and should be useful to anyone teaching phonics. Examiner required. Not suitable for group use.

Untimed: 30 minutes-1 hour

Range: Grades 1-8

Scoring: Examiner evaluated

Cost: Series I $6.50; reading record booklet $3.25; spelling record booklet $4.00; directions for use $.50; Series II $6.50; record booklet $2.50; directions for use $.50.

Publisher: Educators Publishing Service, Inc.

GROUP PHONICS ANALYSIS
Edward B. Fry

child   grades 1-3

Purpose: Diagnoses student use of phonics to determine weaknesses and abilities in reading, listening and speaking. Used as an aid to teacher guidance.

Description: 32 item paper-pencil test measuring the ability to read numbers and letters, to hear consonants, to alphabetize, recognize vowels, to recognize short sounds and long vowel sounds in words, to use vowel-sounding rules, and syllabification. Examiner required. Suitable for group use.

Untimed: Varies

Range: Grades 1-3

Scoring: Self score

Cost: 30 tests and manual $8.00.

Publisher: Jamestown Publishers

GROUP READING ASSESSMENT
F.A. Spooncer

child

Purpose: Measures group achievement of reading ability in the first two years of junior school (students ages 7-9 years). Suitable for less able older juniors and the most backward entrants to secondary schools. Assesses performance of teaching programs at classroom, school or district level.

Description: Multiple item paper-pencil test measures achievement of reading skills which are taught in the first two years of junior school. Norms, derived from testing of over 3,000 children, are provided to cover reading ages 6:3 to 11:7 years, and a table is provided for conversion of raw scores to standardized scores for children ages 7- 9 years. Examiner required. Suitable for group use.
BRITISH PUBLISHER

Untimed: 30 minutes

Range: Ages 7.8-9

Scoring: Examiner evaluated

Cost: Specimen set £1.25; 20 tests £1.75 per set, manual 95p.

Publisher: Hodder & Stoughton

GROUP READING TEST: SECOND EDITION
Dennis Young

child

Purpose: Tests reading achievement of children ages 6- 12 years old. Identifies children reading significantly above or below their age level.

Description: Multiple item paper-pencil test of reading achievement is available in two parallel forms, A and B, which remain unchanged from the original version. The two forms, along with template scoring methods, facilitate use of the test by one teacher with a full class. The second edition of the manual provides new norms for Infants (ages 6:5 to 7:10), first-year Juniors (7:10 to 8:10), and older, less able pupils up to age 12:10, increasing the accuracy of comparison between children of different ages. Examiner required. Suitable for group use.
BRITISH PUBLISHER

Untimed: Not available

Range: Ages 7-12.10

Scoring: Hand key

Cost: Specimen set £1.50; 20 tests (specify form) 95p per set; template (specify form) 75p plus VAT; manual £1.25.

Publisher: Hodder & Stoughton

THE HOLBORN READING SCALE (1980)
A.F. Watts

child

Purpose: Measures progress in word recognition. Used for assessment of reading comprehension.

Description: 33 item paper-pencil test of reading skills. Items are sentences arranged in order of difficulty. Questions based on these sentences are available in the manual, and can be used to measure reading comprehension. Each sentence has a figure next to it indicating a reading age which can be converted into a reading quotient. Examiner required. Suitable for group use. BRITISH PUBLISHER

Untimed: Not available

Range: Ages 5½-11

Scoring: Examiner evaluated

Cost: 25 tests $5.40; manual plus 25 tests $6.60.

Publisher: Harrap, Ltd.-available from The Test Agency and Pendragon House, Inc. (U.S.A.)

INDIVIDUAL PHONICS CRITERION TEST
Edward B. Fry

child   grades 1-6

Purpose: Determines student knowledge of letter sounds to detect reading or speaking deficiences.

Description: 99 item paper-pencil test containing 99 nonsense words, each one testing a phoneme- graph-eme correspondence. The student reads the nonsense words aloud to the examiner from one copy of the test while the examiner uses a separate copy for scoring. Each test item matches a chart in *99 Phonics Charts* by Jamestown. Examiner required. Not suitable for group use.

Untimed: Not available

Range: Grades 1-6

Scoring: Examiner evaluated

Cost: Complete (40 test sheets) $8.00.

Publisher: Jamestown Publishers

THE INSTANT WORDS CRITERION TEST
Edward B. Fry

child   grades K-3

Purpose: Determines a student's ability to read the 300 English words which made up 65 percent of all written material, and indicates the most appropriate place to begin the Complete Diagnostic Test. Used as a teaching tool.

Description: 300 word oral test of knowledge of suffixes and spelling. The student reads each word aloud to the examiner (teacher or parent), who stops the reading after five or ten words have been missed. These are then taught as new words. Examiner required. Not suitable for group use.

Untimed: 30 minutes

Range: Grades K-3

Scoring: Examiner evaluated

Cost: 40 tests $8.00.

Publisher: Jamestown Publishers

JANSKY DIAGNOSTIC BATTERY
Jeannette Jansky

child   Kindergarten

Purpose: Measures reading readiness of kindergarten children. Used for educational planning.

Description: Multiple item battery of 15 verbal, paper-pencil tests of reading readiness abilities. Designed for kindergarten children identified by the Jansky Screening Index as being at risk of not learning to read. Factors assessed include expressive and receptive language, verbal pattern matching, verbal memory, and graphomotor status. Available as a kit which includes cardboard carrying case that fits inside the Jansky Screening Index Kit case, 35 profile forms, 35 nonsense word matching forms, two cartoon sequences, a speech sound discrimination test, pattern tapper, and set of cards for testing word recognition and spelling. Instructions for administering and scoring are presented in Jansky and Hirsch's *Preventing Reading Failure*, published by Harper and Row. Examiner required. Not for group use.

Untimed: 30 minutes

Range: Kindergarten

Scoring: Hand key: examiner evaluated

Cost: Complete kit $25.00; 35 score forms and nonsense word matching forms $3.50.

Publisher: Jeannette Jansky

JANSKY SCREENING INDEX
Jeannette Jansky

child   Kindergarten

Purpose: Identifies kindergarten-age children who may show signs of failing to read by the time they finish second grade. Used to screen those in need of special educational help.

Description: 5 multiple item, paper-pencil and oral language tests of basic readiness skills. Measures ability in design copying, picture naming, lettering naming, word matching and sentence repetition. The Screening Index evolved after research on a preliminary, longer battery, the Predictive Index authored by de Hirsch, Jansky and Langford. Now available in kit form which includes plastic carrying case; 35 score forms; 35 Gates word matching forms (with shield); Bender Motor Gestalt cards A, 1, 2, 4, 6, and 8; a picture naming booklet; and a letter naming booklet. Instructions for administering and scoring are found in *Preventing Reading Failure* by Jansky and de Hirsch; Harper and Row, 1972. Suitable for evaluating large numbers of children. Supervised paraprofessionals may be trained to give tests.

Untimed: 20-30 minutes

Range: Kindergarten

Scoring: Hand key; examiner evaluated

Cost: Complete kit $20.00; 35 score forms and Gates forms $3.50.

Publisher: Jeannette Jansky

LONDON READING TEST (LRT)

child

Purpose: Assesses reading level and pattern of abilities. Used for identifying children in need of remedial teaching.

Description: Multiple item, paper-pencil measure of reading abilities. The two alternate forms (A or B) have three reading passages. Comprehension of the first two passages is tested using the cloze technique, while the third asks questions tapping a wide range of comprehension skills. Scores at both an independent and instructional level are obtained. Examiner required. Suitable for group use. BRITISH PUBLISHER

Untimed: 1 hour

Range: Ages 10.07-12.04

Scoring: Examiner evaluated

Cost: Specimen set £ 2.95; 25 booklets (specify A or B) £4.40; 25 practice sheets A/B £1.45; manual £2.45 (payment in sterling for all overseas orders).

Publisher: NFER-Nelson Publishing Company

METROPOLITAN READING INSTRUCTIONAL TESTS
Roger Farr, George A. Prescott, Irving H. Balow, and Thomas P. Hogan

---

child   grades K.5-9.9

Purpose: Measures reading skills. Used for providing prescriptive information on educational performance of individual pupils.

Description: Multiple item series of paper-pencil tests measuring major components of reading skills including visual discrimination, letter recognition, auditory discrimination, sight vocabulary, phoneme/grapheme: consonants, phoneme/grapheme: vowels, vocabulary in context, word part clues, rate of comprehension, skimming and scanning, and reading comprehension. Divided into six levels: Primer, grade K.5-1.4; Primary 1, grade 1.5-2.4; Primary 2, grade 2.5-3.4; Elementary, grade 3.5-4.9; Intermediate, grade 5.0-6.9; and Advanced 1, grade 7.0-9.9. Each level assesses four to seven of the above components. Materials include two alternate and equivalent forms, JI and KI. One in a series of instructional tests related to the Metropolitan Achievement Tests

Survey Battery. Examiner required. Suitable for group use.

Timed: Varies

Range: Grades K.5-9.9

Scoring: Hand key; may be machine scored; scoring service available

Cost: Specimen sets (includes test, teacher's manual for administering and interpreting; Intermediate and Advanced 1 include handscorable document)-specify level-$6.00 each

Publisher: The Psychological Corporation

MONROE DIAGNOSTIC READING TEST
Marion Monroe

---

child, teen   grades 1-10

Purpose: Assesses reading deficiencies according to chronological and mental age. Used to diagnose special reading difficulties.

Description: 326 item card test is comprised of nine analytic subtests. The analytic tests include: alphabet repeating and reading; iota word test; b, d, p, q, u, n test; recognition of orientation; mirror reading; mirror writing; number reversal; word discrimination; sounding and handedness. The examiner can immediately tell if a child makes the usual mistakes for his grade-level or if he has an excessive amount of a particular type of error. Examiner required. Not suitable for group use.

Timed: 30 minutes

Range: Grades 1-10

Scoring: Hand key

Cost: Complete set (includes test cards, 50 record blanks, manual) $24.00.

Publisher: C.H. Nevins Publishing Company

MONROE READING APTITUDE TESTS
Marion Monroe

child   grades K-1

Purpose: Measures essential skills which determine reading ability. Used by schools to determine reading readiness.

Description: Five subtests assessing factors essential to success in reading: visual test, auditory test, motor control test, test of oral speech and articulation, and language test. Scores are given in percentile terms for each half year. Examiner required. Suitable for group use.

Untimed: 10-15 minutes per subtest

Range: Grades K-1

Scoring: Examiner evaluated

Cost: 35 test booklets (includes teacher's manual, percentile chart, class analysis record, 1 suggestions for special classes) $19.20; test card material $8.05; teacher's manual $1.95; suggestions for special classes $1.50; specimen set $3.45.

Publisher: C.H. Nevins Printing Company

NEALE ANALYSIS OF READING ABILITY
N.B. Neale

child

Purpose: Assesses reading standard of children 6-12 years of age.

Description: Test booklet with three parallel forms, each containing reading passages standardized for six different grades. The test is printed in three different sizes type. Each left hand page has a drawing which sets the scene for the passage to be read. British equivalent reading ages are given for each raw score. Materials include booklet, manual and record

sheets for each form.
BRITISH PUBLISHER

Untimed: 10-15 minutes

Range: Ages 6-12

Scoring: Examiner evaluated

Cost: Contact publisher.

Publisher: Macmillian Education Ltd.

THE O'BRIEN VOCABULARY PLACEMENT TEST
Janet O'Brien

child   grades 1-6

Purpose: Measures the reading ability of elementary school students. Used to identify children who have reading deficiencies.

Description: Ten item paper-pencil test in six sections, one for each grade through the sixth. Each test contains a list of words for which the student selects the antonym from four possible choices. It enables a teacher to find the independent reading level of an entire class in 15 minutes. The test also can be used individually for new students and those in special education classes. Examiner required. Suitable for group use.

Untimed: 15 minutes

Range: Grades 1-6 and special education students

Scoring: Hand key

Cost: Eight dittos and a teacher's manual $5.00.

Publisher: Educational Activities, Inc.

ORAL READING CRITERION TEST
Edward B. Fry

child, teen   grades 1-7

Purpose: Determines student's

independent, instructional and frustration reading ability levels. Used for teacher guidance.

Description: Seven paragraph, paper-pencil test. Examiner has student read the paragraphs aloud and records scores for each one. The number of errors indicates the reading level category: independent, instructional or frustration. A Fry Readability Graph is provided to help the teacher match materials to the student's ability. A minimum first-grade reading level is required. Examiner required. Not suitable for group use.

Untimed: 15-30 minutes

Range: Grades 1-7

Scoring: Examiner evaluated

Cost: 40 tests $8.00.

Publisher: Jamestown Publishers

PERFORMANCE ASSESSMENT IN READING (PAIR)
CTB/McGraw-Hill

teen   grades 7-9

Purpose: Identifies a student's needs in basic reading skills and the instruction required to attain them. Used by junior high school reading teachers.

Description: 72 item, two-part, paper-pencil test consisting of displays such as warning signs, street maps, card catalogs, encyclopedia entries, telephone directories, and bus schedules. Questions are designed to determine reading skills in vocabulary, comprehension, and location/study skills. Examiner required. Suitable for group use.

Untimed: Not available

Range: Junior high school

Scoring: Hand key; computer scoring available

Cost: Specimen set (includes a test book, manual, a hand-score and a computer-score answer sheet, class summary sheet, and a test reviewer's guide) $7.25.

Publisher: CTB/McGraw-Hill

PREREADING EXPECTANCY SCREENING SCALE (PRESS)
Lawrence C. Hartlage and David G. Lucas

child

Purpose: Assesses skills important in reading. Used for predicting reading problems for beginning readers.

Description: Multiple item paper-pencil test of child's recognition of the numbers one through nine and the following shapes: cross, circle, star, square, and diamond. Consists of four subtests: Sequencing, Spatial, Memory, and Letter Identification. Items are read by teacher. Examiner required. Suitable for group use.

Untimed: 35 minutes

Range: Ages 6-9

Scoring: Hand key; examiner evaluated

Cost: Specimen set $7.25; 25 tests $12.50; 100- $49.00; 25 profile sheets (specify boys or girls) $5.50; 100-$21.00; manual $5.50.

Publisher: Psychologists and Educators, Inc.

PRESCRIPTIVE READING INVENTORY (PRI)
CTB/McGraw-Hill

child   grades K-6.5

Purpose: Measures student mastery of reading objectives. Used for diagnosing student needs and prescribing instructional interventions.

Description: Multiple item paper-pencil test of 90 or 30 commonly taught reading objectives. Divided into six levels: Level I, Grades K.0-1.0; Level II, Grades K.5-2.0; Level A, Grades 1.5-2.5; Level B, Grades 2.0-3.5; Level C, Grades 3.0-4.5; and Level D, Grades 4.0-6.5. Levels A-D contain ninety objectives, some of which are tested at more than one level. Objectives are classified in seven process groups: recognition of sound and symbol, phonic analysis, structural analysis, translation, literal comprehension, interpretive comprehension, and critical comprehension. Levels I and II each contain 10 category objectives and 20 specific objectives, which are also classified in seven process groups: auditory discrimination, visual discrimination, alphabet knowledge, language experience, comprehension, attention skills, and initial reading. There is an average of 3-4 items per objective in Levels A-D, and six per objective in Levels I-II. Materials include practice exercises, Examiner's Cassettes for Levels I and II, and a Checklist of Observable Behaviors. Examiner required. Suitable for group use.

Untimed: Varies

Range: Level I, grades K.0-1.0; Level II, grades K.5- 2.0; Level A, grades 1.5-2.5; Level B, grades 2.0-3.5; Level C, grades 3.0-4.5; Level D, grades 4.0- 6.5

Scoring: Hand key; computer scoring available

Cost: Multi-level examination kit $13.45; specimen set (specify level) $7.25.

Publisher: CTB/McGraw-Hill

THE PRIMARY READING TEST
Norman Franck

child

Purpose: Assesses reading comprehension. Used for individual pupil evaluations.

Description: Multiple item paper-pencil test of reading comprehension. Items involve word recognition and sentence completion. Divided into two levels: Level 1 for 6-10 year olds, and Level 2 for 7-12 year olds. Materials include two alternate forms, 1A and 2A. Examiner required. Suitable for group use.

BRITISH PUBLISHER

Untimed: 20-30 minutes

Range: Ages 6-12

Scoring: Hand key

Cost: 25 pupils' booklets (specify level) £3.25; teacher's book (includes scoring keys) £2.10 (payment in sterling for all overseas orders).

Publisher: NFER-Nelson Publishing Company

PRI/RS: SYSTEM 1, GRADED APPROACH, CATEGORY OBJECTIVES TEST
Refer to page 224.

PRI/RS: SYSTEM 2, MULTI-GRADED APPROACH TO ASSESSMENT AND INSTRUCTION
Refer to page 224.

READING CLASSIFICATION TEST
Williamson and Bell

child   grades 2-6

Purpose: Measures reading skills in Australian children grades 2-6.

Description: Multiple item test measures and provides ways of evaluating reading performance in Australian children grades 2-6. Provided in the packet is diagnostic information, pronunciation guide, testcards and manual, and "links with children's literature."

AUSTRALIAN PUBLISHER

Untimed: Not available

Range: Grades 2-6

Scoring: Not available

Cost: Complete kit (includes test cards, manual, pronunciation guide) $2.40; 10 individualized record forms $.40 (Australian currency).

Publisher: Educational Resources

READING LEVEL TESTS (USING CLOZE PROCEDURE)

child

Purpose: Assesses reading skills. Used for selecting appropriate reading materials for pupils.

Description: Multiple item, paper-pencil test of reading comprehension using the cloze technique. Pupils are asked to write in words which have deliberately been left out of prose passages. passages are arranged in increasing order of difficulty. Part 1 consists of four passages for use with children ages 7 to 8; Part 2 is for children in the 9 to 10 year age range, and also has four passages. For use with other standardized tests. Examiner required. Suitable for group use.
BRITISH PUBLISHER

Untimed: Not available

Range: Ages 7-12

Scoring: Examiner evaluated

Cost: 10 Part 1 and 10 Part 2 reading level tests £3.95; manual £0.95 (payment in sterling for all overseas orders).

Publisher: NFER-Nelson Publishing Company

READING READINESS INVENTORY
J. Downing and Derek V. Thackray

child

Purpose: Measures reading readiness of reception-class children ages 4-6. Improves the effectiveness of pre-reading programs.

Description: Paper-pencil observational instrument is designed as both a checklist and a record form. The inventory summarizes the most significant reading readiness factors and provides a convenient and structured basis for classroom observation and for clear, concise recording. Examiner required. Suitable for group use.
BRITISH PUBLISHER

Untimed: Not available

Range: Ages 4-7

Scoring: Examiner evaluated

Cost: Inventory £1.25

Publisher: Hodder & Stoughton

THE READING SKILLS DIAGNOSTIC TEST III, 3RD REVISION (RSDT III)
Richard H. Bloomer

child, teen   grades 2-8

Purpose: Measures content, learning processes and learning capacities necessary for learning how to read. Provides a structure for beginning reading instruction, as well as model for diagnosis and treatment of early learning difficulties related to reading and writing.

Description: 48 paper-pencil subtests measuring mastery of beginning encoding-decoding and word recognition skills, basic processing skills and learning processes. The subtests are arranged in four groups of 12 to measure four levels of response strength: reproduction, recognition, visual-oral, and auditory-motor. Each of the four levels measures content (letter knowledge, simple phonic knowledge, sight words, long vowels, consonant digraphs, and vowel dipthongs); basic processing skills (imitation, copying, multiple discrimination, consonant-vowel blending, and consonant-vowel-consonant blending); and learning capacities (short terms memory for words, short term memory for letters and stimulus magnitude). Context clues at all four levels of response strength help teachers plan specific instructional and remedial approaches. Subtests and levels are arranged sequentially, and the test is designed to be administered one subtest at a time in a test- teach-test format. Levels 1 and 3 are individually administered; Levels 2 and 4 are group administered. Examiner required.

Untimed: Not available

Range: Grades 2-8

Scoring: Hand key; examiner evaluated

Cost: Level 1, manual and answer sheets $16.40; Level 2, manual and answer sheets $19.70; Level 3, manual and test stimuli, record forms $25.50; Level 4, manual and answer sheets $21.80.

Publisher: Brador Publications, Inc.

READING TESTS
F.J. Schonell

child   grades 1-7

Purpose: Measures reading achievement of children grades 1-7.

Description: Four paper-pencil tests measuring four ascending reading levels: Graded Word Reading (R.1), Simple Prose Reading (R.2), Silent Reading Test A (R.3), and Silent Reading Test B (R.4). Handbook for reading tests also available. Examiner required.
BRITISH PUBLISHER

Timed: Varies

Range: Grades 1-7

Scoring: Not available

Cost: 20 R.1 tests £1.25; 20 R.2 tests £1.15; 20 R.3 tests £1.25; 20 R.4 tests £1.25; handbook 60p.

Publisher: Oliver and Boyd/Longman, Inc. (U.S.A.)

READING TESTS SR-A AND SR-B

child

Purpose: Measures reading attainment of primary school children. Used for screening and survey of groups of pupils.

Description: Multiple item, paper-pencil tests of reading achievement. Items are sentence completion tasks, which correlate highly with other reading measures. Examiner required. Suitable for group use.
BRITISH PUBLISHER

Timed: 20 minutes for each test

Range: Ages 7½-12

Scoring: Examiner available

Cost: 10 SR-A and 10 SR-B (specify test) £1.10 each set; combined manual £0.95 (payment in sterling for all overseas orders).

Publisher: NFER-Nelson Publishing Company

SALFORD SENTENCE READING TEST
G.E. Bookbinder

child

Purpose: Measures reading achievement of children having reading ages between 6.0 and 10.6 years.

Description: Multiple item oral response test of reading achievement is available in three parallel forms; A, B and C. Each form consists of a test card containing 13 sentences presented in order of increasing difficulty. Testing ceases when the child has completed the sentence in which the sixth reading error is made. The child's reading age can immediately be read off from the test card. Percentile scores for chronological ages 6.1 to 11.9 are listed separately in the manual. Availability of three parallel forms useful for test-retest situation. The test cards are reusable and are available in sets containing one copy each of forms A, B and C. Examiner required. Not for group use.
BRITISH PUBLISHER

Untimed: 2-3 minutes

Range: Ages 6-12

Scoring: Examiner evaluated

Cost: Specimen test card is available free upon request; test cards (A, B and C) £1.00 per set of 3, manual 80p.

Publisher: Hodder & Stoughton

SIPAY WORD ANALYSIS TEST (SWAT)
Edward R. Sipay

child   grades 1-2

Purpose: Determines a child's strengths and weaknesses in word analysis skills. Used to assess individual progress and program effectiveness.

Description: 17 tests measuring three basic reading skills: visual analysis, phonic analysis and visual blending. SWAT allows for discriminant testing of specific word analysis skills (consonant blends, monosyllabic words, single letters) depending on each student's reading level. The areas the test measure are

sequenced according to the level of difficulty. Examiner required. Not suitable for group use.

Untimed: Total time 3-6 hours; 10-20 minutes for each of the tests

Range: Grades 1 and 2

Scoring: Examiner evaluated

Cost: SWAT kit (includes 1 manual, one of each of the 17 Mini-Manuals, one dozen answer sheets and report forms, 1 complete set of 756 test cards) $80.00; specimen set (includes 1 manual and one test, 6 Mini-Manuals, answer sheet, and report form) $2.75; all tests can be purchased individually.

Publisher: Educators Publishing Service, Inc.

SKILLCORP COMPUTER MANAGEMENT SYSTEM-- READING

child   grades 1-6

Purpose: Assesses reading skill deficiencies. Used to diagnose an individual student's reading base and prescribe resources for reteaching.

Description: 77 tests assessing five strands: phonetic analysis, structural analysis, vocabulary, comprehension and study skills. All skills tested are cross-referenced to basal and supplementary reading programs. Microcomputer prints prescription for individual students or groups to reteach skills not mastered. Materials include test administration manual or test cassettes, and test cards for each grade level. Examiner required. Suitable for group use.

Untimed: Not available

Range: Grades 1-6

Scoring: Hand key; may be computer scored

Cost: Contact publisher.

Publisher: Skillcorp Software, Inc.

SOUTHGATE GROUP READING TESTS
Vera Southgate

child

Purpose: Measures basic reading skills of children ages 5-9 years. Identifies students reading significantly above or below their expected age level.

Description: Two paper-pencil tests of reading ability measure word selection and sentence completion skills. Test 1 is a word selection test suitable for older infants and younger juniors, and for older pupils of low reading ability. Norms are provided for ages 5:9 to 7:9 years. Available in three parallel forms for test-retest purposes. Test 2, a sentence completion test, continues with the assessment of the second stage of learning to read. It has a slight overlap with Test 1 and norms are provided for ages 7:0 to 9:7 years. Two parallel forms are intended to be administered simultaneously, giving alternate children different forms. Test 2 is useful for average 7 and 8 year olds and for bright younger children and slower older ones. Examiner required. Suitable for group use.
BRITISH PUBLISHER

Untimed: Not available

Range: Ages 5-9

Scoring: Examiner evaluated

Cost: Specimen sets 85p each; 20 copies test 1 (specify form) £2.00 per set; 20 copies test 2 (specify form) £1.50 per set; manuals 70p each.

Publisher: Hodder & Stoughton

SOUTHWESTERN SPANISH ARTICULATION TEST (SSAT)
Allen S. Toronto

child

Purpose: Assesses the phonological

skills of Spanish- dominant children. Used to identify phonemes that indicate remediation.

Description: 47 item line drawings elicit verbal responses targeted to a particular phoneme. Reusable stimulus pictures and complete instructions are provided as well as a distinction of Spanish and English articulation assessment. Examiner required. Not suitable for group use. Examiner must have knowledge of Spanish.

Untimed: 10 minutes

Range: Spanish-dominant children

Scoring: Hand key; examiner evaluated

Cost: Complete kit $8.95; 30 scoring forms $3.50.

Publisher: National Educational Laboratory Publishers, Inc.

THE STANDARD READING TESTS
J.C. Daniels and Hunter Diack

child

Purpose: Measures reading ability of children age 9 and older. Used by teachers for placement and for determining remedial needs.

Description: 12 paper-pencil, oral and listening tests: The Standard Test of Reading Skill, Copying Abstract Figures, Copying a Sentence, Visual Discrimination and Orientation Test, Letter- Recognition Test, Aural Discrimination Test, Diagnostic Word-Recognition Tests, Oral Word Recognition, Picture Word Recognition, Silent Prose-Reading and Comprehension, Graded Spelling Test, and Graded Test of Reading Experience. Designed to provide detailed information of reading difficulties for individual children and to indicate steps for improvement. The Standard Test of Reading Skill is the key test and is for students who have not mastered all reading skills. The Graded Spelling and Graded Test of Reading Experience is for high scorers in Test 1. Examiner required. BRITISH PUBLISHER

Untimed: Not available

Range: Ages up to 9

Scoring: Examiner evaluated

Cost: The Standard Reading Tests £4.65; Standard Reading Test 1 (has a set of cards) £2.10 plus VAT; Standard Reading Test 12 (on a set of spirit masters) £2.45 plus VAT.

Publisher: Collins Educational—a division of Collins Publisher.

SUCHER-ALLRED READING PLACEMENT INVENTORY
Floyd Sucher and Ruel A. Allred

child, teen   grades 1-9

Purpose: Assesses students' independent, instructional, and frustrational reading levels. Used for reading placement, identification of reading difficulties and general screening for remedial reading.

Description: Multiple item test measuring word recognition, oral reading, oral reading comprehension, and silent reading comprehension. The Word- Recognition Test is administered first. The child is presented lists of words which he reads orally. The teacher assesses the word-recognition, using the results to select a starting point for administration of the Oral Reading Test. There are two forms available: Form A and Form B. Examiner required. Not suitable for group use.

Untimed: 20 minutes

Range: Grades 1-9

Scoring: Examiner evaluated

Cost: One form and teacher's manual

for class of 35 $12.12, with both forms $18.27.

Publisher: The Economy Company

TEST OF EARLY READING ABILITY (TERA)
D. Kim Reid, Wayne P. Hresko and Donald D. Hammill

child

Purpose: Determines the actual reading ability (not "readiness") of preschool, kindergarten and primary level students. Results can be used to document early reading ability.

Description: Multiple item paper-pencil test examining three areas related to early learning: knowledge of the alphabet, comprehension and the conventions of reading (e.g., book orientation and format). Materials include 50 picture cards and record forms and the manual. Examiner required. Not for group use.

Untimed: Not available

Range: Ages 3.0-7.11

Scoring: Hand key

Cost: Complete (includes manual, 50 picture cards, 50 record forms, storage box) $43.00; components available for separate purchase.

Publisher: PRO-ED

TEST OF LINGUISTIC AWARENESS IN READING READINESS (LARR TEST)
J. Downing, D. Ayers and B. Schaefer

child

Purpose: Assesses a child's conception of language, reading and writing. Used for determining readiness to profit from formal reading instruction.

Description: Three subtest paper-pencil measure of language awareness consisting of Recognising Literacy Behavior, Understanding Literacy Functions and Technical Language of Literacy. Materials include manual with suggestions for instruction. Only preliminary manual is available pending collection of further LARR data. Available to qualified teachers, speech therapists, psychologists, and other professionals concerned with reading education. Examiner required. Suitable for group use. BRITISH PUBLISHER

Untimed: 10 minutes approximately for each subtest

Range: Ages 5-8 and older children who are having difficulties in learning to read.

Scoring: Not available

Cost: Manual ordering information may be obtained through NFER-Nelson.

Publisher: NFER-Nelson Publishing Company

THACKRAY READING READINESS PROFILES
Derek V. Thackray and Lucy Thackray

child

Purpose: Measures reading readiness of reception class children. Diagnoses pre-reading skill deficiencies of older non-readers. Used to develop individualized pre-reading skill programs.

Description: Task assessment and oral response test measures the most important reading readiness indicators. Full instructions for interpreting the profiles and suggestions for developing specific reading readiness skills are contained in the manual. Examiner required. Suitable for group use. BRITISH PUBLISHER

Untimed: Not available

Range: Ages 4-7

Scoring: Examiner evaluated

Cost: Specimen set £1.25; 10 profiles £4.25 per set, manual 95p.

Publisher: Hodder & Stoughton

VISUAL-AURAL DIGIT SPAN TEST (VADS)
Elizabeth M. Koppitz

child

Purpose: Diagnoses specific problems in reading recognition and spelling for children who can read and write digits. Used to develop individual educational programs for learning disabled children.

Description: Multiple item test in which digit sequences on 26 test cards must be reproduced from memory, first orally and then in writing after being presented orally and then, as a separate series, visually. The test measures auditory, visual, visual-auditory and auditory-visual integration, sequence and recall of digits, and organization of written material. There are 11 scores, interpreted individually. Examiner required. Suitable for group use. Available in Spanish.

Untimed: 10 minutes

Range: Ages 5½-12

Scoring: Examiner evaluated

Cost: Manual $23.50; 100 tests $14.50.

Publisher: Grune & Stratton, Inc.

VISUAL DISCRIMINATION TEST
Refer to page 611.

VISUAL MEMORY SCALE (VMS)
James A. Carroll

child

Purpose: Measures short-terms visual memory as aid to diagnosing reading and spelling problems.

Description: 25 card, examiner-led test of child's ability to recognize patterns. The examiner gives the child a five-second look at a card containing a complex geometric design, then has the child pick out the same design among four similar ones on a second card. Examiner required. Not suitable for groups.

Timed: 5 second timed presentation; total test 5-7 minutes

Range: Ages 5-6

Scoring: Hand key

Cost: Set of plates $6.00; manual $3.00; answer blanks $1.50; complete kit $9.50.

Publisher: Carroll Publications

VISUAL MEMORY TEST
Joseph M. Wepman, Anne Morency and Maria Seidl

child

Purpose: Measures a child's ability to remember non-alphabetical, geometric forms. Used to identify any perceptual inadequacy which might reduce the ability to learn to read.

Description: 16 item "point-to" test of a child's ability to recall forms unfamiliar to him which cannot readily be named. The child is shown a design on a "target" page and then is asked to chose it out of four designs shown on a "response" page, thereby testing immediate visual recall. Norms are provided for ages 5, 6, 7, and 8 years. Adequacy threshold

scores indicate the need for additional evaluation. Examiner required. Not for group use.

Untimed: 10-15 minutes

Range: Ages 5-8

Scoring: Hand key

Cost: Complete kit (includes 1 reusable test booklet, 20 score sheets, manual) $28.75.

Publisher: Western Psychological Services

THE WESSEX READING ANALYSIS
A. Hughes, P. Evans and S. Moulton

child, teen

Purpose: Assesses reading accuracy and reading comprehension. Used for diagnosis of reading difficulty by teachers, reading specialists or educational psychologists.

Description: Two component measure of reading skills. The first component is a small book of sentences which provides a quick assessment of oral reading ability. The second component contains passages written in three styles-- narrative, instructional and poetic, which can be used for a more detailed assessment. Tests allow for detailed diagnostic evaluation of reading mistakes. Examiner required. Suitable for group use.
BRITISH PUBLISHER

Untimed: Not available

Range: Ages 7-13

Scoring: Not available

Cost: Contact publisher.

Publisher: NFER-Nelson Publishing Company

WIDE-SPAN READING TEST
Alan Brimer with Herbert Gross

child, teen

Purpose: Measures sentence reading skills. Used for identification of individual students' abilities.

Description: Multiple item, paper-pencil test of reading skills. Items consist of decoding printed symbols, fitting meanings to groups of sounds, and construing the structural relationship of meaning within the context of a sentence. Materials include two parallel forms, A and B. Examiner required. Suitable for group use.
BRITISH PUBLISHER

Timed: 30 minutes

Range: Ages 7-15

Scoring: Hand key

Cost: Specimen set (includes 1 pupil's booklet A & B, 1 pupil's answer sheet and manual) £2.55; introductory set (includes 25 form A and 25 form B tests, 50 answer sheets, 1 teacher's manual) £14.00 (payment in sterling for all overseas orders).

Publisher: NFER-Nelson Publishing Company

WORD DISCRIMINATION TEST
Charles B. Huelsman, Jr.

child   grades 1.2-8.3

Purpose: Measures ability to recognize words. Identifies children (grades 1-8) with word-recognition skill deficiencies.

Description: 92 item paper-pencil, multiple-choice test measures how well students use length, internal design, and external configuration in perceiving words. Each test item consists of a row with one word and four groups of letters that are not words.

The students must recognize and draw a circle around the one word in each row. Grade equivalents are given for all raw scores. Norms based on 1299 sets of scores from children in grades 1-6. Examiner required. Suitable for group use.

Untimed: 15 minutes

Range: Grades 1.2-8.3

Scoring: Hand key; examiner evaluated

Cost: Test $.10.

Publisher: Miami University Alumni Association

High School and Above

ADVANCED READING INVENTORY
Jerry L. Johns

teen, adult   grades 7-College

Purpose: Assesses reading skills. Used to help teachers select appropriate reading materials.

Description: Multiple item paper-pencil test of reading skills. Items are of three types: graded word lists, graded reading passages and cloze tests based on the graded reading passages. In addition, there are two sets of comprehension for each graded reading passage. One set is intended for group administration, one for individual administration. Materials include two alternate forms, A and B. Examiner required. Suitable for group use.

Timed: Varies

Range: Grade 7-college

Scoring: Examiner evaluated

Cost: Test $8.95.

Publisher: William C. Brown Company Publishers

BASIC SKILLS TEST-READING-SECONDARY: FORMS A and B
IOX Assessment Associates

teen   grades 8-11

Purpose: Measures high school minimum competency in the basic reading skills. Useful for minimum competency testing and program evaluation.

Description: 30 item paper-pencil test examines student's ability to understand safety warnings, complete forms and applications, use common reference sources, determine main ideas, and use documents to take action. This test succeeds the IOX Basic Skills Test-Reading-Elementary Level. Examiner required. Suitable for group use.

Untimed: 30-45 minutes

Range: Grades 8-11

Scoring: Hand key

Cost: 25 BR-A1 tests $42.50; 25 BR-B1 tests $42.50; teacher's guide BR-G1 $3.95; test manual BTM-1 $3.95; 50 answer sheets $6.95.

Publisher: IOX Assessment Associates

COMPREHENSION TEST FOR COLLEGE OF EDUCATION STUDENTS
E.L. Black

teen, adult   College

Purpose: Assesses reading comprehension. Used for selection of students for colleges of Education.

Description: 60 item paper-pencil test of reading comprehension. Items are largely multiple-choice based on eight prose passages. Test yields information about the student's comprehension in relation to different subject matter and language styles. Examiner required. Suitable for group use.
BRITISH PUBLISHER

Timed: 45 minutes

Range: College students

Scoring: Examiner evaluated

Cost: Specimen set £1.95; 25 booklets £10.45; manual £1.70 (payment in sterling for all overseas orders).

Publisher: NFER-Nelson Publishing Company

DIAGNOSTIC ANALYSIS OF READING ERRORS (DARE)
Jacquelyn Gillespie and Jacqueline Shohet

teen

Purpose: Identifies adolescents and adults with language-related problems, diagnoses learning disabilities and provides specific data on the visual-auditory coding process for psycho-educational diagnoses. Used to survey school and community populations for educational planning and research.

Description: 46 item paper-pencil, multiple-choice test in which the examiner dictates Wide Range Achievement Test Level II Spelling items and the individual selects one of four choices as being the correct answer. Four measures of visual-auditory transcoding ability are provided: Correct (reading and spelling skills), Sound Substitution (phonic analysis skills), Omission (word structure analysis), and Reversal (Sequencing efficiency). Coordinates with WRAT reading and spelling tests in reading improvement programs and attempts to provide a culture-fair measure of English language skills. Scoring yields diagnostic error patterns, age level norms (ages 12-adult), and standard scores. Free computer scoring available. Restricted to Educational/Psychological professionals. Examiner required. Suitable for group use.

Untimed: 10 minutes

Range: Ages 12-18

Scoring: Hand key; computer scoring available

Cost: Manual $13.50; 50 answer sheets $9.25; free computer scoring available.

Publisher: Jastak Assessment Systems

DIAGNOSTIC SCREENING TEST: READING 3RD EDITION
Thomas D. Gnagey and Patricia A. Gnagey

child, teen   grades 1-13   [☞ ✍]

Purpose: Determines reading achievement levels and diagnoses common reading problems by testing word recognition and reading and listening comprehension.

Description: 84 word paper-pencil recognition items and six comprehension passages to measure six reading levels (comfort, instructional, frustration, comprehension, phonetics-sight, listening comprehension) and seven word attach skills (c- v/c, v/r, v/l, v/v, c/v/c, Sie, Mix). Student reads the word list and comprehension passages aloud and answers prescribed questions. The examiner then reads a passage aloud and the student answers questions. Material includes a consolidation index of how solid or spotty each skill is, a pretest, a measurement of nonsense syllable phonics skill, a phonics sight ratio, a tear sheet of individualized classroom recommendations, equivalent forms 'A' and 'B', percentile ranks, T scores, and grade equivalents. Examiner required. Not suitable for group use.

Untimed: 5-10 minutes

Range: Grades 1-13

Scoring: Hand key

Cost: Manual and 20 test forms "A" $12.00; 100 test forms "A" $21.00; 100 test forms "B" $21.00; 20 test forms "B" $6.50.

Publisher: Facilitation House

EDINBURGH READING TESTS
Godfrey Thomson Unit For Education Research and Moray House College of Education

child, teen

Purpose: Measures general reading abilities of students ages 7-16. Diagnoses the reading strengths and weaknesses of each student, and identifies those in need of special help. Measures success of teaching methods in classes, schools or districts.

Description: Paper-pencil tests of reading achievement are presented in four stages for four different age groups. Each stage is divided into four or more separately timed subtests designed to assess different areas of reading competence. An overall score for the whole test and a separate score for each subtest are obtained for each child. The subtest scores are plotted on a profile, showing which relatively high or low scores are significant and merit further observation. Stage 1 (ages 7.0-9.0) is available in equivalent forms A and B for test-retest programs. Practice items are included in the test forms, which are designed for administration in two sessions of 25 minutes. The profile is printed on the back of each form. Stages 2 (ages 8.6-10.6) and 3 (ages 10.0-12.6) are presented in a single test booklet (test content is the same for both stages). Both tests are designed for administrating in three sessions: Practice Test (30-35 minutes), Part I (40 minutes) and Part II (35 minutes). Stage 4 (ages 12.0-16.0) is designed for administration in two sessions of 35 minutes. The profile is printed on the back of the test booklet. Full details on standardization are given in the manuals. Examiner required. Suitable for group use.
BRITISH PUBLISHER

Timed: 25-35 minutes for each section

Range: Ages 7-16

Scoring: Hand key

Cost: Stage 1 specimen set £1.50; stage 2 specimen set £2.00; stage 3 specimen set £2.25; stage 4 specimen set £1.50.

Publisher: Hodder & Stoughton

IOWA SILENT READING TESTS (ISRT)
Roger Farr, coordinating editor

teen, adult   grades 6-UP

Purpose: Assesses ability to read. Used for diagnosis of student strengths and weakness and for implementation of remedial lesson plans.

Description: Multiple item battery of paper-pencil tests measuring four reading skill areas including Vocabulary, Comprehension, Directed Reading (work- study skills), and Reading Efficiency (rate with comprehension). Directed Reading items measure students ability to use reference sources. Divided into three levels: Level 1 for grades 6 through 9, Level 2 for grades 9 through community college, and Level 3 for accelerated eleventh- and twelfth-graders, college students and professional groups. Level 3 does not include Directed Reading subtest. Materials include two alternate and equivalent forms, E and F. Examiner required. Suitable for group use.

Timed: Level 1, 1 hour 31 minutes; Level 2, 1 hour 26 minutes; Level 3, 56 minutes

Range: Grades 6-12, college

Scoring: Hand key; may be machine scored; scoring service available

Cost: Specimen set (includes test, MRC answer document, hand-scorable answer document, class record, manual of directions, pupil profile) specify Level 1, 2 or 3 $5.00 each.

Publisher: The Psychological Corporation

MAINTAINING READING EFFICIENCY TESTS
Lyle L. Miller

teen, adult   grades 7-UP

Purpose: Measures pre- and posttesting of reading rate, comprehension and efficiency.

Description: Five tests which include content on history, geography, government, culture and people of the following countries: Brazil, Japan, India, New Zealand, and Switzerland. Each reading test contains 5,000 words with each line numbered. Each answer sheet contains 50 items about the content of what has been read. When the timed test is stopped, each student marks the line on which he was reading and is tested only on material read. Examiner required. Suitable for groups.

Timed: 10 minutes per test

Range: Grades 7-adult

Scoring: Hand key

Cost: 20 booklets $15.00; 20 answer sheets $5.00; specimen set $5.00.

Publisher: Developmental-Reading Distributors

MINNESOTA SPEED OF READING TEST
Alvia C. Eruich

teen, adult   grades 12-UP

Purpose: Measures reading speed. Designed for high school seniors, college students, and college graduates.

Description: 38 item paper-pencil test in two forms (A & B) consisting of short paragraphs, each of which contains and "absurd" sentence or phrase which the subject is asked to cross out. The score depends on how many paragraphs are correctly completed within the time limit. Examiner required. Suitable for

group use.

Timed: 6 minutes

Range: Grade 12, college junior, college graduates

Scoring: Hand key

Cost: 100 forms $5.00; specimen set $.35.

Publisher: University of Minnesota Press

MULTIPLE CHOICE ENGLISH and PROGRESSIVE MULTIPLE CHOICE ENGLISH
A. F. Bolt

teen

Purpose: Assesses reading comprehension. Used for familiarizing students with this type of exercise, and as a starting point for creative writing.

Description: Two paper-pencil, multiple-choice tests measuring several aspects of reading comprehension including vocabulary, comprehension, style and summary. Both tests assist students in inquiring about precise meanings and implications. Multiple Choice English (100 pages) consists of 18 reading passages by famous authors, each followed by 15 to 20 questions. Progressive Multiple Choice English (96 pages) consists of 12 longer passages, each followed by 20 to 25 questions. Examiner required. Suitable for group use.

Untimed: Not available

Range: Advanced readers

Scoring: Examiner evaluated

Cost: Each book of tests $5.00.

Publisher: Harrap, Ltd.-available from Pendragon House, Inc. (U.S.A.)

NELSON-DENNY READING TEST: FORMS E AND F
James I. Brown, J. Michael Bennett, and Gerald S. Hanna

teen, adult   grades 9-UP

Purpose: Assesses reading ability of students in grades 9-12. Used to screen for accelerated or special help programs, and for diagnosis.

Description: 136 item paper-pencil test of reading comprehension, vocabulary and reading rate. The test materials include special 26-minute cut-time norms for superior and speed readers. Participants should be representative of the group used in the norming sample for the norms to be of any use in providing evaluation information. Examiner required. Suitable for group use.

Timed: 35 minutes

Range: Grades 9-12, college, adult

Scoring: Hand key; may be machine scored

Cost: 35 test booklets (specify form E or F) $14.94; 35 MRC answer sheets $11.25; manual $3.78.

Publisher: The Riverside Publishing Company

READING/EVERYDAY ACTIVITIES IN LIFE (R/EAL)
Marilyn Lichtman

teen, adult   grades 10-UP

Purpose: Assesses whether or not an individual is functionally literate. Particularly suitable for Blacks, Puerto Ricans, Mexican Americans, rural groups, and other minority groups who have traditionally been singled out by the bias of standardized reading achievement tests. Suitable for adults at basic educational levels and children age 10 years and older. Used for both diagnostic and evaluative purposes.

Description: 45 item paper-pencil free response test measures an individual's ability to read and use language. The test consists of nine reading selections, each representing a general category of daily reading situations encountered by most individuals high-school age and above. The nine passages include: a set of road signs, a TV schedule, a set of directions for preparing cheese pizza, a reading selection on the topic of narcotic drugs, a food market ad, an apartment lease or credit agreement, a road map, a want ad, and a job or credit application. Five questions are asked for each selection based on task analyses of the functions required to deal with reading material involved. A cassette player, headphones (optional), and a test booklet plus cassette are used to administer the test. This method helps insure that subject's inability to understand written directions will not prevent him from understanding what is expected on the test. Constructed responses to open-ended questions provide a more valid measure of the subject's literacy. Available in two equivalent forms, A and B, for pre- and post-testing. Examiner required. Suitable for group use. Available in Spanish.

Untimed: 1 day

Range: High school-adults

Scoring: Examiner evaluated

Cost: Specimen set (includes 1 cassette, 1 test, 1 manual) $8.00; test booklet $1.00; cassettes $6.00 each; manual $6.50 each.

Publisher: Westwood Press, Inc.

READING PROGRESS SCALE: COLLEGE VERSION
Ronald P. Carver

teen, adult   College

Purpose: Estimates reading level of college students. Particularly appropriate for use with those students

who do not read well. Used for academic placement and referral.

Description: 80 item paper-pencil test assessing basic reading abilities. Scoring takes only seconds and provides immediate feedback to community college students regarding which courses they should take. Available in two alternate forms: Form 2C and Form 5C. Examiner required. Suitable for group use.

Timed: 7 minutes

Range: College

Scoring: Hand key

Cost: Specimen set $1.00; 100 tests $30.00; 1 manual free.

Publisher: Revrac Publications, Inc.

SENIOR HIGH ASSESSMENT OF READING PERFORMANCE (SHARP)
CTB/McGraw-Hill

teen   grades 10-12

Purpose: Measures reading skills necessary in everyday life. Used as outcome measure for competency-based reading programs.

Description: 120 item paper-pencil test of minimum competencies in reading. Items consist of 30 displays representing forms and written materials typically encountered everyday. Each display is followed by four multiple-choice items. SHARP is divided into three sections. Section 1 includes a clothing tab, a social security card, a telephone directory index, a job application form, a change of address order, a business letter, a marriage license application, an invitation, a set of directions for hanging wallpaper, and an auto loan application. Section 2 includes a charge account agreement, a newspaper article, a classified newspaper ad, a financial agreement card, a stop payment request, a package label, a recipe, selections from a driver's license handbook, an unemployment insurance claim, and four road signs. Section 3 includes a job resume, a cash register receipt, an area code map, a TV review, a dictionary entry, a magazine article, a street and freeway map, a highway map, a tax form, and a bank statement. Materials include a shortened Form E, consisting of two sections, each with 40 items. Examiner required. Suitable for group use.

Timed: Not available

Range: Senior high school

Scoring: Hand key; computer scoring available

Cost: Specimen set (includes a test book, manual, sample of each answer sheet, class summary sheet, objective matrix, and a test reviewer's guide) $7.25.

Publisher: CTB/McGraw-Hill

Multi-Level

ACER READING TESTS

child, teen   grades 1-12

Purpose: Assesses reading skills. Used for diagnosis of individual strengths and weaknesses as part of an educational evaluation.

Description: 14 multiple-choice, paper-pencil tests of skills important in reading achievement. Tests are ACER Paragraph Reading Test, a screening test for years 6-8; ACER Primary Reading Survey Tests (Levels AA-BB), years 1 and 2. ACER Primary Reading Survey Tests (Levels A-D), years 3-6; ACER Primary Reading Survey Tests (Level D 1A-1C), a three part test of reading achievement for year 6; ACER Silent Reading Test, years 3-6; ACER Word Identification Test, years 1-4;

ACER Word Knowledge Test-Adult Form B; Co-operative Reading Comprehension Test-Form Y, years 11 and above; Co- operative Reading Comprehension Test-L and M, years 8-10; English Skills Assessment; Progressive Achievement Tests-Form A or B; Reading Appraisal Guide; Tests of English for Migrant Students (TEMS). Examiner required. Suitable for group use.

AUSTRALIAN PUBLISHER

Timed: Varies

Range: Grades 1-12

Scoring: Hand key

Cost: Test booklets from $.50-$11.50 for further information write to ACER.

Publisher: The Australian Council for Educational Research Limited

---

ASSESSMENT OF READING GROWTH: LEVELS 9, 13 AND 17

all ages   grades 2-UP

Purpose: Determines silent reading comprehension. Used to enable teachers in predicting how their students will perform on statewide and standardized tests.

Description: 36 item paper-pencil test in three versions: Level 9 (grades 2, 3, 4), Level 13 (grades 6, 7, 8), and Level 17 (grades 10-12, college and adult). There are 18 literal comprehension items and 18 inferential comprehension items which measure vocabulary, reference, facts, main idea, organization, inferences, and ability to read critically. All items are classified by skill type and have been screened for cultural fairness. They are based on material released from the National Assessment of Educational Progress. The test also provides item-by-item average scores of students throughout the nation and total score comparisons for inner city, medium city and suburban school settings as well as national averages. Examiner required. Suitable for

group use.

Untimed: Not available

Range: Grades Level 9 (2-4); Level 13 (6-8); Level 17 (10-adults)

Scoring: Hand key

Cost: 30 tests and manual for one level $8.00.

Publisher: Jamestown Publishers

BASIC WORD VOCABULARY TEST
Harold J. Dupuy

all ages

Purpose: Measures an individual's vocabulary size and development. Used to monitor progress in these areas.

Description: 123 item paper-pencil, multiple-choice test measuring vocabulary in relation to grade level, grade percentile (3-12 and college), chronological age grade placement, vocabulary age, and vocabulary development quotient (similar to IQ). Students mark a varying number of answers depending on their grade level. Examiner required. Suitable for group use.

Untimed: 20 minutes

Range: Ages 4-adult

Scoring: Hand key

Cost: 40 tests and manual $8.00.

Publisher: Jamestown Publishers

BIEMILLER TEST OF READING PROCESSES
Andrew Biemiller

all ages   grades 2-UP

Purpose: Determines why a child is reading at a given level of proficiency and identifies strengths and weaknesses of a child's reading abilities.

Description: Multiple-item, oral read-ing test employing a unique method of monitoring letter speed, word speed out of context, and word speed in context. The test identifies individual differences in three kinds of reading processes: the ability to recognize print quickly, the ability to identify words quickly and the ability to use context to facilitate word identification. Stopwatch required. Examiner required. Not for group use.
CANADIAN PUBLISHER

Untimed: Not available

Range: Grades 2 and above

Scoring: Examiner evaluated

Cost: Examiner kit for 35 (includes administration booklet, test book, 35 record forms) $10.85.

Publisher: Guidance Centre

CLASSROOM READING INVENTORY
Nicholas J. Silvaroli

child, teen   grades 1-UP

Purpose: Assesses student's specific word-recognition and comprehension skills. Used for planning individual skills-oriented reading programs.

Description: Three part, paper-pencil test of reading skills. Subtests are Graded Word Lists, Graded Oral Paragraphs and Graded Spelling Survey. Test items are presented orally by the teacher. Materials include four forms: Forms A, B and C for grades 2 through 8, and Form D for high school and adults. Examiner required. Only Graded Spelling Survey is suitable for group use.

Timed: 12 minutes

Range: Elementary-secondary

Scoring: Examiner evaluated

Cost: Test $9.95.

Publisher: William C. Brown Company Publishers

DIAGNOSTIC READING TESTS: (DRT) SECTION I-VOCABULARY UPPER LEVEL DIAGNOSTIC BATTERY

Committee on Diagnostic Reading Tests, Inc.

teen   grades 7-13

Purpose: Assesses student vocabulary skills in English grammar, literature, math, science, and social studies; useful for text selection, classroom grouping and teacher planning.

Description: 200 item paper-pencil test measuring student's vocabulary familiarity within five subject areas: English grammar and literature, math, science, and social studies. The examiner reads aloud indicated sections from the test directions. Students respond by recording answer on an answer sheet. A stop watch is used and a time limit adhered to exactly. Materials include test booklets, answer sheet, directions for administering, and scoring stencil. Two comparable forms: A and B. Examiner required. Suitable for group use.

Timed: 40 minutes

Range: Grades 7-college freshman year

Scoring: Hand key; computer scoring available

Cost: Test booklet $.25; answer sheet $.07; Directions for Administering $.25; scoring stencil $.25; percentile norms for all tests $2.00; interpretation for all tests $2.50; reading exercises (instructional materials) for all tests, Level 0 (Readiness) $5.00; Level I (4-6) $15.00; Level II (7-9) $25.00; Level III (10-College) $25.00.

Publisher: Committee on Diagnostic Reading Test, Inc.

DIAGNOSTIC READING TESTS: (DRT) SECTION II-COMPREHENSION SILENT AND AUDITORY UPPER LEVEL DIAGNOSTIC BATTERY

Committee on Diagnostic Reading Tests, Inc.

teen   grades 7-13

Purpose: Measures either silent reading or auditory verbal comprehension, or the combination of both. Used to diagnose the verbal abilities of students Grades 7-13.

Description: 50 item paper-pencil test of verbal/reading comprehension measuring the ability to read passages and recognize main ideas, important details, sequences, and relevant conclusions, as well as to draw inferences. Test items were constructed by selecting passages from high school and college texts in science, literature and the social sciences and arranging them in order of difficulty according to the Lorge formula.
There are four methods of administration: Method 1 requires the students to read the passages silently and then answer the questions. Method 2 directs the students to read the passages to themselves as the examiner reads them aloud. The questions are completed in a similar manner with the examiner pausing at appropriate times to allow the students to answer the questions. In Method 3 the students listen without reading as the instructor reads the passages aloud. The questions are then read silently while the instructor reads them aloud, pausing to allow the students time to respond. Method 4 requires the students to listen without reading as both the passages and the questions are read aloud by the examiner. Method 1 measures silent reading comprehension, Methods 2 and 3 measure both silent and auditory reading comprehension, and Method 4 measures auditory comprehension.
Available in four comparable forms: A, B, C, and D. Examiner required. Suitable for group use.

Untimed: Not available

Range: Grades 7-college freshman year

Scoring: Hand key; computer scoring available

Cost: Test booklet $.50, answer sheets $.07. For additional costs contact publisher.

Publisher: Committee on Diagnostic Reading Test, Inc.

DIAGNOSTIC READING TESTS: (DRT) SECTION III- RATE OF READING UPPER LEVEL DIAGNOSTIC BATTERY
Committee on Diagnostic Reading Tests, Inc.

teen   grades 7-13

Purpose: Measures the rate at which a student reads and assesses how well the student comprehends what he is reading at that rate. Used for diagnosis of students Grades 7-13 who have difficulty reading at effective rates.

Description: 60 item paper-pencil test measuring reading speed and comprehension. Arranged in two parts: In the first part the student is asked to read a passage at his normal rate; in the second part the student is given a second passage (comparable in both difficulty and subject matter) which he is asked to read as quickly as possible. Reading speed is scored in words per minute for each part, with a 30 item comprehension check given at the end of each passage. The results identify those students who are unable to read at a higher rate even when strongly urged to do so; those who read more rapidly but with less comprehension; and those who read more rapidly with equivalent or better comprehension. Comparison of a student's performance on the two parts will suggest appropriate remedial reading approaches. Available in two comparable forms, A and B. Examiner required. Suitable for group use.

Untimed: 40 minutes

Range: Grades 7-college freshman year

Scoring: Hand key; computer scoring available

Cost: Per test booklet $.30; per answer sheet $.07; directions for administering $.25; scoring stencil $.25. For additional costs contact publisher.

Publisher: Committee on Diagnostic Reading Test, Inc.

DIAGNOSTIC READING TESTS: (DRT) SECTION IV
Word Attack, Part I, Oral Lower Level and Kindergarten-Fourth Grade Diagnostic Batteries
Committee on Diagnostic Reading Tests, Inc.

child, teen   grades K-8

Purpose: Evaluates oral reading proficiency of elementary school students in order to measure word attack skills, sight vocabulary and use of contextual clues. Used for classroom placement and evaluation.

Description: 96 item verbal test consisting of six paragraphs and three word lists of 30 words each. The examiner and the student each hold a test booklet containing 6 passages on each, grades 1-8 difficulty level. The student reads the materials aloud and the examiner marks errors made, using the system described in the directions, and then summarizes using the Check List of Faulty Habits. Oral reading reveals the student's word attack skills and the adequacy of sight vocabulary. The lists show whether the student confuses words of similar appearance when seen out of context and gives information about other word attack skills such as spelling, sounding and syllabication. Examiner required. Not suitable for group use.

Untimed: Not available

Cost: Test booklet $.20. For additional costs contact publisher.

Publisher: Committee on Diagnostic Reading Test, Inc.

DIAGNOSTIC READING TESTS: (DRT) SECTION IV-WORD ATTACK (PART 1) ORAL UPPER LEVEL DIAGNOSTIC BATTERY

Committee on Diagnostic Reading Tests, Inc.

teen grades 7-13

Purpose: Evaluates a student's ability to read aloud in order to assess word attack skills, sight vocabulary, use of contextual clues, and personal attitudes.

Description: 96 item verbal examination consisting of six paragraphs and three lists of 30 words each. The examiner and the student each hold a test booklet containing 6 passages on each, grades 6-12 difficulty level from which the student reads while the examiner marks errors made using the system described in the directions. The oral reading reveals how a student attacks words and the adequacy of sight vocabulary. Pronouncing the word lists reveals whether the student confuses similar-appearing words when taken out of context, spelling ability, sounding, and syllabication. A comparison of performance with paragraphs and word lists also provides information on how the student uses context clues. Materials include the booklets and a Check List of Faulty Habits. Examiner required. Not for group use.

Untimed: Not available

Range: Grades 7-college freshman year

Scoring: Examiner evaluated

Cost: Per test booklet $.20; directions for administering $.25. For additional costs contact publisher.

Publisher: Committee on Diagnostic Reading Test, Inc.

DIAGNOSTIC READING TESTS: (DRT) SECTION IV-WORD ATTACK PART 2, SILENT. UPPER AND LOWER LEVEL DIAGNOSTIC BATTERIES

Committee on Diagnostic Reading Tests, Inc.

child, teen grades 4-13

Purpose: Helps evaluate the way an individual obtains thought from the printed word when reading silently. Used to diagnose reading habits for possible remediation.

Description: 140 item two-part, verbal test. Part 1 is an individually administered oral reading test, complete instructions for which are in the manual. Part 2 tests the ability to hear sound by means of a matching technique and the ability to divide words into syllables. Remedial exercises are available for students who are deficient in either of the skills tested. The examiner reads aloud indicated sections from the Directions and the student responds on an answer sheet. Examiner required. Suitable for group use.

Untimed: Not available

Range: Grades 4-college freshman year

Scoring: Hand key; computer scoring available

Cost: Per test booklet $.15; per answer sheet $.07 directions for administering $.25; scoring stencil $.25. For additional costs contact publisher.

Publisher: Committee on Diagnostic Reading Test, Inc.

DIAGNOSTIC READING TESTS: (DRT) SURVEY SECTION-BOOKLET I (GRADE 1)

Committee on Diagnostic Reading Tests, Inc.

child grades K-4

Purpose: Assesses the readiness for formal reading instruction of students from Kindergarten through Grade 4.

Description: 422 item paper-pencil test assessing visual discrimination, auditory discrimination, vocabulary, and story reading (including word attach and comprehension). Each child will need a marker (a colored piece of paper about eight inches long and three inches wide), an eraser and a black pencil. The marker is needed so the examiner can see who is or is not following directions and can thus set an appropriate pace for the examination. Performance on this test may be compared to early results on the Reading Readiness Test to monitor growth in reading skills. Materials include: test booklet, directions for administering the test and fan key for scoring. Examiner required. Suitable for group use.

Untimed: Not available

Range: Grades K-4

Scoring: Fan key; computer scoring available

Cost: Test booklet $.30. For additional costs contact publisher.

Publisher: Committee on Diagnostic Reading Test, Inc.

DIAGNOSTIC READING TESTS: (DRT) SURVEY SECTION-BOOKLET II (GRADE 2)
Committee on Diagnostic Reading Tests, Inc.

---

child   grades K-4

Purpose: Measures a child's ability to recognize and comprehend words. Useful for classroom grouping, text selection and teacher planning.

Description: 60 item paper-pencil test divided equally between recognition and comprehension items. Two pages of examples are provided and read to the students by the examiner. The students use a marker (a piece of colored paper about six inches long and three inches wide), an eraser and

a well-sharpened pencil in their response to the sample questions. The same tools may be used by the students in responding to actual test items. The marker is needed so that the examiner can observe who is or is not following directions and can thus set an appropriate pace for the examination. Examiner required. Suitable for group use.

Untimed: Not available

Range: Grades K-4

Scoring: Hand key; computer scoring available

Cost: Test booklet $.30; answer sheet $.07; Directions for Administering $.25; scoring stencil $.25; percentile norms for all tests $2.00; interpretation for all tests $2.50; reading exercises for all tests, Level 0 (Readiness) $5.00; Level I (4-6) $15.00; Level II (7-9) $25.00; Level III (10-College) $25.00.

Publisher: Committee on Diagnostic Reading Test, Inc.

DIAGNOSTIC READING TESTS: (DRT) SURVEY SECTION-BOOKLET III (GRADES 3 AND 4)
Committee on Diagnostic Reading Tests, Inc.

---

teen   grades K-4

Purpose: Measures a child's ability to recognize and comprehend words. Useful for classroom grouping, text selection and teacher planning.

Description: 75 item paper-pencil test consisting of 45 recognition and 30 comprehension items. Two pages of examples are read by the examiner to the students. The students use a marker (a piece of colored paper about six inches long and three inches wide), an eraser and a well-sharpened pencil to respond to sample questions and to actual test items. The marker is needed so the examiner can observe who is or is not following directions and can thus set an appropriate pace for the examination. Examiner required. Suitable for group use.

Untimed: Not available

Range: Grades K-4

Scoring: Hand key; computer scoring available

Cost: Test booklet $.30; answer sheet $.07; Directions for Administering $.25; scoring stencil $.25; percentile norms for all tests $2.00; interpretation for all tests $2.50; reading exercises for all tests, Level 0 (Readiness) $5.00; Level I (4-6) $15.00; Level II (7-9) $25.00; Level III (10-College) $25.00.

Publisher: Committee on Diagnostic Reading Test, Inc.

DIAGNOSTIC READING TESTS: (DRT) SURVEY SEC-TION-LOWER LEVEL, PARTS 1, 2, AND 3
Committee on Diagnostic Reading Tests

child, teen   grades 4-8

Purpose: Measures reading skills of students Grades 4- 8. Identifies students in need of remedial or enriched reading programs. Used to group pupils for classroom teaching and to monitor progress in achievement of important reading skills.

Description: 120 item paper-pencil test arranged in three parts and printed in two booklets. Booklet I contains Part 1, Word Recognition. Booklet II contains Part 2, Vocabulary, and Part 3, Rate of Reading. The 60 item Word Recognition test assesses skills in using phonics, context, and word parts as clues to recognition and meanings of words. The 60 vocabulary words for Part 2 are selected from general literary, social science, science, and mathematics fields. The rate of Reading test is based on a story of natural

science, followed by 15 questions measuring comprehension. The story represents a low fifth-grade reading level according to the Dale-Chall formula. The test as a whole is available in four comparable forms: A, B, C, and D. Examiner required. Suitable for group use.

Untimed: Not available

Range: Grades 4-8

Scoring: Hand key; computer scoring available

Cost: Test booklet $.25, answer sheets $.07. For additional costs contact publisher.

Publisher: Committee on Diagnostic Reading Test, Inc.

DIAGNOSTIC READING TESTS: (DRT) SURVEY SEC-TION-READING READINESS BOOKLET Kindergarten-Fourth Grade Battery
Committee on Diagnostic Reading Tests, Inc.

child   grades K-4

Purpose: Assesses a child's readiness for formal reading instruction.

Description: 229 item paper-pencil test measuring relationships, eye-hand and motor coordination, visual discrimination, auditory discrimination, and vocabulary. Each child will need a marker (a piece of colored paper about six inches long and three inches wide), an eraser and a well-sharpened pencil to respond to sample questions and to actual test items. The marker is needed so the examiner can observe who is or is not following directions and can thus set an appropriate pace for the examination. Examiner required. Suitable for group use.

Untimed: Not available

Range: Grades K-4

Scoring: Fan key; computer scoring available

Cost: Test booklet $.30; answer sheet $.07; Directions for Administering

$.25; scoring stencil $.25; percentile norms for all tests $2.00; interpretation for all tests $2.50; reading exercises for all tests, Level 0 (Readiness) $5.00; Level I (4-6) $15.00; Level II (7-9) $25.00; Level III (10-College) $25.00.

Publisher: Committee on Diagnostic Reading Test, Inc.

DIAGNOSTIC READING TESTS: (DRT) SURVEY SECTION: UPPER LEVEL
Committee on Diagnostic Reading Tests, Inc.

teen, adult   grades 7-13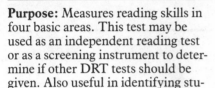

Purpose: Measures reading skills in four basic areas. This test may be used as an independent reading test or as a screening instrument to determine if other DRT tests should be given. Also useful in identifying students in need of remedial programs.

Description: 100 item paper-pencil test with three subtests: General Reading Rates, Vocabulary and Comprehension. May be used as a screening test to identify students to whom the total Upper Level Diagnostic Battery or selected portions of the battery should be administered. The examiner reads aloud indicated sections from the test and students respond on answer sheets. Examiner required. Suitable for group use.

Timed: 40 minutes

Range: Grades 7-college freshman year

Scoring: Hand key; computer scoring available

Cost: Test booklet $.40; answer sheet $.07; Directions for Administering $.25; scoring stencil $.25; percentile norms for all tests $2.00; interpretation for all tests $2.50; reading exercises (instructional material) for all tests, Level 0 (Readiness) $5.00; Level I (4-6) $15.00; Level II (7-9) $25.00; Level III

(10-College) $25.00.

Publisher: Committee on Diagnostic Reading Test, Inc.

DIAGNOSTIC WORD PATTERNS: TESTS 1, 2 AND 3
Evelyn Buckley

all ages

Purpose: Assesses basic phonic knowledge. Used to help classroom teachers determine general word attack concepts to review with an entire class and to identify individual students' strengths and weaknesses in order to develop suitable reading programs.

Description: Three verbal, paper-pencil, 100 word tests, each of which can be used to test spelling and/or word recognition. When used as a spelling test, the words are dictated to the students who then write them on their answer sheets. When used as a word recognition test, the same words are printed on cards for the students to read aloud. As a spelling test, they can be administered to groups; as a word recognition test they must be administered individually. Test 1 deals with short vowels, nonphonetic words, and consonant digraphs. Test 2 covers vowel and dipthong patterns, suffixes, two-syllable words, and non-phonetic words. Materials include Diagnostic Word Patterns Tests, and a teacher's manual. Examiner required. Not suitable for group use.

Untimed: 20-45 minutes

Range: Ages 3-adult

Scoring: Examiner evaluated

Cost: Tests 1, 2 and 3 and teacher's manual $3.85; 50 student charts $3.80; cards for word recognition test $4.40.

Publisher: Educators Publishing Service, Inc.

GATES MacGINITIE READING TEST, CANADIAN ED. (GMRT)
Walter MacGinitie

child, teen   grades K-12

Purpose: Measures reading and vocabulary achievement levels of students K-12. Used for placement and class planning.

Description: Multiple item, paper-pencil test of vocabulary and reading comprehension. The basic level R has 54 items. Levels A-F contain 85-89 items. Examiner required. Suitable for group use.
CANADIAN PUBLISHER

Timed: 55 minutes

Untimed: Level R, 65 minutes

Range: Grades K-12

Scoring: Hand key; computer scoring available

Cost: 35 booklets $14.35; manual $6.00; key $1.25.

Publisher: Nelson Canada Limited

GATES-MacGINITIE READING TESTS-SECOND EDITION
Walter MacGinitie

child, teen   grades 1-12

Purpose: Measures reading achievement of students Grades 3-12. Used to identify those students who would benefit from remedial or accelerated programs, to evaluate instructional programs, and to counsel students and report progress to parents.

Description: Multiple item paper-pencil test assessing basic reading skills. All levels measure vocabulary and reading comprehension; Basic R also measures letter recognition and letter "sounds." Basic R (54 items), for Grade 1, uses hand- or machine-scorable test booklets. Levels A-F (85-89 items each), for Grades 2-12, use scorable test booklets for levels A-C and test booklets with separate

answer sheets for levels D-F. Examiner required. Suitable for group use.

Timed: 55 minutes, Levels A-F

Untimed: 65 minutes, Level Basic R

Range: Grades 1-12

Scoring: Hand key; computer scoring available

Cost: 25 machine-scorable test booklets for Basic R, or levels A, B, C, or D (includes teachers manual) 35 hand-scorable test booklets $12.36 per level; 35 MRC answer sheets for levels D, E or F $8.04 per level; teacher's manual $2.52; MRC scoring templates for levels D, E or F $2.85.

Publisher: The Riverside Publishing Company

GRAY ORAL READING TESTS
William S. Gray and Helen M. Robinson

child, teen   grades K-13

Purpose: Measures growth in oral reading from early first grade to college level and diagnoses oral reading difficulties.

Description: Multiple item paper-pencil test measuring fluency and accuracy of oral reading. The student reads several graded passages, each passage being more difficult in terms of the following: range and density of vocabulary, syllabic length of words, length and complexity of sentence structure, and maturity of concepts. The objective measurements recorded are: the errors, the time and a combination of errors and time. Available in two equivalent forms. Examiner required. Not for group use.

Untimed: Varies

Range: Grades K-13

Scoring: Hand key

Cost: Complete (includes examiner's manual, form A and B passage books,

25 form A and B examination booklets, storage box) $49.00. Separate components, form C and D passage books and examination booklets also available.

Publisher: PRO-ED

INDUSTRIAL READING TEST (IRT)
Refer to page 719.

INFORMAL EVALUATION OF ORAL READING
Deborah Edel

all ages

Purpose: Measures reading ability of individuals of all ages. Used to estimate the student's reading level and diagnose specific reading weaknesses; especially valuable with students learning English as a second language.

Description: Multiple item, oral response test which evaluates reading ability by informally surveying the student's reading performance. Eight reading passages measure the following factors: independent, instructional, frustration, oral comprehension, pattern of reading, type and frequency of reading error, reading style, and behavior. Useful at any level of oral reading ability. Examiner required. Not for group use.

Untimed: 15-35 minutes

Range: Child, adolescent, adult

Scoring: Examiner evaluated

Cost: Complete set (includes 2 reading booklets, 25 evaluation forms, instructions) $9.95.

Publisher: Book Lab

McCARTHY INDIVIDUALIZED DIAGNOSTIC READING INVENTORY
William G. McCarthy

all ages   grades 2-UP

Purpose: Diagnoses the development of student reading skills so the teacher can screen for reading disabilities and select appropriate instructional materials.

Description: 11 brief reading selections ranked from primer to grade 12, read by the student to the examiner. Beginning with Part One, the student's skills are quickly measured by the Controlled Vocabulary List and Basal Reader Graded Selections. All reading errors can be marked on the Teacher Administration Booklet, which is laminated and reusable. The appropriate reading selections are then administered for Parts 2, 3 and 4, based on the student's performance in Part 1. The factors measured are: oral reading, reading comprehension, critical thinking skills, vocabulary, phonics, word recognition, sight vocabulary, and study skills. Hobbies, reading interests and physical health are also evaluated. The last part of the test moves into prescription by providing structure to develop a preliminary plan for reading instruction based on the information gained in the inventory. Examiner required. Not for group use.

Untimed: 1-1½ hours

Range: Grades 2-adult

Scoring: Examiner evaluated

Cost: Information booklet $2.40; teacher booklet $5.90; pupil booklet $1.60; 12 individual record forms $4.90.

Publisher: Educators Publishing Service, Inc.

NATIONAL ACHIEVEMENT TESTS: ENGLISH, READING and VOCABULARY TESTS-- AMERICAN LITERACY TEST
Refer to page 380.

NATIONAL ACHIEVEMENT TESTS: ENGLISH, READING and VOCABULARY TESTS-- READING
Refer to page 381.

POPE INVENTORY OF BASIC READING SKILLS
Lillie Pope

child, teen   grades K-12

Purpose: Evaluates basic reading skills. Appropriate for all students reading below the fourth-grade level. Used to plan reading instruction.

Description: Oral reading, verbal word recognition, and written responses measure 13 basic reading and word recognition skills, such as the ability to match symbols with sounds, knowledge of right and left, and knowledge of basic sight words. Responses are evaluated and summarized in 12 areas. Examiner required. Not for group use.

Untimed: 15-30 minutes

Range: Grades K-12 but below 4th grade reading level

Scoring: Examiner evaluated

Cost: Complete kit (includes 2 card forms, 35 evaluation forms) $7.95.

Publisher: Book Lab

PRESCRIPTIVE READING PER- FORMANCE TEST (PRPT)
Janet B. Fudala

All ages

Purpose: Assesses an individual's

reading level and prereading readiness, and diagnoses a student strengths and weaknesses in word-attack skills. Used for reading or learning disabilities programs and to help comply with P.L. 94-142.

Description: Multiple item paper-pencil and oral response test consisting of graded word lists which are used to quickly assess reading competency. Provides individual assessment of the student's reading and spelling performance and classifies patterns into normal and three atypical patterns suggestive of different types of developmental dyslexia. By evaluation of the spelling of words that are in the student's sight vocabulary and words that are not, the examiner documents strengths and weaknesses in the visual and auditory channels and identifies patterns of performance that have characteristic prescriptive educational implications. The manual presents standardization, validity and reliability data as well as a number of case studies. Examiner required. Not for group use.

Untimed: 15-20 minutes

Range: Grades 1-adult

Scoring: Hand key

Cost: Complete kit (includes one reusable set of word lists, 20 record forms, 20 answer sheets, manual) $18.50.

Publisher: Western Psychological Services

PRI READING SYSTEMS (PRI/ RS)
Refer to page 223.

PRI/RS: SYSTEM 1, GRADED APPROACH, INSTRUCTIONAL OBJECTIVES INVENTORY
Refer to page 224.

READING TEST SERIES

child, teen   grades 1-12

Purpose: Assesses reading skills. Used for screening students and for providing teachers with information regarding the overall reading performance of a class.

Description: Six tests of reading comprehension: Reading Test A, ages 6 to 8; Reading Test AD, ages 8 to 10; Reading Test BD, ages 7 to 10; Reading Comprehension Test DE, ages 10 to 12, Reading Test EH 1-2, ages 11 to 15; and Reading Test EH 3, ages 11 to 15. Reading Tests A, AD, and BD all consist of multiple-choice sentence completion items. Reading Comprehension Test DE is a 50 item test measuring understanding of complex reading passages. Test 1 of Reading Test EH 1-2 consists of 60 sentence completion items. Test 2 has 35 questions based on comprehension passages. Reading Test EH 3 measures comprehension by having pupils silently read prose passages under timed conditions. Examiner required. Suitable for group use. BRITISH PUBLISHER

Timed: Various timings

Range: Primary and secondary grades

Scoring: Hand key

Cost: Primary specimen set (contains one each of pupil forms A, AD, BD, DE and sample manual) £1.20; secondary specimen set (contains one each of pupils forms DE, EH 1-2, EH 3 and a sample manual) £1.40 (payment in sterling for all overseas orders.

Publisher: NFER-Nelson Publishing Company

SPEED SCALE FOR DETERMINING INDEPENDENT READING LEVEL
Ward Cramer and Roger Trent

child, teen   grades 1-12

Purpose: Evaluates the ability of elementary, intermediate and high school students to recognize and understand words. Used as a guide to select textbooks, supplemental reading and library books.

Description: Multiple item, verbal test in two sections: Word Recognition and Comprehension. The examiner has the student read aloud words from a printed card and match words with associated concepts. The stimulus words are presented visually. Conversion tables are provided for translating raw scores into grade level equivalents. Examiner required. Not for group use. Test to be discontinued in Fall of 1983.

Untimed: 15 minutes

Range: Grades 1-12

Scoring: Hand Key

Cost: Manual $2.50; 50 test forms $5.00; specimen set $2.50.

Publisher: Academic Therapy Publications

STANFORD MEASUREMENT SERIES--STANFORD DIAGNOSTIC READING TEST (SDRT)
Refer to page 399.

TEST OF READING COMPREHENSION (TORC)
Virginia L. Brown, Donald D. Hammill and J. Lee Wiederholt

child, teen   grades 2-12

Purpose: Assesses reading comprehension for students in grades 2-12. Used to diagnose reading problems in terms of current psycholinguistic theories of reading comprehension as a constructive process involving both language and cognition.

Description: Eight paper-pencil subtests measuring aspects of reading comprehension. Three of the subtests (General Vocabulary, Syntactic Similarities, and Paragraph Reading) are combined to determine a basic Comprehension Core which is expressed as a Reading Comprehension Quotient (RCQ). Five supplementary subtests include three measuring students' abilities to read the vocabularies of math, science, and social studies; Subtest #7, Reading the Directions of Schoolwork, which is a diagnostic tool for younger or remedial students; and Sentence Sequences. Scaled scores are provided for each subtest. The manual includes: data supporting test-retest and internal consistency reliability, and diagnostic, construct, and criterion-related validity. Examiner required. Not for group use.

Untimed: 1 hour, 45 minutes

Range: Grades 2-12

Scoring: Hand key

Cost: Complete (includes manual, 10 student booklets, 50 answer sheets, 50 profile sheets, set of scoring keys, storage box) $62.00.

Publisher: PRO-ED

WOODCOCK READING MASTERY TESTS (WRMT)
Richard W. Woodcock

child, teen   grades K-12

Purpose: Measures individual reading achievement. Used to detect reading problems. For classroom grouping, program evaluation, clinical and research use.

Description: 400 item verbal test in A and B forms consisting of: 45 identification items, 150 word identification items, 50 word attack items, 70 word comprehension items, and 85 passage comprehension items in an individually administered battery. The examiner shows a test plate to the student and asks a question to which the student responds orally. Only those items within the student's functioning level are administered. Materials include test plates bound into an easel and 25 response forms. The test is norm and criterion referenced. Derived scores are grade equivalents, grade percentile ranks, age equivalents, standard scores and mastery scores. Normal curve equivalents for Chapter I programs are available for grades 2-6. Examiner required. Not for group use.

Untimed: 30-45 minutes

Range: Grades K-12

Scoring: Examiner evaluated; computer scoring available

Cost: Complete kit (form A or B) $37.50; set of 2 forms $67.50; 25 response forms $6.35.

Publisher: American Guidance Service

WORD ANALYSIS DIAGNOSTIC TESTS
Selma E. Herr

child   grades K-3

Purpose: Evaluates word attack abilities for students Grades K-3 and for remedial students through high school. Diagnoses skill deficiencies, assists in placement decisions, and serves as an achievement test.

Description: Multiple item paper-pencil tests assessing proficiency in word analysis and phonics skills. Arranged in four levels: Level A-1 (administered at the end of the reading readiness period), Level A-2 (Grade 1), Level B (Grade 2), and Level C (Grade 3). All levels may be used for appropriate remedial purposes with students of any age. Each level consists of four to six sections measuring skills appropriate to the grade level. Students are provided with a printed form containing familiar objects and spaces for identifying answers by marking the appropriate symbol in response to material presented orally by examiner or tape cassette. Examiner required. Suitable for group use.

Timed: 20-30 minutes per level

Range: Grades K-3; remedial students through Grade 12.

Scoring: Hand key

Cost: Comprehensive Teacher's Guide $52.00.

Publisher: Instructional Materials and Equipment Distributors

WORD ANALYSIS DIAGNOSTIC TESTS--LEVEL A-1/READINESS
Selma E. Herr

child   grades K-1

Purpose: Assesses the readiness of Kindergarten and first-grade students to begin learning the printed symbols (letters and groups of letters) used in reading. Diagnoses skill deficiencies, assists in placement decisions, and measures reading readiness.

Description: 40 item paper-pencil test assessing students' readiness to apply printed symbols to phonetic units. Subtests include: rhyming words, initial consonant sounds, ending consonant sounds, and digraph sounds. Students are provided with a printed form containing familiar objects and spaces for identifying answers by marking the appropriate symbol in response to material presented orally by examiner or tape cassette. Examiner required. Suitable for group use.

Timed: 20 minutes

Range: Kindergarten and 1st grade

Scoring: Hand key

Cost: Class packet (includes 30 tests, Teacher's Guide/keys, cassette containing test) $16.00.

Publisher: Instructional Materials and Equipment Distributors

WORD ANALYSIS DIAGNOSTIC TESTS--LEVEL A2/GRADE 1
Selma E. Herr

child   grades 1-2

Purpose: Measures word attack skills at the end of the first year of phonics instruction. Used with students at the end of Grade 1 or beginning of Grade 2 to diagnose skill deficiencies, assist in placement decisions, and measure achievement.

Description: 79 item paper-pencil, multiple-choice test assessing proficiency in word attack skills and phonics. Subtests include: initial and final consonants, consonant digraphs, four consonant blends, the short vowel sounds, and rhyming words. Students are provided with a printed form containing familiar objects and spaces for identifying answers by marking the appropriate symbol in response to material presented orally by examiner or tape cassette. Examiner required. Suitable for group use.

Timed: 20 minutes

Range: Grades 1 and 2; Grades 3 and 4 for remedial cases

Scoring: Hand key

Cost: Class packet (includes 30 tests, Teacher's Guide/keys, cassette containing test) $16.00.

Publisher: Instructional Materials and Equipment Distributors

WORD ANALYSIS DIAGNOSTIC TESTS--LEVEL B/GRADE 2
Selma E. Herr

child   grades 2-3

Purpose: Measures word attack skills at the end of the second year of phonics instruction. Used with students at the end of Grade 2 or beginning of Grade 3 to diagnose skill deficiencies, assist in placement decisions, and measure achievement.

Description: 76 item paper-pencil, multiple-choice test assessing proficiency in word attack skills and phonics. Subtests include: long and short vowel sounds, vowels followed by r, the sounds of ou, ow, aw, and all, the hard and soft sound of c and g, and the blends and digraphs. Also assesses the ability to pronounce any phonetically based word, use context clues, and understand the meanings of words. Students are provided with a printed form containing familiar objects and spaces for identifying answers by marking the appropriate symbol in response to material presented orally by examiner or tape cassette. Examiner required. Suitable for group use.

Timed: 20 minutes

Range: Grades 2 and 3; Grades 4, 5 and 6 for remedial cases

Scoring: Hand key

Cost: Class packet (includes 30 tests, Teacher's Guide/keys, cassette containing test) $16.00.

Publisher: Instructional Materials and Equipment Distributors

WORD ANALYSIS DIAGNOSTIC TESTS--LEVEL C/GRADE 3
Selma E. Herr

child   grades 3-4

Purpose: Measures word attack skills at the end of Grade 3. Identifies students in need of further training in word analysis before entering Grade 4. Used with older students to diagnose reading disabilities related to word attack skills.

Description: 116 item paper-pencil test assessing proficiency in word analysis skills. Subtests include: vowel sounds, silent letters, syllabications, and structural and phonetic analysis. Students are provided with a printed form containing familiar objects and spaces for identifying answers by marking the appropriate symbol in response to material presented orally by examiner or tape cassette. Examiner required. Suitable for group use.

Timed: 30 minutes

Range: Grades 3 and 4; Grades 5-12 for remedial cases

Scoring: Hand key

Cost: Class packet (includes 30 tests, Teacher's Guide/keys, cassette containing test) $16.00.

Publisher: Instructional Materials and Equipment Distributors

Library Skills

BENNETT LIBRARY USAGE TEST
Alma Bennett and H.E. Schrammel

teen, adult   grades 10-UP

Purpose: Assesses library knowledge of high school and college students. Used as an end-of-course exam.

Description: 130 item paper-pencil test of library knowledge including organization, Dewey Decimal System, vocabulary, reference books, topical locations, and Reader's Guide. Examiner required. Suitable for group use.

Timed: 50 minutes

Range: High school and college

Scoring: Hand key

Cost: Specimen set $1.00; test $.15; manual $.20; key $.20.

Publisher: Bureau of Educational Measurements

LIBRARY SKILLS TEST
IL Association of College and Research Libraries

teen   grades 7-13

Purpose: Assesses student strengths and weaknesses in working with library materials.

Description: Multiple item paper-pencil test covers the following topics: current terminology, card catalog, classification systems, filing, parts of a book, indexes, reference tools, and bibliographic forms. Examiner required. Suitable for group use.

Timed: 45 minutes

Range: Grades 7-college freshmen

Scoring: Hand key; examiner evaluated; computer scoring available

Cost: Complete set (includes 20 test booklets, 1 manual of directions) $16.00; 50 answer sheets $10.00.

Publisher: Scholastic Testing Service, Inc.

LIBRARY SKILLS TEST
Wayne DeMouth

teen

Purpose: Measures student ability to use a library.

Description: 50 item paper-pencil, multiple-choice test in four categories. The Dewey Decimal System and Card Catalog test deals with classification numbers and subject areas and mechanics of the card catalog. The Reader's Guide and Periodicals test focuses on format, abbreviations of terms, and subject areas of periodicals useful in research. The Reference Materials test concentrates on The Dictionary, World Atlas and other sources. The Effective Use of Information in Research test includes useful terms, footnote and bibliography styling, and conventions of correct presentation. Materials include spirit master sets. Examiner required. Suitable for group use.

Untimed: 50 minutes

Range: Ages 9-12

Scoring: Hand key

Cost: Spirit master set $3.95.

Publisher: The Perfection Form Company

TEST OF LIBRARY STUDY SKILLS
Irene Gullette and Francis Hatfield

child, teen   grades 2-12

Purpose: Measures basic essentials of library/media center skills.

Description: 44-50 item paper-pencil test can be self or group administered. Available in three levels for different age groups. The test measures knowledge of arrangement of books, parts of a book, card catalogue, indexes and reference books. It may be used as a diagnostic evaluation of knowledge of library/media center skills. Self-administered. Suitable for group use.

Untimed: 50 minutes (each level)

Range: Grades 2-12 (three levels)

Scoring: Hand key

Cost: Complete kit Level 1 (includes 50 test booklets, 100 answer cards and key) $22.00; complete kit Level 2 or 3, specify level (includes 50 test booklets, 100 answer cards, and key)

$25.00.

Publisher: Larlin Corporation

Sensory-Motor Skills

BENDER-PURDUE REFLEX TEST and TRAINING MANUAL
Miriam Bender

child

Purpose: Determines the presence and/or level of symmetric tonic neck reflex activity in children who are suspected of having learning disabilities. Used to diagnose whether the response interferes with learning and to plan motor-training program.

Description: Six task motor performance test in which six areas are assessed. The child creeps against manual resistance and participates in a variety of movement tasks (such as rocking and creeping backward and forward on hands and knees) as the examiner physically resists the student's progress from varying points of leverage. Scoring is based on the number of deviations from a standard, "perfect" posture and pattern of locomotion. Materials include illustrated instructions for a motor-training program and a book of spirit masters for parents' use at home. The test is also available on videotape. Examiner required. Not suitable for group use.

Untimed: 20 minutes

Range: Ages 6-12

Scoring: Examiner evaluated

Cost: Manual $8.00; 25 recording forms $6.00; book of 12 spirit masters $6.00; specimen set $8.00.

Publisher: Academic Therapy Publications

BENDER VISUAL MOTOR GESTALT TEST
Refer to page 37.

BENTON REVISED VISUAL RETENTION TEST
Refer to page 38.

BRUININKS-OSERETSKY TEST OF MOTOR PROFICIENCY
Robert H. Bruininks

child, teen

Purpose: Determines a child's level of gross and fine motor development. Useful for educational placement, large-group screening, assessing neurological development and evaluating motor training programs.

Description: 46 item physical performance paper-pencil battery grouped into eight subtests: Running Speed and Agility, Balance, Bilateral Coordination, Strength, Upper-Limb Coordination, Response Speed, Visual-Motor Control, and Upper- Limb Speed and Dexterity. The complete battery yields three scores: Gross Motor Composite (large muscles of the shoulders, trunk and legs), Fine Motor Composite (small muscles of the fingers, hand and forearms), and a Battery Composite of general motor performance. Subtest and composite scores can be converted to age-based standard scores, percentile ranks, stanines, and age equivalents. The Short Form test includes 14 items from the complete battery to yield a single score of general motor proficiency which can be converted to an age-based standard score, percentile rank and stanine. Materials include a manual, 25 individual record forms, a sample of alternate Short Form, 25 student booklets, and a set of testing equipment, all in a metal case. The examiner records the child's performance on given tasks, and the student booklet is used for cutting and paper-pencil responses. Examiner required. Not for group use.

Untimed: Short form 15-20 minutes; complete battery 45- 60

Range: Ages 4½-14½

Scoring: Examiner evaluated

Cost: Complete battery $164.50; 25 individual record short forms with complete battery/short form $7.50; 25 short forms $3.00; 25 student booklets $6.75.

Publisher: American Guidance Service

CLOSURE SPEED (GESTALT COMPLETION)
Refer to page 796.

DEVEREUX TEST OF EXTREMITY COORDINATION (DTEC)
The Devereux Foundation

child

Purpose: Assesses level of motor development for children ages 4-10 years. Used to improve student self-image through motor skill development.

Description: 12 item task performance test assessing a child's motor attention span, body image and self- concept. Three tasks assess each of the following factors: sequential motor activity, fine motor ability, static balance, and perceptual motor activity. Examiner required. Not for group use.

Timed: 20 minutes

Range: Ages 4-10

Scoring: Examiner evaluated

Cost: Manual, 50 test sheets and 25 profiles $25.00.

Publisher: The Devereux Foundation

GIBSON SPIRAL MAZE
H.B. Gibson

all ages

Purpose: Measures psychomotor performance in both children and adults. Used for screening and clinical diagnosis.

Description: Paper-pencil test measures psychomotor performance. The test consists of a printed design on a large card which provides a "maze" for the subject to run under timed conditions. Scores of quickness and accuracy are obtained by a standard marking procedure defined in the manual. Characteristic deviations from normal psychomotor performance are used to identify behavioral disturbances such as maladjustment, delinquency and mental ill-health. Restricted to senior staff members of any recognized medical or educational institution, medical doctors, and BPS and APA members. Examiner required. Not for group use. BRITISH PUBLISHER

Untimed: Not available

Range: Child, adult

Scoring: Hand key

Cost: Specimen set £1.65; 20 test cards £2.50 plus VAT per set; manual £1.25.

Publisher: Hodder & Stoughton

JUDGMENT OF LINE ORIENTATION
A.L. Benton, N.R. Varney and K. des Hamsher

adult

Purpose: Measures visuospatial orientation.

Description: Multiple-item, paper-pencil, discrimination- matching test. The response choices consist of 11 lines of different orientation covering a 180 degree range. The stimuli consist of segments from two of the eleven response choices. Normative observations are based on adult hospital controls. Age and sex corrections provided.

Untimed: Not available

Range: Adults

Scoring: Examiner evaluated

Cost: Contact publisher.

Publisher: Oxford University Press

LATERAL AWARENESS AND DIRECTIONALITY TEST (LAD)
August J. Mauser and Joseph F. Lockavitch

child, teen   grades 1-12

Purpose: Determines lateral awareness and directional skills of elementary and secondary school children. Used to identify high-risk, medium-risk and low-risk students for possible program intervention.

Description: 35-illustration, paper-pencil test measuring right-left labeling ability at two levels: lateral awareness and directionality. Items range from single to double commands which require either a unilateral, contralateral, or cross diagonal response. Also measured are such spatial concepts as same direction, 180-degree inversion, 90 degree rotation, and person to person orientation. Materials consist of test plates, recording forms, scoring template and manual, which includes information on screening, diagnosis, and potential program modification. Examiner required. Suitable for group use.

Untimed: 20 minutes

Range: Grades 1-12

Scoring: Hand key

Cost: Manual $7.50; test plates $17.50; 50 record forms $5.00; scoring template $2.00; specimen set $7.50.

Publisher: Academic Therapy Publications

LINCOLN-OSERETSKY MOTOR DEVELOPMENT SCALE
William Sloan

child, teen

Purpose: Measures motor development of children ages 6-14. Used to supplement information obtained from other techniques concerning intellectual, social, emotional, and physical development.

Description: 36 item task-assessment test of a child's motor development. The areas covered are: static coordination, dynamic coordination, speed of movement and asynkinesia (finger dexterity), eye- hand coordination, and gross activity of the hands, arms, legs, and trunk. Both unilateral and bilateral tasks are involved. The test items are arranged in order of difficulty and include: walking backwards, crouching on tiptoe, standing on one foot, touching nose, touching fingertips, tapping rhythmically with feet and fingers, jumping over a rope, finger movement, standing heel to toe, close and open hands alternately, making dots, catching a ball, making a ball, winding thread, balancing a rod crosswise, describing circles in the air, tapping, placing coins and matchsticks, jump and turn about, putting matchsticks in a box, winding thread while walking, throwing a ball, sorting matchsticks, drawing lines, cutting circle, putting coins in a box, tracing mazes, balancing on tiptoe, tapping with feet and fingers, jump and touch heels, tap feet and describe circles, stand on one foot, jumping and clapping, balancing on tiptoe and opening and closing hands, balancing a rod vertically. The manual includes: Complete analysis of test results obtained from boys and girls ages

6-14 years for each item of the scale; percentages passing each item at each age level; correlation of item-scores with age; percentile norms of both sexes, separately and combined; and odd-even reliability for boys and girls. Examiner required. Not for group use.

Untimed: Not available

Range: Ages 6-14

Scoring: Examiner evaluated

Cost: Complete kit (includes all test materials, 50 record blanks and manual) $99.50.

Publisher: Stoelting Co.

MEMORY-FOR-DESIGNS TEST (MFD)
Refer to page 45.

MINNESOTA SPATIAL RELATIONS TEST
American Guidance Service Test Division

teen, adult   grades 10-UP

Purpose: Assesses an individual's ability to visualize spatial relations by matching objects of different shapes and sizes. Used in vocational education, rehabilitation counseling and personnel selection.

Description: Manual test of providing a measure of accurate perception of relationships and speed in manipulating three-dimensional objects. The materials consist of four form boards, A-B and C-D paired. Each board has a different arrangement of 58 cutouts into which blocks of various shapes are fitted. The individual removes blocks from board A and transfers them to the proper places on board B, repeating the process with boards C and D. The kit includes the boards, blocks, two carrying cases, 50 record forms, and a manual. Time

scores are converted to standard scores and percentile ranks, and error scores are expressed as a percentile rank. Examiner required. Not for group use.

Timed: 10-20 minutes

Range: Grades 10-12, adult

Scoring: Examiner evaluated

Cost: Complete $419.50; 50 record forms $6.50.

Publisher: American Guidance Service

MKM PICTURE ARRANGE-MENT TEST (PAT)
Leland Micheal and James King

child   grades K-6

Purpose: Measures the extent to which the subject places information and objects in the left-right sequence common to the United States. Useful in diagnosing poor reading skills and learning disabilities related to directionality problems.

Description: Five item, visual-manual sequencing test in which a poem entitled "A Great Gray Elephant" is read to the subject. Five pictures illustrating the poem are placed before the subject in random order and, as the poem is read, the subject is asked to layout the pictures in the order they occur in the poem. The examiner records the subject's actions. A left-right movement is expected. Examiner required. Not suitable for group use.

Untimed: 3 minute

Range: Grades K-6s

Scoring: Examiner evaluated

Cost: Complete (includes instruction sheet, 5 picture cards, 5 poems) $10.00.

Publisher: MKM

MOORE EYE-HAND COORDI-NATION AND COLOR MATCHING TEST
Joseph E. Moore

all ages

Purpose: Assesses speed of eye-hand movement and ability to match colors. Used to test applicants for jobs requiring hand coordination and color detection, and to identify child deficiencies in these skills.

Description: Basic hand coordination and color matching test using 32 colored marbles and a color marked board. Five norms are evaluated: occupational, college level, pre-school from 24 months to 72 months (separate norms by six month intervals). Ages six to fifteen have separate norms by years and special norms for non-college groups. The speed with which subject places marbles in color-matched slots is calculated from three test trials. Materials consist of marbles, board and manual. Examiner required. Not suitable for group use.

Timed: 4 minutes

Range: Ages 2-adult

Scoring: Examiner evaluated

Cost: Complete $35.00.

Publisher: Joseph E. Moore & Associates

MOTOR-FREE VISUAL PERCEP-TION TEST (MVPT)
Ronald R. Colarusso and Donald D. Hammill

child

Purpose: Assesses visual perception in children and older individuals who have motor problems. Used for screening, diagnostic, and research purposes, especially with those who are learning disabled, motorically impaired, physically handicapped, or mentally retarded.

Description: 36 item point-and-tell test. The subject is shown a line drawing and asked to match the stimulus by pointing to one of a multiple-choice set of other drawings. Materials consist of test plates and recording forms. Examiner required. Not for group use.

Untimed: 10 minutes

Range: Ages 4-8 or older individuals with motor problems

Scoring: Hand key

Cost: Manual $7.50; test plates $17.50; 50 recording forms $5.00; specimen set $7.50.

Publisher: Academic Therapy Publications

ONE-HOLE TEST LEVELS I AND II
Gavriel Salvendy and W. Douglas Seymour

all ages

Purpose: Measures the ability to learn new manipulative tasks. Identifies individuals who are able to learn new skills most rapidly.

Description: Multiple item, task performance test assessing the ability to learn a new task requiring precise and repetitive manipulations. An apparatus is provided containing a power supply, photocell control, counting module, two recepticles, and a number of pins (1" x ⅛"). Pins are automatically positioned in the recepticle nearest to the subject, who grasps the pins one at a time and deposits them in the second recepticle seven inches away. Level I simply records the number of pins deposited per trial. Level II involves the use of stop-clocks and other data collection devices to process "grasp" and "position" factors. Both levels can be administered with either 7- or 15-minute trials. Examiner required. Not for group use.

Timed: 8-20 minutes

Range: Table 1, Industrial Operators; Table 2, College Students; Table 3, Ages 7-96

Scoring: Hand key

Cost: Test unit $220.00 Level I; Level II test unit $378.00.

Publisher: Lafayette Instrument Company, Inc.

PERCEPTUAL MOTOR EDUCATION SCALE
Jack Capon

child

Purpose: Assesses motor skill development and perceptual motor proficiency of young children as a measure of progress and program effectiveness.

Description: Six item physical performance test of basic motor, locomotor and perceptual motor proficiency for pre-Kindergarten through Grade 1 and handicapped children. Measures static and dynamic balance, knowledge of basic body parts, space awareness, hand-eye coordination and locomotor skills (jumping and hopping). Materials required are low balance board, jump box, ball, six chairs, and two cross bars. Designed for teachers and trained aides. Limited training required. Examiner required. Suitable for group use. Available in Spanish.

Untimed: 10-15 minutes

Range: Ages K-6; and handicapped

Scoring: Examiner evaluated

Cost: Complete set (includes test items, directions, scoring, recording sheet, terminology, etc., and activities for program development) $22.50.

Publisher: Pitman Learning, Inc.

PHOTOELECTRIC ROTARY PURSUIT

teen, adult

Purpose: Measures general perceptual motor learning across such parameters as handedness, transfer of training and distribution of practice. Used for vocational evaluation, research, and classroom demonstration of learning principles.

Description: A manual, nonverbal test in which the subject uses a rotary pursuit apparatus to follow a moving light around a pattern (square, circle or triangle). The light moves in either a clockwise or counterclockwise direction at a fixed or variable speed for either a fixed time or a fixed number of revolutions. "On target" time, hits and total test time are measured. Examiner required. Not for group use.

Untimed: Time not standardized

Range: Ages 15 and older

Scoring: Examiner evaluated

Cost: Photo-electric rotary pursuit $475.00; variable speed photo-electric rotary pursuit $650.00; variable speed photo-electric rotary pursuit with tachometer $690.00; basic accessory package $205.00; intermediate accessory package $523.50; deluxe package $739.00.

Publisher: Lafayette Instrument Company, Inc.

THE PRIMARY VISUAL MOTOR TEST
Mary R. Haworth

Mental Age 4-8

Purpose: Assesses visual motor functioning in preschool and primary grade children. Used as a rough measure of intellectual performance skills in deaf or speech-handicapped children.

Description: Multiple task, nonverbal test in which 16 geometrical and simple representational designs are presented by the examiner for the child to copy in designated rectangular spaces marked off on the test sheets. Serves to screen for reading-related difficulties, determine the extent of visual motor deficiencies in retarded children, and assess the general level of functioning in deaf or speech-handicapped children. Test data also available on 130 psychotic children, ages 6-12. Must be administered by persons trained in test administration and interpretation. Suitable for group use.

Untimed: 10-15 minutes

Range: Mental age 4-8 years

Scoring: Examiner evaluated

Cost: Manual $33.00; test cards $10.50; 100 tests $12.00; 50 scoring forms $17.50.

Publisher: Grune & Stratton, Inc.

PURDUE PERCEPTUAL-MOTOR SURVEY (PPMS)
Eugene G. Roach and Newell C. Kephart

child, teen grades PRE-8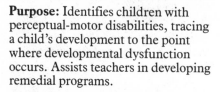

Purpose: Identifies children with perceptual-motor disabilities, tracing a child's development to the point where developmental dysfunction occurs. Assists teachers in developing remedial programs.

Description: 22 item task assessment test measuring laterality, directionality, and perceptual-motor matching skills. Walking board and jumping tests measure balance and posture. Body Image and Differentiation tests include naming ten parts of the body, imitation of movements, obstacle course, Krauss-Weber test, and angels in the snow. A chalkboard test for rhythmic writing, ocular control, and form perception measures

Perceptual- Motor Matching Skills. Examiner required. Not for group use.

Untimed: Varies

Range: Preschool-8

Scoring: Examiner evaluated

Cost: 25 surveys $16.50.

Publisher: Charles E. Merrill Publishing Company

THE RAIL-WALKING TEST
Refer to page 49.

REACTION TIME TESTING

all ages

Purpose: Measures the reaction time component of perceptual motor coordination. Used for psychological research, drug screening, reaction training, and vocational guidance.

Description: A manual, nonverbal test in which the subject faces various stimulus presentations and trials incorporated with the stimulus-response device controlled by the examiner, seated across the table. The devices vary in resolution, stimulus presentation and response requirements, and test auditory or visual simple reaction time, visual discrimination reaction time and reaction-movement time. Examiner required. Not for group use.

Untimed: 1-15 minutes

Range: Ages 5 and older

Scoring: Examiner evaluated

Cost: Multi-Choice Reaction Time Apparatus 1/100th second $455.00, with ready signal $577.00, with Digital 1/100th seconds $850.00, with Digital 1/100th seconds and voice activated RT control $1050.00; Multi-Choice Reaction Time Apparatus 1/100th seconds $975.00, Reaction Movement Timer 1/100th second

$980.00, Digital ¹⁄₁₀₀th second $1400.00.

Publisher: Lafayette Instrument Company, Inc.

RILEY MOTOR PROBLEMS INVENTORY
Refer to page 50.

ROEDER MANIPULATIVE APTITUDE TEST
Wesley S. Roeder

teen, adult

Purpose: Assesses eye, hand and finger coordination or dexterity to provide counselors and personnel professionals with additional evaluation information for educational and vocational guidance.

Description: Four tests measure eye, hand and finger coordination and dexterity, especially thrust and twisting movements, as follows: Part I--insert and twist as many rods as possible in the allotted time into a socket on a styrene-plexiglass board; Part II--use both hands to alternately slide a washer and nut on each side of a T-bar as quickly as possible in the allotted time; Part III--same as Part II, using left hand only. Part IV--same as Parts II and III, using right hand only. Examiner required. Suitable for group use.

Timed: 5 minutes

Range: Ages 15 and older

Scoring: Hand key

Cost: Board and test $98.95; 50 score sheets $4.50.

Publisher: Lafayette Instrument Company, Inc.

SOUTHERN CALIFORNIA SENSORY INTEGRATION TESTS (SCSIT)
A. Jean Ayers

child

Purpose: Measures an individual's ability to see, touch, and move in a coordinated manner. Used to identify the degree and type of disorder often associated with learning and emotional problems, minimal brain dysfunction and cerebral palsy.

Description: 17 paper-pencil and task assessment tests which measure visual, tactile and kinesthetic perception in addition to several different types of motor performance. The battery includes the following tests: Space Visualization, Figure- Ground Perception, Position in Space, Design Copying, Motor Accuracy (Revised), Kinesthesia, Manual Form Perception, Finger Identification, Graphesthesia, Localization of Tactile Stimuli, Double Tactile Stimuli Perception, Imitation of Postures, Crossing Mid-Line of Body, Bilateral Motor Coordination, Right-Left Coordination, Standing Balance (Eyes Open), and Standing Balance (Eyes Closed).
Materials may be ordered separately for the following tests: Space Visualization, Figure-Ground Perception, Position in Space, Design Copying, Motor Accuracy Test (Revised), Form Perception, and Kinesthesia. The Protocol Booklet is used for recording and calculating the scores for all tests except Motor Accuracy and Design Copying. Additional materials available include: profile of standard scores, manual (revised 1980), carrying case, and a 58- page book enterpreting The Southern California Sensory Integration Tests. Each test is standardized on approximately 1,000 subjects, and normative data is given at six-month intervals for ages 4-10 years.

Restricted to qualified personnel. Examiner required. Not suitable for group use.

Untimed: 45-60 minutes

Range: Ages 4-10

Scoring: Hand key; examiner evaluated

Cost: Complete set for 10 $125.00.

Publisher: Western Psychological Services

STANDARDIZED ROAD-MAP TEST OF DIRECTION SENSE
John Money

all ages

Purpose: Assesses directional orientation in children and adults. Used as a quick measure of disability and as part of a full neurophyschological battery to evaluate children suspected of underachieving.

Description: With a marker, the student traces a path through a maze consisting of 32 possible turns. Scoring is on the basis of items-correct-to-total. Conversion tables for percentiles are provided for three age groupings within the 7-18 year range, for males and females. Examiner required. Not for group use.

Untimed: 10 minutes

Range: Ages 8-adult

Scoring: Hand key

Cost: Manual $8.00; 50 test forms $5.00; scoring template $2.00; specimen set $8.00.

Publisher: Academic Therapy Publications

THE TEST OF MOTOR IMPAIRMENT (Henderson Revision)
D.H. Stott, F.A. Moyes and S.E. Henderson

child, teen

Purpose: Detects motor impairment in children above the level of incapacitating spasticity. Used to diagnose motor impairment as a factor in behavior and learning problems.

Description: Eight task, nonverbal test at each of four age bands with yearly norms. The test measures control and balance of body while immobile, control and coordination of upper limbs, control and coordination of entire body while in motion, manual dexterity with emphasis on speed, eye-hand coordination and precision. Child performs eight tasks at own age band and additional tasks at lower levels only in event of failing. Should not be attempted by children who cannot use an upper limb to grasp an object, or are not mobile. New edition includes checklist for observation of coping style and specific faults of motor control. Examiner required. Not suitable for group use.

Untimed: 15 minutes

Range: Ages 5-14

Scoring: Examiner evaluated

Cost: Contact publisher.

Publisher: Brook Educational Publishing Ltd.

TEST OF THREE-DIMENSIONAL CONSTRUCTIONAL PRAXIS

adult

Purpose: Assesses an individual's ability to construct three-dimensional replicas of presented models.

Description: Multiple item paper-pencil test provides two alternate forms for each of two types of stimulus presentations: three-dimensional block models and photographs of these models. The subject constructs three-dimensional replicas for each of the represented stimuli. Normative standards are based on the performance of adult hospital controls and has been collected for children as well.
DUTCH PUBLISHER

Untimed: Not available

Range: Adult

Scoring: Examiner evaluated

Cost: Contact publisher.

Publisher: Oxford University Press

Special Education

Gifted

CREATIVITY ATTITUDE SURVEY (CAS)
Charles E. Schaefer

child   grades 4-6

Purpose: Assesses attitudes important for creative thinking. Used in the evaluation of training programs in creativity.

Description: 32 item paper-pencil test of five dimensions associated with creative thinking: confidence in own ideas; appreciation of fantasy; theoretical and aesthetic orientation; openness to impulse expression; and desire for novelty. Items are statements to which the child indicates agreement or disagreement. Examiner required. Suitable for group use.

Untimed: 10 minutes

Range: Grades 4-6

Scoring: Hand key

Cost: Specimen set $4.00; manual $3.50; 25 tests $12.50; 100-$49.00.

Publisher: Psychologists and Educators, Inc.

CREATIVITY CHECKLIST
David L. Johnson

all ages   grades K-UP

Purpose: Evaluates creativity in people of all educational levels, in any social setting. Used in school, business, family, free play, and training settings to identify gifted individuals and to evaluate creativity programs.

Description: 8 item paper-pencil questionnaire used by an examiner to record observations of eight categories of the subject's creative behavior. The categories are: sensitivity or preference for complexity, fluency, flexibility, resourcefulness, constructional skill, ingenuity or productiveness, independence, and positive self-referencing behavior. The examiner (parent, teacher, counselor) indicates the extent to which he or she has observed (consistently, frequently, occasionally, seldom, never) examples of these characteristics in the individual being evaluated. The sum of the eight items provides a total creativity score. Cut-off points for different levels of creative performance are provided. Examiner required. Suitable for group use.

Untimed: 15 minutes

Range: Kindergarten-graduate school

Scoring: Examiner evaluated

Cost: Complete kit (includes 30 record forms and manual) $8.75.

Publisher: Stoelting Co.

CREATIVITY TESTS FOR CHILDREN (CT)

Refer to page 444.

GIFTED AND TALENTED SCREENING FORM (GTSF)

David L. Johnson

child, teen   grades K-9

Purpose: Identifies gifted and talented children grades K-9. Used in educational, family, and social settings, and by school districts initiating formal, federally-funded programs for the gifted and talented.

Description: 24 item paper-pencil inventory in talent areas of academics, intelligence, creativity, leadership, visual-performing arts, and psychomotor ability. Respondent (parent, teacher, or anyone familiar with the child) is asked to indicate the extent to which he or she has observed (consistently, frequently, occasionally, seldom, never) gifted and talented characteristics in the child being evaluated. GTSF cut-off criterion points are suggested for each of the talent areas. Examiner required. Suitable for group use.

Untimed: 20 minutes

Range: Grades K-9

Scoring: Examiner evaluated

Cost: Complete kit (includes 30 record forms, scorekeys, and manual) $13.00.

Publisher: Stoelting Co.

GROUP INVENTORY FOR FINDING CREATIVE TALENT (GIFT)

Sylvia B. Rinim and Gary A. Davis

child   grades K-6

Purpose: Assesses creativity. Used for identification of gifted students in children in grades Kindergarten through 6.

Description: Multiple item paper-pencil test of interests and attitudes related to creativity. Validation groups include minorities, urban and suburban students, learning disabled and gifted students. Examiner required. Suitable for group use.

Untimed: 20-40 minutes

Range: Grades K-6

Scoring: Machine scored

Cost: Specimen set $6.00; class set of 30 $25.00 (indicate grade level). Scoring included in price and prepayment required.

Publisher: Psychometric Affiliates

GROUP INVENTORY FOR FINDING INTERESTS (GIFFI)

Sylvia B. Rinim and Gary A. Davis

child, teen   grades 6-12

Purpose: Assesses creativity in children in grades 6 through 12. Used for identification of gifted children.

Description: Multiple item paper-pencil test of interests and attitudes related to creativity. Validation groups include minorities, urban and suburban students, learning disabled, and gifted children. Examiner required. Suitable for group use.

Untimed: 20-40 minutes

Range: Grades 6-12

Scoring: Machine scored

Cost: Specimen set $6.00; class set of 30 $35.00 (indicate grade level). Scoring included in price and prepayment required.

Publisher: Psychometric Affiliates

HARDING SKYSCRAPER FORM B-C

Refer to page 479.

HARDING W87 TEST
Refer to page 479.

INTERNATIONAL SOCIETY FOR PHILOSOPHICAL ENQUIRY VOCABULARY FORM A
Refer to page 221.

OREGON ACADEMIC RANKING TEST
Refer to page 483.

THE SIMILES TEST
Charles E. Schaefer

child, teen

Purpose: Identifies children and adolescents who have creative literary talent. Used in educational programs designed to foster creativity and to study the relationship between creativity, personality, and styles of thought.

Description: Ten item, paper-pencil test in which the subject is asked to give three different endings to each of ten incomplete simile forms which appeal to a variety of senses and emotions. An example: "The young girl was as playful as _____." Each completion is scored on a six- point scale for originality. The uniqueness and aptness of a response determine the originality scoring weights. Numerous examples of responses falling within each of the scoring cateogries are provided. Materials include the manual, scoring sheets and two separate forms. Examiner required. Suitable for group use.

Untimed: 15 minutes

Range: Child, adolescent

Scoring: Hand key; examiner evaluated

Cost: Examination kit (includes manual, 10 copies for Form 1 and Form 2, and 20 scoring sheets) $12.00.

Publisher: Research Psychologists Press, Inc.

SOCIAL INTERACTION AND CREATIVITY IN COMMUNICATION SYSTEM (SICCS)
David L. Johnson

all ages grades 1-UP

Purpose: Evaluates creativity, leadership, and communication skills of students from elementary school through college. Used to identify gifted and talented children who might be overlooked due to low academic achievement.

Description: Multiple item paper-pencil inventory provides a system of observation, recording, encoding, and analysis of creativity, leadership, and communication skills. They are: appraisal (expressing a conclusion), prescriptive (expression of concern for control), informational (providing information about characteristics), questioning (asking for response from others), self-reference (making reference to one's own characteristics), self-initiated (spontaneous or uninitiated), productivity (listening or reading the setting dialogue), and quantity (number of verbal acts). The SICCS has been used in a variety of educational, business, training, therapeutic, play, organizational, and community settings. It has also been applied by regular classroom and special education teachers to a variety of work/setting problems. Examiner required. Suitable for group use.

Untimed: Not available

Range: Elementary-college

Scoring: Examiner evaluated

Cost: Complete $13.00

Publisher: Stoelting Co.

A SURVEY OF STUDENTS EDUCATIONAL TALENTS AND SKILLS (ASSETS)
Grand Rapids Public School System

child   grades K-6

Purpose: Identifies gifted and talented students in order to individualize study programs and planning and help parents and teachers discuss the students' needs.

Description: 35 item paper-pencil, test in three parts; one for the student, one for parent, one for teacher. The students respond to statements as 'almost', 'sometime', 'never', and fill in blanks about favorite books, hobbies and activities. Self-administered. Suitable for group use.

Untimed: 40 minutes

Range: Grades K-3 and Grades 4-6

Scoring: Computer scoring available

Cost: Specimen set $5.95; 30 tests $39.60; specify early or later elementary.

Publisher: Learning Publications

TEST OF CREATIVE POTENTIAL (TCP)
R. Hoepfner and J. Hemenway

all ages   grades 2-UP

Purpose: Measures general creative potential. Used with adolescents, adults and children down to the second-grade level. For individual and program evaluation and for research.

Description: Multiple item paper-pencil examination in three separate subtests which assess fluency, flexibility, and elaboration of verbal, symbolic, and figural materials. The "Writing Words" subtest asks the subject to write many words that mean the same as the given words. The "Picture Decoration" section requires the takers to elaboratively decorate simplified pictures. The "License Plate Words" subtest asks takers to make many words that have certain literal qualities. All items are open-ended, restricted only by time. The unique feature of TCP is its scoring guide, which has been developed and checked to minimize subjectivity so that clerks or teachers can score reliably and validly. Scoring procedures, reliability estimates, and norms have been developed on samples of subjects ranging from the second- to the twelfth-grade. Suitable for group uses.

Timed: 22 minutes

Range: Grades 2-adult

Scoring: Hand key; examiner evaluated, scoring service available

Cost: Specimen set (specify form) $6.00; 35 tests $25.00; 100-$55.00; manual $3.00; 35 score rosters $4.00; 100-$10.00; scoring service $1.50 per booklet.

Publisher: Monitor

THINKING CREATIVELY IN ACTION AND MOVEMENT (TCAM)
E. Paul Torrance

child

Purpose: Identifies creative children. Used as part of a program to keep alive and further develop promising creative talent among young children.

Description: Nonverbal, movement test assesses the creativity of young children, especially preschoolers. The responses are appropriate to the developmental characteristics of the younger child, and are physical in nature although verbal responses are acceptable. TCAM Standard Scoring Service (raw scores and T-scores are entered on scoring worksheets) is available. The manual contains a scoring guide for those who wish to self-score the test. Examiner required. Not suitable for group use.

Timed: 10-30 minutes

Range: Ages 3-8

Scoring: Hand key; examiner evaluated

Cost: 20 tests $14.30.

Publisher: Scholastic Testing Service, Inc.

THINKING CREATIVELY WITH SOUNDS AND WORDS (TCSW)
E. Paul Torrance, Joe Khantena and Bert F. Cunnington

all ages   grades 3-UP

Purpose: Measures ability to create images for words and sounds. Use to identify gifted and creative individuals, and to teach imagery.

Description: Two test battery which assesses creativity by measuring the originality of ideas stimulated by abstract sounds and spoken onomatopoeic words. TCSW is a battery of two tests, Sounds and Images, and Onomatopeia and Images. It is available in equivalent forms (A and B) for two levels: Level I (Grades 3-12), and Level II (Adult). Two long-playing records provide the stimuli for each level. May be scored by the examiner with the help of the scoring guide included in the manual; TCSW Standard Scoring Service also available. Examiner required. Suitable for group use.

Timed: 30 minutes/test

Range: Grades Level I, 3-12; Level II, adult

Scoring: Hand key; examiner evaluated

Cost: 20 tests $12.00.

Publisher: Scholastic Testing Service, Inc.

TORRANCE TESTS OF CREATIVE THINKING (TTCT)
E. Paul Torrance

all ages   grades K-UP

Purpose: Assesses the ability to visualize and transform words, meanings and patterns. Used to identify gifted, creative individuals.

Description: Multiple task paper-pencil measure of an individual's creativity which assesses four mental characteristics: fluency, flexibility, originality, and elaboration. The Verbal TTCT uses seven word-based exercises. The Figural TTCT uses three picture-based exercises. The Verbal TTCT can be administered orally to students in the K-3 range, and is easily administered and scored, although persons with psychometric training should interpret the subtest and total scores. "Streamlined" scoring of the figural forms of the overall test is available. This alternative scoring yields norm-referenced measures for fluency, originality, abstractness of titles, elaboration, and resistance to premature closure. It provides an overall Creativity Index and criterion-referenced scores for several creativity indicators. This test is available in two equivalent forms (A and B) for both the verbal and the figural parts. A scoring guide is available in the directions manual; TTCT standard scoring service and stream-lined scoring for figural tests is also available. Examiner required. Suitable for group use.

Timed: Figural 30 minutes; Verbal 45 minutes

Range: Kindergarten-adult

Scoring: Examiner evaluated

Cost: 20 tests (Verbal A, Verbal B, Figural A or Figural B) $12.00.

Publisher: Scholastic Testing Service, Inc.

WATSON-GLASER CRITICAL THINKING APPRAISAL
Goodwin Watson and Edward M. Glaser

teen, adult   grades 9-UP

Purpose: Assesses critical thinking abilities. Used for evaluation of gifted and talented individuals.

Description: 80 item paper-pencil test of five aspects of the ability to think critically, including inferences, recognition of assumptions, deduction, interpretation, and evaluation of arguments. Subject responds to exercises including problems, statements, arguments and interpretation of material encountered on a daily basis. Materials include two alternate and equivalent forms, A and B. Examiner required. Suitable for group use.

Untimed: 50 minutes

Range: Grades 9-12, college, adult

Scoring: Hand key; may be machine scored; scoring service available

Cost: 35 tests (form A or B) $22.00; 35 OPScan answer documents $5.50; key (form A or B) $2.00; manual $1.75; class record $1.00; basic scoring service $1.08 per pupil.

Publisher: The Psychological Corporation

Learning Disabilities

ADELPHI PARENT ADMINISTERED READINESS TEST (A.P.A.R.T.)
Refer to page 440.

ANALYTIC LEARNING DISABILITY ASSESSMENT (ALDA)
Thomas D. Gnagey and Patricia D. Gnagey

child, teen

Purpose: Measures the skills necessary to read, spell, write and work with numbers as an aid to the neuropsychological evaluation of learning disabled, educable mentally retarded and behaviorally disturbed students.

Description: 77 subtests in a spiral-bound book, using pencil, chalk, tape, and worksheets to test fine sound discrimination, short-term sequential verbal memory, verbal word generation, concept formation and generalization, assembling bulk segments, subvocal to vocal motor translation, gross visual discrimination and motoric spatial localization. The test matches students' strengths and weaknesses to the most appropriate teaching methods, helped by age and grade equivalent and criterial norms. The examiner asks questions and gives directions to an individual student. Test forms each include a scoring sheet, student worksheets with tear-out sections, an individualized student learning plan, and a teacher recommendation pamphlet. Other materials are four colored scoring pencils, tape, and a straight-edge ruler, all contained in a leather carrying case. The test is most reliable for ages 8-14. It is not useful unless a learning dysfunction is suspected. Examiner required. Not suitable for group use.

Untimed: 75 minutes

Range: Ages 8-14 learning dysfunction children

Scoring: Hand key

Cost: Complete kit $75.00; 20 additional testing forms $13.50 (includes: testing book, manual, scoring straight edge, 4 colored scoring pencils, tape, chalk, 20 complete testing forms, teaching plan, carrying case).

Publisher: Facilitation House

THE ANSER SYSTEM-AGGRE-GATE NEUROBEHAVIORAL, STUDENT HEALTH AND EDU-CATIONAL REVIEW
Melvin D. Levine

child, teen

Purpose: Gathers information from parents and teachers for the educator or clinician who has questions about a child with learning and/or behavioral problems. Used in schools, health-care and counseling centers to evaluate children with low severity, high prevalence disabilities.

Description: Three separate, short-answer, paper-pencil questionnaires for parents and school personnel to evaluate three age groups: Form 1 (ages 3-5), Form 2 (ages 6-11), and Form 3 (age 12 and over). Form 4 is a self-administered student profile to be completed by students who are nine years or older. The parent questionnaire surveys family history, possible pregnancy problems, health problems, functional problems, early development, early educational experience, skills and interests, activity-attention problems, associated behaviors, and associated strengths. The school questionnaire covers the educational program and setting, special facilities available, and the results of previous testing. The self-administered Student Profile asks the student to rate him or herself on a series of statements in the following categories: fine motor, gross motor, memory, attention, language, general efficiency, visual-spatial processing, sequencing, general academic performance, and social interaction. Examiner required. Not for group use.

Untimed: 30-60 minutes

Range: Ages 3 through 18 years

Scoring: Examiner evaluated

Cost: Form I: parent questionnaire 12 $7.50, school 12 $5.75; Form II: parent 12 $7.50, school 12 $6.50; Form III: parent 12 $7.50, school 12 $6.50; Form IV 12 $5.75; interpreter's guide 1 $5.50; specimen set (includes guide and sample of each form) $5.50.

Publisher: Educators Publishing Service, Inc.

AUDITORY POINTING TEST
Janet B. Fudala, LaVern H. Kunze and John D. Ross

all ages   grades K-UP

Purpose: Measures short-term memory in children and adults through visual-motor responses. Used for remedial planning, especially involving those with oral communication problems.

Description: Multiple item cross-modal test in which the teacher/clinician shows the student ten different stimulus cards, each of which contains eight simple line drawings (from a total stimulus pool of 32 separate drawings). The child is asked to point to the item mentioned by the examiner. Two forms are provided for test and retest. Scoring is on the basis of items-correct-to-ceiling. Materials include recording forms, summary sheets, a set of test cards and plates, and the Manual. Examiner required. Not suitable for group use.

Untimed: 20 minutes

Range: K-adult

Scoring: Hand key

Cost: Manual $5.00; 25 recording forms (specify form A or B) $6.00; 25 student summary sheets $2.00; set of test cards and plates $5.00; specimen set $5.00.

Publisher: Academic Therapy Publications

BASIC NUMBER DIAGNOSTIC TEST
Refer to page 238.

BLOOMER LEARNING TEST (BLT)
Refer to page 476.

THE BODER TEST OF READ-ING-SPELLING PATTERNS
Elena Boder and Sylvia Jarrico

all ages

Purpose: Differentiates specific reading disability, or developmental dyslexia, from nonspecific reading disability through reading and spelling performance. Used to classify dyslexic readers into one of three subtypes, each with its own prognostic and remedial implications.

Description: 300 item paper-pencil tests of reading and spelling ability. The Reading Test uses 13 graded word lists of 20 words each, half phonetic and half nonphonetic. The words are presented in two ways: flash and untimed, requiring from the subject both sight vocabulary and phonic word analysis skills. The Spelling Test uses two individualized spelling lists (10 known words and 10 unknown) based on the student's reading performance. Both the Reading and Spelling tests tap the central visual and auditory processes required for reading and spelling, making it possible to diagnose developmental dyslexia by the joint analysis of reading and spelling as inter-dependent functions. Results should be supplemented with testing that uses instructional materials to which the child already has been and will be exposed. Examiner required. Not suitable for group use.

Timed: 30 minutes

Range: Preprimer-adult

Scoring: Examiner evaluated

Cost: Complete kit $55.00.

Publisher: Grune & Stratton, Inc.

COMPREHENSIVE ASSESS-MENT PROGRAM: DEVELOPING COGNITIVE ABILITIES TEST
Refer to page 477.

DETROIT TESTS OF LEARNING APTITUDE
Refer to page 364.

THE DEVEREUX ELEMENTARY SCHOOL BEHAVIOR RATING SCALE (DESB-II)
Refer to page 617.

DYSLEXIA DETERMINATION TEST: DDT
John R. Griffin and Howard N. Walton

child, teen   grades 2-12

Purpose: Evaluates learning disorders in reading, writing and spelling; differentiates dyslexic patterns from other disorders. Used for diagnostic purposes with students Grades 2-12; also suggests appropriate remedial approaches.

Description: Multiple item paper-pencil test measures and evaluates a student's ability to decode and encode the English language. The test identifies seven specific dyslexic patterns, provides suggestions for therapy, and is particularly useful with students who have normal sensory perceptual, cognitive, and motor abilities, yet have difficulty reading and writing and spelling. The DDT Kit includes: Examiner's Instructional Manual, which provides instructions for administering, scoring, and evaluating the test as well as a discussion of the test's development and objectives; Decoding Wordlist Booklet; Instructional Audio Cassette (a supplement to the manual); Interpretation Recording Forms; and Decoding Patterns Checklists, Form A and Form B (equivalent forms printed in pads of 30 each). Examiner required. Not for group use.

Untimed: 20-25 minutes

Range: Grades 2-12

Scoring: Examiner evaluated

Cost: Complete kit (includes examiner's Instructional Manual, Decoding word list booklet, Instructional Audio Cassettee, 60 Interpretation Recording Forms, 30 Form A, 30 Form B Decoding Patterns checklists) $44.95.

Publisher: Instructional Materials & Equipment Distributors

DYSLEXIA SCHEDULE
John McLeod

child   grades K-1

Purpose: Gathers relevant social data from parents or guardians about a child who has been referred to a specialist due to a reading disability.

Description: 89 item paper-pencil questionnaire to be filled out by the parents or guardians before the child visits a clinic. The results provide the clinician with background data to help evaluate characteristics associated with childhood dyslexia before testing begins.

Untimed: 20-30 minutes

Range: Grades Kindergarten and first

Scoring: Examiner evaluated

Cost: Under 24 $1.00 each; over 24 $.90 each.

Publisher: Educators Publishing Service, Inc.

THE DYSLEXIA SCREENING SURVEY (DSS)
Refer to page 39.

FISHER LANGUAGE SURVEY and WRITE-TO-LEARN PROGRAM
Alyce F. Fisher

child   grades 1-4

Purpose: Identifies students (grades 1-4) in need of special education programs due to learning disabilities. Used to teach language processing, and to evaluate reading and math skills.

Description: Multiple item paper-pencil test of a student's ability to write sentences dictated by the teacher. The sentences include many samples of short vowels, blends, digraphs, and inconsistently-spelled words. The child's responses are evaluated for deficiencies in nine areas: cognition, attention, fine motor, auditory and visual memory, auditory and visual perception, self-image, and integration. The test covers seven levels: Grade 1 (3 sentences), Grade 2-1 (5 sentences), Grade 2-2 (8 sentences, Grade 3-1, 3-2, and 4-1 (10 sentences each), and Grade 4-2 (10 sentences). Examiner required. Not for group use.

Untimed: 10-25 minutes

Range: Grades 1-4

Scoring: Examiner evaluated

Cost: Complete kit (includes 30 record forms, 10 profile forms, manual) $7.00; Write-to-learn Program manual $8.00.

Publisher: Stoelting Co.

THE JESNESS INVENTORY
Refer to page 159.

JORDAN LEFT-RIGHT REVERSAL TEST (JLRRT)
Brian T. Jordan

child

Purpose: Assesses the extent to which a child reverses letters, numbers and words. Used as a screening device by classroom teachers or as one part of a full diagnostic battery.

Description: Multiple item, paper-pencil examination on two levels. Level One tests reversals of capital letters and numerals. Level Two reveals reversed lower-case letters within words, and whole-word reversals within sentences. Manual includes a chapter on remediation techniques and a conversion table to determine developmental age. Examiner required. Suitable for group use.

Untimed: 20 minutes

Range: Ages 5-12

Scoring: Hand key

Cost: Manual $10.00; 25 test forms $6.00; specimen set $10.00.

Publisher: Academic Therapy Publications

KERBY LEARNING MODALITY TEST, REVISED 1980
Maude L. Kerby

child

Purpose: Measures learning abilities of children ages 5-11 in terms of visual, auditory and motor activity skills. Used to identify children with learning disabilities, to plan teaching strategies and to comply with P.L. 94-142.

Description: Multiple item paper-pencil test measuring strengths and weaknesses in three primary learning modalities: visual, auditory and motor activity. The test consists of a variety of classroom work samples in

eight subtests: Visual and Auditory Discrimination, Visual and Auditory Closure, Visual and Auditory Memory, and Visual and Auditory Motor Coordination. Standardized on both black and white subjects with high reliability and validity. Examiner required. Suitable for group use.

Timed: 15 minutes

Range: Ages 5-11

Scoring: Hand key

Cost: Complete kit (includes kindergarten kit 5 years, primary kit ages 6-8 years, intermediate kit ages 8-11 years) $69.80; each kit may be purchased individually as well as the components.

Publisher: Western Psychological Services

LEARNING DISABILITY RATING PROCEDURE (LDRP)
Gerald J. Spadafore and Sharon J. Spadafore

child, teen   grades 1-12

Purpose: Helps evaluate the general mental and social abilities of elementary and secondary school students. Used to determine Learning Disability (LD) placement.

Description: Multiple item paper-pencil evaluation. The examiner rates a student on each of ten indicators ranging from general intelligence and listening comprehension to socially inappropriate behavior and learning motivation. The test provides a basis for discussion during placement meetings as each participant completes the rating form. Total scores are averaged and compared to the criteria which describe each student as a poor, fair, good, or excellent candidate for LD placement. The manual outlines necessary testing and observations which should be made before the meeting. Examiner required. Not for group use.

Untimed: 15 minutes

Range: Grades 1-12

Scoring: Examiner evaluated

Cost: Manual $7.50; 25 rating forms $6.00; specimen set $7.50.

Publisher: Academic Therapy Publications

LEARNING EFFICIENCY TEST (LET)
Raymond E. Webster

all ages

Purpose: Measures visual and auditory memory characteristics of children and adults. Used to determine deficits that may be related to classroom learning problems, for academic placement, and identification of learning handicapped students.

Description: Multiple item paper-pencil measure of visual memory and auditory memory. Both subtests assess these three conditions: immediate recall, short-term recall, and long-term recall. In the Visual Memory subtest, the examiner shows the student non-rhyming letters on stimulus cards. For the Auditory Memory subtest, the examiner reads the letters to the student. Sequences to be remembered range in length from two to nine items. The manual includes an interpretation of the performance and describes remedial activities that can be used to improve learning efficiency. Examiner required. Not suitable for group use.

Untimed: 10-15 minutes

Range: Ages 6-adult

Scoring: Hand key

Cost: Manual $10.00; 25 rating forms $6.00; specimen set $10.00; stimulus cards $7.50.

Publisher: Academic Therapy Publications

NON-READERS INTELLIGENCE TEST-THIRD EDITION and ORAL VERBAL INTELLIGENCE TEST
Dennis Young

child, teen

Purpose: Measures intelligence of students ages 6-14 whose performance would be underestimated if they were required to read the questions. Useful with children suspected of or diagnosed as Educationally Subnormal (ESN). Identifies children in need of special educational assistance.

Description: Multiple item paper-pencil intelligence test is orally administered for use with slow or non-readers and is available in two forms: The Non-Readers Intelligence Test for use with unstreamed children ages 6:7 to 8:11 and with less able children up to the age of 13:11; and the Oral Verbal Intelligence Test for unstreamed children ages 7:6 to 10:11 and with less able children up to the age of 14:11. The third edition of the Non-Readers Intelligence Test Manual offers revised items (replacing words like "pop" which have acquired new meanings) and new norms. The manual for the Oral Verbal Intelligence Test contains details of the test construction and full instructions for administering and scoring the test. Both tests employ the same scoring template. Examiner required. Suitable for group use. BRITISH PUBLISHER

Untimed: Not available

Range: Ages 6.7-13.11

Scoring: Hand key

Cost: Specimen set ;1.25; 20 answer papers 95p plus VAT, marking template 8p plus VAT, manual 95p (specify test).

Publisher: Hodder & Stoughton

THE O'BRIEN VOCABULARY PLACEMENT TEST
Refer to page 500.

PRESCRIPTIVE READING PERFORMANCE TEST (PRPT)
Refer to page 526.

A PSYCHOEDUCATIONAL INVENTORY OF BASIC LEARNING ABILITIES
Refer to page 390.

QUICKSCREEN
Refer to page 391.

SCHOOL PROBLEM SCREENING INVENTORY-FIFTH EDITION
Thomas D. Gnagey

child, teen   grades Nursery-12

Purpose: Diagnoses and classifies learning and behavior problems to help teacher planning and evaluation and to verify the continued eligibility of previously placed special education students.

Description: 38 item paper-pencil test covering ten diagnostic categories: learning disability (visual-motor, auditory-verbal and non-specific), mental retardation, general learning skill deficit, behavior disorder (over or under controlled and general non-specific), educational handicap (social-cultural), and general maladjustment. Teacher uses an inventory sheet to rate the student on the 38 characteristics, then sums the scores in each of the diagnostic categories to obtain ratings of 'not likely', 'possible', and 'very likely'. Examiner

required. Not suitable for group use.

Untimed: 7-10 minutes

Range: Grades Nursery-High school

Scoring: Hand key

Cost: Manual and 20 analysis worksheets $8.65; 100 additional forms $18.00.

Publisher: Facilitation House

SLINGERLAND SCREENING TESTS FOR IDENTIFYING CHILDREN WITH SPECIFIC LANGUAGE DISABILITY
Beth H. Slingerland

child   grades 1-6

Purpose: Screens elementary-school children for indications of specific language disabilities in reading, spelling, handwriting, and speaking in order to identify those who need special tutoring and further evaluation, and to show teachers the strengths and weaknesses of their pupils.

Description: Multiple item, verbal, paper-pencil examination with three forms (A, B, C) for grades 1-4, and a fourth form (D) for grades 5-6. All forms include five subtests which evaluate visual motor coordination and visual memory linked with motor coordination, and three subtests evaluating auditory-visual discrimination and auditory memory-to-motor ability. Form D, which has a ninth subtest to evaluate personal orientation in time and space and the ability to express ideas in writing, helps identify children whose specific language difficulties may have become persistent. All forms have separate Echolalia tests, and include individual auditory tests to identify those who have difficulty recalling words and pronouncing words correctly or who are unable to express their ideas in an organized manner. Examiner required. Suitable for group use.

Untimed: 1½ hours

Range: Forms A, B, and C grades 1-4; Form D for grades 5-6

Scoring: Examiner evaluated

Cost: Screening tests: form A, B, and C for 12 $4.50; form D for 12 $7.00; teacher's manual: form A, B, and C $5.50; form D $4.50. Cards and Charts: Form A, B, and C $8.00; Form D $11.00. Specimen set (teacher's manual and 1 each test): Form A, B, and C $5.50; form D $4.75.

Publisher: Educator Publishing Service, Inc.

S.O.I. LEARNING ABILITIES TEST
Refer to page 466.

SOUTHGATE GROUP READING TESTS
Refer to page 506.

SPATIAL ORIENTATION MEMORY TEST
Joseph M. Wepman and D. Turaids

child

Purpose: Measures a child's ability to retain and recall the orientation of visually presented forms. Used to identify children who face potential learning difficulties.

Description: Multiple item "point-to" response test. The child is shown a "target" page with a non- alphabetic design and then asked to select the same design from the "response" page which has four or five samples of the same design in different rotational positions. This spatial orientation ability prepares the child for individual letter discrimination recall, sequential ordering of letters in words, and related skills essential for reading. Adequacy scores indicated for ages 5, 6, 7, 8, and 9 years. Available in two forms for retesting. Examiner required. Not for group use.

Untimed: 10-15 minutes

Range: Ages 5-9

Scoring: Hand key

Cost: Complete kit (includes 1 reusable test booklet, 20 score sheets, manual) $28.75.

Publisher: Western Psychological Services

STUDENT LEARNING PROFILE
Cuyahoga Special Education Service Center

child, teen   grades K-12

Purpose: Provides an on-going record of basic skills and accomplishments of learning disabled children from grades K-12. Used by teachers, psychologists, counselors, and parents to assess the individual's long and short-terms goals.

Description: 871 item paper-pencil examination administered to small groups over 13 years of schooling. Accomplishment in seven major areas: learning style (modality preferences), progress in study skills, language arts, perceptual development, career development, mathematics, and social/coping skills. The examiner partially fills in squares to the left of performance objects to signify "emergent" behaviors, and completely fills the squares to signify "consistent" behaviors. Each entry is color-coded to correspond to the student's level at the time the objective is met; black for grades K-3, green for grades 4-6, red for 7-8, and blue for 9-12. Materials are contained in a 30-page spiral-bound book which has pages of graduated length to provide easy access to each of the assessment areas. The profile is specifically designed for use with children who have specific learning disabilities, but many of the skills included in it are part of the regular school curricula. Examiner required.

Untimed: Not available

Range: Grades K-12 (children with specific learning disabilities)

Scoring: Examiner evaluated

Cost: 1 copy $4.85; 6 copies $24.85; 100-$2.50 each.

Publisher: Creative Learning Systems, Inc.

SYMBOL DIGIT MODALITIES TEST
Refer to page 52.

TASK ASSESSMENT FOR PRE- SCRIPTIVE TEACHING (TAPT)
Daniel Hofeditz and Duane Wilke

---

all ages

Purpose: Measures an individual's language and math abilities. Used by special education teachers to evaluate students who have learning disabilities, mental impairments, or behavior disorders.

Description: Multiple item paper-pencil test consisting of 12 mathematics and 11 reading booklets which contain all necessary instructions and places for student responses. The Mathematics booklets cover the following 12 areas: pre-skills, addition, subtraction, monetary concepts, time concepts, multiplication, division, fractions, decimals, percentages, weights and measures, and practical skills (including calculators). The Reading booklets cover the following 11 areas: pre- skills, letters, consonant/symbol sound, vowel/symbol sound, blending skills, academic/

instructional words, community/ functional words, word structure analysis, question orientation and context, thought expression, and informational resources. The booklets can be kept in a folder as a permanent part of a student's record. Each booklet contains a Student Progress Sheet which summarizes and graphs performance. TAPT also provides preprinted objective sheets that help meet the local requirements of Individualized Education Programs (IEPs). Examiner required.

Untimed: 20-40 minutes

Range: Ages 6-adult

Scoring: Hand key; examiner evaluated

Cost: Starter set $272.75.

Publisher: Scholastic Testing Service, Inc.

TEST OF CONCEPT UTILIZA- TION (TCU)
Refer to page 486.

WELLER-STRAWSER SCALES OF ADAPTIVE BEHAVIOR: FOR THE LEARNING DISABLED (WSSAB)
Carol Weller and Sherri Strawser

---

child, teen   grades 1-12

Purpose: Assesses the adaptive behavior of elementary and secondary school learning disabled students. Used to determine severity of disabilities and to identify areas requiring remedial attention.

Description: Multiple item paper-pencil form covering the following areas: social coping, relationships, pragmatic language, and production. The scales are completed by a teacher or diagnostician following a period of observation. The total score and subtest scores define the behavior problems as mild to moderate, or moderate to severe. The results, following suggestions in the manual, allow the examiner to develop compensatory teaching techniques to help the student cope with situations in school, home, social, and job environments. Examiner administered. Not suitable for group use.

Untimed: 15 minutes

Range: Grades Elementary, Secondary

Scoring: Examiner evaluated

Cost: Manual $15.00; 25 forms (specify if elementary or secondary) $6.00; specimen set $15.00.

Publisher: Academic Therapy Publications

WORD ORDERS COMPREHENSION TEST
Gillian Fenn

---

all ages

Purpose: Determines ability of learning disabled children to understand word relationships. Used for evaluation by psychologists, speech therapists and teachers of deaf or mentally handicapped children.

Description: Multiple item, verbal test using four picture sets and nine subtests of everyday vocabulary. Test is designed to determine whether children who use words know their meaning when used in sentences. Materials include sentence and answer cards, picture sets, record forms and Manual. Examiner required. Not for group use.
BRITISH PUBLISHER

Untimed: Not available

Range: Ages 4 years and above, including mentally handicapped

Scoring: Examiner evaluated

Cost: Complete kit (includes set of sentence cards, set of answer cards, 25 record forms, 25 scoring sheets for each subtest, 1 picture set A-D) £34.00 (payment in sterling for all overseas orders).

Publisher: NFER-Nelson Publishing Company

Mentally Handicapped

AAMD ADAPTIVE BEHAVIOR SCALE, SCHOOL EDITION (ABS)
K. Nihira, R. Foster, M. Shellhaas, H. Leland, N. Lambert, and M. Windmiller

---

child, teen

Purpose: Assesses children whose adaptive behavior indicates possible mental retardation, emotional disturbance, or other learning handicaps. Used for screening and instructional planning.

Description: 95 item paper-pencil scale, completed by the examiner, measures social and daily living skills and behaviors. Scores are converted to profiles which are used in diagnostic and placement decisions and in formulating general educational goals. Examiner required. Not suitable for group use.

Untimed: 30 minutes

Range: Ages 3-16

Scoring: Examiner evaluated

Cost: Starter set (includes manuals, 2 assessment booklets, 2 each instructional and diagnostic profiles, 2 parent guides) $21.00.

Publisher: CTB/McGraw-Hill

BARSCH LEARNING STYLE INVENTORY
Jeffrey Barsch

teen, adult   grades 9-UP

Purpose: Assesses learning styles of learning disabled and normal high school and college students.

Description: Multiple item paper-pencil test that indicates relative strengths and weaknesses in learning through different sensory channels. The inventory yields scores for visual, auditory, and tactile learning styles. Self-administered. Suitable for group use.

Untimed: 5-10 minutes

Range: Grades 9-adult

Scoring: Examiner evaluated

Cost: 25 record forms $5.00.

Publisher: Academic Therapy Publications

CAIN-LEVINE SOCIAL COMPETENCY SCALE
Leo F. Cain, Samuel Levine and Freeman F. Elzey

child, teen

Purpose: Measures social competence of trainable mentally-retarded children. Used for diagnosis, placement, planning, and training evaluation.

Description: 44 item scale of four aspects of social competence: self-help, initiative, social skills, and communication. Items are administered and evaluated by interviewing parents. Percentile norms based on mentally-retarded children are offered for chronological ages 5-13. Manual includes instructions for use of scales by teachers of clinicians. Examiner required. Not suitable for group use.

Untimed: Open ended

Range: Ages 5-13

Scoring: Examiner evaluated

Cost: Specimen set $2.25; manual $2.00; 25 scales $8.00.

Publisher: Consulting Psychologists Press, Inc.

CAMELOT BEHAVIORAL CHECKLIST
Ray W. Foster

all ages

Purpose: Evaluates adaptive behavior skills in mentally retarded persons. Used to plan and monitor educational programs for such individuals.

Description: 399 item paper-pencil checklist in 10 categories and 40 sub-categories. Among the skills measured are: self-help, physical development, home duties, vocational and economic behaviors, independent travel, numerical and communication skills, and social behavior responsibility. The examiner assigns each description a plus or minus value, to be transferred to a profile sheet which records and displays the student's progress and aids in sequencing of training objectives. The test is of limited use to the severely retarded. Examiner required.

Untimed: 20 minutes

Range: Child, adolescent, adult

Scoring: Hand key

Cost: Manual $3.50, checklist $.45 each.

Publisher: Camelot Behavioral Systems

COMPREHENSIVE LANGUAGE PROGRAM (CLP)
Peoria Association for Retarded Citizens

Mental Age 0-5

Purpose: Evaluates the language and pre-language skills of retarded and handicapped individuals who have language development problems. Used for diagnosis and remediation.

Description: Multiple item, oral response and task assessment test covering eight areas of language development: attending, manipulation of objects, mimicking, matching, identifying, labeling, following directions, and word combinations. A checklist records the student's entry-level achievement. The results provide a basis for subsequent instruction. There are 285 detailed lesson plans covering the eight areas. The plans are designed to be used for 20 to 30 minutes a day, 5 days a week. Record sheets record incremental progress. Examiner required. Not for group use.

Untimed: Varies

Range: 0-5 mental age

Scoring: Hand key

Cost: Starter set $190.00.

Publisher: Scholastic Testing Service, Inc.

COMPREHENSIVE TEST OF ADAPTIVE BEHAVIOR
Gary Adams

all ages

Purpose: Aids in the precise evaluation of handicapped individual's adaptive abilities. Used for placement, to determine where an individual stands in relation to others of the same age or handicap. Also helps in establishing the scope and sequence of training.

Description: 529 item paper-pencil inventory of adaptive behavior in six skill categories: self-help, home living, independent living, social, sensory motor, language concepts, and academic skills. Examiner checks off those skills which the individual has mastered based on observation of the individual's abilities, parent/guardian report, and formal testing. The test is inappropriate for normally developing individuals, since skills are sequenced

in the order handicapped individuals acquire them, not in normal developmental order. Examiner required. Not suitable for group use.

Untimed: Variable

Range: Ages birth-adult handicapped

Scoring: Examiner evaluated

Cost: Contact publisher.

Publisher: Charles E. Merrill Publishing Company

DEVELOPMENTAL LEARNING PROFILE
Cuyahoga Special Education Service Center

child, teen   grades K-12

Purpose: Provides an on-going record of the accomplishment of basic survival skills by educable mentally retarded children from grades K- 12. Used by teachers, psychologists, counselors and parents to determine long and short-term goals.

Description: 1,461 item paper-pencil examination administered to small groups over 13 years of schooling. Measures accomplishments in seven major curriculum areas: language arts, science, social studies, physical and perceptual development, career development, mathematics, and personal-social development. Performance objectives are sequentially arranged to each final objective to prevent skill development gaps. The examiner partially fills in squares to the left of performance objectives to signify "emergent" behaviors, and completely fills the squares to signify "consistent" behaviors. Each entry is color-coded to correspond to the student's level at the time the objective is met; gold for Primary, green for Intermediate, orange for Junior High, and blue for Senior High. Materials are contained in a 42-page spiral-bound book which has pages of graduated length to provide easy access to each of the assessment areas. The profile is specifically designed for educable mentally retarded children, but many of the skills included in it are part of regular school curricula. Examiner required.

Untimed: Not available

Range: Grades K-12 (Educable mentally retarded)

Scoring: Examiner evaluated

Cost: 1 copy-$4.85; 6 copies $24.85

Publisher: Creative Learning Systems, Inc.

THE DEVEREUX CHILD BEHAVIOR RATING SCALE (DCB)
George Spivack and Jules Spotts

child

Purpose: Assesses symptomatic behaviors of children ages 8-12. Used with mentally retarded and emotionally disturbed children for diagnostic and screening procedures, group placement decisions, and assessment of progress in response to specific programs or procedures.

Description: 97 item paper-pencil inventory assessing overt behavior patterns of children. The evaluator (parent or childcare worker living with the child) rates each item according to how he feels the subject's behavior compares to the behavior of normal children his age. Yields 17 scores: distractibility, poor self care, pathological use of senses, emotional detachment, social isolation, poor coordination and body tonus, incontinence, messiness-sloppiness, inadequate need for independence, unresponsiveness to stimulation, proneness to emotional upset, need for adult contact, anxious-fearful ideation, "impulse" ideation, inability to delay, social aggression, and unethical behavior. Self-administered by evaluator. Not for group use.

Untimed: 10-15 minutes

Range: Ages 6-12 years

Scoring: Examiner evaluated

Cost: Examination set (includes 25 scales, manual) $10.50; 1 manual $2.00; 25 scales at $.30 each; 50 scales at $.26 each; 200 scales at $.22 each; 500 scales at $.20 each.

Publisher: The Devereux Foundation

GOODMAN LOCK BOX
Refer to page 451.

KAUFMAN ASSESSMENT BATTERY FOR CHILDREN (K-ABC)
Alan S. Kaufman and Nadeen L. Kaufman

child

Purpose: Measures the intelligence and achievement. Defines intelligence as ability of children to process information and solve problems. Used for psychological and clinical assessment of the learning disabled and mentally retarded, minority group and preschool assessment, and neuropsychological research.

Description: 16 subtests of mental processing skills and achievement. There are: three subtests of sequential processing, seven subtests of simultaneous processing, and six subtests of achievement (acquired knowledge, reading, and arithmetic). Examiner presents to the child a test plate containing a stimulus item, gives a verbal direction, and the child responds. Directions may be given in the child's native language, or with gestures for the hearing impaired. Yields four major scores: sequential processing, simultaneous processing, mental processing composite, and achievement. Each score has a mean of 100 and a standard deviation of 15. National percentile ranks, age and grade equivalents, and sociocultural percentile ranks are also available. Standardization is based on 1980 census data. Separate scales for mental processing and achievement were normed on the same sample. Materials include test plates bound into three easel kits, interpretive manual, 118 photo series cards, seven matrix chips, nine triangles, 25 individual test records, and a container. Examiner must have necessary qualifications to use the test. Not for group use. A Spanish version available in 1984.

Untimed: Varies

Untimed: Preschool, 35-50 minutes; K-1, 50-70 minutes; 2nd and above, 75-85 minutes

Range: Ages 2½-12½

Scoring: Examiner evaluated; computer scored

Cost: Complete test kit $135.00; 25 test records $9.75

Publisher: American Guidance Service

KAUFMAN INFANT AND PRE-SCHOOL SCALE (KIPS)
Refer to page 9.

KHATENA-TORRANCE CREATIVE PERCEPTION INVENTORY
Joe Khantena and E. Paul Torrance

---

teen, adult

Purpose: Identifies creative people and diagnoses their strengths and weaknesses. Used to select individuals for special education programs and job assignments, and to evaluate the effects of instruction which includes creative components.

Description: Two 50 item paper-pencil subtests evaluate individual creativity by measuring the following

biographical components: What Kind Of Person Are You? (WKOPAY); and Something About Myself (SAM). WKOPAY uses 50 pairs of words arranged in forced choice format and requires the individual to choose the word from each pair which is most true for himself. The word pairs are chosen to represent bipolar characteristics (socially desirable versus undesirable, creative versus non-creative) and to measure the following personality characteristics: Acceptance of Authority, Self-Confidence, Inquisitiveness, Awareness of Others, and Disciplined Imagination.

SAM presents 50 statements and asks the takers to check those which apply to themselves. The statements reflect potential for creativity in three areas: Personality Traits, Use of Creative Thinking Strategies, and Creative Productions, and measure the following scales: Environmental Sensitivity, Initiative, Self Strength, Intellectuality, Individuality, and Artistry. WKOPAY and SAM together provide a creative index as well as individual scores for each of the characteristics measured. Suitable for group use.

Untimed: 5-15 minutes

Range: Age 13 and up

Scoring: Examiner evaluated

Cost: Complete kit (includes manual, 30 WKOPAY forms, 30 SAM forms and 30 scoring worksheets) $42.00.

Publisher: Stoelting Co.

LANGUAGE IMITATION TEST (LIT)
Paul Berry and Peter Mittler

Severely Ed. Retarded

Purpose: Assesses the speaking abilities of the severely educationally retarded (ESNS). Used by speech therapists and other teachers with special qualifications in language remediation.

Description: Multiple item oral response test measuring the linguistic competence of the ESNS. Evaluation of elicited imitative responses provided a psycholinguistic assessment of the ESNS individual's speaking abilities. The test has been used only on a limited basis with mildly handicapped (ESNM) and normal children. May be used with other tests of language ability for more complete diagnosis or as part of language remediation programs. Examiner required. Not for group use.
BRITISH PUBLISHER

Untimed: Not available

Range: Severely Educationally Subnormal (ESNS)

Scoring: Examiner evaluated

Cost: Specimen set (includes record form and manual) £4.50; 25 record forms £2.75; manual £4.30 (payment in sterling for all overseas orders.

Publisher: NFER-Nelson Printing Company

PICTORIAL TEST OF INTELLIGENCE
Refer to page 484.

PSYCHOLOGICAL STIMULUS RESPONSE
Refer to page 12.

SCHOOL CHILD STRESS SCALE (SCSS)
Refer to page 89.

SOCIAL AND PREVOCATIONAL INFORMATION BATTERY (SPIB)
A. Halpern, P. Raffeld, L.K. Irvin, and R. Link

EMR Students

Purpose: Assesses an educable mentally retarded student's knowledge of skills and competencies important for community adjustment. Used by educators as an evaluative device in programs for EMR students.

Description: 277 item paper-pencil test, orally administered, consisting of 9 subtests: job search skills, job related behavior, banking, budgeting, purchasing, home management, physical health care, hygiene and grooming, and functional signs. Student's response to each item is either true-false or picture selection. Results can be used to place student's in the Skills for Independent Living resource kit curriculum. Examiner required. Suitable for use with groups not exceeding 20.

Untimed: 15-25 minutes per subtest

Range: Educable mentally retarded junior and senior high school

Scoring: Hand key; computer scoring available

Cost: Specimen set (includes machine and hand scorable test book, manual with key, user's guide, class record sheet, test reviewer's guide) $7.25.

Publisher: CTB/McGraw-Hill

SOCIAL AND PREVOCATIONAL INFORMATION BATTERY- T (SPIB-T)
A. Halpern, R. Raffeld, L.K. Irvin, and R. Link

TMR Students

Purpose: Assesses a mild-to-moderately mentally retarded student's

knowledge of skills and competencies important for community adjustment. Used by educators to evaluate students and programs.

Description: 291 item, orally administered, paper-pencil test comprising nine subtests: job search skills, job related behavior, banking, budgeting, purchasing, home management, physical health care, hygiene and grooming, and functional signs. Results can be used to place students in Skills for Independent Living resource kit curriculum. Examiner required. Suitable for group use, not to exceed 20.

Untimed: 15-25 minutes per subtest

Range: Mild to moderate mentally retarded students

Scoring: Hand key

Cost: Specimen set (includes handscorable test book, pretest, manual with key, and technical summary) $7.25.

Publisher: CTB/McGraw-Hill

SOCIO-SEXUAL KNOWLEDGE AND ATTITUDES TEST (SSKAT)
Refer to page 79.

TARC ASSESSMENT SYSTEM FOR SEVERELY HANDICAPPED CHILDREN
Wayne Sailor and Bonnie Jean Mix

Severe Handicap

Purpose: Measures self-help, motor communication and social skills of severely handicapped children. Used to evaluate rehabilitation programs and to assess effectiveness of specific instruction.

Description: Multiple item observational examination in which the examiner spends several weeks observing a child's behavior in group situations, then uses an assessment inventory to score specific behaviors. The scores are transferred to a profile display sheet which relates behavior to both the child and to a standard sample, pointing out undeveloped and strong skills. Examiner must have professional training. Not suitable for group use.

Untimed: Open ended

Range: Severely and profoundly mentally retarded

Scoring: Examiner evaluated

Cost: Manual and 10 assessment sheets $7.25.

Publisher: H & H Enterprises

TESTS FOR EVERYDAY LIVING (TEL)
Andrew Halpern, Larry Irvin and Janet T. Landman

child, teen   grades 7-12

Purpose: Measures a low-functioning student's knowledge of skills necessary for everyday life. Also used by educators as a curriculum guide.

Description: 245 item, orally administered, paper-pencil test consisting of seven subtests: job search skills, job related behavior, health care, home management, purchasing habits, banking, and budget. A few performance items require reading skill. Results can be used to place students in Skills for Independent Living resource kit curriculum. Examiner required. Suitable for use with groups not exceeding 20.

Untimed: Not available

Range: Grades 7-12, especially low functioning

Scoring: Hand key

Cost: Specimen set $7.25; examiner's set (includes 20 test book, manual with answer key) $27.85.

Publisher: CTB/McGraw-Hill

T.M.R. SCHOOL COMPETENCY SCALES
Samuel Levine, Freeman F. Elzey, Paul Thromahlen, and Leo F. Cain

child, teen

Purpose: Assesses student adaptive skills in trainable mentally retarded (T.M.R.) classroom setting. Used to evaluate strengths and weaknesses and to measure progress.

Description: 91 or 103 item paper-pencil rating scale measuring five school competence skill areas: Perceptual-motor, Initiative-Responsibility, Cognition, Personal-Social, and Language. Items are rated on a 4 point scale by the classroom teacher. Materials include separate scales for each of five age groups: 5-7, 8-10, 11-13, 14-16, and 17 years and over. Scales are published in two forms, one for the two younger age groups (91 items), and one for the three older age groups (103 items). Examiner required. Not suitable for group use.

Untimed: Not available

Range: Ages 5-17 plus

Scoring: Examiner evaluated

Cost: Specimen set $3.75; manual $3.00; 25 scales $13.50 (specify age).

Publisher: Consulting Psychologists Press, Inc.

VALETT DEVELOPMENTAL SURVEY OF BASIC LEARNING ABILITIES
Robert E. Valett

child

Purpose: Assesses the developmental abilities of preschool and early primary children as an aid to formulating individual program plans for special education and remedial teaching.

Description: 233 item paper-pencil, test of a range of developmental abilities, including Motor Integration and Physical Development, Tactile Discrimination, Auditory Discrimination, Visual-Motor Coordination, Visual Discrimination, Language Development and Verbal Fluency, and Concept Development. Materials include a pupil workbook and a small kit of paper materials. Examiner, who should be a special educator or psychologist, selects items appropriate for child's development level and scale scores are plotted to yield a developmental profile. Examiner required. Not suitable for group use.

Untimed: 50 minutes

Range: Ages 2-7

Scoring: Examiner evaluated

Cost: Examiner's kit (includes test materials, record forms, workbook, manual) $17.00.

Publisher: Consulting Psychologists Press, Inc.

VALETT INVENTORY OF CRITICAL THINKING (VICTA)
Refer to page 469.

VOCATIONAL ADAPTATION RATING SCALES (VARS)
Robert G. Malgady, Peter R. Barcher, John Davis and George Towner

Mentally Retarded

Purpose: Measures "problem" behaviors among mentally retarded adolescents and adults in vocational settings. Used for curriculum development, Individualized Education Programs (IEPs) placement and evaluating readiness for "mainstreaming."

Description: 133 item paper-pencil inventory measuring the kind of maladaptive behavior likely to occur in vocational settings such as sheltered workshops, job facilities, or vocational training programs. The examiner (anyone familiar with the individual such as teachers, nurses or parents) responds to statements such as "Talks rudely or impolitely," by indicating the frequency of the behavior's occurance as "Never," "Sometimes," "Often," or "Regularly." The following six scales are measured: Verbal Manners, Communication Skills, Attendance and Punctuality, Interpersonal Behavior, Respect for Property, Rules and Regulations, and Grooming and Personal Hygiene. All six scales and the total score are profiled for both frequency and severity (a useful indicator of potential job impairment) in deciles and T-scores. Standardized on over 600 mildly to severely retarded adolescents and adults with norms which are unbiased with respect to sex, age or IQ. Examiner required. Suitable for group use.

Untimed: 20-30 minutes

Range: Mentally retarded

Scoring: Hand key

Cost: Complete kit (includes 10 booklets and manual) $9.80.

Publisher: Western Psychological Services

VOCATIONAL INFORMATION AND EVALUATION WORK SAMPLES (VIEWS)
Refer to page 683.

VOCATIONAL INTEREST AND SOPHISTICATION ASSESSMENT (VISA)
J.J. Parnicky, H. Kahn and A.D. Burdett

teen, adult

Purpose: Determines the vocational interests and job information of mildly retarded adolescents and young adults. Used for counseling, training projections and job placement.

Description: A verbal, picture book examination. The book for men evaluates aptitudes for work in garages, laundries, food service, maintenance, farm/grounds, materials handling, and industry. The book for women evaluates interests in business/clerical, housekeeping, food service, laundry, and sewing. Examiner required. Not for group use.

Untimed: 30-45 minutes

Range: Mildly retarded adolescents and young adults

Scoring: Examiner evaluated

Cost: Specimen set $10.00; manual $4.00; 75 page male picture book $5.00; 53 page female picture book $4.00; 50 inquiry forms $5.00; 25 male or female response forms $2.00; 25 male or female profile forms $3.00.

Publisher: The Nisonger Center-Ohio State University

VOCATIONAL INTEREST, TEMPERAMENT, AND APTITUDE SYSTEM (VITAS)

EMR Adults

Purpose: Assesses aptitudes, vocational interests, and work-related temperaments of disadvantaged and educably mentally retarded persons. Used for vocational guidance.

Description: Performance test of vocational aptitudes consisting of work samples in 21 areas: nuts, bolts, and washers assembly, packing matchbooks, tile sorting and weighing, collating material samples, verifying numbers, pressing linens, budget book assembly, nail and screw sorting, pipe assembly, filing by letters, lock assembly, circuit board inspection, calculating, message taking, bank teller, proofreading, payroll computation, census interviewing, spot welding, laboratory assistant, and drafting. Assessment process includes orientation, assessment, motivational group session, feedback and interest interview. Requires less than a sixth grade reading level. Materials include individually packaged hardware for all work samples. Examiner required. Suitable for group use, up to ten persons per week.

Untimed: 2½ days

Range: Disadvantaged persons and educable mentally retarded

Scoring: Examiner evaluated

Cost: Contact publisher.

Publisher: Vocational Research Institute-J.E.V.S.

Physically Handicapped

ARTHUR POINT SCALE OF PERFORMANCE TEST: REVISED FORM II
Refer to page 20.

THE BLIND LEARNING APTITUDE TEST (BLAT)
T. Ernest Newland

child, teen

Purpose: Evaluates the academic aptitude of blind children.

Description: 61 item verbal-touch test of tactile discrimination involving patterned dots and lines on 61 embossed plastic pages. The examiner guides the child's hand over the pages and they describe what they feel. Materials include a 39-page examiner's manual, a testing book, embossed pages, and 30 record forms. Examiner required. Not for group use.

Untimed: 20-45 minutes

Range: Ages 6-16 (Blind children)

Scoring: Hand key

Cost: Complete $50.00; manual $7.50.

Publisher: University of Illinois Press

FULL RANGE PICTURE VOCABULARY TEST (FRPV)
Refer to page 22.

GOCHNOUR IDIOM SCREENING TEST (GIST)
Elizabeth A. Gochnour

teen, adult

Purpose: Measures a deaf person's knowledge of figures of speech in the English language. Used by pathologist, audiologist and vocational counselors to assist in program planning.

Description: 20 idiom multiple-choice, pencil-paper test measuring comprehension of idioms by deaf persons. Examiner demonstrates how to mark test. Separate instructions are provided for oral- and manual- communicating subjects. Examiner required. Suitable for group use.

Untimed: 10 minutes

Range: Deaf adolescent, adult

Scoring: Examiner evaluated; may be computer scored

Cost: Manual $1.00; 20 test booklets $2.95.

Publisher: The Interstate Printers & Publishers, Inc.

GRASSI BASIC COGNITIVE EVALUATION
Refer to page 42.

HISKEY-NEBRASKA TEST OF LEARNING APTITUDE
Marshall S. Hiskey

child, teen

Purpose: Evaluates learning potential of deaf children and those with hearing, speech or language handicaps. Used to establish how deaf individuals compare with those who can hear.

Description: A battery of 11 subtests measuring visual- motor coordination, sequential memory, visual retention or stimuli in a series, visual discrimination and matching. The tests are: Bead Patterns, Memory for Color, Picture Identification, Picture Association, Paper Folding Patterns, Visual Attention Span, Block Patterns, Completion of Drawings, Memory for Digits, Puzzle Block Picture Analogies, and Spatial Reasoning. Scales have norms for comparing hearing and deaf children. Examiner required. Not suitable for group use.

Untimed: 50-60 minutes

Range: Ages 2½-18½

Scoring: Examiner evaluated

Cost: Complete set $88.00.

Publisher: The Hiskey-Nebraska Test

KAHN INTELLIGENCE TEST (KIT:EXP): A CULTURE- MINIMIZED EXPERIENCE
Refer to page 26.

KOHS BLOCK DESIGN TEST
Refer to page 481.

MARTIN DEVELOPMENTAL ABILITY TEST FOR THE BLIND
William T. Martin

child, teen

Purpose: Measures developmental level of blind or blind-retarded children, infant to 16 years.

Description: Paper-pencil checklist of basic functional performance measuring factors. Scored on seven subscales: Basic Developmental Skills, Body Imagery-Spatial Orientation, Psychomotor, Math and Problem Solving, Analogies, General Information and Rote Memory-Recall. Administered with several manipulative items. Materials include separate test forms for each subscale and a manual. Examiner required. Not suitable for group use. CANADIAN PUBLISHER

Untimed: Not available

Range: Blind or blind-retarded children

Scoring: Hand key

Cost: Complete test kit $202.62; 25 test forms (specify subtest name) $20.26; replacement manual $20.26.

Publisher: Institute of Psychological Research, Inc.

QUICK NEUROLOGICAL SCREENING TEST
Refer to page 49.

READING FREE VOCATIONAL INTEREST INVENTORY (R-FVII)
Refer to page 679.

(REVISED) PRE-READING SCREENING PROCEDURES
Beth H. Slingerland

child   grades K-1

Purpose: Evaluates young children of average to superior intelligence in order to locate those individuals who have difficulties with hearing, seeing or moving which might indicate a language disability. Used for determining what kinds of special instruction/counseling are needed.

Description: A series of 12 verbal-visual subtests that measure visual perception, visual discrimination, visual recall, visual-motor skills, auditory recall, auditory discrimination, auditory perception, letter knowledge; and language skills such as vocabulary, enunciation, comprehension or oral directions, oral expression, and recall of new words; also evaluates the child's motor coordination, hobbies and interests, attention span, and mental growth.
The test shows: (1) which children are ready for formal instruction in reading, writing and spelling and are ready to learn through conventional methods; (2) which children, who while appearing to be ready, reveal indications of a language disability and who need immediate multi-sensory instruction; (3) those who show language confusion or possible developmental lag but whose maturity indicates a need to begin strengthening their language background; (4) those children, regardless of age, who are unready to begin

reading instruction and who would benefit from more readiness and social development training. Materials consist of a test booklet (including 12 teacher observation/summary sheets and 12 practice pages), teacher's manual (including instructions and detachable answer key), and teacher's cards and chart (two sets of 5 x 10 cards and two copies of a wall chart used in the tests). Many of the tests require students to use a pencil for marking. The examiner first explains the directions to the students and then they proceed with the task. Individually administered, examiner evaluated. Suitable for group use.

Untimed: 2-3 hours

Range: Ages Kindergarten and first grade

Scoring: Hand key, examiner evaluated

Cost: 12 test booklets $12.00; teacher's manual $5.00; teacher's cards and chart $6.50; specimen set (1 includes teacher's manual and 1 test booklet) $5.25.

Publisher: Educator's Publishing Service, Inc.

SEQUIN-GODDARD FORM-BOARDS (TACTUAL PERFORMANCE TEST)
Refer to page 50.

STANFORD-OHWAKI-KOHS BLOCK DESIGN INTELLIGENCE TEST FOR THE BLIND: AMERICAN REVISION
Refer to page 34.

THE TACTILE TEST OF BASIC CONCEPTS
Refer to page 467.

TEST OF SYNTACTIC ABILITIES
Refer to page 599.

VISUAL-AURAL DIGIT SPAN TEST (VADS)
Refer to page 508.

WILLIAMS INTELLIGENCE TEST FOR CHILDREN WITH DEFECTIVE VISION
Refer to page 487.

Special Education

BARCLAY CLASSROOM ASSESSMENT SYSTEMS (BCAS)
Refer to page 632.

BESSEMER SCREENING TEST
Evelyn V. Jones and Gary L. Sapp

child, teen

Purpose: Identifies children ages 7-14 years who may require special education services. Used to screen the learning disabled, emotionally disturbed, mentally retarded, and academically gifted.

Description: Five paper-pencil subtests require the student to: write his own name, produce a human figure drawing, read words or symbols, reproduce abstract designs, and perform mathematic computations. The subtests are arranged in order of increasing difficulty and are similar to tasks the student would encounter in a regular classroom. Examiner required. Suitable for group use.

Timed: Maximum 15 minutes

Range: Ages 7-14

Scoring: Examiner evaluated

Cost: Complete kit (includes 15 student booklets, 30 scoring sheets and manual) $12.00.

Publisher: Stoelting Co.

BRISTOL SOCIAL ADJUSTMENT GUIDES (BSAG)
Refer to page 614.

DIAGNOSTIC SCREENING TEST: ACHIEVEMENT--SOCIAL STUDIES, SCIENCE, LITERATURE and the ARTS (DST: ACHIEVEMENT)
Thomas D. Gnagey and Patricia A. Gnagey

child, teen   grades Nursery-14

Purpose: Measures students' basic knowledge of science, social studies, and literature and the arts to help determine course of study for special education students.

Description: 108 item multiple-choice, paper-pencil test measuring student conceptual level in the three subject areas, along with an approximate mental age. The test also provides a pattern analysis of student motivation, cultural versus organic retardation, cultural deprivation, reading and study skill problems, and possession of practical versus formal knowledge. The examiner explains procedure to individuals or groups, and reads the test if students have poor reading skills. Includes pretest, percentile ranks, T scores and grade equivalents. Examiner required. Suitable for group use.

Untimed: 5-15 minutes

Range: Grades Nursery-14

Scoring: Hand key

Cost: Manual and 20 test forms $14.00; 100 additional test

forms $25.00.
Publisher: Facilitation House

JOSEPH PRE-SCHOOL AND PRI-MARY SELF-CONCEPT SCREENING TEST (JPPSST)
Refer to page 43.

SURVIVAL SKILLS PROFILE
Cuyahoga Special Education Service Center

child, teen   grades K-12

Purpose: Provides an on-going record of the accomplishment of emotionally disturbed children in social survival skills from grades K-12. Used by teachers, psychologists, counselors and parents for planning short and long-term goals.

Description: 412 item paper-pencil examination administered to small groups over 13 years of schooling. Measures skills in two areas: those related directly to daily living, such as telling time, using maps and calendars and nutritional knowledge; and those related to personal development, such as handling criticism and controlling aggression. The examiner marks squares to the left of performance objectives with a slash to indicate "emergent" behavior, or with an 'X' to indicate "mastery." Materials are contained in a spiral-bound 24-page booklet which has pages of graduated length to provide easy access to each of the assessment areas. The profile is designed for use with emotionally disturbed children, so care should be taken to establish guidelines in the recording of behaviors to avoid observer subjectivity. It may be used in conjunction with either the Developmental Learning Profile or the Student Learning Profile. Examiner required.

Untimed: Not available

Range: Grades K-12 (emotionally disturbed children)

Scoring: Examiner evaluated

Cost: 1 copy $4.85; 6 copies $24.85; 100-$2.50 each

Publisher: Creative Learning Systems, Inc.

THE TEST OF PRACTICAL KNOWLEDGE (TPK)
J. Lee Wiederholt and Stephen C. Larsen

teen   grades 8-12

Purpose: Identifies high school students who are less knowledgable than their peers about important daily living skills, determining particular strengths and weaknesses. Used to document student's progress in special programs.

Description: Paper-pencil test consisting of three subtests: Personal Knowledge (relating to information needed to deal independently with day-to-day living), Social Knowledge (relating to social interactions, community services, and leisure activities), and Occupational Knowledge (relating to information needed to operate successfully in job situations). Examiner required. Suitable for group use.

Untimed: 35-40 minutes

Range: Grades 8-12

Scoring: Hand key

Cost: Complete set (includes examiner manual, 25 student booklets, 50 profile sheets, scoring stencil, storage box) $42.00. Components available for separate purchase.

Publisher: PRO-ED

Speech, Hearing and Visual

Auditory

ADVANCED TESTS OF CENTRAL AUDITORY ABILITIES
Arthur Flowers

all ages   grades 2-UP

Purpose: Measures central auditory abilities of low-achieving children and adults to screen them for general hearing-perception problems and to isolate specific auditory phonemic identification deficiencies.

Description: 56 item, two-part, verbal test measuring auditory closure and figure-ground (ability to listen selectively against background noise). Part I has 28 items dealing with competing messages. Part II, also 28 items, assesses low pass filtered speech. All items and examiner instructions are on audio tape. The examiner plays the tape and the individual responds verbally. This is the same as the Flowers-Costello test, only arranged for adults. Examiner required. Not for group use.

Untimed: 8-10 minutes

Range: Grades 2-high school and adult

Scoring: Examiner evaluated

Cost: Tape and 12 booklets $59.50.

Publisher: Perceptual Learning Systems

AUDITORY DISCRIMINATION TEST, 1973
Joseph M. Wepman

child

Purpose: Measures auditory discrimi-

nation ability of children ages 5-8. Used to identify specific auditory learning disabilities for possible remediation.

Description: Oral response test in which children are verbally presented pairs of words and asked to discriminate between them. Predicts articulatory speech defects and certain remedial reading problems. Identical to the 1958 Edition of the same test, except for scoring. In this revised version, scoring is based on a "correct" score basis rather than the "error" basis of the original edition. The new manual contains: standardization tables on 5, 6, 7 and 8-year-olds, a five point rating scale, an interpretation section discussing how the test results may be used, reports on research using the test, and selected references. Examiner required. Not for group use.

Untimed: 10-15 minutes

Range: Ages 5-8

Scoring: Hand key

Cost: Complete kit (includes 20 each form IA and IIA and manual) $13.10.

Publisher: Western Psychological Services

AUDITORY INTEGRATIVE ABILITIES TEST (AIAT)
Carole Grote

child

Purpose: Diagnoses disorders of auditory perceptual as they relate to language-based learning disabilities in children. Used in conjunction with other tests to develop a remedial program.

Description: 30 item paper-pencil test consisting of three subtests. The auditory-motor subtest requires the student to clap hands to sound patterns. The auditory-graphic subtest requires the student to chart sound patterns on index cards. The auditory-verbal subtest requires the student to orally reproduce sound patterns. A cassette tape, included with the material is used to administer the test. The student uses score sheets, also provided, to record his responses. Since the tasks involved may be new and unfamiliar, some pretest training is recommended and provided for in the manual. Examiner required. Suitable for group use.

Untimed: Not available

Range: Ages 6-9

Scoring: Hand key

Cost: Program contains one cassette tape, 25 individual scoring sheets, index cards, and examiner's manual $14.50; 25 additional score sheets $3.30.

Publisher: Educational Activities, Inc.

AUDITORY MEMORY SPAN TEST
Joseph M. Wepman and Anne Morency

child

Purpose: Measures the ability of children ages 5-8 years to retain and recall words as auditory units, an essential capacity for learning how to speak and read accurately. Used to identify specific auditory learning disabilities.

Description: Oral response test assesses the development of a child's ability to retain and recall familiar, isolated words received aurally. The test items are based on the most frequently used words in the spoken vocabulary of five-year-old children. Norms are provided for children ages 5, 6, 7, and 8. Available in two equivalent forms, I and II. Examiner required. Not for group use.

Untimed: 5-10 minutes

Range: Ages 5-8

Scoring: Hand key

Cost: Complete kit (includes 20 each form I and II and manual) $13.10.

Publisher: Western Psychological Services

AUDITORY POINTING TEST
Refer to page 547.

AUDITORY SEQUENTIAL MEMORY TEST
Joseph M. Wepman and Anne Morency

child

Purpose: Measures the ability of children ages 5-8 years to remember and repeat what they have just heard. Used to diagnose specific auditory learning disabilities.

Description: Oral response test assesses a child's ability to repeat from immediate memory an increasing series of digits in the exact order of their verbal presentation. Norms are provided for children ages 5, 6, 7, and 8. Valuable for determining a child's readiness for learning to read and speak with accuracy. Related to spelling and arithmetic achievement. Available in two equivalent forms, I and II. Examiner required. Not for group use.

Untimed: 5 minutes

Range: Ages 5-8

Scoring: Hand key

Cost: Complete kit (includes 20 each forms I and II and manual) $13.10.

Publisher: Western Psychological Services

DENVER AUDIOMETRIC SCREENING TEST (DAST)
Amelia F. Drumwright

all ages

Purpose: Detects those children with

hearing deficiencies to screen for 25dB loss. Those who fail the test are referred for additional examination.

Description: A function test in which a trained examiner creates a tone with an audiometer and checks the child's response. The child is asked to indicate whether it has heard the tone at different decibel levels. Materials consist of test forms and manual. Examiner and audiometer required.

Untimed: 5-10 minutes

Range: Ages 3 years and older

Scoring: Examiner evaluated

Cost: 25 tests $1.75; manual $6.50.

Publisher: Ladoca Publishing Foundation

FLOWERS AUDITORY TEST OF SELECTIVE ATTENTION (FATSA)
Arthur Flowers

child   grades 1-6

Purpose: Determines a child's ability to understand what is being said; a measure of auditory attention deficit to use as a screening tool for possible remedial work.

Description: 35 item paper-pencil test consisting of three practice items and 32 test items which measure central hearing function and selective attention skills. The child is given a directive on tape and then marks one of seven "Simon Says..." statements most appropriate to the recorded directive. An auditory deficit score is thus obtained and remedial instruction is planned. Examiner required. Suitable for group use.

Untimed: 23 minutes

Range: Grades 1-6

Scoring: Hand key

Cost: Complete kit (includes 12 booklets) $69.96.

Publisher: Perceptual Learning Systems

FLOWERS-COSTELLO TESTS OF CENTRAL AUDITORY ABILITY
Arthur Flowers and Mary Rose Costello

child   grades K-6

Purpose: Identifies kindergarten and first-grade children who have hearing-perception problems and establishes probabilities for future reading success. For low-achieving elementary school students, it measures central auditory abilities in order to isolate specific auditory phonemic identification deficiencies.

Description: 48 item, two-part, verbal test measuring auditory closure and figure-ground (ability to listen selectively against background noise). Part I has 24 items dealing with low pass filtered speech. Part II, also 24 items, assesses how the child handles competing messages. All items and examiner instructions are on audio tape. The examiner plays the tape and the taker responds verbally. For kindergarten students, pictures are shown, a statement (i.e., We put a shoe on our...') is made, pictures are shown, and the child points to the object not mentioned. The test is designed for low achieving children whose CAA scores suggest a specific learning disability which may be presumed to interfere with the child's progress. Examiner required. Not for group use.

Untimed: 15 minutes

Range: Grades K-6

Scoring: Examiner evaluated

Cost: Basic kit $89.50; 30 test score sheets $3.50.

Publisher: Perceptual Learning System

GOLDMAN-FRISTOE-WOODCOCK AUDITORY SKILLS TEST BATTERY
Ronald Goldman, Macalyne Fristoe and Richard W. Woodcock

all ages

Purpose: Diagnoses a wide range of auditory skills. Useful for instructional planning.

Description: 12 subtests measure auditory selective attention, diagnostic auditory discrimination, auditory memory, and sound-symbol skills. Examiner presents a test plate to the subject and records the response. The Auditory Selective Attention Test assesses the ability to attend under increasingly difficult listening conditions. The Diagnostic Auditory Discrimination Test-Part 1 meets the need for an assessment of an individual's ability to discriminate between specific speech sounds that are frequently confused. The Diagnostic Auditory Discrimination Test—Part II is used with those who have experienced difficulty with speech—sound discrimination in Part I. The Auditory Memory Tests assess three aspects of auditory memory performance: recognition memory, memory for content, and memory for sequence. The Sound Symbol Tests assess several abilities underlying the development of written language skills. Scores derived are age equivalents, age-based percentile ranks, standard scores, and stanines. Materials include four manuals, 25 response forms in each of the five easels, test plates bound into five easels (diagnostic auditory discrimination tests are in two easels), one test tape per easel, 25 battery profile forms, and technical manual. The prerecorded audiotapes facilitate administration and maintain a standardized presentation procedure. Examiner required. Not for group use.

Untimed: 15 minutes per subtest

Range: Ages 3-80

Scoring: Examiner evaluated

Cost: Complete test battery (5 easel-kits) $142.50; 25 battery profiles

$6.50; 25 record forms $6.00.

Publisher: American Guidance Service

GOLDMAN-FRISTOE-WOODCOCK TEST OF AUDITORY DISCRIMINATION
Ronald Goldman, Macalyne Fristoe and Richard W. Woodcock

all ages

Purpose: Assesses an individual's ability to discriminate speech sounds in quiet and in noise. Screens for deficiencies in speech- sound discrimination that may contribute to learning difficulties.

Description: Two part test. Examiner presents test plate containing four drawings to the subject, using an audio cassette for standardized presentation. The subject responds to a stimulus word by pointing to one of the drawings. Total error scores can be converted to age-based percentile ranks and standard scores. An error analysis may be completed to explore further the types of errors made on either subtest. Materials include test plates bound in an easel, manual, 50 response forms and test audio-cassette. Examiner required. Not for group use.

Untimed: 20-30 minutes

Range: Ages 3-84

Scoring: Examiner evaluated

Cost: Complete kit $36.56; 50 response forms $5.75.

Publisher: American Guidance Service

THE HOLLIEN-THOMPSON GROUP HEARING TEST
Harry Hollien and Carl Thompson

child

Purpose: Identifies children ages 5-8 suffering from a loss of hearing. Used by educators to screen groups of children to determine which children are in need of further individual testing.

Description: Multiple item hearing discrimination test consisting of a 45-page test booklet or original designs in two equated forms for group testing (up to 40 children). Norms for each age group available. Materials consist of manual, guide, cue sheet for administration, scoring template, poster and pack of 50 test forms. Examiner required. Suitable for group use.
CANADIAN PUBLISHER

Untimed: 1-2 minutes

Range: Ages 5-8

Scoring: Hand key; examiner evaluated

Cost: Complete kit (includes manual, administrator's guide cue sheet for administration, scoring template, test poster, 50 test forms-answer sheets) $50.00; 50 additional test forms $8.00.

Publisher: Institute of Pyschological Research, Inc.

LANGUAGE STRUCTURAL AUDITORY RETENTION (LARS)
Luis Carlson

all ages

Purpose: Assesses ability of children and adults to maintain short-term memory for linguistically significant information. Used to detect the inability to recall when there is an unfamiliar or nonsense word in an otherwise familiar sentence.

Description: 58 item test that determines recall of information in a linguistic context when there are two conditions of familiar words, or an unfamiliar word or two nonsense words, in the stimuli. The test provides an estimate of the optimum length of an aural message from which a person may profit during a learning experience. Two equivalent forms allow test-retest without learning effect. Examiner required. Not for group use.

Untimed: 12-15 minutes

Range: Ages 3.7-adult

Scoring: Hand key

Cost: Manual $10.00; 25 form A or B $6.00; specimen set $6.00.

Publisher: Academic Therapy Publications

LINDAMOOD AUDITORY CONCEPTUALIZATION TEST (LAC)
Charles H. and Patricia C. Lindamood

all ages   grades PRE-UP

Purpose: Measures an individual's ability to discriminate one speech sound from another and to perceive the number, order, and sameness or difference of speech sounds in sequences. Used to diagnose auditory-conceptual dysfunctions and to determine the need for remedial training.

Description: 40 item verbal response test in which the subject arranges colored blocks (each symbolizing one speech sound) in a row to represent a sound pattern spoken by the examiner. The color of the blocks indicates sameness or difference with a repeated sound symbolized by the same color block and a different sound by a different color. Materials include the manual, cassette, 24 wooden blocks in six colors, test forms, and examiner's cue sheets. A separate product, "Auditory Discrimination in Depth" provides a training program. The LAC, which is not appropriate for deaf subjects, is to be administered individually by an examiner. Not suitable in group use. Available in Spanish.

Untimed: Not available

Range: Grades Preschool-adult

Scoring: Examiner evaluated

Cost: Complete set $25.00.

Publisher: Teaching Resources Corporation

MONASH DIAGNOSTIC TEST OF LIPREADING ABILITY

all ages   grades K-UP

Purpose: Measures basic lipreading abililites of hearing impaired individuals from Kindergarten to adult age levels. Used for both screening and diagnostic purposes.

Description: Multiple item paper-pencil test administered via color videotape contains three subtests to assess lipreading of words, phonemes or nonsense words, and sentences. Three forms are available: a Screening Test form, and two parallel forms of a Diagnostic Test. The Screening Test is designed for group use and determines basic lipreading ability, while the Diagnostic Test is individually administered and identifies aspects of lipreading requiring special attention or remediation. The tapes include optional soundtracks to examine the usefulness of aided hearing in lipreading. Materials include: (reproduced on request) color videocassette, three training plates, response forms and booklets, record forms, score keys, and manual. Examiner required.
AUSTRALIAN PUBLISHER

Untimed: Not available

Range: Kindergarten-adult

Scoring: Examiner evaluated

Cost: Contact publisher.

Publisher: The Australian Council for Educational Research Limited

NON-LANGUAGE MULTI-MENTAL TEST
Refer to page 28.

OLIPHANT AUDITORY DISCRIMINATION MEMORY TEST
Genevive Oliphant

child, teen   grades 1-8

Purpose: Evaluates the ability of grade school children to hear and discriminate sounds and words. Used to identify those in need of further testing, and to diagnose the relationship between perceptual problems and learning disabilities.

Description: 20 item paper-pencil test measures how well students discriminate sounds and remember what they hear. Each item presents the student with two words, which are either alike or minimally different. A third word is then spoken by the examiner and the student is asked to decide whether that word is the same as the first or second words of if all three words are the same. The words are all single-syllable in a consonant-vowel-consonant format. Examiner required. Suitable for group use.

Untimed: 30-45 minutes

Range: Grades 1-8

Scoring: Examiner evaluated

Cost: Complete kit (includes 12 tests and 2 sheets of teacher directions) $3.30.

Publisher: Educators Publishing Service, Inc.

PEABODY PICTURE VOCABULARY TEST-REVISED (PPVT-R)
Lloyd M. Dunn and Leota M. Dunn

all ages

Purpose: Measures hearing vocabulary for standard American English, estimates verbal ability and scholastic aptitude. Used with non-English speaking students; to screen for mental retardation or giftedness; as part of a comprehensive battery; and to screen applicants for jobs requiring good aural vocabulary.

Description: 175 item "point-to" response test measuring receptive vocabulary in English. Test items, arranged in order of increasing difficulty, consist of plates of four pictures. Subjects are shown a plate and asked to point to the picture which corresponds to the stimulus word. Only those plates within a subject's ability range are administered. Age-based norms include: standard scores, percentile ranks, stanines, and age equivalents. Complete kit includes: 175 test plates bound in an easel, manual, 25 individual record forms, and shelf box. Available in two forms, L and M. Special Plastic Plate Edition available. Examiner required. Not for group use.

Untimed: Not available

Range: Ages 2½-40

Scoring: Examiner evaluated

Cost: Complete kit, form L or M, Regular Edition $29.50; Special Edition $37.50; technical supplement for both forms $15.50; 25 test records, form L or M $4.25.

Publisher: American Guidance Service

SCREENING TEST FOR AUDITORY COMPREHENSION OF LANGUAGE (STACL)
Elizabeth Carrow-Woolfolk

child

Purpose: Identifies young children who have receptive language problems in English or Spanish. Used as a screening instrument for the Test for Auditory Comprehension (TACL).

Description: 25 item oral, paper-pencil test containing items from the TACL covering vocabulary, morphology, and syntax. The child responds to the examiner's oral stimuli by marking correct responses in indi-

vidual booklets. The test is not appropriate for deaf subjects. Examiner required. Suitable for group use. Available in Spanish.

Untimed: Not available

Range: Ages 3.0-7.11

Scoring: Examiner evaluated

Cost: Complete $8.00 (Note: This test will be discontinued in 1984).

Publisher: Teaching Resources Corporation

SCREENING TEST FOR AUDITORY PERCEPTION (STAP): REVISED 1981
Geraldine M. Kimmel and Jack Wahl

child   grades 1-6

Purpose: Assesses weaknesses in five areas of auditory perception in elementary school and remedial students. Used to identify those who are performing below grade or age level.

Description: A series of multiple item paper-pencil subtests measuring ability to discriminate among long versus short vowels, single versus blend initial consonants, rhyming versus non-rhyming words, same versus different rhythmic patterns, and same versus different words. In scoring, abnormal limits indicate a student's need for remedial attention or further testing. Materials include suggested remedial activities for each of the five skill areas tapped. Available on cassette tape for uniform administration. Examiner required. Suitable for group use.

Untimed: 45 minutes

Range: Grades 1-6 and those in remedial classes

Scoring: Hand key

Cost: Manual $7.50; 50 record forms $5.00.

Publisher: Academic Therapy
Publications

SHORT TERM AUDITORY RETRIVAL AND STORAGE TEST (STARS)
Arthur Flowers

child   grades 1-6

Purpose: Identifies a child's short-term ability to remember and use what is heard. Used as a guide to possible remedial help.

Description: 55 item paper-pencil test to isolate auditory retrieval and storage problems. The examiner plays a tape recording, provided with the test materials, the child listens and marks the appropriate pictures in the test booklet. A low score indicates a problem and the need for a remedial program. Examiner required. Suitable for group use.

Untimed: 16 minutes

Range: Grades 1-6

Scoring: Examiner evaluated

Cost: Complete set $69.50.

Publisher: Perceptual Learning Systems

STYCAR HEARING TESTS (REVISED EDITION, 1968)
Mary Sheridan

child

Purpose: Assesses child's capacity to hear with comprehension in common-place situations. Used for preliminary screening of very young or mentally handicapped children.

Description: Multiple item series of simple clinical auditory screening tests. Child responds to toys and pictures. Manual includes drawings of babies and young children responding to the tests. Spoken picture vocabulary cards are laminated to facilitate cleaning. Materials include toy blocks, rattle, plane, boat, cars, and dolls. Available to medical doctors, speech therapists, and teachers of deaf, blind and physically handicapped. Examiner required. Not suitable for group use.
BRITISH PUBLISHER

Untimed: Not available

Range: Ages 6 months-7 years

Scoring: Examiner evaluated

Cost: Complete kit (includes all toys, coloured square card, 5 picture vocabulary cards, children's cutlery set, 25 record forms, manual) £16.25 (payment in sterling for all overseas orders).

Publisher: NFER-Nelson Publishing Company

TEST FOR AUDITORY COMPREHENSION OF LANGUAGE (TACL)
Elizabeth Carrow-Woolfolk

child

Purpose: Analyzes a child's receptive language, including vocabulary, morphology, and syntax. Used for language therapy.

Description: 101 item point-and-tell test. The child responds to pictorial stimuli, each containing three line drawings depicting the correct response, the incorrect response, and a decoy item, by pointing to one of the three items. The test is not appropriate for deaf subjects. Materials include the pictures, and instructions and scoring/analysis forms. Examiner required. Not for group use. Available in Spanish.

Untimed: Not available

Range: Ages 3.0-6.11

Scoring: Examiner evaluated

Cost: $50.00 (Note: Revised edition is currently being developed and standardized for 1984 publication).

Publisher: Teaching Resources Corporation

TEST FOR AUDITORY FIGURE-GROUND DISCRIMINATION (TAFD)-1981

child

Purpose: Measures ability to attend to one sound and to perceive it in relation to, but separate from, competing sounds. Used for educational evaluation.

Description: Seven subtest measure of auditory perception of specific sounds against a variety of background sounds: a bicycle bell against traffic noise, or speech against background music. Child responds verbally to tape recorded stimuli. Materials include a cassette tape recording of the TAFD. Available to professional personnel attached to education departments and to others who can document their expertise. Examiner required. Not suitable for group use.
SOUTH AFRICAN PUBLISHER

Timed: 1 hour

Range: Ages 5-10

Scoring: Examiner evaluated

Cost: Contact publisher (all orders from outside The RSA will be dealt with on merit).

Publisher: Human Sciences Research Council

TESTING-TEACHING MODULE OF AUDITORY DISCRIMINATION (TTMAD)
Victoria Risko

child   grades K-6

Purpose: Determines auditory discrimination in elementary school children and increases proficiency in those skills. Used in developmental, corrective, or remedial programs which focus on auditory discrimination and blending.

Description: Multiple item paper-pencil, verbal assessment in two sections. Section one is a 125 item diagnostic instrument consisting of subtests in these six areas: initial and final consonants, initial and final blends and diagraphs, vowels and vowel combinations. The second section is a series of 450 games and activities to increase proficiency. When skill deficiencies are detected by diagnostic testing, the examiner refers to the teaching activities in the manual. The games and activities, which correspond directly to each skill assessed, are coded by whether they are appropriate for individualized or group instruction, or both. Individual item analysis sheets are provided. Examiner required. Suitable for group use.

Untimed: 20-30 minutes

Range: Grades K-6

Scoring: Examiner evaluated

Cost: Manual $7.50; 25 recording forms $6.00; specimen set $7.50.

Publisher: Academic Therapy Publications

TIP AND DIP TESTS FOR THE HEARING OF SPEECH BY YOUNG CHILDREN
Bruce M. Siegenthaler and George S. Haspiel

child

Purpose: Measures hearing threshold and speech discrimination. Used to evaluate hearing loss with and without amplification, and for medical therapy.

Description: Two test battery. The threshold of hearing test (TIP) contains 25 items in A and B versions which measure hearing threshold by identification of pictures. The test booklet has five pictures per page of objects with names that do not sound alike (blocks, doll, tree, watch). The examiner names an object and the child points to the appropriate picture. The discrimination of speech test (DIP) uses 48 sets of pictures of items the names of which have similar sounds (bear, pear). The child points to the one described by the examiner. The TIP test obtains a threshold of speech hearing score, and DIP contains a discrimination score. Must be administered by a trained audiologist in a sound room. Not for group use.

Untimed: TIP, 5 minutes; DIP, 7 minutes

Range: Ages 3-12, older (when other word tests have not been satisfactory in obtaining responses i.e. stroke victims)

Scoring: Hand key

Cost: Complete (includes picture book with 2 sections, scoring form, response sheets, manual) $15.00.

Publisher: Speech and Hearing Clinic

THE TOKEN TEST FOR CHILDREN
Frank DiSimoni

child

Purpose: Measures functional listening ability in children and identifies receptive language dysfunction. Used in language therapy.

Description: 20 item test in which the child arranged wooden tokens in response to the examiner's oral directions. In addition to the tokens, the materials include the manual and scoring forms. Results can be used to indicate a need for further testing of lexicon and syntax or to rule out language impairment in a child having reading difficulties. Materials include the tokens, manual and scor-

ing forms. The test is not appropriate for deaf subjects. Examiner required. Not for group use.

Untimed: 8 minutes

Range: Ages 3.0-12.5

Scoring: Examiner evaluated

Cost: Complete $25.00.

Publisher: Teaching Resources Corporation

TORONTO TESTS OF RECEPTIVE VOCABULARY-TTRV-(ENGLISH/SPANISH)
Allen S. Toronto

child

Purpose: Measures a child's receptive vocabulary skills in both English and Spanish. Used to identify bilingual children with significantly below age level abilities in both languages.

Description: 40 item oral test with three line drawings for point-response. Standardized to ages 4-10; separate norms are provided for each group and age level. Examiner required. Not suitable for group use. Available in Spanish.

Untimed: 15 minutes

Range: Ages 4-10

Scoring: Hand key; examiner evaluated

Cost: Complete kit (includes stimuli and response pictures, 30 scoring forms) $31.20; 30 scoring forms $3.50.

Publisher: National Educational Laboratory Publisher's, Inc.

TREE/BEE TEST OF AUDITORY DISCRIMINATION (TREE/BEE TEST)
Janet B. Fudala

all ages

Purpose: Measures auditory discrimination abilities in children and adults. Used as a basis for further testing and remediation.

Description: A multiple item, oral response test in which the subjects are shown stimulus pictures and are asked to point to, or mark, the proper picture as the examiner says the word or phrase (e.g., a tree, a bee, or a key). Four equivalent forms are provided for test-retest situation. There are two sets of stimulus pictures and two sets of stimulus items, which can be mixed. A flip-flop book is available for individual administration. No reading or writing is required of the subject. Examiner required. Suitable for group use.

Untimed: 10 minutes

Range: Ages 3-9 (normed) through adults (applications, not normed)

Scoring: Hand key

Cost: Manual $7.50; 10 stimulus pictures form A or form B $7.50; 10 recording forms 1 or form 2 $1.50; flip book of individual stimulus pictures $15.00; specimen set $7.50.

Publisher: Academic Therapy Publications

WEPMAN AUDITORY DISCRIMINATION TEST
Joseph M. Wepman

child

Purpose: Measures auditory discrimination ability of children ages 5-8. Used to identify specific auditory learning disabilities for possible remediation.

Description: Oral response test in which children are verbally presented pairs of words and asked to discriminate between them. Predicts articulatory speech defects and certain remedial reading problems, and has complete phonetic and phonemic balance. Available in two equivalent forms, I and II, for retesting and/or measuring therapy progress. Examiner required. Not for group use.

Untimed: 10-15 minutes

Range: Ages 5-8

Scoring: Hand key

Cost: Complete kit (includes 20 of each form I and II and manual) $13.10.

Publisher: Western Psychological Services

WORD INTELLIGIBILITY BY PICTURE IDENTIFICATION (WIPI)
Mark Ross and Jay Lerman

all ages

Purpose: Measures the ability of the hearing impaired to discriminate between words. Useful in assessing auditory comprehension in young children and stroke patients.

Description: Multiple item picture identification test. Test includes 25 plates of six pictures from which four different but equal word lists are constructed. Examiner reads aloud the name of an object on the card and the subject is asked to identify the object verbally. Examiner required. Not suitable for group use.

Untimed: 20-25 minutes

Range: Ages 6-adult (hearing impaired)

Scoring: Hand key

Cost: Combination set (includes test booklet and 3 pads of score sheets) $23.00.

Publisher: Stanwix House

Speech and Language

ARIZONA ARTICULATION PROFICIENCY SCALE: REVISED
Janet Barker Fudala

child

Purpose: Measures the articulation abilities of children ages 3-12 years. Used to identify those in need of speech therapy.

Description: 48 item oral response measure of articulation performance in which the child responds to pictures and sentences presented on 48 durable plastic-coated stimulus cards. The examiner records all errors in the protocol booklet. A sentence test is provided as an alternative for use with older children. Scores provided include "total articulatory proficiency" and "percentage of improvement." Norms are provided for children ages 3-12 years. A Survey Form is available for compiling an abbreviated articulation record of ten children on a single sheet. Examiner required.

Untimed: 10-15 minutes

Range: Ages 3-12

Scoring: Hand key

Cost: Kit (set of reusable picture test cards, 25 protocol booklets, 10 survey forms, manual) $27.80.

Publisher: Western Psychological Services

ASSESSMENT OF CHILDREN'S LANGUAGE COMPREHENSION (ACLC)
Rochana Foster, Jane J. Giddan and Joel Stark

child

Purpose: Identifies receptive language difficulties in young children to provide guidelines for remediation of language disorders.

Description: 41 item verbal test of language comprehension. Measures understanding of core vocabulary and combination of language elements. Materials include 41 spiral-bound stimulus cards. These are presented to the child, who points to an appropriate picture in response to a word or phrase from the examiner. A 17 item ACLC Group Form has been developed for classroom screening. Examiner required. Not for group use. Available in Spanish.

Timed: 10-15 minutes

Range: Ages 3-6 years 5 months

Scoring: Examiner evaluated

Cost: Complete kit $15.50 (includes card set, manual, 1 pad of recording sheets).

Publisher: Consulting Psychologists Press, Inc.

ASSESSMENT OF FLUENCY IN SCHOOL-AGE CHILDREN (AFSC)
Julia Thompson

child, teen   grades K-12

Purpose: Evaluates a child's speech deficiency. Helpful in assessing those who stutter. Used for therapy and school programs.

Description: 37 item, paper-pencil test measuring expressive language, physiological components, (oral motor and breath control), and self-awareness of disfluencies. Material needed: tape recorder, picture stimulus, stop watch, test form and resource guide. Must be administered by a speech pathologist. Not suitable for group use.

Untimed: 45 minutes

Range: K-12

Scoring: Examiner evaluated

Cost: Complete set (includes resource guide, 32 assessment forms, pad of 32 parent interview forms, pad of 32 teacher evaluation forms, pad of 32 dismissal forms, and carrying case) $32.50.

Publisher: The Interstate Printers & Publishers, Inc.

THE ASSESSMENT OF PHONOLOGICAL PROCESSES
Barbara Williams Hodson

child

Purpose: Helps evaluate the ability to use phonetics by children with severe speech disorders. Used for early childhood intervention and placement.

Description: 55 item test measuring spontaneous utterances naming three-dimensional stimuli. Examiner records speech deviations using narrow phonetic transcription. Materials include four sets of forms: recording, analysis, summary and screening. Examiner required. Not suitable for group use.

Untimed: 20 minutes

Range: Ages 3-8

Scoring: Examiner evaluated; may be computer scored

Cost: Complete kit $24.95 (includes manual, 48 recording forms, 48 analysis sheets, 48 analysis summary sheets, pad of 96 screening forms).

Publisher: The Interstate Printers & Publishers, Inc.

AUSTIN SPANISH ARTICULATION TEST
Elizabeth Carrow-Woolfolk

child

Purpose: Identifies articulation problems in Spanish- speaking children.

Description: 59 item verbal test in which the examiner reads an incomplete sentence and the child completes it. The manual contains reliability and validity data and gives specific instructions for administering and scoring. Examiner must be experienced in articulation testing and have a working knowledge of Spanish. Not suitable for group use.

Untimed: 25 minutes

Range: Ages 3-12 (no norms are provided)

Scoring: Examiner evaluated

Cost: Complete $19.00.

Publisher: Teaching Resources Corporation

BILINGUAL SYNTAX MEASURE (BSM)
Refer to page 230.

BRACKEN BASIC CONCEPT SCALE-DIAGNOSTIC SCALE (BBCS-DIAG.)
Refer to page 442.

THE BZOCH-LEAGUE RECEPTIVE-EXPRESSIVE EMERGENT LANGUAGE SCALE (REEL)
Refer to page 5.

CARROW ELICITED LANGUAGES INVENTORY (CELI)
Elizabeth Carrow-Woolfolk

child

Purpose: Measures the productive control of grammar in young children and diagnoses expressive language delays and disorders. Used to obtain data on a child's grammatical structure.

Description: 52 item test of oral stimuli, based on the technique of eliciting imitation of a sequence of sentences that include basic construction types and specific grammatical morphemes. The stimuli (51 sentences and one phrase) are presented by the examiner. The child's responses are recorded and transcribed from the tape onto a scoring/analysis form, which provides a format for analyzing errors of substitution, addition, omission, transposition, and reversal. A separate verb protocol sheet provides for analyzing production of verb forms. Materials include the test manual, a training guide with practice exercises, the analysis forms, and a cassette or reel training tape. The test is not appropriate for nonverbal subjects. Examiner required. Not for group use.

Untimed: 5 minutes

Range: Ages 3.0-7.11

Scoring: Examiner evaluated

Cost: Complete $53.00.

Publisher: Teaching Resources Corporation

CLINICAL EVALUATION OF LANGUAGE FUNCTIONS- DIAGNOSTIC BATTERY (CELF)
Eleanor Semel and Elisabeth H. Wiig

child, teen   grades K-12

Purpose: Builds a complete picture of a student's language abilities and disabilities. Used in diagnosing language difficulties and making decisions about remediation and intervention.

Description: Eleven category verbal test of language processing and production: phrase and sentence imitation, phrase completion, serial recall, phoneme recall production, abstraction, formulation of attributes, syntax and morphology, semantics, memory, and word finding and retrieval. Examiner required. Not suitable for group use.

Untimed: 60-120 minutes

Range: Grades K-12

Scoring: Examiner evaluated

Cost: Complete battery $89.00; components available individually.

Publisher: Charles E. Merrill Publishing Company

CLINICAL EVALUATION OF LANGUAGE FUNCTIONS- ELEMENTARY AND ADVANCED LEVEL SCREENING (CELF)
Eleanor Semel and Elisabeth Wiig

child, teen   grades K-12

Purpose: Evaluates a student's language processing and production abilities in order to help teachers and school psychologists identify those with language problems.

Description: A multiple item, verbal-visual test of phrase and sentence imitation, phrase completion, serial recall, antonyms, phoneme recall production, abstraction, and formulation of attributes. The grades K-5 version contains 42 items in a "Simon Says" format, and the grades 6-12 test has 52 items in a card game format. Materials include audiotapes, picture stimulus manuals and score forms. Examiner required. Not suitable for group use.

Untimed: 20 minutes

Range: Grades K-12

Scoring: Examiner evaluated

Cost: Elementary package $19.95; advanced level package $19.95; components available individually.

Publisher: Charles E. Merrill Publishing Company

CLINICAL PROBES OF ARTICULATION CONSISTENCY (C-PAC)
Wayne Secord

all ages

Purpose: Provides an in-depth picture of how well an individual speaks and articulates specific sounds; useful for planning and evaluating speech therapy.

Description: Verbal response test of 25 illustrated stories, adult-level reading passages, and duplicating-master articulation probes to elicit responses and check for articulation of target sounds. Specific sounds are assessed in a wide range of contexts: consonants in isolated words, clusters, sentences, and conversational speech; vowels and dipthongs in single words and minimal contrast pairs; and vocalic "R" sounds. Examiner evaluated. Not suitable for group use.

Untimed: 10 minutes

Range: Ages 4-adult

Scoring: Examiner evaluated

Cost: Complete program $45.00; story manual $14.95; spirit masters $15.95; manual $14.95; sounds handbook $6.95.

Publisher: Charles E. Merrill Publishing Company

CRANE ORAL DOMINANCE TEST (CODT)
Barbara J. Crane

child, teen   grades PRE-12

Purpose: Determines if student has a dominant language (Spanish/English) or is bilingual. Used to help instructor prescribe appropriate instructional materials.

Description: Multiple item oral response test that determines which language a student retains best- English or Spanish. Examiner reads four (preschool) or eight (school age) word-pair sets, some of which are in English and some of which are in Spanish. Student responds by repeating as many words as can be remembered. Based on results of eight groups of word-pair sets, the student is classified as Monolingual Non-English, Dominant Non-English, Functionally Bilingual, Dominant English or Monolingual English. Examiner required. Not suitable for group use.

Untimed: 20 minutes

Range: Grades Preschool-high school

Scoring: Examiner evaluated

Cost: Complete for 30 pupils $27.50 (includes test booklets, score sheets, manual).

Publisher: Crane Publishing Co.

A DEEP TEST OF ARTICULATION PICTURE FORM
Eugene McDonald

child   grades K-4

Purpose: Assesses child's ability to produce sounds in various phonetic combinations. Useful for planning therapy.

Description: 60 items per sound for 13 sounds in a verbal test. Examiner places two decks of cards containing pictures before the child. The child names the two pictures and examiner determines if the sounds were correct then flips cards and repeats the process. Trained examiner required. Not suitable for group use.

Untimed: 15-20 minutes

Range: Grades K-4

Scoring: Examiner evaluated

Cost: Test kit (includes instructions and sample cards) $13.50.

Publisher: Stanwix House

A DEEP TEST OF ARTICULA-TION SENTENCE FORM
Eugene McDonald

all ages   grades 3-UP

Purpose: Assesses child's ability to produce sounds in a sentence. Used to determine which sounds need remedial work.

Description: Multiple item verbal test. Examiner flips pages of booklet and child reads sentences containing sound combinations. Trained examiner required. Not suitable for group use.

Untimed: Not available

Range: Grades 3 and above

Scoring: Examiner evaluated

Cost: Test kit (including sample) $10.00.

Publisher: Stanwix House

DEL RIO LANGUAGE SCREEN-ING TEST-DRLST (ENGLISH/SPANISH)

child

Purpose: Assesses both English- and Spanish-dominant children with deviant language skills. Used to place children in bilingual programs according to their proficiency in each

language.

Description: Multiple item flip-card paper-pencil test assessing specific functions essential to learning language. Five subtests address each function: Receptive Vocabulary, Sentence Repetition-Length, Sentence Repetition-Complexity, Oral Commands, and Story Comprehension. Examiner required. Not suitable for group use. Available in Spanish.

Untimed: Not available

Range: Ages 3-7

Scoring: Hand key; examiner evaluated

Cost: Complete kit (includes 30 scoring forms in English and Spanish, manual) $25.00; 30 scoring forms (specify English or Spanish) $3.15 each; manual $19.40.

Publisher: National Educational Laboratory Publishers, Inc.

DENVER ARTICULATION SCREENING EXAM (DASE)
Amelia F. Drumwright

child

Purpose: Detects speech articulation problems in children. Screens for more sophisticated testing.

Description: 22 picture test measuring a child's intelligibility (not its language ability, vocabulary, school readiness, or intelligence). The examiner shows the pictures (displayed on eleven cards) to the child, says a word and the child repeats it. Not recommended for shy or younger children. Examiner required. Not for group use.

Untimed: 5 minutes

Range: Ages 2½-7

Scoring: Examiner evaluated

Cost: 25 tests $1.75; manual $6.50; picture cards $1.25.

Publisher: Ladoca Publishing

Foundation

EXAMINING FOR APHASIA: SECOND EDITION
Jon Eisenson

teen, adult

Purpose: Assesses language functioning of aphasics.

Description: Multiple item procedure for systematically exploring language functioning in aphasics. Materials include manual detailing issues in the assessment of aphasics and fourteen plates of stimulus materials in black and white. Examiner assembles other common objects required for the examination. Examiner required. Not suitable for group use.

Untimed: 30 minutes-2 hours

Range: Adolescent-adult

Scoring: Examiner evaluated

Cost: Complete set (includes manual, 25 record forms) $21.00.

Publisher: The Psychological Corporation

EXPRESSIVE ONE-WORD PICTURE VOCABULARY TEST (EOWPVT)
Refer to page 478.

FLUHARTY PRESCHOOL SPEECH AND LANGUAGE SCREENING TEST
Nancy Buono Fluharty

child

Purpose: Measures vocabulary, articulation, and language performance of preschool children. Used to identify those who need more comprehensive evaluations, and to diagnose delays and disorders.

Description: 35 item verbal test in three categories. Section A evaluates vocabulary level and proficiency of articulation through the child's identification of 15 common objects. Section B indicates receptive language abilities by requiring nonverbal responses to ten sentences, and Section C provides a sample of expressive language as the child repeats ten short sentences stimulated by pictures. Materials include the picture cards, response forms, and a guide. The test, which is not appropriate for nonverbal subjects, is to be individually administered by an examiner. Not suitable for group use.

Untimed: 6 minutes

Range: Ages 2-6

Scoring: Examiner evaluated

Cost: Complete set $18.00.

Publisher: Teaching Resources Corporation

FULLERTON LANGUAGE TEST FOR ADOLESCENTS (EXPERIMENTAL EDITION)
Arden R. Thorum

all ages

Purpose: Measures receptive and expressive language skills. Distinguishes normal from language-impaired adolescents.

Description: 142 item verbal test of eight functions important in the acquisition and effective use of language skills: Auditory Synthesis, Morphology Competency, Oral Commands, Convergent Production, Divergent Production, Syllabication, Grammatic Competency, and Idioms. Each function is identified as being at the competency, instruction, or frustration level. Materials include a set of stimulus items. Examiner required. Not suitable for group use.

Untimed: 45 minutes

Range: Ages 11-adult

Scoring: Hand key; examiner evaluated

Cost: Examiner's kit $20.00 (includes stimulus items, 25 scoring forms and profiles, manual).

Publisher: Consulting Psychologists Press, Inc.

GOLDMAN-FRISTOE TEST OF ARTICULATION
Ronald Goldman and Macalyne Fristoe

child, teen   grades 1-12

Purpose: Assesses an individual's articulation of the consonant. Used as a basis for remedial planning.

Description: Three verbal subtests of articulation of major speech sounds in the initial, medial and final positions; articulatory skills used in connected speech; articulation of sounds known to be difficult for the student. Subtests are: Sound in Words, in which student names pictures of 35 familiar objects; Sounds in Sentences, in which the student retells two stories the examiner has just read; and Stimulability, in which the examiner tests student on the sounds misarticulated in the Sounds in Words subtest. Percentile ranks are provided by age for Sounds in Words and Stimulability subtests. However, interpretation of this test lies more in knowing which sounds an individual produces incorrectly and the type of misproduction than in an overall quantitative score that shows performance in relation to that of other individuals. Materials include test plates in an easel, 50 response forms, and a manual. No reading required. Picture format useful with retarded or easily distractible children. Examiner required. Administer individually only.

Untimed: 15 minutes for Sounds-In-

Words subtest, varied for other two subtests

Range: Grades 1-12

Scoring: Examiner evaluated

Cost: Complete test kit $37.50; 50 response forms $6.50.

Publisher: American Guidance Service

ILLINOIS TEST OF PSYCHO-LINGUISTIC ABILITIES (ITPA)
Samuel A. Kirk, James J. McCarthy and Winifred D. Kirk

child

Purpose: Assesses use and understanding of psycholinguistic abilities in young children; facilitates assessment of a child's abilities for purposes of remediation.

Description: 300 item verbal and paper-pencil test evaluating a child's cognitive and perceptual abilities in three areas: communication, psycholinguistic processes, and levels of organization. There are 12 subtests: Auditory Reception, Visual Reception, Auditory Association, Visual Association, Verbal Expression, Manual Expression, Grammatic Closure, Visual Closure, Auditory Sequential Memory, Visual Sequential Memory, Auditory Closure, and Sound Blending. Test kit includes Examiner's Manual, two picture books, chips, picture sequences, picture strips, six objects for the verbal and manual expression test, 33⅓ rpm record, and carry case. Examiner required. Not for group use. Available in Spanish (from the author only).

Untimed: 60 minutes

Range: Ages 2-10

Scoring: Hand key

Cost: Kit $110.00; record forms and picture strips $12.50; Aids and Precautions in Administering $4.95; Psycholinguistic Learning Disabilities $6.95.

Publisher: University of Illinois Press

ILYIN ORAL INTERVIEW TEST
Donna Ilyin

teen, adult   grades 10-UP

Purpose: Measures the ability of secondary and adult students to communicate accurately in English. Used to assess abilities in English as a first or second language.

Description: 50 item verbal test in which the examiner shows paired pictures to the student, asks questions about them, and the student responds. This enables the examiner to assess student comprehension and ability to use proper English grammar. Examiner required. Suitable for group use.

Untimed: 30 minutes

Range: Secondary and adult students

Scoring: Examiner evaluated

Cost: Test and manual $15.95; 50 score sheets $5.50.

Publisher: Newbury House Publishers, Inc.

LANGUAGE FACILITY TEST
John T. Dailey

child, teen

Purpose: Evaluates how well children ages 3-15 speak in the language or dialect with which they were reared. Assesses gains in language ability. Used for bilingual, early and special education programs, as well as programs for the deaf and physically or mentally handicapped

Description: 12 item oral response test in which children are asked to tell stories about or describe each of three pictures in four forms. Responses are assigned scores on a nine-point scale according to detailed scoring criteria and examples at each level. The scores measure how well children use the language or dialect to which they have been exposed in home or school environment. Provides a measure of language facility which is independent of vocabulary, information, pronunciation, and grammar. Norms are available for ages 3 to 15. Normative data also reported for many subgroups such as the mentally retarded, deaf, physically handicapped, poor readers, and children with behavior problems. Not suitable for adults with better than average language facility. The test kit includes: 12 picture plates, a test administrator's manual, a Spanish supplement to the manual, and Manual Supplement II (Selected Dissertations and other Reports). The test can be administered in Spanish, sign language, or other languages or dialects. Examiner required. Not for group use.

Untimed: 10 minutes

Range: Ages 3-15

Scoring: Examiner evaluated

Cost: Complete kit $22.50; 100 answer booklets $12.00.

Publisher: The Allington Corporation

LANGUAGE IMITATION TEST (LIT)
Refer to page 559.

LANGUAGE SAMPLING AND ANALYSIS (LSA)
Merlin J. Mecham and J. Dean Jones

child, teen

Purpose: Assesses the speaking ability of children ages 2-14 years. Identifies changes in a child's language performance and assesses the effectiveness of professional intervention.

Description: 51 item oral response test measuring the following language domains: mean-length-of utterance, fluency in language production, diversity of vocabulary and lexical categories, diversity of grammatical morphemes, and completeness of grammatical constructions. The manual specifies stimulus and eliciting materials for each test item. The picture stimulus book from the Utah Test of Language Development (UTLD) Kit is used. Responses from the child are tape- recorded and later analyzed for number of responses meeting specified criteria. Administrator must be familiar with language sampling and analysis procedures. Test kit includes: 50 language sample data sheets, 25 summary analysis sheets, and the manual. Can be used with the Utah Test of Language Development for an extended analysis of a child's language structure. Examiner required. Suitable for group use.

Untimed: 90 minutes

Range: Ages 2-14

Scoring: Examiner evaluated

Cost: Complete kit (includes 50 language sample data sheets, 25 summary analysis sheets, manual) $20.00. UTLD and LSA kit $50.00).

Publisher: Communication Research Associates, Inc.

"LET'S TALK" INVENTORY FOR ADOLESCENTS
Elisabeth H. Wiig

---

all ages   grades 4   and UP

Purpose: Evaluates students' ability to communicate by talking; used by speech pathologists, special educators, and psychologists to identify and diagnose students who have social communication problems.

Description: 40 item verbal test in which the examiner gives the description and context of a picture and asks the student to formulate appropriate speech acts for the context, thereby probing four communication functions: ritualizing, informing, controlling, and feeling. Scoring reflects the register and appropriateness of the speech acts formulated. "Drop back" items are included. Subsequent use provides data on progress as a result of intervention. The test is tied to "Let's Talk": Developing prosocial communication skills. Examiner required. Not suitable for group use.

Timed: 30-45 minutes

Range: ages 9-adult

Scoring: Examiner evaluated

Cost: Complete kit $49.00.

Publisher: Charles E. Merrill Publishing Company

MEASUREMENT OF LANGUAGE DEVELOPMENT
Carol Melnick

---

child

Purpose: Measures progress of therapy programs for language-impaired children ages 3-0 to 7-11, including pre-sentence level children. Used with language-delayed (with normal intelligence), mentally retarded, hearing-impaired, and emotionally disturbed children to assess effects of language intervention programs.

Description: 186 item "point-to" and oral response test covering eight subtasks: Primary Verbs, Personal Pronouns, Negatives, Indefinite Pronouns, Interrogative Reversals, Who-Questions, Secondary Verbs, and Conjunctions. The items consist of familiar objects and situations pictured in the stimulus book. The examiner first describes the stimulus pictures and asks the child to point to the one that has been described. The examiner then describes pictures and asks the child to describe them in his own words. The responses are evaluated for both receptive and expressive language, mean length of utterance, word order, and semantic relations. The complete test kit includes a manual, receptive-expressive picture plates and 25 record forms. Examiner required. Not suitable for group use.

Untimed: Not available

Range: Ages 3-0 to 7-11

Scoring: Examiner evaluated

Cost: Complete kit $46.50.

Publisher: Stoelting Co.

MERRILL LANGUAGE SCREENING TEST (MLST)
Nyrna Mumm, Wayne Secord and Katherine Dykstra

child   grades K-1

Purpose: Detects potential language problems in young children by indicating language competencies in comparison to peer performance. Used by teachers and school psychologists to screen groups of children.

Description: Six picture stimulus cards, a manual and an audio-cassette are used to elicit responses from children in order to assess receptive and expressive language skills in five areas: production of complete sentences, utterance length, verb-tense agreement, elaboration, and communication competence. The optional Articulation Screening Inventory can be used to test 16 phonemes. Components available individually. Examiner required. Suitable for group use.

Untimed: 5 minutes

Range: Grades K-1
Scoring: Examiner evaluated

Cost: Complete kit $45.00. Compo-

nents available individually.

Publisher: Charles E. Merrill Publishing Company

MINNESOTA TEST FOR DIFFERENTIAL DIAGNOSIS OF APHASIA
Mildred Schuell

adult

Purpose: Assesses language disturbance due to brain damage; aids in classifying patients and determining prognosis.

Description: Subject responds to questions and cards presented by the examiner, who then evaluates disturbances in hearing, seeing and reading; speech and language; visuomotor and writing; and disturbances of numerical relationships and arithmetic processes. Examiner required. May be administered over several sessions, depending on patient's fatigue. Not suitable for group use.

Untimed: Open ended

Range: Adult

Scoring: Hand key; examiner evaluated

Cost: Manual $2.00; Differential Diagnosis of Aphasia with the Minnesota test $7.95.

Publisher: University of Minnesota Press

MULTILEVEL INFORMAL LANGUAGE INVENTORY (MILI)
Candace L. Goldsworthy

child, teen   grades K-6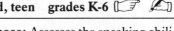

Purpose: Assesses the speaking abilities of children from Kindergarten-Grade 6. Used to identify students with language problems and to provide learning disabilities specialists with informal measures for intervention.

Description: Verbal test which assesses at three levels of speech: spontaneous evoked, indirect imitation, and receptive. Eight oral language functions: verbs, nouns, modification, interrogatives, negations, combining propositions, adverbs and prepositions, and associative language. Using the manual and picture stimuli provided in the test kit, specific types of responses are obtained. Survey scenes elicit short, spontaneous language samples; survey stories elicit more complex language forms through storytelling and paraphrasing; and specific probes focus on key syntactic constructions. Examiner required. Not suitable for group use.

Untimed: Varies

Range: K-6

Scoring: Examiner evaluated

Cost: Complete $45.00; 12 record forms $9.95; picture manual $29.00; examiner's manual $12.95.

Publisher: Charles E. Merrill Publishing Company

NORTHWESTERN SYNTAX SCREENING TEST (NSST)
Laura L. Lee

child

Purpose: Measures a child's syntactic development. Used to identify difficient children who need further evaluation.

Description: Screening test in which the child is asked to respond to short verbal statements by picking out a picture that the statement best describes or by repeating an appropriate statement pertaining to the picture. Receptive and expressive language abilities are evaluated. Examiner required. Not suitable for

group use.

Untimed: 15-25 minutes

Range: Ages 3-7

Scoring: Examiner evaluated

Cost: Test and 100 answer forms $19.95.

Publisher: Northwestern University Press

THE OHIO TEST OF ARTICULATION AND PERCEPTION OF SOUNDS (OTAPS)
Ruth Beckey Irwin and Marcia Stevenson

child, teen   grades K-7

Purpose: Assesses the ability of a child to hear and say various sounds. Useful to determine need for additional therapy.

Description: Multiple item verbal test. Examiner has test booklet containing 59 color plates. Articulation difficulties are tested in four subtests: (1) sound in words, (2) sound in phrases, (3) nonsense words in meaningful sentences, and (4) nonsense words to be imitated. Auditory perception also measured in four subtests: (1) identification of received sounds, (2) comparison of received sounds, (3) identification of self-spoken sounds, and (4) comparison of self-spoken sounds. Trained examiner required. Not suitable for group use.

Untimed: 10-20 minutes per subtest

Range: Grades K-7

Scoring: Examiner evaluated

Cost: Test booklet $13.00; manual $5.00.

Publisher: Stanwix House

ORZECK APHASIA EVALUATION
Refer to page 48.

PHOTO ARTICULATION TEST (PAT)
K. Pendergast, S. Dickey, J. Selma, and A. Soder

child

Purpose: Measures language skills. Used for screening and analysis in schools, clinics and for therapy.

Description: 72 color photographs test arranged with nine pictures on each of eight sheets. Measures language ability on consonants, consonant blends, vowels and diphthongs; categorizes defective sounds as tongue, lip or vowel sounds. The subject names the items in the color photographs as the examiner points to the pictures and records responses on recording sheet. Materials include supplementary test words list. Examiner required. Not suitable for group use.

Untimed: 5 minutes

Range: Ages 3-11

Scoring: Examiner evaluated

Cost: Complete $17.50; 96 recording sheets $2.75.

Publisher: The Interstate Printers & Publishers, Inc.

PICTURE ARTICULATION AND SCREENING TEST (PALST)
Word Making Productions

child   grades PRE-6

Purpose: Screen articulation and language skills of children from preschool to Grade 6. Identifies children in need of further evaluation and assistance.

Description: 13 item oral response

test assessing strengths and weaknesses in articulation. Each test item consists of a picture card showing an activity or scene, such as an Indian shooting an arrow at a rabbit or a child brushing his teeth. The child is asked to describe each card. The examiner evaluates the responses based on the completeness of the child's articulation. Six sounds are emphasized: sh, r, th, s, l, and t. Examiner required. Suitable for group use.

Untimed: 2-3 minutes

Range: Grades Preschool-6

Scoring: Examiner evaluated

Cost: Complete kit (includes test and 1 pad recording forms) $18.95.

Publisher: Word Making Productions

PORCH INDEX OF COMMU-NICATIVE ABILITY (PICA)
Bruce E. Porch

teen, adult

Purpose: Evaluates the ability of aphasic individuals to communicate with other people. Useful for diagnosis and therapy.

Description: 180 item paper-pencil, verbal test of nine modalities of communication: writing, copying, reading, pantomime, verbal, auditory, visual, gestural, and graphic. Measures changes in functioning due to time, treatment and surgery. Items are scored for accuracy, responsiveness, completeness, promptness, and efficiency. Materials include ten pairs of test objects, plastic stimulus cards, and graphic test sheets. Fiber tip pen required for graphic items. Not recommended for children under 12. Examiner required. Not for group use.

Untimed: 30-60 minutes

Range: Ages 13-adult

Scoring: Examiner evaluated

Cost: Complete kit for 25 subjects $100.00 (includes test items and sheets, stimulus cards, manuals, profiles, carrying case).

Publisher: Consulting Psychologists Press, Inc.

PORCH INDEX OF COMMU-NICATIVE ABILITY IN CHILDREN (PICAC)
Bruce E. Porch

child

Purpose: Assesses a child's communicative behavior. Used for diagnosis, prognosis, and treatment planning.

Description: Battery of paper-pencil, verbal tests measuring three modalities of communication: gestural, verbal, and graphic. Visual and auditory level scores are also obtained. The test documents changes in a child's processing ability over time. Items are scored for accuracy, responsiveness, completeness, promptness, and efficiency. The Basic Battery tests preschool children three to six years old; the Advanced Battery is for children six to twelve. Materials include ten pairs of test objects, plastic stimulus cards, and graphic test sheets. A black-tip pen is required for graphic items. Examiner required. Not for group use.

Untimed: 30-60 minutes

Range: Ages 3-12

Scoring: Examiner evaluated

Cost: Deluxe test kit for 25 subjects $85.00; economy test kit complete for 25 subjects without carrying case $69.50; basic battery $5.00; advanced battery $9.00.

Publisher: Consulting Psychologists Press, Inc.

PRESCHOOL LANGUAGE SCALE (PLS)
Irla Lee Zimmerman, Violette G. Steiner and Robert Evatt Pond

child

Purpose: Provides a system for assessment, diagnosis and remediation of early developmental language problems in young children.

Description: A verbal-visual test in which a picture book and program manual are used by an examiner to administer auditory and verbal language tasks. This scale measures receptive and expressive language abilities separately for more accurate diagnosis. Examiner required. Not suitable for group use. Available in Spanish.

Untimed: 20 minutes

Range: Ages Infant to 7 years

Scoring: Examiner evaluated

Cost: Complete $32.95. Components available individually.

Publisher: Charles E. Merrill Publishing Company

PSYCHOLINGUISTIC RATING SCALE
Kenneth L. Hobby

child, teen   grades K-8.9

Purpose: Measures psycholinguistic behaviors relevant to classroom performance of elementary and intermediate school students. Used to screen students for special attention under Public Law 94-142.

Description: Multiple item paper-pencil inventory. A classroom teacher familiar with the child responds to statements about the frequency of classroom behaviors on a one-to-five scale from "seldom" to "frequently." The scale has four different levels: Readiness (Kindergarten to

Grade 1.4), Elementary (Grades 1.5-2.9), Intermediate (Grades 3.0-5.9), and Advanced (Grades 6.0-8.9). The Readiness, Elementary, and Intermediate levels include the following ten subscales (4-5 test items each): auditory reception, auditory association, auditory memory, auditory closure, verbal expression, visual reception, visual association, visual memory, visual closure, and manual expression. The Advanced Level includes all of the above scales except visual closure and manual expression. The scales are based upon the same theoretical structure as the Illinois Test of Psycholinguistic Abilities (ITPA). Scoring yields subscores and a total score. Standardized on 1,200 children with norms provided for each level. Not for group use.

Untimed: 5 minutes

Range: Grades K-8.9

Scoring: Hand key

Cost: Complete kit (includes 5 booklets for each level and manual) $10.90; 25 booklets $7.10 (specify level) manual $6.20.

Publisher: Western Psychological Services

THE PUPIL RATING SCALE: SCREENING FOR LEARNING DISABILITIES (MPRS)
Helmer R. Myklebust

child   grades K-6

Purpose: Measures hearing, speech, motor and social behavior of elementary school children. Used to screen for learning disabilities.

Description: 24 item rating scale covering the following factors: auditory comprehension, spoken language, orientation, motor coordination, and personal- social behavior. The test provides objective data for language disorders as well as for nonverbal behavior. Teachers must be familiar with the children they are rating. Suitable for group use.

Untimed: 5-10 minutes

Range: Grades K-6

Scoring: Examiner evaluated

Cost: Scale and manual $19.50; 50 record forms $17.00.

Publisher: Grune & Stratton, Inc.

QUEENSLAND UNIVERSITY APHASIA AND LANGUAGE TEST (QUALT)

child

Purpose: Meaures language deficiencies in children up to 10 years of age in aphasic or mentally retarded adults. Used for clinical diagnosis.

Description: Multiple item paper-pencil and oral response battery of tests measures deficiencies in the following areas of language usage: oral expression, auditory comprehension, reading, and writing. Three Parallel forms (I, II and III) are available for retesting. Materials include: complete set of materials for Forms I, II and III, handbook, and record form. Examiner required. Not for group use.

AUSTRALIAN PUBLISHER

Untimed: Not available

Range: Children up to 10 years, impaired adults

Scoring: Examiner evaluated

Cost: Contact publisher.

Publisher: The Australian Council for Educational Research Limited

A READING READINESS TEST: REVERSAL TESTS (bilingual)
Ake W. Edfeldt

child   grade 1

Purpose: Measures degree of speech

reversal tendencies in young children before they learn to read. Used by educators and speech therapists to predict reading problems in first grade.

Description: Oral response test based on research into cause and effect of word transposition tendencies of children. The test was developed to diagnose and prevent these difficulties. A child who is scored either as "control case" or "not yet ready to read" is not considered ready to master reading and should, therefore, postpone instruction. Test is said to be easy to administer and score. Materials include manual and test. Examiner required. Not for group use. CANADIAN PUBLISHER

Untimed: Not available

Range: First grade

Scoring: Hand key, examiner evaluated

Cost: Specimen set $5.00; 25 tests $12.00; manual $4.50.

Publisher: Institute of Psychological Research, Inc.

REYNELL DEVELOPMENTAL LANGUAGE SCALES-REVISED EDITION
Refer to page 13.

RILEY ARTICULATION AND LANGUAGE TEST: REVISED
Glyndon D. Riley

child   grades K-2

Purpose: Measures language proficiency of young children. Used to identify those most in need of speech therapy.

Description: Three oral response subtests: Language Proficiency and Intelligibility, Articulation Function,

and Language Function. The tests provide an effective screening device for measuring phonemic similarity, stimulability, number of defective sounds, error consistency, frequency of occurrence, and developmental expectancy. Provides an objective articulation loss score and standardized language loss and language function scores. Standardized on kindergarten, first, and second grade boys and girls from low and middle socioeconomic levels. Examiner required. Not for group use.

Untimed: 2-3 minutes

Range: Grades K-2

Scoring: Hand key

Cost: Complete kit (includes 25 tests, manual) $10.50.

Publisher: Western Psychological Services

SCREENING DEEP TEST OF ARTICULATION
Eugene McDonald

child   grades K-3

Purpose: Assesses child's ability to produce nine consonant sounds in a variety of phonetic contexts. Useful for establishing a profile to determine need for further testing.

Description: 90 item verbal test. Examiner displays pairs of pictures to the child to elicit child's production of bisyllables. Selected consonants occur in different consonant types (single, abutting and in compounds), and in a variety of contexts which require a diversity of overlapping, aritculatory movements. Trained examiner required. Not suitable for group use.

Untimed: 5 minutes

Range: Grades K-3

Scoring: Hand key; examiner evaluated

Cost: Test $13.50.

Publisher: Stanwix House

SCREENING SPEECH ARTIC-ULATION TEST (SSAT)
Merlin J. Mecham, J. Lorin Jex and J. Dean Jones

child   grades PRE-2

Purpose: Identifies children who have significant articulation problems. Used as a screening instrument in Head Start, early education, and early elementary classes; not intended for diagnostic use.

Description: A child is shown pictures designed to elicit specific phonemes when the child is asked to name what he/she sees in the picture. Some prompting is allowed. 47 phonemes are tested in initial, medial, and final word positions. Phonemes produced erroneously are recorded to types of errors on a score sheet. Examiner required. Not suitable for group use.

Untimed: 15 minutes

Range: Grades Preschool-2

Scoring: Examiner evaluated

Cost: Complete kit (includes manual/ picture plates and 25 score sheets).

Publisher: Communications Research Associates, Inc.

SENTENCE COMPREHENSION TEST-SCT-(EXPERIMENTAL EDITION)

child

Purpose: Assesses a young child's ability to use receptive language. Used for remediation by teachers, psychologists and speech therapists.

Description: Multiple item, "point-to" test of sentence comprehension. Examiner shows the child a series of sets of drawings, each with four black

and white drawings which offer a choice in grammatical interpretation when accompanied by the examiner's target sentence. The child can then point to the picture chosen without orally answering. Designed for ages three to five. Materials include reusable picture booklet, score sheets and manual. Examiner required. Not for group use.

CANADIAN PUBLISHER

Untimed: 20 minutes

Range: Ages 3-5

Scoring: Examiner evaluated

Cost: Contact publisher.

Publisher: Institute of Psychological Research, Inc.

SENTENCE IMITATION SCREENING TEST (SIST)
Refer to page 466.

SKLAR APHASIA SCALE: REVISED 1973
Maurice Sklar

adult

Purpose: Diagnoses speech and language disorders resulting from brain damage in adults. Used to plan therapy programs and to measure progress.

Description: Multiple item oral response test of speech and language disorders resulting from brain damage. Quantifies disturbances in four areas: auditory verbal comprehension, reading comprehension, oral expression, and graphic production. Responses are evaluated in each of the four areas for extent of damage and potential responsiveness to therapy. Also provides a Total Impairment Score. Examiner required. Not suitable for group use.

Untimed: 10-15 minutes

Range: Adult

Scoring: Hand key

Cost: Kit (10 protocol booklets, manual, 1 set test materials) $26.50.

Publisher: Western Psychological Services

SLINGERLAND SCREENING TESTS FOR IDENTIFYING CHILDREN WITH SPECIFIC LANGUAGE DISABILITY
Refer to page 552.

SMITH-JOHNSON NONVERBAL PERFORMANCE SCALE
Refer to page 15.

SPECIFIC LANGUAGE DISABILITY TESTS
Neve Malcomesius

teen   grades 6-8

Purpose: Screens entire classroom groups or individual children in grades 6-8 and identifies those who show specific language disability. Used to help design remedial programs and to indicate the need for further testing

Description: Ten paper-pencil subtests are used to identify perceptual language problems through analysis of written performance. Subtests I-V evaluate visual perception: visual discrimination, visual memory, and visual-motor coordination. Subtests VI-X evaluate auditory perception: auditory discrimination, auditory memory, auditory-motor coordination, and comprehension. All tests check handwriting and ability to follow directions. Test materials include the subtests, Teacher's Manual, Test Booklet, Cards and Charts. Examiner required. Suitable for group use.

Untimed: 30-45 minutes

Range: Grades 6-8

Scoring: Examiner evaluated

Cost: 12 tests $6.00; charts and cards $8.00; teacher's manual $1.50; specimen set $1.75.

Publisher: Educators Publishing Service, Inc.

STYCAR LANGUAGE TEST
Mary Sheridan

child

Purpose: Assesses language development. Used for differential diagnosis and management of speech disorders in young children and retardates.

Description: Multiple item series of clinical testing procedures for assessing language and speech skills. Divided into three overlapping procedures: The Common Objects Test, ages 1 to 2; The Miniature Toys Test, ages 21 months to 4 years; and the Picture Book Test, ages 2½ to 7. The examiner has considerable choice in individual application. Tests do not provide pass/fail results; rather, descriptive recording and rating on a 3 to 5 point scale is recommended. Available to speech therapists, medical doctors, and specialist language teachers. Examiner required. Not suitable for group use.
BRITISH PUBLISHER

Untimed: 30 minutes

Range: Children under 7 years old

Scoring: Examiner evaluated

Cost: Complete kit (includes picture card booklet, common objects test, miniature toys, manual) £53.00 (payment in sterling for all overseas orders).

Publisher: NFER-Nelson Publishing Company

SYMBOLIC PLAY TEST-EXPERIMENTAL EDITION (SPT)

Refer to page 16.

TEST FOR ORAL LANGUAGE PRODUCTION (TOLP)

child

Purpose: Measures oral language ability. Used for educational evaluation

Description: Multiple item verbal test of 16 aspects of language production covering productivity, syntactic complexity, correctness, fluency and content. Materials include stimulus materials which subject responds to orally. TOLP available only to professional personnel attached to education departments and others with sufficient knowledge of sentence analysis to score the test. Examiner required. Not suitable for group use. SOUTH AFRICAN PUBLISHER

Untimed: ½-1½ hours

Range: 4½ years-10 years 5 months

Scoring: Hand key; examiner evaluated

Cost: (In Rands) stimulus material 5,40; manual 13,80; 10 scoring sheets 2,20 (orders from outside The RSA will be dealt with on merit).

Publisher: Human Sciences Research Council

TEST OF ADOLESCENT LANGUAGE (TOAL)

Donald D. Hammill, Virginia L. Brown, Stephen C. Larsen, and J. Lee Wiederholt

teen   grades 6-12

Purpose: Assesses the language abilities of students in Grades 6-12. Identifies problems in both spoken and written language and specifies areas in need of intervention. Used to conduct research and to make comparisons between language and cognitive abilities.

Description: Eight paper-pencil and oral response tests measure a broad spectrum of language abilities. The subtests are Vocabulary (semantics) and Grammar (syntax) in Listening, Speaking, Reading, and Writing. The sum of the subtest scores yields an Adolescent Language Quotient (ALQ). Composite scores, each with its own norm- referenced quotient, are yielded for the following ten areas: listening, speaking, reading, writing, spoken language, written language, vocabulary, grammar, receptive language, and expressive language. The examiner's manual presents information on content validity and criterion- related and construct validity research. Examiner required. Not for group use.

Untimed: 1 hours 45 minutes

Range: Grades 6-12

Scoring: Hand key

Cost: Complete (includes examiner's manual, 10 student booklets, 50 student answer sheets, 50 profile sheets, storage box) $66.00.

Publisher: PRO-ED

TEST OF EARLY LANGUAGE DEVELOPMENT (TELD)

Wayne P. Hresko, D. Kim Reid and Donald D. Hammill

child

Purpose: Measures content and form in spoken language abilities of children ages 3-7 years.

Description: 38 item test assessing different aspects of receptive/expressive language using a variety of semantic and syntactic tasks. Materials include picture cards, record forms, and the manual. Examiner required. Not for group use.

Untimed: 15 minutes

Range: Ages 3-0 to 7-11

Scoring: Hand key

Cost: Complete kit (includes soft bound manual, 11 picture cards, 50 record forms) $30.00.

Publisher: PRO-ED

TEST OF GROUP LEARNING SKILLS
Michael A. Watson

child   grades PRE-3

Purpose: Assesses level of general language development and identifies strengths and weaknesses in specific learning skills. Used as a guide for placing pre-kindergarten through third grade children into teaching groups.

Description: 139 item paper-pencil test consisting of visual and auditory subtests. Visual subtests include: Motor, Memory, Association, and Discrimination Factors. Auditory subtests include: Memory, Association and Discrimination Factors. One subtest measures auditory-visual association. Test package includes test sheets, cassette for auditory subtests and film strip for visual subtests. Cassette player, projector, screen, stopwatch, chalk and board, pencils and paper required. Examiner required. Suitable for group use.

Untimed: 4 hours

Range: Grades Pre-kindergarten-3

Scoring: Hand key; examiner evaluated

Cost: Complete program (includes examiner's manual, 2 cassettes of auditory subtests, 3 filmstrips of visual subtests, 8 response booklets or ditto masters, learning profile ditto; ditto kit) $49.00; booklet kit $53.00.

Publisher: Educational Activities, Inc.

TEST OF LANGUAGE DEVELOPMENT (TOLD INTERMEDIATE)
Donald D. Hammill and Phyllis L. Newcomer

child

Purpose: Assesses the speaking abilities of children ages 8-12 years. Identifies those children who have language problems.

Description: 160 item oral response test consisting of five subtests measuring different aspects of spoken language. The Generals (25 items) and Characteristics (50 items) subtests assess the understanding and meaningful use of spoken words. The Sentence Combining (20 items), Word Ordering (25 items), and Grammatic Comprehension (40 items) subtests assess different aspects of grammar. Test results are reported in terms of standard scores, percentiles, age-equivalents, and quotients. By combining various subtest scores, it is possible to diagnose a child's abilities in relation to specific language skills, including: overall spoken language, listening (receptive language), speaking (expressive language), semantics (the meaning of words), and syntax (grammar). Examiner required. Suitable for group use.

Untimed: 40 minutes

Range: Ages 8-6 to 12-11

Scoring: Hand key

Cost: Complete (includes examiner's manual, 50 answer sheets, storage box) $34.00. Components also sold separately.

Publisher: PRO-ED

TEST OF LANGUAGE DEVELOPMENT (TOLD-PRIMARY)
Phillis L. Newman and Donald D. Hammill

child

Purpose: Assesses the speaking abilities of children ages 4-8 years. Used as a language achievement test and to identify children with language problems, including mental retardation, learning disabilities, reading disabilities, speech delays, and articulation problems.

Description: 170 item oral response test consisting of seven subtests measuring different components of spoken language. The Picture Vocabulary (25 items) and Oral Vocabulary (20 items) subtests assess the understanding and meaningful use of spoken words. The Grammatic Understanding, (25 items), Sentence Imitation (30 items), and Grammatic Completion (30 items) subtests assess differing aspects of grammar. The Word Articulation (20 items) and Word Discrimination (20 items) subtests are supplemental tests measuring the ability to say words correctly and to distinguish between words that sound familiar. Test results are reported in terms of standard scores, percentiles, age-equivalents, and quotients. By combining various subtest scores, it is possible to diagnose a child's abilities in relation to specific language skills, including: overall spoken language, listening (receptive language), speaking (expressive language), semantics (the meaning of words), and syntax (grammar). Examiner required. Not for group use.

Untimed: 40 minutes

Range: Ages 4-0 to 8-11

Scoring: Hand key

Cost: Complete (includes examiner's manual, picture plates, 50 answer sheets, storage box) $59.00.

Publisher: PRO-ED

TEST OF MINIMAL ARTICULATION COMPETENCE (T-MAC)
Wayne Secord

all ages

Purpose: Assesses the severity of individual speech disorders. Used to identify children in need of therapy, to monitor speech development against age expectations, and to target the most trainable phonemes for remediation.

Description: Multiple item verbal response test with a procedure choice of picture identification, sentence reading, or sentence repetition. Provides a flexible format for obtaining a diagnostic measure of articulation performance on 24 consonant phonemes, frequently occurring "s", "r", and "l" blends, 12 vowels, 4 diphthongs, and variations of vocalic 'R'. Test kit includes manual and 25 record forms. Examiner required. Suitable for group use.

Untimed: 10 minutes

Range: Ages 5-adult

Scoring: Examiner evaluated

Cost: 25 record forms $7.95; manual $19.95; test kit $25.95.

Publisher: Charles E. Merrill Publishing Company

TEST OF SYNTACTIC ABILITIES
Stephen P. Quigley, Marjorie W. Steinkamp, Desmond J. Power, and Barry W. Jones

child, teen

Purpose: Measures the difficulties which profoundly, prelingually deaf students (ages 10-19 years) may experience in comprehending and using the syntactic structure of standard English. Used for clinical diagnosis and placement in special education programs.

Description: 20 tests measure skills in the use of nine major syntactic structures: negation, conjunction, determiners, question formation, verb processes, pronominalization, relativisation, complementation, and monimalization. A screening test containing items selected from the diagnostic battery is available in two parallel forms to provide a profile of strengths and weaknesses on individual structures as a basis for determining needs for further testing or instruction. The test has been standardized on deaf children, but may also be suitable for diagnostic and normative evaluation of persons with language problems resulting from other causes. Examiner required. Not for group use.

Untimed: Not available

Range: Ages 10-19

Scoring: Examiner evaluated

Cost: Contact publisher.

Publisher: DORMAC, Inc.-distributed by Australian Council for Educational Research Limited

UTAH TEST OF LANGUAGE DEVELOPMENT
Merlin J. Mecham and J. Dean Jones

child, teen

Purpose: Identifies children ages 2-14 years with language-learning disabilities who may be in need of further evaluation and assistance.

Description: 51 item task assessment oral response test measuring the following factors: receptive semantic language, expressive semantic language, receptive sequential language, and expressive sequential language.

Test items are arranged in developmental order. Examiner begins testing at or just below a child's expected level of ability and works down until eight consecutive correct answers are obtained, and then upward from the starting point until eight consecutive incorrect answers are obtained, at which time the test is discontinued. Items are scored as correct (plus) or incorrect (minus). Total score is the total number of pluses. Test kit includes: manual, line-drawing plates, booklet, object kit, and 25 score sheets in a vinyl carrying case. Restricted to persons trained in psychological or educational testing. Examiner required. Not for group use.

Untimed: 20-30 minutes

Range: Ages 2-14

Scoring: Examiner evaluated

Cost: Complete kit $37.50; 25 extra score sheets $3.50.

Publisher: Communication Research Associates, Inc.

THE VANE-L SCALE
Julia R. Vane

child

Purpose: Measures language acquisition of children ages 2-6 years. Used for clinical assessment and diagnosis, and as an instrument to help parents teach concepts to their children that will prepare them for school.

Description: 35 item task assessment test measuring vocabulary, visual and auditory memory, and language concepts. The child is asked to do things that a child their age is expected to do (such as "put your hands on your head") and to repeat a number of sentences. Factors measured include: receptive and expressive language, auditory-verbal and auditory-motor memory, and right- or left-handedness. Standardized scoring procedures provided. Examiner required. Supervision by a psychologist suggested. Not for group use.

Untimed: 10 minutes

Range: Ages 2-6 years

Scoring: Examiner evaluated

Cost: Manual $5.00; 50 record sheets $3.50; test kit $8.00; complete package $15.00.

Publisher: Clinical Psychology Publishing Co., Inc.

WASHINGTON SPEECH SOUND DISCRIMINATION TEST (WSSD)
E. Prather, A Miner, M.A. Addicott, and L. Sunderland

child

Purpose: Evaluates children's speech sound discrimination. Used for pre-kindergarten placement.

Description: 53 item test measures discrimination ability. Child is asked to listen to correct and incorrect productions of five pictured single words. The child signals, by pointing to the picture, each time the word is correctly presented. The test requires no verbal response. Materials include instruction booklet, seven picture cards, and test forms. The child must demonstrate vocabulary and listening ability by completing one of the demonstration items for test administration. Examiner required. Not suitable for group use.

Untimed: 15 minutes

Range: Ages 3½-5

Scoring: Examiner evaluated

Cost: Complete set $11.95; 64 tests $2.50.

Publisher: The Interstate Printers & Publishers, Inc.

WEISS COMPREHENSIVE ARTICULATION TEST (WCAT)
Curtis E. Weiss

child

Purpose: Determines articulation disorders or delays in young children and identifies misarticulation patterns and other problems. Used in articulation therapy.

Description: Multiple item test in two forms: An easel- stand flip book of 85 pictures for subjects who cannot read, and a card with 38 sentences, for those who can. With the pictures, the child supplies the missing word in a sentence spoken by the examiner; with the sentences, the child does the reading of each complete one. Materials include the picture cards and sentence card, manual and response forms. The test is not appropriate for nonverbal subjects and can only be individually administered by an examiner.

Untimed: Not available

Range: Ages 2½-7

Scoring: Examiner evaluated

Cost: Complete $31.00.

Publisher: Teaching Resources Corporation

THE WESTERN APHASIA BATTERY (WAB)
Refer to page 55.

Visual

ALLEN PICTURE TESTS
Henry F. Allen

child

Purpose: Measures visual acuity of children ages 3½-6 years. Used in

Headstart programs, primary grades and Kindergartens, and pediatricians' offices to identify children in need of further diagnosis and assistance.

Description: One test slide and a vision tester measuring preschoolers' visual acuity. Slides measure 20/100, 20/50, 20/40, and 20/30 levels of acuity for both right and left eyes. A training card is used to familiarize the child with the names of the objects used on the test cards (jeep, birthday cake, telephone, and man on a horse). This is an alternate test to the Michigan Pre-school Acuity Tests. Examiner required. Not for group use.

Untimed: 3-5 minutes

Range: Ages 3½-6

Scoring: Hand key; examiner evaluated

Cost: Not available

Publisher: Titmus Optical, Inc.

ANXIETY SCALE FOR THE BLIND

Refer to page 92.

AO PSEUDO-ISOCHROMATIC COLOR TEST

all ages

Purpose: Assesses color perception.

Description: 15 plate test determines red-green vision deficiency. The test utilizes a demonstration plate to explain the numerical plate design. Subject must be able to read. Examiner required. Not suitable for group use. This test to be discontinued in the near future.

Untimed: 5 minutes

Range: All ages

Scoring: Score sheet; examiner evaluated

Cost: Test $62.00.

Publisher: AO Scientific Instruments Division/Warner- Lambert

Technologies, Inc.

CARROW AUDITORY-VISUAL ABILITIES TEST (CAVAT)
Elizabeth Carrow-Woolfolk

child

Purpose: Measures auditory and visual perceptual, motor, and memory skills in children. Used to identify language/learning problems, to analyze sources of auditory and/or visual difficulties, and for instructional programming.

Description: Multiple item set of two paper-pencil verbal- visual batteries containing 14 subtests. They allow comparison of individual performances in auditory and visual abilities by providing data on interrelationships among discrimination, memory and motor skills. In the Visual Abilities battery, the categories are: visual discrimination matching, visual discrimination memory, visual-motor copying, visual-motor memory, and motor speed. In the Auditory Abilities battery, the categories are: picture memory, picture sequence selection, digits forward, digits backward, sentence repetition, word repetition, auditory blending, auditory discrimination in quiet, and auditory discrimination in noise. Materials include test books, response/scoring booklets, cassette, manual, and an entry test for determining which subtests or battery to administer. The visual battery is not appropriate for blind subjects; the auditory is not appropriate for the deaf. Examiner required. Not for group use.

Timed: Motor speed subtest is timed; 1 hour total

Range: Ages 4-10

Scoring: Examiner evaluated

Cost: Complete $85.00.

Publisher: Teaching Resources Corporation

CITY UNIVERSITY COLOR VISION TEST
Robert Fletcher

all ages

Purpose: Diagnoses all types of color deficiencies including the blue/yellow range. Used to assess the depth and degree of color deficiencies.

Description: Ten item paper-pencil test for assessing color deficiencies in children and adults. Four color standards are arranged in a diamond form around a central standard. One of the outer spots is a match or near match to the central one for a color normal. The other three standards are matches for protan, deutan and tritan defectives. Examiner required. Not suitable for group use.

Untimed: 5 minutes

Range: Child-adult

Scoring: Hand key; examiner evaluated

Cost: Complete kit (includes two ring binder, instructions, scoring key, black cards, record charts) $148.00.

Publisher: Keeler Instruments, Inc.

DENVER EYE SCREENING TEST (DEST)
Frankenburg, Goldstein, Arnald, and Barker

child

Purpose: Helps evaluate vision problems in children to determine if a child needs specialized testing.

Description: A performance test in which the examiner shows seven picture cards and asks the child to name the picture at 15 feet. For children six months to two years-five months old, the examiner uses an "E" card and a spinning toy to attract the child's attention and examines its eyes to see if they track, first one eye, then the other. Materials consist of picture cards, cord, toy, plastic occluder, and "E" card. A flashlight is required. Examiner administered. Not for group use.

Untimed: 10 minutes

Range: Ages 6 months-7 years

Scoring: Examiner evaluated

Cost: Complete kit $9.00; manual $6.50; 25 test forms $1.75.

Publisher: Ladoca Publishing Foundation

DVORINE COLOR VISION TEST
Israel Dvorine

teen, adult

Purpose: Identifies individuals with defective color vision. Used for screening for color blindness in industrial settings.

Description: 15 item test for determining type and degree of color vision defect. Subject reads numbers or traces paths made up of multi-colored dots presented against a background of contrasting dots. Materials include 15 plates with 8 auxiliary plates for verification. Examiner required. Not suitable for group use.

Untimed: 2-3 minutes

Range: Job applicants

Scoring: Examiner evaluated

Cost: Booklet of color plates $59.50; 35 record forms, $4.85.

Publisher: The Psychological Corporation

DVORINE PSEUDO-ISOCHROMATIC PLATES
Louis Sloan

all ages   grades PRE-UP

Purpose: Tests for protanoid and

deuteranoid types of red-green color blindness. Used for perceptual screening, vision testing, and drivers tests.

Description: 21 item oral response test assessing red-green color perception. Plates consisting of patterns of colored dots revealing either numbers or trails are held 30 inches in front of the subject who is given approximately five seconds to call out the number or trace the trail formed by the pattern on each plate. Materials consist of a single booklet of color plates containing two demonstration plates, 14 number plates, and 7 trail plates. Examiner required. Not for group use.

Untimed: 3 minutes

Range: Preschool-adult

Scoring: Hand key

Cost: Plates $60.00.

Publisher: Lafayette Instrument Company, Inc.

FARNSWORTH DICHOTOMOUS TEST FOR COLOR BLINDNESS
Dean Farnsworth

teen, adult

Purpose: Assesses color blindness. Used for screening applicants for jobs requiring color vision.

Description: One task test of color vision. Applicant arranges colored caps in order, according to color, on a hinged rack. Pattern of responses is compared to that of normal subjects. Materials include hinged rack with one permanently mounted reference color cap and fifteen movable color caps. Examiner required. Not suitable for group use.

Untimed: 5 minutes

Range: Job applicants

Scoring: Hand key; examiner

evaluated

Cost: Complete set (includes caps, rack, manual, 100 analysis sheets) $178.00; manual $2.00; 100 analysis sheets $8.50.

Publisher: The Psychological Corporation

FARNSWORTH-MUNSELL 100 HUE TEST
Refer to page 712.

HAPTIC INTELLIGENCE SCALE
Refer to page 24.

HILL PERFORMANCE TEST OF SELECTED POSITIONED CONCEPTS
Everett Hill

child

Purpose: Measures the development of spatial concepts in visually-impaired children ages 6-10 years.

Description: 72 item task-assessment test of basic spatial concepts such as front, back, left, and right. The development of these positional concepts is tested through performance on four types of tasks. The children are asked to identify body relationships, demonstrate positional concepts of body parts to one another, demonstrate positional concepts of body parts to other objects, and form object-to-object relationships. The test may be used as a criterion-referenced instrument to identify individual strengths and weaknesses in the area of spatial concepts or as a norm- referenced test. Examiner required. Not for group use.

Untimed: Not available

Range: Ages 6-10

Scoring: Examiner evaluated

Cost: Complete kit (includes 20 record forms and manual) $14.75.

Publisher: Stoelting Co.

ISHIHARA'S TEST FOR COLOUR BLINDNESS
Shinobu Ishihara

all ages   grades PRE-UP

Purpose: Determines whether a patient has normal color vision. Used for school and employee screening.

Description: 24 item visual identification test measuring normal color perception. Each test item consists of a plate of pseudo-isochromatic colors with a number or pattern on each plate. Patient is asked to read the number or trace the pattern on each plate. Children who do not know numbers may trace the numbers. Identifies both protan and deutan type color deficiencies with an indication of whether they are strong or mild. Test materials include: 24-page book of color plates, informational guide, and scoring key. Not limited to English language administration. Examiner required. Suitable for group use.

Untimed: Less than 1 minute

Range: Preschool-adult

Scoring: Hand key; examiner evaluated

Cost: Complete $63.00.

Publisher: Kanehara & Co. Ltd., Japan/Titmus Optical, Inc.

JUDGMENT OF LINE ORIENTATION
Refer to page 533.

KERBY LEARNING MODALITY TEST, REVISED 1980
Refer to page 550.

KNOX'S CUBE TEST (KCT)
Refer to page 453.

MERTENS VISUAL PERCEPTION TEST
Marjorie K. Mertens

child   grades K-1

Purpose: Measures the areas of visual perception which are closely related to reading ability in kindergarten and first-grade students. Used to plan regular classroom and remediation programs and to establish Individualized Education Programs for P.L. 94-142.

Description: Six subtests measure the following areas of visual perception: Design Copying, Design Reproduction, Framed Pictures, Design Completion, Spatial Recognition, and Visual Memory. Reading skill remediation suggestions are provided for each of the six subtests. Standardized on 1,500 kindergarten children and more than 2,900 first graders representing several ethnic groups. Scores have good correlations with the Standford Achievement Test and the Gates-MacGinitie Reading Test. Examiner required. group use.

Untimed: 20-30 minutes

Range: Kindergarten and grade 1

Scoring: Hand key; examiner evaluated

Cost: Kit (10 tests and manual) $7.00.

Publisher: Western Psychological Services

MICHIGAN PRE-SCHOOL ACUITY AND BINOCULARITY TEST

child

Purpose: Measures acuity and screens for binocular vision of children in Headstart, preschool programs and primary grades. Identifies children in need of further evaluation. Used with both handicapped and normally developing children.

Description: Vision tester and four slides comprise two tests: one for visual acuity and one for binocular vision. The test for visual acuity consists of three slides and four training cards. The child is familiarized with the task of determining "which way the table legs point" using the training cards. He then takes the test using the vision tester. The Acuity Test measures both Right Eye and Left Eye Acuity. The Standard Test is 20/30 on a pass/fail basis. 20/20, 20/40, 20/50, and 20/70 levels are also available. The Binocularity Test consists of one slide and uses the "which way do the table legs point" task. It identifies children with amblyopia, suppression and other binocularity problems. Used by pediatricians, family physicians, medical specialists, and school screening programs for purposes of screening and referral. Examiner required. Not suitable for group use.

Untimed: 5 minutes (acuity); 2 minutes (binocularity)

Range: Ages 3¹/₂₀-6

Scoring: Hand key; examiner evaluated

Cost: Complete (3 acuity slides, 1 binocularity slide, manual, accessories) $135.00.

Publisher: Titmus Optical, Inc.

MKM BINOCULAR PRE-SCHOOL TEST
Leland Michael and James King

child   Preschool

Purpose: Helps evaluate the near-point visual performance of preschool and other nonreading children. Used for demonstrating how learning lenses can improve performance and to monitor progress of visual therapy cases.

Description: One card visual-verbal test. The card, used with a stereoscope, contains an array of geometric symbols; some presented to both eyes and others presented to the right or left eye along. If the child has good binocular performance, the symbols will be read in the proper sequence without undue hesitation. If the child tends to see double this factor might suppress the vision of one eye, thus omitting the words presented to that eye. Binocular problems can then be identified. A stereoscope is needed. Examiner required. Not suitable for group use.

Untimed: 2-3 minutes

Range: Preschool

Scoring: Examiner evaluated

Cost: Complete (includes 50 score sheets, instructions, cards) $10.00.

Publisher: MKM

MKM MONOCULAR AND BINOCULAR READING TEST
Leland Michael and James W. King

child   grades 1-2

Purpose: Helps identify children with reading problems related to subtle differences in the vision of one eye or the other. Used for demonstrating how learning lenses can improve performance and to monitor progress of visual therapy cases.

Description: Six card visual-verbal test. The cards are divided into two sets: the first set contains 110 words which most children know by the end of the first grade; the second contains an additional 110 words expected to be known by the end of the second grade. Each set contains three cards. The child reads the first card with the left eye alone. Then, the second card presents the same words in reverse order for the right eye alone. The examiner records errors and time on a score sheet, determining which errors were common to both eyes or which were made with the right or left eye alone. Word reversals, improper vowel sounds and other errors are expected to be about the same for each eye, but if the time for one eye exceeds the other by 20% or more, a binocular visual problem is suspected. The third card contains the same words, with some common to both eyes and others presented just to the right or left eye alone. A stereoscope is needed. Examiner administered. Not suitable for group use.

Untimed: 5-10 minutes

Range: Grades 1 and 2

Scoring: Examiner evaluated

Cost: Complete (includes cards and score pads) $30.00; 50 additional score pads $3.50.

Publisher: MKM

MOTOR-FREE VISUAL PERCEPTION TEST (MVPT)
Refer to page 536.

PEEK-A-BOO TEST
Pat Hill

child

Purpose: Determines vision impairment in normal and retarded children not yet able to read.

Description: Eight target set which presents non-language tests in these six areas: Acuity, Vertical and Lateral Eye Coordination, Fusion, Depth Perception, and Color Discrimination. The cards, which are modern illustrations of familiar objects, are shown one at a time in the Telebinocular (refer to the Visual Survey Telebinocular). Specific questions are asked by the examiner and answers are recorded on a corresponding record form (which is ordered separately). Examiner required. Not for group use.

Timed: 5 minutes

Range: Ages 3-7

Scoring: Hand key

Cost: Complete $54.00; contact publisher for record forms price.

Publisher: Keystone View, Division of Mast Development Company

PROFESSIONAL VISION TESTER

all ages

Purpose: Measures an individual's visual performance. Used to detect vision deficiencies.

Description: 11 test, nonverbal battery. The tests measure: Phoria-Vertical and Lateral at near and far distances (4) tests, Acuity of right and left eyes at near and far distances (6 tests), and one test of Stereopsis and Color Discrimination. Materials include a precision stereoscopic instrument equipped with adjustable viewing aperture height, constant illumination, and a revolving drum to hold test slides. All controls are on the right side of the machine and require a minimum number of manipulations. Questions are simple and direct and the routine can be learned with minimal training. Examiner required. Not suitable for group use.

Untimed: 10 minutes

Range: Ages 5 and older

Scoring: Hand key

Cost: Instrument $995.00.

Publisher: Lafayette Instrument Co., Inc.

RANDOT STEREOPSIS TEST

all ages   Primary-UP

Purpose: Determines whether or not a patient has stereo depth perception and/or binocular vision. Screens children and adults for further evaluation and treatment.

Description: Two stereo vectographs (dot patterns on a homogeneous background) and polaroid glasses are used to measure children's Stereo Depth Perception and Gross Depth Perception. More definitive tests are included for adult patients. The patient wears the polaroid glasses and is asked to view the vectographs and pick out the characters formed by the dot patterns. The test is not practical with very young children and provides no monocular clues. Examiner required. Suitable for group use.

Untimed: 10-15 minutes

Range: Primary grades-adult

Scoring: Hand key; examiner evaluated

Cost: Complete $66.00.

Publisher: Titmus Optical, Inc.

ROUGHNESS DISCRIMINATION TEST
Carson Y. Nolan and June E. Morris

child   grade 1

Purpose: Predicts readiness to learn to read Braille for visually-impaired first-grade students.

Description: 69 item test assessing tactile discrimination. Each item consists of a stimulus card on which is mounted four pieces of sandpaper, of which three are alike and one is different or coarser than the other three. The child is asked to identify which piece of sandpaper feels different from the others. Two practice cards are provided. The complete test kit includes: 71 stimulus cards, test manual, 25 self-scoring answer sheets. Examiner required. Not for group use.

Untimed: 15 minutes

Range: Grade 1-visually impaired students

Scoring: Hand key; examiner evaluated

Cost: Complete $99.90.

Publisher: American Printing House for the Blind, Inc.

SLOAN ACHROMATOPSIA TEST
Refer to page 189.

SOUTHERN CALIFORNIA POSTROTARY NYSTAGMUS TEST
A. Jean Ayres

child

Purpose: Evaluates the normalcy of the duration of nystagmus (involuntary rapid movement of the eyeball) following rotation in children ages 5-9 years. Used to identify disorders of the vestibular system.

Description: The child being evaluated is placed on the Nystagmus Rotation Board and passively rotated to the left and then to the right. At the end of both the left and the right rotations, the duration of nystagmus is observed and recorded. The normalcy of the duration of nystagmus following the rotation is evaluated as an indicator of disorders in the vestibular system. Norms are presented by sex for ages 5-9 years. Examiner required. Not suitable for group use.

Timed: 5 minutes

Range: Ages 5-9

Scoring: Hand key; examiner evaluated

Cost: Complete kit (includes 50 record sheets, Angle Guide Card, board, manual) $49.50.

Publisher: Western Psychological Services

STANFORD-OHWAKI-KOHS BLOCK DESIGN INTELLIGENCE TEST FOR THE BLIND: AMERICAN REVISION
Refer to page 34.

STEREO FLY STEROPSIS TEST

all ages   Preschool-UP

Purpose: Determines whether or not a patient has stereo depth perception and/or binocular vision. Screens children and adults for further evaluation and treatment. Useful with very young children to determine binocular vision.

Description: A house fly vectograph (dot patterns on a homogeneous background) and polaroid glasses are used to measure children's Stereo Depth Perception and Gross Depth Perception. More definitive tests are included for adult patients. The patient wears the polaroid glasses and is asked to view the vectographs and pick out the characters that seem closest. The test contains a picture of a large housefly which is particularly effective with very young children. Useful as screening aid but not for diagnosis. Examiner required. Suitable for group use.

Untimed: 5-10 minutes

Range: Preschool-adult

Scoring: Hand key; examiner evaluated

Cost: Complete $66.00.

Publisher: Titmus Optical, Inc.

STYCAR VISION TESTS
Mary Sheridan

child

Purpose: Assesses vision in children ages 6 months to 7 years. Used for evaluating very young and handicapped children.

Description: Multiple item three performance tests of vision. Stycar Vision Test, ages 2 to 7, uses toys and laminated cards and charts. The Graded Balls Test, ages 6 months to 2 years, also assesses the visual competence or motorically impaired children and those with language difficulties. Use of a reversible occluder is recommended. The Panda Test is for use with children with severe visual or other handicaps. Available to medical doctors and teachers of the blind. Examiner required. Not suitable for group use.
BRITISH PUBLISHER

Untimed: Not available

Range: Ages 6 months-7

Scoring: Examiner evaluated

Cost: Complete kit (includes miniature toys, distant vision cards, 5 letter booklet, 7 letter booklet, Near Vision card and 3 key cards, graded balls, 25 record forms, and manual) £41.60; Panda Test set of cards £7.10; Panda Test set of plastic letters £9.75 (payment in sterling for all overseas orders).

Publisher: NFER-Nelson Publishing Company

TEST OF VISUAL ANALYSIS SKILLS (TVAS)
J. Rosner

child   grades PRE-K

Purpose: Discriminates between those children who are competent and those who are in need of remediation in perceiving the visual relationships necessary for integrating letter and word shapes.

Description: Multiple item paper-pencil test where children are required to copy simple to complex geometric patterns until the task becomes too difficult. Examiner required. Test is to be discontinued some time in 1983.

Untimed: Not available

Range: Preschool-Kindergarten

Scoring: Examiner evaluated

Cost: Contact publisher.

Publisher: Academic Therapy Publications

VISION TESTER: INTERMEDIATE MODEL

child   grades PRE-6

Purpose: Screens visual skills of preschool, Head Start and primary grade students. Identifies students with visual deficits which may affect their performance in school.

Description: A vision tester with 8 test slides are used to screen the visual abilities of young children. Preschool children are tested for Acuity Far, Right Eye, Left Eye, and Binocularity. Primary grade students are tested for Acuity Far, Right Eye, Left Eye, Hyperopia, Heterophorias, far and near, and Color Vision. Test materials include: vision tester with 8 slides, training manual, record forms, and lens unit. Examiner required. Not for group use.

Untimed: 3-5 minutes

Range: Preschool-primary

Scoring: Hand key; examiner evaluated

Cost: Complete $930.00.

Publisher: Titmus Optical, Inc.

VISION TESTER: PROFESSIONAL MODEL

all ages   grades PRE-UP

Purpose: Screens visual skills of preschool, primary and secondary grade students, and adults. Identifies individuals with visual deficits.

Description: A vision tester with 12 slides is used to screen visual skills. Preschool children are tested for Acuity Far, Right Eye, Left Eye, and Binocularity. Primary Grade students are tested for Acuity Far, Right Eye, Left Eye, Hyperopia, Heterophorias, and Color Vision. Secondary Grade students and adults are tested for Acuity Far and Near, Right Eye, Left Eye, Both Eyes, Vertical and Lateral Heterophorias, and Color vision. Test materials include: 12 slides and vision tester, training manual, record forms, and lens unit. Examiner required. Not suitable for group use.

Untimed: 3-5 minutes

Range: Preschool-adult

Scoring: Hand key; examiner evaluated

Cost: Complete $1055.00.

Publisher: Titmus Optical, Inc.

VISION TESTER: SCHOOL MODEL

child   grades 2-6

Purpose: Screens visual skills of children Grades 2-6 to insure that they have adequate vision for study. Identifies children in need of further evaluation and treatment.

Description: Three test slides in a vision tester measuring the following factors: Acuity Far (right eye and left eye), Hyperopia, and Heterophoria (far and near). Complete set includes: three test slides, vision tester, training manual, record forms, and lens unit. Examiner required. Not for group use.

Untimed: 3-5 minutes

Range: Primary grades

Scoring: Hand key; examiner evaluated

Cost: Complete $795.00.

Publisher: Titmus Optical, Inc.

VISUAL DISCRIMINATION TEST
Joseph M. Wepman, Anne Morency and Maria Seidl

child

Purpose: Measures the ability of children ages 5-8 to discriminate visually between similar forms. Used to measure the skills required to learn to read.

Description: 20 item test in which child indicates with "point-to" responses which of four nonalphabetic forms is the same as the example. No verbal responses are required. Separate norms provided for ages 5, 6, 7, and 8 years, along with adequacy threshold scores to indicate need for referral. Materials consist of a 24 page test booklet of original designs, a complete administration and scoring manual, and score sheets marked specifically for the test. Examiner required. Not for group use.

Untimed: 10-15 minutes

Range: Ages 5-8

Scoring: Hand key

Cost: Complete kit (includes 1 reusuable test booklet, 20 score sheets, manual) $28.50.

$28.50.

Publisher: Western Psychological Services

VISUAL FUNCTIONING ASSESSMENT TOOL (VFAT)
Kathleen Costello, Patricia Pinkney and Wendy Scheffers

all ages

Purpose: Assesses visual functioning in the educational setting. Used with low-vision individuals of all ages and levels, including the severely handicapped and to help establish Individualized Education Programs.

Description: An observation test using common classroom materials to assess the following areas of visual functioning: appearance of eyes, basic responses, fixation tracking, saccadic movement, scanning, visual accuity, visual field, depth perception, eye-hand and eye-foot coordination, visual imitation and memory, visual discrimination, visual perception, and concepts of self and others in space, pictures, visual environment, and mobility. It is not necessary to administer the entire VFAT to every student. Specific appropriate areas may be used independently. The test is designed to be administered by an eye specialist or a teacher of the visually-impaired. Examiner required. Not for group use.

Untimed: Not available

Range: Child, adolescent, adult

Scoring: Examiner evaluated

Cost: Complete kit (includes recording forms and manual) $39.00.

Publisher: Stoelting Co.

VISUAL SKILLS TEST

all ages   grades 1-UP

Purpose: Screens basic visual skills as a basis for further optometric examination and diagnosis. Used primarily by optometrists.

Description: Ten cards for use in a standard biopter provide preliminary screening of a patient's visual skills. The cards measure the following factors: Acuity (Far and Near), Right Eye, Left Eye, Both Eyes, Vertical and Lateral Heterophorias, Far; Lateral Heterophorias, Far; Lateral Heterophoria, Near, Central Fusion, Far and Near; Stereopsis and Color Perception, Far, will not stand up under constant use as in school or industrial screening programs. Examiner required. Not suitable for group use.

Untimed: 10-15 minutes

Range: Primary-adult

Scoring: Hand key; examiner evaluated

Cost: Complete $43.00.

Publisher: Titmus Optical, Inc.

VISUAL SKILLS TEST SET
#5100

all ages

Purpose: Determines basic visual patterns, binocular acceptance of prescriptions and need for orthoptic training. Used for vision screening of school children.

Description: Vision test using 15 stereo targets to screen the following visual skills: Phorias, Fusion Readiness, Binocular Visual Efficiency at near and far points, Stereopsis, and Color Discrimination. Cards are shown to the child one at a time in the telebinocular (refer to the Visual Survey Telebinocular), specific questions are asked, and answers are recorded on a corresponding form (which is ordered separately). The test may be too difficult for young children and slow learners. Examiner required. Not for group use.

Untimed: 5 minutes

Range: Ages 8-adult

Scoring: Hand key

Cost: Complete $91.00.

Publisher: Keystone View, Division of Mast Development Company

VISUAL SURVEY TELE-BINOCULAR (VISION SCREENING TELEBINOCULAR)

all ages

Purpose: Measures near-and-far-point vision. Used to screen for remediation.

Description: Vision test using a general purpose telebinocular equipped with the same lens system as the ophthalmic telebinocular, as well as occluder paddles, adjustable viewing head height, and built-in internal slide illumination. During testing, target slides are placed in the instrument, and the individual is asked specific questions about each card. For slide description, refer to the Visual Skills Test Set. The telebinocular can accommodate the Plus Lens attachment. Examiner required. Not for group use.

Untimed: 5 minutes

Range: Ages 3-adult

Scoring: Hand key

Cost: Complete $521.00.

Publisher: Keystone View, Division of Mast Development Company

WILLIAMS INTELLIGENCE TEST FOR CHILDREN WITH DEFECTIVE VISION
Refer to page 487.

Student Evaluation and Counseling

Behavior Problems and Counseling Tools

ANALYSIS OF COPING STYLE (ACS)
Herbert F. Boyd and G. Orville Johnson

child, teen   grades K-12 🖝 ✎

Purpose: Identifies students with behavior problems so teachers, counselors or school psychologists can screen children for further testing, plan counseling approaches or intervention procedures.

Description: 20 item paper-pencil test in which the examiner presents pictures of school situations (with peers and adults) and the students choose one of six possible responses. The responses are analyzed for patterns of coping styles: externalized attack, internalized attack, avoidance, or denial. The test discriminates between normal and disturbed populations. Two versions available: one for elementary school children and one for high school students. Materials include picture stimuli (sheets or overhead transparencies), response forms and manual. Examiner required. Suitable for group use.

Untimed: 10-20 minutes

Range: Grades K-12

Scoring: Hand key

Cost: 25 individual record forms $7.00; 100 group response forms $7.00; elementary transparencies $19.95; secondary transparencies $19.95; manual $19.95.

Publisher: Charles E. Merrill Publishing Company

BEHAVIOR RATING PROFILE (BRP)
Linda L. Brown and Donald D. Hammill

child, teen   grades 1-12 🖝 ✎

Purpose: Identifies elementary and secondary students who are thought to have behavior problems and the settings in which those problems seem prominent. Also identifies individuals who have differing perceptions about the behavior of a student.

Description: Multiple item paper-pencil battery consisting of six independent, individually normed measures. The scales may be used separately or in conjunction with other BRP components. The measures are: the Student Rating Scales, Home, School, and Peer; the Parent Rating Scale, and the Sociogram. May be used with disturbed and learning disabled students. Examiner required. Not suitable for group use.

Untimed: Not available

Range: Grades 1-12

Scoring: Hand key

Cost: Complete kit (includes examiners manual, 50 each of teacher, parent and student rating forms, 50 profile sheets, and storage box) $67.00.

Publisher: PRO-ED

BRISTOL SOCIAL ADJUST-MENT GUIDES, AMERICAN EDITION (BSAG)
D.H. Stott

child, teen

Purpose: Diagnoses nature and extent of behavioral disturbances and social adjustment in children ages 5-16. Used by teachers and school psychologists.

Description: Multiple item paper-pencil observational instrument consisting of short phrases descriptive of a child's behavior. Those phrases which apply to the child being evaluated are underlined by an adult familiar with the child. The guides are concerned with observable behavior rather than inferences based on projective techniques or the child's self-assessment. An overall assessment of maladjustment is provided as well as subscores for five core syndromes (unforthcomingness, withdrawal, depression, inconsequence, and hostility), and four additional associated groupings (peer-maladaptiveness, non-syndromic over-reaction, non-syndromic under-reaction, and neurological symptoms). Available in separate forms for boys and girls. Separate norms provided for boys and girls based on students from city, county, and church schools. Examiner required. Suitable for group use.

Untimed: 10-15 minutes

Range: Ages 5-16

Scoring: Hand key

Cost: Specimen set (includes manual and all forms) $3.50; 25 rating scales $4.50; 100-$16.00 (specify boy or girl form); 25 diagnostic forms $2.00; 100-$7.50 (specify boy or girl form); scoring key $3.50; manual $2.00.

Publisher: Educational and Industrial Testing Service

BRISTOL SOCIAL ADJUST-MENT GUIDES, BRITISH EDITION (BSAG)
D.H. Stott

child, teen

Purpose: Evaluates the behavior patterns of children and adolescents ages 5-15 years. Identifies maladjusted and disturbed children in need of further testing and assistance. Used for clinical diagnosis.

Description: Paper-pencil checklist consists of statements about a child's habits of response to his environment. Designed to be filled out by a teacher, social worker, or other adult familiar with the child's behavior, the inventory provides the clinician with a picture of the child's day-to-day behavior and a system for interpreting that behavior by means of diagnostic forms. Separate guides are provided for the child in the school (boys and girls), in the family, or in residential care. Development of the guides, theoretical implications, and related studies are described in the manual, *The Social Adjustment of Children,* fifth edition. Self-administered by the evaluator under supervision of a psychologist. Not for group use. BRITISH PUBLISHER

Untimed: Open ended

Range: Ages 5-15

Scoring: Examiner evaluated

Cost: Specimen set £1.00 plus VAT; manual £3.50 net c.

Publisher: Hodder & Stoughton

THE BROOK REACTION TEST OF INTERESTS AND TEMPERAMENT
A.W. Heim, K.P. Watts and V. Simmonds

teen, adult

Purpose: Measures interests and temperament of adolescents. Used for individual counseling and vocational guidance.

Description: 80 item paper-pencil test of interests and temperament. Items are ambiguous stimulus words dictated by tape recording. Meanings of stimulus words relate to one or more of 22 interest categories. Adolescent writes the word he associates with each stimulus word. Scoring is determined by the meaning the subject attributes to stimulus word in his response. Examiner required. Suitable for group use.
BRITISH PUBLISHER

Timed: 25 minutes

Range: 13 years and over

Scoring: Hand key

Cost: Complete set (includes part I, part II, part III manuals, 25 score sheets, 25 response sheets, tape) £52.00 plus VAT (payment in sterling for all overseas orders).

Publisher: NFER-Nelson Publishing Company

BUTTONS: A PROJECTIVE TEST FOR PRE- ADOLES-CENTS AND ADOLESCENTS
Esther P. Rothman and Pearl H. Berkowitz

child,   grades Elementary-
teen   High School

Purpose: Evaluates acting-out, maladjusted, disturbed students. Used to identify emotionally and behaviorally disturbed children.

Description: Multiple item oral response test consisting of an eight-page booklet containing 12 cartoon strips of animals in school situations. The last frame in each strip has a blank "balloon" from one of the animals and the child supplies the words for that "balloon." This projective test format uses non-threatening, "fun" cartoons. Exam-

iner required. Not for group use.

Untimed: 15-20 minutes

Range: Elementary-High School

Scoring: Examiner evaluated

Cost: Complete kit (includes 10 tests, 10 protocol booklets, manual) $11.60.

Publisher: Western Psychological Services

CHILD OBSERVATION GUIDE
Mark Stone

child, teen

Purpose: Evaluates a child's behavior. Used in diagnosis of behavior problems.

Description: Multiple item rating scale measure of ten aspects of behavior: appearance, motor ability, orientation, activity level, attention, speech/language, cognitive functioning, emotional state, peer interaction, and adult interaction. Materials include manual with recommendations regarding child observation principles. Examiner required. Not suitable for group use.

Untimed: Observation time

Range: Child-adolescent

Scoring: Examiner evaluated

Cost: Specimen set $5.50; 25 forms $16.50; 100- $65.00; manual $3.50.

Publisher: Psychologists and Educators, Inc.

DECISION MAKING ORGA-NIZER (DMO)
Anna Miller-Tiedeman and Patricia Elenz-Martin

teen, adult   grades 10-UP

Purpose: Diagnoses decision-making problems of high school and college students. Used for counseling and guidance.

Description: 36 item paper-pencil multiple-choice test of self-understanding, educational, career and vocational plans, time use, and barriers to decision making. Subjects are presented with questions followed by five possible responses and asked to check the responses that apply to them (more than one response for each question may be checked). Self-administered. Suitable for group use.

Timed: 10 minutes

Range: Grades High school, college

Scoring: Examiner evaluated

Cost: Starter set (includes manual and 20 organizers) $13.50.

Publisher: Scholastic Testing Service, Inc.

DEMOS D (DROPOUT) SCALE
George D. Demos

teen   grades 7-12

Purpose: Identifies junior and senior high school students who are probable school drop-outs. Used for preventative counseling.

Description: 29 item paper-pencil questionnaire measuring attitudes in four areas: toward teachers, toward education, influences by peers or parents, and school behavior. Minimum fifth-grade reading level required. Gives a total score and basic area scores which are converted to probabilities of dropping out of school. Self-administered. Suitable for group use.

Untimed: 15-20 minutes

Range: Grades 7-12

Scoring: Hand key

Cost: Complete kit (includes 25 forms and manual) $9.60.

Publisher: Western Psychological Services

THE DEVEREUX ADOLESCENT BEHAVIOR RATING SCALE
George Spivack, Peter Haimes and Jules Spotts

teen

Purpose: Assesses the behavior symptoms of normal and emotionally disturbed adolescents ages 13-18 years. Used for diagnostic and screening procedures, group placement decisions, and assessment of progress in response to specific programs or procedures.

Description: 84 item paper-pencil test assessing symptomatic behaviors of adolescents. The evaluator (someone living with the youth) rates each item according to how he feels the subject's behavior compares with the behavior of normal children of the same age. Yields 12 factor scores (unethical behavior, defiant-resistive, domineering-sadistic, heterosexual interest, hyperactive expansive, poor emotional control, need approval and dependency, emotional distance, physical inferiority-timidity, schizoid withdrawal, bizarre speech and cognition, bizarre action), 3 cluster scores (inability to delay, paranoid thought, anxious self-blame), and 11 item scores (persecution, plotting, bodily concern, external influences, compulsive acts, avoids competition, withdrawn, socialization, peer dominance, physical coordination, distraction). Self-administered by evaluator. Not for group use.

Untimed: 10-15 minutes

Range: Ages 13-18 years

Scoring: Examiner evaluated

Cost: Examination set (includes 25 scales; 1 manual) $10.50; manual $2.00; 25 scales at $.30 each; 50 scales at $.26 each; 200 scales at $.22 each; 500 scales at $.20 each.

Publisher: The Devereux Foundation

THE DEVEREUX ELEMEN-
TARY SCHOOL BEHAVIOR
RATING SCALE (DESB-II)
Marshall Swift

child

Purpose: Assesses overt classroom behaviors at the elementary school level. Diagnoses problem behaviors which interfere with classroom performance. Used for screening procedures, group placement decisions, and assessment of progress in response to specific programs or procedures.

Description: 52 item paper-pencil inventory assessing the symptomatic classroom behavior patterns of children grades K-6. The classroom teacher rates each item according to how he feels the subject's behavior compares to the behavior of normal children his age. Yields 11 factor scores (classroom disturbance, impatience, disrespect- defiance, external blame, achievement anxiety, external reliance, comprehension, inattentiveness- withdrawn, irrelevant-responsiveness, creative initiative, need for closeness to the teacher) and 3 item scores (unable to change, quits easily, slow work). Self-administered by teacher. Not for group use.

Untimed: 10-15 minutes

Range: Ages 6-12 years

Scoring: Examiner evaluated

Cost: Examination set $10.50 each (includes 25 scales and manual) $10.50; 1 manual $2.00; 25 scales at $.30 each; 50 scales at $.26 each; 200 scales at $.22 each; 500 scales at $.20 each.

Publisher: The Devereux Foundation

EDUCATION APPERCEPTION
TEST
Jack M. Thompson and Robert A. Sones

child, teen   grades PRE-8

Purpose: Assesses preschool and elementary student attitudes toward school and education. Used to work with acting-out and problem children, including some adolescents.

Description: 72 item oral response test. The examiner uses 18 photographs on sturdy 7" x 9" cards depicting children in school and school related activities to evoke responses in four major areas: reaction to authority, reaction toward learning, peer relationships, and home attitude toward school. Responses to each photograph include "What took place before?", "What is going on now?", "What feelings are involved?", and "What is the outcome?" The test is a projective instrument and yields no scores. Examiner required. Not for group use.

Untimed: 20-30 minutes

Range: Preschool and elementary

Scoring: Examiner evaluated

Cost: Complete set (includes all pictures and manual) $25.10.

Publisher: Western Psychological Services

HOME INDEX
Harrison G. Gough

all ages   grades 6-UP

Purpose: Gathers information from junior high and high school students concerning their home backgrounds and socioeconomic status. Used to forecast educational achievement, as well as to gather biographical data on delinquents and children with behavioral problems.

Description: 22 item paper-pencil true-false inventory assessing students' home and family backgrounds. Measures four categories: social status of family, ownership and material status, socio-civic involvement, and cultural-aesthetic involvement. Scores are provided for each of the categories, as well as a total score reflecting overall socioeconomic status. To encourage accuracy, students are told prior to filling out the inventory that all information will be confidential. College students must be asked to report on their family life at the time they were in junior and senior high school. Norms provided are based on 4,381 junior and senior high school students in a nationwide sample. Test users are furnished with copies of the manual and test from which they can prepare their own. Self- administered. Suitable for group use.

Untimed: 10 minutes

Range: Grades 6-12 and college

Scoring: Hand key

Cost: Free-(manual and copy provided).

Publisher: Harrison G. Gough/ Institute of Personality Assessment and Research

---

INFERRED SELF-CONCEPT SCALE
E.L. McDaniel

child   grades 1-6

Purpose: Evaluates the self-concept of children in grades 1-6 based on their behavior in school.

Description: 30 item paper-pencil inventory presents statements describing various behaviors which a teacher or counselor must rate on a five-point scale from "Never" to "Always" based on observation of the child being evaluated. The assessment of the child's self-concept is inferred from this behavior profile with the aid of standardized scoring and interpretation. Administered by teacher or counselor familiar with the child. Suitable for group use.

Untimed: 15-20 minutes

Range: Grades 1-6

Scoring: Hand key

Cost: Complete kit (includes 50 scales and manual) $8.40.

Publisher: Western Psychological Services

JUNIOR INVENTORY (J.I.)
Hermann H. Remmers and Robert H. Bauernfeind

child, teen   grades 4-8

Purpose: Diagnoses individual problems and concerns among students grades 4-8. Used as a guide for individual needs-assessment counseling and group planning.

Description: Multiple item paper-pencil test similar to the Youth Inventory. The Junior Inventory is designed for grades 4-8, and covers the problems of pre- adolescent boys and girls, with less emphasis on career and college planning and dating problems. The test is in four categories: About Me and My School, About Myself, Getting Along With Others, and Things In General. Computer scoring service and Class Analysis Summary are available. Examiner required. Suitable for group use.

Timed: 35-40 minutes

Range: Grades 4-8

Scoring: Hand key; examiner evaluated; computer scoring available

Cost: 35 test booklets $12.00; 50 answer sheets $10.00.

Publisher: Scholastic Testing Service, Inc.

LEWIS COUNSELING INVENTORY
Refer to page 114.

LIFE ADJUSTMENT INVENTORY
Ronald C. Doll and J. Wayne Wrightstone

teen   grades 9-12

Purpose: Measures general adjustment to high school curriculum. Used for curriculum surveys and diagnosis of individual maladjusted pupils for individual guidance.

Description: Multiple item paper-pencil test of general adjustment to high school curriculum. Also measures feeling of need for additional experiences in thirteen specific areas such as consumer education; religion, morals and ethics; family living; vocational orientation and preparation; reading and study skills; and citizenship education. Conforms with the United States Office of Education's Life Adjustment Program. Examiner required. Suitable for group use.

Untimed: 25 minutes

Range: Grades 9-12

Scoring: Hand key

Cost: Specimen set $2.20; 25 inventories $5.50; 100-$21.00.

Publisher: Psychometric Affiliates

MERRILL-DEMOS DD SCALE (MDDD)
Merril J. Weijola and George D. Demos

child, teen   grades 3-9

Purpose: Identifies potential or actual drug abuse and delinquent behavior on the part of children in grades 3-9. Used to counsel such

children and their parents.

Description: Multiple item paper-pencil attitude scale measures understanding and acceptance of teachers, police, school, and community in order to identify children in need of guidance or counseling. Formerly known as the TPSC scale, the MDDD norms are available for total score and each of the four subscales for both males and females at the primary (grades 3-6) and secondary (grades 6-9) levels. Restricted to A.P.A. members. Examiner required. Suitable for group use.

Untimed: 30 minutes

Range: Grades 3-9

Scoring: Examiner evaluated

Cost: 25 tests $8.50; manual $2.50; 25 profile charts $3.50.

Publisher: Sheridan Psychological Services, Inc.

NORMATIVE ADAPTIVE BEHAVIOR CHECKLIST (NABC)
Gary Adams

all ages

Purpose: Assesses an individual's level of behavioral development; provides a norm-referenced evaluation of skills and abilities and identifies individuals in need of more comprehensive evaluation. Useful for evaluation and placement in special programs and rounding out psycho-educational files.

Description: 160 item paper-pencil checklist (to be filled out by the examiner) of adaptive behavior skills in six categories: self-help skills, home living skills, independent living skills, social skills, sensory/motor skills, and language concepts and academic skills. Examiner checks off those skills which the individual has mastered (most can be done from memory) some interviews may be needed. Can be administered by classroom teacher or school psychologist. Not suitable for group use.

Untimed: 20 minutes

Range: Ages 0-21 years

Scoring: Examiner evaluated

Cost: Contact publisher.

Publisher: Charles E. Merrill Publishing Company

PHSF RELATIONS QUESTIONNAIRE-1970
F.A. Fouché and P.E. Grobbelaar

child, teen

Purpose: Assesses adjustment level of high school students. Used for counseling and guidance.

Description: Paper-pencil questionnaire of 12 aspects of personal adjustment including Self-Confidence, Self-Esteem, Self-Control, Nervousness, Health, Family Influences, Personal Freedom, Sociability-G, Sociability-S, Moral Sense, Formal Relations, and a Desirability Scale. Examiner required. Suitable for group use. Publisher notes that this test is "normed on Whites and Indians only."
SOUTH AFRICAN PUBLISHER

Untimed: 30 minutes

Range: Standards 6-10, college, adult

Scoring: Hand key; examiner evaluated, machine scoring available

Cost: (In Rands) test booklet 0,40; 10 answer sheets 0,60; 10 answer sheets (machine-3881) 1,10; scoring stencil 1, 1,20; scoring stencil 2, 1,20; manual 1,50; annexure to manual 1,80; appendix to manual 2,70 (orders from outside The RSA will be dealt with on merit).

Publisher: Human Sciences Research Council

PRIMARY SELF-CONCEPT INVENTORY
Douglas G. Muller and Robert Leonetti

child grades PRE-6

Purpose: Evaluates social, personal and intellectual self-concepts of elementary school children. Used to assess the role of self-concept in behavior problems for remedial work.

Description: 20 item paper-pencil, verbal test in which the subject marks pictures to indicate feelings about himself in response to a description read aloud by the examiner. Materials include the manual and booklets. Examiner required. Suitable for group use. Available in Spanish.

Untimed: Not available

Range: Preschool-primary

Scoring: Examiner evaluated

Cost: Complete $13.50.

Publisher: Teaching Resources Corporation

SCHOOL BEHAVIOR CHECKLIST
Lovick C. Miller

child, teen

Purpose: Measures a child's classroom behaviors. Used to provide mental health workers with information about behavior in school which might be indicative of psychopathological disorders.

Description: Multiple item paper-pencil inventory consisting of true-false questions and 11 global judgments describing the child's classroom behavior. The teacher completes the questionnaire, which provides an objective and standardized evaluation of classroom behavior in the following areas: Need Achievement, Aggression, Anxiety, Cognitive or Academic Deficit, Hostile Isolation, and Extraversion. Available in two forms: Form Al for children aged 4-6 years which includes three additional clinical scales--Normal Irritability, School Disturbance, and Total Disability; and Form A2 for children aged 7-13 years which includes one additional scale--Total Disability. Norms provided by sex and age for Form A and by sex for Form A2. Completed by the child's teacher. Not for group use.

Untimed: 8-10 minutes

Range: Ages 4-13

Scoring: Hand key

Cost: Complete for both age groups $32.50; Kit Al ages 4-6 and Kit A2 ages 7-13, each $17.20.

Publisher: Western Psychological Services

SCHOOL ENVIRONMENT PREFERENCE SURVEY
Leonard V. Gordon

child, teen grades 1-12

Purpose: Measures work role socialization as it occurs in the traditional school setting for students grades 3-13. Used for academic and disciplinary student counseling, vocational counseling, and instructional planning.

Description: 24 item paper-pencil test of student's levels of commitment to the set of attitudes, values, and behaviors necessary for employment, and which are fostered and rewarded in most school settings. The scales measured are: structured role orientation, self-subordination, traditionalism, rule conformity, and uncriticalness. High and low scores have differential behavioral implications. Norms provided for high school level. Examiner required.

Suitable for group use.

Untimed: 10-15 minutes

Range: Elementary, junior and senior high

Scoring: Hand key; computer scoring available

Cost: Specimen set $2.75; 25 forms $3.75; keys $2.00; manual $2.00.

Publisher: Educational and Industrial Testing Service

SCHOOL/HOME OBSERVATION and REFERRAL SYSTEM (SHORS)
Joyce Evans

child grades PRE-6

Purpose: Identifies children with problems that may interfere with learning. Used by teachers and parents of young children for referral purposes.

Description: Multiple item checklists. The General Checklist describes common physical symptoms of behavioral problems, each of which is keyed to the Specific Checklists. The Specific Checklists (health, motor abilities, vision, hearing, speech and language, learning, and behavior) describe unusual behaviors or physical symptoms. The checklists are marked by the teacher/parent observer. Suitable for group use.

Untimed: Open ended

Range: Preschool-early elementary

Scoring: Examiner evaluated

Cost: Specimen set (includes general checklist, one of each specific checklist, teacher's guide, parent's guide and test reviewer's guide) $7.25; classroom kit for 30 $70.00.

Publisher: CTB/McGraw-Hill

THE SELF-PERCEPTION INVENTORY (SPI)
Anthony Soares and Louise Soares

all ages   grades 1-UP

Purpose: Assesses how an individual sees himself, how he thinks others see him, and how others do see him. Useful to determine the need for counseling and as a counseling tool.

Description: Multiple item paper-pencil test in three categories: students (10 forms), adults (7 forms), and teachers (8 forms). Student forms include (1) self-concept--how individual sees self, (2) reflected self-classmates--how individual thinks classmates see him, (3) reflected self-teachers--how individual thinks teachers see him, (4) reflected self-parents--how individual thinks parents see him, (5) ideal concept--kind of person individual would like to be, (6) perceptions of others--other's rate male individuals, (7) others rate female individuals, (8) student-self--how individual sees self as student, (9) perceptions of others-student self--how others see individual as student (male and female). Adult and teacher forms similar. Students are measured against 20 pairs of bipolar traits; adults and teachers are measured against 36 pairs of traits. Subject rates the subject on each pair of traits by marking appropriately within a four space scale. Examiner required. Suitable for group use. Also available in French, Italian and Spanish.

Untimed: 5-10 minutes per scale

Range: Grades 1-adult

Scoring: Hand key

Cost: Specimen set (indicate level) $5.00.

Publisher: Soares Associates

SELF PROFILE Q-SORT (SPQS)
Alan J. Politte

child, teen   grades 2-UP

Purpose: Assesses student's feelings toward self. Used for elementary school counseling.

Description: 63 item test of self-perception. Items are adjectives. Child indicates whether or not each adjective describes his feelings. Items are administered orally to younger children, older children may read items themselves. Examiner required. Suitable for group use with older children.

Untimed: 10 minutes

Range: Grade 2 or above

Scoring: Examiner evaluated

Cost: Specimen set $3.50; 25 forms $5.50; 100- $21.00.

Publisher: Psychologists and Educators, Inc.

TASKS OF EMOTIONAL DEVELOPMENT TEST (TED)
Haskel Cohen and Geraldine Weil

child, teen

Purpose: Detects potential child behavior problems. Also used to determine reasons for student learning difficulties.

Description: Multiple item oral response projective test consisting of 49 photographs of children, each designed to represent a selected task of emotional development. Measures 13 factors: socialization, aggression, trust, academic learning, conscience of property of others, identification with same sex parent, separation from mother figure, acceptance of limits from adults, acceptance of siblings, acceptance of affection between parents, attitudes toward orderliness/cleanliness, positive self-concept, and positive heterosexual socialization. Responses are rated in five dimensions: perception, outcome, affect, motivation, and spontaneity. Four sets of photographs are provided: 12 photographs each for boys and girls ages 6-11, and 13 photographs each for boys and girls ages 12-18. Each set provides essentially the same stimuli with variations for age and sex. Test kit includes: 49 photo cards and a manual containing instructions and rating scales for each photo. Also available is the book *Tasks of Emotional Development* which discusses construction of the test and rating scales and includes sample stories scored according to the rating scales. Examiner required. Not for group use.

Untimed: Not available

Range: Ages 6-18

Scoring: Examiner evaluated

Cost: Complete set $35.00; textbook $18.00.

Publisher: T.E.D. Associates

WALKER PROBLEM BEHAVIOR IDENTIFICATION CHECKLIST: Revised 1983
Hill M. Walker

child   grades preschool-6

Purpose: Identifies preschool and elementary grade children who have behavior problems. Used to evaluate children for counseling and possible referral.

Description: 50 item paper-pencil inventory consisting of behavior statements which are applied to the child being rated. The checklist can be completed by anyone familiar with the child although it is especially valuable for teachers. Provides a Total Score, with a cut-off to indicate the need for further evaluation or referral. Also provides scores for the following five scales: Acting-Out, Withdrawal, Distractibility, Dis-

turbed Peer Relations, and Immaturity. Standardized on preschool, primary, and intermediate samples, and used for more than 1,-250,000 administrations. Suitable for group use.

Untimed: 5 minutes

Range: Grades preschool-6

Scoring: Hand key

Cost: Complete kit (includes pad of 100 checklists and manual) $12.13.

Publisher: Western Psychological Services

YOUTH INVENTORY (YI)
Hermann H. Remmers and Benjamin Shimberg

teen   grades 7-12

Purpose: Diagnoses individual problems and concerns among students grades 7-12. Used to assess individual student counseling needs and to plan group guidance programs.

Description: Multiple item paper-pencil checklist assessing the needs, problems, and interests of high school students. Topics covered include: My School, After High-School, About Myself, Getting Along With Others, and Things in General. Machine-scoring available for group results only; no individual scores are reported. Examiner required. Suitable for group use. Available in Spanish.

Timed: 30-35 minutes

Range: Grades 7-12

Scoring: Hand key; examiner evaluated; computer scoring available

Cost: 35 booklets $12.00; 50 answer sheets $10.00; general manual $2.25.

Publisher: Scholastic Testing Service, Inc.

Student Attitudes

ARLIN-HILLS ATTITUDE SURVEYS
Marshall Arlin and David Hills

child, teen   grades K-12

Purpose: Assesses student attitudes. Used for research on student attitudes.

Description: 15 item paper-pencil test of student attitudes in four areas: attitude toward teachers, attitude toward learning, attitude toward language, and attitude toward arithmetic. Items are presented in a cartoon format. Since group results are used, four instruments may be distributed at random to students within a classroom. Each instrument divided into three levels: Primary, grades K-3; Elementary, grades 4-6; and High School, grades 7-12. Examiner required. Suitable for group use.

Untimed: 5-10 minutes

Range: Primary (K-3), elementary (4-6), Secondary (7-12) levels

Scoring: Hand key; computer scoring recommended for groups

Cost: Specimen set (includes one survey each for learning processes, teachers, language arts, math, administration card, manual-specify level) $7.25; 25 forms (specify form and level) $6.75; administration/scoring card $1.25; manual $5.50.

Publisher: Psychologists and Educators, Inc.

ATTITUDE TO SCHOOL QUESTIONNAIRE (ASQ)
G.P. Strickland, R. Hoepfner and S.P. Klein

child   grades K-3

Purpose: Assesses the attitudes toward school of children from kindergarten to

grade 3. Used to evaluate affective programs and for research on young children's attitudes toward school.

Description: 15 item paper-pencil test measuring attitudes toward school, school work, show-and-tell activities, reading, math, authority, peers, and playing. Children view cartoons depicting school situations while English narrations are read to them. The children are then asked how they feel about each situation and respond by circling a happy, neutral or unhappy face. Reading and number skills are not required since each item is on a separate page which is colored rather than numbered. In this way, the child need only know five basic colors in order to follow along, and teachers can check to make sure all students are working on the same item. The people in the cartoons are racially ambiguous so that children of various racial groups would be equally likely to identify with the figures. The girls' form and the boys' form feature same-sex main characters. Examiner required. Suitable for group use.

Timed: 20 minutes

Range: Grades K-3

Scoring: Hand key

Cost: Specimen set $9.00; 20 questionnaires (10f, 10m) $23.00; manual $4.00.

Publisher: Monitor

CLASSROOM SOCIOMETRIC ANALYSIS KIT
E. Myers

child, teen   grades 3-12

Purpose: Measures students' attitudes of social acceptance or rejection based on the expressed preferences of their classmates. Used by classroom teachers grades 3-12.

Description: Multiple item paper-pencil test assessing the sociometric aspect of classroom dynamics. Available in two forms, A and B. Form A contains one work and one play question already printed on the pupil questionnaires. In Form B the sociometric questions are left blank in order to allow the teacher to develop hiw own questions and print them on the questionnaire. Manual available. Examiner required. Suitable for group use.

Untimed: Not available

Range: Grades 3-12

Scoring: Examiner evaluated

Cost: Contact publisher.

Publisher: Educational Research Council of America

COMPREHENSIVE ASSESS-MENT PROGRAM: SCHOOL ATTITUDE MEASURE
Lawrence J. Dolan and Marci Morrow Enos

child, teen   grades 4-12

Purpose: Evaluates students' views of their academic environment and of themselves as competent students.

Description: Multiple item measure of five affective dimensions of the student: motivation for schooling; academic self-concept, performance-based; academic self-concept, reference-based; sense of control over performance; and sense of instructional mastery. Available on three levels: grades 4-6, grades 7-8, and grades 9-12. Items may be read to young student with no invalidation provided no interpretive comment is made. National and local percentile ranks are provided. Examiner required. Suitable for group use. Available in Spanish.

Untimed: Not available

Range: Ages 9-18; grades 4-12

Scoring: Computer scoring recommended

Cost: 3 pupil booklets $21.50 (specify level); 35 answer sheets $7.95; manual $6.30; 35 profile $5.90.

Publisher: Scott, Foresman and Company

CONSERVATISM-RADICALISM OPINIONAIRE (C-R)
Theodore F. Lentz and colleagues

teen, adult   grades 13-UP

Purpose: Measures character and disposition along conservatism-radicalism dimension for use in college and adult courses in political psychology and political science.

Description: 60 item paper-pencil test measuring the conservative-radical attitudes of the subject, who is asked to agree or disagree with each statement by marking it plus or minus. Self-administered. Suitable for group use.

Untimed: 30 minutes

Range: College, adult

Scoring: Hand key

Cost: Manual and sample of opinionaire $1.00. Discount available upon request for quantities.

Publisher: Peace Research Laboratory

CORNELL INVENTORY FOR STUDENT APPRAISAL OF TEACHING COURSES
Refer to page 646.

CPRI QUESTIONNAIRES (Q-71, Q-74, Q-75, Q-76)
William Eckhardt

teen, adult   grades 10-UP

Purpose: Measures personality, ideology, and philosophy; for use by high schools, colleges, churches, and civic clubs.

Description: 240 item paper-pencil test in four sections covering the following categories: conformity, nationalism, responsibility, religiosity, impulsivity, bureaucracy, neuroticism, militarism, misanthropy, morality, discipline, capitalism, humanism, egoism, authoritarianism, fatalism, justice, imperialism, and mysticism. The person rates each item on a five-point scale ranging from 'strongly disagree' to 'strongly agree.' Self-administered. Suitable for group use. Available in Spanish, German, Hindi, Dutch, Belgian, Urdu, and Bengali.

Untimed: 15-30 minutes

Range: High school, college, university, adult

Scoring: Hand key

Cost: 77-page manual including background and interpretive material, 4 questionnaires, answer sheets, scoring instructions, and norms $5.00. Questionnaires and answer sheets may be reproduced at no further charge.

Publisher: Peace Research Laboratory

ESTES ATTITUDE SCALE: MEASURES OF ATTITUDE TOWARD SCHOOL SUBJECTS
Thomas H. Estes, Julie Johnstone Estes, Herbert C. Richards, and Doris Roettger

child, teen   grades 2-12

Purpose: Assesses an elementary or secondary school student's attitudes toward reading, mathematics, science, and other subjects. Used to counsel and advise students, to determine the effectiveness of programs designed to influence attitudes, and for research on student attitudes.

Description: Paper-pencil test available in two forms. The elementary form (grades 2-6) includes scales measuring attitudes toward mathematics, reading, and science. The secondary form (grades 7-12) includes these three scales plus English and social studies. Examiner required. Suitable for group use.

Untimed: 10-30 minutes

Range: Grades 2-12

Scoring: Hand key

Cost: Complete (includes examiners manual, 25 elementary booklets, 25 secondary booklets, 50 answer sheets, scoring keys, storage box) $36.00. Components available for separate purchase.

Publisher: PRO-ED

EVALUATED DISPOSITION TOWARD THE ENVIRONMENT (EDEN)
N. Milchus

teen   grades 7-13

Purpose: Assesses the strength of a student's environmental values. Used for self-insight and program evaluation.

Description: 70 item, paired comparison test measures these values: aesthetic, experiential, knowledge-seeking, responsible, prudent (conservation ethic) active, and practical. Students pick one of the pair of activities they prefer. Likert-type 1-5 scale. Examiner required. Suitable for group use.

Untimed: 30-40 minutes

Range: Grades 7-first year college

Scoring: Computer scored

Cost: Specimen set $3.25; 20 inventory booklets $22.00; 20 response sheets $3.25; computer scoring $1.00.

Publisher: Person-O-Metrics, Inc.

G-S-Z INTEREST INVENTORY (GSZ)
Refer to page 666.

KATZ-ZALK OPINION QUESTIONNAIRE
Phyllis Katz and Sue Rosenberg Zalk

child   grades 1-6

Purpose: Measures racial attitudes in children. Used for research to assess change in attitudes.

Description: 55 item paper-pencil test measures the racial attitudes of children. There are 38 race-related questions and 17 "buffer" items to provide a measure of gender attitudes. The child is shown a slide of two or four children interacting (there is a sketch of the slide in the answer book) and asked to put a mark in the box under the child credited with a positive or negative act or attribute. Assesses attitudes towards blacks and whites only, but could be adapted to other groups. Examiner required. Suitable for group use.

Untimed: 30-60 minutes

Range: Grades 1-6

Scoring: Hand key

Cost: Booklet $1.00; slides $75.00 (price on large orders are less).

Publisher: Sue Rosenberg Zalk and Phyllis Katz

MASTER ATTITUDE SCALES
H.H. Remmers

child, teen   grades 7-UP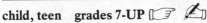

Purpose: Measures attitudes toward a wide range of areas. Used for research purposes.

Description: Nine paper-pencil tests providing formats for assessing attitudes toward the following areas: practice, school subjects, vocations, institutions, defined groups of people, proposed social actions, homemaking activities, individual and group morale, and the high school. Each scale provides a general format for attitudes in that area and leaves the final topic up to the individual examiner. For example, The Scale to Measure Attitudes Toward Any School Subject provides a form that will generally evaluate any academic course, with space provided for the examiner to designate which particular course is to be evaluated. Examiner required. Suitable for group use.

Untimed: 5-10 minutes

Range: Junior high-adult

Scoring: Examiner evaluated

Cost: Contact publisher.

Publisher: Purdue Research Foundation/University Book Store

MOTIVATION ANALYSIS TEST (MAT)
Refer to page 822.

NEW YOUTH RESEARCH SURVEY (NYRS)
Refer to page 256.

PEER ATTITUDES TOWARDS THE HANDICAPPED SCALE (PATHS)
Micheal T. Bayley and John F. Greene

child, teen   grades 4-8

Purpose: Measures an elementary school student's attitudes toward handicapped school-aged children. Used to decide about mainstream placement, to determine a need for intervention to improve attitudes, and to demonstrate that changes in attitudes have occurred.

Description: Multiple item paper-pencil self-report inventory. The student reads a descriptive statement about a peer who has a physical, learning, and/or behavioral handicap and indicates where he thinks that student should be taught. Self-administered; supervision required. Suitable for group use.

Untimed: 20 minutes

Range: Grades 4-8

Scoring: Hand key

Cost: Complete (includes examiner manual, 25 student booklets, 50 record forms, storage box) $35.00. Components available for separate purchase.

Publisher: PRO-ED

PURDUE STUDENT-TEACHER OPINIONAIRE
Refer to page 650.

QUEST: A LIFE CHOICE INVENTORY
N. Milchus, D. Rodwell and O. Mumey

child, teen   grades 9-12

Purpose: Measures the impact on high school students of value clarification in career education, substance abuse prevention and positive group mental health programs. Used to provide an overall assessment of school climate.

Description: 40 item paper-pencil test measures: needs recognition, value clarification, adaptive autonomy, perception of reality, and self worth. Measures on "agree-disagree" Likert-type scale. Self-administered. Suitable for group use.

Untimed: 30 minutes

Range: Grades 9-12

Scoring: Computer scored

Cost: Specimen set $3.00; computer scoring $1.25 each.

Publisher: Person-O-Metrics, Inc.

A SCALE TO MEASURE ATTITUDES TOWARD DISABLED PERSONS
H.E. Yuker and J.R. Block

all ages

Purpose: Assesses attitudes toward disabled persons. Used to evaluate mainstreaming in the schools, hiring of disabled persons and methods of changing attitudes toward the disabled.

Description: Multiple item paper-pencil inventory assessing the attitudes of either disabled or nondisabled persons toward disabled persons. Useful with teachers, employers, counselors, physicians, and students who are involved with disabled individuals. Available in three forms, one form containing 20 items and two forms containing 30 items, including Chinese, Japanese, Hebrew, and Spanish. Self-administered. Suitable for group use.

Untimed: 10 minutes

Range: Student-adult

Scoring: Examiner evaluated

Cost: Free.

Publisher: H.E. Yuker

STUDENT ATTITUDE INVENTORY
D.S. Anderson and J.S. Western

teen

Purpose: Measures attitudes toward school of tertiary students, and assesses the impact of academic environment on these attitudes. Used for student guidance and counseling.

Description: 57 item paper-pencil test requires students to indicate their agreement or disagreement, on a five-point scale, with statements concerning the following dimensions: academic activities, intellectual interests, political-economic liberalism, social liberalism, pragmatism, dogmatism, cynicism. Australian norms provided. Materials include: inventory set of three scoring keys, monograph "Inventory to Measure Students' Attitudes" and specimen set. Self-administered. Suitable for group use. AUSTRALIAN PUBLISHER

Untimed: 15 minutes

Range: Adolescents

Scoring: Hand key; examiner evaluated

Cost: Contact publisher.

Publisher: The Australian Council for Educational Research Limited

---

STUDENT EVALUATION SCALE (SES)
William T. Martin and Sue Martin

all ages

Purpose: Assesses attitudes and behaviors of elementary and secondary school children. Used for evaluating educational and social-emotional responses to school.

Description: 52 item paper-pencil test of two areas of student attitudes: educational response and social-emotional response. Items are rated by teachers or guidance personnel after observing students for a two to three week period. Rating scale ranges from 0-Never to 3-Always. Self-administered. Suitable for group use.

Untimed: 5 minutes

Range: Ages 6-21

Scoring: Examiner evaluated

Cost: Specimen set $4.00; 25 rating and profile forms $5.50; 100-$21.00; manual included with specimen set.

Publisher: Psychologists and Educa-

tors, Inc.

STUDENT ORIENTATIONS SURVEY (S.O.S.)
Barry R. Morstain

teen, adult   College

Purpose: Assesses students' attitudes toward educational policies. Used for research on orientations toward philosophies, purposes and processes related to a college education.

Description: 80 item paper-pencil measure of ten aspects of student orientations toward college: achievement, assignment learning, assessment, affiliation, affirmation, inquiry, independent study, interaction, informal association, and involvement. Items are statements which are rated on a modified Likert scale. Self-administered. Suitable for group use. Available in Spanish.

Untimed: 20 minutes

Range: College students

Scoring: Computer scored

Cost: S.O.S. OpScan form scoring (researcher receives an overall group printout and a scored data deck) $.50.

Publisher: Barry R. Morstain, Ph.D.

STUDENT REACTION TO COLLEGE: TWO YEAR COLLEGE EDITION (SRC/2)
Research staff at Education Testing Service

teen, adult   College

Purpose: Assesses needs and concerns of students in two year colleges. Used for institutional self-assessment for developing programs and services for students.

Description: 150 item paper-pencil assessment of four dimensions of student concerns: Processes of instruction, Program planning, Administrative affairs, and Out-of-class activities. Dimensions are further broken down into areas such as content of courses; appropriateness of course work to occupational goals; satisfaction with teaching procedures; student-faculty relations; educational and occupational decisions; effectiveness of advisers and counselors; registration; regulations; availability of classes; housing; employment; financial aid; and satisfaction with campus environment. Administered by distributing to a random sample of students. Self-administered. Suitable for group use.

Untimed: 50 minutes

Range: College students

Scoring: Computer scored

Cost: Booklets $.65 each; processing $1.75 each.

Publisher: Educational Testing Service

STUDY OF VALUES
G. Allport, P. Vernon and G. Lindzey

teen, adult   grades 10-UP

Purpose: Measures the relative prominence of an individual's basic interests of personality motives. Used for student educational and vocational planning, guidance, personnel selection, and research.

Description: 45 item paper-pencil test measures the following six factors: theoretical, economic, aesthetic, social, political, and religious. The test is designed primarily for use with college students or adults with some college education. It should be used only when there is supervision and guidance in the interpretation by individuals who have had considerable experience in psychological testing and personality theory. Self-

administered. Suitable for group use.

Untimed: 20 minutes

Range: Grades 10-12, college, adult

Scoring: Hand key

Cost: 35 hand-scorable test booklets (includes manual of directions) $11.55.

Publisher: The Riverside Publishing Company

SUBSUMED ABILITIES TEST-- A MEASURE OF LEARNING EFFICIENCY (SAT)
Joseph R. Sanders

teen, adult   grades 7-UP

Purpose: Measures, nonverbally, the subject's ability and willingness to learn; useful for student placement, vocational counseling and job selection.

Description: 60 item paper-pencil test consisting of 30 pairs of items, each of which is composed of four similar' line drawings. The student matches one with another, allowing the examiner to construct a Potential Abilities Score' and a Demonstrated Abilities Score' based on the examinee's ability to conceptualize, form abstractions, and recognize the abstractions in new situations. Designed for persons with at least sixth grade educations. Examiner required. May be self-administered. Suitable for group use.

Timed: 30 minutes

Range: 6th grade-adult

Scoring: Hand key

Cost: Specimen set $5.50; package of tests $17.50; manual $4.10; package of scoring key-tabulation sheets $6.50.

Publisher: Martin M. Bruce, Ph.D. Publisher

SURVEY OF SCHOOL ATTITUDES (SSA)
Thomas P. Hogan

child, teen   grades 1-8

Purpose: Assesses children's reaction to school curriculum. Used for determining objectives of a curriculum program.

Description: Multiple item paper-pencil test of reactions to four areas of school curriculum: reading and language arts, mathematics, science, and social studies. Each area is represented by 15 activities characteristic of the curriculum. Students indicate whether they like, dislike or are neutral toward each activity. Divided into two levels: Primary, grades 1-3, and Intermediate, grades 4-8. Primary level items dictated by teacher. Intermediate items are sentence stems read by student. Materials include two alternate and equivalent forms, A and B. Examiner required. Suitable for group use.

Untimed: Primary, 40 minutes; Intermediate, 30 minutes

Range: Grades 1-8

Scoring: Hand key; scoring service available

Cost: Specimen set (includes test booklets, manual for each level) $5.50; 25 tests (specify Primary or Intermediate) $17.75; keys (specify Primary or Intermediate) $3.30; 35 hand-scorable answer documents for Intermediate $5.00; 35 MRC machine- scorable tests (Primary) $20.00; 35 MRC machine- scorable tests (Intermediate) $17.50.

Publisher: The Psychological Corporation

VALUES INVENTORY FOR CHILDREN (VIC)
Joan S. Guilford, Willa Gupta and Lisbeth Goldberg

child   grades 1-4

Purpose: Measures values of children in grades 1-4 and used to assess their relations to other children, parents and authority figures.

Description: 47 item paper-pencil test measuring seven independent value dimensions: asocial, social conformity, "me first", sociability, academic, masculinity, and adult closeness. Stimuli for all test items are pictorial. Answer sheets may be used at third grade level and above. Items for all seven scales are included in a single test booklet, available in two forms: 'B' for boys and 'G' for girls. One scoring key is required for each sex. Profile charts are available for plotting centile rank by grade level and sex. Norms are provided for grades 1, 2, 3, and 4. The Manual of Interpretations and Administration Manual are necessary. Restricted to A.P.A. members. Examiner required. Suitable for group use.

Untimed: 30 minutes

Range: Grades 1-4

Scoring: Hand key

Cost: 25 tests $25.00 (specify sex); 25 answer sheets $3.50; 25 scoring sheets $3.50; 25 profile charts $3.50; 50 answer sheets are required if entire test is to be used.

Publisher: Sheridan Psychological Services

Student Personality Factors

AAMD ADAPTIVE BEHAVIOR SCALE, SCHOOL EDITION (ABS)
Refer to page 555.

ADAPTIVE BEHAVIOR INVENTORY OF CHILDREN (ABIC)
Refer to page 56.

ADJECTIVE CHECK LIST (ACL)
Refer to page 91.

ADOLESCENT ALIENATION INDEX (AAI)
Refer to page 146.

THE AFFECTIVE PERCEPTION INVENTORY (API)
Anthony T. Soares and Louise Soares

child, teen   grades 1-12

Purpose: Assesses a student's feelings about himself regarding general school experiences and specific curriculum areas. Useful to educators, sociologists and psychologists interested in subject's view of academic world.

Description: Multiple item paper-pencil test for three levels: primary (grades 1-3), intermediate (grades 4-8), and advanced (grades 9-12). Each level is comprised of 9 scales: (1) self as a person; (2) student self; (3) English; (4) math; (5) science; (6) social sciences; (7) the arts; (8) physical education; and (9) school. Student rates himself by marking his perception in the appropriate space on a scale for the various traits. May be necessary for examiner to read test to young children. Examiner required. Suitable for group use. Available in Spanish, Italian and French.

Untimed: 30 minutes

Range: Grades 1-12

Scoring: Hand key

Cost: Specimen set (indicate level) $5.00.

Publisher: Soares Associates

BARCLAY CLASSROOM ASSESSMENT SYSTEM (BCAS)
James R. Barclay

child   grades 3-6

Purpose: Evaluates children in grades 3-6 in relation to classroom situations, their peers, and their teachers. Used by educators and counselors to identify gifted children and children with learning disabilities to plan Individualized Educational Plans (I.E.P.s) and to facilitate compliance with P.L. 94-142.

Description: A multiple-entry paper-pencil Evaluation Booklet is used by the examiner to collect information from the teacher and each child in a class. The results provide a comprehensive report for each child based on sophisticated computer processing of the data gained from the child, classroom peers, and the teacher (who provides demographic information and responds to a brief adjective checklist for each child). The computer report provides for each child the following information: factor scores for Achievement- Motivation, Control-Stability, Introversion- Seclusion, Energy-Activity, Sociability- Affiliation, and Enterprising-Dominance. It also produces an easy-to-read narrative report of the child's self-estimates of his or her Self- Competency Skills, Vocational Awareness, Reinforcers, and Attitude Toward School; peer and teacher estimates; suspected difficulties with problem analysis, general intervention direction and prescriptions. When stanine scores for standardized tests are provided by the teacher, additional relationships between psychosocial variables and academic achievement can be obtained. Intended for group use.

Untimed: 30-45 minutes

Range: Grades 3-6

Scoring: Computer scored

Cost: Introductory kit for 36 students (includes computer processing) $120.00.

Publisher: Western Psychological Services

BECOMING THE GIFT (BTG)
Refer to page 256.

BEHAVIORAL ACADEMIC SELF-ESTEEM (BASE)
Stanley Coopersmith and Ragnar Gilberts

child, teen   grades PRE-8

Purpose: Measures academic self-esteem. Used for counseling and research.

Description: 16 item paper-pencil test which consists of a behavioral rating scale assessing five factors related to self-esteem: Student Initiative, Social Attention, Success/Failure, Social Attraction, and Self-Confidence. Intended for use by teacher, parent, or other professionals. May be used in conjunction with The Coopersmith Self-Esteem Inventory. Self-administered. Suitable for group use.

Untimed: 5 minutes

Range: Grades Preschool-8

Scoring: Hand key; examiner evaluated

Cost: 25 rating scales $6.00; manual, cost not available.

Publisher: Consulting Psychologists Press, Inc.

CHILD BEHAVIOR RATING SCALE
Russell N. Cassel

child   grades PRE-3

Purpose: Measures behavior and personality adjustment of children from preschool through the third grade. Used in counseling both normal and emotionally handicapped children.

Description: 78 item paper-pencil inventory consisting of brief statements about behavior and personality which the evaluator (someone familiar with the child) applies to the child and answers on a 6- point scale ranging from "Yes" to "No." Provides a total personality adjustment score and a profile of the child's adjustment in five areas: Self, Home, Social, School, and Physical. Standardized on 2,000 normal and 200 emotionally handicapped children. Examiner required. Suitable for group use.

Untimed: 30-40 minutes

Range: Preschool-grade 3

Scoring: Hand key

Cost: Complete kit (includes 25 scales and manual) $9.60.

Publisher: Western Psychological Services

CHILDREN'S PERSONALITY QUESTIONNAIRE (CPQ)
Refer to page 83.

COMPREHENSIVE PERSONAL ASSESSMENT SYSTEM: ADJECTIVE SELF-DESCRIPTION (ASD)
Refer to page 97.

COMPREHENSIVE PERSONAL ASSESSMENT SYSTEM: DIRECTED IMAGINATION (DI)
Refer to page 97.

COMPREHENSIVE PERSONAL ASSESSMENT SYSTEM: ONE-WORD SENTENCE COMPLETION (OWSC)
Refer to page 97.

COMPREHENSIVE PERSONAL ASSESSMENT SYSTEM: SELF REPORT INVENTORY (SRI)
Refer to page 97.

CONOLEY-HARRISON PROJECTED SELF-CONCEPT INVENTORY (ENGLISH/SPANISH) (PSCI)

child   grades K-6

Purpose: Measures children's personality development in a test of self-concepts. Used to assess changes in the self-concepts of children exposed to a new curriculum or new environmental setting.

Description: Multiple item test consists of 20 pairs of response pictures and four pairs of practice pictures. Children are instructed to choose between line drawings according to a general statement about the pictures' representation of peer behavior. The test can be administered in Spanish, English, or bilingually. Boy or girl response forms are used. Examiner required. Suitable for group use. Available in Spanish and bilingual.

Untimed: 15 minutes

Range: Kindergarten-grade 6

Scoring: Examiner evaluated

Cost: Response booklet (specify girl or boy) $1.25; manual $15.00.

Publisher: National Educational Laboratory Publishers, Inc.

COOPERSMITH SELF-ESTEEM INVENTORIES (CSEI)
Refer to page 151.

DESCRIBING PERSONALITY
Union College Character Research Project

child, teen   grades PRE-12

Purpose: Determines unique personality characteristics in children from preschool through senior high. Used to aid parent-child and teacher-child relationships.

Description: Paper-pencil projective test of eight personality factors: outstanding characteristics, activities and interests, coaching-school, social relationships, emotional security, imagination and curiosity, vocational interests, and home and family. Designed for eight age levels, for male and female. Parents are required to respond for the preschool age level. Individual descriptions are modified to fit the person being described. Also usable for junior and senior students to increase self-understanding. Materials include forms and instructions. Examiner required. Suitable for group use.

Untimed: 20-30 minutes

Range: Preschool-grade 12

Scoring: Examiner evaluated

Cost: Each form $.25 (specify age and sex); sample set of 16 $3.00.

Publisher: Union College Character Research Project

EARLY SCHOOL PERSON-ALITY QUESTIONNAIRE (ESPQ)
Refer to page 84.

EDUCATIONAL DEVELOP-MENT SERIES (ED SERIES)
Refer to page 367.

EGO STATE INVENTORY
Refer to page 102.

FAMILY PRE-COUNSELING INVENTORY PROGRAM
Refer to page 59.

FROST SELF-DESCRIPTION QUESTIONNAIRE
Refer to page 85.

"GETTING ALONG"-A SITUA-TION-RESPONSE TEST FOR GRADES 7, 8, 9 (FORMS A & B)
Trudys Lawrence

teen   grades 7-9

Purpose: Evaluates the emotional health of Junior High pupils grades 7-9. Used to identify pupils with poor self-image, poor social adjustment and inadequate adjustment in meeting the demands of daily living.

Description: 45 item paper-pencil, multiple-choice test with equivalent Forms A and B. Each form has 45 illustrated situation-response items divided into three sections: Getting Along With One's Self, Getting Along With Others and Getting Along In One's Environment. May be examiner or self-administered. Suitable for group use.

Untimed: 45 minutes

Range: Grades 7, 8, 9

Scoring: Hand key

Cost: Specimen set (form test A, form test B, teacher's manual, scoring key, 2 answer sheets) $1.00; classroom test set (includes 30 tests form A or B or 15 of each form, teacher's manual, scoring key, 30 answer sheets) $4.00; separate prices form A or B tests $.15 each; teacher's manual $.20 each; scoring key $.10 each; answer sheets $.01 each.

Publisher: Trudys Lawrence, Ph.D.

HIGH SCHOOL PERSONALITY QUESTIONNAIRE (HSPQ)
Refer to page 108.

HOW WELL DO YOU KNOW YOURSELF
Refer to page 109.

INCOMPLETE SENTENCES TASK
Refer to page 110.

INTERMEDIATE PERSON-ALITY QUESTIONNAIRE FOR INDIAN PUPILS (IPQI)-1974

child, teen

Purpose: Assesses personality. Used for guidance of children with social and emotional problems. Useful in vocational guidance.

Description: Multiple item paper-pencil measure of ten aspects of personality including social extraversion, verbal intelligence, emotional stability, adventuresomeness, creativity,

dominance, perserverance, relaxedness, spirit of enterprise and environment relatedness. Examiner required. Suitable for group use.
SOUTH AFRICAN PUBLISHER

Untimed: 30-45 minutes

Range: Standards 6-8

Scoring: Hand key

Cost: (In Rands) test booklet 2,00; manual 1,10; scoring stencil 0,20; 10 answer sheets 1,00 (orders from outside The RSA will be dealt with on merit).

Publisher: Human Science Research Council

INTERPERSONAL RELATIONS QUESTIONNAIRE (IRQ)- 1981
Refer to page 110.

IPAT ANXIETY SCALE (or SELF-ANALYSIS FORM)
Refer to page 111.

JESNESS BEHAVIOR CHECKLIST
Refer to page 113.

LUTHER HOSPITAL SENTENCE COMPLETIONS (LHSC)
John R. Thurston

teen, adult

Purpose: Evaluates attitudes and emotional reactions of nursing students and nursing school applicants. Used to predict probable success or failure in nursing school.

Description: 90 item paper-pencil incomplete sentence test. Measures six attitudes related to nursing school performance: nursing, self, home and family, responsibility, academics, and others-love- marriage. Materials

include self-directing test booklet, answer sheet and scoring key. Comprehensive manual covering this and other NRA tests is also available. Test is most relevant to 18-20 year old female applicants. Self- administered. Suitable for group use.

Untimed: 30 minutes

Range: Adults

Scoring: Hand key; scoring service available

Cost: Specimen set $5.00; 25 tests $10.00; manual $15.00.

Publisher: Nursing Research Associates

MARTINEK-ZAICHKOWSKY SELF-CONCEPT SCALE FOR CHILDREN (MZSCS)
Thomas J. Martinek and Leonard D. Zaichkowsky

child, teen   grades 1-8

Purpose: Measures the global self-concept of children in grades 1-8, identifies children with low self-esteem and evaluates the impact of the educational process on a child's self-perception. May be used with non-English speaking children. Used for research and referral.

Description: 25 item paper-pencil forced-choice format test measuring physical, behavioral and emotional aspects of a child's self-confidence. Five factors are covered: satisfaction and happiness; home and family relationships and circumstances; ability in games, recreation and sports; personality traits and emotional tendencies; and behavioral and social characteristics in school. Each test item consists of a page in the test booklet which presents the child with a pair of pictures representing positive and negative roles. The child circles the picture he considers to be most like himself. The test requires little or no reading ability and is culture-free. Examiner required. Suitable for group use.

Untimed: 10-15 minutes

Range: Grades 1-8

Scoring: Hand key; examiner evaluated

Cost: Specimen set $8.25; 25 tests $27.50; 100- $108.00; manual $5.50.

Publisher: Psychologists and Educators, Inc.

MILLON ADOLESCENT PERSONALITY INVENTORY (MAPI)
Refer to page 118.

MOONEY PROBLEM CHECKLIST
Refer to page 121.

MY SELF CHECK LIST (MSCL)
Refer to page 162.

NEW YOUTH RESEARCH SURVEY (NYRS)
Refer to page 256.

NURSE ATTITUDES INVENTORY (NAI)
John R. Thurston

teen, adult

Purpose: Evaluates attitudes and emotional reactions of nursing students and nursing school applicants. Used to predict probable success or failure in nursing school.

Description: 70 item paper-pencil, multiple-choice test in two forms. Evaluates six attitudes related to nursing school performance: nursing, self, home and family, responsibility, academics, and others-love-marriage.

Separate scales evaluate positive and negative attitudes. Materials include self- directing test booklet, answer sheet and scoring key. Comprehensive manual available which covers this and other NRA tests. Test is most relevant to 18-20 year old female applicants. Self- administered. Suitable for group use.

Untimed: 30 minutes

Range: Adult

Scoring: Hand key; examiner evaluated

Cost: Specimen set (excluding key) $10.00; 50 answer sheets $5.00; scoring key $15.00; manual $15.00.

Publisher: Nursing Research Associates

NURSING SENTENCE COMPLETIONS (NSC)
John R. Thurston

teen, adult

Purpose: Evaluates attitudes and emotions of nursing students and applicants to nursing school. Used to predict probably success or failure in nursing school.

Description: 40 item paper-pencil incomplete sentence test. Measures six attitudes related to nursing school performance: nursing, self, home and family, responsibility, academics, and others-love- marriage. Materials consist of a self directing test booklet, answer sheet and scoring key. Comprehensive manual covering this and other NRA tests is also available. Test is most relevant for 18-20 year old female applicants and can be scored with the Nursing Education Scale. Examiner/self-administered. Suitable for group use.

Untimed: 20 minutes

Range: Adults

Scoring: Hand key; scoring service available $5.00.

Cost: Specimen set $5.00; package of 25 $10.00; information regarding deviation and administration $15.00.

Publisher: Nursing Research Associates

THE PERSONAL AUDIT
Refer to page 823.

PERSONALITY DESCRIPTIONS
Refer to page 162.

PERSONALITY RATING SCALE
Refer to page 87.

PICTURE WORLD TEST
Refer to page 163.

THE PRESCHOOL BEHAVIOR QUESTIONNAIRE
Refer to page 87.

PRESCHOOL SELF-CONCEPT PICTURE TEST (PS-CPT)
Rosestellle B. Woolner

child

Purpose: Assesses the opinions a preschooler has of himself in terms of (1) how he perceives himself to be and (2) the way he would like to be. Used to design curriculums which enhance a preschooler's self-concept.

Description: 20 item oral response test measuring a preschooler's opinion of himself in regard to ten pairs of bipolar characteristics: dirty/clean, active/passive, aggressive/non-aggressive, afraid/unafraid, strong/weak, acceptance/rejection, unhappy/happy, group rejection/group acceptance, sharing/non-shar-

ing, and dependence/independence. A set of ten picture plates presents drawings of children representing each of the bipolar characteristics. The child is shown the plates and asked to indicate the drawing with which he identifies and the drawing with which he would like to identify. Variances between the two responses provide the teacher with an opportunity to help the child reduce the degree of difference between the way he sees himself and the way he would like to see himself. Retesting will reveal progress in this direction. Available in four forms for Caucasian and Negro boys and girls. Examiner required. Not for group use.

Untimed: 15 minutes

Range: Ages 4-5

Scoring: Hand key

Cost: Complete (includes 4 sub tests, manual, 25 score sheets) $15.00.

Publisher: Rosestelle B. Woolner, Ed.D.

POLITTE SENTENCE COMPLETION TEST (PSCT)
Alan J. Politte

child, teen   grades 1-12

Purpose: Evaluates personality traits and adjustment of children Grades 1-12. Used to assess personality in the educational, counseling and clinical areas.

Description: 35 item paper-pencil free response projective test of personality. Students are told that the test is a "questionnaire" or an "exercise" in which they are to read the stems and then "complete" the sentence in any way that they feel about the item. Serves as a screening device by which the examiner can gain further insight into the thinking processes of the student and not as an instrument which provides a "score" or normative reference for the student. Persons without training in clinical psychology should use the test as an aid in interview or counseling settings. Clinically trained psychologists can base their interpretations from a psychoanalytic, social, behavioral, or similar approach. Available in two forms: Elementary Form (Grades 1-6) and Secondary Form (Grades 7-12). Self-administered; supervision required. Suitable for group use.

Untimed: 15 minutes

Range: Grades 1-12

Scoring: Examiner evaluated

Cost: Specimen set $3.50; 25 tests (specify elementary or secondary) $6.75; 100-$26.00, manual included.

Publisher: Psychologists and Educators, Inc.

SCAMIN: A SELF CONCEPT AND MOTIVATION INVENTORY: SECONDARY FORM
Milchus, Farrah and Reitz

teen   grades 7-12

Purpose: Determines individual's self-concept and motivation in an academic context.

Description: 64 item paper-pencil test measures: achievement needs, achievement investment, role expectation, and self adequacy. Four levels of the test are available, each with different number of items and length of time necessary for completion. Examiner required. Suitable for group use. Available in Spanish.

Untimed: 30-40 minutes

Range: Grades 7-12

Scoring: Hand key; computer scoring available

Cost: Specimen set $7.00; manual $1.25; key $4.00.

Publisher: Person-O-Metrics

SCAMIN: EARLY ELEMENTARY
Milchus, Farrah and Reitz

child   grades 1-3

Purpose: Measures self-concept and assesses motivation inventory of students in grades 1-3.

Description: 24 item test. The items are responded to on a machine scorable scale of five sad to happy faces to ascertain the child's self-concept strength and to develop a motivational inventory. Examiner required. Suitable for group use.

Untimed: 25 minutes

Range: Grades 1-3

Scoring: Hand key; computer scoring available

Cost: Specimen set $7.00; manual $1.25; key $4.00.

Publisher: Person-O-Metrics, Inc.

SCAMIN: LATER ELEMENTARY
Milchus, Farrah and Reitz

child   grades 3-6

Purpose: Measures self-concept and assesses motivational inventory of students in grades 3-6.

Description: 48 item paper-pencil test measures achievement needs, achievement investment, role expectations, and self adequacy. Items are read orally to class by examiner. Suitable for group use.

Untimed: 30 minutes

Range: Grades 3-6

Scoring: Hand key; computer scoring available

Cost: Specimen set $7.00; manual $1.25; key $4.00.

Publisher: Person-O-Metrics, Inc.

SCAMIN: PRESCHOOL/ KINDERGARTEN
Milchus, Farrah and Reitz

child   grades K-PRE

Purpose: Measures self-concept and assesses motivation of preschool and kindergarten children.

Description: 24 item test using three "face" responses from sad to happy to evaluate self-concept strength. Examiner required. Suitable for group use.

Untimed: 30 minutes

Range: Kindergarten and Preschool

Scoring: Hand key; computer scoring available

Cost: Specimen set $7.00; manual $1.25; key $4.00.

Publisher: Person-O-Metrics, Inc.

SENTENCE COMPLETION TEST
Refer to page 137.

SOCIAL INTELLIGENCE TEST
F.A. Moss, T. Hung and K. Omwake

teen, adult   grades 10-UP

Purpose: Assesses basic social perceptions and judgments of students grade 5 through high school.

Description: Multiple item paper-pencil test measuring five factors: judgment in social situations, recognition of mental state of speaker, observation of human behavior, memory for names and faces, and sense of humor. Percentile norms provided for high school, college and adult populations. Three editions available: Test Second Edition (Long Form); Shortened edition (Omits Memory for Names and Faces factor); Special edition (contains only two parts; Judgment in Social Situations and Observation of Human Behavior). A complete specimen set contains all three forms. Examiner required. Suitable for group use. CANADIAN PUBLISHER

Timed: 50 minutes

Range: High school and above

Scoring: Hand key

Cost: Complete specimen set for all forms $2.00.

Publisher: Institute of Pyschological Research, Inc.

SUINN TEST ANXIETY BEHAVIOR SCALE (STABS)

teen, adult   grades 7-UP

Purpose: Measures a person's anxiety regarding academic testing situations. Used for screening and diagnostic purposes, research on test anxiety, and as a tool in developing anxiety hierarchies for desensitization therapy.

Description: 50 item paper-pencil test assessing the level of a person's test anxiety. Test items refer to experiences related to academic testing that may cause fear or apprehension. The subject rates his anxiety concerning each test item on a five-point scale from "Not At All" to "Very Much." Norms available for college students, adult nonstudents and males and females. Use restricted to APA membership guidelines. Self-administered. Suitable for group use.

Untimed: 20 minutes

Range: Junior high school-college

Scoring: Hand key

Cost: 100 scales $40.00.

Publisher: Rocky Mountain Behavioral Science Institute, Inc.

TEST ANXIETY PROFILE (TAP)
E.R. Oetting and C.W. Cole

teen, adult   grades 10-UP

Purpose: Measures a person's anxieties regarding academic testing situations. Used for screening and counseling purposes.

Description: 77 item paper-pencil test assessing a person's feelings and thoughts in regard to six academic testing situations: multiple-choice exams, math exams, essay exams, unannounced tests, talking in front of a class, and tests with time limits. Each test item consists of a pair of bipolar adjectives separated by a seven-point Likert scale. The subject rates himself on each pair of adjectives according to his thoughts or feelings in each of the testing situation. Two anxiety scores are derived for each testing situation: Feelings of Anxiety (FA) and Thought Inter-ference (TI). Use restricted to APA membership guidelines. Self-administered. Suitable for group use.

Untimed: 10-15 minutes

Range: High school-adult

Scoring: Hand key; examiner evaluated

Cost: 100 tests $50.00; manual and scoring stencil $12.00.

Publisher: Rocky Mountain Behavioral Science Institute, Inc.

THE TEST OF SOCIAL INSIGHT: YOUTH EDITION and ADULT EDITION
Refer to page 148.

Study Skills Attitudes

CAI STUDY SKILLS TEST
William F. Brown

teen, adult   grades 11-UP

Purpose: Measures a student's knowledge of efficient study skills and effective academic attitudes. Used to identify those who need help and, as a post-test, those who fail to learn adequate skills.

Description: 200 item paper-pencil, true-false test of student's knowledge in ten areas: managing time, improving memory, taking lecture notes, reading texts, taking exams, writing themes and reports, giving oral reports, improving scholastic motivation, improving interpersonal relations, and improving concentration. Also available as a computer diskette for Apple II and TRS-80. Self- administered. Suitable for group use.

Untimed: 50 minutes

Range: Grades 11 and up

Scoring: Hand key

Cost: Test $.85 each, 100 $75.00; answer sheet $.35, 250-$75.00; hand key stencil $5.00; direction manual $3.50; computer disk $200.00 for Apple II plus and TRS-80.

Publisher: Effective Study Materials

CORNELL LEARNING AND STUDY SKILLS INVENTORY
Walter Pauk and Russell Cassel

teen, adult   grades 7-12

Purpose: Assesses skills important to effective learning in high school and college. Used for educational counseling.

Description: 120 item paper-pencil test of study skills. Yields scores in seven areas: goal orientation, activity structure, scholarly skills, lecture mastery, textbook mastery, examination mastery, and self mastery, and study efficiency. Twenty Two of the items are included in a Reading Validity Index which determines whether the student has responded thoughtfully. Two forms, College and Secondary School, are available. College Form items are answered on a five point ordinal scale ranging from seldom to always. Secondary School Form items are written in a true-false format. Self-administered. Suitable for group use.

Untimed: 30-45 minutes

Range: Grades 7-12, college

Scoring: Hand key

Cost: Specimen set $7.25; 25 tests $16.50; 100- $65.00; 25 answer sheets, 25 profile sheets $5.50 each; 100-$21.00; keys $5.50; manual $5.50 (specify Secondary or College form).

Publisher: Psychologists and Educators, Inc.

EFFECTIVE STUDY TEST (EST)
William F. Brown

teen, adult   grades 9-UP

Purpose: Identifies students in need of counseling concerning their study skills and habits. Used to monitor student progress in response to counseling and instruction intended to improve study methods.

Description: 125 item paper-pencil true-false test assessing students' knowledge of effective study methods. Measures five sub-scales: reality orientation, study organization, reading behavior, writing behavior, and examination behavior. The test yields a total score for study effectiveness. Use restricted to professional educators. Self-administered. Suitable for group use. Available in Spanish and on computer diskette for Apple II or TRS-80.

Untimed: 35-45 minutes

Range: Grades 9-college

Scoring: Hand key

Cost: Reusable test booklet $.30 each; 200-$55.00; answer sheet $.12 each; 500-$55.00; scoring stencil $.70 each; direction manual $.70 each; specimen set $.175 each; computer diskette $200.00.

Publisher: Effective Study Materials

HOW A CHILD LEARNS
Thomas D. Gnagey

adult

Purpose: Evaluates a student's learning style through teacher observation. Used to organize these observations so that an individualized teaching program may be planned.

Description: Three category paper-pencil test evaluating how students listen and see, how they talk and move, and what they remember. The teacher, using the manual and outlines provided, completes a set of specified observations of regular activities and enters them according to directions. They are then analysed in terms of the students' abilities and a prescriptive teaching plan is written. Especially useful in teacher training programs, student teaching and in-service training. Examiner required. Not suitable for groups.

Untimed: 30-60 minutes

Range: Adult

Scoring: Examiner evaluated

Cost: Training manual and 20 forms $8.95; 100 additional forms $16.00.

Publisher: Facilitation House

STUDY ATTITUDES AND METHODS SURVEY (SAMS)
William B. Michael,
Joan J. Michael and
Wayne S. Zimmerman

teen, adult   grades 7-UP

Purpose: Diagnoses habits and attitudes which may be inhibiting junior high school, high school and college students from achieving full academic potential. Used to identify those students most likely to benefit from individual counseling.

Description: Multiple item paper-pencil inventory assesses dimensions of a motivational, non-cognitive nature which are related to school achievement and which contribute to a student's performance beyond those measured by traditional ability tests. Used for classroom and school-wide screening. The student's profile can provide the requisite insights and guidelines for study habit improvement. Norms provided for high school and college level. Examiner required. Suitable for group use.

Untimed: 20-30 minutes

Range: Junior high, high school and college

Scoring: Hand key; computer scoring available

Cost: Specimen set (includes manual and all forms) $3.00; 25 reusable test booklets $9.50; 50 answer sheets $5.50; 50 profile sheets (specify high school or college) $4.00; keys $4.00; manual $2.00.

Publisher: Educational and Industrial Testing Service

STUDY HABITS EVALUATION AND INSTRUCTION KIT
Peter Jackson, Neil Reid and
Cedric Croft

child, teen

Purpose: Measures and provides instruction on study habits. Used for educational guidance.

Description: Two part paper-pencil test of study habits. Part 1, the Inventory of Study Habits, assists pupils in measuring study habits. The second part, consisting of self-instructional booklets, allows students to work on improving study habits in seven areas: study environment, study time, study organization, reading skills, notetaking skills, exam preparation, and exam technique. Self-administered. Suitable for group use.
PUBLISHED IN NEW ZEALAND

Untimed: 45 minutes

Range: Form 4, 5 and 6 pupils

Scoring: Hand key; examiner evaluated

Cost: Students set $5.50; teacher's specimen set $7.00; 50 response/profile sheet $15.00 (all remittances must be in New Zealand currency).

Publisher: New Zealand Council for Educational Research

STUDY SKILLS COUNSELING EVALUATION
George D. Demos

teen, adult   grades 10-UP

Purpose: Evaluates study habits and attitudes of high school and college students.

Description: 50 item paper-pencil questionnaire asks students to rate themselves with answers ranging from "Very Often" to "Very Seldom" on statements covering the important study areas of time distribution, study conditions, taking notes, examinations, habits, and attitudes. Includes "critical items" which differentiate between "B" and "C" students. Self-administered. Suitable for group use.

Untimed: 10-20 minutes

Range: High school and college

Scoring: Hand key

Cost: Complete kit (includes 20 forms and manual) $8.90.

Publisher: Western Psychological Services

STUDY SKILLS SURVEYS (SSS)
William F. Brown

teen grades 9-13

Purpose: Identifies study skill problems likely to hinder academic achievement; used to counsel students about effective study habits and attitudes.

Description: 60 item paper-pencil, "yes-no" test with three scales designed to evaluate study organization, study techniques and study motivation. Helps students recognize and change poor study habits. Available in Spanish and on computer diskette for Apple II or TRS-80. Self-administered. Suitable for group use.

Untimed: 15-20 minutes

Range: Grades 9-college freshman

Scoring: Hand key

Cost: Reusable test booklet $.30 each; 500-$55.00; student workbook $.20 each; directions manual $.35; specimen set $.85 each; computer disk $200.00.

Publisher: Effective Study Materials

SURVEY OF STUDY HABITS AND ATTITUDES
W.F. Brown and W.H. Holtzman

teen, adult grades 7-UP

Purpose: Identifies students whose study habits and attitudes may prevent them from taking advantage of educational alternatives. Used for educational counseling.

Description: 100 item paper-pencil test of four basic aspects of study habits and attitudes: delay avoidance, work methods, teacher approval, and education acceptance. Also yields Study Habits subtotal, Study Attitude subtotal and total Study Orientation scores. Students rate themselves according to own habits and attitudes. Predictive of academic success. Materials include two forms: Form H for grades 7 through 12, and Form C for college students. Self-administered. Suitable for group use. Available in Spanish.

Untimed: 20-25 minutes

Range: Grades 7-12, college

Scoring: Hand key; may be machine scored

Cost: Specimen set (includes survey, IBM 805 answer document and key, manual) $3.00; 25 surveys $7.75; 50 IBM 805 answer documents $5.25, manual and keys $.250; 50 IBM 1230 answer documents $6.00, manual and keys $3.75.

Publisher: The Psychological Corporation

WRENN STUDY HABITS INVENTORY
C. Gilbert Wrenn

teen, adult grades 10-UP

Purpose: Identifies student study habits and attitudes. Used for academic counseling.

Description: 28 item paper-pencil test of habits and attitudes by which high and low scholarship students are distinquished. A negative item score means response is closer to response given by low scholarship students. Self-administered. Suitable for group use.

Untimed: 10-20 minutes

Range: High school and college

Scoring: Hand key

Cost: Specimen set (includes test, manual, key) $1.00.

Publisher: Consulting Psychologists Press, Inc.

Teacher Evaluation

Student Opinion of Teachers

CLASSROOM ENVIRONMENT SCALE (CES)
Rudolf H. Moos and Edison J. Trickett

teen   grades 7-12

Purpose: Assesses the teaching atmosphere of junior and senior high classrooms to help evaluate the effects of course content, teaching methods, teacher personality, and class composition.

Description: 90 item paper-pencil test measuring nine dimensions of classroom atmosphere: involvement, affiliation, teacher support, task orientation, competition, order and organization, rule clarity, teacher con-

trol, and innovation. These dimensions are grouped into four sets: relationship, personal development, system maintenance, and system change. Materials include four forms: The Real Form (Form R) measuring current perceptions of classroom atmosphere; the Ideal Form (Form I), measuring conceptions of the ideal classroom atmosphere; the Expectations Form (Form E), measuring Expectations about a new classroom, and a 36-item Short Form (Form S). Forms I and E are not published, although reworded instructions and items are listed in the manual. Examiner required. Suitable for group use.

Untimed: 20-30 minutes

Range: Junior and senior high school

Scoring: Examiner evaluated

Cost: Specimen set $4.25; manual $3.25; key $.75.

Publisher: Consulting Psychologists Press, Inc.

COMPREHENSIVE PERSONAL ASSESSMENT SYSTEM: STUDENT EVALUATION OF TEACHERS I (SET I)
Donald J. Veldman and Robert F. Peck

child, teen   grades 3-12

Purpose: Used as student evaluation of teacher behavior. For grades 3 to 12.

Description: Multiple item paper-pencil test consisting of set of ten true-false questions. Test is for research only and is not intended for use in administrative evaluation of teachers. Self-administered; proctor required.

Untimed: 5-15 minutes

Range: Grades 3-12

Scoring: Hand key; computer scoring available

Cost: 100 forms $10.00; manual $1.50.

Publisher: Research and Development Center for Teacher Education

COMPREHENSIVE PERSONAL ASSESSMENT SYSTEM: STUDENT EVALUATION OF TEACHING II (SET II)
Ruth Haak and Robert F. Peck

child   grades 1-3

Purpose: Used for primary student evaluation of teacher behavior.

Description: Three-card choice test. Child is shown card and is presented with a statement; if child agrees, card is put in mailbox; if not, it is put in wastebasket. Cardboard wastebasket and mailbox included in kit with cards. Examiner required. Not suitable for group use.

Untimed: 15-20 minutes

Range: Grades Primary

Scoring: Hand key

Cost: 100 forms $10.00; manual $1.50 (includes cards).

Publisher: Research and Development Center for Teacher Education

CORNELL INVENTORY FOR STUDENT APPRAISAL OF TEACHING COURSES
James A. Maas and Cornell University

teen, adult   College

Purpose: Elicits evaluation from college students of the college class and teacher. Used as evidence for teacher promotion, course guides, and changes in curriculum.

Description: 64 item paper-pencil inventory gathers personal background information from the student and then asks the student to rate from one to five a number of statements concerning the class experience: teacher, course, readings, papers, labs, discussion sections, and exams. The individual instructor can add up to ten questions. Space is

provided for recommendations and personal comments. Self-administered. Suitable for group use.

Untimed: 20 minutes

Range: College students

Scoring: Hand key; computer scoring available

Cost: 100 booklets and answer sheets $15.18.

Publisher: Cornell General Stores

DIAGNOSTIC TEACHER-RATING SCALE
Sister Mary Amatora

teen, adult   grades 7-UP

Purpose: Measures students' perceptions of their teachers. Used to analyze and improve student- teacher relations.

Description: 56 item inventory consisting of two scales. The Area Scale (7 items) consists of a list of attributes related to effective teaching and good student-teacher relations. Students rate their teacher for each attribute on a five-point scale from "worst" to "best". The Diagnostic Checklist (49 items) consists of True-False statements assessing seven factors: liking for teacher; ability to explain; kindness, friendliness, and understanding; fairness in grading; discipline; amount of work required; and liking for lessons. The checklist is available in two similar forms, A and B. Examiner required. Suitable for group use.

Untimed: Not available

Range: Junior high school and up

Scoring: Hand key; examiner evaluated

Cost: Specimen set $1.00; complete kit (includes 35 record sheets for scale and checklist and manual) $4.00.

Publisher: Educators'/Employers' Tests and Services Associates

ENDEAVOR INSTRUCTIONAL RATING SYSTEM
Peter W. Frey

teen, adult   College

Purpose: Measures teacher effectiveness at the college and university level by students.

Description: Seven item paper-pencil measure of the instructor's organizational communication, and interpersonal skills, and the difficulty of the course. A brief rating form is distributed to each student and the students respond to each of seven items. The forms are then collected and processed by computer. The test requires advanced planning and is limited to classes with five or more students. Self-administered. Suitable for groups.

Untimed: 5-7 minutes

Range: College students

Scoring: Computer scored

Cost: Cards $.10-$.20 each depending on quantity; price includes computer processing; minimum order $100.00.

Publisher: Endeavor Information Systems, Inc.

THE PURDUE INSTRUCTOR PERFORMANCE INDICATOR
H.H. Remmers and J.H. Snedeker

teen, adult   College

Purpose: Measures professor's effectiveness as perceived by students. Used for course evaluation.

Description: Multiple item paper-pencil measure of student ratings of professor's effectiveness. Items are forced choice. Rater chooses among four alternatives in each of twelve blocks. All phrases in each block are socially acceptable, half discriminate between effective and ineffective teachers. Materials include two forms, A and B. Self-administered. Suitable for

group use.

Untimed: 10-15 minutes

Range: College level students

Scoring: Hand key

Cost: Contact publisher.

Publisher: Purdue Research Foundation/University Book Store

THE PURDUE RATING SCALE FOR INSTRUCTION
H.H. Remmers and D.N. Elliott

teen, adult   College

Purpose: Measures student perceptions of professors and the classroom teaching situation. Used for research and course evaluation.

Description: Multiple item paper-pencil test of student perceptions of ten characteristics of professors and 14 aspects of the classroom teaching situation. Self-administered. Suitable for group use.

Untimed: 5-10 minutes

Range: College students

Scoring: Machine scorable; computer scoring service available

Cost: Contact publisher.

Publisher: Purdue Research Foundation/University Book Store

THE PURDUE TEACHER EVALUATION SCALE (PTES)
Ralph R. Bentley and Allan R. Starry

teen   grades 7-12

Purpose: Measures student opinions of teachers. Used for providing teachers with information for a program of self-improvement and development.

Description: Multiple item paper-pencil measure of six dimensions of student attitudes toward teachers: ability to motivate students, ability to control students, subject matter orientation of teacher, student-teacher communication, teaching methods and procedures, and fairness of teacher. Examiner required. Suitable for group use.

Untimed: 20 minutes

Range: Junior and senior high students

Scoring: Hand key; computer scoring service available

Cost: Contact publisher.

Publisher: Purdue Research Foundation/University Book Store

STUDENT INSTRUCTIONAL REPORT (SIR)
Research Staff at Educational Testing Service

teen, adult   College

Purpose: Measures student ratings of teacher performance. Used for instructional improvement, administrative decisions and student course selection.

Description: 39 item paper-pencil test of six aspects of teacher performance: course organization and planning; faculty/student interaction; communication; course difficulty and workload; textbooks and readings; and tests and exams. Administered to students in regular class sessions. Examiner required. Suitable for group use. Available in French (Canadian Universities) and Spanish.

Untimed: 50 minutes

Range: College students

Scoring: Computer scored

Cost: First 20,000 forms $.18 each; processing first 5,000 forms $.35 each.

Publisher: Educational Testing Service

Teacher Attitudes

EARLY CHILDHOOD ENVIRONMENT RATING SCALE
Thelma Harms and Richard M. Clifford

adult

Purpose: Evaluates the adequacy of preschool child care settings. Used to assess class daycare, headstart, nursery school and kindergarten programs.

Description: 37 item paper-pencil test. The examiner rates childcare environments in terms of: use of space, materials and experiences to enhance child development, daily schedule and level of supervision provided. A room-by-room evaluation covers: routines for the personal care of the children, room furnishing and display, language- reasoning experiences, fine and gross motor activities, creative activities, social development activities, and adult needs. Materials include Rating Scale Book and Scoring Sheet. Examiner required.

Untimed: Not available

Range: Teachers

Scoring: Examiner evaluated

Cost: Rating scale $5.95; 30 additional scoring sheets $5.50.

Publisher: Teachers College Press

EDUCATIONAL VALUES (VAL-ED)
Will Schutz

adult

Purpose: Assesses an individual's attitudes regarding education. Used to evaluate the working relationships of students, teachers, administrators, or community members.

Description: Multiple item paper-pencil survey of values regarding interpersonal relationships in school settings. Factors included relate to "inclusion, control and affection" at both the feeling and behavioral levels, as well as the purpose and importance of education. Examiner recommended. May be self-administered. Suitable for group use.

Untimed: Not available

Range: Adult

Scoring: Hand key

Cost: Specimen set (including keys) $2.00.

Publisher: Consulting Psychologists Press, Inc.

EMPATHY INVENTORY (EI)
John R. Thurston

adult

Purpose: Measures ability of nursing faculty, counselors and others to empathize with nursing students. Used for self-evaluation.

Description: 75 item paper-pencil test with a dual-choice format. It gives interested individuals an opportunity to check their empathic ability. Materials include a self-directing booklet, answer sheet and scoring key. Comprehensive manual available covering this and other NRA tests. Self-administered. Suitable for group use.

Untimed: 30 minutes

Range: Adults

Scoring: Hand key; scoring service available $2.00 each

Cost: Specimen set (excluding scoring, key) $10.00; 50 EI answer sheets $5.00; EI scoring key $5.00; comprehensive manuals (LHSG, NSC, NAI, & EI) $15.00.

Publisher: Nursing Research Associates

ILLINOIS TESTS IN THE TEACHING OF ENGLISH
William H. Evans and Paul H. Jacobs

adult

Purpose: Measures high school English teachers' achievement of certain professionally established objectives relating to their knowledge and attitudes about English language and literature and how the subject should be taught. Used by schools and colleges for teacher-training evaluation.

Description: Four paper-pencil competency tests involved in the teaching of the English language and literature: Knowledge of Language, Attitude and Knowledge in Written Composition, Knowledge of Literature, and Knowledge of the Teaching of English. Each test is criteria-referenced, and the battery as a whole is based on criteria developed in the form of guidelines and standards by educational specialists and practicing teachers in cooperation with more than 20 universities and colleges. Examiner required. Suitable for group use.

Untimed: Not available

Range: Teachers

Scoring: Hand key; computer scoring available

Cost: Specimen set $5.00; 1-10 individual tests $1.00 each; 11-50 copies $.55 each; 8 keys $8.00; 50 OpScan answer sheets $3.00; individual manuals $2.00 each.

Publisher: Southern Illinois University Press

INSTITUTIONAL FUNCTIONING INVENTORY
Research staff at Educational Testing Services and Earl J. McGrath

adult

Purpose: Evaluates functioning of educational institutions. Used for self-studies for accreditation, planning and research.

Description: 132 item test of 11 dimensions of institutional functioning: intellectual-aesthetic extracurriculum; freedom; human diversity; concern for undergraduate learning; democratic governance; meeting local needs; self-study and planning; concern for advanced knowledge; concern for innovation; and institutional esprit. Inventory is distributed to a random sample of college community members: faculty, administration, students. Self-administered. Suitable for group use. Available in French for Canadian institutions.

Untimed: 45 minutes

Range: Adult

Scoring: Computer scored

Cost: Reusable faculty booklets $.50 each; reusable student booklets $.35 each; answer sheets $.10 each.

Publisher: Educational Testing Service

OPINIONS TOWARD ADOLES-CENTS (OTA SCALE)
William T. Martin

teen, adult   grades 5-7

Purpose: Evaluates attitudes and personality factors which may help or inhibit interpersonal relationships between adults and adolescents. Used to screen persons who will be working with adolescents and to educate current staff members.

Description: 89 item paper-pencil inventory examines bipolar attitudes on the following subscales: Conservative-Liberal, Permissive-Punitive, Morally Accepting-Morally Restrictive, Democratic- Authoritarian, Trust-Mistrust, Acceptance- Prejudice, Misunderstanding-Understanding, and Sincerity-Skepticism (a validity scale reflecting test taking attitude). Norms

provided for various adult and college groups. Fifth- to Seventh-Grade reading level required. Self-administered. Suitable for group use.

Untimed: 20 minutes

Range: Reading level of grade 5-7 is required

Scoring: Hand key

Cost: Specimen set (includes manual, keys, forms) $9.50; examiner's set (includes manual, keys, 25 test books, 25 answer sheets, 25 profile sheets) $32.00; 25 tests $12.50; 25 profile sheets $6.75; 25 answer sheets $5.50; keys $5.50; manual $3.50.

Publisher: Psychologists and Educators, Inc.

PURDUE STUDENT-TEACHER OPINIONAIRE--FORM B (PSTO)
Ralph R. Bentley and JoAnn Price

adult

Purpose: Measures student-teacher morale. Used for providing school with feedback about student- teachers' experiences.

Description: Multiple item paper-pencil measure of nine aspects of student-teacher morale: rapport with supervising teacher, student-teacher rapport with principal, rapport with university supervisor, teaching as a profession, school facilities, professional preparation, rapport with students, rapport with other teachers and student-teacher load. Examiner required. Suitable for group use.

Untimed: 20-30 minutes

Range: Student-teachers

Scoring: Hand key; computer scoring service available

Cost: Contact publisher.

Publisher: Purdue Research Foundation/University Book Store

THE PURDUE TEACHER OPINIONAIRE (PTO)
Ralph R. Bentley and Averno M. Rempel

adult

Purpose: Assesses teacher opinions of school environment. Used for studying teacher morale.

Description: Multiple item paper-pencil measure of ten teacher morale factors: teacher rapport with principal, satisfaction with teaching, rapport among teachers, teacher salary, teacher load, curriculum issues, teacher status, community support of education, school facilities and services, and community pressures. Materials include PTO Supplement with two new factors: teacher rapport with school board and superintendent. Examiner required. Suitable for group use.

Untimed: 20-30 minutes

Range: Adult

Scoring: Hand key; computer scoring service available

Cost: Opinionaire $1.50.

Publisher: Purdue Research Foundation/University Book Store

RUCKER-GABLE EDUCATIONAL PROGRAMMING SCALE
Chauncy N. Rucker and Robert K. Gable

adult

Purpose: Assesses the ability of teachers to measure the attitudes of handicapped children.

Description: 30 item paper-pencil test measures the teacher's ability to place students in the correct educational setting on the basis of a brief description of the student's handicap. Student handicap range includes mildly, moderately and severely handicapped; mental, emtional and learning disability; and total disability. Self-administered by examiner. Suitable for group use. Available in Spanish and Chinese.

Untimed: 20-30 minutes

Range: Teachers

Scoring: Computer scored

Cost: Specimen set $10.00; manual $9.00; scoring service $40.00.

Publisher: Rucker-Gable Associates

A SELF-APPRAISAL SCALE FOR TEACHERS
Howard Wilson

adult

Purpose: Allows teachers to make a self-appraisal of their classroom performance. Used at the close of an academic term, often in conjunction with the Wilson Teacher-Appraisal Scale, to aid in the professional development of classroom instructors.

Description: 102 item paper-pencil inventory allowing instructors to rate themselves in six areas: teacher as a person, teacher as a specialist and educator, teacher's relations with students, course content, classroom performance, and the way teachers feel their students perceive them. Each item in the scale reflects a characteristic of competency as related to teaching methods. The instructor rates himself for each item on a five-point scale from "High" to "Low," circling items of particular importance. Often purchased and supplied by the educational institution and voluntarily used by the instructors as a tool to increase their classroom effectiveness. Self-administered. Suitable for group use.

Untimed: 20 minutes

Range: Teachers

Scoring: Self-evaluated

$1.50 each scale.

Publisher: Administrative Research ciates, Inc.

STAGES OF CONCERN QUESTIONNAIRE (SoCQ)
Gene E. Hall, Archie A. George and William L. Rutherford

adult

Purpose: Assesses faculty concerns regarding the implementation of educational innovations. Used to monitor and evaluate programs implementing educational innovations.

Description: 35 item paper-pencil questionnaire assessing attitudes toward specific educational innovations. Each item is rated on a seven-point scale according to the individual teacher's stage of concern: 0-awareness; 1-informational; 2-personal; 3-management; 4-consequences; 5-collaboration; and 6-refocusing. Self-administered. Suitable for group use. Available in Flemish, Hebrew, Spanish. The translations have new norms and confirming factor analyses.

Untimed: 15 minutes

Range: Teachers and higher education faculty

Scoring: Hand key; examiner evaluated; computer scoring available

Cost: Manual (includes master copy of questionnaire) $4.00.

Publisher: The Research and Development Center for Teacher Evaluation

STRESS PROFILE FOR TEACHERS
Christopher F. Wilson

adult

Purpose: Identifies sources and levels of teacher stress. Used for personal and staff development and awareness, and needs assessment.

Description: 36 item paper-pencil test provides a self-evaluation of the frequency of stress in the following areas: student behavior, intrapersonal conflict, employee/administrator relations, teacher/teacher relations, parent/teacher relations, time management, physical symptoms, psychological symptoms, and stress management techniques. The teacher ranks stress on a five-point scale ranging from "never" to "very often", and then refers to the profile scoring sheet. Self-administered. Suitable for use with groups.

Untimed: 20 minutes

Range: Teachers

Scoring: Hand key

Cost: 50 tests $12.50.

Publisher: The Wright Group

TEACHER OPINIONAIRE ON DEMOCRACY
Enola Ledbetter

adult

Purpose: Assesses teacher's attitudes about what is and is not wise in the way children are treated in school; useful for teacher surveys and college instruction.

Description: 65 item paper-pencil test measuring the "democraticness" of a teacher's philosophy, defined as the extent to which the teacher purports to respect the personality and purpose of the pupil. The teacher is asked to agree or disagree with each statement by marking it plus or minus. Self-administered. Suitable for group use.

Untimed: 30 minutes

Range: Teachers and student teachers

Scoring: Hand key

Cost: Manual and sample opinionaire $1.00.

Publisher: Peace Research Laboratory

THE WILSON TEACHER APPRAISAL SCALE
Howard Wilson

teen, adult   grades 7-16

Purpose: Allows instructors to see how they appear through the eyes of their students. Used at the close of an academic term, often in conjunction with A Self-Appraisal Scale for Teachers, to aid in the professional development of classroom instructors.

Description: 16 item paper-pencil rating scale allowing students to rate the performance of their classroom instructors. Students rate the teacher as person and as an instructor compared to other instructors. Course content and assignments are also rated. The scale is purchased and supplied by the institution and voluntarily used by the instructors as a tool to increase their effectiveness. Self-administered. Suitable for group use.

Untimed: 5 minutes

Range: Grades 7-16

Scoring: Examiner evaluated

Cost: 50 scales $2.50.

Publisher: Administrative Research Associates, Inc.

Vocational

ACADEMIC-TECHNICAL APTITUDE TESTS-ATA and SATA

child, teen

Purpose: Assesses differential job aptitudes. Used for vocational and educational guidance.

Description: Multiple item paper-pencil batteries measuring occupational aptitudes. ATA is for pupils in Standards 6, 7, and 8. SATA is for pupils in Standards 8, 9, and 10. The ATA battery consists of ten tests: Verbal Reasoning, Nonverbal Reasoning, Computations, Spatial Perceptions (2-D), Mechanical Reasoning, Language Comprehension, Spatial Perception (3-D), Comparison, Coordination, and Writing Speed. SATA is available in two forms, A and B. Form A consists of the following ten tests: Verbal Reasoning, Nonverbal Reasoning I: Figure Series, Nonverbal Reasoning II: Dominoes, Computations, Reading Comprehension, Spelling and Vocabulary, Mechanical Reasoning, Spatial Perception (3-D), Comparison, and Price Controlling. Form B has one additional subtest, Filing. Examiner required. Suitable for group use. Publisher notes that this test is "normed on Coloureds only."
SOUTH AFRICAN PUBLISHER

Timed: ATA, 4 hours; SATA 4½ hours

Range: ATA, Standards 6-8; SATA, Standards 8-10

Scoring: Hand key; examiner evaluated

Cost: (In Rands) ATA-test 0,70; manual 3,90; scoring stencils I, II 1,30 each; 10 answer sheets I 0,60; 10 answer sheets II 0,50; SATA-test (specify A or B) 1,60; manual 5,80; scoring stencils I, II (specify A or B) 2,10 each; 10 answer sheets I, II 1,30 each (orders from outside The RSA will be dealt with on merit).

Publisher: Human Sciences Research Council

THE APPLIED BIOLOGICAL AND AGRIBUSINESS INTEREST INVENTORY
Robert W. Walker and Glenn Z. Stevens

teen   grades 8

Purpose: Measures student interest in biological and agribusiness occupations. Used for curriculum planning and career counseling.

Description: 100 item, paper-pencil test measuring general agriculture interest: animals, plants, mechanics, and business. Materials include test booklet, student survey-answer sheet, and summary sheet. Examiner required. Suitable for group use.

Untimed: 20-30 minutes

Range: Grade 8

Scoring: Hand key; examiner evaluated; may be computer scored

Cost: Specimen set (includes single copy of test booklet, answer sheet, scoring key, interest summary form) $2.50.

Publisher: The Interstate Printers & Publishers, Inc.

APTICOM

adult

Purpose: Assesses multiple vocational aptitudes. Used for vocational guidance and counseling.

Description: Multiple item battery of tests measuring ten aptitudes important in vocational performance. Factors measured are general learning, verbal, numerical, spatial, form perception, clerical perception, motor coordination, finger dexterity, manual dexterity, and eye-hand-foot coordination. Items are presented on test panels on APTICOM, a computerized desk-top console. Subject responds by placing a probe beneath the chosen answer, thus illuminating a diode. APTICOM is self-timing and shuts off when allotted time has passed. Examiner required. Suitable for use with groups of four using optional Master Control.

Timed: 70 minutes

Range: Adult

Scoring: Computer scored

Cost: Contact publisher.

Publisher: Vocational Research Institute-J.E.V.S.

APTITUDE TESTS FOR OCCUPATIONS
Wesley S. Roeder

teen, adult   grades 10-UP

Purpose: Assesses aptitudes and potentials related to occupations and careers, in high school students, college students and adults. Used for occupational guidance and counseling.

Description: Six paper-pencil aptitude tests, each of which may be given independently. The tests include: Personal/Social (Test 1), Mechanical (Test 2), General Sales (Test 3), Clerical Routine (Test 4), Computation (Test 5), and Scientific (Test 6). Materials include an examiner's manual for each test. Examiner required. Suitable for group use.

Timed: 1 hour, 17 minutes

Range: High school-adult

Scoring: Hand key; may be computer scored

Cost: Test 1-$18.00; Test 2-$18.00; Test 3-$15.00; Test 4-$13.00; Test 5-$13.00; Test 6-$15.00; each Test includes 35 student booklets, examiner's manual and scoring key.

Publisher: PRO-ED

ARMED SERVICES VOCATIONAL APTITUDE BATTERY (ASVAB)
Department of Defense

teen, adult   grades 9-UP

Purpose: Evaluates high school student's aptitudes. Used for counseling and by the military services to identify eligible graduates for possible recruitment.

Description: 295 item paper-pencil test of aptitudes in various vocational and technical fields. Factors measured include electronics, mechanical comprehension, general science, shop knowledge, automotive information, general information, numerical operations, attention to detail, word knowledge, arithmetic, reasoning, space perception, and mathematics. Indicates academic ability in the following areas: verbal, math, perceptual speed, mechanical ability, and technical trade. A military service recruiter will assist each school in administering the test and Military Entrance Processing Command (MEPLOM) provides the examiner. Individual test results are delivered to school counselors and copies of the scores are given to the recruiting services. Examiner required. Suitable for group use.

Timed: 2 hours, 45 minutes

Range: High school seniors; may be used Grade 9-11 also

Scoring: Computer scored

Cost: No charge to schools for administration, materials and scoring.

Publisher: U.S. Department of Defense

CALIFORNIA LIFE GOALS EVALUATION SCHEDULES
Milton E. Hahn

adult

Purpose: Differentiates "life goals" from "interests" by identifying significant motivational forces in normal individuals 15 years and older. Used for career planning, adjusting to aging or retirement, evoking insights in areas of psychological normaity and college counseling.

Description: 150 item paper-pencil test consisting of "debatable" statements which the subject answers on a five-point acceptance or rejection scale. Measures ten life goals: Esteem, Profit, Fame, Leadership, Power, Security, Social Service, Interesting Experiences, Self-Expression, and Independence. Norms presented based on age, sex, occupation, familial relationships, and projected academic studies. May be self-administered. Suitable for group use.

Untimed: 20-30 minutes

Range: Adult

Scoring: Hand key

Cost: Complete kit (includes 10 profile forms, manual, 5 reusable test booklets, key, 10 answer sheets) $19.50.

Publisher: Western Psychological Services

CAREER ABILITY PLACEMENT SURVEY (CAPS)
Lila Knapp and
Robert R. Knapp

teen, adult   grades 7-UP

Purpose: Measures abilities keyed to entry requirements for the majority of jobs in each of the 14 COPSystem Career Clusters. Used with students from junior high to college level for career and vocational guidance and academic counseling.

Description: Eight paper-pencil subtests measure the following career related abilities: Mechanical Reasoning, Spatial Relations, Verbal Reasoning, Numerical Ability, Language Usage, Word Knowledge, Perceptual Speed and Accuracy, and Manual Speed and Dexterity.

Timed: 51 minutes

Range: Junior high-college

Scoring: Hand key; computer scoring available

Cost: Specimen set (includes one copy each of all the above forms and the manual $2.25; 30 self- scoring test batteries $54.00; 30 self- interpretation guide and profile sheet $9.90; 30 CAPS test forms (specify CAPS test) $4.50; scoring by EdITS $.95 battery; key (set of 7) $7.00; usual aids $14.50; administration tape $7.00.

Publisher: Educational and Industrial Testing Service

CAREER ASSESSMENT INVENTORY (CAI)
Charles B. Johansson

teen, adult   grades 8-UP

Purpose: Evaluates career goals of high school students who want immediate, noncollege-graduate business or technical training. Useful for employment decisions, vocational rehabilitation and self- employment.

Description: 305 item paper-pencil test in a five-response Likert format. Covers six General Occupational Themes (Holland's RIASEC), 22 Basic Occupational Interest Scales, and 91 Occupational Scales. Self-administered. Suitable for group use. Available in French and Spanish.

Untimed: 20-35 minutes

Range: Grades 8-adult

Scoring: Computer scored by NCS

Cost: Profile from $1.90-$4.25; profile and interpretation from $3.10-$10.00; scoring via ARION II teleprocessing from $13.00-$15.00.

Publisher: NCS Interpretive Scoring Systems

CAREER AWARENESS INVENTORY (CAI)
LaVerna M. Fadale

child, teen   grades 3-12

Purpose: Helps students assess how much they know about careers and their own career choices. Used for group discussion and as a pre- and post-test for career awareness.

Description: Multiple item paper-pencil test covers seven areas of career knowledge: related occupations, contact with occupations, job characteristics, functions of occupations, grouping of occupations, work locations of occupations, and self-assessment of career awareness. The Elementary CAI may be used with pupils in Grades 3-6, and the Advanced CAI may be used with pupils in Grades 7-12. CAI was developed under the sponorship of the Cornell Institute for Research and Development in Occupational Education. Self-administered; examiner evaluated. Suitable for group use.

Timed: 60-90 minutes

Range: Elementary grades 3-6; Advanced grades 7-12

Scoring: Hand key; examiner evaluated; computer scoring available

Cost: Complete kit (includes 20 reusable booklets, 1 manual, 1 class record sheet) $20.70; 50 answer sheets $10.00.

Publisher: Scholastic Testing Service, Inc.

CAREER DEVELOPMENT INVENTORY (SCHOOL FORM)
Donald E. Super, Albert S. Thompson, Richard H. Lindeman, Jean Pierre Jordaan, and Roger A. Myers

teen   grades 10-12

Purpose: Assesses individual attitudes, knowledge and skills related to vocational decisions. Used in career counseling courses.

Description: 120 item paper-pencil test of eight dimensions of vocational decision-making: career planning, career exploration, decision-making, world-of-work information, knowledge of preferred occupational group, career development-attitudes, career development-knowledge and skills, and career orientation total. May be administered in one (65 minutes) or two (40 minutes, 25 minutes) sessions. Examiner required. Suitable for group use.

Untimed: 55-65 minutes

Range: Senior high school

Scoring: Computer scored

Cost: Specimen set (includes test booklet, answer sheet, manual) $5.50; computer scoring $2.00 each.

Publisher: Consulting Psychologists Press, Inc.

CAREER GUIDANCE INVENTORY
James E. Oliver

teen, adult   grades 10-12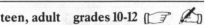

Purpose: Measures comparative strength of interests in 25 trades, services and technologies. Used in educational guidance counseling and career planning for non-baccalaureate bound youth and adults.

Description: 240 item paper-pencil test. Covers 14 engineering-related trades and eleven others: carpentry, masonry, mechanical repair, painting and decorating, plumbing-pipefitting, printing, tool and die making, sheet metal and welding, drafting and design technology, mechanical engineering technology, and industrial production technology, civil and architectural engineering technology, electrical engineering technology and chemical and laboratory technology.

Also covers eleven non-engineering related trades: environmental health technology, agriculture and forestry technology, business management, communications, data processing technology, sales, transportation services, protective services, medical technology—laboratory medical technology—nursing and food services. Suitable for group use.

Untimed: 90 minutes

Range: Junior high-college freshman

Scoring: Hand key

Cost: Specimen set $3.00; booklet $1.25; manual $1.00; 25 answer sheets $20.00.

Publisher: Educational Guidance, Inc.

CAREER INTEREST TEST (CIT)
Refer to page 806.

CAREER MATURITY INVENTORY (CMI)
John O. Crites

teen   grades 6-12

Purpose: Measures student's maturity by examining his attitudes and competencies regarding career decisions. Used by vocational counselors and educators in planning programs.

Description: Two section, paper-pencil test. The Attitude Scale measures the student's maturity with respect to feelings, subjective reactions, and dispositions toward making a career choice; and the (Competency Test assures a competency that is important in career decision making. See CMI: Attitude Scale and CMI: Competence Test. Examiner required. Suitable for group use.

Untimed: Total 3 hours, 5 minutes

Range: Grades 6-12

Scoring: Hand key; computer scoring available

Cost: Specimen set (includes one: attitude scale book, competence test book, manual, theory and research handbook, machine-score answer sheet, maturity profile, and test reviewer's guide) $7.25.

Publisher: CTB/McGraw-Hill

CAREER MATURITY INVENTORY: ATTITUDE SCALE

teen   grades 6-12

Purpose: Measures student's maturity by examining his attitudes and regarding career decisions. Used by vocational counselors and educators in planning programs.

Description: Multiple item paper-pencil test in two forms, A-2 and B-1, that considers five variables (decisiveness, involvement, independence, orientation, and compromise) and measures the student's maturity with respect to feelings, subjective reactions, and dispositions toward making a career choice. The A-2 form is useful for screening or survey purposes, and the B-1 form is useful in counseling situations. Examiner required. Suitable for group use.

Untimed: Screening Form A-2, 25 minutes; Counseling Form B-1, 35 minutes

Range: Grades 6-12

Scoring: Hand key; computer scoring available

Cost: 35 test books, a manual and key (specify form) $22.05.

Publisher: CTB/McGraw-Hill

CAREER MATURITY INVENTORY: COMPETENCE TEST

teen   grades 6-12

Purpose: Measures student's maturity by examining his attitudes and regarding career decisions. Used by vocational counselors and educators in planning programs.

Description: Multiple item paper-pencil test containing five subtests: Self-Appraisal, Occupational Information, Goal Selection, Planning, and Problem Solving. Each test item presents a hypothetical situation and taker must choose one of five answer choices. Examiner required. Suitable for group use.

Untimed: 25 minutes each subtest

Range: Grades 6-12

Scoring: Hand key; computer scoring available

Cost: 35 test books, a manual and key $36.75.

Publisher: CTB/McGraw-Hill

CAREER ORIENTATION PLACEMENT AND EVALUATION SURVEY (COPES)

teen, adult   grades 8-UP

Purpose: Measures personal values related to the type of work one chooses and the satisfactions derived from this occupation. Used for career evaluation and guidance; supplements other types of information used in industrial or educational counseling situations where the goal is improved self-awareness.

Description: Multiple item paper-pencil inventory measuring eight dimensions of personal values related to career evaluation and selection. The values measured are: Investigative, Practical, Independent,

Leadership, Orderliness, Recognition, Aesthetic, and Social. The COPES value dimensions are based on theoretical and factor analytic research and supplement other types of information used in counseling situations where the goal is improved self-awareness. Norms provided for high school and college levels. Self-administered. Suitable for group use.

Untimed: 30 minutes

Range: Grades 8-adult

Scoring: Hand key; computer scoring available

Cost: Specimen set (includes manual and all forms) $2.25; COPES visuals $5.50; 25 reusable test booklets $9.50; 50 computer-scoring answer sheets $5.50; 25 self-scoring booklets $8.25; 25 self- interpretation profiles $2.75; manual $1.25.

Publisher: Educational and Industrial Testing Service

CAREER PLANNING PROGRAM (CPP)
The American College Testing Program

teen, adult   grades 8-adult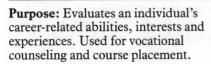

Purpose: Evaluates an individual's career-related abilities, interests and experiences. Used for vocational counseling and course placement.

Description: 436 item paper-pencil test designed to help the subject identify and explore personally relevant occupations and educational programs. Six factors are measured in each of three areas: career-related abilities, interests and experiences. Examiner required. Suitable for group use.

Timed: 150 minutes

Range: Level I, Grades 8-10; Level II, Grades 11- adult

Scoring: Computer scored by ACT

Cost: Complete student set (includes

consummable materials with scoring, 2-page report of results and interpretive booklet for one participant) $4.00; assessment booklet (reusable) $.50; specimen set $6.50. Complete (includes materials including scoring, 2-page report of results, and interpretive booklet for one counselee) $4.00. Per group summary report $40.00; specimen set $6.00.

Publisher: The American College Testing Program

CAREER PATH STRATEGY
Jeffery Siegel

teen, adult

Purpose: Evaluates a person's career potential. Used to develop career guidance programs, recommend career choices or changes and monitor progress toward career goals.

Description: 75 item paper-pencil interview guide assessing an individual's career strategies. Examines the following factors: mental ability, vocational interests, personality testing, ideal career and ideal life style, personal background data (such as educational and employment history), cultural, geographic and economic opportunities and limitations, preliminary career decisions, and strategies for achieving career goals. Includes homework assignments and forms for reassessment and follow-up. The clinician completes the inventory during the counseling session, then evaluates the results and makes appropriate suggestions. Examiner required. Not suitable for group use.

Untimed: 30 minutes

Range: Ages 16-adult

Scoring: Examiner evaluated

Cost: 50 strategy forms $15.00.

Publisher: The Wilmington Press

CHATTERJI'S NON-LANGUAGE PREFERENCE (CNPR)
S. Chatterji

child, teen

Purpose: Determines individual areas of interest for students ages 10-16 years. Used for educational counseling, vocational guidance and career planning.

Description: 150 item multiple-choice paper-pencil test assessing interest in ten broad interest areas: fine arts, literary work, scientific, medical, agricultural, technical, craft, outdoor, sports, and household work. Each test item consists of a three-choice question presented with stick-figure drawings. The non-language presentation is suitable for use with non-English speaking students. The manual provides information on administering, scoring and interpreting the test. Examiner required. Suitable for group use.
PUBLISHED IN INDIA

Untimed: 45 minutes

Range: Ages 10-16

Scoring: Hand key; examiner evaluated

Cost: (In Rupees) specimen set Rs.45; complete kit (includes 25 booklets, 100 answer sheets, 100 profile charts, scoring stencils, manual) Rs.180-00.

Publisher: Manasayan

CHOOSING A CAREER
Refer to page 814.

COMMERCIAL TESTS-1962
Refer to page 198.

COPSYSTEM: CAREER OCCUPATIONAL PREFERENCE SYSTEM
Robert R. Knapp and Lila F. Knapp

teen, adult   grades 7-UP

Purpose: Measures interests, abilities, and work values relevant to occupational and career planing and guidance for students from junior high to college level.

Description: The COPSystem consists of three measuring instruments which can be combined and analyzed in two distinct manners. The three tests are COPSystem Interest Inventory (COPS), the Career Orientation Placement and Evaluation Survey (COPES), and the Career Ability Placement Survey (CAPS). The two methods of analysis and interpretation are the Comprehensive COPSystem and the Summary COPSystem. In the Comprehensive COPSystem, all three tests are administered and the interpreted on a single Comprehensive Career Planning Guide. In the Summary COPSystem, the three tests are administered and interpreted separately by using a Self-Interpretation Profile and Guide for each of the tests and then summarized in the COPSystem Summary Guide. The latter method for separate interpretation and summary is recommended if testing time blocks are such that the three tests are not administered close together during the school year. All tests relate to the following COPSystem Career Clusters: Science, Technology, Consumer Economics, Outdoor, Business, Clerical, Communication, Arts, and Service.

Untimed: Not available

Range: Junior high-college

Scoring: Examiner evaluated

Cost: Specimen set $6.50.

Publisher: Educational and Indus-

COPSYSTEM: INTERMEDIATE INVENTORY (COPS II)
Lila Knapp and Robert R. Knapp

teen   grades 6-7

Purpose: Measures career related interests of sixth- and seventh-grade students. Used for academic counseling and guidance.

Description: Multiple item paper-pencil inventory provides rating of student job related interests based to a large extent on knowledge of school activities. COPS II extends interest measurement to younger students and those at higher grade levels for whom reading or language present difficulties, or where motivational considerations are of special concern. Items are written at a fourth-grade reading level. COPS II can be self-administered and self-scored in one class period. Suitable for group use.

Untimed: One class period, 20-30 minutes for response, 15-20 minutes for student-scoring

Range: Grades 6-7 (4th grade reading level)

Scoring: Hand key

Cost: Specimen set (includes manual) $2.00; 25 self-scoring forms (combined self-scoring booklet and self-interpretation guide) $17.00, 100-$63.00; set of 14 COPSystem occupational cluster charts with COPSystem II cartoons $15.95; 25 pocket size cluster charts $5.00.

Publisher: Educational and Industrial Testing Service

COPSYSTEM INTEREST INVENTORY (COPS)
Robert R. Knapp and Lila Knapp

teen, adult   grades 7-UP

Purpose: Measures job activity interests related to occupational clusters appropriate for college and vocationally oriented individuals. Used for academic counseling, career planning, and vocational guidance.

Description: Multiple item paper-pencil inventory measures interests related to both professional and skilled positions in Science, Technology, Business, Arts, and Service, as well as occupations in Communication, Consumer Economics, Clerical, and Outdoor fields. Each cluster is keyed to curriculum choice and major sources of detailed job information including the "Dictionary of Occupational Titles," VIEW, and the "Occupational Outlook Handbook." On site scoring provides immediate feedback of results. Percentile norms presented separately for high school and college levels. Self-administered. Suitable for group use. Available in Spanish and a Canadian version.

Untimed: 30-40 minutes

Range: Grades 7-adult

Scoring: Hand key; computer scoring available

Cost: Specimen set (includes one copy each of all forms and technical manual) $3.25; 25 expendable self-scoring test booklets $8.25; 25 self-interpretation guides and profile sheets $8.00; 25 machine-scored reusable test booklets $9.75; 50 machine-scored answer sheets $5.00; 14 hand scoring keys $10.00; examiner's manual $1.25; technical manual $1.25.

Publisher: Educational and Industrial Testing Service

COPSYSTEM INTEREST INVENTORY FORM P (COPS-P)
Lisa Knapp, Lee Lila Knapp and Robert R. Knapp

teen, adult   grades 7-UP

Purpose: Measures career-related interests of professionally minded high school and college students. Used for college major and occupational selection and orientation.

Description: Multiple item paper-pencil inventory measures interests related to professional level occupations in the following career clusters: Physical Science, Medical Life Science, Civil Engineering, Electrical Engineering, Mechanical Engineering Agribusiness, Nature, Business Management, Finance, Computation, Written Communication, Oral Communication, Design, Performing Arts, Social Service, and Instructional Service. Separate percentile norms provided for high school and college levels. Self- administered. Suitable for group use.

Untimed: 30-40 minutes

Range: Grades 7-high school, college, adult

Scoring: Hand key; computer scoring available

Cost: Specimen set $3.25; 25 expendable self- scoring test booklets $8.25; 25 self- interpretation guides and profile sheets (specify high school or college norms) $8.00; 25 machine- scored reusable test booklets and answer sheets $9.75.

Publisher: Educational and Industrial Testing Service

COPSYSTEM INTEREST INVENTORY FORM R (COPS-R)
Lila F. Knapp and Robert R. Knapp

teen   grades 6-12

Purpose: Measures job activity interests related to occupational clusters, but in more simplified language than the COPS Interest Inventory. Used for academic counseling, career planning and vocational guidance with students sixth-grade through high school.

Description: Multiple item paper-pencil inventory measures interests related to both professional and skilled positions in Science, Technology, Business, Arts, and Service, as well as occupations in Communications, Consumer Economics, Clerical, and Outdoor fields. COPS Form R is parallel to COPS Interest Inventory but with simpler language and a single norms profile. Items are written at a sixth-grade reading level, and the whole unit is presented in a programmed booklet. May be used with CAPS and COPE as a part of the Summary COPSystem (COPS-R should be the last test administered in this series). A self-scoring form is available, along with a machine-scoring form for processing and scoring by EdITS. Percentile Norms provided at high school level. Self-administered. Suitable for group use.

Untimed: 20 minutes

Range: Grades 6-high school

Scoring: Hand key; computer scoring available

Cost: Specimen set (includes manual and one copy of all forms) $2.75; 25 self-scoring forms $16.00 (includes self-scoring booklet and self- interpretation guide); 25 machine-scored reusable test booklets $9.75; 50 machine-scored answer sheets $5.50; examiner's manual $1.25.

Publisher: Educational and

Industrial Testing Services

CROWLEY OCCUPATIONAL INTERESTS BLANK
Tony Crowley

teen   grades 10-12

Purpose: Evaluates the career and vocational interests of average and below-average students. Used to develop vocational guidance programs.

Description: Multiple item paper-pencil, multiple-choice test in two parts, each covering five areas. Part I ranks general occupational interests: active- outdoor, office, social, practical, and artistic. Part II consists of job comparison statements to determine sources of job satisfaction: financial gain, stability, companionship, working conditions, and interest. Results yield ten scores. Materials include a four-page unisex test form, spiritmaster and manual. Self-administered. Suitable for group use.
BRITISH PUBLISHER

Untimed: 20-30 minutes

Range: Grades high school

Scoring: Hand key

Cost: Spiritmasters £8.97; manual £4.35; 100 questionnaires £9.75.

Publisher: Hobsons Press

CURTIS COMPLETION FORM
Refer to page 100.

DECISION MAKING ORGANIZER (DMO)
Refer to page 615.

DF OPINION SURVEY: AN INVENTORY OF DYNAMIC FACTORS (DFOS)
J.P. Guilford, Paul R. Christensen and Nicholas A. Bond, Jr.

teen, adult   grades 10-UP

Purpose: Measures general motivational factors. May be used for personnel selection, counseling and guidance.

Description: Multiple item paper-pencil inventory measuring ten general motivational factors which were found in an analysis of interest variables. Includes the following ten factors: need for attention, liking for thinking, adventure vs. security, self-reliance vs. dependence, aesthetic appreciation, cultural conformity, need for freedom, realistic thinking, need for precision, and need for diversion. The factors have general implications for personality as well as being related to braod vocational interests. Norms provided for high school and college students. Restricted to A.P.A. members. Examiner required. Suitable for group use.

Untimed: 45 minutes

Range: Ages High school-adult

Scoring: Hand key; may be computer scored

Cost: 25 tests $14.00; 25 answer sheets $4.50; 25 profile charts $3.50; manual $1.50; scoring set $7.50.

Publisher: Sheridan Psychological Services, Inc.

EDUCATIONAL DEVELOPMENT SERIES (ED SERIES)
Refer to page 367.

EDUCATIONAL INTEREST INVENTORY
James E. Oliver

teen, adult   grades 10-UP

Purpose: Measures high school and college students' interests in 22 major areas of study leading to B.A. degrees in colleges and universities. Used for educational guidance counseling and career planning.

Description: 250 item paper-pencil inventory consisting of forced-choice pairs of statements related to interests in fine arts, applied arts, physical and biological science, and social science. Measures interests in the following major areas of study: music, art, communication, education, business administration, engineering, industrial arts, agriculture, nursing, library arts, home economics, botany, zoology, physics, chemistry, geology, earth science, history, political science, sociology, psychology, economics, and mathematics. Self-administered. Proctor required. Suitable for group use.

Untimed: 30-60 minutes

Range: High school, college students

Scoring: Self-score

Cost: Specimen set $3.00; booklet $1.25; manual $1.00; 25 answer sheets $20.00.

Publisher: Educational Guidance, Inc.

EXPERIENCE EXPLORATION
W. Price Ewens

teen, adult   grades 8-UP

Purpose: Identifies possible job alternatives by evaluating a persons's work experience and interests. Used for career planning, vocational guidance and student counseling.

Description: 200 item paper-pencil inventory assessing an individual's abilities and interests in ten occupational areas: outdoor, mechanical, computation, scientific, persuasive, artistic, literary, musical, social service, and clerical. Also includes a 19-item values checklist which identifies the individual's most and least important occupational values: live in a small town/big town, work with hands/ideas, work at a desk/physical activity, work under supervision/unsupervised. Self-administered. Suitable for group use.

Untimed: 45 minutes

Range: Grades 8-adult

Scoring: Examiner evaluated

Cost: 35 survey booklets $14.00; 35 student experience sheets $14.00; interpretative wall chart $2.50; manual $3.50.

Publisher: Chronicle Guidance Publications

FACTORIAL INTEREST BLANK
P.H. Sandall

child, teen

Purpose: Measures degree of interest in basic activities. Used for school counseling and vocational guidance.

Description: Multiple item paper-pencil test of eight fields of basic interest. May be scored by children under supervision. Significant scores derived from a follow-up of 600 school-leavers. The blank also is used for assessment of interest patterns in research projects. Examiner required. Suitable for group use.
BRITISH DISTRIBUTOR

Untimed: 20 to 60 minutes

Range: Ages 11-16 years

Scoring: Hand key

Cost: Contact NFER-Nelson

Publisher: Distributed by NFER-Nelson Publishing Company

FLANAGAN APTITUDE CLASSIFICATION TESTS (FACT)
Refer to page 713.

FORER VOCATIONAL SURVEY: MEN-WOMEN
Bertram R. Forer

teen, adult

Purpose: Evaluates attitudes and goals related to work situations among adolescents and adults; useful for career planning, and vocational guidance.

Description: 80 item paper-pencil, multiple-choice test. The subject completes structured sentence stems that measure three important areas of occupational activity: reactions to specified situations, causes of feelings and actions, and vocational goals. Reveals interpersonal behavior, attitudes toward work, supervision, authority, people, and work dynamics. Self-administered. Suitable for group use.

Untimed: 20-30 minutes

Range: Adolescent, adult

Scoring: Examiner evaluated

Cost: Complete kit (includes 10 men and 10 women forms, 20 record forms, manual) $13.20.

Publisher: Western Psychological Services

GEIST PICTURE INTEREST INVENTORY
Harold Geist

teen, adult   grades 8-UP

Purpose· Identifies an individual's vocational and avocational interests. Used for vocational guidance and placement, especially with culture-limited and educationally deprived persons.

Description: Multiple item paper-pencil, multiple-choice test requiring minimal language skills. The subjects circle one of three pictures depicting vocational and avocational scenes they prefer. Occupational norms are provided from Grade 8 through high school, college and adult levels. A Motivation Questionnaire can be administered separately to explore motivations behind occupational choices. Self-administered. Suitable for group use.

Untimed: 20-30 minutes

Range: Grade 8-adult

Scoring: Hand key

Cost: Complete kit (includes 10 male and 10 female tests, manual) $13.75.

Publisher: Western Psychological Services

GORDON OCCUPATIONAL CHECK LIST II
Leonard V. Gordon

teen, adult   grades 8-UP

Purpose: Identifies areas of job interest. Used for group and individual counseling of non-college bound high school students.

Description: Multiple item paper-pencil test of six broad vocational interest categories including business, arts, outdoors, technical-mechanical, technical- industrial, and service. Categories are further divided in the Area and Work Group classifications used in the Department of Labor's Guide for for Occupational Exploration. Examiner required. Suitable for group use.

Untimed: 20-25 minutes

Range: Grades 8-12, adult

Scoring: Examiner evaluated

Cost: 35 check lists (includes manual, 35 Job Title supplements) $14.00; manual $2.50.

Publisher: The Psychological Corporation

G-S-Z INTEREST INVENTORY (GSZ)
J.P. Guilford, Edwin S. Shneidman and Wayne S. Zimmerman

teen, adult   grades 10-UP

Purpose: Measures individual traits and interests. Used for occupational and acadmic guidance and to select appropriate leisure time activities.

Description: Multiple item paperpencil measure of nine general interest categories, with two traits scored for special interests within each category. The categories are: artistic, linguistic, scientific, mechanical, outdoor, business- political, social activity, personal assistance, and office work. The traits have been selected on the basis of the best evidence available concerning basic and pertinent values or interests common to occupational and professional levels. Vocational interests are distinguished from avocational interests. Norms provided for highschool and college students. Restricted to A.P.A. members. Examiner required. Suitable for group use.

Untimed: 50 minutes

Range: High school-adult

Scoring: Examiner evaluated

Cost: 25 tests $10.00; 25 answer sheets $3.50; 25 profile charts (essential for evaluation) $4.00; manual $1.50.

Publisher: Sheridan Psychological Services, Inc.

GUILFORD-ZIMMERMAN INTEREST INVENTORY (GZII)
Joan S. Guilford and Wayne S. Zimmerman

teen   grade 13

Purpose: Measures broad areas of interest as an aid to vocation guidance.

Description: Multiple item paperpencil test of ten interest areas: Mechanical, Natural, Aesthetic, Service, Clerical, Mercantile, Leadership, Literary, Scientific, and Creative. The inventory is based upon factor analytic findings providing ten extremely homogeneous scales which comprehensively cover the ten interest factors. Unique features include the inclusion of an independent scale of Creative Interest, the porvision for expression of intensity of interest and ease of scoring. Norms provided for college freshmen. Restricted to A.P.A. members. Examiner required. Suitable for group use.

Untimed: 20 minutes

Range: College freshmen

Scoring: Hand key; may be computer scored

Cost: 25 tests $10.00; 25 answer sheets $3.50; manual $1.50; scoring set $4.00; 25 profile charts $3.50.

Publisher: Sheridan Psychological Services, Inc.

HACKMAN-GAITHER INTEREST INVENTORY
Roy Hackman and James W. Gaither

teen, adult   grades 7-UP

Purpose: Determines vocational interests and preferences as a guide to administering aptitude tests. Useful for the handicapped.

Description: 200 item paper-pencil test covering business, sales, scientific and technical, artistic, health and welfare, business clerical, mechanical, service, and outdoor activities. The subjects mark their answers on a four item scale ranging from "like very much" to "do not like at all." Materials consist of a test booklet and answer sheet. Self-administered. Suitable for group

Untimed: 30-45 minutes

Range: Grades 7-adult

Scoring: Hand key

Cost: 20 booklets $16.00; 20 answer sheets $2.40; 20 profile sheets $2.40; 20 work sheets $2.40; 20 comparison charts $2.40; manual $2.50; specimen set $3.00.

Publisher: Psychological Service Center of Philadelphia

HALL OCCUPATIONAL ORIENTATION INVENTORY (HALL)
Lacy G. Hall and Randolph B. Tarrier

---

all ages   grades 3-UP

Purpose: Emphasizes the many possibilities for the student's future and encourages the broadening of the student's perceptions of potentials and priorities. Used for career planning and vocational guidance.

Description: Multiple item, paper-pencil test based on the personality-need theory inspired by Abraham Maslow and adapted by Anne Roe to the area of occupational choice. Assesses psychological needs which are correlated to worker traits and job characteristics identified by the U.S. Department of Labor. Focuses on twenty-two job and personality characteristics: creativity, independence, risk, information-knowledge, belongingness, security, aspiration, esteem, self actualization, personal satisfaction, routine- dependence,

data-orientation, things orientation, people orientation, location concern, aptitude concern, monetary concern, physical abilities concern, environment concern, co-worker concern, qualifications concern, time concern, and defensiveness.

The special carboned response sheet is designed to cumulate responses in meaningful clusters on the inside, which may be easily interpreted by the student with the Interpretive Folder, which guides the student in understanding his or her response patterns. The counselor's manual explains how to use the inventory, with detailed information on interpretation. HALL Levels and Materials include: Intermediate HALL for Grades 3-7 (a shorter inventory with school-focused items, designed to complement awareness/development programs); Young Adult/College HALL for high school and college students and professionals (special focus on jobs and occupations); and Adult Basic HALL for reading-handicapped adults (a shorter inventory with a world-of-work orientation and controlled readability levels.) Separate inventory booklets, interpretive folders, and response sheets are available for each of the three levels.

The counselor's manual includes lesson plans and guidelines for small group/individual counseling strategies and techniques. The HALL Career Education Reader is a supplement to the interpretive folder, detailing DOT occupations which utilize many of the HALL scales according to relative education/training requirements. Videotape training film and STS scoring service also available. Self- administered. Suitable for group use.

Timed: 30-40 minutes

Range: Grades 3-adult

Scoring: Hand key; examiner evaluated; computer scoring available

Cost: 20 inventory booklets $14.00;

20 interpretive folders $8.00; 20 response sheets $8.00.

Publisher: Scholastic Testing Service, Inc.

THE HARRINGTON-O'SHEA CAREER DECISION-MAKING SYSTEM (CDM)
Thomas F. Harrington and Arthur J. O'Shea

teen, adult   grades 7-UP

Purpose: Evaluates the interests and abilities of high and college students to help them select a career. Used to guide study for future occupations and to help adults identify new careers and skills.

Description: Multiple item, short answer paper-pencil examination in which a survey booklet is filled out by the taker, who records personal information about occupational choices, school subject preferences, job values, abilities, and plans for further education or training. Includes a list of 120 items of work activities. The responses contribute to one of six interest scales: Crafts, Scientific Arts, Social, Business, and Clerical. Raw scores on the highest two interest scales are used to identify three or four career clusters for exploration. A Career Clusters Chart shows typical jobs in each cluster, plus related school subjects and abilities. Occupational outlook and training requirements are given for each job listed. The jobs are keyed to the Dictionary of Occupational Titles. In the self-scored edition, an interpretive folder shows the student how to compare the career cluster with the self-reported information. The machine-score edition reports the results in a profile similar to the Interpretive Folder, or in a detailed 12-page personalized narrative report. The student and examiner arrange a counseling session to discuss appropriate careers. Machine-scored users can also order a Group Summary Report, which compiles responses by sex within grade or counselor group. Up to ten locally developed questions can be included in this report. Interpretation is via the raw scores used to find appropriate career clusters. Optional percentile rank norms are available for grades 7-12 and college freshmen. A minimum seventh-grade reading level is required. Counselor required for career session, but the test may be self-administered. Suitable for group use. Available in Spanish.

Untimed: 30-40 minutes

Range: Grades 7-adult

Scoring: Examiner partially evaluates; computer scored

Cost: Specimen set (includes self-scored survey booklet, interpretive folder, machine-scored survey booklet) $2.00.

Publisher: American Guidance Service

HIGH SCHOOL INTEREST QUESTIONNAIRE (HSIQ)- 1973

teen   grades 10-12

Purpose: Measures vocational interests of coloured students. Used for vocational guidance.

Description: 200 item paper-pencil test of eight interest areas: language, performing arts, fine arts, social, science, technical, business and office work. Pupil responds like, indifferent, or dislike to each item. Examiner required. Suitable for group use. Publisher notes that this test is "normed on coloureds only." SOUTH AFRICAN PUBLISHER

Untimed: 45-60 minutes

Range: High school students

Scoring: Hand key; examiner evaluated

Cost: (In Rands) questionnaire 0,30;

manual 3,20; 10 answer sheets 0,50 (orders from outside The RSA will be dealt with on merit).

Publisher: Human Sciences Research Council

HOW WELL DO YOU KNOW YOUR INTERESTS
Thomas N. Jenkins

teen, adult   grades 10-UP

Purpose: Assesses attitudes toward work activities. Used for vocational guidance.

Description: Multiple item paper-pencil test of interests in ten vocational areas: business, mechanical, outdoor, service, research, visual art, amusement, literacy, music, and general work attitudes. Items are rated on a six point scale ranging from Like Tremendously to Dislike Tremendously. Examiner required. Suitable for group use.

Untimed: 10 minutes

Range: High school, college, adult

Scoring: Hand key

Cost: Complete kit (3 test booklets of each edition and manual) $8.25; 25 tests (specify secondary, college, or pesonnel) $16.50; 100-$65.00; keys $5.50; handbook of interpretations $5.50; manual $5.50.

Publisher: Psychologists and Educators, Inc.

IDEAS: INTEREST DETERMINATION AND ASSESSMENT SYSTEM
Charles B. Johansson

teen   grades 6-12

Purpose: Measures vocational interests of junior high and high school students. Used for career and curriculum planning.

Description: 112 item paper-pencil inventory covering 14 vocational interest areas: mechanical/fixing, electronics, nature/outdoors, science, numbers, writing, arts/crafts, social service, child care, medical service, business, sales, office practices, and food service. The test is scored on a seven-point Likert-type scale, and is in a self-contained package which can be scored and interpreted by the student. Self-administered. Suitable for group use.

Untimed: 30-40 minutes

Range: Grades 6-12

Scoring: Hand key

Cost: 25 booklet package $16.00-$19.00.

Publisher: NCS Interpretive Scoring Systems

INDIVIDUAL CAREER EXPLORATION (ICE)
Anna Miller-Tiedeman in consultation with Anne Roe

child, teen   grades 3-12

Purpose: Identifies career areas of interest to students Grades 3-12.

Description: Multiple item paper-pencil inventory designed to help students focus on future occupations in relation to their current interests, experiences, abilities, and ambitions in the following areas: service, business contract, organization, technology, outdoor, science, general culture, and arts and entertainment. It is based on the Roe theory of occupations. Two forms are available: Verbal ICE for Grades 8-12, and Picture form ICE for Grades 3-7. The Picture ICE may also be used with special education classes. Self-administered and scored. Suitable for group use.

Timed: 2 hours

Range: Picture Form Grades 3-7;

Verbal Form Grades 8- 12

Scoring: Hand key

Cost: Starter set (includes 20 inventory booklets, 20 classification of occupation by group and level--for Picture Form, 20 job trends--, 60 job information checklists, 1 manual of directions, 1 technical supplement) $44.30.

Publisher: Scholastic Testing Service, Inc.

INTEREST QUESTIONNAIRE FOR INDIAN SOUTH AFRICANS (IQISA)-1969
S. Oosthuizen

---

teen

Purpose: Assesses interests of Indian pupils. Used for vocational guidance.

Description: 210 item paper-pencil measure of seven categories of interests: language, art, social service, science, mechanical, business and office work. Subject responds like, indifferent, or dislike for each item. Examiner required. Suitable for group use.
SOUTH AFRICAN PUBLISHER

Untimed: 2 hours

Range: Standards 6-10

Scoring: Hand key; examiner evaluated

Publisher: (In Rands) questionnaire 1,50; manual 1,40; 10 answer sheets 0,40 (orders from outside The RSA will be dealt with on merit).

Publisher: Human Sciences Research Council

INVENTORY OF RELIGIOUS ACTIVITIES AND INTERESTS
Sam C. Webb and Richard A. Hunt

---

teen, adult   grades 10-UP

Purpose: Determines whether a person would be interested in the ministry or church related work. Used for United Methodist Church career ministry as a counseling guide.

Description: 240 item paper-pencil test in ten scales that determines interest in United Methodist ministry. Surveys such roles as: counselor, administrator, teacher, scholar, evangelist, spiritual guide, preacher, reformer, priest, and musician. Examiner required. Suitable for group use.

Untimed: 45 minutes

Range: High school and up

Scoring: Hand key; computer scoring available

Cost: Complete specimen set $6.00; hand scoring stencil $5.00; computer scoring $2.00.

Publisher: Datascan

JACKSON VOCATIONAL INTEREST SURVEY (JVIS)
Douglas N. Jackson

---

teen, adult   grades 10-UP

Purpose: Helps evaluate career interest of high school, college students and adults. Used for educational and voctional planning and counseling, and personnel placement.

Description: 289 item paper-pencil inventory consisting of paired statements covering 100 occupational themes: Expressive, Logical, Inquiring, Practical, Assertive, Socialized, Helping, Conventional, Enterprising, and Communicative. The subject marks one of two responses. Scoring yields a sex-fair profile of 34 basic interest scales and 32 occupational clusters. Requires at least a seventh-grade reading level. Suitable for group use. Available in French.

Untimed: 45-60 minutes

Range: High school-adult

Scoring: Hand key; computer scoring available

Cost: Examination kit $16.00; manual $10.50; 25 test booklets $17.25; 25 answer sheets and key $4.25; 25 profiles $4.25.

Publisher: Research Psychologists Press, Inc.

J.E.V.S. WORK SAMPLES: IN-DEPTH VOCATIONAL ASSESSMENT FOR SPECIAL NEEDS GROUPS

adult

Purpose: Assesses aptitudes, vocational interests and work-related behaviors. Used for vocational guidance with individuals for whom paper-pencil tests are inappropriate.

Description: Multiple item performance measure of worker traits consisting of 28 work samples: nut, bolt, and washer assembly, rubber stamping, washer threading, budget book asembly, sign making, tile sorting, nut packing, collating leather samples, grommet assembly, union assembly, belt assembly, ladder assembly, metal square fabrication, hardware assembly, telephone assembly, lock assembly, filing by numbers, proofreading, filing by letters, nail and screw sorting, adding machine, payroll computation, computing postage, resistor reading, pipe assembly, blouse making, vest making, and condensing principle. Assessment process includes group orientation session, instructions, and observations of subject interest and work-related behaviors by the examiner.

Materials include individually packaged hardware for the work samples. Examiner required. Suitable for use with groups of up to 15 with the standard hardware.

Timed: Each of 28 segments are timed; total time 5-7 days

Range: Adult

Scoring: Examiner evaluated

Cost: Contact publisher.

Publisher: Vocational Research Institute-J.E.V.S.

JIIG-CAL OCCUPATIONAL INTERESTS GUIDE and APU OCCUPATIONAL INTEREST GUIDE
S.J. Closs

teen, adult

Purpose: Evaluates personal interests of adults and adolescents over 14 years of age and relates those interests to career orientations. Used by teachers and counselors for career planning and guidance with individuals at all levels of ability.

Description: Multiple item paper-pencil inventory measures six broad types of interests that are related to a number of identified career orientations. The test may be used as a conventional interest test, or as a part of the JIIG-CAL System for Computer Assisted Career Guidance. The system is a set of interlinked computer programs which operate on a file of job information, retrieving from it those jobs which best match details the pupil supplies about his interests, qualifications, health, likes/dislikes, etc. The Jobfile is not a vacancy file but contains coded and descriptive information on the most common jobs. The system provides both students and counselors with ideas (in the form of relevant job titles) and information about each job in the form of a brief description of what it involves, required skills, qualifications, and other relevant features. This is supplemented by references to related careers publications for further information. Restriction code (C) applies. Self-administered but supervision required. Suitable for group use. BRITISH PUBLISHER

Untimed: Not available

Range: Ages 14-adult

Scoring: Hand key; computer scoring available

Cost: Specimen set (templates not included) £15.00.

Publisher: Hodder & Stoughton

JOB AWARENESS INVENTORY
Teen Makowski

teen

Purpose: Evaluates student understanding of common occupations. Used as a prevocational test for special needs students, especially those who are slow or nonreaders.

Description: 100 item paper-pencil test in A and B forms. Measures knowledge of the world of work, occupations, abilities, general information, and interview procedures. Materials include test booklet and manual. May be read to students. Examiner required. Suitable for group use.

Untimed: Not available

Range: Ages 15-17

Scoring: Hand key

Cost: Class set for 10 students $32.95; 20 students $55.95.

Publisher: Mafex Associates, Inc.

KNOWLEDGE OF OCCUPA-TIONS TEST
Leroy G. Baruth

teen   grades 10-12

Purpose: Assesses knowledge of occupations in high school students. Used for vocational guidance.

Description: 96 item multiple-choice paper-pencil measure of what students know about occupations. Item content was drawn from sources including *Occupational Outlook Handbook* and *The Encyclopedia of Career and Vocational Guidance*. Examiner required. Suitable for group use.

Timed: 40 minutes

Range: High school

Scoring: Hand key; machine scoring directions in manual

Cost: Specimen set $7.25; 25 tests $16.50; 100- $65.00; 25 profile sheets, 25 answer sheets $6.75 each; 100-$26.00 each,; key $2.25; manual $5.50.

Publisher: Psychologists and Educators, Inc.

KUDER GENERAL INTEREST SURVEY, FORM E
Frederic Kuder

teen   grades 6-12

Purpose: Assesses student's preferences for various activities related to ten general interest areas. Used with students Grades 6-12 to guide their educational planning toward future employment.

Description: 168 item paper-pencil test measuring preferences in ten general interest areas: outdoor, mechanical, scientific, computational, presuasvie, artistic, literary, musical, social science, and clerical. Scoring and profile construction can be done by student. Sixth-grade reading level required. Self-administered. Suitable for group use.

Untimed: 30-40 minutes

Range: Grades 6-12

Scoring: Hand key; may be machine-scored

Cost: Complete set (includes materials and scoring for 25 students-machine scored version) $47.85; specimen set either version $5.50. No charge for general manual if requested when ordering.

Publisher: Science Research Associates, Inc.

KUDER OCCUPATIONAL INTEREST SURVEY, FORM DD (KOIS)
Refer to page 738.

KUDER PREFERENCE RECORD, VOCATIONAL, FORM CP
Frederic Kuder

teen, adult   grades 9-UP

Purpose: Evaluates occupational interests of students and adults. Used in vocational counseling and employee screening and placement. Identifies reading subject areas of special interest.

Description: 168 item paper-pencil test measuring interests in ten occupational areas: outdoor, mechanical, scientific, computational, persuasive, artistic, literary, musical, social science, and clerical. Subject uses pin to indicate a "most liked" and "least liked" activity for each group of three activities. High school reading level required. Self-administered. Suitable for group use.

Untimed: Not available

Range: Grades 9-12, adult

Scoring: Hand key

Cost: Specimen set $5.50; 25 booklets $30.60; no charge for manual if requested when ordering.

Publisher: Science Research Associates

MILWAUKEE ACADEMIC INTEREST INVENTORY
Andrew R. Baggaley

teen, adult   grades 12-14

Purpose: Measures academic study interests. Used to help college bound high school seniors and college freshmen and sophomores select their college major.

Description: 150 item paper-pencil test compares the student's academic interests with those of typical students in specified fields. Scores provide stanine ranking for six major areas: Physical Science (physics, chemistry, mathematics, engineering), Healing Occupations (medicine, medical technology, pharmacy), Behavioral Science (psychology, sociology, anthropology, social work), Economics (economics, commerce), Humanities-Social Studies (political science, history, philosophy, languages, journalism), and Elementary Education. Test items are designed to minimize response patterns adapted to social desirability rather than the student's real feelings. Self-administered. Suitable for group use.

Untimed: 20 minutes

Range: High school seniors, college freshmen and sophomores

Scoring: Hand key

Cost: Complete kit (includes 5 reusable tests, 20 answer sheets, manual, key) $6.50.

Publisher: Western Psychological Services

19 FIELD INTEREST INVENTORY (19 FII)-1970
F.A. Fouché and N.F. Alberts

teen, adult

Purpose: Assesses vocational interests of high school students. Used for vocational guidance.

Description: Paper-pencil measure of 19 broad areas of vocational interest: fine arts, performing arts, language, historical, service, social work, sociability, public speaking, law, creative thought, science, practical-male, practical- female, numerical, business, clerical, travel, nature, and sport. Scores on two aspects of interests, work-hobby and active-passive, are also obtained. Examiner required. Suitable for group use.
SOUTH AFRICAN PUBLISHER

Untimed: 45 minutes

Range: Standards 8 to 10, college, adult

Scoring: Hand key; examiner evaluated; machine scoring available

Cost: (In Rands) test booklet 1,00; manual 5,20; 10 answer sheets 0,90; 10 machine answer sheets 1,30; student norms 2,80 (orders from outside The RSA will be dealt with on merit).

Publisher: Human Sciences Research Council

NM ATTITUDE TOWARD WORK TEST (NMATWT)
C.C. Healy and S.P. Klein

teen   grades 9-12

Purpose: Measures individual appreciation of the personal and social significance of work. Used for career counseling and program evaluation.

Description: 25 item paper-pencil, multiple-choice test. It evaluates the following factors: attitudes toward preparing for an occupation; feeling that work contributes to self-confidence, self-esteem, and self-actualization; belief that work leads to many benefits, such as security, interpersonal contacts, friends, and things money can buy; acceptance of the desirability of the interdependence of people, of people all "pulling together"; and belief in the value of work for our society. The reliability and norms for this test have been determined from samples of ninth- and twelfth-grade secondary students. Examiner required. Suitable for group use.

Timed: 15 minutes

Range: Grades 9-12

Scoring: Hand key

Cost: Specimen set $5.00; 35 tests $10.00; 100- $27.00; 35 answer sheets $3.00; 100-$6.00; scoring stencil $2.00; manual $3.00.

Publisher: Monitor

NM CAREER DEVELOPMENT TEST (NMCDT)
C.C. Healy and S.P. Klein

teen   grades 9-12

Purpose: Measures an individual's knowledge of what is required to hold a job and to advance in an occupation. Used for career counseling and program evaluation.

Description: 25 item paper-pencil, multiple-choice test of student feelings that success or failure is a function of one's own actions rather than luck. It also measures knowledge of how to conduct oneself properly on the job, and of factors which influence advancement in a chosen field or occupation. The test booklets are reusable, and the scoring is easy and objective, employing a lay-over stencil. The reliability and norms have been determined from samples of ninth- and twelfth-grade secondary students. Examiner required. Suitable for group use.

Timed: 20 minutes

Range: Grades 9-12

Scoring: Hand key

Cost: Specimen set $5.00; 35 tests $10.00; 100- $27.00; 35 answer sheets $3.00; 100-$6.00; scoring stencil $2.00; manual $3.00.

Publisher: Monitor

NM CAREER ORIENTATED ACTIVITIES CHECKLIST (NMCOAC)
C.C. Healy and S.P. Klein

teen   grades 9-12

Purpose: Evaluates an individual's experience in consulting sources of information necessary to plan a career. Used for vocational counseling and planning.

Description: 25 item multiple-choice paper-pencil test of a student's activities in: consulting various sources of information about occupations; acting to provide information about occupations the student is considering; obtaining the high-school training needed for occupations being considered; and making definite plans regarding what will be done upon graduation. Designed for assessment at twelfth-grade level, but has been successfully employed as low as the ninth grade. The test booklets are reusable, and scoring is simple and objective, employing a lay-over scoring stencil. The reliability and norms for the NMCOAC have been determined from samples of ninth-and twelfth-grade students. Examiner required. Suitable for group use.

Timed: 20 minutes

Range: Grades 9-12

Scoring: Hand key

Cost: Specimen set $5.00; 35 tests

$10.00; 100- $6.00; 35 answer sheets $3.00; 100-$6.00; scoring stencils $3.00; manual $3.00.

Publisher: Monitor

NM CAREER PLANNING TEST (NMCPT)
C.C. Healy and S.P. Klein

teen   grades 9-12

Purpose: Measures individual ability to make appropriate decisions about preparing for and selecting an occupation. Used for career counseling and program evaluation.

Description: 20 item paper-pencil, multiple-choice test of student knowledge of sources of information to consult in obtaining knowledge about various occupations, and knowledge of what actions should be taken in order to make a decision related to selecting and preparing for an occupation. Test booklets for the two equivalent forms, A and B, are reusable. Scoring is simple and objective, employing a lay-over stencil. The reliability and norms for both forms of this test have been determined from samples of ninth- and twelfth-grade secondary students. Examiner required. Suitable for group use.

Timed: 20 minutes

Range: Grades 9-12

Scoring: Hand key

Cost: Specimen set $5.00; 35 tests (specify form A or B) $10.00; 100-$27.00; 35 answer sheets (specify form A or B) $3.00; 100-$6.00; scoring stencil (Specify form A or B) $2.00; manual $3.00.

Publisher: Monitor

NM JOB APPLICATION PRO-CEDURES TEST (NMJAPT)
C.C. Healy and S.P. Klein

teen grades 9-12

Purpose: Assesses an individual's knowledge of how to apply for a job. Used for career counseling and program evaluation.

Description: 20 item paper-pencil, multiple-choice test of student ability to make inquiries, read advertisements, and use employment agencies. It also measures ability to complete a job application form satisfactorily, and knowledge of how to conduct oneself during an interview. The test booklets are reusable, and the scoring is easy and objective, employing a lay-over stencil. The reliability and norms have been determined from samples of ninth- and twelfth-grade secondary students. Examiner required. Suitable for group use.

Timed: 20 minutes

Range: Grades 9-12

Scoring: Hand key

Cost: Specimen set $5.00; 35 tests $10.00; 100- $27.00; 35 answer sheets $3.00; 100-$6.00; scoring stencil $2.00; manual $3.00.

Publisher: Monitor

NM KNOWLEDGE OF OCCUPA-TIONS TEST (NMKOOT)
C.C. Healy and S.P. Klein

teen grades 9-12

Purpose: Measures an individual's knowledge of the characteristics and requirements of different occupations. Used for vocational counseling and program evaluation.

Description: 25 item multiple-choice paper-pencil test of a student's knowledge of job characteristics

(hours of work, pay, work environment, tasks, and demand), and of job and personal requirements (training, abilities and interests). The test booklets are reusable, and the scoring is easy and objective, employing a lay-over scoring stencil. The reliability and norms for the NMKOOT have been determined from samples of ninth- and twelfth- grade secondary students. Self-administered. Suitable for group use.

Timed: 20 minutes

Range: Grades 9-12

Scoring: Hand key

Cost: Specimen set $5.00; 35 tests $10.00; 100- $27.00; 35 answer sheets $3.00; 100-$6.00; scoring stencil $2.00; manual $3.00.

Publisher: Monitor

OCCUPATIONAL APTITUDE SURVEY AND INTEREST SCHEDULE
Randall M. Parker

teen grades 8-12

Purpose: Evaluates a high school student's areas of interest, as related to various occupations. Used for occupational guidance and counseling.

Description: Paper-pencil self-rating scale. Interest areas measured are: artistic, scientific, nature, protective, mechanical, industrial, business detail, selling, accommodating, humanitarian, leading/influencing, and physical performing. A companion test is the Aptitude Survey. Scores for both surveys are keyed directly to the Dictionary of Occupational Titles, Guide for Occupational Exploration, and the Worker Trait Group Guide. Examiner required. Suitable for group use.

Untimed: 30 minutes

Range: Grades 8-12

Scoring: Examiner evaluated

Cost: Complete set (includes examiner manual, 25 test booklets, 50 answer sheets, 50 profile sheets, storage box) $39.00. Components available for separate purchase.

Publisher: PRO-ED

OCCUPATIONAL APTITUDE SURVEY AND INTEREST SCHEDULE-APTITUDE SURVEY (OASIS-AS)
Randall M. Parker

teen   grades 8-12

Purpose: Evaluates a high school student's aptitude for various occupations. Used for occupational guidance and counseling.

Description: Multiple item paper-pencil survey measuring the following factors: general ability, verbal, numerical, spatial, perceptual, and manual. A companion test to the Interest Schedule, scores for both surveys are keyed directly to the Dictionary of Occupational Titles, Guide for Occupational Exploration, and the Worker Trait Group Guide. Examiner required. Suitable for group use.

Untimed: 30 minutes

Range: Grades 8-12

Scoring: Examiner evaluated

Cost: Complete set (includes examiner manual, 25 test booklets, 50 answer sheets, 50 profile sheets, storage box) $42.00. Components available for separate purchase.

Publisher: PRO-ED

OCCUPATIONAL CHECK LIST
Tony Crowley

teen, adult

Purpose: Provides a quick indication

of vocational interests of above-average students. Used for career counseling and occupational awareness.

Description: 108 item paper-pencil checklist of a wide variety of jobs grouped into six activity areas: practical, enterprising, scientific, clerical, artistic, and social. Materials include a 16 page manual. Self-administered. Suitable for group use.
BRITISH PUBLISHER

Untimed: 20 minutes

Range: Adolescent, adult

Scoring: Hand key

Cost: Manual £2.00; spiritmaster £6.90; 100 questionnaires £9.75.

Publisher: Hobsons Press

OCC-U-SORT
Lawrence K. Jones

teen, adult   grades 7-UP

Purpose: Determines what things are most important to a person when selecting a career. Used by education counselors.

Description: 60 card set, each card of which contains the name of an occupation, a DOT code, GED level, Holland code, and description of the occupation. Subject sorts the cards in prescribed way to identify and clarify their thoughts about occupations. Card sets are available in three different levels based on educational background of subject. Self-administered. Suitable for use with groups.

Untimed: Not available

Range: Grades 7 and above

Scoring: Examiner or self-evaluated

Cost: Specimen set $7.25; manual $4.00; 20 Self- guided booklets $12.00; 20 Guide to Occupation $12.00; Level Card Deck $8.00 each (specify Plus 3, 4, or 5 level); poster $3.50.

Publisher: CBT/McGraw-Hill

OHIO VOCATIONAL INTEREST SURVEY (OVIS)
Ayres G. D'Costa, David W. Winefordner, John G. Odgers, and Paul B. Koons, Jr.

teen   grades 8-13

Purpose: Assesses occupational and vocational interests. Used for assisting students with educational and vocational plans.

Description: 280 item paper-pencil test of job related interests. Items are work activities to which student indicates degree of interest. Materials include Student Information Questionnaire which gathers background information about student's plans, preferences and interests. Replaced by 1981 OVIS II. Examiner required. Suitable for group use.

Timed: 60-90 minutes

Range: Grades 8-13

Scoring: Scoring service available

Cost: Specimen set (includes test, MRC answer document directions, sample MRC reporting forms) $4.50.

Publisher: The Psychological Corporation

THE ORIENTATION INVENTORY (ORI)
Bernard M. Bass

teen, adult   grades 10-UP

Purpose: Measures attitudes toward achievement and rewards. Used for personnel assessment, high school and college vocational counseling, and group research

Description: 27 item paper-pencil test of three types of orientation toward satisfaction and rewards: self-orientation, interaction-orientation, and task-orientation. Items are forced-choice. Predicts success and performance in various types of work. Based on Bass's theory of interpersonal behavior in organizations. Examiner required. Suitable for group use.

Untimed: 10-15 minutes

Range: High school-college, adult

Scoring: Hand key

Cost: Specimen set (includes manual, key, tests) $4.50.

Publisher: Consulting Pyschologists Press, Inc.

PERSONAL QUESTIONNAIRE/ OCCUPATIONAL VALUES
Educational and Industrial Test Services, Ltd. Staff

child, teen

Purpose: Provides comprehensive details of a person's background. Used for vocational and educational guidance, and to supplement interviews.

Description: Multiple item paper-pencil questionnaire covering the following areas: physical, educational (formal and informal), home and family, social, hobbies, occupational attitudes, occupational achievements (adult form only), occupational check list, and occupational values. The Occupational Values form is a scale for eight important factors in the work situation which indicate the individual's attitude toward various aspects of job security or achievement and risk. The Personal Questionnaire also is available in a juvenile version. Self-administered.
BRITISH PUBLISHER

Untimed: Not available

Range: Juveniles, adult

Scoring: Examiner evaluated

Cost: Contact publisher.

Publisher: Educational and Industrial Test Services, Ltd.

PICTURE VOCATIONAL INTEREST QUESTIONNAIRE FOR ADULTS (PVI)-1981

teen, adult

Purpose: Assesses vocational interests. Used for vocational guidance.

Description: 110 item measure of interest in 11 areas: clerical work, advanced engineering trades, lower engineering trades, woodwork, painting trades, building, domestic work, food preparation, agriculture, tailoring, and leatherwork. Subject indicates preference, dislike or neutral for each item. Examiner required. Suitable for group use. Publisher notes that this test is "normed on adult Blacks only." SOUTH AFRICAN PUBLISHER

Untimed: 30-45 minutes

Range: Standard 5 and above

Scoring: Hand key; examiner evaluated

Cost: (In Rands) manual 7,00; questionnaire 2,30; 10 answer sheets 1,20 (orders from outside The RSA will be dealt with on merit).

Publisher: Human Sciences Research Council

PLANNING CAREER GOALS (PCG)
American Institutes for Research

teen   grades 8-12

Purpose: Provides information to help students make career plans. Used by guidance and counseling personnel to help students make realistic career plans.

Description: 906 item paper-pencil test consisting of an Interest Inventory (300 items), Information Measures (240 items), and Ability Measures (366 items). The Interest Inventory is in three sections: occupations, occupational activities, and current activities. Student indicates his interest in each of 12 career groups by rating job titles, job activities, or job-related youth activities on a 5-point scale. Information Measures samples the student's knowledge about an occupation. Ability Measures evaluate the student in ten areas: reading comprehension, mathematics, abstract reasoning, creativity, mechanical reasoning, English, quantitative reasoning, vocabulary, visualization, and computation. A Life and Career Plans Survey is used to determine the student's present educational and career plans. Examiner required. Suitable for group use.

Untimed: Not available

Range: Grades 8-12

Scoring: Hand key; computer scoring available

Cost: Examination kit (includes one each of the Ability, Interest and Information Measures, answer booklet, handbook, student guide, and a test reviewer's guide) $7.25. The battery may be ordered complete or by component.

Publisher: CTB/McGraw-Hill

OHIO VOCATIONAL INTEREST SURVEY: SECOND EDITION (OVIS II)
Refer to page 413.

READING FREE VOCATIONAL INTEREST INVENTORY (R-FVII)
Ralph Leonard Becker

teen, adult

Purpose: Measures vocational preferences of mentally retarded and developmentally disabled and learning disabled persons in job areas that are realistically within their capabilities. Used for job placement, education and training.

Description: 55 groups of three items each (triad) paper-pencil, forced-choice test measuring 11 vocational interest clusters: automotive, building trades, clerical, animal care, food service, patient care, horticulture, housekeeping, personal service, laundry, and materials handling. Each test triad requires the subject to circle one of three activities (presented in picture form) which most represents the individuals personal job preference. No reading is required. For male or female ages 13 or above; designed especially for persons with language or reading problems. Materials include test booklets, manual, score sheet, and individual profile sheet of job interests. Self-administered. Suitable for group use.

Untimed: 10-20 minutes

Range: Ages 13-adult

Scoring: Hand key

Cost: 20 test booklets $23.80; manual $7.90; sample set $18.75 (10 tests, 1 manual).

Publisher: Elbern Publications

ROTHWELL-MILLER INTEREST BLANK
J. W. Rothwell and K.M. Miller

teen, adult

Purpose: Measures occupational interests of adults and adolescents. Used for occupational guidance and counseling.

Description: Paper-pencil test measures interests in 12 occupational categories: medical, practical, clerical, social service, musical, literary, aesthetic, persuasive, scientific, computational, mechanical, and outdoor.

Nine blocks are presented which list one occupation from each of the 12 categories, and the subject is asked to rank the 12 occupations in each block in order of personal preference without regard to issues of salary and prospects. Australian norms provided. Materials include: test blank-male and female, manual and specimen set. Examiner required. Suitable for group use.
AUSTRALIAN PUBLISHER

Untimed: 20 minutes

Range: Adolescent, adult

Scoring: Examiner evaluated

Cost: Contact publisher.

Publisher: The Australian Council for Educational Research

SAFRAN STUDENT'S INTEREST INVENTORY
C. Safran with D. Feltham and E. Wright

teen   grades 8-12

Purpose: Evaluates vocational interest, goals and grades of junior and senior high school students. Used for counseling and course selection.

Description: 70 item paper-pencil test which categorizes occupational thinking in seven areas: economic, technical, outdoor, service, humane, artistic, and scientific. After brief instruction, inventory may be completed on the students own time. Self-administered. Suitable for group use.
CANADIAN PUBLISHER

Untimed: 45 minutes

Range: Grades 8-12

Scoring: Examiner evaluated

Cost: 35 booklets $21.75; 35 student manuals $12.85; counselor's manual $5.90.

Publisher: Nelson Canada Limited

SELF-DIRECTED SEARCH (SDS)
Refer to page 811.

SIXTEEN PERSONALITY FACTOR QUESTIONNAIRE
Refer to page 138.

SPACE THINKING (FLAGS)
L.L. Thurstone and T.E. Jeffrey

teen, adult

Purpose: Measures the ability to visualize objects in different positions. Used mostly with young people to select those with high mechanical interest and aptitude.

Description: 21 item paper-pencil test of ability to visualize a rigid configuration, of which there is no internal movement, when it is moved into different positions. Each item has six responses. Examiner required. Suitable for group use.

Timed: 5 minutes

Range: Adolescent, adult

Scoring: Hand key

Cost: Specimen set $4.00; 20 tests $7.00; manual $2.00.

Publisher: London House Press

STRONG-CAMPBELL INTEREST INVENTORY (SCII)
Refer to page 811.

STUDY OF VALUES
Refer to page 630.

SUBSUMED ABILITIES TEST-A MEASURE OF LEARNING EFFICIENCY (SAT)
Refer to page 630.

SWEET'S TECHNICAL INFORMATION TEST (STIT)
R. Sweet

teen

Purpose: Measures technical knowledge of students ages 14-17 years. Used in counseling settings to assess suitability for technical and practical occupations at trade and subprofessional levels.

Description: 55 item paper-pencil multiple-choice test measures three areas of technical knowledge: mechanics, electricity and electronics, and woodwork and general tool use. Items are of four main types: identification, use, operation, and component. The test is designed to measure the type of technical information which might be acquired through an interest in this area, rather than as a measure of mechanical aptitude. Australian norms provided for males and females separately. Materials include: reusable test booklet, answer sheet, scoring key, manual, and specimen set. Examiner evaluated. Suitable for group use. Not available to NSW purchasers.
AUSTRALIAN PUBLISHER

Timed: 20 minutes

Range: Ages 14-17

Scoring: Hand key; examiner evaluated

Cost: Contact publisher.

Publisher: The Australian Council for Educational Research Limited

TECHNICAL TESTS-1962
Refer to page 438.

TEST ORIENTATION PROCEDURE
G.K. Bennett and J.E. Doppelt

adult

Purpose: Assists applicants in learning to take tests, reduces test anxiety. Used for vocational counseling; training and evaluating undereducated or Spanish-speaking applicants.

Description: Multiple item paper-pencil test consisting of a simulated job application and five objective tests. Areas covered by objective tests are Speed and Accuracy, Spelling, Vocabulary, Arithmetic, and Information. Tape recording presents instructions and sample questions. After test, tape reviews the answers. Materials include a 20- page booklet of practice tests to be taken home by the applicant. Not suitable for group use.

Untimed: 30 minutes

Range: Adult

Scoring: Hand key

Cost: Complete set (includes tape, manual, 25 tests) reel-to-reel version $33.75; cassette tape version $33.75.

Publisher: The Psychological Corporation

THEOLOGICAL SCHOOL INVENTORY (TSI)
Richard Hunt, Sue Caldwell and James Dittes

adult

Purpose: Assesses an individual's interest, motivation and ability to become a minister. Useful for classes in professional ministry and for educational screening.

Description: 165 item paper-pencil, multiple-choice test covering the following areas: general sources and strength of motivation, view of the processes involved, abilities and preferences, and background and growth. The taker selects one of four answers. Material includes a scale with 12 scale norms and 12 dimension measures. Available in Spanish. Self-administered. Suitable for group use.

Untimed: 60 minutes

Range: Adult

Scoring: Hand key; computer scoring available

Cost: Manual $8.00; question booklet $1.50; answer sheets $.25; hand key $10.00; computer scoring $1.00.

Publisher: Ministry Inventories

TRADE APTITUDE TEST (TRAT)-1982

teen, adult

Purpose: Assesses aptitudes of adult blacks for training in trades. Used for screening prospective trade school students.

Description: 16 subtest paper-pencil measure of skills important to trade training including Skill, Coordination, Patterns, Spare Parts, Classification, Assembling, Calculations, Inspection, Graphs, Mechanical Insight, Mathematics, Spatial Perception (2-D), Vocabulary, Figure Series, Woordeskat and Spatial Perception (3-D). Examiner required. Suitable for group use.
SOUTH AFRICAN PUBLISHER

Untimed: 4³/4 hours

Range: Standard 6 to 8 qualifications

Scoring: Hand key; examiner evaluated; machine scoring available

Cost: (In Rands) test booklet 3,00; manual 9,80; 10 answer sheets 1,00 (specify hand key or machine score);

scoring stencil for answer sheet 2,00; scoring stencil for machine answer sheets 3,70, 2,40 (orders from outside The RSA will be dealt with on merit).

Publisher: Human Sciences Research Council

VOCATIONAL ADAPTATION RATING SCALES (VARS)
Refer to page 562.

VOCATIONAL APPERCEPTION TEST: ADVANCED FORM (VAT:ADV)
R.B. Ammons, M.N. Butler and S.A. Herzig

teen, adult   grades 10-UP

Purpose: Assesses vocational interests and attitudes. Used for vocational guidance and research on development of occupational interests.

Description: Eight or ten item projective measure of occupational attitudes. Items are cards, eight for males and ten for females, showing persons engaged in common occupations. Subjects are asked to tell a story about each picture. Responses are rated as to general preference for occupation, areas of concern to the individual, reason for entering occupation, and outcomes. Materials include set of plates and manual. Examiner required. Not suitable for group use.

Untimed: 25-40 minutes

Range: High school, college level students

Scoring: Examiner evaluated

Cost: Set of plates and manual $14.50.

Publisher: Psychological Test Specialists

VOCATIONAL INFORMATION AND EVALUATION WORK SAMPLES (VIEWS)

adult

Purpose: Assesses vocational interests and abilities of the mentally retarded. Used for vocational guidance.

Description: Multiple item performance tests of abilities consisting of 16 work samples. Tasks performed by adult include sorting, cutting, collating, assembling, weighing, tying, measuring, using hand tools, tending a drill press, and electric machine feeding. Assessment process includes client orientation, demonstration by examiner, training, then timed assessment. Observation of client helps distinguish between learning and performance, and gives information about learning, quality of work and productivity. Requires no reading ability. Examiner required. Not suitable for group use.

Untimed: 4-5 days

Range: Adult mildly-severely retarded

Scoring: Examiner evaluated

Cost: Contact publisher.

Publisher: Vocational Research Institute-J.E.V.S.

VOCATIONAL INTEREST, EXPERIENCE & SKILL ASSESSMENT (VIESA)
The American College Testing Program

teen, adult   grades 8-UP

Purpose: Summarizes high school students' and adults' career interests and experiences. Used for career counseling.

Description: 129 item paper-pencil questionnaire measuring career-related interests, experiences and skills in terms of work tasks involving data, ideas, people, and things. The test is designed to help students expand their self-awareness and to identify career options. A "World-of-Work Map" is used to relate information concerning 500 occupations employing over 95% of the U.S. labor force. A 16-page "Career Guidebook" is used for the test, and an eight-page "Job Family Charts" is provided to identify occupational options. Self- administered and self-scored. Suitable for group use.

Untimed: 45 minutes Level I, Grades 8-10; Level II, Grade 11-adult

Range: Grades 8-12, adult

Scoring: Self-scored

Cost: Participant material $.95; specimen set $4.50.

VOCATIONAL INTEREST INVENTORY (VII)
Patricia W. Lunneborg

teen, adult   grades 11-UP

Purpose: Measures high school students' interest in a number of vocational areas, enabling them to compare their results with those of other high school and college students. Used for vocational and educational guidance.

Description: 112 item paper-pencil inventory. The inventory measures students' relative strengths of interest in eight occupational areas: Service, Business Contact, Organization, Technical, Outdoor, Science, General Culture, and Arts and Entertainment. Each item is a forced-choice statement which pulls apart interests and is especially useful with young adults who are still somewhat undecided about their interests. WPS provides two copies of a 5-6 page narrative report for each student. The report includes: profile of scores by percentile, summary of percentiles and T-scores for each scale, analysis and discussion of all scores at or above the 75th percentile, college majors profile which shows how the individual's scores compare to mean scores of college majors who took the VII when they were in high school, and a discussion of nontraditional areas for exploration if the student scored between the 50th and 75th percentiles in an area considered nontraditional for his or her sex (test items are controlled for sex bias and mixed-sex norms are used). An eight-page student "Guide to Interpretation" describes the types of people typical of each of the eight interest groups. It also gives examples of jobs typical of each group for five levels of education and training: on-the-job training, technical school, community college, bachelor's degree, and post-graduate degree. Standardized on more than 26,000 high school juniors and seniors. Self-administered. Suitable for group use.

Untimed: 30-45 minutes

Range: High school junior-college

Scoring: Computer scored

Cost: Complete kit (includes 2 tests with computer processing and manual) $19.75.

Publisher: Western Psychological Services

VOCATIONAL INTEREST QUESTIONNAIRE FOR PUPILS IN STANDARDS 6-10 (VIQ)-1974

teen

Purpose: Assesses vocational interests. Used for vocational and study guidance.

Description: Paper-pencil test of ten fields of vocational interest including Technical, Outdoor, Social Service, Natural Sciences, Office Work (clerical), Office Work (numerical), Music, Art, Commerce, and Language. Examiner required. Suitable for group use. Publisher notes that this test is "normed on Blacks only." SOUTH AFRICAN PUBLISHER

Untimed: 1 to 1½ hours

Range: Standards 6 through 10

Scoring: Hand key; examiner evaluated; machine scoring available

Cost: (In Rands) questionnaire 0,80; manual 2,75; 10 answer sheets 0,20; 10 machine answer sheets 0,80 (orders from outside The RSA will be dealt with on merit).

Publisher: Human Sciences Research Council

VOCATIONAL OPINION INDEX
Associates for Research in Behavior, Inc.

adult

Purpose: Assesses perceptions and motivations which affect the ability to get and hold a job; useful for counseling, skills training and general diagnosis of work expectations.

Description: 42 item paper-pencil test measuring the person's attractions to work, perceived losses associated with work and possible barriers to employment. Respondents use five point rating scales of agreement on statements of what might happen in the workplace and about problems which might make it difficult for some people to keep a job. The test is not to be used primarily as a screening divice. Examiner required. Suitable for groups. Available in Spanish.

Untimed: 20 minutes

Range: Adult

Scoring: Hand key; examiner evaluated; computer scoring available

Cost: 1-100 booklets $.70 each; 101-500 booklets $.67 each; 501 and more $.63 each; scoring manual $5.00.

Publisher: Associates for Research in Behavior, Inc.

VOCATIONAL PREFERENCE INVENTORY (VPI)
Refer to page 812.

WEBER ADVANCED SPATIAL PERCEPTION TEST (WASP)
P.G. Weber

teen, adult

Purpose: Measures spatial perception abilities of students 13½ and older. Used in counseling settings to assess suitability for technical and practical occupations at trade and subprofessional levels.

Description: Four paper-pencil subtests measure spatial abilities in four

dimensions: the Form Recognition Test measures the ability to identify a stimulus figure which is combined with other figures similar in shape; the Pattern Perception Test requires the student to draw a line around those crosses in a complex pattern which correspond to crosses in a simpler given pattern; the Shape Analysis Test requires the student to indicate which of five small shapes are used to compose a larger shape; and the Reflected Figure Test requires a given figure to be drawn upside down. Australian norms provided. Materials include: reusable test booklet for Form Recognition Test, separate answer booklet containing answer sheet for Form Recognition Test and questions and answer space for the remaining tests, set of score keys, manual, and specimen set. Examiner required. Suitable for group use.
AUSTRALIAN PUBLISHER

Timed: Total administration about 45 minutes

Range: Ages 13½ and older

Scoring: Hand key; examiner evaluated

Cost: Contact publisher.

Publisher: The Australian Council for Educational Research Limited

---

WIDE RANGE EMPLOY-ABILITY SAMPLE TEST (WREST)
Joseph F. Jastak and Sarah Jastak

teen, adult

Purpose: Measures how well a person works at routine manual tasks. Assists in diagnosis of mental retardation and determines the feasibility of competitive employment of the severely handicapped. Used for placement in sheltered workshop or daily activities programs.

Description: Ten item test in which individuals are asked to complete simple manual tasks, such as: folding, stapling, packaging, measuring, assembling, tag stringing, gluing, collating, color or shade and pattern matching (each takes 7-15 minutes to complete). Each of the tasks is carefully taught prior to testing. The tasks measure "horizontal" achievement (the capacity to do the routine operations involved in all jobs regardless of level). Persons with average or above-average scores on WREST are not mentally retarded, even if their scores on "vertical" achievement or intelligence tests rate them as retarded. Scored for speed and accuracy, the results are expressed in scaled scores for each item. Standard scores provided for total production quantity and quality and for a combined technical productivity rating. Norms are provided for three populations: general, sheltered workshop and industrial. Examiner required. Not suitable for group use.

Timed: 60 minutes

Range: Ages 16-adult

Scoring: Examiner evaluated

Cost: Complete including hardwood cabinet $1395.00.

Publisher: Jastak Assessment Systems

WIDE RANGE INTEREST-OPINION TEST (WRIOT)
Joseph F. Jastak and Sarah Jastak

all ages

Purpose: Provides information about vocational interests (without language requirements). Assesses levels of self-projected ability, aspiration level and social conformity. Used in vocational/career planning and counseling, employee selection and placement, and to help coordinate instruction/

therapy plans with interest/attitude patterns.

Description: 150 item paper-pencil test measuring an individual's occupational motivation according to his likes and dislikes. The test booklet contains 150 pages with three pictures on each page. Each picture shows an individual or group performing a specific job. The subject must select the picture he likes the most and the picture he likes the least for each page. The results are presented on a report form which graphically shows an individual's strength of interest in 18 interest and eight attitude clusters (normed on seven age groups from five-adult, separately for males and females). Occupational range is from unskilled labor to the highest levels of training. Useful with the educationally and culturally disadvantaged, the learning disabled, the mentally retarded, and the deaf. The picture titles can be read to the blind. Individual administration is necessary for those unable to complete a separate answer sheet. 35 mm film strip is available (used instead of picture book), as well as a supplementary Job Title Lists. Examiner required. Suitable for group use (except where noted).

Untimed: 40 minutes

Range: Ages 5-adult

Scoring: Hand key; computer scoring available

Cost: Manual $21.80; 50 test forms $9.25; 50 report forms $9.25; key $35.95; film strip $80.00; job title list $39.95.

Publisher: Jastak Assessment Systems

Miscellaneous

CHANGE FACILITATOR STAGES OF CONCERN QUESTIONNAIRE (CFSoCQ)
William L. Rutherford, Gene E. Hall and Archie A. George

adult

Purpose: Assesses stages of concern of group discussion leaders (change facilitators) when they are involved in facilitating educational changes. Used for training and monitoring the progress of change facilitators.

Description: 35 item paper-pencil questionnaire. Measures seven stages of concern: awareness, information, personal, management, consequence, collaboration, and refocusing. All scales are assessed in relation to the generic role of being a change facilitator. Normed for educational setting only. May be mailed to the respondent. Self-administered. Suitable for group use. Available in Dutch and Flemish.

Untimed: 15 minutes

Range: Adult educators

Scoring: Hand key; examiner evaluated; computer scoring available

Cost: Manual (includes master copy of questionnaire) $5.00.

Publisher: The Research and Development Center for Teacher Education.

COMMUNITY COLLEGE GOALS INVENTORY (CCGI)
Research staff of Educational Testing Service

teen, adult   College

Purpose: Assesses educational goals of community colleges. Used for establishing priorities and giving direction to present and future planning.

Description: 90 item paper-pencil test of 20 goal areas divided into two types, Outcome Goals and Process Goals. Outcome Goals include academic development, intellectual orientation, individual personal development, humanism/altruism, cultural/aesthetic awareness, traditional religiousness, vocational preparation, advanced training, research, meeting local needs, public service, social egalitarianism, and social criticism/activism. Process Goals include freedom, democratic governance, community, intellectual/aesthetic environment, innovation, off-campus learning, and accountability/efficiency. Administered by distributing to a random sample of students. Materials include space for 20 additional locally written goals. Self-administered. Suitable for group use.

Untimed: 45 minutes

Range: College students

Scoring: Computer scored

Cost: Booklets $.65 each; processing $1.75 each.

Publisher: Educational Testing Service

COUNTRY SCHOOL EXAMINATIONS
Michigan Department of Public Instruction

all ages

Purpose: Compares current elementary school examinations of basic skills and competency with similar tests given in the early 20th century. Used to develop student, parent and community appreciation for early standards of educational achievement.

Description: A paper-pencil collection of six reprints from historic educational achievement tests given in the early 1900s in a one-room schoolhouse in Michigan. One is the State of Michigan Examination Questions of 1921 for a city teachers' examination, and three are the State of Michigan Examination Questions used in 1919, 1920 and 1921 for eighth grade graduation. The other two are the Michigan Winter Term Examination of 1913, and the Michigan Fall Term Examination of 1914, for grades one through eight. Materials include a specimen set and packages of 25 booklets for each of the six tests which can be ordered separately. Self-administered. Suitable for group use. 45 minutes

Untimed:

Range: Student, adult

Scoring: Examiner evaluated

Cost: Specimen set (includes all examinations) $5.95; 25 individual test booklets $5.75.

Publisher: Research Concepts

CURETON MULTI-APTITUDE TEST (CMAT)
E.E. Cureton and L. W. Cureton et al.

adult

Purpose: Demonstrates group testing. Used for introductory and advanced classes in testing or with conferences or nonprofessional groups.

Description: Ten part paper-pencil test using vocabulary, general information, arithmetic, number series, figure classification, mechanical comprehension, word recognition, scrambled letters checking (clerical), and paper form board subtests are typical of longer tests in current use. The CMAT may be used with five kinds of groups; introductory classes in general or applied psychology and in related fields such as personnel administration; advanced measurement, statistics and test construction classes; conferences, institutes and seminars; nonprofessional groups such as service clubs or parents for instructional or public relations purposes; and individuals or groups with little experience in testing. Not used in counseling and selection.

Examiner required. Suitable for group use.

Untimed: 1-5 minutes per test; 45-50 minutes for full battery

Range: Adult

Scoring: Hand key

Cost: Complete study kit for one $3.50 (test and key).

Publisher: The Psychological Corporation

EDUCATIONAL GOAL ATTAIN-MENT TESTS
Bruce W. Tuckman and Alberto P.S. Montare

teen   grades 7-12

Purpose: Assesses a broad range of educational goals, both cognitive and affective, that are common to many communities. Used to assess and revise a school system's instructional program.

Description: 1430 item paper-pencil battery of ten tests designed to assess school and district needs rather than a diagnostic tool of individual student performance. Three types of test items are used in the EGAT: knowledge items, to measure information that a student has acquired and retained; attitude items, to measure a student's orientation or feelings as reflected by his inclination to agree or disagree with a given attitude statement; behavior items, to indicate how students will behave--these items describe a behavior and ask the student to indicate whether and to what degree he performs this behavior. Each student takes one subtest; retesting may be performed by giving different subtests to the student. Tests are designed for use in the 7th through the 12th grades. Examiner required. Suitable for group use. Available in Spanish.

Timed: 1 hour 40 minutes

Range: Grades 7-12

Scoring: Hand key; scoring service available

Cost: Test booklet $.60; answer sheet $.05; manual $.60; no charge for Information Booklet and Handbook for Test Administrators.

Publisher: Phi Delta Kappa

EDUCATIONAL GOAL ATTAIN-MENT TESTS: ARTS AND LEISURE
Bruce W. Tuckman and Alberto P.S. Montare

teen   grades 7-12

Purpose: Assesses knowledge, attitudes and behavior related to hobbies, leisure activities, music, art, and literature. Used for curriculum planning in the Arts and Leisure area.

Description: 150 item test designed to assess the arts and leisure programs of a community school program and indicate needed areas for improvement or growth. Eight areas are evaluated: knowledge related to hobbies and leisure activities, attitudes toward outdoor pastimes, attitudes toward indoor pastimes, behavior in hobbies and leisure, knowledge of music, knowledge of art and literature, attitude toward value of aesthetics, and behavior of creative expression. Examiner required. Suitable for group use.

Timed: 1 hour 40 minutes

Range: Grades 7-12

Scoring: Hand key; scoring service available

Cost: Test booklet $.60; answer sheet $.05; manual $.60; no charge for Information Booklet and Handbook for Test Administrators.

Publisher: Phi Delta Kappa

EDUCATIONAL GOAL ATTAINMENT TESTS: CAREERS
Bruce W. Tuckman and Alberto P.S. Montare

teen   grades 7-12

Purpose: Assessed knowledge, attitudes and behavior related to careers. Used for curriculum planning in career development and vocational areas.

Description: 139 item paper-pencil test designed to assess the careers programs of a community school and indicate needed areas for improvement. Eight areas are evaluated: knowledge of trades, knowledge of business, attitudes toward good workmanship, behavior related to jobs, knowledge of career information sources, knowledge of job opportunity, attitude of career maturity, and behavior of career, and self awareness. Examiner required. Suitable for group use. Available in Spanish.

Timed: 1 hour 40 minutes

Range: Grades 7-12

Scoring: Hand key; scoring service available

Cost: Test booklet $.60; answer sheet $.05; manual $.60; no charge for Information Booklet and Handbook for Test Administrators.

Publisher: Phi Delta Kappa

EDUCATIONAL GOAL ATTAINMENT TESTS: CIVICS
Bruce W. Tuckman and Alberto P.S. Montare

teen   grades 7-12

Purpose: Assesses knowledge and attitudes toward citizenship and democratic ideas. Used for curriculum planning in civics.

Description: 172 item paper-pencil test designed to assess the civics programs of a community school and indicate needed areas for improvement. Eight areas are evaluated: knowledge of civic rights, knowledge of civic responsibilities, attitude toward productive citizenship, attitude toward respect for property, knowledge of rights and privileges, knowledge of American heritage, behavior of loyalty to country, and behavior of patriotism. Examiner required. Suitable for group use. Available in Spanish.

Timed: 1 hour 40 minutes

Range: Grades 7-12

Scoring: Hand key; scoring service available

Cost: Test booklets $.60; answer sheet $.05; manual $.60; no charge for Information Booklet and Handbook for Test Administrators.

Publisher: Phi Delta Kappa

EDUCATIONAL GOAL ATTAINMENT TESTS: ENGLISH LANGUAGE
Bruce W. Tuckman and Alberto P.S. Montare

teen   grades 7-12

Purpose: Assesses language art skills. Used for curriculum development in English.

Description: 127 item paper-pencil test designed to assess the English Language program of a community school and indicate needed areas for improvement. Three areas are evaluated: knowledge of word meaning; knowledge of language mechanics; and knowledge of reading comprehension. Examiner required. Suitable for group use.

Timed: 1 hour 40 minutes

Range: Grades 7-12

Scoring: Hand key; scoring service available

Cost: Test booklet $.60; answer sheet $.05; manual $.60; no charge for Information Booklet and Handbook for Test Administrators.

Publisher: Phi Delta Kappa

EDUCATIONAL GOAL ATTAINMENT TESTS: GENERAL KNOWLEDGE
Bruce W. Tuckman and Alberto P.S. Montare

teen   grades 7-12

Purpose: Assesses general knowledge of math, science, current and historical events, and culture. Used for curriculum planning in general.

Description: 126 item paper-pencil test is designed to assess the general knowledge of student in a community school. Five areas are evaluated, knowledge of: math, science, current and historical events, family in culture, and culture in general. Examiner required. Suitable for group use. Available in Spanish.

Timed: 1 hour 40 minutes

Range: Grades 7-12

Scoring: Hand key; scoring service available

Cost: Test booklet $.60; answer sheet $.05; manual $.60; no charge for Information Booklet and Handbook for Test Administrators.

Publisher: Phi Delta Kappa

EDUCATIONAL GOAL ATTAINMENT TESTS: HUMAN RELATIONS
Bruce W. Tuckman and Alberto P.S. Montare

teen   grades 7-12

Purpose: Assesses knowledge, attitudes and behavior related to cultures and change. Used for curriculum planning in human relations programs.

Description: 152 item paper-pencil test is designed to assess the human relation programs of a community school. Nine areas are evaluated: knowledge of others, knowledge of group process, attitudes of tolerance toward others, attitude toward human relations, behavior of positive human relations, knowledge related to change, attitude of tolerance of ambiguity, attitude of internal control, and behavior of nonconformity. Examiner required. Suitable for group use.

Timed: 1 hour 40 minutes

Range: Grades 7-12

Scoring: Hand key; scoring service available

Cost: Test booklet $.60; answer sheet $.05; manual $.60; no charge for Information Booklet and Handbook for Test Administrators.

Publisher: Phi Delta Kappa

EDUCATIONAL GOAL ATTAINMENT TESTS: LATIN AMERICA
Bruce W. Tuckman and Alberto P.S. Montare

teen   grades 7-12

Purpose: Assesses the knowledge of the Puerto Rican culture and Spanish language arts skills. Used for Latin American curriculum planning.

Description: 123 item paper-pencil test designed to assess the understanding of Latin American culture, foreign language programs of a community school, and to indicate areas for improvement. EGAT is written ½ in English and ½ in Spanish to test facility in the language. Four areas are evaluated: knowledge of history and culture; knowledge of people, places and arts; knowledge of language mechanics; knowledge of vocabulary reading comprehension. Examiner required. Suitable for group use.

Timed: 1 hour 40 minutes

Range: Grades 7-12

Scoring: Hand key; scoring service available

Cost: Test booklet $.60; answer sheet $.05; manual $.60; no charge for Information Booklet and Handbook for Test Administrators.

Publisher: Phi Delta Kappa

EDUCATIONAL GOAL ATTAINMENT TESTS: LIFE SKILLS
Bruce W. Tuckman and Alberto P.S. Montare

teen   grades 7-12

Purpose: Assesses knowledge, attitudes and behavior toward family and resource-management and health practices. Used for curriculum planning for life skills classes.

Description: 181 item paper-pencil test designed to assess the life skills programs of a community school. Ten areas are evaluated: knowledge of family management, attitudes toward family management, behavior of family management, knowledge of personal economics, knowledge of environment, behavior of resource management, knowledge of health practices, attitudes toward health practices, behavior of personal hygiene, and behavior of exercise and diet. Examiner required. Suitable for group use. Available in Spanish.

Timed: 1 hour 40 minutes

Range: Grades 7-12

Scoring: Hand key; scoring service available

Cost: Test booklet $.60; answer sheet $.05; manual $.60; no charge for Information Booklet and Handbook for Test Administrators.

Publisher: Phi Delta Kappa

EDUCATIONAL GOAL ATTAINMENT TESTS: REASONING
Bruce W. Tuckman and Alberto P.S. Montare

teen   grades 7-12

Purpose: Assesses the ability to use logical and scientific reasoning. Used to assess the need for development of logical reasoning within a curriculum.

Description: 49 item paper-pencil test designed to assess the "reasoning developmental programs" of a community school and indicate needed areas for improvement. The two areas measured are: knowledge of scientific methods and problems solving skills. Examiner required. Suitable for group use.

Timed: 1 hour 40 minutes

Range: Grades 7-12

Scoring: Hand key; scoring service available

Cost: Test booklet $.60; answer sheet $.05; manual $.60; no charge for Information Booklet and Handbook for Test Administrators.

Publisher: Phi Delta Kappa

EDUCATIONAL GOAL ATTAINMENT TESTS: SELF TEST
Bruce W. Tuckman and Alberto P.S. Montare

teen   grades 7-12

Purpose: Assesses a student's attitudes towards himself and his values, and how his behavior reflects these values. Used to enhance a curriculum so a student develops pride in work, a feeling of self-worth, good character, and self-respect.

Description: 208 item paper-pencil test is designed to assess the self-development programs of a community school and indicate areas needed for improvement. Ten areas are evaluated: attitudes toward one's achievements, attitudes of self- awareness, attitudes of self-worth, attitude of moral values, attitude of character, behaving ethically, behaving with self-discipline, attitude of curiosity, attitude toward learning, and behavior of self-improvement. Examiner required. Suitable for group use.

Timed: 1 hour 40 minutes

Range: Grades 7-12

Scoring: Hand key; scoring service available

Cost: Test booklet $.60; answer sheet $.05; manual $.60; no charge for Information Booklet and Handbook for Test Administrators.

Publisher: Phi Delta Kappa

INSTITUTIONAL GOALS INVENTORY (IGI)
Research staff at Educational Testing Service

teen, adult   College

Purpose: Assesses educational goals of educational institutions. Used for establishing priorities and giving direction to present and future planning.

Description: 90 item paper-pencil test of 20 goal areas divided into two types, Outcome Goals and Process Goals. Outcome Goals include academic development, intellectual orientation, individual personal development, humanism/altruism, cultural/aesthetic awareness, traditional religiousness, vocational preparation, advanced training, research, meeting local needs, public service, social egalitarianism, and social criticism/activism. Process Goals include freedom, democratic governance, community, intellectual/aesthetic environment, innovation, off-campus learning, and accountability/efficiency. Administered by distributing to a random sample of students. Materials include space for 20 additional locally written goals. Self-administered. Suitable for group use. Available in French (Canadian Universities) and Spanish.

Untimed: 45 minutes

Range: College students

Scoring: Computer scored

Cost: Booklets $.65 each; processing $1.75 each.

Publisher: Educational Testing Service

LIGHT'S RETENTION SCALE
H. Wayne Light

---

child, teen   grades 1-12

Purpose: Determines whether an elementary or secondary school student would benefit from grade retention. Used for counseling and to guide parents and school staff.

Description: 19 category paper-pencil scale calling attention to such areas of concern as age, emotional and behavior problems, motivation, absenteeism, and presence of learning disabilities. Each factor is evaluated on a one- to-five scale with the total score reduced into several "retention candidacy" categories that indicate whether the student is likely to benefit from retention. Among the materials is the Parent Guide to Grade Retention, a statement of factors to be considered in making the decision. Examiner required. Not for group use.

Untimed: 10-15 minutes

Range: Grades 1-12

Scoring: Examiner evaluated

Cost: Manual $7.50; 25 recording forms $6.00; 25 parent guides $6.00; specimen set $7.50.

Publisher: Academic Therapy Publications

SMALL COLLEGE GOALS INVENTORY (SCGI)
Research staff at Educational Testing Service

teen, adult   College

Purpose: Assesses educational goals of small colleges. Used for establishing priorities and giving direction to present and future planning.

Description: 90 item paper-pencil test of 20 goal areas divided into two types, Outcome Goals and Process Goals. Outcome Goals include academic development, intellectual orientation, individual personal development, humanism/altruism, cultural/aesthetic awareness, traditional religiousness, vocational preparation, advanced training, research, meeting local needs, public service, social egalitarianism, and social criticism/activism. Process Goals include freedom, democratic governance, community, intellectual/aesthetic environment, innovation, off-campus learning, and accountability/efficiency. Administered by distributing to a random sample of students. Materials include space for 20 additional locally written goals. Self-administered. Suitable for group use.

Untimed: 45 minutes

Range: College students

Scoring: Computer scored

Cost: Booklets $.65 each; processing $1.75 each.

Publisher: Educational Testing Service

STUDENT REACTIONS TO COLLEGE: FOUR YEAR COLLEGE EDITION (SRC/4)
Research staff at Educational Testing Service

teen, adult   College

Purpose: Assesses needs and concerns of students in four year colleges. Used for institutional self-assessment for developing programs and services for students.

Description: 150 item paper-pencil assessment of four dimensions of student concerns: Processes of instruction, Program planning, Administrative affairs, and Out-of-class activities. Dimensions are further broken down into areas such as content of courses, appropriateness of course work to occupational goals, satisfaction with teaching procedures, student-faculty relations, educational and occupational decisions, effectiveness of advisors and counselors, registration, regulations, availability of classes, housing, employment, financial aid, and satisfaction with campus environment. Administered by distributing to a random sample of students. Self-administered. Suitable for group use.

Untimed: 50 minutes

Range: College students

Scoring: Computer scored

Cost: Booklet $.65 each; processing $1.75 each.

Publisher: Educational Testing Service

UNIVERSITY RESIDENCE ENVIRONMENT SCALE (URES)
Rudolf H. Moos and Marvin S. Gerst

teen, adult   College

Purpose: Assesses the social environment of university residence halls and dormitories.

Description: 100 item paper-pencil true-false test of ten dimensions of social climate: involvement, emotional support, independence, traditional social orientation, competition, academic achievement, intellectuality, order and organization, student influence, and innovation. Materials consist of the Real Form (Form R) which measures current perceptions of a residence; the 40 item Short Form (Form S); the Expectations Form (Form E), measuring expectations of a new residence; and the Ideal Form (Form I), which measures conceptions of an ideal residence hall environment. Forms I and E are not in published form, but items and instructions appear in the Appendix of the URES manual. One of a series of nine Social Climate Scales. Examiner required. Suitable for group use.

Untimed: 20-30 minutes

Range: College students

Scoring: Hand key; examiner evaluated

Cost: Specimen set $4.00; 25 reusable tests $4.00; 50 answer sheets $3.00; 50 profiles $3.00; key $.75; manual $3.00.

Publisher: Consulting Psychologists Press, Inc.

Driving and Safety Education

HOW TO DRIVE
American Automobile Association

teen, adult

Purpose: Measures students' knowledge of many aspects of the safe operation of an automobile. Used by driver education teachers.

Description: 178 multiple-choice items in 12 paper-pencil tests accompanying the book *How to Drive* published by the American Automobile Association. Each test consists of 12 to 20 items and covers one chapter of the book: "Driving Laws and Controls," "Car Control, Skills and Habits," "Basic Maneuvers," "Driving an Automobile with a Manual Shift," "Vision and Perception," "Management of Time and Space," "Interacting with Other Users," "Adverse Driving Conditions and Emergencies," "Keeping Fit to Drive," "Consumer's Guide to Trouble-Free and Economical Driving," "Driving with a Trailer," and "Collisions and Insurance." Self-administered. Suitable for group use.

Untimed: 20 minutes per chapter

Range: 14 years and up

Scoring: Hand key; examiner evaluated

Cost: 24 test booklets $10.00; 100 answer sheets $2.75.

Publisher: American Automobile Association

SAFE DRIVER ATTITUDE TEST (SDAT)
Russell L. Carey, Dawn Bashara and Harry Schmadeke

adult

Purpose: Measures attitudes of drivers, including handicapped and learning disabled adolescents, toward certain driving situations.

Description: 19 item paper-pencil multiple-choice test of driving predicaments, designed to reflect such attitudes as self-centeredness, egoism, cautiousness, rashness, and general acceptance of, and compliance with, the law. In each of two filmstrips, actual and model simulation of driving dilemmas are shown, followed by three illustrative, narrated alternatives. Students view the filmstrips at separate sittings and enter responses on an answer sheet. Examiner required. Designed for use with groups.

Untimed: 2 parts--10 to 11 minutes each of showing time plus time to record responses

Range: Adult

Scoring: Hand key

Cost: Program includes 2 full color filmstrips, cassette, teacher's guide, and a ditto for student answers and profiles $34.00.

Publisher: Educational Activities, Inc.

THEORY TESTS FOR LICENSES

adult

Purpose: Assesses knowledge of driving skills. Used for issuance of driver's and learner's licenses.

Description: Multiple item paper-pencil measure of vehicle driver's knowledge of the rules of the road, road traffic signs and vehicle controls. Tests also cover relevant portions of the Road Traffic Ordinances of the Provinces. Materials include three equivalent forms. These tests are available only to licensing authorities with the power to issue learner's and driver's licenses, and who have examiners with certificates of competency issued by the HSRC. Examiner required. Suitable for group use. SOUTH AFRICAN PUBLISHER

Untimed: Driver's, 45 minutes; Learner's, 1 hour

Range: Adult

Scoring: Hand key; examiner evaluated

Cost: (In Rands) Driver's test 1,48; scoring stencils 0,54; instructions 0,19; 10 answer sheets 0,21; manual

1,00 net; Learner's test 1,70; scoring stencils 0,54; instructions 0,21; 10 answer sheets 0,21; manual 1,00 (orders from outside The RSA will be dealt with on merit).

Publisher: Human Sciences Research Council

WILSON DRIVER SELECTION TEST
Clark L. Wilson

adult

Purpose: Evaluates ability to perceive speed and spatial relationships as a way to screen personnel to reduce the risk of operator caused accidents. Used by driver selection and evaluation companies and schools.

Description: Six category, paper-pencil, nonverbal test measuring visual attention, depth visualization, recognition of simple and complex details, eye- hand coordination, and steadiness. Booklet includes norms for males and females as well as items on the adult's accident record and personal history. Examiner required. Suitable for group use.

Timed: 26 minutes

Range: Adult

Scoring: Hand key

Cost: Specimen set $5.23; manual $4.35; key $.66; package of tests $16.45.

Publisher: Martin M. Bruce, Ph.D., Publisher

Business and Industry

The tests that have been placed and described in the Business Section are generally used in the business world for the purpose of assessments in personnel selection, development and promotion.

The reader is encouraged to consult the Psychology Section and Education Section for other helpful assessment techniques which may also be of value in the area of business.

Business and Industry Section Index

Business and Industry Section

Aptitude and Skills Screening

ACER WORD KNOWLEDGE TEST-ADULT FORM B
Refer to page 761.

ADULT BASIC LEARNING EXAMINATION (ABLE)
Bjorn Karlsen, Richard Madden and Eric F. Gardner

teen, adult

Purpose: Measures adult achievement in basic learning. Used for evaluating job applicants.

Description: Multiple item paper-pencil measure of vocabulary knowledge, reading comprehension, spelling and arithmetic computation and problem-solving skills. Divided into three levels: Level I, yields grade scores 1 to 6; Level II, yields grade scores 3 to 9; and Level III, yields percentile ranks and stanines for grades 9 to 12. Vocabulary test is dictated, no reading required. Arithmetic Problem-Solving test is dictated at Level I. Materials include a short screening test, SelectABLE, for use in determining the appropriate level of ABLE for each applicant. ABLE available in two alternate forms, A and B, at each level. SelectABLE has only one form. Examiner required. Suitable for group use.

Untimed: SelectABLE, 15 minutes; Levels I and II, 2 hours, Level III, 3 hours 25 minutes

Range: Ages 17-adult

Scoring: Hand key; may be machine scored

Cost: Specimen set (includes test, handbook, group record, booklet key except Level III) $6.00 (specify level); cassettes for Level I and Level III $16.50 each.

Publisher: The Psychological Corporation

ADVANCED TEST BATTERY (ATB)
Saville & Holdsworth, Ltd. Staff

adult

Purpose: Evaluates verbal, numerical and spatial reasoning at the very top range of ability. Used in the selection, development and guidance of personnel at the graduate level or in management positions.

Description: Seven paper-pencil multiple-choice tests measuring verbal, numerical and diagramming skills. There are five main tests which are arranged in two levels. Level 1 is somewhat easier and consists of three aptitude tests: Verbal Concepts (VA1), Number Series (NA2) and Diagramming (DA5). Level 2 has a higher perceived relevance (face validity) and consists of two tests in which skills are applied in context: Verbal Critical Reasoning (VA3) and Numerical Critical Reasoning (NA4). These five tests can be given in various combinations to suit a number of contexts. For some applications, the Technical Test Battery Diagrammatic Reasoning Test (DTB) and and TTB Spatial Reasoning Test (ST7) are used with the ATB tests. Range: from good 'O' level standard to the top end of the graduate population. Examiner required. Suitable for group use.

BRITISH PUBLISHER

Timed: 150 minutes

Range: Adult

Scoring: Hand key; examiner evaluated; may be computer scored

Cost: Complete (includes 10 level 1 booklets, 10 level 2 booklets, set of keys, set of administration cards, 50 profile charts, 25 score sheets, 25 testing logs) £370.00.

Publisher: Saville and Holdsworth, Ltd.

ADVANCED TEST BATTERY: DIAGRAMMATIC REASONING (ATB:DT8)
Saville and Holdsworth, Ltd. Staff

adult

Purpose: Measures diagrammatical reasoning ability. Used for selection and placement for technical occupations and jobs involving systems design, flow charting and engineering fault diagnosis.

Description: 40 item paper-pencil multiple-choice test requiring the candidate to discover logical rules governing sequences occurring in rows of three related symbols and diagrams, and choose a fourth related symbol from the selections in the answer booklet. Range: from GCE 'O' level to degree. Examiner required. Suitable for group use.
BRITISH PUBLISHER

Timed: 15 minutes

Range: Adult

Scoring: Hand key; examiner evaluated; may be computer scored

Cost: 10 question booklets £12.50; 50 answer sheets £21.00; key £4.00.

Publisher: Saville and Holdsworth, Ltd.

ADVANCED TEST BATTERY: DIAGRAMMING (ATB:DA5)
Saville and Holdsworth, Ltd. Staff

adult

Purpose: Measures logical analysis by assessing the ability to follow complex instructions within a given command system in order to arrive at a solution. Used to select personnel for computer programming and data processing, as well as engineering, chemical processing and related industries.

Description: 50 item paper-pencil multiple-choice test measuring diagramming skills. Each item consists of a column of figures or symbols within boxes, each of which has a command attached. The actual instruction conveyed by each command (represented by coded symbols) is explained on a separate card. The task is to carry out the commands in order to arrive at a new column of figures. The commands involve inverting figures, omitting figures, exchanging figures, or changing the complete order of figures in a specified way. Initial items are simple, but the complexity steadily increases. The diagrams provide a nonverbal task similar to flow-charting. Range: from GCE 'O' level upwards. Examiner required. Suitable for group use.
BRITISH PUBLISHER

Timed: 20 minutes

Range: Adult

Scoring: Hand key; examiner evaluated; may be computer scored

Cost: 10 question booklets £25.00; 10 command cards £17.00; 50 answer sheets £21.00.

Publisher: Saville and Holdsworth, Ltd.

ADVANCED TEST BATTERY: NUMBER SERIES (ATB:NA2)
Saville and Holdsworth, Ltd. Staff

adult

Purpose: Measures the ability to reason with numbers at a high degree of difficulty. Used in selection and development of management staff and graduate recruitment.

Description: 30 item paper-pencil multiple-choice test. Each item consists of a number series with one missing number. The candidates must select from five possible answers the one which completes the series. Emphasizes developing appropriate strategies and the recognition of relationships between numbers, rather than long calculations. Range: from GCE 'A' level upwards. Examiner required. Suitable for group use. BRITISH PUBLISHER

Timed: 15 minutes

Range: Adult

Scoring: Hand key; examiner evaluated; may be computer scored

Cost: 10 question booklets £17.50; 50 answer sheets £21.00; key £4.00.

Publisher: Saville and Holdsworth, Ltd.

ADVANCED TEST BATTERY: NUMERICAL CRITICAL REASONING (ATB:NA4)
Saville and Holdsworth, Ltd. Staff

adult

Purpose: Measures the ability to make correct inferences from numerical or statistical data. Used for selection and placement for jobs involving control systems, selection and development of management staff and graduate recruitment.

Description: 40 item paper-pencil multiple-choice test consisting of a series of statistical tables and a number of inferences made from each of them. For each item, the candidates must select the correct inference from five possible answers. The data used in the tables samples a number of areas: production costs, exchange rates, results from a market research survey. The test has a high degree of apparent relevance to management decision-making. Range: from GCE 'A' level upwards. Examiner required. Suitable for group use. BRITISH PUBLISHER

Timed: 35 minutes

Range: Adult

Scoring: Hand key; examiner evaluated; may be computer scored

Cost: 10 question booklets £25.00; Data card £17.00; 50 answer sheets £21.00; key £4.00.

Publisher: Saville and Holdsworth, Ltd.

ADVANCED TEST BATTERY: SPATIAL REASONING (ATB:ST7)
Saville and Holdsworth, Ltd. Staff

adult

Purpose: Measures ability to visualize and manipulate shapes in three dimensions, given a two-dimensional drawing. Used in selection and development of advanced personnel: engineers, designers, architects, and draftsmen.

Description: 40 item paper-pencil multiple-choice test consisting of a series of folded-out cubes and perspective drawings of assembled cubes. Subjects must identify the assembled cubes which could be made from the folded-out cube, each face of which has a different pattern. Range: from GCE 'O' level to degree.

Examiner required. Suitable for group use.
BRITISH PUBLISHER

Timed: 20 minutes

Range: Adult

Scoring: Hand key; examiner evaluated; may be computer scored

Cost: 10 question booklets £12.50; 50 answer sheets £21.00; key £4.00.

Publisher: Saville and Holdsworth, Ltd.

ADVANCED TEST BATTERY: VERBAL CONCEPTS (ATB:VA1)
Saville and Holdsworth, Ltd. Staff

adult

Purpose: Measures general verbal skills at an advanced level. Used in selection and development with management, senior specialist staff and graduate entrants.

Description: 40 item paper-pencil multiple-choice test measuring knowledge of the meanings of words and the relationships between them. Candidates are required to identify the relationship between a pair of words and to select, from five possible words, the one which relates in the same way to a third given word. The vocabulary used is general and non-specialist, but the range of relationships is very diverse. Range: from GCE 'A' level upwards. Examiner required. Suitable for group use.
BRITISH PUBLISHER

Timed: 15 minutes

Range: Adult

Scoring: Hand key; examiner evaluated; may be computer scored

Cost: 10 question booklets £17.50; 50 answer sheets £21.00; key £4.00.

Publisher: Saville and Holdsworth, Ltd.

ADVANCED TEST BATTERY: VERBAL CRITICAL REASONING (ATB-VA3)
Saville and Holdsworth, Ltd. Staff

adult

Purpose: Measures the ability to evaluate the logic of various kinds of arguments. Used for management selection and graduate recruitment.

Description: 60 item paper-pencil multiple-choice test consisting of argumentative passages and a number of statements which might be made in connection with each of them. The statements must be evaluated in terms of whether they, their opposite, or neither, logically follow from the passage in question. The passages sample a wide range of material from politics to medicine, all of which could be on the agenda of a management meeting. The test has a high degree of apparent relevance to the assessment of managerial skills.
Range: from GCE 'A' level upwards.
Examiner required. Suitable for group use.
BRITISH PUBLISHER

Timed: 30 minutes

Range: Adult

Scoring: Hand key; examiner evaluated; may be computer scored

Cost: 10 question booklets £25.00; 50 answer sheets £21.00; key £4.00.

Publisher: Saville and Holdsworth, Ltd.

APTICOM
Refer to page 654.

ARMED SERVICES VOCATIONAL APTITUDE BATTERY (ASVAB)

Refer to page 655.

BASIC OCCUPATIONAL LITERACY TEST (BOLT)
U.S. Employment Service

adult

Purpose: Measures basic reading and arithmetic skills of educationally disadvantaged adults. Used for occupational training and counseling.

Description: Multiple item paper-pencil test divided into four subtests of reading and arithmetic. Reading section assesses vocabulary and comprehension at four levels of difficulty: advanced, high intermediate, basic intermediate, and fundamental. Arithmetic section assesses computation and reasoning at advanced, intermediate and fundamental levels. Examiner determines the appropriate testing level for each individual using BOLT Wide Range Scale and the individual's reported years of education. Alternate forms A, B and C are available for each subtest at each level of difficulty except the advanced level. Alternate forms A and B are available for the advanced level. Raw scores can be converted to standard scores and General Education Degree GED levels. Materials include test booklet and manuals. Examiner required. Suitable for group use.

Timed: Each reading test, 15 minutes; each arithmetic test, 30 minutes

Range: Adult

Scoring: Hand key; maybe computer scored

Cost: Available only through State Employment agencies.

Publisher: U.S. Dept. of Labor

BASIC OCCUPATIONAL LITERACY TEST: (BOLT) WIDE RANGE SCALE

adult

Purpose: Measures individual's reading and arithmetic abilities. Used as a pretest to determine whether the individual should be given the General Aptitude Test Battery or the Non-Reading Aptitude Test Battery as a preliminary to taking the Basic Occupational Literacy Test. Used for employment counseling.

Description: 15 item paper-pencil examination in two subtests, reading and arithmetic, with eight items in each subtest. Available only through State Employment Agencies. Examiner required. Suitable for group use.

Untimed: 15 minutes

Range: Adult

Scoring: Hand key

Cost: Available through State Employment Agency only.

Publisher: U.S. Dept. of Labor

CLASSIFICATION TEST BATTERY (CTB)

adult

Purpose: Evaluates general thinking and adaptability skills of illiterate and semi-literate applicants for unskilled and semiskilled mining jobs.

Description: Four paper-pencil and task assessment tests measure non-verbal reasoning and spatial ability. The battery contains: Pattern Reproduction Test, Circles Test, Forms Series Test (Mines Version), and Colored Peg Board Test. The battery was devised as a unit and can only be used as described in the manual. Pre-test instructions available in any of nine African languages and English. The test itself is administered by a silent film. Administered at centers established by firms employing the publisher's consultation and training services; use restricted to competent persons properly registered with either the South African Medical and Dental Council or Test Commission of the Republic of South Africa. Examiner required. Suitable for group use.

SOUTH AFRICAN PUBLISHER

Untimed: Not available

Range: Illiterate and semi-literate job applicants

Scoring: Examiner evaluated

Cost: (In Rands) Complete battery 73,00; manual 7,20; instructional film 400,00.

Publisher: National Institute for Personnel Research

COLOR MATCHING APTITUDE TEST
Inter-society Council

adult

Purpose: Measures color perception for vocational placement. Used to screen for positions in paint factories, coatings industries such as varnishes, paints and lacquers.

Description: 48 item task performance test measuring ability to discriminate between various shades of color. One set of 48 color chips is mounted on an easel. An identical set is in a dispenser on the easel. The subject must match color chips in the dispenser with those on the easel. Materials include two sets of chips, scoring card and scoring key. Examiner required. Not suitable for group use.

Untimed: 45 minutes-1 hour

Range: Adult

Scoring: Hand key

Cost: Complete kit (includes 2 sets of 48 chips, scoring card, key) $400.00.

Publisher: Federation of Societies of Coating Technologies

COMPREHENSIVE ABILITY BATTERY (CAB)
A. Ralph Hakstian and Raymond B. Cattell

teen, adult grades 10-UP

Purpose: Measures a variety of abilities important in industrial settings for individuals high school age and above. Used in career and vocational counseling and employee selection and placement.

Description: 20 paper-pencil subtests each measure a single primary ability factor related to performance in industrial settings. The tests in the battery may be used individually or in combination. The subtests are grouped and presented in four test booklets (CAB-1, 2, 3/4, and 5). CAB-1 contains: Verbal Ability, Numerical Ability, Spatial Ability, and Perceptual Completion. CAB-2 contains: Clerical Speed and Accuracy, Reasoning, Hidden Shapes, Rote Memory, and Mechanical Ability. CAB-3/4 contains: Meaningful Memory, Memory Span, Spelling, Auditory Ability, and Esthetic Judgment. CAB-5 contains: Organizing Ideas, Production of Ideas, Verbal Fluency, Originality, Tracking, and Drawing. Percentile norms are provided for males, females and combined for each test at the high school level. Additional norms for college students, convicts and general population adults are provided for selected tests. Examiner required. Suitable for group use.

Untimed: Battery, 1 hour 20 minutes

Range: High school students and adults

Scoring: Hand key; computer scoring available

Cost: Specimen set (includes 4 test

booklets, answer and profile sheets for all tests, manual) $8.00.

Publisher: Institute for Personality and Ability Testing, Inc.

CRITICAL REASONING TEST BATTERY (CRTB)
Saville and Holdsworth, Ltd. Staff

adult

Purpose: Measures skills of evaluation and reasoning among individuals of average and above ability (GCE O' level and above). Used in the selection and development of 'A' level entrants and supervisory and junior management personnel. Also used for guidance and placement of students sixth form and above.

Description: Three paper-pencil multiple-choice tests measuring the following skills: Verbal evaluation, interpreting data, and diagrammatic reasoning. The Verbal Evaluation Test (VC1) is 60 items measuring the ability to understand and evaluate the logic of various types of arguments. The Interpreting Data Test (NC2) is 40 items measuring the ability to make correct decisions or inferences from numerical or statistical data, presented as tables or diagrams. The Diagrammatic Series Test (DC3) is 40 items measuring the ability to reason with diagrams and requires the candidate to discover logical rules governing sequences of symbols and diagrams. Together these tests provide information on important abilities related to junior management. Examiner required. Suitable for group use.
BRITISH PUBLISHER

Timed: over 1 hour

Range: Adult

Scoring: Hand key; examiner evaluated; may be computer scored

Cost: Complete (includes question

booklets, answer sheets, key, data cards, profile charts, test logs) £185.00.

Publisher: Saville and Holdsworth, Ltd.

DVORINE COLOR VISION TEST
Refer to page 603.

EMPLOYEE APTITUDE SURVEY TEST #1--VERBAL COMPREHENSION (EAS #1)
G. Grimsley, F.L. Ruch, N.D. Warren, and J.S. Ford

adult

Purpose: Measures ability to use and understand the relationships between words. Used for selection and placement of executives, secretaries, professional personnel, and high level office workers. Also helpful in career counseling.

Description: 30 item paper-pencil multiple-choice test measuring word-relationship recognition, reading speed, and ability to understand instructions. Each item consists of a word followed by a list of four other words, from which the examinee must select the one which means the same or about the same as the first word. Available in two equivalent forms. Examiner required. Suitable for group use. Available in Polish and German.

Timed: 5 minutes

Range: Adult

Scoring: Hand key; computer scored

Cost: 25 tests $.35 each.

Publisher: Psychological Services, Inc.

EMPLOYEE APTITUDE SURVEY TEST #2--NUMERICAL ABILITY (EAS #2)
G. Grimsley, F.L. Ruch and N.D. Warren

adult

Purpose: Measures basic mathematical skill. Used for selection and placement of executives, supervisors, engineers, accountants, sales and clerical workers.

Description: 75 item paper-pencil multiple-choice test arranged in three parts of 25 items each. All three parts test the skills of addition, subtraction, multiplication, and division. Part I deals with whole numbers, Part II with decimal fractions and Part III with common fractions. Available in two equivalent forms. Examiner required. Suitable for group use. Available in Spanish, French, German, Polish, Farsee and Indonesian.

Timed: 10 minutes

Range: Adult

Scoring: Hand key; computer scored

Cost: 25 tests $.35 each.

Publisher: Psychological Services, Inc.

EMPLOYEE APTITUDE SURVEY TEST #3--VISUAL PURSUIT (EAS #3)
G. Grimsley, F.L. Ruch, N.D. Warren, and J.S. Ford

adult

Purpose: Measures speed and accuracy in visually tracing lines through complex designs. Used with draftsmen, design engineers, technicians and related workers. Helpful in employee selection and in career counseling.

Description: 30 item paper-pencil multiple-choice test consisting of a maze of lines that weave their way from their starting points (numbered 1 to 30) on the right-hand side of the page to a column of boxes on the left. The task is to identify for each starting point the box on the left at which the line ends. Examinees are encouraged to trace with their eyes, not their pencils. Available in two equivalent forms. Examiner required. Suitable for group use. Available in Spanish, Polish, French, German, and Indonesian.

Timed: 10 minutes

Range: Adult

Scoring: Hand key; computer scored

Cost: 25 tests $.35 each.

Publisher: Psychological Services, Inc.

EMPLOYEE APTITUDE SURVEY TEST #4--VISUAL SPEED AND ACCURACY (EAS #4)
G. Grimsley, F.L. Ruch and N.D. Warren

adult

Purpose: Measures ability to see details quickly and accurately. Used for selection of bookkeepers, accountants, general office clerks, stenographers, and machine operators. Helpful in career planning.

Description: 90 item paper-pencil multiple-choice test. Each test item consists of two series of numbers and symbols which must be compared and determined to be "the same" or "different." May be administered to sales supervisors and executives with the expectations that their scores will be above the average for other groups. Available in two equivalent forms. Examiner required. Suitable for group use. Available in Spanish, Polish, French, German, and Indonesian.

Timed: 5 minutes

Range: Adult

Scoring: Hand key; computer scored

Cost: 25 tests $.35 each.

Publisher: Psychological Services, Inc.

EMPLOYEE APTITUDE SURVEY TEST #5--SPACE VISUALIZATION (EAS #5)
G. Grimsley, F.L. Ruch, N.D. Warren, and J.S. Ford

adult

Purpose: Measures ability to visualize and manipulate objects in three dimensions on a two-dimensional drawing. Used for employee selection for jobs which require mechanical aptitude, such as draftsmen, engineers and technicians. Also helpful in career planning.

Description: 50 item paper-pencil multiple-choice test consisting of ten perspective line-drawings of stacks of blocks. The blocks are all the same size and of rectangular shape so that they appear to stack neatly and distinctly. Five of the blocks in each stack are lettered. Subjects must look at each lettered block and determine how many other blocks in the stack the lettered block touches. Available in two equivalent forms. Examiner required. Suitable for group use. Available in Spanish, Polish, German, and Indonesian.

Timed: 5 minutes

Range: Adult

Scoring: Hand key; computer scored

Cost: 25 tests $.35 each.

Publisher: Psychological Services, Inc.

EMPLOYEE APTITUDE SURVEY TEST #6--NUMERICAL REASONING (EAS #6)
G. Grimsley, F.L. Ruch, N.D. Warren, and J.S. Ford

adult

Purpose: Measures ability to analyze and find relationships within series of numbers and predicts trainability for technical, supervisory and executive positions. Used for employee selection and career counseling.

Description: 20 item paper-pencil multiple-choice test. Each item consists of a series of seven numbers followed by a question mark where the next number of the series should be. Examinees must determine the pattern of each series, and select (from five choices) the number which correctly fills the blank. Emphasis is on logic and deduction rather than computation. Available in two equivalent forms. Examiner required. Suitable for group use. Available in Spanish, Polish, French, German, Farsee, and Indonesian.

Timed: 5 minutes

Range: Adult

Scoring: Hand key; computer scored

Cost: 25 tests $.35 each.

Publisher: Psychological Services, Inc.

EMPLOYEE APTITUDE SURVEYTEST #7--VERBAL REASONING (EAS #7)
G. Grimsley, F.L. Ruch, N.D. Warren, and J.S. Ford

adult

Purpose: Measures ability to analyze information and draw valid conclusions from that information. Used for employee selection for jobs which require the ability to organize, evaluate, and use information, such as administrative and technical decision making, supervisory, scientific, and accounting. Helpful in career counseling.

Description: 30 item paper-pencil multiple-choice test consisting of six lists of facts (one-sentence statements) with five possible conclusions for each list of facts. The task is to read each list of facts and then look at each conclusion and decide whether it is definitely true, definitely false, or unknown from the given facts. Available in two equivalent forms. Examiner required. Suitable for group use. Available in Spanish, Polish, French, and German.

Timed: 5 minutes

Range: Adult

Scoring: Hand key; computer scored

Cost: 25 tests $.35 each.

Publisher: Psychological Services, Inc.

EMPLOYEE APTITUDE SURVEY TEST #8--WORD FLUENCY (EAS #8)
G. Grimsley, F.L. Ruch, N.D. Warren, and J.S. Ford

adult

Purpose: Measures flexibility in language. Used for selection of salespersons, journalists, representatives, writers, receptionists, secretaries, and executives. Helpful in career planning.

Description: Open-ended (75 answer spaces provided) paper- pencil test which measures word fluency by determining how many words beginning with one specific letter (given at the beginning of the test) a person can produce in a five minute test period. Examiner required. Suitable for group use.

Timed: 5 minutes

Range: Adult

Scoring: Hand key; computer scored

Cost: 25 tests $.35 each.

Publisher: Psychological Services, Inc.

EMPLOYEE APTITUDE SURVEY TEST #9--MANUAL SPEED AND ACCURACY (EAS #9)
G. Grimsley, F.L. Ruch, N.D. Warren, and J.S. Ford

adult

Purpose: Measures ability to make fine finger movements rapidly and accurately. Used for selection of clerical workers, machine operators, technicians, repairmen, precision jobs, repetitive tasks. Also useful in career planning.

Description: Multiple item paper-pencil test consisting of a straight forward array of evenly-spaced lines of small circles (750 "O"'s in all). Applicant must place a pencil dot in as many "O"'s as possible in five minutes. Examiner required. Suitable for group use. Available in Spanish, Polish and Indonesian.

Timed: 5 minutes

Range: Adult

Scoring: Hand key; computer scored

Cost: 25 tests $.35 each.

Publisher: Psychological Services, Inc.

EMPLOYEE APTITUDE SURVEY TEST #10--SYMBOLIC REASONING (EAS #10)
G. Grimsley, F.L. Ruch, N.D. Warren, and J.S. Ford

adult

Purpose: Measures ability to manipulate abstract symbols and use them to make valid decisions. Evaluates high levels of reasoning required for science and technology, trouble-shooters, data programmers, accountants, and engineers. Helpful in career planning.

Description: 30 item paper-pencil multiple-choice test consisting of a list of abstract symbols (and their coded meanings) which are used to establish relationships in the form of "A" to "B" to "C". Given this statement, the examinee must decide whether a proposed relationship between "A" and "C" is true, false, or unknown from the given statement. Available in two equivalent forms. Examiner required. Suitable for group use. Available in Spanish, Polish, French, German, and Indonesian.

Timed: 5 minutes

Range: Adult

Scoring: Hand key; computer scored

Cost: 25 tests $.35 each.

Publisher: Psychological Services, Inc.

EMPLOYMENT BARRIER IDENTIFICATION SCALE (EBIS)
John M. McKee

teen, adult

Purpose: Measures the ability of an unemployed individual to gain and retain employment. Identifies areas and skills in which the job seeker may need training and assesses employment training programs. Used with CETA participants and rehabilitational clients, as well as the general unemployed population.

Description: 19 item paper-pencil test evaluates an individual's employability. Topics covered include job skills, education, environmental support, and personal survival skills. The test may be presented as an oral interview for use with illiterate examinees. Examiner required. Suitable for group use (except when orally presented).

Untimed: 30 minutes

Range: Ages 15-adult

Scoring: Hand key

Cost: Complete (includes 25 scales and manual) $30.00.

Publisher: Behavior Science Press

ENGLISH LANGUAGE ACHIEVEMENT TEST

teen, adult   grades 12-UP

Purpose: Measures achievement of basic English language skills. Suitable for use with matriculants and higher. Used in employee selection and placement.

Description: Multiple item paper-pencil test assesses English language abilities in spelling, comprehension and vocabulary. Norms are based on a group of matriculants. Restricted to competent persons properly registered with either the South African Medical and Dental Council or Test Commission of the Republic of South Africa. Examiner required. Suitable for group use. Afrikaans version available.
SOUTH AFRICAN PUBLISHER

Timed: 19 minutes

Range: Matriculants and higher

Scoring: Hand key; examiner evaluated

Cost: Contact publisher.

Publisher: National Institute for Personnel Research

ETSA TESTS
George A. W. Stouffer, Jr. and S. Trevor Hadley

teen, adult   grades 10-UP

Purpose: Measures general and specific job aptitudes. Used for employee selection, placement, promotion, and measurement of training progress.

Description: Eight paper-pencil aptitude tests measuring: General Mental Ability, Office Arithmetic, General Clerical Ability, Stenographic Skills, Mechanical Familiarity, Mechanical Knowledge, Sales Aptitude, and Personal Adjustment Index. General Mental Ability and Personal Adjustment Index may be combined with one of the specific skills tests to give comprehensive information about an applicant. Available only to qualified test users: personnel managers, counselors, psychologists, and educators. Examiner required. Suitable for group use.

Timed: Varies

Range: High school-adult

Scoring: Hand key; examiner evaluated

Cost: Complete sample set (test 1-A and 8-A with manual and keys) $6.00; sample set, any one test $5.00.

Publisher: Employers' Tests and Services Associates

ETSA TESTS 1-A--GENERAL MENTAL ABILITY
George A. W. Stouffer, Jr., and S. Trevor Hadley

teen, adult   grades 10-UP 👉 ✍️

Purpose: Measures general intelligence and learning ability. Used for employee selection, placement and promotion.

Description: 75 item paper-pencil test of general learning ability consisting of both verbal and nonverbal items. May be used in conjunction with ETSA 8-A, Personal Adjustment Index, and any ETSA test of specific skill areas. Examiner required. Suitable for group use.

Untimed: 45 minutes

Range: High school-adult

Scoring: Hand key; examiner evaluated; scoring service available

Cost: 10 tests with key $12.00; manual $2.50; handbook $2.50.

Publisher: Employers' Tests and Services Associates

ETSA TESTS 2-A--OFFICE ARITHMETIC TEST
George A. W. Stouffer, Jr., and S. Trevor Hadley

teen, adult   grades 10-UP 👉 ✍️

Purpose: Measures ability to use office arithmetic. Used for employee selection, placement and promotion.

Description: 50 item paper-pencil test assessing arithmetic skills used in office work. Areas tested include: whole number computation, mixed number computation, written problems, reading tables, reading graphs, and advanced office computation. One in a series of ETSA tests. Examiner required. Suitable for group use.

Timed: 40 minutes

Range: High school-adult

Scoring: Hand key; examiner evaluated; scoring service available

Cost: 10 tests with key $12.00; manual $2.50; handbook $2.50.

Publisher: Employers' Tests and Services Associates

ETSA TESTS 3-A--GENERAL CLERICAL ABILITY TEST
George A. W. Stouffer, Jr., and S. Trevor Hadley

teen, adult   grades 10-UP 👉 ✍️

Purpose: Measures general skills required of clerks in routine office work. Used for employee selection, placement and promotion.

Description: 131 item paper-pencil test assessing general clerical skills. Items include alphabetizing, checking lists of numbers and names, spelling, office vocabulary, and basic information. Emphasis is on speed and accuracy. One in a series of ETSA tests. Examiner required. Suitable for group use.

Timed: 20 minutes

Range: High school-adult

Scoring: Hand key; examiner evaluated; scoring service available

Cost: 10 tests with key $12.00; manual $2.50; handbook $2.50.

Publisher: Employers' Tests and Services Associates

ETSA TESTS 4-A-- STENOGRAPHIC SKILLS TEST
George A. W. Stouffer, Jr., and S. Trevor Hadley

teen, adult   grades 10-UP

Purpose: Measures typing, shorthand and general skills required of secretaries and stenographers. Used for employee selection, placement and promotion.

Description: 120 item paper-pencil test measuring four basic office skills: spelling, filing, grammar, and general office information. Materials include supplemental performance evaluations of typing and shorthand, either or both of which may be used with the basic scale. One in a series of ETSA tests. Examiner required. Suitable for group use.

Untimed: 45 minutes; Typing Test Supplement, 5 minutes; Shorthand Test, 18 minutes

Range: High school-adult

Scoring: Hand key; examiner evaluated; scoring service available

Cost: 10 tests with key $12.00; manual $2.50; handbook $2.50.

Publisher: Employers' Tests and

Services Associates

ETSA TESTS 5-A-- MECHANICAL FAMILIARITY
George A. W. Stouffer, Jr., and S. Trevor Hadley

teen, adult   grades 10-UP

Purpose: Measures ability to recognize common tools and instruments. Used for employee selection, placement and promotion.

Description: 50 item paper-pencil, nonverbal test of background in mechanical activities. Items are commonly used tools which applicant identifies. One in a series of ETSA tests. Examiner required. Suitable for group use.

Untimed: 60 minutes

Range: High school-adult

Scoring: Hand key; examiner evaluated; scoring service available

Cost: 10 tests with key $12.00; manual $2.50; handbook $2.50.

Publisher: Employers' Tests and Services Associates

ETSA TESTS 6-A-- MECHANICAL KNOWLEDGE
George A. W. Stouffer, Jr., and S. Trevor Hadley

teen, adult   grades 10-UP

Purpose: Measures mechanical insight and understanding. Used for employee selection, placement and promotion.

Description: 121 item paper-pencil test assessing six areas of mechanical knowledge. Discriminates between novices, journeymen and experts. One in a series of ETSA tests. Examiner required. Suitable for group use.

Untimed: 90 minutes

Range: High school-adult

Scoring: Hand key; examiner evaluated; scoring service available

Cost: 10 tests with key $12.00; manual $2.50; handbook $2.50.

Publisher: Employers' Tests and Services Associates

ETSA TESTS 7-A--SALES APTITUDE
George A. W. Stouffer, Jr., and S. Trevor Hadley

teen, adult   grades 10-UP

Purpose: Measures abilities and skills required in effective selling. Used for employee selection, placement and promotion.

Description: 100 item paper-pencil test assessing seven aspects of sales aptitude: sales judgment, interest in selling, personality factors, identification of self with selling occupation, level of aspiration, insight into human nature, and awareness of sales approach. One in a series of ETSA tests. Examiner required. Suitable for group use.

Untimed: 60 minutes

Range: High school-adult

Scoring: Hand key; examiner evaluated; scoring service available

Cost: 10 tests with key $12.00; manual $2.50; handbook $2.50.

Publisher: Employers' Tests and Services Associates

ETSA TESTS 8-A--PERSONAL ADJUSTMENT INDEX
George A. W. Stouffer, Jr., and S. Trevor Hadley

teen, adult   grades 10-UP

Purpose: Measures personality traits for all types of jobs. Used for employee selection, placement and promotion.

Description: 105 item paper-pencil test measuring seven components of personal adjustment: community spirit, attitude toward cooperation with employer, attitude toward health, attitude toward authority, lack of nervous tendencies, leadership, and job stability. May be used in conjunction with ETSA 1-A, General Mental Ability, and any ETSA test of a specific skill area. Examiner required. Suitable for group use.

Untimed: 60 minutes

Range: High school-adult

Scoring: Hand key; examiner evaluated; scoring service available

Cost: 10 tests with key $12.00; manual $2.50; handbook $2.50.

Publisher: Employers' Tests and Services Associates

FARNSWORTH DICHOTOMOUS TEST FOR COLOR BLINDNESS
Refer to page 604.

FARNSWORTH-MUNSEL 100 HUE TEST
Munsell Color

all ages

Purpose: Determines color vision anomalies and color aptitude. Used to screen workers in such fields as electronics where color determination is a part of the job.

Description: Manual-visual apparatus test consisting of four trays each containing a segment of 85 color reference disks recessed in individual black plastic caps. The subject is asked to place color caps in true order, with the results posted on score sheets to yield numerical and graphic results. Material consists of the trays, a wood carrying case, instruction manual, and 100 score sheets. Examiner required. Not suitable for group use.

Untimed: 10 minutes

Range: Ages 6-adult

Scoring: Hand key

Cost: Complete (includes 4 trays, wooden carrying case, instruction manual, 100 score sheets) $340.00.

Publisher: Munsell Color

FINE FINGER DEXTERITY WORK TASK UNIT
Refer to page 853.

FLANAGAN APTITUDE CLASSIFICATION TESTS (FACT)
John C. Flanagan

teen, adult

Purpose: Assesses skills necessary for the successful completion of particular occupational tasks. Used for vocational counseling, curriculum planning, and selection and placement of employees.

Description: Multiple-item paperpencil battery of 16 aptitude tests designed to assess the subjects abilities relative to others in the total population and in specific occupations. Tests are:
Inspection: measures ability to spot flaws or imperfections in a series of articles quickly and accurately.
Mechanics: measures ability to understand mechanical principles and to analyze mechanical movements (2 equivalent forms).
Tables: measures ability to read tables and charts quickly and accurately.
Reasoning: measures ability to understand basic mathematical concepts and relationships.
Assembly: measures ability to visualize the appearance of an object

assembled from a number of separate parts.
Judgment and Comprehension: measures ability to read with understanding, to reason logically and to use good judgment in practical situations.
Components: measures ability to locate and identify simple parts of a complex whole.
Arithmetic: measures ability to work quickly and accurately with numbers in addition, subtraction, multiplication, and division problems.
Ingenuity: measures creative or inventive skills and ability to devise ingenious procedures, equipment or presentations.
Scales: measures ability to read scales, graphs and charts quickly and accurately.
Expression: measures knowledge of correct English grammar and sentence structure.
Precision: measures ability to do precision work with small objects and speed and accuracy in making appropriate finger movements with one or both hands.
Coordination: measures ability to coordinate hand and arm movements in a smooth and accurate manner.
Patterns: measures ability to perceive and reproduce simple pattern outlines in a precise and accurate way.
Coding: measures ability to code typical office information quickly and accurately (2 equivalent forms).
Memory: measures ability to learn and recall the classification or identifying symbols for various materials or groups of items (2 equivalent forms).

Each test is printed as a separate non-reusable booklet and may be given singly or in combination. The FACT battery differs from the FIT battery in that the tests are generally lower level and have longer time limits. Self-administered. Suitable for group use.

Timed: 5-40 minutes per test

Range: Students and adults

Scoring: Hand scored. Carbon insert (answers transfer to scoring key on inside of test booklet)

Cost: 25 test booklets (specify test) $28.00; reasoning manual $2.10; ingenuity manual $2.10; examiner's manual $2.60.

Publisher: Science Research Associates, Inc.

FLANAGAN INDUSTRIAL TESTS (FIT)
John C. Flanagan

adult

Purpose: Predicts success for given job elements in adults. Used for employee screening, hiring and placing in a wide variety of jobs.

Description: A paper-pencil battery of 18 tests designed for use with adults in personnel selection programs. Tests are:
Arithmetic (Ar): Measures ability to add, subtract, multiply and divide.
Assembly (As): Measures ability to visualize the appearance of an object assembled form a number of separate parts.
Components (Com): Measures ability to locate and identify important parts of a whole, which involves an ability to change visual patterns.
Coordination (Co): Measures ability to coordinate hand and arm movements smoothly and accurately.
Electronics (El): Measures ability to understand electrical and electronic

principals and to analyze diagrams of electrical circuits.
Expression (Ex): Measures feeling for and knowledge of correct English in writing and talking.
Ingenuity (Ing): Measures creative or inventive skills and the ability to devise ingenious procedures, equipment or presentations.
Inspection (Ins): Measures ability to spot flaws or imperfections in a series of articles quickly and accurately.
Judgment and Comprehension: Measures ability to read with understanding, to reason logically, and to use good judgment in interpreting materials.
Mathematics and Reasoning (M-R): Measures ability to understand basic math concepts and to translate ideas and operations into brief mathematical notations.
Mechanics (Me): Measures ability to understand mechanical principles and to analyze mechanical movements.
Memory (Mem): Measures ability to learn and recall a term associated with an unfamiliar one.
Patterns (Pat): Measures ability to perceive and reproduce simple pattern outlines precisely and accurately.
Planning (Pl): Measures ability to plan, organize and schedule.
Precision (Pre): Measures ability to do precision work with small objects and speed and accuracy in making appropriate finger movements.
Scales (Sc): Measures ability to read scales, graphs and charts quickly and accurately.
Tables (Ta): Measures ability to read tables quickly and accurately.
Vocabulary (Va): Measures ability to choose the right word to convey an idea and knowledge of words used in business and government matters.
Each test is printed as a separate booklet and may be given singly or in combination. Self-administered. Suitable for group use.

Timed: 5-15 minutes per test

Range: Adults

Scoring: Hand key (except for

Coordination and Precision tests)

Cost: 25 test booklets (specify test $15.00; scoring stencils $6.00 each; inspection scoring stencil $12.00.

Publisher: Science Research Associates, Inc.

FOOT OPERATED HINGED BOX WORK TASK UNIT
Refer to page 853.

GENERAL ABILITY TESTS: NUMERICAL (GAT-NUMERICAL)
Refer to page 798.

GENERAL ABILITY TESTS: PERCEPTUAL (GAT-PERCEPTUAL)
Refer to page 799.

GENERAL ABILITY TESTS: VERBAL (GAT-VERBAL)
Refer to page 799.

GENERAL APTITUDE SERIES (GAS)
Saville and Holdsworth, Ltd. Staff

adult

Purpose: Assesses a wide range of general abilities. Used in the counseling and placement of general managerial personnel, the measurement of abilities in cases of job dissatisfaction, personnel transfers, occupational counseling, and occupational research.

Description: Seven paper-pencil multiple-choice tests measuring verbal, numerical, spatial, mechanical, diagrammatic, clerical, and diagramming skills. The tests include: Verbal Concepts (VA1), Number series (NA2), Spatial Recognition (ST9), Mechanical Comprehension (MT4), Diagrammatic Reasoning (DT8), Classification (CP4), and Diagramming (DA5). Provides a high degree of relevance to occupational work in relation to the amount of testing time required. Examiner required. Suitable for group use.
BRITISH PUBLISHER

Timed: 1 hour 42 minutes

Range: Adult

Scoring: Hand key; examiner evaluated; may be computer scored

Cost: Complete (includes all tests, score sheets, manual, keys) £295.00.

Publisher: Saville and Holdsworth, Ltd.

GENERAL APTITUDE TEST BATTERY (GATB)
U.S. Employment Service

teen, adult   grades 9-UP

Purpose: Measures vocational aptitudes of literate individuals who need help in choosing an occupation. Used for counseling.

Description: 434 item paper-pencil test consisting of 284 multiple-choice, 150 dichotomous choice (same- different) questions, and two dexterity form boards. Twelve subtests measure nine vocational aptitudes: General Learning Ability, Verbal, Numerical, Spatial, Form Perception, Clerical Perception, Motor Coordination, Finger Dexterity, and Manual Dexterity. Raw scores are converted to aptitude scores by use of conversion tables. Occupational Aptitude Patterns (OAP) indicate the aptitude requirements for groups of occupations. There are 66 OAPs covering 97% of all non-supervisory occupations. The

GATB is scored in terms of OAPs. A letter grade of "H", "M", or "L" is assigned for each OAP. Results of the battery indicate the individual's likelihood of being successful in the various occupations. Use in the U.S. must be authorized by State Employment Security Agencies, and in Canada by the Canadian Employment and Immigration Commission. Examiner required. Suitable for group use. Available in Spanish and French.

Untimed: 1 hour

Range: Grades 9-12 and adults

Scoring: Hand key; computer scoring available

Cost: 100 test I.D. sheets $14.00; 250 answer sheets $22.00; scoring stencil $5.50; computer scoring $1.25.

Publisher: United States Department of Labor

GOTTSCHALDT FIGURES TEST

---

adult

Purpose: Measures visual perception and analytical ability. Used with job applicants with at least ten years of education for purposes of employee screening and selection.

Description: Multiple item paper-pencil test requires the applicant to find given embedded figures in more complex diagrams. Restricted to competent persons properly registered with either the South African Medical and Dental Council or Test Commission of the Republic of South Africa. Examiner required. Suitable for group use. Afrikaans version available.
SOUTH AFRICAN PUBLISHER

Timed: 20 minutes

Range: Job applicants with at least 10 years of education

Scoring: Hand key

Cost: Contact publisher.

Publisher: National Institute for Personnel Research

GUILFORD-ZIMMERMAN APTITUDE SURVEY (GZAS)
J.P. Guilford and Wayne S. Zimmerman

---

teen, adult   grades 10-UP

Purpose: Measures mental abilities as a test of aptitude for many areas of employment and academic pursuit.

Description: Six paper-pencil tests measuring abilities in the areas of verbal and abstract intelligence, numerical facility, and perception. The aptitudes fit into the Structure-of-Intellect categories. Code letters after the GZAS test name indicate the category to which the test belongs. Battery includes the following six tests: Verbal Comprehension, General Reasoning, Numerical Operations, Perceptual Speed, Spatial Orientation, and Spatial Visualization. The tests may be used singly or in combination, depending on the needs of the situation. The score on each test has a definite meaning and are generally independent in function. Examiner required. Restricted to A.P.A. members. Suitable for group use.

Timed: 93 minutes

Range: High school-adult

Scoring: Hand key; may be computer scored

Cost: Specimen set $3.50.

Publisher: Sheridan Psychological Services

GUILFORD-ZIMMERMAN APTITUDE SURVEY: GENERAL REASONING (GZAS:GR)
J.P. Guilford and Wayne S. Zimmerman

teen, adult   grades 10-UP

Purpose: Evaluates reasoning abilities through arithmetic-reasoning items. Used as an aptitude test for a variety of problem-solving tasks.

Description: Multiple item paper-pencil test consists of arithmetic-reasoning items graded in difficulty. Numerical computation is kept to a minimum, removing most of the numerical-facility component from the measure. Results yield C-scale, centile and T-scale norms for college groups. Manual, answer sheets, profile charts, and scoring stencils must be ordered separately. Restricted to A.P.A. members. Examiner required. Suitable for group use.

Timed: 35 minutes

Range: High school-adult

Scoring: Hand key; may be computer scored

Cost: 25 tests $10.00; 25 answer sheets $3.50; manual $4.00; hand key $4.50.

Publisher: Sheridan Psychological Services

GUILFORD-ZIMMERMAN APTITUDE SURVEY: NUMERICAL OPERATIONS (GZAS:NO)
J.P. Guilford and Wayne S. Zimmerman

teen, adult   grades 10-UP

Purpose: Measures ability to work with numbers. Used with accountants, salespersons and many types of clerical workers.

Description: Multiple item paper-pencil, multiple-choice test includes simple problems of addition, subtraction and multiplication. Results yield C- scale, centile and T-scale norms for college groups. Manual, profile charts and scoring keys must each be ordered separately. Restricted to A.P.A. members. Examiner required. Suitable for group use.

Timed: 8 minutes

Range: High school-adult

Scoring: Hand key; may be computer scored

Cost: 25 tests $7.50; manual $4.00; hand key $4.00.

Publisher: Sheridan Psychological Services

GUILFORD-ZIMMERMAN APTITUDE SURVEY: PERCEPTUAL SPEED (GZAS:PS)
J.P. Guilford and Wayne S. Zimmerman

teen, adult   grades 10-UP

Purpose: Measures ability to compare details quickly and accurately. Used in selection of inspectors, clerks and machine operators.

Description: Multiple item paper-pencil, multiple-choice test which measures speed and accuracy in comparing visual details. Evaluates judgment of identity or difference. The skill assessed is evaluation of "figural units." Results yield C-scale, centile and T-scale norms for college groups. Manual, profile charts and scoring keys must each be ordered separately. Restricted to A.P.A. members. Examiner required. Suitable for group use.

Timed: 5 minutes

Range: High school-adult

Scoring: Hand key; may be computer scored

Cost: 25 tests $7.50; manual $4.00; hand key $4.00.

Publisher: Sheridan Psychological Services

GUILFORD-ZIMMERMAN APTITUDE SURVEY: SPATIAL ORIENTATION (GZAS:SO)
J.P. Guilford and Wayne S. Zimmerman

teen, adult   grades 10-UP

Purpose: Measures ability to perceive spatial arrangements. Relevant to the operation of machines in which there is a choice of direction of movement in response to signals.

Description: Paper-pencil, multiple-choice test which measures the cognition of figural systems. Results yield C-scale, centile and T-scale norms for college groups. Manual, answer sheets, profile charts, and scoring stencils must each be ordered separately. Restricted to A.P.A. members. Examiner required. Suitable for group use.

Timed: 10 minutes

Range: High school-adult

Scoring: Hand key; may be computer scored

Cost: 25 tests $14.00; 25 answer sheets $3.50; manual $4.00; hand key $4.50.

Publisher: Sheridan Psychological Services

GUILFORD-ZIMMERMAN APTITUDE SURVEY: SPATIAL VISUALIZATION (GZAS:SV)
J.P. Guilford and Wayne S. Zimmerman

teen, adult   grades 10-UP

Purpose: Measures the ability to mentally manipulate ideas visually. Used to screen engineers, architects and draftsmen. May be used for situations involving work with mechanical devices.

Description: Multiple item paper-pencil, multiple-choice test which measures the "cognition of figural transformations." Results yield C-scale, centile and T-scale norms for college groups. Manual, answer sheets, profile charts, and scoring stencils must each be ordered separately. Restricted to A.P.A. members. Examiner required. Suitable for group use.

Timed: 10 minutes

Range: High school-adult

Scoring: Hand key; may be computer scored

Cost: 25 tests $14.00; 25 answer sheets $3.50; manual $4.00; hand key $4.50.

Publisher: Sheridan Psychological Services

GUILFORD-ZIMMERMAN APTITUDE SURVEY: VERBAL COMPREHENSION (GZAS:VC)
J.P. Guilford and Wayne S. Zimmerman

teen, adult   grades 10-UP

Purpose: Measures verbal comprehension. Assesses academic aptitude and suitability for fields in which reading ability is an important factor.

Description: 72 item paper-pencil, multiple-choice test which measures verbal comprehension. Test items are constructed to maintain a uniform level of difficulty for all alternative responses to each item. Therefore, the chance of arriving at correct answers simply by eliminating the more familiar wrong answers may be minimized. Results yield C-scale, centile and T-scale norms for college groups. Manual, answer sheets, profile charts, and scoring stencils must each be ordered separately. Restricted to A.P.A. members. Examiner required. Suitable for group use.

Timed: 25 minutes

Range: High school-adult

Scoring: Hand key; may be computer scored

Cost: 25 tests $10.00; 25 answer sheets $3.50; manual $4.00; hand key $4.50.

Publisher: Sheridan Psychological Services

HAND DYNAMOMETER (DYNAMOMETER GRIP STRENGTH TEST)

child, teen

Purpose: Measures general body strength and provides an index of right versus left handedness. Used for vocational evaluation, employee screening and fitness evaluation.

Description: A task performance test measuring grip strength. A millimeter rule and grip dynamometer with adjustable stirrup are adjusted until the inside scale equals half the distance from where the subject's thumb joins the hand to the end of the fingers. The subject then squeezes with full strength which is measured by the dynamometer. Examiner required. Not for group use.

Untimed: 1 minute

Range: Ages 6-18 years

Scoring: Hand key

Cost: Model 78010 and 78011 $130.00 each.

Publisher: Lafayette Instrument Co., Inc.

HINGED BOX WORK TASK UNIT

Refer to page 854.

INDEX CARD WORK TASK UNIT

Refer to page 854.

INDUSTRIAL READING TEST (IRT)

teen, adult   grades 10-UP

Purpose: Measures reading comprehension. Used for selecting job applicants and screening trainees for vocational or technical programs.

Description: 38 item paper-pencil test of reading comprehension covering nine reading passages of graded difficulty. Some passages are sections of technical manuals; others are in the form of company memoranda. Materials include two forms, A and B. Sales of Form A restricted to business and industry; Form B available to both schools and businesses. Examiner required. Suitable for group use.

Timed: 40 minutes

Range: Vocational High school students and adults

Scoring: Hand key; may be machine scored

Cost: Specimen set (includes test, IBM 805/OpScan answer document, key, manual) $4.50; 25 tests (form A or B) $10.00; 50 IBM 805/OpScan answer documents $5.75; keys $1.75 each; manual $2.85.

Publisher: The Psychological Corporation

I.P.I. APTITUDE-INTEL-LIGENCE TEST SERIES: BLOCKS

Industrial Psychology, Inc.

adult

Purpose: Measures apptitude to visualize objects on the basis of three-dimensional cues. Used to screen applicants for positions in the mechanical and technical job fields.

Description: 32 item paper-pencil test of spatial relations and quantitative ability. Examiner required. Suitable for group use. Available in French and Spanish.

Timed: 5 minutes

Range: Adult

Scoring: Hand key

Cost: 20 tests $17.00.

Publisher: Industrial Psychology, Inc.

I.P.I. APTITUDE-INTEL-LIGENCE TEST SERIES: DEXTERITY
Industrial Psychology, Inc.

adult

Purpose: Determines ability to rapidly perform routine motor tasks involving eye-hand coordination. Used to screen applicants for mechanical and technical jobs.

Description: Three one-minute paper-pencil subtests (maze, checks, dots) to demonstrate ability to perform routine motor tasks. Examiner required. Suitable for group use. Available in French and Spanish.

Timed: 3 minutes

Range: Adult

Scoring: Hand key

Cost: 20 tests $17.00.

Publisher: Industrial Psychology, Inc.

I.P.I. APTITUDE-INTEL-LIGENCE TEST SERIES: DIMENSION
Industrial Psychology, Inc.

adult

Purpose: Evaluates ability to visualize objects when seen from different angles. Used to screen applicants for positions in the mechanical and technical job fields.

Description: 48 item paper-pencil test that is a third measure of spatial relations at a high level. Examiner required. Suitable for group use. Available in French and Spanish.

Timed: 5 minutes

Range: Adult

Scoring: Hand key

Cost: 20 tests $17.00.

Publisher: Industrial Psychology, Inc.

I.P.I. APTITUDE-INTEL-LIGENCE TEST SERIES: FACTORY TERMS
Industrial Psychology, Inc.

adult

Purpose: Determines ability to understand the words and information used in factory and mechanical settings. Used to screen applicants for mechanical and technical jobs.

Description: 54 item paper-pencil test of comprehension of high-level mechanical, engineering and factory information. Examiner required. Suitable for group use.

Timed: 10 minutes

Range: Adult

Scoring: Hand key

Cost: 20 tests $17.00.

Publisher: Industrial Psychology, Inc.

I.P.I. APTITUDE-INTELLIGENCE TEST SERIES: FLUENCY
Industrial Psychology, Inc.

adult

Purpose: Assesses aptitude to use words with ease. Used to screen applicants for clerical, sales and supervisory jobs.

Description: Three two-minute paper-pencil subtests measuring ability to write or talk without mentally blocking or searching for the right word. Examiner required. Suitable for group use. Available in French and Spanish.

Timed: 6 minutes

Range: Adult

Scoring: Hand key

Cost: 20 tests $17.00.

Publisher: Industrial Psychology, Inc.

I.P.I. APTITUDE-INTELLIGENCE TEST SERIES: JUDGMENT
Industrial Psychology, Inc.

adult

Purpose: Evaluates an individual's ability to solve difficult problems. Used to screen applicants for clerical, sales and supervisory positions.

Description: 54 item paper-pencil test of aptitude to think logically, to plan and to deal with abstract relations. Examiner required. Suitable for group use. Available in French and Spanish.

Timed: 6 minutes

Range: Adult

Scoring: Hand key

Cost: 20 tests $17.00.

Publisher: Industrial Psychology, Inc.

I.P.I. APTITUDE-INTELLIGENCE TEST SERIES: MEMORY
Industrial Psychology, Inc.

adult

Purpose: Determines ability to remember visual, verbal and numerical materials. Used to screen applicants for clerical, sales and supervisory jobs.

Description: Three two-minute paper-pencil subtests demonstrating aptitude to recognize and recall associations such as names, faces, numbers, and prices. Examiner required. Suitable for group use. Available in French and Spanish.

Timed: 6 minutes

Range: Adult

Scoring: Hand key

Cost: 20 tests $30.00.

Publisher: Industrial Psychology, Inc.

I.P.I. APTITUDE-INTELLIGENCE TEST SERIES: MOTOR APPARATUS
Industrial Psychology, Inc.

adult

Purpose: Measures ability of adults to coordinate eye and hand movements in a specific motor task. Used to screen applicants for positions in the mechanical and technical fields.

Description: Three item test requiring a special motor apparatus for administration. The examination consists of three trials of the same task. The examiner reviews instructions and sample questions with the subjects, sets timer and the test begins. The procedure is repeated two more times. Examiner required. Can be administered to groups only if more than one apparatus is available.

Available in French and Spanish.

Timed: 6 minutes

Range: Adult

Scoring: Hand key

Cost: 20 tests $17.00; Motor Board $125.00.

Publisher: Industrial Psychology, Inc.

I.P.I. APTITUDE-INTELLIGENCE TEST SERIES: NUMBERS
Industrial Psychology, Inc.

adult

Purpose: Measures ability to work rapidly and accurately with numbers. Used to screen applicants for clerical and mechanical positions.

Description: Multiple-item paper-pencil test measuring aptitude for working with number systems such as files, codes, symbols, standard procedures, etc. Examiner required. Suitable for group use.

Timed: 6 minutes

Range: Adult

Scoring: Hand key

Cost: 20 tests $17.00.

Publisher: Industrial Psychology, Inc.

I.P.I. APTITUDE-INTELLIGENCE TEST SERIES: OFFICE TERMS
Industrial Psychology, Inc.

adult

Purpose: Measures ability to understand special terms used in business and industry. Used to screen applicants for positions in the clerical, sales and supervisory job fields.

Description: 54 item paper-pencil

test measures comprehension of information of an office or business nature and general mental ability. It also indicates overqualification for routine, repetitive assignments. Examiner required. Suitable for group use. Available in French and Spanish.

Timed: 6 minutes

Range: Adult

Scoring: Hand key

Cost: 20 tests $17.00.

Publisher: Industrial Psychology, Inc.

I.P.I. APTITUDE-INTELLIGENCE TEST SERIES: PARTS
Industrial Psychology, Inc.

adult

Purpose: Assesses ability to see the whole in relation to its parts. Used to screen applicants for clerical, mechanical, technical, sales, and supervisory positions.

Description: 48 item paper-pencil test of aptitude for visualizing size, shape and spatial relations of objects in two and three dimensions. Reveals the subject's sense of layout and organization. Examiner required. Suitable for group use. Available in French and Spanish.

Timed: 6 minutes

Range: Adult

Scoring: Hand key

Cost: 20 tests $17.00.

Publisher: Industrial Psychology, Inc.

I.P.I. APTITUDE-INTELLIGENCE TEST SERIES: PERCEPTION
Industrial Psychology, Inc.

adult

Purpose: Measures ability to perceive differences in written words and numbers. Used to screen applicants for clerical, sales and supervisory jobs.

Description: 54 item paper-pencil test of ability to rapidly scan and locate details in words and numbers, and to recognize likenesses and differences. Examiner required. Suitable for group use. Available in French and Spanish.

Timed: 6 minutes

Range: Adult

Scoring: Hand key

Cost: 20 tests $17.00.

Publisher: Industrial Psychology, Inc.

I.P.I. APTITUDE-INTELLIGENCE TEST SERIES: PRECISION
Industrial Psychology, Inc.

adult

Purpose: Determines ability to see details in pictures. Used by employers in screening applicants for technical and mechanical jobs with inspection duties.

Description: 48 item paper-pencil test using pictures to test ability to identify objects and rapidly recognize differences and likenesses. Examiner required. Suitable for group use. Available in French and Spanish.

Timed: 5 minutes

Range: Adult

Scoring: Hand key

Cost: 20 tests $17.00.

Publisher: Industrial Psychology, Inc.

I.P.I. APTITUDE-INTELLIGENCE TEST SERIES: SALES TERMS
Industrial Psychology, Inc.

adult

Purpose: Measures ability to understand words and information. Used to assist employers in screening applicants for positions in clerical, sales and supervisory job fields.

Description: 54 item paper-pencil test of comprehension of sales related information. Indicates if a person is overqualified for routine or repetitive assignments. Examiner required. Suitable for group use. Available in French and Spanish.

Timed: 5 minutes

Range: Adult

Scoring: Hand key

Cost: 20 tests $17.00.

Publisher: Industrial Psychology, Inc.

I.P.I. APTITUDE-INTELLIGENCE TEST SERIES: TOOLS
Industrial Psychology, Inc.

adult

Purpose: Evaluates comprehension of simple tools and mechanical equipment. Used to screen applicants for positions in mechanical and technical job fields

Description: 48 item paper-pencil test of ability to recognize pictures of common tools, equipment and machines. Does not require the ability to read or write. Examiner required. Suitable for group use. Available in French and Spanish.

Timed: 5 minutes

Range: Adult

Scoring: Hand key

Cost: 20 tests $17.00.

Publisher: Industrial Psychology, Inc.

I.P.I. EMPLOYEE APTITUDE SERIES: CONTACT PERSONALITY FACTOR (CPF)
IPI Staff, R.B. Cattell, J.E. King, and A.K. Schuettler

adult

Purpose: Determines contact versus non-contact factor in personality. Used for screening, placement and promotion of employees.

Description: 40 item paper-pencil personality test of extroversion versus introversion. Examiner required. Suitable for group use. Available in French and Spanish.

Timed: 10 minutes

Range: Adult

Scoring: Hand key

Cost: 20 tests $17.00.

Publisher: Industrial Psychology, Inc.

I.P.I. EMPLOYEE APTITUDE SERIES: NEUROTIC PERSONALITY FACTOR (NPF)
IPI Staff, R.B. Cattell, J.E. King, and A.K. Schuettler

adult

Purpose: Measures emotional balance and/or the lack of neurotic tendencies in personality. Used to screen applicants for a variety of positions and to place and promote employees.

Description: 40 item paper-pencil test of an individual's general stability

and emotional balance. Examiner required. Suitable for group use. Available in French and Spanish.

Timed: 10 minutes

Range: Adult

Scoring: Hand key

Cost: 20 tests $17.00.

Publisher: Industrial Psychology, Inc.

I.P.I. EMPLOYEE APTITUDE SERIES: SIXTEEN PERSONALITY FACTOR (16PF) TEST
IPI Staff, R.B. Cattell, J.E. King, and A.K. Schuettler

adult

Purpose: Measures 16 basic factors of personality. Used to screen applicants for a variety of positions.

Description: 102 item paper-pencil test of the following traits: bright, mature, dominant, enthusiastic, participating, consistent, adventurous, tough-minded, trustful, conventional, sophisticated, self-confident, liberal, self-sufficient, controlled, and stable. Examiner required. Suitable for group use. Available in French and Spanish.

Timed: 20 minutes

Range: Adult

Scoring: Hand key

Cost: 20 tests $30.00.

Publisher: Industrial Psychology, Inc.

I.P.I. JOB TEST FIELD SERIES: CONTACT CLERK
Industrial Psychology, Inc.

adult

Purpose: Assesses skills and personality of applicants for public relations positions. Used in screening for complaint, information, receptionists, and reservation positions.

Description: Multiple item paper-pencil battery of four aptitude and one personality test. Tests are: Memory, Fluency, Sales Terms, Perception, and Contact Personality factor. For individual test descriptions, see I.P.I. Aptitude-Intelligence Test Series. Examiner required. Suitable for group use. Available in French and Spanish.

Timed: 45 minutes

Range: Adult

Scoring: Hand key

Cost: Complete instruction kits $15.00; test package $8.00; aptitude instruction kits $10.00; aptitude test packages $6.00.

Publisher: Industrial Psychology, Inc.

I.P.I. JOB TEST FIELD SERIES: DENTAL OFFICE ASSISTANT
Industrial Psychology, Inc.

adult

Purpose: Assesses skills of applicants for dental office assistants. Used to screen assistants who will work chairside, doing light secretarial duties, and along with patients and dentist.

Description: Multiple item paper-pencil battery of four aptitude and two personality tests. Tests are: Office Terms, Numbers, Judgment, Perception, Neurotic Personality Factor, and Contact Personality Factor. For individual test descriptions, see I.P.I. Aptitude-Intelligence Test Series. Examiner required. Suitable for group use. Available in French and Spanish.

Timed: 60 minutes

Range: Adult

Scoring: Hand key

Cost: Instruction kits $10.00; test packages $6.00.

Publisher: Industrial Psychology, Inc.

I.P.I. JOB TEST FIELD SERIES: DENTAL TECHNICIAN
Industrial Psychology, Inc.

adult

Purpose: Assesses skills of applicants for a position as a dental technician. Used in screening laboratory worker in four classification levels: cast metal, denture, crown and bridge, porcelain and acrylic.

Description: Multiple item paper-pencil battery of two achievement tests and two personality tests. Tests are: Dexterity, Dimension, Neurotic Personality Factor, and Contact Personality Factor. For individual test descriptions, see I.P.I. Aptitude-Intelligence Test Series. Examiner required. Suitable for group use. Available in French and Spanish.

Timed: 25 minutes

Range: Adult

Scoring: Hand key

Cost: Instruction kits $10.00; test packages $6.00.

Publisher: Industrial Psychology, Inc.

I.P.I. JOB TEST FIELD SERIES: DESIGNER
Industrial Psychology, Inc.

adult

Purpose: Assesses skills and personality of applicants for designer positions. Used in screening for artists, architects, draftsmen, layout men, and photographers.

Description: Multiple item paper-pencil battery of six aptitude and three personality tests. Tests are:

Sales Terms, Precision, Parts, Blocks, Dimension, Dexterity, 16 Personality Factors, Neurotic Personality Factor, and Contact Personality Factor. For individual test descriptions, see I.P.I. Aptitude-Intelligence Test Series. Examiner required. Suitable for group use. Available in French and Spanish.

Timed: 75 minutes

Range: Adult

Scoring: Hand key

Cost: Complete kit $15.00; test packages $8.00 each; aptitude kit $10.00; aptitude test packages $6.00 each.

Publisher: Industrial Psychology, Inc.

I.P.I. JOB TEST FIELD SERIES: ENGINEER
Industrial Psychology, Inc.

adult

Purpose: Assesses skills and personality of applicants seeking various engineering positions. Used in screening for automotive, chemical, electrical, mechanical, and production engineering.

Description: Multiple item paper-pencil battery of seven aptitude and three personality tests. Tests are: Office Terms, Factory Terms, Tools, Numbers, Judgment, Precision, Dimension, 16 Personality Factors, Neurotic Personality Factor, and Contact Personality Factor. For individual test descriptions, see I.P.I. Aptitude-Intelligence Test Series. Examiner required. Suitable for group use. Available in French and Spanish.

Timed: 90 minutes

Range: Adult

Scoring: Hand key

Cost: Complete kit $15.00; test packages $8.00 each; aptitude kits $10.00; aptitude test packages $6.00 each.

Publisher: Industrial Psychology, Inc.

I.P.I. JOB TEST FIELD SERIES: FACTORY MACHINE OPERATOR
Industrial Psychology, Inc.

adult

Purpose: Assesses skills and personality of applicants for various factory machine-oriented positions. Used in screening for cutter, dental lab, lathe, press, sewing, and welder jobs.

Description: Multiple item paper-pencil battery of five aptitude and two personality tests. Tests are: Motor, Precision, Tools, Blocks, Dexterity, Neurotic Personality Factor, and Contact Personality Factor. For individual test descriptions, see I.P.I. Aptitude-Intelligence Test Series. Examiner required. Suitable for group use. Available in French and Spanish.

Timed: 45 minutes

Range: Adult

Scoring: Hand key

Cost: Complete kit $15.00; test packages $8.00 each; aptitude kit $10.00; aptitude test packages $6.00 each.

Publisher: Industrial Psychology, Inc.

I.P.I. JOB TEST FIELD SERIES: FACTORY SUPERVISOR
Industrial Psychology, Inc.

adult

Purpose: Assesses skills and personality for supervisory positions in a factory setting. Used for evaluating the achievement and personality of maintenance and production people, foremen and superintendents.

Description: Multiple item paper-

pencil battery of eight aptitude and three personality tests. Tests are: Office Terms, Factory Terms, Tools, Numbers, Judgment, Fluency, Memory, 16 Personality Factors, Neurotic Personality Factor, and Contact Personality Factor. For individual test descriptions, see I.P.I. Aptitude-Intelligence Test Series. Examiner required. Suitable for group use. Available in French and Spanish.

Timed: 120 minutes

Range: Adult

Scoring: Hand key

Cost: Complete kit $15.00; test packages $8.00 each; aptitude kit $10.00; aptitude test packages $6.00 each.

Publisher: Industrial Psychology, Inc.

I.P.I. JOB TEST FIELD SERIES: GENERAL CLERK
Industrial Psychology, Inc.

adult

Purpose: Assesses skills of applicants for general clerical positions. Used in evaluating skills of typing, filing, billing, transcribing, sorting, writing, and answering the phone.

Description: Multiple item paper-pencil battery of seven aptitude tests. The tests are: Office Terms, Numbers, Perception, Judgment, Fluency, Memory, and Parts. For individual test descriptions, see I.P.I. Aptitude-Intelligence Test Series. Examiner required. Suitable for group use. Available in French and Spanish.

Timed: 40 minutes

Range: Adult

Scoring: Hand key

Cost: Aptitude instruction kit $10.00; aptitude test packages $6.00.

Publisher: Industrial Psychology, Inc.

I.P.I. JOB TEST FIELD SERIES: INSPECTOR
Industrial Psychology, Inc.

adult

Purpose: Assesses skills and personality of applicants for inspector-oriented positions. Used in evaluating skills of checking, classifying, examining, grading, pairing, scaling, and sorting.

Description: Multiple item paper-pencil battery of five aptitude and two personality tests. Tests are: Tools, Precision, Dimension, Parts, Blocks, Neurotic Personality Factor, and Contact Personality Factor. For individual test descriptions, see I.P.I. Aptitude-Intelligence Test Series. Examiner required. Suitable for group use. Available in French and Spanish.

Timed: 60 minutes

Range: Adult

Scoring: Hand key

Cost: Complete kit $15.00; test packages $8.00 each; aptitude kit $10.00; aptitude test packages $6.00 each.

Publisher: Industrial Psychology, Inc.

I.P.I. JOB TEST FIELD SERIES: INSTRUCTOR
Industrial Psychology, Inc.

adult

Purpose: Assesses skills and personality of applicants for various teaching positions. Used in screening for counselors, instructors, safety directors, teachers, and training directors.

Description: Multiple item paper-pencil battery of six aptitude and three personality tests. Tests are: Fluency, Sales Terms, Parts, Memory, Judgment, Perception, 16 Personality

Factors, Neurotic Personality Factor, and Contact Personality Factor. For individual test descriptions, see I.P.I. Aptitude-Intelligence Test Series. Examiner required. Suitable for group use. Available in French and Spanish.

Timed: 90 minutes

Range: Adult

Scoring: Hand key

Cost: Complete kit $15.00; test packages $8.00 each; aptitude kit $10.00; aptitude test packages $6.00 each.

Publisher: Industrial Psychology, Inc.

I.P.I. JOB TEST FIELD SERIES: JUNIOR CLERK
Industrial Psychology, Inc.

adult

Purpose: Assesses skills and personality of entry-level clerical applicants. Used in evaluating skills of checking, coding, indexing, mailing, shipping, sorting, and stocking.

Description: Multiple item paper-pencil battery of three timed aptitude and one untimed personality tests. Tests are: Perception, Office Terms, Numbers, and Contact Personality Factor. For individual test descriptions, see I.P.I. Aptitude-Intelligence Test Series. Examiner required. Suitable for group use. Available in French and Spanish.

Timed: 45 minutes

Range: Adult

Scoring: Hand key

Cost: Complete kit $15.00; test packages $8.00 each; aptitude kit $10.00; aptitude test packages $6.00 each.

Publisher: Industrial Psychology, Inc.

I.P.I. JOB TEST FIELD SERIES: NUMBERS CLERK
Industrial Psychology, Inc.

adult

Purpose: Assesses skills and personality of applicants seeking numerically oriented positions. Used in screening for accounting, billing, insurance, inventory, payroll, and statistical positions.

Description: Multiple item paper-pencil battery of four aptitude and two personality tests. Tests are: Numbers, Perception, Office Terms, Judgment, Neurotic Personality Factor, and Contact Personality Factor. For individual test descriptions, see I.P.I. Aptitude-Intelligence Test Series. Examiner required. Suitable for group use. Available in French and Spanish.

Timed: 45 minutes

Range: Adult

Scoring: Hand key

Cost: Complete kit $15.00; test packages $8.00 each; aptitude kit $10.00; aptitude test packages $6.00 each.

Publisher: Industrial Psychology, Inc.

I.P.I. JOB TEST FIELD SERIES: OFFICE MACHINE OPERATOR
Industrial Psychology, Inc.

adult

Purpose: Assesses skills and personality of applicants for positions utilizing office machines. Used in screening for accounting, billing, IBM, keypunch, and typist positions.

Description: Multiple item paper-pencil battery of four aptitude and two personality tests. Tests are: Office Terms, Perception, Parts, Dexterity, Neurotic Personality Factor, and Contact Personality Factor.

For individual test descriptions, see I.P.I. Aptitude-Intelligence Test Series. Examiner required. Suitable for group use. Available in French and Spanish.

Timed: 45 minutes

Range: Adult

Scoring: Hand key

Cost: Complete kit $15.00; test packages $8.00 each; aptitude kit $10.00; aptitude test packages $6.00 each.

Publisher: Industrial Psychology, Inc.

I.P.I. JOB TEST FIELD SERIES: OFFICE SUPERVISOR
Industrial Psychology, Inc.

adult

Purpose: Assesses skills and personality of applicants for supervisory positions in an office setting. Used in screening for administrator, controller, department head, and vice-president.

Description: Multiple item paper-pencil battery of seven aptitude and three personality tests. Tests are: Office Terms, Numbers, Perception, Judgment, Fluency, Memory, Parts, 16 Personality Factors, Neurotic Personality Factor, and Contact Personality Factor. For individual test descriptions, see I.P.I. Aptitude-Intelligence Test Series. Examiner required. Suitable for group use. Available in French and Spanish.

Timed: 120 minutes

Range: Adult

Scoring: Hand key

Cost: Complete kit $15.00; test packages $8.00 each; aptitude kit $10.00; aptitude test packages $6.00 each.

Publisher: Industrial Psychology, Inc.

I.P.I. JOB TEST FIELD SERIES: OFFICE TECHNICAL
Industrial Psychology, Inc.

adult

Purpose: Assesses skills and personality of applicants for various office technical positions. Used for evaluating the achievement and personality of such people as accountants, estimators, methods clerks, statisticians, and time study experts.

Description: Multiple item paper-pencil battery of six aptitude and three personality tests. Tests are: Office Terms, Numbers, Perception, Parts, Memory, Judgment, 16 Personality Factors, Neurotic Personality Factor, and Contact Personality Factor. For individual test descriptions, see I.P.I. Aptitude-Intelligence Test Series. Examiner required. Suitable for group use. Available in French and Spanish.

Timed: 90 minutes

Range: Adult

Scoring: Hand key

Cost: Complete kit $15.00; test packages $8.00 each; aptitude kit $10.00; aptitude test packages $6.00 each.

Publisher: Industrial Psychology, Inc.

I.P.I. JOB TEST FIELD SERIES: OPTOMETRIC ASSISTANT
Industrial Psychology, Inc.

adult

Purpose: Assesses skills and personality of applicants for positions of optometric assistant. Used in screening those who will act as a support person for optometrists, working with practitioner and patients and doing reception and light secretarial duties.

Description: Multiple item paper-

pencil battery of five aptitude and two personality tests. Tests are: Office Terms, Numbers, Perception, Judgment, Fluency, Neurotic Personality Factor, and Contact Personality Factor. For individual test descriptions, see I.P.I. Aptitude-Intelligence Test Series. Examiner required. Suitable for group use. Available in French and Spanish.

Timed: 45 minutes

Range: Adult

Scoring: Hand key

Cost: Instruction kits $10.00; test packages $6.00.

Publisher: Industrial Psychology, Inc.

I.P.I. JOB TEST FIELD SERIES: SALES CLERK
Industrial Psychology, Inc.

adult

Purpose: Assesses skills and personality of applicants for low level sales positions. Used in screening for department store, post office, teller, ticketer, and waitress positions.

Description: Multiple item paper-pencil battery of five aptitude and one personality tests. Tests are: Sales Terms, Numbers, Perception, Fluency, Memory, and Contact Personality Factor. For individual test descriptions, see I.P.I. Aptitude-Intelligence Test Series. Examiner required. Suitable for group use. Available in French and Spanish.

Timed: 45 minutes

Range: Adult

Scoring: Hand key

Cost: Complete kit $15.00; test packages $8.00 each; aptitude kit $10.00; aptitude test packages $6.00 each.

Publisher: Industrial Psychology, Inc.

I.P.I. JOB TEST FIELD SERIES: SALES ENGINEER
Industrial Psychology, Inc.

adult

Purpose: Assesses skills and personality of applicants for technically oriented sales positions. Used for screening for claims work, adjusting, purchasing, technical sales, underwriting.

Description: A paper-pencil battery of six aptitude and three personality tests. Tests are: Sales Terms, Numbers, Judgment, Fluency, Memory, Parts, 16 Personality Factors, Neurotic Personality Factor, and Contact Personality Factor. For individual test descriptions, see I.P.I. Aptitude-Intelligence Test Series. Examiner required. Suitable for group use. Available in French and Spanish.

Timed: 75 minutes

Range: Adult

Scoring: Hand key

Cost: Complete kit $15.00; test packages $8.00 each; aptitude kit $10.00; aptitude test packages $6.00 each.

Publisher: Industrial Psychology, Inc.

I.P.I. JOB TEST FIELD SERIES: SALES PERSON
Industrial Psychology, Inc.

adult

Purpose: Assesses skills of applicants for various sales positions. Used in screening for agent, demonstrator, insurance, retail, wholesale, and route sales positions.

Description: Multiple item paper-pencil battery of five aptitude and two personality tests. Tests are: Sales Terms, Numbers, Perception, Fluency, Memory, 16 Personality Factors, and Contact Personality Factor. For individual test descriptions, see I.P.I. Aptitude-Intelligence Test Series. Examiner required. Suitable for group use. Available in French and Spanish.

Timed: 75 minutes

Range: Adult

Scoring: Hand key

Cost: Complete kit $15.00; test packages $8.00 each; aptitude kit $10.00; aptitude test packages $6.00 each.

Publisher: Industrial Psychology, Inc.

I.P.I. JOB TEST FIELD SERIES: SALES SUPERVISOR
Industrial Psychology, Inc.

adult

Purpose: Assesses skills and personality of applicants for supervisory positions in the sales field. Used in screening for advertising, credit, merchandise, service, and store sales positions.

Description: Multiple item paper-pencil battery of seven aptitude and three personality tests. Tests are: Sales Terms, Numbers, Perception, Parts, Fluency, Judgment, Memory, 16 Personality Factors, Neurotic Personality Factor, and Contact Personality Factor. For individual test descriptions, see I.P.I. Aptitude-Intelligence Test Series. Examiner required. Suitable for group use. Available in French and Spanish.

Timed: 120 minutes

Range: Adult

Scoring: Hand key

Cost: Complete kit $15.00; test packages $8.00 each; aptitude kit $10.00; aptitude test packages $6.00 each.

Publisher: Industrial Psychology, Inc.

I.P.I. JOB TEST FIELD SERIES: SCIENTIST
Industrial Psychology, Inc.

adult

Purpose: Assesses skills and personality of applicants for various positions in the science field. Used in screening for biologist, chemist, economist, inventory, physicist, and research fields.

Description: Multiple item paper-pencil battery of seven aptitude and three personality tests. Tests are: Factory Terms, Office Terms, Numbers, Judgment, Precision, Dimension, Dexterity, 16 Personality Factors, Neurotic Personality Factor, and Contact Personality Factor. For individual test descriptions, see I.P.I. Aptitude-Intelligence Test Series. Examiner required. Suitable for group use. Available in French and Spanish.

Timed: 90 minutes

Range: Adult

Scoring: Hand key

Cost: Complete kit $15.00; test packages $8.00 each; aptitude kit $10.00; aptitude test packages $6.00 each.

Publisher: Industrial Psychology, Inc.

I.P.I. JOB TEST FIELD SERIES: SECRETARY
Industrial Psychology, Inc.

adult

Purpose: Assesses skills of applicants for secretarial positions. Used in screening for stenographers, executive, legal, private and social secretaries.

Description: Multiple item paper-pencil battery of six aptitude and three personality tests. Tests are: Sales Terms, Perception, Judgment,

Parts, Fluency, Memory, 16 Personality Factor, Contact Personality Factor, and Neurotic Personality Factor. For individual test descriptions, see I.P.I. Aptitude-Intelligence Test Series. Examiner required. Suitable for group use. Available in French and Spanish.

Timed: 75 minutes

Range: Adult

Scoring: Hand key

Cost: Complete kit $15.00; test packages $8.00 each; aptitude kit $10.00; aptitude test packages $6.00 each.

Publisher: Industrial Psychology, Inc.

I.P.I. JOB TEST FIELD SERIES: SEMI-SKILLED WORKER
Industrial Psychology, Inc.

adult

Purpose: Assesses skills and personality of applicants for semi-skilled mechanical positions. Used in screening for assembler, construction, helper, and production positions.

Description: Multiple item paper-pencil battery of four aptitude and two personality tests. Tests are: Precision, Motor, Blocks, Tools, Neurotic Personality Factor, and Contact Personality Factor. For individual test descriptions, see I.P.I. Aptitude-Intelligence Test Series. Examiner required. Suitable for group use. Available in French and Spanish.

Timed: 75 minutes

Range: Adult

Scoring: Hand key

Cost: Complete kit $15.00; test packages $8.00 each; aptitude kit $10.00; aptitude test packages $6.00 each.

Publisher: Industrial Psychology, Inc.

I.P.I. JOB TEST FIELD SERIES: SENIOR CLERK
Industrial Psychology, Inc.

adult

Purpose: Assesses skills and personality of applicants for high level clerical or administrative positions. Used in screening for administrative, bookkeeping, correspondence, cost, and production positions.

Description: Multiple item paper-pencil battery of five aptitude and two personality tests. Tests are: Office Terms, Perception, Numbers, Judgment, Fluency, 16 Personality Factors, and Contact Personality Factor. For individual test descriptions, see I.P.I. Aptitude-Intelligence Test Series. Examiner required. Suitable for group use. Available in French and Spanish.

Timed: 60 minutes

Range: Adult

Scoring: Hand key

Cost: Complete kit $15.00; test packages $8.00 each; aptitude kit $10.00; aptitude test packages $6.00 each.

Publisher: Industrial Psychology, Inc.

I.P.I. JOB TEST FIELD SERIES: SKILLED WORKER
Industrial Psychology, Inc.

adult

Purpose: Assesses skills of applicants for various skilled worker positions. Used in screening for linemen, machinists, maintenance workers, mechanics, and tool-makers.

Description: Multiple item paper-pencil battery of seven aptitude and two personality tests. Tests are: Office Terms, Factory Terms, Tools, Numbers, Precision, Motor, Blocks, 16 Personality Factors, and Neurotic

Personality Factor. For individual test descriptions, see I.P.I. Aptitude-Intelligence Test Series. Examiner required. Suitable for group use. Available in French and Spanish.

Timed: 75 minutes

Range: Adult

Scoring: Hand key

Cost: Complete kit $15.00; test packages $8.00 each; aptitude kit $10.00; aptitude test packages $6.00 each.

Publisher: Industrial Psychology, Inc.

I.P.I. JOB TEST FIELD SERIES: UNSKILLED WORKER
Industrial Psychology, Inc.

adult

Purpose: Assesses skills and personality of applicants for positions in the low level mechanical job field. Used for screening janitors, laborers, loaders, material handlers, packers, and truckers.

Description: Multiple item paper-pencil battery of three aptitude and one personality test. Tests are: Tools, Precision, Motor, and Neurotic Personality Factor. For individual test descriptions, see I.P.I. Aptitude-Intelligence Test Series. Examiner required. Suitable for group use. Available in French and Spanish.

Timed: 30 minutes

Range: Adult

Scoring: Hand key

Cost: Complete kit $15.00; test packages $8.00 each; aptitude kit $10.00; aptitude test packages $6.00 each.

Publisher: Industrial Psychology, Inc.

I.P.I. JOB TEST FIELD SERIES: VEHICLE OPERATOR
Industrial Psychology, Inc.

adult

Purpose: Assesses skills and personality of applicants for various vehicle operator positions. Used in screening for crane, elevator, motorman, taxi, teamster, tractor, and truck driving positions.

Description: Multiple item paper-pencil battery of five aptitude and two personality tests. Tests are Tools: Precision, Dimension, Dexterity, Motor, Neurotic Personality Factor, and Contact Personality Factor. For individual test descriptions, see I.P.I. Aptitude-Intelligence Test Series. Examiner required. Suitable for group use. Available in French and Spanish.

Timed: 45 minutes

Range: Adult

Scoring: Hand key

Cost: Complete kit $15.00; test packages $8.00 each; aptitude kit $10.00; aptitude test packages $6.00 each.

Publisher: Industrial Psychology, Inc.

I.P.I. JOB TEST FIELD SERIES: WRITER
Industrial Psychology, Inc.

adult

Purpose: Assesses skills and personality of applicants for writing positions. Used in screening for advertising, author, copywriter, critic, editor, journalist, and public relations positions.

Description: Multiple item paper-pencil battery of six aptitude and three personality tests. Tests are: Sales Terms, Perception, Judgment, Fluency, Memory, Parts, 16

Personality Factors, Neurotic Personality Factor, and Contact Personality Factor. For individual test descriptions, see I.P.I. Aptitude-Intelligence Test Series. Examiner required. Suitable for group use. Available in French and Spanish.

Timed: 90 minutes

Range: Adult

Scoring: Hand key

Cost: Complete kit $15.00; test packages $8.00 each; aptitude kit $10.00; aptitude test packages $6.00 each.

Publisher: Industrial Psychology, Inc.

year study in over 100 insurance companies, batteries have been developed for each entry-level position in each JEPS member company. Use restricted to insurance companies. Examiner required. Suitable for group use.

Timed: Each subtest varies

Range: Adult

Scoring: Hand key

Cost: Test $.30-$.50 per applicant depending on number of subtests and volume ordered.

Publisher: Life Office Management Association

JOB EFFECTIVENESS PREDICTION SYSTEM (JEPS)
Personnel Decisions Research Institute for Life Office Management Association

adult

Purpose: Measures a variety of skills required for a wide range of clerical, technical, and professional positions. Used for selection and placement of entry-level employees in life and property/casualty insurance companies.

Description: 11 multiple item paper-pencil tests measuring verbal, mathematical, and clerical skills. The tests are: Numerical Ability-1, Numerical Ability-2, Mathematical Skill, Spelling, Language Usage, Reading Comprehension-1, Reading Comprehension-2, Verbal Comprehension, Filing, Coding and Converting, and Comparing and Checking. Not all of the tests are required for each selection decision. In many cases, two, three or four of the tests used in combination will accurately predict potential job performance. Each of the eleven tests is independent. Developed following the Uniform Guidelines on Employee Selection Procedures during a five

JOB EFFECTIVENESS PREDICTION SYSTEM: CODING AND CONVERTING (JEPS: TEST CODE K)
Personnel Decisions Research Institute for Life Office Management Association

adult

Purpose: Measures the ability to quickly and accurately use conversion tables and coding guides. Used for selection and placement of entry-level clerical/technical employees in life and property/casualty insurance companies.

Description: 85 item paper-pencil multiple-choice test consisting of three sections. In the first section the examinee indicates the correct annual premium for 20 monthly premiums using a table that converts monthly premiums to annual premiums. In the second section the examinee indicates the correct letter code for 25 annual premiums using a table of letter codes for annual premiums. In the last section both tables are presented, and the examinee must indicate the correct code for 40 monthly premiums. Use restricted to insurance companies. Examiner required. Suitable for group use.

Timed: 8 minutes

Range: Adult

Scoring: Hand key

Cost: Test $.30-$.50 per applicant depending on volume ordered.

Publisher: Life Office Management Association

JOB EFFECTIVENESS PREDICTION SYSTEM: COMPARING AND CHECKING (JEPS: TEST CODE L)

Personnel Decisions Research Institute for Life Office Management Association

adult

Purpose: Measures clerical checking abilities with numbers and words. Used for selection and placement of entry-level clerical/technical employees in life and property/casualty insurance companies.

Description: 40 item paper-pencil multiple-choice test measuring the ability to compare words and numbers and detect differences. The examinee is presented with "correct" lists of words and numbers (names, addresses, dollar amounts, etc.) and "lists to be checked." Subjects are asked to count the number of errors per line. Use restricted to insurance companies. Examiner required. Suitable for group use.

Timed: 7 minutes

Range: Adult

Scoring: Hand key

Cost: Test $.30-$.50 per applicant depending on volume ordered.

Publisher: Life Office Management Association

JOB EFFECTIVENESS PREDICTION SYSTEM: FILING (JEPS: TEST CODE J)

Personnel Decisions Research Institute for Life Office Management Association

adult

Purpose: Measures general filing skills. Used for selection and placement of entry-level clerical/technical employees in life and property/casualty insurance companies.

Description: 60 item paper-pencil multiple-choice test measuring the ability to file materials according to given instructions. The examinee is presented with "existing files" with numbered slots between entries and lists of entries "to be filed." The examinee indicates the number of the slot into which each of the entries should be filed. Use restricted to insurance companies. Examiner required. Suitable for group use.

Timed: 5 minutes

Range: Adult

Scoring: Hand key

Cost: Test $.30-$.50 per applicant depending on volume ordered.

Publisher: Life Office Management Association

JOB EFFECTIVENESS PREDICTION SYSTEM: LANGUAGE USAGE (JEPS: TEST CODE E)

Personnel Decisions Research Institute for Life Office Management Association

adult

Purpose: Measures knowledge of the proper usage of the English language. Used for selection and placement of entry-level clerical/technical employees in life and property/casualty insurance companies.

Description: 94 item paper-pencil test measuring knowledge of grammar, punctuation, capitalization, and the formation of plurals. A reading selection is divided into two parts, and for each part the subject indicates whether or not there are any errors. Use restricted to insurance companies. Examiner required. Suitable for group use.

Timed: 12 minutes

Range: Adult

Scoring: Hand key

Cost: Test $.30-$.50 per applicant depending on volume ordered.

Publisher: Life Office Management Association

JOB EFFECTIVENESS PREDICTION SYSTEM: MATHEMATICAL SKILL (JEPS: TEST CODE C)

Personnel Decisions Research Institute for Life Office Management Association

adult

Purpose: Measures ability to work with mathematical relationships and formulas. Used for selection and placement of entry-level clerical/technical employees in life and property/casualty insurance companies.

Description: 23 item paper-pencil multiple-choice test measuring skill in solving and manipulating mathematical relationships and formulas. One section involves solving formulas and the other requires selecting the appropriate formula to use in solving problems. Use restricted to insurance companies. Examiner required. Suitable for group use.

Timed: 20 minutes

Range: Adult

Scoring: Hand key

Cost: Test $.30-$.50 per applicant depending on volume ordered.

Publisher: Life Office Management Association

JOB EFFECTIVENESS PREDICTION SYSTEM: NUMERICAL ABILITY-1 (JEPS: TEST CODE A)

Personnel Decisions Research Institute for Life Office Management Association

adult

Purpose: Measures ability to add, subtract, multiply, and divide. Used for selection and placement of entry-level clerical/technical employees in life and property/casualty insurance companies.

Description: 50 item paper-pencil multiple-choice test measuring the ability to perform basic arithmetic operations. Test items include addition, subtraction, multiplication, and division with whole numbers, fractions, decimals, and percentages. Use restricted to insurance companies. Examiner required. Suitable for group use.

Timed: 8 minutes

Range: Adult

Scoring: Hand key

Cost: Test $.30-$.50 per applicant depending on volume ordered.

Publisher: Life Office Management Association

JOB EFFECTIVENESS PREDICTION SYSTEM: NUMERICAL ABILITY-2 (JEPS: TEST CODE B)

Personnel Decisions Research Institute for Life Office Management Association

adult

Purpose: Measures ability to work with decimals and percentages. Used for selection and placement of entry-level clerical/technical employees in life and property/casualty insurance companies.

Description: 50 item paper-pencil multiple-choice and true- false test measuring numerical ability with problems requiring work with percentages, rounding off decimal numbers and approximating correct answers. Use restricted to insurance companies. Examiner required. Suitable for group use.

Timed: 15 minutes

Range: Adult

Scoring: Hand key

Cost: Test $.30-$.50 per applicant depending on volume ordered.

Publisher: Life Office Management Association

JOB EFFECTIVENESS PREDICTION SYSTEM: READING COMPREHENSION 1 (JEPS: TEST CODE F)
Personnel Decisions Research Institute for Life Office Management Association

adult

Purpose: Measures ability to understand written instructions. Used for selection and placement of entry-level clerical/technical employees in life and property/casualty insurance companies.

Description: 30 item paper-pencil multiple-choice test measuring the ability to understand written directions, definitions and procedures. There are several reading passages, each followed by questions about the passage. Use restricted to insurance companies. Examiner required. Suitable for group use.

Timed: 30 minutes

Range: Adult

Scoring: Hand key

Cost: Test $.30-$.50 per applicant

depending on volume ordered.

Publisher: Life Office Management Association

JOB EFFECTIVENESS PREDICTION SYSTEM: READING COMPREHENSION-2 (JEPS: TEST CODE G)
Personnel Decisions Research Institute for Life Office Management Association

adult

Purpose: Measures level of general reading comprehension. Used for selection and placement of entry-level clerical/technical employees in life and property/casualty insurance companies.

Description: 35 item paper-pencil multiple-choice test measuring reading comprehension at approximately a grade ll-13 reading level. There are several reading passages, each followed by questions about the passage. Use restricted to insurance companies. Examiner required. Suitable for group use.

Timed: 30 minutes

Range: Adult

Scoring: Hand key

Cost: Test $.30-$.50 per applicant depending on volume ordered.

Publisher: Life Office Management Association

JOB EFFECTIVENESS PREDICTION SYSTEM: SPELLING (JEPS: TEST CODE D)
Personnel Decisions Research Institute for Life Office Management Association

adult

Purpose: Measures ability to recognize whether or not words are correctly spelled. Used for selection and placement of entry-level clerical/technical employees in life and property/casualty insurance companies.

Description: 85 item paper-pencil test consisting of a list of words, some spelled correctly, some incorrectly. The examinee indicates whether each word is spelled correctly or not. Use restricted to insurance companies. Examiner required. Suitable for group use.

Timed: 7 minutes

Range: Adult

Scoring: Hand key

Cost: Test $.30-$.50 per applicant depending on volume ordered.

Publisher: Life Office Management Association

JOB EFFECTIVENESS PREDICTION SYSTEM: VERBAL COMPREHENSION (JEPS: TEST CODE H)
Personnel Decisions Research Institute for Life Office Management Association

adult

Purpose: Measures general word knowledge. Used for selection and placement of entry-level clerical/technical employees in life and property/casualty insurance companies.

Description: 35 item paper-pencil multiple-choice test measuring vocabulary and word knowledge. All the words are general in nature rather than taken from specialized or esoteric vocabularies. Use restricted to insurance companies. Examiner required. Suitable for group use.

Timed: 6 minutes

Range: Adult

Scoring: Hand key

Cost: Test $.30-$.50 per applicant depending on volume ordered.

Publisher: Life Office Management Association

KUDER OCCUPATIONAL INTEREST SURVEY, FORM DD (KOIS)
Frederic Kuder

teen, adult   grades 11-UP

Purpose: Measures how an individual's interests compare with those of satisfied workers or students in a number of occupational fields. Used with high school and college students and adults for career planning, vocational guidance and academic counseling.

Description: 100 item paper-pencil inventory assessing subject's interests in a number of areas related to occupational fields and educational majors. Test items consist of a list of three activities. Subject indicates for each item which activity he likes the most and which he likes the least. Compares subject's interests with those of satisfied workers in 126 specific occupational groups and satisfied students in 48 college major groups. The Report of Scores lists scores on occupational and college major scales separately, in rank order for each student. All respondents receive scores on all scales, including some non- traditional occupations for men and women. The interpretive leaflet helps subjects understand and use these scores. A revised General Manual provides technical data regarding reliability, validity, scoring, interpretation, and compliance with Title IX regulations. Optional interpretive guides include: Expanding Your Future (a guide to help subjects interpret and use their scores) and Counseling with the Kuder Occupational Interest Survey Form DD (a handbook for counselors). Sixth-grade reading level required. Self-administered. Suitable for group use.

Timed: 30-40 minutes

Range: Grades 11-adult

Scoring: Computer scoring available

Cost: Specimen set (includes survey booklet, interpretive leaflet, general manual, and scoring for 1 individual) $5.90; materials and scoring for 20 persons $59.90. No charge for general manual if requested when ordering.

Publisher: Science Research Associates, Inc.

LICENSURE, CERTIFICATION, REGISTRATION, AND QUALIFYING EXAMINATIONS: PROFESSIONAL EXAMINATION DIVISION
The Psychological Corporation

---

adult

Purpose: Assesses skills and competence of professionals in various areas. Used by local, state, and national organizations and agencies for licensing, certifying, registering, and qualifying members of their respective occupations.

Description: Multiple item, paper-pencil tests used to establish credentials attesting to the skill and competence of those professionals meeting or exceeding minimum standards. Some of the programs administered by the Professional Examination Division are:
Medical Record Registration and Accreditation Examinations: for medical record administrators and technicians for the American Medical Record Association.
Certification Examinations for Nurse Anesthetists: for initial certification by the Council of Nurse Anesthetists.
Certification Examinations for Computer Professionals: including Certificates in Data Processing and Computer Programming for the Institute for Certification of Computer Professionals.
Certification Examinations for

Occupational Therapists and Occupational Therapy Assistants: for the American-Occupational Therapy Association.
Accreditation Examinations for Personnel and Industrial Relations Professionals: for the Personnel Accreditation Institute.
Cosmetology Licensure Examinations: for cosmetologists, cosmetology teachers, manicurists, and estheticians by the National-Interstate Council of State Boards of Cosmetology.
Psychiatric Technician Licensing Examinations: for Arkansas and Colorado.
Certifying Examination for Surgical Technologists: for the Association of Surgical Technologists.
Certification Examination for Critical-Care Nurses: for the AACN Certification Corporation of the American Association of Critical-Care Nurses.
Certification Examinations for Employment Consultants: for the National Association of Personnel Consultants.
Certification Examination for Neurosurgical Nurses: for the American Board of Neurosurgical Nursing.
Registration Examination for Electroencephalographic Technologists: for the American Board of Registration of Electroencephalographic Technologists.
Certification Examination for Professional Marketing Communicators: for the Business/Professional Advertising Association.
Certification Examination for Enterostomal Therapists: for the International Association of Enterostomal Therapy.
Registration Examination for Radiography Technologists and Radiography Career Challenge Examination: for the American Registry of Clinical Radiography Technologists.
Certification Examination for Professional Code Administrators: for the

National Academy of Code Administration.

Certification Examination for Emergency Nurses: for the Board of Certification for Emergency Nursing. Registration Examinations for Optometric Technicians and Optometric Assistants: for the American Optometric Association. Certification Examination for Orthopedic Physician Assistants: for the National Board for Certification of Orthopedic Physician Assistants. Certification Examination for Medical Staff Coordinators: for the National Association--Medical Staff Services. Examination Series for Membership: by The American Institute of Real Estate Appraisers. Certification Examination for Tumor Registrars: for the National Tumor Registrars Association, Inc. Certification Examination for Practitioners in Infection Control: for the Certification Board of Infection Control.

Tests are given in designated test centers. Applicants must complete and file an application and the appropriate fee by specific deadlines. For specific content and cost information, contact the publisher or the relevant association. Examiner required. Suitable for group use.

Timed: Approximately 4 hours per test

Range: Adults

Scoring: Computer scoring service provided

Cost: Contact publisher.

Publisher: The Professional Examinations Division/The Psychological Corporation

LIGONDE EQUIVALENCE TEST
Paultre Ligondé

adult

Purpose: Measures grade level ability of adults who have been out of school 20-30 years. Used when determination of school grade level is relevant to employment qualifications and for placement in adult education programs.

Description: Multiple item paper-pencil test assessing the grade level of adults who have long been out of school. Scoring is based on what students from a particular grade level should retain in terms of verbal and numerical skills. Used for employee selection for positions requiring verbal communication or clerical skills, in determination of school levels for trade or labor unions, and for issuance of competency cards. Normed on 3,000 French and English Canadians who left school 20-30 years ago. Available in two forms: GE and HE both including questions on knowledge of the second language. Examiner required. Suitable for group use.
CANADIAN PUBLISHER

Timed: 15 minutes

Range: Adults

Scoring: Hand key

Cost: Specimen key $3.00.

Publisher: Institute of Psychological Research, Inc.

MATHEMATICAL ACHIEVEMENT TEST

adult

Purpose: Measures general skills of algebra, geometry and mathematics at the secondary school level. Used in employee selection for clerical and technical positions.

Description: Multiple item paper-pencil achievement test assesses to what extent the subject can apply the principles of algebra, geometry and general mathematics as taught in secondary schools. Norms are based on a group of matriculated boys and girls. Restricted to competent persons properly registered with either the South African Medical and Dental Council or Test Commission of The Republic of South Africa. Examiner required. Suitable for group use. Afrikaans version available.
SOUTH AFRICAN PUBLISHER

Timed: 23 minutes

Range: Job applicants with at least 10 years of education

Scoring: Hand key; examiner evaluated

Cost: Contact publisher.

Publisher: National Institute for Personnel Research

MECHANICAL ABILITY TEST
J.R. Morrisby

all ages

Purpose: Measures natural mechanical aptitude (not learned knowledge) in adults. Used to predict potential in most areas of engineering, especially electrical and mechanical, in assembly work, carpentry and building trades.

Description: 35 item paper-pencil test. Each item consists of an illustrated mechanical principle and a question with five alternative answers. A knowledge of theoretical physics is not required since the test is not intended to measure the level of mechanical knowledge the subject has attained. Materials include the booklet, manual, specimen set, answer sheets, and scoring key. The test is restricted to examiners who provide evidence of adequate training and practical experience in the use of such tests. Examiner required. Suitable for group use.
BRITISH PUBLISHER

Timed: 15 minutes

Range: Average 11-superior adult

Scoring: Hand key; examiner evaluated.

Cost: Contact publisher.

Publisher: Educational and Industrial Test Services Ltd.

MINNESOTA ENGINEERING ANALOGIES TEST
Refer to page 411.

MINNESOTA SPATIAL RELATIONS TEST
Refer to page 535.

MORRISBY DIFFERENTIAL TEST BATTERY (DTB)
Refer to page 801.

MULTIFUNCTIONAL WORK TASK UNIT
Refer to page 857.

NATIONAL ACADEMIC APTITUDE TESTS-VERBAL INTELLIGENCE
Refer to page 380.

NATIONAL BUSINESS ENTRANCE TESTS
Refer to page 200.

NATIONAL BUSINESS ENTRANCE TESTS-BOOK-KEEPING TEST
Refer to page 200.

NATIONAL BUSINESS ENTRANCE TESTS-BUSINESS FUNDAMENTALS AND GENERAL INFORMATION TEST
Refer to page 201.

NATIONAL BUSINESS ENTRANCE TESTS-MACHINE CALCULATION TEST
Refer to page 201.

NATIONAL BUSINESS ENTRANCE TESTS-STENOGRAPHIC TEST
Refer to page 201.

NON-READING APTITUDE BATTERY (NATB)
U.S. Employment Service

adult

Purpose: Measures vocational aptitudes of individuals with low level of literacy skills. Used for vocational counseling and employment screening.

Description: 14 verbal subtests of nine aptitudes to help individuals with low reading skills choose an occupation. The test measures the following aptitudes: General Learning Ability, Verbal Ability, Numerical Ability, Spatial Aptitude, Form Perception, Clerical Perception, Motor Coordination, Finger Dexterity, and Manual Dexterity. The aptitudes are tested orally through procedures which involve neither reading nor writing. The subjects performance is interpreted according to the Occupational Aptitude Patterns (OAPs). The subject's scores are compared to those of successful individuals in various occupations. High, medium or low probability of success in different employment settings is estimated for the individual. Materials consist of test booklets in which all answers are marked, a pegboard for place and turn tests and a Finger Dexterity Board. Use must be authorized in the U.S. by State Employment Security Agencies, and in Canada by the Canadian Employment and Immigration Commission. Examiner required. Suitable for group use.

Timed: 2 hours

Range: Adult

Scoring: Hand key

Cost: Available through State Employment Agency only.

Publisher: U.S. Dept. of Labor

NORMAL, INTERMEDIATE AND HIGH LEVEL BATTERIES

adult

Purpose: Measures mental abilities and verbal skills related to many clerical and technical positions. Suitable for matriculants and higher.

Description: Three batteries of paper-pencil tests measure three levels of mental and verbal abilities. The Normal Battery, used with standards 6-10 and job applicants with 8-11 years of education, contains five tests: mental alertness, reading comprehension, vocabulary, spelling, and computation. The Intermediate Battery, used with standards 7-10 and job applicants with 9-12 years of education, contains seven tests: mental alertness, arithmetical problems, computation, spot-the-error, reading comprehension, vocabulary, and spelling. The High Level Battery, used with a wide range of groups at matric and higher levels, contains six tests: mental alertness, arithmetical problems, reading comprehension (English, Afrikaans) and vocabulary (English, Afrikaans). Norms provided for all three batteries for their appropriate levels. Restricted to competent persons properly registered with either the South African medical and Dental Council or Test Commission of the Republic of South Africa. Examiner required. Suitable for group use. Afrikaans version available. SOUTH AFRICAN PUBLISHER

Timed: Normal, 120 minutes; Intermediate, 165 minutes; High Level, 117 minutes

Range: Job applicants with 8 years of education and up

Scoring: Hand key; examiner evaluated

Cost: Contact publisher.

Publisher: National Institute for Personnel Research

ONE MINUTE PER-FLU-DEX TESTS
F.J. Holmes

---

adult

Purpose: Measures abilities desired in factory and office jobs. Used for evaluation of applicants for employment.

Description: Seven paper-pencil test battery measuring office and industrial skills: Per-Symb, measuring symbol number substitution; Per-Verb, letter perception and counting; Per-Numb, number perception and counting; Flu-Verb, word completion, verbal fluency; Flu-Num, arithmetical computation; Dex-Man, manual speed of movement; and Dex-Aim, aiming accuracy and speed. Materials include profile-guidance sheets. Each test may be purchased and used separately. Examiner required. Suitable for

group use.

Timed: 1 minute per test

Range: Adult

Scoring: Hand scoring

Cost: Specimen set $2.20; 25 tests $2.20; 100-$7.70 (specify form); 25 profiles $2.20; 100-$7.70; examination kit for 25 $16.50.

Publisher: Psychometric Affiliates

PERSONNEL TEST BATTERY (PTB)
Saville and Holdsworth, Ltd.

---

adult

Purpose: Evaluates skills relevant to any job which requires the quick and accurate routine use of numbers, words and other symbols. Assesses skills required for clerks, bookkeepers, typists, data processors, sales persons, nurses, and others.

Description: Six paper-pencil multiple-choice aptitude tests arranged in two levels. Both levels assess language proficiency, numeracy, and perceptual accuracy. Level 1 measures these abilities in terms of basic skills and comprehension and includes the following tests: Verbal Usage (VP1), Numerical Computation (NP2), and Checking (CO3). Level 2 measures similar skills at a more advanced level involving higher order reasoning and includes the following tests: Verbal meaning (VP5), Numerical Reasoning (NP6), and Classification (CP4). Together, the tests cover a wide range of abilities for persons with no formal educational background through the GCE 'O' level and 'A' level. Two optioal tests are available which measure basic clerical checking skills: Basic Checking (CP7) and Audio Checking (CP8). The combination of PTB tests administered will depend on the specific job and its context. Examiner required. Suitable for group use.

BRITISH PUBLISHER

Timed: 71 minutes complete battery; 7-10 minutes per test

Range: Adult

Scoring: Hand key; may be computer scored

Cost: 10 question booklets £16.00; 50 answer sheets (specify level) £16.00; key £3.00.

Publisher: Saville and Holdsworth, Ltd.

PERSONNEL TEST BATTERY: AUDIO CHECKING (PTB:CP8)
Saville and Holdsworth, Ltd.

adult

Purpose: Tests an individual's ability to receive and check information which is presented orally. Used for selection of clerical staff who must process information presented orally as in tele-sales or airline/hotel bookings.

Description: 60 item paper-pencil multiple-choice test in which the task is to listen to a string of numbers or letters presented on an audio-tape and select the identical string from the five choices presented in the question booklet. There are three sub-tests: letters, numbers, and letters and numbers mixed. Range: from minimal educational qualifications to GCE 'A' level. Examiner required. Suitable for group use.
BRITISH PUBLISHER

Timed: 10 minutes

Range: Adult

Scoring: Hand key; examiner evaluated; maybe computer scored

Cost: Audio cassette £12.00; 50 answer sheets £16.00; key £3.00.

Publisher: Saville and Holdsworth, Ltd.

PERSONNEL TEST BATTERY: BASIC CHECKING (PTB:CP7)
Saville and Holdsworth, Ltd.

adult

Purpose: Tests for speed and accuracy in checking a variety of materials at a very basic level. Used for selection of clerical and general staff concerned with simple routine checking.

Description: 80 item paper-pencil multiple-choice test consisting of two sub-tests: one involves checking a list of numbers, the other involves a list of letters. In each list a series of strings of numbers (or letters) is presented and these are compared with another page where the identical string must be selected (from five choices). Range: from minimal educational qualifications to GCE 'A' level. Examiner required. Suitable for group use.
BRITISH PUBLISHER

Timed: 10 minutes

Range: Adult

Scoring: Hand key; examiner evaluated; maybe computer scored

Cost: 10 question booklets £16.00; 50 answer sheets £16.00; key £3.00.

Publisher: Saville and Holdsworth, Ltd.

PERSONNEL TEST BATTERY: CHECKING (PTB:CP3)
Saville and Holdsworth, Ltd.

adult

Purpose: Measures ability to perceive and check a variety of material quickly and accurately. Used for personnel selection of office, sales or general staff positions.

Description: 40 item paper-pencil proof-reading test. Two lists of information about hotels are provided.

One list is handwritten and the other printed, and the material contained in the lists includes names, numbers, and symbols. Candidates must compare the two lists and note any errors in accordance with a given code (designed to represent a real clerical task). Range: from minimal educational qualifications to GCE 'A' level. Examiner required. Suitable for group use.
BRITISH PUBLISHER

Timed: 7 minutes

Range: Adult

Scoring: Hand key; examiner evaluated; maybe computer scored

Cost: 10 question booklets £16.00; 50 answer sheets £16.00; key £3.00.

Publisher: Saville and Holdsworth, Ltd.

PERSONNEL TEST BATTERY: CLASSIFICATION (PTB:CP4)
Saville and Holdsworth, Ltd.

adult

Purpose: Measures the ability to perceive and classify material in accordance with a set of instructions. Used for personnel decisions when data handling, filing or the following of instructions are important.

Description: 60 item paper-pencil test representing a real clerical task. A number of sales order forms must be filed, requiring the candidate to classify each order and then record the order in coded form. Some orders ("account sales") must be filed alphabetically, and others ("cash sales") must be classified under seven categories of goods purchased. Range: from minimal educational qualifications to GCE 'A' level. Examiner required. Suitable for group use.
BRITISH PUBLISHER

Timed: 7 minutes

Range: Adult

Scoring: Hand key; examiner evaluated; maybe computer scored

Cost: 10 question booklets £16.00; 50 answer sheets £16.00; key £3.00.

Publisher: Saville and Holdsworth, Ltd.

PERSONNEL TEST BATTERY: NUMERICAL COMPUTATION (PTB:NP2)
Saville and Holdsworth, Ltd.

adult

Purpose: Measures ability to work with numbers. Used for selection of clerical, sales and general staff.

Description: 30 item paper-pencil multiple-choice test measuring the understanding of relationships between numbers and operations, as well as quick and accurate calculation. In each item one number has been omitted from an equation, and the task is to select (from five choices) the number which will correctly complete the equation. Simple fractions and decimals are used, and some problems are expresses in £'s, but more complex notation or operations are deliberately omitted. Range: from minimal educational qualifications to GCE 'A' level. Examiner required. Suitable for group use.
BRITISH PUBLISHER

Timed: 7 minutes

Range: Adult

Scoring: Hand key; examiner evaluated; maybe computer scored

Cost: 10 question booklets £16.00; 50 answer sheets £16.00; key £3.00.

Publisher: Saville and Holdsworth, Ltd.

PERSONNEL TEST BATTERY: NUMERICAL REASONING (PTB:NP6)
Saville and Holdsworth, Ltd.

adult

Purpose: Measures simple numerical reasoning skills. Used for selection of clerical, sales or general staff.

Description: 30 item paper-pencil multiple-choice test consisting of word problems with numerical answers. Some calculation is involved, but the emphasis is on understanding, reasoning and recognizing short cut methods. The problems cover basic arithmetic operations, simple percentages, fractions, decimals, and graphs. The questions are all given a commercial slant, and involve working out sale or purchase prices, profit margins, mark-ups, change, weights, times, and areas. Range: from minimal educational qualifications to GCE 'A' level. Examiner required. Suitable for group use.
BRITISH PUBLISHER

Timed: 10 minutes

Range: Adult

Scoring: Hand key; examiner evaluated; maybe computer scored

Cost: 10 question booklets £16.00; 50 answer sheets £16.00; key £3.00.

Publisher: Saville and Holdsworth, Ltd.

PERSONNEL TEST BATTERY: VERBAL MEANING (PTB:VP5)
Saville and Holdsworth, Ltd.

adult

Purpose: Assesses an individual's knowledge of the meaning of words and the relationships between them. Used for selection with any job where verbal communication skills are important.

Description: 30 item paper-pencil multiple-choice test requiring the candidate to identify the relationship (same or opposite) between one pair of words and to select (from five choices) the word which relates in the same way to a third given word. The vocabulary used is non- specialist, everyday language. VP5 is more difficult than VP1 of the same battery. Range: from minimal educational qualifications to GCE 'A' level. Examiner required. Suitable for group use.
BRITISH PUBLISHER

Timed: 10 minutes

Range: Adult

Scoring: Hand key; examiner evaluated; maybe computer scored

Cost: 10 question booklets £16.00; 50 answer sheets £16.00; key £3.00.

Publisher: Saville and Holdsworth, Ltd.

PERSONNEL TEST BATTERY: VERBAL USAGE (PTB:VP1)
Saville and Holdsworth, Ltd.

adult

Purpose: Measures ability for spelling, grammar and choice of words. Used in job placement which involves the receipt, processing or drafting of correspondence.

Description: 30 item paper-pencil multiple-choice test. Each item consists of a sentence from which two words have been omitted. The candidate must choose (from five choices) the correct pair of words to complete the sentence. The sentences consist of words and phrases commonly found in commercial correspondence. Range: from minimal educational qualifications to GCE 'A' level. Examiner required. Suitable for group use.
BRITISH PUBLISHER

Timed: 10 minutes

Range: Adult

Scoring: Hand key; examiner evaluated; maybe computer scored

Cost: 10 question booklets £16.00; 50 answer sheets £16.00; key £3.00.

Publisher: Saville and Holdsworth, Ltd.

PERSONNEL TESTS FOR INDUSTRY (PTI)
A.G. Wesman and J.E. Doppelt

adult

Purpose: Assesses general ability. Used in the selection of workers for jobs requiring verbal and numerical competence.

Description: Multiple item paper-pencil tests of two dimensions of general ability, verbal and numerical competence. Items are multiple-choice and problem solving. Materials include four equivalent forms. Tapes for administering the PTI are available. Examiner required. Suitable for group use.

Timed: Verbal, 5 minutes; numerical, 20 minutes

Range: Adults

Scoring: Hand key

Cost: Specimen set (includes all forms of V and N booklets, keys, manual, with manual for PTI-ODT) $3.50; 25 tests (specify Verbal or Numerical, Form A or B) $6.50.

Publisher: The Psychological Corporation

PERSONNEL TESTS FOR INDUSTRY-ORAL DIRECTIONS TEST (PTI-ODT)
C.R. Langmuir

adult

Purpose: Measures ability to understand and follow oral directions. Used in the selection of applicants with a limited knowledge of English.

Description: Multiple item paper-pencil test of ability to follow oral directions. Applicant responds to dictated instructions on tape by marking answer document. Materials include two equivalent forms, S and T. Examiner required. Suitable for group use. Form S available in a Spanish-American edition.

Timed: 15 minutes

Range: Adults

Scoring: Hand key

Cost: Complete set (includes recording, manual, script, key, 100 answer documents) $22.75; reel- to-reel tape version $24.50; cassette tape version $24.75.

Publisher: The Psychological Corporation

PRESS TEST
Refer to page 844.

PROGRAMMER APTITUDE SERIES: LEVEL 1 (PAS-1)
Saville and Holdsworth, Ltd.

adult

Purpose: Measures aptitudes for the very diverse range of activities and levels of skills required for programmer jobs. Used for entry-level data processing staff selections.

Description: Five paper-pencil multiple-choice tests measuring the acquisition of skills that are involved in most business programming functions. The tests include: Advanced Testing Battery (ATB) Diagramming (DA5), ATB Verbal Concepts (VA1), ATB Number Series (NA2), Personnel Test Battery (PTB) Basic Checking (CP7), and Technical Test Battery (TTB) Spatial Recognition (ST7). Provides a good over-view of diagramming, verbal, numerical, clerical, and spatial abilities.

Examiner required. Suitable for group use.
BRITISH PUBLISHER

Timed: 75 minutes

Range: Adult

Scoring: Hand key; examiner evaluated; may be computer scored.

Cost: Complete (includes test booklets, 50 answer sheets, keys, profiles, manual) £265.00.

Publisher: Saville and Holdsworth, Ltd.

PROGRAMMER APTITUDE SERIES: LEVEL 2 (PAS-2)
Saville and Holdsworth, Ltd.

---

adult

Purpose: Measures aptitudes for the very diverse range of activities and levels of skills required for programmer jobs at an intermediate level. Useful for intermediate data processing staff selections.

Description: Five paper-pencil multiple-choice tests measuring the acquisition of skills that are involved in most business programming functions, but at a higher level of difficulty than the basic level. Tests include: ATB Diagramming (DA5), ATB Verbal Critical Reasoning (VA3), ATB Number Series (NA2), PTB Basic Cecking (CP7), and TTB Spatial Reasoning (ST7). This combination of tests is useful where more "top" is required, for example when dealing with good GCE 'O' and 'A' level applicants. Examiner required. Suitable for group use.
BRITISH PUBLISHER

Timed: 75 minutes

Range: Adult

Scoring: Hand key; examiner evaluated; may be computer scored.

Cost: Complete (includes test booklets, 50 answer sheets, keys, profiles, manual) £265.00.

Publisher: Saville and Holdsworth, Ltd.

PROGRAMMER APTITUDE SERIES: LEVEL 3 (PAS-3)
Saville and Holdsworth, Ltd.

---

adult

Purpose: Measures aptitudes for the very diverse range of activities and levels of skills required for data processing staff selection at higher levels, including graduates.

Description: Five paper-pencil multiple-choice tests measuring the acquisition of skills that are involved in most business programming functions by higher staff members and graduates. Tests include: ATB Verbal Concepts (VA1), ATB Number Series (NA2), ATB Verbal Critical Reasoning (VA3), ATB Numerical Critical Reasoning (NA4), and TTB Diagrammatic Reasoning (DT8). Examiner required. Suitable for group use.
BRITISH PUBLISHER

Timed: 75 minutes

Range: Adult

Scoring: Hand key; examiner evaluated; may be computer scored.

Cost: Complete (includes test booklets, 50 answer sheets, keys, profiles, manual) £306.00.

Publisher: Saville and Holdsworth, Ltd.

PURDUE BLUEPRINT READING TEST
H. F. Owen and J. N. Arnold

---

teen, adult

Purpose: Assesses ability to read standard blueprints. Used for applicant and student selection.

Description: Multiple item paper-

pencil test of knowledge of fundamental principles of reading blueprints. Sale restricted to companies employing qualified personnel administrators and to psychologists using the test for instruction or vocational guidance. Examiner required. Suitable for group use.

Untimed: Not available

Range: Vocational students and adults

Scoring: Hand key

Cost: Specimen set $1.00; 25 tests, manual, key $6.00.

Publisher: Purdue Research Foundation/University Book Store

PURDUE INTERVIEW AIDS
C.H. Lawshe

adult

Purpose: Measures skill in reading working drawings, micrometers, and standard scales. Used for evaluating qualifications of job applicants.

Description: Three verbal tests of specific skills: Can You Read a Working Drawing?, Can You Read a Micrometer? and Can You Read a Scale?. Administered as part of the interview. Sale restricted to companies employing qualified personnel administrators and to psychologists using tests for instruction or vocational guidance. Examiner required. Not suitable for group use.

Untimed: Not available

Range: Adults

Scoring: Examiner evaluated

Cost: Specimen set (includes 3 aids plus instruction sheet) $1.00; 25 tests and instruction sheet (specify test) $4.50.

Publisher: Purdue Research Foundation/University Book Store

PURDUE TRADE INFORMATION TESTS

teen, adult

Purpose: Assesses knowledge of various trades. Used for selection of applicants.

Description: Four paper-pencil tests of knowledge in the following trades: Welding, Carpentry, Sheet Metal Workers, and Engine Lathe Operators. Sale restricted to companies employing qualified personnel administrators and to psychologists using the tests for instructional or vocational guidance. Examiner required. Suitable for group use.

Untimed: Not available

Range: Vocational school and adult

Scoring: Hand key

Cost: Specimen set (specify test) $1.00; 25 tests, manual, scoring key (specify test) $6.00.

Publisher: Purdue Research Foundation/University Book Store

REVISED BETA EXAMINA-
TION-SECOND EDITION
(BETA-II)
D.E. Kellogg and N.W. Morton

adult

Purpose: Measures mental ability of non-reading applicants. Used for testing applicants in settings with large numbers of unskilled workers.

Description: Six separately timed paper-pencil tests of mental ability including mazes, coding, paper formboards, picture completion, clerical checking, and picture absurdities. Directions are given orally to applicant. Examiner required. Suitable for group use. Available in Spanish.

Untimed: 30 minutes

Range: Job applicants

Scoring: Hand key

Cost: Specimen set (includes test, demonstration booklet, manual, key) $2.75; 25 tests (includes demonstration booklet, manual, key) $11.25.

Publisher: The Psychological Corporation

REVOLVING ASSEMBLY TABLE
Refer to page 861.

THE SHAPES ANALYSIS TEST
Alice Heim, K.P. Watts and V. Simmonds

teen, adult

Purpose: Assesses ability of subject to mentally manipulate different shapes and sizes of geometric figures. Used for screening for job placement or training.

Description: 36 item paper-pencil multiple-choice test of spatial perception. Each item is comprised of several figures. Subject must visualize how each figure will appear if turned over or around, estimate area and assess spatial relations. Six items are presented cyclically in order of increasing difficulty. 18 items are two-dimensional figures and the rest are three-dimensional figures. Materials include re-usable test booklet. Examiner required. Suitable for group use.
BRITISH PUBLISHER

Timed: 25 minutes

Range: 13-Adult

Scoring: Hand key; examiner evaluated; scoring service available

Cost: Booklet $2.50; answer sheet $1.50; manual $8.00.

Publisher: The Test Agency

SHAPES TEST
J.R. Morrisby

all ages

Purpose: Measures spatial-perceptual ability. Used in such occupations as design work, drafting, and die-making which involve diagrammatic representation of real objects and systems.

Description: 60 item paper-pencil multiple-choice instrument following the principle of spatial tests in which the subject is required to manipulate figures mentally in three dimensions. Materials include the booklet and manual, specimen set, answer sheets, and the scoring key. The test is restricted to examiners who provide evidence of adequate training and practical experience in the use of such tests. Examiner required. Suitable for group use.
BRITISH PUBLISHER

Timed: 10 minutes

Range: Average 11-superior adult

Scoring: Hand key

Cost: Contact publisher.

Publisher: Educational and Industrial Test Services, Ltd.

SHORT OCCUPATIONAL KNOWLEDGE TESTS (SOKT)
Bruce A. Campbell and Suellen O. Johnson

adult

Purpose: Measures knowledge of the content and concepts involved in various jobs. Distinguishes between knowledgeable workers and those with only a superficial knowledge of specific occupational areas. Used for employee screening and placement.

Description: 13 paper-pencil tests measuring knowledge of the following jobs: auto mechanics, bookkeepers, carpenters, drafters, electricians, machinists, office machine operators, plumbers, secretaries, tool and die makers, truck drivers, and welders. Examiner required. Suitable for group use. Test to be discontinued some time in 1983.

Untimed: 10-15 minutes

Range: Adults

Scoring: Hand scored-carbon insert (answers transfer to key on inside of test booklet).

Cost: 25 test booklets (specify test) $20.00; Examiner's Manual $2.70.

Publisher: Science Research Associates, Inc.

SKILLS AND ATTRIBUTES INVENTORY
M.E. Baehr

adult

Purpose: Assesses the relative importance of skill and attribute factors necessary for successful job performance. Used for job selection, placement, diagnosis of training needs, and systematic job and self analysis.

Description: 96 item paper-pencil test of the following areas: general functioning, intelligence, visual activity, visual coordination skills, physical coordination, mechanical skills, graphic clerical skills, general clerical skills, leadership ability, tolerance in inter-personal relations, organization identification, conscientiousness and reliability, efficiency under stress, and solitary work. Each item is rated on importance to the job, on a scale of six, from "little or none" to "outstanding." Basic reading skills are required. Examiner required. Suitable for group use.

Untimed: 45 minutes

Range: Adult

Scoring: Hand key; computer scoring available

Cost: Specimen set $4.00; 20 tests $8.00.

Publisher: London House Press

SOUTH AFRICAN PERSONALITY QUESTIONNAIRE
Refer to page 139.

SPACE THINKING (FLAGS)
Refer to page 681.

SPECIFIC APTITUDE TEST BATTERY (SATB)
U.S. Employment Service

adult

Purpose: Measures aptitude for specific occupations. Used to select untrained or inexperienced applicants for referrals to specific jobs or occupational training.

Description: Multiple item paper-pencil test reflecting the aptitude requirements for specific occupations against which an individual's scores can be matched. Two to four aptitude test batteries derived from the General Aptitude Test Battery (GATB). The SATB score matching process is similar to the Occupational Aptitudes Patterns (OAPs). Available only to State Employment Security Agencies. Examiner required. Suitable for group use. Available in Spanish.

Timed: Each subtest is timed

Range: Adult

Scoring: Hand Key

Cost: Available through State Employment agencies only.

Publisher: U.S. Department of Labor

SRA READING-ARITHMETIC INDEX
SRA Industrial Test Development Staff

teen, adult

Purpose: Assesses general reading and computational achievement for those over 14 years old. Used for entry level positions and training programs where basic skills of applicants are often too low to be reliably evaluated by typical selection tests.

Description: Two paper-pencil self-scoring tests measuring reading skills (picture-word association, word decoding, comprehension of phrases, sentences, and paragraphs) and arithmetic skills (addition and subtraction, multiplication and division, fractional operations, decimals and percentages). Score reflects highest developmental level passed. Examiner required. Suitable for group use.

Untimed: 25 minutes per index

Range: 14-adult

Scoring: Hand scored-carbon insert (answers transfer to key on inside of test booklet).

Cost: 25 test booklets (specify form) $16.00; examiner's manual $2.10.

Publisher: Science Research Associates, Inc.

SRA VERBAL FORM
L.L. Thurstone and Thelma Gwinn Thurstone

adult

Purpose: Measures an individual's overall adaptability and flexibility in comprehending and following instructions and in adjusting to alternating types of problems on the job. Used in both school and industry for selection and placement.

Description: Paper-pencil short-answer test of general mental abilities. Measures both linguistic (vocabulary) and quantitative (arithmetic) factors. Items of both types are interspersed with a time limit. Test is similar to Thurstone Test of Mental Alertness but shorter and more appropriate for persons of slightly lower general ability. Manual revised in 1983. Mostly self-administered. Suitable for group use.

Timed: 15 minutes

Range: Adult

Scoring: Hand scored-carbon insert (answers transfer to key on inside of test booklet)

Cost: 25 test booklets $16.50; examiner's manual $1.40.

Publisher: Science Research Associates, Inc.

SURVEY OF SPACE RELATIONS ABILITY (SSRA)
Harry W. Case and Floyd Ruch

adult

Purpose: Measures the ability of an individual to perceive rapidly and accurately the relationships among objects in space. Used to measure skills associated with assembly work, inspections, drafting, and tool and die making.

Description: 32 item paper-pencil multiple-choice test. Each item consists of a geometric design constructed of smaller parts, followed by a series of ten possible parts. The task is to select from the series those parts which would go together to make up the original design (the number of correct parts for each item ranges from two to seven). Examiner required. Suitable for group use.

Timed: 15 minutes

Range: Adult

Scoring: Hand key

Cost: Test booklet (minimum order of 25) $.45 each; optional answer sheet (minimum order of 25) $.25 each; manual $1.35; specimen set (includes 1 booklet and manual) $4.75.

Publisher: Psychological Services, Inc.

TECHNICAL AND SCIENTIFIC INFORMATION TEST, TECHNICAL READING COMPREHENSION TEST and GENERAL SCIENCE TEST

teen, adult

Purpose: Measures technical and scientific knowledge and technical reading comprehension. Used with matriculated students standards 7-9.

Description: The General Science Test consists of two paper-pencil subtests: The Technical and Scientific Information Test which contains informational questions over general science topics; and The Technical Reading Comprehension Test which contains a number of paragraphs with questions to determine to what extent articles of a technical nature can be understood. The two tests are administered in separate booklets. Restricted to competent persons properly registered with either the South African medical and Dental Council or Test Commission of the Republic of South Africa. Examiner required. Suitable for group uses. Available in Afrikaans.
SOUTH AFRICAN PUBLISHER

Untimed: Not available

Range: Standards 7 to 9; General Science Test, matriculants and higher

Scoring: Hand key; examiner evaluated

Cost: (In Rands) Reusable book 0,60; 25 answer sheet (specify test) 1,80; answer keys 2,40; manual 7,20; General Science Test reusable book 3,60; General Science Test manual 7,20.

Publisher: National Institute for Personnel Research

TECHNICAL TEST BATTERY (TTB)
Saville and Holdsworth, Ltd.

adult

Purpose: Measures comprehension and reasoning skills. Used as a test of aptitude for a wide range of apprentice, technical and technologist categories.

Description: Eight paper-pencil multiple-choice aptitude tests arranged in two levels of four scales each. Level One is intended for craft apprentice, operator, foreman, and similar occupations. The Level One Scales measure comprehension skills: Verbal Comprehension (VT1), Numerical Computation (NT2), Visual Estimation (ET3), and Mechanical Comprehension (MT4). Level One's range extends from those with no formal educational qualifications through CSE and GCE 'O' level. Level Two overlaps Level One, but is more extensive and difficult. Suitable for technician, HNC/HND, supervisory, technologist, technical sales, and some degree-level candidates. The following Level Two scales measure higher order reasoning skills: Verbal Reasoning (VT5), Numerical Reasoning (NT6), Spatial Reasoning (ST7), and Diagrammatic Reasoning (DT8). The range for Level Two extends from good CSE to GCE 'O' and 'A' level upward. Also available is an optional Spatial Recognition test (ST9), designed to measure spatial ability through complete shape recognition. Examiner required. Suitable for group use.
BRITISH PUBLISHER

Timed: 110 minutes

Range: Adult

Scoring: Hand key; examiner evaluated; may be computer scored.

Cost: Complete (includes 10 question booklets for level 1 and 20 for level 2, set of keys, set of administration cards, 50 profile charts, 25 score sheets, 25 test logs) £260.00.

Publisher: Saville and Holdsworth, Ltd.

TECHNICAL TEST BATTERY: DIAGRAMMATIC REASONING (TTB:DT8)
Saville and Holdsworth, Ltd. Staff

adult

Purpose: Measures diagrammatical reasoning ability. Used for personnel selection for technical occupations and jobs involving systems design, flow charting and similar skills.

Description: 40 item paper-pencil multiple-choice test consisting of a series of abstract designs in logical sequences. Respondents must select, from five choices, the design which completes the logical sequence. Candidates must think logically and flexibly. Range: from CSE to GCE 'A' level and above. Examiner required. Suitable for group use.
BRITISH PUBLISHER

Timed: 15 minutes

Range: Adult

Scoring: Hand key; examiner evaluated; may be computer scored

Cost: 10 question booklets £12.50; 50 answer sheets £12.50; key £3.00.

Publisher: Saville and Holdsworth, Ltd.

TECHNICAL TEST BATTERY: MECHANICAL COMPREHENSION (TTB:MT4)
Saville and Holdsworth, Ltd. Staff

adult

Purpose: Measures understanding of basic mechanical principles. Used in selection and development of craftsmen and technicians

Description: 40 item paper-pencil multiple-choice test measuring knowledge of the classic mechanical elements such as gears, pulleys, and levers, as well as a wide range of domestic and leisure applications of physics and mechanics, from electric ovens to billiard balls. Each item consists of a three-choice question about a technical drawing. The drawings are presented in technical workshop style without demanding any specific pre-knowledge to interpret the. Range: from minimal educational qualifications to GCE 'A' level. Examiner required. Suitable for group use.
BRITISH PUBLISHER

Timed: 10 minutes

Range: Adult

Scoring: Hand key; examiner evaluated; may be computer scored

Cost: 10 question booklets £12.50; 50 answer sheets £12.50; key £3.00.

Publisher: Saville and Holdsworth, Ltd.

TECHNICAL TEST BATTERY: NUMERICAL COMPUTATION (TTB:NT2)
Saville and Holdsworth, Ltd. Staff

adult

Purpose: Measures basic ability to work with numbers. Used for craft apprentice selection.

Description: 40 item paper-pencil multiple-choice test assessing the understanding of mathematical relationships and operations and the ability to calculate quickly and accurately. In each item one number or operation has been omitted from an equation, and the task is to select the missing element from five possible answers. Fractions, decimals and percentages are included, but more complex notations or operations are deliberately omitted (NT2 is slightly more advanced than NP2 in this respect). Range: from minimal educational qualifications to GCE 'A' level. Examiner required. Suitable for group use.
BRITISH PUBLISHER

Timed: 10 minutes

Range: Adult

Scoring: Hand key; examiner evaluated; may be computer scored

Cost: 10 question booklets £12.50; 50 answer sheets £12.50; key £3.00.

Publisher: Saville and Holdsworth, Ltd.

TECHNICAL TEST BATTERY: NUMERICAL REASONING (TTB:NT6)
Saville and Holdsworth, Ltd. Staff

adult

Purpose: Measures simple numerical reasoning skills. Used in the selection and development of technical staff, including apprentices

Description: 30 item paper-pencil multiple-choice test consisting of short word problems with numerical answers. Some calculation is involved, but the emphasis is on understanding, reasoning and recognizing short cut methods. The problems cover the basic arithmetic operations, percentages, fractions, decimals, angles, graphs, simple technical drawings, metric lengths, areas, and volumes. The questions are all given a technical slant, dealing with materials, output, production methods, etc. Range: from GCE 'O' level to 'A' level. Examiner required. Suitable for group use.
BRITISH PUBLISHER

Timed: 10 minutes

Range: Adult

Scoring: Hand key; examiner evaluated; may be computer scored

Cost: 10 question booklets £12.50; 50 answer sheets £12.50; key £3.00.

Publisher: Saville and Holdsworth, Ltd.

TECHNICAL TEST BATTERY: SPATIAL REASONING (TTB:ST7)
Saville and Holdsworth, Ltd. Staff

adult

Purpose: Measures ability to visualize and manipulate shapes in three dimensions when given a two- dimensional drawing. Used in selection and development work with many technical occupations.

Description: 40 item paper-pencil multiple-choice test consisting of a series of folded-out cubes and perspective drawings of assembled cubes. Respondents must identify the assembled cubes which could be made from the folded-out cube, each face of which has a different pattern. Range: from GCE 'O' level to degree. Examiner required. Suitable for group use.
BRITISH PUBLISHER

Timed: 20 minutes

Range: Adult

Scoring: Hand key; examiner evaluated; may be computer scored

Cost: 10 question booklets £12.50; 50 answer sheets £12.50; key £3.00.

Publisher: Saville and Holdsworth, Ltd.

TECHNICAL TEST BATTERY: SPATIAL RECOGNITION (TTB:ST9)

Saville and Holdsworth, Ltd. Staff

adult

Purpose: Measures generalized spatial ability. Used for apprentice, programmer or operator selection.

Description: 40 item paper-pencil multiple-choice test measuring the ability to recognize shapes in two dimensions. A series of shapes is presented, and for each one the identical shape must be selected from five choices. The emphasis is on the recognition of a complete shape when rotated rather than the more specific angle or length estimation required in ET3. Requires less complex spatial skills than those measured in ST7. Range: from CSE to GCE 'A' level. Examiner required. Suitable for group use.
BRITISH PUBLISHER

Timed: 15 minutes

Range: Adult

Scoring: Hand key; examiner evaluated; may be computer scored

Cost: 10 question booklets £12.50; 50 answer sheets £12.50; key £3.00.

Publisher: Saville and Holdsworth, Ltd.

TECHNICAL TEST BATTERY: VERBAL COMPREHENSION (TTB:VT1)

Saville and Holdsworth, Ltd. Staff

adult

Purpose: Measures vocabulary and basic word skills in a technical con-

text. Used in selecting and counseling apprentices in engineering and other industries.

Description: 40 item paper-pencil multiple-choice test assessing basic verbal skills, including: sentence completion, same and opposite words, analogies, etc. The language has been deliberately chosen to reflect the comprehension requirements of technical occupations and crafts. Range: from minimal educational qualifications to GCE 'O' level Examiner required. Suitable for group use.
BRITISH PUBLISHER

Timed: 10 minutes

Range: Adult

Scoring: Hand key; examiner evaluated; may be computer scored

Cost: 10 question booklets £12.50; 50 answer sheets £12.50; key £3.00.

Publisher: Saville and Holdsworth, Ltd.

TECHNICAL TEST BATTERY: VERBAL REASONING (TTB:VT5)

Saville and Holdsworth, Ltd. Staff

adult

Purpose: Measures a high order of verbal skills. Used for technical selection and development, from craft apprentice level upwards.

Description: 35 item paper-pencil multiple-choice test concerning the meaning of words and the relationships between them. Respondents must identify the relationship between one pair of words and then select (from five possible words) the one which relates in the same way to a third given word. The vocabulary used has a scientific and technical bias. Range: from GCE 'O' levels to 'A' level. Examiner required. Suitable

for group use.
BRITISH PUBLISHER

Timed: 10 minutes

Range: Adult

Scoring: Hand key; examiner evaluated; may be computer scored

Cost: 10 question booklets £12.50; 50 answer sheets £12.50; key £3.00.

Publisher: Saville and Holdsworth, Ltd.

TECHNICAL TEST BATTERY: VISUAL ESTIMATION (TTB:ET3)
Saville and Holdsworth, Ltd. Staff

adult

Purpose: Measures important elements of spatial perception relating to craft and design operations. Used for selection and development of all technical grades, especially craft and operator levels.

Description: 40 item paper-pencil multiple-choice test involving the estimation of lengths, angles and shapes. In each item the respondent must select the two figures from a set of five which are identical in form although in many cases they are rotated on the page. Of the eight tests in the TTB, this is the most independent, suggesting that it measures a special aptitude, relatively free from overlap with general intellectual capacity. Range: from minimal educational qualifications to GCB 'A' level. Examiner required. Suitable for group use.
BRITISH PUBLISHER

Timed: 10 minutes

Range: Adult

Scoring: Hand key; examiner evaluated; may be computer scored

Cost: 10 question booklets £12.50; 50 answer sheets £12.50; key £3.00.

Publisher: Saville and Holdsworth, Ltd.

TEST A/8: ARITHMETIC

teen, adult

Purpose: Measures general arithmetic ability. Used in employee selection and placement with technical college students and applicants for clerical and trade positions with 8-12 years of education.

Description: Multiple item paper-pencil test measures general arithmetic ability. Matriculants are allowed 30 minutes to complete the test; non-matriculants are allowed 40 minutes. Norms are available for technical college students and matriculated males. Restricted to competent persons properly registered with either the South African Medical and Dental Council or Test Commission of the Republic of South Africa. Examiner required. Suitable for group use. Available in English and Afrikaans.
SOUTH AFRICAN PUBLISHER

Timed: Varies

Range: Technical college students; adults with 8-12 years of education

Scoring: Hand key; examiner evaluated

Cost: Contact publisher.

Publisher: National Institute for Personnel Research

TEST OF ENGLISH FOR INTERNATIONAL COMMUNICATION (TOEIC)

adult

Purpose: Assesses English language abilities. Used for assessment of English language proficiency in placement position for international business.

Description: 200 item test of English

listening and reading abilities. Listening items are administered by audio tape. Materials include test booklets and audio tape. Examiner required. Suitable for group use.

Timed: Sections 104, 45 minutes; Sections 5-7, 75 minutes

Range: Adult

Scoring: Computer scoring available

Cost: Contact publisher.

Publisher: Educational Testing Service

THURSTONE TEST OF MENTAL ALERTNESS
Refer to page 804.

UNDERSTANDING COMMUNICATION
T.G. Thurstone

adult

Purpose: Measures comprehension of verbal material in short sentences and phrases. Used for industrial screening and selection of skilled occupational groups that need to understand written material and communications.

Description: 40 item paper-pencil single-score test. Basic reading skills are required. Examiner required. Suitable for use with groups.

Timed: 15 minutes

Range: Adult

Scoring: Hand key

Cost: 20 tests $4.00.

Publisher: London House Press

VISION TESTER: AEROMEDICAL MODEL

adult

Purpose: Screens visual abilities of people involved in aviation to insure that they meet minimum standards established by the Federal Aviation Administration.

Description: Five slides in a vision tester measure the following factors: Acuity Far (right eye, left eye, both eyes), Vertical and Lateral Heterophorias, Color Vision, and Acuity Near (right eye, left eye, both eyes). Approved by FAA for aeromedical use. Materials include: tester, 5 slides, training manual, and record forms. Examiner required. Not for group use.

Untimed: 5-10 minutes

Range: Adult

Scoring: Hand key; examiner evaluated

Cost: Complete $845.00.

Publisher: Titmus Optical, Inc.

VISION TESTER-INDUSTRIAL MODEL

adult

Purpose: Measures the visual skills of job applicants and employees to insure that they meet minimum vision standards for their jobs. Used for industrial and commercial employee screening.

Description: 12 slides in a vision tester measuring the following factors: Acuity Far (right eye, left eye, both eyes), Vertical and Lateral Heterophorias (far), Color Vision, Depth perception, Acuity Near (right eye, left eye, both eyes), and Lateral Phoria (near). Job standards book provided based on recommendations of Occupational Research Center,

Purdue University. Complete set includes: 12 slides and vision tester, training manual, record forms, and job standards book. Examiner required. Not for group use.

Untimed: 8-10 minutes

Range: Adult

Scoring: Hand key; examiner evaluated

Cost: Complete $1055.00.

Publisher: Titmus Optical, Inc.

WESMAN PERSONNEL CLASSIFICATION TEST
A. G. Wesman

teen, adult

Purpose: Assesses general mental ability. Used for selection of employees for clerical, sales, supervisory, and managerial positions.

Description: Multiple item paper-pencil test of two major aspects of mental ability, verbal and numerical. Verbal items are analogies. Numerical items test basic math skills plus processes and understanding of quantitative relationships. Materials include three forms, A, B and C. Verbal part of Form C is somewhat more difficult than the Verbal parts of Forms A and B. Examiner required. Suitable for group use.

Timed: Part I, 18 minutes; Part II, 10 minutes

Range: Job applicants

Scoring: Hand key

Cost: Specimen set (one each of materials for all 3 forms) $3.50; 25 tests (includes manual, booklet, key) $7.85. (specify Form A, B or C).

Publisher: The Psychological Corporation

WESTERN MICHIGAN UNIVERSITY ENGLISH USAGE- ORIENTATION FORM (EUO)
Bernadine P. Carlson

teen, adult   College

Purpose: Measures level of English language skills. Used for pre- and post-testing in business and technical seminars in effective writing.

Description: 75 item paper-pencil multiple-choice test consisting of three parts. Part I (30 items) includes three subtests: grammatical errors, spelling and diction. Part II (30 items) consists of two subtests: punctuation for meaning and sentence structure. Part III (15 items) consists of two subtests: reading comprehension and rhetorical style evaluation. Examiner required. Suitable for group use.

Timed: 45 minutes

Range: College

Scoring: Hand key; computer scoring available

Cost: Contact publisher.

Publisher: Bernadine P. Carlson

WIDE RANGE ACHIEVEMENT TEST (WRAT)
Refer to page 408.

THE WONDERLIC PERSONNEL TEST
E. F. Wonderlic

adult

Purpose: Measures level of mental ability in business, educational and industrial situations. Used for selection and placement of business personnel and for vocational guidance.

Description: 50 item paper-pencil

test measuring general learning ability in verbal, spatial and numerical reasoning to predict ability to adjust to complex and rapidly changing job requirements and ability to complete complex job training. The test also measures potential turnover and dissatisfaction on routinized or simplex labor intensive jobs. Test items include Analogies, Analysis of geometric Figures, Arithmetic Problems, Disarranged Sentences, Sentence Parallelism with Proverbs, Similarities, Logic, Definitions, Judgment, Direction Following, and others. Materials include eight equivalent test forms for employer use; four equivalent forms for personnel agency use; two equivalent forms for scholastic use; and one form for the visually handicapped. Examiner administered. Suitable for group use. Available in Spanish and French.

Timed: 12 minutes; may also be untimed

Range: Adult

Scoring: Hand key

Cost: Introductory package (includes 20 Form I, 20 Form II) $35.00; 25 forms $18.75.

Publisher: E.F. Wonderlic & Associates

WORD FLUENCY
R.J. Corsini

adult

Purpose: Determines the speed of relevant verbal associations and individual's ability to produce appropriate words rapidly. Used for vocational counseling and personnel selection in such fields as supervision, management and sales which require communication skills.

Description: 80 item paper-pencil fill-in test of verbal fluency of expression. Examiner required. Suitable for group use. Can be verbally

administered in any language.

Timed: 10 minutes

Range: Adult

Scoring: Hand key

Cost: 20 tests $3.00.

Publisher: London House Press

Clerical

ACER NUMBER TEST

teen, adult

Purpose: Measures addition and multiplication skills. Used for employee selection for clerical positions and occupational guidance.

Description: Multiple item paper-pencil test measures speed and accuracy in addition and multiplication. The first part contains items involving the addition of three 2-digit numbers; the second part involves the multiplication of two digits by one digit. Items in each part are nearly equal in difficulty. In addition to age norms, data is presented for university, senior technical college and national service trainee groups-the latter provides the basis for tentative occupational norms. Materials include: four-page expendable test booklet, scoring key, manual, and specimen set. Examiner required. Suitable for group use.
AUSTRALIAN PUBLISHER

Timed: 5 minutes for each part plus 5 minutes for instruction

Range: 13.6 years and older

Scoring: Hand key

Cost: Contact publisher.

Publisher: The Australian Council for Educational Research Limited

ACER SHORT CLERICAL TEST (FORM C)

teen, adult

Purpose: Measures basic skills of checking and arithmetic as a test of clerical aptitude. Useful in employee selection where these skills are important.

Description: Multiple item paper-pencil test measures a person's ability to perceive, remember and check written or printed material (both verbal and numerical), and to perform arithmetic operations. These abilities are important in accounting, general clerical work, business machine operating. Also valid for occupations such as printing, pharmacy, engineering, counter sales, etc., in which speed and accuracy of perception of similar material could be factors of efficient performance. Australian norms provided. British norms available in British Supplement of Norms for Tests Used in clerical selection. Examiner required. Suitable for group use.
AUSTRALIAN PUBLISHER

Timed: 5 minutes for each part plus 5 minutes for administration

Range: 15 years and older

Scoring: Hand key

Cost: Contact publisher.

Publisher: The Australian Council for Educational Research Limited

ACER SPEED AND ACCURACY TESTS-FORM A

teen, adult

Purpose: Measures checking skills of individuals age 13 years and older. Useful in selection of clerical personnel.

Description: Multiple item paper-pencil test measures the ability to perceive, retain and check relatively familiar material in the form of printed numbers and names while working in a limited amount of time. The test contains two sections: Name Checking and Number Checking. Australian norms available for school, university, adult, and some occupational groups. British normative data available in *British Supplement of Norms for Tests Used in Clerical Selection.* Examiner required. Suitable for group use.
AUSTRALIAN PUBLISHER

Timed: 6 minutes for each part

Range: 13.6 years and older

Scoring: Hand key

Cost: Contact publisher.

Publisher: The Australian Council for Educational Research Limited

ACER WORD KNOWLEDGE TEST-ADULT FORM B

teen, adult

Purpose: Evaluates a person's reading vocabulary. Used for employee selection and placement for clerical and business positions which require verbal facility.

Description: 100 item paper-pencil multiple-choice test measures a person's reading vocabulary and provides a useful measure of general education. Norms are based on the results of a sample of Victorian national (Australian) service trainees (ages 18 years and older). Materials include: four-page expendable booklet, score key, manual, and specimen set. Examiner required. Suitable for group use.
AUSTRALIAN PUBLISHER

Timed: 8 minutes

Range: 18 years and older

Scoring: Hand key

Cost: Contact publisher.

Publisher: The Australian Council for Educational Research Limited

BLOX TEST (PERCEPTUAL BATTERY)

teen, adult

Purpose: Measures visual perception. Used with subjects with 10-12 years of schooling for purposes of employee selection and placement in a variety of clerical and technical positions.

Description: Multiple item paper-pencil test measures spatial relations and visualization. The subject must analyze given geometric figures and then find them in a series as seen from another angle. Popularly known as the Perceptual Battery. Restricted to competent persons properly registered with either the South African Medical and Dental Council or Test Commission of the Republic of South Africa. Examiner required. Suitable for group use. Afrikaans version available.
SOUTH AFRICAN PUBLISHER

Timed: 30 minutes

Range: Job applicants with at least 10 years of education

Scoring: Hand key; examiner evaluated

Cost: Contact publisher.

Publisher: National Institute for Personnel Research

CLERICAL APTITUDE TESTS
Andrew Kobal, J. Wayne Wrightstone and Andrew J. MacElroy

teen, adult   grades 7-UP

Purpose: Assesses aptitude for clerical work. Used for screening job applicants.

Description: Three part paper-pencil test of clerical aptitudes. Factors measured include: business practice; number checking; and date, name, and address checking. Scores correlate with job success. Examiner required. Suit-

able for group use.

Timed: 40 minutes

Range: 7-12, adult

Scoring: Hand key

Cost: Specimen set $2.20; 25 tests $5.50; 100 tests $21.00.

Publisher: Psychometric Affiliates

CLERICAL SKILLS SERIES
Martin M. Bruce

adult

Purpose: Assesses language, physical coordination and math abilities necessary for various clerical jobs. Used for screening prospective employees, measuring student skills and evaluating current employees.

Description: Ten category paper-penciltest series covering: Alphabetizing—Filing, Arithmetic, Clerical Speed and Accuracy, Coding, Eye-Hand Accuracy, Grammar and Punctuation, Spelling—Vocabulary, and Word Fluency. The series consists of ten short tests, six of which are timed. They can be given separately or as a unit, and each can be scored and interpreted independently. Examiner required. Suitable for group use.

Timed: 2-8 minutes per section

Range: Adult

Scoring: Hand key

Cost: Specimen set $10.90; manual $4.25; package of profile sheets $6.50; Keys $.70 each.

Publisher: Martin M. Bruce, Ph.D., Publisher

CLERICAL SKILLS TEST
U.S. Employment Service

adult

Purpose: Assesses the clerical skills required to perform a variety of occupational tasks. Used for job placement.

Description: Six paper-pencil, performance subtests of the subject's ability to: type from plain copy, take dictation, spell, do statistical typing, and spell medical and legal terms. Materials required include a typewriter, typing paper and pencils. It is necessary to give only those subtests which relate to significant job skill needs. An experienced worker will score higher than an inexperienced worker. Norm tables are used to convert raw scores to deciles based on representative samples of experienced workers. Examiner required. Suitable for group use.

Timed: Varies

Range: Adult

Scoring: Hand key

Cost: Available through State Employment Agencies only.

Publisher: U.S. Department of Labor

CLERICAL TASK INVENTORY-FORM C
C.H. Lawshe

adult

Purpose: Assesses tasks performed by clerical and office personnel. Used for job evaluation of clerical positions and redesigning clerical jobs.

Description: 163 item standardized check list of frequently performed tasks. Tasks are clustered into 13 performance domains such as Performing Mathematical Computations and Understanding Printed/Written Communication. Rater checks tasks frequently performed in clerical position of interest. Self-administered. Suitable for group use.

Untimed: Not available

Range: Adults

Scoring: Examiner evaluated; may be machine scored

Cost: 10 inventories $15.00.

Publisher: Purdue Research Foundation/University Book Store

CLERICAL TEST 1
E.I.T.S. Staff

adult

Purpose: Measures speed and accuracy of basic skills in routine clerical and office occupations that require the employee to check information, especially printed material. Used to screen persons for office work and for positions such as checking clerks, checkout operators and data checkers.

Description: 140 item paper-pencil test divided in two parts: Number Checking and Name Checking. The task is to determine if two sets of numbers, or two names, are exactly the same or different. A minimal level of reasoning, measuring conceptual speed or mental alertness is required. The use of number words has increased the discrimination of Part 1, and, similarly in Part 2, the inclusion of random letters and words has the same effect. Materials include booklets, scoring key, specimen set, and manual. Tests in arithmetic and language usage also are available in this three-part clerical series. Examiner required. Suitable for group use. BRITISH PUBLISHER

Timed: 7 minutes

Range: Adult

Scoring: Hand key

Cost: Contact publisher.

Publisher: Educational and Industrial Test Services Ltd.

CLERICAL TEST 2
E.I.T.S. Staff

adult

Purpose: Assesses individual skill in ordinary arithmetic processes and the ability to apply this skill to everyday problems. Used to screen for a variety of clerical occupations, such as data checking, routine accounts and shop work.

Description: 50 item paper-pencil, two-part test. Part 1 consists of 32 computations in addition, subtraction, multiplication, and division, arranged in order of difficulty, with the answers to be calculated by the subject. Part 2 consists of 18 arithmetic problems, expressed verbally, to be solved. Materials include booklets, scoring key, specimen set, and manual. Tests in speed and accuracy and in spelling, grammar and language usage also available in this three-part clerical series. Examiner required. Suitable for group use. BRITISH PUBLISHER

Timed: 14 minutes

Range: Adult

Scoring: Hand key; examiner evaluated

Cost: Contact publisher.

Publisher: Educational & Industrial Test Services Ltd.

CLERICAL TEST 3
E.I.T.S. Staff

adult

Purpose: Evaluates a person's ability in spelling, grammar and language usage. Used to screen for most office jobs, especially those involving the processing of information.

Description: 91 item paper-pencil test of three parts. Part 1 is a 60-word spelling test, in which the subject indicates if a given word is spelled correctly or incorrectly. Part 2 consists of 30 short sentences, in which the subject identifies a word which makes the grammar incorrect. Part 3 is a short business letter, in which the subject marks the errors and rewrites the letter. Materials include booklets, scoring key, specimen set, and manual. Tests in speed and accuracy and in arithmetic also are available in this three- part clerical series. Examiner required. Suitable for group use. BRITISH PUBLISHER

Timed: 15½ minutes

Range: Adult

Scoring: Hand key; examiner evaluated

Cost: Contact publisher.

Publisher: Educational and Industrial Test Services Ltd.

CLERICAL TEST, SERIES N
Stevens, Thurow and Associates

adult

Purpose: Measures ability to think and to use words and numbers accurately. Used to screen candidates for such clerical positions as payroll, accounting, receiving, inventory control, warehouse, and filing.

Description: 206 item, five-test battery of paper-pencil tests of detail and numerical skills. The tests are: Mental Abilities (Inventory II), a 50-item multiple-choice and free response test of general mental ability; Inventory E, a 96-item test requiring the subjects to evaluate a pair of words or numbers for each test item and decide whether they are the same or different; Inventory F, a 30- item test in which subjects copy a list of four- to ten-digit numbers in order and in the properly numbered spaces provided on the back of the sheet on which the list is printed; Inventory G, an 80- item free response test of basic addition and multiplication skills; and Inventory H, a 30-item test in which the examinees must copy a list of names in order and in the properly numbered spaces provided on the back of the sheet on which the list is printed. Test kit also includes application forms and rating charts. Examiner required. Suitable for group use.

Timed: 33 minutes

Range: Adult

Scoring: Hand key

Cost: 5 test battery with application form and rating chart (pkg. of 10) $8.50; manual of instructions, including scoring keys $1.00.

Publisher: Stevens, Thurow and Associates

CLERICAL TESTS, SERIES V
Stevens, Thurow and Associates

adult

Purpose: Measures ability to use and spell words and type accurately. Used to screen candidates for clerical positions, such as secretaries, typists, clerks, dictaphone operators, and stenographers.

Description: 233 item battery of four paper-pencil tests and one test of typing ability. Mental Abilities (Inventory II), a 50-item multiple-choice and free response test of general mental abilities; Inventory A, a 30-item test in which subjects evaluate sentences as being grammatically correct or incorrect; Inventory B, a 100-item test in which the subject must decide whether or not words are spelled correctly; Inventory C, a 52-item test in which phrases are presented with one word capitalized and subjects are asked to choose one of five words following each phrase which has very nearly the same meaning as the capitalized word; and Inventory D, a 10-minute test of

speed and accuracy in typing a standard business letter from provided copy. The battery is highly discriminating throughout its range. Test kit includes application forms and rating charts. Examiner required. Suitable for group use.

Timed: 45 minutes (no limit on vocabulary test)

Range: Adult

Scoring: Hand key

Cost: 5 test battery with application form and rating chart $8.50; manual of instructions, including scoring keys $1.00.

Publisher: Stevens, Thurow and Associates

CURTIS VERBAL-CLERICAL SKILLS TESTS
James W. Curtis

teen, adult

Purpose: Assesses clerical and verbal abilities. Used for evaluation of job applicants.

Description: Four multiple item paper-pencil tests of clerical abilities: Computation, measuring practical arithmetic; Checking, measuring perceptual speed and accuracy; Comprehension, measuring reading vocabulary; and Capacity, measuring logical reasoning ability. Examiner required. Suitable for group use.

Timed: 2 minutes per test

Range: 16-adult

Scoring: Hand key

Cost: Specimen set $2.20; 25 tests $2.20; 100-$7.70 (specify which form).

Publisher: Psychometric Affiliates

ETSA TESTS 2-A OFFICE ARITHMETIC TEST
Refer to page 710.

ETSA TESTS 3-A GENERAL CLERICAL ABILITY TEST
Refer to page 710.

ETSA TESTS 4-A STENOGRAPHIC SKILLS TEST
Refer to page 711.

GENERAL CLERICAL TEST (GCT)

teen, adult

Purpose: Assesses clerical aptitude. Used for selecting applicants and evaluating clerical employees for promotion.

Description: Multiple item paper-pencil test of three types of abilities needed for clerical jobs: clerical speed and accuracy, numerical ability, and verbal ability, GCT-Clerical test involves finding errors by comparing copy with original and using an alphabetical file. GCT-Numerical test requires applicant to solve arithmetic problems, find numerical errors and solve numerical word problems. GCT-Verbal involves correcting spelling errors, answering questions about a reading passage, understanding word meanings and correcting grammatical errors. GCT is also published in two partial booklets: Booklet A, Clerical and Numerical subtests, and Booklet B, Verbal subtests. Examiner required. Suitable for group use.

Timed: Varies

Range: Job applicants

Scoring: Hand key

Cost: Specimen set (includes test booklet for complete battery, manual, key) $2.00; 25 tests $15.00; 25 test booklet A (Clerical, Numerical) $9.50; 25 test booklet B (Verbal) $9.50.

Publisher: The Psychological Corporation

GUILFORD-ZIMMERMAN APTITUDE SURVEY: NUMERICAL OPERATIONS (GZAS:NO)
Refer to page 717.

GUILFORD-ZIMMERMAN APTITUDE SURVEY: PERCEPTUAL SPEED (GZAS:PS)
Refer to page 717.

THE HARVARD BANK TELLER PROFICIENCY TEST
Steven Stanard

adult

Purpose: Measures a person's aptitude and skills for work as a bank teller. Used to screen tellers at banks and savings and loans.

Description: Six section paper-pencil test that measures accuracy, speed, customer relations, judgment, numerical ability, initiative, and communicative skills. Examiner required. Suitable for group use.

Timed: 30 minutes

Range: Adult

Scoring: Computer scored

Cost: Complete (includes test and computer report) $35.00 per person

Publisher: Harvard Personnel Testing

HAY APTITUDE TEST BATTERY
Edward N. Hay

adult

Purpose: Identifies job applicants with the greatest aptitude for handling clerical deail and working with numbers. Used to select personnel for office and clerical positions, trainee positions requiring innate perceptual skills and positions requiring quick recognition of numbers.

Description: Four paper-pencil tests assessing clerical and numerical aptitude. Tests include: Test 1 "The Warm-Up" (unscored), the Hay Number Perception Test (NP), the Hay Name Finding Test (NF), and the Hay Number Series Completion Test (NS). Predicts aptitude for a variety of positions: accounting, bookkeeping, typing, filing, keypunch, proof- reading, general office, shipping departments, mail departments, warehouses, stockroom workers, and printing personnel. Optional cassette tapes available for administration and timing of all four tests. Examiner required. Suitable for group use. Available in French.

Timed: 15 minutes

Range: Adult

Scoring: Hand key

Cost: Complete (includes 5 tapes and test books) $55.00.

Publisher: E.F. Wonderlic and Associates, Inc.

HAY APTITUDE TEST BATTERY: NAME FINDING
Edward N. Hay

adult

Purpose: Measures ability to check and verify names quickly and accurately. Used for selection of office and clerical personnel.

Description: 32 item paper-pencil multiple-choice test assessing the ability to read names and hold them in memory long enough to accurately identify them from four similarly spelled names on the back of the same sheet. Similar to many clerical tasks, such as making bookkeeping entries, typing invoices or typing checks. May be administered and timed via optional cassette tape. Examiner required. Suitable for group use. Available in French.

Timed: 4 minutes

Range: Adult

Scoring: Hand key

Cost: 25 forms $18.00.

Publisher: E.F. Wonderlic & Associates, Inc.

HAY APTITUDE TEST BATTERY: NUMBER PERCEPTION
Edward N. Hay

adult

Purpose: Measures ability to check pairs of numbers and identify those which are the same. Used for selection of office and clerical personnel.

Description: 200 item paper-pencil measuring speed and accuracy of numerical checking. Each test item consists of a pair of numbers which the applicant must decide are either the same or different. Test items designed to include most common clerical errors. May be administered and timed via optional cassette tape. Examiner required. Suitable for group use. Available in French.

Timed: 4 minutes

Range: Adult

Scoring: Hand key

Cost: 25 forms $17.00.

Publisher: E.F. Wonderlic & Associates, Inc.

HAY APTITUDE TEST BATTERY: NUMBER SERIES COMPLETION
Edward N. Hay

adult

Purpose: Measures the ability to deduce the pattern in a series of six numbers and provide the seventh and eighth numbers in the series. Used for selection of office and clerical personnel.

Description: 30 item paper-pencil test assessing numerical reasoning abilities. Each test item presents a series of six numbers (1-3 digits) related by an unknown pattern. Applicants must provide the next two numbers in the series. Good clerks can find the additional numbers more readily than poor ones. May be administered and timed via optional cassette tape. Examiner required. Suitable for group use. Available in French.

Timed: 4 minutes

Range: Adult

Scoring: Hand key

Cost: 25 forms $17.00.

Publisher: E.F. Wonderlic & Associates, Inc.

HAY APTITUDE TEST BATTERY: WARM-UP
Edward N. Hay

adult

Purpose: Introduces job applicants to the testing procedures of the Hay Aptitude Test Battery.

Description: 20 item unscored paper-pencil test provides a warm up for the other Hay Aptitude tests. The exercise is intended to quiet nervous applicants and to familiarize applicants with the format of the other tests. May be administered and timed via optional cassette tape. Examiner required. Suitable for group use. Available in French.

Timed: 4 minutes

Range: Adult

Scoring: Hand key

Cost: 25 forms $12.50.

Publisher: E.F. Wonderlic & Associates, Inc.

INVENTORY OF RELIGIOUS ACTIVITIES AND INTERESTS
Refer to page 670.

I.P.I. APTITUDE-INTELLIGENCE TEST SERIES: FLUENCY
Refer to page 721.

I.P.I. APTITUDE-INTELLIGENCE TEST SERIES: MEMORY
Refer to page 721.

I.P.I. APTITUDE-INTELLIGENCE TEST SERIES: NUMBERS
Refer to page 722.

I.P.I. APTITUDE-INTELLIGENCE TEST SERIES: PERCEPTION
Refer to page 723.

I.P.I. JOB TEST FIELD SERIES: GENERAL CLERK
Refer to page 727.

JOB EFFECTIVENESS PREDICTION SYSTEM: SPELLING (JEPS: TEST CODE D)
Refer to page 737.

JOB EFFECTIVENESS PREDICTION SYSTEM: VERBAL COMPREHENSION (JEPS: TEST CODE H)
Refer to page 738.

MATHEMATICAL ACHIEVEMENT TEST
Refer to page 740.

MINNESOTA CLERICAL TEST (MCT)
D.M. Andrew, D.G. Paterson and H.P. Longstaff

adult

Purpose: Measures ability to see differences or errors in pairs of names and pairs of numbers. Used in selecting clerical applicants.

Description: Multiple item paper-pencil test of speed and accuracy of visual perception. Items are pairs of names and numbers. Applicant checks each pair that is identical. Predicts performance in numerous jobs including adding-machine operators, clerical employees, key machine operators, and personnel trust department employees. Materials include optional tapes for test administration. Examiner required. Suitable for group use.

Timed: 15 minutes

Range: Adults

Scoring: Hand key; examiner evaluated

Cost: Specimen set (includes test, manual, key) $2.25; 25 tests (includes manual and key) $7.25; key $1.25;

manual $1.25.

Publisher: The Psychological Corporation

NATIONAL BUSINESS ENTRANCE TESTS-BOOK-KEEPING TEST
Refer to page 200.

NATIONAL BUSINESS ENTRANCE TESTS-STE-NOGRAPHIC TEST
Refer to page 201.

NFER CLERICAL TESTS

teen, adult

Purpose: Assesses clerical skills. Used for selection of applicants and for vocational guidance.

Description: Four paper-pencil tests of clerical skills: Group Test 20, Group Test 61A, Group Test 64, and Group Test 66A. Group Test 20 measures speed and accuracy in checking numbers and names. Group Test 61A measures speed and accuracy in filing, classifying, and checking. Group Test 64 assesses spelling, and Group Test 66A tests attainment level in arithmetic. Examiner required. Suitable for group use.
BRITISH PUBLISHER

Timed: Varies

Range: 15 and older

Scoring: Hand key

Cost: Contact publisher.

Publisher: NFER-Nelson Publishing Company

OFFICE SKILLS ACHIEVEMENT TEST
Paul L. Mellenbruch

teen, adult   grades 10-UP

Purpose: Assesses clerical skills. Used for educational and vocational guidance and for screening applicants for employment.

Description: Multiple item paper-pencil test of several important office and clerical skills. Abilities measured include business letter writing, English usage, checking, filing, simple arithmetic, and following written instructions. Developed in office work situations using clerical employees. Examiner required. Suitable for group use.

Timed: 20 minutes

Range: High school-adult

Scoring: Hand key

Cost: Specimen set (includes one test, manual and key) $3.30; 25 tests $5.50; 100-$21.00.

Publisher: Psychometric Affiliates

OFFICE SKILLS TESTS
Science Research Associates, Inc.

adult

Purpose: Assesses clerical ability of entry level job applicants. Used for employee selection and placement.

Description: 12 short tests comprising five batteries suitable for screening clerks, accounting clerks, typists, secretary/stenographers, library assistants and other office personnel. Tests are: Checking, Coding, Filing, Forms Completion, Grammar, Numerical Skills, Oral Directions, Punctuation, Reading Comprehension, Spelling, Typing, and Vocabulary. Each test has two equivalent forms. Norms provided for timed and untimed tests. Examiner

required. Suitable for group use.

Untimed: 3 to 10 minutes per test

Range: Adults

Scoring: Hand key

Cost: Office Skills kit (includes 5 copies of each test, answer stencils, file folders, audio cassette for oral directions test, 2 manuals, and normative data) $117.00; 25 test booklets (specify test) $16.50; scoring stencils $5.80 each; oral directions cassette $27.00; administrator's manual $4.60; technical manual $5.40.

Publisher: Science Research Associates, Inc.

PERCEPTUAL SPEED (IDENTICAL FORMS)
L.L. Thurstone and T.E. Jeffrey

adult

Purpose: Measures ability to identify rapidly the similarities and differences in visual configurations. Used to select clerical personnel or workers in occupations that require rapid perception of inaccuracies in written materials and diagrams.

Description: 140 item paper-pencil test of perceptual skill. The subject selects the figure among five choices which appears to be most similar to the illustration. Examiner required. Suitable for group use.

Timed: 5 minutes

Range: Adult

Scoring: Hand key

Cost: Specimen set $4.00.

Publisher: London House Press

PERSONNEL RESEARCH INSTITUTE CLERICAL BATTERY: ALPHABETIZING TEST
Personnel Research Institute

adult

Purpose: Measures an individual's ability to alphabetize lists of names. Used to train and place clerical workers.

Description: 45 item paper-pencil test of speed and accuracy in alphabetizing names. The subject is asked to place five names in alphabetical order in each of the 45 problems. Used as a compliment to the PRI Filing Test. Available in equivalent A and B forms. Examiner required. Suitable for group use.

Timed: 6 minutes

Range: Adult

Scoring: Hand key

Cost: 100 tests $35.00.

Publisher: Personnel Research Institute

PERSONNEL RESEARCH INSTITUTE CLERICAL BATTERY: ARITHMETIC REASONING TEST
Personnel Research Institute

adult

Purpose: Measures an individual's ability to solve arithmetic problems. Used for clerical training and job placement.

Description: 20 item paper-pencil test measuring speed and accuracy in solving basic arithmetic procedures. The subject decides what procedure is used for the problems presented. Examiner required. Suitable for group use.

Timed: 10 minutes

Range: Adult

Scoring: Hand key

Cost: 100 tests $35.00.

Publisher: Personnel Research Institute

PERSONNEL RESEARCH INSTITUTE CLERICAL BATTERY: CLASSIFICATION TEST
Personnel Research Institute

adult

Purpose: Evaluates a person's ability to use words, numbers and solve problems. Used for office and personnel placement.

Description: 100 item, multiple-choice, paper-pencil test. Measures vocabulary, arithmetic, and 40 items on analogy and general information. Available in two equivalent forms A and B. Examiner required. Suitable for group use.

Timed: 15 minutes

Range: Adult

Scoring: Hand key

Cost: 100 tests $35.00.

Publisher: Personnel Research Institute

PERSONNEL RESEARCH INSTITUTE CLERICAL BATTERY: FILING TEST
Personnel Research Institute

adult

Purpose: Measures an individual's ability to file names alphabetically. Used for clerical job placement.

Description: 50 item paper-pencil test measuring speed and accuracy in filing. Subject is presented with an illustration of five file drawers containing 50 file folders arranged alphabetically and labeled; "Aa-Am", "An-Az", etc. Subject must indicate which one of the file folders should be filed. Available in equivalent A and B forms. Examiner required. Suitable for group use.

Timed: 10 minutes

Range: Adult

Scoring: Hand key

Cost: 100 tests $35.00.

Publisher: Personnel Research Institute

PERSONNEL RESEARCH INSTITUTE CLERICAL BATTERY: NAME COMPARISON TEST
Personnel Research Institute

adult

Purpose: Measures ability to recognize misspelled names. Used for clerical job placement.

Description: Multiple item paper-pencil test measuring ability to recognize transposed letters, substitution of one letter for another, and addition of a letter to a name. The subject compares a list of names printed on one page and refers to second page as a measure of speed and accuracy in identifying whether two names are identical or different. Examiner required. Suitable for group use.

Timed: 7 minutes

Range: Adult

Scoring: Hand key

Cost: 100 tests $35.00.

Publisher: Personnel Research Institute

PERSONNEL RESEARCH INSTITUTE CLERICAL BATTERY: NUMBER COMPARISON TEST
Personnel Research Institute

adult

Purpose: Measures an individual's ability to accurately recognize errors in lists of numbers. Used for clerical training and job placement.

Description: 200 item paper-pencil test of ability to perform the monotonous task of scanning lists of numbers for transposition, substitution and additions. Subject is asked to compare two series of numbers from 3-12 digits, and indicate which pairs are not identical. Examiner required. Suitable for group use.

Timed: 9 minutes

Range: Adult

Scoring: Hand key

Cost: 100 tests $35.00.

Publisher: Personnel Research Institute

PERSONNEL RESEARCH INSTITUTE CLERICAL BATTERY: SPELLING TEST
Personnel Research Institute

adult

Purpose: Measures an individual's spelling ability. Used for training and placement in stenographics.

Description: 73 item paper-pencil test arranged in cycles of ten on varying levels of difficulty. Each item is a phonetic spelling with a brief definition of a misspelled business word. The individual spells the word correctly. Examiner required. Suitable for group use.

Timed: 15 minutes

Range: Adult

Scoring: Hand key

Cost: 100 tests $35.00.

Publisher: Personnel Research Institute

PERSONNEL RESEARCH INSTITUTE CLERICAL BATTERY: TABULATION TEST
Personnel Research Institute

adult

Purpose: Measures ability to classify items. Used for office-record placement.

Description: 15 item paper-pencil test measures basic arithmetic skills and classification ability. Each problem contains a list of items typical of those in office records. Subject is asked to assign items to appropriate categories. Available in two equivalent forms A and B. Examiner required. Suitable for group use.

Timed: 10 minutes

Range: Adult

Scoring: Hand key

Cost: 100 tests $35.00.

Publisher: Personnel Research Institute

PERSONNEL RESEARCH INSTITUTE CLERICAL BATTERY: TEST OF SHORTHAND SKILLS
Personnel Research Institute

adult

Purpose: Measures stenographic proficiency in transcription. Used to screen applicants for secretarial placement.

Description: 386 item paper-pencil test. Page 1 consists of an ordinary business letter with space between the lines. Subject is asked to translate the letter into shorthand. Page 2 is a carbon of the shorthand notes. Page 3 reproduces parts of the original letter, with 60 key words left blank to be completed from the shorthand notes. Materials include booklet that may be used for any method of shorthand.

Examiner required. Suitable for group use.

Timed: 20 minutes

Range: Adult

Scoring: Hand key

Cost: 100 tests $65.00.

Publisher: Personnel Research Institute

PERSONNEL TEST BATTERY: AUDIO CHECKING (PTB:CP8)
Refer to page 744.

PERSONNEL TEST BATTERY: BASIC CHECKING (PTB:CP7)
Refer to page 744.

PERSONNEL TEST BATTERY: CHECKING (PTB:CP3)
Refer to page 744.

PERSONNEL TEST BATTERY: CLASSIFICATION (PTB:CP4)
Refer to page 745.

PERSONNEL TEST BATTERY: NUMERICAL COMPUTATION (PTB:NP2)
Refer to page 745.

PERSONNEL TEST BATTERY: NUMERICAL REASONING (PTB:NP6)
Refer to page 746.

PERSONNEL TEST BATTERY: VERBAL USAGE (PTB:VP1)
Refer to page 746.

PSI BASIC SKILLS TESTS FOR BUSINESS, INDUSTRY, AND GOVERNMENT: CLASSIFYING (BST #11)
W.W. Ruch, A.N. Shub, S.M. Moinat, and D.A. Dye

adult

Purpose: Measures ability to place information into predetermined categories. Used in selection of clerical and office workers.

Description: 48 item paper-pencil multiple-choice test presenting four sets of codes (Time and Motion Study codes, Building Visitor Codes, Employee Identification Codes, and Benefits Booklet Contents) with 12 items for each set which must be properly categorized. Test items have a high degree of apparent relevancy to clerical duties. Validated against job performance of clerical and office workers in a nationwide cooperative study. Examiner required. Suitable for group use.

Timed: 5 minutes

Range: Adult

Scoring: Hand key

Cost: 25 tests $.50 each

Publisher: Psychological Services, Inc.

PSI BASIC SKILLS TESTS FOR BUSINESS, INDUSTRY, AND GOVERNMENT: CODING (BST #12)
W.W. Ruch, A.N. Shub, S.M. Moinat, and D.A. Dye

adult

Purpose: Measures ability to code information according to a prescribed system. Used in selection of clerical and office workers.

Description: 18 item paper-pencil multiple-choice test in which subjects are given systems for coding information (each system codes four categories of related information). For each test item, the subject must code the given information into the four coded categories. The coding systems and the information to be coded have a high degree of apparent relevancy to actual clerical duties. Validated against job performance of clerical and office workers in a nationwide cooperative study. Examiner required. Suitable for group use.

Timed: 5 minutes

Range: Adult

Scoring: Hand key

Cost: 25 tests $.50 each

Publisher: Psychological Services, Inc.

PSI BASIC SKILLS TESTS FOR BUSINESS, INDUSTRY, AND GOVERNMENT: COMPUTATION (BST #4)
W.W. Ruch, A.N. Shub, S.M. Moinat, and D.A. Dye

adult

Purpose: Measures ability to solve arithmetic problems. Used in selection of clerical and office workers.

Description: 40 item paper-pencil multiple-choice test measuring the ability to add, subtract, multiply, and divide, using whole numbers, fractions and decimals. Validated against job performance of clerical and office workers in a nationwide cooperative study. Examiner required. Suitable for group use.

Timed: 5 minutes

Range: Adult

Scoring: Hand key

Cost: 25 tests $.50 each

Publisher: Psychological Services, Inc.

PSI BASIC SKILLS TESTS FOR BUSINESS, INDUSTRY, AND GOVERNMENT: DECISION MAKING (BST #6)
W.W. Ruch, A.N. Shub, S.M. Moinat, and D.A. Dye

adult

Purpose: Measures ability to read a set of procedures and apply them to new situations. Used in selection of clerical and office workers.

Description: 20 item paper-pencil multiple-choice test in which sets of procedures (related to clerical or office duties) are described, and a set of action codes for implementing the procedures. The examinee is then presented with a number of problems in which he must decide the course of action for each item and mark the appropriate answer code. Validated against job performance of clerical and office workers in a nationwide cooperative study. Examiner required. Suitable for group use.

Timed: 5 minutes

Range: Adult

Scoring: Hand key

Cost: 25 tests $.50 each

Publisher: Psychological Services, Inc.

PSI BASIC SKILLS TESTS FOR BUSINESS, INDUSTRY, AND GOVERNMENT: FILING NAMES (BST #13)
W.W. Ruch, A.N. Shub, S.M. Moinat, and D.A. Dye

adult

Purpose: Measures ability to file simple entries alphabetically. Used in selection of clerical and office workers.

Description: 50 item paper-pencil multiple-choice test in which subjects are presented with a name, followed by a list of four other names (alphabetically arranged). The task is to "file" the given name at the beginning, between two of the names, or at the end of the list. Validated against job performance of clerical and office workers in a nationwide cooperative study. Examiner required. Suitable for group use.

Timed: 1½ minutes

Range: Adult

Scoring: Hand key

Cost: 25 tests $.50 each

Publisher: Psychological Services, Inc.

PSI BASIC SKILLS TESTS FOR BUSINESS, INDUSTRY, AND GOVERNMENT: FILING NUMBERS (BST #14)
W.W. Ruch, A.N. Shub, S.M. Moinat, and D.A. Dye

adult

Purpose: Measures ability to file numbers in numerical order. Used in selection of clerical and office workers.

Description: 75 item paper-pencil multiple-choice test. Each test item consists of a 6-digit number to be filed numerically in a list of four other 6-digit numbers (already arranged in numerical order). Validated against job performance of clerical and office workers in a nationwide cooperative study. Examiner required. Suitable for group use.

Timed: 2 minutes

Range: Adult

Scoring: Hand key

Cost: 25 tests $.50 each

Publisher: Psychological Services, Inc.

PSI BASIC SKILLS TESTS FOR BUSINESS, INDUSTRY, AND GOVERNMENT: FOLLOWING ORAL DIRECTIONS (BST #7)
W.W. Ruch, A.N. Shub, S.M. Moinat, and D.A. Dye

adult

Purpose: Measures ability to listen to information and instructions presented orally and answer questions about what is heard. Used in selection of clerical and office workers.

Description: 24 item paper-pencil multiple-choice test in which subjects listen to a 6½ minute prerecorded cassette tape and then answer questions about the content of the tape. The tape is played only once (no rewinding or stopping of the tape is allowed) and subjects are encouraged to take written notes during the playing of the tape. The content of the tape has a high degree of apparent relevancy to clerical and office duties. Validated against job performance of clerical and office workers in a nationwide cooperative study. Examiner required. Suitable for group use.

Timed: 5 minutes

Range: Adult

Scoring: Hand key

Cost: 25 tests $.50 each

Publisher: Psychological Services, Inc.

PSI BASIC SKILLS TESTS FOR BUSINESS, INDUSTRY, AND GOVERNMENT: FOLLOWING WRITTEN DIRECTIONS (BST #8)
W.W. Ruch, A.N. Shub, S.M. Moinat, and D.A. Dye

adult

Purpose: Measures ability to read, understand and apply sets of written instructions. Used in selection of cler-

ical and office workers.

Description: 36 item paper-pencil multiple-choice test requiring examinees to read sets of rules and apply them to a number of case examples. The rules and case examples have a high degree of apparent relevancy to clerical and office duties. Validated against job performance of clerical and office workers in a nationwide cooperative study. Examiner required. Suitable for group use.

Timed: 5 minutes

Range: Adult

Scoring: Hand key

Cost: 25 tests $.50 each

Publisher: Psychological Services, Inc.

PSI BASIC SKILLS TESTS FOR BUSINESS, INDUSTRY, AND GOVERNMENT: FORMS CHECKING (BST #9)
W.W. Ruch, A.N. Shub, S.M. Moinat, and D.A. Dye

adult

Purpose: Measures ability to verify the accuracy of completed forms by comparison to written information. Used in selection of clerical and office workers.

Description: 42 item paper-pencil True-False test with paragraphs of information followed by clerical forms apparently filled out using the information in the paragraph. Examinees must check a number of the entries on each form to determine if they are correct or incorrect. Validated against job performance of clerical and office workers in a nationwide cooperative study. Examiner required. Suitable for group use.

Timed: 5 minutes

Range: Adult

Scoring: Hand key

Cost: 25 tests $.50 each

Publisher: Psychological Services, Inc.

PSI BASIC SKILLS TESTS FOR BUSINESS, INDUSTRY, AND GOVERNMENT: LANGUAGE SKILLS (BST #1)
W.W. Ruch, A.N. Shub, S.M. Moinat, and D.A. Dye

adult

Purpose: Measures ability to recognize correct spelling, punctuation, capitalization, grammar, and usage. Used in selection of clerical and office workers.

Description: 25 item paper-pencil multiple-choice test. Each test item consists of one sentence, part of which is underlined. The underlined section may contain errors in spelling, punctuation, capitalization, grammar, or usage. The examinee must select one of three possible changes for the underlined section as correct, or indicate that no change is necessary. Validated against job performance of clerical and office workers in a nationwide cooperative study. Examiner required. Suitable for group use.

Timed: 5 minutes

Range: Adult

Scoring: Hand key

Cost: 25 tests $.50 each

Publisher: Psychological Services, Inc.

PSI BASIC SKILLS TESTS FOR BUSINESS, INDUSTRY, AND GOVERNMENT: MEMORY (BST #16)
W.W. Ruch, A.N. Shub, S.M. Moinat, and D.A. Dye

adult

Purpose: Measures ability to recall names and categories after being allowed a short period of time to study a chart in which the information is listed. Used in selection of clerical and office workers.

Description: 25 item paper-pencil multiple-choice test in which applicants are given five minutes to study a Reference List, and then five minutes to recall the information. The Reference List presents the names of five building supply companies in each of five categories: plumbing, heating lighting, roofing, and flooring. The task is to recall for each of the 25 companies the category in which it was listed. Validated against job performance of clerical and office workers in a nationwide cooperative study. Examiner required. Suitable for group use.

Timed: 5 minutes

Range: Adult

Scoring: Hand key

Cost: 25 tests $.50 each

Publisher: Psychological Services, Inc.

PSI BASIC SKILLS TESTS FOR BUSINESS, INDUSTRY, AND GOVERNMENT: PROBLEM SOLVING (BST #5)
W.W. Ruch, A.N. Shub, S.M. Moinat, and D.A. Dye

adult

Purpose: Measures the ability to solve "story" problems requiring the application of arithmetic operations.

Used in selection of clerical and office workers.

Description: 24 item paper-pencil multiple-choice test. Each item is a short word problem which requires a numerical answer. Emphasis is on determining the arithmetic problem contained in the "story" rather than on lengthy computations. Validated against job performance of clerical and office workers in a nationwide cooperative study. Examiner required. Suitable for group use.

Timed: 10 minutes

Range: Adult

Scoring: Hand key

Cost: 25 tests $.50 each

Publisher: Psychological Services, Inc.

PSI BASIC SKILLS TESTS FOR BUSINESS, INDUSTRY, AND GOVERNMENT: READING COMPREHENSION (BST #2)
W.W. Ruch, A.N. Shub, S.M. Moinat, and D.A. Dye

adult

Purpose: Measures basic reading comprehension. Used in selection of clerical and office workers.

Description: 23 item paper-pencil multiple-choice test measuring the ability to read short passages and then answer literal and inferential questions about them. Validated against job performance of clerical and office workers in a nationwide cooperative study. Examiner required. Suitable for group use.

Timed: 10 minutes

Range: Adult

Scoring: Hand key

Cost: 25 tests $.50 each

Publisher: Psychological Services, Inc.

PSI BASIC SKILLS TESTS FOR BUSINESS, INDUSTRY, AND GOVERNMENT: REASONING (BST #10)
W.W. Ruch, A.N. Shub, S.M. Moinat, and D.A. Dye

adult

Purpose: Measures ability to analyze factual information and draw valid logical conclusions from that information. Used in selection of clerical and office workers.

Description: 30 item paper-pencil multiple-choice test consisting of six lists of facts (one-sentence statements), with five possible conclusions for each list of facts. The task is to read each list of facts and then look at each conclusion and decide whether it is definitely true, definitely false or unknown from the given facts. Validated against job performance of clerical and office workers in a nationwide cooperative study. Examiner required. Suitable for group use.

Timed: 5 minutes

Range: Adult

Scoring: Hand key

Cost: 25 tests $.50 each

Publisher: Psychological Services, Inc.

PSI BASIC SKILLS TESTS FOR BUSINESS, INDUSTRY, AND GOVERNMENT: TYPING: PRACTICE COPY (BST #17)
W.W. Ruch, A.N. Shub, S.M. Moinat, and D.A. Dye

adult

Purpose: Familiarizes subject with the typewriter they will be using during testing (an unscored warm-up exercise. May be administered prior to any of the three BST typing tests.

Description: Unscored typing exercise in which examinees become familiar with the location of all keys (including margin release and backspace) and make all necessary adjustments. Practice copy is typed double-space with a five-space paragraph indentation and 60-character lines. Validated against job performance of clerical and office workers in a nationwide cooperative study. Examiner required. Suitable for group use.

Timed: 2 minutes

Range: Adult

Scoring: Hand key

Cost: 25 tests $.50 each

Publisher: Psychological Services, Inc.

PSI BASIC SKILLS TESTS FOR BUSINESS, INDUSTRY, AND GOVERNMENT: TYPING: REVISED COPY (BST #19)
W.W. Ruch, A.N. Shub, S.M. Moinat, and D.A. Dye

---

adult

Purpose: Measures ability to type from printed copy with handwritten corrections. Used in selection of clerical and office workers.

Description: Typing proficiency test in which examinees are given five minutes to type as much of the Revised Copy as possible, making the indicated changes and corrections as they type (double-spaced 60-character lines with 5-space paragraph indentations and 10-space tab setting for headings). Revised Copy is scored for accuracy, speed and how correctly the handwritten changes are made in the final typed copy. Validated against job performance of clerical and office workers in a nationwide cooperative study. Examiner required. Suitable for group use.

Timed: 5 minutes

Range: Adult

Scoring: Hand key

Cost: 25 tests $.50 each

Publisher: Psychological Services, Inc.

PSI BASIC SKILLS TESTS FOR BUSINESS, INDUSTRY, AND GOVERNMENT: TYPING: STRAIGHT COPY (BST #18)
W.W. Ruch, A.N. Shub, S.M. Moinat, and D.A. Dye

---

adult

Purpose: Measures ability to type straight copy (word-for-word with no revisions) with speed and accuracy. Used in selection of clerical and office workers.

Description: Typing proficiency test in which applicants are given five minutes to type as much of a given passage as possible. The passage is typed exactly as it is printed, line for line (double-spaced 60-character lines with 5-space paragraph indentation). Applicants are given time to set up their typewriters before the test begins. Straight copy is scored for speed and accuracy. Validated against job performance of clerical and office workers in a nationwide cooperative study. Examiner required. Suitable for group use.

Timed: 5 minutes

Range: Adult

Scoring: Hand key

Cost: 25 tests $.50 each

Publisher: Psychological Services, Inc.

PSI BASIC SKILLS TESTS FOR BUSINESS, INDUSTRY, AND GOVERNMENT: TYPING: TABLES (BST #20)
W.W. Ruch, A.N. Shub, S.M. Moinat, and D.A. Dye

adult

Purpose: Measures ability to set up and type tables according to specific directions. Used in selection of clerical and office workers.

Description: Typing proficiency test in which examinees are given seven minutes to type as much of three given tables as possible. The copy and directions for each of the three tables is given in handwritten form. Requires extensive use of tabulator, with each table having its own specified settings. Final copy is scored on speed, accuracy and skill at correctly following the handwritten instructions. Validated against job performance of clerical and office workers in a nationwide cooperative study. Examiner required. Suitable for group use.

Timed: 7 minutes

Range: Adult

Scoring: Hand key

Cost: 25 tests $.50 each

Publisher: Psychological Services, Inc.

PSI BASIC SKILLS TESTS FOR BUSINESS, INDUSTRY, AND GOVERNMENT: VISUAL SPEED AND ACCURACY (BST #15)
W.W. Ruch, A.N. Shub, S.M. Moinat, and D.A. Dye

adult

Purpose: Measures ability to see details quickly and accurately. Used in selection of clerical and office workers.

Description: 150 item paper-pencil multiple-choice test. Each test item consists of two series of numbers and symbols which must be compared and determined to be the same or different. Validated against job performance of clerical and office workers in a nationwide cooperative study. Examiner required. Suitable for group use.

Timed: 5 minutes

Range: Adult

Scoring: Hand key

Cost: 25 tests $.50 each

Publisher: Psychological Services, Inc.

PSI BASIC SKILLS TESTS FOR BUSINESS, INDUSTRY, AND GOVERNMENT: VOCABULARY (BST #3)
W.W. Ruch, A.N. Shub, S.M. Moinat, and D.A. Dye

adult

Purpose: Measures the ability to recognize the correct meaning of words. Used in selection of clerical and office workers.

Description: 45 item paper-pencil multiple-choice test in which each item consists of a sentence with one word underlined, followed by four words. The examinee must select the word which means the same or about the same as the word that is underlined in the sentence. Validated against job performance of clerical and office workers in a nationwide cooperative study. Examiner required. Suitable for group use.

Timed: 5 minutes

Range: Adult

Scoring: Hand key

Cost: 25 tests $.50 each

Publisher: Psychological Services, Inc.

PURDUE CLERICAL ADAPT-ABILITY TEST (REVISED)

teen, adult

Purpose: Assesses clerical abilities. Used for selection of clerical and office personnel.

Description: Multiple item paper-pencil measure of six aspects of clerical work: spelling, arithmetic computation, checking of names and numbers, word meaning, copying, and arithmetic reasoning. Sale restricted to companies employing qualified personnel administrators and to psychologists using tests for instruction or vocational guidance. Examiner required. Suitable for group use.

Untimed: Not available

Range: Job applicants

Scoring: Hand key

Cost: Specimen set $1.00; 25 tests, manual, key $9.50.

Publisher: Purdue Research Foundation/University Book Store

SEASHORE-BENNETT STENOGRAPHIC PROFICIENCY TEST
G.K. Bennett and H.G. Seashore

adult

Purpose: Measure stenographic skills. Used for employment and promotion of stenographers.

Description: Five task test of ability to type dictated commercial letters. Five letters are contained in each form: two are short and slow, two are medium in both length and dictation speed, and one is long and fast. Materials include two parallel, alternate forms, B-1 and B-2. Tapes with dictation are available on record, tape and cassette. Sold only to personnel departments of business and indus-trial firms for the testing of applicants and employees. Not sold to schools or employment agencies. Examiner required. Suitable for group use.

Timed: Dictation, 15 minutes; Transcription, 30 minutes

Range: Adults

Scoring: Examiner evaluated

Cost: Complete set (includes recordings for both forms, manual, script, 100 summary charts) record version $27.00; reel-to-reel tape version $29.00; cassette tape version $31.00.

Publisher: The Psychological Corporation

SHORT EMPLOYMENT TESTS
G.K. Bennett and Marjorie Gelink

adult

Purpose: Measures clerical skills. Used in applicant selection.

Description: Three paper-pencil scales measuring skills related to performance in clerical jobs: SET- Verbal (V), SET-Numerical (N), and SET-Clerical Aptitude (CA). Predicts performance of bank tellers, accounting clerks, hospital clerical workers, and airline reservation agents. Materials include four equivalent forms. Tapes are available for test administration. Sold only to personnel departments of business and industrial firms for testing applicants and employees. Not sold to schools or employment agencies. Form 1 restricted to member banks of the American Banker's Association (ABA). Examiner required. Suitable for group use.

Timed: 5 minutes per scale

Range: Adults

Scoring: Hand key

Cost: Specimen set (includes booklet and key for each of three tests, manual, form 1) $1.95; forms 2, 3, 4 combined specimen set $2.75; 25 V tests (specify form) $6.85; 25 N tests (specify form) $6.85; 25 CA tests (specify form) $6.85.

Publisher: The Psychological Corporation

SHORTHAND APTITUDE TEST
Queensland Department of Education

teen, adult   grades 10-UP

Purpose: Measures aptitude for the clerical skill of taking shorthand dictation. Used for employee selection and placement for secretarial and clerical positions which require shorthand dictation methods.

Description: Four paper-pencil subtests measure skills involved in taking shorthand notes. The four subtests include: a test of speed in writing a typical shorthand symbol, a multiple-choice spelling test, a test of phonetic association requiring the correct spelling of phonetically written words, and a test in which the correct English word is to be translated from phonetic symbols. Australian norms provided for high school level and above. Materials include: 4- page expendable booklet, manual and specimen set. Examiner required. Suitable for group use.
AUSTRALIAN PUBLISHER

Timed: 31 minutes

Range: High school and above

Scoring: Hand key

Cost: Specimen set $3.75; 10 tests $2.50; manual $3.50 (all remittances must be in Australian currency).

Publisher: The Australian Council for Educational Research Limited

SHORT TESTS OF CLERICAL ABILITY (STCA)
Jean Maier Palormo

adult

Purpose: Assesses aptitudes and abilities which are important to the successful completion of typical office tasks. Used for selection and placement in different office job classifications: secretary- stenographer, office clerk, specialized clerk (accounting, statistical and billing).

Description: Multiple item paper-pencil test consisting of seven parts. The battery includes arithmetic skills, business vocabulary, checking accuracy, coding, oral and written directions, filing, and language (grammar and spelling). Norm referenced including minority groups. Examiner required. Suitable for group use.

Untimed: 3-6 minutes per test

Range: Adult

Scoring: Hand key

Cost: 25 test booklets (specify test $15.50; scoring stencils (specify test) $2.40 each; examiner's manual $1.60.

Publisher: Science Research Associates, Inc.

SRA CLERICAL APTITUDES
Richardson, Bellows, Henry & Co., Inc., New York

adult

Purpose: Assesses general aptitudes necessary for clerical work. Used in employee screening and placing.

Description: Three paper-pencil tests measure: office vocabulary, office arithmetic and office checking. Indicates ability to learn tasks usually performed in various clerical jobs. Office vocabulary is a 48 item test measuring command of basic vocabulary and verbal relations. The arithmetic test consists of 24 items requiring application of basic math processes to the solution of practical problems. The checking section consists of 144 items measuring the ability to perceive details easily and rapidly. Examiner required. Suitable for group use.

Timed: 25 minutes

Range: Adults

Scoring: Hand scored--carbon insert (answers transfer to scoring key on inside of answer sheet)

Cost: 25 reusable test booklets $62.00; 25 answer sheets $12.00; 100 profile sheets $14.50; examiner's manual $1.00.

Publisher: Science Research Associates, Inc.

SRA TYPING 5
Steven J. Stanard and LaVonne Macaitis

adult

Purpose: Measures a person's ability to type a particular kind of assignment. Used with a variety of typing positions requiring different skills.

Description: Three forms measure speed and accuracy in the performance of different typing tasks. Form A (Typing Speed) consists of a letter with approximately 215 words measuring key-stroking speed and accuracy. Form B (Business Letter) measures ability to set up a business letter and type it quickly and accurately for the more experienced typist. Form C (Numerical), 115 + words and 40 number test, measures speed and accuracy in typing complex material containing words, symbols, and numbers in columns with headings. Examiner required. Suitable for group use.

Timed: 5 minutes for each test (after practice time)

Range: Adult

Scoring: Hand key

Cost: 25 test booklets (specify test) $14.50; 25 practice sheets $5.40; examiner's manual $1.30.

Publisher: Science Research Associates, Inc.

SRA TYPING SKILLS TEST
Marion W. Richardson and Ruth A. Pedersen

adult

Purpose: Assesses typing skills. Used by teachers and managers to evaluate the skills of students, typists, clerical help, and job applicants.

Description: Test of typing speed and accuracy consisting of a business letter approximately 225 words to be copied as often as possible in an accurately timed 10 minute period. Scored according to International Typewriting Contest Rules. Available in two equivalent forms. Examiner required. Suitable for group use. Examiner required. Suitable for group use.

Timed: 10 minutes (after practice time)

Range: Adult

Scoring: Hand key

Cost: 25 form A test booklets (spaced for use with standard manual and electric typewriters) $15.50; 25 form B test booklets (spaced for use with standard manual typewriters only) $15.50; examiner's manual $1.60.

Publisher: Science Research Associates, Inc.

STENOGRAPHIC TEST
E.F. Wonderlic & Associates, Inc.

adult

Purpose: Measures speed and accuracy in taking shorthand notes. Used for selection and placement of stenographers.

Description: 26 item paper-pencil test assessing shorthand- stenographic skills. Test items consist of 100 word letters of various "syllable densities" dictated at speeds ranging from 40-160 words per minute. The Vari-Speed Guide quickly determines an applicant's approximate level of skill. From this point, successively more difficult and faster letters are dictated until the applicant's best performance is determined. May be administered and timed via optional cassette tape, which includes: all 26 letters dictated at their proper rate, warm-up exercises and directions. Examiner required. Suitable for group use.

Timed: 15 minutes

Range: Adult

Scoring: Hand key

Cost: Complete $96.00; individual tapes (text not included) $24.00; printed text $19.00.

Publisher: E.F. Wonderlic & Associates, Inc.

TEST A/8: ARITHMETIC
Refer to page 757.

TYPING TEST
E.F. Wonderlic & Associates, Inc.

adult

Purpose: Assesses typing speed and accuracy. Used to select entry level typists and keypunch operators.

Description: Multiple item typing performance test consisting of five forms. Warm Up Form, Straight Copy Forms C and D measure typing speed in copying straight printed material. Random Numbers Form 2 is used to screen typists who will be asked to do significant amounts of typing for accounting, address files, and computer input, Random Alphabet Form K (no verbal knowledge required) is used to screen typists involved in CRT and other operations using letter codes. May be administered and timed with optional cassette tape. Examiner required. Suitable for group use.

Timed: 5 minutes

Range: Adult

Scoring: Hand key

Cost: Reusable complete package $26.00; test with cassette tape $24.00.

Publisher: E.F. Wonderlic & Associates, Inc.

TYPING TEST FOR BUSINESS (TTB)
J.E. Doppelt, A.D. Hartman and F.B. Krawchick

adult

Purpose: Assesses typing skills. Used to test applicants for typist positions, key punch operators, secretaries, or any position where typing skill is necessary.

Description: Test of five kinds of typing used in business: Straight Copy, Letters, Revised Manuscript, Numbers, and Tables. Warm-up Practice Copy administered first. Practice Copy and Straight Copy may be given as a quick screening test. Materials include two alternate forms, A and B. Sold only to personnel departments of business and industrial firms for the testing of applicants and employees. Not sold to schools or employment agencies. Examiner required. Suitable for

group use.

Timed: Varies

Range: Adults

Scoring: Hand key

Cost: Specimen set (includes test booklet and key for each test, both forms, manual) $5.75; 25 Practice Copy tests $3.25; 25 Straight Copy tests $6.75; 25 Letters tests $6.75; 25 Revised Manuscript tests $6.75; 25 Numbers tests $6.75; 25 Tables tests $6.75 (specify form A or B on all).

Publisher: The Psychological Corporation

Computer

ADVANCED TEST BATTERY: DIAGRAMMING (ATB:DA5)
Refer to page 700.

ADVANCED TEST BATTERY: DIAGRAMMATIC REASONING (ATB:DT8)
Refer to page 700.

APTITUDE ASSESSMENT BATTERY: PROGRAMMING (AABP)
Jack M. Wolfe

adult

Purpose: Determines a person's aptitude for computer programming. May be used in selecting job candidates, as a guide for training programs and for revealing work habits and task preferences.

Description: Five problem paper-pencil tests that measure ability to draw deductions, understand complicated instructions, interpret intricate specifications, reason, desk-check, debug,

and document and annotate work. Examiner required. Suitable for group use. Available in French, Spanish and Braille.

Untimed: 120 minutes

Range: Adult

Scoring: Scoring service provided

Cost: Complete (includes test and evaluation) $85.00.

Publisher: Wolfe Computer Personnel Testing, Inc.

COMPUTER OPERATOR APTITUDE BATTERY (COAB)
A. Joanne Holloway

adult

Purpose: Helps predict job performance of computer operators. Used by data processing managers and personnel directors in selection of applicants for computer operator positions.

Description: Paper-pencil test predicting success as a computer programmer. Consists of three separately timed subtests: Sequence Recognition, Format Checking, and Logical Thinking. Examiner required. Suitable for group use.

Timed: 45 minutes

Range: Adult

Scoring: Hand scored--carbon insert (answers transfer to scoring key on inside of answer sheet).

Cost: 5 reusable test booklets $49.00; 25 answer sheets $24.00; examiner's manual $3.10.

Publisher: Science Research Associates, Inc.

COMPUTER PROGRAMMER APTITUDE BATTERY (CPAB)
Jean Maier Palormo

adult

Purpose: Measures potential for success in the computer programming field. Used by data processing managers and personnel directors to identify people with the aptitude for computer programming.

Description: Five separately timed paper-pencil tests measuring verbal meaning, reasoning, letter series, number ability, and diagramming (problem analysis and logical solution). Examiner required. Suitable for group use.

Timed: 75 minutes

Range: Adult

Scoring: Hand scored--carbon insert (answers transfer to scoring key on inside of answer sheet)

Cost: 5 reusable test booklets $49.00; 25 answer sheets $24.00; examiner's manual $5.20.

Publisher: Science Research Associates, Inc.

PROGRAMMER APTITUDE COMPETENCE TEST SYSTEM (PACTS)
C.A. Haverly and Pete Seiner

adult

Purpose: Measures an individual's ability to write good computer programs, regardless of experience. Used for job screening.

Description: Multiple item test of 4-6 problems with up to 20 total problems possible. The subject is given an instruction book to study for 30-50 minutes, which describes a general computer programming language for a hypothetical computer. The subject is then given a book of problems, with difficulty based on programming experience. Completed programs are evaluated by computer scoring on correctness, efficiency, compactness, problem difficulty, and completion time. Materials include the computer installation, manual and problems. Examiner required. Suitable for group use.

Untimed: 2-3 hours

Range: Adults

Scoring: Computer scored

Cost: Computer installation $8,-200.00; PACTS is available on service basis: $100.00 per test for the first five tests, $80.00 per test for additional five tests.

Publisher: Haverly Systems, Inc.

PROGRAMMER APTITUDE SERIES: LEVEL 1 (PAS-1)
Refer to page 747.

PROGRAMMER APTITUDE SERIES: LEVEL 2 (PAS-2)
Refer to page 748.

PROGRAMMER APTITUDE SERIES: LEVEL 3 (PAS-3)
Refer to page 748.

SYSTEMS PROGRAMMING APTITUDE TEST (SPAT)
Jack Wolfe

adult

Purpose: Measures a person's aptitude for systems and software programming. May be used for hiring, training, and promotion decisions at all levels of skill.

Description: Five part paper-pencil test that measures accuracy, reasoning, ability to deal with complex relationships, and skills in deductive, interpretive and analytic reasoning. Examiner required. Suitable for group use.

Untimed: 180 minutes

Range: Adult

Scoring: Scoring service provided

Cost: Complete (test and computer report) $175.00.

Publisher: Wolfe Computer Personnel Testing, Inc.

SYSTEMS ANALYST APTITUDE TEST (SAAT)
Jack M. Wolfe

adult

Purpose: Measures a person's aptitude for business systems design. Useful for hiring, training and promotion of computer analysts and programmers.

Description: Single item (case study) test that evaluates interpretation of specifications, ability to plan a logical procedure, recognition of alternative solutions, clarity of explanation, quality of organization, attention to detail, effectiveness and efficiency of design. Available in French. Examiner required. Suitable for group use.

Untimed: 180 minutes

Range: Adult

Scoring: Scoring service provided

Cost: Complete (includes test and computer report) $225.00 per person.

Publisher: Wolfe Computer Personnel Training, Inc.

TECHNICAL TEST BATTERY: DIAGRAMMATIC REASONING (TTB:DT8)
Refer to page 754.

WOLFE COMPUTER OPERATOR APTITUDE TEST (WCOAT)
Jack M. Wolfe

adult

Purpose: Measures a person's aptitude as a computer operator. Useful for selecting best qualified candidates.

Description: 20 item, short answer, paper-pencil test measuring attention to detail, ability to detect and correct errors in a job stream, and problem solving ability. Available in French. Examiner required. Suitable for group use.

Timed: 120 minutes

Range: Adult

Scoring: Scoring service provided

Cost: Complete (includes test and computer report) $55.00 per person

Publisher: Wolfe Computer Personnel Testing, Inc.

WOLFE DATA ENTRY OPERATOR APTITUDE TEST (WDEOAT)
S. Berke

adult

Purpose: Determines a person's aptitude for work as a data entry operator or terminal operator. May be used for hiring or training purposes.

Description: Six item, multi-part, paper-pencil test that measures manual dexterity, coding, accuracy, numerical skills, editing, and work speed. Examiner required. Suitable for group use.

Timed: 30 minutes

Range: Adult

Scoring: Scoring service provided

Cost: Complete (includes test and

computer report) $45.00 per person.

Publisher: Wolfe Computer Personnel Testing, Inc.

WOLFE-PROGRAMMING APTITUDE TEST (WPAT)
Jack Wolfe

adult

Purpose: Determines a person's aptitude for computer programming. Useful as a screening instrument.

Description: Ten problem paper-pencil test. A 64-page booklet with answers provided so that respondents can score their own tests. Self-administered. Suitable for group use.

Untimed: 60 minutes

Range: Adult

Scoring: Hand key; scored by candidate (optional)

Cost: $49.00 each.

Publisher: Wolfe Computer Personnel Testing, Inc.

WOLFE PROGRAMMING LANGUAGE TEST: COBOL (WCOBL)
Jack M. Wolfe

adult

Purpose: Assesses a person's knowledge of COBOL. Useful for screening experienced programmers.

Description: 47 item paper-pencil test that measures speed of work and evaluates coding skills, documentation and knowledge of COBOL. Suitable for junior and intermediate programmers with detailed knowledge of COBOL manual. Examiner required. Suitable for group use.

Timed: 120 minutes

Range: Adult

Scoring: Scoring service provided

Cost: Complete (includes test and computer report) $55.00 per person.

Publisher: Wolfe Computer Personnel Testing, Inc.

WOLFE SCREENING TEST FOR PROGRAMMING APTITUDE (WPT)
Jack W. Wolfe

adult

Purpose: Measures a person's aptitude for computer programming. Used by schools and placement agencies.

Description: Three part paper-pencil test that measures attention to detail, ability to solve problems, and ability to interpret specifications. Examiner required. Suitable for group use. Available in French.

Timed: 40 minutes

Range: Adult

Scoring: Hand key; examiner evaluated

Cost: 1-9 test booklets and key $12.50 each.

Publisher: Wolfe Computer Personnel Testing, Inc.

WOLFE-SPENCE PROGRAMMING APTITUDE TEST (WSPAT)
Jack M. Wolfe and R. J. Spence

adult

Purpose: Screens entry level candidates for computer programming work. May be used for hiring or selecting candidates for training classes.

Description: 8 item paper-pencil test

that measures a person's logical capabilities and ability to interpret intricate specifications. Candidates passing the WSPAT should be given the AABP test prior to making hiring decisions. Examiner required. Suitable for group use.

Timed: 120 minutes

Range: Adult

Scoring: Scoring service provided

Cost: Complete (includes test and computer report) $35.00 per person.

Publisher: Wolfe Computer Personnel Testing, Inc.

WOLFE-WINROW CICS/VS COMMAND LEVEL PROFICIENCY TEST (WWCICS)
B. W. Winrow

adult

Purpose: Measures a person's knowledge of IBM CICS/VS Command Level. Used for hiring, training and promoting applications programmers and software specialists.

Description: Five part paper-pencil test that in addition to measuring general knowledge of CICS/VS concepts, facilities and commands, also assesses ability to code CICS/VS commands from specifications and to debug and test in a CICS/VS environment. Test also includes an optional measure of specific knowledge of Basic Mapping Support and related commands. Examiner required. Suitable for group use.

Timed: 30 minutes

Range: Adult

Scoring: Scoring service provided

Cost: Complete (includes detailed report) $55.00.

Publisher: Wolfe Computer Personnel Testing, Inc.

WOLFE-WINROW DOS/VS JCL PROFICIENCY TEST
B. Winrow

adult

Purpose: Measures a person's knowledge of DOS, DOS/VS or DOS/VSE JCL language. May be used for hiring, training and promotion purposes.

Description: Five part paper-pencil test that measures ability to identify common JCL errors, ability to code, ability to overwrite catalogued procedures, and specific knowledge of JCL parameters. Suitable for examining computer operators, DOS JCL analysts, and applications programmers at all experience levels. Examiner required. Suitable for group use.

Timed: 30 minutes

Range: Adult

Scoring: Scoring service provided

Cost: Complete (includes test and computer report) $55.00 per person.

Publisher: Wolfe Computer Personnel Testing, Inc.

WOLFE-WINROW OS JCL PROFICIENCY TEST
B. W. Winrow

adult

Purpose: Measures a person's knowledge of IBM OS/JCL language. Used for hiring, promoting and training computer operators, analysts and programmers.

Description: Five part paper-pencil test that measures the following skills: general knowledge of JCL statements and parameters as well as specific understanding of JCL parameters, catalogued procedures, symbolic parameters, GDGs and overriding JCL. Test also assesses ability to identify OS/JCL errors and ability to code OS/JCL. Examiner required. Suitable for group use.

Timed: 30 minutes

Range: Adult

Scoring: Scoring service provided

Cost: Complete (includes test and computer report) $55.00 per person.

Publisher: Wolfe Computer Personnel Testing, Inc.

WOLFE-WINROW STRUCTURED COBOL
B. Winrow

adult

Purpose: Assesses a person's knowledge of structured COBOL. Used for hiring, evaluating existing staff, evaluating training needs and effectiveness, and promotion.

Description: Five question paper-pencil test that measures ability to identify structured programming tools for COBOL, use concepts such as table look-up and debugging aids, define storage attributes and code PICTURE clauses for COBOL, code from specifications, and understand arithmetic operations and programming efficiencies. Examiner required. Suitable for group use.

Timed: 30 minutes

Range: Adult

Scoring: Scoring service provided

Cost: Complete (includes report) $55.00 per person.

Publisher: Wolfe Computer Personnel Testing, Inc.

WOLFE-WINROW TSO/SPF PROFICIENCY TEST (WWTSO)
B. W. Winrow

adult

Purpose: Assesses a person's knowledge of IBM TSO/SPE. Useful for hiring, training and promoting programmers and software specialists.

Description: Five part paper-pencil test evaluating an applicant's knowledge of TSO/SPE features and commands. Examiner required. Suitable for group use.

Timed: 30 minutes

Range: Adult

Scoring: Scoring service provided

Cost: Complete (includes test and detailed report) $55.00.

Publisher: Wolfe Computer Personnel Testing, Inc.

THE WORD PROCESSING OPERATOR ASSESSMENT BATTERY
S. Berke

adult

Purpose: Determines a person's suitability for work as a word processor operator. Used to supplement interviews, reference checking and machine tests in the hiring process.

Description: Five item paper-pencil test measuring attention to detail, ability to solve problems, manual dexterity, numerical skill, alphabetizing, filing, and coding. Examiner required. Suitable for group use. Available in French.

Timed: 30 minutes

Range: Adult

Scoring: Scoring service provided

Cost: Complete (test kit and

evaluation) $55.00.

Publisher: Harvard Personnel Testing

Engineering

ADVANCED TEST BATTERY: DIAGRAMMING (ATB:DA5)
Refer to page 700.

ADVANCED TEST BATTERY: SPATIAL REASONING (ATB:ST7)
Refer to page 701.

CLOSURE FLEXIBILITY (CONCEALED FIGURES)
L.L. Thurstone and T.E. Jeffrey

adult

Purpose: Measures visual and space perception skills. Used by vocational counselors to predict mechanical skills and possible success in the engineering and drafting professions.

Description: 49 item paper-pencil test of ability to hold a configuration in mind despite distraction, as indicated by seeing a given figure embedded in a larger, more complex drawing. (Example: with a figure shown, test subject indicates in which of four drawings that figure appears.) Examiner required. Suitable for group use.

Timed: 10 minutes

Range: Adult

Scoring: Hand key, may be computer scored

Cost: Specimen set $4.00.

Publisher: London House Press

ELECTRICAL SOPHISTICATION TEST
Stanley Ciesla

adult

Purpose: Assesses electrical knowledge. Used for evaluation of job applicants.

Description: Multiple item paper-pencil test of sophistication of electrical knowledge. Discriminates between persons with electrical know-how and those with none, as well as discriminates between electrical engineers and other types of engineers. Examiner required. Suitable for group use.

Untimed: 10 minutes

Range: Adult

Scoring: Hand key

Cost: Specimen set $2.00; 25 tests $.275; 100- $10.00

Publisher: Psychometric Affiliates

ENGINEER PERFORMANCE DESCRIPTION FORM (EPDF)
John C. South

adult

Purpose: Evaluates on-the-job performance of non- supervisory engineers who have less than five years professional experience. Used to counsel and develop junior engineering staff and to assess training programs.

Description: Multiple item paper-pencil observational instrument. Six performance factors are measured: communication, relating to others, administrative ability, motivation, technical knowledge ability, and self-sufficiency. The supervisory manual contains instructions on how to use and complete the inventory with guidelines for interpreting the results. Ratings are provided for each of the six factors, along with an index of overall performance. Percentiles are given for overall scores. Ratings completed by supervisor.

Untimed: 20-45 minutes

Range: Adult

Scoring: Hand key; scoring service available

Cost: Test $.45; scoring service $.20 per test; manual $.40.

Publisher: John C. South

GARNETT COLLEGE TEST IN ENGINEERING SCIENCE (REVISED EDITION)
Refer to page 411.

GUILFORD-ZIMMERMAN APTITUDE SURVEY: SPATIAL VISUALIZATION (GZAS:SV)
Refer to page 718.

INDIVIDUAL QUALIFICATION FORM
Morris I. Stein

adult

Purpose: Determines a profile of the type of individual needed for a specific job in technical industries and research and development (R & D) organizations. Used to improve placement procedures with scientists, engineers and research personnel.

Description: 30 item paper-pencil questionnaire elicits an accurate statement from the supervisor of a job's requirements, opportunities and limitations. Items are specified in terms of role requirements in order to facilitate the screening of job applicants. Self-administered by supervisor or administrator. Restricted to R & D personnel.

Untimed: 20 minutes

Range: Adult

Scoring: Examiner evaluated

Cost: $2.50 each.

Publisher: Morris I. Stein

I.P.I. APTITUDE-INTELLIGENCE TEST SERIES: DIMENSION
Refer to page 720.

I.P.I. JOB TEST FIELD SERIES: ENGINEER
Refer to page 726.

MINNESOTA ENGINEERING ANALOGIES TEST
Refer to page 411.

NIIP TESTS-ENGINEERING SELECTION TEST BATTERY
Refer to page 412.

PRIMARY MECHANICAL ABILITY TEST
Refer to page 859.

PURDUE BLUEPRINT READING TEST
Refer to page 748.

PURDUE CREATIVITY TEST
Douglas Harris and C.H. Lawshe

teen, adult

Purpose: Measures creativity in engineering. Used for identifying engineers with capacity for production of new ideas.

Description: Multiple item paper-pencil measure of creative potential in design production, research and development. Tests yield three scores: fluency, flexibility and total creativity. Materials include two equivalent forms, G and H. Restricted to companies with qualified personnel administrators and to psychologists using tests for instruction or vocational guidance.

Untimed: Not available

Range: Engineering applicants

Scoring: Hand key

Cost: Specimen set (includes form G and H and manual) $1.00; 25 tests (form G or H) and manual $11.00.

Publisher: Purdue Research Association/University Book Store

RESEARCH PERSONNEL REVIEW FORM
Morris I. Stein

adult

Purpose: Evaluates the performance of personnel in research and development organizations. Measures strengths and weaknesses of scientists and engineers in this field.

Description: 120 item paper-pencil questionnaire assesses a scientist's or engineer's work in terms of quantity, quality and creativity. Test items cover administrative, employee, social, scientific, and professional factors involved in the individual's performance. Self-administered by the individual being reviewed. Suitable for group use.

Untimed: 30 minutes

Range: Adult

Scoring: Examiner evaluated

Cost: $2.50 per copy

Publisher: Morris I. Stein

SENIOR ENGLISH TEST
Refer to page 430.

SURVEY OF OBJECT VISUALIZATION (SOV)
Refer to page 804.

SURVEYS OF RESEARCH ENVIRONMENTS
Morris I. Stein

adult

Purpose: Obtains information from scientists and engineers concerning their job situations and the demands being placed upon them. Evaluates and identifies problem areas in Research and Development (R & D) organizations.

Description: 189 item paper-pencil inventory asks research and administrative personnel to evaluate the organization and factors that lead to success and creativity on the job. Items are presented in terms of role requirements: scientific, professional, administrative, social and employee. Self-administered. Suitable for group use. Restricted to R & D organizations.

Untimed: 45 minutes

Range: Adult

Scoring: Examiner evaluated

Cost: $2.50 per copy.

Publisher: Morris I. Stein

TECHNICAL TEST BATTERY: VERBAL COMPREHENSION (TTB:VT1)
Refer to page 756.

Intelligence and Related

ADAPTABILITY TEST
Joseph Tiffin and C.H. Lawshe

adult

Purpose: Measures mental adaptability and alertness. Distinguishes between people who should be placed in jobs requiring more learning ability and those who should be in more simple or routine jobs.

Description: 70 item paper-pencil test consisting primarily of verbal items and word match problems. Predicts success in a variety of business and industrial situations. Predicative validity information given for clerical employees, general foreman, first line supervisors and other employees and supervisors. Examiner required. Suitable for group use.

Timed: 15 minutes

Range: Adult

Scoring: Hand key

Cost: 25 test booklets (specify form A or B) $15.50; examiner's manual $1.60.

Publisher: Science Research Associates, Inc.

ADULT BASIC LEARNING EXAMINATION (ABLE)
Refer to page 699.

ADVANCED PERSONNEL TEST
W.S. Miller

adult

Purpose: Assesses verbal reasoning ability. Used for employee selection in business, industry and government.

Description: Multiple item paper-pencil test of verbal reasoning ability. Business test comparable to the Miller Analogies Test and Mathematical Reasoning Test. Examiner required. Suitable for group use.

Untimed: Not available

Range: Adult

Scoring: Scoring service available

Cost: Contact publisher.

Publisher: The Psychological Corporation

BRUCE VOCABULARY INVENTORY
Martin M. Bruce

adult

Purpose: Determines how a subject's vocabulary compares with others in various business occupations.

Description: 100 item paper-pencil multiple-choice test in which the subject matches one of four alternative words with a key vocabulary word. Measures the ability to recognize and comprehend words. The score can be compared to those of executives, middle-managers, white collar workers, engineers, blue collar workers, and a "total employed population." Self-administered. Suitable for group use.

Untimed: 15-20 minutes

Range: Adult

Scoring: Hand key

Cost: Specimen set with IBM scoring stencil $4.95; specimen set with hand key $4.30; package of tests $15.30; manual $2.37; hand key $.66; IBM scoring stencils $2.37; IBM answer sheets $6.05.

Publisher: Martin M. Bruce, Ph.D., Publisher

CLOSURE SPEED (GESTALT COMPLETION)
L.L. Thurstone and T.E. Jeffery

adult

Purpose: Evaluates visual and space perception skills, ideational fluency and inductive reasoning ability.

Description: 24 item paper-pencil, fill-in test of the subject's ability to construct a total picture from incomplete or ambiguous material. Basic reading and writing skills are required. Examiner required. Suitable for group use.

Timed: 3 minutes

Range: Adult

Scoring: Hand key

Cost: Specimen set $4.00; 20 test booklets $4.00; scoring key, no charge; manual $2.50.

Publisher: London House Press

COMPOUND SERIES TEST (CST)
J.R. Morrisby

all ages

Purpose: Assesses general intelligence by measuring the capacity to learn through the systematic analysis of a problem. Used in industry for personnel selection, placement and promotion.

Description: 60 item paper-pencil test requiring persistence, concentration, and directed effort in order to solve problems. Each item presents a pattern drawn as a string of beads varying in size, shape and color. The subject indicates which two beads from a choice of eight continue the pattern. The same type of item, increasing in difficulty and complexity, is used through-out, thereby measuring the ability to direct and

control the investment of intellectual effort. Since the test does not depend on such acquired skills as the use of words or numbers, it is suitable for use with educationally and socially disadvantaged subjects. In addition, the colors are arranged so that color-blind subjects can distinguish them. If the CST is to be used in screening for higher-level occupations, it is recommended that it be supplemented by other tests, such as the full Differential Test Battery of E.I.T.S. The CST is restricted to examiners who provide evidence of adequate training and practical experience in the use of such tests. Examiner required. Suitable for group use.
BRITISH PUBLISHER

Timed: 20-30 minutes

Range: Ages 6-adult

Scoring: Hand key; examiner evaluated

Cost: Contact publisher.

Publisher: Educational and Industrial Test Services Ltd.

CONCEPT ATTAINMENT TEST
J.M. Schepers

teen, adult   College

Purpose: Measures conceptual and rational mental abilities of science and technical graduates. Used for employee screening and selection.

Description: Multiple item paper-pencil test measures the ability to attain concepts through the use of rational strategies of thought. The test consists of ten problems in which solutions can only be obtained provided a well-defined and logical strategy is followed consistently. Norms provided for science graduates. Restricted to competent persons properly registered with either the South African Medical and Dental Council or Test Commission of the Republic of South Africa. Examiner

required. Suitable for group use. Afrikaans version available.
SOUTH AFRICAN PUBLISHER

Timed: 50 minutes

Range: College and adult

Scoring: Hand key; examiner evaluated

Cost: Contact publisher

Publisher: National Institute for Personnel Research

DEDUCTIVE REASONING TEST

teen, adult

Purpose: Measures logical thinking abilities. Used with matriculants and higher for purposes of employee screening and selection for a wide variety of technical positions.

Description: Multiple item paper-pencil test is based on formal syllogisms. Each syllogism contains either factual, contra-factual, or non-sense premises. The test provides a measure of the ability to deduce logically correct conclusions from the information contained in the premises. Restricted to competent persons properly registered with the South African Medical and Dental Council or Test Commission of the Republic of South Africa. Examiner required. Suitable for group use. Afrikaans version available.
SOUTH AFRICAN PUBLISHER

Timed: 40 minutes

Range: Job applicants who are matriculants and higher

Scoring: Hand key; examiner evaluated

Cost: Contact publisher

Publisher: National Institute for Personnel Research

FIGURE CLASSIFICATION TEST

teen, adult

Purpose: Measures abstract reasoning ability. Used with examinees who have 7-9 years of schooling for purposes of employee selection and placement.

Description: Multiple item paper-pencil test measures conceptual reasoning ability by requiring the examinee to analyze sets of figures and to deduce the basic relationships which divide each set into two groups. The relationships are indicated by uniformity, symmetry, inversion, repetition, and series. Restricted to competent persons properly registered with the South African Medical and Dental Council or Test Commission of the Republic of South Africa. Examiner required. Suitable for group use. Afrikaans version available.
SOUTH AFRICAN PUBLISHER

Timed: 60 minutes

Range: Job applicants with 7-9 years of schooling

Scoring: Hand key; examiner evaluated

Cost: Contact publisher

Publisher: National Institute for Personnel Research

EMPLOYEE APTITUDE SURVEY TEST #10--SYMBOLIC REASONING (EAS #10)
Refer to page 708.

ETSA TESTS 1-A: GENERAL MENTAL ABILITY
Refer to page 710.

FORM SERIES TEST A

teen, adult

Purpose: Measures non-verbal reasoning ability. Used with groups with 0-8 years of schooling for purposes of employee selection and placement.

Description: Multiple item task assessment test measures nonverbal reasoning ability using a board on which is printed a series of patterns made up of forms of different sizes, shapes and colors. Each pattern must be completed by inferring from the given series of shapes and colors what the next two must be. Restricted to competent persons properly registered with the South African Medical and Dental Council or Test Commission of the Republic of South Africa. Examiner required. Suitable for group use. Afrikaans version available.

SOUTH AFRICAN PUBLISHER

Untimed: Not available

Range: Job applicants with no schooling to eight years of schooling

Scoring: Hand key; examiner evaluated

Cost: Contact publisher

Publisher: National Institute for Personnel Research

GENERAL ABILITY TESTS: NUMERICAL (GAT NUMERICAL)
J.R. Morrisby

all ages

Purpose: Measures numerical intelligence. Used for personnel selection in most occupations, especially those in which numerical concepts are involved and the ability to think quantitatively is at a premium. Also used as a predictor of academic success.

Description: Multiple item paper-pencil test in three parts. Part 1 requires the subject to indicate whether simple addition and multiplication calculations, worked out, are correct or incorrect. Part 2 consists of a number series in which the degree of computation required is reduced, but the dependence on the subject's ability to see numerical relationships is increased. In Part 3, the subject completes matrixes with one element missing. The computational requirement on Part 3 is small, but the requirement to see into numerical relationships is at a maximum. The mental functions involved in each sub-test are arranged to give a progression throughout the test, from a loading of speed of apprehension in Part 1 to a heavy loading of insight or intuitive power in Part 3. Materials include booklets, scoring keys, specimen set, and the manual. Tests of verbal intelligence and of nonverbal, or perceptual intelligence are also available in this three-part GAT series. The series has been constructed as a matched trio to give differential assessment of the main areas of mental ability, but any one may be used alone. The GAT is restricted to examiners who provide evidence of adequate training and practical experience in the use of such tests. Examiner required. Suitable for group use.

BRITISH PUBLISHER

Timed: 35 minutes

Range: Ages 11 and older

Scoring: Hand key; examiner evaluated; computer scoring available

Cost: Contact publisher.

Publisher: Educational and Industrial Test Service Ltd.

GENERAL ABILITY TESTS: PERCEPTUAL (GAT PERCEPTUAL)

J.R. Morrisby

all ages

Purpose: Measures nonverbal, perceptual intelligence. Used for personnel selection in most occupations, especially engineering, design, and scientific work which deals with real objects rather than verbal or numerical concepts.

Description: Multiple item paper-pencil, multiple-choice test in three categories. Part 1, requires the subject to determine which meaningless figures shown are identical with a given example. In Part 2, the subject classifies four of six figures shown in each item and indicates the two that do not belong. In Part 3, the subject selects a pair of figures analogous with a given pair, to test insight into relationships between perceptual forms. The mental functions involved in each sub-test are arranged to give a progression throughout the test, from a loading of speed of apprehension in Part 1 to a heavy loading of insight or intuitive power in Part 3. Materials include booklets, scoring keys, specimen set, and the manual. Tests of verbal intelligence and numerical intelligence are also available in this three-part GAT series. The series has been constructed as a matched trio to give differential assessment of the main areas of mental ability, but any one may be used alone. The GAT is restricted to examiners who provide evidence of adequate training and practical experience in the use of such tests. Examiner required. Suitable for group use.
BRITISH PUBLISHER

Timed: 27 minutes

Range: Ages 11 and older

Scoring: Hand key; examiner evaluated

Cost: Contact publisher.

Publisher: Educational and Industrial Test Service Ltd.

GENERAL ABILITY TESTS: VERBAL (GAT VERBAL)

J.R. Morrisby

all ages

Purpose: Measures verbal intelligence. Used as a selection tool in most occupations, especially those which emphasize communicating skills and written work, and as a predictor of academic success.

Description: Multiple item paper-pencil, multiple-choice instrument consisting of three separately times subtests. Part 1 measures speedy understanding of verbal concepts, expressed as synonyms and antonyms. Performance depends upon an adequate vocabulary and language insight. Part 2 is based on classification of words with vocabulary requirement reduced and dependence on insight into relationships between verbal concepts increased. Part 3 tests ability to make up pairs of words, from a multiple-choice array, which are analogous with a given pair. In this section, demands on vocabulary are low and demands on insight are maximal. The mental functions involved in each sub-test are arranged to give a progression throughout the test, from a loading of speed of apprehension in Part 1 to a heavy loading of insight or intuitive power in Part 3. Materials include booklets, scoring keys, specimen set, and the manual. Tests of numerical intelligence and nonverbal, or perceptual intelligence are also available in this three-part GAT series. The series has been constructed as a matched trio to give differential assessment of the main areas of mental ability, but any one may be used alone. The GAT is restricted to examiners who provide evidence of adequate training and practical experience in the use of such tests. Examiner required. Suitable for group use.

BRITISH PUBLISHER

Timed: 16 minutes

Range: Ages 11-intelligently superior adult

Scoring: Hand key; examiner evaluated; computer scoring available

Cost: Contact publisher.

Publisher: Educational and Industrial Test Service Ltd.

GUILFORD-ZIMMERMAN APTITUDE SURVEY (GZAS)
Refer to page 716.

GUILFORD-ZIMMERMAN APTITUDE SURVEY: GENERAL REASONING (GZAS:GR)
Refer to page 717.

GUILFORD-ZIMMERMAN APTITUDE SURVEY: VERBAL COMPREHENSION (GZAS:VC)
Refer to page 718.

INVENTORY NUMBER II
Jack Harris Hazlehurst

teen, adult

Purpose: Measures mental ability of people over the age of 16 regardless of educational level. Used for employee selection and placement.

Description: 50 item paper-pencil multiple-choice and free response test. Measures an individual's ability to solve problems involving word meanings and verbally constructed conceptual relations, and those which require the manipulations of number relationships. Problems are included which are designed to sample the creative, reproductive and relational aspects of imagination. The test is standardized on a carefully structured sampling, according to age, education and level of vocational adjustment. Examiner required. Suitable for group use.

Timed: 15 minutes

Range: Adult

Scoring: Hand key

Cost: 25 tests $3.00; monograph of instructions and critical statistical evaluation plus scoring key $1.00.

Publisher: Stevens, Thurow and Associates

LEARNING ABILITY PROFILE (LAP)
Margarita Henning

adult

Purpose: Assesses a person's ability to learn. May be used in determine the potential for job success.

Description: 80 item paper-pencil test measuring overall learning ability, flexibility, frustration level, problem solving ability and decisiveness. Examiner required. Suitable for group use. Available in French.

Untimed: 60 minutes

Range: Adult

Scoring: Hand key; examiner evaluated

Cost: Complete set (2 test booklets, answer sheets and manual) $100.00.

Publisher: Harvard Personnel Testing

MENTAL ALERTNESS--
ADVANCED AND
INTERMEDIATE

adult

Purpose: Measures general intelligence for purposes of employee screening and selection. Used with matriculants and higher, and people with 10-12 years of schooling.

Description: Two paper-pencil tests measure general intelligence, mainly verbal, at two levels of education. The Advanced test is suitable for matriculants and higher, while the Intermediate test is for candidates with 10-12 years of schooling. Both tests are available in two parallel forms. Norms are provided for each test. Restricted to competent persons properly registered with the South African Medical and Dental Council or Test Commission of the Republic of South Africa. Examiner required. Suitable for group use. Afrikaans version available.
SOUTH AFRICAN PUBLISHER

Timed: 35 minutes each

Range: Adults

Scoring: Hand key; examiner evaluated

Cost: Contact publisher

Publisher: National Institute for Personnel Research

MORRISBY DIFFERENTIAL
TEST BATTERY (DTB)
J.R. Morrisby

teen, adult

Purpose: Evaluates a person's intellectual structure and basic personality characteristics. Used to predict the likelihood of success in a large number of occupations and modes of behavior in a variety of situations. Widely used for career guidance.

Description: A paper-pencil battery of 12 intelligence and personality tests, designed to give a total assessment of an individual as well as meaningful single test scores. The four intelligence tests are the Compound Series Test, a measure of basic intellectual power, and three General Ability Tests: Verbal, Numerical and Perceptual. The Shapes Test and Mechanical Ability Test provide measures of spatial and mechanical ability to show the subject's level of practicality and analysis and overview abilities. The six Speed Tests: Conceptual Speed, Perserverance, Word Fluency, Ideational Fluency, Motor Speed, and Motor Skill, measure qualities such as leadership, confidence, flexibility, resistance to change, speed of awareness, personal commitment, tenacity, and initiative. Materials include one-time test forms, reusable booklets, manual, and scoring keys. A scoring service, an interpretation service, and a grading service are also available. The battery is restricted to examiners who provide evidence of adequate training and practical experience in the use of such tests. Examiner required. Suitable for group use.
BRITISH PUBLISHER

Untimed: 3 hours, 10 minutes

Range: Ages 13 and up

Scoring: Examiner evaluated; computer prepared interpretative reports available

Cost: Contact publisher

Publisher: Educational and Industrial Test Services Ltd.

NON-VERBAL REASONING
R.J. Corsini

adult

Purpose: Assesses logical reasoning ability in nonverbal situation. Used for industrial job screening and selection, and for vocational counseling.

Description: 44 item paper-pencil test of capacity to reason logically. Subject studies one picture, then selects from among four others the one which best compliments it. Examiner required. Suitable for group use.

Untimed: 20 minutes

Range: Adult

Scoring: Hand key, machine scoring available

Cost: Specimen set $3.00.

Publisher: London House Press

PATTERN RELATIONS TEST

adult

Purpose: Measures inductive reasoning abilities. Suitable for use with university level and graduate job applicants for a variety of science and technical positions.

Description: Multiple item paper-pencil test measures the ability to recognize associated concepts that fit sets of data and the consequent-forming and testing of hypotheses. The test is similar to Raven's Progressive Matrices. Norms established on scientific research workers with degrees and first-year engineering students. Restricted to competent persons properly registered with the South African Medical and Dental Council or Test Commission of the Republic of South Africa. Examiner required. Suitable for group use. Afrikaans version available.
SOUTH AFRICAN PUBLISHER

Timed: 50 minutes each

Range: Job applicants with university level or college degree

Scoring: Hand key; examiner evaluated

Cost: Contact publisher

Publisher: National Institute for Personnel Research

PERSONNEL RESEARCH INSTITUTE: FACTORY SERIES B
Personnel Research Institute

adult

Purpose: Measures an individual's general mental ability. Used for factory job placement.

Description: 50 item paper-pencil test measuring: general factual knowledge, arithmetic, numerical reasoning, and spatial relations. The test questions simulate problems found in routine industrial jobs. Examiner required. Suitable for group use.

Timed: 10 or 15 minutes

Range: Adult

Scoring: Hand key

Cost: 100 tests $35.00

Publisher: Personnel Research Institute

PURDUE NON-LANGUAGE PERSONNEL TEST
Joseph Tiffin

teen, adult

Purpose: Assesses general mental ability. Used for evaluation of applicants who cannot be fairly tested using verbal tests.

Description: Multiple item paper-pencil, nonverbal measure of intelligence. Items consist entirely of geometric forms. Materials include two forms, A-S and B-S. Sales restricted to companies employing qualified personnel administrators and to psychologists using tests for instruction or vocational guidance. Examiner required. Suitable for group use.

Untimed: Not available

Range: Job applicants

Scoring: Hand key

Cost: Specimen set (includes form A-S, form B-S, manual and keys) $1.00; 25 tests, manual, key (specify form) $7.50.

Publisher: Purdue Research Foundation/University Book Store

SHIP DESTINATION TEST (SD)
Paul R. Christensen and J.P. Guilford

---

teen, adult   grades 10-UP

Purpose: Measures general reasoning ability among high school students, college students and adult. Used for job selection when arithmetic reasoning is important.

Description: 48 item paper-pencil multiple-choice test measuring the cognition of semantic systems by means of a well-disguised arithmetic-reasoning test. The test items are steeply graded in complexity and difficulty, with nine practice problems included. Emphasis is on problem solving that involves seeing interrelationships of variables or elements, rather than numerical computation. Test materials consist of answer sheets and reusable test booklets. Norms provided for college groups. Restricted to A.P.A. membership or equivalent. Examiner required. Suitable for group use.

Timed: 15 minutes

Range: High school-adult

Scoring: Hand key; may be computer scored

Cost: 25 tests $7.00; 25 answer sheets $3.50; manual $.75; hand key $2.00.

Publisher: Sheridan Psychological Services, Inc.

SRA NONVERBAL FORM
Robert N. McMurry and Joseph E. King

---

adult

Purpose: Assesses general learning ability. Measures learning potential of individuals who have difficulty in reading or understanding the English language. Used for employee selection and placement.

Description: 60 item paper-pencil test consisting or five drawings, each measuring recognition of differences. Examiner required. Suitable for group use.

Timed: 10 minutes

Range: Adults with a high school education or less

Scoring: Hand scored--carbon insert (answers transfer to key on inside of test booklet).

Cost: 25 test booklets $16.00; examiner's manual $1.20.

Publisher: Science Research Associates, Inc.

SRA PICTORIAL REASONING TEST (PRT)
Robert N. McMurry and Phyllis D. Arnold

---

teen, adult

Purpose: Measures general reasoning ability of students, especially older non-readers. Useful for predicting job success and as a basic screening test for entry level jobs.

Description: 80 item paper-pencil pictorial test measuring aspects of learning ability. Test is culturally unbiased and does not require previously learned reading skills. Examiner required. Suitable for group use.

Timed: 15 minutes (may also be given

untimed)

Range: High school education or less

Scoring: Hand scored--carbon insert (answers transfer to key on inside of test booklet).

Cost: 25 test booklets $23.50; examiner's manual $3.40.

Publisher: Science Research Associates, Inc.

SURVEY OF OBJECT VISUALIZATION (SOV)
Daniel R. Miller

adult

Purpose: Measures ability to perceive spatial relationships, a skill required in technically oriented positions such as draftsmen, engineers, architects, and mechanics. Used in career planning and employee selection and placement.

Description: 44 item paper-pencil multiple-choice test. Each test item consists of a drawing of a flat geometric pattern on which dotted lines have been drawn. Each test item is followed by four perspective drawings. The examinees must select the perspective drawing which is actually the flat pattern after it has been folded on the dotted lines. Examiner required. Suitable for group use.

Timed: 25 minutes

Range: Adult

Scoring: Hand key

Cost: Test booklet (minimum order of 25) $.25 each; optional answer sheet (minimum order of 25) $.25 each; manual $1.35; key $.75; specimen set (includes booklet and manual) $4.75.

Publisher: Psychological Services, Inc.

THURSTONE TEST OF MENTAL ALERTNESS
L.L. Thurstone and Thelma Gwinn Thurstone

adult

Purpose: Measures an individual's capacity to acquire new knowledge and skills and to use what they have learned in problem solving. Measures individual differences in ability to learn and perform mental tasks of varying type and complexity. Used for employee selection and vocational counseling.

Description: 126 item paper-pencil test measuring four general areas: arithmetic reasoning, number series, same-opposite and definition. Average educational opportunities and familiarity with English language requisite. Two equivalent forms available. Examiner required. Suitable for group use.

Timed: 20 minutes

Range: Adult

Scoring: Hand scored--carbon insert (answers transfer to key on inside of test booklet).

Cost: 25 test booklets $23.50; examiner's manual $1.60.

Publisher: Science Research Associates

VERBAL REASONING
Raymond J. Corsini and Richard Renck

adult

Purpose: Assesses individual capacity to reason logically as indicated by solutions to verbal problems. Used for industrial job selection and vocational counseling.

Description: 36 item paper-pencil test of mental reasoning consisting of 12 statements with three questions each. A knowledge of basic English is required. Examiner required. Suitable for group use.

Timed: 15 minutes

Range: Adult

Scoring: Hand key

Cost: Specimen set $3.00; 20 tests $4.00.

Publisher: London House Press

WATSON-GLASER CRITICAL THINKING APPRAISAL
Refer to page 546.

WESTERN PERSONNEL TESTS
Robert L. Gunn and Morse P. Manson

adult

Purpose: Measures general intelligence. Used for personnel screening.

Description: Multiple item paper-pencil test providing a quick measure of general intelligence. Available in four equivalent forms: A, B, C, and D. Norms are provided for general population as well as professional, college, clerical, skilled and unskilled populations. The test has a high correlation with longer personnel tests. Examiner required. Suitable for group use.

Timed: 5 minutes

Range: Adult

Scoring: Hand key

Cost: Kit (25 tests, manual, key) $9.85.

Publisher: Western Psychological Services

THE WONDERLIC PERSONNEL TEST
Refer to page 759.

Interests

ADVANCED OCCUPATIONAL INTEREST INVENTORY
Saville and Holdsworth, Ltd.

---

adult

Purpose: Collects information about job related interests from school leavers and adults with education from 'O' level upwards including graduates and managerial personnel. Used for counseling, vocational guidance, career planning, redundancy and retirement counseling, and selection and placement decisions.

Description: Multiple item paper-pencil inventory asking respondents to state their liking for activities related to graduate and managerial positions. Consists of 19 scales (distinct from the General inventory) which can be organized into a hierarchy of interests to provide derived scores. The scales are: medical, welfare, education, control, commercial, managerial, administration, legal, financial, data processing, information, media, art and design, biological, physical, process, mechanical, electrical, and construction. Examiner required. Suitable for group use.

BRITISH PUBLISHER

Timed: Not available

Range: Adult

Scoring: Hand key; examiner evaluated; may be computer scored

Cost: 10 booklets £8.50; manual and guide £15.00; key £4.00.

Publisher: Saville and Holdsworth, Ltd.

CANADIAN OCCUPATIONAL INTEREST INVENTORY (COII)
G. Booth and Luc Begin

adult

Purpose: Identifies an adult's attitudes toward occupationally related activities.

Description: 70 item paper-pencil measure of attitudes as they relate occupationally to activities. Interests and activities are measured by the following bi-polar factors: things vs. people, business contact vs. scientific, routine vs. creative, social vs. solitary, and prestige vs. production. Test relates to the computer guidance program CHOICES. Examiner required. Suitable for group use. Available in French.

Untimed: 40 minutes

Range: Adult

Scoring: Hand key

Cost: 25 booklets $20.50; manual $8.50; 500 sheets and charts $77.95; key $3.25.

Publisher: Nelson Canada Limited

CAREER INTEREST TEST (CIT)
Educational and Industrial Test Services Ltd. Staff

teen, adult

Purpose: Determines the vocational interests of young people and adults. Used for vocational and educational guidance.

Description: Multiple item paper-pencil forced choice test. The score reveals the subject's interests in or aversions to occupations in these six catagories of interests: outdoor-physical, scientific- theoretical, social service, aesthetic-literary, commercial-clerical, and practical technical. Materials include booklets, scoring key, specimen set, and manual. Examiner required. Suitable for group use.

BRITISH PUBLISHER

Untimed: 20 minutes

Range: Adolescent-adult

Scoring: Examiner evaluated

Cost: Contact publisher.

Publisher: Educational and Industrial Test Services Ltd.

CURTIS INTEREST SCALE
James W. Curtis

teen, adult   grades 10-UP

Purpose: Assesses individual vocational interest patterns. Used for vocational guidance, screening and selection.

Description: 55 item paper-pencil test of vocational interests in ten occupational areas: applied arts, business, computation, direct sales, entertainment, farming, inter-personal, mechanics, production, and science. Estimate of "level of responsibility" is also obtained. Self- administered. Suitable for group use.

Untimed: 10 minutes

Range: High school and older

Scoring: Examiner evaluated; scoring service available

Cost: Specimen set (includes one test, manual, profile sheet) $3.00; 25 scales $4.00; 100 scales $14.00; 25 profiles $2.50; 100 scales $8.00.

Publisher: Psychometric Affiliates

EXPERIENCE EXPLORATION
Refer to page 664.

FORER VOCATIONAL SURVEY: MEN-WOMEN
Refer to page 665.

GENERAL OCCUPATIONAL INTEREST INVENTORY
Saville and Holdsworth, Ltd.

adult

Purpose: Collects information about job-related interests among school leavers and adults with education up to the 'O' level. Used for counseling, vocational guidance, career planning, redundancy and retirement counseling as well as selection and placement decisions.

Description: Multiple item paper-pencil inventory asking respondents to state their liking for activities which are related to specific occupations relevant to this level, including: child care workers, waiter/tress, sales representative, security officers, chargehand, secretary, farmer, graphic designer, dressmaker, maintenance electrician, and plumber. Scores are grouped for 18 main categories: medical, welfare, personal services, selling goods, selling services, supervision, clerical, office equipment, control, leisure, art and design, crafts, plants, animals, transport, construction, electrical and mechanical. Evaluation of the scores for the 18 groups provides derived scores which indicate specific interests. Examiner required. Suitable for group use.
BRITISH PUBLISHER

Untimed: Not available

Range: Adult

Scoring: Hand key; examiner evaluated; may be computer scored.

Cost: 10 booklets £8.50; manual and guide £15.00; key £4.00.

Publisher: Saville and Holdsworth, Ltd.

HACKMAN-GAITHER INTEREST INVENTORY
Refer to page 666.

THE INTEREST CHECK LIST (ICL)

adult

Purpose: Determines an individual's employment interests. Used as a guide to vocational counseling and self-assessment.

Description: 210 item paper-pencil checklist of sample tasks which have been keyed to the work groups listed in the Guide for Occupational Exploration. It permits the evaluation of the applicant's likes and dislikes, leading to an understanding of why they are interested in the subjects indicated. Especially useful for persons who have no firmly stated interests or who are not aware of the variety of existing occupations. Self-administered. Suitable for group use. Available in Spanish.

Untimed: 20 minutes

Range: Adult

Scoring: Hand key

Cost: Available through State Employment agencies only.

Publisher: U.S. Department of Labor

INVENTORY OF VOCATIONAL INTERESTS
Andrew Kobal, J. Wayne Wrightstone, Karl Kunze, edited by Andrew J. MacElroy

teen, adult   grades 10-UP

Purpose: Assesses vocational interests. Used for vocational guidance.

Description: 25 subject paper-pencil test of occupational interests. There are ten responses under each of the 25 topics. Provides insight into both major and minor interests. Areas measured include academic, artistic, mechanical, business and economic, and farm-agricultural. Materials include an inventory and occupation index arranged by vocational categories in the manual. Examiner required. Suitable for group use.

Timed: 35 minutes

Range: High school and older

Scoring: Examiner evaluated

Cost: Specimen set $2.20; 25 tests $3.85; 100- $12.00; 25 answer sheets $2.20; 100-$7.70.

Publisher: Psychometric Affiliates

JACKSON VOCATIONAL INTEREST SURVEY (JVIS)
Refer to page 670.

THE JOB ANALYSIS AND INTEREST MEASUREMENT (JAIM)
Regis H. Walther

teen, adult

Purpose: Measures the skills and attitudes important to coping with adult work roles. May be used for vocational counseling, determining job requirements, evaluating personnel and job applicants, and the study of occupational and organizational personalities.

Description: 154-item multiple-choice paper-pencil test scored on 32 scales relating to self-management, interpersonal style, reaction to aggression, cognitive style, relation to authority, supervisory style, work preferences and values. It is based on the assumption that individuals develop coping skills for particular situations which may or may not be effective in new circumstances. The respondent reads each question, selects the most appropriate response and enters the choice number on an answer sheet. Self-administered. Suitable for group use.

Untimed: 30-45 minutes

Range: Ages 16-adult

Scoring: Computer scored

Cost: Specimen set $4.00; scoring costs: minimum charge of $20 for scoring 1 to 2 subjects; $8.00 per subject for 6-10; scoring services are provided at cost to student and faculty conducting properly designed nonfunded research.

Publisher: JAIM Research, Inc.

JIIG-CAL OCCUPATIONAL INTERESTS GUIDE AND APU OCCUPATIONAL INTEREST GUIDE
Refer to page 671.

KUDER PREFERENCE RECORD, VOCATIONAL, FORM CP
Refer to page 673.

INFORMATION SYSTEM SKILLS
Malcolm J. Morrisby

adult

Purpose: Measures basic aptitudes required in operating terminal based information systems. Used to predict success in such occupations as: Word Processing, On-line Data Enquiries, Computerized Stock Control Systems, Data Entry etc.

Description: Consists of four subtests: Part 1 Reasoning, 60 verbal and numerical items measure ability in these areas, equivalent to 'general intelligence'; Part 2 Form recognition: 70 items of embedded figures measuring spatial skill and perceptual ability; Part 3 Clerical Speed and Accuracy. Two documents containing words and figures are presented each with a copy, which the subject marks for errors; Part 4 A short test of manual speed, in the form of a controlled dotting test. Materials include booklets, scoring keys, specimen set and manual. Examiner required. Suitable for group use.
BRITISH PUBLISHER

Untimed: 40 minutes

Range: Adult

Scoring: Hand keys

Cost: Contact publisher

Publisher: Educational and Industrial Test Services Ltd.

LIFE STYLE QUESTIONNAIRE
James Barrett

teen, adult

Purpose: Provides insight regarding interests, attitudes and behaviors of people about to begin work or already working. Used for vocational guidance, counseling and management development.

Description: 132 item paper-pencil test for self-assessment of vocational interests and attitudes. Items are statements about work activities. Scores are provided on thirteen scales: six dealing with general motivation, five examining consistency of outlook with interests, and two estimating the degree of certainty about questionnaire responses. The test booklet contains instructions on how to respond to test items. Self-administered. Suitable for group use. BRITISH PUBLISHER

Timed: 20 minutes

Range: Ages 15-adult

Scoring: Hand key; scoring service available

Cost: Booklet $2.50; answer sheet and graphs set $1.50; manual $8.00.

Publisher: The Test Agency

MINNESOTA IMPORTANCE QUESTIONNAIRE (MIQ)

adult

Purpose: Measures vocational needs and relates them to occupational reinforcers. Assesses need-reinforcer correspondence as a supplement to standard measures of occupational interests and abilities.

Description: Multiple item paper-pencil inventory assessing vocational needs in terms of preferred occupational reinforcers. Two forms are available: The Paired Form (102 items) presents pairs of vocational needs statements, and the examinee indicates the more important need in each pair; and the Ranking Form (42 items), which presents vocational need statements in groups of five, and the individual ranks the five needs in each group according to their importance. Both forms measure the following need dimensions: ability, utilization, achievement, activity, advancement, authority, company policies and practices, compensation, co-workers, creativity, independence, moral values, recognition, responsibility, security, social service, social status, supervision-human relations, supervision-technical, variety, and working conditions. A computer-generated profile and interpretation are provided for each examinee, which includes: scores on each dimension (Ranked Form also includes Autonomy Scale) in the form of a profile, correspondence of examinee's need pattern to Occupational Reinforcer Patterns (ORP's), lists (50 each) of occupations with ORP's most similar and least similar to the examinee's MIQ profile, predictions of job satisfaction for each occupation listed, references for further information, a validity score, and an error factor for each score. A technical manual (available at no charge to qualifed users) discusses development, reliability, validity, normative data, and interpretations of sample MIQ profiles. Self-administered with clinical supervision. Suitable for group use. Restricted to APA members only. Available in Spanish and French.

Untimed: Varies

Range: Adult

Scoring: Computer scored

Cost: 10-99 booklets $.40 each (specify ranked or paired form); 10-499 answer sheets $.05 each (specify ranked or paired form); computer scoring $1.30 per report.

Publisher: Vocational Psychology Research, University of Minnesota

OHIO VOCATIONAL INTEREST SURVEY: SECOND EDITION (OVIS II)

teen, adult   grades 7-UP

Purpose: Assesses occupational and vocational interests. Used for educational and vocational counseling.

Description: 253 item paper-pencil test of job-related interests. Items are job activities to which student responds on a five point scale ranging from "Like very much" to "Dislike very much." Used in conjunction with the Dictionary of Occupational Titles, OVIS II classifies occupations according to three elements; data, people and things. Materials include Career Planner Workbook, Handbook for Exploring Careers, and filmstrips to aid counselors in administering and interpreting OVIS II. Supersedes 1969 OVIS. Examiner required. Suitable for group use.

Untimed: 45 minutes

Range: Grades 7-12, college-adult

Scoring: Hand key, may be machine scored, scoring service available

Cost: 35 tests $20.00; 35 hand-scorable answer documents $17.25; 35 MRC machine-scorable answer documents $9.50; 35 NCS machine-scorable answer documents $11.25; basic scoring service $1.50 per pupil.

Publisher: The Psychological Corporation

ROTHWELL-MILLER INTEREST BLANK
J. W. Rothwell and K.M. Miller

teen, adult   grades 10-UP

Purpose: Assesses the vocational interests of secondary school students and adults. Used for vocational and educational guidance.

Description: Multiple item paper-pencil test in which the subject ranks representative titles in order of preference in 12 occupational areas: outdoor, mechanical, computational, scientific, persuasive, aesthetic, literary, musical, social services, clerical, practical, and medical. The pattern of scores indicates the relative strengths of a person's interests and may be compared with extensive norm tables given in the manual. Separate male and female test forms are available, and a unisex version is to be ready soon. Examiner required. Suitable for group use.
BRITISH PUBLISHER

Untimed: 20 minutes

Range: Secondary students-adults

Scoring: Examiner evaluated

Cost: Contact publisher.

Publisher: N.F.E.R.—Nelson Publishing Co. Ltd.

SELF-DESCRIPTION INVENTORY (SDI)
Charles B. Johansson

teen, adult   grades 9-UP

Purpose: Evaluates an individual's personal attitudes and vocational interests. Used for personnel selection and vocational needs assessment.

Description: 200 item paper-pencil inventory covering 11 personal description and six vocational scales. The personal scales include the following factors: Caution/

Adventurous, Nonscientific/ Analytical, Tense/Relaxed, Insecure/ Confident, Conventional/Imaginative, Impatient/Patient, Unconcerned/Altruistic, Reserved/ Outgoing, Softspoken/Forceful, Lackadaisical/Industrious, Unorganized/Orderly. The vocational scales include the following: Realistic, Investigative, Artistic, Social, Enterprising, Conventional. Self-administered. Suitable for group use.

Untimed: 15-20 minutes

Range: Grades 9-adult

Scoring: Computer scored

Cost: Profile form $2.15-$4.25 each (scoring included).

Publisher: NCS Interpretive Scoring Systems

SELF-DIRECTED SEARCH (SDS)
John L. Holland

teen, adult   grades 10-UP

Purpose: Helps explore an individual's work world. Used for vocational guidance counseling and personnel work.

Description: Multiple-item paper-pencil test of six interest types: realistic (R), investigative (I), artistic (A), social (S), enterprising (E), and conventional (C). Stimulates discussion of vocational possibilities and resolution of vocational problems. The test-takers obtain a three letter code reflecting their major interest types. This code can then be used to identify appropriate vocational options. Materials include a Counselor's Guide, assessment books, occupations finders, and an interpretive booklet. A separate form (Form E) is available for examinees with a limited command of written English. Form E yields simplified two letter codes. Self-administered. Suitable for group

use. Available in Spanish and Vietnamese.

Untimed: 2-3 hours

Range: High school-adult

Scoring: Hand key

Cost: Specimen set (no manual, includes counselor's guide) $2.25; manual $8.00.

Publisher: Consulting Psychologists Press, Inc.

STRONG-CAMPBELL INTEREST INVENTORY (SCII)
E.K. Strong, Jr. and David P. Campbell

teen, adult   grades 8-UP

Purpose: Measures occupational interests in a wide range of career areas requiring, for the most part, advanced technical or college training. Used to make long-range curricular and occupational choices, as well as for employee selection and placement, and vocational rehabilitation placement.

Description: 325 item paper-pencil multiple-choice test asking the examinee to respond either "like", "indifferent", or "dislike" to items covering a broad range of familiar occupational tasks and day-to-day activities. General topics include: occupations, school subjects, activities, amusements, types of people, preference between two activities, and "your characteristics". Responses are then analyzed by computer to yield a profile that presents scores on a number of scales and offers interpretive advice. Specifically, the respondent is scored on: Six General Occupational Themes (based on Holland's RIASEC themes), 23 Basic Interest Scales (measuring strength and consistency of specific interest areas), and 162 Occupational Scales (refelecting degree of similarity between respondent and people employed in particular occupations). The scoring services also provide 11 additional non-occupational and administrative indexes as a further guide to interpreting the results. Computer scoring required and available from a number of sources (test results available immediately via ARION II Teleprocessing). Self-administered. Suitable for group use. Available in Spanish.

Untimed: 30-40 minutes

Range: Grades 8-adult

Scoring: Computer scored

Cost: Profile only $1.90-$4.25 depending on quantity and turnaround time via mail; profile and interpretation $3.10-$10.00 depending on quantity and turnaround time via mail; scoring via ARION II teleprocessing $13.00-$15.00 depending upon turnaround time.

Publisher: Stanford University Press

U.S. EMPLOYMENT SERVICE (USES) INTEREST INVENTORY
U.S. Employment Service

adult

Purpose: Measures an individual's general occupational interests as a guide to vocational counseling.

Description: 162 item paper-pencil examination of 12 interest areas listed in the USES Guide for Occupational Exploration: artistic, scientific, plants and animals, protective, mechanical, industrial, business retail, selling, accommodating, humanitarian, leading-influencing, physical performance. Available only to State Employment Services or to organizations which have approval from such Services. Self-administered. Suitable for group use.

Untimed: 20 minutes

Range: Adult

Scoring: Hand key; computer scoring available

Cost: Available only through State Employment Agencies.

Publisher: U.S. Department of Labor

VOCATIONAL PREFERENCE INVENTORY (VPI)
John L. Holland

teen, adult   grades 10-UP

Purpose: Essentially a personality test that uses occupational item contents. Used to assess vocational and occupational interests.

Description: 160 item paper-pencil test of 11 dimensions related to a person's interpersonal relationships, interests, and values. The inventory includes the following dimensions: Realistic, Intellectual, Social, Conventional, Enterprising, Artistic, Self-Control, Masculinity, Status, Infrequency, Acquiscence. Items are all occupational titles and the subject's indicate which they like or dislike. Highest scores on the first six scales may be used to search Holland's Occupations Finder for career suggestions. Examiner/self-administered. Suitable for group use.

Untimed: 15-30 minutes

Range: Grades High school-adult

Scoring: Hand key

Cost: Specimen set $5.00; manual $4.00; key $1.00; 25 reusable tests $2.75; 50 answer sheets and profiles $5.50.

Publisher: Consulting Psychologists Press, Inc.

WIDE RANGE INTEREST-OPINION TEST (WRIOT)
Refer to page 686.

WORK ENVIRONMENT PREFERENCE SCHEDULE
Leonard V. Gordon

adult

Purpose: Measures an individual's commitment to the kinds of attitudes, values and behaviors rewarded by bureaucratic organizations. Used for selecting persons for suitable employment positions.

Description: Multiple item paper-pencil test of work environment preference. Items are statements of values, attitudes and behaviors. Applicants rate each statement on a five-point scale from strongly agree to strongly disagree. Individuals with high scores may be best suited for highly structured environments. Low-scoring applicants may be best suited for positions where initiative and independent judgment are required. Examiner required. Suitable for group use.

Untimed: 10 minutes

Range: Adult

Scoring: Hand key

Cost: Contact publisher.

Publisher: The Psychological Corporation

WORK INTEREST INDEX
M.E. Baehr, R. Renck, R.K. Burns, and R.W. Pranis

adult

Purpose: Measures an individual's interest in 12 vocational areas, as well as flexibility of interest and vocational aspiration through a nonverbal procedure. Used for industrial job screening and selection as well as vocational counseling.

Description: 96 item paper-pencil, pictorial examination of the following factors: professional and technical,

social and verbal, authority and prestige, artistic and interpretative, artistic and stylized, artistic and creative, technical and scientific, clerical and routine, business contact and structured, personal service and persuasive, mechanical and productive, control of massive equipment. The test booklet consists of a series of pictures which the subject marks with "L" for "like" or "D" for "dislike." Self-administered. Suitable for group use.

Untimed: 15-20 minutes

Range: Adult

Scoring: Hand key; computer scoring available

Cost: Specimen set $5.00.

Publisher: London House Press

THE WORLD OF WORK INVENTORY
Robert E. Ripley, original author and Karen Hudson, revision

teen, adult

Purpose: Measures career interests from professional through industrial levels, temperaments and aptitudes related to careers and vocations. Used for employee selection, career counseling, vocational rehabilitation, and adult/career education classes.

Description: 518 item paper-pencil inventory. 98 multiple-choice items assess the following achievement-aptitude areas: abstractions, spatial-form, verbal, mechanical, electrical, and clerical. 420 rating items (subject responds "like," "dislike," or "neutral") assess 12 job-related temperament factors and interests in 17 professional and industrial career areas. Cassette tape available for instruction of examiners. Self-administered. Suitable for group use. Available in Spanish.

Untimed: 2 hours, 15 minutes

Range: Ages 13-65

Scoring: Computer scored

Cost: Reusable test booklet $5.00; answer sheets $5.50; interpretation manual $19.95; computer service included with cost of answer sheets. Non-profit price schedule available.

Publisher: World of Work, Inc.

Interpersonal Skills and Attitudes

BIOGRAPHICAL INDEX
Willard A. Kerr

adult

Purpose: Quantifies background data. Used for predicting success in managerial and sales positions and in recruitment programs for general business.

Description: Multiple item paper-pencil measure of personal background information. Yields five scores: stability, drive to excel, human relations, financial status, and personal adjustment. Three middle scores provide estimate of basic energy level. Predicts annual salary increment of executives. Examiner required. Suitable for group use.

Untimed: Not available

Range: Adult

Scoring: Hand key

Cost: Specimen set $3.30; 25 indices $5.50; 100- $21.00; 25 answer sheets $2.20; 100-$7.70.

Publisher: Psychometric Affiliates

BUSINESS JUDGMENT TEST
Martin M. Bruce

adult

Purpose: Evaluates the subject's sense of 'good social judgment' and 'social intelligence' in business-related situations. Used for employee selection and training.

Description: 25 item paper-pencil multiple-choice test in which the subject selects one of four ways to complete a stem' statement, allowing the examiner to gauge the subject's sense of socially accepted and desirable ways to behave in business relationships. The score suggests the degree to which the subject agrees with the general opinion of persons in business as to the optimal way to handle various relationships. Self-administered. Suitable for group use.

Untimed: 10-15 minutes

Range: Adult

Scoring: Hand key

Cost: Specimen set $5.25; manual $4.10; key $.70 each; package of tests $16.50.

Publisher: Martin M. Bruce, Ph.D., Publishers

CHOOSING A CAREER
J.W. Rothwell and K.M. Miller

teen, adult

Purpose: Evaluates individual attitudes towards work. Used for vocational and educational guidance.

Description: Multiple item paper-pencil test supplement to the Rothwell-Miller Interest Blank. The taker is asked to rank a series of statements in order of their importance, thereby determining the subject's attitudes towards five factors: rewards, interests, security, pride and recognition, and autonomy. Norms are given in the manual. Examiner required. Suitable for group use.
BRITISH PUBLISHER

Untimed: 10 minutes

Range: Secondary school students-adults

Scoring: Examiner evaluated

Cost: Contact publisher.

Publisher: Educational and Industrial Test Services Ltd.

COMMUNICATING EMPATHY
Refer to page 835.

COMREY PERSONALITY SCALES (CPS)
Refer to page 98.

A CREATIVITY MEASURE-- THE SRT SCALE
William C. Kosinar

teen, adult   grades 10-UP

Purpose: Assesses level of creativity. Used for career guidance with youths and selection of research and scientific personnel.

Description: Multiple item paper-pencil test of creativity. Items are forced choice. Manual provides norms on scientific personnel, National Science Talent Search winners, college students, and high school students. Examiner required. Suitable for group use.

Untimed: 5 minutes

Range: High school-adult

Scoring: Examiner evaluated

Cost: Specimen set $3.30; 25 tests $5.50; 100- $21.00.

Publisher: Psychometric Affiliates

CULTURE SHOCK INVENTORY (CSI)
W.J. Reddin

adult

Purpose: Assesses a person's susceptibility to cultural shock. Used to acquaint those who expect to work outside their own culture with potentially difficult areas.

Description: Multiple item paper-pencil test consisting of scales that test for western ethnocentrism, cross cultural experience, cognitive flex, behavioral flex, cultural knowledge (specific and general), customs acceptance, and interpersonal sensitivity. May be used with managers, wives, older children and in colleges. Self-administered. Suitable for group use. CANADIAN PUBLISHER

Untimed: 20-30 minutes

Range: Adult

Scoring: Hand key

Cost: Sample kit (contains 21 test samples, fact sheet and one test user's guide) $75.00; test kit (10 test copies plus fact sheet and user's guide) $40.00

Publisher: Organizational Tests (Canada) Ltd.

CURTIS COMPLETION FORM
Refer to page 100.

DEPRESSION ADJECTIVE CHECK LIST (DACL)
Refer to page 100.

DF OPINION SURVEY: AN INVENTORY OF DYNAMIC FACTORS (DFOS)
Refer to page 663.

DIMOCK L. INVENTORY (DLI)
Hedly G. Dimock

teen, adult   grades 10-UP

Purpose: Measures how well leaders work with the people they are supposed to lead. Used to select camp counselors and other leaders, and to measure changes in attitudes as a function of human relations and sensitivity training.

Description: Paper-pencil test of the extent to which a potential leader has a flexible, cooperative, participative orientation toward working with others. Norms provided for high school students and adults. Restricted to A.P.A. members. Examiner required. Suitable for group use.

Untimed: 25 minutes

Range: High school-adult

Scoring: Hand key; may be computer scored

Cost: 25 tests $10.00; 25 answer sheets $3.50; manual $1.50; scoring set $4.00.

Publisher: Sheridan Psychological Services, Inc.

THE EMPATHY TEST
W.A. Kerr and B.J. Speroff

teen, adult   grades 10-UP

Purpose: Measures empathic ability. Used for selection of managerial and supervisory personnel and graduate students.

Description: Multiple item paper-pencil test of ability to put oneself in another person's position, establish rapport, and anticipate another person's reactions, feelings and behavior. Empathy is measured as a variable unrelated to intelligence and most other attitudes. Materials include three forms: Form A, Blue collar emphasis; Form B, White collar emphasis; and Form C, Canadian emphasis. Examiner required. Suitable for group use.

Timed: 15 minutes

Range: High school-adult

Scoring: Examiner evaluated

Cost: Specimen set $2.20; 25 tests

$2.20; 100-$7.70 (specify form).

Publisher: Psychometric Affiliates

EMPLOYEE ATTITUDE INVENTORY
London House Press

adult

Purpose: Identifies employees who might steal or engage in costly antisocial acts in the workplace. Used in investigation and organizational assessment of honesty and as a guide for in-house promotions.

Description: 179 item paper-pencil test of the following factors: theft admissions, attitudes, and suspicions, drug-abuse tendencies, and job dissatisfaction and burnout. Validity scale is included. Anonymous mail or computer scoring by phone. Self-administered, although it can be given orally to illiterates. Suitable for group use.

Untimed: 30 minutes

Range: Adult

Scoring: Computer scored

Cost: Complete $12.00.

Publisher: London House Press

ETSA TESTS 8-A PERSONAL ADJUSTMENT INDEX
Refer to page 712.

EYSENCK PERSONALITY INVENTORY (EPI)
Refer to page 103.

FAMOUS SAYINGS (FS)
Bernard M. Bass

teen, adult   grades 10-UP

Purpose: Assesses personality. Used

for industrial and professional screening, and for research in social psychology.

Description: 131 item paper-pencil test of four vocationally important aspects of personality including hostility, fear of failure, social acquiescence, and acceptance of conventional mores. Items are general statements consisting mainly of famous sayings, proverbs and adages. Instructions are read aloud by examiner while subjects read them silently. Subjects indicate whether they agree, disagree or are uncertain. Examiner required. Suitable for group use.

Untimed: 15-30 minutes

Range: High school-adult

Scoring: Hand key; examiner evaluated

Cost: Complete kit (includes general manual, 50 test blanks, Form 1, scoring stencil Form 1) $13.00; 50 tests $10.00; general manual $3.00.

Publisher: Psychological Test Specialists

GROUP ENVIRONMENT SCALE
Refer to page 106.

HOW SUPERVISE?
Refer to page 837.

INTERPERSONAL COMMUNICATION INVENTORY (ICI)
Millard Bienvenu

teen, adult

Purpose: Evaluates interpersonal communication skills. Used in counseling and teaching communication skills.

Description: 40 item paper-pencil multiple-choice test. Measures the following communication skills: self-disclosure, expression of feelings, listening skills, non-verbal communication, acceptance of feelings, confrontation. Materials include: questionnaire, answer sheet, manual. Self- administered. Suitable for group use.

Untimed: 15 minutes

Range: Ages 15 and older

Scoring: Hand key; examiner evaluated

Cost: Test $.35 each; guide $2.50.

Publisher: Counseling and Self-Improvement Programs/Millard Bienvenu, Ph.D.

INTER-PERSON PERCEPTION TEST (IPPT)
Refer to page 159.

INVENTORY OF INDIVIDUALLY-PERCEIVED GROUP COHESIVENESS (IIPGC)
David L. Johnson

teen, adult   grades 10-UP

Purpose: Measures an individual's sense of cooperation in group activities. Used for counseling in school, business, family, training, research, organizational, and community settings.

Description: 20 item paper-pencil inventory of an individual's perception of cooperation, control and task influence processes operating in a group and resulting in some degree of cohesiveness. This questionnaire is particularly useful before and after group sessions. Self-administered. Suitable for group use.

Untimed: 15 minutes

Range: High school-adult

Scoring: Self-scored

Cost: Complete kit (includes 30 record forms, 3 feedback sheets, manual) $13.25.

Publisher: Stoelting Co.

I.P.I. EMPLOYEE ATTITUDE SERIES: CONTACT PERSONALITY FACTOR (CPF)
Refer to page 724.

I.P.I. EMPLOYEE ATTITUDE SERIES: NEUROTIC PERSONALITY FACTOR (NPF)
Refer to page 724.

I.P.I. EMPLOYEE ATTITUDE SERIES: SIXTEEN PERSONALITY FACTOR (16PF) TEST
Refer to page 724.

JENKINS ACTIVITY SURVEY (JAS)
Refer to page 180.

A JOB ANALYSIS BASED TEST BATTERY FOR THE EVALUATION OF POTENTIAL OF HIGHER LEVEL PERSONNEL

adult

Purpose: Assesses a person's potential for successful performance in high level management, professional and sales positions. Used for career counseling and employee selection.

Description: Nine paper-pencil tests assessing attributes required of management, professional and sales personnel. The battery includes: motivational measures derived from qualified background data, language facility, perceptual skills, creative potential, sales potential, personal insight, self-reliance, ability to work under pressure, and personal emotional adjustment. Test batteries consisting of six to eight tests have been developed for predicting successful performance at three levels in the line management hierarchy, as a staff professional or manager of such personnel, or as a sales representative or manager of sales personnel. Scores for each battery include individual test scores and associated estimates of potential for successful performance. Examiner required. Suitable for group use.

Untimed: 30 minutes for each test

Range: Adult

Scoring: Hand key; examiner evaluated for career counseling; computer scoring available for screening key industrial positions

Cost: Per test battery $3.00-$5.00.

Publisher: London House Press

JOB ATTITUDE SCALE (JAS)
Shoukry Saleh

adult

Purpose: Evaluates an employee's job preferences and attitudes. Used in business and industry to evaluate programs and individual orientations toward the workplace.

Description: 120 item long form and 60 item short form paper-pencil, forced-choice test of attitudes towards these 16 qualities: praise and recognition, growth in skills, creative work, responsibility, advancement, achievement, salary, security, personnel policies, competent supervision, relations-peers, relations- subordinant, relations-supervisor, working conditions, status, and family needs. The long form yields one general score and 16 subscores. The short form yeilds an intrinsic score. Self-administered. Suitable for group use. Available in French.

Untimed: 30 minutes

Range: Adult

Scoring: Hand key

Cost: Specimen set (includes manual and test sheet key) $7.00; 100-$20.00.

Publisher: Shouksy Saleh

KIPNIS-SCHMIDT PROFILES OF ORGANIZATIONAL INFLUENCE STRATEGIES: INFLUENCING YOUR CO-WORKERS (POIS-FORM C)
David Kipnis and Stuart M. Schmidt

adult

Purpose: Assesses which strategies a person uses in attempting to influence co-workers. Used for organizational communication assessment, organizational and human resources development, team building, and managerial training.

Description: 27 item paper-pencil test describing various influence tactics which a subject rates on a six point scale from 1 (never) to 6 (almost always) in two columns: How frequently one uses this tactic when first trying to influence a co-worker; How frequently the tactic is used in a second attempt when the co-worker resists cooperating. Self- administered; facilitator helpful. Suitable for group use.

Untimed: 20-25 minutes

Range: Adult

Scoring: Hand key

Cost: Complete set (materials for 10 participants) $45.00.

Publisher: University Associates, Inc.

KIPNIS-SCHMIDT PROFILES OF ORGANIZATIONAL INFLUENCE STRATEGIES: INFLUENCING YOUR MANAGER (POIS: FORM M)
David Kipnis and Stuart M. Schmidt

adult

Purpose: Assesses which strategies a person uses in attempting to influence his manager. Used for organizational communication assessment, organization and human resource development, team building, and managerial training.

Description: 27 item paper-pencil test describing various influence tactics which a subject rates on a six point scale from 1 (never) to 6 (almost always) in two columns: How frequently one uses this tactic when first trying to influence a manager; How frequently the tactic is used in a second attempt when the manager resists cooperating. Self- administered; facilitator helpful. Suitable for group use.

Untimed: 20-25 minutes

Range: Adult

Scoring: Hand key

Cost: Complete set (materials for 10 participants) $45.00.

Publisher: University Associates, Inc.

KIPNIS-SCHMIDT PROFILES OF ORGANIZATIONAL INFLUENCE STRATEGIES: INFLUENCING YOUR SUBORDINATES (POIS: FORM S)
David Kipnis and Stuart M. Schmidt

adult

Purpose: Assesses which strategies a person uses in attempting to influence subordinates. Used for organizational communication assessment, organization and human resource development, team building, and managerial training.

Description: 33 item paper-pencil test describing various influence tactics which a subject rates on a six point scale from 1 (never) to 6 (almost always) in two columns: How frequently one uses this tactic when first trying to influence a subordinate; How frequently the tactic is used in a second attempt when the subordinate resists cooperating. Self- administered; facilitator helpful. Suitable for group use.

Untimed: 25-30 minutes

Range: Adult

Scoring: Hand key

Cost: Complete set (materials for 10 participants) $45.00.

Publisher: University Associates, Inc.

MANSON EVALUATION
Morse P. Manson

adult

Purpose: Identifies maladjusted individuals. Used for personnel screening, diagnosis, therapy, and research.

Description: Multiple item paper-pencil measure of seven personality characteristics: anxiety, depressive fluctuations, emotional sensitivity, resentfulness, incompleteness, aloneness and interpersonal relations. Identifies three types of maladjusted individuals: alcoholics, inadequates and immature. Norms provided for men and women. Examiner required. Suitable for group use.

Untimed: 5-10 minutes

Range: Adult

Scoring: Hand key

Cost: Kit (20 tests, manual, key)

$9.80.

Publisher: Western Psychological Services

MASLACH BURNOUT INVENTORY (MBI)
Refer to page 182.

MAUDSLEY PERSONALITY INVENTORY (MPI)
Refer to page 117.

McCORMICK JOB PERFORMANCE MEASUREMENT "RATE-$-SCALE" (RATE-$-SCALE)
Ronald R. McCormick

adult

Purpose: Measures employee performance in terms of the dollar value of a successfully completed job. Used for employee compensation, training, promotion, and recruitment. Useful in all industries and public agencies which have professional personnel office staff.

Description: Multiple item paper-pencil inventory assessing four areas of employee performance: responsibility, attitude, time in labor grade, and efficiency. The employee's supervisor completes the form, which provides a rating scale in terms of the critical tasks and duties which the employee performs for pay. Comparisons of employee job performance are based upon the dollar value of the successful performance of a fully qualified worker. Local validation is required since employee job performance ratings are based upon the individual firm's compensation schedule. Results of employee evaluations can be readily entered into a computer for the detailed analysis required for rating form validation and payroll cost projections.

Self-administered.

Untimed: 5 minutes

Range: Adult

Scoring: Examiner evaluated

Cost: 25 rating forms $7.50.

Publisher: Trademark Design Products, Inc.

MINNESOTA JOB DESCRIPTION QUESTIONNAIRE (MJDQ)

adult

Purpose: Evaluates an employee's or supervisor's perception of the reinforcer characteristics of an occupation. Also used for research.

Description: 42 item paper-pencil test covering: ability, advancement, creativity, co-workers, security, and independence. Subjects rate groups of five statements from one to five according to how well each statement describes their job. Five additional questions regarding the supervisory experience are included as well. The MJDQ may also be used for obtaining a subject's perception of jobs in terms of expected or perceived reinforcer patterns. Materials include test booklet and manual. Self-administered. Suitable for group use.

Untimed: Open ended

Range: Adult

Scoring: Examiner evaluated

Cost: Contact publisher.

Publisher: Vocational Psychology Research, University of Minnesota

MINNESOTA SATISFACTION QUESTIONNAIRE (MSQ)

adult

Purpose: Evaluates an employees satisfaction with his job. Used for occupational and social research.

Description: 100 item paper-pencil questionnaire consisting of statements about various aspects of a person's job which he is asked to rate on a five-point scale from "not satisfied" to "extremely satisfied." Twenty scales of five items each measure the following factors: ability, utilization, achievement, activity, advancement, authority, company policies and practices, compensation, co-workers, creativity, independence, moral values, recognition, responsibility, security, social science, social status, supervision-human relations, supervision- technical, variety, and working conditions. Optional 20-item General Satisfaction scale is also available. The alternative Short-Form MSQ consists of one item from each of the 20 scales and yields Intrinisic, Extrinsic and General Satisfaction Scores. The manual includes: descriptions of the development and and scoring of both forms, reliability and validity data and norms. Examiner required. Suitable for group use. Restricted to APA members only.

Untimed: Varies

Range: Adult

Scoring: Hand key; computer scoring available

Cost: Specimen set $9.00 (photocopy of manual, single copies of: long-form, long-form 1967 revision, short form).

Publisher: Vocational Psychology Research, University of Minnesota

MINNESOTA SATISFACTORINESS SCALE (MSS)

adult

Purpose: Measures an employee's satisfactoriness on a job. Used as a research instrument.

Description: 28 item paper-pencil

inventory assessing an employee's behavior on the job. The employee's supervisor completes the form. Scores are provided for five scales: Performance, Conformance, Dependability, Personal Adjustment, and General Satisfactoriness. Additional data analysis also available. The manual includes: information on development and scoring of the test, reliability and validity data, and norms. Self-administered by supervisor. Use restricted to APA members.

Untimed: Varies

Range: Adult

Scoring: Hand key; computer scoring available

Cost: 30 scales $.15 each; manual $5.45.

Publisher: Vocational Psychology Research, University of Minnesota

MOTIVATION ANALYSIS TEST (MAT)
Arthur B. Sweney, Raymond B. Cattell, John L. Horn, and IPAT Staff

teen, adult   grades 10-UP

Purpose: Measures motivational patterns in high school seniors and adults. Used in a variety of counseling situations in education and business.

Description: 208 item paper-pencil multiple-choice test provides ten measures of comfort, social and achievement needs. Five are basic drives: caution, sex, self-assertion, aggressiveness, and self-indulgence. Five are interests that develop and mature through learning experience: career, affection, dependency, responsibility, self- fulfillment. For each of the ten interest areas, scores measure drive or need level, satisfaction level, degree of conflict, and total motivational strength. Standard

scores are provided for men and women together. Self-administered. Suitable for group use.

Untimed: 50-60 minutes

Range: High school seniors and adult

Scoring: Hand key; computer scoring service available

Cost: MAT professional examination kit $15.80; MAT specimen set $11.50; 25 test booklets $19.25; 50 machine-scorable answer sheets $8.00, 50 handscored answer sheets $7.00; 50 profile sheets $5.50; 4 scoring keys $5.50; MAT handbook/assessment manual $10.00; MAT individual scoring report certificates $2.28-$3.80 each depending on quantity and MAT score rosters $.96- $1.60 each depending on quantity.

Publisher: Institute for Personality and Ability Testing, Inc.

MYERS-BRIGGS TYPE INDICATOR (MBTI)
Refer to page 122.

OPINIONS TOWARD ADOLESCENTS (OTA SCALE)
Refer to page 650.

ORGANIZATION SURVEY
Human Resource Center, University of Chicago

adult

Purpose: Analyzes job problems, as seen by employees, in order to develop plans for greater organization effectiveness. Used to diagnose problems in key areas by regional location, department or work category.

Description: 120 item paper-pencil test in three categories: Motivation and Morale (40 items), Organization and Effectiveness (50 items), and "Optional," which includes up to 30 items. Factors measured include organization identification, job satisfaction, material rewards, supervisory leadership, and work associates; in the second, work organization, administrative effectiveness, supervisory practices, communication effectiveness, performance and development, and work efficiency. The procedure is by anonymous mail or group administration, followed by machine scoring which produces profiles comparing the organization group/department respectively with company, industry and national norms. The test, which may be given orally to illiterates, offers flexibiity to the choice of categories, items and demographic classifications. Surveys also are available for hospital and school personnel. Self-administered. Suitable for group use.

Untimed: 20 minutes

Range: Adult

Scoring: Computer scored

Cost: Complete $6.00 per employee.

Publisher: London House Press

THE PERSONAL AUDIT
*Clifford R. Adams and
William M. Lepley*

teen, adult   grades 7-UP

Purpose: Assesses an individual's personality as a factor of how well that person will perform in school or industry. Also used for clinical diagnosis of maladjustment.

Description: 450 item paper-pencil objective personality tests. Nine scales of 50 items each measure relatively independent components of personality: Seriousness-Impulsiveness, Firmness-Indecision, Tranquility-Irritability, Frankness-Evasion, Stability-Instability,

Tolerance-Intolerance, Steadiness-Emotionality, Persistence-Fluctuation, Contentment-Worry. Acquaints teachers with personality characteristics of students as an aid to vocational and educational counseling, and provides an index of employees' job satisfaction and success in terms of their personal adjustment. Two forms available: Form LL, used with adults having the equivalent of a grammar school education and senior high school students: Form SS (the first six scales of Form LL) used with junior high school students or where administration time is limited. Self-administered. Suitable for group use.

Untimed: Form LL, 40-50 minutes; Form SS, 30-40 minutes

Range: Junior high school-adult

Scoring: Hand key

Cost: 25 test booklets Form LL $29.00; 25 test booklets Form SS $24.00; examiner's manual $1.90.

Publisher: Science Research Associates, Inc.

PERSONAL DATA FORM
Morris I. Stein

adult

Purpose: Assesses job applicants in terms of the following roles: scientist, professional, administrative, employee, and social. Used to place individuals in positions where they can work creatively and productively.

Description: 80 item paper-pencil questionnaire serves as a job application form for technical and administrative positions with Research and Development organizations. Test items elicit information concerning the applicant's self- concept, abilities, and self-perception in terms of the roles required by the job for which he is applying. Self-administered. Suitable for group use.

Untimed: 30 minutes

Range: Adult

Scoring: Examiner evaluated

Cost: $2.50 per copy.

Publisher: Morris I. Stein

PERSONAL HISTORY INDEX
M.E. Baehr, R.K.Burns and
R.N. McMurry

---

adult

Purpose: Evaluates an individual's achievement in ten motivational areas based on quantified personal background data. Used for career counseling of higher-level personnel and for job screening in conjunction with a structured interview form.

Description: 87 item paper-pencil, multiple-choice test. It measures the following ten factors: school achievement, school activities, higher education achievement, drive, leadership and group participation, financial responsibility, parental family adjustment, successful professional parents, and job and personal stability. Different combinations of factors can be used in the selection of various types of industrial personnel. Basic reading skills are required. Different versions of the test are available for males, females, high-level, and entry-level personnel. Self-administered. Suitable for group use.

Untimed: 15-20 minutes

Range: Adult

Scoring: Hand key; computer scoring available

Cost: Specimen set $5.00; 20 tests $10.00.

Publisher: London House Press

PERSONALITY RESEARCH FORM (PRF)
Refer to page 163.

PERSONAL QUESTIONNAIRE/ OCCUPATIONAL VALUES
Refer to page 678.

THE PERSONAL SKILLS MAP (PSM)
Darwin B. Nelson and Gary R. Low

---

teen, adult

Purpose: Evaluates self-perceived skill levels key to personal and career effectiveness. Used for counseling and to plan individual and group intervention strategies.

Description: 300 item paper-pencil test. Evaluates two intrapersonal skills: self-esteem, and growth motivation; three interpersonal skills: assertion, interpersonal awareness and empathy; and six career/life skills: drive strength, decision-making, time management, sales orientation, commitment ethic, and stress management. There are three response categories: most descriptive, sometimes descriptive, and least descriptive, with no right or wrong answers. The test is designed to benefit the person using it, not for screening purposes. Self-administered. Suitable for group use.

Untimed: 60 minutes

Range: Adolescent, adult

Scoring: Computer scored; self-score version available

Cost: Booklet $5.00 (specify adolescent or adult); manual $20.00; specimen set $75.00.

Publisher: Institute for the Development of Human Resources

PERSONNEL SELECTION INVENTORY (PSI)
London House Press

adult

Purpose: Identifies job applicants who might engage in counterproductive behavior in the workplace.

Description: 108 item paper-pencil test examining behavior that could result in theft, violence or drug-abuse on the job. A distortion scale is included. Basic literacy is required. Self-administered. Suitable for group use. Available in Spanish.

Untimed: 30-40 minutes

Range: Adult

Scoring: Computer scored by phone

Cost: Complete $8.00-$14.00 depending on volume.

Publisher: London House Press

PICTURE SITUATION TEST

adult

Purpose: Measures an individual's response to aggression provoking stimuli within an everyday context. Used for personnel screening and placement and clinical research on aggression.

Description: 20 item paper-pencil test measures the type of aggression an individual displays and the effect is is likely to have on the interpersonal situation in which aggression appears. The test items consist of partially structured pictures depicting aggression provoking situations. The individual must complete the situation by giving his own responses. Responses are scored for type of aggression (direct, denial) and effect of response (constructive, destructive). A method for standardized scoring is provided. Restricted to competent persons properly regis-

tered with either the South African Medical and Dental Council or Test Commission of the Republic of South Africa. Examiner required. Suitable for group use. Afrikaans version available.

SOUTH AFRICAN PUBLISHER

Untimed: No time limit

Range: Adult males

Scoring: Hand key; examiner evaluated

Cost: Contact publisher.

Publisher: National Institute for Personnel Research

POSITION ANALYSIS QUESTIONNAIRE (PAQ)
Ernest J. McCormick, P.R. Jeanneret and Robert C. Meacham

adult

Purpose: Analyzes jobs in terms of job elements that reflect directly or infer the basic human behaviors involved, regardless of their specific technological areas or functions. Used with jobs at all levels, including: managerial, supervisory staff, professional, technical, skilled public contact, office, production and operation, service, and semiskilled.

Description: 187 item paper-pencil job analysis rating scale. Examiner/analyst indicates the degree of involvment of each of the elements listed using appropriate rating scales such as importance, frequency, etc. The job elements are organized so that they provide for a logical analysis of the jobs structure. Six broad areas are assessed: information input, mental processes, work output, relationships with other persons, job context, and other job characteristics. Examples of specific job elements are: the use of written materials, the level of decision-making, the use of mechanical devices, working in a hazardous environment, and working at a specified pace. Analysis of the questionnaire is in terms of job dimensions (clusters of related elements). Results are used as the basis for job aptitude requirements, as the basis for deriving "point" values for jobs that in turn can be used to establish compensation rates, and as the basis for classifying jobs into clusters which have statistically similar profiles. Also available on an experimental basis is the Job Activity Preference Questionnaire (JAPQ) which measures an individual's career interests in terms of the PAQ job dimensions. Self-administered by analyst, personnel staff, job supervisors, and in some cases the workers. themselves.

Untimed: Not available

Range: Adult

Scoring: Examiner evaluated; computer processing available

Cost: Complete kit (PAQ, record form, technical manual, job analysis manual, users manual, binder) $27.00; computer processing from PAQ services $1.60 to $100.00 based on processing option.

Publisher: Purdue Research Foundation/University Book Store

POWER PERCEPTION PROFILE--SELF/OTHER
Paul Hersey and Walter E. Natemeyer

adult

Purpose: Evaluates the way an individual uses power as the basis for asserting leadership. Used for leadership-management training, HRD and team building.

Description: 21 item paper-pencil test of seven power bases: coercion, connection, expert, information, legitimate, referent, and reward. The profiles include two separate instruments "Perception of Self" and

"Perception of Other." The individual answers questions on one form about himself and has someone else complete an observer's form. They then chart and compare scores and draw a profile of the results for discussion. Materials contain profiles, scoring and interpretation. Self-administered. Suitable for group use.

Untimed: No available

Range: Adult

Scoring: Hand key

Cost: 1-9 complete kits (includes profiles, scoring interpretation) $2.95 each (specify form for Self or Other).

Publisher: Center for Leadership Studies

PROBLEM-SOLVING DECISION-MAKING STYLE INVENTORY
Refer to page 844.

THE PURDUE HANDICAP PROBLEMS INVENTORY
H.H. Remmers and G.N. Wright

adult

Purpose: Measures self-perceived problems of the handicapped adult. Used for counseling and research.

Description: Paper-pencil self-report of perceived problems in four areas: Social, Family, Vocational, and Personal. Examiner required. Suitable for group use.

Untimed: 25-35 minutes

Range: Adult handicapped

Scoring: Hand key; may be machine scored

Cost: Contact publisher.

Publisher: Purdue Research Foundation/University Book Store

REACTION TO EVERYDAY SIT-UATIONS-TEST
Sheena M.A. Waterhouse

teen, adult

Purpose: Measures general anxiety shown by individuals in their day-to-day lives. Used for employee selection and screening and clinical research.

Description: 50 item paper-pencil questionnaire measures the general anxiety shown by examinees in everyday situations. Each test item relates to a particular situation in which anxiety might be shown. Restricted to competent persons properly registered with either the South African Medical and Dental Council or Test Commission of the Republic of South Africa. Examiner required. Suitable for group use. Afrikaans version available.
SOUTH AFRICAN PUBLISHER

Untimed: Not time limit

Range: Ages 16 and older

Scoring: Hand key

Cost: Contact publisher.

Publisher: National Institute for Personnel Research

REID REPORT

adult

Purpose: Evaluates the honesty of job applicants. Identifies individuals most likely to steal at work if given the opportunity. Does not discriminate on the basis of sex, race or age.

Description: Multiple item paper-pencil questionnaire consists of three sections. The first section contains 90 Yes-No questions which measure the applicant's attitudes toward theft and the punishment of theft. The second section contains a detailed biographical data blank covering previous

employment, education and social history which includes drug and alcohol abuse and excessive gambling as they relate to a need to steal. The third section is an admissions list of previous thefts. Based on the section-one score and the evaluation of the bio-data and admission-of-theft questions, the applicant is recommended or not recommended for employment. Results available by phone or mail. Examiner required. Suitable for group use. Available in Spanish, Portugese, Italian, Polish, and French.

Untimed: Not available

Range: Adult

Scoring: Computer scored.

Cost: 5-99 tests and evaluation $12.00 each.

Publisher: Reid Psychological Systems

REID SURVEY

adult

Purpose: Evaluates the honesty of current employees. Identifies employees most likely to be responsible for thefts within the company. Used to screen employees for promotion to sensitive positions. Does not discriminate on the basis of sex, race or age.

Description: Multiple item paper-pencil questionnaire consists of three sections. The first section contains 90 Yes-No questions which measure the employee's attitudes toward theft and the punishment of theft. The second section contains a detailed biographical data blank covering previous employment, education and social history which includes drug and alcohol abuse and excessive gambling as they relate to a need to steal. The third section is an admissions list of previous thefts. Based on the section-one score and the evaluation of the bio-data and admission- of-theft, employees with a tendency toward theft are identified. Results available by phone or mail. Examiner required. Suitable for group use. Available in Spanish, Portugese, and French.

Untimed: Not available

Range: Adult

Scoring: Computer scored.

Cost: 5-99 tests and evaluation $15.00 each.

Publisher: Reid Psychological Systems

A SCALE TO MEASURE ATTITUDES TOWARD DISABLED PERSONS
Refer to page 682.

THE SCHUTZ MEASURES: ELEMENT F--FEELINGS
Refer to page 133.

THE SCHUTZ MEASURES: ELEMENT J--JOB (JOB HOLDER, CO-WORKER)
Will Schutz

adult

Purpose: Measures perceptions of personal and interpersonal aspects of a job. Used for analysis of personal growth, job clarification, career planning, training and development.

Description: A 54 item paper-pencil test which contains forms for "job or job holder" and "co-workers." For personal feedback, the job holder and co- worker(s) complete the forms and compare results. For job definition, the forms are evaluated by persons evaluating or planning the job. Factors measured include Expressed- Received and Perceived- Wanted

aspects of the behavioral dimensions of Inclusion, Control, and Openness, and the feelings dimensions of Significance, Competence, and Likeability. Self-administered; facilitator helpful. Suitable for group use.

Untimed: 15-20 minutes

Range: Adult

Scoring: Hand key

Cost: Complete set (includes material for 10 participants) $30.00; trainer's package (includes manual and each of 5 instruments) $50.00.

Publisher: University Associates, Inc.

THE SCHUTZ MEASURES: ELEMENT R-- RELATIONSHIPS
Refer to page 134.

SELF ACTUALIZATION INVENTORY (SAI)
W.J. Reddin

adult

Purpose: Measures the degree to which a person's needs are fulfilled. Used to compare responses of managers and their subordinates.

Description: A paper-pencil test covering the following needs: physical, security, relationships, respect, independence, self-actualization. Self-administered. Suitable for group use. CANADIAN PUBLISHER

Untimed: 20-30 minutes

Range: Adult

Scoring: Hand key

Cost: Sample kit (contains 21 test samples, fact sheet and one test user's guide) $75.00; test kit (10 test copies plus fact sheet and user's guide) $40.00.

Publisher: Organizational Tests (Canada) Ltd.

SIXTEEN PERSONALITY FACTOR QUESTIONNAIRE
Refer to page 138.

THE STANTON INVENTORY
Carl S. Klump

adult

Purpose: Assesses problems of theft in businesses. Used for identification of responsible parties.

Description: 96 item paper-pencil questionnaire regarding company dishonesty, morale, personal attitudes and general company, information. The questionnaire assists in identifying problem areas, i.e. management weaknesses, theft, etc. Self-administered. Suitable for group use.

Untimed: Not available

Range: Adult

Scoring: Scoring service available

Cost: 1-99 inventory sheets and evaluation $25.00 each.

Publisher: The Stanton Corporation

THE STANTON SURVEY
Carl S. Klump

adult

Purpose: Measures honesty. Used for screening and evaluating job applicants.

Description: Multiple item paper-pencil test of honesty divided into two major sections. The first section includes one page of biographical items covering educational and vocational history, as well as social habits. Second part consists of 84 multiple-choice questions about attitudes toward honesty and about actual events involving honest and dishonest behaviors. Self-administered. Suitable for group use.

Untimed: Not available

Range: Adult

Scoring: Hand key; may be computer scored; computer scoring available

Cost: 1-499 hand scorable surveys $8.00 each; 1-99 phone in or computer scored surveys $12.00 each; 1-22 computer scored surveys, including analysis $12.00 each.

Publisher: The Stanton Corporation

THE STANTON SURVEY PHASE II
Carl S. Klump

adult

Purpose: Measures honesty. Used for screening and evaluating job applicants.

Description: Paper-pencil test divided into two parts. First part consists of 36 agree-disagree items covering attitudes toward honesty and about actual events involving honest and dishonest behaviors. Second part consists of multiple-choice and short answer items probing social habits such as drinking, gambling and drug use. Similar to Stanton Survey, but omits personal history and biographical information. Self-administered. Suitable for group use.

Untimed: Not available

Range: Adult

Scoring: Scoring service available, hand key, may be computer scored

Cost: $7.00 per booklet including evaluation.

Publisher: The Stanton Corporation

SUPERVISORY COMMUNICA-TION RELATIONS TEST (SCOM)

Refer to page 847.

SUPERVISORY HUMAN RELA-TIONS TEST (SHR)
W.J. Reddin

adult

Purpose: Measures a person's attitude toward others. Can be used before or after instruction in human relations.

Description: 80 item, true-false, paper-pencil test that measures attitude toward superiors, co-workers and subordinates. Nor recommended as a test-retest device to discover the effects of training. Suitable for white or blue collar supervision. Self-administered. Suitable for group use. CANADIAN PUBLISHER

Untimed: 20-30 minutes

Range: Adult

Scoring: Hand key

Cost: Sample kit (contains 21 test samples, fact sheet and one test user's guide) $75.00; test kit (10 test copies plus fact sheet and user's guide) $30.00.

Publisher: Organizational Tests (Canada) Ltd.

SURVEY OF INTERPERSONAL VALUES

Refer to page 142.

SURVEY OF PERSONAL VALUES
Leonard V. Gordon

teen, adult   grades 10-UP

Purpose: Measures an individual's

critical values that help determine coping ability with everyday problems. Used for employee screening and placement, vocational guidance and counseling.

Description: 30 item paper-pencil test consisting of forced-choice triads of value statements. Subjects indicate which statement they find personally most important in each triad. Six values are measured: practical mindedness, achievement, variety, decisiveness, orderliness, and goal orientation. Manual to be revised in 1983. Self-administered. Suitable for group use.

Untimed: 15 minutes

Range: High school and older

Scoring: Hand key

Cost: 25 test booklets $19.00; scoring stencil $3.40; examiner's manual $1.60.

Publisher: Science Research Associates, Inc.

TAV SELECTION SYSTEM
R.R. Morman

adult

Purpose: Measures normal interpersonal reactions "toward," "away from," and "versus" people. Used as an occupational selection tool and a counseling aid.

Description: Multiple item paper-pencil test consisting of seven subtests: Personal Data, Proverbs and Sayings, Preferences, Sales Reactions, Judgments, Adjective Check List, and Mental Agility. Predictive validity scores given for a number of typical professions: traffic officers, teachers, salesmen, nurses, and others. Self-administered. Suitable for group use.

Timed: 3 hours

Range: Adult

Scoring: Hand key

Cost: Contact publisher.

Publisher: TAV Selection System

TEMPERAMENT AND VALUES INVENTORY (TVI)
Charles B. Johansson

teen, adult grades 9-UP

Purpose: Measures an individual's attitudes and work values. Used for career development, personnel counseling, and training needs assessment.

Description: 230 item paper-pencil test containing 133 true-false statements and 97 five-point scale items. The test covers seven bipolar temperament scales: Routine-Flexible, Quiet-Active, Attentive-Distractible, Serious-Cheerful, Consistent-Changeable, Reserved-Sociable, and Reticent-Persuasive. The test also contains seven reward value scales: Social Recognition, Managerial Sales Benefits, Leadership, Social Service, Task Specificity, Philosophical Curiosity, and Work Independence. Self-administered. Suitable for group use.

Untimed: 20-30 minutes

Range: Grades 9-12, adult

Scoring: Computer scored

Cost: Profile $1.90-$4.25; Profile and interpretation $3.50-$10.00; scoring via ARION II $13.00-$14.00.

Publisher: NCS Interpretive Scoring Systems

TEST OF WORK COMPETENCY AND STABILITY
A. Gaston Leblanc

adult

Purpose: Measures stress levels in motor coordination and mental concentration. Used to evaluate

psychological capacity for work performance.

Description: Multiple item paper-pencil interview and manual dexterity test of six factors related to work competency in industry. The test includes the following factors: work stability, assertiveness, persistence and concentration, psychomotor steadiness, capacity and stress tolerance. Scores screen workers and provide information for rehabilitation. Materials come in a set which includes manual, interview questionnaire sheets, mirror tracing patterns, tapping patterns (a tremometer and tapping apparatus with 24-volt impulse counter) and record blanks. Examiner required. Not suitable for group use. Available in French. CANADIAN PUBLISHER

Untimed: Varies

Range: Adult (21-67 years)

Scoring: Hand key

Cost: Complete set (includes manual, test materials of tremometer and tapping apparatus, tapping board, mirror tracing apparatus, picture arrangement test, 25 record blanks, 25 questionnaires, key, 25 mirror tracing patterns, 25 tapping patterns) $150.00; 25 record blanks $4.80; 25 interview sheets $4.80; 25 mirror tracing patterns $2.80; 25 tapping patterns $2.80; mirror tracing apparatus $24.00; manual $8.00.

Publisher: Institute of Psychological Research, Inc.

THURSTONE TEMPERAMENT SCHEDULE
L.L. Thurstone and Thelma Gwinn Thurstone

adult

Purpose: Evaluates permanent aspects of personality and how normal, well-adjusted people differ from one another. Used by managers to determine employee suitability for particular jobs.

Description: 140 item paper-pencil questionnaire assessing seven areas of temperament: active, vigorous, impulsive, dominant, stable, sociable, reflective. Limited to use by individuals with advanced training in personality instruments. Self- administered. Suitable for group use.

Untimed: 15-20 minutes

Range: Adult

Scoring: Hand scored--carbon insert (answers transfer to scoring key on inside of test booklet)

Cost: 25 booklets $18.50; examiner's manual $1.60.

Publisher: Science Research Associates, Inc.

TRAIT EVALUATION INDEX
Alan R. Nelson

adult

Purpose: Assesses adult personality traits in any and all environments. Useful for job placement and career counseling.

Description: 125 item paper-pencil two-choice test measuring 24 personality dimensions, including: social orientation, elation, self-control, sincerity, compliance, ambition, dynamism, caution, propriety, and intellectual orientation. Material consists of a manual and academic-industrial-business profile sheets. Available in German. Self-administered. Suitable for group use.

Untimed: 30-40 minutes

Range: Adult

Scoring: Hand key

Cost: Specimen set with scoring stencils $10.90; specimen set without scoring stencils $5.77; 25 tests $15.30; manual $5.10; 24 IBM scoring stencils $9.02; 25 profile sheets

$6.05.

Publisher: Martin M. Bruce, Ph.D., Publishers

TRIADAL EQUATED PERSONALITY INVENTORY
Refer to page 144.

TRUSTWORTHINESS ATTITUDE SURVEY (T.A. SURVEY)
Alan Strand and Robert W. Cormack

adult

Purpose: Measures attitudes and personality characteristics related to trustworthiness. Used to screen applicants for jobs involving security, money and product handling.

Description: 118 item paper-pencil, multiple-choice and short answer test of attitudes and beliefs. Must be administered by a qualified, licensed company or government agency examiner. Suitable for group use.

Untimed: 20-30 minutes

Range: Adult

Scoring: Hand key

Cost: Specimen set, no charge; 25 tests $6.00; scoring templates leased yearly $60.00.

Publisher: Psychological Systems Corporation

WARD ATMOSPHERE SCALE (WAS)
Rudolf H. Moos

teen, adult

Purpose: Assesses the social environments of hospital- based psychiatric treatment programs. Used to evaluate organizational effectiveness.

Description: 100 item paper-pencil,

true-false test of ten aspects of social environment yielding ten scores: Involvement, Support, Spontaneity, Autonomy, Practical Orientation, Personal Problem Orientation, Anger and Aggression, Order and Organization, Program Clarity, Staff Control. Three "treatment outcome" scales may be used as well: Dropout, Release Rate, Community Tenure. Materials include the Real Form (Form R), which measures perceptions of a current program; the 40 item Short Form (Form S); the Ideal Form (Form I), measuring conceptions of an ideal program; and the Expectations Form (Form E), measuring expectations of a new program. Forms I and E are not published, but items and instructions appear in the Appendix of the WAS manual. One of nine Social Climate Scales. Examiner required. Suitable for group use.

Untimed: 20 minutes

Range: Adolescent, adult

Scoring: Hand key; examiner evaluated

Cost: Specimen set $5.00; 25 reusable tests $4.00; 50 answer sheets $3.00; 50 profiles $3.00; key $.75; manual $3.75.

Publisher: Consulting Psychologists Press, Inc.

WESTERN PERSONALITY INVENTORY
Refer to page 145.

THE WHISLER STRATEGY TEST
Lawrence Whisler

adult

Purpose: Assesses strategy used in approaching problems. Used for evaluating applicants for employment.

Description: Multiple item paper-pencil measure of seven aspects of strategy: solutions, speed, boldness, caution, hypercaution, and net strategy. Test detects both risk-takers and risk-avoiders. Evaluates subject with respect to the wisdom of his strategy. Examiner required. Suitable for group use.

Timed: 25 minutes

Range: Adult

Scoring: Hand key

Cost: Specimen set $2.20; 25 tests $5.50; 100- $21.00; 25 answer sheets $2.20; 100-$7.70.

Publisher: Psychometric Affiliates

WORK ENVIRONMENT SCALE (WES)
Paul Insel and Rudolf Moos

adult

Purpose: Evaluates the social climate of work units. Used to assess correlates of productivity, worker satisfaction, and supervisory methods.

Description: 90 item paper-pencil measure of ten dimensions of work social environments: involvement, peer cohesion, supervisor support, autonomy, task orientation, work pressure, clarity, control, innovation, and physical comfort. These dimensions are grouped into three sets: relationship, personal growth, and system maintenance and change. Materials include three forms: The Real Form (Form R), which measures perceptions of existing work environments; the Ideal Form (Form I), measuring conceptions of deal work environments; and the Expectations Form (Form E), measuring expectations about work settings. Forms I and E are not published, although items and instructions will be provided upon request. Examiner required. Suitable for group use.

Untimed: 20 minutes, approximately

Range: Adult

Scoring: Hand key

Cost: Specimen set $6.00; manual $5.00; key $.75.

Publisher: Consulting Psychologists Press, Inc.

WORK ENVIRONMENT PREFERENCE SCHEDULE
Refer to page 813.

Management and Supervision

ADVANCED TEST BATTERY (ATB)
Refer to page 699.

ADVANCED TEST BATTERY: NUMERICAL CRITICAL REASONING (ATB:NA4)
Refer to page 701.

ADVANCED TEST BATTERY: NUMBER SERIES (ATB:NA2)
Refer to page 701.

ADVANCED TEST BATTERY: VERBAL CONCEPTS (ATB:VA1)
Refer to page 702.

ADVANCED TEST BATTERY: VERBAL CRITICAL REASONING (ATB:VA3)
Refer to page 702.

COMMUNICATION KNOWLEDGE INVENTORY
W.J. Reddin

adult

Purpose: Assesses a manager's general knowledge of communication.

Description: 40 item paper-pencil test covering verbal and nonverbal communication fallacies. Self- administered. Suitable for group use. CANADIAN PUBLISHER

Untimed: 20-30 minutes

Range: Adult

Scoring: Hand key

Cost: Sample kit (contains 21 test samples, fact sheet and one test user's guide) $75.00; test kit (10 test copies plus fact sheet and user's guide) $40.00; cash orders postpaid.

Publisher: Organizational Tests (Canada) Ltd.

COMMUNICATION SENSITIVITY INVENTORY
W.J. Reddin

adult

Purpose: Determines the characteristic response of a manager to whom others come with problems. Used as a pretest in courses in listening, coaching and communication.

Description: Ten item paper-pencil multiple choice test that measures a manager's reaction to problems expressed by subordinates. Responses are categorized as feeling, challenge, more information or recommendation. Self-administered. Suitable for group use. CANADIAN PUBLISHER

Untimed: 20-30 minutes

Range: Adult

Scoring: Hand key

Cost: Sample kit (contains 21 test

samples, fact sheet and one test user's guide) $75.00; test kit (10 test copies plus fact sheet and user's guide) $40.00; cash orders postpaid.

Publisher: Organizational Tests (Canada) Ltd.

COMMUNICATING EMPATHY
John Milnes and Harvey Bertcher

adult

Purpose: Assesses verbal empathic responses of adults nad helps teach them to develop empathic communication skills. Used for communication skills training. Appropriate for use by counselors, therapists, trainers, and those requiring management and leadership training.

Description: Assessment consists of an Introduction, nine aurally administered paper-pencil exercises, and a Conclusion, all of which comprise a full day's training program in empathic communication skills. Package includes: two cassette tapes, a facilitator's guide in a 6 x 9 album, and 25 copies of the Participant's Response Form. Cassette player and quiet room required. Examiner required. Suitable for small group use.

Untimed: 1 day

Range: Adult

Scoring: Tape key

Cost: Complete (includes 2 cassette tapes, 25 response forms, manual) $44.95.

Publisher: University Associates, Inc.

CREE QUESTIONNAIRE
T.G. Thurstone and J.J. Mellinger

adult

Purpose: Evaluates an individual's

overall creative potential and the extent to which his behavior resembles that of identified creative individuals. Used for placement of managerial and professional personnel and career counseling.

Description: 145 item paper-pencil test in two alternate forms. It measures the following 13 factorially determined dimensions of the creative personality: dominance vs. submission, indifference vs. involvement, independence vs. conformity, unstructured vs. structured work situation, selective vs. prescribed activity, involved vs. detached attitude, pressures vs. relaxed situation, high vs. low energy level, fast vs. slow reaction time, high vs. low ideational spontaneity, and strength of theoretical, artistic, and mechanical interests. Basic reading skills are required. Self-administered. Suitable for group use.

Untimed: 15-20 minutes

Range: Adult

Scoring: Hand key; computer scoring available

Cost: 20 tests $7.00; score sheet, no charge; manual $4.00.

Publisher: London House Press

DIMOCK L. INVENTORY (DLI)
Refer to page 815.

EDUCATIONAL ADMINISTRATIVE STYLE DIAGNOSIS TEST
W.J. Reddin

adult

Purpose: Measures the styles of educational administrators. Used as a training tool.

Description: Multiple item paper-pencil test designed to give scores on many styles based on the 3-D Theory of Leadership Effectiveness. Relates the administrator's scores to such styles as deserter, missionary, autocrat, compromiser, bureaucrat, developer, benevolent autocrat, task orientation, relationships orientation, and effectiveness. The administrator responds to items such as, "He sees students as sources of competent help and welcomes suggestions from them." Self-administered. Suitable for group use.

CANADIAN PUBLISHER

Untimed: 20-30 minutes

Range: Adult

Scoring: Hand key

Cost: Sample kit (contains 21 test samples, fact sheet and one test user's guide) $75.00; test kit (10 test copies plus fact sheet and user's guide) $40.00; cash orders postpaid.

Publisher: Organizational Test (Canada) Ltd.

EMO QUESTIONNAIRE (EMOTIONAL ADJUSTMENT)
G.O. Baehr and M.E. Baehr

---

adult

Purpose: Determines an individual's personal-emotional adjustment. Used to evaluate the potential of managerial and professional personnel, and to screen applicants for jobs requiring efficient performance under pressure.

Description: 140 item paper-pencil examination of ten traditional psychodiagnostic categories (rationalization, inferiority feelings, hostility, depression, fear and anxiety, organic reaction, projection, unreality, sex, withdrawal), and four composite adjustment factors (internal, external, somatic, general). The results reflect both the individual's internal psychodynamics and his relationship with the external environment. In combination with

other instruments, the test has been validated for selection of sales persons, police and security guards, and transit operators. In hospital settings, it is useful as a diagnosis of emotional health and to chart the course of psycho-therapy. Basic reading skills are required. Scoring is by hand or machine, depending upon the purpose for which the test is being used. Examiner required. Suitable for group use. Available in French.

Untimed: 20-30 minutes

Range: Adult

Scoring: Examiner evaluated (for full diagnosis); computer scored (for screening and selection)

Cost: 20 tests $8.00.

Publisher: London House Press

EMPLOYEE APTITUDE SURVEY TEST #6--NUMERICAL REASONING (EAS #6)
Refer to page 707.

EMPLOYEE APTITUDE SURVEY TEST #7--VERBAL REASONING (EAS #7)
Refer to page 707.

EXECUTIVE PROFILE SURVEY (EPS)
Virgil R. Lang

---

adult

Purpose: Measures executive potential and identifies individuals likely to succeed. Assesses an organization's executive strengths and identifies future needs. Used for employee evaluation and placement, screening job applicants and professional development.

Description: 94 item (61 on a 7-point Likert scale and 33 multiple-choice) paper-pencil test measures self- attitudes, values, and beliefs of individuals in comparison with over 2,000 top-level executives. Based on a 10-year study of the "executive personality," EPS measures the 11 personality- profile dimensions most important in business, management and executive settings. The profile dimensions include: ambitious, self-assertive, enthusiastic, creative, innovative, self-directed, receptive, adaptable, composed, perceptive, and systematic traits of the individual. The Survey also provides two validity scales. Norms, reliability, validity, and developmental background are explained in "Perspectives on the Executive Personality." Self-administered. Suitable for group use.

Untimed: 60 minutes

Range: Adult

Scoring: Computer scored and interpreted

Cost: Profile (prepaid answer sheet) and interpretation via mail $20.00; via ARION II depending on turnaround time $24.00-$26.00.

Publisher: Institute for Personality and Ability Testing, Inc.

GENERAL APTITUDE SERIES (GAS)
Refer to page 715.

===

GUILFORD-HOLLEY L. INVENTORY (GHL)
J.P. Guilford and J.W. Holley

---

adult

Purpose: Measures qualities of leadership and suggests possible leadership styles which may be adopted based on an individual's personality.

Description: Multiple item paper-

pencil inventory measures five motivational (hormetic) traits: benevolence, ambition, meticulousness, need for discipline, and aggressiveness. The test was developed in the context of a study of the psychological qualities of leaders and may be used to indicate how leaders, or other individuals, stand with respect to some commonly accepted characteristics of some types of leaders. Suggestions for leadership styles to be adopted are based on high and low scoring on individual traits. C-scale and centile norms provided for adults. Restricted to A.P.A. members. Examiner required. Suitable for group use.

Untimed: 25 minutes

Range: Adult

Scoring: Hand key; may be computer scored

Cost: 25 tests $10.00; 25 answer sheets $3.50; manual $1.50; scoring key $2.00.

Publisher: Sheridan Psychological Services, Inc.

HOW SUPERVISE?
Q.W. File and H.H. Remmers

---

adult

Purpose: Measures a supervisor's knowledge of human relations in work situations. Used for training, promoting and counseling supervisors.

Description: Multiple item paper-pencil test of beliefs about human relations in business and industry. Subjects indicate whether they believe certain supervisory practices, company policies and supervisor opinions are desirable or undesirable. Materials include two alternate forms, A and B, that deal with problems of supervisors. Form M consists of items from Forms A and B which are applicable to higher management levels. Examiner required. Suitable for group use.

Untimed: 40 minutes

Range: Adult

Scoring: Hand key

Cost: 25 tests (specify form A, B or M) includes manual and key $7.25; key (specify form A, B or M) $1.00; manual $1.25.

Publisher: The Psychological Corporation

INTERACTION INFLUENCE ANALYSIS
Paul Hersey and Joseph W. Keilty

adult

Purpose: Evaluates supervisor-subordinate relationship by charting the ways they listen and respond to each other.

Description: 125 item paper-pencil test in which observers record behavior during 1-5 leader-follower interactions. Three types of interaction are evaluated: leader behavior (directing, open or closed questionning, supporting); effective follower behavior (attentive listening, accepting, rational responding); ineffective follower behavior (nonattentive listening, rejecting irrational responding). Examiner required. Suitable for group use.

Untimed: Not available

Range: Adult

Scoring: Hand key

Cost: 1-9 score sheets $2.95 each; 10-99 score sheets $2.65 each.

Publisher: Center for Leadership Studies

I.P.I. APTITUDE-INTELLIGENCE TEST SERIES: JUDGMENT
Refer to page 721.

I.P.I. JOB TEST FIELD SERIES: FACTORY SUPERVISOR
Refer to page 726.

I.P.I. JOB TEST FIELD SERIES: OFFICE SUPERVISOR
Refer to page 729.

I.P.I. JOB TEST FIELD SERIES: SALES SUPERVISOR
Refer to page 731.

A JOB ANALYSIS TEST BATTERY FOR THE EVALUATION OF POTENTIAL OF HIGHER LEVEL PERSONNEL
Refer to page 818.

JOB FUNCTIONS INVENTORY FOR HIGHER LEVEL PERSONNEL
M.E. Baehr, W.G. Lonergan and B.A. Hunt

adult

Purpose: Determines the relative importance of functions performed on the job and the ability to perform them. Used for job description and design, job clarification, diagnosis of individual and group training needs, and vocational and career counseling.

Description: 140 item paper-pencil test. It provides a standardized and quantified procedure for measuring the following factors: objective- setting, financial planning and review, work procedures and practices, inter-departmental coordination, development and implementing technical ideas, judgment and decision-making, group cooperation and teamwork, coping with difficulties, promoting safety, communications, developing employee potential, supervisory practices, personal practices, self-development, communication-organization relations, and outside contacts. The test requires high school reading ability and has been validated for selection of police and higher level personnel. Self-administered. Suitable for group use. New test title to be Managerial And Professional Job Functions Inventory.

Untimed: 45 minutes

Range: Adult

Scoring: Hand key; computer scoring available

Cost: 20 tests $8.00.

Publisher: London House Press

THE JONES-MOHR LISTENING TEST
John E. Jones and Lawrence Mohr

adult

Purpose: Provides feedback on listening accuracy. Used for manager and leadership assessment, interviewing, communication skills training, counseling, and family therapy training.

Description: Aurally administered paper-pencil test measuring how well a person understands intended meanings. Subject listens to tape cassette and respond to test items. The subject then scores his own form according to taped instructions. Materials includes: cassette tape, 25 copies each of parallel forms A and B, and a Facilitator's Guide in a 6 x 9 inch album. Cassette player and quiet room required. Self-administered. Suitable for group use.

Timed: 30 minutes

Range: Adult

Scoring: Tape key

Cost: Complete (includes cassette tape, 25 recording form A and B, manual) $44.95.

Publisher: University Associates, Inc.

KIPNIS-SCHMIDT PROFILES OF ORGANIZATIONAL INFLUENCE STRATEGIES: INFLUENCING YOUR SUBORDINATES (POIS:FORM S)
Refer to page 819.

LEADER EFFECTIVENESS AND ADAPTABILITY DESCRIPTION (LEAD)-SELF/OTHER
Paul Hersey and Kenneth H. Blanchard

adult

Purpose: Evaluates a leader's style in terms of "directing, selling, participating, or telling" and ascertains it's appropriatness to certain situations and employees.

Description: 12 item situational, two-form, paper-pencil test. A LEAD Self form is filled out by the leader, and a LEAD Other form is filled out by the leader's superiors, associates or subordinates. Each form contains 12 situations to which the respondent chooses one of four alternative actions which the leader might select. The answers are transferred to a self-scoring sheet, then transferred onto a graph providing a three-dimensional display of the results. A data- profile sheet is used for interpretation. A facilitator is recommended for interpretation, directions and theory. Available in French. Self-administered. Suitable for groups.

Untimed: Not available

Range: Adult

Scoring: Hand key

Cost: 1-9 forms $2.95 each; 10-99 forms $2.65 each (specify LEAD Self form or LEAD Other form); 1-9 directs for self-scoring $1.95 each; 1-9 profiles $2.95 each.

Publisher: Center for Leadership Studies

LEADERSHIP ABILITY EVALUATION
Russell N. Cassel and Edward J. Stancik

teen, adult   grades 9-UP

Purpose: Measures leadership abilities, behavior and style in adults and high school students. Used for counseling and self-analysis.

Description: 50 item paper-pencil multiple-choice test. Each test item consists of a leadership-decision problem, each with four possible solutions. Responses reflect specific decision modes or social climate structures and classify decision- making patterns into one of four types: Laissez Faire, Democratic-Cooperative, Autocratic- Submissive, and Autocratic-Aggressive. The test items are presented in an eight-page test booklet. Normed on 2,000 individuals with additional norms provided for 400 outstanding leaders and 100 U.S. Air Force officers. Self-administered. Suitable for group use.

Untimed: 15 minutes

Range: Grades 9-12, adult

Scoring: Hand key

Cost: Kit (10 tests, manual) $7.90.

Publisher: Western Psychological Services

LEADERSHIP EVALUATION AND DEVELOPMENT SCALE (LEADS)
Harley W. Mowry

adult

Purpose: Measures a person's ability as a supervisor to make decisions and lead others. Used for management selection, placement and advancement.

Description: 44 item paper-pencil multiple-choice test consisting of eight supervisory problems which are described with enough background information to allow for in-depth analysis through a series of multiple-choice questions that follow each presentation. The cases presented are taken from the Armstrong Cork Company's filmstrip, "Human Relations in Supervision," and were selected on the basis of being typical of real problems, importance to effective supervision, and the opportunities offered for analysis in depth. All questions have been item-analyzed against both total score and an outside criterion of supervisory success. Test materials consist of a Casebook and a Question and Response Book, both with complete instructions. Self-administered. Suitable for group use.

Untimed: Not available

Range: Adult

Scoring: Hand key

Cost: 10 casebooks $1.75 each; 10 question and response booklets $1.00 each; scoring key $2.75; manual $.50; specimen set (one each: casebook, question booklet, manual) $8.75.

Publisher: Psychological Services, Inc.

LEADERSHIP OPINION QUESTIONNAIRE (LOQ)
Edwin A. Fleishman

adult

Purpose: Measures supervisory leadership abilities. Provides a brief measure of leadership attitudes and is useful in a variety of industrial and other organizational settings for selection, appraisal, counseling, and training of employees.

Description: 40 item paper-pencil test measuring two aspects of leadership: Consideration (how likely an individual's job relationship with subordinates is characterized by mutual trust, respect, consideration) and Structure (how likely an individual is to define and structure his and subordinates' roles toward goal attainment. Self- administered. Suitable for group use.

Untimed: 10-15 minutes

Range: Adult

Scoring: Hand scored--carbon insert (answers transfer to scoring key on inside of test booklet)

Cost: 25 test booklets $19.50; examiner's manual $1.30.

Publisher: Science Research Associates, Inc.

LEADERSHIP SCALE--MANAGER/STAFF MEMBER
Paul Hersey, Kenneth H. Blanchard and Ronald K. Hambleton

adult

Purpose: Assesses a leader's task and relationship behavior toward staff member. Aids in leadership and managerial training, HRD, team building and problem solving.

Description: Scale in two forms: Manager Form, manager selects staff member's most important objectives and rates task and relationship behaviors in relation to those objectives. Staff Member's Form, staff member selects his most important objectives and rates the manager's behavior in relation to them. Two dimensions are measured: task dimension (goal-setting, organizing, setting time lines, directing, controlling); relationship dimension (giving support, communicating, facilitating interactions, active listening, providing feedback).

Untimed: Not available

Range: Adult

Scoring: Hand key

Cost: 1-9 scales $2.95 each; 10-99 scales $2.65 each (specify Manager or Staff Member's form).

Publisher: Center for Leadership Studies

MANAGEMENT CHANGE INVENTORY
W.J. Reddin

adult

Purpose: Measures a manager's knowledge of sound methods of introducing change at a worker and supervisory level. Used before or after training in change techniques.

Description: 80 item true-false paper-pencil test that assesses the likelihood of a manager to obtain cooperation in support of proposed changes. Topics covered include participation, speed degree of information, training, resistance, and planning. Self-administered. Suitable for group use.
CANADIAN PUBLISHER

Untimed: 20-30 minutes

Range: Adult

Scoring: Hand key

Cost: Sample kit (contains 21 test samples, fact sheet and one test user's guide) $75.00; test kit (10 test copies plus fact sheet and user's guide)

$40.00; cash orders postpaid.

Publisher: Organizational Tests (Canada) Ltd.

MANAGEMENT COACHING RELATIONS TEST (MCR)
W.J. Reddin

adult

Purpose: Measures a manager's knowledge of sound methods of coaching subordinates who may be supervisors or managers. Can be used before or after a discussion of coaching.

Description: 80 item true-false paper-pencil test measuring knowledge of performance appraisal, effectiveness criteria, coaching interview, and training. Self-administered.
CANADIAN PUBLISHER

Untimed: 20-30 minutes

Range: Adult

Scoring: Hand key

Cost: Sample kit (contains 21 test samples, fact sheet and one test user's guide) $75.00; test kit (10 test copies plus fact sheet and user's guide) $40.00; cash orders postpaid.

Publisher: Organizational Tests (Canada) Ltd.

MANAGEMENT STYLE DIAGNOSIS TEST
W.J. Reddin

adult

Purpose: Measures managers and supervisors against the eight styles of the 3-D Theory of Leadership Effectiveness. Used in management and supervisory training seminars.

Description: Multiple item paper-pencil which asks the manager to agree/disagree with descriptive state-ments of a hypothetical manager's actions. Test scores relate to styles such as deserter, missionary, autocrat, compromiser, bureaucrat, developer, benevolent autocrat, task orientation, relationships orientation, and effectiveness. Self-administered. Suitable for group use.
CANADIAN PUBLISHER

Untimed: 20-30 minutes

Range: Adult

Scoring: Hand key

Cost: Sample kit (contains 21 test samples, fact sheet and one test user's guide) $75.00; test kit (10 test copies plus fact sheet and user's guide) $40.00; cash orders postpaid.

Publisher: Organizational Tests (Canada) Ltd.

MANAGERIAL STYLE QUESTIONNAIRE (MSQ-M) AND (MSQ-S)
Bruce A. Kirchhoff

adult

Purpose: Evaluates the use of objectives and goals among managers. Identifies managers with goal related problems. Used for management staff development.

Description: 47 item paper-pencil test measuring the extent to which managers use objectives in performing their managerial duties. Assesses seven dimensions: controlling, coordinating, motivating, appraisal, compensation, personnel selection, training, and developing. Two forms available: a manager self-evaluation form (MSQ-M) and a form for subordinate-evaluation of the manager (MSQ-S). Application limited to managerial and professional personnel. Self- administered. Suitable for group use. Available in Swedish, Dutch, French, and German.

Untimed: 10-15 minutes

Range: Adult

Scoring: Hand key; computer scoring available

Cost: 25 evaluation forms or profiles $35.00; punch card of computer program and instructions $125.00; computer score service $12.50 per form.

Publisher: BJK Associates

MATURITY SCALE--SELF/ MANAGER
Ronald K. Hambleton, Kenneth H. Blanchard and Paul Hersey

adult

Purpose: Determines a person's willingness and ability to be self-directed. Used for leadership and managerial training, team building and HRD.

Description: Paper-pencil test measuring job maturity in terms of: job experience and knowledge; ability to solve problems; ability to take responsibility; meet deadlines. Measures psychological maturity in terms of: willingness to take responsibility; achievement motivation; persistence; work attitudes; and independence. The employee and the manager each fill out a form, selecting up to five of the individual's most important objectives, rating each other on the above characteristics. Charting and interpretation materials are included with each test form, although a facilitator is recommended for theory, interpretation and follow-up. Self- administered. Suitable for groups.

Untimed: Not available

Range: Adult

Scoring: Hand key

Cost: 1-9 forms $2.95 each; 10-99 forms $2.65 each; 100-299 forms $2.30 each; 300 or more forms $1.95 each (specify Self-Rating Form or Manager Form).

Publisher: Center for Leadership Studies

MATURITY STYLE MATCH-- STAFF MEMBER/MANAGER
Paul Hersey, Kenneth H. Blanchard and Joseph W. Keilty

adult

Purpose: Evaluates the relationship between manager's leadership style and employee's maturity. Used for management and leadership training, HRD, team building and conflict resolution.

Description: Multiple item paper-pencil test of four leadership-style dimensions rated against employee's major objectives or responsibilities (1-6) compared with the employee's psychological and job maturity. Materials consist of four-page rating forms, to be completed by manager and staff member and result in matrix comparison of employee's and manager's ratings. A facilitator is recommended for theory and interpretation although an interpretation text is included in materials. Self-administered. Suitable for group use.

Untimed: Not available

Range: Adult

Scoring: Hand key

Cost: 1-9 complete kit (includes rating forms and interpretation text) $2.95 each (specify Manager form or Staff form).

Publisher: Center For Leadership Studies

ORGANIZATION HEALTH SURVEY (OHS)
W.J. Reddin

adult

Purpose: Reveals the attitudes of managers in an organization. Used as a training device or as feedback to top management.

Description: 80 item true-false

paper-pencil test providing a separate score on productivity, leadership, organization structure, communication, conflict management, participation, human resource management, and creativity. Self-administered. Suitable for group use. CANADIAN PUBLISHER

Untimed: 20-30 minutes

Range: Adult

Scoring: Hand key

Cost: Sample kit (contains 21 test samples, fact sheet and one test user's guide) $75.00; test kit (10 test copies plus fact sheet and user's guide) $40.00; cash orders postpaid.

Publisher: Organizational Tests (Canada) Ltd.

POWER PERCEPTION PROFILE--SELF/OTHER
Refer to page 826.

PRESS TEST
M.E. Baehr and R.J. Corsini

adult

Purpose: Assesses ability of adults to work under pressure by providing objective measures of reaction time. Used for career counseling and placement of high-level personnel, especially in occupations where efficiency must be maintained under pressure.

Description: 600-item paper-pencil test measuring speed of reaction to verbal stimuli, speed of reaction to color stimuli, and speed of reaction to color stimuli under distraction caused by interfering verbal stimuli. For valid results, stop-watch time limits and strict monitoring must be employed in the administration of the test, which is not designed to be completed in the allotted time. Reading skills are not required. Has been

used in selection of airline pilots. Examiner-required. Suitable for group use. Can be given in any language.

Timed: 90 seconds each part

Range: Adult

Scoring: Hand key

Cost: 20 tests $16.00.

Publisher: London House Press

PROBLEM-SOLVING DECISION-MAKING STYLE INVENTORY--SELF/OTHER
Paul Hersey and Walter E. Natemeyer

adult

Purpose: Evaluates individual problem-solving and decision-making styles as an aid to management training, team-building, HRD, and organizational development.

Description: 12 item paper-pencil, multiple-choice form. The test measures directive behavior (how the individual solves problems, makes decisions and spells out others' duties), and supportive behavior (how the individual engages in two-way communication and provides social and emotional support). The person completes the Self Inventory and an associate completes the Other Inventory. The two profiles are then compared and discussed. The test package includes score sheets, profile analysis and interpretation materials. Self-administered. Suitable for group use.

Untimed: Not available

Range: Adult

Scoring: Hand key

Cost: 1-9 forms $2.95 each; 10-99 forms $2.65 each; 100-299 forms $2.30 each; 300 or more forms $1.95 each (specify Self Inventory or Other Inventory).

Publisher: Center for Leadership Studies

PROFESSIONAL AND MANAGERIAL POSITION QUESTIONNAIRE (PMPQ)
J.L. Mitchell and Ernest J. McCormick

adult

Purpose: Assesses characteristics of jobs. Used for analysis of professional, managerial and related positions.

Description: Multiple item paper-pencil measure of job characteristics. There are five scales: Part-of- the-job, Complexity, Impact, Responsibility, and Special. PMPQ items are divided into three sections: Job Functions, Personal Requirements and Other Information. Analyst rates each item in terms of its relevance to the job. Special features include numerous computer processing options. Self-administered. Suitable for group use.

Untimed: 30 minutes

Range: Adult

Scoring: Examiner evaluated; computer processing available

Cost: Questionnaire $1.40; computer processing from PAQ Services $1.60 to $100.00 based on processing option.

Publisher: Purdue Research Foundation/University Book Store

PURDUE INDUSTRIAL SUPERVISORS WORD-MEANING TEST
Joseph Tiffin and Donald A. Long

adult

Purpose: Measures supervisors' understanding of words which appear frequently in material directed to them. Used for personnel evaluation.

Description: Multiple item paper-pencil test of word comprehension. Used in conjunction with the Purdue Reading Test for Industrial Supervisors. Sale restricted to companies employing qualified personnel administrators and to psychologists using tests for instruction or vocational guidance. Examiner required. Suitable for group use.

Untimed: Not available

Range: Adult supervisors

Scoring: Hand key

Cost: Specimen set $1.00; 25 tests, manual, key $6.00.

Publisher: Purdue Research Foundation/University Book Store

PURDUE RATING SCALE FOR ADMINISTRATORS AND EXECUTIVES
H.H. Remmers and R.L. Hobson

adult

Purpose: Assesses effectiveness of executives/administrators based on ratings of subordinates and co-workers. Used for providing feedback on performance.

Description: 36 item paper-pencil test of three dimensions of executive and administrative effectiveness: fairness to subordinates, administrative achievement and democratic orientation. The employee rates the administrator on each of 36 characteristics. Self-administered. Suitable for group use.

Untimed: 5 minutes

Range: Adult

Scoring: Examiner evaluated

Cost: Contact publisher.

Publisher: Purdue Research Foundation/University Book Store

PURDUE READING TEST FOR INDUSTRIAL SUPERVISORS
Joseph Tiffin and Roy Dunlap

adult

Purpose: Measures reading comprehension of paragraphs. Used for evaluation of supervisory personnel.

Description: Multiple item paper-pencil test of ability to understand material frequently encountered by supervisors. Used in conjunction with the Purdue Industrial Supervisors Word-Meaning Test. Sale restricted to companies employing qualified personnel administrators and to psychologists using tests for instruction or vocational guidance. Examiner required. Suitable for group use.

Untimed: Not available

Range: Adult supervisor

Scoring: Hand key

Cost: Specimen set $1.00; 25 tests, manual, key $7.50.

Publisher: Purdue Research Foundation/University Book Store

STEIN SURVEY FOR ADMINISTRATORS
Morris I. Stein

adult

Purpose: Determines a supervisor's or administrator's view of his role in research and development (R & D) organizations. Used to assess the organization from a supervisor's point of view.

Description: 95-item paper-pencil questionnaire measures an individual's perception of his status and role requirements as a supervisor or administrator working with research and development organizations. Self-administered. Suitable for group use. Restricted to R & D organizations.

Untimed: 35 minutes

Range: Adult

Scoring: Examiner evaluated

Cost: $2.50 per copy.

Publisher: Morris I. Stein

SUPERVISORY CHANGE RELATIONS TEST (SCHR)
W.J. Reddin

adult

Purpose: Measures a supervisor's knowledge of sound methods of introducing change. Can be used before or after training in change techniques.

Description: 80 item true-false paper-pencil test which measures a supervisor's understanding of how change can be affected by participation, speed, degree of information, training, resistance, and planning. Suitable for blue or white collar supervision. Test is based on chapter 13 of Reddin, W.J., *Managerial Effectiveness*, McGraw- Hill, 1970. Self-administered. Suitable for group use. CANADIAN PUBLISHER

Untimed: 20-30 minutes

Range: Adult

Scoring: Hand key

Cost: Sample kit (contains 21 test samples, fact sheet and one test user's guide) $75.00; test kit (10 test copies plus fact sheet and user's guide) $30.00; cash orders postpaid.

Publisher: Organizational Tests (Canada) Ltd.

SUPERVISORY COACHING RELATIONS TEST (SCORE)
W.J. Reddin

adult

Purpose: Measures a supervisor's knowledge of the methods of coaching subordinates. Can be used before or after coaching training.

Description: 80 item true-false paper-pencil test covering performance appraisal, effectiveness criteria, coaching interview, and training. Suitable for white or blue collar supervision. Self- administered. Suitable for group use.
CANADIAN PUBLISHER

Untimed: 20-30 minutes

Range: Adult

Scoring: Hand key

Cost: Sample kit (contains 21 test samples, fact sheet and one test user's guide) $75.00; test kit (10 test copies plus fact sheet and user's guide) $30.00; cash orders postpaid.

Publisher: Organizational Tests (Canada) Ltd.

SUPERVISORY COMMUNICATION RELATIONS TEST (SCOM)
W.J. Reddin

adult

Purpose: Measures a person's understanding of sound communication methods. Can be used before or after coaching training.

Description: 80 item true-false paper-pencil test covering communication with subordinates, co-workers and superiors. Also assesses ability to give orders and introduce change. Test covers verbal and non-verbal communication. Suitable for either blue or white collar supervision. Self-administered. Suitable for group use.
CANADIAN PUBLISHER

Untimed: 20-30 minutes

Range: Adult

Scoring: Hand key

Cost: Sample kit (contains 21 test samples, fact sheet and one test user's guide) $75.00; test kit (10 test copies plus fact sheet and user's guide) $30.00; cash orders postpaid.

Publisher: Organizational Tests (Canada) Ltd.

SUPERVISORY HUMAN RELATIONS TEST (SHR)
Refer to page 830.

SUPERVISORY JOB DISCIPLINE TEST (SJD)
W.J. Reddin

adult

Purpose: Determines a person's knowledge of accepted disciplinary techniques. Used before or after training in disciplinary training techniques.

Description: 80 item true-false paper-pencil test covering lateness, horseplay, appropriate punishments, corrective interview techniques, handling errors, long coffee breaks, visiting other departments, eating lunch at desk. Suitable for either blue or white collar supervision. Self-administered. Suitable for group use.
CANADIAN PUBLISHER

Untimed: 20-30 minutes

Range: Adult

Scoring: Hand key

Cost: Sample kit (contains 21 test samples, fact sheet and one test user's guide) $75.00; test kit (10 test copies plus fact sheet and user's guide) $30.00; cash orders postpaid.

Publisher: Organizational Tests (Canada) Ltd.

SUPERVISORY JOB INSTRUCTION TEST (SJI)
W.J. Reddin

adult

Purpose: Measures a person's knowledge of how to instruct others on the job. Used before or after job instruction training.

Description: 80 item true-false paper-pencil test measuring understanding of learning principles, teacher- learner relationships, learning aids, learning environment. Suitable for either blue or white collar supervision. Self-administered. Suitable for group use.
CANADIAN PUBLISHER

Untimed: 20-30 minutes

Range: Adult

Scoring: Hand key

Cost: Sample kit (contains 21 test samples, fact sheet and one test user's guide) $75.00; test kit (10 test copies plus fact sheet and user's guide) $30.00; cash orders postpaid.

Publisher: Organizational Tests (Canada) Ltd.

SUPERVISORY JOB SAFETY TEST (SJS)
W.J. Reddin

adult

Purpose: Measures a person's attitudes toward an understanding of good safety practices. Used before or after safety training.

Description: 80 question true-false paper-pencil test over safety instruction, safety devices, safety responsibilities, safety causes, corrective practices, work methods, types of accidents, hazard analysis, accident investigation, and role of supervisors. Suitable for either blue or white collar supervision. Self-

administered. Suitable for group use.
CANADIAN PUBLISHER

Untimed: 20-30 minutes

Range: Adult

Scoring: Hand key

Cost: Sample kit (contains 21 test samples, fact sheet and one test user's guide) $75.00; test kit (10 test copies plus fact sheet and user's guide) $30.00; cash orders postpaid.

Publisher: Organizational Tests (Canada) Ltd.

SUPERVISORY POTENTIAL TEST (SPT)
W.J. Reddin

adult

Purpose: Measures a person's understanding of supervisory methods, principles and techniques. Used as a training tool.

Description: 80 item true-false paper-pencil test covering subordinate evaluation techniques, disciplinary principles, promotion criteria, change introduction, superior relations, new supervisor attachment and subordinate motivation. Suitable for either blue or white collar supervision. Self-administered. Suitable for group use.
CANADIAN PUBLISHER

Untimed: 20-30 minutes

Range: Adult

Scoring: Hand key

Cost: Sample kit (contains 21 test samples, fact sheet and one test user's guide) $75.00; test kit (10 test copies plus fact sheet and user's guide) $30.00; cash orders postpaid.

Publisher: Organizational Tests (Canada) Ltd.

SUPERVISORY PRACTICE TEST (REVISED)
Martin M. Bruce

adult

Purpose: Evaluates supervisory ability and potential in a business-world setting to aid in means of personnel selection, evaluation and training.

Description: 50 item paper-pencil multiple-choice test which indicates the extent to which the taker is able to perceive the desired course of action in making business decisions as compared with the perceptions and attitudes of managers and subordinates. Minority group data are available. Self-administered. Suitable for group use. Available in French, Spanish, and German.

Untimed: 20 minutes

Range: Adult

Scoring: Hand key

Cost: Specimen set $4.95; manual $3.85; key $.66; package of tests $15.29.

Publisher: Martin M. Bruce, Ph.D., Publisher

SUPERVISORY UNION RELATIONS TEST (SUR)
W.J. Reddin

adult

Purpose: Measures a supervisor's attitudes toward unions. Used for evaluating supervisor's and manager's attitudes.

Description: 80 item true-false paper-pencil test covering motives of union leadership, why men join unions, how best to work with unions, management rights, role of shop steward, foreman-union relationship, labor benefits and company benefits. Respondents answer on the basis of what they believe is best for

their position or company at the present time. Suitable for either blue or white collar supervision. Self-administered. Suitable for group use. CANADIAN PUBLISHER

Untimed: 20-30 minutes

Range: Adult

Scoring: Hand key

Cost: Sample kit (contains 21 test samples, fact sheet and one test user's guide) $75.00; test kit (10 test copies plus fact sheet and user's guide) $30.00; cash orders postpaid.

Publisher: Organizational Tests (Canada) Ltd.

TEMPERAMENT COMPARATOR
M.E. Baehr

adult

Purpose: Determines the relatively permanent temperament traits which are characteristic of an individual's behavior. Used for evaluation of the potential of higher-level managerial and professional personnel, job screening, and vocational counseling.

Description: 153 item paper-pencil test consisting of trait pairs derived from application of a paired comparison technique to 18 individual traits. Emphasis is on individual variations in significant dimensions within the "normal" range of behavior. Factors measured are the 18 individual traits and five factorially determined behavior factors: extroversive vs. reserved, emotionally responsive vs. emotionally controlled, self-reliant/individually oriented vs. dependent/group oriented, excitable vs. placid, socially oriented vs. not socially oriented. The test provides a measure of internal consistency of response. Basic reading skills are required. A mechanical procedure (disk and insert) is available for hand scoring. Examiner required. Suitable for

group use.

Untimed: 20-30 minutes

Range: Adult

Scoring: Hand key; examiner evaluated (for full diagnosis); computer scored (for screening and selection).

Cost: Specimen set $6.00.

Publisher: London House Press

TEST OF PRACTICAL JUDGMENT-FORM 62
Alfred J. Cardall

adult

Purpose: Determines employee ability to use practical judgment in solving problems. Used to screen for management and sales positions.

Description: Multiple item paper-pencil multiple-choice test of judgment factors which may be used in conjunction with intelligence testing. May be used for screening, selection and placement of individuals whose work involves thinking, planning or getting along with people. Examines such factors as empathy, drive and social maturity. Materials include five tests, key and manual. Examiner required. Suitable for group use. Available in French.
CANADIAN PUBLISHER

Untimed: 30 minutes

Range: Adult

Scoring: Hand key

Cost: Review set (includes 5 tests, key and manual) $5.00; 25 booklets $15.00.

Publisher: Institute of Psychological Research, Inc.

VALUES INVENTORY (VI)
W.J. Reddin

teen, adult   College-UP

Purpose: Reveals a manager's value

system. Used in college and industry.

Description: Multiple item paper-pencil test consisting of quotations among which the manager chooses preferred statements. Values tested are theoretical, power, effectiveness, achievement, human, industry, and profit. Self-administered. Suitable for group use.
CANADIAN PUBLISHER

Untimed: 20-30 minutes

Range: College student and adult

Scoring: Hand key

Cost: Sample kit (contains 21 test samples, fact sheet and one test user's guide) $75.00; test kit (10 test copies plus fact sheet and user's guide) $40.00; cash orders postpaid.

Publisher: Organizational Tests (Canada) Ltd.

X-Y-Z INVENTORY
W.J. Reddin

adult

Purpose: Reveals a manager's basic, underlying, philosophical assumptions about man. Used in business to help understand a manager's frame-of- reference in assessing employees performance.

Description: Multiple item inventory which reveals some elements of a manager's assumptions that man is: a Beast (X), a Self-Actualizing Being (Y), or a Rational Being (Z). Used prior to discussion of X, Y, and Z theories.
CANADIAN PUBLISHER

Untimed: 20-30 minutes

Range: Adult

Scoring: Hand key

Cost: Sample kit (contains 21 test samples, fact sheet and one test user's guide) $75.00; test kit (10 test copies plus fact sheet and user's guide) $40.00; cash orders postpaid.

Publisher: Organizational Tests (Canada) Ltd.

Mechanical Abilities and Manual Dexterity

ACER MECHANICAL COMPREHENSION TEST

teen, adult

Purpose: Measures mechanical aptitude. Used for employee selection and placement for positions requiring some degree of mechanical aptitude.

Description: 45 item paper-pencil multiple-choice test consists of problems in the form of diagrams which illustrate various mechanical principles and mechanisms. Australian norms provided for various age groups as well as university and technical college groups. Materials include: reusable booklet, separate answer sheet, scoring key, manual, and specimen set. Examiner required. Suitable for group use. AUSTRALIAN PUBLISHER

Timed: 30 minutes

Range: 13.6 years and older

Scoring: Hand key

Cost: Contact publisher.

Publisher: The Australian Council for Educational Research Limited

ACER MECHANICAL REASONING TEST (REVISED EDITION)

teen, adult

Purpose: Measures basic mechanical reasoning abilities. Used for employee selection and placement for positions requiring some degree of mechanical aptitude.

Description: Multiple item paper-pencil, multiple-choice test consists of problems in the firm of diagrams which illustrate various mechanical principles and mechanisms. This test is a shortened version of the ACER Mechanical Comprehension Test with some different items and less verbal content. Australian norms are provided for apprenticeship applicants for a variety of trades and for apprentices beginning training. Materials include: reusable booklet, answer sheet, score key, manual, and specimen set. Examiner required. Suitable for group use. AUSTRALIAN PUBLISHER

Timed: 20 minutes

Range: 15 years and older

Scoring: Hand key

Cost: Contact publisher.

Publisher: The Australian Council for Educational Research Limited

BENNETT MECHANICAL COMPREHENSION TEST (BMCT)
G.K. Bennett, et al.

adult

Purpose: Measures ability to understand mechanical relationships and physical laws in practical situations. Used to screen job applicants for positions requiring practical application of mechanical principles, complex machine operation and repair.

Description: Multiple item paper-pencil test assessing understanding of mechanical relationships. Items are multiple-choice. Materials include two equivalent forms, S and T. Previous forms, AA, BB, CC, and W1 are still available. Tapes of questions read aloud are available to aid in accurate testing of applicants with limited reading skills. Examiner required. Suitable for group use. Forms S and T available in Spanish.

Timed: 30 minutes

Range: Adult

Scoring: Hand key

Cost: Specimen set (includes tests, answer document, keys, manual) $3.75; 25 tests $14.75; 50 answer documents $6.75; key (specify S or T) $2.00; manual $2.00; tape recording (specify reel-to-reel or cassette) $17.25.

Publisher: The Psychological Corporation

CLOSURE FLEXIBILITY (CONCEALED FIGURES)
Refer to page 792.

CRAWFORD SMALL PARTS DEXTERITY TEST (CSPDT)
John Crawford

teen, adult

Purpose: Measures fine eye-hand coordination. For use in selecting applicants for jobs such as engravers, watch repairers and telephone installers.

Description: Two part performance measure of dexterity. Part 1 measures dexterity in using tweezers to assemble pin and collar assemblies. Part 2 measures dexterity in placing small screws in threaded holes in a plate and screwing them down with a screwdriver. The CSPDT may be administered in two ways. In the work-limit method, subject completes task and total time is the score. Using time-limit procedure, the score is the amount of work done in a specified time. Materials include assembly plate, pins, collars, and screws. Examiner required. Suitable for group use.

Timed: 10 to 15 minutes

Range: Job applicants

Scoring: Examiner evaluated

Cost: Complete set (includes manual and spare parts) $134.00.

Publisher: The Psychological Corporation

CURTIS SPATIAL TESTS: OBJECT COMPLETION TEST AND SPACE-FORM TEST
James W. Curtis

adult

Purpose: Assesses perceptual efficiency. Used for screening applicants for jobs requiring manual skills.

Description: Two paper-pencil tests of perceptual efficiency, one two-dimensional and one three- dimensional. May be used in conjunction with Holmes' One Minute Per-Flu-Dex Tests for screening on factory aptitudes. Examiner required. Suitable for group use.

Timed: 1 minute per test

Range: Adult

Scoring: Hand key

Cost: Specimen set $2.00; 25 tests $2.20; 100-$7.70 (specify form).

Publisher: Psychometric Affiliates

EMPLOYEE APTITUDE SURVEY TEST #9--MANUAL SPEED AND ACCURACY (EAS #9)
Refer to page 708.

FINE DEXTERITY TEST
E.I.T.S. Staff

adult

Purpose: Measures fine finger and small tool dexterity as a skill needed in small parts assembly work. Used for personnel selection and placement.

Description: Two task test of fine dexterity. The test is taken on a wooden board containing a row of pins and a collection of collars and washers located in storage cups on the board. The subject uses fingers and forceps to place the collars and washers on the pins. Other materials include a sorting tray and a collar-removing plate to speed administration. Spare washers, collars and forceps also are available. Examiner required. Suitable for group use. BRITISH PUBLISHER

Timed: 7 minutes

Range: Adult

Scoring: Examiner evaluated

Cost: Contact publisher.

Publisher: Educational and Industrial Test Services Ltd.

FINE FINGER DEXTERITY WORK TASK UNIT

adult

Purpose: Assesses kinesthetic memory, bi-manual coordination, finger dexterity, and frustration tolerance. Used for vocational evaluation and job placement of blind and visually impaired multiply handicapped persons.

Description: Multiple task test to evaluate a variety of work abilities. The individual is taught the task, then works for a 50 minute period and receives feedback on this rate and accuracy of work. Provides an objective method of comparing a blind or visually impaired person's performance to that of an average sighted person. Materials include assembled testing equipment and a manual. Examiner required. Not suitable for group use.

Timed: 50 minutes

Range: Adult

Scoring: Examiner evaluated

Cost: Manual $15.00; testing apparatus, contact: George Aarons, Royal Maid Association for the Blind, P.O. Drawer 30, Hazlehurst, MS 39083; (601) 894-1771.

Publisher: Mississippi State University Rehabilitation Research & Training Center/National Industries for the Blind

FOOT OPERATED HINGED BOX WORK TASK UNIT

adult

Purpose: Assesses hand-foot coordination, bi-manual coordination and finger dexterity. Used for vocational evaluation and job placement of blind and visually impaired multiply handicapped persons.

Description: Multiple task test to evaluate a variety of work abilities. The individual is taught the task, then works for a 50 minute period and receives feedback on this rate and accuracy of work. Provides an objective method of comparing a blind or visually impaired person's performance to that of an average sighted person. Materials include assembled testing equipment and a manual. Examiner required. Not suitable for group use.

Timed: 50 minutes

Range: Adult

Scoring: Examiner evaluated

Cost: Manual $15.00; testing apparatus, contact: George Aarons, Royal Maid Association for the Blind, P.O. Drawer 30, Hazlehurst, MS 39083; (601) 894-1771.

Publisher: Mississippi State University Rehabilitation Research & Training Center/National Industries for the Blind

HAND-TOOL DEXTERITY TEST
G.K. Bennett

adult

Purpose: Measures skill in using

ordinary mechanic's tools, wrenches and screwdrivers. Used in selection of applicants for mechanical and industrial jobs.

Description: A task test of mechanical skill. Subject takes apart twelve assemblies of nuts, bolts and washers from wooden frame, then reassembles them. Score is time required. Materials include wooden frame, nuts, bolts, washers, and tools. Examiner required. Not suitable for group use.

Timed: 7 minutes

Range: Adult

Scoring: Score obtained by timing

Cost: Complete set (includes manual) $133.00; manual $1.85.

Publisher: The Psychological Corporation

HINGED BOX WORK TASK UNIT

adult

Purpose: Assesses tactual perception, material control, bi-manual coordination, and frustration tolerance. Used for vocational evaluation and job placement of blind and visually impaired multiply handicapped persons.

Description: Multiple task test to evaluate a variety of work abilities. The individual is taught the task, then works for a 50 minute period and receives feedback on this rate and accuracy of work. Provides an objective method of comparing a blind or visually impaired person's performance to that of an average sighted person. Materials include assembled testing equipment and a manual. Examiner required. Not suitable for group use.

Timed: 50 minutes

Range: Adult

Scoring: Examiner evaluated

Cost: Manual $15.00; testing apparatus, contact: George Aarons, Royal Maid Association for the Blind, P.O. Drawer 30, Hazlehurst, MS 39083; (601) 894-1771.

Publisher: Mississippi State University Rehabilitation Research & Training Center/National Industries for the Blind

INDEX CARD WORK TASK UNIT

adult

Purpose: Assesses bi-manual coordination, finger dexterity, frustration tolerance, and memory for sequence of operations. Used for vocational evaluation and job placement of blind and visually impaired multiply handicapped persons.

Description: Multiple task test to evaluate a variety of work abilities. The individual is taught the task, then works for a 50 minute period and receives feedback on this rate and accuracy of work. Provides an objective method of comparing a blind or visually impaired person's performance to that of an average sighted person. Materials include assembled testing equipment and a manual. Examiner required. Not suitable for group use.

Timed: 50 minutes

Range: Adult

Scoring: Examiner evaluated

Cost: Manual $15.00; testing apparatus, contact: George Aarons, Royal Maid Association for the Blind, P.O. Drawer 30, Hazlehurst, MS 39083; (601) 894-1771.

Publisher: Mississippi State University Rehabilitation Research & Training Center/National Industries for the Blind

INTUITIVE MECHANICS (WEIGHTS AND PULLEYS)
L.L. Thurstone and T.E. Jeffrey

adult

Purpose: Assesses mechanical aptitude, especially of engineering students. Used for vocational counseling.

Description: 32 item paper-pencil measure of ability to understand mechanical relationships and visualize internal movement in a mechanical system. Test assesses, for instance, students' ability to judge whether a diagrammed system is stable and/or stationary. Examiner required. Suitable for group use.

Timed: 3 minutes

Range: Adult

Scoring: Hand key

Cost: Specimen set $3.00.

Publisher: London House Press

I.P.I. APTITUDE-INTELLIGENCE TEST SERIES: DEXTERITY
Refer to page 720.

I.P.I. APTITUDE-INTELLIGENCE TEST SERIES: MOTOR APPARATUS
Refer to page 721.

I.P.I. JOB TEST FIELD SERIES: INSPECTOR
Refer to page 727.

MANUAL DEXTERITY TEST
E.I.T.S. Staff

adult

Purpose: Measures manual dexterity as a skill needed in assembly and packaging tasks. Used for personnel placement and selection.

Description: Multiple item paper-pencil test consisting of one subtest in manual speed and a second in manual skill. Materials include booklets, specimen set and the manual. Examiner required. Suitable for group use. BRITISH PUBLISHER

Timed: Part I, 45 seconds; Part II, 90 seconds

Range: Adult

Scoring: Examiner evaluated

Cost: Contact publisher.

Publisher: Educational and Industrial Test Services Ltd.

MECHANICAL ABILITY TEST
Refer to page 741.

MECHANICAL APTITUDE TEST
Andrew Kobal, J. Wayne Wrightstone, Karl R. Kunze, and edited by Andrew J. MacElroy

teen, adult   grades 10-UP

Purpose: Measures interests and abilities in skilled trades. Used for educational and vocational guidance and for selecting applicants for apprenticeships and industrial training.

Description: Four paper-pencil tests of mechanical aptitudes. Factors measured include: comprehension of mechanical tasks; use of tools and materials; matching tools and operations; and use of tools and materials. Examiner required. Suitable for group use.

Timed: 45 minutes

Range: High school and adult

Scoring: Hand key

Cost: Specimen set $2.20; 25 tests $5.50; 100-$21.00.

Publisher: Psychometric Affiliates

MECHANICAL MOVEMENTS
L.L. Thurstone and T.E. Jeffrey

adult

Purpose: Determines degree of mechanical interest and experience. Used for vocational counseling and to select persons for mechanical occupations in industry.

Description: 38 item paper-pencil, multiple-choice measure of mechanical comprehension. Indicates the ability to visualize a moving mechanical system where there is internal movement or displacement of the parts. Basic reading skills are required. Examiner required. Suitable for group use.

Timed: 14 minutes

Range: Adult

Scoring: Hand key

Cost: Specimen set $3.00; 20 tests $4.00.

Publisher: London House Press

MINNESOTA MANUAL DEXTERITY TEST

teen, adult

Purpose: Measures an individual's capacity for the kind of rapid, simple hand-eye coordination needed for such semi-skilled shop and clerical operations as wrapping, sorting and packing.

Description: Two phase, nonverbal, manual dexterity test measuring rate of hand movement and finger manipulation. Materials consist of a 36 x 12 inch board with 58 holes 1⅜″ in diameter spaced 2¼″ apart, arranged in four rows containing 58 round

pegs painted red on one side and black on the other. In the placing test, the taker is presented with the empty board and asked to transfer the pegs, presented same color up, back to the board using only one hand. In the turning test, the pegs are left in the board and the taker removes each peg one at a time with one hand, turns it over, transfers it to the other hand, and replaces it in the same position on the board until all pegs have been turned. Both tests are timed for four complete trials. Examiner required. Suitable for group use.

Untimed: 6-10 minutes

Range: Age 13-adult

Scoring: Hand key

Cost: Complete test $99.00; replacement wooden cylinder $.75 each; 50 record blanks $3.50.

Publisher: Lafayette Instrument Company, Inc.

MINNESOTA RATE OF MANIPULATION TESTS
Employment Stabilization Research Institute, University of Minnesota

adult

Purpose: Measures finger-hand-arm dexterity. Used for employee selection for jobs requiring manual dexterity, and in vocational and rehabilitation training programs.

Description: Five test battery measuring: Placing, Turning, Displacing, One Hand Turning and Placing, and Two Hand Turning and Placing. Materials consist of two test boards, each with 60 round holes in four rows, and 60 round blocks, painted orange on the top half and yellow on the lower half. Two blocks are transferred from one board to the other, being turned and moved in various ways. The subject is then instructed to transfer all pegs back to the board using only one hand. In the turning test, the pegs are left in the board and the subject removes each block one at a time with one hand, turns it over, transfers it to the free hand and replaces it in the same position on the board. All tests are timed and repeated for four complete trials. The Displacing and Turning Tests are suitable for use with the Blind. The board, blocks, and 50 individual record forms, and a manual are included in a vinyl carrying case. Examiner required. Suitable for group use.

Timed: 10 minutes or less for each test

Range: Adult

Scoring: Examiner evaluated

Cost: Complete $147.50.

Publisher: American Guidance Service

MOORE EYE-HAND COORDI-NATION AND COLOR MATCHING TEST
Refer to page 536.

MULTIFUNCTIONAL WORK TASK UNIT

adult

Purpose: Assesses bi-manual coordination, material control, and kinesthetic memory. Used for vocational evaluation and job placement of blind and visually impaired multiply handicapped persons.

Description: Multiple task test to evaluate a variety of work abilities. The individual is taught the task, then works for a 50 minute period and receives feedback on this rate and accuracy of work. Provides an objective method of comparing a blind or visually impaired person's perform-

ance to that of an average sighted person. Materials include assembled testing equipment and a manual. Examiner required. Not suitable for group use.

Timed: 50 minutes

Range: Adult

Scoring: Examiner evaluated

Cost: Manual $15.00; testing apparatus, contact: George Aarons, Royal Maid Association for the Blind, P.O. Drawer 30, Hazlehurst, MS 39083; (601) 894-1771.

Publisher: Mississippi State University Rehabilitation Research & Training Center/National Industries for the Blind

O'CONNOR FINGER DEXTERITY TEST
Johnson O'Connor

adult

Purpose: Measures finger dexterity. Used to determine individual aptitude for small assembly jobs requiring rapid hand work.

Description: Multiple-operation, manual test. Materials are an 11" x 5½" board containing a shallow well and 100 ³⁄₁₆" holes (arranged in 10 rows) and a set of 300 pins. The individual is required to place three pins in each hole. The time required to fill the first 50 holes and the time for the second 50 holes are recorded separately. The test has been found useful in predicting success in the assembling of armatures, miniature parts, clocks, watches, the filling of vials and small lathe and machine work. Examiner required. Suitable for group use.

Untimed: 8-16 minutes

Range: Adult

Scoring: Hand key; examiner evaluated

Cost: Complete $62.00; set of 310

replacement pins $20.50.

Publisher: Stoelting Co.

O'CONNOR TWEEZER DEXTERITY TEST
Johnson O'Connor

teen, adult

Purpose: Measures fine eye-hand coordination and the ability to use small hand tools precisely and steadily. Used to identify vocational aptitude.

Description: Multiple-operation, manual test. The materials are an 11" x 5½" board containing a shallow well and 100 small holes (arranged in 10 rows) and 100 one-inch pins. The individual is required to put a pin in each of the holes using only small tweezers. The total elapsed time is recorded. High score indicates an aptitude for tasks involving the use of small hand tools e.g., forceps, needle-nose pliers and tweezers used by laboratory workers, medical personnel, watch repairers, and stamp collectors. Examiner required. Suitable for group use.

Untimed: 8-10 minutes

Range: Ages 14 and older

Scoring: Hand key; examiner evaluated

Cost: Complete $62.00; set of 105 replacement pins $12.50.

Publisher: Stoelting Co.

O'CONNOR WIGGLY BLOCK
Johnson O'Connor

adult

Purpose: Measures ability to visualize structured design and three-dimensional space. Assesses aptitudes associated with machinists, tool and die makers, draftsmen, engineers, and architects.

Description: Task assessment test measuring an individual's ability to visualize a completed project from the disassembled pieces. The test consists of assembling a 10" x 6" x 6" wooden block which has been cut on two planes into nine irregular pieces. The subject assembles the block three times. The average time for the three trials is recorded. Examiner required. Suitable for group use.

Untimed: 15-30 minutes

Range: Adult

Scoring: Hand key

Cost: Complete test $65.00; package of 50 record blanks $3.75.

Publisher: Lafayette Instrument Co., Inc.

PEG BOARD
E.I.T.S. Staff

adult

Purpose: Determines manual dexterity as a skill needed in assembly work of a fine nature, such as in electrical and light engineering assembly tasks and packaging tasks. Used for personnel selection and placement.

Description: Multiple task examination covering two primary movements. The first consists of placing pins in holes on a peg board, using right and left hands separately and both hands together. The second involves assembling a washer and a collar on a pin and placing it on the board, using both hands. The peg board is set with a line of nine holes for practice and, for the test proper, and additional 29 holes, arranged in an ellipse. The hole diameters vary to produce a large range of results without increasing the performance time with every fifth hole marked to facilitate fast scoring. For the test task, there are pins, collars, washers located in the appropriate cups on the board. A manual and test materials are included with the kit. Examiner required. Suitable for group use. BRITISH PUBLISHER

Timed: 7 minutes

Range: Adult

Scoring: Examiner evaluated

Cost: Contact publisher.

Publisher: Educational and Industrial Test Services Ltd.

PENNSYLVANIA BI-MANUAL WORKSAMPLE
John R. Roberts

teen, adult

Purpose: Measures manual dexterity and eye-hand coordination. Used for employee placement.

Description: A multiple-operation manual dexterity test. Employee is presented with an 8 x 24 inch board containing 100 holes (arranged in 10 rows) and a set of nuts and bolts, to test finger dexterity of both hands, whole movement of both arms, eye-hand coordination, and bi-manual coordination. The employee grasps a nut between thumb and index finger of one hand and a bolt between the thumb and index finger of the other hand, then turns the bolt into the nut and places both in a hole in the board. Twenty practice motions are allowed, and 80 motions are timed. Disassembly reverses the process and involves timing 100 motions. Up to four persons can be tested at once provided each has a separate board. Assembly and disassembly times can be converted to percentage ranks and standard scores. A special supplement contains directions for administering test to blind persons. Materials include the board, nuts and bolts, 50 record forms and a vinyl carrying case. Examiner required. Suitable for group use.

Timed: 12 minutes

Range: Ages 16-39 years

Scoring: Examiner evaluated

Cost: Complete kit $93.50; 50 record forms $2.50.

Publisher: American Guidance Service

PRIMARY MECHANICAL ABILITY TEST
Jack Harris Hazlehurst

adult

Purpose: Measures mechanical aptitude. Used to select and classify shop personnel from highly skilled engineers, draftsmen and machinists to relatively unskilled workers and apprentices.

Description: 119 item paper-pencil multiple-choice, four part test. Each section measures a separate aspect of mechanical aptitude: CROSSES for size discrimination, BOLTS for space perception, TOOLS for tool knowledge, and MISSING LINES for visualization. These tests have been standardized on a large sampling of the population including senior and technical high school students, college students in liberal arts and engineering courses, mechanics and craftsmen with limited formal education, professional engineers, and men from a large number of non-technical vocations. Examiner required. Suitable for group use.

Timed: 22 minutes

Range: Adult

Scoring: Hand key

Cost: 25 batteries $11.00; manual listing technical data, instructions for administering and scoring and norms $1.00.

Publisher: Stevens, Thurow and Associates

PURDUE MECHANICAL ADAPTABILITY TEST
C.H. Lawshe and Joseph Tiffin

teen, adult

Purpose: Assesses mechanical interests and abilities. Used for selection of job applicants.

Description: Multiple item paper-pencil test identifying subjects who are "mechanically inclined." Restricted to companies employing qualified personnel administrators and to psychologists using tests for instruction or vocational guidance. Examiner required. Suitable for group use.

Untimed: Not available

Range: Males 15 and over

Scoring: Hand key

Cost: Specimen set $1.00; 25 tests, manual, key $7.50.

Publisher: Purdue Research Foundation/University Book Store

PURDUE PEGBOARD TEST
Developed by Purdue Research Foundation under the direction of Joseph Tiffin

all ages

Purpose: Measures hand-finger-arm dexterity required for certain types of manual work. Used in the selection of business and industrial personnel.

Description: A multiple-operation manual test of gross and fine motor movements of hands, fingers, arms, and "tip of fingers." Measures dexterity needed in assembly work , electronic production work and similarly related jobs. The materials consist of a test board with two vertical rows of holes and four storage wells holding 50 pegs, 40 washers and 20 collars. To test the right hand, the subject inserts as many pegs as possi-

ble in the holes, starting at the top of the right hand row. Left hand test uses the left row, moving top to bottom. Both hands then are used together to fill both rows top to bottom. The Assembly Test has the subject pick up a peg with the right hand, insert it in the top right hole, then place a washer over the peg with the left hand, followed by a collar with the right hand and a second washer with the left hand. This procedure consititutes one assembly. The subject must complete as many assemblies as possible in the allotted time. Examiner required. Suitable for group use.

Timed: 5-10 minutes

Range: Original, adult; Revised, ages 5-15 years 11 months

Scoring: Hand key

Cost: Complete $130.00 (board, manual); 100 profiles $32.00; complete replacement set $35.00 (pegs, washers, collars); manual $1.70.

Publisher: Science Research Associates, Inc.

REVISED MINNESOTA PAPER FORM BOARD TEST
Rensis Likert and W.H. Quasha

adult

Purpose: Measures ability to visualize and manipulate objects in space. For use in selecting applicants for jobs requiring mechanical-spatial ability.

Description: Multiple item paper-pencil test of spatial perception. Applicant required to visualize the assembly of two-dimensional geometric shapes into a whole design. Related to both mechanical and artistic ability. Materials include two equivalent forms, AA and BB (hand scoring); MA and MB (machine scoring). Examiner required. Suitable for group use. Available in a French-Canadian edition.

Timed: 20 minutes

Range: Adult

Scoring: Hand key; may be machine scored; computer scoring service available

Cost: 25 tests (includes manual, key) $7.65; 25 tests for use with separate answer documents $9.00; 50 IBM 805 answer documents for use with form MA or MB $5.50.

Publisher: The Psychological Corporation

REVOLVING ASSEMBLY TABLE

adult

Purpose: Assesses bi-manual coordination, finger dexterity, kinesthetic memory, and ability to work with others. . Used for vocational evaluation and job placement of blind and visually impaired multiply handicapped persons.

Description: Multiple task test to evaluate a variety of work abilities. The individual is taught the task, then works for a 50 minute period and receives feedback on this rate and accuracy of work. Provides an objective method of comparing a blind or visually impaired person's performance to that of an average sighted person. Materials include assembled testing equipment and a manual. Examiner required. Not suitable for group use.

Timed: 50 minutes

Range: Adult

Scoring: Examiner evaluated

Cost: Manual $15.00; testing apparatus, contact: George Aarons, Royal Maid Association for the Blind, P.O.

Drawer 30, Hazlehurst, MS 39083; (601) 894-1771.

Publisher: Mississippi State University Rehabilitation Research & Training Center/National Industries for the Blind

ROEDER MANIPULATIVE APTITUDE TEST
Wesley S. Roeder

teen, adult

Purpose: Assesses eye, hand and finger coordination. Used to screen employees and trainees for jobs requiring eye-hand coordination, including: typing, mechanics, radio/TV repair, machinists, draftsmen, and machine operators.

Description: Task performance test measuring speed and dexterity in executing certain movements with the hands, arms and fingers, particularly thrusting and twisting movements. Four tasks are provided using the following materials: one styrene- plexiglass board with T-bar, four trays containing 10 sockets each, and a supply of rods, caps, washers, and nuts. Part 1 requires the subject to insert and twist a rod into a socket on the board and place a cap on the top of each rod, completing as many assemblies as possible in three minutes. Part 2 involves alternately sliding a washer and nut on each side of the T-bar as quickly as possible for 40 seconds. Part 3 repeats the washer/nut task, using the left hand only. Part 4 repeats the washer/nut task with the right hand only. Examiner required. Suitable for group use (limited only by availability of materials).

Timed: 5 minutes

Range: 15 years and older

Scoring: Hand key

Cost: Board and parts $98.95; 50 score sheets $4.50.

Publisher: Lafayette Instrument

Company, Inc.

SRA MECHANICAL APTITUDES
Richardson, Bellows, Henry and Company, Inc.

teen, adult   grades 10-UP

Purpose: Evaluates an individual's mechanical aptitude. Used for employee selection and placement.

Description: Three paper-pencil aptitude tests measuring Mechanical Knowledge, Space Relations and Shop Arithmetic. Mechanical Knowledge test consists of 46 pictures of common tools measuring general mechanical background. Space Relations test consists of 40 items measuring ability to visualize and mentally manipulate objects in space. The Shop Arithmetic test consists of 24 problems measuring application of quantitative reasoning and fundamental math operations. All three tests presented in one booklet. Examiner required. Suitable for group use.

Timed: 35 minutes

Range: High school-older

Scoring: Hand scored--carbon insert (answers transfer to scoring key on inside of answer sheet)

Cost: 25 reusable test booklets $62.00; 25 answer sheets $12.00; 100 profile sheets $14.50.

Publisher: Science Research Associates, Inc.

SRA TEST OF MECHANICAL CONCEPTS
Steven J. Stanard and Kathleen A. Bode

adult

Purpose: Measures an individual's ability to visualize and understand basic mechanical and spatial interrelationships. Useful for employee selection and screening for such jobs as assembler, maintenance mechanic, machinist, and factory production worker.

Description: Three paper-pencil subtests measuring separate skills or abilities necessary for jobs requiring mechanical ability. The Mechanical Interrelationships test consists of 24 drawings depicting mechanical movements and interrelationships. The Mechanical Tools and Devices subtest consists of 30 items measuring knowledge of common mechanical tools and devices. The Spatial Relations subtest consists of 24 items measuring ability to visualize and manipulate objects in space. Examiner required. Suitable for group use.

Untimed: 35-40 minutes

Range: Adult

Scoring: Hand scored--carbon insert (answers transfer to scoring key on inside of test booklet).

Cost: 25 test booklets (Form A or Form B) $38.00; examiner's manual $1.70.

Publisher: Science Research Associates, Inc.

STROMBERG DEXTERITY TEST (SDT)
E.L. Stromberg

adult

Purpose: Measures manipulative skill in sorting by color and by sequence.

Description: Two trial performance test of manual dexterity. Applicant is asked to discriminate and sort the biscuit-sized discs as well as to move and place them as fast as possible. Score is number of seconds required to complete the two trials. Materials include assembly board and discs.

Examiner required. Not suitable for group use.

Timed: 5-10 minutes

Range: Adult

Scoring: Score obtained by timing

Cost: Complete set (includes manual) $151.00; manual $1.50.

Publisher: The Psychological Corporation

Municipal Services

APTITUDE TEST FOR POLICEMEN
McCann Associates, Inc.

adult

Purpose: Assesses ability and learning aptitude of police officer candidates. Used for police department personnel selection.

Description: 100 item paper-pencil, multiple-choice test in two forms: 60 and 72. Form 72 has an additional 30 verbal learning-ability questions and is the easier of the two. It covers ability to learn verbal and quantitative skills, total learning ability, interest in police work, common sense in police situations, and sense of public relations in the performance of police duties. Materials include test booklet, answer sheets, scoring stencil, and instruction manual with several norm tables for interpreting scores. Also available is a 50-item, multiple-choice observation test which covers candidate ability to observe obvious and deduced facts about a picture of an accident scene. These tests are available only to qualified municipal officials and Civil Service Commissions. Suitable for group use. Examiner required.

Timed: 3 hours

Range: Adult

Scoring: Hand key

Cost: 10 sets or less $50.00; 11-24 sets $4.40 each.

Publisher: McCann Associates, Inc.

THE DRIVER ATTITUDE SURVEY (DAS)
Donald H. Schuster and J.P. Guilford

teen, adult   grades 10-UP

Purpose: Discriminates between safe and unsafe drivers. Used to screen employees for jobs that involve driving.

Description: Paper-pencil inventory discriminates between safe, law-abiding drivers and two classes of problem drivers: those who violate motor-vehicle codes and those who have accidents for which they are responsible. Includes a Violations Score, and Accidents Score, and three validation keys: a Faking Score, a Deviance Score, and an X Score. The X Score indicates if the subject is violation- or accident-prone. There are also scales measuring excessive use of alcoholic beverages and personal relations with others. Centile norms are provided for high school students and adults. Restricted to A.P.A. members. Examiner required. Suitable for group use.

Untimed: 30 minutes

Range: High school-adult

Scoring: Hand key; computer scorable

Cost: 25 tests $10.00; 25 answer sheets $3.50; manual $1.50; scoring key $4.00.

Publisher: Sheridan Psychological Services, Inc.

ECONOMY FIRE PROMOTION
McCann Associates, Inc.

adult

Purpose: Assesses candidate skills for promotion within a municipal fire department. Used for promotion to the positions of driver engineer, lieutenant, captain, battalion chief, deputy chief, assistant chief, and chief.

Description: 100 item paper-pencil, multiple-choice test of: fire attack knowledge, fire extinguishment knowledge, overhaul, salvage and rescue, fire prevention and investigation, supervision and administration. Materials include test booklets, answer sheets, scoring key, and manual. Available only to Civil Service Commissions or qualified municipal officials. Examiner required. Suitable for group use.

Timed: 3½ hours

Range: Adult

Scoring: Hand key

Cost: First 5 candidates $200.00; next 5 candidates $8.00 each.

Publisher: McCann Associates, Inc.

ECONOMY POLICE PROMOTION
McCann Associates, Inc.

adult

Purpose: Assesses candidate skills for police promotion. Used for positions of sergeant, lieutenant, captain, assistant chief, chief, and detective.

Description: 100 item paper-pencil, multiple-choice test of: patrol, other police knowledge, crime investigation, police supervision, police administration, and legal knowledge (i.e., laws generally acceptable in most states). The number of questions in each section varies according to rank being tested. Materials include test booklets, answer sheets, identification sheets, scoring stencil, charts for tabulating scores, and a manual. Deluxe tests available in which law questions have been specifically checked with the state laws where the test is to be given. Available only on rental basis to qualified municipal officials and Civil Service Commissions. Examiner required. Suitable for group use.

Timed: 3½ hours

Range: Adult

Scoring: Hand key; may be computer scored

Cost: First 5 candidates a minimum of $200.00; next 5 candidates $8.00 each.

Publisher: McCann Associates, Inc.

ESV FIREFIGHTER
McCann Associates, Inc.

adult

Purpose: Assesses candidates' skills in firefighting. Used by fire departments for job screening.

Description: 125 item paper-pencil, multiple-choice test covering: interest in firefighting, compatibility, map reading, spatial visualization, visual pursuit, understanding and interpreting table and test material about firefighting, basic building construction, and mechanical aptitude. Materials include test booklets, answer sheet, scoring key, and manual. Available only to Civil Service Commissions or qualified municipal officials. Examiner required. Suitable for group use.

Timed: 2 hours

Range: Adult

Scoring: Hand key

Cost: The first 5 candidates $150.00; the next 5 candidates $10.00 each.

Publisher: McCann Associates, Inc.

EXPERIENCE AND BACK-GROUND QUESTIONNAIRE (EBQ)
M.E. Baehr and R.E. Penny

adult

Purpose: Identifies job applicants whose backgrounds indicate that they are well suited for employment as transit bus operators or municipal police patrolmen. Used in validated test batteries for employee screening and selection.

Description: 86 item paper-pencil multiple-choice inventory assessing the following background areas: group participation and school achievement, drive, mobility, financial responsibility, family responsibility, job and personal stability, parental family adjustment, successful parents, and general health. Quantified background scores are provided for each areas as an index of predicted job performance. Basic adult reading skills required. Examiner required. Suitable for group use.

Untimed: 30-45 minutes

Range: Adult

Scoring: Hand key; computer scoring available

Cost: 20 tests $8.00.

Publisher: London House Press

FIRE COMPANY OFFICER FORMS 1, 2, AND A
McCann Associates, Inc.

adult

Purpose: Assesses abilities of candidates for promotion in municipal fire departments.

Description: 100 item paper-pencil, multiple-choice criterion-related validity test. The following areas are assessed: fire attack knowledge, fire extinguishment knowledge, chemistry and physics of fire, and fireground supervision and management. Materials include test booklets, answer sheets, scoring key, and manual. Available only to Civil Service Commissions or qualified municipal officials. Examiner required. Suitable for group use.

Timed: 3½ hours

Range: Adult

Scoring: Hand key

Cost: The first 5 candidates $450.00; the next 5 candidates $26.00 each.

Publisher: McCann Associates, Inc.

FIREMAN ENTRANCE APTITUDE TESTS
McCann Associates, Inc.

adult

Purpose: Assesses aptitude for firefighting and ability to learn. Used by fire departments to select entrance level personnel

Description: 100 and 130 item paper-pencil, multiple-choice test in two forms: 62A and 70A. Booklet I of both tests includes 55 questions on verbal and quantitative learning ability. Booklet II of form 62A contains 45 questions in three subtests: Common Sense, Interest in Firefighting Situations, and Mechanical Aptitude. Book II of 70A includes the same 45 questions plus 30 easy-learning ability questions. Form 70A is easier and is intended for users who are legally required to use 70-75% as the minimum passing score. Materials include test booklets, answer sheets, scoring stencil, and manual. The format is identical to the McCann policeman test, so they can be given simultaneously. Available only to Civil Service Commissions or competent municipal officials. Examiner required. Suitable for group use.

Timed: 3 hours

Range: Adult

Scoring: Hand key

Cost: 10 sets or less $50.00; 11-24 sets $4.40 each.

Publisher: McCann Associates, Inc.

FIRE PROMOTION TEST
McCann Associates, Inc.

adult

Purpose: Measures knowledge of fire-fighting and job responsibilities. Used to evaluate candidates for promotion within fire departments.

Description: 100 item paper-pencil test of: knowledge of fire attack, fire extinguishment, rescue, salvage, fire inspection, fire supervision, fire administration, first aid practices, and many others per request of individual departments. Tests are individually prepared according to job analysis, with separate tests available for positions of driver, engineer, lieutenant, captain, battalion chief, deputy chief, assistant chief, and chief. Materials include test booklet, answer sheets, identification sheets, envelopes, candidate study guides, and administration instructions. Computer scored and analyzed. Available only to Civil Service Commissions or qualified municipal officials. Examiner required. Suitable for group use.

Timed: 3½ hours

Range: Adult

Scoring: Hand key; computer scored

Cost: First 5 candidates $450.00; next 5 candidates $27.00 each.

Publisher: McCann Associates, Inc.

LAW ENFORCEMENT ASSESSMENT AND DEVELOPMENT REPORT (LEADR)
Rita Dee-Burnett, Edgar F. Johns and Samuel E. Krug

adult

Purpose: Identifies individuals who are most likely to succeed as law enforcement officers in enforcement, investigative, or protective services. Allows lay persons or hiring commissions to make personnel decisions.

Description: Paper-pencil test measures four psychological areas which are related to law enforcement capabilities: emotional maturity, integrity/control, intellectual efficiency, and interpersonal relations. Scores are developed for each of the four areas which show how candidates compare with one another in overall performance and likelihood of adjustment to policing activities. The computer-based report is presented in a clear, concise, narrative form. The scoring service provides group scores in alphabetical lists, as well as optional rankings on the basis of sex, race, overall scores, and scores on each of the four dimensions tested. The manual documents the basic research and technology on which LEADR was developed and validated. Examiner required. Suitable for group use.

Untimed: Not available

Range: Adult

Scoring: Computerized scoring and interpretive service is available

Cost: LEADR Certificates $17.50-$25.00 each depending upon quantity.

Publisher: Institute for Personality and Ability Testing, Inc.

POLICE OFFICER ESV-100
McCann Associates, Inc.

adult

Purpose: Assesses abilities of candidates for police officer. Used by municipal police departments for job screening.

Description: 100 item paper-pencil, multiple-choice test assessing: observational ability, ability to exercise judgment and common sense, interest in police work, map reading, dealing with people, ability to read and comprehend policy text material, and reasoning ability. Materials include test booklets, answer sheet, scoring key, and manual. Available only to Civil Service Commissions or qualified municipal officials. Examiner required. Suitable for group use.

Timed: 2 hours, 40 minutes

Range: Adult

Scoring: Hand key

Cost: The first 5 candidates $150.00; the next 5 candidates $10.00 each.

Publisher: McCann Associates, Inc.

POLICE OFFICER ESV-125
McCann Associates, Inc.

adult

Purpose: Assesses abilities of candidates for police officer. Used by municipal police departments for job screening.

Description: 125 item paper-pencil, multiple-choice test assessing: observational ability, police aptitude, police public relations and police judgment. Materials include test booklets, answer sheet, scoring key, and manual. Available only to Civil Service Commissions or qualified municipal officials. Examiner required. Suitable for group use.

Timed: 3 hours

Range: Adult

Scoring: Hand key

Cost: The first 5 candidates $150.00; the next 5 candidates $10.00 each.

Publisher: McCann Associates, Inc.

POLICE PROMOTION TEST
McCann Associates, Inc.

adult

Purpose: Assesses abilities of candidates for police promotion. Used by municipal police departments to promote to the level of sergeant, lieutenant, captain, assistant chief, chief, and detective.

Description: 100 item paper-pencil, multiple-choice test. Each test is individually prepared according to analysis of job for which the subject is being tested. The test may include: patrol techniques, investigative techniques, supervisory, and administrative knowledge. Materials include test booklets, answer sheet, scoring key, and manual. Available only to Civil Service Commissions or qualified municipal officials. Examiner required. Suitable for group use.

Timed: 3½ hours

Range: Adult

Scoring: Hand key

Cost: The first 5 candidates $450.00; the next 5 candidates $27.00 each.

Publisher: McCann Associates, Inc.

POLICE SERGEANT (ESV)
McCann Associates, Inc.

adult

Purpose: Assesses candidates for promotion to police sergeant. Used by municipal police departments.

Description: 100 item paper-pencil, multiple-choice test of: knowledge of police supervisory principles and practices; legal knowledge; technical police knowledge; police judgment; and understanding and interpreting police table and text materials. Publisher scores each area and gives a total score, norms, mean scores, standard deviations, reliability coefficient, and narrative evaluation report. Materials include test booklets, candidate study guide, answer sheet, identification sheet, envelope and manual. Available on a rental basis only to qualified municipal officials and Civil Service Commissions. Examiner required. Suitable for group use.

Timed: 3½ hours

Range: Adult

Scoring: Hand key

Cost: For the first 5 candidates $450.00; the next 5 candidates $26.00 each.

Publisher: McCann Associates, Inc.

TRANSIT BUS OPERATOR SELECTION TEST BATTERY
M.E. Baehr, G.O. Baehr and R.E. Penny

adult

Purpose: Identifies males and females with good potential for long-term successful performance as bus operators.

Description: Three paper-pencil tests measuring aptitude for operating buses: Emo Questionnaire Test Booklet (140 items), Skills and Attributes Inventory Test Booklet, (96 items), and Experience and Background Questionnaire (86 items). Combination of the three test scores which best predict bus operator road performance was determined through a performance criterion validation implemented separately for men and women. Examiner required. Suitable for group use.

Timed: 90 minutes for total battery

Range: Adult

Scoring: Hand key; computer scoring available

Cost: Booklets only-$1.20 per test battery.

Publisher: London House Press

Sales

APTITUDES ASSOCIATES TEST OF SALES APTITUDE
Martin M. Bruce

adult

Purpose: Aids in the appraisal of sales aptitude, provides an objective measure of one important aspect of that aptitude, namely knowledge and understanding of basic principles of selling. Useful as a sales selection aid in evaluation and training, as well as vocational guidance.

Description: 50 item paper-pencil test measuring the subject's knowledge and understanding of the principles of selling a wide variety of goods ranging from heavy industrial capital items to door-to-door housewares. Norms are available to compare a person's score with salespeople, men, women, and selected 'special sales groups.'

Untimed: 20-30 minutes

Range: Adult

Scoring: Hand key

Cost: Specimen set $4.95; manual $3.85; key $.66; package of tests $15.30.

Publisher: Martin M. Bruce, Ph.D., Publisher

APTITUDE INDEX BATTERY (AIB)
LIMRA

adult

Purpose: Indicates the success potential of individuals considering a career selling life insurance. Used as a guide for management to select candidates likely to be successful.

Description: 278 item paper-pencil, multiple-choice and true-false test (A) for applicants who have not had previous insurance sales experience and (B) for those with prior insurance sales experience. The higher the score, the higher the probability of success. A similar version is available in Canada (both English and French). Self-administered. Suitable for group use.

Untimed: 1l/2 hours

Range: Adult

Scoring: Computer scored

Cost: Test book $5.00; answer sheets $8.50 each; (Sold only in lots of 100); cost of scoring test included; scoring service $10.00.

Publisher: Life Insurance Marketing and Research Association, Inc.

DIPLOMACY TEST OF EMPATHY
Willard A. Kerr

adult

Purpose: Measures empathic ability. Used for selecting applicants for sales positions.

Description: Multiple item paper-pencil test measures the ability to sell, to be persuasive, tactful, and diplomatic. Items correlate with mean salary increases of executives, but have little or no relationship with intelligence. Norms on general adults, management, sales, and sales management. Examiner required. Suitable for group use.

Untimed: 20 minutes

Range: Adult

Scoring: Hand key

Cost: Specimen set $3.30; 25 tests $3.85; 100- $12.00; 25 answer sheets $2.20; 100-$7.70.

Publisher: Psychometric Affiliates

ETSA TESTS 7-A SALES APTITUDE
Refer to page 712.

GUILFORD-ZIMMERMAN APTITUDE SURVEY: NUMERICAL OPERATIONS (GZAS:N.O.)
Refer to page 717.

I.P.I. APTITUDE-INTELLIGENCE TEST SERIES: JUDGMENT
Refer to page 721.

I.P.I. APTITUDE-INTELLIGENCE TEST SERIES: SALES TERMS
Refer to page 723.

I.P.I. JOB TEST FIELD SERIES: SALES CLERKS
Refer to page 730.

PERSONNEL TEST BATTERY: NUMERICAL COMPUTATION (PTB:NP2)
Refer to page 745.

SALES ATTITUDE CHECKLIST
Erwin K. Taylor

adult

Purpose: Measures attitudes and behaviors involved in sales and selling. Used for sales selection programs.

Description: 31 item paper-pencil test assessing basic attitudes toward selling and habits in the selling situation. Norms provided for applicants for the following positions: sales and sales managerial positions, automobile salespersons, freight traffic salespersons, office equipment salespersons, and utility salespersons. Examiner required. Suitable for group use.

Untimed: 10-15 minutes

Range: Adult

Scoring: Hand scored--carbon insert

(answers transfer to scoring key on inside of test booklet)

Cost: 25 test booklets $27.00; examiner's manual $2.10.

Publisher: Science Research Associates, Inc.

SALES COMPREHENSION TEST
Martin M. Bruce

adult

Purpose: Measures sales ability and potential based on the subject's understanding of the principles of selling. Used for evaluating prospective salespeople, vocational counseling and training projects for salespeople.

Description: 30 item paper-pencil, multiple-choice test aiding in measuring the applicant's potential for selling. Standard test procedures are used. Available in French, Italian and German. Self-administered. Suitable for group use.

Untimed: 15-20 minutes

Range: Adult

Scoring: Hand key

Cost: Specimen set $5.25; manual $4.10; key $.70; package of profile sheets $6.50; package of tests $16.50.

Publisher: Martin M. Bruce, Ph.D., Publisher

SALES MOTIVATION INVENTORY
Martin M. Bruce

adult

Purpose: Assesses interest in and motivation for sales work, particularly commission, wholesale and insurance selling.

Description: 75 item paper-pencil multiple-choice test measuring sales motivation and drive. Consists of stem

statements to be completed by choosing one of several alternative endings. Not intended for clerking or order-taking positions. Self- administered. Suitable for groups. Available in French.

Untimed: 20-30 minutes

Range: Adult

Scoring: Hand key

Cost: Specimen set $5.25; manual $4.10; key $.70; package of profile sheets $6.50; package of tests $16.50.

Publisher: Martin M. Bruce, Ph.D., Publisher

THE SALES SENTENCE COMPLETION BLANK
Norman Geroski and Karl Geisinger

adult

Purpose: Aids in the selection of competent sales personnel by providing insight into how the applicant thinks, his social attitudes and his probable reactions in sales situations.

Description: 40 item paper-pencil test consisting of sentence fragments to be completed by the subject. The examiner assesses the results by scoring the responses on a 1 to 7 scale, allowing a "projection" of the subject's attitudes about life, self and others. Self-administered. Suitable for group use.

Untimed: 20-35 minutes

Range: Adult

Scoring: Hand key

Cost: Specimen set $5.25; manual $4.25; package of tests $16.50.

Publisher: Martin M. Bruce, Ph.D., Publisher

SALES STYLE DIAGNOSIS TEST
W.J. Reddin and David Forman

adult

Purpose: Measures a salesperson's

selling style and effectiveness. Used to screen, coach and train salespersons.

Description: Multiple item paper-pencil test designed to give scores on the eight selling styles of deserter, missionary, autocrat, compromiser, bureaucrat, developer, benevolent autocrat and executive. Task orientation, relationships orientation and effectiveness are assessed as well. The individual responds to actions of a hypothetical salesperson and receives a score indicative of selling style. Self-administered. Suitable for group use. CANADIAN PUBLISHER

Untimed: 20-30 minutes

Range: Adult

Scoring: Hand key

Cost: Sample kit (contains 21 test samples, fact sheets and one test user's guide) $75.00; test kit (10 test copies plus fact sheet and user's guide) $40.00; cash orders postpaid.

Publisher: Organizational Tests (Canada) Ltd.

TEST OF PRACTICAL JUDGMENT--FORM 62
Refer to page 850.

TEST OF RETAIL SALES INSIGHT (TRSI)
Russell N. Cassel

adult

Purpose: Assesses degree of knowledge about retail selling. Used for in-service education of retail sales clerks and assessing progress in distributive education courses.

Description: 60 item paper-pencil test of five areas: general sales knowledge, customer motivation and need, merchandise procurement and adaptation, sales promotion procedures,

and sales closure. Items provide five alternative multiple-choice answers. The subject must have a fifth grade reading ability. Examiner required. Suitable for group use.

Untimed: 30 minutes

Range: Adult

Scoring: Hand key

Cost: Specimen set $7.25; 25 tests $22.00; 100- $86.00; 25 answer sheets $5.50; 100-$21.00; 25 profile sheets $6.75; 100-$26.00; keys $5.50; manual $5.50.

Publisher: Psychologists and Educators, Inc.

Teachers

TEACHER OCCUPATIONAL COMPETENCY TESTS (TOCT)

adult

Purpose: Assesses competency in skilled trades and occupations. Used for providing evidence of competence to become a teacher or obtain academic credit at participating educational institutions.

Description: Multiple item paper-pencil tests of skills and knowledge in 40 vocational fields: Air Conditioning and Refrigeration, Airframe and Power Plant, Architectural Drafting, Audio Visual Communication, Automotive Body and Fender, Auto Body Repair, Baking, Brick Masonry, Building Construction Occupations, Building Trades Maintenance, Cabinet Making and Millwork, Carpentry, Civil Technology, Commercial Art, Commercial Photography, Computer Technology, Cosmetology, Diesel Engine Repair, Drafting Occupations, Electrical Installation, Electronics Communications, Electronics Technology, Heating, Industrial Electronics, Machine Drafting, Machine Trades, Major Appliance Repair, Masonry, Materials Handling, Mechanical Technology, Medical Technology, Painting and Decorating, Plumbing, Power Sewing, Printing, Quantity Food Preparation, Radio/TV Repair, Refrigeration, Sheet Metal, Small Engine Repair, Textile Production/Fabrication, Tool and Die Making, Welding. Each TOCT consists of two parts, written and performance. Written tests are multiple-choice and cover factual knowledge, technical information, understanding of principles, and problem solving abilities related to the occupation. The performance tests are administered in a laboratory, school shop, or clinical setting, and enables the applicant to demonstrate knowledge and skills of competent craft persons. Examiner required. Suitable for group use.

Untimed: Time varies with tests

Range: Adult

Scoring: Scoring service provided

Cost: Contact publisher.

Publisher: National Occupational Competency Testing Institute

---

TEACHER OCCUPATIONAL COMPETENCY TESTING: AIR CONDITIONING AND REFRIGERATION EXAMINATION

adult

Purpose: Assesses competency in air conditioning and refrigeration. Used for providing evidence of competence to become a teacher or obtain academic credit at participating educational institutions.

Description: Two part test of skills and knowledge important in air conditioning and refrigeration work. The written test has approximately 200 multiple-choice items and covers the following areas: domestic systems installation, domestic systems servicing, commercial systems installation, commercial system servicing, residential air conditioning and heating installation, residential air conditioning and heating service, industrial refrigeration installation, and industrial refrigeration service. Performance test is evenly divided between three areas: domestic systems installation and service, commercial system installation and servicing, and residential air conditioning and heating. Handbook and references will be provided for preparation. Personal tools may be used. Examiner required. Written test suitable for group use.

Timed: Written test, 3 hours; Performance test, 5 hours

Range: Adult

Scoring: Computer scoring provided

Cost: Contact publisher.

Publisher: National Occupational Competency Testing Institute

---

TEACHER OCCUPATIONAL COMPETENCY TESTING: AIRFRAME AND POWER PLANT EXAMINATION

adult

Purpose: Assesses competency in airframe and power plant trades. Used for providing evidence of competence to become a teacher or obtain academic credit at participating educational institutions.

Description: Two part test of skills and knowledge important in airframe and power plant work. The written test has approximately 200 multiple-choice items and covers the following areas: general knowledge, airframe--systems and components, and power plant operation and maintenance: systems and components. Performance test measures skills in seven areas: sheet metal work, generator service, use of airworthiness directives, hydraulic components and systems, engine ignition timing, engine valve service, and carburetor service. Shop manuals and specification will be provided for preparation. Personal tools may be used. Examiner required. Written test suitable for group use.

Timed: Written test, 3 hours; Performance test, 5½ hours

Range: Adult

Scoring: Computer scoring provided

Cost: Contact publisher.

Publisher: National Occupational Competency Testing Institute

TEACHER OCCUPATIONAL COMPETENCY TESTING: ARCHITECTURAL DRAFTING EXAMINATION

adult

Purpose: Assesses competency in architectural drafting. Used for providing evidence of competence to become a teacher or obtain academic credit at participating educational institutions.

Description: Two part test of skills and knowledge important in architectural drafting positions. The written test has approximately 200 multiple- choice items and covers the following areas: basic architectural data, planning and design, materials and methods of construction, structural systems, and administration. The performance test measures skills in six areas: sections, working drawings, structural items, electrical items, heating, and perspective and rendering. Applicant should bring a set of drawing instruments, drawing pencils (lead holder and leads), slide rule, architect's erasers, erasing shields. The applicant can bring a lettering guide and Kidder's Handbook and Standards if desired. Examiner required. Written test suitable for group use.

Timed: Written test, 3 hours; Perform-

ance test, 5 hours

Range: Adult

Scoring: Computer scoring provided

Cost: Contact publisher.

Publisher: National Occupational Competency Testing Institute

TEACHER OCCUPATIONAL COMPETENCY TESTING: AUDIO-VISUAL COMMUNICATIONS TECHNOLOGY

adult

Purpose: Assesses competency in audio-visual communications technology. Used for providing evidence of competence to become a teacher or obtain academic credit at participating educational institutions.

Description: Two part test of skills and knowledge important in audio-visual communications technology. The written test has approximately 200 multiple-choice items and covers the following areas: general information and theory, design and construction of visuals, catalog, storage, and distribution of audio-visual materials, and equipment identification and operation. The performance test measures skills in four areas: motion picture operation, photography, tape recorder operation, and transparency design. Over one half of the performance test focuses on Photography. Examiner required. Written test suitable for group use.

Timed: Written test, 3 hours; Performance test, 3 hours, 40 minutes

Range: Adult

Scoring: Computer scoring provided

Cost: Contact publisher.

Publisher: National Occupational Competency Testing Institute

TEACHER OCCUPATIONAL COMPETENCY TESTING: AUTOMOTIVE BODY AND FENDER

adult

Purpose: Assesses competency in automotive body and repair. Used for providing evidence of competence to become a teacher or obtain academic credit at participating educational institutions.

Description: Two part test of skills and knowledge important in automotive body and fender work. The written test has approximately 200 multiple-choice items and covers the following areas: metal forming, alignment, welding, refinishing, estimating, synthetics, accessory systems and glass and trim. The performance test measures skills in three areas: metal forming, welding, and refinishing. Examiner required. Written test suitable for group use.

Timed: Written test, 3 hours; Performance test, 4 hours

Range: Adult

Scoring: Computer scoring provided

Cost: Contact publisher.

Publisher: National Occupational Competency Testing Institute

TEACHER OCCUPATIONAL COMPETENCY TESTING: AUTO BODY REPAIR EXAMINATION

adult

Purpose: Assesses competency in auto body repair. Used for providing evidence of competence to become a teacher or obtain academic credit at participating educational institutions.

Description: Two part test of skills and knowledge important in auto body repair. The written test has approximately 200 multiple-choice items and covers the following areas: welding, sheet metal repair, refinishing, glass: trim and hardware, panel sections, frame alignment, electrical circuits, estimating and safety. The performance test measures skills in four areas: sheet metal repair, refinishing, body construction, and electrical. One half of the performance test focuses on sheet metal repair. Handbooks and reference material will be provided. Examiner required. Written test suitable for group use.

Timed: Written test, 3 hours; Performance test, 6 hours

Range: Adult

Scoring: Computer scoring provided

Cost: Contact publisher.

Publisher: National Occupational Competency Testing Institute

TEACHER OCCUPATIONAL COMPETENCY TESTING: AUTO MECHANIC EXAMINATION

adult

Purpose: Assesses competency in auto mechanics. Used for providing evidence of competence to become a teacher or obtain academic credit at participating educational institutions.

Description: Two part test of skills and knowledge important in auto mechanics. The written test has approximately 200 multiple-choice items and covers the following areas: basic shop principles and practices, engines, emission systems, engine system analysis and repair, suspension, steering and braking, fuel systems, electrical, drive line and components, accessories, and shop management and control. The performance test measures skills in 12 areas: engines, basic automotive practices, fuel systems, electrical, batteries, air conditioning, charging systems, emission systems, engine analysis and repair, drive lines and components, suspension and steering, and brakes. Test equipment, shop manuals and specifications will be provided. Personal tools may be used. Examiner required. Written test suitable for group use.

Timed: Written test, 3 hours; Performance test, 5 hours

Range: Adult

Scoring: Computer scoring provided

Cost: Contact publisher.

Publisher: National Occupational Competency Testing Institute

TEACHER OCCUPATIONAL COMPETENCY TESTING: BRICK MASONRY

adult

Purpose: Assesses competency in brick masonry. Used for providing evidence of competence to become a teacher or obtain academic credit at participating educational institutions.

Description: Two part test of skills and knowledge important in brick masonry. The written test has approximately 200 multiple-choice items and covers the following areas: brick, block, tile, and stone. The performance test measures skills in these same four areas. The emphasis on both the written and performance tests is on brick. Examiner required. Written test suitable for group use.

Timed: Written test, 3 hours; Performance test, 4 hours

Range: Adult

Scoring: Computer scoring provided

Cost: Contact publisher.

Publisher: National Occupational Competency Testing Institute

TEACHER OCCUPATIONAL COMPETENCY TESTING: BUILDING CONSTRUCTION OCCUPATIONS EXAMINATION

adult

Purpose: Assesses competency in building construction occupations. Used for providing evidence of competence to become a teacher or obtain academic credit at participating educational institutions.

Description: Two part test of skills and knowledge important in building construction occupations. The written test has approximately 200 multiple- choice items and covers the following areas: carpentry, electrical, plumbing, painting, masonry, building code and safety, and sheet metal. The performance test measures skills in six areas: masonry, carpentry, painting, sheet metal, plumbing, and electrical. Examiner required. Written test suitable for group use.

Timed: Written test, 3 hours; Performance test, 6 hours

Range: Adult

Scoring: Computer scoring provided

Cost: Contact publisher.

Publisher: National Occupational Competency Testing Institute

TEACHER OCCUPATIONAL COMPETENCY TESTING: BUILDING TRADES MAINTENANCE EXAMINATION

adult

Purpose: Assesses competency in building trade maintenance occupations. Used for providing evidence of competence to become a teacher or obtain academic credit at participating educational institutions.

Description: Two part test of skills and knowledge important in building trades maintenance occupations. The written test has approximately 200 multiple-choice items and covers the following areas: heating, air conditioning and refrigeration, carpentry, masonry, custodial, electrical, painting and wallpapering, plumbing, management practices, sheet metal and welding. The performance test measures skill in nine areas: masonry, welding, carpentry, surface coating, electrical installation, plumbing, door hardware, glass installation, and custodial services. Examiner required. Written test suitable for group use.

Timed: Written test, 3 hours; Performance test, 5 hours, 35 minutes

Range: Adult

Scoring: Computer scoring provided
Cost: Contact publisher.

Publisher: National Occupational Competency Testing Institute

TEACHER OCCUPATIONAL COMPETENCY TESTING: CABINET MAKING AND MILLWORK EXAMINATION

adult

Purpose: Assesses competency in cabinet making and millwork occupations. Used for providing evidence of competence to become a teacher or obtain academic credit at participating educational institutions.

Description: Two part test of skills and knowledge important in carpentry. The written test consists of approximately 200 multiple-choice items covering the following areas: planning, safety, machines, hand tools, wood/stock selection, joinery, assembly, and finishing. The performance test measures skills in eight areas: planning and layout, wood/stock selection, hand tools, safety, machine, joinery, assembly, and finish. References will be provided.

Personal tools may be used. Examiner required. Written test suitable for group use.

Timed: Written test, 3 hours; Performance test, 5 hours

Range: Adult

Scoring: Computer scoring provided
Cost: Contact publisher.

Publisher: National Occupational Competency Testing Institute

TEACHER OCCUPATIONAL COMPETENCY TESTING: CARPENTRY EXAMINATION

adult

Purpose: Assesses competency in carpentry. Used for providing evidence of competence to become a teacher or obtain academic credit at participating educational institutions.

Description: Two part test of skills and knowledge important in carpentry. The written test has approximately 200 multiple-choice items and covers the following areas: surveying, layout, and blueprint reading, foundation work, concrete walks, floors, and step construction, floor framing, wall and ceiling framing, estimating scaffolding, roof framing and roofing, stair construction, interior finish, cabinetry, and exterior finish. The performance test measures skills in five areas: floor framing, wall framing, roof framing, roofing, and exterior finish. Personal tools may be used. It is recommended that you bring your own portable power saw. Examiner required. Written test suitable for gorup use.

Timed: Written test, 3 hours; Performance test, 5 hours

Range: Adult

Scoring: Computer scoring provided
Cost: Contact publisher.

Publisher: National Occupational Competency Testing Institute

TEACHER OCCUPATIONAL COMPETENCY TESTING: CIVIL TECHNOLOGY EXAMINATION

adult

Purpose: Assesses competency in civil technology occupations. Used for providing evidence of competence to become a teacher or obtain academic credit at participating educational institutions.

Description: Two part test of skills and knowledge important in civil technology occupations. The written test has approximately 200 multiple-choice items and covers the following areas: asphalt, soil, concrete, surveying, instrumentation, steel structures, general engineering information, and drafting. The performance test measures skills in five areas: concrete, soils, asphalt, surveying, and drafting. All necessary tools, machinery and handbooks will be provided. Candidates are to bring slide rules and drafting instruments. Examiner required. Written test suitable for gorup use.

Timed: Written test, 3 hours; Performance test, 5 hours

Range: Adult

Scoring: Computer scoring provided
Cost: Contact publisher.

Publisher: National Occupational Competency Testing Institute

TEACHER OCCUPATIONAL COMPETENCY TESTING: COMMERCIAL ART

adult

Purpose: Assesses competency in commercial art. Used for providing evidence of competence to become a teacher or obtain academic credit at participating educatioal institutions.

Description: Two part test of skills and knowledge important in commercial art. The written test has approximately 200 multiple-choice items and covers the following areas: production art, drawing, color, design, rendering, and potpourri. The performance test measures skills in six areas: production art, color, rendering, drawing, design, and potpourri. Examiner required. Written test suitable for group use.

Timed: Written test, 3 hours; Performance test, 4 hours

Range: Adult

Scoring: Computer scoring provided
Cost: Contact publisher.

Publisher: National Occupational Competency Testing Institute

TEACHER OCCUPATIONAL COMPETENCY TESTING: COMPUTER TECHNOLOGY EXAMINATION

adult

Purpose: Assesses competency in computer technology. Used for providing evidence of competence to become a teacher or obtain academic credit at participating educational institutions.

Description: Two part test of skills and knowledge important in computer technology. The written test has approximately 200 multiple-choice items and covers the following areas: general information, data processing machine operations, computer programming, and system analysis and design. The performance test measures skills in three areas: file preparation, flowcharting, and source listing and output. Majority of performance test deals with source listing and output. Examinee must be able to operate keypunch or CRT with keyboard. Examiner required. Written test suitable for group use.

Timed: Written test, 3 hours; Performance test, 5 hours

Range: Adult

Scoring: Computer scoring provided

Cost: Contact publisher.

Publisher: National Occupational Competency Testing Institute

TEACHER OCCUPATIONAL COMPETENCY TESTING: COSMETOLOGY EXAMINATION

adult

Purpose: Assesses competency in cosmetology. Used for providing evidence of competence to become a teacher or obtain academic credit at participating educational institutions.

Description: Two part test of skills and knowledge important in cosmetology. The written test has approximately 200 multiple-choice items and covers the following areas: care of hands, shampoos and rinses, permanent waving, hair styling, hair-coloring, hair pieces, care of hair and scalp, hair straightening, hair shaping, facial treatments, removal of superfluous hair, professional makeup, and shop operation and management. The performance test measures skills in six areas: manipulative techniques of hairstyling, haircutting, hair styling, permanent waving orchemical hair straightening, hair coloring orthermal curling, and manicure or facial makeup. One live model and one mannequin are required for performance examination. Candidate supplies haircutting tools, lotions, rollers, makeup, and curling irons. Towels, shampoo, cotton and standard shop equipment will be furnished. Candidate must submit to examiner at time of testing a published plan and photograph of hair style he intends to execute. Examiner required. Written test suitable for group use.

TEACHER OCCUPATIONAL COMPETENCY TESTING: DIESEL ENGINE REPAIR EXAMINATION

adult

Purpose: Assesses competency in diesel engine repair. Used for providing evidence of competence to become a teacher or obtain academic credit at participating educational institutions.

Description: Two part test of skills and knowledge important in diesel engine repair. The written test has approximately 200 multiple-choice items and covers the following areas: fuel injection pumps and nozzle repair and adjustment, hydraulic systems troubleshooting, electrical systems diagnosis and repair, power train operation and repair, basic engine diagnosis and repair. Performance test includes: fuel injection pump and nozzle repair, testing and callibrating pump systems, basic engine diagnosis and repair, electrical systems diagnosis and repair, power train operation and repair. Examiner required. Written test suitable for group use.

Timed: Written test, 3 hours

Range: Adult

Scoring: Computer scoring provided

Cost: Contact publisher.

Publisher: National Occupational Competency Testing Institute

TEACHER OCCUPATIONAL COMPETENCY TESTING: DRAFTING OCCUPATIONS EXAMINATION

adult

Purpose: Assesses competency in drafting occupations. Used for providing evidence of competence to become a teacher or obtain academic credit at participating educational institutions.

Description: Two part test of skills and knowledge important in drafting occupations. The written test has approximately 200 multiple-choice items and covers the following areas: fundamentals, related trades, related mathematics and related sciences. The performance test measures skills in nine areas: orthographics, sectioning, any projection, revolutions, isometric and oblique, threads and fasteners, intersections, development and drawing dimension. Examiner required. Written test suitable for group use.

Timed: Written test, 3 hours; Performance test, 5 hours

Range: Adult

Scoring: Computer scoring provided

Cost: Contact publisher.

Publisher: National Occupational Competency Testing Institute

TEACHER OCCUPATIONAL COMPETENCY TESTING: ELECTRICAL INSTALLATION

adult

Purpose: Assesses competency in electrical installation. Used for providing evidence of competence to become a teacher or obtain academic credit at participating educational institutions.

Description: Two part test of skills and knowledge important in electrical installation. The written test has approximately 200 multiple-choice items and covers the following areas: basic principles of electricity and magnetism and their application in the trade, reading working instructions and trade calculations, lighting, motors and generators, wiring practices and procedures, transformers, and general trade information. The performance test measures skills in six areas: layout and print reading, installation, testing and operation of controls, code applications, installation of residential, commercial wiring, testing and trouble-shooting of installations, and safety. Applicants may bring own reference materials and handbooks. Personal tools may also be used. Examiner required. Written test suitable for group use.

Timed: Written test, 3 hours; Performance test, 5 hours

Range: Adult

Scoring: Computer scoring provided

Cost: Contact publisher.

Publisher: National Occupational Competency Testing Institute

TEACHER OCCUPATIONAL COMPETENCY TESTING: ELECTRONICS COMMUNICATIONS EXAMINATION

adult

Purpose: Assesses competency in electronics communications. Used for providing evidence of competence to become a teacher or obtain academic credit at participating educational institutions.

Description: Two part test of skills and knowledge important in electronics communications. The written test has approximately 200 multiple-choice items and covers the following areas: basic electricity, measurements, standards and tolerances, conductors, insulators, and semi- conductors, batteries, sources of voltage, vacuum tube and solid state devices, amplifiers in cascade for RF and AF, other concepts in electronics, inductive devices, alternating current, single phase circuits, electronic circuits, and methods and procedures. The performance test measures skills in three areas: radio equipment, recording equipment, and television service. Television service accounts for one half of the performance test. Personal tools may be used. Allied Data Handbook may be consulted. Examiner required. Written test suitable for group use.

Timed: Written test, 3 hours; Performance test, 4 hours

Range: Adult

Scoring: Computer scoring provided

Cost: Contact publisher.

Publisher: National Occupational Competency Testing Institute

---

TEACHER OCCUPATIONAL COMPETENCY TESTING: ELECTRONICS TECHNOLOGY U.S.O.E. CODE 16.0108 PENNSYLVANIA NUMBER 2111

adult

Purpose: Assesses competency in electronics technology. Used for providing evidence of competence to become a teacher or obtain academic credit at participating educational institutions.

Description: Two part test of skills and knowledge important in electronics technology. The written test has approximately 200 multiple-choice items and covers the following areas: analysis, troubleshooting and repair, instrumentation, electronic components, and basic theory. The performance test measures skills in six areas: analysis, troubleshooting

and repair, instrumentation, electronics components, basic theory, and fabrication and inspection. Examiner required. Written test suitable for group use.

Untimed: Not available

Range: Adult

Scoring: Computer scoring provided

Cost: Contact publisher.

Publisher: National Occupational Competency Testing Institute

---

TEACHER OCCUPATIONAL COMPETENCY TESTING: HEATING EXAMINATION

adult

Purpose: Assesses competency in heating occupations. Used for providing evidence of competence to become a teacher or obtain academic credit at participating educational institutions.

Description: Two part test of skills and knowledge important in heating occupations. The written test has approximately 200 multiple-choice items and covers the following areas: systems, heating plants, controls, and service and testing. The performance test measures skills in four areas: systems, heating plants, controls, and service and testing. Examiner required. Written test suitable for group use.

Timed: Written test, 3 hours; Performance test, 4 hours

Range: Adult

Scoring: Computer scoring provided

Cost: Contact publisher.

Publisher: National Occupational Competency Testing Institute

TEACHER OCCUPATIONAL COMPETENCY TESTING: INDUSTRIAL ELECTRICIAN EXAMINATION #014

adult

Purpose: Assesses competency of industrial electricians. Used for providing evidence of competence to become a teacher or obtain academic credit at participating educational institutions.

Description: Two part test of skills and knowledge important of industrial electricians. The written test has approximately 200 multiple-choice items and covers the following areas: fundamental knowledge of electronics and electricity applied by the industrial electrician, basic concepts and application of direct current to the operation, testing, maintenance, and repair of electric power equipment, basic concepts and application of alternating current to the operation, testing, maintenance and repair of electric power equipment, operating principles and concepts of power generation and distribution, and operating principles and concepts of motors and controls. The performance test measures skills in four areas: conduit and tubing, connect distribution system, installation, service and repair of fluorescent light system, and wiring. Personal tools may be used. Examiner required. Written test suitable for group use.

Timed: Written test, 3 hours; Performance test, 5 hours

Range: Adult

Scoring: Computer scoring provided

Cost: Contact publisher.

Publisher: National Occupational Competency Testing Institute

TEACHER OCCUPATIONAL COMPETENCY TESTING: INDUSTRIAL ELECTRONICS EXAMINATION #016

adult

Purpose: Assesses competency in industrial electronics occupations. Used for providing evidence of competence to become a teacher or obtain academic credit at participating educational institutions.

Description: Two part test of skills and knowledge important in industrial electronics. The written test has approximately 200 multiple-choice items and covers the following areas: basic electronic fundamentals, digital circuits, network (passive), electronic control devices, amplifiers, detectors, and active circuits, components, use of instruments, troubleshooting, electronic assembly precautions, computer technology, energy conversion, and transducers. The performance test measures skills in four areas: use of measuring instruments, measure, observe, and record, use of test equipment, and program simple problems. Candidate must bring his own slide rule. Handbook, manuals, and other reference materials will be provided. Examiner required. Written test suitable for group use.

Timed: Written test, 3 hours; Performance test, 2½ hours

Range: Adult

Scoring: Computer scoring provided

Cost: Contact publisher.

Publisher: National Occupational Competency Testing Institute

TEACHER OCCUPATIONAL COMPETENCY TESTING: MACHINE DRAFTING EXAMINATION

adult

Purpose: Assesses competency in machine drafting occupations. Used for providing evidence of competence to become a teacher or obtain academic credit at participating educational institutions.

Description: Two part test of skills and knowledge important in machine drafting. The written test has approximately 200 multiple-choice items and covers the following areas: drafting room practice, orthographic and pictorial drawings, dimensions, tolerance and symbols, threads and fasteners, cams, gears and pulley, trade computations, shop information, and applied science. The performance test measures eight skill areas: orthographic projection, sectioning, auxiliary projection, revolutions, isometric, intersections, developments, and drawing and dimension. Examiner required. Written test suitable for group use.

Timed: Written test, 3 hours; Performance test, 4 hours

Range: Adult

Scoring: Computer scoring provided

Cost: Contact publisher.

Publisher: National Occupational Competency Testing Institute

---

TEACHER OCCUPATIONAL COMPETENCY TESTING: MACHINE TRADES EXAMINATION

adult

Purpose: Assesses competency in machine trades. Used for providing evidence of competence to become a teacher or obtain academic credit at participating educational institutions.

Description: Two part test of skills and knowledge important in machine trades occupations. The written test has approximately 200 multiple-choice items and covers the following areas: bench assembly work, layout and inspection; machine sawing, filing and multiple parts processing; milling processes and machines; drilling, tapping, lapping--machines and attachments; grinding and precision finishing--processes and machines; applied math and science; shaping and planning processes; turning; and electrical discharge machining. The performance test measures skills in five areas: bench and assembly, layout and inspection; milling processes and machines; grinding and precision finishing; drilling, tapping, reaming-- machines and attachments; and turning and processing. Personal tools (micrometors and scales) may be used. Safety glasses are required and candidates may bring their own. Examiner required. Written test suitable for group use.

Timed: Written test, 3 hours; Performance test, 5 hours

Range: Adult

Scoring: Computer scoring provided

Cost: Contact publisher.

Publisher: National Occupational Competency Testing Institute

---

TEACHER OCCUPATIONAL COMPETENCY TESTING: MAJOR APPLIANCE REPAIR EXAMINATION

adult

Purpose: Assesses competency in major appliance repair. Used for providing evidence of competence to become a teacher or obtain academic credit at participating educational institutions.

Description: Two part test of skills

and knowledge important in major appliance repair. The written test has approximately 200 multiple-choice items and covers the following areas: fundamentals, power tools and small appliances, kitchen equipment, major heating devices, laundry equipment, and refrigeration. The performance test measures skills in three areas: major heating devices, laundry equipment, and refrigeration. Personal tools may be used. Handbooks and references will be provided. Examiner required. Written test suitable for group use.

Timed: Written test, 3 hours; Performance test, 6 hours

Range: Adult

Scoring: Examiner evaluated; scoring service provided

Cost: Contact publisher.

Publisher: National Occupational Competency Testing Institute

TEACHER OCCUPATIONAL COMPETENCY TESTING: MASONRY EXAMINATION

adult

Purpose: Assesses competency in masonry occupations. Used for providing evidence of competence to become a teacher or obtain academic credit at participating educational institutions.

Description: Two part test of skills and knowledge important in masonry. The written test has approximately 200 multiple-choice items and covers the following areas: trade tools, terminology, estimating procedures, layout procedures, masonry practices, safety, and materials of the trade. The performance test measures skills in four areas: layout procedures, work practices, quality of completed work, and observation of safe practices. Personal hand tools will be required.

Examiner required. Written test suitagroup use.

Timed: Written test, 2 hours; Performance test, 3 hours

Range: Adult

Scoring: Examiner evaluated; scoring service available

Cost: Contact publisher.

Publisher: National Occupational Competency Testing Institute

TEACHER OCCUPATIONAL COMPETENCY TESTING: MASONRY OCCUPATIONS

adult

Purpose: Assesses competency in masonry occupations. Used for providing evidence of competence to become a teacher or obtain academic credit at participating educational institutions.

Description: Two part test of skills and knowledge important in masonry occupations. The written test has approximately 200 multiple-choice items and covers the following areas: concrete, stone, estimating, tile, plaster and brick/block. The performance test measures skills in four areas: block, brick, stone, and tile. Examiner required. Written test suitable for group use.

Untimed: Not available

Range: Adult

Scoring: Examiner evaluated; scoring service provided

Cost: Contact publisher.

Publisher: National Occupational Competency Testing Institute

TEACHER OCCUPATIONAL COMPETENCY TESTING: MATERIALS HANDLING EXAMINATION

adult

Purpose: Assesses competency in materials handling. Used for providing evidence of competence to become a teacher or obtain academic credit at participating educational institutions.

Description: Two part test of skills and knowledge important in materials handling. The written test has approximately 200 multiple-choice items and covers the following areas: warehousing, purchasing, shipping and distribution, transportation, receiving, materials handling equipment, material storage, inventory control. The performance test measures skills in seven areas: purchasing, shipping, equipment, receiving, storage, warehouse, and inventory. Examiner required. Written test suitable for group use.

Timed: Written test, 3 hours; Performance test, 4 hours, 25 minutes

Range: Adult

Scoring: Examiner evaluated; scoring service available

Cost: Contact publisher.

Publisher: National Occupational Competency Testing Institute

TEACHER OCCUPATIONAL COMPETENCY TESTING: MECHANICAL TECHNOLOGY EXAMINATION

adult

Purpose: Assesses competency in mechanical technology occupations. Used for providing evidence of competence to become a teacher or obtain academic credit at participating educational institutions.

Description: Two part test of skills and knowledge important in machine technology occupations. The written test has approximately 200 multiple-choice items and covers the following areas: machine tool operations, metallurgy, statics, fluid mechanics, thermodynamics, flectricity, strength of materials, physics, mathematics, and computer. The performance test measures skills in four areas: design, drawing, testing, and evaluation and reporting. The following personal tools will be required: set of drawing instruments, drawing pencils, copy of Machinery Handbook, slide rule, lettering guide, ball point or other pen. Examiner required. Written test suitable for group use.

Timed: Written test, 3 hours; Performance test, 6 hours

Range: Adult

Scoring: Examiner evaluated; scoring service provided

Cost: Contact publisher.

Publisher: National Occupational Competency Testing Institute

TEACHER OCCUPATIONAL COMPETENCY TESTING: PAINTING AND DECORATING EXAMINATION

adult

Purpose: Assesses competency in painting and decorating. Used for providing evidence of competence to become a teacher or obtain academic credit at participating educational institutions.

Description: Two part test of skills and knowledge important in painting and decorating occupations. The written test has approximately 200 multiple- choice items and covers the following areas: exterior and interior painting, wood finishing, wall covering, estimating, color and color harmony, and special wall finishes. The performance test measure abilities in five areas: exterior and interior painting, wood finishing, wall covering, color and color harmony, and clean up. Examiner required. Written test suitable for group use.

Timed: Written test, 3 hours; Performance test, 4 hours

Range: Adult

Scoring: Examiner evaluated; scoring service provided

Cost: Contact publisher.

Publisher: National Occupational Competency Testing Institute

---

TEACHER OCCUPATIONAL COMPETENCY TESTING: PLUMBING EXAMINATION

adult

Purpose: Assesses competency in plumbing. Used for providing evidence of competence to become a teacher or obtain academic credit at participating educational institutions.

Description: Two part test of skills and knowledge important in plumbing. The written test has approximately 200 multiple-choice items and covers the following areas: water supply and distribution--fixture units; physical properties and characteristics of commonly used material and supplies; operating principles and installation of commonly used materials and supplies; installation and principles of operation of building drains and sewers; installation and operation of storm water drains; plumbing fixtures; industrial and special wastes; inspection and tests; and general trade information. The performance test measures abilities in four areas: work from builder's or architect's drawings; rough-in standard installation; install fixtures and accessories on a variety of materials; and testing systems. Personal

tools may be used. Handbooks and reference material may also be brought to the session. Installation will be done on available facilites. Examiner required. Written test suitable for group use.

Timed: Written test, 3 hours; Performance test, 5 hours

Range: Adult

Scoring: Examiner evaluated; scoring service provided

Cost: Contact publisher.

Publisher: National Occupational Competency Testing Institute

---

TEACHER OCCUPATIONAL COMPETENCY TESTING: POWER SEWING EXAMINATION

adult

Purpose: Assesses competency in power sewing. Used for providing evidence of competence to become a teacher or obtain academic credit at participating educational institutions.

Description: Two part test of skills and knowledge important in power sewing. The written test has approximately 200 multiple-choice items and covers the following areas: Power machine operation, apparel assembly, terminology, needle trade industry, and tools and attachments. The performance test measures abilities in five areas: assembling techniques, sewing machines, tools and attachments, finishing techniques, materials, and safety and clean up. Examiner required. Written test suitable for group use.

Timed: Written test, 3 hours; Performance test, 4 hours

Range: Adult

Scoring: Examiner evaluated; scoring service provided

Cost: Contact publisher.

Publisher: National Occupational

TEACHER OCCUPATIONAL COMPETENCY TESTING: PRINTING EXAMINATION

adult

Purpose: Assesses competency in printing. Used for providing evidence of competence to become a teacher or obtain academic credit at participating educational institutions.

Description: Two part test of skills and knowledge important in printing. The written test has approximately 200 multiple-choice items and covers the following areas: design and composition, trade information, job safety, photography, platemaking, stripping, image transfer, and finishing. The performance test measures abilities in four areas: design and composition, photo preparatory-image carriers, image transfer, and bindery/finishing. Examiner required. Written test suitable for group use.

Timed: Written test, 3 hours; Performance test, 5 hours

Range: Adult

Scoring: Examiner evaluated; scoring service provided

Cost: Contact publisher.

Publisher: National Occupational Competency Testing Institute

TEACHER OCCUPATIONAL COMPETENCY TESTING: QUANTITY FOOD PREPRATIONS EXAMINATION

adult

Purpose: Assesses competency in quantity food preparation. Used for providing evidence of competence to become a teacher or obtain academic credit at participating educational institutions.

Description: Two part test of skills and knowledge important in quantity food preparation. The written test has approximately 200 multiple-choice items and covers the following areas: appetizers, soup stocks and salads; hot foods; vegetables; beverages; equipment; baking; cheeses; buffet, lunch, breakfast; and administration. The performance test measures abilities in seven areas: recipes and menus; assemble and portion ingredients; methods of food preparation; use of utensils and hand tools; use of equipment; use of preparation areas; and general knowledge. All items needed will be furnished. Examiner required. Written test suitable for group use.

Timed: Written test, 3 hours; Performance test, 3 hours

Range: Adult

Scoring: Examiner evaluated; scoring service provided

Cost: Contact publisher.

Publisher: National Occupational Competency Testing Institute

TEACHER OCCUPATIONAL COMPETENCY TESTING: QUANTITY FOODS EXAMINATION

adult

Purpose: Assesses competency in quantity foods. Used for providing evidence of competence to become a teacher or obtain academic credit at participating educational institutions.

Description: Two part test of skills and knowledge important in quantity foods. The written test has approximately 200 multiple-choice items and covers the following areas: cost control and menu planning; safety and cleanliness; waitressing and customer service; food service occupations nutrition; food purchasing; food receiving and storage; and food preparation. The performance test measures abilities in two areas: work organization and food preparation. Ninety percent of the performance test deals with food preparation. Examiner required. Written test suitable for group use.

Timed: Written test, 3 hours; Performance test, 4 hours

Range: Adult

Scoring: Examiner evaluated; computer scoring provided

Cost: Contact publisher.

Publisher: National Occupational Competency Testing Institute

TEACHER OCCUPATIONAL COMPETENCY TESTING: RADIO/TV REPAIR EXAMINATION

adult

Purpose: Assesses competency in radio/TV repair. Used for providing evidence of competence to become a teacher or obtain academic credit at participating educational institutions.

Description: Two part test of skills and knowledge important in radio/TV repair. The written test has approximately 200 multiple-choice items and covers the following areas: fundamental electronics theory, solid state and tube circuitry, basic electronic circuits, communications systems, and radio and TV servicing. The performance test measures abilities in four areas: use of test equipment, receiver alignment, solid state radio troubleshooting, and TV service and troubleshooting. Examiner required. Written test suitable for group use.

Timed: Written test, 3 hours; Performance test, 5 hours

Range: Adult

Scoring: Examiner evaluated; scoring service provided

Cost: Contact publisher.

Publisher: National Occupational Competency Testing Institute

TEACHER OCCUPATIONAL COMPETENCY TESTING: REFRIGERATION

adult

Purpose: Assesses competency in refrigeration. Used for providing evidence of competence to become a teacher or obtain academic credit at participating educational institutions.

Description: Two part test of skills and knowledge important in refrigeration occupations. The written test has approximately 200 multiple-choice items and covers the following areas: domestic service, commercial service, industrial service, commercial installation, and industrial installation. The performance test consists entirely of skills in assembly, installation, and service. Examiner required. Written test suitable for group use.

Timed: Written test, 3 hours; Performance test, open ended

Range: Adult

Scoring: Examiner evaluated; scoring service provided

Cost: Contact publisher.

Publisher: National Occupational Competency Testing Institute

TEACHER OCCUPATIONAL COMPETENCY TESTING: SHEET METAL EXAMINATION

adult

Purpose: Assesses competency in sheet metal occupations. Used for providing evidence of competence to become a teacher or obtain academic credit at participating educational institutions.

Description: Two part test of skills

and knowledge important in sheet metal work. The written test has approximately 200 multiple-choice items and covers the following areas: layout and drafting; sheet metal machinery; bench and hand tools-processing; welding; computations; hazards; materials; building code and regulations; fluxes; application of trade science; and sheet metal fabrication. The performance test measures abilities in five areas: pattern development; fabrication and assembly; welding and fastening; identification and protection of materials; and grinding and drilling. Candidate may bring own tools. Examiner required. Written test suitable for group use.

Timed: Written test, 3 hours; Performance test, 5 hours

Range: Adult

Scoring: Examiner evaluated; scoring service provided

Cost: Contact publisher.

Publisher: National Occupational Competency Testing Institute

---

TEACHER OCCUPATIONAL COMPETENCY TESTING: SMALL ENGINE REPAIR EXAMINATION #005

adult

Purpose: Assesses competency in small engine repair. Used for providing evidence of competence to become a teacher or obtain academic credit at participating educational institutions.

Description: Two part test of skills and knowledge important in small engine repair. The written test has approximately 200 multiple-choice items and covers the following areas: benchwork, testing and inspection; engine operation; cylinder block servicing and overhaul; lubrication system and lubrication; cooling and

exhaust systems; transmission of power and drive units; troubleshooting; fuel systems and carburetion; ignition and starting systems; trade related information; preventive maintenance; trade application of science, and trade computations. The performance test measures abilities in nine areas: benchwork, testing and inspection; engine analysis; cooling and exhaust system; preventive maintenance; cylinder block servicing and overhaul; lubricating systems and lubrication; fuel systems and carburetion; ignition and starting systems; and troubleshooting. Personal tools may be used. Handbooks and references will be provided; however, candidate may bring his own. Examiner required. Written test suitable for group use.

Timed: Written test, 3 hours; Performance test, 5 hours

Range: Adult

Scoring: Examiner evaluated; scoring service provided

Cost: Contact publisher.

Publisher: National Occupational Competency Testing Institute

---

TEACHER OCCUPATIONAL COMPETENCY TESTING: SMALL ENGINE REPAIR EXAMINATION #056

adult

Purpose: Assesses competency in small engine repair. Used for providing evidence of competence to become a teacher or obtain academic credit at participating educational institutions.

Description: Two part test of skills and knowledge important in small engine repair. The written test has approximately 200 multiple-choice items and covers the following areas: related information and functioning of engines; basic troubleshooting; fuel system; electrical system; lubrication, exhaust, cooling and transmission. The performance test measures abilities in four areas: tune-up, engine repair, cutting components, and electrical. Examiner required. Written test suitable for group use.

Timed: Written test, 3 hours; Performance test, 3 hours

Range: Adult

Scoring: Examiner evaluated; scoring service provided

Cost: Contact publisher.

Publisher: National Occupational Competency Testing Institute

TEACHER OCCUPATIONAL COMPETENCY TESTING: TEXTILE PRODUCTION/FABRICATION

adult

Purpose: Assesses competency in textile production/fabrication. Used for providing evidence of competence to become a teacher or obtain academic credit at participating educational institutions.

Description: Two part test of skills and knowledge important in textile production/fabrication. The written test has approximately 200 multiple-choice items and covers the following areas: power machine operations, apparel assembly, pattern making, alterations, and textiles. The performance test measures abilities in the same five areas. Candidate should bring: trousers with cuffs and fly-type zipper, skirt, coat or jacket with vented sleeve, seam binding to match skirt, trouser zipper, hand sewing needles, fabric shears, nippers, ripping instrument, and thimble. Examiner required. Written test suitable for group use.

Timed: Written test, 3 hours; Performance test, 4 hours

Range: Adult

Scoring: Examiner evaluated; scoring service provided

Cost: Contact publisher.

Publisher: National Occupational Competency Testing Institute

TEACHER OCCUPATIONAL COMPETENCY TESTING: TOOL AND DIE MAKING EXAMINATION

adult

Purpose: Assesses competency in tool and die making. Used for providing evidence of competence to become a teacher or obtain academic credit at participating educational institutions.

Description: Two part test of skills and knowledge important in tool and die making. The written test has approximately 200 multiple-choice items and covers the following areas: inspection work, tool design and cost estimating, characteristics of metals, math, metallurgy/heat treat, physical mechanics, metal fabrication, profiling machines, surface finish pages, and extruding and molding. The performance test measures abilities in three areas: die making, tooling, and jig and fixture work. Examiner required. Written test suitable for group use.

Timed: Written test, 3 hours; Performance test, 5 hours

Range: Adult

Scoring: Examiner evaluated; scoring service provided

Cost: Contact publisher.

Publisher: National Occupational Competency Testing Institute

TEACHER OCCUPATIONAL COMPETENCY TESTING: WELDING EXAMINATION #021

adult

Purpose: Assesses competency in welding. Used for providing evidence of competence to become a teacher or obtain academic credit at participating educational institutions.

Description: Two part test of skills and knowledge important in welding. The written test has approximately 200 multiple-choice items and covers the following areas: general welder qualifications; welding symbols; joint design; welding defects and causes; testing; electricity; basic metallurgy; oxyfuel welding; brazing; hard surfacing; other processes; shielded arc welding; gas metal arc welding; and gas tungsten arc welding. The performance test measures abilities in four areas: shielded metal arc welding; oxyfuel welding; gas metal arc welding; and gas tungsten arc welding. Personal tools may be used. Candidate furnishes appropriate work clothes and safety equipment. Examiner required. Written test suitable for group use.

Timed: Written test, 3 hours; Performance test, 4 hours

Range: Adult

Scoring: Examiner evaluated; scoring service provided

Cost: Contact publisher.

Publisher: National Occupational Competency Testing Institute

TEACHER OCCUPATIONAL COMPETENCY TESTING: WELDING EXAMINATION #057

adult

Purpose: Assesses competency in welding occupations. Used for providing evidence of competence to become a teacher or obtain academic credit at participating educational institutions.

Description: Two part test of skills and knowledge important in welding occupations. The written test has approximately 200 multiple-choice items and covers the following areas: general knowledge, shielded metal arc, oxyfuel welding, torch brazing, gas metal arc, and basic metallurgy. The performance test measures abilities in four areas: shielded metal arc welding, oxyfuel welding, gas-metal arc welding, and gas-tungsten arc welding. Examiner required. Written test suitable for group use.

Timed: Written test, 3 hours; Performance test, 4 hours, 10 minutes

Range: Adult

Scoring: Examiner evaluated; scoring service provided

Cost: Contact publisher.

Publisher: National Occupational Competency Testing Institute

Publisher Index

Academic Therapy Publications, 20 Commercial Blvd., Novato, California 94947; (415) 883-3314

Administrative Research Associates, Inc., Irvine Town Center, Box 4211, Irvine, California 92644; no business phone

Allington Corporation, (The), P.O. Box 125, Remington, Virginia 22734; (703) 825-5722

American Association of Bible Colleges, P.O. Box 1523, Fayetteville, Arkansas 72701; (501) 521-8164

American Automobile Association (AAA), Traffic Safety Department, 8111 Gatehouse Road, Falls Church, Virginia 22047; (703) AAA-6621

American College Testing Program, (The), 2201 North Dodge Street, P.O. Box 168, Iowa City, Iowa 52243; (319) 337-1000

American Dental Association, 211 East Chicago Avenue, Chicago, Illinois 60611; (312) 440-2500

American Foundation for the Blind, 15 West 16th Street, New York, New York 10011; (212) 620-2000

American Guidance Service, Publishers' Building, Circle Pines, Minnesota 55014; (800) 328-2560, in Minnesota (612) 786-4343

American Optical (AO) Scientific Instruments Division, Warner-Lambert Technologies, Inc., P.O. Box 123, Buffalo, New York 14240; (716) 891-3000

American Orthopsychiatric Association, (The), Inc., 1775 Broadway, New York, New York 10019; (212) 586-5690

American Printing House for the Blind, 1839 Frankfort Avenue, P.O. Box 6085, Louisville, Kentucky 40206-0085; (502) 895-2405

Associates for Research in Behavior, Inc. (ARBOR), The Science Center, 34th & Market Streets, Philadelphia, Pennsylvania 19104: (215) 387-5300

Association of American Medical Colleges, 1 Dupont Circle NW, Suite 200, Washington, D.C. 20036; (202) 828-0400

Aurora Publishing, 1709 Bragaw St., Suite B, Anchorage, Alaska 99504; (907) 279-5251

Australian Council for Educational Research Ltd. (ACER), Frederick Street, Hawthorn, Victoria 3122, Australia; (03) 818-1271

Bardis (Panos D.), The Univeristy of Toledo, Toledo, Ohio 43606; (419) 537-4242

Behar (Lenore), Division Mental Health, Albemarle Building, 325 N. Salisbury Street, Raleigh, North Carolina 27611; (919) 733-4660

Behavior Science Press, P.O. Box BV, University, Alabama 35486; (205) 759-2089

Behavior Science Systems, Inc., Box 1108, Minneapolis, Minnesota 55440; no business phone

Belwin-Mills Publishing Company, 25 Deshon Drive, Melville, New York 11747; (516) 293-3400

Bingham Button Test, 46211 North 125th Street East, Lancaster, California 93534; (805) 943-3241

Biometrics Research, Research Assessment and Training Unit, New York State Psychiatric Institute, 722 West 168th Street, Room 341, New York, New York 10032; (212) 960-5534

BJK Associates, 2104 South 135th Avenue, Omaha, Nebraska 68144; (402) 330-3726

Bobbs-Merrill Educational Publishing, 4300 West 62nd Street, P.O. Box 7080, Indianapolis, Indiana 46206; (317) 298-5479

Bond Publishing Company, 787 Willett Ave., Riverside, Rhode Island 02915-9990; (401) 437-0421

Book-Lab, 500 74th Street, North Bergen, New Jersey 07047; (201) 861-6763

Brador Publications Inc., Education Division, 36 Main Street, Livonia, New York 14487; (716) 346-3191

Brandywine Associates, P.O. Box 1, Concordville, Pennsylvania 19331; (215) 358-3957

Brook Educational Publishing Ltd., Box 1171, Guelph, Ontario, Canada NIH 6N3; (519) 836-2920

Brown, (William C.), Company Publishers, 2460 Kemper Boulevard, Dubuque, Iowa 52001; (319) 588-1451

Bruce, (Martin M.), Ph.D., Publishers, 50 Larchwood Road, Larchmont, New York 10538; (914) 834-1555

Bureau of Business and Economic Research, College of Business Administration, University of Iowa, Iowa City, Iowa 52242; (319) 353-2121

Bureau of Educational Measurements, Emporia State Univeristy, Emporia, Kansas 66801; (316) 343-1200

Camelot Behavioral Systems, P.O. Box 3447, Lawrence, Kansas 66044; (913) 843-9159

Carlson, (Bernadine P.), c/o Western Michigan University, 720 Sprau Tower, Kalamazoo, Michigan 49008; (616) 383-0788

Carroll Publications, 704 South University, Mount Pleasant, Michigan 48858; (517) 772-3956

Center for Epidemiologic Studies, Department of Health and Human Services, 5600 Fishers Lane, Rockville, Maryland 20857; (301) 443-4513

Center for Improvement of Undergraduate Education, (The), 115 Rand Hall, Cornell University,

Ithaca, New York 14850; (607) 256-1000

Center for Leadership Studies (available from Learning Resources Corp.), 8517 Production Avenue, P.O. Box 26240, San Diego, California 92126; (714) 578-5900

Chambers, (Jay L.), College of William and Mary, Williamsburg, Virginia 23185; (703) 253-4000

Childcraft Education Corp., 20 Kilmer Road, Edison, New Jersey 08818; (800) 631-5652, in New Jersey (201) 572-6100

Chronicle Guidance Publications, Inc., Moravia, New York 13118; (315) 497-0330

Clinical Psychology Publishing Company, Inc., 4 Conant Square, Brandon, Vermont 05733; (802) 247-6871

Coddington (R. Dean), School of Medicine in New Orleans, Louisiana State University Medical Center, 1542 Tulane Avenue, New Orleans, Louisiana 70112; (504) 568-4006.

Coffin Associates, 21 Darling Street, Marblehead, Massachusetts 01945; (617) 631-9491

College Board Publications, (The), Box 2815, Princeton, New Jersey 08541; (609) 771-7600

Collins Educational/A Division of Collins Publisher, Box 9, 29 Frogmore, St. Albans, Hertfordshire, AL2 2NF; England

Committee on Diagnostic Reading Tests, (The), Inc., Mountain Home, North Carolina 28758; (704) 693-5223

Communication Research Associates, Inc., P.O. Box 11012, Salt Lake City, Utah 84147; (801) 292-3880

Consulting Psychologists Press, Inc., 577 College Avenue, P.O. Box 11636, Palo Alto, California 94306; (415) 857-1444

Counseling and Self-Improvement Programs, 710 Watson Drive, Natchitoches, Louisiana 71457; (318) 352-5313

C.P.S. Inc., Box 83, Larchmont, New York 10538; no business phone

CRAC Publications, Hobsons Press (Cambridge) Ltd., Bateman Street, Cambridge CB2 1LZ, England; (0223) 354551

Crane Publishing Company, Division of MLP, 1301 Hamilton Avenue, P.O. Box 3713, Trenton, New Jersey 08629; (609) 393-1111

Creative Learning Systems, Inc., 936 C Street, San Diego, California 92101; (619) 231-3599

Croft Inc., 4922 Harford Road, Baltimore, Maryland 21214; (301) 254-5082

CTB/McGraw-Hill, Del Monte Research Park, Monterey, California 93940; (408) 649-8400, (800) 538-9547, in California (800) 682-9222

Datascan, 1134 Bobbie lane, Garland, Texas 75042; (214) 276-3978

Delaware County Intermediate Unit, State Building, Sixth and Olive Streets, Media, Pennsylvania 10963; (215) 565-4880

Developmental Reading Distributors, P.O. Box 1451, Cape Coral, Florida 33910; (813) 549-6562

Devereux Foundation, (The), 19 South Waterloo Road, Devon, Pennsylvania 64112; (215) 964-3000

Economy Company, (The), P.O. Box 25308, 1901 North Walnut Street, Oklahoma City, Oklahoma 73125; (405) 528-8444

Educational Activities, Inc., P.O. Box 392, Freeport, New York 11520; (516) 223-4666

Educational and Industrial Testing Service (EDITS), P.O. Box 7234, San Diego, California 92107; (619) 222-1666

Educational and Industrial Test Services Ltd. (EITS), 83, High Street, Hemel Hempstead, Herts. HP1 3AH. England; (0442) 56773/68645

Educational Guidance, Inc., P.O. Box 511, Main Post Office, Dearborn, Michigan 48121; (313) 274-0682

Educational Records Bureau Inc., Bardwell Hall, 37 Cameron Street, Wellesley, Massachusetts 02181; (617) 235-8920

Educational Research Council of America, Rockefeller Building, 614 West Superior Avenue, Cleveland, Ohio 44113; (216) 696-8222

Educational Resources, 19 Peacedale Grove, Nunawading, Victoria 3131, Australia; no business phone

Educational Studies & Development, 1357 Forest Park Road, Muskegon, Michigan 49441; (616) 780-2053/755-1041

Educational Testing Service (ETS), Rosedale Road, Princeton, New Jersey 08541; (609) 921-9000

Educators Publishing Service, Inc., (EPS), 75 Moulton Street, Cambridge, Massachusetts 02238-9101; (800) 225-5750, in Massachusetts (800) 792-5166

Effective Study Materials, P.O. Box 603, San Marcos, Texas 78666; (512) 442-7979

Elbern Publications, P.O. Box 09497, Columbus, Ohio 43209; (614) 235-2643

El Paso Rehabilitation Center, 2630 Richmond, El Paso, Texas 79930; (915) 566-2956

Employers' Tests and Services Associates (ETSA), 120 Detzel Place-Dept. G-180, Cincinnati, Ohio 45219; (513) 281-5389

Endeavor Information Systems, Inc., 1317 Livingston Street, Evanston, Illinois 60201; no business phone

Examinations Committee, American Chemical Society (ACS), University of South Florida, Chemistry, Room 112, Tampa, Florida 33620; (813) 974-2730

Facilitation House, Box 611-E, Ottawa, Illinois 61350; (815) 434-2353

Family Life Publications, Inc., Box 427, Saluda, North Carolina 28773; (704) 749-4971

Fast, (Charles C.), Northeast Missouri State University, Kirksville, Missouri 63501; (816) 785-4000

Federation of Societies of Coatings Technology, 1315 Walnut Street, Philadelphia, Pennsylvania 19107; (215) 545-1506

Fetler & Associates, P.O. Box 3473, Arlington Station, Poughkeepsie, New York 12603; (914) 471-9340

Frost, (Brian), University of Calgary, 2500 University Drive N.W., Calgary, Alberta, Canada T2N 1N4; (403) 284-5651

Gibson, (Robert), Publisher, 17, Fitzroy Place, Glasgow, Scotland G3 7BR; (041) 248-5674

Girona, (Ricardo), 428 Columbus Avenue, Sandusky, Ohio 44870; no business phone

Gleser, (Goldine C.), 7710 Medical Sciences Building, 231 Bethesda Avenue, Cincinnati, Ohio 45267; no business phone

Gough, (Harrison G.)/ Institute of Personality and Research, University of California, Berkeley, California 94720; (415) 642-6000

Goyer, (Robert S.), Center for Communication Studies, Ohio University, Athens, Ohio 45701; (602) 965-5095

Grassi, (Joseph R.), Inc., Mailman Center for Child Development, P.O. Box 016820, University of Miami, Miami, Florida 33101; (305) 547-6631

Grune & Stratton, Inc., 111 Fifth Avenue, New York, New York 10003; (212) 741-6800

Guidance Centre, Faculty of Education, University of Toronto, 252 Bloor Street West, Toronto, Ontario, Canada M5S 2Y3; (416) 978-3206/3210

H & H Enterprises, Box 1070-T, Lawrence, Kansas 66044; (913) 843-4793

Halgren Tests, 873 Persimmon Avenue, Sunnyvale, California 94087; (408) 738-1342

Harding, (Christopher), Harding Tests, Box 271, North Rockhampton Mail Centre, 04701, Australia; no business phone

Harrap Ltd., 19-23 Ludgate Hill, London, England EC4M 7PD; (01) 248-6444; USA: Pendragon House, Inc., 2898 Joseph Avenue, Campbell, California 95008; (408) 371-2737

Harvard Personnel Testing, Box 319, Oradell, New Jersey 07649; (201) 265-5393

Harvard University Press, 79 Garden Street, Cambridge, Massachusetts 02138; (617) 495-2600

Haverly Systems, Inc., 78 Broadway, P.O. Box 919, Denville, New Jersey 07834; (201) 627-1424

Hayes Educational Tests, 7040 North Portsmouth Avenue, Portland, Oregon 97203; (503) 285-3745

Heath, (Roy D.), 1193 South East Street, Amherst, Massachusetts 01002; (413) 253-7756

Hill, (William Fawcett), California State Polytechnic University, Pomona, 3801 West Temple Avenue, Pomona, California 91768; (714) 626-0128

Hiskey-Nebraska Test, (The), 5640 Baldwin, Lincoln, Nebraska 68507; (402) 466-6145

Hodder & Stoughton Educational, A Division of Hodder & Stoughton Ltd., P.O. Box 702, Mill Road, Dunton Green, Sevenoaks, Kent, TN13 2YD, England; (0732) 50111

Human Sciences Research Council, Private Bag X41, 0001 Pretoria, South Africa; (012) 28-3944

Illinois Thinking Project, Education Building, Univeristy of Illinois, Urbana, Illinois 61801; (217) 333-1000

Indstrial Psychology Incorporated (IPI), 515 Madison Avenue, New York, New York 10022; (212) 355-5330

Institute for Personality and Ability Testing, Inc. (IPAT), P.O. Box 188, 1602 Coronado Drive, Champaign, Illinois 61820; (217) 352-4739

Institute for Psycho-Imagination Therapy, c/o Joseph Shorr, Ph.D., 111 North La Cienega Blvd. #108, Beverly Hills, California 90211; (213) 652-2922

Institute for Psychosomatic & Psychiatric Research & Training/Daniel Offer, Michael Reese Hospital and Medical Center, 29th Street and Ellis Avenue, Chicago, Illinois 60616; (312) 791-3826

Institute for the Development of Human Resources, 1201 Second Street, Corpus Christi, Texas 78404; (512) 883-6442

Institute of Psychological Research, Inc., 34, Fleury Street West, Montreal, Quebec, Canada, H3L 929; (514) 382-3000

Instructional Materials & Equipment Distributors (IMED), 1520 Cotner Avenue, Los Angeles, California 90025; (213) 879-0377

Instructional Materials Laboratory, The Ohio State University, 1885 Neil Avenue, Columbus, Ohio 43210; (614) 422-2345

Interstate Printers and Publishers, Inc., (The), (IPP), P.O. Box 594, Jackson at Van Buren, Danville, Illinois 61832; (217) 446-0500

Intran Corporation, 4555 West 77th Street, Minneapolis, Minnesota 55435; (612) 835-5422

IOX Assessment Associates, 11411 West Jefferson Boulevard, Culver City, California 90230; (213) 391-6295

JAIM Research, Inc., 1808 Collingwood Road, Alexandria, Virginia 22308; (703) 765-5903

Jamestown Publishers, P.O. Box 6743, 544 Douglas Avenue, Providence, Rhode Island, 02940; (401)

351-1915
Jansky, (Jeannette J.), 120 East 89th Street, New York, New York 10028; (212) 876-8894
Jastak Associates, Inc., 1526 Gilpin, Wilmington, Delaware 19806; (302) 652-4990
Joint Council on Economic Education, 1212 Avenue of the Americas, New York, New York 10036; (212) 582-5150
Kahn, (Marvin W.), Department of Psychology, The University of Arizona, Tucson, Arizona, Tucson, Arizona 85721; (602) 626-2921
Karger, (S.), AG, Basel, P.O. Box, Postfach, CH-4009 Basel, Switzerland
Katz, (Martin M.), 6305 Walhonding Road, Bethesda, Maryland 20816; (301) 229-1511
Keeler Instruments Inc., 456 Parkway, Lawrence Park Industrial District, Broomall, Pennsylvania; (215) 353-4350, (800) 523-5620
Kew, (Clifton E.), 245 East 19th Street, New York, New York 10003; (212) 473-3082
Keystone View, Division of Mast Development Company, 2212 East 12th Street, Davenport, Iowa 52803; (319) 326-0141
Knobloch, (Hilda), 230 E. Oglethorpe Avenue, Savannah, Georgia 31401;
Kreiger, (Robert E.), Publishing Company, Incorporated, P.O. Box 9542, Melbourne, Florida 32901; (305) 724-9542
Kundu, (Ramanath), Department of Psychology, University of Calcutta, 92, Acharya Prafulla Chandra Road, Calcutta 700009, India; (35) 9666/7089
Ladoca Publishing Foundation, Laradon Hall Training and Residential Center, East 51st Avenue & Lincoln Street, Denver, Colorado 80216; (303) 629-6379
Lafayette Instrument Company, P.O. Box 5729, Lafayette, Indiana 47903; (317) 423-1505
LaForge, (Rolfe), 83 Homestead Blvd., Mill Valley, California 94941; (415) 388-8121
Larlin Corporation, P.O. Box 1523, 1119 Cobb Parkway, South Marietta, Georgia 30061; (404) 424-6210
Lawrence, (Trudys), 5916 Del Loma Avenue, San Gabriel, California 91775; (213) 286-2027
Leach, (Glenn C.,), Wagner College, 631 Howard Avenue, Staten Island, New York 10301; (212) 390-3100
Learning Publications, Inc., P.O. Box 1326, Dept. C-1, Holmes Beach, Florida 33509; (616) 372-1045
Leonard, (Hal), Publishing Corporation, 960 E. Mark Street, Winona, Minnesota 55987; (507) 454-2920
Lewis, (H.K.), & Co. Ltd., 136 Gower Street, London, England WC1E 6BS; (01) 387-4282
Life Insurance Marketing and Research Association, Inc. (LIMRA), P.O. Box 208, Hartford, Connecticut 06141; (203) 677-0033
Life Office Management Association, Inc. (LOMA), 100 Colony Square, Atlanta, Georgia 30361; (404) 892-7272
London House Press, 1550 Northwest Highway, Park Ridge, Illinois 60068; (312) 298-7311
M.A.A. Committee on High School Contests, Department of Mathematics and Statistics, 917 Oldfather Hall, University of Nebraska, Lincoln, Nebraska 68588; (402) 472-7211
Macmillan Education Ltd., Houndmills, Basinstoke, Hants, RG21 2XS, England
Mafex Associates, Inc., 90 Cherry Street, Box 519, Johnston, Pennsylvania 15907; (800) 458-0151, in Pennsylvania (814) 535-3597
Manasayan, 32 Netaji Subhash Marg, Delhi 110006, India; no business phone
Marriage Council of Philadelphia, Inc., 4025 Chestnut Street, Suite 210, Philadelphia, Pennsylvania 19104; (215) 222-7574
Martinus Nijhoff, Postbuss 566, 2501 CN, Lange Voorhout, 9-11, The Hague, Netherlands; (070) 469460
McCann Associates, 2755 Philmont Avenue, Huntingdon Valley, Pennsylvania 19006; (215) 947-5775
McCartney, (William A.), P.O. Box 507, Kaneohe, Hawaii 96744; (808) 239-8071
Medical Research Council, Department of Psychological Medicine, Royal Free Hospital, Pond Street, London, NW3 20G, England; (01) 794-0500
Meeting Street School, The Easter Seal Society of Rhode Island, Inc., 667 Waterman Avenue, East Providence, Rhode Island 02914; (401) 438-9500
Merrell-National Laboratories, Division of Richardson-Merrell Inc., 2110 East Galbraith Road, Cincinnatti, Ohio 45215; (513) 948-9111
Merrill, (Charles E.), Publishing Company, 1300 Alum Creek Drive, Box 508, Columbus, Ohio 43216; (614) 258-8441
Miami University Alumni Association, Murstein Alumni Center, Oxford, Ohio 45056; (513) 529-5211
Midwest Music Tests, c/o Newell H. Long, 1304 East University Street, Bloomington, Indiana 47401; (812) 332-0211
Ministry Inventories, P.O. Box 8265, Dallas, Texas 75205; (214) 276-3978
Ministry of Education, The Ontario Institute for Studies in Education, 252 Bloor Street West,

Toronto, Ontario, Canada M5S 1V6; (416) 965-6789
Mississippi State University Rehabilitation Research & Training Center, P.O. Drawer 5365, Mississippi State, Mississippi 39762; (601) 325-2001
MKM, 809 Kansas City Street, Rapid City, South Dakota 57701; (605) 342-7223
Monitor, P.O. Box 2337, Hollywood, California 90028; no business phone
Moore, (Joseph E.), and Associates, Perry Drive, R.F.D. 12, Box 309, Gainesville, Georgia 30501; no business phone
Morrison, (James H.), 9804 Hadley, Overland Park, Kansas 66212; (913) 642-2258
Morstain, (Barry R.), Department of Urban Affairs, University of Delaware, Neward, Delaware 19711; (302) 738-2394
Munsell Color, Macbeth, A Division of Kollmorgen Corporation, 2441 N. Calvert Street, Baltimore, Maryland 21218; (301) 243-2171
National Business Education Association, 1914 Association Drive, Reston, Virginia 22091; (703) 860-8300
National Educational Laboratory Publishers, Inc., 813 Airport Boulevard, Austin, Texas 78702; (512) 385-7084
National Institute for Personnell Research, P.O. Box 32410, Braamfontein, 2017 South Africa; (011) 39-4451
National Occupational Competency Testing Institute, 45 Colvin Avenue, Albany, New York 12206; (518) 482-8864
NCS Interpretive Scoring Systems, P.O. Box 1416, Minneapolis, Minnesota 55440; (612) 830-7730, or (800) 328-6116
Nelson Canada Limited, 1120 Birchmount Road, Scarborough, Ontario, Canada M1K 5G4; (416) 752-9100
Nevins, (C.H.), Printing Company, 311 Bryn Mawr Island, Bayshore Gardens, Bradenton, Florida 33507; (813) 755-5330
Newbury House Publishers, Inc., 54 Warehouse Lane, Rowley, Massachusetts 01969; (617) 948-2840
New Zealand Council for Educational Research (NZCER), P.O. Box 3237, Wellington, New Zealand
NFER-Nelson Publishing Company LTD., Darville House, 2 Oxford Road East, Windsor, Berkshire, SL4 1DF, England; (07535) 58961
Nisonger Center, (The), Ohio State University, 1580 Cannon Drive, Columbus, Ohio 43210; (614) 422-0825
Northwestern University Press, Dept. SLD-82, 1735 Benson Avenue, Evanston, Illinois 60201; (312) 492-5313
Nursing Research Associates, 3752 Cummings Street, Eau Claire, Wisconsin 54701; (715) 836-4731
Oliver and Boyd, Robert Stevenson House, 1-3 Baxter's Place, Leith Walk, Edinburg EH1 3AF, Scotland. U.S. Representative: Longman Inc., 19 West 44th Street, New York, New York 10036; (212) 764-3950
Organizational Tests (Canada) Ltd., Box 324, Fredericton, New Brunswick, Canada E3B 4Y9; (506) 455-8366
Oxford University Press, 200 Madison Avenue, New York, New York 10016; (212) 679-7300
Peace Research Laboratory, 6251 San Bonita, St. Louis, Missouri 63105; (314) 721-8219
Perceptual Learning Systems, P.O. Box 864, Dearborn, Michigan 48121; (313) 277-6480
Perfection Form Company, (The), 8350 Hickman Road, Suite 15, Des Moines, Iowa 50322; (800) 831-4190, in Iowa (800) 432-5831
Personnel Research Institute (PRI), Psychological Research Services, Case Western Reserve University, 11220 Bellflower Road, Cleveland, Ohio 44106; (216) 368-3546
Person-O-Metrics, Inc., Evaluation & Development Services, 20504 Williamsburg Road, Dearborn Heights, Michigan 48127; no business phone
Phi Delta Kappa, Eighth and Union, P.O. Box 789, Bloomington, Indiana 47402; (812) 339-1156
Phoenix Institute of California, (The), 248 Blossom Hill Road, Los Gatos, California 95030; (408) 354-6122
Phonovisual Products, Inc., 12216 Parklawn Drive, P.O. Box 2007, Rockville, Maryland 20852; (301) 881-4888
Pikunas, (Justin), 335 Briggs Building, University of Detroit, Detroit, Michigan 48221; (313) 927-1000
Pitman Learning, Inc., 6 Davis Drive, Belmont, California 94002; (415) 592-7810
Priority Innovations, Inc., P.O. Box 792, Skokie, Illinois (60076); (312) 729-1434
Pro-Ed, 5341 Industrial Oaks Boulevard, Austin, Texas 78735; (512) 892-3142
Professional Examinations Division/ The Psychological Corporation, 7500 Old Oak Boulevard, Cleveland, Ohio 44130
Programs for Education, Inc., Dept. W-16, 82 Park Avenue, Flemington, New Jersey 08822; (212) 689-3911
Psychodiagnostic Test Company, Box 859, East Lansing, Michigan 48823; no business phone
Psychodynamic Instruments, c/o Gerald S. Blum, Department of Psychology, University of Califor-

nia, Santa Barbara, Califoria 93106; no business phone

Psychological Assessment and Services, Inc., P.O. Box 1031, Iowa City, Iowa 52240; no business phone

Psychological Assessment Resources, Inc., P.O. Box 98, Odessa, Florida 33556; (813) 920-6357

Psychological Corporation, (The), (Psy Cor), A Subsidiary of Harcourt Brace Jovanovich, Inc., 7500 Old Oak Boulevard, Cleveland, Ohio 44130;

Psychological Development Publications, P.O. Box 3198, Aspen, Colorado 81612; (303) 925-4432

Psychological Publications, Inc., 5300 Hollywood Boulevard, Los Angeles, California 90027; (213) 465-4163

Psychological Service Center of Philadelphia, Suite 904, 1422 Chestnut Street, Philadelphia, Pennsylvania 19102; (215) 568-2555

Psychological Services, Inc., Suite 1200, 3450 Wilshire Boulevard, Los Angeles, California 90010; (213) 738-1132

Psychological Systems Corporation, 1301 West 22nd Street, Oak Brook, Illinois 60521; (312) 325-8000

Psychological Test Specialists, Box 9229, Missoula, Montana 59807; no business phone

Psychologists and Educators, Inc., 211 West State Street, Jacksonville, Illinois 62650; (217) 243-2135

Psychometric Affiliates, Box 3167, Munster, Indiana 46321; (219) 836-1661

Pumroy, (Donald K.), College of Education, University of Maryland, College Park, Maryland 20742; (301) 454-2027

Purdue University Bookstore, P.O. Box 3028, Station 11, 360 State Street, West Lafayette, Indiana 47906; (317) 743-9618

Reid Psychological Systems, 233 North Michigan Avenue, Chicago, Illinois 60601; (312) 938-9200

Reitan, (Ralph M.), Department of Psychology, University of Arizona, Tucson, Arizona 85721; (602) 626-2493

Research and Development Center for Teacher Education, The University of Texas at Austin, Education Annex 3.203, Austin, Texas 78712-1288; (512) 471-1343

Research Concepts, A Division of Test Maker, Inc., 1368 East Airport Road, Muskegon, Michigan 49444; (616) 739-7401

Research Press, Box 317760, Champaign, Illinois 61820; (217) 352-3273

Research Psychologists Press, Inc., P.O. Box 984, Port Huron, Michigan 48060; (313) 982-4556

Revrac Publications, Inc., 207 West 116th Street, Kansas City, Missouri 64114; no business phone

Riverside Publishing Company, (The), P.O. Box 1970, Iowa City, Iowa 52244; (319) 354-5104

Rocky Mountain Behavioral Science Institute, Inc. (RMBSI), P.O. Box 1066, Fort Collins, Colorado 80522; no business phone

Rosenzweig, (Saul), 8029 Washington Avenue, St. Louis, Missouri 63114; no business phone

Rucker-Gable Associates, P.O. Box 927, Storrs, Connecticut 06268; (203) 423-7880

Saleh (S.D.), University of Waterloo, Faculty of Engineering, Department of Management Sciences, Waterloo, Ontario, Canada N2L 3G1; (519) 885-1211

Sauls, (Charles), Department of Curriculum and Instruction, Louisiana State University, Baton Rouge, Louisiana 70803; (504) 388-3202

Saville & Holdsworth Ltd. (SHL), 18 Malbrook Road, London, England SW15 6UF; (01) 788-5182

Schmidt, (Paul F.), 1209 West Main Street, Shelbyville, Kentucky 40065; (502) 456-1990

Scholastic Testing Service, Inc., 480 Meyer Road, P.O. Box 1056, Bensenville, Illinois 60106; (312) 766-7150

Science Research Associates, Inc. (SRA), 155 North Wacker Drive, Chicago, Illinois 60606; (800) 621-0664, in Illinois (312) 984-2000

Scott, Foresman and Company, Test Division, 1900 East Lake Avenue, Glenview, Illinois 60025; (312) 729-3000

Search Institute, 122 West Franklin, Suite 215, Minneapolis, Minnesota 55404-2466; (612) 870-3664

Sheridan Psychological Services, Inc., P.O. Box 6101, Orange, California 92667; (714) 639-2595

Skillcorp Software, Inc., 1711 McGraw Avenue, Irvine, California 92714; (714) 549-3246

Slosson Educational Publications, Inc., P.O. Box 280, East Aurora, New York 14052; (716) 652-0930

SOARES Associates, 111 Teeter Rock Road, Trumbull, Connecticut 06611; (203) 375-5353

South, (John C.), Duquesne University, Pittsburgh, Pennsylvania 15282; (412) 434-6000

Southern Illinois University Press, P.O. Box 3697, Carbondale, Illinois 62901; (618) 453-2281

Speech and Hearing Clinic, 110 Moore Building, University Park, Pennsylvania 16802; (814) 865-5414

Springer Publishing Company, 200 Park Avenue South, New York, New York 10003; (212) 475-2494

Stanford University Press, Stanford, California 94305; (415) 497-9434

Stanton Corporation, (The), 417 South Dearborn Street, Chicago, Illinois 60605; (800) 621-4152, in Illinois (312) 922-0970

Stanwix House, Inc., 3020 Chartiers Avenue, Pittsburgh, Pennsylvania 15204; (412) 771-4233

Statistical Publishing Society, Indian Statistical Institute, 203 Barrackpore Trunk Road, Calcutta, India 700 035

Steck-Vaughn Company, P.O. Box 2028, Austin, Texas 78768; (800) 531-5015, in Texas (800)

252-9317

Stein, (Morris), Graduate School of Arts and Science, Research Center for Human Relations, New York University, 6 Washington Place, 7th Floor, New York, New York 10003; (212) 598-1212

Stevens, Thurow and Associates, 100 West Monroe Street, Chicago, Illinois 60603; (312) 332-6277

Stoelting Co., 1350 S. Kostner Avenue, Chicago, Illinois 60623; (312) 522-4500

Stratton-Christian Press, Inc., Box 1055, University Place Station, Des Moines, Iowa 50311; no business phone

SWETS Test Services, Heereweg 347b, 2161 CA Lisse, The Netherlands; 02521-19113

Tabin, (Johanna Krout), 162 Park Avenue, Glencoe, Illinois 60022; (312) 835-0162

TAV Selection System, 12807 Arminta Street, North Hollywood, California 91605; no business phone

Teachers College Press, Teachers College, Columbia University, 1234 Amsterdam Avenue, New York, New York 10027; (212) 678-3929

Teaching Resources Corporation, 50 Pond Park Road, Hingham, Massachusetts 02043; (617) 749-9461

T.E.D. Associates, 42 Lowell Road, Brookline, Massachusetts 02146; (617) 734-5868

Test Agency, (The), Cournswood House, North Dean, High Wycombe, Bucks, HP14 4NW, England; (024) 3384

Titmus Optical Company, Petersburg, Virginia 23803; (800) 446-1802, in Virginia (800) 552-1869

Trademark Design Products, Inc., P.O. Box 2010, Boca Raton, Florida 33432; no business phone

Twitchell-Allen, (Doris), Bangor Mental Health Institute, Maine Department of Mental Health and Mental Retardation, Box 926, Bangor, Maine 04401; (207) 947-6981

Union College, Character Research Project, 207 State Street, Schenectady, New York 12305; (518) 370-6012

United States Department of Defense, Testing Directorate, Headquarters, Military Enlistment Processing Command, Attn: MEPCT, Fort Sheridan, Illinois 60037; (312) 926-4111

United States Department of Labor, Division of Testing, Employment and Training Administration, Washington, D.C. 20213; (202) 376-6270

University Associates, Inc., Learning Resources Corporation, 8517 Production Avenue, P.O. Box 26240, San Diego, California 92126; (714) 578-5900

University of Illinois Press, 54 E. Gregory Drive, Box 5081, Station A, Champaign, Illinois 61820; (800) 233-4175/638-3030

University of Minnesota Press, 2037 University Avenue S.E., Minneapolis, Minnesota 55414; (612) 373-3266. Tests are distributed by NCS Interpretive Scoring Systems, P.O. Box 1416, Minneapolis, Minnesota 55440; (612) 830-7730

University of Washington Press, P.O. Box 85569, Seattle, Washington 98105; (206) 543-8870

University Park Press Inc., 300 North Charles Street, Baltimore, Maryland 21201; (301) 547-0700 or (800) 638-7511

University Press of America, University of Detroit, 4001 W. McNichols Road, Detroit, Michigan 48221; (313) 927-1000

Vocational Psychology Research, University of Minnesota, Elliott Hall, 75 East River Road, Minneapolis, Minnesota 55455; (612) 376-7377

Vocational Research Institute, 1700 Sansom, Suite 900, Philadelphia, Pennsylvania 19103-5281; (213) 893-5911

Warner/Chilcott, 201 Tabor Raod, Morris Plains, New Jersey 07950; (201) 540-2000

Weider, (Arthur), 300 Central Park West, New York, New York 10024; (212) 873-2322

Western Psychological Services, 12031 Wilshire Boulevard, Los Angeles, California 90025; (213) 478-2061

Westwood Press Inc., 770 Broadway, 3rd Floor, New York, New York 10003; (212) 420-8008

Wilmington Collection, (The), 13315 Wilmington Drive, Dallas, Texas 75234; (214) 620-8431

Williams, (Robert L.), & Associates, Inc., 6372 Delmar Boulevard, St. Louis, Missouri 63130; (314) 862-0055

Winch, (B.L.), & Associates, 45 Hitching Post Drive, Building 21B, Rolling Hills Estates, California 90274; (213) 539-6430

Wolfe Computer Aptitude Testing LTD., P.O. Box 1104, St. Laurent Station, Montreal, Canada H4L 4W6; (514) 337-4139

Wonderlic, (E.F.), & Associates, Inc., P.O. Box 7, Northfield, Illinois 60093; (312) 446-8900

Woolner, (Rosestelle B.), 3551 Aurora Circle, Memphis, Tennessee 38111; (901) 454-2365

Word Making Productions, P.O. Box 15038, Salt Lake City, Utah 84115-0038; (801) 484-3092

World of Work, Inc., 2923 N. 67th Place, Scottsdale, Arizona 85251; (602) 946-1884

Wright Group, (The), 7620 Miramar Road, Suite 4100, San Diego, California 92126; (614) 464-7811

Yuker, (H.E.), Hofstra University, Hempstead, New York 11550; (516) 560-5635

Zalk, (Susan Rosenberg), Hunter College, 695 Park Avenue, New York, New York 10021; (212) 570-5118

Zung, (William W.K.), Veterans Administration Medical Center, 508 Fulton Street, Durham, North Carolina 27705; (919) 286-0411

Test Title Index

XLVI

L

LII

Author Index

Scoring Service Index

The following sources provide scoring services for various tests and/or market test-related computer hardware and software. The type of service available (i.e. computer or machine scoring, software or hardware programs) is listed in italics following the source or firm name. For scoring information on a specific test refer to the descriptive entry in the main body of **TESTS.**

Academic Therapy Publications *software* 20 Commercial Blvd., Novato, California 94947; (415) 883-3314.

American College Testing Program, (The) *computer scoring service* 2201 North Dodge Street, P.O. Box 168, Iowa City, Iowa 52243; (319) 337-1000.

American Dental Association *computer scoring service* 211 East Chicago Avenue, Chicago, Illinois 60611; (312) 440-2500.

American Guidance Service *computer scoring service* Publishers' Building, Circle Pines, Minnesota 55014; (800) 328-2560, in Minnesota (612) 786-4343.

Associates for Research in Behavior, Inc. (ARBOR) *computer scoring service* The Science Center, 34th & Market Streets, Philadelphia, Pennsylvania 19104; (215) 387-5300.

Behaviordyne *computer scoring service* 599 College Avenue, Suite One, Palo Alto, California 94306; (415) 857-0111.

Biometrics Research *software* Research Assessment and Training Unit, New York State Psychiatric Institute, 722 West 168th Street, Room 341, New York, New York 10032; (212) 960-5534.

BJK Associates *computer scoring service* 2104 South 135th Avenue, Omaha, Nebraska 68144; (402) 330-3726.

Bureau of Educational Measurements *machine scoring service* Emporia State University, Emporia, Kansas 66801; (316) 343-1200.

Caldwell Report *computer scoring service* 3122 Santa Monica Boulevard, Santa Monica, California 90404; (213) 829-3644.

Carlson, (Bernadine P.) *computer scoring service* c/o Western Michigan University, 720 Sprau Tower, Kalamazoo, Michigan 49008; (616) 383-0788.

Center for Applied Psychology *software* 2245 Manhattan Boulevard, Harvey, Louisiana 70058; (504) 361-3330.

Center for Improvement of Undergraduate Education *computer scoring service* 115 Rand Hall, Cornell University, Ithaca, New York 14850; (607) 256-1000.

Chambers, (Jay L.) *computer scoring service* College of William and Mary, Williamsburg, Virginia 23185; (703) 253-4000.

College Board Publications, (The) *computer scoring service* Box 2815, Princeton, New Jersey 08541; (609) 771-7600.

Compu-Psych, Inc. *hardware and software* Dept. M, One Liberty Plaza, P.O. Box 458, Liberty, Missouri 64068; (800) 821-2461, in Missouri (816) 781-8202.

CTB/McGraw-Hill *computer scoring service* Del Monte Research Park, Monterey, California 93940; (408) 649-8400, (800) 538-9547, in California (800) 682-9222.

Datascan *computer scoring service* 1134 Bobbie Lane, Garland, Texas 75042; (214) 276-3978.

Delphic Systems, Ltd. *computer scoring service* P.O. Box 1019, Coconut Grove, Florida 33133; no business phone.

Educational and Industrial Testing Service (EdITS) *computer scoring service* P.O. Box 7234, San Diego, California 92107; (619) 222-1666.

Educational and Industrial Test Services Ltd. (EITS) *computer scoring service* 83, High Street, Hemel Hempstead, Herts. HPI 3AH England; (0442) 56773.

Educational Records Bureau Inc. *computer scoring service* Bardwell Hall, 37 Cameron Street, Wellesley, Massachusetts 02181; (617) 235-8920.

Educational Testing Service (ETS) *computer scoring service* Rosedale Road, Princeton, New Jersey 08541; (609) 921-9000.

Employers' Tests and Services Associates (ETSA) *computer scoring service* 120 Detzel Place—Dept. G—180, Cincinnati, Ohio 45219; (513) 281-5389.

Endeavor Information Systems, Inc. *computer scoring service* 1317 Livingston Street, Evanston, Illinois 60201; no business phone.

Grassi, (Joseph R.), Inc. *scoring service* Mailman Center for Child Development, P.O. Box 016820, University of Miami, Miami, Florida 33101; (305) 547-6631.

Grune & Stratton, Inc. *scoring service* 111 Fifth Avenue, New York, New York 10003; (212) 741-6800.

Hartley Software *software* 1776 Thornapple River Drive, Grand Rapids, Michigan 49506; (616) 676-9176.

Harvard Personnel Testing *computer scoring service* Box 319, Oradell, New Jersey 07649; (201) 265-5393.

Haverly Systems Inc. *computer scoring service* 78 Broadway, P.O. Box 919, Denville, New Jersey 07834; (201) 627-1424.

Hill, (William Fawcett) *computer scoring service* California State Polytechnic University, Pomona, 3801 West Temple Avenue, Pomona, California 91768; (714) 626-0128.

Illinois Thinking Project *scoring service* Education Building, University of Illinois, Urbana, Illinois 61801; (217) 333-1000.

Institute for Personality and Ability Testing, Inc. (IPAT) *computer scoring service* P.O. Box 188, 1602 Coronado Drive, Champaign, Illinois 61820; (217) 352-4739.

Institute for Psychosomatic & Psychiatric Research & Training/Daniel Offer *scoring service* Michael Reese Hospital and Medical Center, 29th Street and Ellis Avenue, Chicago, Illinois 60616; (312) 791-3826.

Institute for the Development of Human Resources *computer scoring service* 1201 Second Street, Corpus Christi, Texas 78404; (512) 883-6442.

Institute of Psychological Research, Inc. *computer scoring service* 34, Fleury Street West, Montreal, Quebec H3L 929; (514) 382-3000.

Instructional Materials Laboratory *computer scoring service* The Ohio State University, 1885 Neil Avenue, Columbus, Ohio 43210; (614) 422-2345.

Integrated Professional Systems *computer scoring service, hardware and software* 5211 Mahoning Avenue, Austintown, Ohio 44515; (216) 799-3282.

Intran Corporation *computer scoring service* 4555 West 77th Street, Minneapolis, Minnesota 55435; (612) 835-5422.

JAIM Research, Inc. *computer scoring service* 1808 Collingwood Road, Alexandria, Virginia 22308; (703) 765-5903.

Jansky, (Jeannette J.) *computer scoring service* 120 East 89th Street, New York, New York 10028; (212) 876-8894.

Learning Publications, Inc. *computer scoring service* P.O. Box 1326, Dept. C-1, Holmes Beach, Florida 33509; (616) 372-1045.

Life Insurance Marketing and Research Association, Inc. (LIMRA) *computer scoring service* P.O. Box 208, Hartford, Connecticut 06141; (203) 677-0033.

London House Press *computer scoring service* 1550 Northwest Highway, Park Ridge, Illinois 60068; (312) 298-7311.

M.A.A. Committee on High School Contests, Department of Mathematics and Statistics *computer scoring service* 917 Oldfather Hall, University of Nebraska, Lincoln, Nebraska 68588; (402) 472-7211.

McCann Associates *computer scoring service* 2755 Philmont Avenue, Huntingdon Valley, Pennsylvania 19006; (215) 947-5775.

Medical Research Council, Department of Psychological Medicine, Royal Free Hospital *scoring service* Pond Street, London NW3, England 2QG; (01) 794-0500.

Merrill, Charles E., Publishing Company *computer scoring service* 1300 Alum Creek Drive, Box 508, Columbus, Ohio 43216; (614) 258-8441.

Ministry Inventories *computer scoring service* P.O. Box 8265, Dallas, Texas 75205; (214) 276-3978.

Monitor *scoring service* P.O. Box 2337, Hollywood, California 90028; no business phone.

Morstain (Barry R.) *computer scoring service* Department of Urban Affairs, University of Delaware, Newark, Delaware 19711; (302) 738-2394.

Nisonger Center (The), Ohio State University *scoring service* 1580 Cannon Drive, Columbus, Ohio 43210; (614) 422-0825.

Nursing Research Associates *scoring service* 3752 Cummings Street, Eau Claire, Wisconsin 54701; (715) 836-4731.

National Occupational Competency Testing Institute *scoring service* 45 Colvin Avenue, Albany, New York 12206; (518) 482-8864.

NCS Interpretive Scoring Systems *computer scoring service* P.O. Box 1416, Minneapolis, Minnesota 55440; (612) 830-7730 or (800) 328-6116.

Nelson Canada Limited *computer scoring service* 1120 Birchmount Road, Scarborough, Ontario, Canada M1K 5G4; (416) 752-9100.

NFER-Nelson Publishing Company Ltd. *computer scoring service* Darville House, 2 Oxford Road East, Windsor, Berkshire 5L4 1DF, England; (07535) 58961.

Person-O-Metrics, Inc., Evaluation & Development Services *scoring service* 20504 Williamsburg Road, Dearborn Heights, Michigan 48127; no business phone

Phoenix Institute of California (The) *computer scoring service* 248 Blossom Hill Road, Los Gatos, California 95030; (408) 354-6122.

Precision People, Inc. *software* 3452 North Ride Circle S., Jacksonville, Florida 32217; (904) 262-1096.

Professional Examinations Division/The Psychological Corporation *computer scoring service* 757 Third Avenue, New York, New York 10017; (212) 888-3171.

Psychological Assessment Resources, Inc. *computer scoring service and software* P.O. Box 98, Odessa, Florida 33556; (813) 920-6357.

Psychological Corporation Scoring Center (The) *MRC Answer Documents scoring service* Highway 1 and Interstate 80, Iowa City, Iowa 52240; (212) 888-3602 or

The Psychological Corporation Scoring Service (for Arizona, California, Idaho, Nevada, Oregon, Utah and Washington) 770 Lucerne Way, Sunnyvale, California 94086; (212) 888-3602.

Psychological Corporation Scoring Service (The) *OpScan scoring service* 7500 Old Oak Boulevard, Cleveland, Ohio 44130.

Psychological Corporation (The) *software* 7500 Old Oak Boulevard, Cleveland, Ohio 44130.

Psychological Software Specialists *software* 1776 Fowler, Richland, Washington 99352; (509) 735-3427.

Psych Systems *hardware and software* 600 Reisterstown Road, Baltimore, Maryland 21208; (301) 486-2206.

Purdue University Bookstore *computer scoring service* P.O. Box 3028, Station 11, 360 State Street, West Lafayette, Indiana 47906; (317) 743-9618.

Reid Psychological Systems *computer scoring service* 233 North Michigan Avenue, Chicago, Illinois 60601; (312) 938-9200.

Research Concepts, A Division of Test Maker, Inc. *computer scoring service* 1368 East Airport Road, Muskegon, Michigan 49444; (616) 739-7401.

Research Psychologists Press Inc. *computer scoring service* P.O. Box 984, Port Huron, Michigan 48060; (313) 982-4556.

Riverside Publishing Company (The) *computer scoring service* P.O. Box 1970, Iowa City, Iowa 52244; (319) 354-5104.

Rucker-Gable Associates *computer scoring service* P.O. Box 927, Storrs, Connecticut 06268; (203) 423-7880.

Saville & Holdsworth Ltd. (SHL) *scoring service* 18 Malbrook Road, London SW15 6UF England; (01) 788-5182.

Scholastic Testing Service, Inc. *computer scoring service* 480 Meyer Road, P.O. Box 1056, Bensenville, Illinois 60106; (312) 766-7150.

Science Research Associates, Inc. (SRA) *computer scoring service* 155 North Wacker Drive, Chicago, Illinois 60606; (800) 621-0664, in Illinois (312) 984-2000.

Scientific Software Associates, Ltd. *software* Box 208, Wausau, Wisconsin 54401; (715) 845-2066.

Scott, Foresman and Company, Test Division *computer scoring service* 1900 East Lake Avenue, Glenview, Illinois 60025; (312) 729-3000.

Search Institute *computer scoring service* 122 West Franklin, Suite 215, Minneapolis, Minnesota 55404-2466; (612) 870-3664.

South (John C.) *scoring service* Duquesne University, Pittsburgh, Pennsylvania 15282; (412) 434-6000.

Southern Illinois University Press *computer scoring service* P.O. Box 3697, Carbondale, Illinois 62901; (618) 453-2281.

Stanford University Press *computer scoring service* Stanford, California 94305; (415) 497-9434.

Stanton Corporation (The) *computer scoring service* 417 South Dearborn Street, Chicago, Illinois 60605; (800) 621-4152, in Illinois (312) 922-0970.

Sysdata International Inc. *computer scoring service* 7671 Old Central Avenue NE, Minneapolis, Minnesota 55432; (612) 780-1750.

United States Department of Defense, Testing Directorate *computer scoring service* Headquarters, Military Enlistment Processing Command, Attn: MEPCT, Fort Sheridan, Illinois 60037; (312) 926-4111.

United States Department of Labor, Division of Testing *computer scoring service* Employment and Training Administration, Washington, D.C. 20213; (202) 376-6270.

Vocational Psychology Research *scoring service* University of Minnesota, Elliott Hall, 75 East River Road, Minneapolis, Minnesota 55455; (612) 376-7377.

Vocational Research Institute *software* 1700 Sansom, Suite 900, Philadelphia, Pennsylvania 19103-5281; (213) 893-5911.

Western Psychological Services *computer scoring service* 12031 Wilshire Boulevard, Los Angeles, California 90025; (213) 478-2061.

Wolfe Computer Personnel Testing Inc. *scoring service* P.O. Box 319, Oradell, New Jersey 07649; (201) 265-5393.

Visually Impaired Index